Toyota Hi-Lux & 4Runner
Automotive Repair Manual

**by Bob Henderson
and John H Haynes**
Member of the Guild of Motoring Writers

Models covered:
All Toyota Hi-Lux and 4Runner models
with petrol and diesel engines
1979 – 1997

Haynes Australia Pty Limited
haynes.com

92736-7Y9

Acknowledgements

We are grateful for the help and cooperation of Toyota Motor Company for their assistance with technical information and certain illustrations. Technical writers who contributed to this project include John Raffa, Jeff Killingsworth and Larry Warren.

A book in the Haynes Automotive Repair Manual Series

ISBN-13: 978-1-62092-295-8

ISBN-10: 1-62092-295-9

Contents

Haynes mechanic, author and photographer with Toyota Hi-Lux

About this manual

Its purpose

The purpose of this manual is to help you get the best value from your vehicle. It can do so in several ways. It can help you decide what work must be done, even if you choose to have it done by a dealer service department or a repair shop; it provides information and procedures for routine maintenance and servicing; and it offers diagnostic and repair procedures to follow when trouble occurs.

We hope you use the manual to tackle the work yourself. For many simpler jobs, doing it yourself may be quicker than arranging an appointment to get the vehicle into a shop and making the trips to leave it and pick it up. More importantly, a lot of money can be saved by avoiding the expense the shop must pass on to you to cover its labor and overhead costs. An added benefit is the sense of satisfaction and accomplishment that you feel after doing the job yourself.

Using the manual

The manual is divided into Chapters. Each Chapter is divided into numbered Sections, which are headed in bold type between horizontal lines. Each Section consists of consecutively numbered paragraphs.

At the beginning of each numbered Section you will be referred to any illustrations which apply to the procedures in that Section. The reference numbers used in illustration captions pinpoint the pertinent Section and the Step within that Section. That is, illustration 3.2 means the illustration refers to Section 3 and Step (or paragraph) 2 within that Section.

Procedures, once described in the text, are not normally repeated. When it's necessary to refer to another Chapter, the reference will be given as Chapter and Section number. Cross references given without use of the word "Chapter" apply to Sections and/or paragraphs in the same Chapter. For example, "see Section 8" means in the same Chapter.

References to the left or right side of the vehicle assume you are sitting in the driver's seat, facing forward.

Even though we have prepared this manual with extreme care, neither the publisher nor the author can accept responsibility for any errors in, or omissions from, the information given.

NOTE

A **Note** provides information necessary to properly complete a procedure or information which will make the procedure easier to understand.

CAUTION

A **Caution** provides a special procedure or special steps which must be taken while completing the procedure where the Caution is found. Not heeding a Caution can result in damage to the assembly being worked on.

WARNING

A **Warning** provides a special procedure or special steps which must be taken while completing the procedure where the Warning is found. Not heeding a Warning can result in personal injury.

Introduction to the Toyota Hi-Lux and 4Runner

The Toyota Hi-Lux and 4Runner models are conventional front engine/rear wheel drive layout with optional four-wheel drive (4WD) .

Petrol engines are available in an inline four-cylinder with either overhead valve (OHV) cylinder head configuration or, on later four-cylinders and V6 models, overhead camshafts (OHC) with either a carburettor or port-type fuel injection.

Diesel engines are equipped with either a 2.2 litre (L), 2.4 litre (2L) or 2.8 litre (3L) engine.

The engine drives the rear wheels through either a four or five-speed manual transmission or an automatic transmission via a driveshaft and solid rear axle. On 4WD models, a transfer case and driveshaft are used to drive the front wheels through independent driveaxles.

Front suspension on 2WD models is independent, featuring torsion bars, with power-assisted steering available on later models. Leaf springs are used in the rear.

The front suspension on 4WD models uses either a solid front axle or, on some later models, independent front suspension, similar to that of the 2WD version.

Some models use drum brakes on the front and rear wheels. Most models, though, have power assisted discs at the front and self-adjusting drums at the rear.

Vehicle identification numbers

The VIN is stamped into the right side frame rail, and is visible through the right front wheel opening

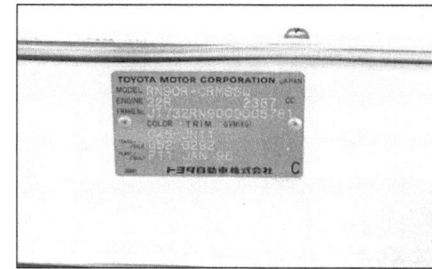

The Compliance plate is attached to the firewall

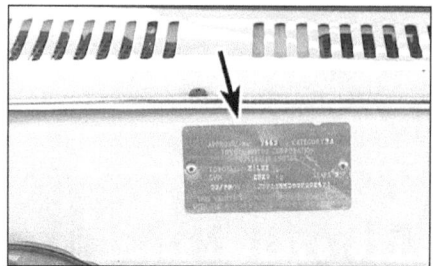

The manufacturer's data plate is also affixed to the firewall

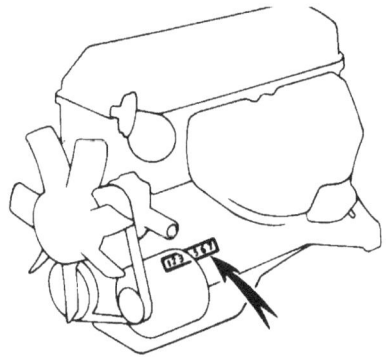

The engine identification number on R-series petrol engines is stamped into the block on the left side

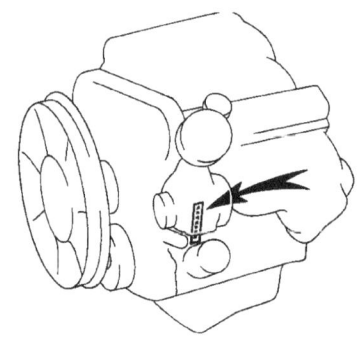

The engine identification number on Y-series petrol engines is stamped into the block on the right side

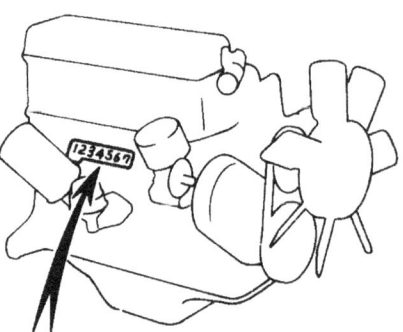

The V6 petrol engine identification number can be found on the left side of the block, just above the oil filter

Modifications are a continuing and unpublicized process in vehicle manufacturing. Since spare parts manuals and lists are compiled on a numerical basis, the individual vehicle numbers are essential to correctly identify the component required.

Vehicle Identification Number (VIN)

The VIN is very important because it's used for title and registration purposes. The VIN is stamped onto the compliance plate fastened to the firewall (see illustration) and also to the RH side chassis rail (see illustration). It contains valuable information such as where and when the vehicle was manufactured, the model year and the body style.

Compliance Plate

The compliance plate is located on the firewall in the engine compartment (see illustration). The compliance plate certifies the vehicle has met the specific safety, environmental and consumer protection requirements required by the Australian Design Rules (ADR). The Compliance Plate also contains the VIN and must never be removed from the vehicle.

Data Plate

The manufacturer's data plate is attached to the firewall in the engine compartment next to the Compliance Plate (see illustration). The Data Plate contains such information as the name of the manufacturer, the month and year of production, the trim and paint codes and the option codes. The trim, paint and option codes should be referred to when ordering spare parts.

Engine identification numbers - Petrol models

The engine identification number on R-series engines is stamped on a pad on the left side of the block (see illustration). On Y-series engines it's stamped on a pad on the right side of the block (see illustration). On the V6 engine, the ID number is found on the left side of the block, just above the oil filter (see illustration).

Engine identification numbers - Diesel models

The engine identification number is stamped on a pad on the right hand side of the cylinder block (L engines) or on the left side of the block (2L and 3L engines) (see illustrations).

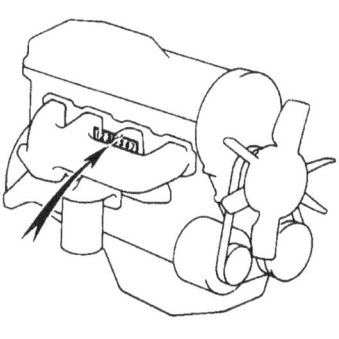

On L (2.2 litre) diesel engines, the engine identification number is stamped on a pad on the right side of the cylinder block, behind the exhaust manifold

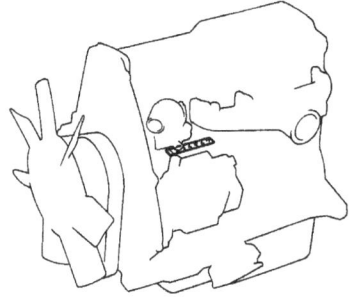

On 2L (2.4 litre) and 3L (2.8 litre) diesel engines, the engine identification number is stamped on a pad on the left side of the cylinder block, near the thermostat housing

Buying parts

Spare parts are available from many sources, which generally fall into one of two categories - authorized dealer parts departments and independent retail auto parts stores. Our advice concerning these parts is as follows:

Retail auto parts stores: Good auto parts stores will stock frequently needed components which wear out relatively fast, such as clutch components, exhaust systems, brake parts, tune-up parts, etc. These stores often supply new or reconditioned parts on an exchange basis, which can save a considerable amount of money. Discount auto parts stores are often very good places to buy materials and parts needed for general vehicle maintenance such as oil, grease, filters, spark plugs, belts, touch-up paint, bulbs, etc. They also usually sell tools and general accessories, have convenient hours, charge lower prices and can often be found not far from home.

Authorized dealer parts department: This is the best source for parts which are unique to the vehicle and not generally available elsewhere (such as major engine parts, transmission parts, trim pieces, etc.).

Warranty information: If the vehicle is still covered under warranty, be sure that any spare parts purchased - regardless of the source - do not invalidate the warranty!

To be sure of obtaining the correct parts, have engine and chassis numbers available and, if possible, take the old parts along for positive identification.

Maintenance techniques, tools and working facilities

Maintenance techniques

There are a number of techniques involved in maintenance and repair that will be referred to throughout this manual. Application of these techniques will enable the home mechanic to be more efficient, better organized and capable of performing the various tasks properly, which will ensure that the repair job is thorough and complete.

Fasteners

Fasteners are nuts, bolts, studs and screws used to hold two or more parts together. There are a few things to keep in mind when working with fasteners. Almost all of them use a locking device of some type, either a lockwasher, locknut, locking tab or thread adhesive. All threaded fasteners should be clean and straight, with undamaged threads and undamaged corners on the hex head where the spanner fits. Develop the habit of renewing all damaged nuts and bolts. Special locknuts with nylon or fiber inserts can only be used once. If they are removed, they lose their locking ability and must be renewed.

Rusted nuts and bolts should be treated with a penetrating fluid to ease removal and prevent breakage. Some mechanics use turpentine in a spout-type oil can, which works quite well. After applying the rust penetrant, let it work for a few minutes before trying to loosen the nut or bolt. Badly rusted fasteners may have to be chiseled or sawed off or removed with a special nut breaker, available at tool stores.

If a bolt or stud breaks off in an assembly, it can be drilled and removed with a special tool commonly available for this purpose. Most automotive machine shops can perform this task, as well as other repair procedures, such as the repair of threaded holes that have been stripped out.

Flat washers and lockwashers, when removed from an assembly, should always be refit exactly as removed. Renew any damaged washers. Never use a lockwasher on any soft metal surface (such as aluminium), thin sheet metal or plastic.

Fastener sizes

For a number of reasons, automobile manufacturers are making wider and wider use of metric fasteners. Therefore, it is important to be able to tell the difference between standard (sometimes called U.S. or SAE) and metric hardware, since they cannot be interchanged.

All bolts, whether standard or metric, are sized according to diameter, thread pitch and length. For example, a standard M12 - 1.75 x 25 metric bolt is 12 mm in diameter, has a thread pitch of 1.75 mm (the distance between threads) and is 25 mm long. The two bolts are nearly identical, and easily confused, but they are not interchangeable.

In addition to the differences in diameter, thread pitch and length, metric and standard bolts can also be distinguished by examining the bolt heads. To begin with, the distance across the flats on a standard bolt head is measured in inches, while the same dimension on a metric bolt is sized in millimeters (the same is true for nuts). As a result, a standard spanner should not be used on a metric bolt and a metric spanner should not be used on a standard bolt. Also, most standard bolts have slashes radiating out from the centre of the head to denote the grade or strength of the bolt, which is an indication of the amount of torque that can be applied to it. The

greater the number of slashes, the greater the strength of the bolt. Grades 0 through 5 are commonly used on automobiles. Metric bolts have a property class (grade) number, rather than a slash, molded into their heads to indicate bolt strength. In this case, the higher the number, the stronger the bolt. Property class numbers 8.8, 9.8 and 10.9 are commonly used on automobiles.

Strength markings can also be used to distinguish standard hex nuts from metric hex nuts. Many standard nuts have dots stamped into one side, while metric nuts are marked with a number. The greater the number of dots, or the higher the number, the greater the strength of the nut.

Metric studs are also marked on their ends according to property class (grade).

Larger studs are numbered (the same as metric bolts), while smaller studs carry a geometric code to denote grade.

It should be noted that many fasteners, especially Grades 0 through 2, have no distinguishing marks on them. When such is the case, the only way to determine whether it is standard or metric is to measure the thread pitch or compare it to a known fastener of the same size.

Standard fasteners are often referred to as SAE, as opposed to metric. However, it should be noted that SAE technically refers to a non-metric fine thread fastener only. Coarse thread non-metric fasteners are referred to as USS sizes.

Since fasteners of the same size (both standard and metric) may have different

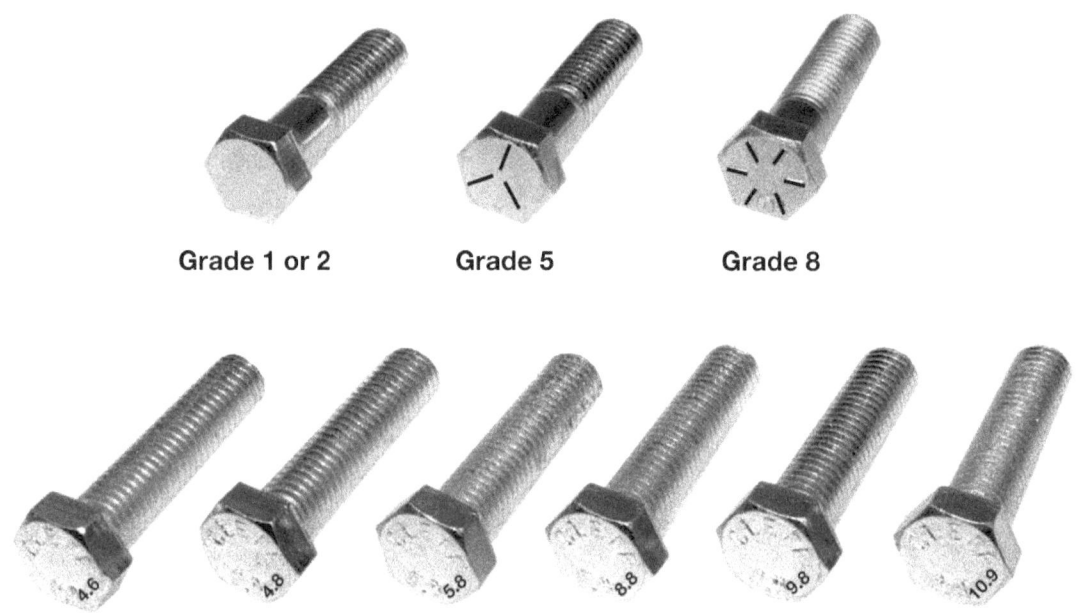

Grade 1 or 2   Grade 5   Grade 8

Bolt strength marking (standard/SAE/USS; bottom - metric)

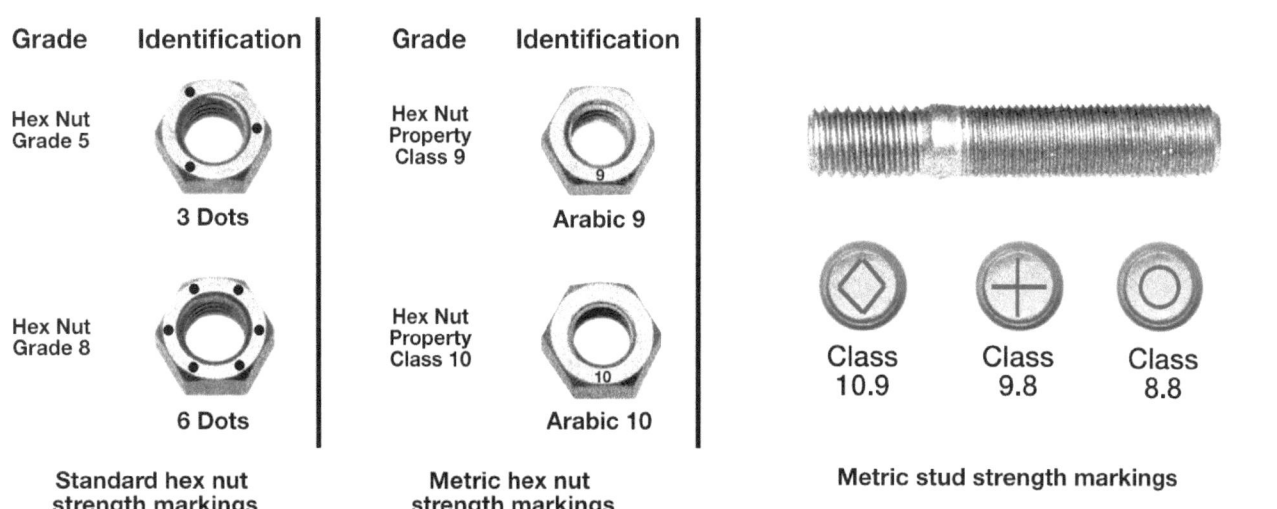

Grade	Identification
Hex Nut Grade 5	3 Dots
Hex Nut Grade 8	6 Dots

Standard hex nut strength markings

Grade	Identification
Hex Nut Property Class 9	Arabic 9
Hex Nut Property Class 10	Arabic 10

Metric hex nut strength markings

Class 10.9   Class 9.8   Class 8.8

Metric stud strength markings

strength ratings, be sure to refit any bolts, studs or nuts removed from your vehicle in their original locations. Also, when renewing a fastener, make sure that the new one has a strength rating equal to or greater than the original.

Tightening sequences and procedures

Most threaded fasteners should be tightened to a specific torque value (torque is the twisting force applied to a threaded component such as a nut or bolt). Overtightening the fastener can weaken it and cause it to break, while undertightening can cause it to eventually come loose. Bolts, screws and studs,

depending on the material they are made of and their thread diameters, have specific torque values, many of which are noted in the Specifications at the beginning of each Chapter. Be sure to follow the torque recommendations closely. For fasteners not assigned a specific torque, a general torque value chart is presented here as a guide. These torque values are for dry (unlubricated) fasteners threaded into steel or cast iron (not aluminium). As was previously mentioned, the size and grade of a fastener determine the amount of torque that can safely be applied to it. The figures listed here are approximate for Grade 2 and Grade 3 fasteners. Higher grades can

tolerate higher torque values.

Fasteners laid out in a pattern, such as cylinder head bolts, sump bolts, differential cover bolts, etc., must be loosened or tightened in sequence to avoid warping the component. This sequence will normally be shown in the appropriate Chapter. If a specific pattern is not given, the following procedures can be used to prevent warping.

Initially, the bolts or nuts should be assembled finger-tight only. Next, they should be tightened one full turn each, in a crisscross or diagonal pattern. After each one has been tightened one full turn, return to the first one and tighten them all one-half turn, follow-

Metric thread sizes	Nm	Ft-lbs
M-6	9 to 12	6 to 9
M-8	19 to 28	14 to 21
M-10	38 to 54	28 to 40
M-12	68 to 96	50 to 71
M-14	109 to 154	80 to 140
Pipe thread sizes		
1/8	7 to 10	5 to 8
1/4	17 to 24	12 to 18
3/8	30 to 44	22 to 33
1/2	34 to 47	25 to 35
U.S. thread sizes		
1/4 - 20	9 to 12	6 to 9
5/16 - 18	17 to 24	12 to 18
5/16 - 24	19 to 27	14 to 20
3/8 - 16	30 to 43	22 to 32
3/8 - 24	37 to 51	27 to 38
7/16 - 14	55 to 74	40 to 55
7/16 - 20	55 to 81	40 to 60
1/2 - 13	75 to 108	55 to 80

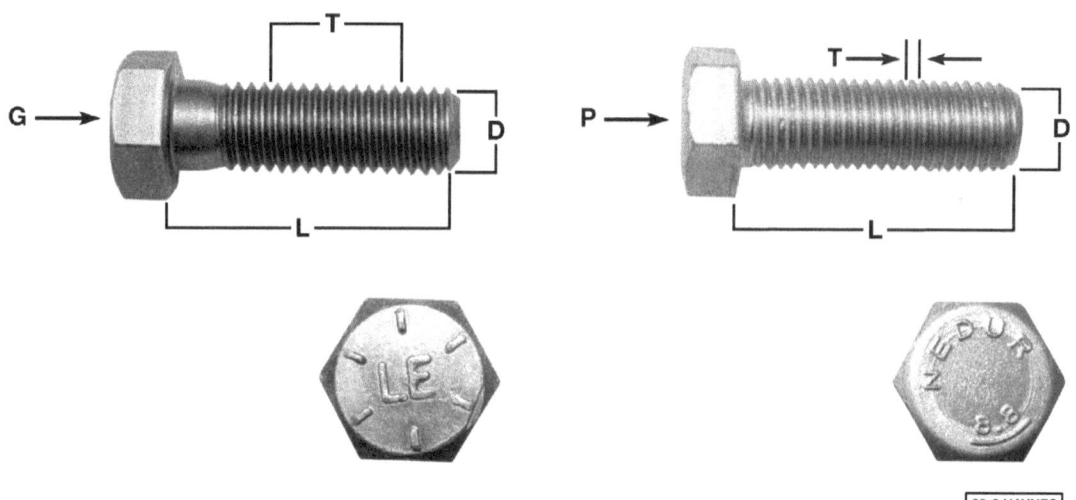

00-2 HAYNES

Standard (SAE and USS) bolt dimensions/grade marks

G   Grade marks (bolt strength)
L   Length (in inches)
T   Thread pitch (number of threads per inch)
D   Nominal diameter (in inches)

Metric bolt dimensions/grade marks

P   Property class (bolt strength)
L   Length (in millimeters)
T   Thread pitch (distance between threads in millimeters)
D   Diameter

ing the same pattern. Finally, tighten each of them one-quarter turn at a time until each fastener has been tightened to the proper torque. To loosen and remove the fasteners, the procedure would be reversed.

Component disassembly

Component disassembly should be done with care and purpose to help ensure that the parts go back together properly. Always keep track of the sequence in which parts are removed. Make note of special characteristics or marks on parts that can be refitted more than one way, such as a grooved thrust washer on a shaft. It is a good idea to lay the disassembled parts out on a clean surface in the order that they were removed. It may also be helpful to make sketches or take instant photos of components before removal.

When removing fasteners from a component, keep track of their locations. Sometimes threading a bolt back in a part, or putting the washers and nut back on a stud, can prevent mix-ups later. If nuts and bolts cannot be returned to their original locations, they should be kept in a compartmented box or a series of small boxes. A cupcake or muffin tin is ideal for this purpose, since each cavity can hold the bolts and nuts from a particular area (i.e. sump bolts, valve cover bolts, engine mount bolts, etc.). A pan of this type is especially helpful when working on assemblies with very small parts, such as the carburettor, alternator, valve train or interior dash and trim pieces. The cavities can be marked with paint or tape to identify the contents.

Whenever wiring looms, harnesses or connectors are separated, it is a good idea to identify the two halves with numbered pieces of masking tape so they can be easily reconnected.

Gasket sealing surfaces

Throughout any vehicle, gaskets are used to seal the mating surfaces between two parts and keep lubricants, fluids, vacuum or pressure contained in an assembly.

Many times these gaskets are coated with a liquid or paste-type gasket sealing compound before assembly. Age, heat and

pressure can sometimes cause the two parts to stick together so tightly that they are very difficult to separate. Often, the assembly can be loosened by striking it with a soft-face hammer near the mating surfaces. A regular hammer can be used if a block of wood is placed between the hammer and the part. Do not hammer on cast parts or parts that could be easily damaged. With any particularly stubborn part, always recheck to make sure that every fastener has been removed.

Avoid using a screwdriver or bar to prise apart an assembly, as they can easily mar the gasket sealing surfaces of the parts, which must remain smooth. If levering is absolutely necessary, use an old broom handle, but keep in mind that extra clean up will be necessary if the wood splinters.

After the parts are separated, the old gasket must be carefully scraped off and the gasket surfaces cleaned. Stubborn gasket material can be soaked with rust penetrant or treated with a special chemical to soften it so it can be easily scraped off. A scraper can be fashioned from a piece of copper tubing by flattening and sharpening one end. Copper is recommended because it is usually softer than the surfaces to be scraped, which reduces the chance of gouging the part. Some gaskets can be removed with a wire brush, but regardless of the method used, the mating surfaces must be left clean and smooth. If for some reason the gasket surface is gouged, then a gasket sealer thick enough to fill scratches will have to be used during reassembly of the components. For most applications, a non-drying (or semi-drying) gasket sealer should be used.

Hose removal tips

Warning: *If the vehicle is equipped with air conditioning, do not disconnect any of the A/C hoses without first having the system depressurized by a dealer service department or a service station.* .

Hose removal precautions closely parallel gasket removal precautions. Avoid scratching or gouging the surface that the hose mates against or the connection may leak. This is especially true for radiator hoses.

Because of various chemical reactions, the rubber in hoses can bond itself to the metal spigot that the hose fits over. To remove a hose, first loosen the hose clamps that secure it to the spigot. Then, with slip-joint pliers, grab the hose at the clamp and rotate it around the spigot. Work it back and forth until it is completely free, then pull it off. Silicone or other lubricants will ease removal if they can be applied between the hose and the outside of the spigot. Apply the same lubricant to the inside of the hose and the outside of the spigot to simplify refitting.

As a last resort (and if the hose is to be renewed anyway), the rubber can be slit with a knife and the hose peeled from the spigot. If this must be done, be careful that the metal connection is not damaged.

If a hose clamp is broken or damaged, do not reuse it. Wire-type clamps usually weaken with age, so it is a good idea to renew them with screw-type clamps whenever a hose is removed.

Tools

A selection of good tools is a basic requirement for anyone who plans to maintain and repair his or her own vehicle. For the owner who has few tools, the initial investment might seem high, but when compared to the spiraling costs of professional auto maintenance and repair, it is a wise one.

To help the owner decide which tools are needed to perform the tasks detailed in this manual, the following tool lists are offered: *Maintenance and minor repair, Repair/overhaul* and *Special*.

The newcomer to practical mechanics should start off with the *maintenance and minor repair* tool kit, which is adequate for the simpler jobs performed on a vehicle. Then, as confidence and experience grow, the owner can tackle more difficult tasks, buying additional tools as they are needed. Eventually the basic kit will be expanded into the *repair and overhaul* tool set. Over a period of time, the experienced do-it-yourselfer will assemble a tool set complete enough for most repair and overhaul procedures and will add tools

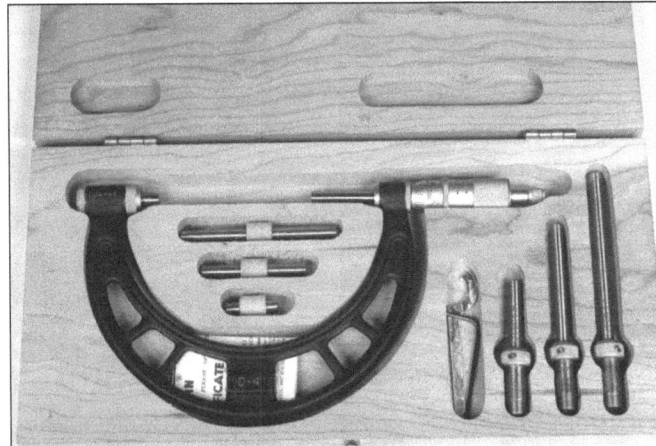

Micrometer set

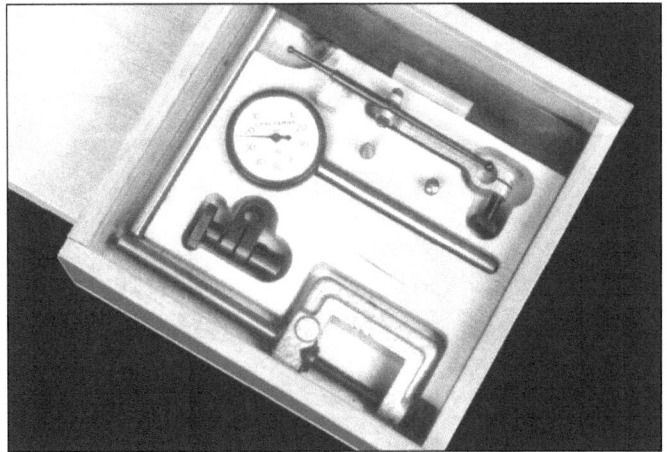

Dial indicator set

Dial caliper

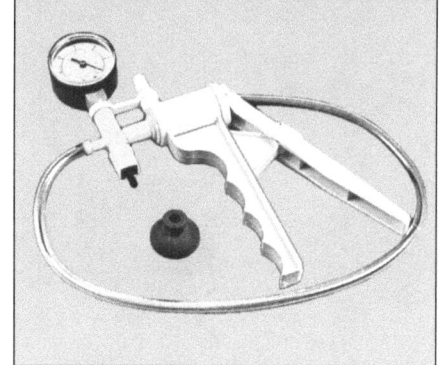

Hand-operated vacuum pump

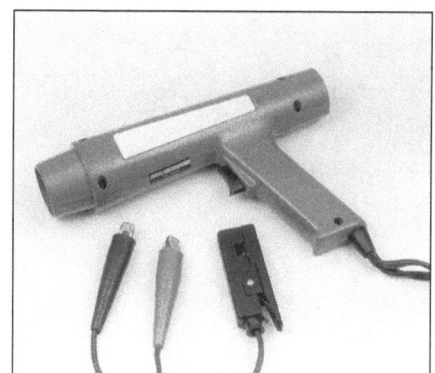

Timing light

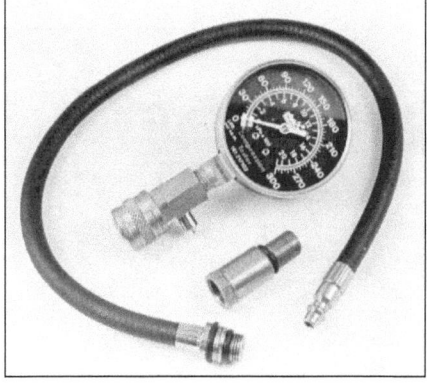

Compression gauge with adapter

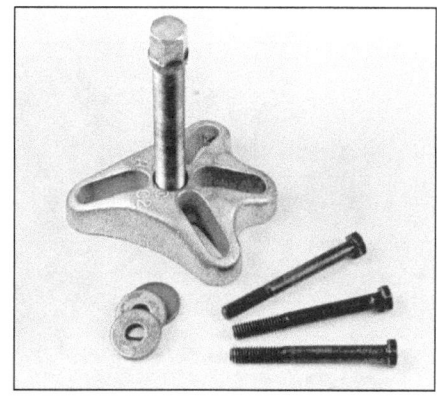

Damper/steering wheel puller

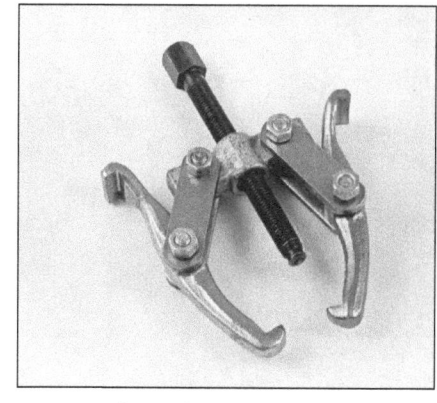

General purpose puller

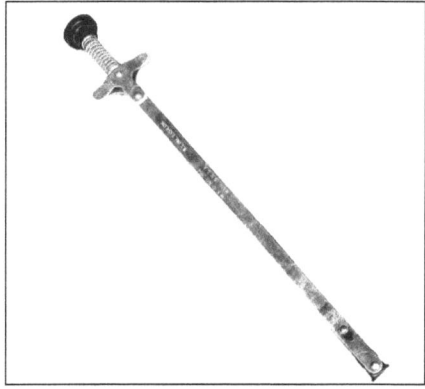

Hydraulic lifter removal tool

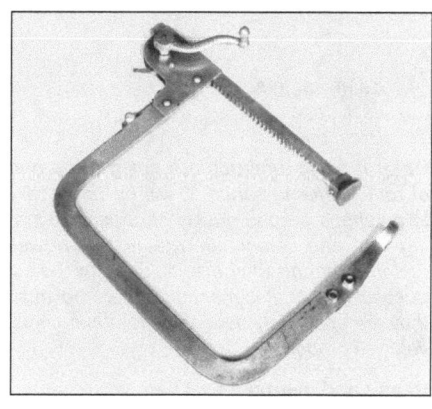

Valve spring compressor

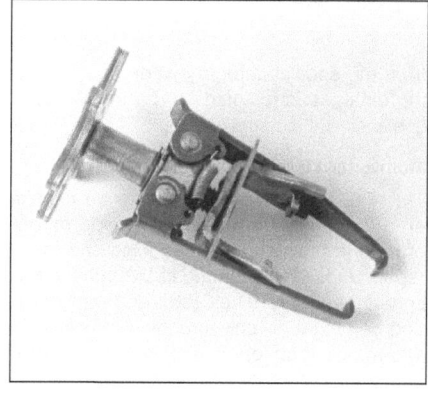

Valve spring compressor

Ridge reamer

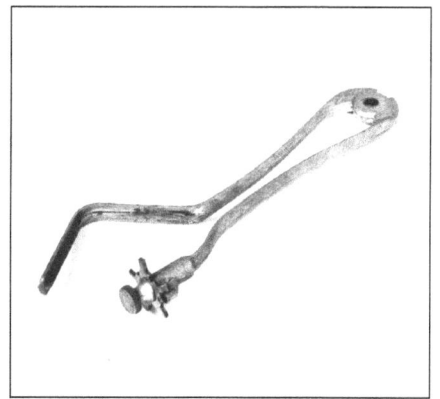

Piston ring groove cleaning tool

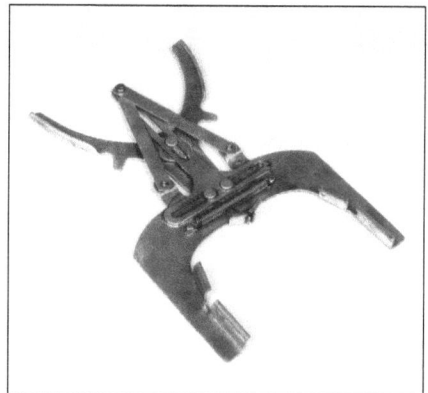

Ring removal/refitting tool

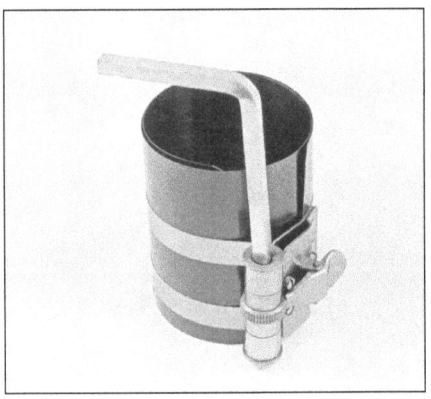

Ring compressor

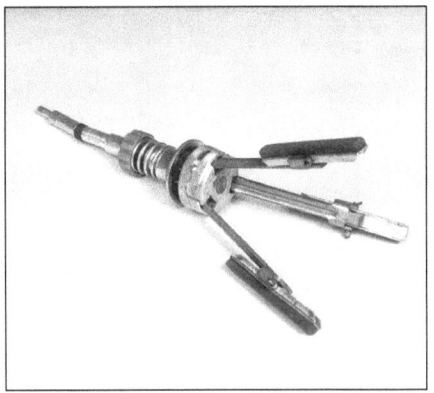

Cylinder hone

Brake hold-down spring tool

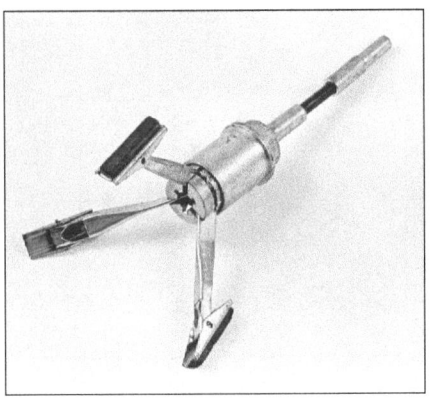

Brake cylinder hone

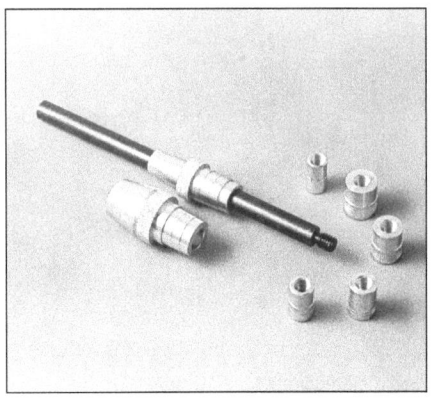

Clutch plate alignment tool

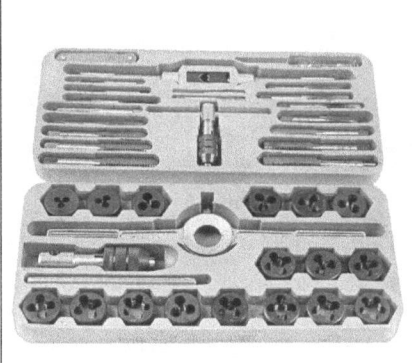

Tap and die set

from the special category when it is felt that the expense is justified by the frequency of use.

Maintenance and minor repair tool kit

The tools in this list should be considered the minimum required for performance of routine maintenance, servicing and minor repair work. We recommend the purchase of combination wrenches (box-end and open-end combined in one spanner). While more expensive than open end wrenches, they offer the advantages of both types of spanner.

> Combination spanner set (6 mm to 19 mm)
> Adjustable spanner
> Spark plug wrench with rubber insert
> Spark plug gap adjusting tool
> Feeler gauge set
> Brake bleeder wrench
> Standard screwdriver
> Phillips screwdriver
> Combination pliers
> Hacksaw and assortment of blades
> Tyre pressure gauge
> Grease gun
> Oil can
> Fine emery cloth
> Wire brush
> Battery post and cable cleaning tool
> Oil filter wrench
> Funnel (medium size)

> Safety goggles
> Jackstands (2)
> Drain pan

Note: *If basic tune-ups are going to be part of routine maintenance, it will be necessary to purchase a good quality stroboscopic timing light and combination tachometer/dwell meter. Although they are included in the list of special tools, it is mentioned here because they are absolutely necessary for tuning most vehicles properly.*

Repair and overhaul tool set

These tools are essential for anyone who plans to perform major repairs and are in addition to those in the maintenance and minor repair tool kit. Included is a comprehensive set of sockets which, though expensive, are invaluable because of their versatility, especially when various extensions and drives are available. We recommend the 1/2-inch drive over the 3/8-inch drive. Although the larger drive is bulky and more expensive, it has the capacity of accepting a very wide range of large sockets. Ideally, however, the mechanic should have a 3/8-inch drive set and a 1/2-inch drive set.

> Socket set(s)
> Reversible ratchet
> Extension
> Universal joint
> Torque wrench (same size drive as

> sockets)
> Ball peen hammer
> Soft-face hammer (plastic/rubber)
> Standard screwdriver
> Standard screwdriver (stubby)
> Phillips screwdriver
> Phillips screwdriver (stubby - No. 2)
> Pliers - vise grip
> Pliers - lineman's
> Pliers - needle nose
> Pliers - snap-ring (internal and external)
> Cold chisel
> Scribe
> Scraper (made from flattened copper tubing)
> Centrepunch
> Pin punches
> Steel rule/straightedge
> Allen wrench set (4 mm to 10 mm)
> A selection of files
> Wire brush (large)
> Jackstands (second set)
> Jack (scissor or hydraulic type)

Note: *Another tool which is often useful is an electric drill with a chuck capacity of 10 mm and a set of good quality drill bits.*

Special tools

The tools in this list include those which are not used regularly, are expensive to buy, or which need to be used in accordance with their manufacturer's instructions.

Unless these tools will be used frequently, it is not very economical to purchase many of them. A consideration would be to split the cost and use between yourself and a friend or friends. In addition, most of these tools can be obtained from a tool rental shop on a temporary basis.

This list primarily contains only those tools and instruments widely available to the public, and not those special tools produced by the vehicle manufacturer for distribution to dealer service departments. Occasionally, references to the manufacturer's special tools are included in the text of this manual. Generally, an alternative method of doing the job without the special tool is offered. However, sometimes there is no alternative to their use. Where this is the case, and the tool cannot be purchased or borrowed, the work should be turned over to the dealer service department or an automotive repair shop.

> *Valve spring compressor*
> *Piston ring groove cleaning tool*
> *Piston ring compressor*
> *Piston ring refitting tool*
> *Cylinder compression gauge*
> *Cylinder ridge reamer*
> *Cylinder surfacing hone*
> *Cylinder bore gauge*
> *Micrometers and/or dial calipers*
> *Hydraulic lifter removal tool*
> *Balljoint separator*
> *Universal-type puller*
> *Impact screwdriver*
> *Dial indicator set*
> *Stroboscopic timing light (inductive pick-up)*
> *Hand operated vacuum/pressure pump*
> *Tachometer/dwell meter*
> *Universal electrical multimeter*
> *Cable hoist*
> *Brake spring removal and refitting tools*
> *Floor jack*

Buying tools

For the do-it-yourselfer who is just starting to get involved in vehicle maintenance and repair, there are a number of options available when purchasing tools. If maintenance and minor repair is the extent of the work to be done, the purchase of individual tools is satisfactory. If, on the other hand, extensive work is planned, it would be a good idea to purchase a modest tool set from one of the large retail chain stores. A set can usually be bought at a substantial savings over the individual tool prices, and they often come with a tool box. As additional tools are needed, add-on sets, individual tools and a larger tool box can be purchased to expand the tool selection. Building a tool set gradually allows the cost of the tools to be spread over a longer period of time and gives the mechanic the freedom to choose only those tools that will

actually be used.

Tool stores will often be the only source of some of the special tools that are needed, but regardless of where tools are bought, try to avoid cheap ones, especially when buying screwdrivers and sockets, because they won't last very long. The expense involved in renewing cheap tools will eventually be greater than the initial cost of quality tools.

Care and maintenance of tools

Good tools are expensive, so it makes sense to treat them with respect. Keep them clean and in usable condition and store them properly when not in use. Always wipe off any dirt, grease or metal chips before putting them away. Never leave tools lying around in the work area. Upon completion of a job, always check closely under the bonnet for tools that may have been left there so they won't get lost during a test drive.

Some tools, such as screwdrivers, pliers, wrenches and sockets, can be hung on a panel mounted on the garage or workshop wall, while others should be kept in a tool box or tray. Measuring instruments, gauges, meters, etc. must be carefully stored where they cannot be damaged by weather or impact from other tools.

When tools are used with care and stored properly, they will last a very long time. Even with the best of care, though, tools will wear out if used frequently. When a tool is damaged or worn out, renew it. Subsequent jobs will be safer and more enjoyable if you do.

How to repair damaged threads

Sometimes, the internal threads of a nut or bolt hole can become stripped, usually from overtightening. Stripping threads is an all-too-common occurrence, especially when working with aluminium parts, because aluminium is so soft that it easily strips out.

Usually, external or internal threads are only partially stripped. After they've been cleaned up with a tap or die, they'll still work. Sometimes, however, threads are badly damaged. When this happens, you've got three choices:

1) *Drill and tap the hole to the next suitable oversize and fit a larger diameter bolt, screw or stud.*
2) *Drill and tap the hole to accept a threaded plug, then drill and tap the plug to the original screw size. You can also buy a plug already threaded to the original size. Then you simply drill a hole to the specified size, then run the threaded plug into the hole with a bolt and jam nut. Once the plug is fully seated, remove the jam nut and bolt.*

3) *The third method uses a patented thread repair kit like Heli-Coil or Slimsert. These easy-to-use kits are designed to repair damaged threads in straight-through holes and blind holes. Both are available as kits which can handle a variety of sizes and thread patterns. Drill the hole, then tap it with the special included tap. refit the Heli-Coil and the hole is back to its original diameter and thread pitch.*

Regardless of which method you use, be sure to proceed calmly and carefully. A little impatience or carelessness during one of these relatively simple procedures can ruin your whole day's work and cost you a bundle if you wreck an expensive part.

Working facilities

Not to be overlooked when discussing tools is the workshop. If anything more than routine maintenance is to be carried out, some sort of suitable work area is essential.

It is understood, and appreciated, that many home mechanics do not have a good workshop or garage available, and end up removing an engine or doing major repairs outside. It is recommended, however, that the overhaul or repair be completed under the cover of a roof.

A clean, flat workbench or table of comfortable working height is an absolute necessity. The workbench should be equipped with a vise that has a jaw opening of at least 100 mm.

As mentioned previously, some clean, dry storage space is also required for tools, as well as the lubricants, fluids, cleaning solvents, etc. which soon become necessary.

Sometimes waste oil and fluids, drained from the engine or cooling system during normal maintenance or repairs, present a disposal problem. To avoid pouring them on the ground or into a sewage system, pour the used fluids into large containers, seal them with caps and take them to an authorized disposal site or recycling centre. Plastic jugs, such as old antifreeze containers, are ideal for this purpose.

Always keep a supply of old newspapers and clean rags available. Old towels are excellent for mopping up spills. Many mechanics use rolls of paper towels for most work because they are readily available and disposable. To help keep the area under the vehicle clean, a large cardboard box can be cut open and flattened to protect the garage or shop floor.

Whenever working over a painted surface, such as when leaning over a fender to service something under the bonnet, always cover it with an old blanket or bedspread to protect the finish. Vinyl covered pads, made especially for this purpose, are available at auto parts stores.

Jacking and towing

Jacking

The jack supplied with the vehicle should only be used for raising the vehicle for changing a tyre or placing jackstands under the frame. **Warning:** *Never crawl under the vehicle or start the engine when the jack is being used as the only means of support.*

All vehicles are supplied with a jack. It should be placed under the rear axle for raising the rear of the vehicle and under the front siderail (2WD and 4WD with independent front suspension) or front axle housing (4WD with a solid front axle) for raising the front of the vehicle **(see illustrations)**.

The vehicle should be on level ground with the wheels blocked and the transmission in Park (automatic) or Reverse (manual). On 4WD vehicles, the transfer case should be in the Neutral position. Prise off the hub cap (if equipped) using the tapered end of the lug wrench. Loosen the lug nuts one half turn and leave them in place until the wheel is raised off the ground.

Place the jack under the side of the vehicle in the indicated position. Use the supplied spanner to turn the jackscrew clockwise until

the wheel is raised off the ground. Remove the lug nuts, pull off the wheel and renew it with the spare.

With the beveled side in, replace the lug nuts and tighten them until snug. Lower the vehicle by turning the jackscrew counterclockwise. Remove the jack and tighten the nuts in a diagonal pattern. refit the hubcap by placing it in position and using the heel of your hand or a rubber mallet to seat it.

Towing

The vehicle can be towed with all four wheels on the ground, provided speeds do not exceed 55 kph and the distance is not over 80 kilometers, otherwise transmission damage can result.

Towing equipment specifically designed for this purpose should be used and should be attached to the main structural members of the vehicle, not the bumper or brackets **(see illustrations)**.

Safety is a major consideration when towing and all applicable state and local laws must be obeyed. A safety chain system must be used for all towing.

While towing, the parking brake should be released and the transmission and transfer case should be in Neutral. The steering must be unlocked (ignition switch in the Off position). Remember that power steering and power brakes will not work with the engine off.

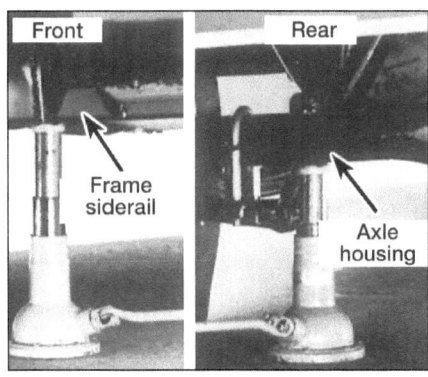

Recommended 2WD (and 4WD with independent front suspension) jacking locations

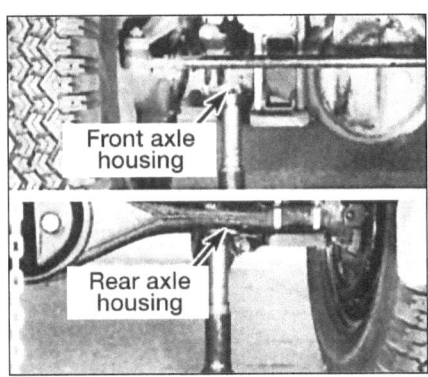

Recommended jacking locations - 4WD with solid front axle

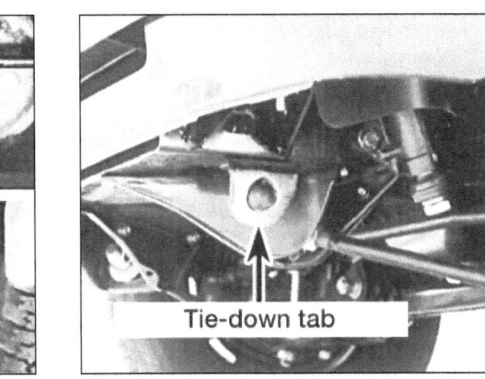

2WD vehicles have towing/tie-down tabs attached to the frame

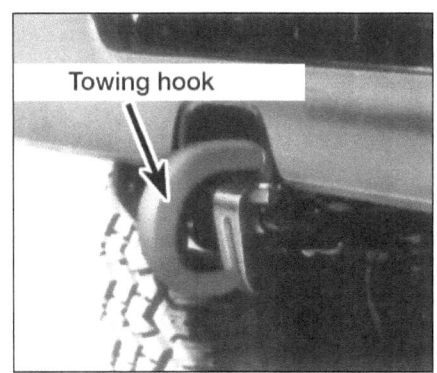

4WD vehicles are equipped with heavy-duty tow hooks

Booster battery (jump) starting

Observe these precautions when using a booster battery to start a vehicle:

a) Before connecting the booster battery, make sure the ignition switch is in the Off position.

b) Turn off the lights, heater and other electrical loads.

c) Your eyes should be shielded. Safety goggles are a good idea.

d) Make sure the booster battery is the same voltage as the dead one in the vehicle.

e) The two vehicles MUST NOT TOUCH each other!

f) Make sure the transaxle is in Neutral (manual) or Park (automatic).

g) If the booster battery is not a maintenance-free type, remove the vent caps and lay a cloth over the vent holes.

Connect the red jumper cable to the positive (+) terminals of each battery **(see illustration)**.

Connect one end of the black jumper cable to the negative (-) terminal of the booster battery. The other end of this cable should be connected to a good earth on the vehicle to be started, such as a bolt or bracket on the body.

Start the engine using the booster battery, then, with the engine running at idle speed, disconnect the jumper cables in the reverse order of connection.

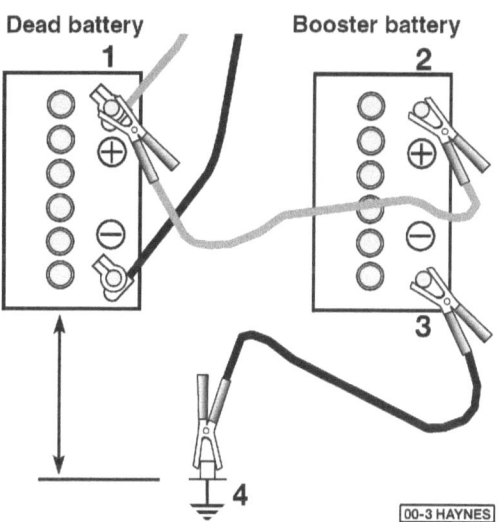

Make the booster battery cable connections in the numerical order shown (note that the negative cable of the booster battery is NOT attached to the negative terminal of the dead battery)

Automotive chemicals and lubricants

A number of automotive chemicals and lubricants are available for use during vehicle maintenance and repair. They include a wide variety of products ranging from cleaning solvents and degreasers to lubricants and protective sprays for rubber, plastic and vinyl.

Cleaners

Carburettor cleaner and choke cleaner is a strong solvent for gum, varnish and carbon. Most carburettor cleaners leave a dry-type lubricant film which will not harden or gum up. Because of this film it is not recommended for use on electrical components.

Brake system cleaner is used to remove grease and brake fluid from the brake system, where clean surfaces are absolutely necessary. It leaves no residue and often eliminates brake squeal caused by contaminants.

Electrical cleaner removes oxidation, corrosion and carbon deposits from electrical contacts, restoring full current flow. It can also be used to clean spark plugs, carburettor jets, voltage regulators and other parts where an oil-free surface is desired.

Demoisturants remove water and moisture from electrical components such as alternators, voltage regulators, electrical connectors and fuse blocks. They are non-conductive, non-corrosive and non-flammable.

Degreasers are heavy-duty solvents used to remove grease from the outside of the engine and from chassis components. They can be sprayed or brushed on and, depending on the type, are rinsed off either with water or solvent.

Lubricants

Motor oil is the lubricant formulated for use in engines. It normally contains a wide variety of additives to prevent corrosion and reduce foaming and wear. Motor oil comes in various weights (viscosity ratings) from 5 to 80. The recommended weight of the oil depends on the season, temperature and the demands on the engine. Light oil is used in cold climates and under light load conditions. Heavy oil is used in hot climates and where high loads are encountered. Multi-viscosity oils are designed to have characteristics of both light and heavy oils and are available in a number of weights from 5W-20 to 20W-50.

Gear oil is designed to be used in differentials, manual transmissions and other areas where high-temperature lubrication is required.

Chassis and wheel bearing grease is a heavy grease used where increased loads and friction are encountered, such as for wheel bearings, balljoints, tie-rod ends and universal joints.

High-temperature wheel bearing grease is designed to withstand the extreme temperatures encountered by wheel bearings in disc brake equipped vehicles. It usually contains molybdenum disulfide (moly), which is a dry-type lubricant.

White grease is a heavy grease for metal-to-metal applications where water is a problem. White grease stays soft under both low and high temperatures (usually from -56 to +106-degrees C), and will not wash off or dilute in the presence of water.

Assembly lube is a special extreme pressure lubricant, usually containing moly, used to lubricate high-load parts (such as main and rod bearings and cam lobes) for initial start-up of a new engine. The assembly lube lubricates the parts without being squeezed out or washed away until the engine oiling system begins to function.

Silicone lubricants are used to protect rubber, plastic, vinyl and nylon parts.

Graphite lubricants are used where oils cannot be used due to contamination problems, such as in locks. The dry graphite will lubricate metal parts while remaining uncontaminated by dirt, water, oil or acids. It is electrically conductive and will not foul electrical contacts in locks such as the ignition switch.

Moly penetrants loosen and lubricate seized, rusted and corroded fasteners and prevent future rusting or freezing.

Heat-sink grease is a special electrically non-conductive grease that is used for mounting electronic ignition modules where it is essential that heat is transferred away from the module.

Sealants

RTV sealant is one of the most widely used gasket compounds. Made from silicone, RTV is air curing, it seals, bonds, waterproofs, fills surface irregularities, remains flexible, doesn't shrink, is relatively easy to remove, and is used as a supplementary sealer with almost all low and medium temperature gaskets.

Anaerobic sealant is much like RTV in that it can be used either to seal gaskets or to form gaskets by itself. It remains flexible, is solvent resistant and fills surface imperfections. The difference between an anaerobic sealant and an RTV-type sealant is in the curing. RTV cures when exposed to air, while an anaerobic sealant cures only in the absence of air. This means that an anaerobic sealant cures only after the assembly of parts, sealing them together.

Thread and pipe sealant is used for sealing hydraulic and pneumatic fittings and vacuum lines. It is usually made from a Teflon compound, and comes in a spray, a paint-on liquid and as a wrap-around tape.

Chemicals

Anti-seize compound prevents seizing, galling, cold welding, rust and corrosion in fasteners. High-temperature ant-seize, usually made with copper and graphite lubricants, is used for exhaust system and exhaust manifold bolts.

Anaerobic locking compounds are used to keep fasteners from vibrating or working loose and cure only after refitting, in the absence of air. Medium strength locking compound is used for small nuts, bolts and screws that may be removed later. High-strength locking compound is for large nuts, bolts and studs which aren't removed on a regular basis.

Oil additives range from viscosity index improvers to chemical treatments that claim to reduce internal engine friction. It should be noted that most oil manufacturers caution against using additives with their oils.

Fuel additives perform several functions, depending on their chemical makeup. They usually contain solvents that help dissolve gum and varnish that build up on carburettor, fuel injection and intake parts. They also serve to break down carbon deposits that form on the inside surfaces of the combustion chambers. Some additives contain upper cylinder lubricants for valves and piston rings, and others contain chemicals to remove condensation from the fuel tank.

Miscellaneous

Brake fluid is specially formulated hydraulic fluid that can withstand the heat and pressure encountered in brake systems. Care must be taken so this fluid does not come in contact with painted surfaces or plastics. An opened container should always be resealed to prevent contamination by water or dirt.

Weatherstrip adhesive is used to bond weatherstripping around doors, windows and luggage compartment lids. It is sometimes used to attach trim pieces.

Undercoating is a petroleum-based, tar-like substance that is designed to protect metal surfaces on the underside of the vehicle from corrosion. It also acts as a sound-deadening agent by insulating the bottom of the vehicle.

Waxes and polishes are used to help protect painted and plated surfaces from the weather. Different types of paint may require the use of different types of wax and polish. Some polishes utilize a chemical or abrasive cleaner to help remove the top layer of oxidized (dull) paint on older vehicles. In recent years many non-wax polishes that contain a wide variety of chemicals such as polymers and silicones have been introduced. These non-wax polishes are usually easier to apply and last longer than conventional waxes and polishes.

Conversion factors

Length (distance)

Inches (in)	X 25.4	= Millimetres (mm)	X 0.0394	= Inches (in)
Feet (ft)	X 0.305	= Metres (m)	X 3.281	= Feet (ft)
Miles	X 1.609	= Kilometres (km)	X 0.621	= Miles

Volume (capacity)

Cubic inches (cu in; in^3)	X 16.387	= Cubic centimetres (cc; cm^3)	X 0.061	= Cubic inches (cu in; in^3)
Imperial pints (Imp pt)	X 0.568	= Litres (l)	X 1.76	= Imperial pints (Imp pt)
Imperial quarts (Imp qt)	X 1.137	= Litres (l)	X 0.88	= Imperial quarts (Imp qt)
Imperial quarts (Imp qt)	X 1.201	= US quarts (US qt)	X 0.833	= Imperial quarts (Imp qt)
US quarts (US qt)	X 0.946	= Litres (l)	X 1.057	= US quarts (US qt)
Imperial gallons (Imp gal)	X 4.546	= Litres (l)	X 0.22	= Imperial gallons (Imp gal)
Imperial gallons (Imp gal)	X 1.201	= US gallons (US gal)	X 0.833	= Imperial gallons (Imp gal)
US gallons (US gal)	X 3.785	= Litres (l)	X 0.264	= US gallons (US gal)

Mass (weight)

Ounces (oz)	X 28.35	= Grams (g)	X 0.035	= Ounces (oz)
Pounds (lb)	X 0.454	= Kilograms (kg)	X 2.205	= Pounds (lb)

Force

Ounces-force (ozf; oz)	X 0.278	= Newtons (N)	X 3.6	= Ounces-force (ozf; oz)
Pounds-force (lbf; lb)	X 4.448	= Newtons (N)	X 0.225	= Pounds-force (lbf; lb)
Newtons (N)	X 0.1	= Kilograms-force (kgf; kg)	X 9.81	= Newtons (N)

Pressure

Pounds-force per square inch (psi; lbf/in^2; lb/in^2)	X 0.070	= Kilograms-force per square centimetre (kgf/cm^2; kg/cm^2)	X 14.223	= Pounds-force per square inch (psi; lbf/in^2; lb/in^2)
Pounds-force per square inch (psi; lbf/in^2; lb/in^2)	X 0.068	= Atmospheres (atm)	X 14.696	= Pounds-force per square inch (psi; lbf/in^2; lb/in^2)
Pounds-force per square inch (psi; lbf/in^2; lb/in^2)	X 0.069	= Bars	X 14.5	= Pounds-force per square inch (psi; lbf/in^2; lb/in^2)
Pounds-force per square inch (psi; lbf/in^2; lb/in^2)	X 6.895	= Kilopascals (kPa)	X 0.145	= Pounds-force per square inch (psi; lbf/in^2; lb/in^2)
Kilopascals (kPa)	X 0.01	= Kilograms-force per square centimetre (kgf/cm^2; kg/cm^2)	X 98.1	= Kilopascals (kPa)

Torque (moment of force)

Pounds-force inches (lbf in; lb in)	X 1.152	= Kilograms-force centimetre (kgf cm, kg cm)	X 0.868	= Pounds-force inches (lbf in; lb in)
Pounds-force inches (lbf in; lb in)	X 0.113	= Newton metres (Nm)	X 8.85	= Pounds-force inches (lbf in; lb in)
Pounds-force inches (lbf in; lb in)	X 0.083	= Pounds-force feet (lbf ft; lb ft)	X 12	= Pounds-force inches (lbf in; lb in)
Pounds-force feet (lbf ft; lb ft)	X 0.138	= Kilograms-force metres (kgf m; kg m)	X 7.233	= Pounds-force feet (lbf ft; lb ft)
Pounds-force feet (lbf ft; lb ft)	X 1.356	= Newton metres (Nm)	X 0.738	= Pounds-force feet (lbf ft; lb ft)
Newton metres (Nm)	X 0.102	= Kilograms-force metres (kgf m; kg m)	X 9.804	= Newton metres (Nm)

Vacuum

Inches mercury (in. Hg)	X 3.377	= Kilopascals (kPa)	X 0.2961	= Inches mercury
Inches mercury (in. Hg)	X 25.4	= Millimeters mercury (mm Hg)	X 0.0394	= Inches mercury

Power

Horsepower (hp)	X 745.7	= Watts (W)	X 0.0013	= Horsepower (hp)

Velocity (speed)

Miles per hour (miles/hr; mph)	X 1.609	= Kilometres per hour (km/hr; kph)	X 0.621	= Miles per hour (miles/hr; mph)

Fuel consumption*

Miles per gallon, Imperial (mpg)	X 0.354	= Kilometres per litre (km/l)	X 2.825	= Miles per gallon, Imperial (mpg)
Miles per gallon, US (mpg)	X 0.425	= Kilometres per litre (km/l)	X 2.352	= Miles per gallon, US (mpg)

Temperature

Degrees Fahrenheit = (°C x 1.8) + 32   Degrees Celsius (Degrees Centigrade; °C) = (°F - 32) x 0.56

It is common practice to convert from miles per gallon (mpg) to litres/100 kilometres (l/100km), where mpg (Imperial) x l/100 km = 282 and mpg (US) x l/100 km = 235

Safety first!

Regardless of how enthusiastic you may be about getting on with the job at hand, take the time to ensure that your safety is not jeopardized. A moment's lack of attention can result in an accident, as can failure to observe certain simple safety precautions. The possibility of an accident will always exist, and the following points should not be considered a comprehensive list of all dangers. Rather, they are intended to make you aware of the risks and to encourage a safety conscious approach to all work you carry out on your vehicle.

Essential DOs and DON'Ts

DON'T rely on a jack when working under the vehicle. Always use approved jackstands to support the weight of the vehicle and place them under the recommended lift or support points.

DON'T attempt to loosen extremely tight fasteners (i.e. wheel lug nuts) while the vehicle is on a jack - it may fall.

DON'T start the engine without first making sure that the transmission is in Neutral (or Park where applicable) and the parking brake is set.

DON'T remove the radiator cap from a hot cooling system - let it cool or cover it with a cloth and release the pressure gradually.

DON'T attempt to drain the engine oil until you are sure it has cooled to the point that it will not burn you.

DON'T touch any part of the engine or exhaust system until it has cooled sufficiently to avoid burns.

DON'T siphon toxic liquids such as petrol, antifreeze and brake fluid by mouth, or allow them to remain on your skin.

DON'T inhale brake lining dust - it is potentially hazardous (see *Asbestos* below).

DON'T allow spilled oil or grease to remain on the floor - wipe it up before someone slips on it.

DON'T use loose fitting wrenches or other tools which may slip and cause injury.

DON'T push on wrenches when loosening or tightening nuts or bolts. Always try to pull the spanner toward you. If the situation calls for pushing the spanner away, push with an open hand to avoid scraped knuckles if the spanner should slip.

DON'T attempt to lift a heavy component alone - get someone to help you.

DON'T rush or take unsafe shortcuts to finish a job.

DON'T allow children or animals in or around the vehicle while you are working on it.

DO wear eye protection when using power tools such as a drill, sander, bench grinder, etc. and when working under a vehicle.

DO keep loose clothing and long hair well out of the way of moving parts.

DO make sure that any hoist used has a safe working load rating adequate for the job.

DO get someone to check on you periodically when working alone on a vehicle.

DO carry out work in a logical sequence and make sure that everything is correctly assembled and tightened.

DO keep chemicals and fluids tightly capped and out of the reach of children and pets.

DO remember that your vehicle's safety affects that of yourself and others. If in doubt on any point, get professional advice.

Asbestos

Certain friction, insulating, sealing, and other products - such as brake linings, brake bands, clutch linings, torque converters, gaskets, etc. - may contain asbestos. Extreme care must be taken to avoid inhalation of dust from such products, since it is hazardous to health. If in doubt, assume that they do contain asbestos.

Fire

Remember at all times that petrol is highly flammable. Never smoke or have any kind of open flame around when working on a vehicle. But the risk does not end there. A spark caused by an electrical short circuit, by two metal surfaces contacting each other, or even by static electricity built up in your body under certain conditions, can ignite petrol vapours, which in a confined space are highly explosive. Do not, under any circumstances, use petrol for cleaning parts. Use an approved safety solvent.

Always disconnect the battery earth (-) cable at the battery before working on any part of the fuel system or electrical system. Never risk spilling fuel on a hot engine or exhaust component. It is strongly recommended that a fire extinguisher suitable for use on fuel and electrical fires be kept handy in the garage or workshop at all times. Never try to extinguish a fuel or electrical fire with water.

Fumes

Certain fumes are highly toxic and can quickly cause unconsciousness and even death if inhaled to any extent. Petrol vapour falls into this category, as do the vapours from some cleaning solvents. Any draining or pouring of such volatile fluids should be done in a well ventilated area.

When using cleaning fluids and solvents, read the instructions on the container carefully. Never use materials from unmarked containers.

Never run the engine in an enclosed space, such as a garage. Exhaust fumes contain carbon monoxide, which is extremely poisonous. If you need to run the engine, always do so in the open air, or at least have the rear of the vehicle outside the work area.

If you are fortunate enough to have the use of an inspection pit, never drain or pour petrol and never run the engine while the vehicle is over the pit. The fumes, being heavier than air, will concentrate in the pit with possibly lethal results.

The battery

Never create a spark or allow a bare light bulb near a battery. They normally give off a certain amount of hydrogen gas, which is highly explosive.

Always disconnect the battery earth (-) cable at the battery before working on the fuel or electrical systems.

If possible, loosen the filler caps or cover when charging the battery from an external source (this does not apply to sealed or maintenance-free batteries). Do not charge at an excessive rate or the battery may burst.

Take care when adding water to a non maintenance-free battery and when carrying a battery. The electrolyte, even when diluted, is very corrosive and should not be allowed to contact clothing or skin.

Always wear eye protection when cleaning the battery to prevent the caustic deposits from entering your eyes.

Household current

When using an electric power tool, inspection light, etc., which operates on household current, always make sure that the tool is correctly connected to its plug and that, where necessary, it is properly earthed. Do not use such items in damp conditions and, again, do not create a spark or apply excessive heat in the vicinity of fuel or fuel vapour.

Secondary ignition system voltage

A severe electric shock can result from touching certain parts of the ignition system (such as the spark plug wires) when the engine is running or being cranked, particularly if components are damp or the insulation is defective. In the case of an electronic ignition system, the secondary system voltage is much higher and could prove fatal.

Troubleshooting

Contents

This Section provides an easy reference guide to the more common problems that may occur during the operation of your vehicle. Various symptoms and their probable causes are grouped under headings denoting components or systems, such as Engine, Cooling system, etc. They also refer to the Chapter and/or Section that deals with the problem.

Remember that successful troubleshooting isn't a mysterious 'black art' practiced only by professional mechanics, it's simply the result of knowledge combined with an intelligent, systematic approach to a problem. Always use a process of elimination starting with the simplest solution and working through to the most complex - and never overlook the obvious. Anyone can run the fuel tank dry or leave the lights on overnight, so don't assume that you're exempt from such oversights.

Finally, always establish a clear idea why a problem has occurred and take steps to ensure that it doesn't happen again. If the electrical system fails because of a poor connection, check all other connections in the system to make sure they don't fail as well. If a particular fuse continues to blow, find out why - don't just go on renewing fuses. Remember, failure of a small component can often be indicative of potential failure or incorrect functioning of a more important component or system.

Engine and performance

1 Engine will not rotate when attempting to start

1   Battery terminal connections loose or corroded. Check the cable terminals at the battery; tighten cable clamp and/or clean off corrosion as necessary (see Chapter 1).
2   Battery discharged or faulty. If the cable ends are clean and tight on the battery posts, turn the key to the On position and switch on the headlights or windscreen wipers. If they won't run, the battery is discharged.
3   Automatic transmission not engaged in park (P) or Neutral (N).
4   Broken, loose or disconnected wires in the starting circuit. Inspect all wires and connectors at the battery, starter solenoid and ignition switch (on steering column).
5   Starter motor pinion jammed in flywheel ring gear. If manual transmission, place transmission in gear and rock the vehicle to manually turn the engine. Remove starter (see Chapter 5) and inspect pinion and flywheel (see Chapter 2) at earliest convenience.
6   Starter solenoid faulty (see Chapter 5).
7   Starter motor faulty (see Chapter 5).
8   Ignition switch faulty (see Chapter 13).
9   Engine seized. try to turn the crankshaft with a large socket and breaker bar on the pulley bolt.

2 Engine rotates but will not start

1   Fuel tank empty.
2   Battery discharged (engine rotates slowly). Check the operation of electrical components as described in previous Section.
3   Battery terminal connections loose or corroded. See previous Section .
4   Fuel not reaching carburettor or fuel injectors. Check for clogged fuel filter or lines and defective fuel or injection pump. Also make sure the tank vent lines aren't clogged (see Chapter 4B) or (see Chapter 4B).
5   On petrol engines:
  a   Choke not operating properly (see Chapter 1).
  b   Faulty distributor components. Check the cap and rotor (see Chapter 1).
  c   Defective IC ignition unit (Chapter 5).
  d   Dirty or clogged carburettor jets or fuel injector. Carburettor out of adjustment.
  e   Wet or damaged ignition components (Chapters 1 and 5).
  f   Worn, faulty or incorrectly gapped spark plugs (Chapter 1).
  g   Broken, loose or disconnected wires in the starting circuit (see previous Section).
  h   Loose distributor (changing ignition timing). Turn the distributor body as necessary to start the engine, then adjust the ignition timing as soon as possible (Chapter 1).
  i   Broken, loose or disconnected wires at the ignition coil or faulty coil (Chapter 5).
6   On diesel engines:
  a   Fuel cut-off solenoid faulty (see Chapter 4B).
  b   Air in injection pipes. Bleed the fuel system (see Chapter 4B).
  c   Defective injection pump (see Chapter 4B).
  d   Incorrect injection pump timing (see Chapter 4B).
7   Dirty or clogged fuel injectors.
8   Low cylinder compression. Check as described in (see Chapter 2E).
9   Valve clearances not properly adjusted (see Chapter 1).
10   Water in fuel. Drain tank and fill with new fuel. Also drain fuel filter/sedimenter (see Chapter 1).
11   Broken, loose or disconnected wires in the starting circuit.
12   Timing belt (see Chapter 2C) or (see Chapter 2D) or timing chain (see Chapter 2A) or (see Chapter 2B) failure or wear affecting valve timing.

3 Starter motor operates without turning engine

1   Starter pinion sticking. Remove the starter (see Chapter 5) and inspect.
2   Starter pinion or flywheel/driveplate teeth worn or broken. Remove the inspection cover on the left side of the engine and inspect.

4 Engine hard to start when cold

1   Battery discharged or low. Check as described in Chapter 1.
2   Fuel not reaching the carburettor or fuel injectors. Check the fuel filter and lines (see Chapter 1) and (see Chapter 4A) or (see Chapter 4B).

Petrol models

3   Choke inoperative (see Chapter 1) or (see Chapter 4A).
4   Defective spark plugs (see Chapter 1).

Diesel models

5   Fuel heater inoperative (see Chapter 4B).
6   Pre-heating system (glow plugs) not operating (see Chapter 6).

5 Engine hard to start when hot

1   Air filter dirty (see Chapter 1).

Petrol models

2   Air in the fuel system or defective fuel injection pump or pump timing (see Chapter 4B).

Diesel models

3   Fuel not reaching carburettor or fuel injectors (see Section 4). Check for a vapour lock situation, brought about by clogged fuel tank vent lines.
4   Bad engine earth connection.
5   Choke sticking (Chapter 1).
6   Defective pick-up coil in distributor (Chapter 5).
7   Float level too high (Chapter 4).

6 Starter motor noisy or engages roughly

1   Pinion or flywheel/driveplate teeth worn or broken. Remove the inspection cover on the left side of the engine and inspect.
2   Starter motor mounting bolts loose or missing.
3   Defective starter (see Chapter 5).

7 Engine starts but stops immediately

Petrol models

1   Loose or damaged wire harness connections at distributor, coil or alternator.
2   Inlet manifold vacuum leaks. Make sure all mounting bolts/nuts are tight and all vacuum hoses connected to the manifold are attached properly and in good condition.

Diesel models

3   Fault in the fuel heater system (see

Chapter 4B).
4   Air in the fuel system or defective fuel injection pump or pump timing (see Chapter 4B).

8   Engine "lopes" while idling or idles erratically

1   Air filter clogged (see Chapter 1).
2   Leaking head gasket. Perform a cylinder compression check (see Chapter 2E).

Petrol models

3   Vacuum leaks. Check mounting bolts at the inlet manifold for tightness. Make sure that all vacuum hoses are connected and in good condition. Use a stethoscope or a length of fuel hose held against your ear to listen for vacuum leaks while the engine is running. A hissing sound will be heard. A soapy water solution will also detect leaks. Check the inlet manifold gasket surfaces.
4   Leaking EGR valve or plugged PCV valve (see Chapter 1) (see Chapter 6).
5   Timing chain or belt worn (see Chapter 2A) or (see Chapter 2B).
6   Camshaft lobes worn (see Chapter 2A), or (see Chapter 2B).
7   Valve clearance out of adjustment (see Chapter 1). Valves burned or otherwise leaking (see Chapter 2A), (see Chapter 2B).
8   Ignition timing out of adjustment (see Chapter 1).
9   Ignition system not operating properly (see Chapter 1), (see Chapter 5).
10   Thermostatic air cleaner not operating properly (see Chapter 1).
11   Choke not operating properly (see Chapter 1).
12   Dirty or clogged injectors. Carburettor dirty, clogged or out of adjustment (see Chapter 4A).
13   Idle speed out of adjustment (see Chapter 1) and (see Chapter 4A).

Diesel models

14   Timing belt worn (see Chapter 2C) or (see Chapter 2D).
15   Camshaft lobes worn (see Chapter 2C) or (see Chapter 2D).
16   Valve clearance out of adjustment (see Chapter 1). Valves burned or otherwise leaking (see Chapter 2C) or (see Chapter 2D).
17   Injection pump out of adjustment (see Chapter 4B).
18   Dirty or clogged injectors (see Chapter 4B).
19   Air in the fuel system or defective injection pump (see Chapter 4B).
20   Incorrect injection pump timing (see Chapter 4B).

9   Engine misses at idle speed

1   Clogged fuel filter and/or foreign matter in fuel. Remove the fuel filter (see Chapter 1) and inspect. On diesel models, service the

sedimenter.
2   Low or uneven cylinder compression (see Chapter 2E).
3   Clogged or dirty fuel injectors (see Chapter 4A) or (see Chapter 4B).

Petrol models

1   Spark plugs faulty or not gapped properly (see Chapter 1).
2   Faulty spark plug wires (see Chapter 1).
3   Wet or damaged distributor components (see Chapter 1).
4   Short circuits in ignition, coil or spark plug wires.
5   Sticking or faulty emissions systems (see Chapter 6).
7   Vacuum leaks at inlet manifold or hose connections. Check as described in Section 8.
8   Incorrect idle speed (see Chapter 1) or idle mixture.
9   Incorrect ignition timing (see Chapter 1).
10   Choke not operating properly (see Chapter 1).

Diesel models

11   Air in the fuel system or defective fuel injection pump or injector (see Chapter 4B).
12   Incorrect fuel injection pump timing (see Chapter 4B).

10   Excessively high idle speed

1   Idle speed incorrectly adjusted (see Chapter 1).
2   Valve clearances incorrectly adjusted (see Chapter 1).
3   Sticking throttle cable or linkage (see Chapter 4A) or (see Chapter 4B).

Petrol models

4   Choke opened excessively at idle (see Chapter 4B).
5   Dash pot out of adjustment (see Chapter 6).

11   Battery will not hold a charge

1   Alternator drivebelt defective or not adjusted properly (see Chapter 1).
2   Battery cables loose or corroded (see Chapter 1).
3   Alternator not charging properly (see Chapter 5).
4   Loose, broken or faulty wires in the charging circuit (see Chapter 5).
5   Short circuit causing a continuous drain on the battery (see Chapter 12).
6   Battery defective internally.
7   Faulty voltage regulator (see Chapter 5).

12   Alternator light stays on

1   Fault in alternator or charging circuit (see Chapter 5).

2   Alternator drivebelt defective or not properly adjusted (see Chapter 1).

13   Alternator light fails to come on when key is turned on

1   Faulty bulb (see Chapter 12).
2   Defective alternator (see Chapter 5).
3   Fault in the printed circuit, dash wiring or bulb holder (see Chapter 12).

14   Engine misses throughout driving speed range

1   Fuel filter clogged and/or impurities in the fuel system. Renew fuel filter (see Chapter 1) and/or clean sedimenter (see Chapter 1) or clean system (see Chapter 4B).
2   Low or uneven cylinder compression pressures (see Chapter 2E).
3   Dirty or clogged fuel injectors (see Chapter 4A) or (see Chapter 4B).

Petrol models

4   Incorrect ignition timing (see Chapter 1).
5   Cracked distributor cap, disconnected distributor wires or damaged distributor components (see Chapter 1) .
6   Defective spark plug wires (see Chapter 1).
7   Emissions system components faulty (see Chapter 6).
8   Weak or faulty ignition coil (see Chapter 5).
9   Weak or faulty ignition system (see Chapter 5).
10   Vacuum leaks at inlet manifold or vacuum hoses (see Section 8).
11   Dirty or clogged carburettor or fuel injector (see Chapter 4A).
12   Leaky EGR valve (see Chapter 6).
13   Carburettor out of adjustment (see Chapter 4A).
14   Idle speed out of adjustment (see Chapter 1).

Diesel models

15   Air in the fuel system or defective fuel injection pump or injector (see Chapter 4B).
16   Incorrect fuel injection pump timing (see Chapter 4B).

15   Hesitation or stumble during acceleration

Petrol models

1   Ignition timing incorrect (see Chapter 1).
2   Ignition system not operating properly (see Chapter 5).
3   Dirty or clogged carburettor or fuel injector (see Chapter 4A).
4   Low fuel pressure. Check for proper operation of the fuel pump and for restrictions in the fuel filter and lines (see Chapter 4A).

5   Carburettor out of adjustment (see Chapter 4A).

Diesel models

6   Air in the fuel system or defective fuel injection pump or injector (see Chapter 4B).
7   Incorrect fuel injection pump timing (see Chapter 4B).

16   Engine stalls

1   Idle speed incorrect (see Chapter 1).
2   Fuel filter clogged and/or water and impurities in the fuel system (see Chapter 1).
3   Valve clearances incorrect (see Chapter 1).

Petrol models

4   Choke not operating properly (see Chapter 1).
5   Damaged or wet distributor cap and wires.
6   Emissions system components faulty (see Chapter 6).
7   Faulty or incorrectly gapped spark plugs (see Chapter 1). Also check the spark plug wires (see Chapter 1).
8   Vacuum leak at the carburettor, inlet manifold or vacuum hoses (see Section 8).

Diesel models

9   Air in the fuel system or defective fuel injection pump or injector (see Chapter 4B).
10   Incorrect fuel injection pump timing (see Chapter 4B).

17   Engine lacks power

1   Air filter dirty (see Chapter 1).
2   Brakes binding (see Chapter 1) and (see Chapter 9).
3   Automatic transmission fluid level incorrect, causing slippage (see Chapter 1).
4   Clutch slipping (see Chapter 8).
5   Fuel filter clogged and/or impurities in the fuel system. Renew fuel filter (see Chapter 1) and/or clean sedimenter (see Chapter 1) or clean system (see Chapter 4B).
6   Use of sub-standard fuel. Fill tank with correct octane fuel.
7   Low or uneven cylinder compression pressures (see Chapter 2E).

Petrol models

8   Incorrect ignition timing (see Chapter 1).
9   Excessive play in distributor shaft. At the same time check for faulty distributor cap, wires, etc. (see Chapter 1).
10   Faulty or incorrectly gapped spark plugs (see Chapter 1).
11   Spark timing control system not operating properly (see Chapter 6).
12   Faulty ignition coil (see Chapter 5).
13   EGR system not functioning properly (see Chapter 6).
14   Air leak at carburettor or inlet manifold (check as described in Section 8).

15   Dirty or clogged carburettor jets or malfunctioning choke (see Chapter 1).

Diesel models

16   Incorrect fuel injection pump timing (see Chapter 4B).
17   Air in the fuel system or defective fuel injection pump or injector (see Chapter 4B).

18   Engine backfires

1   Valve clearances incorrect (see Chapter 1).
2   Damaged valve springs or sticking valves (see Chapter 2).

Petrol models

3   EGR system not functioning properly (see Chapter 6).
4   Ignition timing incorrect (see Chapter 1)
5   Thermostatic air cleaner system not operating properly (see Chapter 6).
6   Vacuum leak (see Section 8).
7   Intake air leak (see Section 8).
8   Carburettor float level out of adjustment.

Diesel models

9   Injection timing incorrect (see Chapter 4B).
10   Camshaft lobe(s) worn (see Chapter 2A).
11   Timing belt stretched (see Chapter 2A).

19   Engine surges while holding accelerator steady

Petrol models

1   Intake air leak (see Section 8).
2   Fuel pump not working properly.

Diesel models

3   Internal injection pump fault or air in the fuel system (see Chapter 4B).

20   Pinging or knocking engine sounds when engine is under load

1   Incorrect grade of fuel. Fill tank with the proper fuel.

Petrol models

2   Ignition timing incorrect (see Chapter 1).
3   Carbon build-up in combustion chambers. Remove cylinder head(s) and clean combustion chambers (see Chapter 2A), (see Chapter 2B).
4   Incorrect spark plugs (see Chapter 1).

Diesel models

5   Injection timing incorrect (see Chapter 4B).

21   Engine continues to run after being turned off

Petrol models

1   Idle speed too high (see Chapter 1).
2   Ignition timing incorrect (see Chapter 1) .
3   Incorrect spark plug heat range (see Chapter 1).
4   Intake air leak (see Section 8).
5   Carbon build-up in combustion chambers. Remove the cylinder head(s) and clean the combustion chambers (see Chapter 2A), (see Chapter 2B).
6   Valves sticking (see Chapter 2A), (see Chapter 2B).
7   BCDD or FICD system not operating properly (see Chapter 6).
8   Valve clearance incorrect (see Chapter 1).
9   EGR system not operating properly (see Chapter 6).
10   Fuel shut-off system not operating properly (see Chapter 6).
11   Check for causes of overheating (Section 27).

Diesel models

12   Fuel cut-off solenoid faulty (see Chapter 4B).

22   Low oil pressure

1   Improper grade of oil.
2   Oil pressure regulator valve not operating properly (see Chapter 2A), (see Chapter 2B).
3   Oil pump worn or damaged (see Chapter 2A), (see Chapter 2B), (see Chapter 2C) or (see Chapter 2D).
4   Engine overheating (refer to Section 27).
5   Clogged oil filter (see Chapter 1).
6   Clogged oil strainer (see Chapter 2A), (see Chapter 2B), (see Chapter 2C) or (see Chapter 2D).
7   Oil pressure gauge not working properly (see Chapter 2E).
8   Main and/or connecting rod bearings worn (see Chapter 2E).

23   Excessive oil consumption

1   Loose oil drain plug.
2   Loose bolts or damaged sump gasket (see Chapter 2).
3   Loose bolts or damaged oil pump/front cover gasket (see Chapter 2A).
4   Front or rear crankshaft oil seal leaking (see Chapter 2A).
5   Loose bolts or damaged valve cover gasket (see Chapter 2A).
6   Loose oil filter (see Chapter 1).
7   Loose or damaged oil pressure switch (see Chapter 2B).
8   Pistons and cylinders excessively worn (see Chapter 2B).

9 Piston rings not fitted correctly on pistons (see Chapter 2B).
10 Worn or damaged piston rings (see Chapter 2B).
11 Intake and/or exhaust valve oil seals worn or damaged (see Chapter 2A).
12 Worn or damaged valves/guides (see Chapter 2B).

24 Excessive fuel consumption

1 Dirty or clogged air filter element (see Chapter 1).
2 Incorrect idle speed (see Chapter 1).
3 Low tyre pressure or incorrect tyre size (see Chapter 10).
3 Fuel leakage. Check all connections, lines and components in the fuel system (see Chapter 4A) or (see Chapter 4B).

Petrol models

4 Choke not operating properly (see Chapter 1).
5 Dirty or clogged carburettor jets or fuel injectors (see Chapter 4A).

Diesel models

6 Air in the fuel system or defective fuel injection pump or injector (see Chapter 4B).
7 Incorrect fuel injection pump timing (see Chapter 4B).

25 Fuel odor

1 Fuel leakage. Check all connections, lines and components in the fuel system (see Chapter 4A) or (see Chapter 4B).
2 Fuel tank overfilled. Fill only to automatic shut-off.

Petrol models

3 Charcoal canister filter in Evaporative Emissions Control system clogged (see Chapter 1).
4 Vapour leaks from Evaporative Emissions Control system lines (see Chapter 6).

26 Miscellaneous engine noises

1 A strong dull noise that becomes more rapid as the engine accelerates indicates worn or damaged crankshaft bearings or an unevenly worn crankshaft. To pinpoint the trouble spot, start the engine and loosen the injection pipe fittings at the injectors, one at a time. If the noise stops, the cylinder with the loosened injector fitting indicates the problem area. Renew the bearing and/or service or renew the crankshaft (see Chapter 2).
2 A similar (yet slightly higher pitched) noise to the crankshaft knocking described in the previous paragraph, that becomes more rapid as the engine accelerates, indicates worn or damaged connecting rod bearings (see Chapter 2). The procedure for locating

the problem cylinder is the same as described in Paragraph 1.
3 An overlapping metallic noise that increases in intensity as the engine speed increases, yet diminishes as the engine warms up indicates abnormal piston and cylinder wear (see Chapter 2). To locate the problem cylinder, use the procedure described in Paragraph 1.
4 A rapid clicking noise that becomes faster as the engine accelerates indicates a worn piston pin or piston pin hole. This sound will happen each time the piston hits the highest and lowest points in the stroke. The procedure for locating the problem piston is described in Paragraph 1.
5 A metallic clicking noise coming from the water pump indicates worn or damaged water pump bearings or pump. Renew the water pump (see Chapter 3).
6 A rapid tapping sound or clicking sound that becomes faster as the engine speed increases indicates "valve tapping" or improperly adjusted valve clearances. This can be identified by holding one end of a section of hose to your ear and placing the other end at different spots along the valve cover. The point where the sound is loudest indicates the problem valve. Adjust the valve clearance (see Chapter 1).
7 A steady metallic rattling or rapping sound coming from the area fo the timing chain cover indicates a worn, damaged or out-of-adjustment timing chain. Service or renew the chain and related components. (Chapter 2B).

Cooling system

27 Overheating

1 Insufficient coolant in system (see Chapter 1).
2 Drivebelt defective or not adjusted properly (see Chapter 1).
3 Radiator core blocked or radiator grille dirty and restricted (see Chapter 3)
4 Thermostat faulty (see Chapter 3).
5 Fan not functioning properly (see Chapter 3).
6 Radiator cap not maintaining proper pressure. Have cap pressure tested by service station or repair shop.
7 Ignition timing incorrect (see Chapter 1).
8 Defective water pump (see Chapter 3).
9 Improper grade of engine.
10 Inaccurate temperature gauge (see Chapter 12).

28 Overcooling

1 Thermostat faulty (see Chapter 3).
2 Inaccurate temperature gauge (see Chapter 12).

29 External coolant leakage

1 Deteriorated or damaged hoses. Loose clamps at hose connections (see Chapter 1).
2 Water pump seals defective. If this is the case, water will drip from the weep hole in the water pump body (see Chapter 3).
3 Leakage from radiator core or header tank. This will require the radiator to be professionally repaired (see Chapter 3 for removal procedures).
4 Engine drain plugs or water jacket freeze plugs leaking (see Chapters 1 and 2).
5 Leak from coolant temperature switch (see Chapter 3).
6 Leak from damaged gaskets or small cracks (see Chapter 2).
7 Damaged head gasket. This can be verified by checking the condition of the engine oil as noted in Section 30.

30 Internal coolant leakage

Note: Internal coolant leaks can usually be detected by examining the oil. Check the dipstick and inside the valve cover for water deposits and an oil consistency like that of a milkshake.
1 Leaking cylinder head gasket. Have the system pressure tested or remove the cylinder head (see Chapter 2) and inspect.
2 Cracked cylinder bore or cylinder head. Dismantle engine and inspect (see Chapter 2).
3 Loose cylinder head bolts (tighten as described in Chapter 2).

31 Abnormal coolant loss

1 Overfilling system (see Chapter 1).
2 Coolant boiling away due to overheating (see causes in Section 27).
3 Internal or external leakage (see Sections 29 and 30).
4 Faulty radiator cap. Have the cap pressure tested.
5 Cooling system being pressurised by engine compression. This could be due to a cracked head or block or leaking head gasket(s).

32 Poor coolant circulation

1 Inoperative water pump. A quick test is to pinch the top radiator hose closed with your hand while the engine is idling, then release it. You should feel a surge of coolant if the pump Is working properly (see Chapter 3).
2 Restriction in cooling system. Drain, flush and refill the system (see Chapter 1). If necessary, remove the radiator (see Chapter 3) and have it reverse flushed or professionally cleaned.
3 Loose water pump drivebelt (see Chapter 1).

4   Thermostat sticking (see Chapter 3).
5   Insufficient coolant (see Chapter 1).

33 Corrosion

1   Excessive impurities in the water. Soft, clean water is recommended. Distilled or rainwater is satisfactory.
2   Insufficient antifreeze solution (refer to Chapter 1 for the proper ratio of water to antifreeze).
3   Infrequent flushing and draining of system. Regular flushing of the cooling system should be carried out at the specified intervals as described in Chapter 1.

Clutch

Note: *All clutch related service information is located in Chapter 8, unless otherwise noted.*

34 Fails to release (pedal pressed to the floor - shift lever does not move freely in and out of Reverse)

1   Clutch contaminated with oil. Remove clutch plate and inspect.
2   Clutch plate warped, distorted or otherwise damaged.
3   Diaphragm spring fatigued. Remove clutch cover/pressure plate assembly and inspect.
4   Leakage of fluid from clutch hydraulic system. Inspect master cylinder, release cylinder and connecting lines.
5   Air in clutch hydraulic system. Bleed the system.
6   Insufficient pedal stroke. Check and adjust as necessary.
7   Piston seal in operating cylinder deformed or damaged.
8   Lack of grease on pilot bush.
9   Damaged transmission input shaft splines.

35 Clutch slips (engine speed increases with no increase in vehicle speed)

1   Worn or oil soaked clutch plate.
2   Clutch plate not broken in. It may take 30 or 40 normal starts for a new clutch to seat.
3   Diaphragm spring weak or damaged. Remove clutch cover/pressure plate assembly and inspect.
4   Flywheel warped or scored (see Chapter 2).
5   Debris in master cylinder preventing the piston from returning to its normal position.
6   Clutch hydraulic line damaged.

36 Grabbing (chattering) as clutch is engaged

1   Oil on clutch plate. Remove and inspect. Repair any leaks.
2   Worn or loose engine or transmission mounts. They may move slightly when clutch is released. Inspect mounts and bolts.
3   Worn splines on transmission input shaft. Remove clutch components and inspect.
4   Warped pressure plate or flywheel. Remove clutch components and inspect.
5   Diaphragm spring fatigued. Remove clutch cover/pressure plate assembly and inspect.
6   Clutch linings hardened or warped.
7   Clutch lining rivets loose.
8   Engine and transmission not in alignment. Check for foreign object between bellhousing and engine block. Check for loose bellhousing bolts.

37 Squeal or rumble with clutch engaged (pedal released)

1   Improper pedal adjustment. Adjust pedal free play.
2   Release bearing binding on transmission shaft. Remove clutch components and check bearing. Remove any burrs or nicks, clean and relubricate before refitting.
3   Clutch rivets loose.
4   Clutch plate cracked.
5   Fatigued clutch plate torsion springs. Renew clutch plate.

38 Squeal or rumble with clutch disengaged (pedal depressed)

1   Worn or damaged release bearing.
2   Worn or broken pressure plate diaphragm fingers.
3   Worn or damaged pilot bearing.

39 Clutch pedal stays on floor when disengaged

1   Binding linkage or release bearing. Inspect linkage or remove clutch components as necessary.
2   Linkage springs being over extended. Adjust linkage for proper free play. Make sure proper pedal stop (bumper) is fitted.

Manual transmission

Note: *All manual transmission service information is located in Chapter 7A, unless otherwise noted.*

40 Noisy in Neutral with engine running

1   Input shaft bearing worn.
2   Damaged main drive gear bearing.
3   Insufficient transmission oil (see Chapter 1).
4   Transmission oil in poor condition. Drain and fill with proper grade oil. Check old oil for water and debris (see Chapter 1).
5   Noise can be caused by variations in engine torque. Change the idle speed and see if noise disappears.

41 Noisy in all gears

1   Any of the above causes, and/or:
2   Worn or damaged output gear bearings or shaft.

42 Noisy in one particular gear

1   Worn, damaged or chipped gear teeth.
2   Worn or damaged synchroniser.

43 Slips out of gear

1   Transmission loose on clutch housing.
2   Stiff shift lever seal.
3   Shift linkage binding.
4   Broken or loose input gear bearing retainer.
5   Dirt between clutch lever and engine housing.
6   Worn linkage.
7   Damaged or worn check balls, fork rod ball grooves or check springs.
8   Worn mainshaft or countershaft bearings.
9   Loose engine mounts (see Chapter 2).
10   Excessive gear end play.
11   Worn synchronisers.

44 Oil leaks

1   Excessive amount of lubricant in transmission (see Chapter 1 for correct checking procedures). Drain lubricant as required.
2   Side cover loose or gasket damaged.
3   Rear oil seal or speedometer oil seal damaged.
4   To pinpoint a leak, first remove all built-up dirt and grime from the transmission. Degreasing agents and/or steam cleaning will achieve this. With the underside clean, drive the vehicle at low speeds so the air flow will

not blow the leak far from its source. Raise the vehicle and determine where the leak is located.

45 Difficulty engaging gears

1   Clutch not releasing completely.
2   Loose or damaged shift linkage. Make a thorough inspection, renewing parts as necessary.
3   Insufficient transmission oil (see Chapter 1).
4   Transmission oil in poor condition. Drain and fill with proper grade oil. Check oil for water and debris (see Chapter 1).
5   Worn or damaged striking rod.
6   Sticking or jamming gears.

46 Noise occurs while shifting gears

1   Check for proper operation of the clutch (see Chapter 8).
2   Faulty synchroniser assemblies. Measure baulk ring-to-gear clearance. Also, check for wear or damage to baulk rings or any parts of the synchromesh assemblies.

Automatic transmission

Note: *Due to the complexity of the automatic transmission, it's difficult for the home mechanic to properly diagnose and service. For problems other than the following, the vehicle should be taken to a reputable mechanic.*

47 Fluid leakage

1   Automatic transmission fluid is a deep red colour, and fluid leaks should not be confused with engine oil which can easily be blown by airflow to the transmission.
2   To pinpoint a leak, first remove all built-up dirt and grime from the transmission. Degreasing agents and/or steam cleaning will achieve this. With the underside clean, drive the vehicle at low speeds so the air flow will not blow the leak far from its source. Raise the vehicle and determine where the leak is located. Common areas of leakage are:
   a) *Fluid pan: tighten mounting bolts and/ or renew pan gasket as necessary (see Chapter 1).*
   b) *Rear extension: tighten bolts and/or renew oil seal as necessary.*
   c) *Filler pipe: renew the rubber oil seal where pipe enters transmission case.*
   d) *Transmission oil lines: tighten fittings where lines enter transmission case and/ or renew lines.*
   e) *Vent pipe: transmission overfilled and/or water in fluid (see checking procedures, Chapter 1).*

   f) *Speedometer connector: renew the O-ring where speedometer cable enters transmission case.*

48 General shift mechanism problems

Chapter 7B deals with checking and adjusting the shift linkage on automatic transmissions. Common problems which may be caused by out of adjustment linkage are:
   a) *Engine starting in gears other than P (park) or N (Neutral).*
   b) *Indicator pointing to a gear other than the one actually engaged.*
   c) *Vehicle moves with transmission in P (Park) position.*

49 Transmission will not downshift with the accelerator pedal pressed to the floor

Chapter 7B deals with adjusting the throttle valve cable to enable the transmission to downshift properly.

50 Engine will start in gears other than Park or Neutral

Chapter 7B deals with adjusting the Neutral start switch fitted on automatic transmissions.

51 Transmission slips, shifts rough, is noisy or has no drive in forward or Reverse gears

1   There are many probable causes for the above problems, but the home mechanic should concern himself only with one possibility; fluid level.
2   Before taking the vehicle to a shop, check the fluid level and condition as described in Chapter 1. Add fluid, if necessary, or change the fluid and filter if needed. If problems persist, have a professional diagnose the transmission.

Driveshaft

52 Leaks at front of driveshaft

Defective transmission rear seal. See Chapter 7 for renewal procedure. As this is done, check the splined yoke for burrs or roughness that could damage the new seal. Remove burrs with crocus cloth.

53 Knock or clunk when transmission is under initial load (just after transmission is put into gear)

1   Loose or disconnected rear suspension components. Check all mounting bolts and bushes (see Chapters 1 and 11).
2   Loose driveshaft bolts. Inspect all bolts and nuts and tighten them securely.
3   Worn or damaged universal joint bearings. Renew driveshaft (see Chapter 8).
4   Worn sleeve yoke and mainshaft spline.
5   Defective centre bearing or insulator.

54 Metallic grating sound consistent with vehicle speed

Pronounced wear in the universal joint bearings. Renew U-joints or driveshafts, as necessary.

55 Vibration

Note: *Before blaming the driveshaft, make sure the tyres are perfectly balanced and perform the following test.*
1   Connect a tachometer inside the vehicle to monitor engine speed as the vehicle is driven. Drive the vehicle and note the engine speed at which the vibration (roughness) is most pronounced. Now shift the transmission to a different gear and bring the engine speed to the same point.
2   If the vibration occurs at the same engine speed (rpm) regardless of which gear the transmission is in, the driveshaft is NOT at fault since the driveshaft speed varies.
3   If the vibration decreases or is eliminated when the transmission is in a different gear at the same engine speed, refer to the following probable causes.
4   Bent or dented driveshaft. Inspect and renew as necessary.
5   Undercoating or built-up dirt, etc. on the driveshaft. Clean the shaft thoroughly.
6   Worn universal joint bearings. Renew the U-joints or driveshaft as necessary.
7   Driveshaft and/or companion flange out of balance. Check for missing weights on the shaft. Remove driveshaft and refit 180° from original position, then recheck. Have the driveshaft balanced if problem persists .
8   Loose driveshaft mounting bolts/nuts.
9   Defective centre bearing, if so equipped.
10   Worn transmission rear bush (see Chapter 7A).

56 Scraping noise

Make sure the dust cover on the sleeve yoke isn't rubbing on the transmission extension housing.

57   Whining or whistling noise

Defective centre bearing, if so equipped.

Rear axle and differential

Note: *For differential servicing information, refer to Chapter 8, unless otherwise specified.*

58   Noise - same when in drive as when vehicle is coasting

1   Road noise. No corrective action available.
2   Tyre noise. Inspect tyres and check tyre pressures (see Chapter 1).
3   Front wheel bearings loose, worn or damaged (see Chapter 1).
4   Insufficient differential oil (see Chapter 1).
5   Defective differential.

59   Knocking sound when starting or shifting gears

Defective or incorrectly adjusted differential.

60   Noise when turning

Defective differential.

61   Vibration

See probable causes under *Driveshaft*. Proceed under the guidelines listed for the driveshaft. If the problem persists, check the rear wheel bearings by raising the rear of the vehicle and spinning the wheels by hand. Listen for evidence of rough (noisy) bearings. Remove and inspect (see Chapter 8).

62   Oil leaks

1   Pinion oil seal damaged (see Chapter 8).
2   Axleshaft oil seals damaged (see Chapter 8).
3   Differential cover leaking. Tighten mounting bolts or renew the gasket as required.
4   Loose filler or drain plug on differential (see Chapter 1).
5   Clogged or damaged breather on differential.

Transfer case (4WD models)

Note: *All transfer case service information is located in Chapter 7C unless otherwise noted.*

63   Gear jumping out of mesh

1   Incorrect control lever free play.
2   Interference between the control lever and the console.
3   Play or fatigue in the transfer case mounts.
4   Internal wear or incorrect adjustments.

64   Difficult shifting

1   Lack of oil (see Chapter 1).
2   Internal wear, damage or incorrect adjustment.

65   Noise

1   Lack of oil in transfer case (see Chapter 1).
2   Noise in 4H and 4L, but not in 2H indicates cause is in the front differential or front axle.
3   Noise in 2H, 4H and 4L indicates cause is in rear differential or rear axle.
4   Noise in 2H and 4H but not in 4L, or in 4L only, indicates internal wear or damage in transfer case.

Brakes

Note: *Before assuming a brake problem exists, make sure the tyres are in good condition and inflated properly, the front end alignment is correct and the vehicle is not loaded with weight in an unequal manner. All service procedures for the brakes are included in Chapter 9, unless otherwise noted.*

66   Vehicle pulls to one side during braking

1   Defective, damaged or oil contaminated brake pad or shoe on one side. Inspect as described in Chapter 1. Refer to Chapter 9 if renewal is required.
2   Excessive wear of brake pad material or disc on one side. Inspect and repair as necessary.
3   Loose or disconnected front suspension components. Inspect and tighten all bolts securely (see Chapters 1 and 11).
4   Defective caliper assembly. Remove caliper and inspect for stuck piston or damage.
5   Scored or out-of-round disc.
6   Loose caliper mounting bolts.
7   Incorrect wheel bearing adjustment.

67   Noise (high-pitched squeal)

1   Front brake pads worn out. This noise comes from the wear sensor rubbing against the disc. Renew pads immediately!
2   Glazed or contaminated pads.
3   Dirty or scored disc.
4   Bent support plate.

68   Excessive brake pedal travel

1   Partial brake system failure. Inspect entire system (see Chapter 1) and correct as required.
2   Insufficient fluid in master cylinder. Check and add fluid (see Chapter 1) - bleed system if necessary (see Chapter 9).
3   Air in system. Bleed system.
4   Brakes out of adjustment. Check the operation of the automatic adjusters .
5   Defective check valve. Renew valve and bleed system.

69   Brake pedal feels spongy when depressed

1   Air in brake lines. Bleed the brake system.
2   Deteriorated rubber brake hoses. Inspect all system hoses and lines. Renew parts as necessary.
3   Master cylinder mounting nuts loose. Inspect master cylinder bolts (nuts) and tighten them securely.
4   Master cylinder faulty.
5   Incorrect shoe or pad clearance.
6   Clogged reservoir cap vent hole.
7   Deformed rubber brake lines.
8   Soft or swollen caliper seals.
9   Poor quality brake fluid. Bleed entire system and fill with new approved fluid.

70   Excessive effort required to stop vehicle

1   Power brake booster or vacuum pump not operating properly, or vacuum reservoir or hoses leaking.
2   Excessively worn linings or pads. Check and renew if necessary.
3   One or more caliper pistons seized or sticking. Inspect and rebuild as required.
4   Brake pads or linings contaminated with oil or grease. Inspect and renew as required.
5   New pads or linings fitted and not yet seated. It'll take a while for the new material to seat against the disc or drum.
6   Worn or damaged master cylinder or caliper assemblies. Check particularly for seized pistons.
7   Also see causes listed under Section 69.

71 Pedal travels to the floor with little resistance

Little or no fluid in the master cylinder reservoir caused by leaking caliper piston(s) or loose, damaged or disconnected brake lines. Inspect entire system and repair as necessary.

72 Brake pedal pulsates during brake application

1   Wheel bearings damaged, worn or out of adjustment (see Chapter 1).
2   Caliper not sliding properly due to improper refitting or obstructions. Remove and inspect.
3   Disc not within specifications. Remove the disc and check for excessive lateral runout and parallelism. Have the discs resurfaced or renew them. Also make sure that all discs are the same thickness.
4   Out of round rear brake drums. Remove the drums and have them resurfaced or renew them.

73 Brakes drag (indicated by sluggish; engine performance or wheels being very hot after driving)

1   Output rod adjustment incorrect at the brake pedal.
2   Obstructed master cylinder compensator. Disassemble master cylinder and clean.
3   Master cylinder piston seized in bore. Overhaul master cylinder.
4   Caliper assembly in need of overhaul.
5   Brake pads or shoes worn out.
6   Piston cups in master cylinder or caliper assembly deformed. Overhaul master cylinder.
7   Disc not within specifications (Section 72).
8   Parking brake assembly will not release.
9   Clogged or internally split brake lines.
10   Wheel bearings out of adjustment (see Chapter 1).
11   Brake pedal height improperly adjusted.
12   Wheel cylinder needs overhaul.
13   Improper shoe-to-drum clearance. Adjust as necessary.

74 Rear brakes lock up under light brake application

1   Tyre pressures too high.
2   Tyres excessively worn (see Chapter 1).
3   Defective LSPV valve.

75 Rear brakes lock up under heavy brake application

1   Tyre pressures too high.
2   Tyres excessively worn (see Chapter 1).
3   Front brake pads contaminated with oil, mud or water. Clean or renew the pads.
4   Front brake pads excessively worn.
5   Defective master cylinder or caliper assembly.

Suspension and steering

Note: *All service procedures for the suspension and steering systems are included in Chapter 10, unless otherwise noted.*

76 Vehicle pulls to one side

1   Tyre pressures uneven (see Chapter 1).
2   Defective tyre (see Chapter 1).
3   Excessive wear in suspension or steering components (see Chapter 1).
4   Front end alignment incorrect.
5   Front brakes dragging. Inspect as described in Section 73.
6   Wheel bearings improperly adjusted (see Chapter 1).
7   Wheel lug nuts loose.
8   Worn upper or lower link or tension rod bushes.

77 Shimmy, shake or vibration

1   Tyre or wheel out-of-balance or out-of-round. Have them balanced on the vehicle.
2   Loose, worn or out of adjustment wheel bearings (see Chapter 1).
3   Shock absorbers and/or suspension components worn or damaged. Check for worn bushes in the upper and lower links.
4   Wheel lug nuts loose.
5   Incorrect tyre pressures.
6   Excessively worn or damaged tyre.
7   Loosely mounted steering gear housing.
8   Steering gear improperly adjusted.
9   Loose, worn or damaged steering components.
10   Damaged idler arm.
11   Worn balljoint.

78 Excessive pitching and/or rolling around corners or during braking

1   Defective shock absorbers. Renew as a set.
2   Broken or weak springs and/or suspension components.
3   Worn or damaged stabiliser bar or bushes.
4   Worn or damaged upper or lower links or bushes.

79 Wandering or general instability

1   Improper tyre pressures.
2   Worn or damaged upper and lower link or strut bar bushes.
3   Incorrect front end alignment.
4   Worn or damaged steering linkage or upper or lower link.
5   Improperly adjusted steering gear.
6   Out of balance wheels.
7   Loose wheel lug nuts.
8   Worn rear shock absorbers.
9   Fatigued or damaged rear leaf springs.

80 Excessively stiff steering

1   Lack of lubricant in power steering fluid reservoir, where appropriate (see Chapter 1).
2   Incorrect tyre pressures (see Chapter 1).
3   Lack of lubrication at balljoints (see Chapter 1).
4   Front end out of alignment.
5   Steering gear out of adjustment or lacking lubrication.
6   Improperly adjusted wheel bearings.
7   Worn or damaged steering gear.
8   Interference of steering column with turn signal switch.
9   Low tyre pressures.
10   Worn or damaged balljoints.
11   Worn or damaged steering linkage.
12   See also Section 79.

81 Excessive play in steering

1   Loose wheel bearings (see Chapter 1).
2   Excessive wear in upper or lower link or strut bar bushes (see Chapter 1)
3   Steering gear improperly adjusted.
4   Incorrect front end alignment.
5   Steering gear mounting bolts loose.
6   Worn steering linkage.

82 Lack of power assistance

1   Steering pump drivebelt faulty or not adjusted properly (see Chapter 1).
2   Fluid level low (see Chapter 1).
3   Hoses or pipes restricting the flow. Inspect and renew parts as necessary.
4   Air in power steering system. Bleed system.
5   Defective power steering pump.

83 Steering wheel fails to return to straight-ahead position

1   Incorrect front end alignment.
2   Tyre pressures low.
3   Steering gears improperly engaged.
4   Steering column out of alignment.
5   Worn or damaged balljoint.
6   Worn or damaged steering linkage.

7 Improperly lubricated idler arm.
8 Insufficient oil in steering gear.
9 Lack of fluid in power steering pump.

84 Steering effort not the same in both directions (power system)

1 Leaks in steering gear.
2 Clogged fluid passage in steering gear.

85 Noisy power steering pump

1 Insufficient oil in pump.
2 Clogged hoses or oil filter in pump.
3 Loose pulley.
4 Improperly adjusted drivebelt (see Chapter 1).
5 Defective pump.

86 Miscellaneous noises

1 Improper tyre pressures.
2 Insufficiently lubricated balljoint or steering linkage.

3 Loose or worn steering gear, steering linkage or suspension components.
4 Defective shock absorber.
5 Defective wheel bearing.
6 Worn or damaged upper or lower link or strut bar bush.
7 Damaged spring.
8 Loose wheel lug nuts.
9 Worn or damaged rear axleshaft spline.
10 Worn or damaged rear shock absorber mounting bush.
11 Incorrect rear axle end play.
12 See also causes of noises at the rear axle and driveshaft.
13 Worn or damaged driveaxle joints (4WD models).

87 Excessive tyre wear (not specific to one area)

1 Incorrect tyre pressures.
2 Tyres out of balance. Have them balanced on the vehicle.
3 Wheels damaged. Inspect and renew as necessary.
4 Suspension or steering components worn (see Chapter 1).

88 Excessive tyre wear on outside edge

1 Incorrect tyre pressure.
2 Excessive speed in turns.
3 Front end alignment incorrect (excessive toe-in and/or camber).

89 Excessive tyre wear on inside edge

1 Incorrect tyre pressure.
2 Front end alignment incorrect (toe-out and/or negative camber).
3 Loose or damaged steering components (see Chapter 1).

90 Tyre tread worn in one place

1 Tyres out of balance. Have them balanced on the vehicle.
2 Damaged or buckled wheel. Inspect and renew if necessary.
3 Defective tyre.

Chapter 1
Tune-up and routine maintenance

Contents

Specifications

Recommended lubricants and fluids

Note: *Listed here are manufacturer recommendations at the time this manual was written. Manufacturers occasionally upgrade their fluid and lubricant specifications, so check with your local auto parts store for current recommendations*

Engine oil	
Type	
Petrol	Petroleum-based or synthetic multigrade engine oil
Diesel	API grade CE or SG/CE multigrade and low sulphate ash limit engine oil
Viscosity	See accompanying chart
Coolant	50/50 mixture of ethylene glycol based anti-freeze
Brake fluid	DOT 3
Clutch fluid	DOT 3 brake fluid
Automatic transmission fluid	DEXRON II ATF
Power steering fluid	DEXRON II ATF
Suspension and steering balljoint grease (2WD)	Molybdenum-disulfide lithium base, NLGI No.1 or No.2 (DO NOT use multi-purpose or chassis grease)

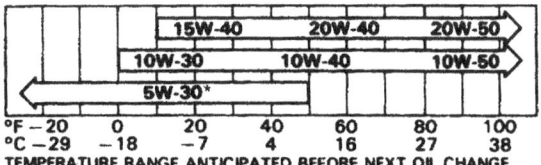

Engine oil viscosity chart

*Not recommended for continuous high-speed operation

Recommended lubricants and fluids (continued)

Suspension and steering component grease (4WD)
    Steering knuckle.. Molybdenum-disulfide lithium base, NLGI No.2
    Drag link and steering shaft slide yoke .... Lithium base chassis grease, NLGI No.0
    Driveshaft
        U-joints and slide yokes.. Lithium base multi-purpose, NLGI No.1
        Double cardan U-joints .... Molybdenum-disulfide base, NLGI No.2
Steering gearbox oil.. API GL-4 (90 weight)
Wheel bearing grease .... Lithium base multi-purpose, NLGI No.2
Manual transmission oil .... API GL-4 SAE 75W90 or 80W90 hypoid gear oil
Differential oil .... API GL-5 SAE 80W90 hypoid gear oil
Transfer case oil .... API GL-4 or GL-5 SAE 80W or 90W hypoid gear oil

Capacities*

Engine oil (with filter change)
    Petrol
        12R engine .... 4.2 litres
        18R, 20R, 22R engines .... 4.5 litres
        Y-series engines
            2WD models... 3.5 litres
            4WD models... 4.0 litres
        V6 engine.. 4.5 litres
    Diesel
        L, 1988 and earlier 2L engines .... 5.8 litres
        Later 2L and 3L engines .... 6.0 litres
Automatic transmission
    With 4-cylinder engine.. 2.5 litres
    With V6 engine.. 4.5 litres
Manual transmission
    4-speed .... 1.9 litres
    5-speed .... 3.9 litres
Differential
    Rear axle.. 2.2 litres
    Front axle
        With independent front suspension .... 1.6 litres
        With solid front axle .... 2.3 litres
Transfer case
    With manual transmission... 1.6 litres
    With automatic transmission .... 1.1 litres
Cooling system
    Petrol
        12R engine .... 7 litres
        18R, 20R and 22R engines .... 8 litres
        Y-series engines .... 7.4 litres
        V6 engine.. 10.5 litres
    Diesel
        L, 1988 and earlier 2L engines .... 10.5 litres
        Later 2L and 3L engines .... 9.2 litres

All capacities approximate. Add as necessary to bring appropriate level.

Brakes

Pedal height
    RN30/LN30, 40 series.. 162 to 172 mm
    YN50/LN50, 60 series .... 151 to 156 mm
    YN/RN/LN80, 90, 105, 106, 110 series
        2WD... 148 to 153 mm
        4WD
            Regular and double cab .... 147 to 152 mm
            Xtra cab.. 145 to 150 mm
    4Runner .... 145 mm
Pedal freeplay (all models)... 3 to 6 mm
Pedal reserve distance (at 50 kg)
    RN/LN30, 40 series.. At least 80 mm
    RN/LN50, 60 series
        With front disc brakes
            2WD .... At least 60 mm
            4WD .... At least 55 mm
        With front drum brakes .... At least 75 mm

Pedal reserve distance (at 50 kg)
   YN/RN/LN80, 90, 105, 106, 110 series
      2WD
         With front drum brakes .... At least 75 mm
         With front disc brakes
            Regular cab .... At least 76.5 mm
            Double cab .... At least 72 mm
            Xtra cab .... At least 77 mm
      4WD
         Regular and double cab .... At least 61 mm
         Xtra cab .... At least 59 mm
      4Runner .... At least 54 mm
Disc brake pad lining thickness (minimum) .... 3 mm
Drum brake shoe lining thickness (minimum)...................................... 1.5 mm

Engine

Idle speed - Petrol
   L,1988 and earlier 2L engines... 700 rpm
   Later 2L and 3L engines
      Manual transmission... 700 rpm
      Automatic transmission... 800 rpm
   Maximum engine speed
      L and all 2L engines .... 4,900 rpm
      3L engine .... 4,600 rpm
Idle speed - Diesel... See Chapter 4B
Valve clearances
   Petrol
      12R, 20R, 22R engines (hot)
         Intake.. 0.2 mm
         Exhaust .... 0.3 mm
      18R engine (hot)
         Intake.. 0.2 mm
         Exhaust .... 0.36 mm
      V6 engine (cold)
         Intake.. 0.18 to 0.28 mm
         Exhaust .... 0.22 to 0.32 mm
   Diesel
      L, 1988 and earlier 2L engines (hot)
         Intake.. 0.25 mm
         Exhaust .... 0.36 mm
      Later 2L and 3L engines (cold)
         Intake.. 0.20 to 0.30 mm
         Exhaust .... 0.40 to 0.50 mm
Spark plug type and gap
   12R, 18R, 20R, carburetted Y-series engines............................... N11YC @ 0.8 mm
   22R engine.. RN11YC4 @ 0.9 mm
   Fuel-injected Y-series engines .... RN11YCC4 @ 1.1 mm
   V6 engine .... RC10YCC4 @ 0.9 mm
Spark plug wire resistance .... Less than 25000 ohms
Ignition timing
   12R engine.. 8-degrees BTDC @ 700 rpm
   18R engine.. 7-degrees BTDC @ 750 rpm
   20R engine.. 8-degrees BTDC @ 750 rpm
   22R engine.. 5-degrees BTDC @ 950 rpm (max)
   1Y, 2Y, 3Y engines .... 8-degrees BTDC @ 850 rpm
   4Y engines
      Carburetted... 4-degrees BTDC @ 650 rpm
      Fuel-injected .... 12-degrees BTDC @ 700 rpm (M/T) or 750 rpm (A/T)
   V6 engine .... 10-degrees BTDC @ 800 rpm
Ignition points
   Gap (between cam and rubbing block) .... 0.45 mm
   Dwell angle... 52-degrees
Firing order
   Four-cylinder engines.. 1-3-4-2
   V6 engine 1-2-3-4-5-6

Clutch

Pedal freeplay... 5 to 13 mm
Pedal height.. 150 to 163 mm

Torque specifications

	Nm
Automatic transmission fluid pan bolts	4 to 6
Automatic transmission filter/strainer bolts	8
Front wheel bearing adjusting nut*	
2WD	34
4WD (manual locking hub only)	58
Fuel filter banjo bolts (EFI only)	30
Spark plugs	
Four-cylinder engines	15 to 20
V6 engine	24
Oxygen sensor nuts	19
Wheel lug nuts	88 to 118

* Initial torque only - see text (Sections 23 and 24) for complete tightening procedure

Engine compartment components - 22R-E petrol engine (typical); left-hand drive shown, right-hand drive similar

1 Air intake plenum	5 Air filter housing	8 Radiator cap
2 PCV hose	6 Distributor	9 Engine oil filler cap
3 Spark plug wires	7 Engine oil dipstick	10 Upper radiator hose
4 Brake fluid reservoir		

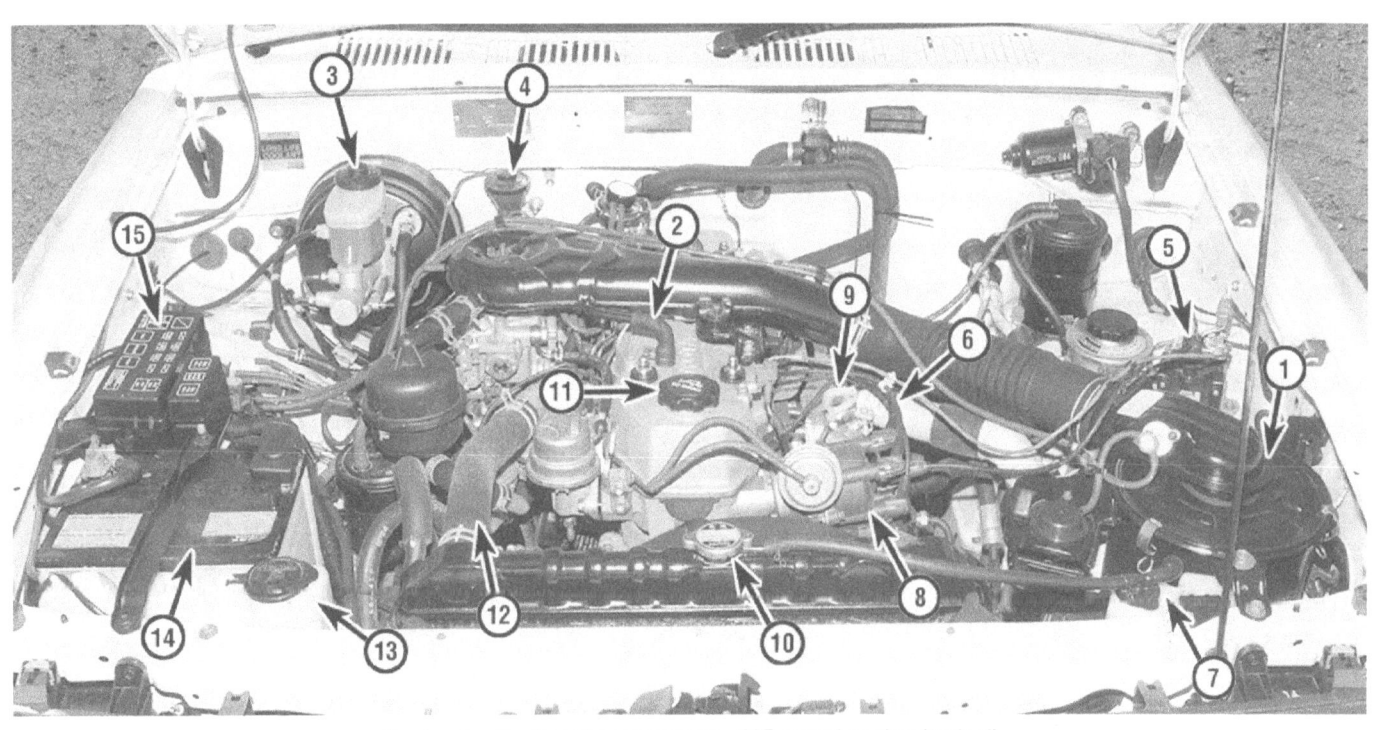

Engine compartment components - 22R petrol engine (typical)

1 Air filter housing	5 Ignition coil	9 Engine oil dipstick	13 Windscreen washer
2 PCV hose	6 Spark plug wires	10 Radiator cap	fluid reservoir
3 Brake fluid reservoir	7 Coolant reservoir	11 Engine oil filler cap	14 Battery
4 Clutch fluid reservoir	8 Distributor	12 Upper radiator hose	15 Fuse box

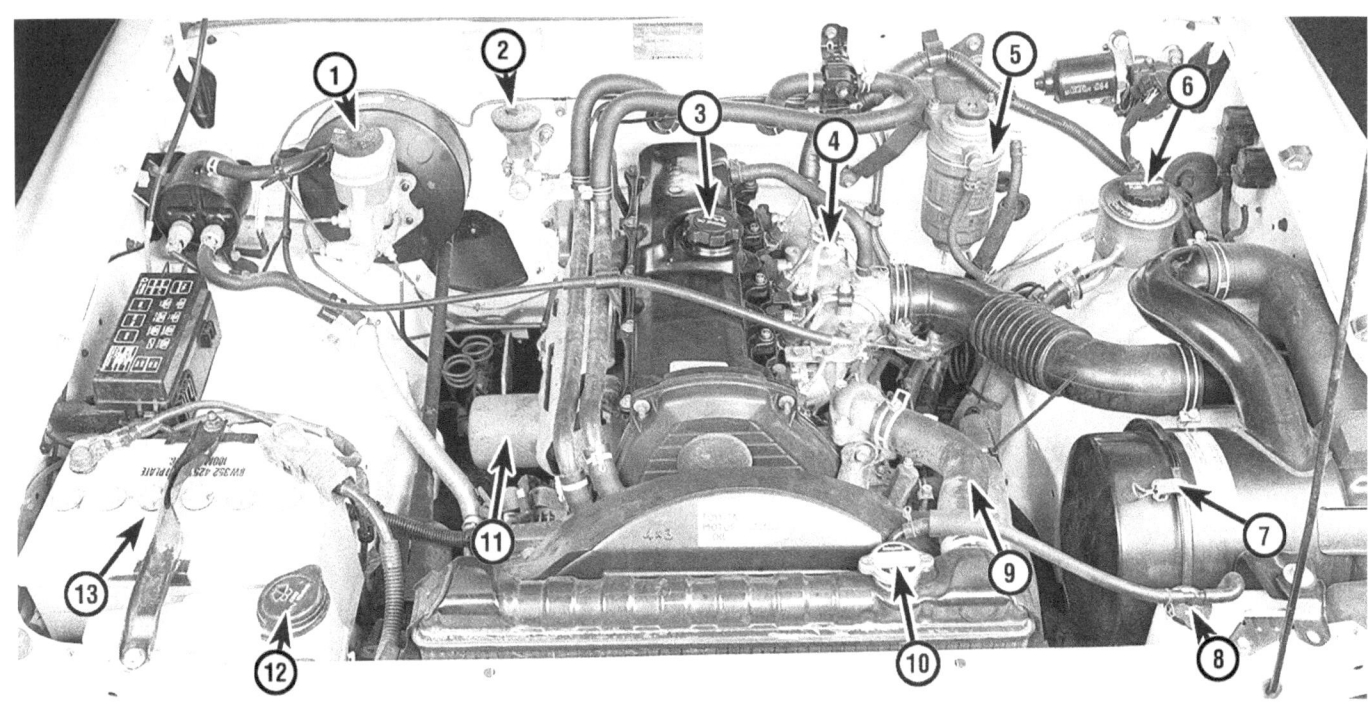

Engine compartment components - V6 petrol engine; left-hand drive shown, right-hand drive similar

1 Throttle body	5 Distributor	9 Upper radiator hose
2 Brake fluid reservoir	6 Air cleaner housing	10 Power steering fluid reservoir
3 Clutch fluid reservoir	7 Alternator	11 Battery
4 Engine oil filler cap	8 Spark plug wires	12 EVAP system canister

Engine compartment components - 3L (2.8 litre) engine

1 Brake fluid reservoir	5 Fuel filter	8 Coolant reservoir	12 Windscreen washer
2 Clutch fluid reservoir	6 Power steering fluid	9 Upper radiator hose	fluid reservoir
3 Engine oil filler cap	reservoir	10 Radiator cap	13 Battery
4 Engine oil dipstick	7 Air cleaner housing	11 Engine oil filter	

Underside view of
engine compartment
components -
typical 2WD

1 Steering balljoints
2 Radiator drain
3 Alternator
4 Suspension
   balljoint
5 Brake caliper
6 Brake hose
7 Manual
   transmission oil
   check/fill plug
8 Manual
   transmission drain
   plug
9 Engine oil drain
   plug

Underside view of the
components at the
rear of the vehicle -
typical 2WD

1 Exhaust pipe
2 Brake hose
3 Shock absorber
4 Differential oil
   check/fill plug
5 Differential drain
   plug
6 Muffler

1   Toyota Hi-Lux and 4Runner Maintenance schedule

The following maintenance intervals are based on the assumption that the vehicle owner will be doing the maintenance or service work, as opposed to having a dealer service department do the work. Although the time/distance intervals are based on factory recommendations, most have been shortened to ensure, for example, that such items as lubricants and fluids are checked/changed at intervals that promote maximum engine/driveline service life. Also, subject to the preference of the individual owner interested in keeping the vehicle in peak condition at all times and with the vehicle's ultimate resale in mind, many of the maintenance procedures may be performed more often than recommended in the following schedule. We encourage such owner initiative.

Every 400 kilometres/weekly, whichever comes first

Check the engine oil level (see Section 4)
Check the coolant level (see Section 4)
Check the windscreen washer fluid level (see Section 4)
Check the brake and clutch fluid levels (see Section 4)
Check the battery electrolyte level (see Section 4)
Check the automatic transmission fluid level (see Section 5)
Check the power steering fluid level (see Section 6)
Check the tyres and tyre pressures (see Section 7)

Every 12,000 kilometres/6 months, whichever comes first

All items listed above plus:
Inspect/renew the windscreen wiper blades (see Section 8)
Check/adjust the brake pedal (see Section 9)
Check and service the battery (see Section 10)
Check the cooling system (see Section 11)
Inspect/renew all underbonnet hoses (see Section 12)
Inspect the exhaust system (see Section 13)
Lubricate the chassis components (see Section 14)
Change the engine oil and filter (see Section 15)

Every 24,000 kilometres/12 months, whichever comes first

All items listed above plus:
Check/adjust the engine drivebelts (see Section 16)
Check/adjust the engine idle speed and maximum speed (see Section 17)
Inspect the suspension and steering components (see Section 19)
Check the fuel system (see Section 20)
Rotate the tyres (see Section 21)
Check the brakes (see Section 22)
Check and repack the front wheel bearings (Sections 23 and 24)
Check the manual transmission oil level (see Section 25)
Check the differential oil level (see Section 26)
Check the transfer case oil level (see Section 27)

Petrol
Check the Throttle Positioner (TP) (if equipped) (see Chapter 6)
Check/adjust the valve clearances (four-cylinder engine only) (see Section 18)
Renew the ignition points, if equipped (see Section 42)

Diesel
Renew the fuel filter and, if equipped, service the sedimenter (see Section 28)

Every 48,000 kilometres/24 months, whichever comes first

All items listed above plus:

All models
Renew the fuel tank cap gasket (see Section 29)
Check the clutch pedal freeplay (see Section 30)
Renew the air filter (see Section 31)
Check the PCV system (see Section 32)
Service the cooling system (drain, flush and refill) (see Section 33)
Change the manual transmission oil (see Section 34)
Change the automatic transmission fluid (see Section 35)
Change the differential oil (see Section 36)
Change the transfer case oil (see Section 37)

Petrol
Renew the EVAP system canister(s) (see Section 38)
Renew the spark plugs (see Section 44)
Check/renew the spark plug wires (see Section 45)
Check/renew the distributor cap and rotor (see Section 41)
Check the thermostatic air cleaner (see Section 39)
Check the carburettor choke operation (see Section 40)
Check/adjust the ignition timing (see Section 43)
Check the Spark Control (SC) system (see Chapter 6)
Check the Air Injection (AI) system (see Chapter 6)
Renew the fuel filter (see Section 28)

Diesel
Check/adjust the valve clearances (1989 and later 2L and 3L engines) (see Section 18)

Every 96,000 kilometres/48 months, whichever comes first

Renew the oxygen sensor (four-cylinder petrol models with fuel injection) (see Section 46)
Check/adjust the V6 petrol engine valve clearances (see Section 18)
Renew the timing belt (see Chapter 2C - V6 petrol engine); (see Chapter 2D - diesel engines).

Severe operating conditions

Severe operating conditions are defined as follows:
A) *Pulling a trailer*
B) *Repeated short trips*
C) *Driving on rough or muddy roads*
D) *Driving on dusty roads*
E) *Operating in extremely cold weather and/or driving in areas using road salt*
F) *Repeated short trips in extremely cold weather*

If your vehicle is operated under severe conditions, the maintenance schedule must be amended as follows:

Every 6,000 kilometres or 3 months, whichever occurs first:

Change the engine oil and filter if condition(s) A, D, F exist (see Section 15)

Lubricate the steering knuckle and chassis if condition C exists (see Section 14)

Check the steering linkage, gearbox oil and steering wheel freeplay if condition C exists (see Section 19)

Check the balljoints and dust covers (2WD vehicles) if conditions C, D, E exist (see Section 19)

Check the air filter if condition D exists (see Section 31)

Every 12,000 kilometres or 6 months, whichever occurs first:

Check the exhaust pipes and brackets if conditions(s) A, B, C, E exist (see Section 13)

Lubricate the driveshaft (4WD vehicles) if condition(s) A and C exist (see Section 14)

Check the brake linings and drums if condition(s) A, B, C, D, exist (see Section 22)

Every 24,000 kilometres or 12 months, whichever occurs first:

Renew the air filter if condition D exists (see Section 31)

Change the manual transmission lubricant if condition(s) A and C exist (see Section 34)

Change the automatic transmission fluid if condition(s) A and C exist (see Section 35)

Change the differential lubricant if condition(s) A and C exist (see Section 36)

Change the transfer case lubricant (4WD vehicles) if condition(s) A and C exist (see Section 37)

2 Introduction

This Chapter is designed to help the home mechanic maintain the Toyota Hi-Lux/4Runner with the goals of maximum performance, economy, safety and reliability in mind.

Included is a master maintenance schedule, followed by procedures dealing specifically with each item on the schedule. Visual checks, adjustments, component renewal and other helpful items are included. Refer to the accompanying illustrations of the engine compartment and the under side of the vehicle for the locations of various components.

Servicing your vehicle in accordance with the planned distance/time maintenance schedule and the step-by-step procedures should result in maximum reliability and extend the life of your vehicle. Keep in mind that it's a comprehensive plan - maintaining some items but not others at the specified intervals will not produce the same results.

As you perform routine maintenance procedures, you'll find that many can, and should, be grouped together because of the nature of the procedures or because of the proximity of two otherwise unrelated components or systems.

For example, if the vehicle is raised for chassis lubrication, you should inspect the exhaust, suspension, steering and fuel systems while you're under the vehicle. When you're rotating the tyres, it makes good sense to check the brakes since the wheels are already removed. Finally, let's suppose you have to borrow or rent a torque wrench. Even if you only need it to tighten the lug nuts, you might as well check the torque of as many critical fasteners as time allows.

The first step in this maintenance program is to prepare yourself before the actual work begins. Read through all the procedures you're planning to do, then gather up all the parts and tools needed. If it looks like you might run into problems during a particular job, seek advice from a mechanic or experienced do-it-yourselfer.

3 Tune-up general information

The term tune-up is used in this manual to represent a combination of individual operations rather than one specific procedure.

If, from the time the vehicle is new, the routine maintenance schedule is followed closely and frequent checks are made of fluid levels and high wear items, as suggested throughout this manual, the engine will be kept in relatively good running condition and the need for additional work will be minimised.

More likely than not, however, there will be times when the engine is running poorly due to lack of regular maintenance. This is even more likely if a used vehicle, which has not received regular and frequent maintenance checks, is purchased. In such cases, an engine tune-up will be needed outside of the regular routine maintenance intervals.

The first step in any tune-up or diagnostic procedure to help correct a poor running engine is a cylinder compression check. A compression check (see Chapter 2 Part B) will help determine the condition of internal engine components and should be used as a guide for tune-up and repair procedures. If, for instance, a compression check indicates serious internal engine wear, a conventional tune-up will not improve the performance of the engine and would be a waste of time and money. Because of its importance, the compression check should be done by someone with the right equipment and the knowledge to use it properly.

The following procedures are those most often needed to bring a generally poor running engine back into a proper state of tune.

Minor tune-up

Check all engine related fluids (see Section 4)

Check the cylinder compression (see Chapter 2E)

Clean and check the battery (see Section 10)

Check and service the cooling system (see Section 11)

Check all underbonnet hoses (see Section 12)

Check and adjust the drivebelts (see Section 16)

Check and adjust the idle and maximum engine speeds (see Section 17)

Adjust the valve clearances (R-series engines), (L, 1988 and earlier 2L engines) (see Section 18)

Renew the fuel filter/service the sedimenter (see Section 28)

Renew the air filter (see Section 31)

Check the PCV hose (see Section 32)

Renew the spark plugs (see Section 44)

Inspect the distributor cap and rotor (see Section 41)

Inspect the spark plug and coil wires (see Section 45)

Check and adjust the ignition timing (see Section 43)

Major tune-up

All items listed under Minor tune-up plus

Check the charging system (see Chapter 5)

Check the ignition system (petrol) (see Chapter 5)

Check the EGR system (petrol) (see Chapter 6)

Check the fuel system (see Section 20 and see Chapter 4A or Chapter 4B)

4 Fluid level checks

Note: *The following are fluid level checks to be done on a 400 kilometre or weekly basis. Additional fluid level checks can be found in specific maintenance procedures which follow. Regardless of how often the fluid levels are checked, watch for puddles under the vehicle - if leaks are noted, make repairs immediately.*

1 Fluids are an essential part of the lubrication, cooling, brake, clutch and windscreen washer systems. Because the fluids gradually become depleted and/or contaminated during normal operation of the vehicle, they must be periodically replenished. See Recommended lubricants and fluids at the beginning of this

4.4a Location of the engine oil dipstick (right arrow) and filler cap (left arrow)

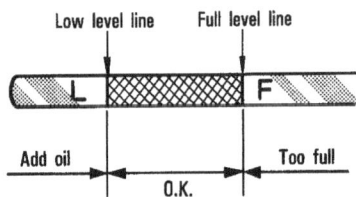

4.4b The engine oil level MUST be kept between the Low and Full marks on the dipstick or serious and costly engine damage could occur!

Chapter before adding fluid to any of the following components. **Note:** *The vehicle must be on level ground when fluid levels are checked.*

Engine oil

Refer to illustrations 4.4a and 4.4b

2   The engine oil level is checked with a dipstick that extends through a tube and into the sump at the bottom of the engine.

3   The oil level should be checked before the vehicle has been driven, or about 15 minutes after the engine has been shut off. If the oil is checked immediately after driving the vehicle, some of the oil will remain in the upper engine components, resulting in an inaccurate reading on the dipstick.

4   Pull the dipstick out of the tube **(see illustration)** and wipe all the oil from the end with a clean rag or paper towel. Insert the clean dipstick all the way back into the tube, then pull it out again. Note the oil at the end of the dipstick. Add oil as necessary to keep the level between the L (low) mark and the F (full) mark on the dipstick **(see illustration)**.

5   Don't overfill the engine by adding too much oil since this may result in oil leaks or oil seal failures. If the level is too high, the oil could be aerated by the crankshaft and severe engine damage may result.

6   Oil is added to the engine after removing a threaded cap from the valve cover **(see illustration 4.4a)**. A funnel will help reduce spills.

7   Checking the oil level is an important preventive maintenance step. A consistently low oil level indicates oil leakage through damaged seals, defective gaskets or past

worn rings or valve guides. If the oil looks milky in colour or has water droplets in it, the cylinder head gasket(s) may be blown or the head(s) or block may be cracked. The engine should be checked immediately. The condition of the oil should also be checked. Whenever you check the oil level, slide your thumb and index finger up the dipstick before wiping off the oil. If you see small dirt or metal particles clinging to the dipstick, the oil should be changed (see Section 15).

Engine coolant

Refer to illustrations 4.9a and 4.9b

Warning: *Don't allow antifreeze to come in contact with your skin or painted surfaces of the vehicle. Flush contaminated areas immediately with plenty of water. Don't store new coolant or leave old coolant lying around where it's accessible to children or pets - they're attracted by its sweet smell. Ingestion of even a small amount of coolant can be fatal! Wipe up garage floor and drip pan coolant spills immediately. Keep antifreeze containers covered and repair leaks in your cooling system as soon as they are noticed.*

8   All vehicles covered by this manual are equipped with a pressurised coolant recovery system. A white plastic coolant reservoir located in the engine compartment is connected by a hose to the radiator filler neck. If the engine overheats, coolant escapes through a valve in the radiator cap and travels through the hose into the reservoir. As the engine cools, the coolant is automatically drawn back into the cooling system to maintain the correct level.

9   The coolant level in the reservoir should be checked regularly. **Warning:** *Do not remove the radiator cap to check the coolant level when the engine is warm.* The level in the reservoir varies with the temperature of the engine. When the engine is cold, coolant level should be at or slightly above the Low mark on the reservoir. Once the engine has warmed up, the level should be at or near the Full mark **(see illustration)**. If it isn't, allow the engine to cool, then remove the cap from the reservoir and add a 50/50 mixture of ethylene glycol-based antifreeze and water

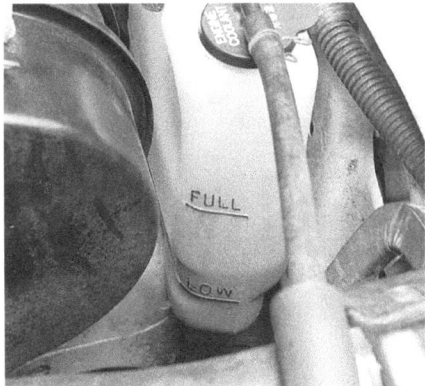

4.9a If the coolant level in the reservoir isn't between the two marks . . .

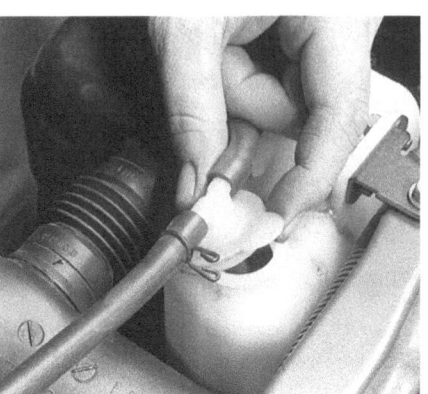

4.9b . . . prise up on the cap to remove it and add more coolant to the reservoir - DO NOT overfill it!

(see illustration).

10   Drive the vehicle and recheck the coolant level. If only a small amount of coolant is required to bring the system up to the proper level, water can be used. However, repeated additions of water will dilute the antifreeze and water solution. In order to maintain the proper ratio of antifreeze and water, always top up the coolant level with the correct mixture. An empty plastic milk jug or bleach bottle makes an excellent container for mixing coolant. Do not use rust inhibitors or additives.

11   If the coolant level drops consistently, there may be a leak in the system. Inspect the radiator, hoses, filler cap, drain plugs and water pump (see Section 11). If no leaks are noted, have the radiator cap pressure tested by a service station.

12   If you have to remove the radiator cap, wait until the engine has cooled, then wrap a thick cloth around the cap and turn it to the first stop. If coolant or steam escapes, let the engine cool down longer, then remove the cap.

13   Check the condition of the coolant as well. It should be relatively clear. If it's brown or rust coloured, the system should be drained, flushed and refilled. Even if the coolant appears to be normal, the corrosion inhibitors wear out, so it must be renewed at the specified intervals.

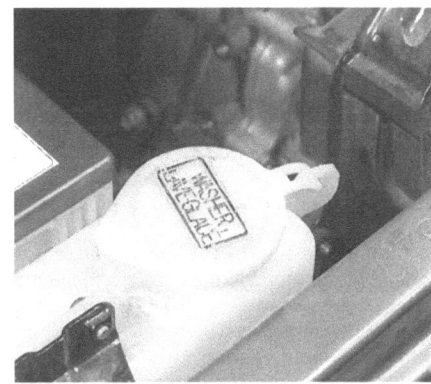

4.14 The windscreen washer fluid level should be kept near the top of the reservoir - don't confuse the windscreen washer and engine coolant reservoirs

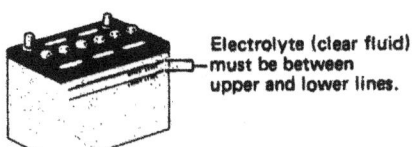

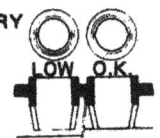

Electrolyte (clear fluid) must be between upper and lower lines.

TRANSLUCENT BATTERY

LOW   O.K.

OPAQUE BATTERY

4.17 On some batteries, the electrolyte level can be checked without removing the cell caps - it must be maintained between the lines on the case

4.19a The brake fluid level should be kept near the upper (MAX) mark on the reservoir - it's translucent so the cover doesn't have to be removed for the check

4.19b The clutch fluid level should be maintained at the line on the reservoir (arrow)

Windscreen washer fluid

Refer to illustration 4.14

14   Fluid for the windscreen washer system is stored in a plastic reservoir located near the battery **(see illustration)**. If necessary, refer to the underbonnet component illustration(s) at the beginning of this Chapter to locate the reservoir.
15   In milder climates, plain water can be used in the reservoir, but it should be kept no more than 2/3 full to allow for expansion if the water freezes. In colder climates, use windscreen washer system antifreeze, available at any auto parts store, to lower the freezing point of the fluid. Mix the antifreeze with water in accordance with the manufacturer's directions on the container. **Caution:** *Don't use cooling system antifreeze - it will damage the vehicle's paint.*
16   To help prevent icing in cold weather, warm the windscreen with the defroster before using the washer.

Battery electrolyte

Refer to illustration 4.17

17   To check the electrolyte level in the battery, remove all of the cell caps. If the level is low, add distilled water until it's above the plates. Some batteries are translucent so the electrolyte level can be checked by looking at the side of the case **(see illustration)**. Most aftermarket renewal batteries have a split-ring indicator in each cell to help you judge when enough water has been added - don't overfill the cells!

Brake and clutch fluid

Refer to illustrations 4.19a and 4.19b

18   The brake master cylinder is mounted on the front of the power booster unit in the engine compartment. The clutch cylinder used on manual transmission models is mounted adjacent to it on the firewall.
19   The fluid inside is readily visible. The level should be between the MIN and MAX marks on the reservoirs **(see illustrations)**. If a low level is indicated, be sure to wipe the top of the reservoir cover with a clean rag to prevent contamination of the brake and/or clutch system before removing the cover.

20   When adding fluid, pour it carefully into the reservoir to avoid spilling it onto surrounding painted surfaces. Be sure the specified fluid is used, since mixing different types of brake fluid can cause damage to the system. See *Recommended lubricants and fluids* at the front of this Chapter or your owner's manual. **Warning:** *Brake fluid can harm your eyes and damage painted surfaces, so be very careful when handling or pouring it. Don't use brake fluid that's been standing open or is more than one year old. Brake fluid absorbs moisture from the air. Excess moisture can cause a dangerous loss of brake efficiency.*
21   At this time the fluid and master cylinder can be inspected for contamination. The system should be drained and refilled if deposits, dirt particles or water droplets are seen in the fluid.
22   After filling the reservoir to the proper level, make sure the cover is on tight to prevent fluid leakage.
23   The brake fluid level in the master cylinder will drop slightly as the pads and the brake shoes at each wheel wear down during normal operation. If the master cylinder requires repeated additions to keep it at the proper level, it's an indication of leakage in the brake system, which should be corrected immediately. Check all brake lines and connections (see Section 22 for more information).

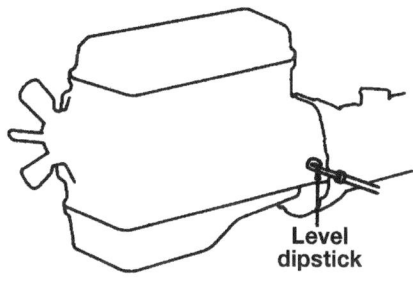

5.3 The automatic transmission fluid dipstick is located at the rear of the engine, on the left side

Level dipstick

24   If, upon checking the master cylinder fluid level, you discover one or both reservoirs empty or nearly empty, the brake system should be bled (see Chapter 9).

5   Automatic transmission fluid level check

Refer to illustrations 5.3 and 5.6

1   The automatic transmission fluid level should be carefully maintained. Low fluid level can lead to slipping or loss of drive, while overfilling can cause foaming and loss of fluid.
2   With the parking brake set, start the engine, then move the shift lever through all the gear ranges, ending in Park. The fluid level must be checked with the vehicle level and the engine running at idle. **Note:** *Incorrect fluid level readings will result if the vehicle has just been driven at high speeds for an extended period, in hot weather in city traffic, or if it has been pulling a trailer. If any of these conditions apply, wait until the fluid has cooled (about 30 minutes).*
3   With the transmission at normal operating temperature, remove the dipstick from the filler tube. The dipstick is located at the rear of the engine compartment, usually on the left side **(see illustration)**.
4   Carefully touch the fluid at the end of the dipstick to determine if it's cool (30 to 50-degrees C) or hot (51 to 80-degrees C). Wipe the fluid from the dipstick with a clean rag and push it back into the filler tube until the cap seats.
5   Pull the dipstick out again and note the fluid level.
6   If the fluid felt cool, the level should be within the COLD range (between the cutouts) **(see illustration)**. If the fluid was hot, the level should be within the HOT range.
7   If additional fluid is required, add it directly into the tube using a funnel. It takes about 0.5 litre to raise the level from the L mark to the H mark with a hot transmission, so add the fluid a little at a time and keep checking the level until it's correct.

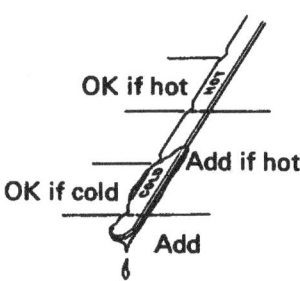

5.6 The fluid level on the dipstick will change, depending on the temperature of the transmission and fluid

8   The condition of the fluid should also be checked along with the level. If the fluid at the end of the dipstick is a dark reddish-brown colour, or if it smells burned, it should be changed. If you are in doubt about the condition of the fluid, purchase some new fluid and compare the two for colour and smell.

6   Power steering fluid level check

Refer to illustration 6.2

1   Unlike manual steering, the power steering system relies on fluid which may, over a period of time, require replenishing.
2   The fluid reservoir for the V6 engine power steering pump is located on the pump body at the front of the engine. On vehicles with a four-cylinder engine, the reservoir is separate from the pump and is mounted on the left side inner fender panel **(see illustration)**.

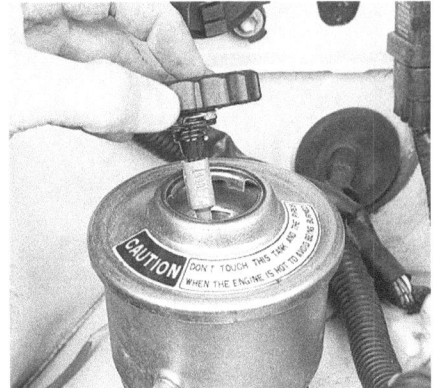

6.2 The power steering pump reservoir is mounted on the left side inner fender panel in the engine compartment - the dipstick has marks for checking the fluid level hot or cold

3   For the check, the front wheels should be pointed straight ahead and the engine should be off. The power steering fluid should be warm (although the dipstick for some models is graduated for hot or cold checking). The fluid can be considered cold if the engine hasn't been run for at least five hours.
4   Use a clean rag to wipe off the reservoir cap and the area around it. This will help prevent any foreign matter from entering the reservoir during the check.
5   Twist off the cap - it has a dipstick attached to it.
6   Wipe off the fluid with a clean rag, reinsert the dipstick, then withdraw it and note the fluid level. The level should be within the range marked on the dipstick **(see illustra-**

7.2 A tyre tread depth indicator should be used to monitor tyre wear - they're available at auto parts stores and service stations and cost very little

tion). Never allow the fluid level to drop below the lower range mark.
7   If additional fluid is required, pour the specified type directly into the reservoir, using a funnel to prevent spills.
8   If the reservoir requires frequent fluid additions, all power steering hoses, hose connections and the power steering pump should be carefully checked for leaks.

7   Tyre and tyre pressure checks

Refer to illustrations 7.2, 7.3, 7.4a, 7.4b and 7.8

1   Periodic inspection of the tyres may spare you the inconvenience of being stranded with a flat tyre. It can also provide you with vital information regarding possible problems in the steering and suspension systems before major damage occurs.
2   The original tyres on this vehicle are equipped with wear indicator bars that will appear when tread depth reaches a predetermined limit, usually about 1.5 mm. Tread wear can be monitored with a simple, inexpensive device known as a tread depth indicator **(see illustration)**.
3   Note any abnormal tread wear **(see illustration)**. Tread pattern irregularities such as cupping, flat spots and more wear on one side than the other are indications of front end alignment and/or balance problems. If any of these conditions are noted, take the vehicle to a tyre shop or service station to correct the problem.
4   Look closely for cuts, punctures and embedded nails or tacks. Sometimes a tyre will hold air pressure for a short time or leak down very slowly after a nail has embedded itself in the tread. If a slow leak persists, check the valve stem core to make sure it's tight **(see illustration)**. Examine the tread for an object that may have embedded itself in the tyre or for a "plug" that may have begun to leak (radial tyre punctures are repaired with a plug that's fitted in a puncture). If a puncture is suspected, it can be easily verified by spray-

UNDERINFLATION

INCORRECT TOE-IN OR EXTREME CAMBER

CUPPING

Cupping may be caused by:
● Underinflation and/or mechanical irregularities such as out-of-balance condition of wheel and/or tyre, and bent or damaged wheel.
● Loose or worn steering tie-rod or steering idler arm.
● Loose, damaged or worn front suspension parts.

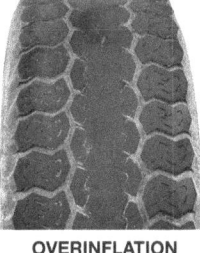

OVERINFLATION

FEATHERING DUE TO MISALIGNMENT

7.3 This chart will help you determine the condition of your tyres, the probable cause(s) of abnormal wear and the corrective action necessary

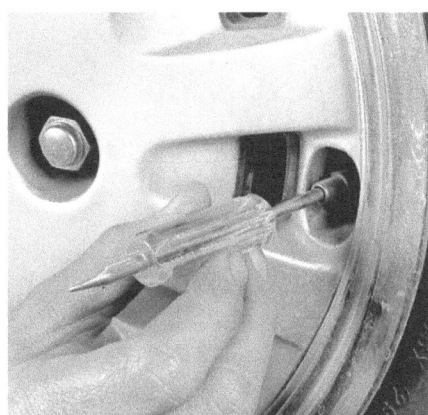

7.4a If a tyre loses air on a steady basis, check the valve core first to make sure it's snug (special inexpensive wrenches are commonly available at auto parts stores)

7.4b If the valve core is tight, raise the corner of the vehicle with the low tyre and spray a soapy water solution onto the tread as the tyre is turned - slow leaks will cause small bubbles to appear

7.8 To extend the life of the tyres, check the air pressure at least once a week with an accurate gauge (don't forget the spare!)

ing a solution of soapy water onto the tread area **(see illustration)**. The soapy solution will bubble if there's a leak. Unless the puncture is unusually large, a tyre shop or service station can usually repair the tyre.

5   Carefully inspect the inner sidewall of each tyre for evidence of brake fluid leakage. If you see any, inspect the brakes immediately.

6   Correct air pressure adds to the life span of the tyres, improves fuel economy and enhances overall ride quality. Tyre pressure cannot be accurately estimated by looking at a tyre, especially if it's a radial. A tyre pressure gauge is essential. Keep an accurate gauge in the vehicle. The pressure gauges attached to the nozzles of air hoses at service stations are often inaccurate.

7   Always check tyre pressure when the tyres are cold. Cold, in this case, means the vehicle has not been driven over two kilometres in the three hours preceding a tyre pressure check. A pressure rise of 30 to 50 kPa is not uncommon once the tyres are warm.

8   Unscrew the valve cap protruding from the wheel or hubcap and push the gauge firmly onto the valve stem **(see illustration)**. Note the reading on the gauge and compare the figure to the recommended tyre pressure

shown on the placard on the glove compartment door. Be sure to refit the valve cap to keep dirt and moisture out of the valve stem mechanism. Check all four tyres and, if necessary, add enough air to bring them up to the recommended pressure.

9   Don't forget to keep the spare tyre inflated to the specified pressure (refer to your owner's manual or the tyre sidewall).

8   Wiper blade check and renewal

Refer to illustrations 8.5 and 8.6

1   The windscreen wiper and blade assembly should be inspected periodically for damage, loose components and cracked or worn blade elements.

2   Road film can build up on the wiper blades and affect their efficiency, so they should be washed regularly with a mild detergent and water solution.

3   The action of the wiping mechanism can loosen the fasteners, so they should be checked and tightened, as necessary, at the same time the wiper blades are checked.

4   If the wiper blade elements (sometimes called inserts) are cracked, worn or warped,

they should be renewed.

5   Pull the top of the rubber element in until it's free of the end slot, revealing the renewal hole **(see illustration)**. Pull the rubber blade element out of the hole.

6   To fit the new one, insert the end of the element with the small protrusions into the renewal hole and work the rubber along the slot into the frame **(see illustration)**. Once the entire blade is in the frame slot, allow it to expand and fill in the end.

9   Brake pedal check and adjustment

Pedal height

Refer to illustration 9.1

1   Make sure the pedal height is correct by measuring the distance from the floor board to the top of the pedal **(see illustration)**. See the Specifications at the front of this Chapter. If incorrect, adjust the pedal height.

2   Loosen the brake light switch.

3   Adjust the pedal height by turning the pushrod until the specified height is attained.

4   Tighten the brake light switch until the switch body lightly contacts the pedal stop.

5   After adjusting the pedal height, check and adjust the pedal freeplay.

Pedal freeplay

Refer to illustration 9.8

6   With the engine off, depress the brake pedal several times until there is no more vacuum left in the booster.

7   Depress the pedal by hand until resistance is felt.

8   Measure the distance the pedal travels before resistance is felt **(see illustration)**. Compare the results to the Specifications.

9   If incorrect, adjust the pedal freeplay by turning the pushrod.

10   Start the engine and confirm that the pedal freeplay is correct.

8.5 Pull the wiper blade element out of the end slot, then through the renewal hole

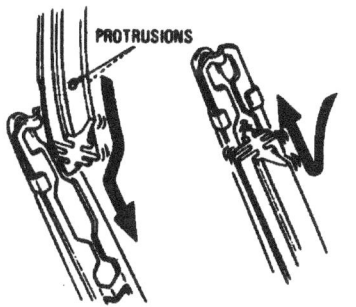

8.6 Insert the end of the new blade element with the protrusions into the renewal hole and slide the element into place

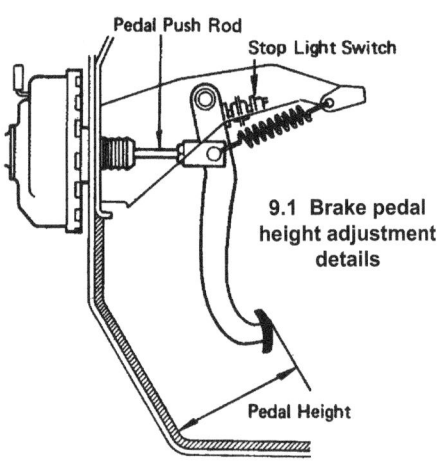

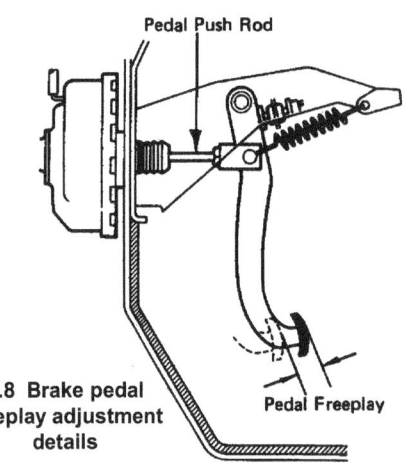

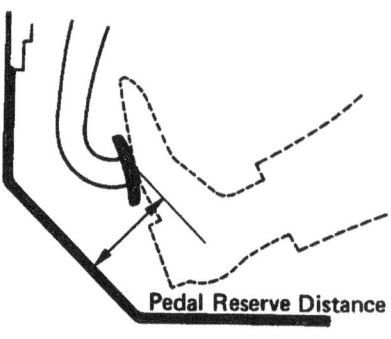

9.1 Brake pedal height adjustment details

9.8 Brake pedal freeplay adjustment details

9.13 Brake pedal reserve distance must be as specified

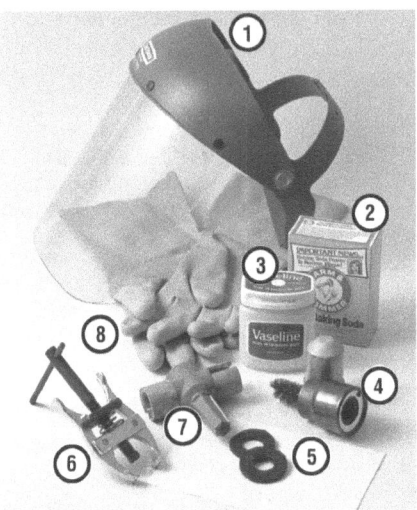

10.1 Tools and materials required for battery maintenance

1 *Face shield/safety goggles - When removing corrosion with a brush, the acidic particles can easily fly up into your eyes*

2 ***Baking soda*** *- A solution of baking soda and water can be used to neutralise corrosion*

3 ***Petroleum jelly*** *- A layer of this on the battery posts will help prevent corrosion*

4 ***Battery post/cable cleaner*** *- This wire brush cleaning tool will remove all traces of corrosion from the battery posts and cable clamps*

5 ***Treated felt washers*** *- Placing one of these on each post, directly under the cable clamps, will help prevent corrosion*

6 ***Puller*** *- Sometimes the cable clamps are very difficult to pull off the posts, even after the nut/bolt has been completely loosened. This tool pulls the clamp straight up and off the post without damage*

7 ***Battery post/cable cleaner*** *- Here is another cleaning tool which is a slightly different version of number 4 above, but it does the same thing*

8 ***Rubber gloves*** *- Another safety item to consider when servicing the battery; remember, that's acid inside the battery!*

11   After adjusting the pedal freeplay, recheck the pedal height.

12   Recheck the clearance between the brake light switch and the pedal stop. There should be a clearance of 0.51 to 2.29 mm. If adjustment is necessary, loosen the brake light switch locknut and turn the brake light switch body until the correct amount is obtained. Tighten the locknut.

Pedal reserve distance

Refer to illustration 9.13

13   With the brake pedal fully depressed, measure the distance from the floor board to a line parallel with the floor board at the centre of the brake pedal **(see illustration)**. Confirm that this measurement is within the specified limits.

10   Battery check and maintenance

Refer to illustrations 10.1, 10.5a, 10.5b, 10.5c and 10.5d

Warning: *Several precautions must be followed when checking and servicing the battery. Hydrogen gas, which is highly flammable, is always present in the battery cells, so keep lighted tobacco and all other open flames and sparks away from the battery. The electrolyte in the cells is actually dilute sul-*

10.5a Battery terminal corrosion usually appears as light, fluffy powder

phuric acid, which will cause injury if splashed on your skin or in your eyes. It'll also ruin clothes and painted surfaces. When removing the battery cables, always detach the negative cable first and hook it up last!

Check

1   Battery maintenance is an important procedure which will help ensure that you aren't stranded because of a dead battery. Several tools are required for this procedure **(see illustration)**.

2   The electrolyte level should be checked every week (see Section 4).

3   Periodically clean the top and sides of the battery. Remove all dirt and moisture. This will help prevent corrosion and ensure that the battery doesn't become partially discharged by leakage through moisture and dirt. Check the case for cracks and distortion.

4   Check the tightness of the battery cable bolts to ensure good electrical connections. Inspect the entire length of each cable, looking for cracked or abraded insulation and frayed conductors. Battery cable removal and refitting is covered in Chapter 5.

5   If corrosion, which usually appears as white, fluffy deposits, is evident, remove the cables from the terminals, clean them with

10.5b Removing the cable from the battery post with a spanner - sometimes special battery pliers are required for this procedure if corrosion has caused deterioration of the nut hex (always remove the earth cable first and hook it up last!)

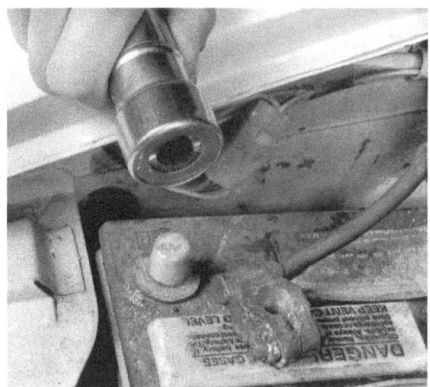

10.5c Regardless of the type of tool used to clean the battery posts, a clean, shiny surface should be the result

10.5d When cleaning the cable clamps, all corrosion must be removed (the inside of the clamp is tapered to match the taper of the post, so don't remove too much material)

Check for a chafed area that could fail prematurely.

Check for a soft area indicating the hose has deteriorated inside.

Overtightening the clamp on a hardened hose will damage the hose and cause a leak.

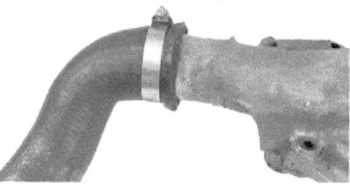

Check each hose for swelling and oil-soaked ends. Cracks and breaks can be located by squeezing the hose.

11.4 Hoses, like drivebelts, have a habit of failing at the worst possible time - to prevent the inconvenience of a blown radiator or heater hose, inspect them carefully as shown here

a battery brush and refit them **(see illustrations)**. Corrosion can be kept to a minimum by applying a layer of petroleum jelly to the terminals after the cables are in place.

6   Make sure the battery carrier is in good condition and the hold-down clamp is tight. If the battery is removed, make sure that nothing is in the bottom of the carrier when it's refitted and don't overtighten the clamp nuts.

7   The freezing point of electrolyte depends on its specific gravity. Since freezing can ruin a battery, it should be kept in a fully charged state to protect against freezing.

8   If you frequently have to add water to the battery and the case has been inspected for cracks that could cause leakage, but none are found, the battery is being overcharged; the charging system should be checked as described in Chapter 5.

9   If any doubt exists about the battery state of charge, a hydrometer should be used to test it by withdrawing a little electrolyte from each cell, one at a time.

10   The specific gravity of the electrolyte at 27-degrees C will be approximately 1.270 for a fully charged battery. For every 5.5-degrees C that the electrolyte temperature is above 27-degrees C, add 0.04 to the specific gravity. Subtract 0.04 if the temperature is below 27-degrees C.

11   A specific gravity reading of 1.240 with an electrolyte temperature of 27-degrees C indicates a half-charged battery.

12   Some of the common causes of battery failure are:

a) *Accessories, especially headlights, left on overnight or for several hours.*

b) *Slow average driving speeds for short intervals.*

c) *The electrical load of the vehicle being more than the alternator output. This is very common when several high draw accessories are being used simultaneously (such as radio/stereo, air conditioning, window defoggers, lights, etc.).*

d) *Charging system problems such as short circuits, slipping drivebelt, defective alternator or faulty voltage regulator.*

e) *Battery neglect, such as loose or corroded terminals or loose battery hold-down clamp.*

Battery charging

13   In winter when heavy demand is placed upon the battery, it's a good idea to occasionally have it charged from an external source.

14   When charging the battery, the negative cable should be disconnected. The charger leads should be connected to the battery before the charger is plugged in or turned on. If the leads are connected to the battery terminals after the charger is on, a spark could occur and the hydrogen gas given off by the battery could explode!

15   The battery should be charged at a low rate of about 4 to 6 amps, and should be left on for at least three or four hours. A trickle charger charging at the rate of 1.5 amps can be safely used overnight.

16   Special rapid boost charges which are claimed to restore the power of the battery in a short time can cause serious damage to the battery plates and should only be used in an emergency situation.

17   The battery should be left on the charger only until the specific gravity is brought up to a normal level. Don't overcharge the battery! **Note:** *Some battery chargers will automatically shut off after the battery is fully charged, making it unnecessary to keep a close watch on the state of charge.*

18   When disconnecting the charger, unplug it before disconnecting the charger leads from the battery.

---

11   Cooling system check

Refer to illustration 11.4

1   Many major engine failures can be attributed to a faulty cooling system. If the vehicle is equipped with an automatic transmission, the cooling system also cools the transmission fluid, prolonging transmission life.

2   The cooling system should be checked with the engine cold. Do this before the vehicle is driven for the day or after it has been shut off for at least three hours.

3   Remove the radiator cap by turning it counterclockwise until it reaches a stop. If you hear a hissing sound (indicating there's still pressure in the system), wait until it stops. Now press down on the cap with the palm of your hand and continue turning until it can be removed. Thoroughly clean the cap, inside and out, with clean water. Also clean the filler neck on the radiator. All traces of corrosion should be removed. The coolant inside the radiator should be relatively transparent. If it's rust coloured, the system should be drained and refilled (see Section 33). If the coolant level is not up to the top, add additional anti-freeze/coolant mixture (see Section 4).

4   Carefully check the large upper and lower radiator hoses along with the smaller diameter heater hoses which run from the engine to the firewall. Inspect each hose along its entire length, renewing any hose that's cracked, swollen or deteriorated.

Cracks may become more apparent if the hose is squeezed **(see illustration)**. Regardless of condition, it's a good idea to renew hoses every two years.

5   Make sure that all hose connections are tight. A leak in the cooling system will usually show up as white or rust coloured deposits on the areas adjoining the leak. If wire-type clamps are used at the ends of the hoses, it may be a good idea to renew them with more secure screw-type clamps.

6   Use compressed air or a soft brush to remove bugs, leaves, etc. from the front of the radiator or air conditioning condenser. Be careful not to damage the delicate cooling fins or cut yourself on them.

7   Every other inspection, or at the first indication of cooling system problems, have the cap and system pressure tested. If you don't have a pressure tester, most service stations and repair shops will do this for a minimal charge.

12   Underbonnet hose check and renewal

General

1   **Caution:** *Renewal of air conditioning hoses must be left to a dealer service department or air conditioning shop that has the equipment to depressurise the system safely. Never remove air conditioning components or hoses until the system has been depressurised.*

2   High temperatures in the engine compartment can cause the deterioration of the rubber and plastic hoses used for engine and accessory operation. Periodic inspection should be made for cracks, loose clamps, material hardening and leaks. Information specific to the cooling system hoses can be found in Section 11.

3   Some, but not all, hoses are secured to the fittings with clamps. Where clamps are used, check to be sure they haven't lost their tension, allowing the hose to leak. If clamps aren't used, make sure the hose has not expanded and/or hardened where it slips over the fitting, allowing it to leak.

Vacuum hoses

4   It's quite common for vacuum hoses, especially those in the emissions system, to be colour coded or identified by coloured stripes moulded into them. Various systems require hoses with different wall thicknesses, collapse resistance and temperature resistance. When renewing hoses, be sure the new ones are made of the same material.

5   Often the only effective way to check a hose is to remove it completely from the vehicle. If more than one hose is removed, be sure to label the hoses and fittings to ensure correct refitting.

6   When checking vacuum hoses, be sure to include any plastic T-fittings in the check. Inspect the fittings for cracks and the hose where it fits over the fitting for distortion,

which could cause leakage.

7   A small piece of vacuum hose can be used as a stethoscope to detect vacuum leaks. Hold one end of the hose to your ear and probe around vacuum hoses and fittings, listening for the "hissing" sound characteristic of a vacuum leak. **Warning:** *When probing with the vacuum hose stethoscope, be very careful not to come into contact with moving engine components such as the drivebelts and fan.*

Fuel hose

Warning: *There are certain precautions which must be taken when inspecting or servicing fuel system components. Work in a well ventilated area and don't allow open flames (cigarettes, appliance pilot lights, etc.) or bare light bulbs near the work area. Mop up any spills immediately and don't store fuel soaked rags where they could ignite. On vehicles equipped with fuel injection, the fuel system is under pressure, so if any fuel lines are to be disconnected, the pressure in the system must be relieved first* (see Chapter 4A).

8   Check all rubber fuel lines for deterioration and chafing. Check carefully for cracks in areas where the hose bends and where it's attached to fittings.

9   High quality fuel line should be used for fuel line renewal. **Warning:** *Never, under any circumstances, use unreinforced vacuum line, clear plastic tubing or water hose for fuel lines!*

10   Spring-type clamps are commonly used on fuel lines. They often lose their tension over a period of time, and can be "sprung" during removal. Renew all spring-type clamps with screw clamps whenever a hose is renewed.

Metal lines

11   Sections of metal line are used between the fuel pump and the fuel injectors. Check carefully to be sure the line has not been bent or crimped and look for signs of leakage. These lines must only be renewed with genuine factory injection pipes due to the extremely high pressures developed by the fuel injection pump.

12   If a section of metal fuel line must be renewed, only seamless steel tubing should be used, since copper and aluminium tubing don't have the strength necessary to withstand normal engine vibration.

13   Check the metal brake lines where they enter the master cylinder and brake proportioning unit (if used) for cracks in the lines and loose fittings. Any sign of brake fluid leakage means an immediate thorough inspection of the brake system should be done.

13   Exhaust system check

1   With the engine cold (at least three hours after the vehicle has been driven), check the complete exhaust system from the manifold to the end of the tailpipe.

Warning: *On petrol models, be careful around the catalytic converter, which may be hot even after three hours.*

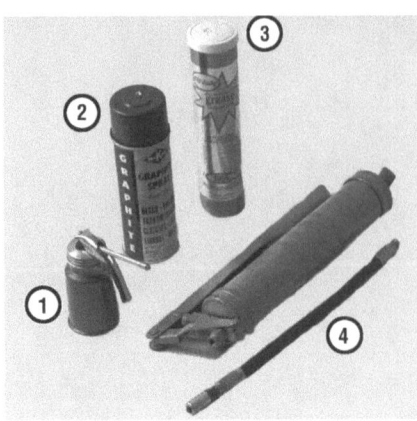

14.1 Materials required for chassis and body lubrication

1   *Engine oil - Light engine oil in a can like this can be used for door and bonnet hinges*
2   **Graphite spray** *- Used to lubricate lock cylinders*
3   *Grease - Grease, in a variety of types and weights, is available for use in a grease gun. Check the Specifications for your requirements*
4   **Grease gun** *- A common grease gun, shown here with a detachable hose and nozzle, is needed for chassis lubrication. After use, clean it thoroughly!*

2   Raise the vehicle and support it securely on jackstands.

3   Check the exhaust pipes and connections for signs of leakage and/or corrosion indicating a potential failure. Make sure that all brackets and hangers are in good condition and tight.

4   Inspect the underside of the body for holes, corrosion, open seams, etc. which may allow exhaust gases to enter the passenger compartment. Seal all body openings with silicone sealant or body putty.

5   Rattles and other noises can often be traced to the exhaust system, especially the hangers, mounts and heat shields. Try to move the pipes, muffler(s) and on petrol models, the catalytic converter. If the components can come in contact with the body or suspension parts, secure the exhaust system with new brackets and hangers.

14   Chassis lubrication

Refer to illustrations 14.1, 14.3, 14.5 and 14.6

1   A grease gun and cartridge filled with the recommended grease are the only items required for chassis lubrication other than some clean rags and equipment needed to raise and support the vehicle safely **(see illustration)**.

2   For easier access under the vehicle, raise it with a jack and place jackstands under the frame. Make sure the vehicle is safely supported by the stands!

3   Locate the grease fittings on the chassis and driveline components **(see illustration)**.

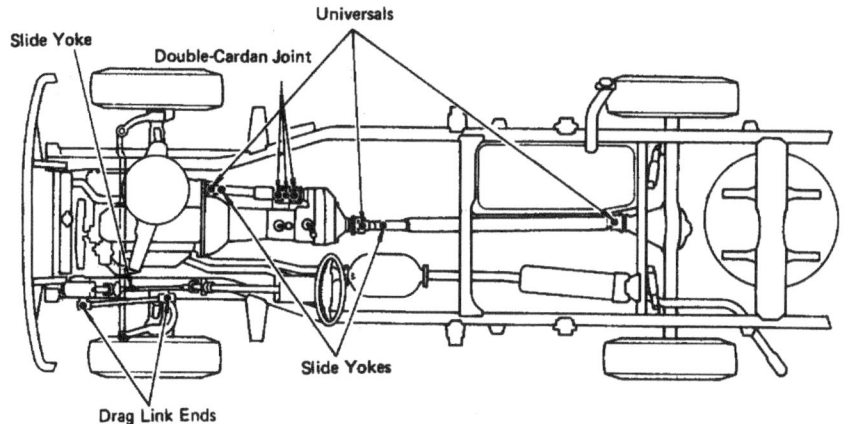

14.3 Chassis lubrication points

14.5 Suspension balljoint grease fitting locations - you may have to unscrew the plugs and fit fittings

4   Force a little of the grease out of the nozzle to remove any dirt from the end of the gun, then wipe it off with a rag.

5   To lubricate the suspension balljoints (2WD vehicles), remove the threaded plug and fit a grease fitting in each hole, then pump grease into the balljoints (see illustration). If the grease seeps out around the gun nozzle, the fitting is clogged or the nozzle isn't seated all the way. Resecure the gun nozzle to the fitting and try again. If necessary, use another grease fitting.

6   On 4WD vehicles with solid front axles only, remove the threaded plug from each steering knuckle and repack them with lubricant (see illustration). Refit the screw plugs. Lubricate the remaining chassis components (see illustration 14.3). Before pumping in any grease, wipe mud and dust off the grease fittings. Note: To lubricate the driveshaft U-joints, use the grease charger attachment included with the vehicle tool kit.

7   Wipe excess grease from the components and grease fittings.

8   While you're under the vehicle, clean and lubricate the parking brake cable, cable guides and levers.

9   Lower the vehicle to the ground.

14.6 Remove the 4WD screw plugs to lubricate the steering knuckles - later models have two plugs per wheel

10   Open the bonnet and smear a little chassis grease on the bonnet latch mechanism. Have an assistant pull the release knob from inside the vehicle as you lubricate the cable at the latch.

11   Lubricate all the hinges (door, bonnet, tailgate) with a few drops of light engine oil.

12   The key lock cylinders can be lubricated with spray-on graphite, which is available at auto parts stores.

15   Engine oil and filter change

Refer to illustrations 15.3, 15.9, 15.14a, 15.14b, 15.14c and 15.18

1   Frequent oil changes are the most important preventive maintenance procedures that can be done by the home mechanic. As engine oil ages, it becomes diluted and contaminated, which leads to premature engine wear.

2   Although some sources recommend oil filter changes every other oil change, the minimal cost of an oil filter and the fact that it's easy to renew dictate that a new filter be used every time the oil is changed.

3   Gather all necessary tools and materials before beginning this procedure (see illustration).

4   You should have plenty of clean rags and newspapers handy to mop up any spills. Access to the underside of the vehicle is greatly improved if the vehicle can be lifted on a hoist, driven onto ramps or supported by jackstands. Warning: Do not work under a vehicle which is supported only by a bumper, hydraulic or scissors-type jack!

5   If this is your first oil change, get under the vehicle and familiarise yourself with the locations of the oil drain plug and the oil filter. The engine and exhaust components will be warm during the actual work, so note how they're situated to avoid touching them when working under the vehicle.

6   Warm the engine to normal operating temperature. If the new oil or any tools are needed, use the warm-up time to obtain everything necessary for the job. The correct oil

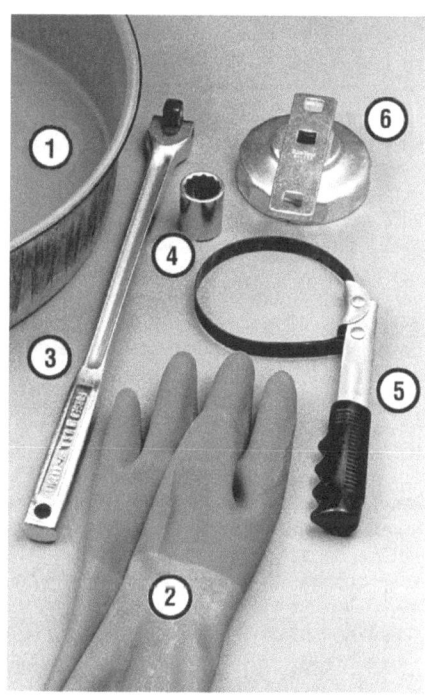

15.3 These tools are required when changing the engine oil and filter

1 Drain pan - It should be fairly shallow in depth, but wide in order to prevent spills

2 Rubber gloves - When removing the drain plug and filter it is inevitable that you will get oil on your hands (the gloves will prevent burns)

3 Breaker bar - Sometimes the oil drain plug is pretty tight and a long breaker bar is needed to loosen it

4 Socket - To be used with the breaker bar or a ratchet (must be the correct size to refit the drain plug)

5 Filter wrench - This is a metal band-type wrench, which requires clearance around the filter to be effective

6 Filter wrench - This type fits on the bottom of the filter and can be turned with a ratchet or breaker bar (different size wrenches are available for different types of filters)

15.9 The engine oil drain plug is located at the bottom of the pan and should be removed with a box-end spanner or socket - DO NOT use an open-end spanner, as the corners on the bolt hex are easily rounded off

15.14a The four-cylinder petrol engine oil filter is located on the right side of the block (arrow)

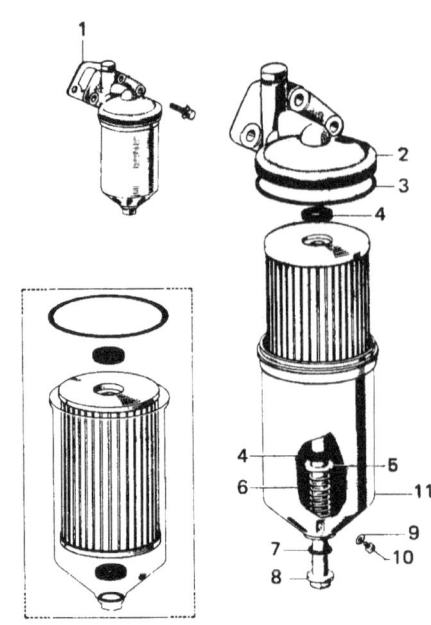

15.14b Details of the cartridge-type oil filter some petrol models use

1 Gasket	7 O-ring
2 Filter base	8 Centre bolt
3 O-ring	9 Washer
4 Seal	10 Plug
5 Washer	11 Filter bowl
6 Spring	

for your application can be found in *Recommended lubricants and fluids* at the beginning of this Chapter.

7   With the engine oil warm (warm engine oil will drain better and more built-up sludge will be removed with it), raise and support the vehicle. Make sure it's safely supported!

8   Move all necessary tools, rags and newspapers under the vehicle. Set the drain pan under the drain plug. Keep in mind that the oil will initially flow from the pan with some force; position the pan accordingly.

9   Being careful not to touch any of the hot exhaust components, use a spanner to remove the drain plug near the bottom of the sump **(see illustration)**. Depending on how hot the oil is, you may want to wear gloves while unscrewing the plug the final few turns.

10   Allow the old oil to drain into the pan. It may be necessary to move the pan as the oil flow slows to a trickle.

11   After all the oil has drained, wipe off the drain plug with a clean rag. Small metal particles may cling to the plug and would immediately contaminate the new oil.

12   Clean the area around the drain plug opening and refit the plug. Tighten the plug securely with the spanner.

13   Move the drain pan into position under the oil filter.

14   Most models are equipped with a canister-type filter. Use a filter wrench to loosen the oil filter **(see illustration)**. Chain or metal band filter wrenches may distort the filter canister, but it doesn't matter since the filter will be discarded anyway. Some early models are equipped with a cartridge-type filter unit **(see illustration)**. On these models, remove the bolt and allow the oil to drain, then remove the filter bowl and take out the filter element. Be sure to recover the O-ring from the filter base. Also, make sure the upper seal for the bolt isn't stuck to the filter base.

15   Completely unscrew the old filter. Be careful; it's full of oil. Empty the oil inside the filter into the drain pan. If you're renewing a cartridge-type filter, wash all of the components with solvent.

16   Compare the old filter with the new one to make sure they're the same type.

17   Use a clean rag to remove all oil, dirt and sludge from the area where the oil filter mounts to the engine. Check the old filter to

make sure the rubber gasket isn't stuck to the engine. If the gasket is stuck to the engine, remove it.

18   Apply a light coat of clean oil to the rubber gasket on the new oil filter **(see illustration)**.

19   If you're fitting a canister-type filter, attach the new filter to the engine, following the tightening directions printed on the filter canister or packing box. Most filter manufacturers recommend against using a filter wrench due to the possibility of overtightening and damage to the seal. If you're renewing a cartridge-type filter, be sure to use new O-rings and seals and lubricate them with clean engine oil. Finally, fit the filter assembly and tighten the centre bolt securely, but don't overtighten it.

20   Remove all tools, rags, etc. from under the vehicle, being careful not to spill the oil in the drain pan, then lower the vehicle.

21   Move to the engine compartment and locate the oil filler cap.

22   Pour the fresh oil through the filler cap opening. A funnel may be needed to avoid spills.

23   Pour three litres (petrol models) or five litres (diesel models) of fresh oil into the engine. Wait a few minutes to allow the oil to drain into the pan, then check the level on the oil dipstick (see Section 4 if necessary). If the oil level is above the L mark, start the engine and allow the new oil to circulate.

24   Run the engine for only about a minute

15.14c Removing the oil filter from the right side of the block - diesel engines

15.18 Lubricate the oil filter gasket with clean engine oil before fitting the filter on the engine

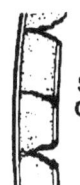
SMALL CRACKS

GREASE

GLAZED

ALWAYS CHECK the underside of the belt.

16.3a Here are some of the more common problems associated with drivebelts (check the belts very carefully to prevent an untimely breakdown)

ACCEPTABLE

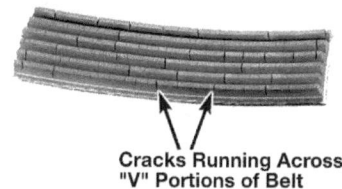

Cracks Running Across "V" Portions of Belt

UNACCEPTABLE

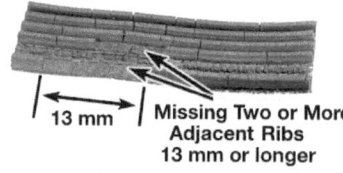

13 mm | Missing Two or More Adjacent Ribs 13 mm or longer

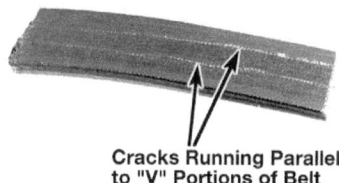

Cracks Running Parallel to "V" Portions of Belt

16.3b Small cracks in the underside of a V-ribbed belt are acceptable - lengthwise cracks, or missing pieces that cause the belt to make noise, are cause for renewal

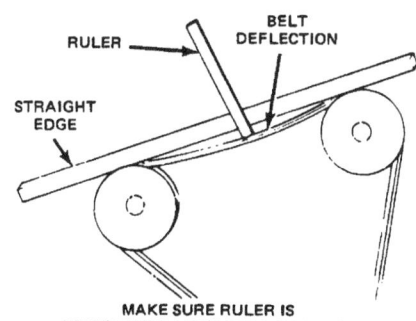

BELT DEFLECTION
RULER
STRAIGHT EDGE
MAKE SURE RULER IS PERPENDICULAR TO STRAIGHT EDGE

16.5 Measuring drivebelt deflection with a straightedge and ruler

16.6 Some components have an adjusting bolt that can be used to tension the drivebelt very accurately

and then shut it off. Immediately look under the vehicle and check for leaks at the sump drain plug and around the oil filter. If either one is leaking, tighten it a little more.

25 With the new oil circulated and the filter now completely full, recheck the level on the dipstick and add more oil as necessary.

26 During the first few trips after an oil change, make it a point to check frequently for leaks and correct oil level.

27 The old oil drained from the engine cannot be reused in its present state and should be disposed of. Oil reclamation centres, auto repair shops and service stations will normally accept the oil, which can be refined and used again. After the oil has cooled it can be poured into a container (capped plastic jugs or bottles, milk cartons, etc.) for transport to a disposal site.

16 Drivebelt check, adjustment and renewal

Refer to illustrations 16.3a, 16.3b, 16.5 and 16.6

1 The drivebelts, or V-belts as they are often called, are located at the front of the engine and play an important role in the overall operation of the engine and accessories. Due to their function and material makeup, the belts are prone to failure after a period of time and should be inspected and adjusted periodically to prevent major engine damage.

2 The number of belts used on a particular vehicle depends on the accessories fitted. Drivebelts are used to turn the alternator, smog pump, power steering pump, water pump and air conditioning compressor. Depending on the pulley arrangement, more than one of the components may be driven by a single belt.

3 With the engine off, locate the drivebelts at the front of the engine. Using your fingers (and a flashlight, if necessary), move along the belts checking for cracks and separation of the belt plies. Also check for fraying and glazing, which gives the belt a shiny appearance **(see illustration)**. Check V-ribbed belts

for longitudinal cracks and adjacent missing ribs longer than 13 mm **(see illustration)**. Small cracks running across V-ribbed belts are acceptable. Both sides of each belt should be inspected, which means you'll have to twist each belt to check the underside. Check the pulleys for nicks, cracks, distortion and corrosion.

4 To check the tension of each belt in accordance with factory recommendations, fit a drivebelt tension gauge. Measure the tension in accordance with the tension gauge instructions and compare your measurement to the specified drivebelt tension for either a used or new belt. **Note:** *A "new" belt is defined as any belt which has not been run; a "used" belt is one that has been run for more than ten minutes.*

5 The special gauge is the most accurate way to check belt tension. However, if you don't have a gauge, and cannot borrow one, the following "rule-of-thumb" method is recommended as an alternative. Lay a straightedge across the longest free span (the distance between two pulleys) of the belt. Push down firmly on the belt at a point half way between the pulleys and see how much the belt moves (deflects). Measure the deflection with a ruler **(see illustration)**. The belt should deflect 3 mm to 6 mm if the distance from pulley centre-to-pulley centre is less than 30 cm; for V-belts it should deflect from 3 mm to 9 mm if the distance from pulley centre-to-pulley centre is over 30 cm, slightly less for V-ribbed belts.

6 If adjustment is needed, either to make the belt tighter or looser, it's done by moving the belt-driven accessory on the bracket. Each component usually has an adjusting bolt and a pivot bolt. Both bolts must be loosened slightly to enable you to move the component. Some components have an adjusting bolt that can be turned to change the belt tension after the lock bolt is loosened **(see illustration)**.

7 After the two bolts have been loosened, move the component away from the engine to tighten the belt or toward the engine to loosen the belt. Hold the accessory in position and check the belt tension. If it's correct, tighten the two bolts until just snug, then recheck the tension. If the tension is correct, tighten the bolts.

8 You may have to use some sort of lever to move the accessory while the belt is adjusted. If this must be done to gain the proper leverage, be very careful not to damage the component being moved or the part being pried against (especially the smog pump).

9 To renew a belt, follow the above procedures for drivebelt adjustment but slip the belt off the pulleys and remove it. Since belts tend to wear out more or less at the same time, it's a good idea to renew all of them at the same time. Mark each belt and the corresponding pulley grooves so the new belts can be fitted properly.

10 Take the old belts with you when purchasing new ones in order to make a direct comparison for length, width and design.

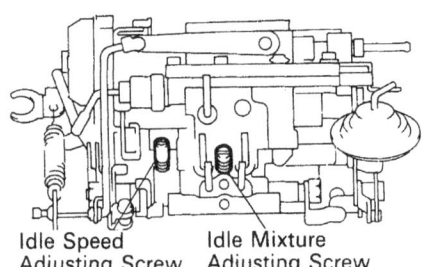

17.7a Carburettor idle speed and mixture adjusting screw locations (Y-series engines)

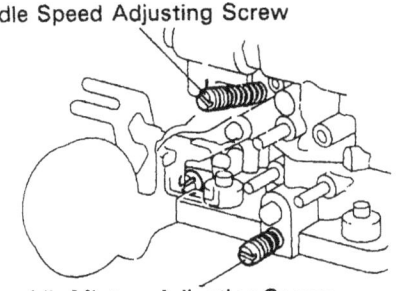

17.7b Carburettor idle speed and mixture adjusting screw locations (typical 22R engine)

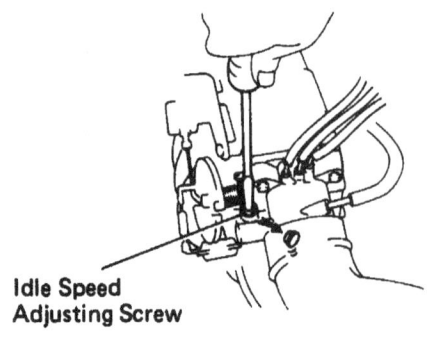

17.10 EFI idle speed adjusting screw location

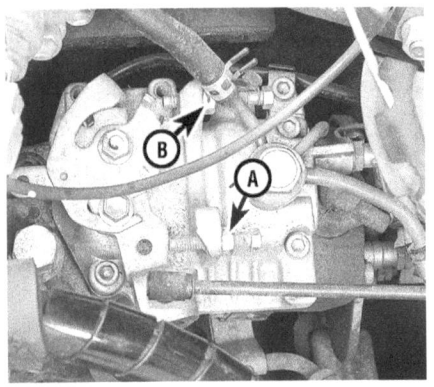

17.17 To adjust the idle speed, loosen locknut (A) and turn the adjusting screw; to adjust the maximum engine speed, loosen locknut (B) and turn the maximum speed screw in or out (only a little at a time) then recheck the maximum engine speed

11   Adjust the belts as described earlier in this Section.

17   Idle speed/maximum engine speed check and adjustment

Petrol models

1   Engine idle speed is the speed at which the engine operates when no accelerator pedal pressure is applied. The idle speed is critical to the performance of the engine itself, as well as many accessories.
2   To get an accurate reading, a hand-held tachometer must be used when adjusting idle speed. The exact hook-up for these meters depends on the manufacturer, so follow the directions included with the tachometer.
3   Apply the parking brake and block the wheels. Be sure the transmission is in Neutral (manual transmission) or Park (automatic transmission).
4   Turn off the air conditioner (if equipped), the headlights and all other accessories.
5   Start the engine and allow it to reach normal operating temperature.

Carburetted models

Refer to illustrations 17.7a and 17.7b

6   Check the engine idle speed with the tachometer and compare it to the VECI label under the bonnet.
7   If the idle speed is incorrect, turn the idle speed adjusting screw to change it **(see illustrations)**.

Fuel-injected models

Refer to illustration 17.10

8   Run the engine at 2500 rpm for about two minutes, then allow it to return to idle.
9   Check the engine idle speed with the tachometer and compare it to the VECI label under the bonnet.
10   If the idle speed is incorrect, remove the rubber plug (if equipped) from the throttle body and turn the idle speed adjusting screw to change it **(see illustration)**.

Diesel models

Refer to illustration 17.17

11   Engine idle speed is the speed at which the engine operates when no accelerator pedal pressure is applied. The idle speed is critical to the performance of the engine itself, as well as many accessories.
12   A special diesel tachometer must be used when adjusting idle speed. The exact hook-up for these meters depends on the manufacturer, so follow the directions included with the tachometer.
13   Apply the parking brake and block the wheels. Be sure the transmission is in Neutral (manual transmission) or Park (automatic transmission).
14   Turn off the air conditioner (if equipped), the headlights and all other accessories.
15   Start the engine and allow it to reach normal operating temperature.
16   Check the engine idle speed with the tachometer and compare it to the value listed in this Chapter's Specifications.
17   If the idle speed is incorrect, loosen the locknut and turn the idle speed adjusting screw to change it **(see illustration)**.
18   Make sure the accelerator cable still has the proper amount of slack in it. If it doesn't, adjust the cable (see Chapter 4).

19   To adjust the maximum engine speed, first make sure the throttle bellcrank travels all the way to the maximum speed stop when an assistant fully depresses the accelerator pedal (do this with the engine OFF). If it does not, adjust the accelerator cable (see Chapter 4).
20   Start the engine and watch the tachometer as you turn the throttle bellcrank all the way until it contacts the maximum speed screw.
Warning: *Hold the throttle in this position only long enough to obtain a steady reading, and make sure your body is not positioned in line with the cooling fan. Compare your reading with the value listed in this Chapter's Specifications. If necessary, loosen the locknut and turn the maximum speed screw in or out as necessary* **(see illustration 17.17),** *the recheck the maximum engine speed.*

18   Valve clearance check and adjustment

Petrol models

Refer to illustrations 18.5, 18.7 and 18.10

R-Series four-cylinder engines

1   Start the engine and allow it to reach normal operating temperature, then shut it off.
2   Remove the air cleaner (Chapter 4) and the valve cover (Chapter 2).
3   Position the number one piston at TDC on the compression stroke (Chapter 2).
4   Make sure the rocker arms for the number one cylinder valves are loose and number four are tight. If they aren't, the number one piston is not at TDC on the compression stroke.
5   Check/adjust only the open valves **(see illustration for 20R and 22R engines)**. The valve clearances can be found in the Specifications at the beginning of this Chapter. If you're working on a 12R or 18R engine, check/adjust valve numbers 1 and 5 (exhaust) and 2 and 3 (intake) (the valves are numbered from front-to-rear).
6   The clearance is measured by inserting the specified size feeler gauge between the end of the valve stem and the adjusting

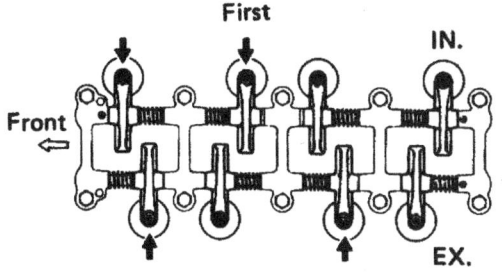

First

IN.

Front

EX.

18.5 Adjust the valves indicated by the arrows with the number one piston at TDC on the compression stroke - 20R and 22R petrol engines

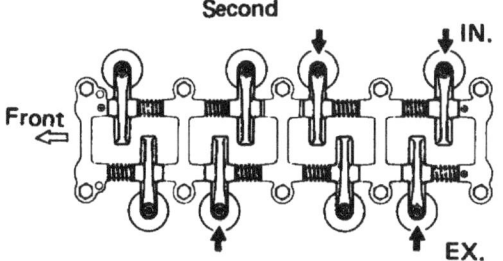

Second

IN.

Front

EX.

18.10 Turn the crankshaft one complete revolution (360-degrees), then adjust the valves marked here with an arrow - 20R and 22R petrol engines

18.7 The valve clearance can be changed by turning the adjusting screw with a screwdriver - once the clearance is set, tighten the locknut with a spanner and withdraw the feeler gauge

screw. You should feel a slight amount of drag when the feeler gauge is moved back-and-forth.

7   If the gap is too large or too small, loosen the locknut and turn the adjusting screw to obtain the correct gap (**see illustration**).

8   Once the gap has been set, hold the screw in position with a screwdriver and retighten the locknut. Recheck the valve clearance - sometimes it'll change slightly when the locknut is tightened. If so, readjust it until it's correct.

9   Repeat the procedure for the remaining valves (see illustration 18.5), then turn the crankshaft one complete revolution (360-degrees) and realign the notch in the pulley with the zero on the engine.

10   If you're working on a 20R or 22R engine, adjust the valves indicated by the arrows (**see illustration**). If you're working on a 12R or 18R engine, adjust valve numbers 6 and 7 (intake) and numbers 4 and 5 (exhaust).

11   Refit the valve cover and the air cleaner assembly.

V6 engine

Refer to illustrations 18.17a, 18.17b, 18.18a, 18.18b, 18.20a, 18.20b and 18.21

Note: *The following procedure requires the use of a special valve lifter tool. It is impossible to perform this task without it.*

12   Disconnect the negative cable from the battery.

13   Disconnect the cruise control cable, air cleaner duct or other components which will interfere with cylinder head cover removal.

14   Mark and remove the spark plug wires, then blow out the recessed area between the camshafts with compressed air, if available, to remove any debris that might fall into the cylinders. Remove the spark plugs (Section 34).

15   Remove the valve covers (see Chapter 2C).

16   Refer to Chapter 2C and position the number 1 piston at TDC on the compression stroke.

17   Measure the clearances of the indicated valves with a feeler gauge of the specified thickness (**see illustrations**).

18   Turn the crankshaft 2/3-turn (240 degrees) and measure the valve clearances shown (**see illustration**). Turn the crankshaft a further 2/3-turn and measure the remaining valves (**see illustration**).

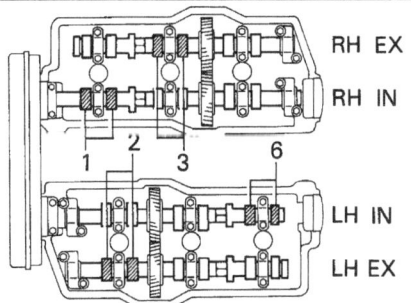

RH EX
RH IN

1   2   3   6

LH IN
LH EX

18.17a When the No.1 piston is at TDC on the compression stroke, the clearances for the valves indicated can be measured

18.17b Measure the clearance for each valve with a feeler gauge of the specified thickness - if the clearance is correct, you should feel a slight drag on the gauge as you pull it out

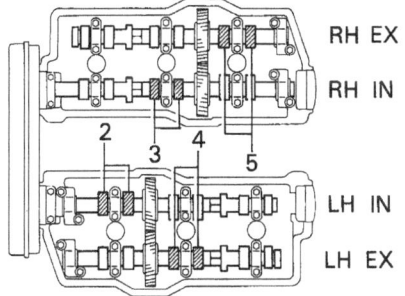

RH EX
RH IN

2   3   4   5

LH IN
LH EX

18.18a Make sure the No.1 piston is at TDC on the compression stroke, then rotate the engine 2/3 of a revolution (240°) and measure the clearances for the valves indicated

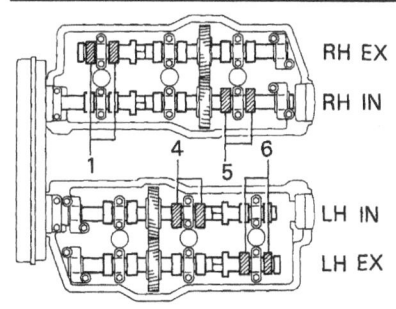

RH EX
RH IN

1   4   6
5

LH IN
LH EX

18.18b Rotate the crankshaft an additional 2/3-turn (240°) and measure the valve clearances for the remaining valves

18.20a Refit the valve lifter tool as shown and squeeze the handles together to lower the valve lifter so the shim can be removed

18.20b Remove the shim with a small screwdriver, a pair of tweezers or a magnet

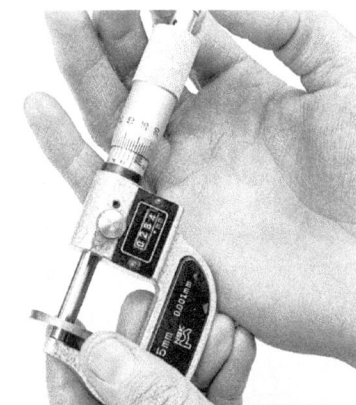

18.21 Measure the shim thickness with a micrometer

19   After all the valve clearances have been measured, turn the crankshaft pulley until the camshaft lobe above the first valve which you intend to adjust is pointing upward, away from the shim.

20   Position the notch in the valve lifter toward the spark plug. Then press down the valve lifter with the special valve lifter tool **(see illustration)**. Place the special valve lifter tool in position as shown, with the longer jaw of the tool gripping the lower edge of the cast lifter boss and the upper, shorter jaw gripping the upper edge of the lifter itself. Press down the valve lifter by squeezing the handles of the valve lifter tool together and remove the adjusting shim with a small screwdriver or a pair of tweezers **(see illustration)**. Note that the wire hook on the end of one valve lifter tool handle can be used to clamp both handles together to keep the lifter depressed while the shim is removed.

21   Measure the thickness of the shim with a micrometer **(see illustration)**. To calculate the correct thickness of a shim that will place the valve clearance within the specified value, use the following formula:

Intake side: $N = T + (A - 0.20 \text{ mm})$
Exhaust side: $N = T + (A - 0.25 \text{ mm})$
T = thickness of the shim used
A = valve clearance measured
N = thickness of the new shim

22   Select a shim with a thickness as close as possible to the valve clearance calculated. Shims, which are available in 17 sizes in increments of 0.050 mm (0.0020 in), range in size from 2.500 mm (0.0984 in) to 3.300 mm (0.1299 in). **Note:** *Through careful analysis of*

the shim sizes needed to bring all the out-of-specification valve clearances within specification, it is often possible to simply move a shim that has to come out anyway to another valve lifter requiring a shim of that particular size, thereby reducing the number of new shims that must be purchased.

23   Place the special valve lifter tool in position as shown **(see illustration 18.20a)**, with the longer jaw of the tool gripping the lower edge of the cast lifter boss and the upper, shorter jaw gripping the upper edge of the lifter itself, press down the valve lifter by squeezing the handles of the valve lifter tool together and fit the new adjusting shim (note that the wire hook on the end of one valve lifter tool hand can be used to clamp the handles together to keep the lifter depressed while the shim is inserted). Measure the clearance with a feeler gauge to make sure that your calculations are correct.

24   Repeat this procedure until all the valves which are out of clearance have been corrected.

25   Refitting of the spark plugs, valve covers, spark plug wires and boots, accelerator cable bracket, etc. is the reverse of removal.

Diesel models

All L model engines and 2L engines before 1988

Refer to illustrations 18.30, 18.32 and 18.35

26   Start the engine and allow it to reach normal operating temperature, then shut it off.

27   Remove the valve cover (see Chapter 2A).

28   Position the number one piston at TDC on the compression stroke (see Chapter 2A).

29   Make sure the rocker arms for the number one cylinder valves are loose and number four are tight. If they aren't, the number one piston is not at TDC on the compression stroke (rotate the crankshaft one full turn to bring cylinder No.1 to TDC on the compression stroke).

30   Check/adjust only the indicated valves **(see illustration)**. The valve clearances can be found in the Specifications at the beginning of this Chapter.

31   The clearance is measured by inserting the specified size feeler gauge between the end of the valve stem and the adjusting screw. You should feel a slight amount of drag when the feeler gauge is moved back-and-forth.

32   If the gap is too large or too small, loosen the locknut and turn the adjusting screw to obtain the correct gap **(see illustration 18.7)**.

33   Once the gap has been set, hold the screw in position with a screwdriver and retighten the locknut. Recheck the valve clearance - sometimes it'll change slightly when the locknut is tightened. If so, readjust it until it's correct.

34   Repeat the procedure for the remaining valves **(see illustration 18.30)**, then turn the crankshaft one complete revolution (360-degrees) and realign the notch in the pulley with the pointer on the engine.

35   Adjust the remaining valves indicated by the arrows **(see illustration)**.

36   Refit the valve cover and the air cleaner assembly.

1989 and later 2L and 3L engines

Refer to illustrations 18.4a, 18.4b, 18.5, 18.7a, 18.7b and 18.8

Note: *The following procedure requires the use of a special valve lifter tool. It is impossible to perform this task without it.*

37   Disconnect the negative cable from the battery.

38   Remove the valve cover (see Chapter 2D).

39   Refer to Chapter 2D and position the No.1 piston at TDC on the compression stroke.

40   Measure the clearances of the indicated valves with a feeler gauge of the specified thickness **(see illustrations)**.

41   Turn the crankshaft one full turn (360 degrees) and measure the remaining valve clearances **(see illustration)**.

42   After all the valve clearances have been

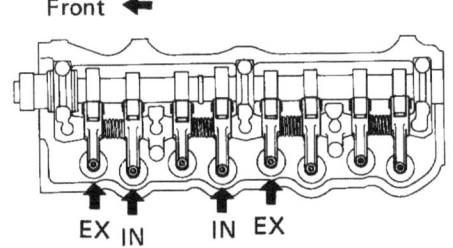

18.30 Adjust the valves indicated by the arrows with the number one piston at TDC on the compression stroke

18.35 Turn the crankshaft one complete revolution (360-degrees), then adjust the valves marked here with an arrow

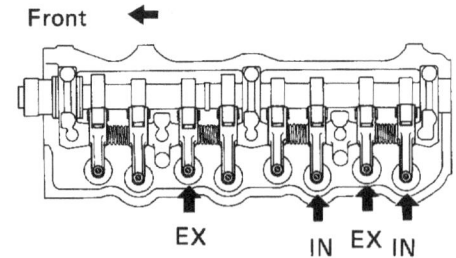

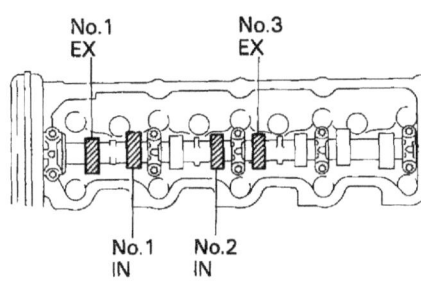

18.40a When the No.1 piston is at TDC on the compression stroke, the clearances for the valves indicated can be measured

18.40b Measure the clearance for each valve with a feeler gauge of the specified thickness - if the clearance is correct, you should feel a slight drag on the gauge as you pull it out

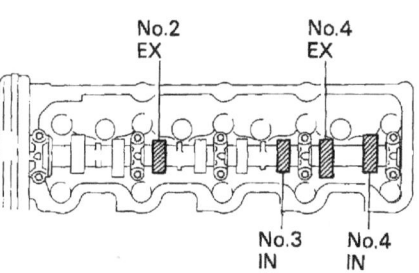

18.41 When the No.4 piston is at TDC on the compression stroke, measure the clearances for the valves indicated

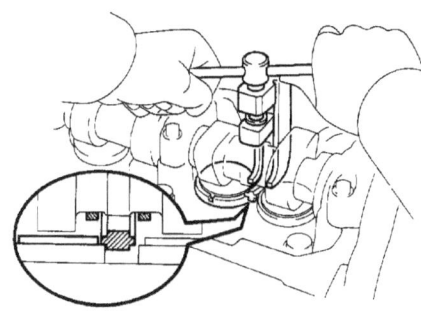

18.43a Refit a special valve lifter tool and turn the handle to depress the lifters ...

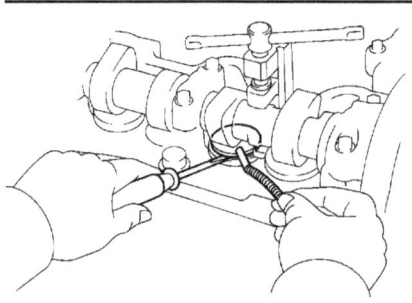

18.43b ... then remove the adjusting shim with a magnet and a small screwdriver

measured, turn the crankshaft pulley until the camshaft lobe above the first valve which you intend to adjust is pointing upward, away from the shim.

43   Press down the valve lifter with a special valve lifter tool **(see illustration)**. Remove the adjusting shim with a small screwdriver and a magnet **(see illustration)**.

44   Measure the thickness of the shim with a micrometer **(see illustration 18.21)**. To calculate the correct thickness of a renewal shim that will place the valve clearance within the specified value, use the following formula:

>   Intake side: N = T + (A-0.25 mm)
>   Exhaust side: N = T + (A-0.45 mm)
>   T = thickness of the shim used
>   A = valve clearance measured
>   N = thickness of the new shim

45   Select a shim with a thickness as close as possible to the valve clearance calculated. Shims, which are available in 17 sizes in increments of 0.050 mm (0.0020 in), range in size from 2.500 mm (0.0984 in) to 3.300 mm (0.1299 in). **Note:** *Through careful analysis of the shim sizes needed to bring all the out-of-specification valve clearances within specification, it is often possible to simply move a shim that has to come out anyway to another valve lifter requiring a shim of that particular size, thereby reducing the number of new shims that must be purchased.*

46   Place the special valve lifter tool in posi-

tion **(see illustration 18.43a)**. Depress the valve lifter and fit the new adjusting shim. Measure the clearance with a feeler gauge to make sure that your calculations are correct.

47   Repeat this procedure until all the valves which are out of clearance have been corrected.

48   Refit the valve cover.

19   Suspension and steering check

Refer to illustration 19.6

1   Whenever the front of the vehicle is raised for any reason, it's a good idea to visu-

ally check the suspension and steering components for wear.

2   Indications of steering or suspension problems include excessive play in the steering wheel before the front wheels react, excessive swaying around corners or body movement over rough roads and binding at some point as the steering wheel is turned.

3   Before the vehicle is raised for inspection, test the shock absorbers by pushing down aggressively at each corner. If the vehicle doesn't come back to a level position within one or two bounces, the shocks are worn and should be renewed. As this is done listen for squeaks and other noises from the suspension components. Information on shock absorber and suspension components can be found in Chapter 10.

4   Raise the front end of the vehicle and support it on jackstands. Make sure it's safely supported!

5   Crawl under the vehicle and check for loose bolts, broken or disconnected parts and deteriorated rubber bushes on all suspension and steering components. Look for grease or fluid leaking from around the steering gear assembly and shock absorbers. If equipped, check the power steering hoses and connections for leaks. On 4WD models with independent front suspension, check the balljoint dust covers and driveaxle boots for damage.

6   The balljoint seals should be checked at this time. This includes not only the upper and lower suspension balljoints, but those connecting the steering linkage parts as well. After cleaning around the balljoints, inspect

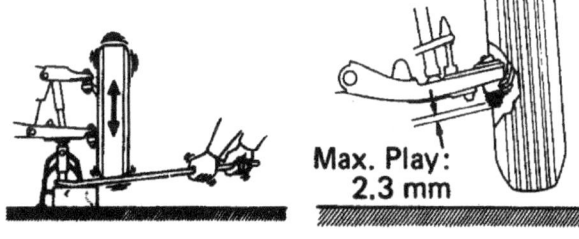

19.6 Check the suspension balljoints for wear by levering up on the tyres as shown here - note that the lower control arm must be supported by a jackstand and the tyre must be off the ground

Max. Play: 2.3 mm

the seals for cracks and damage. Check the balljoints (2WD vehicles) for wear **(see illustration)**.

7   Grip the top and bottom of each wheel and try to move it in and out. It won't take a lot of effort to be able to feel any play in the wheel bearings. If the play is noticeable it would be a good idea to adjust it right away or it could confuse further inspections.

8   Grip each side of the wheel and try rocking it laterally. Steady pressure will, of course, turn the steering, but back and forth pressure will reveal a loose steering joint. If some play is felt it would be easier to get assistance from someone so while one person rocks the wheel from side-to-side, the other can look at the joints, bushes and connections in the steering linkage.

9   To check the steering box, first make sure the bolts holding the steering box to the frame are tight. Then get another person to help examine the mechanism. One should look at, or hold onto, the arm at the bottom of the steering box while the other turns the steering wheel a little from side to side. The amount of lost motion between the steering wheel and the gear arm indicates the degree of wear in the steering box. Check the gearbox oil level as well. On 2WD models it should be about 25 mm from the top. On 4WD models it should be about 13 mm from the top. Refer to the *Recommended lubricants and fluids* section in the Specifications if oil is needed.

10   Moving to the vehicle interior, check the play in the steering wheel by turning it slowly in both directions until the wheels can just be felt turning. The steering wheel freeplay should be less than 28 mm. Excessive play is another indication of wear in the steering gear or linkage.

11   Following the inspection of the front, a similar inspection should be made of the rear suspension components, again checking for loose bolts, damaged or disconnected parts and deteriorated rubber bushes.

20   Fuel system check

Warning: *Fuel is extremely flammable, so take extra precautions when you work on any part of the fuel system. Don't smoke or allow open flames or bare light bulbs near the work area, and don't work in a garage where a natural gas-type appliance (such as a water heater or a clothes dryer) is present. Since fuel is carcinogenic, wear latex gloves when there's a possibility of being exposed to fuel, and, if you spill any fuel on your skin, rinse it off immediately with soap and water. Mop up any spills immediately and do not store fuel-soaked rags where they could ignite. The fuel system on fuel-injected petrol models is under constant pressure, so, if any fuel lines are to be disconnected, relieve the fuel system pressure first (see Chapter 4A). When you perform any kind of work on the fuel*

system, wear safety glasses and have a Class B type fire extinguisher on hand.

1   On most models the main fuel tank is located along the left frame rail.

2   The fuel system should be checked with the vehicle raised on a hoist so the components underneath the vehicle are readily visible and accessible.

3   If the smell of fuel is noticed while driving or after the vehicle has been in the sun, the system should be thoroughly inspected immediately.

4   Remove the fuel tank cap and check for damage, corrosion and an unbroken sealing imprint on the gasket. Renew the cap or gasket if necessary.

5   With the vehicle raised, check the fuel tank and filler neck for punctures, cracks and other damage. The connection between the filler neck and the tank is especially critical. Sometimes a rubber filler neck will leak due to loose clamps or deteriorated rubber, problems a home mechanic can usually rectify. **Warning:** *Do not, under any circumstances, try to repair a fuel tank yourself (except rubber components). A welding torch or any open flame can easily cause the fuel vapours to explode if the proper precautions are not taken!*

6   Carefully check all rubber hoses and metal lines leading away from the fuel tank. Look for loose connections, deteriorated hoses, crimped lines and other damage. Follow the lines to the front of the vehicle, carefully inspecting them all the way. Repair or renew damaged sections as necessary.

7   If a fuel odour is present on petrol models, check the EVAP system (see Chapter 6).

21   Tyre rotation

Refer to illustration 21.2

1   The tyres should be rotated at the specified intervals and whenever uneven wear is noticed. Since the vehicle will be raised and the tyres removed, it would be a good time to check the brakes and repack the wheel bearings as well.

2   Refer to the accompanying illustration for the preferred tyre rotation pattern.

3   Refer to the information in *Jacking and towing* at the front of this manual for the proper procedures to follow when raising the vehicle and changing a tyre. If the brakes are to be checked, don't apply the parking brake as stated. Make sure the tyres are blocked to prevent the vehicle from rolling as it's raised.

4   Preferably, the entire vehicle should be raised at the same time. This can be done on a hoist or by jacking up each corner and then lowering the vehicle onto jackstands placed under the frame rails. Always use four jackstands and make sure the vehicle is safely supported!

5   After rotation, check and adjust the tyre pressures as necessary and be sure to check the lug nut tightness.

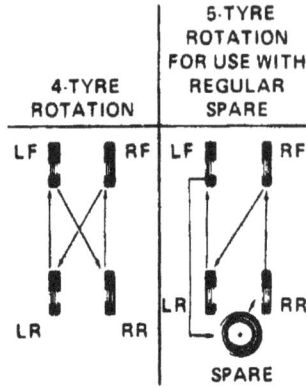

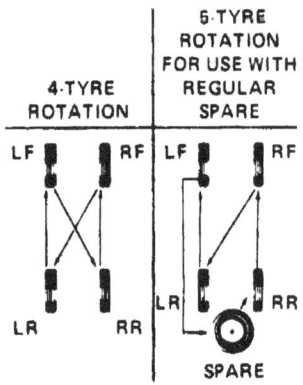

21.2 Tyre rotation diagram

6   For additional information on the wheels and tyres, refer to Chapter 10.

22   Brake check

Refer to illustrations 22.6a, 22.6b, 22.10, 22.11, 22.12 and 22.14

Note: *For detailed photographs of the brake system, refer to Chapter 9.*

Warning: *Brake system dust may contain asbestos, which is hazardous to your health. DO NOT blow it out with compressed air and DO NOT inhale it. DO NOT use petrol or petroleum-based solvents to remove the dust. Use brake system cleaner only!*

1   In addition to the specified intervals, the brakes should be inspected every time the wheels are removed.

2   To check the brakes, the vehicle must be raised and supported securely on jackstands.

Disc brakes

3   Disc brakes are used on the front wheels of most models. Extensive disc damage can occur if the pads are allowed to wear beyond the specified limit.

4   Raise the vehicle and support it securely

22.6a To check the brake pads on models with fixed calipers, remove the inspection cover (if equipped) and note the thickness of the pad lining (arrow) on both pads in each caliper

22.6b Floating calipers don't have an inspection cover - the pad lining material (arrows) is visible through the large opening

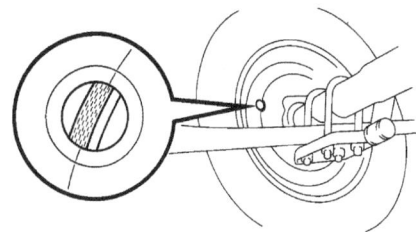

22.10 Remove the plug and look through the inspection hole with a flashlight to check the rear brake lining thickness (later models only)

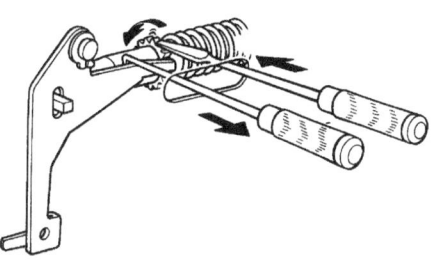

22.11 Hold the locking lever out of the way with a hooked tool and turn the star wheel with a screwdriver to move the brake shoes away from the drum

on jackstands, then remove all four wheels (see *Jacking and towing* at the front of the manual if necessary).

5   The disc brake calipers, which contain the pads, are visible with the wheels removed. There's an outer pad and an inner pad in each caliper. All four pads should be inspected.

6   Each caliper has an opening, which will allow you to inspect the pads **(see illustrations)**. If the pad material has worn to about 3 mm or less, the pads should be renewed.

7   If you're unsure about the exact thickness of the remaining lining material, remove the pads for further inspection or renewal (refer to Chapter 9).

8   Before refitting the wheels, check for leakage and/or damage (cracks, splitting, etc.) around the brake hose connections. Renew the hose or fittings as necessary, referring to Chapter 9.

9   Check the condition of the disc. Look for score marks, deep scratches and burned spots. If these conditions exist, the hub/disc assembly should be removed for servicing.

Drum brakes

10   **Note:** On later models, the brake shoe

22.12 Stuck brake drums can be removed by screwing bolts into the threaded holes and tightening them a little at a time

lining thickness can be checked without removing the drum - simply prise the inspection hole plug out of the backing plate **(see illustration)** and check the lining through the hole. A comprehensive inspection requires removal of the brake drum as described below. Remove the drum by pulling it off the axle and brake assembly. If it's stuck, make sure the parking brake is released, then squirt penetrating oil into the joint between the hub and drum. Allow the oil to soak in and try to pull the drum off again.

11   If the drum still can't be pulled off, the brake shoes will have to be retracted. This is done by first removing the dust cover from the backing plate. With the cover removed, use a small screwdriver to turn the star wheel, which will move the brake shoes away from the drum **(see illustration)**.

12   As a last resort, thread a bolt into each of the holes in the drum **(see illustration)** and tighten the bolts a little at a time to force the drum off.

13   With the drum removed, be careful not to touch any brake dust (see the Warning at the beginning of this Section).

14   Note the thickness of the lining material on both the front and rear brake shoes. If the material has worn away to within 1.5 mm of the recessed rivets or metal backing, the shoes should be renewed **(see illustration)**. The shoes should also be renewed if they're cracked, glazed (shiny surface) or contaminated with brake fluid.

15   Make sure that all the brake assembly springs are connected and in good condition.

16   Check the brake components for signs of fluid leakage. Carefully prise back the rubber cups on the wheel cylinders located at the top of the brake shoes with your finger. Any leakage is an indication that the wheel cylinders should be overhauled immediately (see Chapter 9). Also check the brake hoses and connections for leakage.

17   Wipe the inside of the drum with a clean rag and brake cleaner or denatured alcohol. Again, be careful not to breath the asbestos dust.

18   Check the inside of the drum for cracks, score marks, deep scratches and hard spots, which will appear as small discolourations. If imperfections cannot be removed with fine emery cloth, the drum must be taken to a machine shop equipped to resurface the drums.

19   If all parts are in good working condition, refit the brake drum.

20   Refit the wheels and lower the vehicle.

Parking brake

21   The parking brake operates from a hand lever and locks the rear brakes. The easiest, and perhaps most obvious method of periodically checking the operation of the parking brake assembly is to park the vehicle on a steep hill with the parking brake set and the transmission in Neutral. If the parking brake cannot prevent the vehicle from rolling, it's in need of adjustment (see Chapter 9).

Vacuum system

Note: *A vacuum pump is used on diesel models as the engine vacuum is insufficient on diesel engines to provide a vacuum supply for the braking system.*

22   The vacuum pump (mounted on the alternator), reservoir and associated hoses play an important role in the operation of the brakes. A failure in any of these components will cause a lack of power assistance, which will require a much greater effort by the driver to slow the vehicle.

23   Check the vacuum hoses and the vacuum reservoir for cracking, deteriorated hoses

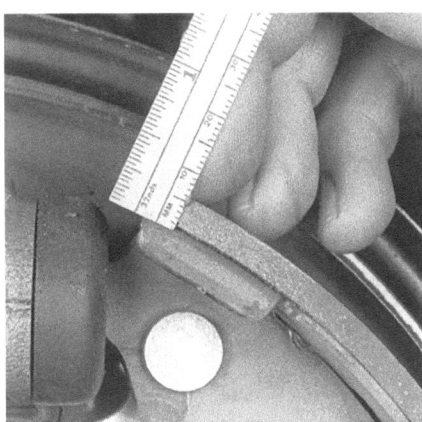

22.14 On bonded linings, measure the distance to the backing plate - on riveted linings, measure the depth of the rivet hole to determine the amount of lining remaining

and vacuum leaks (refer to Section 12 for the vacuum leak checking procedure). Refer to Chapter 9 for the location of the vacuum reservoir and the vacuum pump. Renew any parts that have failed or appear questionable.

23   Front wheel bearing check, repack and adjustment (2WD models)

Refer to illustrations 23.1, 23.6, 23.11, 23.15, 23.19 and 23.23

1   In most cases the front wheel bearings will not need servicing until the brake pads are changed. However, the bearings should be checked whenever the front of the vehicle is raised for any reason. Several items, including a torque wrench and special grease, are required for this procedure **(see illustration)**.
2   With the vehicle securely supported on jackstands, spin each wheel and check for noise, rolling resistance and freeplay.
3   Grasp the top of each tyre with one hand and the bottom with the other. Move the wheel in-and-out on the spindle. If there's any noticeable movement, the bearings should be

checked and then repacked with grease or renewed if necessary.
4   Remove the wheel(s).
5   Fabricate a wood block to slide between the brake pads to keep them separated. Remove the brake caliper (see Chapter 9) and hang it out of the way on a piece of wire. Be careful not to kink or stretch the brake hose.
6   Prise the cap out of the hub using a screwdriver or hammer and chisel **(see illustration)**.
7   Straighten the bent ends of the split pin, then pull the split pin out. Discard the split pin and use a new one during reassembly.
8   Remove the nut lock, adjusting nut and thrust washer from the end of the spindle.
9   Pull the hub out slightly, then push it back into its original position. This should force the outer wheel bearing off the spindle enough so it can be removed.
10   Pull the hub/disc assembly off the spindle.
11   Use a screwdriver to prise the seal out of the rear of the hub **(see illustration)**. As this is done, note how the seal is fitted.
12   Remove the inner wheel bearing from the hub.
13   Use solvent to remove all traces of the old grease from the bearings, hub and spindle. A small brush may prove helpful; however make sure no bristles from the brush embed themselves inside the bearing rollers. Allow the parts to air dry.
14   Carefully inspect the bearings for cracks, heat discolouration, worn rollers, etc. Check the bearing races inside the hub for wear and damage. If the bearing races are defective, the hubs should be taken to a machine shop with the facilities to remove the old races and press new ones in. Note that the bearings and races come as matched sets and old bearings should never be refitted on new races.
15   Use high-temperature front wheel bearing grease to pack the bearings. Work the grease completely into the bearings, forcing it between the rollers, cone and cage from the back side **(see illustration)**.
16   Apply a thin coat of grease to the spindle at the outer bearing seat, inner bearing seat, shoulder and seal seat.

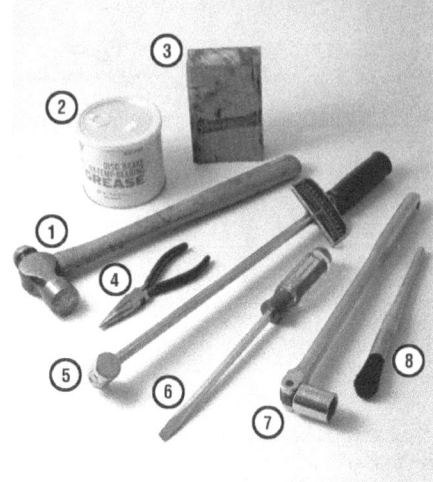

23.1 Tools and materials needed for front wheel bearing maintenance

1 Hammer - A common hammer will do just fine
*2 **Grease** - High-temperature grease which is formulated specially for front wheel bearings should be used*
*3 **Wood block** - If you have a scrap piece of wood, it can be used to drive the new seal into the hub*
*4 **Needle-nose pliers** - Used to straighten and remove the split pin in the spindle*
*5 **Torque wrench** - This is very important in this procedure; if the bearing is too tight, the wheel won't turn freely - if it is too loose, the wheel will "wobble' on the spindle. Either way, it could mean extensive damage*
*6 **Screwdriver** - Used to remove the seal from the hub (a long screwdriver would be preferred)*
*7 **Socket/breaker bar** - Needed to loosen the nut on the spindle if it is extremely tight*
*8 **Brush** - Together with some clean solvent, this will be used to remove old grease from the hub and spindle*

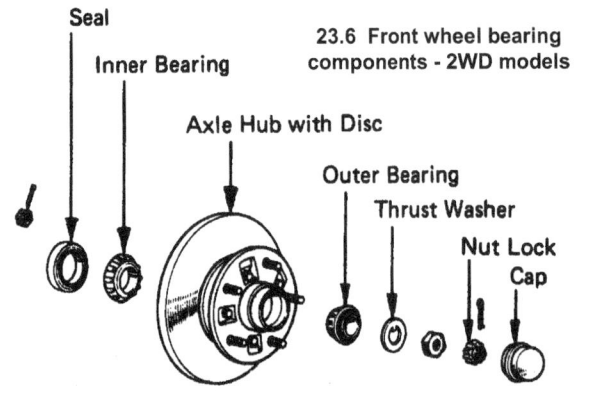

23.6 Front wheel bearing components - 2WD models

Seal
Inner Bearing
Axle Hub with Disc
Outer Bearing
Thrust Washer
Nut Lock
Cap

23.11 Use a large screwdriver to prise the seal out of the rear of the hub

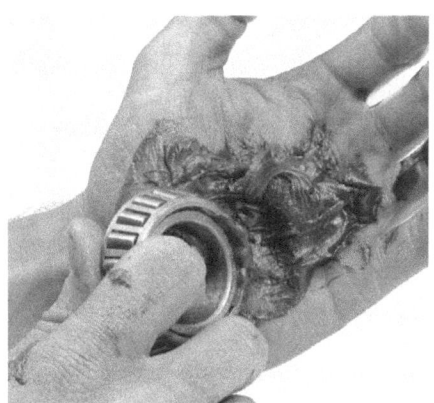

23.15 Work clean grease of the recommended type into each bearing until it's full

23.19 Tap the seal into place with a block of wood and a hammer

23.23 The wheel bearing preload is checked with a spring scale as shown here

17   Put a small quantity of grease behind each bearing race inside the hub. Using your finger, form a dam at these points to provide for extra grease and to keep thinned grease from flowing out of the bearing.
18   Place the grease-packed inner bearing into the rear of the hub and put a little more grease outside of the bearing.
19   Place a new seal over the inner bearing and tap the seal evenly into place with a hammer and block of wood until it's flush with the hub **(see illustration)**.
20   Carefully place the hub assembly onto the spindle and push the grease-packed outer bearing into position.
21   Refit the thrust washer and adjusting nut. Tighten the nut to the initial specified torque.
22   Spin the hub in a forward direction to seat the bearings and remove any grease or burrs which could cause excessive bearing play later.
23   Loosen the nut until there is 0.5 to 1.0 mm axial (in-and-out) play in the hub. Attach a spring scale to one of the lug bolts and measure the force required to start the hub turning **(see illustration)**. This is the oil seal frictional drag. Record the measurement. Tighten the nut until the bearing preload is 0.6 to 1.8 kg (5.9 to 18 N) greater than the oil seal frictional drag. The bearing preload is the force required to start the hub turning (as measured with the spring scale). The hub axial play should be less than 0.05 mm.
24   Refit the nut lock and a new split pin.
25   Bend the ends of the split pin until they're flat against the nut. Cut off any extra length which could interfere with the dust cap.
26   Refit the dust cap. Tap it into place with a hammer.
27   Place the brake caliper near the disc and carefully remove the wood spacer. Refit the caliper (see Chapter 9).
28   Refit the wheel and tighten the lug nuts.
29   Grasp the top and bottom of the tyre and check the bearings in the manner described earlier in this Section.
30   Lower the vehicle. Tighten the lug nuts to the torque listed in this Chapter's Specifications.

24 Front wheel bearing check, repack and adjustment (4WD models)

Refer to illustrations 24.4, 24.7a, 24.7b and 24.7c

1   In most cases, the front wheel bearings will not need servicing until the brake pads are changed. However, the bearings should be checked whenever the front wheels are raised for any reason. Several items, including a torque wrench and special grease, are required for this procedure **(see illustration 23.1)**.
2   Refer to Section 23 and follow the instructions in Steps 2 through 5.
3   Remove the free-wheel or locking hub assembly (see Chapter 8).
4   Remove the locknut, lock washer, adjusting nut and thrust washer **(see illustration)**.
5   Refer to Section 23 and follow the instructions in Steps 9 through 20.

6   Refit the thrust washer and adjusting nut.
7   On models with a solid front axle:
a) *Tighten the adjusting nut to 58 Nm* **(see illustration)**.
b) *Loosen the adjusting nut until it can be turned by hand* **(see illustration)**.
c) *Retighten the adjusting nut to 4-to-7 Nm, then turn the hub two or three times to ensure that it moves smoothly with no play in the bearings.*
d) *Using a spring tension gauge, check for the correct preload (2.8 to 3.9 kg [27 to 38 N] on YN/LN 50 and 60 series, or 2.9-to-5.7 kg [28 to 56 N] on YN/RN/LN30, 40, 80, 90, 105, 106 and 110 series and 4Runner)* **(see illustration)**. *If the preload is incorrect, loosen or tighten the nut accordingly.*
e) *Refit the lock washer and locknut.*
f) *Tighten the nut to 79-to-98 Nm (RN/ LN30, 40 series) or 35 Nm (all others).*

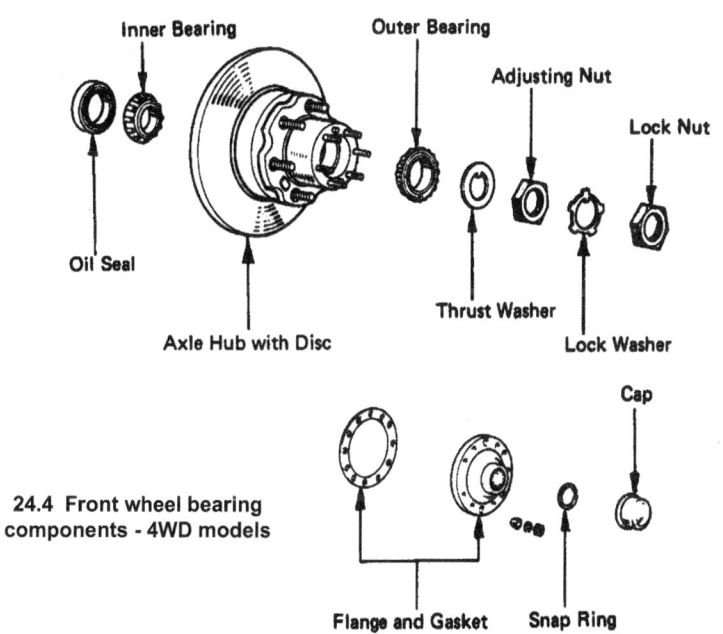

24.4 Front wheel bearing components - 4WD models

Inner Bearing   Outer Bearing   Adjusting Nut   Lock Nut

Oil Seal   Axle Hub with Disc   Thrust Washer   Lock Washer

Cap   Flange and Gasket   Snap Ring

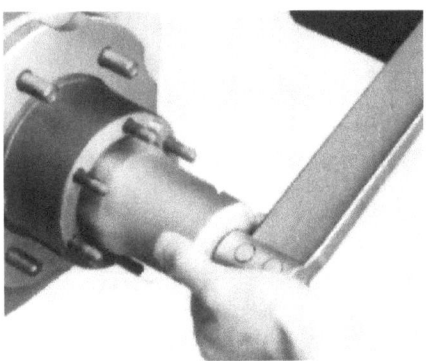

24.7a On 4WD models, tighten the front wheel bearing adjusting nut with a torque wrench . . .

g) *Secure the locknut by bending one of the lock washer tabs over the adjusting nut and one over the locknut.*
h) *Refit the free-wheel or locking hub assembly (see Chapter 8).*

8   On models with independent front suspension:

a) *This procedure applies only to vehicles with manual locking hubs. For vehicles with automatic locking hubs, refer to Chapter 8.*
b) *Tighten the adjusting nut to 59 Nm (see illustration 24.7a).*
c) *Loosen the adjusting nut until it can be turned by hand (see illustration 24.7b).*
d) *Using a spring scale attached to one of the lug bolts, measure the frictional drag of the oil seal and record it for use later in the procedure (see illustration 24.7c). The force required to get the hub to turn (measured on the scale) is the oil seal drag.*
e) *Retighten the adjusting nut to 25 Nm, then refit the lock washer and locknut. Tighten the locknut to 47 Nm.*
f) *Make sure the bearing has no play, then check the preload with the spring scale. Preload is the force required to get the hub to turn. It should be 28-to-56 N. If the preload is not as specified, tighten or loosen the adjusting nut as required.*

25.1 The manual transmission check/fill plug is accessible from under the vehicle

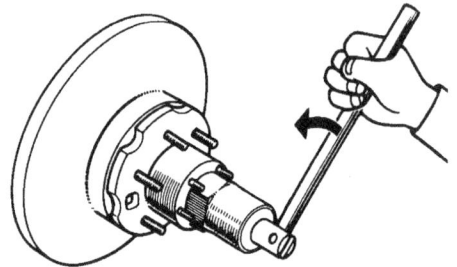

24.7b . . . then loosen the nut again until it can just be turned by hand . . .

g) *Secure the locknut by bending one of the lock washer tabs over the adjusting nut and one over the locknut.*
h) *Refit the free-wheel or locking hub assembly (see Chapter 8).*

9   Refer to Section 23 and follow the instructions in Steps 28 through 31.

25 Manual transmission oil level check

Refer to illustration 25.1

1   Manual transmissions don't have a dipstick. The oil level is checked by removing a plug from the side of the transmission case **(see illustration)**. Locate the plug and use a rag to clean the plug and the area around it. If the vehicle is raised to gain access to the plug, be sure to support it safely on jackstands - DO NOT crawl under the vehicle when it's supported only by a jack!
2   With the engine and transmission cold, remove the plug. If lubricant immediately starts leaking out, thread the plug back into the transmission - the level is correct. If it doesn't, completely remove the plug and reach inside the hole with your little finger. The level should be even with the bottom of the plug hole.
3   If the transmission needs more lubricant, use a syringe or small pump to add it through the plug hole.
4   Thread the plug back into the transmis-

26.2 Remove the check/fill plug to determine the differential oil level

24.7c . . . and check the bearing preload with a spring scale

sion and tighten it securely. Drive the vehicle, then check for leaks around the plug.

26 Differential oil level check

Refer to illustration 26.2

1   The differential has a check/fill plug which must be removed to check the oil level. If the vehicle is raised to gain access to the plug, be sure to support it safely on jackstands - DO NOT crawl under the vehicle when it's supported only by a jack!
2   Remove the oil check/fill plug from the differential **(see illustration)**.
3   The oil level should be at the bottom of the plug opening. If not, use a syringe or pump to add the recommended lubricant until it just starts to run out of the opening.
4   Refit the plug and tighten it securely. Check for leaks after the first few kilometres of driving.

27 Transfer case oil level check

Refer to illustration 27.1

1   The transfer case oil level is checked

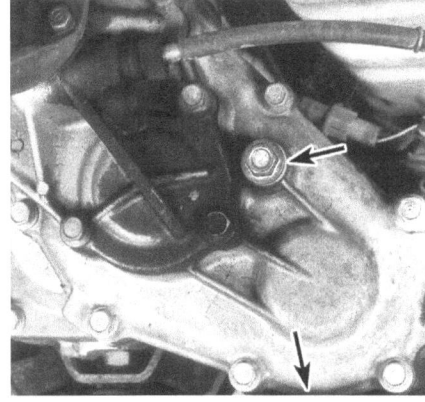

27.1 The transfer case check/fill plug (upper arrow) and drain plug (lower arrow) are accessible from under the vehicle (typical)

28.5 The arrow on the fuel filter indicates the outlet side (carburetted models)

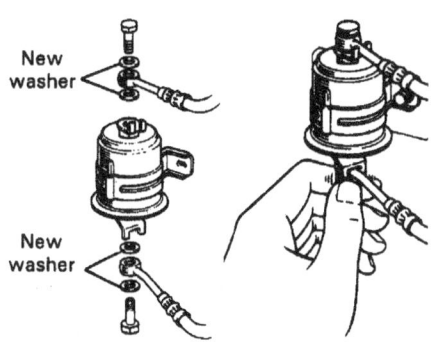

28.6 EFI fuel filter mounting details - always tighten the banjo bolts by hand before using a spanner

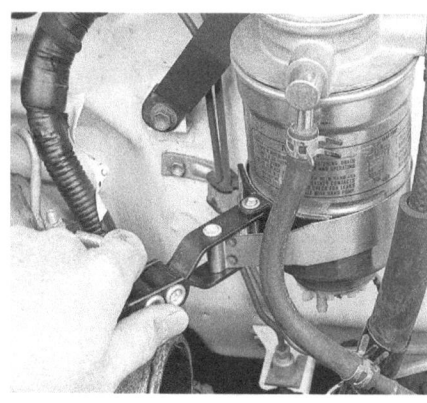

28.14 Unscrew the fuel filter with an oil filter wrench

by removing a plug from the side of the case **(see illustration)**. Remove the rock guard (if equipped), then locate the plug and use a rag to clean the plug and the area around it. If the vehicle is raised to gain access to the plug, be sure to support it safely on jackstands - DO NOT crawl under the vehicle when it's supported only by a jack!

2   With the engine and transfer case cold, remove the plug. If lubricant immediately starts leaking out, thread the plug back into the case - the level is correct. If it doesn't, completely remove the plug and reach inside the hole with your little finger. The level should be within 5 mm of the bottom of the plug hole.

3   If more oil is needed, use a syringe or small pump to add it through the opening.

4   Thread the plug back into the case and tighten it securely. Drive the vehicle, then check for leaks around the plug. refit the rock guard.

28 Fuel filter renewal

Warning: *Fuel is extremely flammable, so take extra precautions when you work on any part of the fuel system. Don't smoke or allow open flames or bare light bulbs near the work area, and don't work in a garage where a natural gas-type appliance (such as a water heater or a clothes dryer) with a pilot light is present. Since fuel is carcinogenic, wear latex gloves when there's a possibility of being exposed to fuel, and, if you spill any fuel on your skin, rinse it off immediately with soap and water. The fuel system on fuel-injected models is under constant pressure, so, if any fuel lines are to be disconnected, the fuel pressure in the system must be relieved first. Mop up any spills immediately and do not store fuel-soaked rags where they could ignite. When you perform any kind of work on the fuel system, wear safety glasses and have a Class B type fire extinguisher on hand.*

1   This job should be done with the engine cold (after sitting at least three hours). Place a metal container, rags or newspapers under the filter to catch spilled fuel.

Petrol engines
Carburetted models

Refer to illustration 28.5

2   The fuel filter is located under the vehicle, near the fuel tank or in the engine compartment. If the vehicle must be raised to change the filter, be sure to support it safely on jackstands!

3   To renew the filter, release the clamps and slide them down the hoses, past the fittings on the filter.

4   Carefully twist and pull on the hoses to separate them from the filter. If the hoses are in bad shape, now would be a good time to renew them. Slide off the old clamps and fit new ones.

5   Pull the filter out of the clip and fit the new one, then hook up the hoses and reposition the clamps. Note that the arrow on the filter must point in the direction of fuel flow (toward the carburettor) **(see illustration)**. Start the engine and check carefully for leaks at the filter hose connections.

Fuel-injected models

Refer to illustration 28.6

Warning: *Depressurise the fuel system before removing the filter (see Chapter 4A).*

6   Loosen the banjo bolts on both ends of the fuel filter **(see illustration)** with a flare nut spanner. Disconnect both lines.

7   Remove both bracket bolts and detach the old filter and the filter support bracket.

8   Remove the filter clamp bolt and separate the old filter from the bracket. Note that the inlet and outlet lines are clearly labelled and that the flanged end of the filter faces down.

9   Fit the new filter and bracket assembly and tighten the bracket bolts securely. Make sure that the new filter is fitted flanged end down.

10   Using the new sealing washers - two per banjo fitting - provided by the filter manufacturer, refit the inlet and outlet banjo bolts and tighten them to the specified torque.

11   The remainder of refitting is the reverse of the removal procedure.

Diesel engines
Fuel filter renewal

Refer to illustrations 28.14, 28.15 and 28.18

12   Disconnect the cable from the negative terminal of the battery.

13   If equipped, detach the clamp from the filter body.

14   Unplug the water sensor electrical connector (if equipped). Place several old rags under the fuel filter area to catch any fuel that may spill when the fuel filter is removed. Using an oil filter wrench, unscrew the filter from the filter adapter **(see illustration)**.

15   If equipped, unscrew the water sensor/drain valve from the bottom of the filter canister **(see illustration)**.

16   Refit a new O-ring onto the water sensor. Lubricate the O-ring with fuel and thread it into the bottom of the new filter canister, tightening it by hand only. Reconnect the electrical connector.

17   Lubricate the rubber gasket on the filter canister with clean fuel and screw it onto the filter adapter, tightening it by hand only (approximately 3/4 of a turn after the gasket makes contact with the adapter).

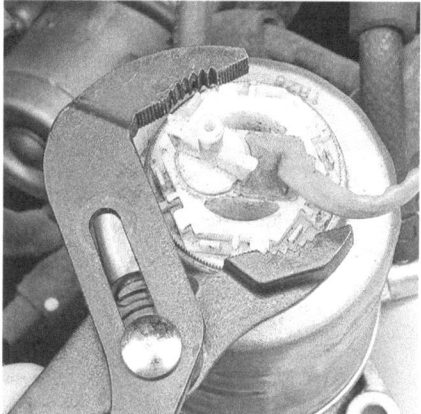

28.15 Unscrew the water sensor from the bottom of the fuel filter (on models so equipped)

28.18 After fitting the new filter, operate the priming pump until it becomes harder to push

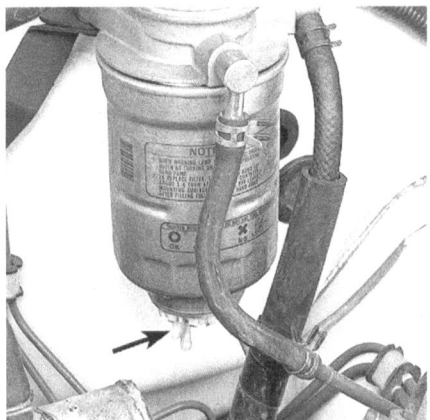

28.20 Location of the fuel filter drain tap (arrow) (models without a sedimenter)

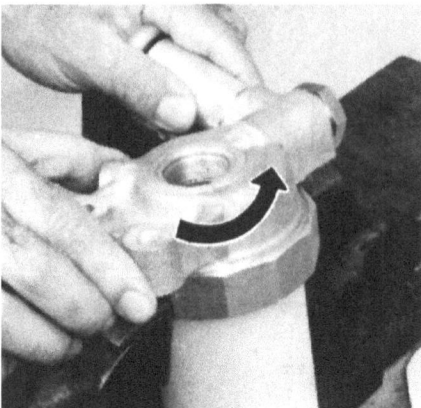

28.26 Mount the sedimenter nut in a vise and unscrew the adapter from the case

18   To prime the filter, depress the plunger on the top of the filter adapter **(see illustration)** (or on models with a sedimenter, on top of the sedimenter assembly) until the resistance required to do so becomes noticeably stronger.

Fuel filter draining

Refer to illustration 28.20

19   Occasionally it may become necessary to drain out any water that has accumulated in the fuel filter (or, on models with a sedimenter, from the sedimenter). A light on the instrument panel should alert you when an unacceptable amount of water has built up.

20   Place rags under the drain tap at the bottom of the filter (or sedimenter, on models so equipped) **(see illustration)**. An alternative to this would be to attach a length of tubing to the fitting on the tap and run the hose into a container placed under the vehicle.

21   Open the tap a couple of turns and operate the plunger until clean, uncontaminated fuel flows from the tap **(see illustration 28.20)**. Tighten the drain tap securely.

Fuel sedimenter servicing

Refer to illustrations 28.26 and 28.27

22   Early models are equipped with a separate device for catching water in the fuel system. This device, called a sedimenter, is mounted on the firewall.

23   If a warning light on the instrument panel alerts you of the accumulation of water in the sedimenter, drain the water following Steps 8 through 10. Occasionally, the sedimenter should be disassembled to clean the body of dirt and other accumulated contaminants.

24   Loosen the hose clamps and detach the hoses from the sedimenter. Plug the hoses to prevent fuel spillage.

25   Unscrew the water sensor from the adapter.

26   Mount the sedimenter in a vise, with the jaws of the vise clamping on the large nut holding the adapter to the case **(see illustration)**. Unscrew the adapter from the nut.

27   Wash all of the components in solvent and dry them thoroughly **(see illustration)**. Check all parts for signs of deterioration, renewing as necessary.

28   Reassemble the sedimenter, making sure the tab on the case is in alignment with the cutout in the adapter. Tighten the large nut by hand only.

29   Refit the sedimenter and prime the system by operating the pump until resistance increases.

30   Reconnect the battery cable, start the engine and check for fuel leaks.

---

29   Fuel tank cap gasket renewal

1   Obtain a new gasket.

2   Remove the tank cap and carefully prise the old gasket out of the recess. Be careful not to damage the sealing surface inside the cap.

3   Work the new gasket into the cap recess.

4   Refit the cap, then remove it and make sure the gasket seals all the way around.

28.27 Exploded view of the sedimenter

1 *Fuel sedimenter case and nut*
2 *Water level warning switch*
3 *Adapter*
4 *Fuel fitting and sealing washers*
5 *Fuel fitting and sealing washers*

31.3a Release the spring clips (arrows) and remove the wing nut to detach the air cleaner top plate, then lift out the filter element - carburettored petrol models

31.3b Release the spring clips to detach the air cleaner cover . . .

31.4a . . . unscrew the wing nut . . .

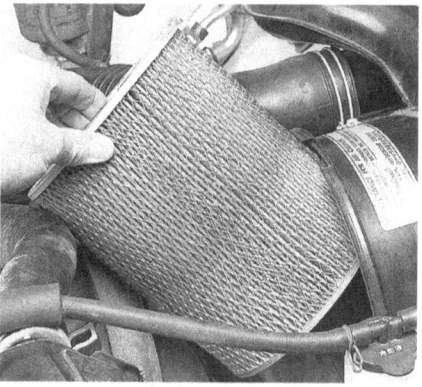

31.4b . . . and pull the filter element out of the air cleaner housing - diesel models

30   Clutch pedal freeplay check and adjustment

1   On vehicles equipped with a manual transmission, the clutch pedal height and freeplay must be correctly adjusted.
2   The height of the clutch pedal is the distance the pedal sits off the floor (measured from the centre of the rubber pad). The distance should be as specified. If the pedal height is not within the specified range, loosen the locknut on the pedal stop and turn the stop in or out until the pedal height is correct. Retighten the locknut.
3   The freeplay is the pedal slack, or the distance the pedal can be depressed before it begins to have any effect on the clutch. The distance should be as specified. If it isn't, loosen the locknut on the clutch master cylinder pushrod, turn the pushrod until the freeplay is correct, then retighten the locknut.

31   Air filter renewal

Refer to illustrations 31.3a, 31.3b, 31.4a and 31.4b

1   At the specified intervals, the air filter

should be renewed. A thorough program of preventive maintenance would also call for the filter to be inspected periodically between changes, especially if the vehicle is often driven in dusty conditions.
2   The air filter is located inside the air cleaner housing, which is mounted in the engine compartment.
3   Release the clips that hold the top of the air cleaner housing, then remove it **(see illustrations)**.
4   Remove the wing nut and guide the air filter out of the housing **(see illustrations)**. If it's covered with dirt, it should be renewed.
5   Wipe the inside of the air cleaner housing with a rag.
6   Place the old filter (if in good condition) or the new filter (if renewal is necessary) into the air cleaner housing. Install and tighten the wing nut.
7   On EFI models, the air filter case is located in the front corner of the engine compartment. Release the wire clips and carefully lift up on the cover to expose the filter element **(see illustration)**. Remove the filter and clean the seat area, then fit the new filter. Make sure it's properly seated in the case.
8   Refit the cover on the air cleaner and snap the clips into place.

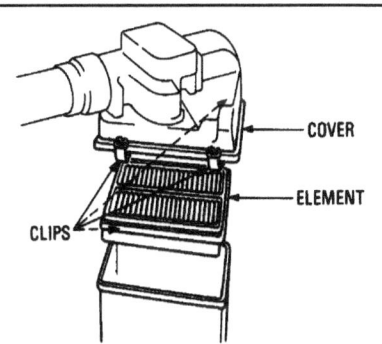

31.7 On EFI (or MPI) equipped vehicles, the air filter element can be removed after releasing the spring clips and pulling the housing cover up

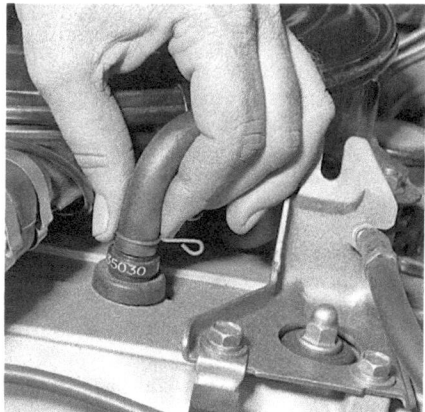

32.2 The PCV valve is located in the valve cover

32   PCV check and renewal

Petrol models

Refer to illustration 32.2

1   The PCV valve is usually located in the valve cover.
2   With the engine idling at normal operating temperature, pull the valve (with hose attached) from the rubber grommet in the cover **(see illustration)**.
3   Place your finger over the valve opening. If there's no vacuum at the valve, check for a plugged hose, manifold port, or the valve itself. Renew any plugged or deteriorated hoses.
4   Turn off the engine and shake the PCV valve, listening for a rattle. If the valve doesn't rattle, renew it.
5   To renew the valve, release the clamp and pull it from the end of the hose, noting its fitted position and direction.
6   When purchasing a new PCV valve, make sure it's for your particular vehicle and engine type. Compare the old valve with the new one to make sure they're the same.
7   Push the valve into the end of the hose until it's seated, then reposition the clamp.
8   Inspect the rubber grommet for damage and renew it if necessary.

32.10 Location of the PCV hose

9   Push the PCV valve and hose into the grommet until the valve is seated.

Diesel models

Refer to illustration 32.10

10   The PCV hose runs between the valve cover and the inlet manifold **(see illustration)**.

11   At the specified interval, loosen the hose clamps and detach the hose from its fittings. Blow through the hose to check for any obstructions. If the hose is blocked, use a long, thin screwdriver or a piece of wire to remove all accumulations of carbon and burned oil residue. If this can't be achieved satisfactorily, renew the hose.

12   Also check the ports on the valve cover and the inlet manifold for obstructions.

---

33   Cooling system servicing (draining, flushing and refilling)

Refer to illustration 33.4a. 33.4b and 33.4c

Warning: *Do not allow antifreeze to come in contact with your skin or painted surfaces of the vehicle. If you do, rinse it off immediately with plenty of clean water. Consult local authorities regarding proper disposal of antifreeze before draining the cooling system. In many areas, reclamation centres have been established to collect used oil and coolant mixtures.*

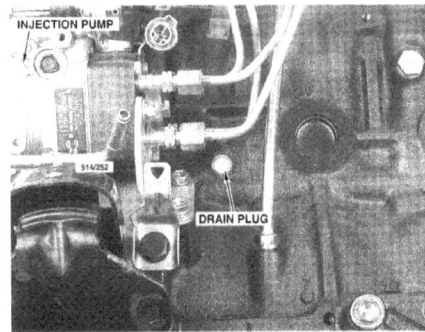

33.4c Location of the diesel engine block drain plug. The radiator drain is on the passenger side of lower radiator tank

33.4a Four-cylinder petrol engine coolant drain plug location. The radiator drain is on the drivers side of lower radiator tank

1   Periodically, the cooling system should be drained, flushed and refilled to replenish the antifreeze mixture and prevent formation of rust and corrosion, which can impair the performance of the cooling system and cause engine damage. When the cooling system is serviced, all hoses and the radiator cap should be checked and renewed if necessary.

2   Apply the parking brake and block the wheels. If the vehicle has just been driven, wait several hours to allow the engine to cool down before beginning this procedure.

3   Once the engine is completely cool, remove the radiator cap. Place the heater temperature control in the maximum heat position.

4   Move a large container under the radiator drain to catch the coolant, then unscrew the drain plug (a pair of pliers may be required to turn it) **(see illustration)**.

5   After the coolant stops flowing out of the radiator, move the container under the engine block drain plug **(see illustration 33.4a. 33.4b or 33.4c)**. Remove the plug(s) and allow the coolant in the block to drain.

6   While the coolant is draining, check the condition of the radiator hoses, heater hoses and clamps (refer to Section 11 if necessary).

7   Renew any damaged clamps or hoses.

8   Once the system is completely drained, flush the radiator with fresh water from a garden hose until it runs clear at the drain. The flushing action of the water will remove sediments from the radiator but will not remove rust and scale from the engine and cooling tube surfaces.

9   These deposits can be removed with a chemical cleaner. Follow the procedure outlined in the manufacturer's instructions. If the radiator is severely corroded, damaged or leaking, it should be removed (see Chapter 3) and taken to a radiator repair shop.

10   Remove the overflow hose from the coolant recovery reservoir. Drain the reservoir and flush it with clean water, then reconnect the hose.

11   Refit and tighten the radiator drain plug. Install and tighten the block drain plug(s).

12   Slowly add new coolant (a 50/50 mixture of water and antifreeze) to the radiator until it's full. Add coolant to the reservoir up to the lower mark.

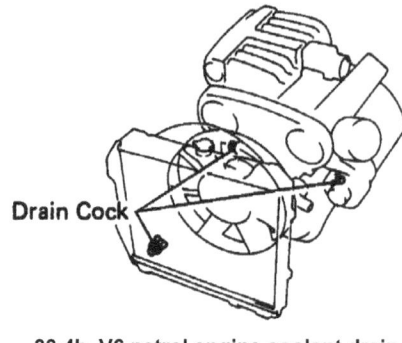

33.4b V6 petrol engine coolant drain plug locations

13   Leave the radiator cap off and run the engine in a well-ventilated area until the thermostat opens (coolant will begin flowing through the radiator and the upper radiator hose will become hot).

14   Turn the engine off and let it cool. Add more coolant mixture to bring the level back up to the lip on the radiator filler neck.

15   Squeeze the upper radiator hose to expel air, then add more coolant mixture if necessary. Renew the radiator cap.

16   Start the engine, allow it to reach normal operating temperature and check for leaks.

---

34   Manual transmission oil change

Refer to illustration 34.3

1   Drive the vehicle for a few kilometres to thoroughly warm up the transmission oil.

2   Raise the vehicle and support it securely on jackstands.

3   Move a drain pan, rags, newspapers and a wrench under the vehicle. With the drain pan and newspapers in position under the transmission, use the wrench to remove the check/fill plug from the side of the transmission **(see illustration 25.1)**. Loosen the drain plug located in the bottom of the transmission case **(see illustration)**.

4   Once loosened, carefully unscrew it with your fingers until you can remove it from the

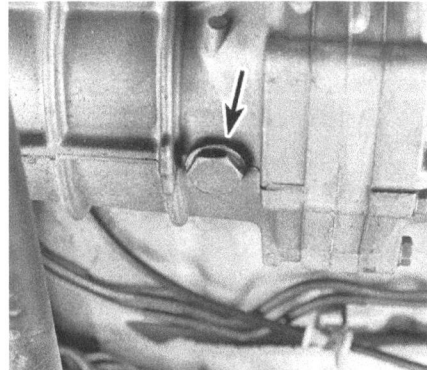

34.3 The manual transmission drain plug is located at the bottom of the case (arrow)

35.5 The automatic transmission fluid can be drained by removing the plug from the pan

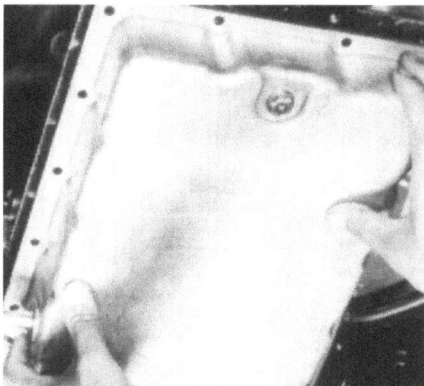

35.6 Lower the pan carefully - it'll still have some fluid in it

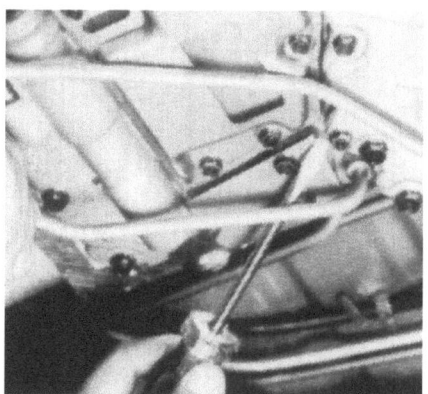

35.7 Use a screwdriver to carefully prise the tubes loose

transmission. Allow all of the oil to drain into the pan. If the plug is too hot to touch, use the wrench to remove it.

5   If the transmission is equipped with a magnetic drain plug, see if there are bits of metal clinging to it. If there are, it's a sign of excessive internal wear, indicating that the transmission should be carefully inspected in the near future. If the transmission isn't equipped with a magnetic drain plug, allow the oil in the pan to cool, then feel with your hands along the bottom of the drain pan for debris.

6   Clean the drain plug, then refit it in the transmission and tighten it securely.

7   Using a hand pump or syringe, fill the transmission with the correct amount and grade of oil (see Specifications), until the level is just at the bottom of the plug hole (see Section 25).

8   Refit the check/fill plug and tighten it securely.

35   Automatic transmission fluid and filter change

Refer to illustrations 35.5, 35.6, 35.7 and 35.8

1   At the specified time intervals, the trans-

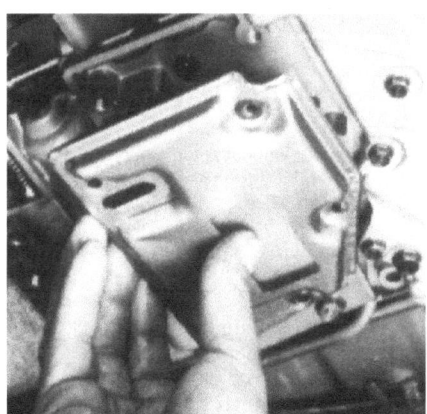

35.8 The filter is held in place with several bolts

mission fluid should be drained and renewed and a new filter fitted. Since the fluid should be hot when it's drained, drive the vehicle for 15 or 20 minutes before proceeding.

2   Before beginning work, purchase the specified transmission fluid (see *Recommended lubricants and fluids* at the front of this Chapter).

3   Other tools necessary for this job include jackstands to support the vehicle in a raised position, a drain pan capable of holding at least four litres, newspapers and clean rags.

4   Raise the vehicle and support it securely on jackstands.

5   With a drain pan in place, remove the plug and let the fluid drain into the pan **(see illustration)**. Be careful not to burn yourself on anything- it may be wise to wear gloves.

6   Remove the bolts and detach the transmission pan and filler tube **(see illustration)**. Discard the gasket. If the pan must be pried off, be very careful not to distort the pan or damage the transmission gasket surface!

7   Carefully prise the tubes loose with a screwdriver **(see illustration)**.

8   Remove the bolts and detach the filter/ strainer from the transmission **(see illustration)**.

9   Refit the new filter/strainer and tighten the bolts securely, then press the tubes into place very carefully by hand only.

10   Carefully clean the gasket surface of the transmission to remove all traces of the old gasket and sealant.

11   Drain the fluid from the transmission pan, clean it with solvent and dry it with compressed air.

12   Apply a thin layer of RTV sealant to the transmission case side of the new gasket.

13   Make sure the gasket surface on the transmission pan is clean, then apply a thin layer of RTV sealant to it and position the new gasket on the pan. Put the pan in place against the transmission, refit the bolts and, working around the pan, tighten each bolt a little at a time until the final torque figure is reached.

14   Lower the vehicle and add new automatic transmission fluid through the filler tube (see Section 5). The amount should be equal

to the amount of fluid that was drained (you don't want to overfill it).

15   With the transmission in Park and the parking brake set, run the engine at a fast idle, but don't race it.

16   Move the gear selector through each range and back to Park, then check the fluid level (see Section 5). Add more fluid as required.

17   Check under the vehicle for leaks during the first few kilometres of driving.

36   Differential oil change

Note: *The following procedure can be used for the rear differential as well as the front differential on 4WD vehicles.*

1   Drive the vehicle for several kilometres to warm up the differential oil, then raise the vehicle and support it securely on jackstands.

2   Move a drain pan, rags, newspapers and a spanner under the vehicle.

3   With the drain pan under the differential, use the spanner to loosen the drain plug. It's the lower of the two plugs **(see illustration 26.2)**.

4   Once loosened, carefully unscrew it with your fingers until you can remove it from the case.

5   Allow all of the oil to drain into the pan, then renew the drain plug and tighten it securely.

6   Feel with your hands along the bottom of the drain pan for any metal bits that may have come out with the oil. If there are any, it's a sign of excessive wear, indicating that the internal components should be carefully inspected in the near future.

7   Remove the differential check/fill plug (see Section 26). Using a hand pump, syringe or funnel, fill the differential with the correct amount and grade of oil (see the Specifications) until the level is just at the bottom of the plug hole.

8   Install the plug and tighten it securely.

9   Lower the vehicle. Check for leaks at the drain plug after the first few kilometres of driving.

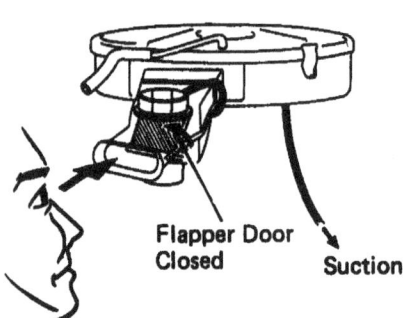

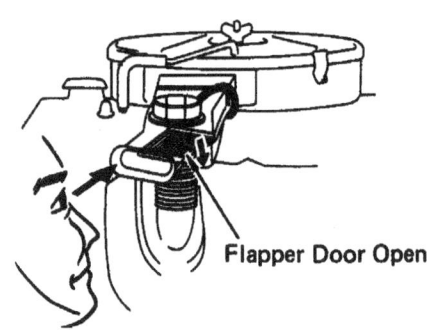

39.4 Position of the thermostatically controlled flapper door with the engine cold

39.6 Position of the thermostatically controlled flapper door with the engine at normal operating temperature

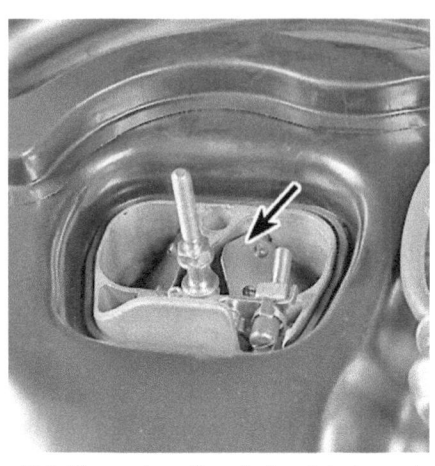

40.3 The carburettor choke plate (arrow) is visible after removing the air cleaner top plate or air intake duct

37   Transfer case oil change

1   Drive the vehicle for at least 15 minutes in 4WD to warm up the oil in the case.
2   Raise the vehicle and support it securely on jackstands. Remove the rock guard (if equipped).
3   Move a drain pan, rags, newspapers and a breaker bar or ratchet (to refit the square drive hole in the transfer case drain plug) under the vehicle.
4   Remove the check/fill plug **(see illustration 27.1)**.
5   Remove the drain plug from the lower part of the case and allow the old oil to drain completely.
6   Carefully clean and refit the drain plug after the case is completely drained. Tighten the plug securely.
7   Fill the case with the specified lubricant until it's level with the lower edge of the filler hole.
8   Refit the check/fill plug and tighten it securely.
9   Refit the rock guard, then lower the vehicle.
10   Check carefully for leaks around the drain plug after the first few kilometres of driving.

38   Fuel Evaporative Control (EVAP) system canister renewal

Note: *Refer to the Emissions chapter (see Chapter 6) for illustrations showing the EVAP system canister location(s).*
1   The function of the EVAP system is to draw fuel vapours from the tank and carburettor, store them in a charcoal canister and route them to the cylinders to be burned during normal engine operation. Depending on the vehicle year and model, more than one canister may be used (one for the fuel tank and one for the carburettor).
2   The canister(s) should be renewed at the specified intervals. However, if a fuel odour is detected, the canister(s) and system hoses should be inspected immediately.

3   Locate the canister(s) by tracing the lines from the carburettor and/or fuel tank.
4   Remove the canister(s) after disconnecting the hoses (mark the hoses and fittings to ensure correct refitting).
5   Refit the canister(s) by reattaching the hoses.
6   The EVAP system is explained in more detail in the Emission Control chapter (see Chapter 6).

39   Thermostatic air cleaner check

Refer to illustrations 39.4 and 39.6
1   All models are equipped with a thermostatically controlled air cleaner, which draws air to the carburettor from different locations depending on engine temperature.
2   This is a simple visual check. However, if access is tight, a small mirror may have to be used.
3   Open the bonnet and find the air control valve (flapper door) in the air cleaner assembly. It's located inside the long snorkel portion of the air cleaner housing.
4   If there's a flexible air duct attached to the end of the snorkel, disconnect it so you can look through the end of the snorkel and see the flapper door inside **(see illustration)**. A mirror may be needed if you can't safely look directly into the end of the snorkel.
5   The check should be done when the engine and outside air are cold. Start the engine and watch the flapper door, which should move up and close off the snorkel air passage. With the door closed, air can't enter through the end of the snorkel, but instead enters the air cleaner through the hot air duct attached to the exhaust manifold.
6   As the engine warms up to operating temperature, the door should open to allow air through the snorkel end **(see illustration)**. Depending on outside air temperature, this may take 10 to 15 minutes. To speed up the check you can reconnect the snorkel air duct, drive the vehicle and then check the position of the flapper door.
7   If the thermostatic air cleaner isn't operating properly, see Chapter 6 for more information.

40   Carburettor choke check

Refer to illustration 40.3
1   The choke operates only when the engine is cold, so this check should be performed before the engine has been started for the day.
2   Open the bonnet and remove the top plate of the air cleaner assembly, or loosen the clamp and remove the air intake duct. If any vacuum hoses must be disconnected, tag them to ensure refitting in their original positions.
3   Look at the centre of the carburettor. You'll notice a flat plate at the carburettor opening **(see illustration)**.
4   Have an assistant press the throttle pedal to the floor. The plate should close completely. Start the engine while you watch the plate at the carburettor. Don't position your face near the carburettor, as the engine could backfire, causing serious burns! When the engine starts, the choke plate should open slightly.
5   Allow the engine to continue running at an idle speed. As the engine warms up to operating temperature, the plate should slowly open, allowing more air to enter through the top of the carburettor.
6   After a few minutes, the choke plate should be completely open to the vertical position. Blip the throttle to make sure the fast idle cam disengages.
7   You'll notice that engine speed corresponds to the plate opening. With the plate closed, the engine should run at a fast idle speed. As the plate opens and the throttle is moved to disengage the fast idle cam, the engine speed will decrease.
8   With the engine off and the throttle held half-way open, open and close the choke several times. Check the linkage to see if it's hooked up correctly and make sure it doesn't bind.

9   If the choke or linkage binds, sticks or works sluggishly, clean it with choke cleaner (an aerosol spray available at auto parts stores). If the condition persists after cleaning, renew the troublesome parts.
10   Visually inspect all vacuum hoses to be sure they're securely connected and look for cracks and deterioration. Renew as necessary.
11   If the choke fails to operate normally, but no mechanical causes can be found, refer to Chapter 4.

---

41 Distributor cap and rotor check and renewal

Refer to illustrations 41.4 and 41.6
Note: *It's common practice to fit a new distributor cap and rotor whenever new spark plug wires are fitted.*

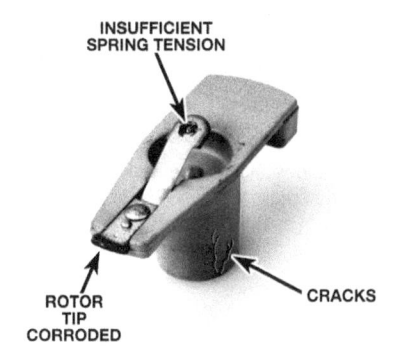

41.4 The ignition rotor should be checked for wear and corrosion as indicated here (if in doubt about its condition, buy a new one)

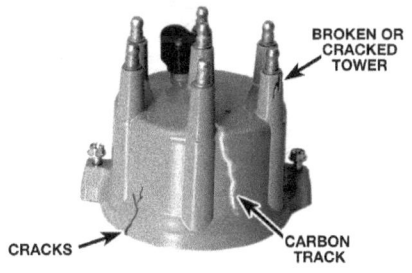

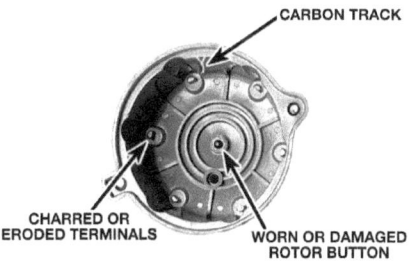

41.6 Shown here are some of the common defects to look for when inspecting the distributor cap (if in doubt about its condition, replace it)

1   Although the breakerless distributor used on these vehicles requires much less maintenance than a conventional distributor, periodic inspections should be performed at the intervals specified in the routine maintenance schedule and whenever any work is performed on the distributor.
2   Disconnect the ignition coil wire from the coil, then loosen the screws that hold the cap to the distributor body. Detach the distributor cap and wires.
3   Place the cap, with the spark plug and coil wires still attached, out of the way. Use a length of wire or rope to secure it, if necessary.
4   The rotor is now visible on the end of the distributor shaft. Check it carefully for cracks and carbon tracks. Make sure the centre terminal spring tension is adequate and look for corrosion and wear on the rotor tip **(see illus-**

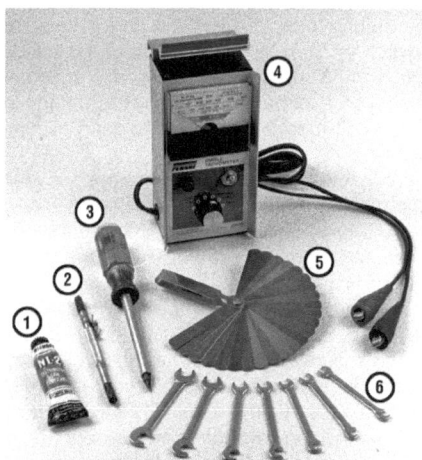

42.1 Tools and materials needed for contact point renewal and dwell angle adjustment

1   *Distributor cam lube - Sometimes this special lubricant comes with the new points; however, it's a good idea to buy a tube and have it on hand*
2   *Screw starter - This tool has special claws which hold the screw securely as it's started, which helps prevent accidental dropping of the screw*
3   *Magnetic screwdriver - Serves the same purpose as 2 above. If you don't have one of these special screwdrivers, you risk dropping the point mounting screws down into the distributor body*
4   *Dwell meter - A dwell meter is the only accurate way to determine the point setting (gap). Connect the meter according to the instructions supplied with it.*
5   *Blade-type feeler gauges - These are required to set the initial point gap (space between the points when they are open)*
6   *Ignition spanners - These special spanners are made to work within the tight confines of the distributor. Specifically, they are needed to loosen the nut/bolt which secures the leads to the points.*

tration). If in doubt about its condition, renew it.
5   If renewal is required, detach the rotor from the shaft and fit a new one. The rotor is indexed to the shaft so it can only be fitted one way.
6   Check the distributor cap for carbon tracks, cracks and other damage. Closely examine the terminals on the inside of the cap for excessive corrosion and damage **(see illustration)**. Slight deposits are normal. Again, if in doubt about the condition of the cap, renew it. Apply a small dab of silicone lubricant to each terminal before refitting the cap. Also, make sure the carbon brush (centre terminal) is correctly fitted in the cap - a wide gap between the brush and rotor will result in rotor burn-through and/or damage to the distributor cap.
7   When renewing the cap, simply transfer the spark plug and coil wires, one at a time, from the old cap to the new cap. Be very careful not to mix up the wires!
8   Reattach the cap to the distributor, then tighten the screws.

---

42 Ignition points renewal and adjustment

Renewal

Refer to illustrations 42.1, 42.6 and 42.7
1   The ignition points must be renewed at regular intervals on vehicles not equipped with electronic ignition. Several special tools are required for this procedure **(see illustration)**.
2   After removing the distributor cap and rotor (see Section 41), the ignition points are plainly visible. They can be examined by gently levering them open to reveal the condition of the contact surfaces. If they're rough, pitted, covered with oil or burned, they should be renewed along with the condenser (if equipped; later models don't have a condenser). **Caution:** *This procedure requires the removal of small screws which can easily fall down into the distributor. To retrieve them, the distributor would have to be removed and disassembled. Use a magnetic or spring-loaded screwdriver and be extra careful.*
3   If not already done, remove the distributor cap by releasing the clips or loosening the retaining screws.
4   Position the cap (with the spark plug wires still attached) out of the way. Use a length of wire to hold it out of the way, if necessary.
5   Remove the rotor and (if equipped) dust shield by pulling straight up and off the shaft.
6   Noting how they are routed, disconnect the wires from the points and loosen the screws which secure the ignition points to the breaker plate **(see illustration)**. Lift the points out of the distributor.
7   On earlier models, the condenser, mounted on the side of the distributor hous-

42.6 The ignition points are secured to the breaker plate with two screws (arrows)

42.7 On models so equipped, the condenser is located on the side of the distributor and is secured by one screw

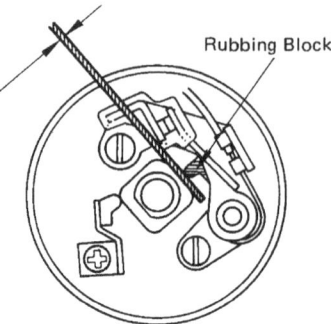

42.14 Insert the feeler gauge between the rubbing block and the flat side of the distributor cam

ing **(see illustration)**, must be renewed along with the points. Remove the terminal mounting nut and washer. Remove the mounting screw and lift the condenser off. Refitting is the reverse of removal.

8   Before fitting the new points, clean the breaker plate and the cam on the distributor shaft to remove all dirt, dust and oil.

9   Apply a small amount of distributor cam lube (usually supplied with the new points, but also available separately) to the cam lobes.

10   Place the new point set into position, then tighten the screws securely.

11   Attach the wires to the new points. Make sure the wires are routed so they don't interfere with breaker plate or advance weight movement.

12   Although the gap between the contact points (dwell angle) will be adjusted later, make the initial adjustment now, which will allow the engine to be started.

Adjustment

Refer to illustrations 42.14 and 42.15

13   Make sure that the point rubbing block positioned above one of the flat sides of the

42.15 After loosening the screws that secure the points to the breaker plate, insert a screwdriver into the slot and turn it slightly to obtain the desired gap

distributor cam. If it isn't, turn the ignition switch to Start in short bursts to reposition the cam. You can also turn the crankshaft with a breaker bar and socket attached to the large bolt that holds the crankshaft pulley in place.

14   Insert a 0.45 mm feeler gauge between the rubbing block and the flat side of the cam **(see illustration)**. The gap is correct when a slight amount of drag is felt as the feeler gauge is withdrawn.

15   If no drag is felt or the gauge can't be inserted, loosen the point hold-down screw, insert a screwdriver into the adjustment slot **(see illustration)** and turn it until the point gap is equal to the thickness of the feeler gauge. Tighten the hold-down screw.

16   Inspect the rotor and distributor cap as described in Section 36 and refit them.

17   Start the engine and check the dwell angle and ignition timing.

18   Whenever new ignition points are used or the original points are cleaned, the dwell angle must be checked and adjusted.

19   Precise adjustment of the dwell angle requires an instrument called a dwell meter. Combination tachometer dwell meters are commonly available at reasonable cost from auto parts stores. An approximate setting can be obtained if a meter isn't available.

20   If a dwell meter is available, hook it up following the manufacturer's instructions.

21   Start the engine and allow it to run at idle until normal operating temperature is reached (the engine must be warm to obtain an accurate reading).

22   Compare the dwell reading on the meter with those in the Specifications Section at the beginning of this Chapter or the VECI label in the engine compartment. If there's a discrepancy between the two, assume the VECI label or tune-up decal is correct.

23   If the dwell is not as specified, turn off the engine, remove the distributor cap, readjust the point gap, refit the cap and check it again.

43   Ignition timing check and adjustment

Refer to illustrations 43.1, 43.2 and 43.6

1   The proper ignition timing setting for your vehicle is printed on the VECI label located on the underside of the bonnet or listed in the Specifications at the beginning of this Chapter. Some special tools will be required for this procedure **(see illustration)**.

2   Locate the timing plate on the front of

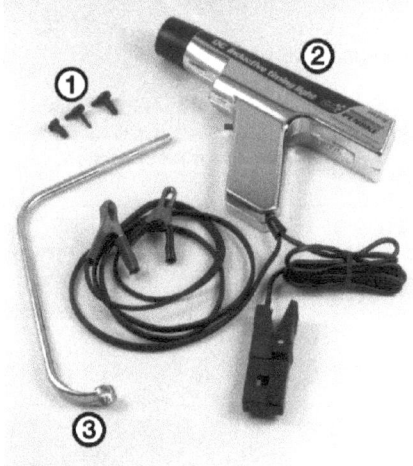

43.1 Tools needed to check and adjust the ignition timing

1   *Vacuum plugs - Vacuum hoses will, in most cases, have to be disconnected and plugged. Moulded plugs in various shapes and sizes are available for this*

2   *Inductive pick-up timing light - Flashes a bright concentrated beam of light when the number one spark plug fires. Connect the leads according to the instructions supplied with the light*

3   *Distributor wrench - On some models, the hold-down bolt for the distributor is difficult to reach and turn with conventional wrenches or sockets. A special wrench like this must be used*

43.2 The timing plate and pulley notch (arrow) are located low on the front of the engine - be careful of moving engine parts when checking the timing!

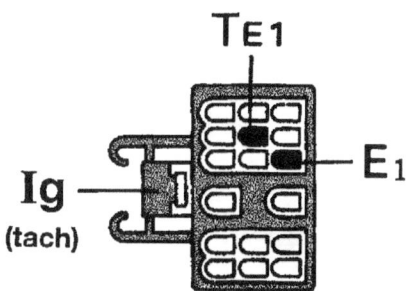

43.6 Connect a jumper wire between terminals TE1 and E1 before checking or adjusting timing on later models

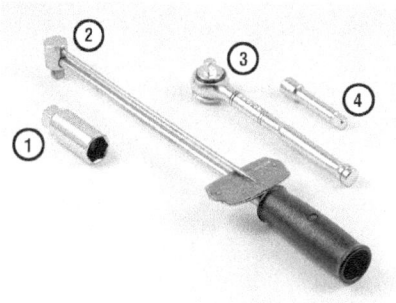

44.2 Tools required for changing spark plugs

1 Spark plug socket - This will have special padding inside to protect the spark plug porcelain insulator
2 Torque wrench - Although not mandatory, use of this tool is the best way to ensure that the plugs are tightened properly
3 Ratchet - Standard hand tool to fit the plug socket
4 Extension - Depending on model and accessories, you may need special extensions and universal joints to reach one or more of the plugs
5 Spark plug gap gauge - This gauge for checking the gap comes in a variety of styles. Make sure the gap for your engine is included

the engine, near the crankshaft pulley **(see illustration)**. The 0 mark is Top Dead Centre (TDC). To locate which mark the notch in the pulley must line up with for the timing to be correct, count back from the 0 mark the number of degrees BTDC (Before Top Dead Centre) noted on the VECI label or as listed in this Chapter's Specifications.

3   Locate the timing notch in the pulley and mark it with a dab of paint or chalk so it'll be visible under the strobe light. To locate the notch it may be necessary to have an assistant temporarily turn the ignition off and on in short bursts to turn the crankshaft. **Warning:** *Stay clear of all moving engine components if the engine is turned in this manner!*

4   Before attempting to check/adjust the timing, make sure the air gap is correct (Chapter 5).

5   Connect a tachometer according to the manufacturer's instructions and make sure the idle speed is correct. Adjust it if necessary as described in Section 17.

Note: *The tachometer may be connected to the Ig terminal of the check connector* **(see illustration 43.6)**

6   Allow the engine to reach normal operating temperature. Be sure the air conditioner, if equipped, is off. On some models, as noted on the VECI label, you must disconnect the distributor vacuum advance hose and plug it or connect a jumper wire between terminals TE1 and E1 of the check connector **(see illustration)**.

7   With the ignition switch off, connect the pick-up lead of the timing light to the number one spark plug wire. On four-cylinder engines, it's the front one. On V6 engines it's the first spark plug on the right side as viewed from the driver's seat. Use either a jumper lead between the wire and plug or an inductive-type pick up. Don't pierce the wire or attempt to insert a wire between the boot and plug wire. Connect the timing light power leads according to the manufacturer's instructions.

8   Make sure the wiring for the timing light is clear of all moving engine components, then start the engine. Race the engine two or three times, then allow it to idle for a minute.

9   Point the flashing timing light at the timing marks, again being careful not to come in contact with moving parts. The marks you highlighted should appear stationary. If the marks are in alignment, the timing is correct. If the marks aren't aligned, turn off the engine.

10   Loosen the distributor locknut until the distributor can be rotated.

11   Start the engine and slowly rotate the distributor until the timing marks are aligned.

12   Shut off the engine and tighten the distributor locknut, being careful not to move the distributor.

13   Restart the engine and recheck the timing to make sure the marks are still in alignment.

14   Disconnect the timing light.

15   Race the engine two or three times, then allow it to run at idle. Recheck the idle speed with the tachometer. If it has changed from the correct setting readjust it.

16   Drive the vehicle and listen for "pinging" noises. They'll be noticeable when the engine is hot and under load (climbing a hill, accelerating from a stop). If you hear engine pinging, the ignition timing is too far advanced (Before Top Dead Centre). Reconnect the timing light and turn the distributor to move the mark 1-degree or 2-degrees in the retard direction (clockwise). Road test the vehicle again to check for proper operation.

17   To keep "pinging" at a minimum, yet still allow you to operate the vehicle at the specified timing setting, use petrol of the same octane at all times. Switching fuel brands and octane levels can decrease performance and economy, and possibly damage the engine.

44 Spark plug renewal

Refer to illustrations 44.2, 44.5a, 44.5b, 44.6 and 44.10

1   Renew the spark plugs at the intervals recommended in the *Routine maintenance schedule*.

2   In most cases, the tools necessary for spark plug renewal include a spark plug socket which fits onto a ratchet (spark plug sockets are padded inside to prevent damage to the porcelain insulators on the new plugs), various extensions and a gap gauge to check and adjust the gaps on the new plugs **(see illustration)**. A special plug wire removal tool is available for separating the wire boots from the spark plugs, but it isn't absolutely necessary. A torque wrench should be used to tighten the new plugs.

3   The best approach when renewing the spark plugs is to purchase the new ones in advance, adjust them to the proper gap and renew them one at a time. When buying the new spark plugs, be sure to obtain the correct plug type for your particular engine. This information can be found on the *Emission Control Information* label located under the bonnet and in the factory owner's manual. If differences exist between the plug specified on the emissions label and in the owner's manual, assume the emissions label is correct.

4   Allow the engine to cool completely before attempting to remove any of the plugs. While you're waiting for the engine to cool, check the new plugs for defects and adjust the gaps.

5   The gap is checked by inserting the proper thickness gauge between the electrodes at the tip of the plug **(see illustration)**. The gap between the electrodes should be

44.5a Spark plug manufacturers recommend using a wire-type gauge when checking the gap - if the wire doesn't slide between the electrodes with a slight drag, adjustment is required

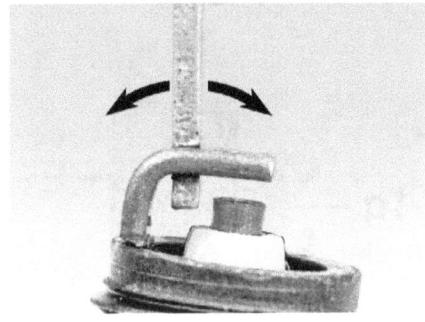

44.5b To change the gap, bend the side electrode only, as indicated by the arrows, and be very careful not to crack or chip the porcelain insulator surrounding the centre electrode

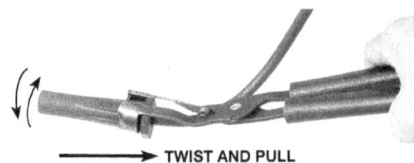

TWIST AND PULL

44.6 When removing the spark plug wires, grip the boot only and use a twisting/pulling motion

the same as the one specified on the *Emissions Control Information* label. The wire should just slide between the electrodes with a slight amount of drag. If the gap is incorrect, use the adjuster on the gauge body to bend the curved side electrode slightly until the proper gap is obtained **(see illustration)**. If the side electrode is not exactly over the centre electrode, bend it with the adjuster until it is. Check for cracks in the porcelain insulator (if any are found, the plug shouldn't be used).

6   With the engine cool, remove the spark plug wire from one spark plug. Pull only on the boot at the end of the wire - don't pull on the wire **(see illustration)**. A plug wire removal tool should be used if available.

7   If compressed air is available, use it to blow any dirt or foreign material away from the spark plug hole. A common bicycle pump will also work. The idea here is to eliminate the possibility of debris falling into the cylinder as the spark plug is removed.

8   Place the spark plug socket over the plug and remove it from the engine by turning it in a anti-clockwise direction.

9   Compare the spark plug to those shown in the photos on the inside of the back cover to get an indication of the general running condition of the engine.

10   Thread one of the new plugs into the hole until you can no longer turn it with your fingers, then tighten it with a torque wrench (if available) or the ratchet. It might be a good idea to slip a short length of rubber hose over the end of the plug to use as a tool to thread it into place **(see illustration)**. The hose will grip the plug well enough to turn it, but will start to slip if the plug begins to cross-thread in the hole - this will prevent damaged threads and the accompanying repair costs.

11   Before pushing the spark plug wire onto the end of the plug, inspect it following the procedures outlined in Section 35.

12   Attach the plug wire to the new spark plug, again using a twisting motion on the boot until it's seated on the spark plug.

13   Repeat the procedure for the remaining spark plugs, renewing them one at a time to prevent mixing up the spark plug wires.

45   Spark plug wire check and renewal

1   The spark plug wires should be checked at the recommended intervals and whenever new spark plugs are fitted in the engine.

2   The wires should be inspected one at a time to prevent mixing up the order, which is essential for proper engine operation.

3   Disconnect the plug wire from one spark plug. To do this, grab the rubber boot, twist slightly and pull the wire free. Do not pull on the wire itself, only on the rubber boot **(see illustration 45.6)**.

4   Check inside the boot for corrosion, which will look like a white crusty powder. Push the wire and boot back onto the end of the spark plug. It should be a tight fit on the plug. If it isn't, remove the wire and use a pair of pliers to carefully crimp the metal connector inside the boot until it fits securely on the end of the spark plug.

5   Using a clean rag, wipe the entire length of the wire to remove any built-up dirt and grease. Once the wire is clean, check for holes, burned areas, cracks and other damage. Don't bend the wire excessively or the conductor inside might break.

6   Disconnect the wire from the distributor cap (and plug, if still attached). Again, pull only on the rubber boot. Check for corrosion and a tight fit in the same manner as the spark plug end. Using an ohmmeter, check the resistance of the plug wire and compare it to the Specifications. If it's greater than specified, renew the wire (it would be a good idea to renew all of the wires, even if only one is bad).

7   Check the remaining spark plug wires one at a time, making sure they are securely fastened at the distributor and the spark plug when the check is complete.

8   If new spark plug wires are required, purchase a new set for your specific engine model. Wire sets are available pre-cut, with the rubber boots already fitted. Remove and fit the wires one at a time to avoid mix-ups in the firing order. The wire routing is extremely

44.10 A length of snug-fitting rubber hose will save time and prevent damaged threads when refitting the spark plugs

important, so be sure to note exactly how each wire is situated before removing it.

46   Oxygen sensor renewal

Refer to illustration 46.2

1   The oxygen (exhaust gas) sensor, if so equipped, should be renewed at the specified intervals.

2   The sensor is mounted in the exhaust manifold and can be identified by the wires attached to it **(see illustration)**. Renewal consists of disconnecting the wire harness and removing the mounting nuts. Detach the old sensor (and gasket), position the new one over the studs, along with a new gasket, then refit the mounting nuts. Tighten the nuts to the specified torque, then reconnect the wire harness.

3   The sensor operation/feedback control should be checked by a dealer service department.

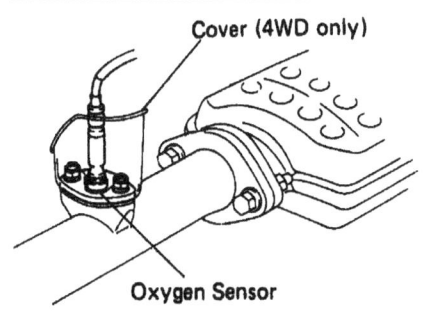

Cover (4WD only)

Oxygen Sensor

46.2 Typical oxygen sensor mounting details

Chapter 2 Part A Four-cylinder Overhead valve (OHV) petrol engines

Contents

Specifications

12R engine

General
Displacement	1587 cc
Cylinder numbers (front-to-rear)	1-2-3-4
Firing order	1-3-4-2

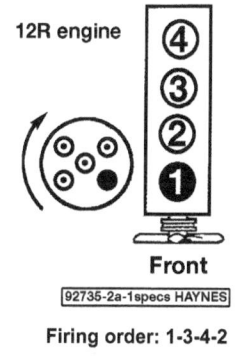

12R engine

Front

92735-2a-1specs HAYNES

Firing order: 1-3-4-2

Cylinder location and distributor rotation

Camshaft, lifters and rocker arms
Lobe height	
Intake	6.365 to 6.415 mm
Exhaust	6.475 to 6.525 mm
Thrust clearance (endplay)	
Standard	0.05 to 0.13 mm
Limit	0.2 mm
Timing gear backlash (maximum)	0.03 mm
Journal-to-bearing (oil) clearance	
Standard	0.025 to 0.066 mm
Limit	0.1 mm
Journal out-of-round limit	0.01 mm
Journal diameter STD (journals numbered from front-to-rear of engine)	
No. 1	46.459 to 46.475 mm
No. 2	46.209 to 46.225 mm
No. 3	45.959 to 45.995 mm
Rocker arm-to-shaft oil clearance	
Standard	0.020 to 0.035 mm
Limit	0.05 mm
Rocker shaft diameter	18.474 to 18.487 mm

12R engine (continued)

Cylinder head
Warpage limit... 0.15 mm

Oil pump
Driven gear-to-oil pump body clearance
     Standard.. 0.10 to 0.15 mm
     Limit.. 0.20 mm
Inner rotor tip clearance
     Standard.. 0.07 to 0.12 mm
     Limit.. 0.20 mm
Gear side clearance
     Standard.. 0.03 to 0.07 mm
     Limit.. 0.15 mm

Torque specifications
	Nm
Camshaft thrust plate bolts	15
Camshaft sprocket bolt	Not available
Crankshaft pulley bolt	48
Cylinder head bolts	
Stage 1	41
Stage 2	82
Stage 3	116
Flywheel/driveplate-to-crankshaft bolts	64
Intake/exhaust manifold bolts	41
Sump mounting bolts	12
Oil pump bolt	15
Oil pump cover bolts	7.8
Rocker arm bolts	25
Valve cover bolts	10
Timing cover bolts	15

Y-series engines

General
Displacement
     1Y.. 1626 cc
     2Y.. 1812 cc
     3Y.. 1998 cc
     4Y.. 2237 cc
Cylinder numbers (front-to-rear) 1-2-3-4
Firing order 1-3-4-2

Cylinder head
Warpage limit... 0.15 mm

Camshaft, lifters and rocker arms
Lobe height
     Intake .... 38.620 to 38.720
     Exhaust .... 38.629 to 38.729
Lobe height limit
     Intake .... 38.26 mm
     Exhaust .... 38.27 mm
Thrust clearance (endplay)
     Standard.. 0.07 to 0.22 mm
     Limit.. 0.30 mm
Journal-to-bearing (oil) clearance
     Standard.. 0.025 to 0.111 mm
     Limit.. 0.14 mm
Journal out-of-round limit .... 0.01 mm
Camshaft bearing inside diameter
     No. 1.. 46.500 to 46.570 mm
     No. 2.. 46.250 to 46.320 mm
     No. 3.. 46.000 to 46.070 mm
     No. 4.. 45.750 to 45.820 mm
     No. 5.. 45.500 to 45.570 mm

1Y, 2Y, 3Y, 4Y
(carburetted)
engines

④
③
②
①

Front
Firing Order: 1-3-4-2

4Y-E engine

④
③
②
①

Front
Firing Order: 1-3-4-2

92735-2a specs HAYNES

Cylinder location and distributor rotation

Journal diameter (standard)
    No. 1.. 46.459 to 46.475 mm
    No. 2.. 46.209 to 46.225 mm
    No. 3.. 45.960 to 45.970 mm
    No. 4.. 45.709 to 45.725 mm
    No. 5.. 45.459 to 45.475 mm
Rocker arm-to-shaft oil clearance
    Standard.. 0.013 to 0.041 mm
    Limit.. 0.08 mm
Rocker shaft diameter .... 18.474 to 18.487 mm
Rocker arm inside diameter.. 18.500 to 18.515 mm

Timing chain and sprockets
Timing chain length (maximum) .... 291.4 mm
Timing chain sprocket wear limit (measured with chain)
    Crankshaft.. 59 mm
    Camshaft.. 114 mm
Timing chain slack (chain refitted) .... 13.5 mm @ 98 N (10 kg)
Timing chain tensioner thickness
    Standard.. 15 mm
    Minimum.. 12.5 mm
Timing chain damper thickness
    Standard.. 6.6 mm
    Minimum.. 5.0 mm
Valve lifter diameter... 21.387 to 21.404 mm
Valve lifter bore diameter... 21.417 to 21.443 mm
Valve lifter oil clearance
    Standard.. 0.013 to 0.056 mm
    Maximum... 0.10 mm

Oil pump
Driven gear-to-oil pump body clearance
    Standard.. 0.10 to 0.15 mm
    Limit.. 0.20 mm
Inner rotor tip clearance
    Standard.. 0.07 to 0.12 mm
    Limit.. 0.20 mm
Gear side clearance
    Standard.. 0.03 to 0.07 mm
    Limit.. 0.15 mm

Torque specifications   **Nm**
Camshaft thrust plate bolts 18
Camshaft sprocket bolt.. 90
Crankshaft pulley bolt.. 157
Cylinder head bolts
    12 mm bolt head 19
    14 mm bolt head 88
Flywheel-to-crankshaft bolts.. 83
Driveplate-to-crankshaft bolts.. 74
Inlet/exhaust manifold bolts... 49
Sump mounting bolts... 13
Oil pump mounting bolt.. 18
Oil pump cover bolts.. 7.8
Rocker arm bolts 24
Valve cover-to-cylinder head nuts .... Not available
Timing chain case-to-block bolts 18
Timing chain cover-to-case bolts 5.9
Timing chain tensioner 18
Rear main oil seal retainer... 12

1   General information

This Part of Chapter 2 is devoted to in-vehicle engine repair procedures for the 12R and Y-series pushrod engines.

All information concerning engine removal and installation can be found in Chapter 2E.

The following repair procedures are based on the assumption that the engine is refitted in the vehicle. If the engine has been removed from the vehicle and mounted on a stand, many of the steps included in this Part of Chapter 2 will not apply.

The Specifications included in this Part of Chapter 2 apply only to the procedures included in this Part. Additional Specifications necessary for removing and overhauling the engine are found in Part E.

2   Repair operations possible with the engine in the vehicle

Many major repair operations can be accomplished without removing the engine from the vehicle.

Clean the engine compartment and the exterior of the engine with some type of pressure washer before any work is done. A clean engine will make the job easier and will help keep dirt out of the internal areas of the engine.

If vacuum, exhaust, oil or coolant leaks develop, indicating a need for gasket or seal renewal, the repairs can generally be made with the engine in the vehicle. The intake and exhaust manifold gaskets, sump gasket and cylinder head gasket are all accessible with the engine in place.

Exterior engine components such as the inlet and exhaust manifolds, the sump (and the oil pump), the water pump, the starter motor, the alternator, the distributor and the carburettor or fuel injection components can be removed for repair with the engine in place.

Since the cylinder head can be removed without pulling the engine, valve component servicing can also be accomplished with the engine in the vehicle.

In extreme cases caused by a lack of necessary equipment, repair or renewal of piston rings, pistons, connecting rods and rod bearings is possible with the engine in the

vehicle. However, this practice is not recommended because of the cleaning and preparation work that must be done to the components involved.

3   Top Dead Centre (TDC) for number one piston - locating

Refer to Chapter 2 Part B, Section 3 for this procedure.

4   Valve cover - removal and refitting

Refer to illustration 4.6

1   Disconnect the negative cable from the battery.

2   Rotate the throttle bellcrank and pass the end of the accelerator cable through the slot. Loosen the adjusting nuts and detach the accelerator cable casing from its bracket.

3   If the vehicle is equipped with an automatic transmission, also disconnect the kickdown cable the same way.

4   Detach the PCV hose and crankcase breather hose from the valve cover.

5   Label and remove any other hoses and/or wires necessary to provide clearance for valve cover removal.

6   Remove the valve cover retaining nuts and washers and lift off the cover **(see illustration)**. If the valve cover is stuck to the cylinder head, bump the end with a wood block and hammer to jar it loose. If that doesn't work, try to detach the cover by breaking the seal with a putty knife or razor blade. **Caution:** *Don't prise at the valve cover-to-cylinder head joint or damage to the sealing surfaces may occur, leading to oil leaks after the valve cover is refitted.*

7   Prior to refitting, remove all traces of dirt, oil and old gasket material from the cover and cylinder head. Clean the mating surfaces with lacquer thinner or acetone and a clean rag.

8   Inspect the mating surface on the cover for damage and warpage. Correct or renew as necessary.

9   If a rubber sealing gasket was used, it can be reused unless it has high number of kilometres and the rubber has hardened or cracked. Composition-type gaskets must always be renewed. It's a good idea to coat these types of gaskets with a thin film of RTV sealant.

10   Place the valve cover on the cylinder head while the sealant (if used) is still wet and refit the washers and mounting nuts. Tighten the nuts a little at a time until the torque listed in this Chapter's Specifications is reached. **Note:** *Be sure to fit new rubber seals into the washers if they are cracked, hardened or otherwise deteriorated.*

11   Complete the refitting procedure by reversing the removal procedure.

12   Start the engine and check for oil leaks.

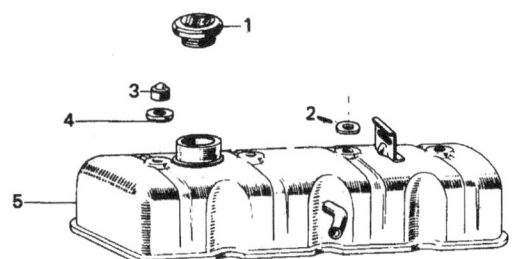

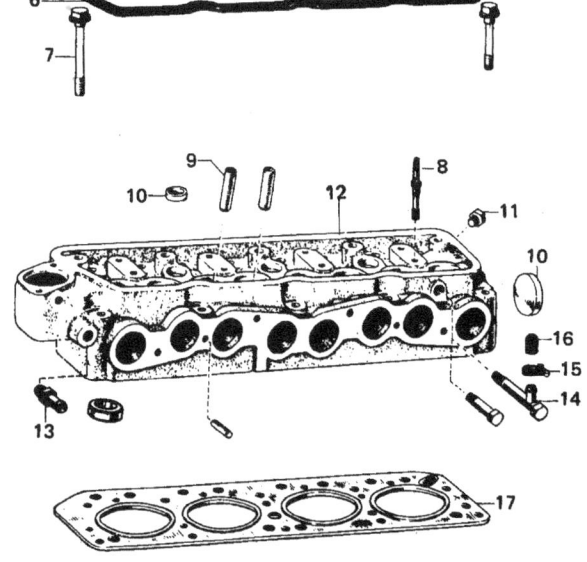

4.6   Valve cover and cylinder head details (12R engine)

1   *Oil filler cap*
2   *Washer*
3   *Nut*
4   *Grommet*
5   *Valve cover*
6   *Gasket*
7   *Cylinder head bolt*
8   *Valve cover stud*
9   *Valve guide*
10   *Core plug*
11   *Plug*
12   *Cylinder head*
13   *Water bypass fitting*
14   *Heater hose fitting*
15   *Hose clamp*
16   *Plug*
17   *Gasket*

5 Pushrod cover (12R engine) - removal and refitting

Refer to illustration 5.2

1   Disconnect the negative cable at the battery.

2   Remove the pushrod cover bolts **(see illustration)** and carefully prise the pushrod cover from the side of the block, using a thin-blade knife if necessary to release it from the block. Use caution not to distort the cover sealing flanges.

3   Scrape all old gasket and sealant from the pushrod cover and the block.

4   Using a thin film of RTV sealant to hold it in place, fit a new gasket on the pushrod cover.

5   Place the cover against the block and refit the bolts, washers and gaskets. Tighten the bolts securely.

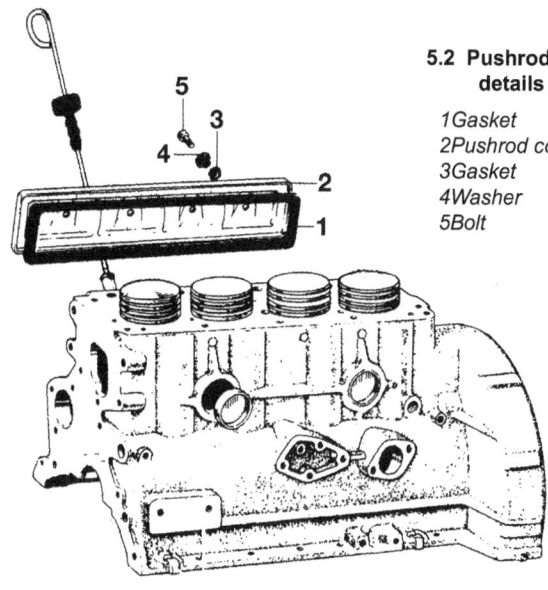

5.2 Pushrod cover installation details (12R engine)

1 Gasket
2 Pushrod cover
3 Gasket
4 Washer
5 Bolt

6 Rocker arms and pushrods - removal, inspection and refitting

Refer to illustrations 6.2a, 6.2b, 6.4 and 6.12

Removal

1   Detach the valve cover from the cylinder head, referring to Section 4.

2   Loosen the rocker arm bolts in the sequence shown, a little at a time, to allow the rocker shaft to remain level to the plane of the cylinder head **(see Illustrations)**.

3   Remove the rocker arm assembly as a single unit. Be careful to not allow any of the components slide off the rocker shaft.

4   Remove the pushrods and store them separately to make sure they don't get mixed up during refitting **(see illustration)**.

Inspection

5   Try to wiggle each rocker arm on the shaft. If movement is felt, disassemble the shaft and rocker arm assembly, laying the parts out in order so as to prevent confusion on reassembly. Check each rocker arm for wear, cracks and other damage, especially the pushrod pocket and where the valve

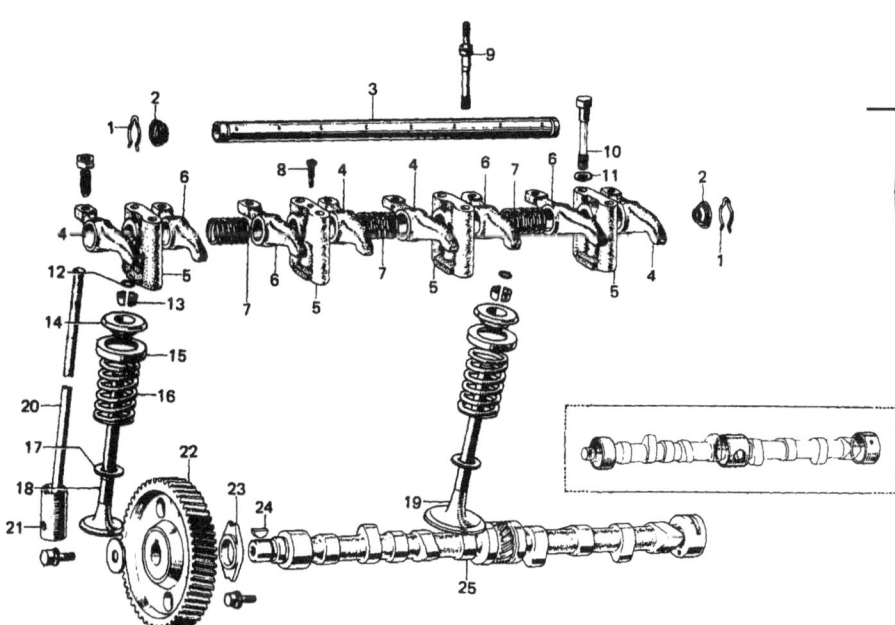

6.2a Camshaft and valve gear details (12R engine)

1 Spring clip	10 Rocker arm mounting bolts	18 Exhaust valve
2 Coil spring	11 Washer	19 Intake valve
3 Rocker shaft	12 O-ring	20 Pushrod
4 Rocker arm	13 Keepers	21 Valve lifter
5 Rocker pillar	14 Valve spring retainer	22 Timing gear
6 Rocker arm	15 Oil shield	23 Thrust plate
7 Spring	16 Valve spring	24 Woodruff key
8 Locking screw	17 Washer	25 Camshaft
9 Valve cover stud		

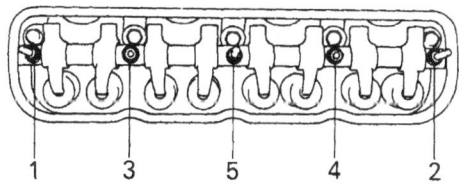

6.2b Loosen the rocker arm bolts in this order (Y-series engine shown; on 12R engines, loosen each pair of pillar bolts starting on the outer pillars, then the inner pillars)

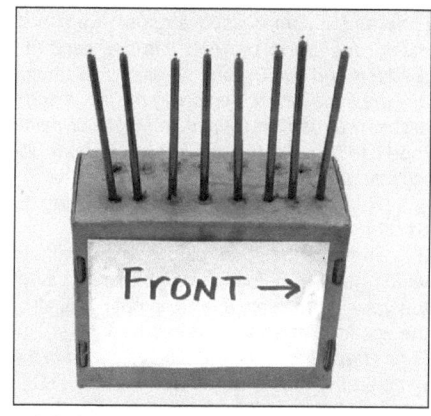

6.4 A perforated cardboard box can be used to store the pushrods in order

stems contact the rocker arm faces.

6   Make sure the hole at the pushrod end of each rocker arm is open.

7   Check each rocker arm inside diameter with an inside micrometer and compare your readings with the values listed in this Chapter's Specifications. Also check for cracks and galling. If the rocker arms are worn or damaged, renew them and use new pivots as well. Measure the diameter of the rocker shafts, too, and compare with the Specifications. Renew the rocker shaft if necessary.

8   Inspect the pushrods for cracks and excessive wear at the ends. Roll each pushrod across a piece of plate glass to see if it's bent (if it wobbles, it's bent).

Refitting

9   Lubricate the lower ends of the pushrods with clean engine oil or moly-base grease and refit them in their original locations. Make sure each pushrod seats completely in the lifter socket.

10   Apply moly-base grease to the ends of the valve stems and the upper ends of the pushrods.

11   Assemble the rocker arms, springs and washers onto the shaft. Apply moly-base grease to the pivots to prevent damage to the mating surfaces before engine oil pressure builds up.

12   Refit the rocker arm assembly, making sure the pushrods seat in the pockets of the rocker arms. Tighten the bolts, a little at a time in the proper sequence **(see illustration)**, to the torque listed in this Chapter's Specifications.

13   If you're working on a 12R engine, adjust the valve clearances (see Chapter 1).

14   Refit the valve cover and run the engine. Check for oil leaks and unusual valve train noises.

---

7   Valve springs, retainers and seals - renewal

Refer to illustrations 7.4, 7.9, 7.15 and 7.17

Note: *Broken valve springs and defective valve stem seals can be renewed without removing the cylinder heads. Two special tools and a compressed air source are normally required to perform this operation, so read through this Section carefully and rent or buy the tools before beginning the job. If compressed air isn't available, a length of nylon rope can be used to keep the valves from falling into the cylinder during this procedure.*

1   Remove the valve cover referring to Section 4.

2   Remove the spark plug from the cylinder which has the defective component. If all of the valve stem seals are being renewed, all of the spark plugs should be removed.

3   Turn the crankshaft until the piston in the affected cylinder is at top dead centre (TDC) on the compression stroke (see Section 3 for instructions). If you're renewing all of the valve stem seals, begin with cylinder number

one and work on the valves for one cylinder at a time. Move from cylinder-to-cylinder following the firing order sequence (see the Specifications listed at the beginning of this Chapter).

4   Thread an adaptor into the spark plug hole **(see illustration)** and connect an air hose from a compressed air source to it. Most auto parts stores can supply the air hose adaptor. **Note:** *Many cylinder compression gauges utilise a screw-in fitting that may work with your air hose quick-disconnect fitting.*

5   Remove the rocker arm and shaft assembly (see Section 6).

6   Apply compressed air to the cylinder. **Warning:** *The piston may be forced down by compressed air, causing the crankshaft to turn suddenly. If the wrench used when positioning the number one piston at TDC is still attached to the bolt in the crankshaft nose, it could cause damage or injury when the crankshaft moves.*

7   The valves should be held in place by the air pressure. If the valve faces or seats are in poor condition, leaks may prevent air pressure from retaining the valves - refer to the alternative procedure below.

8   If you don't have access to compressed air, an alternative method can be used. Position the piston at a point approximately 45-degrees (1/4-turn) before TDC on the compression stroke, then feed a long piece of nylon rope through the spark plug hole until it fills the combustion chamber. Be sure to leave the end of the rope hanging out of the engine so it can be removed easily. Use a large ratchet and socket to rotate the crank-

shaft in the normal direction of rotation until slight resistance is felt.

9   Stuff shop rags into the cylinder head holes above and below the valves to prevent parts and tools from falling into the engine, then use a valve spring compressor to compress the spring **(see illustration)**. Remove the collets with small needle-nose pliers or a magnet.

10   Remove the spring retainer, oil shield and valve spring, then remove the guide seal. **Note:** *If air pressure fails to hold the valve in the closed position during this operation, the valve face and/or seat is probably damaged. If so, the cylinder head will have to be removed for additional repair operations.*

11   Wrap a rubber band or tape around the top of the valve stem so the valve won't fall into the combustion chamber, then release the air pressure. **Note:** *If a rope was used instead of air pressure, turn the crankshaft slightly in the direction opposite normal rotation.*

12   Inspect the valve stem for damage. Rotate the valve in the guide and check the end for eccentric movement, which would indicate that the valve is bent.

13   Move the valve up-and-down in the guide and make sure it doesn't bind. If the valve stem binds, either the valve is bent or the guide is damaged. In either case, the head will have to be removed for repair.

14   Reapply air pressure to the cylinder to retain the valve in the closed position, then remove the tape or rubber band from the valve stem. If a rope was used instead of air pressure, rotate the crankshaft in the normal

---

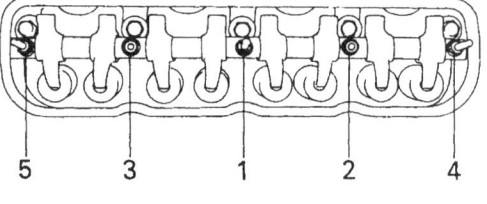

6.12 Tighten the rocker arm bolts in this sequence (Y-series engine shown; on the 12R engine, start from the center pillars, then the outer pillars)

5   3   1   2   4

7.4 This is what the air hose adapter that threads into the spark plug hole looks like - they're commonly available from auto parts stores

7.9 Once the spring is compressed, the keepers can be removed with a small magnet or needle-nose pliers

direction of rotation until slight resistance is felt.

15   Lubricate the valve stem with engine oil and fit a new guide seal **(see illustration)**.

16   Refit the spring and shield in position over the valve.

17   Refit the valve spring retainer. Compress the valve spring and carefully position the collets in the groove. Apply a small dab of grease to the inside of each collet to hold it in place **(see illustration)**.

18   Remove the pressure from the spring tool and make sure the collets are seated.

19   Disconnect the air hose and remove the adaptor from the spark plug hole. If a rope was used in place of air pressure, pull it out of the cylinder.

20   Refer to Section 6 and refit the pushrods and the rocker shaft assembly.

21   Refit the spark plug(s) and hook up the wire(s).

22   Refer to Section 4 and refit the valve cover.

23   Start and run the engine, then check for oil leaks and unusual sounds coming from the valve cover area.

8   Inlet and exhaust manifolds - removal and refitting

Refer to illustrations 8.9a, 8.9b and 8.10

Warning: *Allow the engine to cool completely before performing this procedure.*

1   Disconnect the negative cable from the battery.

2   Detach the air intake duct from the carburettor or throttle body.

3   On carburetted models, remove the carburettor (see Chapter 4A). Be sure to carefully mark all hoses and wires.

4   On fuel-injected models, remove the air intake plenum (see Chapter 4A).

5   On fuel-injected models, relieve the fuel system pressure (see Chapter 4A), then disconnect the fuel feed and return lines from the fuel rail (see Chapter 4A).

6   If equipped, detach the water pipe from the manifold studs.

7   Raise the vehicle and support it securely on jackstands placed under the frame.

8   Unscrew the exhaust pipe-to-manifold

7.15 The valve guide seals can be installed with a deep socket

nuts. **Note:** *It's good idea to spray some penetrating oil onto these nuts before attempting to unscrew them, as they're usually rusted.*

9   Lower the vehicle and unscrew the manifold nuts and bolts **(see illustrations)**. Pull the manifolds away from the engine to disengage them from the studs cylinder head, then lift the manifolds from the engine. If the manifolds stick to the engine after all the fasteners are removed, tap them with a soft-faced hammer or a block of wood and a hammer while supporting them.

10   If it is necessary to separate the inlet and exhaust manifolds, remove the four Allen-head bolts holding the manifolds together **(see illustration)**.

11   Thoroughly clean the mating surfaces, removing all traces of gasket material. Check the mating surfaces with a straightedge and a feeler gauge; if warpage exceeds 0.4 mm, the manifold(s) should be resurfaced or, if severely warped, renewed.

12   If the inlet manifold is being renewed, transfer all fittings to the new one. If the exhaust manifold is being renewed, transfer the heat shield to the new manifold.

13   If the manifolds were separated from each other, rejoin them and refit the bolts, but don't tighten the bolts yet.

14   Position the new gasket on the cylinder head and refit the manifold assembly.

15   Refit the manifold assembly on the cylinder head studs. Refit the fasteners and

7.17 Apply a small dab of grease to each keeper as shown here before installation - it'll hold them in place on the valve stem as the spring is released

tighten them in two or three stages, to the torque listed in this Chapter's Specifications.

16   If the manifolds were separated, tighten the attaching bolts securely. Refit the heat shield.

17   Refit the remaining parts in the reverse order of removal.

18   Run the engine and check for vacuum and fuel leaks.

9   Cylinder head - removal and refitting

Refer to illustrations 9.6, 9.7, 9.11a and 9.11b

Warning: *The engine must be completely cool before performing this procedure.*

1   Remove the valve cover (see Section 4) and the rocker arms and pushrods (see Section 6).

2   Drain the cooling system (see Chapter 1).

3   Remove the inlet and exhaust manifolds (see Section 8).

4   Remove the drivebelt(s) as described in Chapter 1.

5   Mark and detach any other wires and hoses that would interfere with removal.

6   Unscrew the cylinder head bolts by reversing the tightening sequence shown

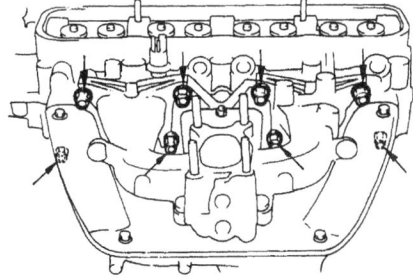

8.9a Inlet/exhaust manifold mounting nuts (carbureted Y-series engine)

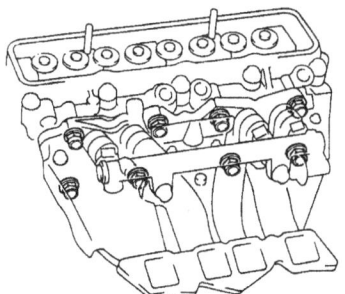

8.9b Inlet/exhaust manifold mounting nuts (fuel-injected Y-series engine)

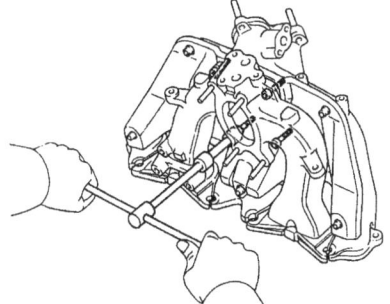

8.10 The manifolds are held together by four bolts

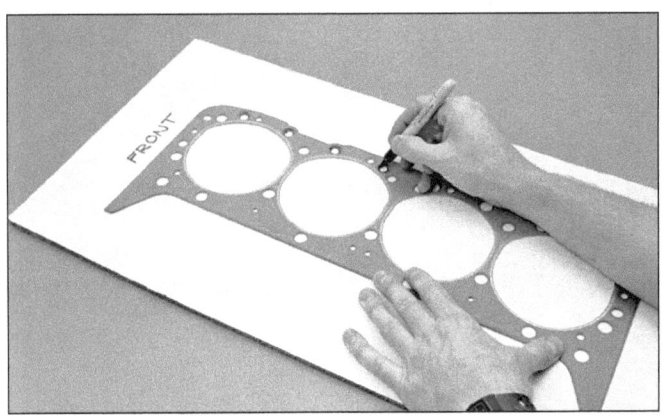

9.6 To avoid mixing up the head bolts, use a new gasket to transfer the bolt hole pattern to a piece of cardboard, then punch holes to accept the bolts

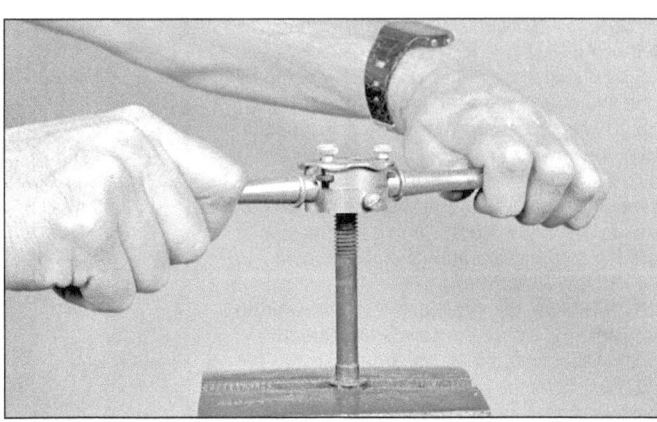

9.7 A die should be used to remove sealant and corrosion from the head bolt threads prior to installation

in **illustration 9.11a or 9.11b**, then lift it off the engine. If the head is stuck to the engine block, it may be necessary to tap it with a soft-face hammer or a block of wood and a hammer to break the seal. Keep the head bolts in order, as different size bolts may be used in these engines **(see illustration)**.

7   Stuff clean shop towels into the cylinders. Thoroughly clean the gasket surfaces, removing all traces of gasket material. Run an appropriate sized tap into the bolt holes in the cylinder head and run a die over the bolt threads **(see illustration)**. Ensure all bolt holes are clean and dry.

8   Inspect the cylinder head for cracks and check it for warpage.

9   These engines use a composition gasket. Fit it dry (without any sealing compound).

10   Refit the head gasket, making sure all coolant and oil passages line up. Look for marks such as TOP or FRONT. Place the cylinder head on the engine.

11   Refit the bolts and tighten them in the sequence shown **(see illustrations)**. Tighten them in the steps and to the torque listed in this Chapter's Specifications.

12   Refit the remaining components in the reverse order of removal.

13   If you're working on a 12R engine, adjust the valve clearances (see Chapter 1).

14   Change the engine oil and filter (see

Chapter 1).

15   Refill the cooling system (see Chapter 1) and run the engine, checking for leaks and proper operation.

10   Valve lifters - removal, inspection and refitting

12R engine

Removal

1   Remove the valve cover (see Section 4).
2   Remove the rocker arm assembly and the pushrods (see Section 6).
3   Remove the pushrod cover (see Section 5).
4   Arrange to store the lifters in order so they can be returned to their original bores, if reused. A small, partitioned box or an egg carton works well.
5   Using a hooked tool, a magnet or a piece of bent coat hanger **(see illustration 10.14)**, pull each lifter up and out of its bore, then retrieve it through the pushrod cover.

Inspection

6   Check the lifters as described in Steps 16 and 17.

Refitting

7   Lubricate the bearing surfaces of the lifter bores with clean engine oil. Coat the lifter walls, the lifter foot and the pushrod pocket with moly-based grease or engine assembly lube, then refit the lifters in their original bores.

8   The remainder of refitting is the reverse of removal.

9   Adjust the valve clearances (see Chapter 1).

Y-series engines

10   A noisy hydraulic lifter can be isolated when the engine is idling. Place a length of hose or tubing on the valve cover near the position of each valve while listening at the other end. Or remove the valve cover and, with the engine idling, place a finger on each of the valve spring retainers, one at a time. If a valve lifter is defective, it'll be evident from the shock felt at the retainer as the valve opens.

11   The most likely cause of a noisy valve lifter is a piece of dirt trapped between the plunger and the lifter body.

Removal

Refer to illustration 10.14

12   Remove the valve cover (see Section 4).

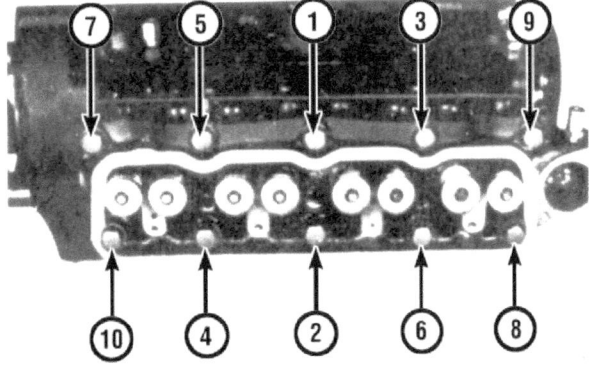

9.11a Cylinder head bolt TIGHTENING sequence (12R engine)

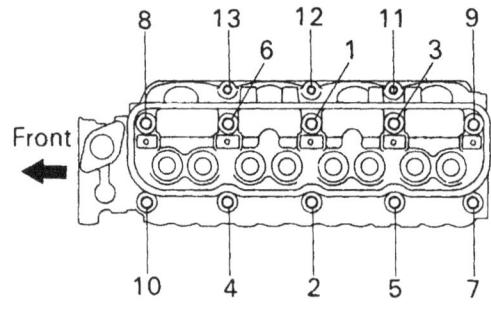

9.11b Cylinder head bolt TIGHTENING sequence (Y-series engines)

13   Remove the rocker arm assembly and pushrods (see Section 6).

14   Using a magnet, a hooked tool or a piece of bent coat hanger, remove the lifters through the openings in the cylinder head **(see illustration)**.

15   Store the lifters in a clearly labelled box to insure their refitting in the same lifter bores.

Inspection

Refer to illustrations 10.17a, 10.17b, 10.17c and 10.17d

16   Clean the lifters with solvent and dry them thoroughly. Do this one lifter at a time to avoid mixing them up.

17   Check each lifter wall, pushrod seat and foot for scuffing, score marks and uneven wear. Each lifter foot (the surface that rides on the cam lobe) must be slightly convex, although this can be difficult to determine by eye. If the base of the lifter is concave or rough **(see illustrations)**, the lifters and camshaft must be renewed. If the lifter walls are damaged or worn (which isn't very likely), inspect the lifter bores in the engine block as well. If the pushrod seats **(see illustration)** are worn, check the pushrod ends.

18   If new lifters are being fitted, a new camshaft must also be fitted. If a new camshaft is fitted, then use new lifters as well. Never fit used lifters unless the original camshaft is used and the lifters can be refitted in their original locations!

Refitting

19   The used lifters must be refitted in their original bores. Coat them with moly-base grease or engine assembly lube.

20   Lubricate the bearing surfaces of the lifter bores with clean engine oil.

21   Refit the lifter(s) in the lifter bore(s).

22   Refit the pushrods and the rocker arm assembly (see Section 6).

23   Refit the valve cover (Section 4).

10.14 The lifters can be removed with a piece of hooked wire

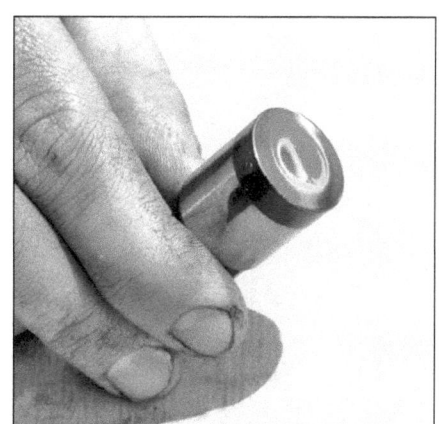

10.17a If the bottom of any lifter is worn concave, scratched or galled, replace the entire set with new lifters

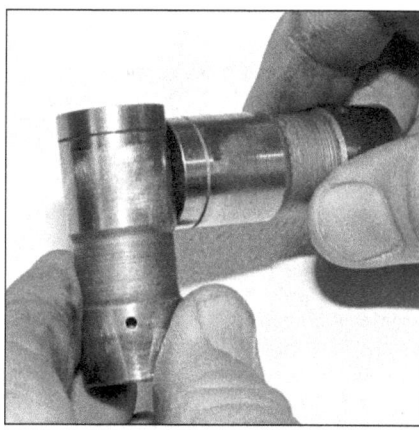

10.17b The foot of each lifter should be slightly convex - the side of another lifter can be used as a straightedge to check it; if it appears flat, it is worn and must not be reused

11   Crankshaft pulley - removal and refitting

Refer to illustration 11.6

1   Disconnect the cable from the negative battery terminal.

2   Remove the drivebelts (see Chapter 1). Tag each belt as it's removed to simplify refitting. If the vehicle is equipped with a fan shroud, unscrew the mounting bolts and position the shroud out of the way.

3   Raise the vehicle and place it securely on jackstands.

4   If the vehicle is equipped with a manual

transmission, apply the parking brake and put the transmission in gear to prevent the crankshaft from turning. If your vehicle is equipped with an automatic transmission, it may be necessary to remove the starter motor (see Chapter 5) and immobilise the starter ring gear with a large screwdriver.

5   With the crankshaft immobilised, unscrew the pulley retaining bolt.

6   Remove the crankshaft pulley. If the pulley is stuck, it will necessary to use a puller. Use only a puller that attaches to the hub of the pulley (such as a steering wheel puller) **(see illustration)**, NOT a jaw-type puller that bears on the outer diameter of the pulley, as this would destroy it.

10.17c If the lifters are pitted or rough, they shouldn't be reused

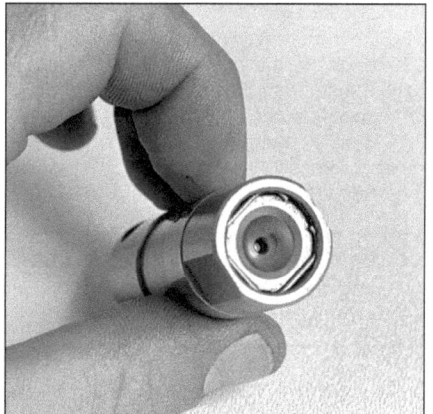

10.17d Check the pushrod seat (arrow) in the top of each lifter for wear

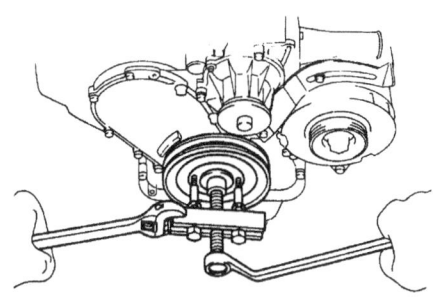

11.6 Remove the crankshaft pulley with a puller that bears on the pulley hub - not on the outer edge of the pulley

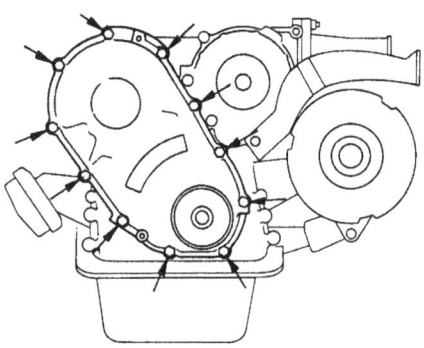

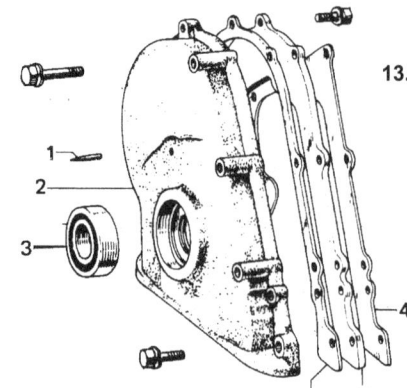

13.3b Timing cover details - 12R engine

1 Timing pointer
2 Timing cover
3 Oil seal
4 Gasket
5 Plate

13.3a Timing cover bolt locations - Y-series engines

7   Refer to Section 12 for the front oil seal renewal procedure.

8   Apply a thin layer of multi-purpose grease to the seal contact surface of the pulley.

9   Slide the pulley onto the crankshaft. Note that the slot in the hub must be aligned with the Woodruff key in the end of the crankshaft. Once the key is aligned with the slot, tap the pulley onto the crankshaft with a soft-face hammer. The retaining bolt can also be used to press the pulley into position.

10   Tighten the pulley bolt to the torque listed in this Chapter's Specifications.

11   The remainder of refitting is the reverse of the removal procedure.

12   Crankshaft front oil seal - renewal

Refer to Chapter 2 Part B, Section 14 for this procedure.

13   Timing cover - removal and refitting

Refer to illustrations 13.3a and 13.3b

1   Remove the crankshaft pulley (see Section 11).

2   Remove the engine cooling fan (see Chapter 3).

3   Remove the timing cover bolts and, on 12R engines, the sump-to-timing cover bolts **(see illustrations)**.

4   Separate the timing cover from the engine. Avoid damaging the sealing surfaces; do not force tools between the cover and block.

5   Cut off the sump gasket end tabs flush with the front face of the cylinder block and trim off the end seal tabs.

6   Thoroughly clean the cover and all sealing surfaces, removing any traces of gasket material. On 12R engines, clean the sump mating surface also. Drive the old oil seal out from the rear of the timing gear cover and renew it.

7   Apply RTV sealant to both sides of the new timing cover gasket and position the gas-

14.8 Timing sprocket alignment - the thrust plate bolts are accessible through the holes in the camshaft sprocket (12R engine)

ket on the engine block.

8   On 12R engines, cut off the front portion of a new sump gasket to fit the exposed apart of the sump, then stick the gasket in place with RTV sealant. Apply an extra bead of sealant to each end of the gasket, where the timing cover meets the block and sump.

9   Apply a film of clean engine oil or multi-purpose grease to the crankshaft front oil seal.

10   Position the timing cover on the engine block. If you're working on a 12R engine, take care not to disturb the sump gasket.

11   Refit the crankshaft pulley to centre the timing gear cover.

12   Refit the cover mounting bolts and, on 12R engines, the sump-to-cover bolts and tighten them to the torque listed in this Chapter's Specifications.

13   Refit the remaining parts in the reverse order of removal.

14   Run the engine and check for oil leaks.

14   Camshaft and timing gears (12R engine) - removal, inspection and refitting

Removal

Refer to illustrations 14.8 and 14.9

1   Set the number one piston at Top Dead Centre (TDC) (see Section 3).

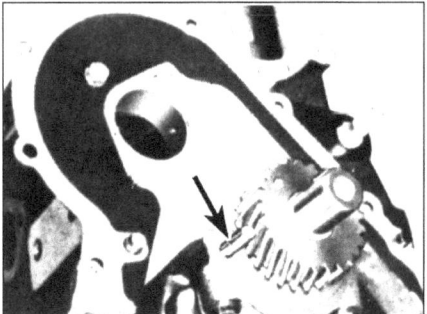

14.9 Make sure the oil hole in the nozzle (arrow) points towards the area where the gears mesh

2   Remove the valve cover (see Section 4) and the rocker arm assembly and pushrods (see Section 6).

3   Remove the valve lifters (see Section 10). Remove the fuel pump (see Chapter 4A).

4   Remove the timing cover (see Section 13).

5   Mark the relationship of the distributor body to the engine block. Remove the distributor cap and mark the relationship of the rotor to the distributor body. Now remove the distributor (see Chapter 5).

6   Check the timing gear backlash using a dial indicator positioned against one of the camshaft gear teeth. **Note:** *If you don't have a dial indicator, you can use feeler gauges.* If the backlash is excessive, renew both the crankshaft gear and the camshaft gear. Refer to the Specifications listed in the beginning of this Chapter. Also check the endplay (thrust clearance) with a dial indicator, comparing your reading with the value listed in this Chapter's Specifications. The endplay can also be checked with a feeler gauge after the camshaft has been removed **(see illustration 16.2)**. If the endplay is excessive, renew the thrust plate and, if necessary, the camshaft.

7   Remove the radiator (see Chapter 3). If equipped with air conditioning, it will be necessary to remove the condenser also.

8   Remove the thrust plate mounting bolts **(see illustration)** and carefully remove the camshaft from the engine block. Don't allow the cam lobes to contact the camshaft bearings in the engine block.

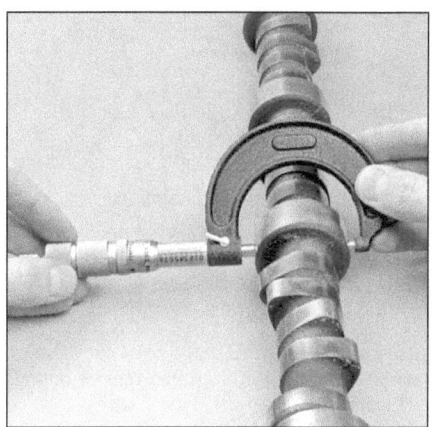

14.13 Check the diameter of each camshaft bearing journal to pinpoint excessive wear and out-of-round conditions

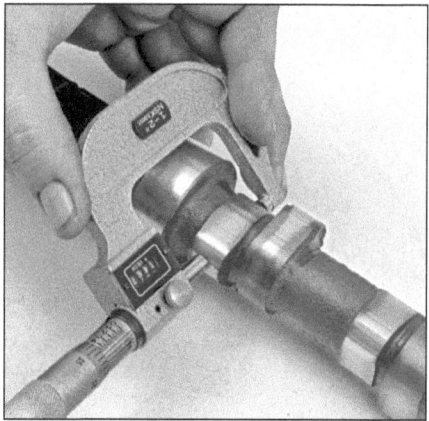

14.14 Measure the lobe height with a micrometer, then measure the base circle (smallest diameter of the lobe); subtract the smaller measurement from the larger to calculate lobe lift

9   Check the oil nozzle in the front main bearing cap **(see illustration)**. Make sure the oil hole is pointing up towards the intersection of the two gears. This is very important for refitting otherwise the gears will not receive the proper lubrication if the direction is misguided.

10   Remove the Woodruff key for the crankshaft pulley. Remove the crankshaft gear using a puller.

Inspection

Refer to illustrations 14.13 and 14.14

11   Clean the components and inspect for wear and damage. Timing gear teeth that are deformed, chipped, pitted or discoloured call for renewal. Always renew the timing gears as a set. Make sure the engine block is clean and the crankshaft does not have any burrs, scratches or damage that will prevent the timing gear from sliding over the surface easily. If the camshaft gear must be renewed, mount the camshaft in a vice lined with rags and unscrew the gear mounting bolt. When fitting the new gear, make sure the timing mark faces out.

12   Clean the camshaft with solvent and dry

it, then inspect the bearing journals for uneven wear and pitting. If the bearing journals are damaged, the bearing inserts in the block are probably damaged as well. Both the camshaft and bearings (and the lifters) will have to be renewed. Renewal of the camshaft bearings requires special tools and techniques which place it beyond the scope of the home mechanic.

13   Measure the bearing journals with a micrometer to determine if they are excessively worn or out-of-round **(see illustration)**. The camshaft bearings in the block can be measured with an inside micrometer, but this is very difficult to do without removing the engine and disassembling it first (camshaft journal oil clearance can be calculated by subtracting the journal diameter from the bearing inside diameter).

14   Measure the height of the cam lobes with a micrometer **(see illustration)**, then measure the smallest diameter (base circle). Subtract the smaller diameter from the lobe height to calculate lobe lift. Compare your findings with the values listed in this Chapter's Specifications.

15   Check the camshaft lobes for heat discolouration, score marks, chipped areas, pitting and uneven wear. If the lobes are in good condition and the lobe lift measurements are as specified, the camshaft can be reused.

Refitting

16   Refit the crankshaft timing gear with the mark facing out. Be sure to align the timing gear with the key in the crankshaft.

17   Lubricate the camshaft bearing journals and lobes with camshaft refitting lube. Refit the camshaft, making sure the gears mesh with the timing marks properly aligned **(see illustration 14.8)**. Tighten the thrust washer bolts to the torque listed in this Chapter's Specifications.

18   Make sure the camshaft timing gear and the crankshaft timing gear teeth mesh correctly and that they do not bind when rotating.

19   Refit the crankshaft pulley key.

20   Refit the remaining parts in the reverse order of removal. Refer to the appropriate Sections for instructions.

21   Change the engine oil and filter, adjust the valve clearances and set the ignition timing (see Chapter 1).

15   Timing chain and sprockets (Y-series engines) - removal, inspection and refitting

Removal

Refer to illustrations 15.2, 15.3, 15.4 and 15.5

1   Set the engine at top dead centre (TDC) for the No. 1 cylinder (see Section 3). Remove the timing cover (see Section 13).

2   Before removing the timing chain and sprockets, check the chain slack using a spring scale and a ruler **(see illustration)**. compare your measurement with the value listed in this Chapter's Specifications. If the chain slack is excessive, renew the chain and sprockets as a set.

3   Unbolt the timing chain tensioner from the engine **(see illustration)**.

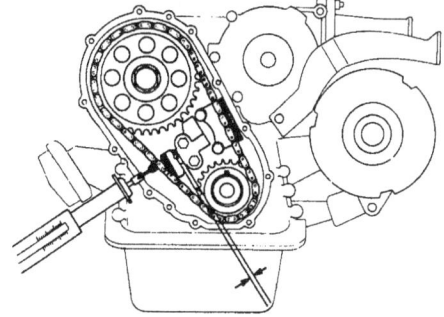

15.2 Attach a spring scale to the timing chain and pull with a force of 10 kg (98 N), then measure the space between the tensioner body and the tensioner foot, as shown (Y-series engine)

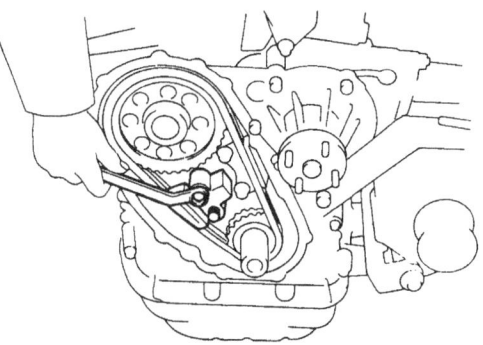

15.3 The timing chain tensioner is retained by two bolts (Y-series engine)

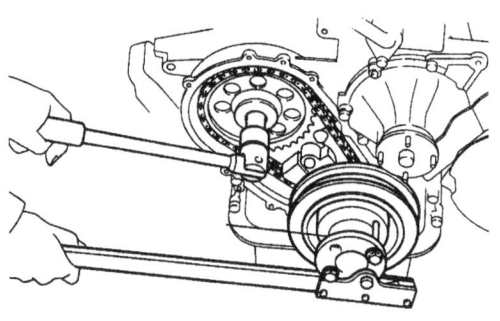

15.4 Immobilize the crankshaft and loosen the camshaft sprocket bolt (Y-series engine)

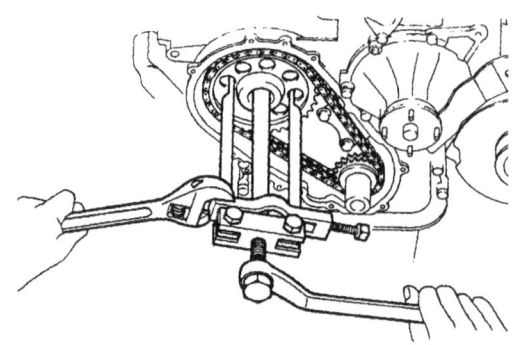

15.5 Remove the camshaft sprocket with a puller, if necessary (Y-series engine)

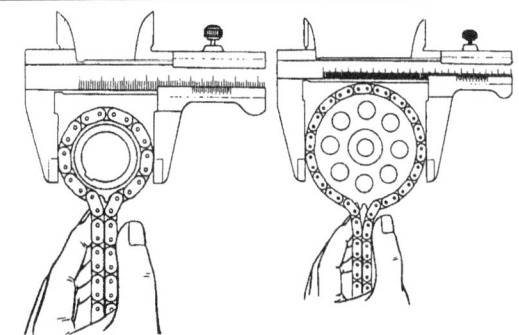

15.6 Loop the timing chain around each sprocket and measure the combined diameter, comparing your measurements with the values listed in this Chapter's Specifications (Y-series engine)

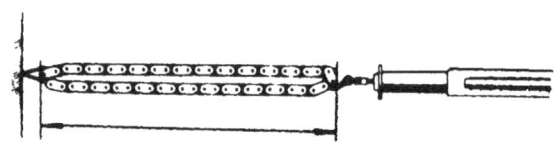

15.7 Using a spring scale, pull on the timing chain with a force of 5 kg (48 N) and measure the length of the chain (Y-series engine)

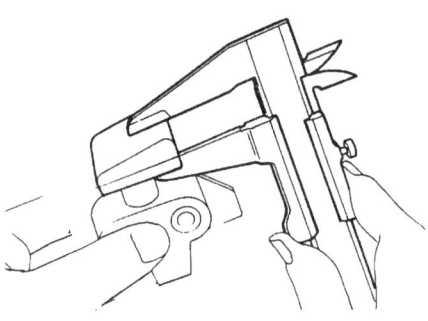

15.8 Measure the thickness of the chain tensioner foot - replace it if wear is excessive (Y-series engine)

15.10 The camshaft and crankshaft marks must be aligned like this before the sprockets and timing chain are installed (Y-series engine)

4   Refit the crankshaft pulley and, immo-bilising the crankshaft with a suitable holding tool, unscrew the camshaft sprocket bolt **(see illustration)**. An alternative method would be to hold the crankshaft pulley with a strap wrench, or wedge a large screwdriver in the flywheel or driveplate ring gear teeth.
5   Remove the camshaft sprocket, timing chain and crankshaft sprocket as an assem-bly. If the camshaft sprocket is stuck to the camshaft, remove it with a gear puller **(see illustration)**.

Camshaft Set Key

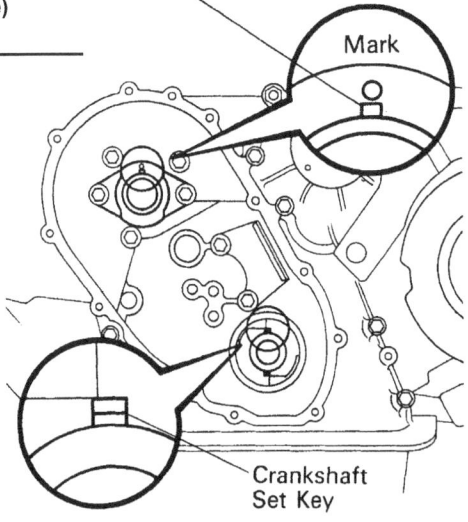
Mark

Crankshaft Set Key

Inspection

Refer to illustrations 15.6, 15.7 and 15.8

6   Check the sprockets for wear by wrap-ping the timing chain around them and meas-uring the diameter of the sprocket/chain com-bination **(see illustration)**. Compare your measurement with the values listed in this Chapter's Specifications. If either sprocket measurement is less than specified, the sprockets and chain must be renewed as a set.
7   Check the timing chain for excessive wear by measuring its length under a load of 5 kg (48 N) **(see illustration)**. Compare your measurement with the value listed in this Chapter's Specifications and renew the chain if wear is excessive.
8   Check the thickness of the tensioner foot **(see illustration)**, comparing your measure-ment with the value listed in this Chapter's Specifications.
9   Renew the tensioner if necessary.

Refitting

Refer to illustrations 15.10 and 15.11

10   Make sure the camshaft and crankshaft are still properly positioned **(see illustration)**.
11   Loop the timing chain over the cam sprocket, making sure the marked links on the chain engage with the marks on the sprockets **(see illustration)**.
12   Refit the sprockets and chain. Refit the camshaft sprocket bolt and tighten it to the torque listed in this Chapter's Specifications,

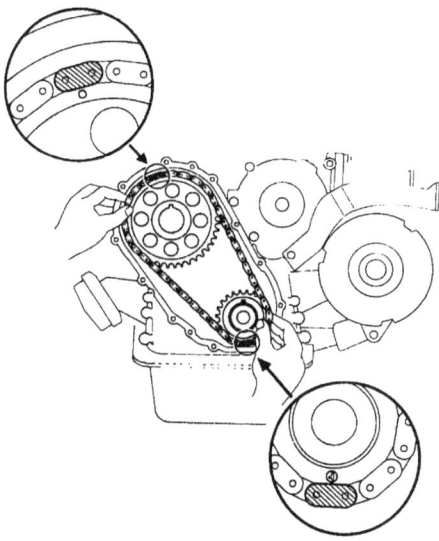

15.11 The marked links on the timing chain must mesh with the marks on the sprockets (Y-series engine)

using the method described in Step 4 to prevent the crankshaft from turning.

13   Refit the chain tensioner, tightening the bolts to the torque listed in this Chapter's Specifications.

14   The remainder of refitting is the reverse of removal.

16 Camshaft and bearings (Y-series engines) - removal, inspection and refitting

Removal

Refer to illustration 16.2, 16.3a and 16.3b

1   Following the procedure in Section 14, remove the timing chain and sprockets. Remove the valve lifters (see Section 10). On carburetted models, remove the fuel pump (see Chapter 4A).

2   Before removing the camshaft, check the endplay (thrust clearance) with a dial indicator, comparing your reading with the value listed in this Chapter's Specifications. The endplay can also be checked with a feeler gauge after the camshaft has been removed **(see illustra-**

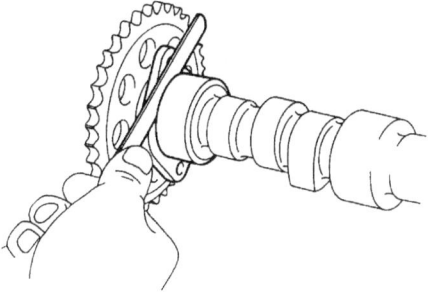

16.2 Checking the thrust plate clearance with a feeler gauge

tion). If the endplay is excessive, renew the thrust plate and, if necessary, the camshaft.

3   Unscrew the thrust plate bolts and remove the camshaft, being careful not to let the cam lobes contact the camshaft bearings in the block **(see illustration)**. If necessary, remove the timing chain case from the front of the engine **(see illustration)**.

Inspection

4   Inspect the camshaft as described in Section 14, Steps 12 through 15, renewing parts as necessary.

5   Check the timing chain and sprockets as described in Section 15, renewing parts as necessary.

Refitting

6   Lubricate the camshaft bearing journals and lobes with camshaft refitting lube. Refit the camshaft, making sure the mark on the camshaft is aligned with the mark on the thrust plate **(see illustration 15.10)**. **Note:** *The mark on the thrust plate must be pointing up.*

7   Refit the timing chain and sprockets, following the procedure described in Section 15.

8   The remainder of refitting is the reverse of removal. Change the engine oil and filter (see Chapter 1).

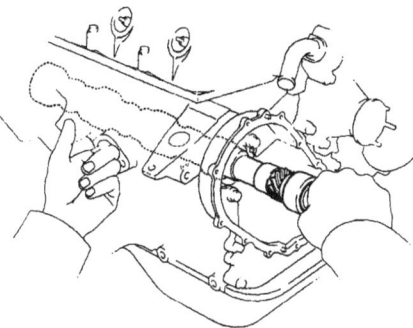

16.3a When removing the camshaft, be very careful not to let the cam lobes contact the camshaft bearings in the block

17 Sump - removal and refitting

Refer to Chapter 2 Part B, Section 11 for the sump removal and refitting procedure, as it is very similar. Simply ignore the steps which do not apply.

18 Oil pump - removal and refitting

Note: *It is advisable to renew the oil pump with a new unit when the engine is rebuilt. If you suspect low oil pressure, be sure to check the oil pressure before removing the sump (see Chapter 2E for information concerning the oil pressure check).*

Removal

1   Remove the sump (see Section 17).

2   Unbolt the oil strainer assembly from the block.

3   Remove the oil pump attaching bolt and remove the oil pump.

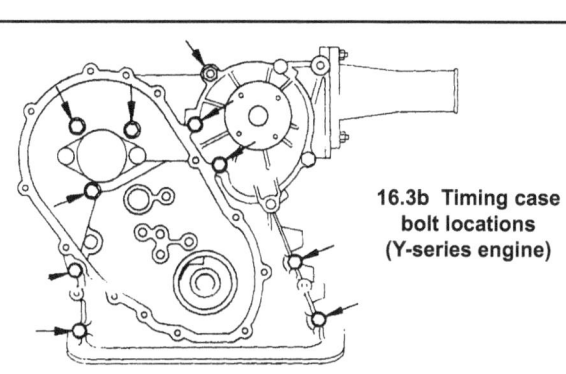

16.3b Timing case bolt locations (Y-series engine)

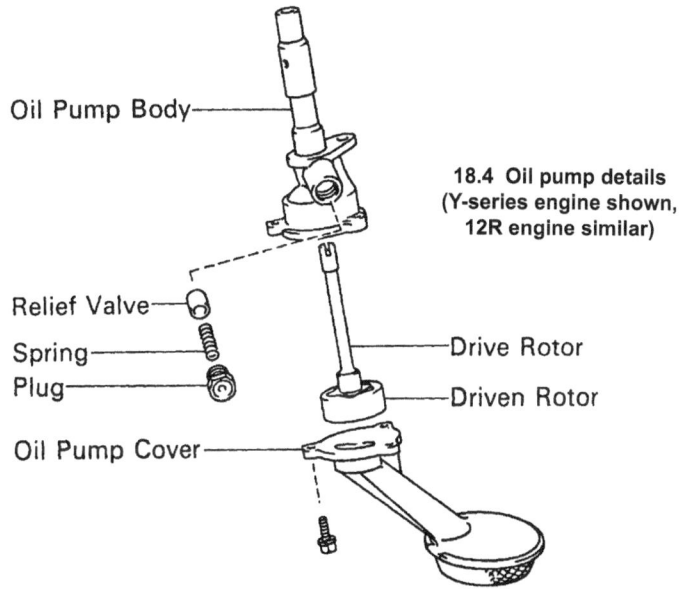

Oil Pump Body

Relief Valve

Spring

Plug

Oil Pump Cover

Drive Rotor

Driven Rotor

18.4 Oil pump details (Y-series engine shown, 12R engine similar)

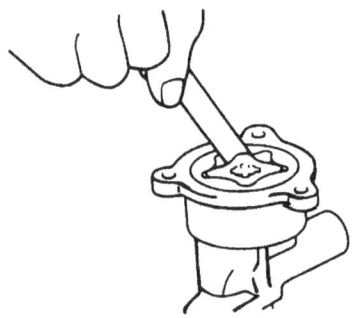

18.7 Measuring the oil pump rotor tip clearance

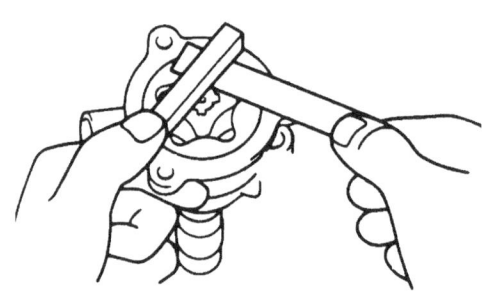

18.8 Measuring the oil pump rotor end clearance

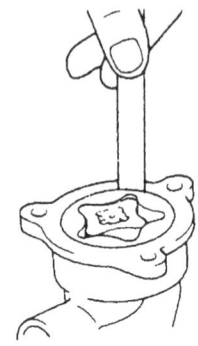

18.9 Measuring the oil pump driven rotor-to-housing clearance

Inspection

Refer to illustrations 18.4, 18.7, 18.8, 18.9 and 18.10

4   Remove the three retaining bolts and separate the cover from the pump body **(see illustration)** .

5   Separate the drive shaft and rotors from the pump body.

6   Wash the components in solvent and inspect them as follows:

7   Using a feeler gauge, measure the clearance between the tips of the drive and the driven rotors and compare your measurement to the clearance listed in this Chapter's Speci-

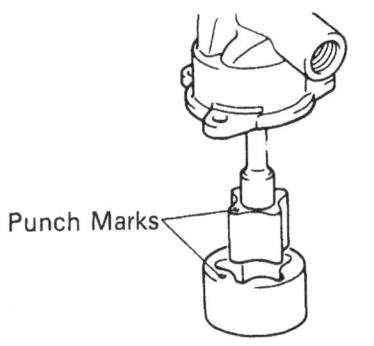

18.10 When assembling the oil pump, make sure the marks on the drive and driven rotors are in alignment

fications **(see illustration)**. If the indicated clearance is not within the specified range, renew the oil pump.

8   Using a straightedge, check the clearance between the end faces of the rotors and the body flange and compare your measurement to the clearance listed in this Chapter's Specifications **(see illustration)**. If the indicated clearance is not within the specified range, renew the oil pump.

9   Again, using a feeler gauge, measure the clearance between the outer rotor and the inside of the pump body and compare your measurement to the clearance listed in this Chapter's Specifications **(see illustration)**. If the indicated clearance is not within the specified range, renew the oil pump.

10   To assemble the pump, refit the shaft and driven rotor, aligning the marks on the rotors **(see illustration)**. Refit the cover and tighten the bolts to the torque listed in this Chapter's Specifications.

11   If the engine is being completely overhauled, fit a new oil pump - don't reuse the original or attempt to rebuild it.

Refitting

12   To refit the pump, turn the shaft so the gear tang mates with the slot on the lower end of the distributor drive. The oil pump should slide easily into place. If it doesn't, pull it off and turn the tang until it's aligned with the distributor drive.

13   Refit the pump attaching bolt. Tighten it to the torque listed in this Chapter's Specifications.

14   Refit the sump.

15   Add oil, run the engine and check for leaks.

19   Flywheel/driveplate - removal and refitting

Refer to Chapter 2 Part B for the flywheel/driveplate removal and refitting procedure, but use the torque specifications listed at the beginning of this Chapter.

20   Rear main oil seal - renewal

Refer to Chapter 2 Part B for the rear main oil seal renewal procedure, but use the torque specifications at the beginning of this Chapter for the oil seal retainer bolts (if the retainer is removed).

21   Engine mounts - check and renewal

Refer to Chapter 2 Part B for the engine mount check and renewal procedure.

Chapter 2 Part B Four-cylinder Overhead cam (OHC) petrol engines

Contents

Specifications

General

Cylinder numbers (front-to-rear)	1-2-3-4
Firing order	1-3-4-2

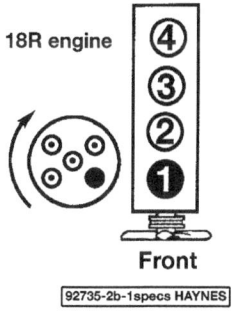

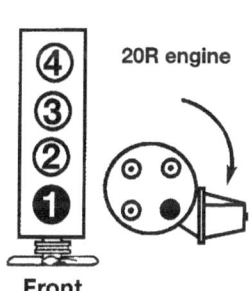

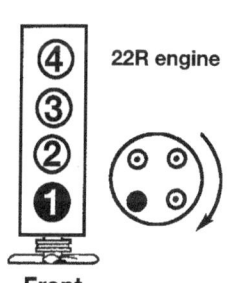

Cylinder location and distributor rotation

Manifold warpage limits

Intake..	0.2 mm
Exhaust...	0.7 mm

Rocker arm assembly

Rocker arm-to-shaft (oil) clearance

Standard..	0.01 to 0.05 mm
Service limit..	0.08 mm

Camshaft

Endplay

Standard..	0.08 to 0.18 mm
Service limit..	0.25 mm

Bearing journal diameter

18R	34.92 to 34.996 mm
20R, 22R...	32.98 to 33.00 mm

Bearing oil clearance

Standard..	0.01 to 0.05 mm
Service limit..	0.1 mm
Runout limit..	0.2 mm

Lobe lift (18R)

Intake	8.04 mm
Exhaust	8.10 mm

Lobe height (20R, 22R)

Intake	42.63 to 42.72 mm
Exhaust	42.69 to 42.78 mm

Cylinder head

Warpage limit..	0.15 mm

Timing chain and sprockets

Length

18R..	147.12 mm
20R, 22R (17 links)	147 mm maximum

Minimum sprocket diameters (with chain meshed in teeth)

18R

Camshaft sprocket...	78.2 mm
Crankshaft sprocket...	60.0 mm
Auxiliary driveshaft sprocket...	114.5 mm
Auxiliary driveshaft-to-camshaft sprocket....................................	78.2 mm

20R, 22R

Camshaft sprocket...	113.8 mm
Crankshaft sprocket...	59.4 mm

Minimum tensioner slipper thickness

18R..	11.5 mm
20R, 22R...	11.0 mm

Minimum damper thickness **(see illustrations 16.16a and 16.16b)**

18R..	6.8 mm

20R, 22R

No. 1	5.0 mm
No. 2	4.5 mm

Oil pump

Driven gear-to-oil pump body clearance

Standard..	0.09 to 0.15 mm
Service limit..	0.2 mm

Driven gear-to-crescent clearance (20R, 22R)

Standard..	0.15 to 0.21 mm
Service limit..	0.3 mm

Drive gear-to-crescent clearance (20R, 22R)

Standard..	0.22 to 0.25 mm
Service limit..	0.3 mm
Inner rotor tip clearance (18R)..	0.10 to 0.15 mm

Gear side clearance

Standard..	0.03 to 0.09 mm
Service limit..	0.15 mm

Torque specifications

	Nm
Inlet manifold bolts/nuts (20R, 22R)	19
Exhaust manifold bolts/nuts (20R, 22R)	44
Manifold bolts (18R)	48
Camshaft bearing cap bolts	
18R	22
20R, 22R	20
Cylinder head bolts	
18R	118
20R, 22R	78
Camshaft sprocket bolt	
18R	22
20R, 22R	78
Crankshaft pulley bolt	
18R	110
20R, 22R	157
Timing chain cover bolts	
18R	15
20R, 22R	
8 mm	13
10 mm	39
Sump bolts	
18R	7
20R, 22R	13
Oil pump mounting bolts	
18R	Not available
20R, 22R **(see illustration 12.30)**	
Bolt A	25
Bolt B	19
Bolt C	13
Oil pick-up tube mounting bolts	13
Flywheel/driveplate mounting bolts	
18R	75
20R, 22R	108

1 General information

This Part of Chapter 2 is devoted to in-vehicle repair procedures for the 18R, 20R and 22R engines.

All information concerning engine removal and installation can be found in Chapter 2E.

The following repair procedures are based on the assumption that the engine is refitted in the vehicle. If the engine has been removed from the vehicle and mounted on a stand, many of the steps included in this Part of Chapter 2 will not apply.

The Specifications included in this Part of Chapter 2 apply only to the engines and procedures in this Part. Additional Specifications necessary for removing and overhauling the engine are found in Part E.

2 Repair operations possible with the engine in the vehicle

Many major repair operations can be accomplished without removing the engine from the vehicle.

Clean the engine compartment and the exterior of the engine with some type of pressure washer before any work is done. It'll make the job easier and help keep dirt out of the internal areas of the engine.

Remove the bonnet to improve access to the engine as repairs are performed (see Chapter 11 if necessary).

If vacuum, exhaust, oil or coolant leaks develop, indicating a need for gasket or seal renewal, the repairs can generally be made with the engine in the vehicle. The sump gasket, cylinder head gasket, intake and exhaust manifold gaskets, timing chain cover gaskets and the crankshaft oil seals are accessible with the engine in place.

Exterior engine components, such as the water pump, the starter motor, the alternator, the distributor and the fuel system components, as well as the intake and exhaust manifolds, can be removed for repair with the engine in place.

Since the cylinder head can be removed without pulling the engine, camshaft and valve component servicing can also be accomplished with the engine in the vehicle.

Renewal of, repairs to or inspection of the timing chain and sprockets and the oil pump are all possible with the engine in place.

In extreme cases caused by a lack of necessary equipment, repair or renewal of piston rings, pistons, connecting rods and rod bearings is possible with the engine in the vehicle. However, this practice is not recommended because of the cleaning and preparation work that must be done to the components involved.

3 Top Dead Centre (TDC) for number one piston - locating

Refer to illustrations 3.4 and 3.5

1   Top Dead Centre (TDC) is the highest point in the cylinder that each piston reaches as it travels up-and-down when the crankshaft turns. Each piston reaches TDC on the compression stroke and again on the exhaust stroke, but TDC generally refers to piston position on the compression stroke. The timing marks on the pulley refitted on the front of the crankshaft are referenced to the number one piston at TDC on the compression stroke.

2   Positioning the piston(s) at TDC is an essential part of many procedures such as camshaft and timing chain/sprocket removal and distributor removal.

3   In order to bring any piston to TDC, the crankshaft must be turned using one of the methods outlined below. When looking at the front of the engine, normal crankshaft rotation is clockwise. **Warning:** *Before beginning this procedure, be sure to place the transmission in Neutral. Also, detach the coil wire from the centre terminal of the distributor cap and earth it on the block with a jumper wire.*

a) *The preferred method is to turn the crankshaft with a large socket and breaker bar attached to the crankshaft pulley hub bolt threaded into the front of the crankshaft.*

3.4 Make a mark on the distributor directly below the number one spark plug wire terminal on the cap (arrow)

3.5 Align the notch in the crankshaft pulley with the 0 (zero) on the timing plate

b) *A remote starter switch, which may save some time, can also be used. Attach the switch leads to the solenoid terminals. Once the piston is close to TDC, use a socket and breaker bar as described in the previous paragraph.*

c) *If an assistant is available to turn the ignition switch to the Start position in short bursts, you can get the piston close to TDC without a remote starter switch. Use a socket and breaker bar as described in Paragraph a) to complete the procedure.*

4   Note the position of the terminal for the number one spark plug wire on the distributor cap. Use a felt-tip pen or chalk to make a mark on the distributor directly under the terminal **(see illustration)**. Detach the cap from the distributor and set it aside.

5   Turn the crankshaft (see Step 3 above) until the notch in the crankshaft pulley is aligned with the 0 on the timing plate (located

at the front of the engine) **(see illustration)**.

6   Look at the distributor rotor - it should be pointing directly at the mark you made on the distributor body. If the rotor is pointing at the terminal for the number four spark plug, the number one piston is at TDC on the exhaust stroke.

7   To get the piston to TDC on the compression stroke, turn the crankshaft one complete turn (360-degrees) clockwise. The rotor should now be pointing at the mark on the distributor. When the rotor is pointing at the number one spark plug wire terminal in the distributor cap and the ignition timing marks are aligned, the number one piston is at TDC on the compression stroke.

8   After the number one piston has been positioned at TDC on the compression stroke, TDC for any of the remaining pistons can be located by turning the crankshaft 180-degrees at a time and following the firing order.

4   Valve cover - removal and refitting

Refer to illustrations 4.3a, 4.3b, 4.4a, 4.4b and 4.9

1   On carburetted models, remove the air cleaner (see Chapter 4A). Disconnect the negative battery cable from the battery.

2   Remove the spark plug wire supports from the valve cover. Don't disconnect the wires from the supports.

3   Label and disconnect all vacuum hoses, wires and PCV hoses attached to the valve cover. Remove the bolts and detach the throttle cable bracket **(see illustrations)**.

4   Remove the valve cover mounting bolts or nuts **(see illustrations)**. Don't lose the washers.

5   Detach the valve cover and discard the old gasket. **Caution:** *If the cover is stuck to the head, bump the end with a block of wood and a hammer to jar it loose. If that doesn't work, try to slip a flexible putty knife between the head and cover to break the gasket seal. Don't prise at the cover-to-head joint or damage to the sealing surfaces may occur, leading to oil leaks in the future.*

6   The mating surfaces of the head and valve cover must be perfectly clean when the cover is refitted. Use a gasket scraper to remove all traces of sealant and old gasket material, then clean the mating surfaces with lacquer thinner or acetone. If there's sealant or oil on the mating surfaces when the cover is refitted, oil leaks may develop.

7   Inspect the rubber grommets in the valve cover (the rubber insulators under each bolt/nut and washer). If they're cracked or deteriorated, renew them.

8   If the valve cover uses a conventional gasket, apply a thin, uniform layer of sealant to the head mating surface of the cover and the surface of the new gasket that will be against the head, place the new gasket

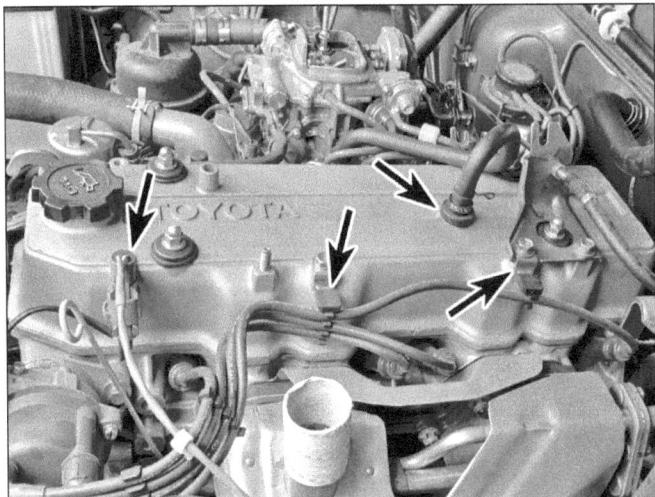

4.3a Detach the PCV hose, spark plug wire holders, ignition system primary wire and throttle cable bracket (arrows) before attempting to remove the valve cover

4.3b On fuel-injected models, remove the vacuum and breather hoses as well (arrows)

4.4a 18R valve covers are attached to the head with nuts (arrows) along the cover flange

4.4b Some 20R and 22R valve covers use bolts, others use nuts, but they all use washers and rubber grommets - remove the grommets after you've removed the valve cover and inspect each one for cracks and deterioration

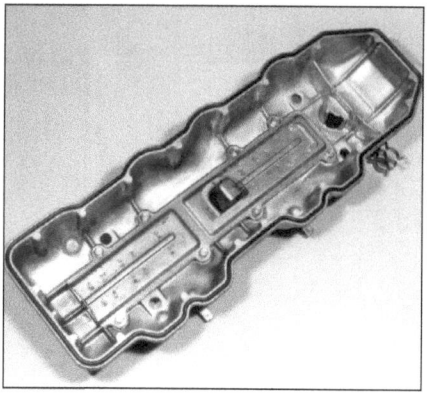

4.9 Some valve covers use conventional gaskets; others, like this one, use an O-ring-type gasket that seats into a groove in the perimeter of the valve cover

in position with the sealant against the cylinder head, then place the valve cover on the gasket. While the sealant is still wet, refit the mounting bolts and tighten them securely. Use new rubber seals on the bolts.

9   If the valve cover uses an O-ring-type gasket, it's not necessary to use sealant, but make sure the new gasket is seated properly into the groove in the perimeter of the valve cover **(see illustration)**. A little bit of grease will prevent it from falling out and getting mashed (if this happens, it will leak). Refit the valve cover washers and bolts/nuts and tighten them securely.

10   Complete the refitting by reversing the removal procedure.

5   Inlet manifold - removal and refitting

Removal

Refer to illustrations 5.6a, 5.6b, 5.6c and 5.7

Note: *On 18R engines, it's easier to remove the intake and exhaust manifolds as a single assembly, then separate them.*

1   On fuel-injected models, relieve the fuel system pressure (see Chapter 4A), then remove the throttle body and plenum (see Chapter 4A). On carburetted models, the car-

burettor does not have to be removed from the manifold.

2   Disconnect the cable from the negative terminal of the battery.

3   Drain the cooling system (see Chapter 1), then detach the upper radiator hose.

4   Loosen the clamp on the air injection check valve, if equipped (see Chapter 6). Remove the EGR valve and vacuum modulator, if equipped (see Chapter 6).

5   Label and detach all hoses and wires attached to the manifold and throttle body or carburettor. Don't forget the accelerator rod or cable (see Chapter 4A).

6   Remove the bolts and nuts that attach the manifold to the head **(see illustrations)**. Start at the ends and work toward the middle, loosening each one a little at a time until they

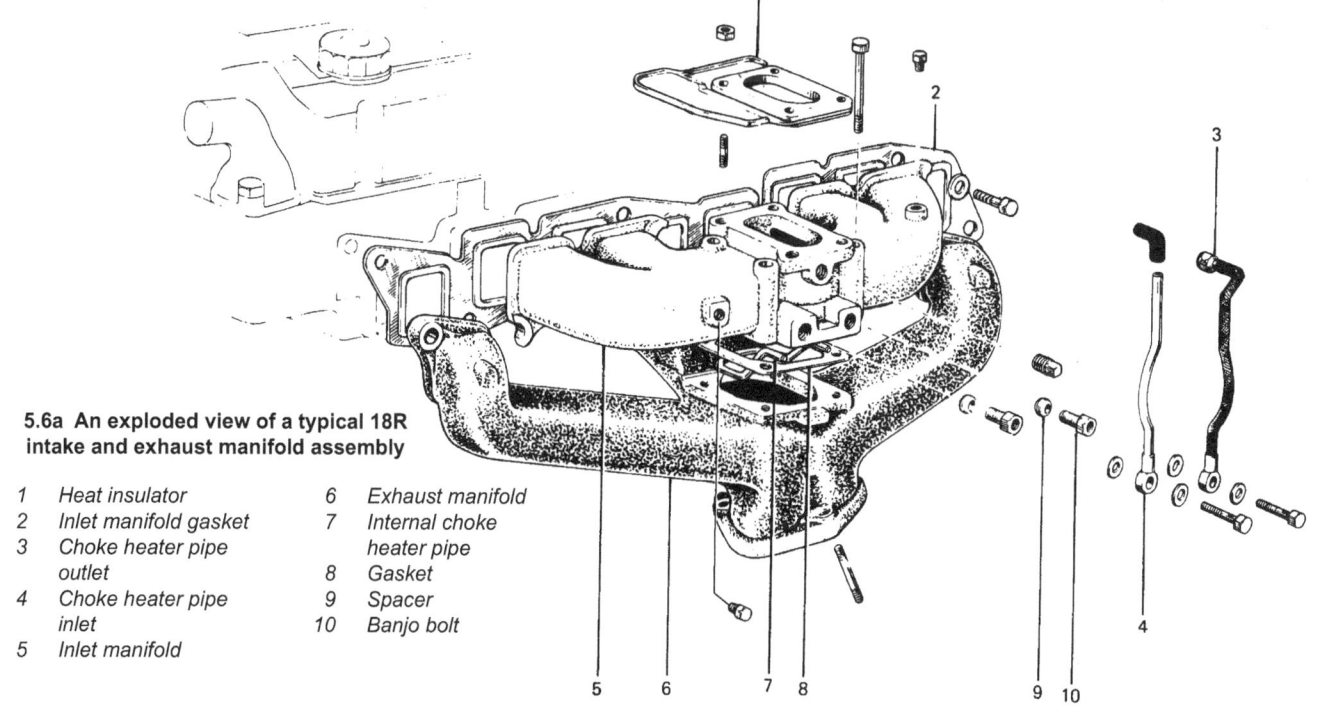

5.6a An exploded view of a typical 18R intake and exhaust manifold assembly

1	Heat insulator	6	Exhaust manifold
2	Inlet manifold gasket	7	Internal choke
3	Choke heater pipe		heater pipe
	outlet	8	Gasket
4	Choke heater pipe	9	Spacer
	inlet	10	Banjo bolt
5	Inlet manifold		

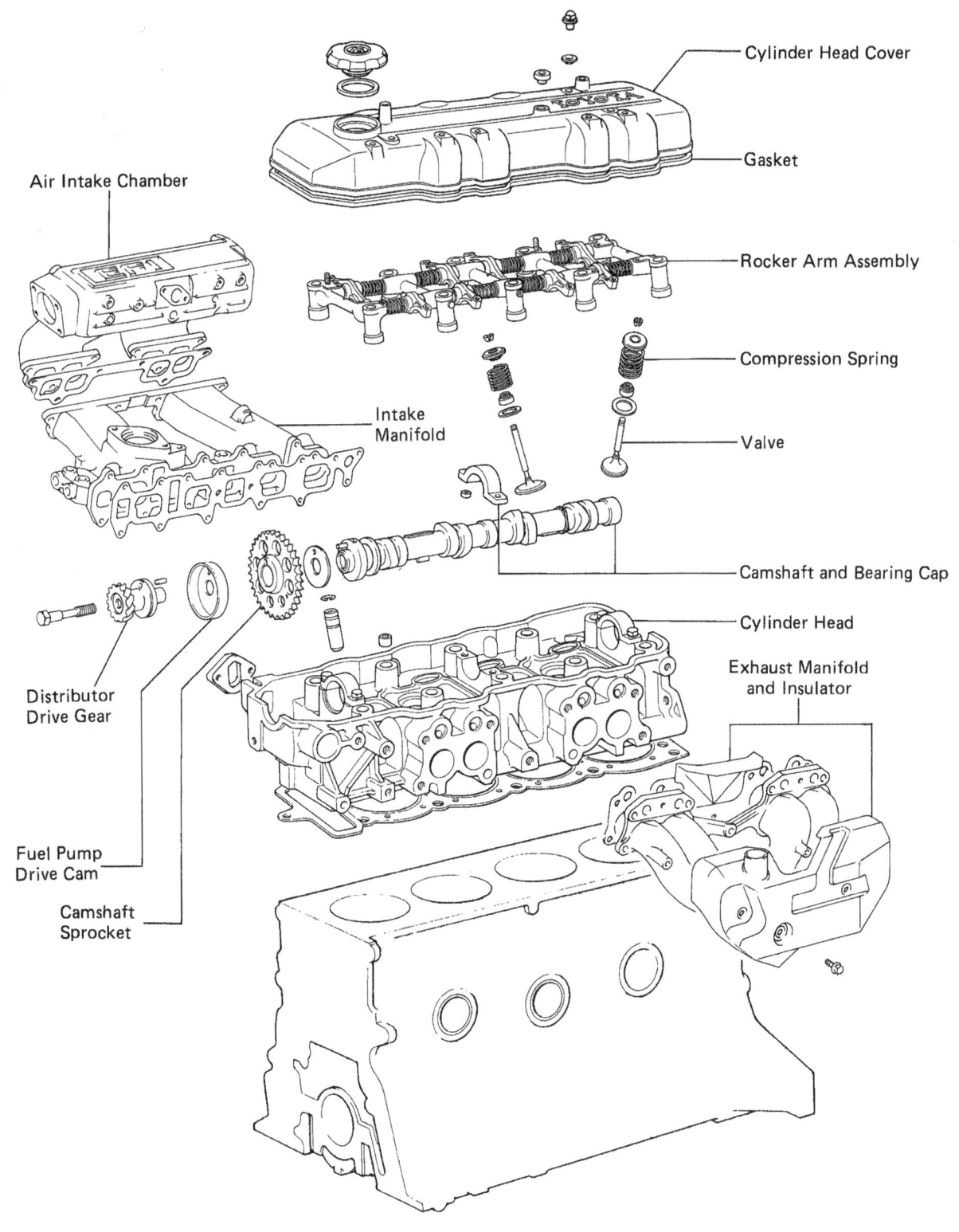

5.6b An exploded view of a typical 22R cylinder head assembly

can be removed.

7   Move the manifold up-and-down to break the gasket seal, then detach it from the head. Remove and discard the old gasket. **Note:** *On some models, you'll have to remove the ther-*

mostatic valve **(see illustration)** *before you can remove the old gasket.*

8   If you're removing the inlet manifold on an 18R engine, separate the intake and exhaust manifolds **(see illustration 5.6a).**

Refitting

Refer to illustrations 5.10 and 5.14
Note: *The mating surfaces of the cylinder head and manifold must be perfectly clean*

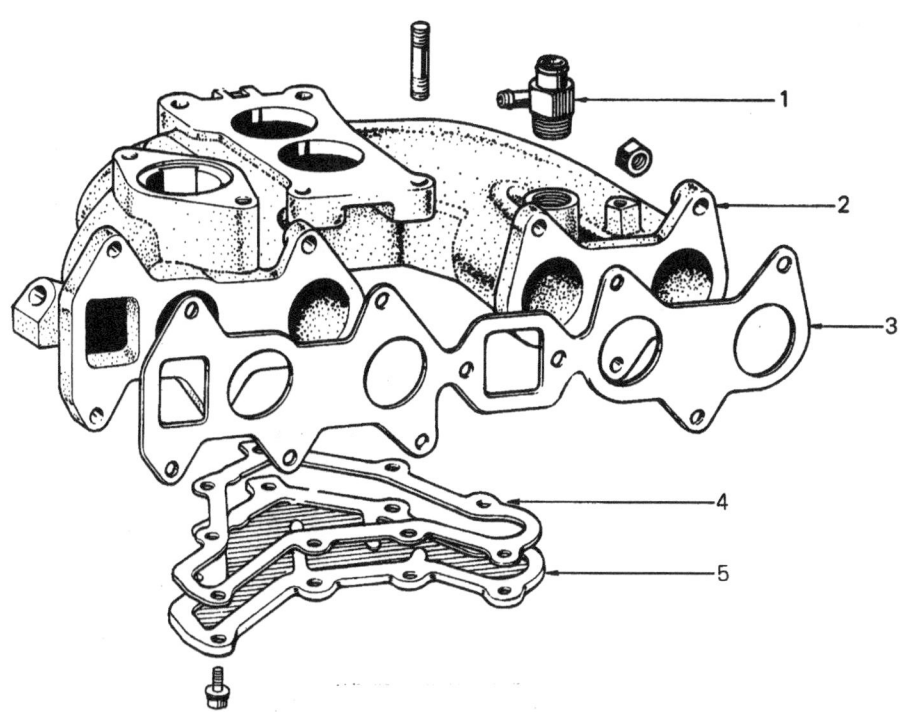

5.7 On some models, the thermostatic valve is mounted between the two middle intake runners; you'll have to detach it from the head to remove the old gasket (and make sure you fit the new gasket before you reattach the valve)

5.6c An exploded view of a typical 20R inlet manifold assembly (22R inlet manifold similar)

1	Hose junction	3	Gasket	5	Cover plate
2	Inlet manifold	4	Gasket		

when the manifold is refitted. Gasket removal solvents in aerosol cans are available at most auto parts stores and may be helpful when removing old gasket material that's stuck to the head and manifold (since they're made of aluminium, aggressive scraping can cause damage). Be sure to follow the directions printed on the container.

9   Use a gasket scraper to remove all traces of sealant and old gasket material, then clean the surfaces with lacquer thinner or acetone. If there is old sealant or oil on the mating surfaces when the manifold is refitted, vacuum leaks may develop.

10   Check the manifold-to-cylinder head gasket surface for warpage. Lay a straight-edge along the manifold and try to slip a feeler gauge between the manifold and the straightedge at each runner **(see illustration)**. If the manifold is warped beyond the specified limit, it must be resurfaced or renewed.

11   Check the manifold for corrosion (at the coolant passages), cracks and other dam-

age. If defects are found, have the manifold repaired or renewed as necessary. If a new manifold is fitted, transfer all brackets and fittings to the new one. Be sure to use a new thermostat (see Chapter 3).

12   Use a tap of the correct size to chase the threads in the bolt holes, then use compressed air (if available) to remove the debris from the holes. **Warning:** *Wear safety glasses or a face shield to protect your eyes when using compressed air!* Clean the stud threads with a die.

13   If you're refitting the inlet manifold on an 18R engine, reattach the inlet and exhaust manifolds to each other now **(see illustration 5.6a)** so they can be refitted as a single assembly.

14   Apply a thin, uniform layer of RTV sealant to the manifold mating surfaces and the cylinder head side of the gasket and fit the gasket on the head. If the thermostatic valve is mounted on the head, between the middle

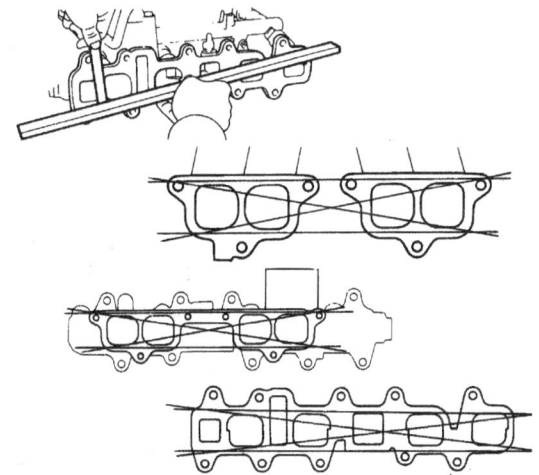

5.10 Use a straightedge and feeler gauges to check the inlet manifold for warpage - make the check lengthwise and diagonally

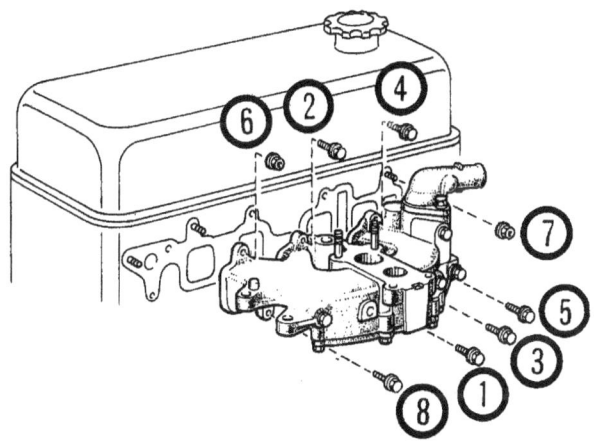

5.14 Typical inlet manifold bolt TIGHTENING sequence

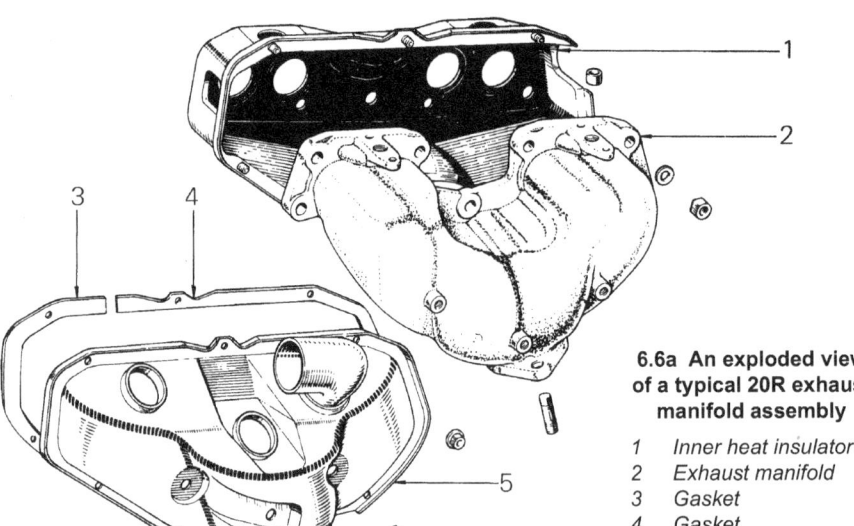

6.6a An exploded view of a typical 20R exhaust manifold assembly

1   Inner heat insulator
2   Exhaust manifold
3   Gasket
4   Gasket
5   Outer heat insulator

6.6b Remove the heat shield bolts (arrows) and the heat shield (22R shown, others similar)

intake runners of the manifold, refit it now and tighten the bolts securely. Refit the inlet manifold, hand tighten all fasteners, then tighten them in the recommended sequence to the torque listed in this Chapter's Specifications **(see illustration)**. Work up to the final torque in three steps.

15   The rest of refitting is the reverse of removal.

6   Exhaust manifold - removal and refitting

Refer to illustrations 6.6a, 6.6b, 6.7, 6.8 and 6.11

Note: *On 18R engines, it's easier to remove the intake and exhaust manifolds as a single assembly, then separate them* (see Section 5).

Removal

1   Make sure the engine is completely cool before beginning this procedure.

2   On carburetted models, remove the air cleaner assembly (see Chapter 4A).
3   Raise the front of the vehicle and support it on jackstands.
4   Disconnect the front exhaust pipe from the exhaust manifold (see Chapter 4A).
5   Unplug the oxygen sensor wire, if equipped (see Chapter 6).
6   Remove the heat shield bolts and detach the shield **(see illustrations)**.
7   Remove the air injection tube bolts/nuts, if equipped **(see illustration)**, but don't separate the tube assembly from the manifold.
8   Loosen the bolts and nuts that retain the exhaust manifold to the cylinder head **(see illustration)**. Work from the ends toward the centre in a criss-cross pattern.
9   Remove the bolts/nuts and detach the exhaust manifold and air injection tube assembly. Remove the inner heat shield, if equipped.

Refitting

10   Before refitting the manifold, remove all traces of the old gasket with a scraper. Clean

the mating surfaces with lacquer thinner or acetone.
11   Using a straightedge and feeler gauge, check the manifold-to-cylinder head mating surface for warpage **(see illustration)**. If it's warped beyond the service limit, the manifold must be resurfaced or renewed.
12   Check for corrosion, cracks and other damage. Repair or renew the manifold as necessary.
13   Place a new exhaust manifold gasket in position on the cylinder head, then hold the manifold in place and fit the mounting bolts/nuts finger tight.
14   Tighten the mounting bolts/nuts, in three or four steps, to the specified torque. Work from the centre out toward the ends to prevent distortion of the manifold.
15   The remainder of refitting is the reverse of the removal procedure.
16   Start the engine and check for exhaust leaks between the manifold and cylinder head and between the manifold and exhaust pipe.

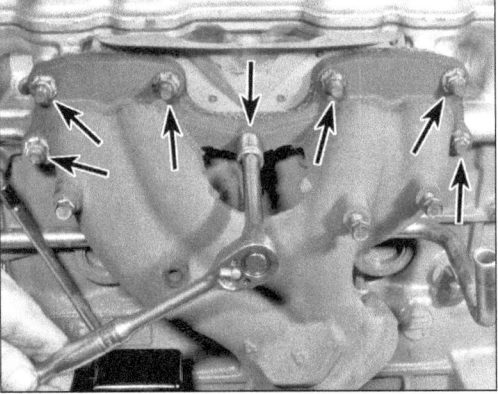

6.7 If the engine uses an air injection system, remove the air injection tube mounting bolts (arrows), but don't separate the tube assembly from the manifold (22R shown, others similar)

6.8 A typical exhaust manifold, ready for removal - loosen the bolts from the ends toward the centre in a criss-cross pattern

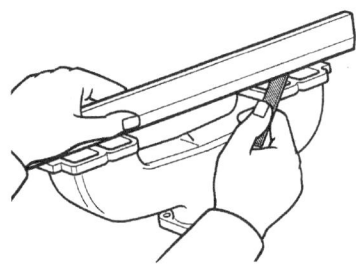

6.11 The exhaust manifold can be checked for warpage by trying to slip a feeler gauge under a straightedge as shown here

7.10a This dimple on the camshaft sprocket (arrow) should at the 12 o'clock position when the number one piston is at TDC (on newer models, the dimple will be positioned between two shiny links)

7.10b If there's no dimple on the camshaft sprocket, or if it's hard to see, paint or scribe alignment marks on the sprocket and timing chain before removing the sprocket from the camshaft

7.11a Remove this semi-circular plug . . .

7.11b . . . then remove the camshaft sprocket bolt and the distributor drive gear, the fuel pump eccentric (carburetted models) and the camshaft thrust plate

7   Cylinder head - removal and refitting

Removal

Refer to illustrations 7.10a, 7.10b, 7.11a, 7.11b, 7.12, 7.13, 7.14 and 7.15

1   Detach the cable from the negative battery terminal, drain the engine oil and drain the cooling system (see Chapter 1). Detach the upper radiator hose (see Chapter 3).
2   If the engine is carburetted, remove the air cleaner, then disconnect the accelerator rod or cable (see Chapter 4A). If the vehicle has an automatic transmission, disconnect the throttle rod or cable (see Chapter 7B).
3   Remove the valve cover (see Section 4).
4   Remove the distributor (see Chapter 5).
5   On carburetted models, remove the fuel pump (see Chapter 4A).
6   Remove the earth cable bolts and detach the earth cables from the front and rear of the head.
7   Remove the power steering pump (see

Chapter 10). Leave the hoses attached and position the pump upright, out of the way.
8   Remove the intake and exhaust manifolds (see Sections 5 and 6). If the engine is equipped with an Air Suction (AS) system, remove the rear air suction pipe.
9   Position the number one piston at TDC on the compression stroke (see Section 3).
10   When the number one piston is at TDC, a dimple on the camshaft sprocket **(see illustration)** is centred between two timing chain links (these two links are shiny on newer models). If there's no dimple, or if it's hard to see, use a permanent marker or white paint to mark the camshaft sprocket and chain **(see illustration)**.
11   Remove the semi-circular rubber seal from the front of the head and unscrew the camshaft sprocket bolts (three bolts on 18R engines, single large bolt on 20R and 22R engines) **(see illustrations)**. Detach the distributor drive gear and, on carburetted models, the fuel pump eccentric from the end of the camshaft **(see illustration)**.
12   Pull the sprocket and chain off the camshaft and rest the sprocket on the upper ends of the chain dampers **(see illustration)**. Leave the chain meshed with the sprocket.

13   Remove the small cylinder head-to-timing chain cover bolt, if applicable **(see illustration)**.
14   Loosen the cylinder head bolts in 1/4-turn increments until they can be removed by hand. Follow the recommended sequence **(see illustration)** to avoid warping or cracking the head. **Note:** *DO NOT pull the bolts out of the rocker arm shaft supports. Once all of the bolts are loose, lift up on the shafts to remove the rocker arms, shafts and bolts as an assembly.*
15   Lift the head off the engine. The head

7.12 Pull the sprocket off the camshaft and rest it on the upper ends of the chain dampers - leave the chain meshed with the sprocket

7.13 Don't forget to remove the small cylinder head-to-timing chain cover bolt from the front of the head

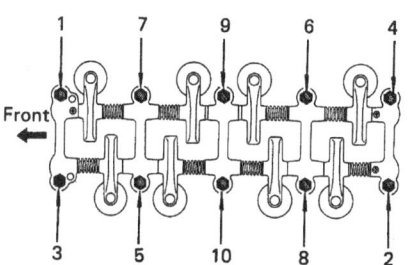

7.14 Cylinder head bolt LOOSENING sequence

7.15 The cylinder head can usually be lifted off the block using a rocking motion

7.22a Apply sealant to the cylinder head at both front corners

7.22b When you fit the new head gasket, make sure it's right-side-up (the oil and coolant passage holes in the gasket and the block won't match up if the gasket is upside down) and make sure it's positioned by the dowel pins (arrows) at each end of the block

7.23 Position the camshaft with the dowel pin (arrow) at the top (12 o'clock position)

may stick to the engine block, but this can usually be overcome by rocking one side of the head up first **(see illustration)**. If this technique doesn't work, DO NOT prise between the head and block - damage to the mating surfaces will result! Instead, position a lever or large screwdriver between the block and a casting projection on the head and prise the head loose.

16   The timing chain and camshaft sprocket will remain in place, resting on the chain dampers.

17   Place the head on blocks of wood to prevent damage to the gasket surface. Remove the head gasket from the block.

18   To remove and inspect the rocker arm assembly, see Section 8. To remove and inspect the camshaft, see Section 9.

Refitting

Refer to illustrations 7.22a, 7.22b, 7.23, 7.24 and 7.26

19   The mating surfaces of the cylinder head and block must be perfectly clean when the head is refitted. Use a gasket scraper to remove all traces of carbon and old gasket material, then clean the mating surfaces with lacquer thinner or acetone. If there's oil on the mating surfaces when the head is refitted, the gasket may not seal correctly and leaks could

develop. When working on the block, stuff the cylinders with clean shop rags to keep out debris. Use a vacuum cleaner to remove any debris that falls into the cylinders.

20   Check the block and head mating surfaces for nicks, deep scratches and other damage. If damage is slight, it can be removed with a file; if it's excessive, machining may be the only alternative. Also check the head and block deck for warpage.

21   Use a tap of the correct size to chase the threads in the head bolt holes. Mount each bolt in a vice and run a die down the threads to remove corrosion and restore the threads. Dirt, corrosion, sealant and damaged threads will affect torque readings.

22   Apply sealant to the two front corners of the block **(see illustration)**. Place the gasket in place over the engine block dowel pins **(see illustration)**. If the camshaft sprocket has been removed, reattach it to the chain with the marks aligned. Make sure the number one piston is still at TDC, then carefully lower the cylinder head onto the engine, over the dowel pins and the gasket. Be careful not to move the gasket.

23   If you removed it, refit the camshaft (see Section 9). Turn the camshaft to position the dowel at the top **(see illustration)**.

24   While holding up the sprocket and chain,

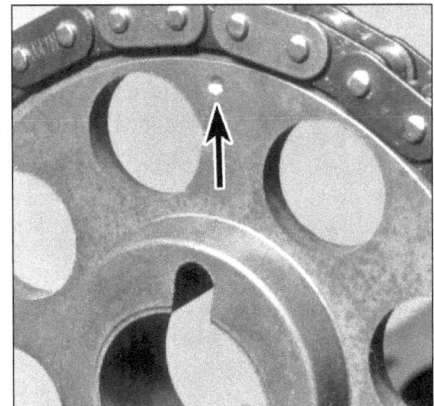

7.24 Refit the camshaft sprocket with the two bright chain links (or previously-applied matchmarks) on either side of the dimple (arrow) and the groove or hole at the top (12 o'clock position) so it mates with the dowel in the camshaft flange

turn the crankshaft until the cam sprocket groove or hole is at the top and centred between the two shiny links **(see illustration)**.

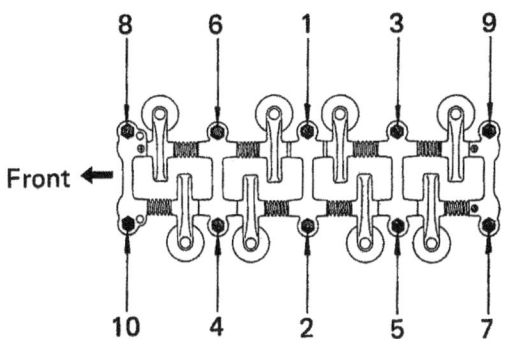

7.26 Cylinder head bolt TIGHTENING sequence

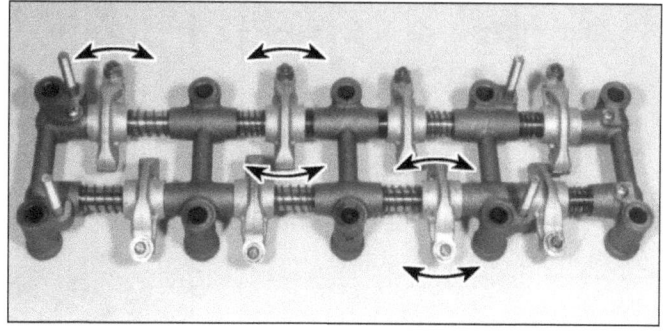

8.1 To check for play in the rocker arms, try to wiggle each rocker arm from side-to-side on the shaft

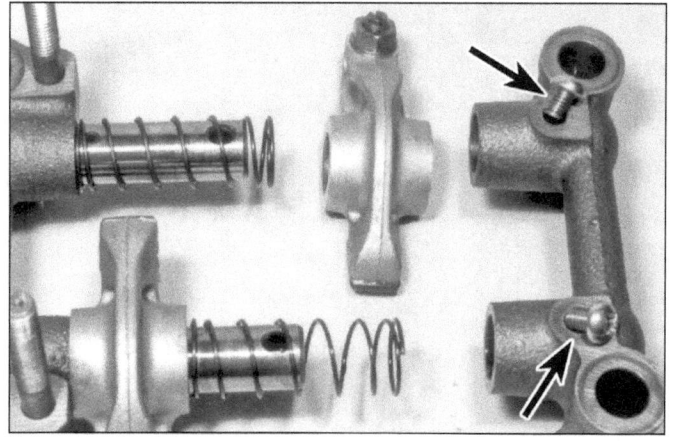

8.2a To disassemble the rocker arm assembly for inspection or servicing, remove these small screws (arrows) from each rocker end stand

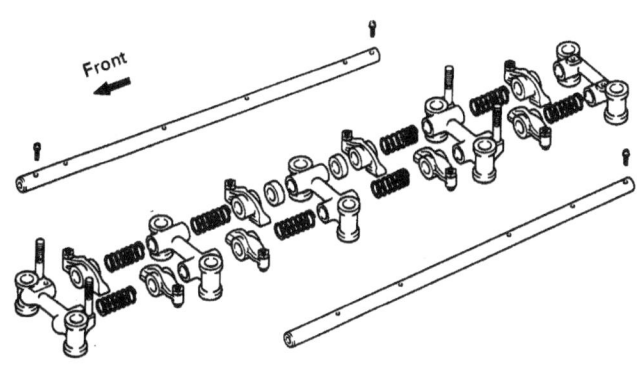

8.2b An exploded view of the rocker arm assembly (it's a good idea to lay out the parts just like this on a clean workbench during inspection or servicing to prevent mix-ups during reassembly

25   Loosen the locknut and adjuster screw in each rocker arm. Place the rocker arm shaft/ head bolt assembly over the dowels on the cylinder head. Thread the head bolts in by hand.

26   Tighten the head bolts in four equal steps to the torque listed in this Chapter's Specifications. Be sure to follow the recommended sequence (see illustration).

27   Refit the cylinder head-to-timing chain cover bolt (if applicable) and tighten it to the torque listed in this Chapter's Specifications.

28   Align the groove or hole in the cam sprocket with the dowel on the cam flange and attach the sprocket to the camshaft. Note: If the chain doesn't seem long enough, turn the crankshaft back-and-forth slightly while pulling up on the chain and sprocket until the sprocket fits over the dowel.

29   On 18R engines, tighten the three camshaft sprocket bolts to the torque listed in this Chapter's Specifications. On 20R and 22R engines, place the distributor drive gear and (on carburetted 20R and 22R engines) the fuel pump eccentric over the sprocket and tighten the sprocket bolt to the torque listed in this Chapter's Specifications.

30   Adjust the valves (see Chapter 1).

31   On carburetted models, refit the fuel pump (see Chapter 4A).

32   Refit the distributor (see Chapter 5).

33   Apply RTV sealant to the front and rear semi-circular rubber seals and refit them in the cylinder head.

34   Refit the valve cover (see Section 4) and any brackets or parts removed from it.

35   Refit the rear air suction pipe, if equipped.

36   Refit the intake and exhaust manifolds (see Sections 5 and 6). Refit the carburettor on the inlet manifold if you removed it (see Chapter 4A).

37   Attach the exhaust pipe to the exhaust manifold and tighten the three nuts.

38   Connect the accelerator rod or cable (see Chapter 4A).

39   If the vehicle has an automatic transmission, connect the throttle valve rod or cable (see Chapter 7B).

40   Refit the air cleaner housing or duct.

41   Add the correct amount of engine oil (see Chapter 1).

42   Fill the radiator with the correct amount of coolant (see Chapter 1).

43   Adjust the spark plug gaps and refit and tighten the spark plugs to the torque listed in the Chapter 1 Specifications.

44   Attach the cable to the negative battery terminal.

45   Start the engine and allow it to reach normal operating temperature.

46   Reset the ignition timing (see Chapter 1).

47   Readjust the valves (see Chapter 1).

8   Rocker arm assembly - removal, inspection and refitting

Note: The cylinder head bolts also hold the rocker arm assembly in place, so cylinder head removal and refitting is always part of removing and fitting the rocker arm assembly. If the rocker arm assembly is detached for any reason, be sure to remove the head as well so a new gasket can be fitted. Once the head bolts are loosened, the seal between the head and block is compromised and leaks could result if a new gasket isn't fitted.

Removal

See the "Removal" portion of Section 7.

Inspection

Refer to illustrations 8.1, 8.2a, 8.2b and 8.4

1   Try to twist each rocker arm from side-to-side on the shaft (see illustration). Very little play should be detected. If excessive play is evident, disassemble the rocker arms and shafts. Note: If the parts are removed from the shafts, be sure to mark them or lay them out in the correct order- they MUST be refitted in their original locations and with the same orientation.

2   Remove the spring clips or screws from the rear ends of the shafts (see illustration)

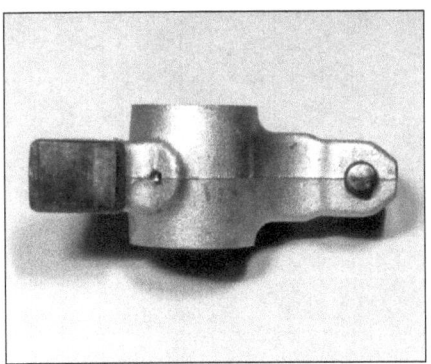

8.4 Check the rocker arm pads and the ends of the adjusting screws for wear and damage

9.1 Check the camshaft endplay with a feeler gauge between the flange and the front bearing cap of the camshaft

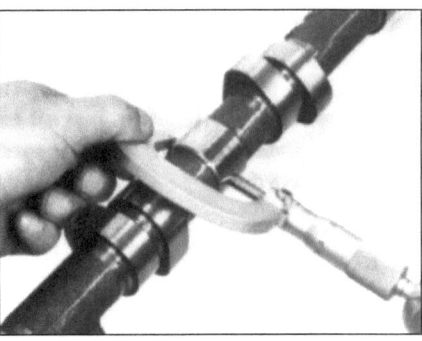

9.6 Measure each camshaft bearing journal with a micrometer

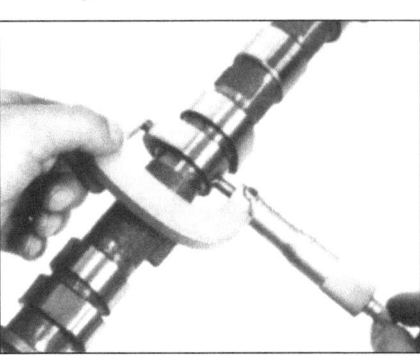

9.8 Measure the height of each camshaft lobe with a micrometer

and the bolts from the front shaft support. Slide the shaft supports, rocker arms and springs off the shafts, but keep all the parts in order so they can be returned to their original locations during reassembly **(see illustration)**. The shaft supports have different configurations and must not be interchanged.

3   Using a micrometer and a small telescoping gauge, measure the diameter of the shafts (where each rocker arm makes contact) and the rocker arm bore diameters. Subtract the shaft diameter from the corresponding rocker arm bore diameter to obtain the rocker arm oil clearance. Repeat the procedure for each rocker arm and compare the results to the Specifications.

4   Check the rocker arm faces (that contact the camshaft lobes) and the ends of the adjusting screws (that contact the valve stems) for pitting, excessive wear and roughness **(see illustration)**. Check the adjusting screw threads for damage. Make sure they can be threaded in and out of the rocker arms.

5   Any damaged or excessively worn parts should be renewed. It should be noted that the rocker arm bores have bushes in them that can be renewed (a job which should be done by an automotive machine shop). If the bushes are renewed, make sure the oil holes in each rocker arm and bush are aligned before assembling the rocker arm components.

Refitting

See the "Refitting" portion of Section 7.

---

9   Camshaft - removal, inspection and refitting

Removal

Refer to illustration 9.1

1   Remove the rocker arm assembly (see Section 8). With the camshaft still in place, check the endplay with a feeler gauge or dial indicator **(see illustration)**. If it's greater than specified, a new cylinder head will be required.

2   Remove the bolts and detach the bearing caps from the head, then lift out the camshaft. Be careful not to nick or gouge the bearing surfaces in the caps or head.

3   Refit the bearing caps in their original locations and thread the bolts in finger tight.

Inspection

Refer to illustrations 9.6 and 9.8

4   Clean the camshaft with solvent and dry it with compressed air. Clean the bearing surfaces in the head and caps as well.

5   Inspect the camshaft bearing journals for excessive wear and evidence of seizure. If the journals are damaged, the bearing surfaces in the head and bearing caps are probably damaged as well. Both the camshaft and cylinder head (as well as the bearing caps) will have to be renewed with new parts.

6   Using a micrometer, measure the diameter of each of the cam bearing journals **(see illustration)**. Take the measurement at two locations on each journal (90-degrees apart). If the journal diameters are less than the service limit, the camshaft must be renewed.

7   The camshaft runout should also be checked (to determine if it's bent). This measurement requires a dial indicator and a special jig (or V-blocks) so it should be done by an automotive machine shop.

8   Check the cam lobes for pitting, grooves, scoring or flaking. Measure the cam lobe height and compare it to the Specifications **(see illustration)**. If the lobe height is less than the minimum specified, and/or the lobes are damaged, a new camshaft must be obtained.

9   Examine the bearing surfaces in the head and the bearing caps. Look for scoring, galling and burned areas. If damage is evident, the cylinder head and bearing caps (as well as the camshaft) will have to be renewed.

10   Check the bearing oil clearances with Plastigage when the camshaft is refitted.

Refitting

Refer to illustrations 9.16, 9.17, 9.18 and 9.22

11   If the inspection reveals no excessive wear or damage, the cam bearing oil clearance should be checked before deciding to refit the original camshaft. **Note:** *The cylinder head should be thoroughly cleaned before checking the bearing oil clearance, but it's not absolutely necessary if extra care is taken during the following steps.*

12   Clean the camshaft and bearing caps with solvent and dry them thoroughly.

13   The bearing oil clearances should be checked with Plastigage, which is available at auto parts stores. Type HPG-1 (green) should be used for this procedure.

14   Make sure the cam bearing journals and the bearing surfaces in the caps and cylinder head are clean and oil free (if the cylinder head hasn't been cleaned, wipe the bearing surfaces with a clean lint-free cloth). **Note:** *DO NOT apply oil or any other lubricant to the cylinder head, camshaft or bearing caps during this procedure.*

15   Carefully lay the camshaft in position in the cylinder head.

16   Cut three pieces of Plastigage the same length as the bearing journal width. Lay a piece of Plastigage on each bearing journal, parallel to the camshaft centre-line **(see illustration)**.

17   Refit the bearing caps in their original locations with the marks facing forward. Tighten the bolts in each cap very gradually (about 1/4-turn at a time), alternating between the two until you reach the torque listed in this

9.16 Lay a strip of Plastigage on each camshaft bearing journal . . .

9.17 . . . then refit the caps and tighten the bolts to the specified torque - DO NOT turn the camshaft

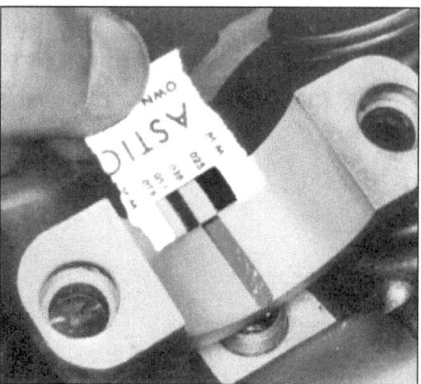

9.18 Compare the width of the crushed Plastigage to the scale on the envelope to determine the oil clearance - always take the measurement at the widest point

9.22 Make sure the arrows on the camshaft bearing caps all face toward the front of the engine

Chapter's Specifications **(see illustration)**. **Note:** *DO NOT turn the camshaft at any time during this procedure!*

18   Remove the bolts (loosen them gradually to avoid distortion of the caps), lift off the caps and compare the widest portion of the crushed Plastigage on each bearing journal to the scale printed on the Plastigage envelope. Locate the line on the scale that's the same width as the Plastigage, then read the number opposite the line. This number is the bearing oil clearance **(see illustration)**.

19   If the oil clearance is greater than the service limit, the bearing surfaces in the head and caps are excessively worn. Since the cylinder head must be renewed to restore the oil clearances, check with your dealer parts department and an automotive machine shop for advice before proceeding.

20   Once the procedure is complete, remove all traces of the Plastigage material from the cam journals and the bearing caps. Use a soft, blunt instrument such as a piece of wood (a credit card also works well) to avoid scratching the bearings. Clean the journals and the bearing caps with solvent to complete the clean-up.

21   Prior to final refitting of the camshaft, lubricate the bearing surfaces and the lobes with moly-base grease or engine assembly lube.

22   Carefully lay the camshaft in the head. Make sure the bearing surfaces in the caps are clean, then refit them on the head. They should be numbered one through three (front-to-rear) and the arrows must point toward the front of the engine **(see illustration)**.

23   Refit and tighten the bolts as described in Step 11.

24   After the cap bolts have been tightened, turn the camshaft by hand and check for obvious binding.

10   Valve springs, retainers and seals - renewal

On many engines, broken valve springs and defective valve stem seals can be renewed with the cylinder head still fitted. However, on this engine, the cylinder head is already detached from the block by the time you have removed the rocker arm assembly because the head bolts also retain the rocker arm assembly. Since you have to remove the head anyway to renew the head gasket, you might as well perform a complete top end inspection and overhaul.

11   Sump - removal and refitting

Refer to illustrations 11.4, 11.5, 11.8a and 11.8b

1   Drain the engine oil.

2   Raise the front of the vehicle and support it on jackstands placed under the frame.

3   Remove the splash shield, if equipped.

4   Disconnect the relay rod (see the steering linkage removal and refitting section in Chapter 10), then remove the front crossmember **(see illustration)**.

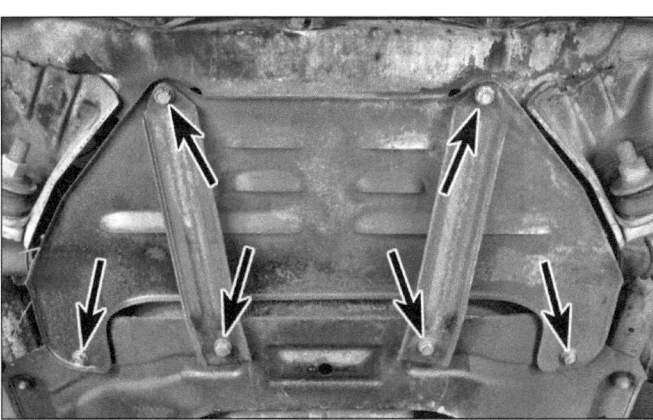

11.4 Remove the crossmember retaining bolts (arrows) and the crossmember to provide access to the sump

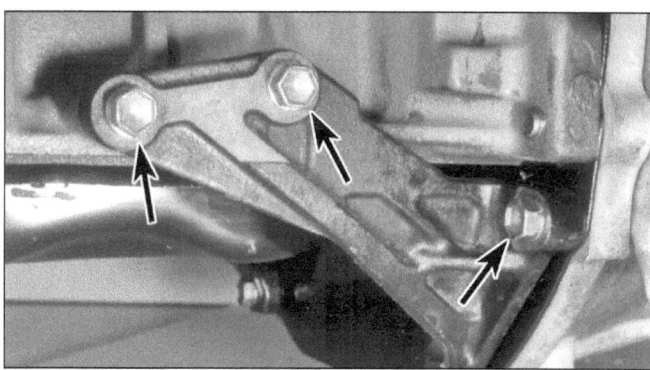

11.5 Some models use reinforcement brackets between the bottom of the block and the transmission bellhousing; you may have to remove these brackets to gain access to the rear sump flange bolts and/or to detach the pan from the block

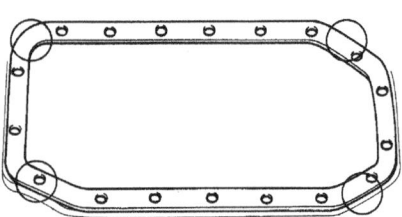

11.8a On 1984 and earlier models, apply gasket sealant to the corner areas of the sump gasket as indicated

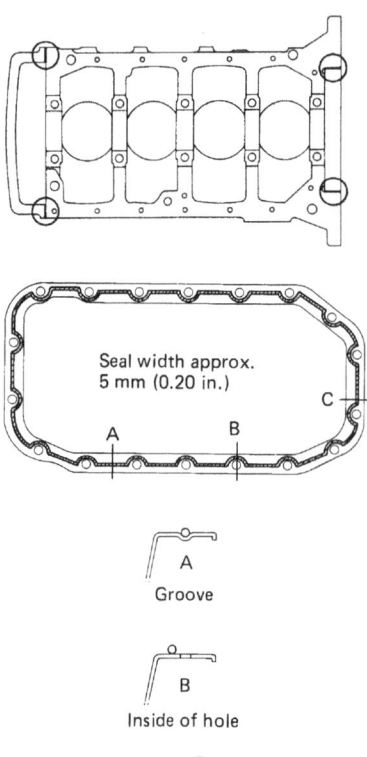

Seal width approx. 5 mm (0.20 in.)

A

Groove

B

Inside of hole

C ⊢→ 5 mm (0.20 in.)

11.8b On 1985 and later models, apply sealant as shown to both sides of the new sump gasket (top) and the joints in the block (bottom)

5   If there are reinforcement brackets between the pan and the transmission bell-housing **(see illustration)**, it may be necessary to remove them to get at the rear pan bolts. Also, on some models it may be necessary to raise the engine slightly to provide enough clearance between the engine and the frame to allow sump removal. Where this is the case, unbolt the radiator fan shroud, remove the engine mount-to-frame bolts and raise the engine, preferably with a hoist from above. Remove the sump bolts and detach the pan. Don't prise between the block and pan or damage to the sealing surfaces may result and oil leaks could develop. Use a block of wood and a hammer to dislodge the pan if it's stuck.

6   Use a scraper to remove all traces of old gasket material and sealant from the block, timing chain cover, rear oil seal housing and sump. Clean the gasket sealing surfaces with lacquer thinner or acetone and make sure the bolt holes in the block are clean.

7   Check the sump flange for distortion, particularly around the bolt holes. If necessary, place the pan on a block of wood and use a hammer to flatten and restore the gasket surface.

8   On 1984 and earlier models, apply a thin coat of gasket sealant to the corner areas of the sump flange **(see illustration)** and fit a new gasket on the flange. Make sure the bolt holes are aligned. The sump on 1985 models doesn't require a gasket - liquid sealant (Toyota no. 08826-00080 or equivalent) is used instead. Cut the nozzle on the sealant tube to provide a 5 mm opening, then apply the sealant to the pan and block **(see illustration)**. Avoid excessive amounts of sealant and be sure to attach the sump within five minutes or the sealant will have to be scraped off and reapplied.

9   Position the sump against the engine block and refit the mounting bolts. Tighten them in a criss-cross pattern to the torque listed in this Chapter's Specifications.

10   Wait at least 30 minutes before filling the engine with oil, then start the engine and check the pan for leaks.

11   Refit the parts removed for access to the sump.

12   Oil pump and pick-up tube - removal, inspection and refitting

18R engines

Refer to illustration 12.3

1   Remove the sump (see Section 11).

2   Remove the three oil pump retaining bolts and remove the pump.

3   Unscrew and remove the pressure relief valve **(see illustration)**.

4   Unbolt and detach the oil strainer.

5   Remove the three retaining bolts and separate the cover from the pump body.

6   Separate the oil pump shaft and driven rotor from the body.

7   Wash the components in solvent and inspect them as follows:

8   Using a feeler gauge, measure the clearance between the tips of the drive and the driven rotors and compare your measurement to the clearance listed in this Chapter's Specifications. If the indicated clearance is not within the specified range, renew the rotors as a set.

9   Using a straightedge, check the clearance between the end faces of the rotors and the body flange and compare your measurement to the clearance listed in this Chapter's Specifications. If the indicated clearance is not within the specified range, renew the rotors as a set.

10   Again, using a feeler gauge, measure the clearance between the outer rotor and the inside of the pump body and compare your measurement to the clearance listed in

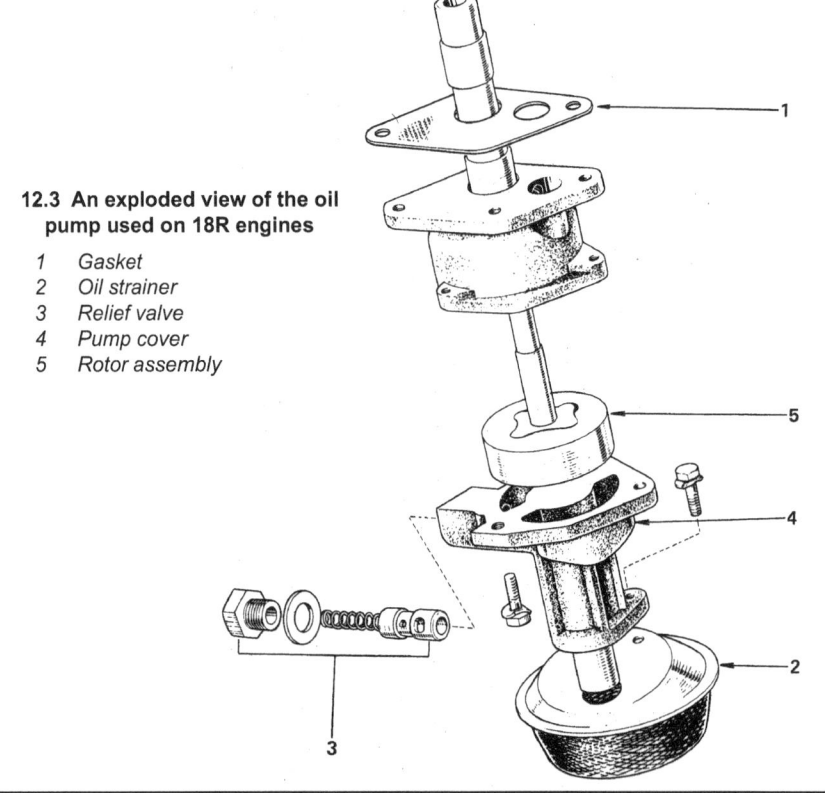

12.3 An exploded view of the oil pump used on 18R engines

1   *Gasket*
2   *Oil strainer*
3   *Relief valve*
4   *Pump cover*
5   *Rotor assembly*

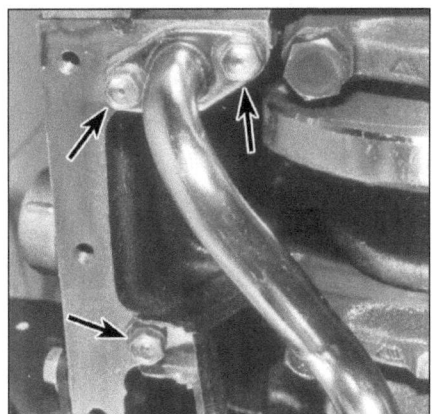

12.15 The oil pick-up tube is held in place by three bolts (arrows) on 20R and 22R engines

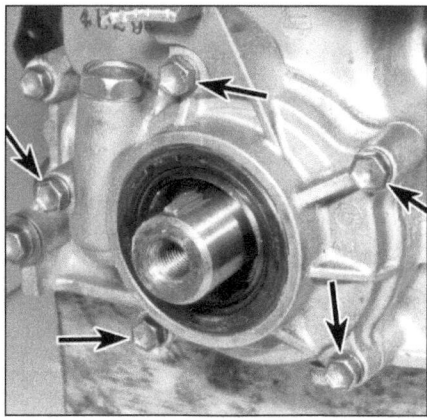

12.17 Remove the oil pump bolts (arrows) (20R 22R engines)

12.18a Remove the O-ring . . .

12.18b . . . then remove the oil pump drive spline (20R and 22R engines)

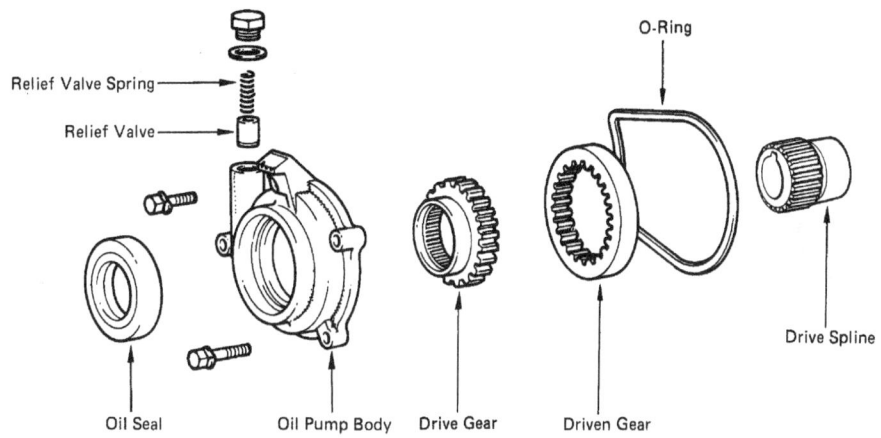

12.19 An exploded view of the oil pump assembly (20R and 22R engines)

this Chapter's Specifications. If the indicated clearance is not within the specified range, renew the pump body.

11   If you're overhauling the engine, it's a good idea to renew the relief spring and valve.
12   Reassembly is the reverse of disassembly.
13   Refitting is the reverse of removal. Make sure the rotor punch marks face down when the pump is refitted. Always use a new gasket when fitting the pump to the crankcase.

20R and 22R engines

Refer to illustrations 12.15, 12.17, 12.18a, 12.18b, 12.19, 12.21, 12.22a, 12.22b, 12.23 and 12.30

14   Remove the sump (see Section 11).
15   Remove the bolts and detach the oil pick-up tube **(see illustration)**.
16   Remove the crankshaft pulley (see Section 13).
17   Remove the bolts and detach the oil pump assembly from the timing chain cover **(see illustration)**.
18   Remove the O-ring and oil pump drive spline **(see illustrations)**.
19   Unscrew the plug and remove the spring

and relief valve from the oil pump **(see illustration)**.
20   Check the drive spline, drive gear, driven gear, pump body and timing chain cover for wear and damage. If wear or damage is found, renew the pump.
21   Measure the clearance between the driven gear and body with a feeler gauge

(see illustration). If the clearance is greater than the specified maximum, renew the pump.
22   Measure the clearance between both gears and the crescent with feeler gauges **(see illustrations)**. If the clearance is greater than the specified maximum, renew the pump.

12.21 Measure the clearance between the driven gear and the oil pump body with a feeler gauge (20R and 22R engines)

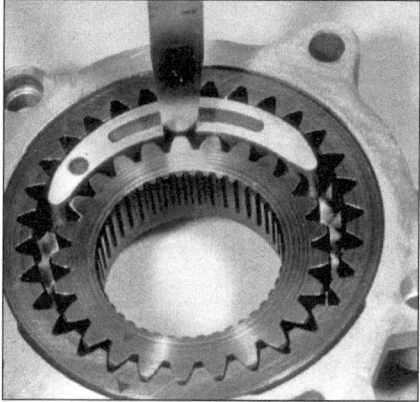

12.22a Measure the clearance between the drive gear and the crescent with a feeler gauge (20R and 22R engines)

12.22b　Measure the clearance between the driven gear and the crescent with a feeler gauge (20R and 22R engines)

12.23　Measure the oil pump gear side clearance with a straightedge and a feeler gauge (20R and 22R engines)

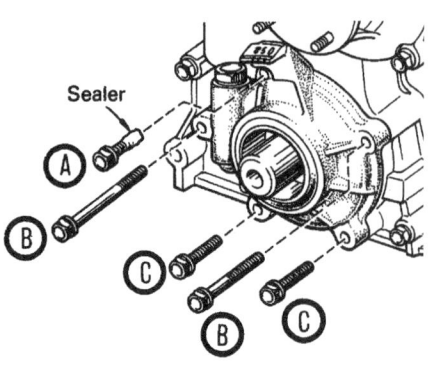

12.30　Apply sealant to the upper left bolt and tighten bolts A, B and C to their respective torques listed in this Chapter's Specifications (20R and 22R engines)

23　Measure the side clearance with a straightedge and feeler gauge **(see illustration)**. If the clearance is greater than the specified maximum, renew the pump.

24　Check the relief valve piston and bore for scuffing and score marks. Make sure the valve moves freely in the bore without excessive side play. If any defects are found, renew the appropriate parts.

25　Check the crankshaft front oil seal for wear and damage. If a new one is required, prise out the old one and fit a new one (see Section 14).

26　To reassemble the pump, lubricate and insert the relief valve piston and spring, then refit the plug (with a new gasket).

27　Coat them with clean oil, then insert the drive and driven gears into the pump body.

28　Slide the pump drive spline onto the crankshaft.

29　Fit a new O-ring in the groove. **Note:** *Failure to renew this O-ring can result in a leak which can be mistaken for a crankshaft front seal leak.*

30　Apply sealant to the upper oil pump bolt, then refit the pump and the mounting bolts **(see illustration)**. Tighten the bolts in a criss-cross pattern to the torque listed in this Chapter's Specifications.

31　Clean and refit the oil pick-up tube and screen. Tighten the bolts securely.

32　Refit the sump (see Section 11).

33　Refit the crankshaft pulley (see Section 13).

34　Refit the drivebelts and add engine oil (see Chapter 1).

13　Crankshaft pulley - removal and refitting

Refer to illustration 13.6

1　Disconnect the negative battery cable from the battery.

2　Remove the radiator and shroud (see Chapter 3).

3　Unbolt the splash shield, if equipped.

4　Remove the drivebelts (see Chapter 1).

5　Remove the flywheel/driveplate inspection cover and wedge a screwdriver in the starter ring gear teeth to prevent the crankshaft from turning. Remove the pulley mounting bolt. They're usually very tight, so use a six-point socket and a 1/2-inch drive breaker bar.

6　Use a puller to remove the pulley from the crankshaft **(see illustration)**. DO NOT use a gear puller that applies force to the outer edge of the pulley!

7　The lip of the crankshaft front oil seal can eventually wear a groove in the surface of the pulley hub that it seals. Before refitting the old pulley, be sure to inspect this seal surface for groove damage. If the pulley groove is mild, you can usually polish it out with crocus or emery cloth. If it's badly grooved, renew the pulley and fit a new seal (see Section 14). Otherwise, the seal will eventually leak.

8　Refitting is the reverse of removal. Be sure to apply moly-base grease or clean engine oil to the seal contact surface on the pulley hub before refitting the pulley on the crankshaft. Also, be sure to align the keyway in the pulley hub with the key in the crankshaft or the pulley won't slide into place.

9　Tighten the pulley bolt to the torque listed in this Chapter's Specifications.

14　Crankshaft front oil seal - renewal

Refer to illustrations 14.2 and 14.3

1　Remove the crankshaft pulley (see Section 13). Inspect the seal surface of the pulley hub as described in Step 7 of Section 13. If the seal groove is serious, renew the crank pulley, or the new seal will spring a leak when the groove tears up the seal lip.

2　If you're careful, you can prise the oil seal out of the timing chain cover (18R engines) or the oil pump (20R and 22R engines) with a seal removal tool or screwdriver. Don't scratch the crank seal bore or damage the crankshaft

PULLER

13.6　Use the recommended tool to remove the crankshaft pulley - if a puller that applies force to the outer edge is used, the pulley may be damaged

in the process (if the crankshaft is damaged, the new seal will leak). On 18R engines, this strategy is preferable to removing the entire timing cover (anytime you have to remove the timing cover, always renew the front oil seal). But on later model (20R and 22R) engines, you may find it easier to remove the oil pump (see Section 12) and prise out the seal on the workbench **(see illustration)**.

3　Clean the bore in the cover or oil pump and coat the outer edge of the new seal with engine oil or multi-purpose grease. Using a socket with an outside diameter slightly smaller than the outside diameter of the seal (and with a bore big enough to clear the nose of the crankshaft), carefully drive the new seal into place with a hammer. If a socket isn't available, a short section of large diameter pipe will work. Check the seal after refitting to be sure that the spring didn't pop out of place. If you're fitting a new seal on the bench, the same procedure applies **(see illustration)**, except you don't have to worry about clearing the nose of the crank.

4　Refit the pulley (see Section 13). Make sure the seal surface of the pulley hub is free of grooves from the old seal lip.

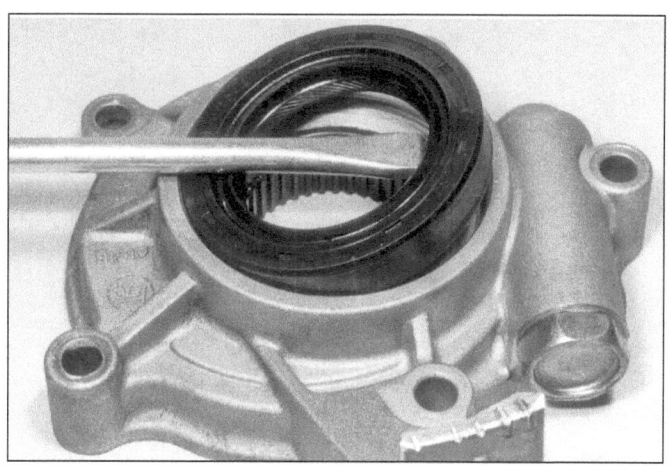

14.2 Prise out the old seal from the oil pump with a screwdriver - make sure you don't nick or gouge the seal bore or the new seal will leak

14.3 To fit the new seal, tap it into place with a large socket or section of pipe with an outside diameter slightly smaller than the inside diameter of the bore

5   The parts removed to gain access to the pulley can now be refitted.
6   Run the engine and check for leaks.

15 Timing chain cover - removal and refitting

Refer to illustrations 15.9a, 15.9b, 15.10, 15.12a and 15.12b

1   Remove the cylinder head (see Section 7).
2   Remove the sump (see Section 11).
3   On some later models, you may want to remove the radiator to give yourself more room to work (see Chapter 3).
4   Remove the accessory drivebelts (see Chapter 1).
5   On models with air injection, remove the air pump and, if necessary, the pump mounting bracket(s) (see Chapter 6).
6   On air-conditioned models, unbolt the compressor and set it aside without discon-

necting the hoses. If the mounting bracket(s) are bolted to the timing cover, or in the way, detach it.
7   If the alternator adjustment or mounting bracket is attached to the timing chain cover, detach it, then move the bracket toward the alternator (see Chapter 5).
8   Remove the crankshaft pulley (see Section 13).
9   If coolant bypass or heater tubes are attached to the timing cover, remove the bolts **(see illustrations)** and detach the tubes.
10   Remove the timing chain cover mounting bolts **(see illustration)**. On 20R and 22R engines, note that different length bolts are used - they must be returned to their original locations! Tap on the cover with a soft-face hammer to separate it from the engine block. If the cover is stuck, recheck for any remaining bolts. DO NOT prise the cover off - the gasket surfaces are easily damaged and oil leaks could result!

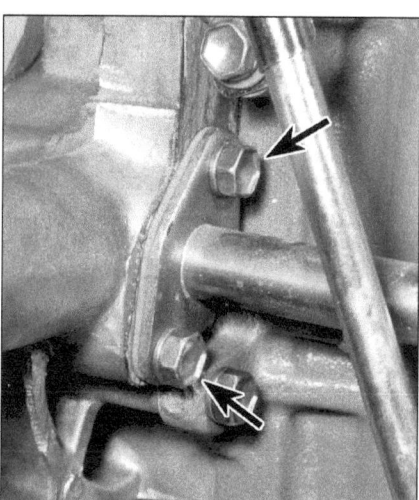

15.9a On 20R engines, the heater tube is attached to the back side of the timing cover with two bolts (arrows)

15.9b On 20R and 22R engines, the coolant bypass tube is attached to the timing cover with two bolts (arrows)

15.10 Timing chain cover bolt locations (arrows) (22R engine shown, 20R engine similar)

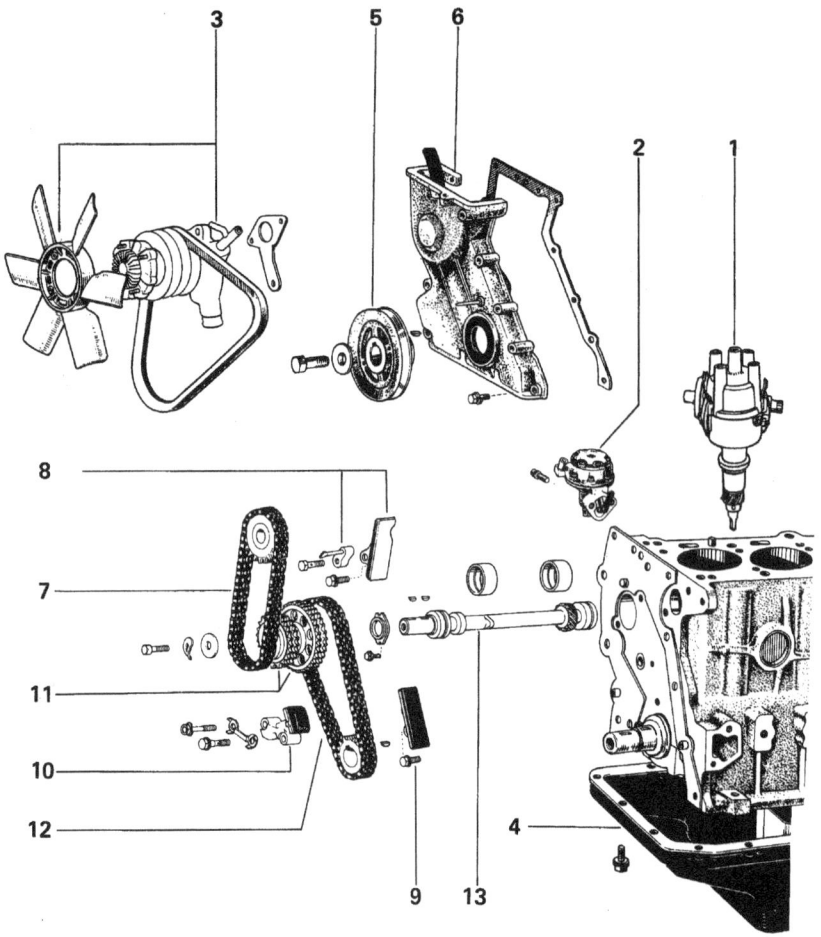

15.12a An exploded view of the timing chain cover and timing chain assembly (18R engine)

1 Distributor
2 Fuel pump
3 Fan and water pump
4 Sump
5 Crankshaft pulley
6 Timing cover
7 Camshaft timing chain and camshaft sprocket
8 No. 2 chain damper and oil jet
9 No. 1 chain damper
10 No. 1 chain tensioner
11 Camshaft timing chain drive sprocket (front) and oil pump driveshaft sprocket (rear)
12 Oil pump drive chain and crankshaft sprocket
13 Oil pump driveshaft

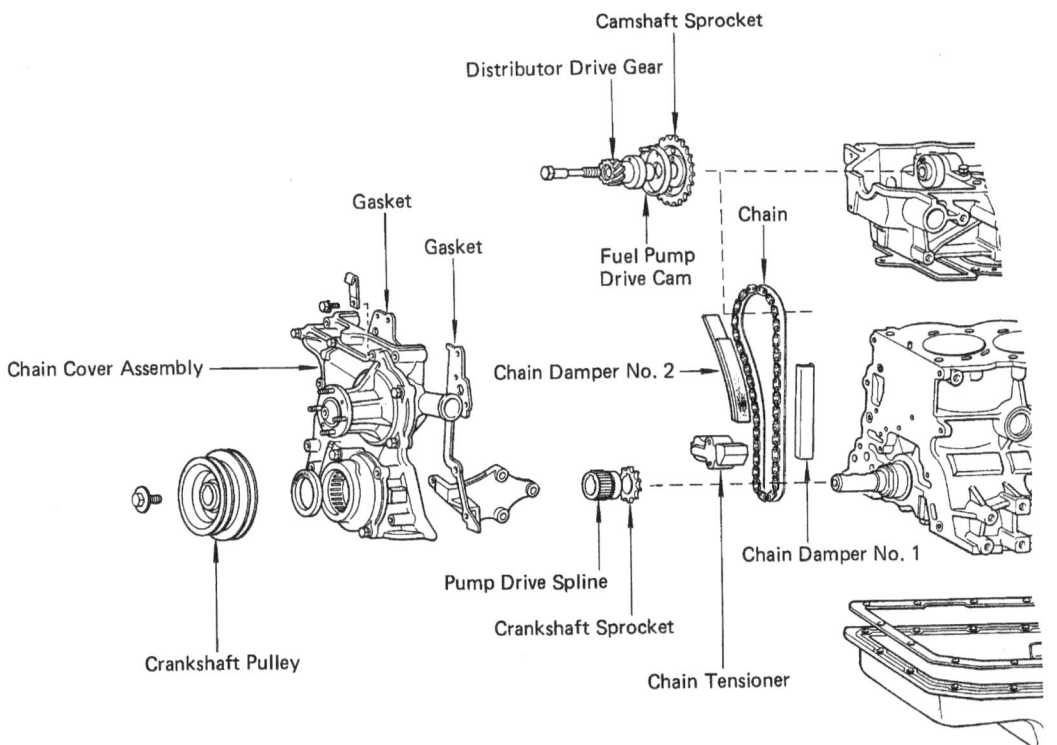

15.12b An exploded view of the timing chain cover and timing chain on 22R engine (20R engine similar)

16.8 To remove the timing chain tensioner on 18R engines, bend down the tangs on the lockplate and remove the two bolts (arrows)

16.9 When the number one piston is at TDC on a 20R or 22R engine, this shiny link should be at six o'clock - put a mark on the crankshaft sprocket next to this link to ensure proper refitting

16.12 When you remove the crankshaft sprocket from a 20R or 22R engine, make sure you don't lose the key - note the position of the keyways: pointing to 12 o'clock (straight up, toward the cylinder head); this is where they should be pointing when you refit the sprocket and chain

11   Remove all traces of gasket material and sealant from the cover and block, then clean the surfaces with lacquer thinner or acetone. Be careful not to nick or gouge the timing chain cover with the gasket scraper.

12   Apply a thin film of RTV sealant to the block side of the new gaskets, then position them on the block. The dowel pins and sealant will hold them in place. Apply a thin layer of RTV sealant to the timing chain cover gasket surfaces, then attach the cover to the block. Don't disturb the gaskets and (on 20R and 22R engines) make sure the oil pump drive spline engages in the pump (**see illustrations**).

13   Refit the bolts and tighten them in 1/4-turn increments to the torque listed in this Chapter's Specifications.

14   The remaining refitting steps are the reverse of removal.

16   Timing chain and sprockets - removal, inspection and refitting

Removal

1   Position the number one piston at TDC on the compression stroke (see Section 3).

2   Remove the cylinder head (see Section 7).

3   Remove the sump (see Section 11).

4   Remove the radiator (see Chapter 3).

5   Remove the crankshaft pulley (see Section 13).

6   Remove the timing cover (see Section 15).

18R engines

Refer to illustration 16.8

7   Remove the camshaft drive chain, the camshaft drive sprocket (the front oil pump driveshaft sprocket) and the camshaft drive chain tensioner (**see illustration 15.12a**).

8   Loosen or remove the oil pump drive chain tensioner (**see illustration**) and remove the oil pump driveshaft sprocket, the crankshaft sprocket and the oil pump drive chain as a single assembly (**see illustration 15.12a**).

20R and 22R engines

Refer to illustrations 16.9 and 16.12

9   If you're planning to use the same chain on a late-model engine, mark the sprocket tooth adjacent to the shiny link (**see illustration**) to ensure proper refitting (this step isn't absolutely necessary, since you have already marked the relationship of the cam sprocket to the timing chain; however, it does give you one more alignment reference mark to use during refitting of the chain, which simplifies the task of timing the camshaft to the crankshaft).

10   Remove the oil pump drive spline, if you haven't already done so (**see illustration 12.18b**). You may need to use a puller if it's seized on the crank.

11   Disengage the cam chain from the tensioner and dampers and remove it from the crankshaft sprocket.

12   Remove the crankshaft sprocket from the end of the crankshaft (**see illustration**). You may also need a puller for the crank sprocket if it's stuck.

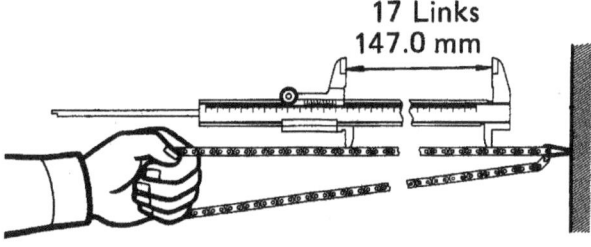

**17 Links
147.0 mm**

16.13 To check for timing chain stretch on a 20R or 22R engine, measure the length of 17 links and compare your measurement to the dimension listed in this Chapter's Specifications

Inspection

Refer to illustrations 16.13, 16.15a, 16.15b, 16.16a and 16.16b

13   To check for chain stretch, clean the chain(s) and inspect them as follows: Measure the length of 17 links with the chain stretched tight (**see illustration**). Repeat your measurement on three other chain areas selected at random. If any measurement exceeds the limit listed in this Chapter's Specifications, even at one location, renew the chain. If you don't have a caliper handy, here's another way to check the chain(s): Hold the chain with its rollers in a vertical position. If the chain is worn, it will bow (dip) in the middle; if it's still in reasonably good condition, it will bow only slightly or not at all. **Note:** *Generally speaking, it's a good idea to renew the chain(s) anytime you remove the timing cover, regardless of the outcome of the above inspection procedures.*

14   Inspect the teeth on the camshaft and crankshaft sprockets (and, on 18R engines, the two sprockets on the oil pump driveshaft). If they're worn, renew the sprockets and chain. **Note:** *Even if the chain appeared to be in satisfactory condition in Step 13, it's essential that you renew it if any of the sprockets are worn. Otherwise, the old chain may shorten the service life of the new sprockets.*

16.15a To remove a 20R or 22R timing chain tensioner for inspection, remove these two bolts

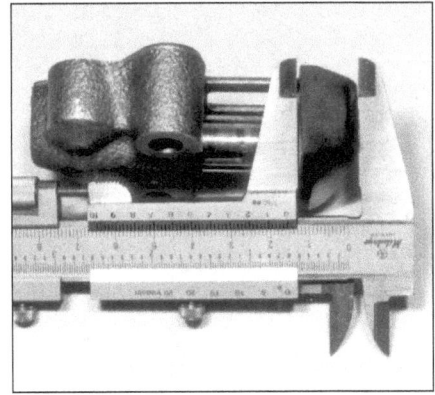

16.15b Measure the thickness of the tensioner slipper pad with vernier calipers and compare your measurement to the dimension listed in this Chapter's Specifications

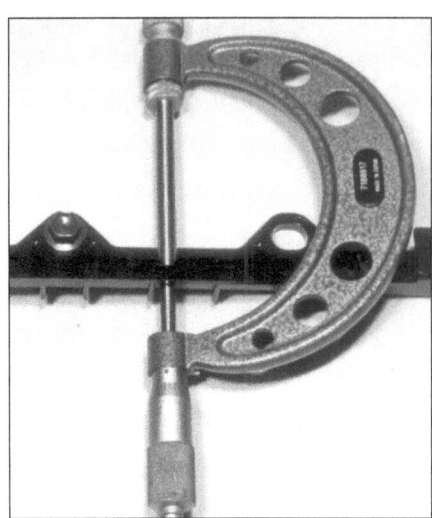

16.16a Measure the No. 1 (straight) timing chain damper on a 20R or 22R engine with a micrometer or vernier caliper and compare your measurement to the dimension listed in this Chapter's Specifications

16.16b Measure the No. 2 (curved) timing chain damper on a 20R or 22R engine with a micrometer or vernier caliper and compare your measurement to the dimension listed in this Chapter's Specifications

16.18 On an 18R engine, the keyways in the crankshaft and oil pump driveshaft must be pointing toward the 12 o'clock position (toward the cylinder head) before you refit the chain and sprockets

16.19 On an 18R engine, the mark on the crankshaft sprocket must be aligned with the single shiny link and the dimple or mark on the camshaft sprocket must be centred between the two shiny links at top

15   On 18R engines, bend down the lock-plate tangs on the chain tensioner slipper **(see illustration 16.8)**. Remove the chain tensioner slipper bolts **(see illustration)** and remove the tensioner. Check the tensioner slipper pad for wear and damage. The pad should move in and out of its bore without binding or excessive play. If the pad on 18R engines is worn or damaged, renew it. On 20R and 22R engines, measure the thickness of the pad **(see illustration)**. If it's less than the thickness listed in this Chapter's Specifications, renew the chain tensioner.

16   Check the chain dampers (guides) for wear and damage. If the damper on an 18R engine is worn, renew it. On 20R and 22R engines, measure the thickness of each damper with a vernier caliper or micrometer **(see illustrations)**. If they're worn beyond the limits listed in this Chapter's Specifications, fit new ones. **Note:** *If you fit new dampers on a 20R or 22R engine, make sure the top of the left (no. 2) damper is all the way to the left before tightening the bolt (the bolt should be in the right end of the slot).*

Refitting

18R engines

Refer to illustrations 16.18, 16.19 and 16.23

17   If you removed them, refit the chain tensioner and damper and tighten the mounting bolts securely.

18   If you haven't turned the crankshaft or oil pump driveshaft while the chain was removed, their keyways should both be pointing to 12 o'clock (toward the top of the cylinder head) **(see illustration)**. Make sure the keys are in their respective keyways.

19   Lay the chain out on a workbench and place the crankshaft and oil pump driveshaft sprockets so that their dimples or timing marks are aligned correctly (dimple or timing mark on the cam sprocket centred between two shiny links at the top; mark on the crank sprocket aligned with the single shiny link or mark on the chain) **(see illustration)**, then carefully fit the sprockets and chain as a single assembly, maintaining the above alignment.

20   Apply a coat of gasket sealant to the back of the new timing cover gasket and refit the gasket onto the front of the block.

21   Refit the upper chain damper and tensioner, if removed.

22   Refit the camshaft drive sprocket onto the oil pump driveshaft and tighten the bolt to the torque listed in this Chapter's Specifications.

23   Place the camshaft drive chain on the oil pump driveshaft sprocket so that the timing mark is at the six o'clock position, centred on the two shiny links of the chain **(see illustration)**, then refit the sprocket onto the shaft. Use a hooked piece of wire to keep the chain engaged with the sprocket teeth until the timing cover and cylinder head are refitted.

16.23 On an 18R engine, the mark on the camshaft drive sprocket (the outer, smaller sprocket on the oil pump driveshaft) must be centred between the two shiny links below

20R and 22R engines

Refer to illustration 16.26

24 Before refitting the chain and sprockets, make sure the key in the crankshaft is in the 12 o'clock position (facing up).
25 Refit the sprocket and oil pump drive spline on the crankshaft. **Note:** *The sprocket must be refitted with the hub collar facing in (against the engine).*
26 Mesh the timing chain and camshaft sprocket. The mark on the sprocket must be between the two bright chain links **(see illustration)**.
27 Align the bright link on the chain with the timing mark on the crankshaft sprocket **(see illustration 16.9)**, then attach the chain to the sprocket.
28 Position the chain between the dampers and engage the tensioner, then attach the sprocket to the camshaft and tighten the bolt (see Section 9). Make sure the fuel pump eccentric (if used) and the distributor drive gear are in place before refitting the bolt.
29 Turn the camshaft sprocket counterclockwise to take up the slack in the chain.
30 Double-check to make sure the timing marks on the sprockets and the bright links on the chain are aligned properly.

All engines

31 Refit the timing chain cover.
32 Refit the crankshaft pulley (see Section 13).
33 Refit the radiator (see Chapter 3).
34 Refit the sump (see Section 11).
35 Refit the cylinder head (see Section 7).

17 Oil pump driveshaft (18R engines) - removal, inspection and refitting

Removal

1 Remove the cylinder head (see Section 7).
2 Remove the sump (see Section 11).

16.26 Align the two bright chain links with the timing mark on the camshaft sprocket

3 Remove the crankshaft pulley (see Section 13).
4 Remove the timing chain cover (see Section 15).
5 Remove the timing chains and sprockets (see Section 16).
6 Remove the two bolts from the thrust plate that retains the oil pump driveshaft and pull the shaft out of the block **(see illustration 15.12a)**.

Inspection

7 Clean the oil pump driveshaft with solvent, then inspect it as follows: Examine the teeth on the spiral bevel drive gear for the oil pump. If they're chewed up, or the hard facing is worn off the thrust side of each tooth, renew the driveshaft. Inspect the bearings for wear. If they're worn, renew the driveshaft.

Refitting

8 Refitting is the reverse of removal.

18 Flywheel/driveplate - removal and refitting

1 Remove the manual transmission, pressure plate and clutch disc as described in Chapters 7A and 8, or the automatic transmission as described in Chapter 7B.
2 Flatten the lockplate tabs (if used) and remove the bolts that secure the fly-wheel/driveplate to the crankshaft rear flange. Be careful - the flywheel is very heavy and should not be dropped. If the crankshaft turns as the bolts are loosened, wedge a screwdriver in the starter ring gear teeth.
3 Detach the flywheel/driveplate from the crankshaft flange.
4 If the teeth on the flywheel/driveplate starter ring gear are badly worn, or if some are missing, fit a new flywheel or driveplate. If this is the case, be sure to renew the starter (see Chapter 5).
5 Refer to Chapter 8 for the flywheel inspection procedure and the pilot bearing check and renewal procedure.

6 Before refitting the flywheel/driveplate, clean the mating surfaces.
7 If removed, refit the rear plate.
8 Position the flywheel/driveplate against the crankshaft and refit the mounting bolts. Use a thread locking compound on the bolts.
9 Tighten the bolts in a criss-cross pattern to the torque listed in this Chapter's Specifications.
10 The remainder of refitting is the reverse of removal.

19 Rear main oil seal - renewal

Note: *The rear main oil seal can be renewed without removing the seal retainer. However, the preferred method is to remove the retainer first, then renew the seal on the bench.*
1 Raise the front of the vehicle and place it securely on jackstands.
2 Remove the transmission (see Chapter 7A) or (see Chapter 7B).
3 If equipped with a manual transmission, remove the pressure plate and clutch disc (see Chapter 8).
4 Remove the flywheel or driveplate (see Section 18).
5 If you're removing the seal retainer, remove the sump (see Section 11). **Note:** *The retainer can be removed without actually removing the sump - you can simply remove the bolts that attach the sump flange to the retainer - but we don't recommend this approach because an oil leak between the retainer and the sump flange may develop at this point.*

Retainer removed

Refer to illustrations 19.6, 19.7 and 19.10
6 Remove the rear main oil seal retainer **(see illustration)**. Discard the old gasket.
7 Place the retainer on a clean workbench and carefully prise out the old seal with a

19.6 Typical rear main oil seal retainer bolts (arrows) (22R engine shown, other engines similar)

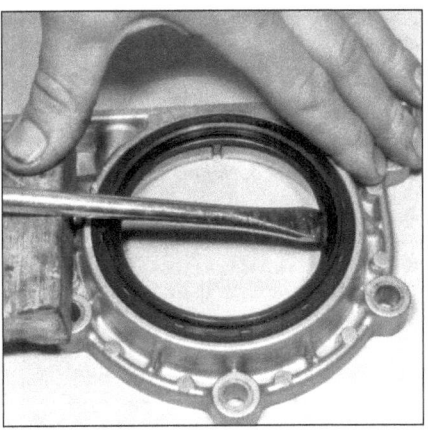

19.7 Prise the old seal out of the retainer with a large screwdriver - use a block of wood as a fulcrum (instead of the edge of the seal bore) to prevent damage to the retainer - make sure you don't nick or gouge the seal bore surface or the seal will leak

19.10 Coat the new retainer gasket with RTV sealant and carefully place it in position on the block

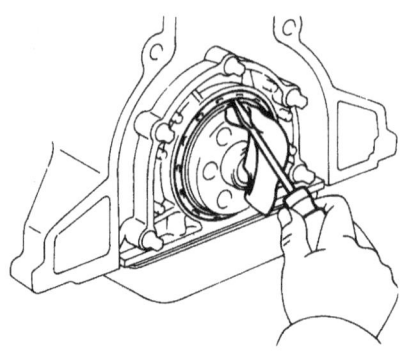

19.13 When removing the rear main oil seal from the housing, wrap the screwdriver with a rag to protect the crankshaft

20.5 Remove the mount-to-chassis bolts/ nuts and the mount-to-engine bracket bolt/nut (arrow) to detach the engine mount

large screwdriver **(see illustration)**. Make sure you don't nick or gouge the seal bore.

8   Using a gasket scraper, carefully remove all traces of old gasket material from the mating surfaces of the block and the seal retainer. Make sure you don't nick or gouge either surface.

9   Using a large socket with an outside diameter slightly smaller than the inside diameter of the seal bore, carefully drive the new seal into place until it's fully seated in the retainer.

10   Coat the rear (block side) of the new gasket with RTV sealant and place it in position **(see illustration)**.

11   Refit the retainer and the retainer bolts. Tighten the bolts evenly and securely. Don't over torque them or you may crack the aluminium retainer.

12   The remainder of refitting is the reverse of removal.

Retainer on the engine

Refer to illustration 19.13

13   Using a seal removal tool or a large screwdriver, carefully prise the seal out of the housing **(see illustration)**. Don't scratch or nick the crankshaft in the process!

14   Clean the bore in the housing and the seal contact surface on the crankshaft. Check the crankshaft surface for scratches and nicks that could damage the new seal lip and cause oil leaks. If the crankshaft is damaged, the only

alternative is a new or different crankshaft.

15   Apply a light coat of engine oil or multi-purpose grease to the outer edge of the new seal. Also lubricate the seal lip.

16   The seal lip must face toward the front of the engine. Carefully work the seal lip over the end of the crankshaft and tap the seal in with a hammer and punch until it's seated in the bore. **Caution:** *Be extremely careful - take your time and drive the seal gently and evenly into place. Damaging a new seal will result in an oil leak.*

17   The remainder of refitting is the reverse of removal.

---

20   Engine mounts - renewal

Refer to illustration 20.5

Warning: *Improper lifting methods or devices are potentially dangerous. DO NOT place any part of your body under the engine/transmission when it's supported only by a jack. Failure of the lifting device could result in serious injury or death.*

1   If the rubber mounts have hardened, cracked or separated from the metal backing plates, they must be renewed. This operation may be carried out with the engine/transmission still in the vehicle.

2   Disconnect the negative cable from the battery.

3   Raise the front of the vehicle and support it securely on jackstands. Apply the parking brake and block the rear wheels.

4   Support the engine with a jack. Position a block of wood between the jack head and the sump.

5   Remove the engine mount-to-chassis bolts/nuts **(see illustration)**.

6   Remove the mount-to-engine bracket bolts. It's not necessary to detach the bracket from the engine.

7   Raise the engine just enough to clear the bracket, then remove the engine mount.

8   Place the new mount in position.

9   Refit the mount-to-engine bracket bolts and tighten them securely.

10   Tighten the mount-to-chassis bolts/nuts securely. Remove the jackstands and lower the vehicle.

Chapter 2 Part C
V6 petrol engine

Contents

Specifications

General

Cylinder numbers (front-to-rear)

Right side	1-3-5
Left side	2-4-6
Firing order	1-2-3-4-5-6

Camshaft and related components

Lifters

Outside diameter	37.922 to 37.932 mm
Bore diameter	37.960 to 37.975 mm
Lifter-to-bore clearance	
Standard	0.028 to 0.053 mm
Service limit	0.1 mm

Cylinder head

Warpage limit	0.10 mm

Cylinder location and
distributor rotation

Camshaft

Valve clearances (engine cold)

    Intake .... 0.18 to 0.28 mm

    Exhaust .... 0.22 to 0.32 mm

Bearing journal diameter .... 33.959 to 33.975 mm

Bearing oil clearance

    Standard... 0.025 to 0.066 mm

    Service limit.. 0.1 mm

Lobe height

    Standard... 47.83 to 47.93 mm

    Service limit.. 47.50 mm

Endplay

    Standard... 0.08 to 0.19 mm

    Service limit.. 0.25 mm

Runout limit (total indicator reading)... 0.06 mm

Timing belt tension spring free length .... 56.275 mm

Oil pump

Driven gear-to-pump body clearance

    Standard... 0.100 to 0.130 mm

    Service limit.. 0.30 mm

Gear-to-gear clearance

    Standard... 0.11 to 0.24 mm

    Service limit.. 0.35 mm

Gear side clearance

    Standard... 0.03 to 0.09 mm

    Service limit.. 0.15 mm

Torque specifications

                                                                           Nm

Inlet manifold bolts/nuts.. 18

Exhaust manifold nuts 39

Vibration damper bolt 245

Timing belt cover bolts

    No. 1 (lower) cover... 5.4

    No. 2 (upper) cover... 5.4

    No. 3 (rear) cover... 8.3

Fan pulley bracket bolts... 40

Moveable timing belt idler pulley (tensioner) bolt 37

Camshaft sprocket bolts 108

Camshaft bearing cap bolts... 16

Cylinder head bolts

    Step 1.. 44

    Step 2.. Turn an additional 90-degrees (1/4-turn)

    Step 3.. Turn an additional 90-degrees (1/4-turn)

Cylinder head bolt A.. 37

Sump bolts... 5.9

Oil pump mounting bolts.. 20

Oil strainer tube mounting bolts.. 6.9

Flywheel/driveplate bolts 88

Rear main oil seal retainer mounting bolts 7.8

Apply a non-hardening thread locking compound to the threads before refitting

1 General information

This Part of Chapter 2 is devoted to in-vehicle repair procedures for the V6 engine. All information concerning engine removal and refitting and engine block and cylinder head overhaul can be found in Part E of this Chapter.

The following repair procedures are based on the assumption that the engine is refitted in the vehicle. If the engine has been removed from the vehicle and mounted on a stand, many of the steps outlined in this Part of Chapter 2 will not apply.

The Specifications included in this Part of Chapter 2 apply only to the procedures contained in this Part. Additional Specifications necessary for removing and overhauling the engine are found in Part E.

2 Repair operations possible with the engine in the vehicle

Many major repair operations can be accomplished without removing the engine from the vehicle.

Clean the engine compartment and the exterior of the engine with some type of pressure washer before any work is done. It will

3.4 Mark the distributor housing (arrow) directly below the number one cylinder spark plug wire terminal in the distributor cap

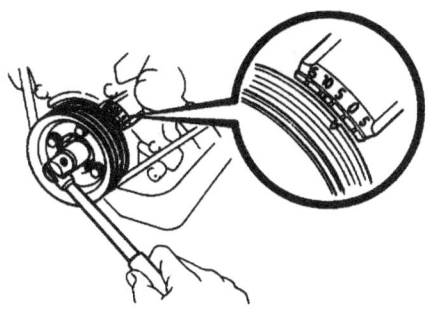

3.6 When the notch in the pulley is aligned with the zero on the timing plate as shown here and the rotor is pointing at the number one cylinder spark plug wire terminal in the distributor cap, the number one piston is at TDC on the compression stroke

make the job easier and help keep dirt out of the internal areas of the engine.

Remove the bonnet, if necessary, to improve access to the engine as repairs are performed (refer to Chapter 11 if necessary).

If vacuum, exhaust, oil or coolant leaks develop, indicating a need for gasket or seal renewal, the repairs can generally be made with the engine in the vehicle. The intake and exhaust manifold gaskets, cylinder head cover gaskets, sump gasket, crankshaft oil seals and cylinder head gaskets are all accessible with the engine in place.

Exterior engine components, such as the intake and exhaust manifolds, the sump (and the oil pump), the water pump, the starter motor, the alternator, the distributor and the fuel system components can be removed for repair with the engine in place.

Since the cylinder heads can be removed without pulling the engine, valve component servicing can also be accomplished with the engine in the vehicle. Renewal of the timing belt and sprockets is also possible with the engine in the vehicle.

In extreme cases caused by a lack of necessary equipment, repair or renewal of piston rings, pistons, connecting rods and rod bearings is possible with the engine in the vehicle. However, this practice is not recommended because of the cleaning and preparation work that must be done to the components involved.

3 Top Dead Centre (TDC) for number one piston - locating

Refer to illustrations 3.4 and 3.6

1 Top Dead Centre (TDC) is the highest point in the cylinder that each piston reaches as it travels up-and-down when the crankshaft turns. Each piston reaches TDC on the compression stroke and again on the exhaust stroke, but TDC generally refers to piston position on the compression stroke. The tim-

ing marks on the vibration damper refitted on the front of the crankshaft are referenced to the number one piston at TDC on the compression stroke.

2 Positioning the piston(s) at TDC is an essential part of many procedures such as cylinder head removal, timing belt and sprocket renewal and distributor removal.

3 In order to bring any piston to TDC, the crankshaft must be turned using one of the methods outlined below. When looking at the front of the engine, normal crankshaft rotation is clockwise. **Warning:** *Before beginning this procedure, be sure to place the transmission in Neutral and unplug the wire connector at the distributor to disable the ignition system.*

a) *The preferred method is to turn the crankshaft with a large socket and breaker bar attached to the vibration damper bolt threaded into the front of the crankshaft.*

b) *A remote starter switch, which may save some time, can also be used. Attach the switch leads to the S (switch) and B (battery) terminals on the starter solenoid. Once the piston is close to TDC, use a socket and breaker bar as described in the previous paragraph.*

c) *If an assistant is available to turn the ignition switch to the Start position in short bursts, you can get the piston close to TDC without a remote starter switch. Use a socket and breaker bar as described in Paragraph a) to complete the procedure.*

4 Make a mark on the distributor housing directly below the number one spark plug wire terminal on the distributor cap **(see illustration)**.

5 Remove the distributor cap as described in Chapter 1.

6 Turn the crankshaft (see Paragraph 3 above) until the line on the vibration damper is aligned with the zero mark on the timing plate **(see illustration)**. The timing plate and vibration damper are located low on the front of the

engine, combined with the pulley that turns the drivebelt.

7 The rotor should now be pointing directly at the mark on the distributor housing. If it isn't, the piston is at TDC on the exhaust stroke.

8 To get the piston to TDC on the compression stroke, turn the crankshaft one complete turn (360°) clockwise. The rotor should now be pointing at the mark. When the rotor is pointing at the number one spark plug wire terminal in the distributor cap (which is indicated by the mark on the housing) and the ignition timing marks are aligned, the number one piston is at TDC on the compression stroke.

9 After the number one piston has been positioned at TDC on the compression stroke, TDC for any of the remaining cylinders can be located by turning the crankshaft 120° at a time and following the firing order (refer to the Specifications).

4 Cylinder head covers - removal and refitting

1 Disconnect the negative cable from the battery.

Removal

Right side cover

Refer to illustration 4.3

2 Remove the air intake chamber and related components as described in Chapter 4.

3 Remove the mounting bolts **(see illustration)**.

4 Detach the cover from the head. **Caution:** *If the cover is stuck to the head, bump one end with a block of wood and a hammer to jar it loose. If that doesn't work, try to slip a flexible putty knife between the head and cover to break the gasket seal. Don't prise at the cover-to-head joint or damage to the sealing surfaces may occur (leading to oil leaks in the future).*

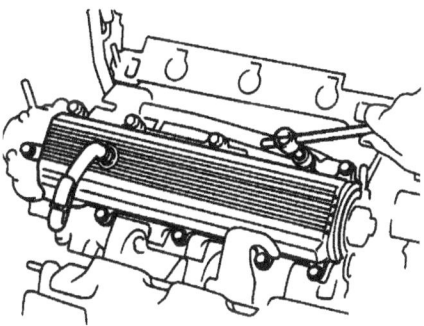

4.3 The cylinder head covers are held in place with several bolts around the edge

4.5 Detach the air intake tube and breather hose (arrow) before attempting to remove the left side cylinder head cover

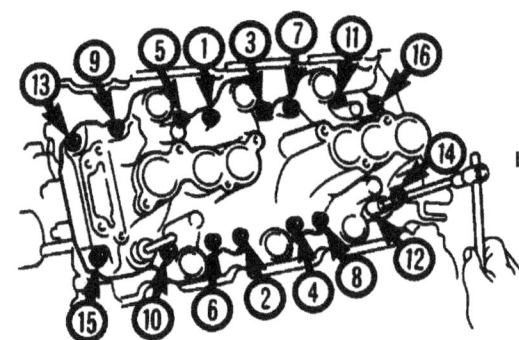

5.12 Tighten the inlet manifold bolts/nuts from the centre out in a criss-cross pattern

Left side cover

Refer to illustration 4.5

5   Remove the breather hose from the cover **(see illustration)**.

6   Remove the air cleaner-to-throttle body tube (Chapter 4A).

7   Remove the engine wire brackets that overlap the cover.

8   Remove the mounting bolts and lift off the cover. Read the **Caution** in Step 4.

Refitting

9   The mating surfaces of each cylinder head and cover must be perfectly clean when the covers are refitted. Use a gasket scraper to remove all traces of sealant and old gasket material, then clean the mating surfaces with lacquer thinner or acetone. If there's sealant or oil on the mating surfaces when the cover is refitted, oil leaks may develop.

10   Clean the mounting bolt threads with a die to remove any corrosion and restore damaged threads. Make sure the threaded holes in the head are clean - run a tap into them to remove corrosion and restore damaged threads.

11   Position a new gasket on the cylinder head.

12   Carefully position the cover on the head and refit the bolts.

13   Tighten the bolts in three or four steps until they're snug. Don't overtighten them or oil leaks could develop.

14   The remaining refitting steps are the reverse of removal.

15   Start the engine and check carefully for oil leaks as the engine warms up.

---

5   Inlet manifold - removal and refitting

Removal

1   Remove the air intake chamber (Chapter 4).

2   Disconnect the negative cable from the battery.

3   Drain the cooling system (Chapter 1).

4   Remove any remaining hoses, wires or cables attached to the manifold or its components.

5   Loosen the manifold mounting bolts/nuts in 1/4-turn increments until they can be removed by hand.

6   The manifold will probably be stuck to the cylinder heads and force may be required to break the gasket seal. **Caution:** *Don't prise between the manifold and the heads or damage to the gasket sealing surfaces may occur, leading to vacuum leaks.*

Refitting

Refer to illustration 5.12

Note: *The mating surfaces of the cylinder heads and manifold must be perfectly clean when the manifold is refitted. Gasket removal solvents in aerosol cans are available at most auto parts stores and may be helpful when removing old gasket material that's stuck to the heads and manifold (since they're made of aluminium, aggressive scraping can cause damage). Be sure to follow the directions printed on the container.*

7   Use a gasket scraper to remove all traces of sealant and old gasket material, then clean the mating surfaces with lacquer thinner or acetone. If there's old sealant or oil on the mating surfaces when the manifold is refitted, oil or vacuum leaks may develop. Use a vacuum cleaner to remove any material that falls into the intake ports in the heads.

8   Use a tap of the correct size to chase the threads in the bolt holes, then use compressed air (if available) to remove the debris from the holes. **Warning:** *Wear safety glasses or a face shield to protect your eyes when using compressed air!*

9   Position the gaskets on the cylinder heads. No sealant is required; however, follow the instructions included with the new gaskets.

10   Make sure all intake port openings, coolant passage holes and bolt holes are aligned correctly.

11   Carefully set the manifold in place. **Caution:** *Don't disturb the gaskets.*

12   Refit the bolts/nuts and tighten them to the specified torque following the recommended sequence **(see illustration)**. Work

up to the final torque in two steps.

13   The remaining refitting steps are the reverse of removal. Start the engine and check carefully for oil and coolant leaks at the inlet manifold joints.

---

6   Exhaust manifolds - removal and refitting

---

1   Disconnect the negative cable from the battery.

2   Raise the vehicle and support it securely on jackstands.

3   Working underneath the vehicle, unbolt the exhaust pipes from the manifold(s) (Chapter 4A).

4   Unbolt the exhaust crossover pipe and the manifold heat shield(s).

5   If you're removing the *left* manifold, detach the air cleaner-to-throttle body tube.

6   If you're removing the *right* manifold, detach the EGR tube and air suction reed valve (see Chapter 6).

7   Apply penetrating oil to the threads, then remove the mounting nuts and detach the manifold from the head.

8   Prior to refitting of either manifold, clean all gasket mating surfaces.

9   Fit a new gasket on the studs.

10   Refit the manifold and tighten the nuts to the specified torque. Work from the centre of the manifold to the ends in a spiral pattern.

11   Refitting of the remaining components is the reverse of removal.

---

7   Vibration damper - removal and refitting

Refer to illustration 7.6

1   Disconnect the negative cable from the battery.

2   Remove the fan shroud and radiator (Chapter 3).

3   Remove the drivebelts (Chapter 1).

4   Remove the bolts and detach the power steering pump pulley.

5   Remove the starter bolts and push the starter away from the flywheel gear. Wedge a lever between the flywheel/driveplate teeth to prevent the crankshaft from turning while loosening the large vibration damper bolt.

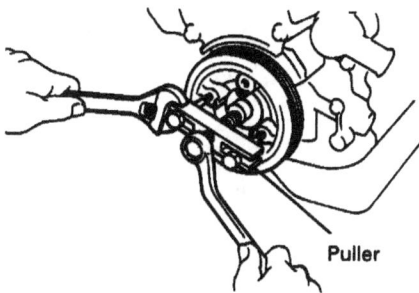

7.6 Use the recommended puller to remove the vibration damper - if a puller that applies force to the outer edge is used, the damper may be damaged!

6   Leave the damper bolt in place to provide the gear puller with something to push against. Use a puller to remove the damper **(see illustration). Caution:** *Don't use a puller with jaws that grip the outer edge of the damper! The puller must be the type shown in the illustration that utilises bolts to apply force to the damper hub only.*
7   To refit the damper, position it on the nose of the crankshaft, align the keyway and refit the bolt. Tighten the bolt to the specified torque.
8   The remaining refitting steps are the reverse of the removal procedure.

8   Timing belt – removal and refitting

Removal

Refer to illustrations 8.9, 8.11, 8.13, 8.15, 8.16 and 8.17

1   Disconnect the negative cable from the battery.
2   Remove the radiator and shroud as described in Chapter 3.
3   On vehicles so equipped, remove the power steering pulley and drivebelt (see Chapter 10) and unbolt the pump from the brackets without disconnecting the hoses. Set the pump aside.

4   Remove the spark plugs (see Chapter 1).
5   Disconnect the air hoses from the air pipe.
6   Remove the water outlet from the front of the engine.
7   On air-conditioned models, remove the compressor drivebelt (see Chapter 1).
8   Detach the alternator drivebelt, belt guide and fan pulley (see Chapter 5). Remove the fan/clutch assembly (see Chapter 3).
9   Detach the spark plug wire looms from the top edge of the no. 2 timing belt cover, then remove the bolts and detach the cover **(see illustration).**
10   Position the number one piston at TDC

on the compression stroke (see Section 3). **Caution:** *Once this has been done, DO NOT turn the crankshaft until the sprockets and timing belt have been refitted!*
11   Be sure that the marks on the camshaft sprockets and rear timing belt cover are aligned **(see illustration).**
12   If the crankshaft sprocket marks are In alignment but the camshaft sprocket marks are not, rotate the crankshaft two complete revolutions and recheck the marks.
13   Remove the fan pulley bracket **(see illustration).**
14   Remove the crankshaft pulley, vibration damper (see Section 7) and the number one timing belt cover.

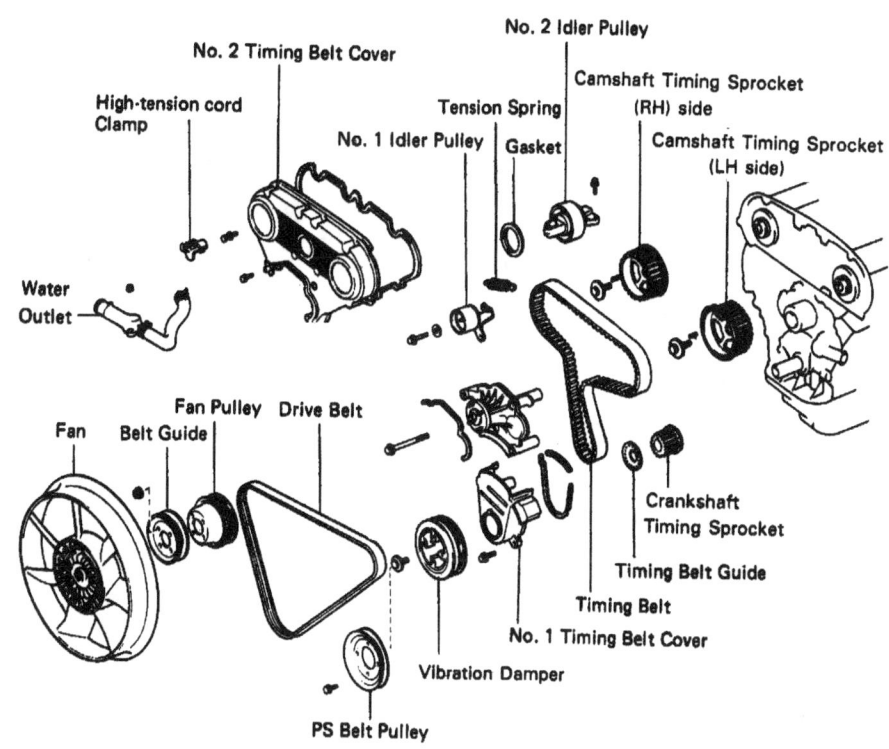

8.9 Timing belt and related components - exploded view

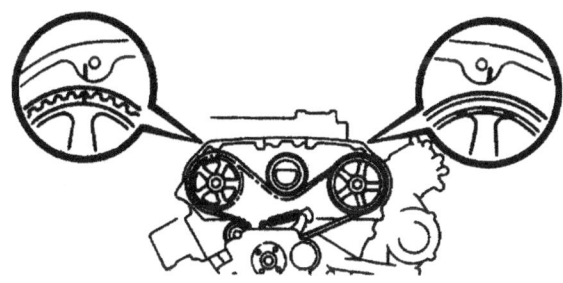

8.11 Align the marks on the rear cover with the marks on the sprockets before removing the belt

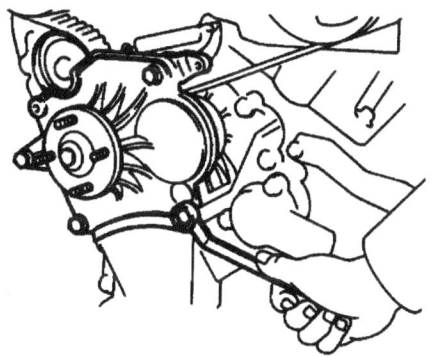

8.13 Remove the fan pulley bracket

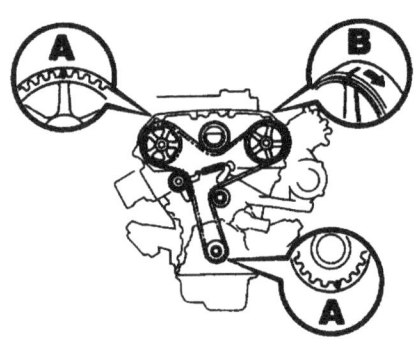

8.15 Make match marks on the belt and sprockets (A) and apply an arrow (B) to the timing belt indicating normal direction of rotation

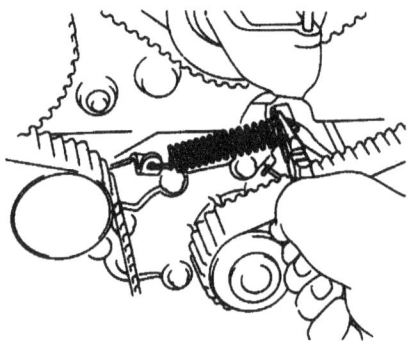

8.16 Detach the tension spring with a pair of needle nose pliers

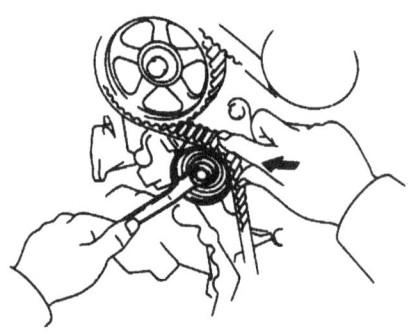

8.17 Loosen the idler pulley bolt and shift the pulley to the left as far as possible

15   If the timing belt is to be reused, mark the belt position at each camshaft sprocket, mark the belt at the crankshaft sprocket and apply an arrow indicating the direction of rotation **(see illustration)**.
16   Remove the timing belt guide and tension spring **(see illustration)**.
17   To relieve the timing belt tension, loosen the bolt and shift the idler pulley to the left as far as it will go, then temporarily retighten the bolt **(see illustration)**.
18   Slip the timing belt off the sprockets. If you plan to reuse the belt, check it carefully for wear and damage and make sure it hasn't been contaminated with oil, fuel or coolant. Don't twist, bend or turn the belt inside out. **Caution:** *It's a very good idea to fit a new belt rather than reuse the old one, regardless of it's condition. If the belt fails during engine operation, extensive damage may occur!*

Inspection

Refer to illustrations 8.19 and 8.20

19   Check the idler and fan pulley bearings to see if they turn smoothly **(see illustration)**.
20   Measure the free length of the tension spring **(see illustration)**. Compare your measurements with this Chapter's Specifications. Renew the spring if it's not as specified.

8.19 Check the idler bearings for smooth operation

Refitting

Refer to illustrations 8.21, 8.22, 8.24, 8.26, 8.27a, 8.27b and 8.28

21   Align the groove in the crankshaft sprocket with the mark on the oil pump **(see illustration)**.
22   Align the camshaft sprocket timing marks with the marks on the rear (no. 3) timing belt cover **(see illustration)**.
23   Refit the timing belt over the camshaft sprockets, idler pulleys, fan pulley and crankshaft sprocket. **Note:** *If the old belt is being refitted, align the marks made during removal*

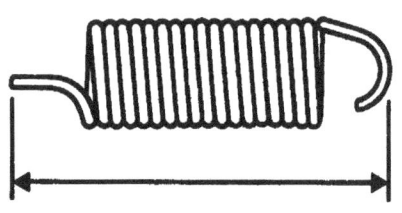

8.20 Measure the tension spring free length

and make sure the arrow **(see illustration 8.15)** *is pointing in the direction of crankshaft rotation (clockwise).*
24   Loosen the idler pulley bolt and prise the idler pulley to the right, as far as it will go, then temporarily tighten the bolt **(see illustration)**.
25   Refit the tension spring and loosen the idler pulley bolt slightly to allow the tension spring to tension the idler.
26   Refit the damper bolt and rotate the crankshaft clockwise, two complete revolutions **(see illustration)**.
27   Recheck the timing mark alignment **(see illustration)**. If the marks aren't aligned exactly as shown, the timing belt will have to be removed, the pulleys realigned, the belt refitted and the check redone. Once you are

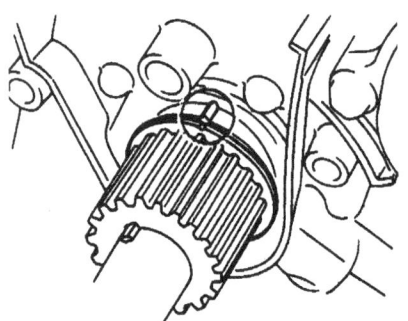

8.21 Align the groove in the crankshaft sprocket with the mark on the oil pump

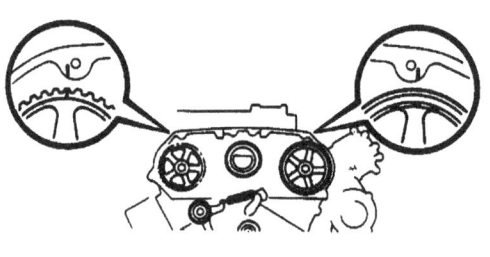

8.22 Align the marks on the camshaft sprockets with the stationary marks on the rear timing belt cover

8.24 Loosen the bolt and prise the idler pulley to the right, then tighten the bolt

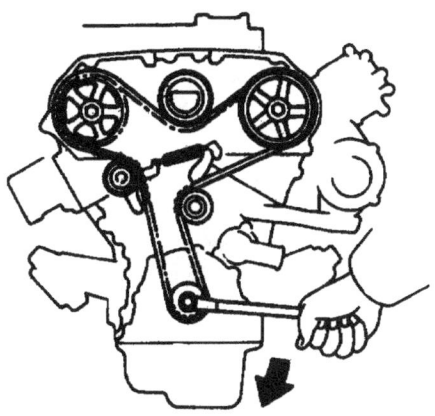

8.26 Slowly turn the crankshaft through two complete revolutions . . .

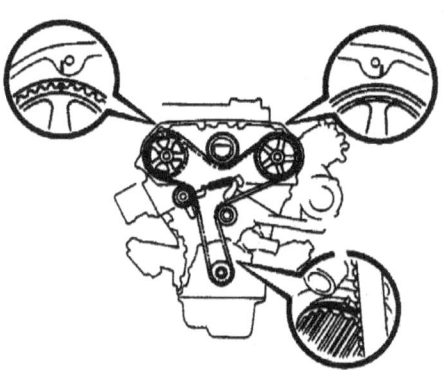

8.27a . . . then recheck the alignment of the marks - after exactly two revolutions, they should be aligned as shown here

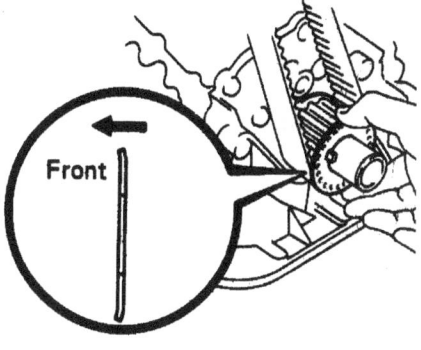

8.27b Be sure the curved lip on the timing belt guide faces away from the belt

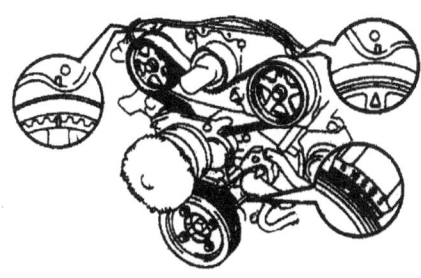

8.28 Recheck the alignment of the timing marks - after two revolutions, they should be aligned as shown here

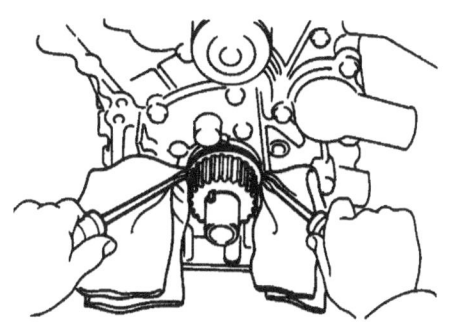

9.3 Cushion the oil pump housing with shop rags, then carefully prise the sprocket off the end of the crankshaft (a puller may be needed)

9.6 Prise out the seal with a screwdriver - be careful not to scratch or nick the crankshaft!

satisfied the belt is refitted properly, tighten the idler/tensioner pulley bolt to the torque listed in this Chapter's specifications, remove the crankshaft damper bolt and refit the timing belt guide (see illustration), the number one timing cover and the fan pulley bracket. Refit the vibration damper and tighten the damper bolt to the torque listed in this Chapter's Specifications.

28 Using the damper bolt, rotate the crankshaft clockwise two complete revolutions. Recheck the timing mark alignment (see illustration). If the marks aren't aligned exactly as shown, the belt will have to be removed, the pulleys realigned and the check redone.

29 Refit the remaining components in the reverse order of removal.

9 Crankshaft front oil seal - renewal

Refer to illustrations 9.3, 9.6, 9.7 and 9.8

1 Disconnect the negative cable from the battery.

2 Remove the fan shroud and radiator (Chapter 3), drivebelts (Chapter 1), vibration

damper (Section 7) and timing belt (Section 8).

3 Wedge two screwdrivers behind the crankshaft sprocket (see illustration). Carefully prise the sprocket off the crankshaft. Some timing belt sprockets can be pried off easily with screwdrivers. Others are more difficult to remove because corrosion fuses them to the nose of the crankshaft. If the sprocket on your engine is difficult to prise off, don't try to get it all the way off with screwdrivers. instead, slide it off just far enough to grip it with a puller.

4 Once there's enough space between the sprocket and the oil pump housing to refit a small gear puller, thread the vibration damper bolt into the nose of the crankshaft and refit the puller. The bolt provides something solid for the puller screw to push against and protects the crankshaft threads.

5 Turn the bolt of the puller until the sprocket comes off.

6 Carefully prise the oil seal out with a screwdriver (see illustration). Don't scratch or nick the crankshaft in the process!

7 Before refitting, apply assembly lube or grease to the inside of the seal (see illustration).

8 Clean the bore in the oil pump housing

and coat the outer edge of the new seal with grease. Using a socket with an outside diameter slightly smaller than the outside diameter of the seal, carefully drive the seal into place

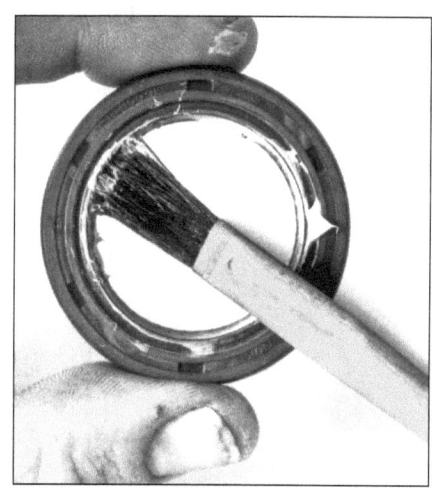

9.7 Coat the seal lip with grease . . .

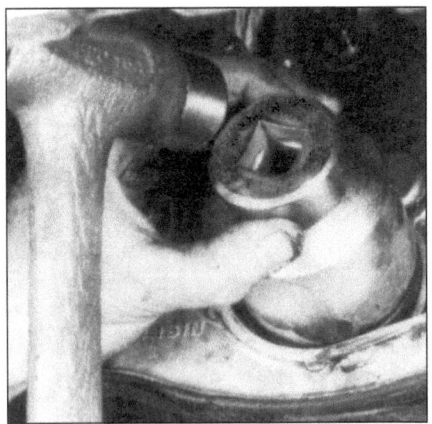

9.8 . . . then drive the new seal into the opening with a large socket and hammer - DO NOT damage the seal in the process!

10.3 Use the special tool when loosening the sprocket bolt - DO NOT use the timing belt to prevent the sprocket from moving!

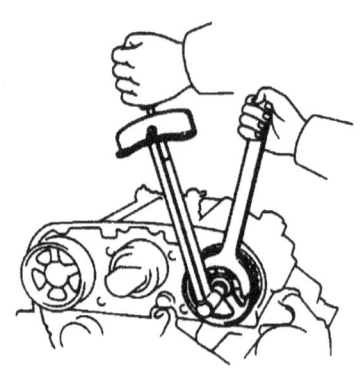

10.6 Be sure to tighten the sprocket bolt with a torque wrench - note the special tool used to hold the sprocket

with a hammer **(see illustration)**. If a socket isn't available, a short section of pipe will also work.

9   Make sure the Woodruff key is in place in the crankshaft.

10   Apply a thin coat of assembly lube to the inside of the crankshaft sprocket and slide it onto the crankshaft. If necessary, tap it into place with a section of pipe and a hammer.

11   Refitting of the remaining components is the reverse of removal. Tighten all bolts to the specified torque.

10   Camshaft oil seal - renewal

Refer to illustrations 10.3 and 10.6

Note: *Renew both camshaft oil seals at the same time. If one seal has failed, the other one will probably fail soon.*

1   Remove the timing belt as described in Section 8.

2   To remove the camshaft sprockets a special holding tool is needed (Toyota no. SST 09278-54012 or equivalent). **Caution:** *Don't use the timing belt to keep the camshaft from turning when loosening or tightening the*

sprocket bolts!

3   While holding the sprocket with the special tool, remove the mounting bolt **(see illustration)** and detach the sprocket. **Note:** *Do one side at a time so the sprockets don't get mixed up.*

4   Using a screwdriver or seal removal tool, carefully prise the seal out of the housing. Don't nick or scratch the camshaft in the process. Clean the bore in the housing.

5   To fit the new seal, first apply multi-purpose grease to the outer edge and the seal lip, then use a length of pipe or large socket and a hammer to tap the new seal into place.

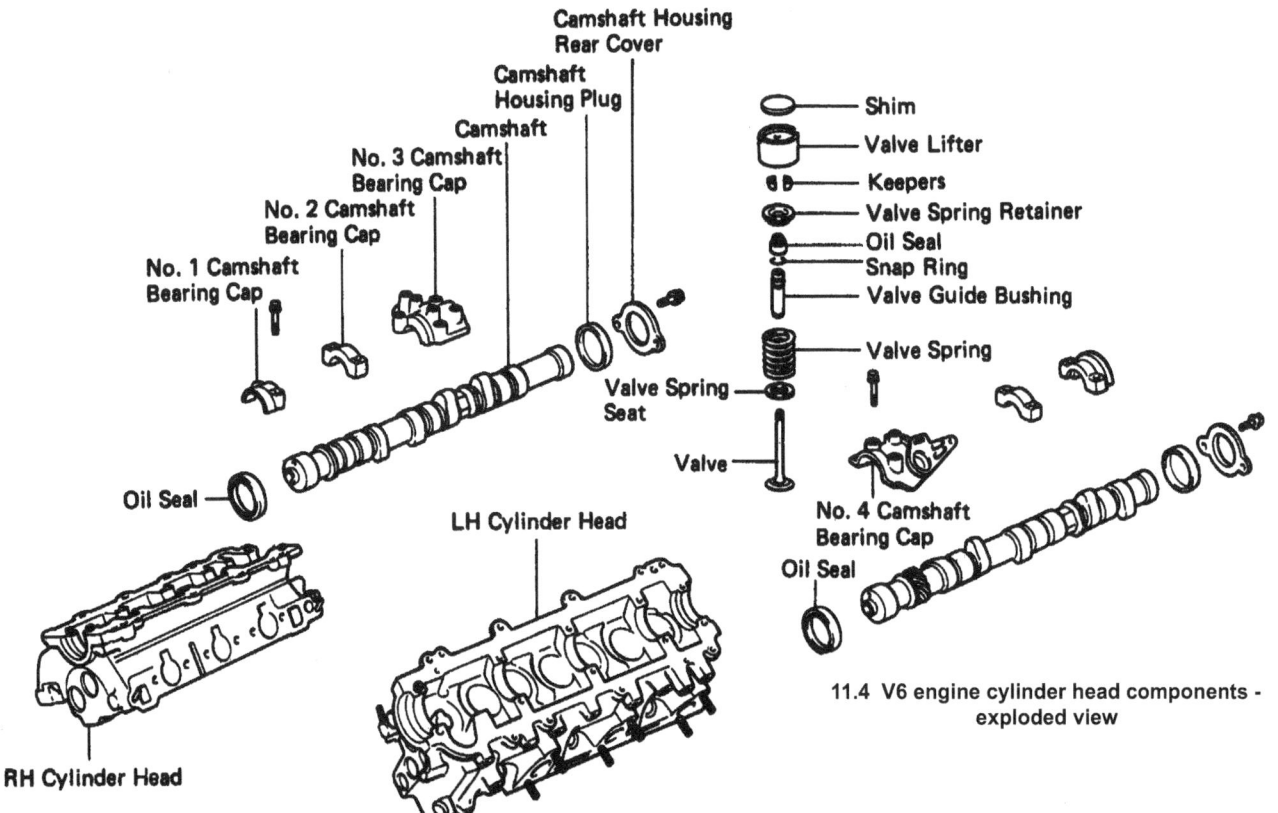

11.4 V6 engine cylinder head components - exploded view

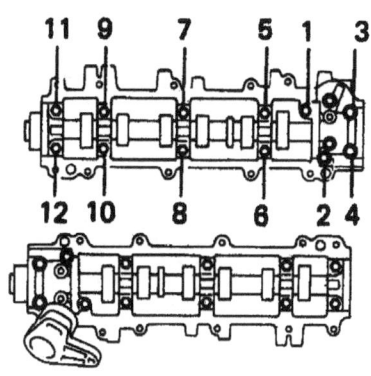

11.5 LOOSEN the camshaft bearing cap bolts a little at a time in the sequence shown here

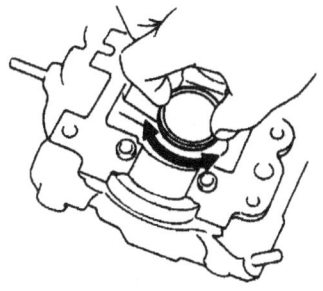

11.8 Turn the lifters back-and-forth while pulling them out

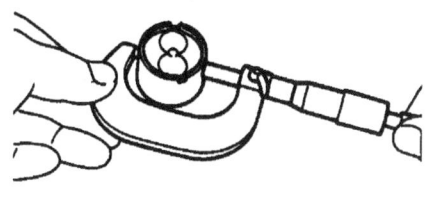

11.10a Measure the lifter diameter at several points . . .

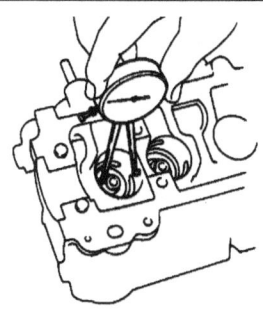

11.10b . . . then measure the corresponding lifter bore inside diameter - subtract the lifter diameter from the bore diameter to obtain the clearance

11.14 Lay a strip of Plastigage on each camshaft bearing journal, parallel to the camshaft centre-line

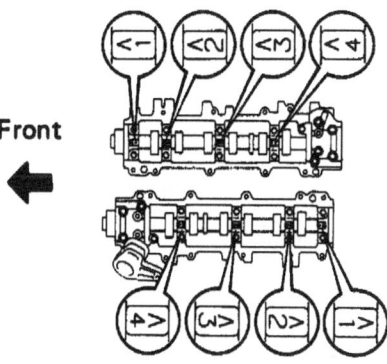

11.15 Refit the bearing caps with the arrow on each cap pointing toward the front (RH head) or rear (LH head)

Be sure the seal is seated properly.

6   Refit the sprocket(s) and tighten the bolt(s) to the specified torque **(see illustration)**.

7   Refit the timing belt and related parts, following the procedure outlined in Section 8.

8   Run the engine and check for oil leaks.

11 Camshafts and lifters - removal, inspection and refitting

Removal

Refer to illustrations 11.4, 11.5 and 11.8

1   Remove the cylinder head cover(s) as described in Section 4.

2   Remove the timing belt (see Section 8).

3   Remove the camshaft sprockets as described in Section 10.

4   Remove the two bolts and detach the rear cover(s) **(see illustration)**.

5   Loosen the bearing cap bolts in 1/4-turn increments. Follow the factory recommended sequence **(see illustration)**.

6   Remove the camshaft bearing caps, camshaft housing plug and oil seal, then lift out the camshaft **(see illustration 11.4)**.

7   Obtain a divided storage container, such as an empty egg carton, for the valve lifters

and shims. Mark the container so the lifters will be returned to their original locations during refitting.

8   Grasp each lifter and work it back-and-forth while pulling it out **(see illustration)**. Store the lifters and shims in the divided container.

Inspection

Refer to illustrations 11.10a, 11.10b, 11.14, 11.15, 11.16, 11.17 and 11.19

9   Clean the lifters and shims with solvent and dry them thoroughly without mixing them up.

10   Check each lifter wall, shim and shim seat for scuffing, score marks and uneven wear. Measure the diameter of each lifter and the corresponding lifter bore in the head **(see illustrations)**. Compare the results to the Specifications.

11   Clean the camshaft and bearing caps with solvent and dry them. Inspect the bearing journals for uneven wear, pitting and evidence of seizure. The camshaft runout should also be checked (to determine if it's bent). This measurement requires a special jig (or V-blocks) and a dial indicator, so it should be done by an automotive machine shop.

12   If the bearing journals appear to be in good condition, measure them with a micrometer to determine their sizes and whether or not they're out-of-round.

13   Using a micrometer, measure the cam

lobe height. Compare the results to the Specifications.

14   To measure camshaft bearing oil clearance, place the camshaft in the cylinder head dry (without lubrication). Don't refit the lifters. Place a strip of Plastigage across each bearing journal **(see illustration)**.

15   Refit the bearing caps with the arrow on each cap pointing toward the front (RH head) or rear (LH head) and in numerical order from front-to-rear **(see illustration)**.

16   Refit and tighten the cap bolts following the recommended sequence **(see illustration)**. Work up to the specified torque in three

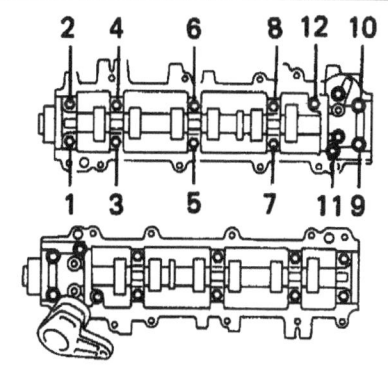

11.16 Camshaft bearing cap bolt TIGHTENING sequence

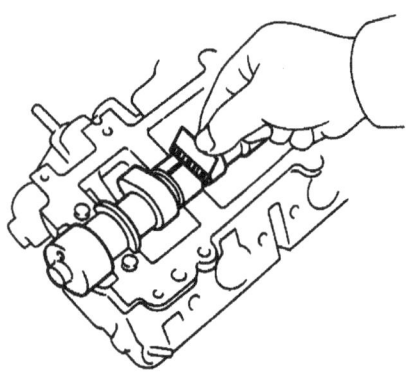

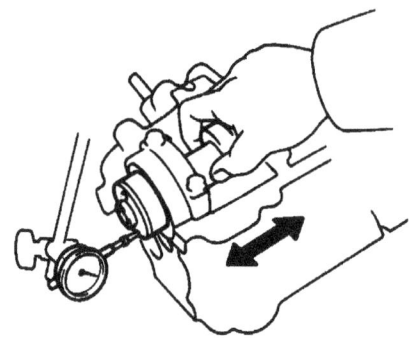

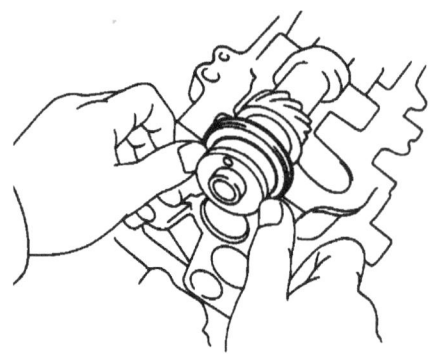

11.17 Compare the width of the crushed Plastigage to the scale on the Plastigage envelope to obtain the clearance - be sure to use the correct scale (inch and metric scales are included)

11.19 Move the camshaft back-and forth and read the end play on the dial indicator

11.22 Before refitting the camshafts, slip the oil seals into place . . .

steps. **Caution:** *DO NOT turn the camshaft at any time during this procedure!*

17   Remove the caps and measure the Plastigage at its widest point **(see illustration)**. Compare the readings to the Specifications.

18   Remove the Plastigage with a fingernail or the edge of a credit card. Lubricate the journals with camshaft refitting lube and refit the bearing caps.

19   Using a dial indicator, check the end play by moving the camshaft back-and-forth **(see illustration)**. Compare the measurement to the Specifications.

20   If any parts fail the inspection, renew them as necessary.

Refitting

Refer to illustrations 11.22 and 11.23

21   The lifters and shims must be returned to their original bores. Coat them with moly-base grease or engine assembly lube and refit them in the head.

22   Coat the camshaft and the lip of the new seal with camshaft refitting assembly lube. Place the camshaft in the head. Refit the oil seal **(see illustration)** and camshaft housing plug.

23   Apply a bead of sealant (Toyota no. 08826-00080 or equivalent) to the number one and three bearing caps **(see illustration)**. Refit the bearing caps immediately and tighten the bolts as described in Steps 15 and 16.

24   Compare the valve clearances to the Specifications. See Chapter 1 for the valve adjustment procedure.

25   Refit the timing belt and sprockets as described in Sections 8 and 10.

26   Refit the remaining parts in the reverse order of removal.

12   Cylinder heads - removal and refitting

Removal

Refer to illustrations 12.11, 12.12, 12.17, 12.20, 12.25 and 12.26

1   Relieve the fuel system pressure as described in Chapter 4A.

2   Disconnect the negative cable from the battery.

3   Remove the air cleaner hose and case (see Chapter 4A).

4   Drain the coolant from the radiator and

block (see Chapter 1).

5   Remove the radiator (see Chapter 3).

6   If you're removing the right head, detach the power steering pump (see Chapter 10).

7   Remove the air conditioning drivebelt, if equipped (see Chapter 1).

8   Remove the cooling fan/clutch assembly and pulley (see Chapter 3), then remove the drivebelt.

9   Clearly label, then disconnect the wires, fuel lines and coolant, vacuum and emissions hoses that run between the cylinder heads and/or manifolds and the body.

10   Detach the throttle cable, transmission cable (automatic transmission only) and cruise control cable (if equipped) from the throttle body. Refer to Chapter 4A for additional information

11   On manual transmission equipped models, disconnect the clutch release cylinder hose **(see illustration)**. Place a drain pan under it to catch the fluid.

12   Disconnect the exhaust crossover pipe **(see illustration)** from the exhaust manifolds.

13   Remove the timing belt as described in Section 8.

14   Remove the distributor (Chapter 5) and the spark plug wires (Chapter 1).

15   Remove the air intake chamber (see Chapter 4A).

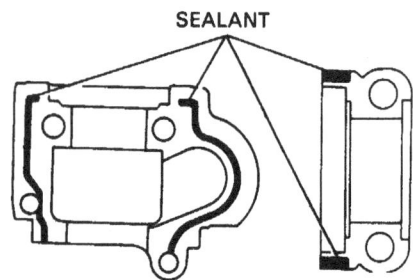

11.23 . . . and apply sealant to the number one and three caps

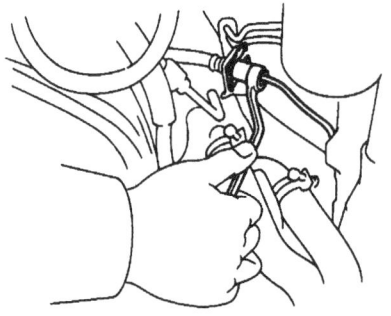

12.11 Disconnect the clutch release cylinder hose at the rear of the engine

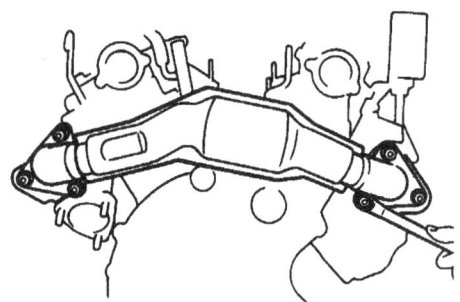

12.12 The crossover pipe, viewed here from the firewall looking forward, connects both exhaust manifolds

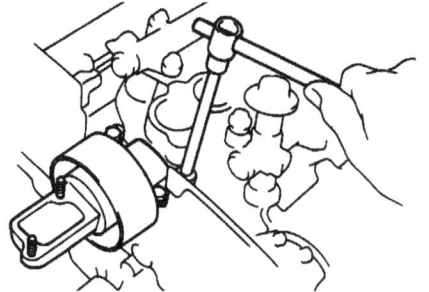

12.17 Unbolt the upper timing belt idler pulley

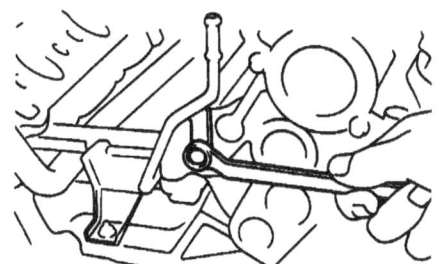

12.20 Remove the coolant bypass pipe

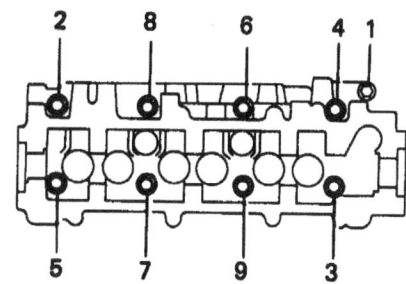

12.25 Cylinder head bolt LOOSENING sequence

16   Unbolt and remove the rear centre (no. 4) timing belt cover.
17   Remove the upper (no. 2) idler pulley **(see illustration)**.
18   Remove the rear main (no. 3) timing belt cover.
19   Remove the inlet manifold (see Section 5).
20   Unbolt the coolant bypass tube from the front of the left cylinder head **(see illustration)**.
21   If you're removing the left cylinder head, remove the alternator (see Chapter 5) and unbolt the dipstick tube.
22   The exhaust manifold(s) may be removed at this point, if desired (see Section 6). The cylinder heads will be easier to remove if the manifolds are detached.
23   Remove the cylinder head cover(s) as described in Section 4.
24   Remove the camshaft(s), following the procedure outlined in Section 11.
25   Using a 12-point socket and a breaker bar, loosen the head bolts in 1/4-turn increments until they can be removed by hand. Follow the factory recommended sequence **(see illustration). Caution:** *The head could warp or crack if the sequence isn't followed.*
26   Remove the cylinder head(s). If resistance is felt, double-check to make sure all bolts have been removed, then try to dislodge the head by striking it with a wood block and hammer. If levering is required, be very careful not to damage the head or block gasket surfaces **(see illustration)**.
27   Refer to Section 11 for the camshaft and lifter removal and refitting procedure. Cyl-

inder head disassembly, inspection and reassembly should be carried out by an engine machine shop.

Refitting

Refer to illustrations 12.32, 12.33 and 12.34
28   The mating surfaces of the cylinder head(s) and block must be perfectly clean when the head is refitted. Use a gasket scraper to remove all traces of carbon and old gasket material, then clean the mating surfaces with lacquer thinner or acetone. If there's oil on the mating surfaces when the head is refitted, the gasket may not seal correctly and leaks may develop. Use a vacuum cleaner to remove any debris that falls into the cylinders.
29   Check the block and head mating surfaces for nicks, deep scratches and other damage. If damage is slight, it can be removed with a file - if it's excessive, machining may be the only alternative.
30   Use a tap of the correct size to chase the threads in the head bolt holes. Remove the debris with compressed air. **Warning:** *Wear eye protection when using compressed air! Mount each bolt in a vice and run a die down the threads to remove corrosion and restore damaged threads. Dirt, corrosion, sealant and damaged threads will affect torque readings.*
31   Position a new head gasket on the engine block.
32   Lightly oil the head bolts, then refit them in their original locations. Using a 12-point socket, tighten the bolts to the Specified torque in three steps. Follow the recom-

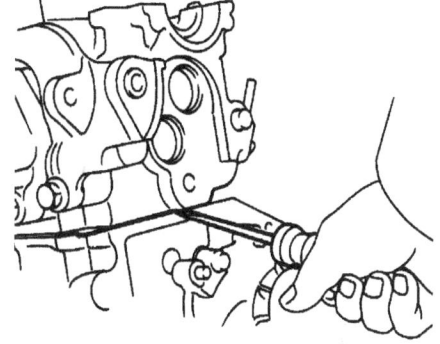

12.26 Prise only on the cast protrusions to dislodge the cylinder head - DO NOT prise between the gasket surfaces!

mended sequence **(see illustration)**. Don't tighten bolt A at this time.
33   Apply a dab of paint to the front of each head bolt (except bolt A) **(see illustration)**.
34   Following the same tightening sequence, turn each head bolt an additional 90° (1/4-turn) **(see illustration)**.
35   As a final step, turn each bolt yet another 90° (1/4-turn), so that each numbered head bolt has been turned a total of 180° (1/2-turn).
36   Tighten bolt A.
37   Refit the remaining parts in the reverse order of removal.
38   Change the oil and filter (see Chapter 1) and check all fluid levels. Run the engine and check for leaks and proper operation.

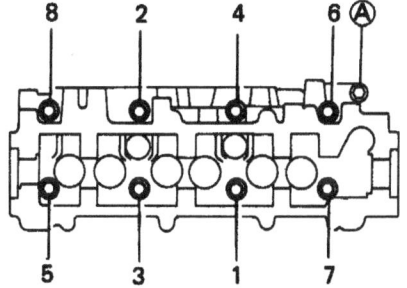

12.32 Cylinder head bolt TIGHTENING sequence

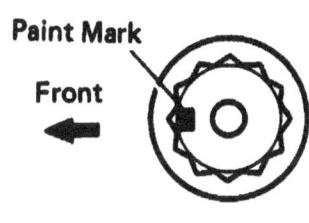

12.33 Apply a dab of paint to the front of each head bolt . . .

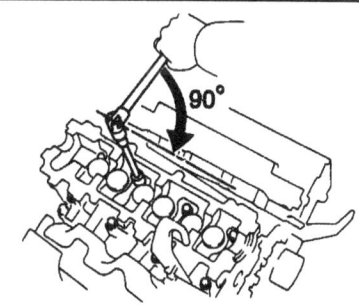

12.34 . . . so you can tell when they have been turned an additional 180-degrees total (in two 90-degree steps)

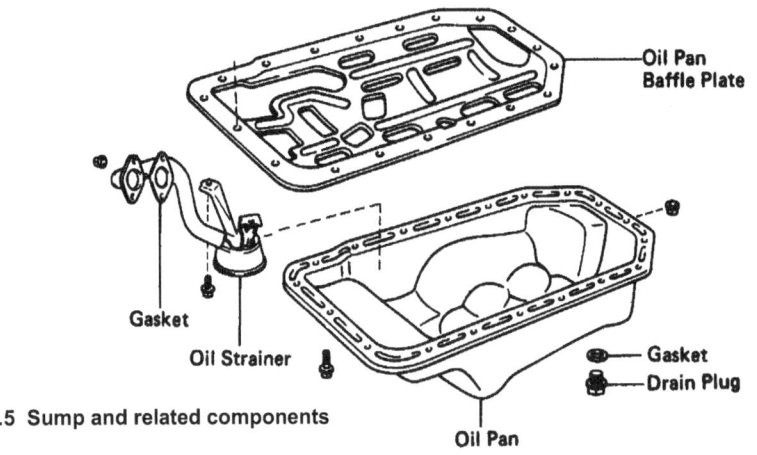

13.5 Sump and related components

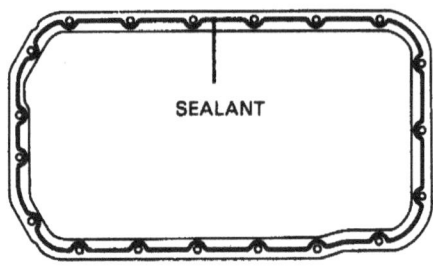

13.8 Apply sealant to the sump (and baffle) flanges - make sure it goes around the inside of the bolt holes

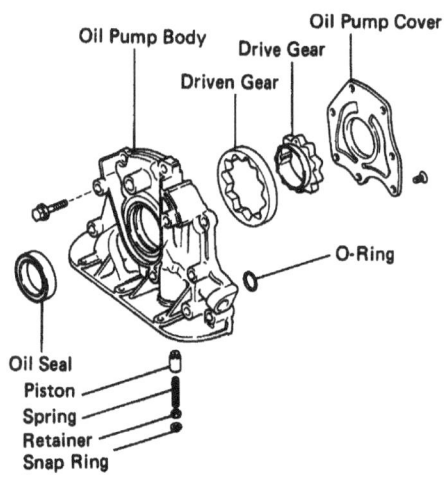

14.3 Oil pump components - exploded view

13 Sump - removal and refitting

Refer to illustrations 13.5 and 13.8

1   Disconnect the negative cable from the battery.
2   Raise the vehicle and support it securely on jackstands.
3   Remove the undercover (belly-pan).
4   Drain the engine oil (Chapter 1).
5   Remove the bolts and detach the sump. Don't prise between the pan and the block or damage to the sealing surfaces may result and oil leaks could develop. If the pan is stuck, dislodge it with a block of wood and a hammer. Detach the baffle plate from the sump **(see illustration)**.
6   Use a gasket scraper to remove all traces of old sealant from the pan and block. Clean the mating surfaces with lacquer thinner or acetone.
7   Make sure the holes in the block are clean (use a tap to remove any sealant or corrosion from the threads).
8   Apply sealant (Toyota no. 08826-00080 or equivalent) to the sump mating surface, then position the baffle plate on the pan and apply sealant to the baffle plate-to-block mating surface (a 3 mm wide bead should be sufficient) **(see illustration)**.
9   Position the pan against the block and refit the bolts. Tighten the bolts in three or four steps, working from the centre of the pan

toward the ends in a spiral pattern.
10   The remaining refitting steps are the reverse of removal.

14 Oil pump - removal, inspection and refitting

Removal

Refer to illustration 14.3

1   Remove the timing belt as described in Section 8. Remove the crankshaft sprocket (Section 9).
2   Remove the sump, baffle and oil strainer (see Section 13).
3   Remove the oil pump-to-engine block bolts **(see illustration)**.
4   Use a block of wood and a hammer to break the oil pump gasket seal, then detach the pump from the block.
5   Remove the O-ring **(see illustration 14.3)**.
6   Use a scraper to remove old sealant from the oil pump and engine block mating surfaces. Clean them with lacquer thinner or acetone.

Inspection

Refer to illustrations 14.7a, 14. 7b, 14.10a, 14.10b and 14.10c

7   Remove the snap-ring and slide out the

retainer, spring and oil pressure relief valve piston **(see illustration)**. Use a large Phillips screwdriver to remove the screws holding the oil pump cover to the body **(see illustration)**. Lift out the gears.
8   Clean all components with solvent, then inspect them for wear and damage.
9   Lubricate the oil pressure relief valve piston with oil and see if it falls smoothly into the bore by its own weight.
10   Check the following clearances with a feeler gauge **(see illustrations)** and compare

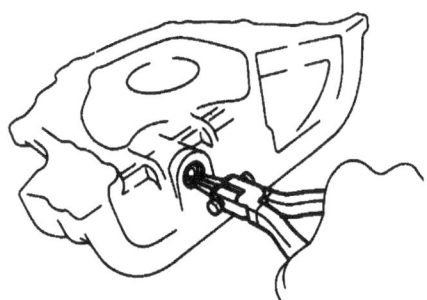

14.7a Remove the snap-ring to release the oil pressure relief valve components from the bore in the pump body

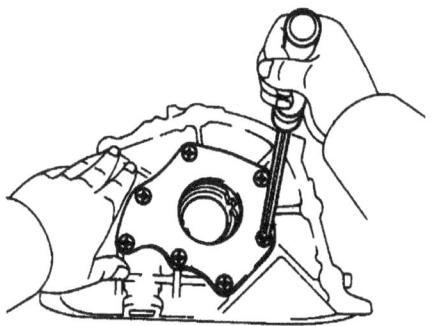

14.7b Remove the screws and detach the cover to remove the gears from the pump

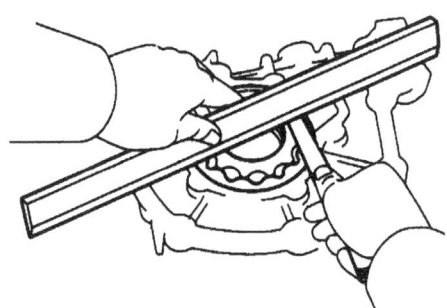

14.10a Measuring gear side clearance with a precision straightedge and feeler gauge

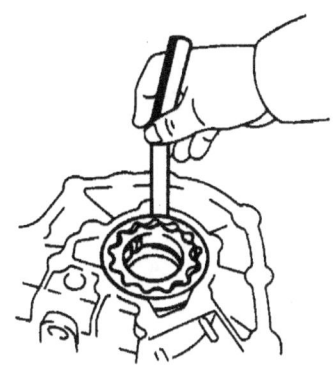

14.10b Measuring driven gear-to-pump body clearance with a feeler gauge

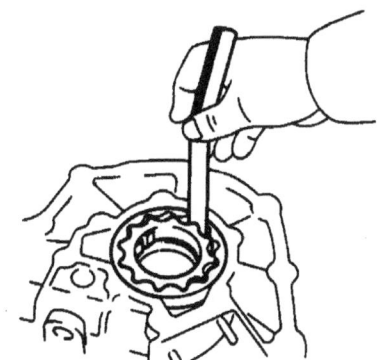

14.10c Measuring drive gear-to-driven gear clearance with a feeler gauge

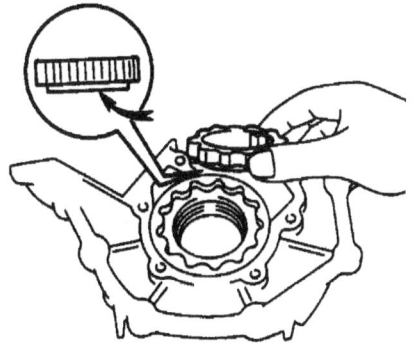

14.13 Be sure the drive gear is refitted with the shoulder facing in

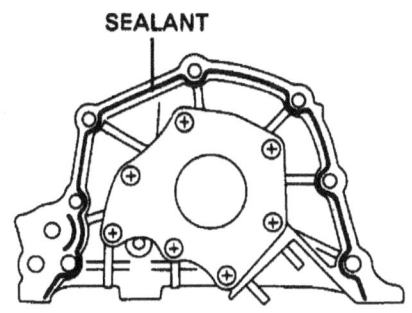

14.14 Apply sealant to the oil pump body-to-engine block mating surface before refitting the pump

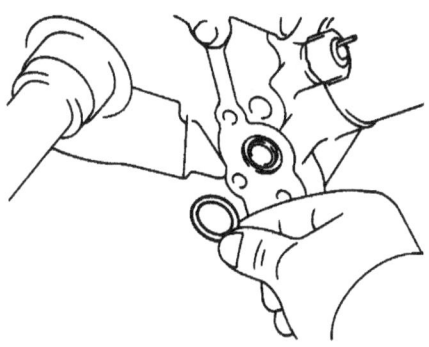

14.15 Use heavy grease to hold the O-ring in the block groove . . .

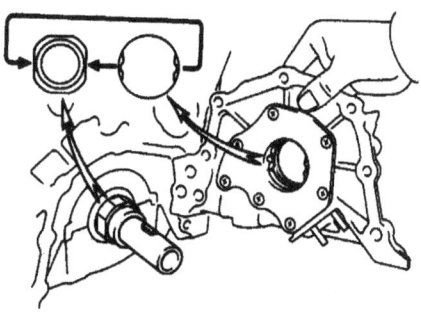

14.16 . . . then align the crankshaft and drive gear flats and refit the oil pump

the measurements to the Specifications:

    Gear side clearance
    Driven gear-to-pump body
    Drive gear-to-driven gear

If the clearances aren't as specified, fit a new oil pump.

Refitting

Refer to illustrations 14.13, 14.14, 14.15 and 14.16

11   Prise out the oil seal with a large screwdriver.

12   Apply multi-purpose grease to the outer edge of the new seal. Lay the oil pump body on a workbench and carefully drive the seal into place with a large socket and hammer.

13   Position the drive and driven gears in the oil pump body **(see illustration)**. Pack the cavities around the gears with petroleum jelly and refit the cover.

14   Apply a 2 mm wide bead of sealant (Toyota no. 08826-00080 or equivalent) to the pump-to-block mating surface **(see illustration)**.

15   Fit a new O-ring in the engine block groove **(see illustration)**.

16   Refit the oil pump over the crankshaft with the spline teeth engaged with the oil pump drive gear **(see illustration)**.

17   Refit the oil pump bolts and tighten them to the Specified torque in a criss-cross pattern.

18   Refit the remaining parts in the reverse order of removal.

19   Be sure to add oil, then run the engine and check for oil leaks.

15 Flywheel/driveplate - removal and refitting

Refer to illustrations 15.3 and 15.9

1   Raise the vehicle and support it securely on jackstands, then refer to Chapter 7 and remove the transmission.

2   Remove the pressure plate assembly and clutch disc (Chapter 8) (manual transmission equipped vehicles).

3   Use paint to draw a line from the flywheel to the end of the crankshaft for correct alignment during refitting **(see illustration)**.

4   Remove the bolts that secure the flywheel to the crankshaft rear flange. If difficulty is experienced in removing the bolts due to movement of the crankshaft, wedge a screwdriver through the starter opening to keep the flywheel from turning.

5   Remove the flywheel/driveplate from the crankshaft flange.

6   Clean any grease or oil from the flywheel. Inspect the surface of the flywheel for rivet grooves, burned areas and score marks. Light scoring can be removed with emery

15.3 To ensure proper balance, mark the flywheel/driveplate in relationship to the crankshaft

cloth. Check for cracked or broken teeth. Lay the flywheel on a flat surface and use a straightedge to check for warpage.

7   Clean the mating surfaces of the flywheel/driveplate and the crankshaft.

8   Position the flywheel/driveplate against the crankshaft, matching the alignment marks made during removal. Before refitting the bolts, apply a non-hardening thread locking compound to the threads.

9   Wedge a screwdriver through the starter motor opening to keep the flywheel from turning. Tighten the bolts to the specified torque in two or three steps. Follow the recommended

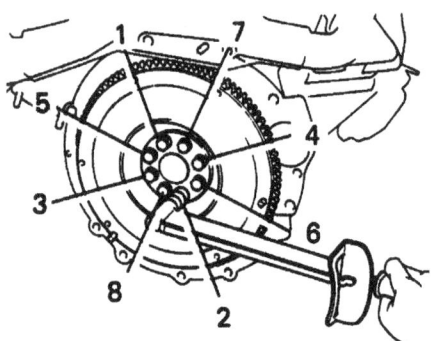

15.9 Flywheel/driveplate bolt TIGHTENING
sequence

sequence (see illustration).
10   The remainder of refitting is the reverse
of the removal procedure.

16   Rear main oil seal - renewal

*Refer to illustrations 16.2a, 16.2b, 16.5, 16.6
and 16.7*

1   The transmission must be removed from
the vehicle for this procedure (see Chapter
7) and the flywheel/driveplate must be separated from the engine (see Section 15).
2   The seal can be renewed without dropping the sump or removing the seal retainer.
However, this method is not recommended
because the lip of the seal is quite stiff and it's
possible to cock the seal in the retainer bore or
damage it during refitting. If you want to take
the chance, prise out the old seal with a screwdriver (see illustration). Apply multi-purpose
grease to the crankshaft seal journal and the
lip of the new seal and carefully push the new
seal into place. The lip is stiff, so carefully work
it onto the crankshaft with a smooth object like
the end of an extension (see illustration) as
you tap the seal into place. Don't rush it or you
may damage the seal.
3   The following method is recommended
but requires removal of the sump (see Section 13) and the seal retainer.

16.2a The quick way to renew the
crankshaft rear oil seal is to simply prise
the old one out with a screwdriver and
push the new one into the retainer bore
- the trouble is, the seal lip is stiff and
can easily be damaged during refitting if
you're not careful

4   After the sump has been removed,
remove the bolts, detach the seal retainer and
peel off all the old sealant.
5   Position the seal and retainer assembly
on a couple of wood blocks on a workbench
and drive the old seal out with a punch (see
illustration).
6   Drive the new seal into the retainer with
a block of wood (see illustration) or a section
of pipe slightly smaller in diameter than the
outside diameter of the seal.
7   Apply a 2 mm wide bead of sealant
(Toyota no. 08826-00080 or equivalent) to
the seal retainer-to-block mating surface (see
illustration).
8   Lubricate the crankshaft seal journal
and the lip of the new seal with multi-purpose
grease.
9   Slowly and carefully push the seal onto
the crankshaft. The seal lip is stiff, so work it
onto the crankshaft with a smooth object such
as the end of an extension (see illustration
16.2b) as you push the retainer against the
block.
10   Refit and tighten all the retainer bolts to

16.2b The seal is quite stiff and won't
slide over the end of the crankshaft very
easily, so lubricate the lip with multi-
purpose grease and carefully work it over
the crankshaft journal with a smooth.
blunt object, to avoid damaging it

the specified torque.
11   The remaining steps are the reverse of
removal.

17   Engine mounts - check and
renewal

1   Engine mounts should be periodically
inspected for hardening or cracking of the
rubber and separation of the rubber from the
metal backing.
2   Renew the front mounts by loosening the nuts and bolts retaining them to the
engine mounting bracket and chassis on both
sides of the engine.
3   Take the weight of the engine off the
mounts by placing a jack and wooden block
under the sump. Carefully raise the engine
enough to allow removal of the mount(s).
Extreme caution should be exercised during
this procedure.
4   If you intend to use the old mounts
again, mark them clearly to ensure that they
are refitted, right side up, on the same side as
before. Remove the nuts and bolts retaining
the mounts and detach the mounts, noting the
correct refitted position.
5   Refitting is the reverse of the removal
procedure.

16.5 After removing the retainer from the
engine, support it on a couple of wood
blocks and drive out the old seal with
a punch and hammer

16.6 Drive the new seal into the retainer
with a block of wood or a section of
pipe, if you have one large enough -
make sure that you don't cock the
seal in the retainer bore

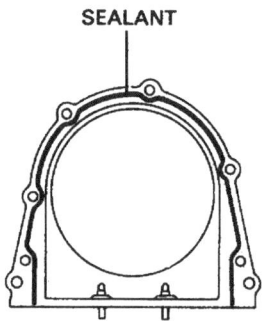

16.7 Apply sealant to the oil seal retainer-
to-block mating surface before bolting
it to the engine

Chapter 2 Part D   Diesel engines

Contents

Specifications

Note: *References to early 2L engines refer to 1988 and earlier 2L engines (with rocker arms).*

General
Cylinder numbers (front-to-rear)	1-2-3-4
Injection order	1-3-4-2
Displacement	
L engine	2.2 litres
2L engine	2.4 litres
3L engine	2.8 litres

Manifold warpage limits
Inlet	0.2 mm
Exhaust	0.7 mm

Cylinder head
Warpage limit	0.20 mm

Rocker arm assembly (L engine)
Shaft diameter (service limit)... 18.44 mm
Rocker arm bore diameter (service limit)... 18.60 mm
Rocker arm-to-shaft (oil) clearance
    Standard.. 0.017 to 0.051 mm
    Service limit .... 0.10 mm

Camshaft
Endplay
    L and early 2L engines
        Standard .... 0.055 to 0.155 mm
        Service limit .... 0.3 mm
    Later 2L and 3L engines
        Standard .... 0.080 to 0.280 mm
        Service limit .... 0.35 mm
Bearing journal diameter
    L and early 2L engines... 34.969 to 34.985 mm
    Later 2L and 3L engines
        No. 1 journal .... 34.969 to 34.985 mm
        All others... 27.969 to 27.985 mm
Bearing oil clearance
    Standard.. 0.022 to 0.074 mm
    Service limit .... 0.1 mm
Runout limit
    L and early 2L engines... 0.05 mm
    Later 2L and 3L engines... 0.1 mm
Lobe height
    L and early 2L engines
        Standard
            Inlet.. 43.048 mm
            Exhaust .... 43.232 mm
        Service limit
            Inlet.. 42.70 mm
            Exhaust .... 42.90 mm
    Later 2L engine
        Standard
            Inlet.. 53.850 to 53.870 mm
            Exhaust .... 54.990 to 55.010 mm
        Service limit
            Inlet.. 53.35 mm
            Exhaust .... 53.49 mm
    3L engine
        Standard
            Inlet.. 54.290 to 54.310 mm
            Exhaust .... 54.990 to 55.010 mm
        Service limit
            Inlet.. 53.79 mm
            Exhaust .... 53.49 mm

Valve lifters
Diameter... 40.892 to 40.902 mm
Bore diameter.. 40.960 to 40.980 mm
Oil clearance
    Standard.. 0.058 to 0.088 mm
    Service limit .... 0.10 mm

Timing belt tensioner
Tensioner spring free length
    L and early 2L engines... 39.7 mm
    Later 2L and 3L engines... 44.4 to 45.4 mm

Oil pump
Driven gear-to-oil pump body clearance
    L and early 2L engines
        Standard .... 0.06 to 0.15 mm
        Service limit .... 0.2 mm
    Later 2L and 3L engines
        Standard .... 0.144 to 0.219 mm
        Service limit .... 0.4 mm

Driven gear-to-crescent clearance (L and early 2L engines)
    Standard... 0.15 to 0.21 mm
    Service limit... 0.3 mm
Drive gear-to-crescent clearance (L and early 2L engines)
    Standard... 0.22 to 0.25 mm
    Service limit... 0.3 mm
Inner rotor tip clearance (Later 2L and 3L engines)
    Standard... 0.110 to 0.240 mm
    Service limit... 0.30 mm
Gear side clearance
    L and early 2L engines
        Standard .... 0.03 to 0.09 mm
        Service limit .... 0.15 mm
    Later 2L and 3L engines
        Standard .... 0.035 to 0.085 mm
        Service limit .... 0.15 mm

Torque specifications

	Nm
Inlet manifold bolts/nuts	
L engine	11 to 15
2L, 3L engines	24
Exhaust manifold bolts/nuts	
L engine	15 to 20
Later 2L and 3L engines	52
Early 2L engine	39
Rocker arm bolts shaft support bolts (L and early 2L engines)	15 to 20
Camshaft bearing cap bolts (Later 2L and 3L engines)	25
Cylinder head bolts	
L and early 2L engines	114 to 122
Later 2L and 3L engines	
Step 1	78
Step 2	Turn an additional 90-degrees
Step 3	Turn an additional 90-degrees
Camshaft oil seal retainer (Later 2L and 3L engines)	18
Camshaft sprocket bolt	98
Crankshaft pulley bolt	
L engine	93 to 102
Later 2L and 3L engines	167
Early 2L engine	137
Injection pump sprocket nut	64
Sump bolts	18
Oil pickup tube mounting bolts	12
Oil cooler-to-oil filter bracket	14
Oil filter bracket assembly-to-engine	
Bolts	19
Nuts	21
Oil pump (front cover) mounting bolts	
L and early 2L engines	19
Later 2L and 3L engines	23
Rear main oil seal retainer	13
Flywheel mounting bolts	
L and early 2L engines	114 to 122
Later 2L and 3L engines	123
Driveplate mounting bolts	
L and early 2L engines	114 to 122
Later 2L and 3L engines	98

1 General information

This Part of Chapter 2 is devoted to in-vehicle repair procedures for the L, 2L and 3L engines.

All information concerning engine removal and installation can be found in Chapter 2E.

The following repair procedures are based on the assumption that the engine is fitted in the vehicle. If the engine has been removed from the vehicle and mounted on a stand, many of the steps included in this Part of Chapter 2 will not apply.

The Specifications included in this Part of Chapter 2 apply only to the engines and procedures in this Part. Additional Specifications necessary for removing and overhauling the engine are found in Part E.

2 Repair operations possible with the engine in the vehicle

Many major repair operations can be accomplished without removing the engine from the vehicle.

Clean the engine compartment and the exterior of the engine with some type of pressure washer before any work is done. It'll make the job easier and help keep dirt out of the internal areas of the engine.

Remove the bonnet to improve access to the engine as repairs are performed (see Chapter 11 if necessary).

If vacuum, exhaust, oil or coolant leaks develop, indicating a need for gasket or seal renewal, the repairs can generally be made with the engine in the vehicle. The sump gasket, cylinder head gasket, inlet and exhaust manifold gaskets, front cover gaskets and the crankshaft oil seals are accessible with the engine in place.

Exterior engine components, such as the oil filter bracket, the water pump, the starter motor, the alternator and the fuel injection pump, as well as the inlet and exhaust manifolds, can be removed for repair with the engine in place.

Since the cylinder head can be removed without pulling the engine, camshaft and valve component servicing can also be accomplished with the engine in the vehicle.

Renewal or inspection of the timing belt and sprockets and the oil pump are all possible with the engine in place.

In extreme cases caused by a lack of necessary equipment, repair or renewal of piston rings, pistons, connecting rods and rod bearings is possible with the engine in the vehicle. However, this practice is not recommended because of the cleaning and preparation work that must be done to the components involved.

3   Top Dead Centre (TDC) for number one piston - locating

Refer to illustration 3.4

1   Top Dead Centre (TDC) is the highest point in the cylinder that each piston reaches as it travels up-and-down when the crankshaft turns. Each piston reaches TDC on the compression stroke and again on the exhaust stroke, but TDC generally refers to piston position on the compression stroke. The timing marks on the pulley fitted on the front of the crankshaft are referenced to the number one piston at TDC on the compression stroke.
2   Positioning the piston(s) at TDC is an essential part of many procedures such as camshaft and timing belt/sprocket removal and injection pump removal.
3   In order to bring any piston to TDC, the crankshaft must be turned using one of the methods outlined below. When looking at the front of the engine, normal crankshaft rotation is clockwise. **Warning:** *Before beginning this procedure, be sure to place the transmission in Neutral. Also, detach the wire from the terminal of the fuel cut solenoid if you plan to turn the engine over with the starter motor.*

a) *The preferred method is to turn the crankshaft with a large socket and breaker bar attached to the crankshaft pulley hub bolt threaded into the front of the crankshaft.*

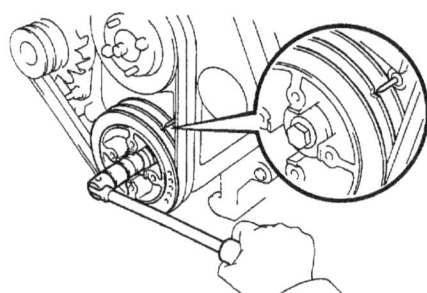

3.4 Align the notch in the crankshaft pulley with the pointer on the front cover

b) *A remote starter switch, which may save some time, can also be used. Attach the switch leads to the solenoid terminals. Once the piston is close to TDC, use a socket and breaker bar as described in the previous paragraph.*
c) *If an assistant is available to turn the ignition switch to the Start position in short bursts, you can get the piston close to TDC without a remote starter switch. Use a socket and breaker bar as described in Paragraph a) to complete the procedure.*

4   Turn the crankshaft (see Step 3 above) until the notch in the crankshaft pulley is aligned with the 0 on the timing plate (located at the front of the engine) **(see illustration)**.
5   Remove the valve cover (see Section 4). Make sure the rocker arms (L and early 2L engines) for the no. 1 cylinder are loose or, on later 2L and 3L engines, make sure the cam lobes are pointing away from the lifters. If not, the no. 1 piston is on the exhaust stroke (proceed to the next step).
6   To get the piston to TDC on the compression stroke (if it wasn't in the previous step), turn the crankshaft one complete turn (360-degrees) clockwise.
7   After the number one piston has been positioned at TDC on the compression stroke, TDC for any of the remaining pistons can be located by turning the crankshaft 180-degrees at a time and following the injection order.

4   Valve cover - removal and refitting

Refer to illustrations 4.4 and 4.8

1   Disconnect the negative battery cable from the battery.
2   Detach the accelerator cable from the throttle bellcrank and its brackets (see Chapter 4B).
3   Disconnect the PCV hose from the valve cover.
4   Remove the valve cover mounting bolts and nuts **(see illustration)**. Don't lose the washers. **Note:** *Some engines have a cover mounted to the top of the primary valve cover.*
5   Detach the valve cover and discard the old gasket. **Caution:** *If the cover is stuck to the head, bump the end with a block of wood*

4.3 Location of the valve cover bolts and nuts (1989 and later 2L and 3L engines)

and a hammer to jar it loose. If that doesn't work, try to slip a flexible putty knife between the head and cover to break the gasket seal. Don't prise at the cover-to-head joint or damage to the sealing surfaces may occur, leading to oil leaks in the future. **Note:** *On L and early 2L engines, be careful not to lose the rubber half-moon seal at the rear mating surface of the cylinder head.*
6   The mating surfaces of the head and valve cover must be perfectly clean when the cover is refitted. Use a gasket scraper to remove all traces of sealant and old gasket material, then clean the mating surfaces with lacquer thinner or acetone. If there's sealant or oil on the mating surfaces when the cover is refitted, oil leaks may develop.
7   If the valve cover uses a conventional gasket, apply a thin, uniform layer of sealant to the cover and the surface of the new gasket that will be against the head, place the new gasket in position with the sealant against the cylinder head, then place the valve cover on the gasket. While the sealant is still wet, refit the mounting bolts and nuts and tighten them

4.8 Before refitting the valve cover, apply a bead of RTV sealant to the area where the cam seal retainer mates with the cylinder head

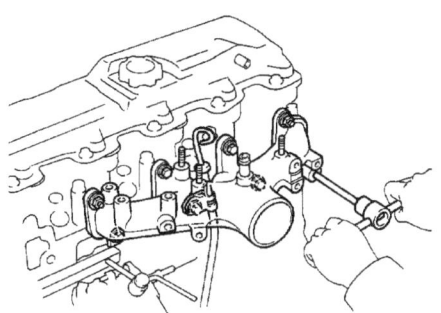

5.6 Inlet manifold bolt/nut locations

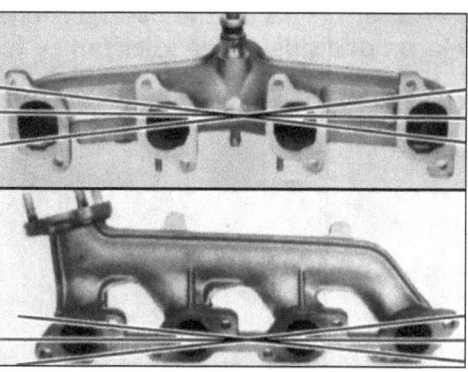

5.9 Use a straightedge and feeler gauges to check the manifolds for warpage - make the check lengthwise and diagonally

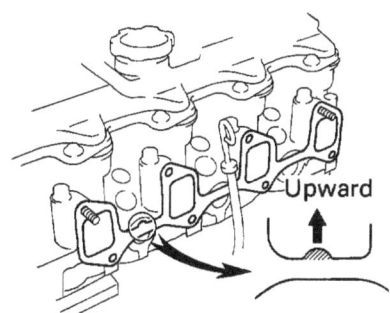

5.12 On 1989 and later 2L and 3L engines, the projection on the inlet manifold gasket must face up

securely. If you're working on an L engine or 1988 and earlier 2L engine, make sure the half-moon seal at the rear of the cylinder head is in place.

8   If the valve cover uses an O-ring-type gasket, it's not necessary to use sealant, but make sure the new gasket is fitted properly into the groove in the perimeter of the valve cover. A little bit of grease will prevent it from falling out during refitting. A small bead of sealant should be applied to the area where the camshaft seal retainer mates to the cylinder head (see illustration).

9   refit the valve cover bolts and nuts and tighten them securely.

10   Complete the refitting by reversing the removal procedure.

5   Inlet manifold - removal and refitting

Removal

Refer to illustration 5.6

1   Disconnect the cable from the negative terminal of the battery.

2   Detach the accelerator cable from the throttle bellcrank, then prise the linkage off the post on the bottom of the bellcrank (see Chapter 4B).

3   Remove the injection pipes.

4   Unscrew the nut and detach the glow plug strap from the post on the inlet manifold (see Chapter 6).

5   Detach the PCV hose from the inlet manifold.

6   Remove the bolts and nuts that attach the manifold to the head (see illustrations). Start at the ends and work toward the middle, loosening each one a little at a time until they can be removed.

7   Move the manifold up-and-down to break the gasket seal, then detach it from the head. Remove and discard the old gasket.

Refitting

Refer to illustrations 5.9 and 5.12

Note: *The mating surfaces of the cylinder head and manifold must be perfectly clean when the manifold is refitted. Gasket removal solvents in aerosol cans are available at most auto parts stores and may be helpful when*

removing old gasket material that's stuck to the head and manifold (since they're made of aluminium, aggressive scraping can cause damage). Be sure to follow the directions printed on the container.

8   Use a gasket scraper to remove all traces of sealant and old gasket material, then clean the surfaces with lacquer thinner or acetone. If there is old sealant or oil on the mating surfaces when the manifold is refitted, vacuum leaks may develop.

9   Check the manifold-to-cylinder head gasket surface for warpage. Lay a straightedge along the manifold and try to slip a feeler gauge between the manifold and the straightedge at each runner (see illustration). If the manifold is warped beyond the specified limit, it must be resurfaced or renewed.

10   Check the manifold for corrosion (at the coolant passages), cracks and other damage. If defects are found, have the manifold repaired or renewed as necessary. If a new manifold is fitted, transfer all brackets and fittings to the new one. Be sure to use a new thermostat (see Chapter 3).

11   Use a tap of the correct size to chase the threads in the bolt holes, then use compressed air (if available) to remove the debris from the holes. **Warning:** *Wear safety glasses or a face shield to protect your eyes when using compressed air!* Clean the stud threads with a die.

12   Apply a thin, uniform layer of RTV seal-

ant to the manifold mating surfaces and the cylinder head side of the gasket and fit the gasket on the head (see illustration). refit the inlet manifold, hand tighten all fasteners, then tighten them to the torque listed in this Chapter's Specifications, starting with the four centre bolts and then the four outer bolts. Work up to the final torque in three steps.

13   The rest of refitting is the reverse of removal.

6   Exhaust manifold - removal and refitting

Refer to illustrations 6.4 and 6.5

Removal

1   Make sure the engine is completely cool before beginning this procedure.

2   Raise the front of the vehicle and support it on jackstands.

3   Disconnect the front exhaust pipe from the exhaust manifold (see Chapter 4B).

4   Remove the heat shield bolts and detach the shield (see illustration).

5   Loosen the bolts and nuts that retain the exhaust manifold to the cylinder head (see illustration). Work from the ends toward the centre in a criss-cross pattern.

6   Remove the bolts/nuts and detach the exhaust manifold.

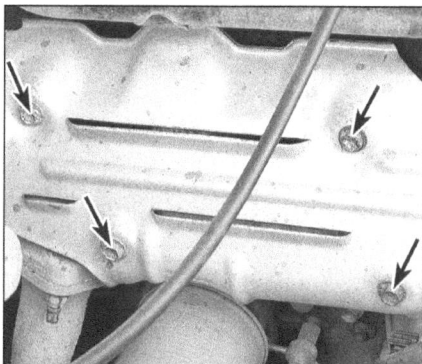

6.4 The exhaust manifold heat shield is retained by four bolts (arrows)

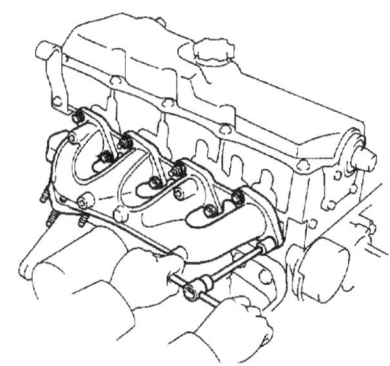

6.5 Locations of the exhaust manifold mounting nuts/bolts

7.5 Use a puller that applies force to the hub of the crankshaft pulley, like this steering wheel puller, not one that grasps the outer circumference of the pulley

8.6a On 1989 and later 2L and 3L engines, the heater pipes are secured to the side of the block with two bolts (arrows) . . .

8.6b . . . and to the thermostat housing with one bolt

Refitting

7   Before refitting the manifold, remove all traces of the old gasket with a scraper. Clean the mating surfaces with lacquer thinner or acetone.

8   Using a straightedge and feeler gauge, check the manifold-to-cylinder head mating surface for warpage **(see illustration 5.9)**. If it's warped beyond the service limit, the manifold must be resurfaced or renewed.

9   Check for corrosion, cracks and other damage. Repair or renew the manifold as necessary.

10   Place a new exhaust manifold gasket in position on the cylinder head, then hold the manifold in place and refit the mounting bolts/nuts finger tight.

11   Tighten the mounting bolts/nuts, in three or four steps, to the specified torque. Work from the centre out toward the ends to prevent distortion of the manifold.

12   The remainder of refitting is the reverse of the removal procedure.

13   Start the engine and check for exhaust leaks between the manifold and cylinder head and between the manifold and exhaust pipe.

7   Crankshaft pulley - removal and refitting

Refer to illustration 7.5

1   Disconnect the negative battery cable from the battery. Drain the cooling system (see Chapter 1).

2   Remove the fan, shroud and radiator (see Chapter 3).

3   Remove the drivebelts (see Chapter 1).

4   Remove the flywheel/driveplate inspection cover and wedge a screwdriver in the starter ring gear teeth to prevent the crankshaft from turning. Remove the pulley mounting bolt. It's usually very tight, so use a six-point socket, if available, and a 1/2-inch drive breaker bar.

5   Use a puller to remove the pulley from the crankshaft **(see illustration)**. DO NOT use a gear puller that applies force to the outer edge of the pulley!

6   Refitting is the reverse of removal. Be sure to apply grease or clean engine oil to the seal contact surface on the pulley hub before refitting the pulley on the crankshaft. Also, be sure to align the keyway in the pulley hub with the key in the crankshaft or the pulley won't slide into place.

7   Tighten the pulley bolt to the torque listed in this Chapter's Specifications.

8   The remainder of refitting is the reverse of removal. Refill the cooling system (see Chapter 1), start the engine and check for leaks.

8   Timing belt and sprockets - removal, inspection and refitting

Removal

Refer to illustrations 8.6a, 8.6b, 8.7, 8.8a, 8.8b, 8.8c, 8.8d, 8.9, 8.10a, 8.10b and 8.11

1   Position the number one piston at TDC on the compression stroke (see Section 3). **Caution:** *Once this has been done, DO NOT*

8.7 Timing belt cover bolt/nut locations (arrows) (1989 and later 2L and 3L engines)

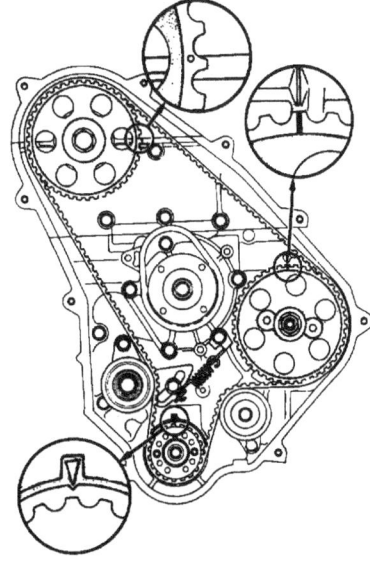

8.8a When the engine is at TDC on the compression for the number one cylinder, the camshaft sprocket, crankshaft sprocket and injection pump sprocket must be aligned with their corresponding marks (L and 1988 and earlier 2L engine shown)

8.8b On 1989 and later 2L and 3L engines, the mark on the cam sprocket must be in alignment with the arrow on the timing belt rear cover . . .

8.8c . . . the notch on the crankshaft sprocket must be in alignment with the projection on the front cover (arrows) . . .

8.8d . . . and the mark on the injection pump sprocket must be aligned with the projection on the front cover

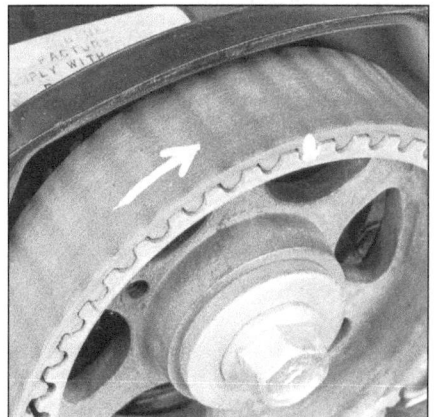

8.9 If you plan on using the original belt, mark its relationship to each sprocket and draw an arrow on it to indicate its direction of travel

8.10a Loosen the tensioner pulley bolt (arrow) . . .

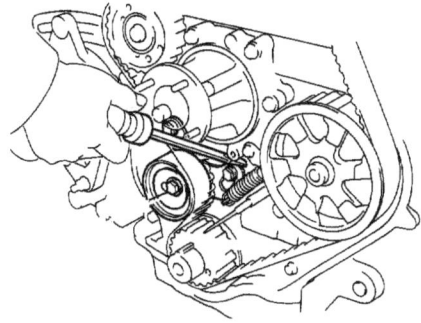

8.10b . . . then prise the tensioner pulley away from the belt and retighten the bolt

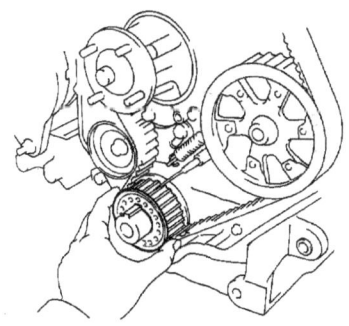

8.11 Remove the timing belt guide from the nose of the crankshaft

turn the crankshaft until the timing belt has been refited!

2   Disconnect the negative cable from the battery. Drain the cooling system (see Chapter 1).

3   Remove the fan, shroud and radiator as described in Chapter 3.

4   Remove the drivebelts (see Chapter 1).

5   Remove the crankshaft pulley (see Section 7).

6   On 1989 and later 2L and 3L engines, remove the bolts from the heater pipes and reposition the pipes over the valve cover **(see illustrations)**.

7   Remove the nuts and bolts and detach the timing belt cover **(see illustration)**.

8   Be sure that the timing marks on the camshaft sprocket, crankshaft sprocket and injection pump are aligned with their corresponding marks **(see illustrations)**. If the crankshaft sprocket marks are in alignment but the camshaft and injection pump sprocket marks are not, rotate the crankshaft one complete revolution and recheck the marks.

9   If the timing belt is to be reused, mark the belt position at each sprocket and apply an arrow indicating the direction of rotation

(see illustration).

10   To relieve the timing belt tension, loosen the bolt and prise the tensioner pulley away from the belt, then retighten the bolt **(see illustrations)**.

11   Remove the timing belt guide **(see illustration)** and tension spring.

12   Slip the timing belt off the sprockets. If you plan to reuse the belt, check it carefully for wear and damage and make sure it hasn't been contaminated with oil, fuel or coolant. Don't twist, bend or turn the belt inside out. **Caution:** *It's a very good idea to fit a new belt rather than reuse the old one, regardless of it's condition. If the belt fails during engine operation, extensive damage may occur!*

Inspection

Refer to illustration 8.14

13   Check the tensioner pulley to see if it turns smoothly. If not, renew it. On models so equipped, also check the idler pulley.

14   Measure the free length of the tension spring **(see illustration)**. Compare your measurements with this Chapter's Specifications. Renew the spring if it's not as specified.

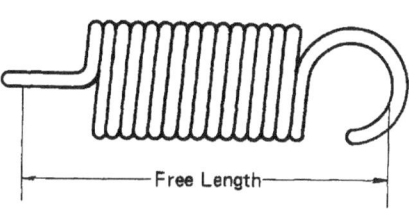

8.14 Measure the free length of the tensioner spring and compare it to the specifications at the front of this Chapter

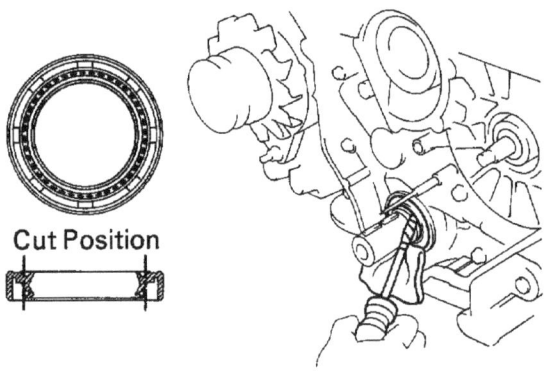

9.3 Cut the lip of the crankshaft front oil seal off, then carefully prise the seal from the front cover/oil pump

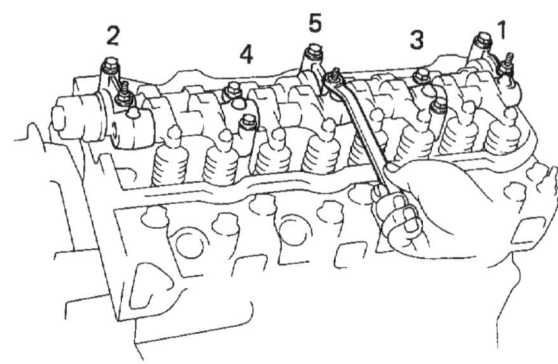

10.2 Loosen each pair of rocker arm support bolts, a little at a time, in the order shown

15   Check the sprockets for wear and damage. If it's necessary to remove a camshaft or injection pump sprocket, prevent it from turning by fitting two bolts of the proper diameter and thread pitch into the threaded holes in the sprocket, then place a large screwdriver or lever across the bolts as you loosen the sprocket bolt or nut. Attach a puller to the sprocket to draw it off. To remove a crankshaft sprocket, use a screw-type puller with bolts threaded into the holes in the sprocket (a steering wheel puller will work).

Refitting

16   Align the notch in the crankshaft sprocket with the mark on the oil pump/front cover **(see illustration 8.8c)**. Align the camshaft and injection pump sprocket timing marks **(see illustrations 8.8b and 8.8d)**. If the camshaft or injection pump sprocket was removed, refit it and tighten it using the same method that was used to loosen it. **Caution:** *Don't use the timing belt to hold the sprocket from turning when loosening or tightening the sprocket bolt or nut!*

17   Refit the timing belt over the camshaft sprocket, injection pump sprocket, idler pulley (if equipped), crankshaft sprocket, tensioner pulley and the idler sprocket (if equipped). There should be no slack in the belt run between the camshaft sprocket and the injection pump sprocket, or between the injection pump sprocket and the crankshaft sprocket. **Note:** *If the old belt is being refited, align the marks made during removal and make sure the arrow **(see illustration 8.9)** is pointing in the direction of crankshaft rotation (clockwise).*

18   Loosen the tensioner pulley bolt and prise the pulley to your right (to apply tension to the belt), as far as it will go, then temporarily tighten the bolt.

19   Refit the tension spring and loosen the tensioner pulley bolt slightly to allow the tension spring to tension the idler.

20   Refit the crankshaft pulley bolt and rotate the crankshaft clockwise, two complete revolutions.

21   Recheck the timing mark alignment **(see illustrations 8.8a, 8.8b, 8.8c and 8.8d)**. If the marks aren't aligned exactly as shown, the timing belt will have to be removed, the pulleys realigned, the belt refited and the check redone. Once you are satisfied the belt is fitted properly, tighten the tensioner pulley bolt to the torque listed in this Chapter's specifications, remove the crankshaft pulley bolt and refit the timing belt guide **(see illustration 8.11)** and the timing belt cover. refit the crankshaft pulley and tighten the bolt to the torque listed in this Chapter's Specifications.

22   Refit the remaining components in the reverse order of removal. Refill the cooling system as described in Chapter 1.

9   Crankshaft front oil seal - renewal

Refer to illustration 9.3

1   Remove the crankshaft pulley (see Section 7).

2   Remove the timing belt and the crankshaft sprocket (see Section 8).

3   If you're careful, you can prise the oil seal out of the oil pump/front cover with a seal removal tool or screwdriver. Don't scratch the crankshaft in the process (if the crankshaft is damaged, the new seal will leak) It's a good idea to cut off the lip of the seal before trying to prise it out **(see illustration)**.

4   Clean the bore in the cover or oil pump and coat the outer edge of the new seal with engine oil or multi-purpose grease. Using a seal driver or a socket with an outside diameter slightly smaller than the outside diameter of the seal (and with a bore big enough to clear the nose of the crankshaft), carefully drive the new seal into place with a hammer. If a socket isn't available, a short section of large diameter pipe will work. Check the seal after refitting to be sure that the spring didn't pop out of place. If you're fitting a new seal on the bench, the same procedure applies, except you don't have to worry about clearing the nose of the crank.

5   Refit the crankshaft sprocket and timing belt (see Section 8) and the crankshaft pulley (see Section 7).

6   The parts removed to gain access to the pulley can now be refited.

7   Refill the cooling system (see Chapter 1), run the engine and check for leaks.

10   Rocker arm assembly - removal, inspection and refitting

Refer to illustrations 10.2, 10.4 and 10.5
Note: *This procedure applies to all L engines, and to 2L engines through 1988.*

Removal

1   Position the engine at TDC on the compression stroke for the number 1 cylinder (see Section 3). Remove the valve cover (see Section 4).

2   Unscrew the rocker arm shaft support bolts, a little at a time, in the recommended sequence **(see illustration)**.

3   Lift the rocker arm assembly from the cylinder head. **Note:** *The shaft supports carry the upper halves of the camshaft bearings - be careful not to drop them.*

Inspection

4   Try to twist each rocker arm from side-to-side on the shaft. Very little play should be detected. If excessive play is evident, disassemble the rocker arms and shaft. Remove the bolts from the front and rear shaft supports. Slide the shaft supports, rocker arms and springs off the shaft, but keep all the parts in order so they can be returned to their original locations during reassembly **(see illustration)**. The shaft supports have different configurations and must not be interchanged. **Note:** *If the parts are removed from the shafts, be sure to mark them or lay them out in the correct order- they MUST be refited in their original locations and with the same orientation.*

5   Using a micrometer and a bore gauge, measure the diameter of the shafts (where each rocker arm makes contact) and the rocker arm bore diameters **(see illustration)**. Subtract the shaft diameter from the corresponding rocker arm bore diameter to obtain

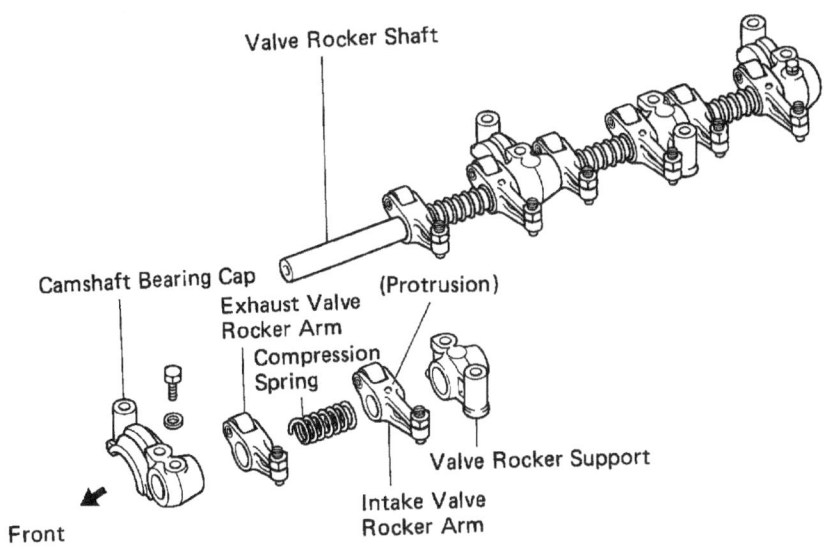

10.4 Rocker arm and shaft details (L and 1988 and earlier 2L engines)

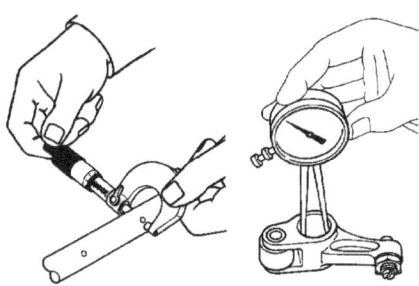

10.5 Measure the diameter of the rocker arm shaft (in the areas where the rocker arms ride) and the diameter of the rocker arm bore to calculate the rocker arm oil clearance

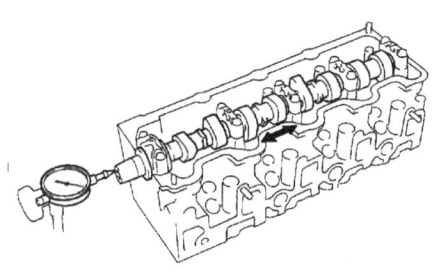

11.2 Attach a dial indicator to the front of the engine, prise the camshaft toward the rear of the head, zero the dial indicator and prise the camshaft towards the front of the engine - the reading on the indicator is the camshaft endplay

the rocker arm oil clearance. Repeat the procedure for each rocker arm and compare the results to the Specifications.

6 Check the rocker arm rollers (that contact the camshaft lobes) and the ends of the adjusting screws (that contact the valve stems) for pitting, excessive wear and roughness. Check the adjusting screw threads for damage. Make sure they can be threaded in and out of the rocker arms.

7 Any damaged or excessively worn parts should be renewed.

Refitting

8 Assemble the rocker arms and supports on the shaft, making sure the oil hole in the shaft is aligned with the oil hole in the front shaft support. Loosen the nuts and back out the valve adjuster screws a couple of turns each.

9 Lubricate the camshaft bearing surfaces with clean engine oil or engine assembly lube. Making sure the camshaft bearing shells are in place in the shaft supports, refit the rocker

arm assembly. refit the bolts, tightening them a little at a time, in the reverse order of that shown in **illustration 10.2**.

10 Adjust the valve clearances (see Chapter 1).

11 The remainder of refitting is the reverse of removal.

11 Camshaft and lifters - removal, inspection and refitting

Note: *The information in this Section related to valve lifters applies to 1989 and later 2L and 3L engines only.*

Removal

Refer to illustrations 11.2, 11.3, 11.4a, 11.4b, 11.6a and 11.6b

1 Drain the cooling system (see Chapter 1). Position the engine at TDC on the compression stroke (see Section 3). Remove the valve cover (see Section 4) and the timing belt and

cam sprocket (see Section 8).

2 With the camshaft still in place, check the endplay with a feeler gauge or dial indicator **(see illustration)**. If it's greater than specified, a new cylinder head will be required.

3 If you're working on a 1989 or later 2L or 3L engine, remove the rear timing belt cover **(see illustration)**.

4 Remove the camshaft oil seal retainer **(see illustrations)**.

11.3 The timing belt rear cover on 1989 and later 2L and 3L engines is retained by four bolts (arrows)

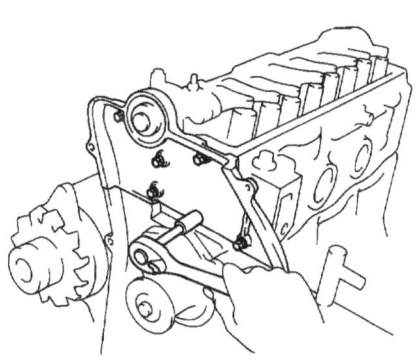

11.4a Camshaft oil seal retainer details - 1988 and earlier L and 2L engines

11.4b Camshaft oil seal retainer details - 1989 and later 2L and 3L engines

11.6a Locations of the camshaft bearing cap bolts - 1989 and later 2L and 3L engines

5   If you're working on an L engine (or a 1988 or earlier 2L engine), remove the rocker arm assembly (see Section 10).

6   If you're working on a 1989 or later 2L engine or a 3L engine, check the valve clearance (see Chapter 1) and record your measurements. Remove the camshaft bearing cap bolts, a little at a time, and detach the bearing caps from the head **(see illustration)**. Lay the bearing caps out in order - they must be returned to their original locations. **Note:** *The bearing caps are numbered from front to rear, and arrowed to indicate which side of the cap faces forward* **(see illustration)**.

7   Lift out the camshaft. Be careful not to nick or gouge the bearings in the head.

8   Refit the bearing caps in their original locations and thread the bolts in finger tight.

9   On 1989 and later 2L and 3L engines, remove the valve lifters from their bores and arrange them in order. It's a good idea to mark the lifters with a felt-tip pen to avoid mixing them up.

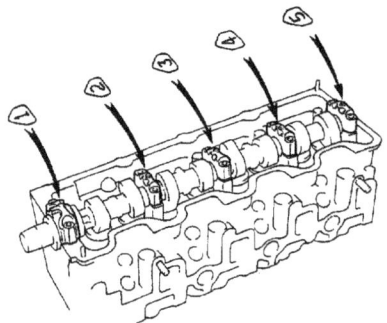

11.6b The camshaft bearing cap bolts are numbered front-to-rear and have arrows indicating which side faces the front of the engine

Inspection

Refer to illustrations 11.12, 11.14 and 11.17

10   Clean the camshaft with solvent and dry it with compressed air. Clean the bearings in the head and caps as well.

11   Inspect the camshaft bearing journals for excessive wear and evidence of seizure. If the journals are damaged, the bearing surfaces in the head and bearing caps are probably damaged as well. Both the camshaft and cylinder head (as well as the bearing caps) will have to be renewed.

12   Using a micrometer, measure the diameter of each of the cam bearing journals **(see illustration)**. Take the measurement at two locations on each journal (90-degrees apart). If the journal diameters are less than the service limit, the camshaft must be renewed.

13   The camshaft runout should also be checked (to determine if it's bent). This measurement requires a dial indicator and a special jig (or V-blocks) so it should be done by an automotive machine shop.

14   Check the cam lobes for pitting, grooves, scoring or flaking. Measure the cam lobe height and compare it to the Specifications **(see illustration)**. If the lobe height is less than the minimum specified, and/or the

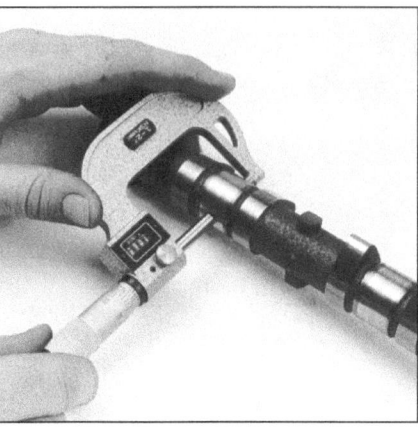

11.12 Measure each journal diameter with a micrometer (if any journal measures less than the specified limit, renew the camshaft)

lobes are damaged, a new camshaft must be obtained.

15   Examine the bearings in the head and in the bearing caps. Look for scoring, flaking and burned areas. If damage is evident, the bearings will have to be renewed.

16   Check the bearing oil clearances with Plastigage when the camshaft is refitted (see Step 18).

17   On 1989 and later 2L and 3L engines, check each lifter for scuffing and score marks **(see illustration)**. Measure the outside diameter of each lifter and the inside diameters of the corresponding lifter bores. Subtract the lifter diameter from the lifter bore diameter to determine the oil clearance. Compare it to this Chapter's Specifications. If the oil clearance is excessive, a new cylinder head and/or new lifters will be required.

Refitting

Refer to illustrations 11.23 and 11.25

18   If the inspection reveals no excessive wear or damage, the cam bearing oil clearance should be checked before deciding to refit the original camshaft.

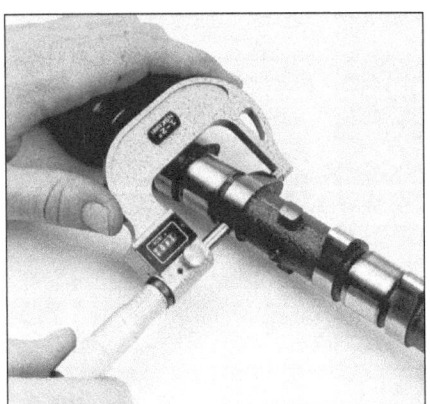

11.14 Measure the camshaft lobe heights - if any lobe height is less than the specified allowable minimum, renew the camshaft

11.17 Wipe off the oil and inspect each lifter for wear and scuffing

11.23 Lay a strip of Plastigage on each camshaft bearing journal, then refit the bearing caps and tighten them to the torque listed in this Chapter's Specifications

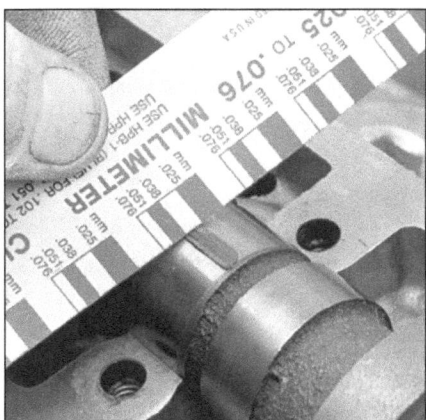

11.25 Compare the width of the crushed Plastigage to the scale on the envelope to determine oil clearance

19   Clean the camshaft, bearings and bearing caps with solvent and dry them thoroughly. refit the bearing shells into their bearing caps (or rocker arm stands).

20   The bearing oil clearances should be checked with Plastigage, which is available at auto parts stores. Type HPG-1 (green) should be used for this procedure.

21   Make sure the cam bearing journals and the bearings in the caps (or rocker arm stands) and cylinder head are clean and oil free. **Note:** *DO NOT apply oil or any other lubricant to the cylinder head, camshaft or bearing caps during this procedure.*

22   Carefully lay the camshaft in position in the cylinder head.

23   Cut five pieces of Plastigage the same length as the bearing journal width. Lay a piece of Plastigage on each bearing journal, parallel to the camshaft centerline **(see illustration)**.

24   Refit the bearing caps in their original locations with the marks facing forward, or on L engines and 1988 and earlier 2L engines, refit the rocker arm assembly. Tighten the bolts in each cap very gradually (about 1/4-turn at a time), alternating between the two until you reach the torque listed in this Chapter's Specifications. **Note:** *DO NOT turn the camshaft at any time during this procedure!*

25   Remove the bolts (loosen them gradually to avoid distortion of the caps), lift off the caps or rocker arm assembly and compare the widest portion of the crushed Plastigage on each bearing journal to the scale printed on the Plastigage envelope **(see illustration)**. Locate the line on the scale that's the same width as the Plastigage, then read the number opposite the line. This number is the bearing oil clearance.

26   If the oil clearance is greater than the service limit, and the camshaft bearing journal diameters are within specification, the bearings are excessively worn and must be renewed.

27   Once the procedure is complete, remove all traces of the Plastigage material from the cam journals and the bearings. Use a soft, blunt instrument such as a piece of wood (a

credit card also works well) to avoid scratching the bearings. Clean the journals and the bearings with solvent to complete the clean-up.

28   Prior to final refitting of the camshaft, lubricate the bearing surfaces and the lobes with camshaft refitting lube.

29   If you're working on a later 2L or 3L engine, lubricate the valve lifters with clean engine oil and refit them in their original bores. If the valve clearances were within specification when checked in Step 6, the same shims can be used. If not, adjust the valve clearances as described in Chapter 1.

30   Make sure the bearings in the head are in place, then carefully lay the camshaft in the head, with the keyway in the 12 o'clock position. Make sure the bearings in the caps are clean, then refit them on the head in their proper positions. If you're working on an L engine or a 1988 or earlier 2L engine, refit the rocker arm assembly (see Section 10).

31   On later 2L and 3L engines, refit and tighten the bolts as described in Step 24.

32   Check the camshaft endplay (see Step 2).

33   Lubricate the lip of the camshaft oil seal, then fit the oil seal retainer and tighten the bolts to the torque listed in this Chapter's Specifications. If the seal is in need of renewal, refer to Section 12.

34   If you're working on an L engine or a 1988 or earlier 2L engine, adjust the valve clearances (see Chapter 1).

35   The remainder of refitting is the reverse of removal. Refill the cooling system (see Chapter 1), run the engine and check for leaks.

12   Camshaft oil seal - renewal

1   Remove the timing belt and camshaft sprocket as described in Section 11.

2   Remove the rear timing belt cover (1989 and later 2L and 3L engines only) **(see illustration 11.3)**.

3   You can attempt to prise out the old seal without removing the seal retainer, but if that proves too difficult, you'll have to remove the retainer and prise the seal out on the workbench **(see illustrations 11.4a and 11.4b)**. Using a screwdriver or seal removal tool, carefully prise the seal out of the housing. Don't nick or scratch the camshaft in the process. Clean the bore in the housing.

4   To fit the new seal, first apply multi-purpose grease to the outer edge and the seal lip, then use a length of pipe or large socket and a hammer to tap the new seal into place. Be sure the seal is seated properly.

5   Refit the sprocket and tighten the bolt to the torque listed in this Chapter's Specifications. Prevent the sprocket from turning by using the method described in Section 8, Step 15.

6   Refit the timing belt and related parts, following the procedure outlined in Section 8.

8   Run the engine and check for oil leaks.

13   Valve springs, retainers and seals - renewal

Refer to illustrations 13.4, 13.9, 13.15 and 13.17

Note 1: *This procedure applies to L engines and 1988 and earlier 2L engines (with rocker arms) only. The valve springs on later 2L and 3L engines are recessed in the head, making in-vehicle renewal of the valve springs, retainers and seals too difficult.*

Note 2: *Broken valve springs and defective valve stem seals can be renewed without removing the cylinder head. Two special tools and a compressed air source are normally required to perform this operation, so read through this Section carefully and rent or buy the tools before beginning the job. If compressed air isn't available, a length of nylon rope can be used to keep the valves from falling into the cylinder during this procedure.*

1   Remove the valve cover referring to Section 4.

2   Remove the glow plug from the cylinder which has the defective component. If all of the valve stem seals are being renewed, all of the glow plugs should be removed.

3   Turn the crankshaft until the piston in the affected cylinder is at top dead centre (TDC) on the compression stroke (see Section 3 for instructions). If you're renewing all of the valve stem seals, begin with cylinder number one and work on the valves for one cylinder at a time. Move from cylinder-to-cylinder following the injection order sequence (see the Specifications listed at the beginning of this Chapter).

4   Thread an adapter into the glow plug hole **(see illustration)** and connect an air hose from a compressed air source to it. Most auto parts stores can supply the air hose adapter. **Note:** *Many cylinder compression gauges utilize a screw-in fitting that may work with your air hose quick-disconnect fitting.*

5   Remove the rocker arm assembly (see Section 10).

6   Apply compressed air to the cylinder. Warning: The piston may be forced down by compressed air, causing the crankshaft to

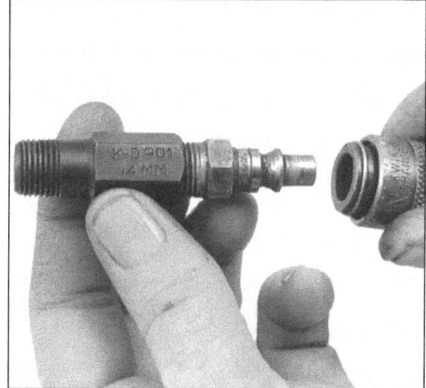

13.4 This is what the air hose adapter that threads into the glow plug hole looks like

13.9 Once the spring is compressed, the collets can be removed with a small magnet or needle-nose pliers

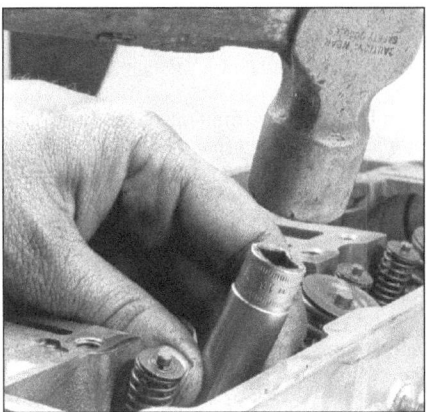

13.15 The valve guide seals can be removed with a deep socket

13.17 Apply a small dab of grease to each collet before refitting - it'll hold them in place on the valve stem as the spring is released

turn suddenly. If the spanner used when positioning the number one piston at TDC is still attached to the bolt in the crankshaft nose, it could cause damage or injury when the crankshaft moves.

7   The valves should be held in place by the air pressure.

8   If you don't have access to compressed air, an alternative method can be used. Position the piston at a point approximately 45-degrees (1/4-turn) before TDC on the compression stroke, then feed a long piece of nylon rope through the glow plug hole until it fills the combustion chamber. Be sure to leave the end of the rope hanging out of the engine so it can be removed easily. Use a large ratchet and socket to rotate the crankshaft in the normal direction of rotation until slight resistance is felt.

9   Stuff shop rags into the cylinder head holes above and below the valves to prevent parts and tools from falling into the engine, then use a valve spring compressor to compress the spring **(see illustration)**. Remove the collets with small needle-nose pliers or a magnet.

10   Remove the spring retainer, oil shield and valve spring, then remove the guide seal. **Note:** *If air pressure fails to hold the valve in the closed position during this operation, the valve face and/or seat is probably damaged. If so, the cylinder head will have to be removed for additional repair operations.*

11   Wrap a rubber band or tape around the top of the valve stem so the valve won't fall into the combustion chamber, then release the air pressure. **Note:** *If a rope was used instead of air pressure, turn the crankshaft slightly in the direction opposite normal rotation.*

12   Inspect the valve stem for damage. Rotate the valve in the guide and check the end for eccentric movement, which would indicate that the valve is bent.

13   Move the valve up-and-down in the guide and make sure it doesn't bind. If the valve stem binds, either the valve is bent or the guide is damaged. In either case, the head will have to be removed for repair.

14   Reapply air pressure to the cylinder to retain the valve in the closed position, then remove the tape or rubber band from the valve stem. If a rope was used instead of air pressure, rotate the crankshaft in the normal direction of rotation until slight resistance is felt.

15   Lubricate the valve stem with engine oil and fit a new guide seal **(see illustration)**.

16   Refit the spring and shield in position over the valve.

17   Refit the valve spring retainer. Compress the valve spring and carefully position the collets in the groove. Apply a small dab of grease to the inside of each collet to hold it in place **(see illustration)**.

18   Remove the pressure from the spring tool and make sure the collets are seated.

19   Disconnect the air hose and remove the adapter from the glow plug hole. If a rope was used in place of air pressure, pull it out of the cylinder.

20   Refer to Section 10 and refit the rocker arm assembly.

21   Refit the glow plug(s) and hook up the glow plug strap.

22   Adjust the valve clearances (see Chapter 1).

23   Refer to Section 4 and refit the valve cover.

24   Start and run the engine, then check for oil leaks and unusual sounds coming from the valve cover area.

14   Cylinder head - removal and refitting

Caution: *The engine must be completely cool before starting this procedure.*

Removal

Refer to illustrations 14.8, 14.9a and 14.9b

1   Position the engine at TDC on the compression stroke (see Section 3).

2   Detach the cable from the negative battery terminal, drain the engine oil and the cooling system (see Chapter 1). Detach the upper radiator hose from the thermostat hous-

ing cover (see Chapter 3).

3   Remove the valve cover (see Section 4).

4   Remove the timing belt and camshaft sprocket (see Section 8).

5   On 1989 and later 2L and 3L engines, remove the rear timing belt cover **(see illustration 11.3)**.

6   Remove the inlet and exhaust manifolds (see Sections 5 and 6).

7   If you're working on an L engine or a 1988 or earlier 2L engine, remove the rocker arm assembly (see Section 10) and the camshaft (see Section 11). If you're working on a later 2L or a 3L engine, the camshaft can stay in place.

8   Loosen the cylinder head bolts in 1/4-turn increments until they can be removed by hand. Loosen them in the order opposite that of the tightening sequence **(see illustrations 14.20a and 14.20b)** to avoid warping or cracking the head. Keep the head bolts in order so they can be returned to their original locations **(see illustration)**.

9   Lift the head off the engine **(see illustrations)**. The head may stick to the engine block, but this can usually be overcome by rocking one side of the head up first. If this technique doesn't work, DO NOT prise between the head and block - damage to the mating surfaces will result! Instead, position a

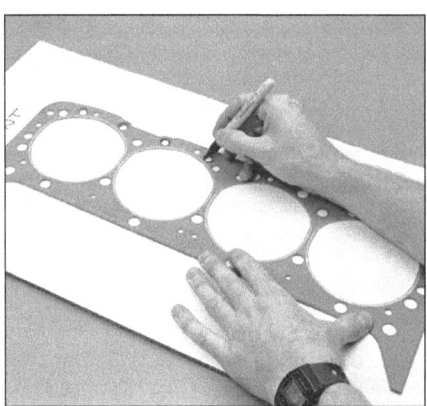

14.8 To avoid mixing up the head bolts, use a new gasket to transfer the bolt hole pattern to a piece of cardboard, then punch holes to accept the bolts

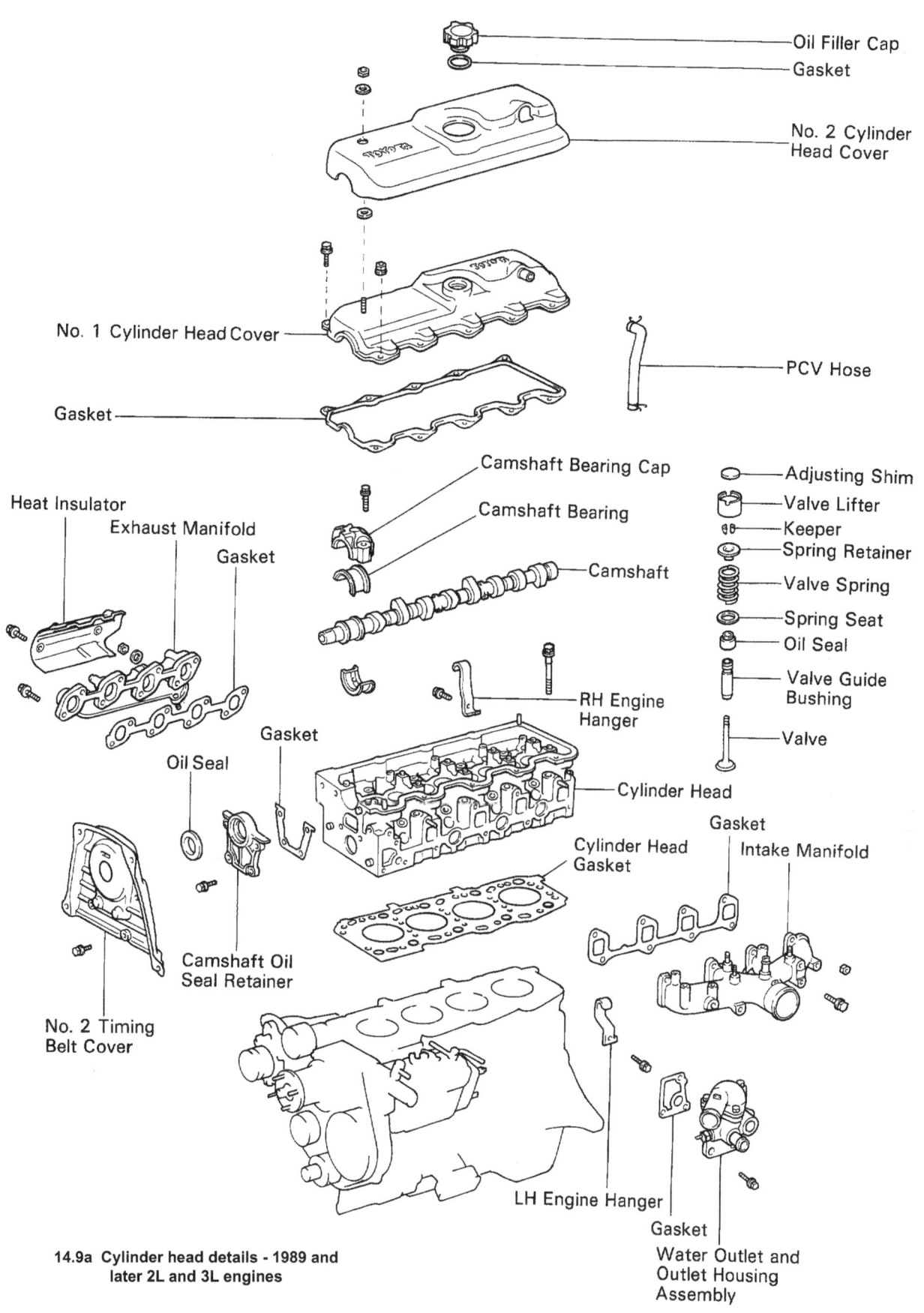

Oil Filler Cap

Gasket

No. 2 Cylinder Head Cover

No. 1 Cylinder Head Cover

PCV Hose

Gasket

Camshaft Bearing Cap

Camshaft Bearing

Camshaft

Heat Insulator

Exhaust Manifold

Gasket

Adjusting Shim

Valve Lifter

Keeper

Spring Retainer

Valve Spring

Spring Seat

Oil Seal

Valve Guide Bushing

Valve

RH Engine Hanger

Gasket

Oil Seal

Cylinder Head

Cylinder Head Gasket

Gasket

Intake Manifold

Camshaft Oil Seal Retainer

No. 2 Timing Belt Cover

LH Engine Hanger

Gasket

Water Outlet and Outlet Housing Assembly

14.9a Cylinder head details - 1989 and later 2L and 3L engines

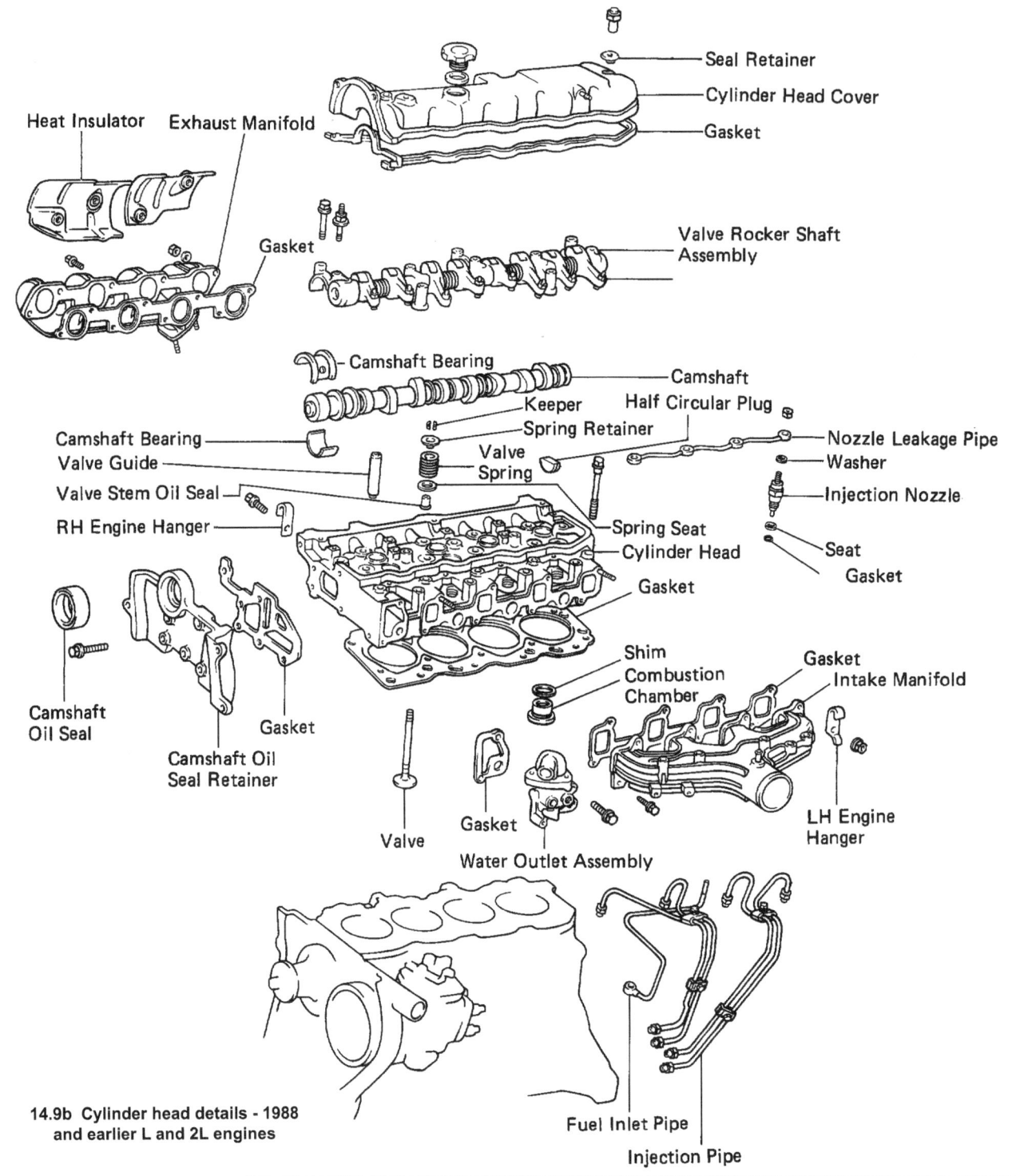

**14.9b Cylinder head details - 1988
and earlier L and 2L engines**

lever or large screwdriver between the block and a casting projection on the head and prise the head loose.

10   Place the head on blocks of wood to prevent damage to the gasket surface. Remove the head gasket from the block.

11   To remove and inspect the rocker arm assembly, see Section 8. To remove and inspect the camshaft, see Section 11.

Refitting

Refer to illustrations 14.12, 14.15, 14.16a, 14.16b, 14.17a, 14.17b, 14.20a and 14.20b

12   The mating surfaces of the cylinder head and block must be perfectly clean when the head is refitted. Use a gasket scraper to remove all traces of carbon and old gasket material, then clean the mating surfaces with lacquer thinner or acetone. If there's oil on the mating surfaces when the head is refitted, the gasket may not seal correctly and leaks could

develop. When working on the block, stuff the cylinders with clean shop rags to keep out debris. Use a vacuum cleaner to remove any debris that falls into the cylinders.

13   Check the block and head mating surfaces for nicks, deep scratches and other damage. If damage is slight, it can be removed with a file; if it's excessive, machining may be the only alternative. Also check the head and block deck for warpage.

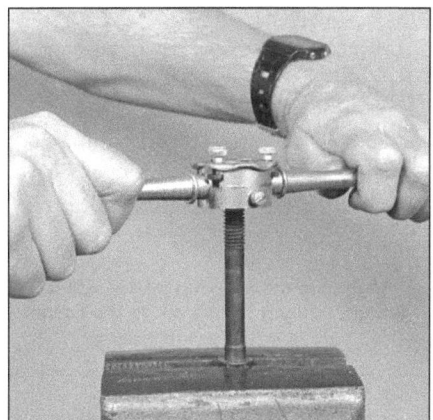

14.14 A die should be used to remove sealant and corrosion from the head bolt threads prior to refitting

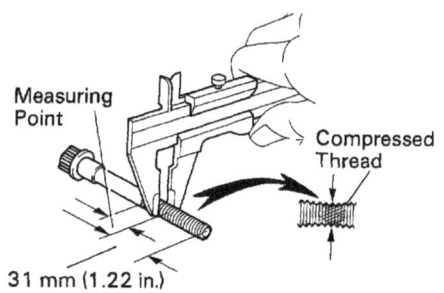

14.15 On 1989 and later 2L and 3L engines, measure the diameter of each head bolt, 31 mm from the end of the bolt, to see if the bolt is still usable - the minimum allowable diameter is 11.6 mm

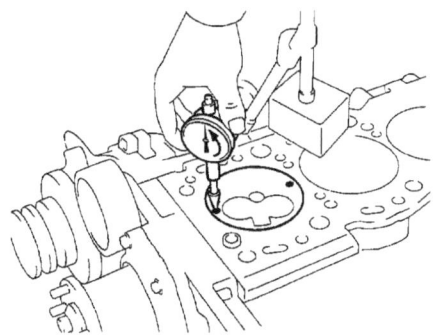

14.16a Find the highest point (greatest protrusion) of the piston and zero the dial indicator . . .

14   Use a tap of the correct size to chase the threads in the head bolt holes. Blow out the head bolt holes with compressed air to remove any debris. **Warning:** *Wear eye protection.* Mount each bolt in a vise and run a die down the threads to remove corrosion and restore the threads **(see illustration)**. Dirt, corrosion, sealant and damaged threads will affect torque readings.

15   If you're working on a 1989 or later 2L or 3L engine, measure the diameter of the head bolt threads. If any have "necked down" past the minimum allowable diameter, renew them.

16   Also, if you're working on a 1989 or later 2L or 3L engine, measure the protrusion of piston number 1, using a dial indicator while turning the crankshaft slightly before and slightly past TDC **(see illustration)**. Find the point where the piston protrudes the most, zero the dial indicator, then carefully slide the dial indicator to the side so the plunger drops off the piston and contacts the block deck **(see illustration)**. Record this measurement, then repeat the procedure on the number 4 piston. Rotate the engine 180-degrees and repeat the procedure on piston numbers 2 and 3, recording their protrusions.

17   Compare the greatest piston protrusion with the accompanying chart to select the proper thickness head gasket **(see illustration)**. The head gaskets are coded to indicate

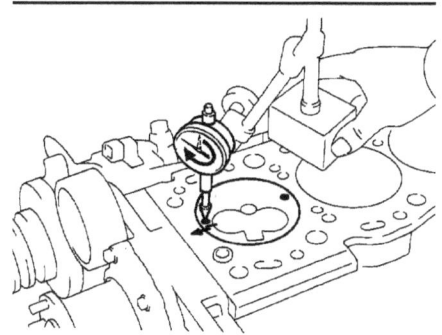

14.16b . . . then carefully slide the indicator plunger off the edge of the piston onto the block deck - the reading on the gauge is the amount of piston protrusion

their thicknesses **(see illustration)**.

18   Return the engine to TDC, aligning the notch on the crankshaft sprocket with the mark on the oil pump/front cover. refit the head gasket on the engine block, aligning all of the bolt holes. Check to make sure the gasket is the correct one, and that none of the oil or coolant passages are blocked.

19   Refit the cylinder head, being careful not to disturb the gasket. Lightly lubricate the head bolts with clean engine oil, then refit them in their proper locations, threading them in by hand. **Caution:** *If you're working on a*

Piston protrusion mm (in.)	Gasket size
0.68 – 0.77 (0.0268 – 0.0303)	Use B
0.78 – 0.87 (0.0307 – 0.0343)	Use D
0.88 – 0.97 (0.0316 – 0.0382)	Use F

14.17a Compare the greatest piston protrusion to this chart to determine which size head gasket to use (1989 and later 2L and 3L engines)

1989 or later 2L or a 3L engine, make sure the keyway in the end of the camshaft is in the 12 o'clock position.

20   Tighten the head bolts in four equal steps to the torque listed in this Chapter's Specifications. Be sure to follow the recommended sequence **(see illustrations)**.

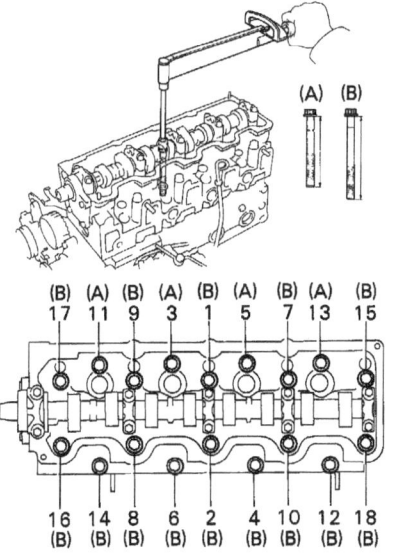

14.20b Head bolt TIGHTENING sequence (1989 and later 2L and 3L engines) - note the fitted positions of the different length bolts

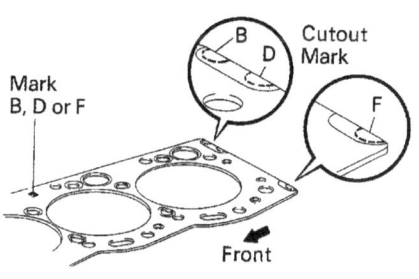

14.17b Head gasket coding details (1989 and later 2L and 3L engines)

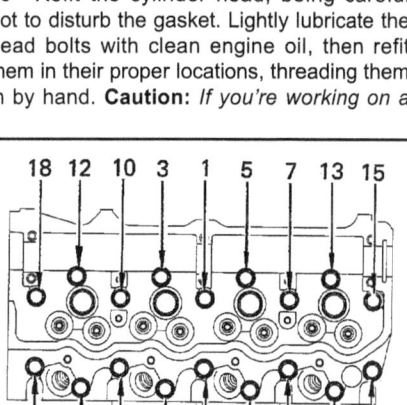

14.20a Head bolt TIGHTENING sequence (1988 and earlier L and 2L engines)

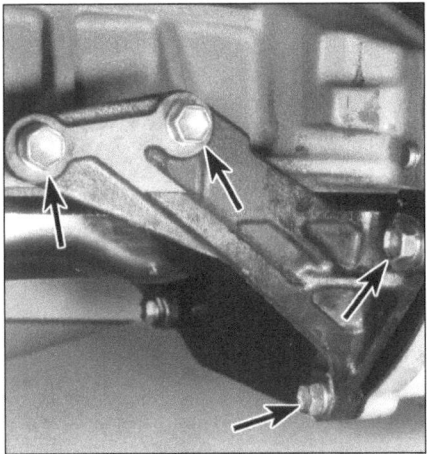

15.5 Remove the reinforcement brackets before attempting to remove the sump

21   If you removed it, refit the camshaft (see Section 11). Turn the camshaft to position the keyway at the 12 o'clock position.
22   Refit the cam sprocket (see Section 8). Make sure the mark on the sprocket is in alignment with its corresponding mark on the rear timing belt cover (1989 and later 2L and 3L engines) **(see illustration 8.8b)** or, on L and early 2L engines, with the top surface of the cylinder head **(see illustration 8.8a)**.
23   If you're working on a L engine or a 1988 or earlier 2L engine, loosen the adjuster screws and refit the rocker arm assembly (see Section 10).
24   Refit the timing belt (see Section 8).
25   If you're working on a L engine or a 1988 or earlier 2L engine, adjust the valves (see Chapter 1).
26   If you're working on a L engine or a 1988 or earlier 2L engine, apply RTV sealant to the rear half-moon rubber seal and refit it in the cylinder head.
27   Refit the valve cover (see Section 4).
28   Refit the inlet and exhaust manifolds (see Sections 5 and 6).
29   Attach the exhaust pipe to the exhaust manifold and tighten the three nuts.
30   The remainder of refitting is the reverse of removal. Refill the cooling system, fit new engine oil and change the oil filter (see Chapter 1). Start the engine and check for leaks and proper operation.
31   If you're working on a L engine or a 1988 or earlier 2L engine, readjust the valves (see Chapter 1).

15 Sump - removal and refitting

Refer to illustrations 15.5, 15.9a, 15.8b and 15.9c

Note: *The sump can be removed with the engine in the vehicle on 4WD models with a solid front axle, and on 2WD models. On 4WD models with independent front suspension, the engine must be removed from the vehicle in order to remove the sump.*

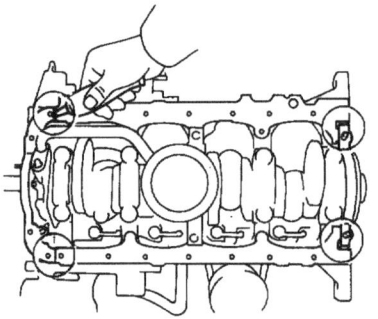

15.9a Apply a bead of RTV sealant to the areas where the rear main oil seal retainer and the front cover/oil pump mate to the cylinder block

1   Drain the engine oil (see Chapter 1).
2   Raise the front of the vehicle and support it on jackstands placed under the frame.
3   Remove the splash shield, if equipped.
4   If you're working on a 2WD model, disconnect the relay rod (see the steering linkage removal and refitting section in Chapter 10), then remove the front crossmember.
5   If there are reinforcement brackets between the pan and the transmission bell-housing **(see illustration)**, it may be necessary to remove them to get at the rear pan bolts. Also, on some models it may be necessary to raise the engine slightly to provide enough clearance between the engine and the frame to allow sump removal. Where this is the case, unbolt the radiator fan shroud, remove the engine mount-to-frame bolts and raise the engine, preferably with a hoist from above, then place wood blocks between the mounts and the frame.
6   Remove the sump bolts and detach the pan. Don't prise between the block and pan or damage to the sealing surfaces may result and oil leaks could develop. Use a block of wood and a hammer to dislodge the pan if it's stuck.
7   Use a scraper to remove all traces of old gasket material and sealant from the block, timing chain cover, rear oil seal housing and sump. Clean the gasket sealing surfaces with lacquer thinner or acetone and make sure the bolt holes in the block are clean.
8   Check the sump flange for distortion, particularly around the bolt holes. If necessary, place the pan on a block of wood and use a hammer to flatten and restore the gasket surface.
9   Apply a bead of RTV sealant to the areas where the rear main oil seal retainer and the oil pump/front cover meet the engine block **(see illustration)**. Also apply a thin coat of gasket sealant to the corner areas of the sump flange **(see illustration)** and fit a new gasket on the flange. Make sure the bolt holes are aligned. On models that don't use a gasket apply a 5mm bead of RTV sealant to the sump flange **(see illustration)**, and to the areas shown in **illustration 15.9a**. Avoid excessive amounts of sealant and be sure to attach the sump within five minutes or

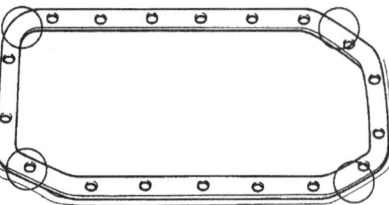

15.9b On models that use an sump gasket, apply RTV sealant to the corner areas of the sump gasket

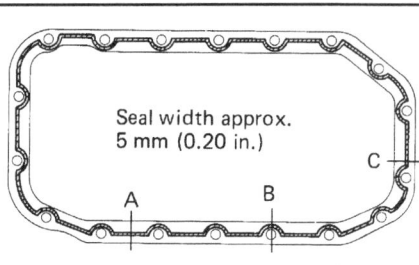

Seal width approx. 5 mm (0.20 in.)

A
Groove

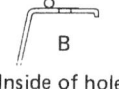
B
Inside of hole

C   5 mm (0.20 in.)

15.9c On models that don't use an sump gasket, apply a continuous bead of RTV sealant to the sump flange

the sealant will have to be scraped off and reapplied.
10   Position the sump against the engine block and refit the mounting bolts. Tighten them in a criss-cross pattern to the torque listed in this Chapter's Specifications.
11   Wait at least 30 minutes before filling the engine with oil (see Chapter 1), then start the engine and check the pan for leaks.
12   Refit the parts removed for access to the sump.

16 Oil pump and pick-up tube - removal, inspection and refitting

Removal

Refer to illustrations 16.7 and 16.8

1   Position the engine at TDC on the compression stroke for cylinder no. 1 (see Section 3).
2   Drain the cooling system and the engine oil (see Chapter 1).

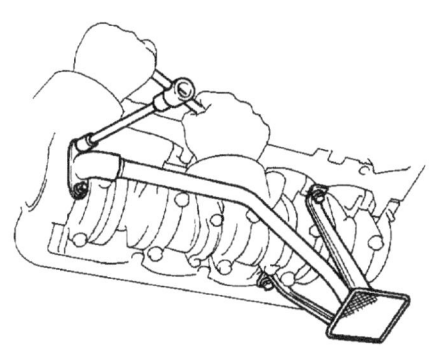

16.7 Unbolt the oil pump pick-up tube and screen

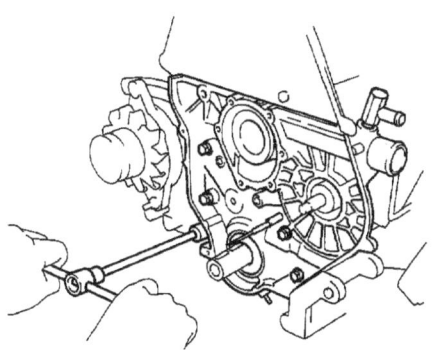

16.8 Oil pump/front cover bolt locations (1989 and later 2L and 3L engine shown, others similar)

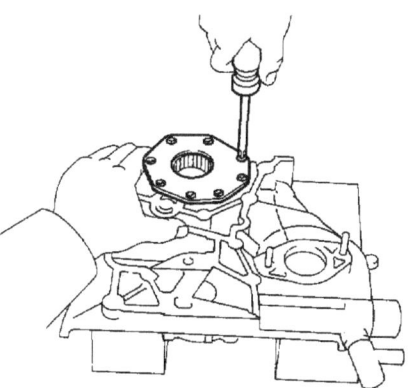

16.9a Remove the screws and lift off the pump body cover

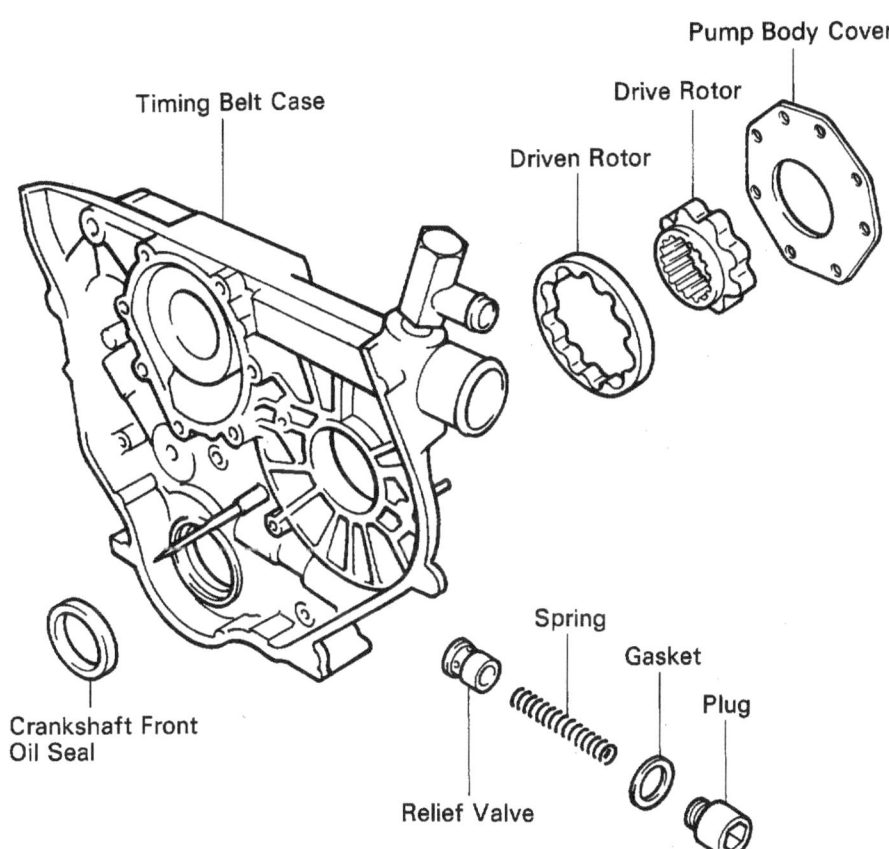

16.9b Oil pump details - exploded view (1989 and later 2L and 3L engine shown, others similar)

Labels: Timing Belt Case, Driven Rotor, Drive Rotor, Pump Body Cover, Crankshaft Front Oil Seal, Spring, Gasket, Plug, Relief Valve

16.11 Measuring the driven gear-to-pump body clearance

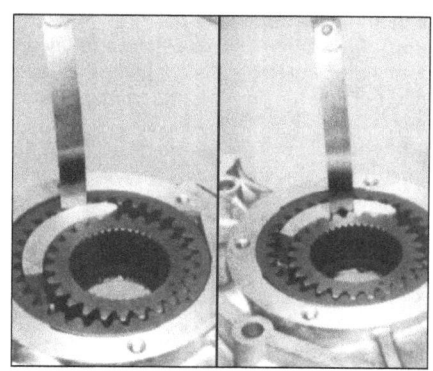

16.12 Measuring the driven and drive gear-to-crescent clearance (1988 and earlier L and 2L engines)

3   Remove the timing belt (see Section 8).
4   Remove the water pump (see Chapter 3).
5   Remove the fuel injection pump (see Chapter 4B).
6   Remove the sump (see Section 15).
7   Remove the bolts and detach the oil pick-up tube **(see illustration)**.
8   Remove the bolts and detach the oil pump/front cover assembly **(see illustration)**.

Inspection

Refer to illustrations 16.9a, 16.9b, 16.11, 16.12, 16.13, 16.14 and 16.18

9   Remove the screws and detach the cover to expose the oil pump gears **(see illustrations)**.
10   Unscrew the plug and remove the spring and relief valve from the oil pump, if equipped **(see illustration 16.9b)**.
11   Measure the clearance between the

driven gear and body with a feeler gauge **(see illustration)**. If the clearance is greater than the specified maximum, renew the pump.
12   On L engines and 1988 and earlier 2L engines, measure the clearance between both gears and the crescent with feeler gauges **(see illustration)**. If the clearance is greater than the specified maximum, renew the pump.
13   If you're working on a 1989 or later 2L or 3L engine, measure the tip clearance between the drive and driven gears **(see illustration)**. If the clearance is greater than

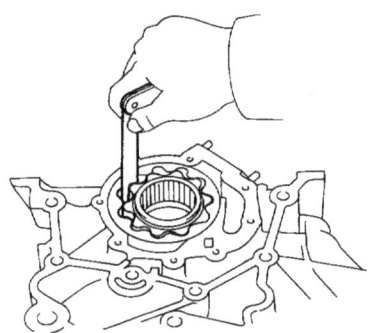

16.13 Measuring the pump rotor tip clearance (1989 and later 2L and 3L engines)

16.14 Measuring the oil pump gear side clearance

16.18 When refitting the gear in the pump body, be sure to align the marks on the gears

the specified maximum, renew the pump.

14   Measure the side clearance with a straightedge and feeler gauge **(see illustration)**. If the clearance is greater than the specified maximum, renew the pump.

15   On models so equipped, check the relief valve piston and bore for scuffing and score marks. Make sure the valve moves freely in the bore without excessive side play. If any defects are found, renew the appropriate parts.

16   Check the crankshaft front oil seal for wear and damage. If a new one is required, prise out the old one and fit a new one.

17   To reassemble the pump, lubricate and insert the relief valve piston and spring, then refit the plug (with a new gasket).

18   Coat them with clean oil, then insert the drive and driven gears into the pump body, aligning their matchmarks **(see illustration)**. Pack the recesses between the gears with petroleum jelly - this will prime the pump and help the engine to build up oil pressure quickly when it is first started.

19   Refit the cover over the gears. Coat the threads of each screw with a non-hardening thread locking compound and refit them, tightening them securely.

Refitting

20   Using a new gasket, refit the oil pump/front cover assembly to the engine. Tighten the bolts in a criss-cross pattern to the torque listed in this Chapter's Specifications.

21   Clean and refit the oil pick-up tube and screen. refit the pick-up tube and tighten the bolts to the torque listed in this Chapter's Specifications.

22   The remainder of refitting is the reverse of removal.

23   Refill the engine with oil and refit new coolant (see Chapter 1).

---

17   Flywheel/driveplate - removal and refitting

1   Remove the manual transmission, pressure plate and clutch disc as described in Chapters 7A and 8, or the automatic transmission as described in Chapter 7B.

18.6 Typical rear main oil seal retainer bolts (arrows)

2   Flatten the lockplate tabs (if used) and remove the bolts that secure the flywheel/driveplate to the crankshaft rear flange. Be careful - the flywheel is very heavy and should not be dropped. If the crankshaft turns as the bolts are loosened, wedge a screwdriver in the starter ring gear teeth.

3   Detach the flywheel/driveplate from the crankshaft flange.

4   If the teeth on the flywheel/driveplate starter ring gear are badly worn, or if some are missing, fit a new flywheel or driveplate. If this is the case, be sure to renew the starter (see Chapter 5).

5   Refer to Chapter 8 for the flywheel inspection procedure and the pilot bearing check and renewal procedure.

6   Before refitting the flywheel/driveplate, clean the mating surfaces.

7   If removed, refit the rear plate.

8   Position the flywheel/driveplate against the crankshaft and refit the mounting bolts. Use a non-hardening thread locking compound on the bolts.

9   Tighten the bolts in a criss-cross pattern to the torque listed in this Chapter's Specifications.

10   The remainder of refitting is the reverse of removal.

---

18   Rear main oil seal - renewal

Note: *The rear main oil seal can be renewed without removing the seal retainer. However, the preferred method is to remove the retainer first, then renew the seal on the bench.*

1   Raise the front of the vehicle and place it securely on jackstands.

2   Remove the transmission (see Chapter 7).

3   If equipped with a manual transmission, remove the pressure plate and clutch disc (see Chapter 8).

4   Remove the flywheel or driveplate (see Section 17).

5   If you're removing the seal retainer, remove the sump (see Section 15). **Note:** T*he retainer can be removed without actually removing the sump - you can simply remove the bolts that attach the sump flange to the retainer - but we don't recommend this approach because an oil leak between the retainer and the sump flange may develop at this point.*

Retainer removed

Refer to illustrations 18.6, 18.7 and 18.10

6   Remove the rear main oil seal retainer **(see illustration)**. Discard the old gasket.

7   Place the retainer on a clean workbench and carefully prise out the old seal with a large screwdriver **(see illustration)**. Make sure you don't nick or gouge the seal bore.

8   Using a gasket scraper, carefully remove all traces of old gasket material from the mating surfaces of the block and the seal retainer. Make sure you don't nick or gouge either surface.

9   Using a large socket with an outside diameter slightly smaller than the inside diameter of the seal bore, carefully drive the new seal into place until it's fully seated in the retainer.

10   Coat the rear (block side) of the new gasket with RTV sealant and place it in position **(see illustration)**.

11   Refit the retainer and the retainer bolts, tightening them to the torque listed in this

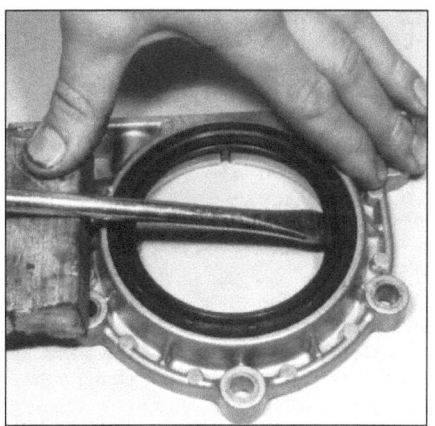

18.7 Prise the old seal out of the retainer with a large screwdriver - use a block of wood as a fulcrum (instead of the edge of the seal bore) to prevent damage to the retainer - make sure you don't nick or gouge the seal bore surface or the seal will leak

18.10 Coat the new retainer gasket with RTV sealant and carefully place it in position on the block

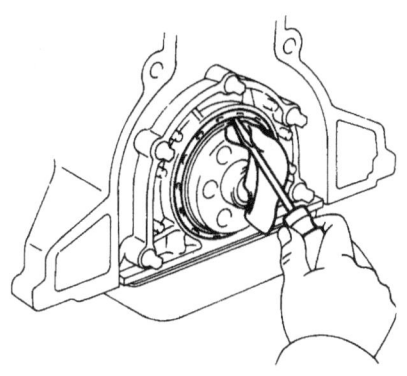

18.13 When removing the rear main oil seal from the housing, wrap the screwdriver with a rag to protect the crankshaft

Chapter's Specifications.

12   The remainder of refitting is the reverse of removal.

Retainer on the engine

Refer to illustration 18.13

13   Using a seal removal tool or a large screwdriver, carefully prise the seal out of the housing **(see illustration)**. Don't scratch or nick the crankshaft in the process!

14   Clean the bore in the housing and the seal contact surface on the crankshaft. Check the crankshaft surface for scratches and nicks that could damage the new seal lip and cause oil leaks. If the crankshaft is damaged, the only alternative is a new or different crankshaft.

15   Apply a light coat of engine oil or multipurpose grease to the outer edge of the new seal. Also lubricate the seal lip.

16   The seal lip must face toward the front of the engine. Carefully work the seal lip over the end of the crankshaft and tap the seal in with a hammer and punch until it's seated in the bore. **Caution:** *Be extremely careful - take your time and drive the seal gently and evenly into place. Damaging a new seal will result in an oil leak.*

17   The remainder of refitting is the reverse of removal.

---

19   Oil filter bracket and oil cooler - removal and refitting

Refer to illustrations 19.3 and 19.4

1   Drain the engine oil and remove the oil filter (see Chapter 1). Also drain the engine coolant (see Chapter 1).

2   Remove the exhaust manifold (see Section 6).

3   Remove the bolts and detach the oil filter bracket/oil cooler assembly from the engine

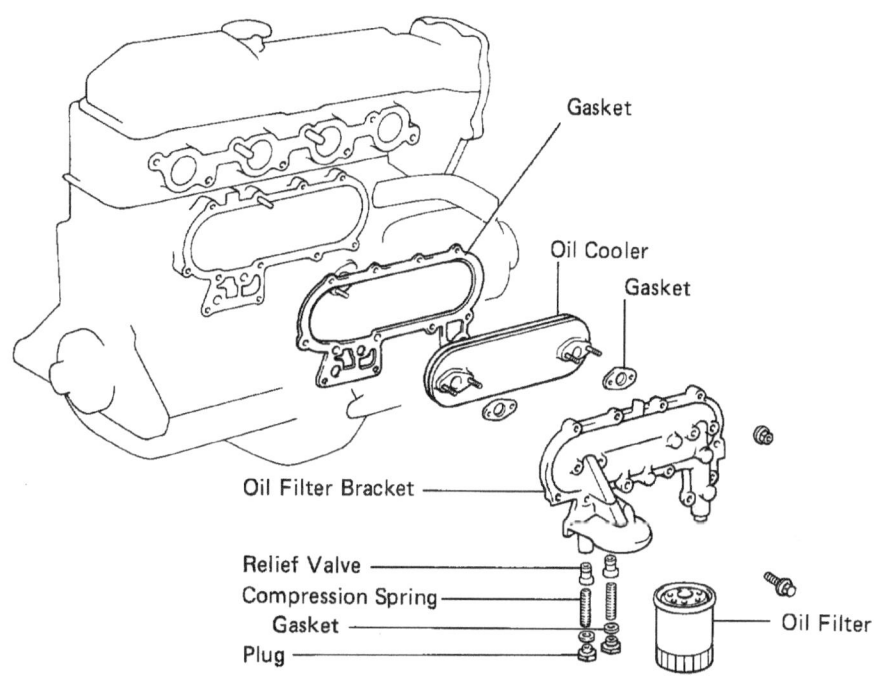

19.3 Oil filter bracket/oil cooler details

block **(see illustration)**. Be prepared for coolant spillage. **Note:** *Make an illustration showing the length of each bolt and its position on the filter bracket, as the bolts are of three different lengths.*

4   Remove the nuts and detach the oil cooler from the filter bracket **(see illustration)**.

5   Clean all of the gasket mating surfaces of sealant and old gasket material.

6   Check the oil cooler for signs of leakage, renewing it if necessary.

7   Unscrew the plugs and remove the relief valves and springs. Insert each valve into its hole and see that it falls to the bottom of its hole under its own weight. If it doesn't renew the valve or the filter bracket, as necessary.

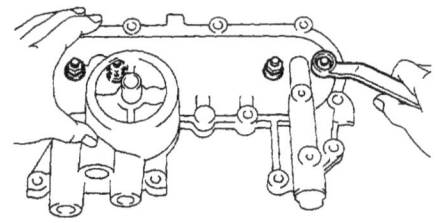

19.4 Remove the four nuts and detach the oil cooler from the filter bracket

20.5 Remove the mount-to-chassis bolts/ nuts and the mount-to-engine bracket bolt/nut (arrow) to detach the engine mount

8   Using new gaskets, connect the oil cooler to the filter bracket. refit the nuts and tighten them to the torque listed in this Chap-ter's Specifications.

9   Apply a thin coat of RTV sealant to the new gasket, then fit the gasket and oil filter bracket/cooler assembly to the engine block. refit the nuts and bolts, tightening them in a criss-cross pattern to the torque listed in this Chapter's Specifications.

10   refit the exhaust manifold (see Sec-tion 6).

11   Refill the engine with oil and coolant and fit a new oil filter (see Chapter 1).

20   Engine mounts - renewal

Refer to illustration 20.5

Warning: *Improper lifting methods or devices are potentially dangerous. DO NOT place any part of your body under the engine/transmis-sion when it's supported only by a jack. Fail-ure of the lifting device could result in serious injury or death.*

1   If the rubber mounts have hardened, cracked or separated from the metal backing plates, they must be renewed. This operation may be carried out with the engine/transmis-sion still in the vehicle.

2   Disconnect the negative cable from the battery.

3   Raise the front of the vehicle and sup-port it securely on jackstands. Apply the park-ing brake and block the rear wheels.

4   Support the engine with a jack. Position a block of wood between the jack head and the sump.

5   Remove the engine mount-to-chassis bolts/nuts **(see illustration)**.

6   Remove the mount-to-engine bracket bolts. It's not necessary to detach the bracket from the engine.

7   Raise the engine just enough to clear the bracket, then remove the engine mount.

8   Place the new mount in position.

9   Refit the mount-to-engine bracket bolts and tighten them securely.

10   Tighten the mount-to-chassis bolts/nuts securely. Remove the jackstands and lower the vehicle.

Chapter 2 Part E
General engine overhaul procedures

Contents

Specifications – petrol engines

Four-cylinder engines

General

Oil pressure
- 12R engine .... Not available (but should have at least 69 kPa for every 1000 rpm)
- Y-series engines .... 245 to 490 kPa at 3000 rpm
- 18R engine .... 372 kPa at 2500 rpm
- 20R engine .... 440 kPa at 2500 rpm
- 22R engine .... 490 kPa at 3000 rpm

Compression pressure
- Standard .... 1,177 kPa
- Minimum .... 883 kPa
- Maximum difference between cylinders .... 98 kPa

Camshaft, lifters and rocker arms .... See Chapter 2A, see Chapter 2B, see Chapter 2C

Four-cylinder engines (continued)

Cylinder head warpage limit
Block surface .... 0.15 mm
Manifold surface .... 0.20 mm

Valves
Valve stem diameter
  Intake
      12R engine .... 7.970 to 7.990 mm
      18R engine .... 7.975 to 7.985 mm
      20R, 22R, Y-series engines .... 7.970 to 7.985 mm
  Exhaust
      12R engine .... 7.870 to 7.980 mm
      18R engine .... 7.955 to 7.975 mm
      20R, 22R, Y-series engines .... 7.965 to 7.980 mm
Valve face angle 44.5-degrees
Valve margin width
  R-series engines .... 0.6 mm
  Y-series engines
    Intake .... 0.5 mm
    Exhaust .... 0.8 mm
Valve spring free length
  12R engine
    Inner .... Not available
    Outer .... 43.9 mm
  18R engine
    Inner .... 44.1 mm
    Outer .... 46.5 mm
  20R, 22R engines .... 48.5 mm
  Y-series engines .... 47.0 mm
Valve spring fitted height
  12R engine .... Not available
  18R engine .... Not available
  20R, 22R, Y-series engines .... 40.5 mm
Valve spring out-of-square limit
  12R engine .... Not available
  20R engine .... 1.9 mm
  18R, 22R engines .... 1.6 mm
  Y-series engine .... 2.0 mm
Valve guide inside diameter .... 8.01 to 8.03 mm
Valve stem-to-guide clearance
  Standard
    Intake .... 0.025 to 0.06 mm
    Exhaust .... 0.03 to 0.065 mm
  Limit
    Intake .... 0.08 mm
    Exhaust .... 0.10 mm
Valve seat
  Angle 45-degrees
  Width .... 1.2 to 1.6 mm

Engine block
Deck distortion limit .... 0.05 mm
Cylinder bore diameter
  12R engine .... 80.5 to 80.55 mm
  18R engine .... 88.5 to 88.55 mm
  1Y engine .... 86.0 to 86.03 mm
  2Y engine .... 86.0 to 86.03 mm
  3Y engine .... 86.0 to 86.03 mm
  4Y engine .... 91.0 to 91.03 mm
  20R engine .... 88.50 to 88.53 mm
  22R engine .... 92.00 to 92.03 mm
Cylinder bore out-of-round limit .... 0.02 mm
Cylinder bore taper limit .... 0.02 mm
Piston-to-bore clearance
  12R engine .... 0.01 to 0.05 mm
  18R engine .... 0.05 to 0.07 mm
  1Y engine .... 0.075 to 0.095 mm
  2Y engine .... 0.075 to 0.095 mm

3Y engine	0.075 to 0.095 mm
4Y engine	0.065 to 0.085 mm
20R engine	0.03 to 0.05 mm
22R engine	0.02 to 0.04 mm

Pistons and rings

Diameter (standard)

12R engine	80.45 to 80.50 mm
18R engine	88.44 to 88.49 mm
1Y engine	85.915 to 85.945 mm
2Y engine	85.915 to 85.945 mm
3Y engine	85.915 to 85.945 mm
4Y engine	90.925 to 90.955 mm
20R engine	88.46 to 88.49 mm
22R engine	91.970 to 92.000 mm

Piston ring end gap

12R, 18R, 20R engines	0.1 to 0.3 mm
22R engine	
Top compression ring..	0.25 to 0.47 mm
Second compression ring	0.60 to 0.82 mm
Oil ring	0.20 to 0.57 mm
1Y, 2Y, 3Y engines	
Top compression ring..	0.22 to 0.51 mm
Second compression ring	0.15 to 0.47 mm
Oil ring	0.13 to 0.50 mm
4Y engine	
Top compression ring..	0.23 to 0.51 mm
Second compression ring	0.16 to 0.47 mm
Oil ring	0.13 to 0.50 mm
Piston ring side clearance (maximum for new rings)............................	0.2 mm

Crankshaft, connecting rods and main bearings

Connecting rod endplay (side clearance)

12R engine	0.08 to 0.24 mm
18R, 20R, 22R engines	
Standard	0.16 to 0.26 mm
Limit	0.30 mm
Y-series engines	
Standard	0.16 to 0.312 mm
Limit	0.35 mm

Crankshaft endplay

12R engine	0.04 to 0.13 mm
18R, 20R, 22R, Y-series engines	
Standard	0.02 to 0.20 mm
Limit	0.30 mm
Crankshaft runout limit...	0.1 mm

Main bearing journal diameter (standard)

12R engine	49.976 to 50.000 mm
18R, 20R, 22R engines..	59.98 to 60.00 mm
Y-series engines..	57.985 to 58.000 mm

Connecting rod journal diameter

12R engine	Not available
18R, 20R, 22R engines..	52.99 to 53.00 mm
Y-series engines..	47.985 to 48.000 mm

Journal taper/out-of-round limit

18R, 20R, 22R engines..	0.01 mm
12R, Y-series engines	0.02 mm

Main bearing oil clearance

Standard

18R engine	0.016 to 0.040 mm
12R, 20R, 22R engines	0.025 to 0.055 mm
Y-series engines	0.020 to 0.051 mm

Limit

R-series engines..	0.08 mm
Y-series engines	0.10 mm

Four-cylinder engines (continued)

Connecting rod bearing oil clearance

    Standard

        12R engine .... 0.024 to 0.050 mm

        18R, 20R, 22R engines .... 0.025 to 0.055 mm

        Y-series engines .... 0.020 to 0.051 mm

    Limit.. 0.1 mm

Flywheel runout limit... 0.2 mm

Torque specifications*   **Nm**

Main bearing cap bolts

    12R engine.. 109

    18R engine.. 112

    20R engine.. 112

    22R engine.. 103

    Y-series engines... 78

Connecting rod cap nuts

    12R engine.. 48

    18R engine.. 61

    20R engine.. 53

    22R engine.. 69

    Y-series engines... 49

*Note: *Refer to Part A or B for additional torque specifications.*

V6 engine

General

Oil pressure

    At idle .... 29 kPa

    At 3000 rpm... 245 to 520 kPa

Compression pressure at 300 rpm

    Standard.. 1,177 kPa

    Minimum.. 981 kPa

    Maximum difference between cylinders .... 98 kPa

Camshaft and lifters .... See Chapter 2, Part C

Cylinder head warpage limit.. 0.10 mm

Valves and seats

Valve stem diameter

    Intake .... 7.970 to 7.985 mm

    Exhaust .... 7.965 to 7.980 mm

Valve guide inside diameter... 8.010 to 8.030 mm

Valve stem-to-guide clearance

    Standard

        Intake .... 0.025 to 0.060 mm

        Exhaust... 0.030 to 0.065 mm

    Limit

        Intake .... 0.08 mm

        Exhaust... 0.10 mm

Valve margin width limit .... 1.3 mm

Valve length .... 104.0 to 104.3 mm

Valve stem end grinding limit.. 0.5 mm

Valve spring free length .... 47.01 mm

Valve spring pressure/height .... 40.0 mm @ 26 Kg

Valve spring out-of-square limit .... 1.23 mm

Valve spring refitted height .... 40.0 mm

Valve seats

    Angle (intake and exhaust) 45-degrees

    Width .... 1.2 to 1.6 mm

Engine block

Deck distortion limit .... 0.05 mm

Cylinder bore

    Diameter (standard)

        Grade no. 1 - std. size .... 87.500 to 87.510 mm

        Grade no. 2.. 87.511 to 87.520 mm

        Grade no. 3.. 87.520 to 87.530 mm

    Wear limit .... 0.2 mm

    Taper/out-of-round limit .... 0.02 mm

Pistons and rings

Piston diameter	
Grade no. 1 - std. size	87.410 to 87.420 mm
Grade no. 2	87.421 to 87.430 mm
Grade no. 3	87.431 to 87.440 mm
Piston-to-bore clearance	0.080 to 0.10 mm
Piston ring side clearance (compression rings only)	
Standard	0.03 to 0.07 mm
Limit	0.2 mm
Piston ring end gap	
Top compression ring	
Standard	0.23 to 0.33 mm
Limit	0.83 mm
Second compression ring	
Standard	0.38 to 0.48 mm
Limit	0.93 mm
Oil control ring	
Standard	0.15 to 0.40 mm
Limit	0.90 mm

Crankshaft and connecting rods

Connecting rod endplay (side clearance)	
Standard	0.15 to 0.33 mm
Limit	0.38 mm
Crankshaft end play	
Standard	0.02 to 0.22 mm
Limit	0.30 mm
Main journal diameter	
Grade no. 0	63.996 to 64.000 mm
Grade no. 1	63.990 to 63.995 mm
Grade no. 2	63.985 to 63.989 mm
Connecting rod journal diameter	54.987 to 55.000 mm
Journal taper/out-of-round limit	0.020 mm
Crankshaft runout limit	0.06 mm
Main bearing oil clearance	
Standard	0.024 to 0.042 mm
Limit	0.080 mm
Connecting rod bearing oil clearance	
Standard	0.024 to 0.054 mm
Limit	0.080 mm

Torque specifications*

	Nm
Main bearing cap bolts	
Step 1	61
Step 2	Turn an additional 90° (1/4-turn)
Connecting rod cap nuts	
Step 1	25
Step 2	Turn an additional 90° (1/4-turn)
Rear oil seal retainer bolts	8

*__Note:__ *Refer to Part C for additional torque specifications.*

Specifications – diesel engines

Note: *References to early 2L engines refer to 1988 and earlier 2L engines (with rocker arms).*

General

Oil pressure	
At idle	29 kPa or more
At 3000 rpm	294 to 539 kPa
Compression pressure (@ 250 rpm)	
Standard	3,138 kPa or more
Minimum	1,961 kPa
Maximum difference between cylinders	490 kPa
Camshaft, lifters and rocker arms	See Chapter 2D

Cylinder head warpage limit

All engines	0.20 mm

Diesel engines (continued)

Combustion chamber

Protrusion
    L and early 2L engines .... 0.01 to 0.07 mm
    Later 2L and 3L engines... -0.03 to 0.03 mm
Available shim thicknesses
    L and early 2L engines .... 0.05 mm
                                                                         0.10 mm
                                                                       0.15 mm
                                                                       0.20 mm
    Later 2L and 3L engines... 0.03 mm

Valves

Valve stem diameter
    Inlet
        L engine, early 2L engine... 8.473 to 8.489 mm
        Later 2L and 3L engines .... 7.975 to 7.990 mm
    Exhaust
        L engine, early 2L engine... 8.454 to 8.470 mm
        Later 2L and 3L engines .... 7.960 to 7.975 mm
Valve face angle 44.5-degrees
Valve margin width (minimum)
    L engine, early 2L engine
        Inlet.. 0.9 mm
        Exhaust... 1.0 mm
    Later 2L and 3L engines
        Inlet.. 1.1 mm
        Exhaust... 1.2 mm
Valve spring free length
    L engine, early 2L engine .... 47.98 mm
    Later 2L and 3L engines
        Yellow mark .... 46.20 mm
        Blue mark.. 49.14 mm
Valve spring fitted height
    L engine, early 2L engine .... 39.3 mm
    Later 2L and 3L engines... 37.0 mm
Valve spring out-of-square limit .... 2.0 mm
Valve guide inside diameter
    L engine, early 2L engine .... 8.51 to 8.53 mm
    Later 2L and 3L engines... 8.01 to 8.03 mm
Valve stem-to-guide clearance
    L engine, early 2L engine
        Standard
            Inlet.. 0.021 to 0.057 mm
            Exhaust .... 0.040 to 0.076 mm
        Limit
            Inlet.. 0.10 mm
            Exhaust .... 0.12 mm
    Later 2L and 3L engines
        Standard
            Inlet.. 0.020 to 0.055 mm
            Exhaust .... 0.035 to 0.070 mm
        Limit
            Inlet.. 0.08 mm
            Exhaust .... 0.10 mm
Valve seat
    Angle 45-degrees
    Width
        L engine, early 2L engine... 1.2 to 1.6 mm
        Later 2L and 3L engines .... 1.8 to 2.2 mm

Engine block

Deck distortion limit .... 0.20 mm
Cylinder bore diameter
    L and 2L engines
        Standard .... 92.00 to 92.030 mm
        Limit .... 92.23 mm

3L engine
    Standard .... 96.00 to 96.030 mm
    Limit .... 96.23 mm
Cylinder bore out-of-round limit .... 0.02 mm
Cylinder bore taper limit.. 0.02 mm
Piston-to-bore clearance
    Standard .... 0.050 to 0.070 mm
    Limit... 0.14 mm

Pistons and rings

Diameter (standard)
    L, 2L engines.. 91.940 to 91.970 mm
    3L engine .... 95.940 to 95.970 mm
Piston ring end gap
    L, early 2L engines
        Top compression ring... 0.35 to 0.62 mm
        Second compression ring .... 0.20 to 0.47 mm
        Oil ring .... 0.20 to 0.52 mm
    Later 2L and 3L engines
        Top compression ring... 0.35 to 0.65 mm
        Second compression ring .... 0.30 to 0.60 mm
        Oil ring .... 0.20 to 0.50 mm
Piston ring side clearance (maximum for new rings)
    L, early 2L engines
        Top compression ring... 0.020 to 0.065 mm
        Second compression ring .... 0.040 to 0.080 mm
        Oil ring .... 0.030 to 0.070 mm
    Later 2L and 3L engines
        Top compression ring... 0.028 to 0.077 mm
        Second compression ring .... 0.060 to 0.105 mm
        Oil ring .... 0.030 to 0.070 mm

Crankshaft, connecting rods and main bearings

Connecting rod endplay (side clearance)
    L, early 2L engines
        Standard .... 0.08 to 0.20 mm
        Limit 0.3
    Later 2L and 3L engines
        Standard .... 0.80 to 0.30 mm
        Limit .... 0.35 mm
Crankshaft endplay
    Standard.. 0.04 to 0.250 mm
    Limit .... 0.30 mm
Crankshaft runout limit... 0.06 mm
Main bearing journal diameter (standard)............................... 61.985 to 62.000 mm
Connecting rod journal diameter
    L, 2L engines.. 52.988 to 53.000 mm
    3L engine .... 54.988 to 55.000 mm
Journal taper/out-of-round limit.. 0.02 mm
Main bearing oil clearance
    Standard.. 0.034 to 0.065 mm
    Limit .... 0.10 mm
Connecting rod bearing oil clearance
    Standard.. 0.036 to 0.064 mm
    Limit .... 0.1 mm

Torque specifications*

Nm
Main bearing cap bolts 103
Connecting rod cap nuts
    L, early 2L engines... 59
    Later 2L and 3L engines
        Step 1 54
        Step 2 .... Turn an additional 90-degrees

*Note: Refer to Part D for additional torque specifications.

2.4a Typical oil pressure switch (22R engine shown, other engines similar - all switches are located near the oil filter)

2.4b To check the oil pressure, remove the oil pressure switch and fit a pressure gauge in the hole (when you refit the switch, coat the threads with Teflon tape or thread sealant to prevent leaks)

3.4 A compression gauge with a threaded fitting for the spark plug hole is preferred over the type that requires hand pressure to maintain the seal - be sure to open the throttle and choke valves as far as possible during the compression check!

1   General information - engine overhaul

Overhauling an engine is a difficult and time-consuming task. Special tools and knowledge are required. For these reasons, we recommend that engine overhaul is best left to a professional engine rebuilder. A competent engine rebuilder will handle the inspection of your old parts and offer advice concerning the reconditioning or replacement of the original engine.

Be aware that some engine builders can only rebuild the engine you bring them, which can take several weeks, while other rebuilders have rebuilt exchange engines in stock. If time is an issue, an exchange engine may be the best solution. If an exchange engine is fitted, check with your state registry authority as some insist the engine number on the new engine is included on your registration and insurance details.

An engine overhaul involves restoring the internal parts to the specifications of a new engine. During an overhaul, the piston rings are replaced and the cylinder walls are reconditioned (rebored and/or honed). If a rebore is done by an automotive machine shop, new oversize pistons will also be installed. The main bearings and connecting rod bearings are generally replaced with new ones and, if necessary, the crankshaft may be reground to restore the journals. Generally, the valves are serviced as well, since they're usually in less-than-perfect condition at this point. The end result should be a like-new engine that will give many trouble-free miles.

Included in this chapter are general information and diagnostic testing procedures for determining the overall mechanical condition of your engine.

It is important to establish the condition of the cylinder block. Never purchase parts or have machine work done on other components until the block has been thoroughly inspected by a professional machine shop.

The following Sections have been written

to help you determine whether your engine needs to be overhauled and how to remove and install it once you've determined it needs to be rebuilt. For information concerning in-vehicle engine repair, see Chapter 2A or 2B.

It's not always easy to determine when, or if, an engine should be completely overhauled, because a number of factors must be considered.

High mileage is not necessarily an indication that an overhaul is needed, while low mileage doesn't preclude the need for an overhaul. Frequency of servicing is probably the most important consideration. An engine that has had regular and frequent oil and filter changes, as well as other required maintenance, will most likely give many thousands of kilometres of reliable service. Conversely, a neglected engine may require an overhaul very early in its service life.

Excessive oil consumption is an indication that piston rings, valve seals and/or valve guides are in need of attention. Make sure that oil leaks aren't responsible before deciding that the rings and/or valve guides are bad. Perform a cylinder compression check to determine the extent of the work required (see Section 3).

Check the oil pressure with a gauge installed in place of the oil pressure sending unit and compare it to this chapter's Specifications (see Section 2). If it's extremely low, the bearings and/or oil pump are probably worn out.

Loss of power, rough running, knocking or metallic engine noises, excessive valve train noise and high fuel consumption rates may also point to the need for an overhaul, especially if they're all present at the same time. If a complete tune-up doesn't remedy the situation, major mechanical work is the only solution.

Note: *Critical cooling system components such as the hoses, drivebelts, thermostat and water pump should be replaced with new parts when an engine is overhauled. The radiator should be checked carefully to ensure that it isn't clogged or leaking (see Chapter 3).*

If you purchase a rebuilt engine or short block, some rebuilders will not warranty their engines unless the radiator has been professionally flushed.

2   Oil pressure check

Refer to illustrations 2.4a and 2.4b

1   Low engine oil pressure can be a sign of an engine in need of rebuilding. A low oil pressure warning lamp is not a test of the lubrication system. Such indicators only come on when the oil pressure is dangerously low. Even a factory oil pressure gauge in the dashboard is only a relative indication, although much better for driver information than a warning light. A better test is with a mechanical (not electrical) oil pressure gauge.

2   Locate the oil pressure indicator sending unit on the engine block **(see illustrations)**.

Note: *It is near the crankshaft pulley on all engines.*

3   Unscrew and remove the oil pressure sending unit, then screw in the hose for your oil pressure gauge. If necessary, install an adapter fitting. Use Teflon tape or thread sealant on the threads of the adapter and/or the fitting on the end of your gauge's hose.

4   Connect an accurate tachometer to the engine, according to the tachometer manufacturer's instructions.

5   Check the oil pressure with the engine running (normal operating temperature) at the specified engine speed, and compare it to this chapter's Specifications. If it's extremely low, the bearings and/or oil pump are probably worn out.

3   Compression check

Refer to illustration 3.4

Warning: *Use only a compression gauge specifically designed for diesel engines on diesel engine models.*

1 A compression check will tell you what mechanical condition the upper end (pistons, rings, valves, head gaskets) of your engine is in. Specifically, it can tell you if the compression is down due to leakage caused by worn piston rings, defective valves and seats or a blown head gasket.

Note: *The engine must be at normal operating temperature and the battery must be fully charged for this check.*

Note: *On petrol engines, if the engine is equipped with a carburettor, the choke valve must be all the way open to get an accurate compression reading (if the engine's warm, the choke should be open).*

2 Begin by cleaning the area around the spark or glow plugs before you remove them (compressed air should be used, if available, otherwise a small brush or even a bicycle tyre pump will work). The idea is to prevent dirt from getting into the cylinders as the compression check is being done. Remove all of the spark or glow plugs from the engine (see Chapter 1) - petrol engines or (see Chapter 4B) - diesel engines.

3 On petrol engines, block the throttle wide open. Detach the large coil wire from the distributor cap and earth it on the engine block. Use a heavy jumper wire with alligator clips at both ends to ensure a good earth. On models with the coil mounted in the distributor, disconnect the primary (low voltage) wiring from the distributor.

4 On diesel engines, detach the wire from the terminal on the fuel cut solenoid (see Chapter 4B). Also remove the glow plug fuses or relays(s) (see Chapter 6).

5 With the compression gauge in the number one spark or glow plug hole **(see illustration)**, depress the accelerator pedal all the way to the floor to open the throttle valve. Crank the engine over at least four compression strokes and watch the gauge. The compression should build up quickly in a healthy engine. Low compression on the first stroke, followed by gradually increasing pressure on successive strokes, indicates worn piston rings. A low compression reading on the first stroke, which doesn't build up during successive strokes, indicates leaking valves or a blown head gasket (a cracked head could also be the cause). Record the highest gauge reading obtained.

6 Repeat the procedure for the remaining cylinders and compare the results to the Specifications.

7 Add some engine oil (about three squirts from a plunger-type oil can) to each cylinder, through the spark plug hole, and repeat the test.

8 If the compression increases after the oil is added, the piston rings are definitely worn. If the compression doesn't increase significantly, the leakage is occurring at the valves or head gasket. Leakage past the valves may be caused by incorrect clearances, burned valve seats and/or faces or warped, cracked or bent valves.

9 If two adjacent cylinders have equally low compression, there's a strong possibility that the head gasket between them is blown. The appearance of coolant in the combustion chambers or the crankcase would verify this condition.

10 If the compression is unusually high, the combustion chambers are probably coated with carbon deposits. If that's the case, the cylinder head should be removed and decarbonised.

11 If compression is way down or varies greatly between cylinders, it would be a good idea to have a leak-down test performed by an automotive repair shop. This test will pinpoint exactly where the leakage is occurring and how severe it is.

4 Engine - removal and refitting

Warning: *The air conditioning system is under high pressure. Do not loosen any fittings or remove any components until after the system has been discharged by a dealer service department or service station. Air conditioning refrigerant should be properly discharged into an approved container at a dealer service department or an automotive air conditioning repair facility. Always wear eye protection when disconnecting air conditioning system fittings.*

Removal

Refer to illustration 4.13

1 The engine can be removed from the vehicle in one of two ways. One is with the engine and transmission handled as a unit. The other is with the engine separated from the transmission before removal from the vehicle. If you're working on a 4WD model, it is recommended that you separate the engine from the transmission and remove the engine by itself. The procedure outlined here is for removing the engine and transmission as a unit. If you choose to remove only the engine, leaving the transmission in place in the vehicle, refer to Chapter 7 for the procedure to follow when separating the engine from the transmission.

2 Before proceeding, read Section 4, *Engine removal - methods and precautions.*

3 The following sequence of operations doesn't have to be performed in any specific order. It's simply a checklist of everything that must be disconnected or removed before the engine and transmission can be lifted out of the vehicle. It's very important that all linkages, electrical wires, hoses and cables be removed or disconnected before attempting to lift the engine out, so double-check everything carefully. **Warning:** *If the vehicle is equipped with air conditioning, have the system discharged by a service station before disconnecting any of the lines. DO NOT attempt it at home - serious injury or damage could result!*

4 Scribe or paint around the bonnet hinge brackets on the bonnet (to ensure proper alignment of the bonnet during refitting).

Remove the bolts and lift the bonnet carefully away from the vehicle (with the help of an assistant) (see Chapter 11).

5 On fuel injected models, relieve the fuel system pressure (see Chapter 4A) or (see Chapter 4B).

6 Raise the vehicle and support it on jackstands. Remove the engine undercover.

7 Disconnect both battery cables from the battery (negative first, then positive), remove the battery hold-down and lift the battery out of the vehicle. Disconnect the battery cable from the starter motor terminal.

8 Drain the engine oil and the transmission lubricant (see Chapter 1).

9 Remove the fan shroud and radiator (see Chapter 3).

10 If the vehicle is equipped with power steering or air conditioning, remove the drivebelt and pump or compressor mounting bolts. Lay the pump or compressor aside without disconnecting the hoses.

11 Remove the fan, fan pulley and drivebelt (see Chapter 3).

12 Remove the air cleaner (refer to Chapter 4A) or (see Chapter 4B).

13 Clearly label, then detach all coolant, vacuum, fuel and emissions hoses, electrical wires and earth straps that connect the engine/transmission to the vehicle **(see illustration)**.

14 Clearly label and disconnect all control cables and linkages from the carburettor, throttle body or injection pump and the transmission (see Chapter 4A), (see Chapter 4B), (see Chapter 7A) or (see Chapter 7B).

15 If the transmission is to be removed with the engine, remove the driveshaft (see Chapter 8).

16 Disconnect the speedometer cable.

17 Disconnect the exhaust pipe clamp from the transmission housing.

18 Disconnect the exhaust pipe from the exhaust manifold (see Chapter 4A) or (see Chapter 4B).

19 Disconnect the shift lever linkage (automatic transmission).

20 Remove the clutch release cylinder and hose bracket mounting bolts (manual trans-

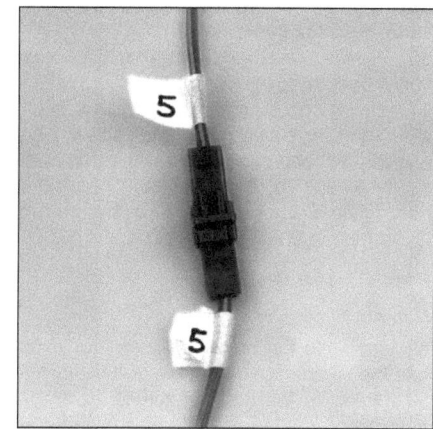

4.13 Label each wire before unplugging the connector

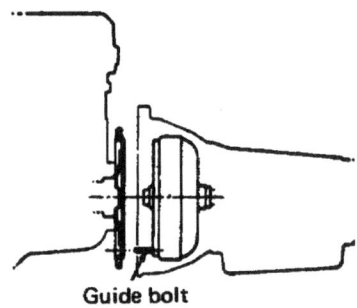

Guide bolt

4.29 Use guide bolts to ensure correct alignment of the engine and transmission

4.33 The stiffener plates are attached to the transmission with two bolts

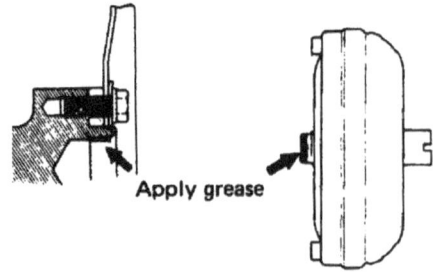

Apply grease

4.39 Apply grease to the areas indicated before rejoining the engine and automatic transmission

mission) and lay the cylinder alongside the frame.

21   Remove the bolts from the mounts at the front of the engine.

22   Position a jack under the transmission. Be sure to place a block of wood between the jack and the transmission to prevent damage.

23   Unbolt the rear engine mount bracket from the crossmember.

24   Attach the engine hoist chain to the engine's lift brackets.

25   Slowly and carefully lift the engine out of the vehicle. Make sure that all wires and hoses are disconnected.

Separating the engine and transmission

Automatic transmission

Refer to illustration 4.29

26   Remove the starter motor.

27   Remove the cover and stiffener plates from the lower part of the converter housing.

28   Make sure the transmission fluid is completely drained, then remove the six bolts that attach the torque converter to the driveplate. The bolts are accessible through the opening in the lower half of the converter housing and can only be removed one at a time. The driveplate will have to be rotated by turning the crankshaft pulley bolt with a spanner.

29   Cut the heads off two bolts and thread them into two of the holes vacated by the converter bolts **(see illustration)**.

30   Remove the bolts that attach the converter housing to the engine block.

31   Using one guide bolt as a pivot, insert a screwdriver between the engine rear plate and the bolt and prise the transmission away from the engine. A detailed and illustrated description of automatic transmission removal is included in Chapter 7 (see Chapter 7B).

Manual transmission

Refer to illustration 4.33

32   Remove the mounting bolts and separate the starter motor from the bellhousing.

33   Remove the bolts attaching the transmission to the engine block and stiffener plates **(see illustration)**.

34   Support the transmission near the front and pull straight back until it's free. Don't let

the transmission slip and fall, as damage to the input shaft could result.

35   Refer to Chapter 8 and remove the clutch assembly from the flywheel. A detailed and illustrated description of manual transmission removal is included in Chapter 7, (see Chapter 7A).

Rejoining the engine and transmission

Automatic transmission

Refer to illustration 4.39

36   This procedure is basically the reverse of removal.

37   Make sure the torque converter is properly refitted in the converter housing. The driveplate mounting bosses should be the specified distance from the housing-to-engine block mating surface.

38   Refit one of the guide bolts (used when separating the transmission from the engine) in one of the lower torque converter-to-driveplate bolt holes.

39   Apply a layer of multi-purpose grease to the recess in the end of the crankshaft **(see illustration)**.

40   Support the transmission and carefully guide it into position on the engine. The guide bolt should pass through the lower driveplate hole and the torque converter should enter the crankshaft recess.

41   Align the engine block dowel pins with the holes in the housing, then refit the mounting bolts and tighten them securely.

42   Refit the torque converter-to-driveplate mounting bolts and tighten them in several steps, using a criss-cross pattern, to the specified torque. Turn the crankshaft as required to expose the bolts.

43   Refit the cover and stiffener plates and tighten the bolts securely.

44   Attach the starter motor to the housing and tighten the bolts securely.

Manual transmission

45   This procedure is basically the reverse of removal. Refer to Chapter 8 and attach the

clutch assembly to the flywheel before proceeding.

46   Apply multi-purpose grease to the splines of the transmission input shaft, then carefully guide the input shaft into the clutch assembly until the bellhousing seats against the engine block. The splines on the shaft must mesh with the splines in the clutch disc and the end of the shaft must fit into the pilot bearing in the crankshaft.

47   Refit the bolts securing the bellhousing to the engine and tighten them securely.

48   Attach the starter motor and tighten the bolts.

49   Refit and tighten the stiffener plate bolts.

Refitting

50   Raise the vehicle and support it securely on jackstands.

51   Attach the engine to the hoist just like it was during removal and raise the engine until it clears the front of the vehicle. Don't let the engine swing freely.

52   Angle the transmission steeply toward the back of the vehicle and carefully lower the engine into place. Work slowly and use the transmission and hoist to direct the engine to its proper location on the motor mounts.

53   With the engine in place (still attached to the hoist), support the transmission with a jack and refit the front motor mount bolts. Tighten them finger tight only.

54   Remove the hoist and move it out of the way.

55   Refit the transmission support crossmember by raising or lowering the jack as necessary. Tighten the nuts attaching the transmission to the crossmember and the bolts holding the crossmember to the frame.

56   Tighten the engine mount bolts securely.

57   Refit and connect the remaining parts in the reverse order of removal.

58   Refill the crankcase with oil and add coolant as outlined in Chapter 1. Refill the transmission as required.

59   Run the engine and check for proper operation and leaks.

60   Recheck all fluid levels.

Chapter 3
Cooling, heating and air conditioning systems

Contents

Specifications

General

Coolant capacity	See Chapter 1
Radiator cap pressure rating	75 to 103 kPa
Thermostat opening temperature	
Diesel	86 to 90-degrees C
Petrol	Not specified

Torque specifications

	Nm
Thermostat housing cover bolts/nuts	
Petrol	
Y-series engines	12
R-series engines	Not available; tighten securely
V6 engine	20
Diesel	19
Water pump mounting bolts/nuts	
Petrol	
Y-series engines	
All except bolt holding alternator bracket	16
Bolt holding alternator bracket	39
R-series engines	8.8
V6 engine	
Small bolts	18
Large bolts	20
Diesel	
L (2.2L) engine	19
2L (2.4L) and 3L (2.8L) engines	23

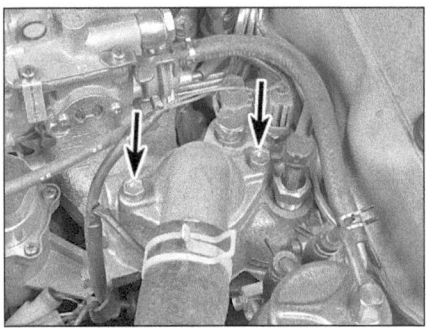

3.9a Typical R-series petrol engine thermostat housing bolts (arrows)

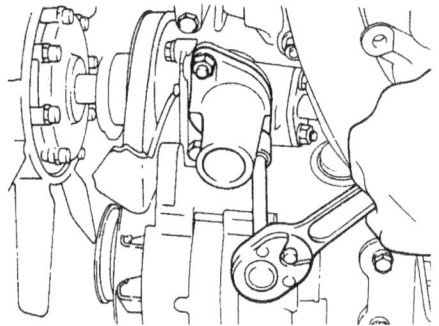

3.9b Location of the thermostat housing cover on Y-series petrol engines

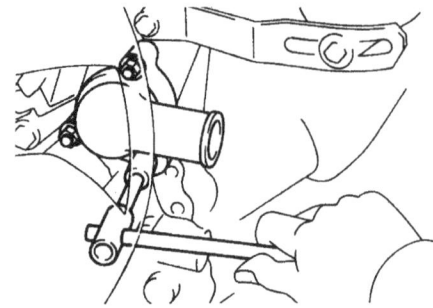

3.9c The V6 thermostat housing is located adjacent to the water pump

1   General information

The cooling system used on the models covered by this manual comprises the radiator, water pump, cooling fan and its fluid drive clutch, coolant reserve system and a thermostat.

The radiator is of conventional vertical flow design, mounted behind the vehicle's front grille. Two coolant hoses join it to the engine block.

The water pump is located at the front of the engine and is driven through a pulley and belt which also drives the alternator.

The fan clutch is located at the front of the water pump pulley and is attached to the pulley/water pump assembly by four nuts which secure it to studs screwed into the face of the water pump drive flange. The fan clutch serves to conserve engine power by disengaging the fan at high engine speeds, causing the fan to free-wheel. As engine speeds drop to a predetermined level, the fluid drive re-engages and the fan resumes driven rotation. The fan is attached to studs protruding from the front of the fan clutch.

The coolant reserve tank, which serves to make the cooling system a closed one, is located near the front of the engine compartment and is attached to the radiator through a hose that connects with an outlet just below the radiator cap.

The thermostat is located in a housing atop the inlet manifold. In its closed position, it serves to keep coolant in the cylinder block and head until the engine has reached an efficient operating temperature. As this temperature is reached, the thermostat opens, allowing coolant to pass from the head into the top radiator hose and into the radiator tank.

The heater utilises heat generated from circulated engine coolant by drawing air through a passenger compartment-mounted heater core. Heater controls are mounted in the vehicle's dashboard and the system's blower employs an electric motor mounted in the under-dash located central heater unit. The blower circulates air through the system's heat and defroster ducts. 4Runner models are equipped with a duct that carries heat under the centre console to a blower unit for the passengers in the back seat.

Air conditioning is an available option. Most of the system's components, except the evaporator/expansion valve (cooling unit) and controls, which are contained in the passenger compartment, are mounted in the engine compartment. Special refrigerant lines transfer R-134a, the cooling agent, back and forth between the passenger and engine compartment components.

Warning: *If any component of the air conditioning system needs to be removed, the system must be depressurised first. Do not attempt to discharge the system yourself, as the system contains gas under very high pressure. This could result in physical injury as well as damage to the system.*

2   Antifreeze - general information

Warning: *Don't allow antifreeze to come in contact with your skin or painted surfaces of the vehicle. Rinse off spills immediately with plenty of water. Antifreeze is highly toxic if ingested. Never leave antifreeze lying around in an open container or in puddles on the floor; children and pets are attracted by its sweet smell and may drink it. Check with local authorities about disposing of used antifreeze. Many communities have collection centres which will see that antifreeze is disposed of safely. Never dump antifreeze on the ground or into drains.*
Note: *Non-toxic antifreeze is now manufactured and available at local auto parts stores, but even these types should be disposed of properly.*

The cooling system should be filled with a water/ethylene glycol based antifreeze solution which will prevent freezing down to at least -29-degrees C. It also provides protection against corrosion and increases the coolant boiling point.

The cooling system should be drained, flushed and refilled at least every other year (see Chapter 1). The use of antifreeze solutions for periods of longer than two years is likely to cause damage and encourage the formation of rust and scale in the system.

Before adding antifreeze to the system, check all hose connections. Antifreeze can leak through very minute openings.

The exact mixture of antifreeze to water which you should use depends on the relative weather conditions. The mixture should contain at least 50-percent antifreeze, but should never contain more than 70-percent antifreeze. Refer to the antifreeze ratio table on the coolant container.

3   Thermostat - check and renewal

Refer to illustrations 3.9 and 3.10
Note: *Don't drive the vehicle without a thermostat! Models equipped with oxygen sensors may stay in open loop and emissions and fuel economy will suffer.*

Check

1   Before condemning the thermostat, check the coolant level, drivebelt tension and temperature gauge (or light) operation.
2   If the engine takes a long time to warm up, the thermostat is probably stuck open. Renew the thermostat.
3   If the engine runs too hot, check the temperature of the upper radiator hose. If the hose isn't hot, the thermostat is probably stuck shut. Renew the thermostat.
4   If the upper radiator hose is hot, it means the coolant is circulating and the thermostat is open. Refer to the *Troubleshooting* section at the front of this manual for the cause of overheating.
5   If an engine has been overheated, you may find damage such as leaking head gaskets, scuffed pistons and warped or cracked heads.

Renewal

Warning: *The engine must be completely cool before beginning this procedure!*
6   Disconnect the negative battery cable from the battery.
7   Drain about two quarts of coolant from the cooling system (see Chapter 1).
8   Loosen the hose clamp and detach the upper radiator hose from the thermostat housing cover.
9   Remove the bolts, then detach the thermostat housing cover and gasket **(see illustrations)**. **Note:** *If the cover is difficult to remove, tap it gently with a soft-face ham-*

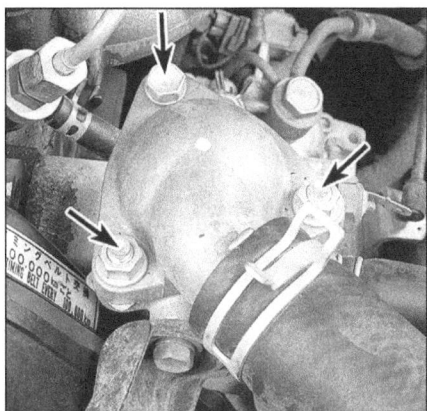

3.9d Diesel engine thermostat housing fasteners (arrows)

3.10 Removing the thermostat - make sure the spring end faces down during refitting

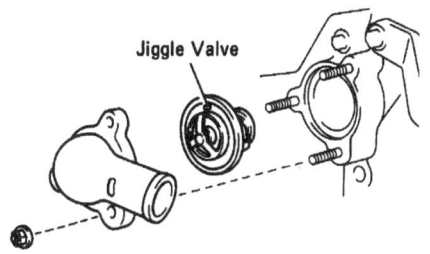

3.12a On models with vertically mounted thermostats, make sure the jiggle valve is in the 12 o'clock position

3.12b The thermostat gasket, which is actually a grooved sealing ring, fits around the edge of the thermostat

mer or a block of wood. Don't try to prise the cover loose or damage to the gasket sealing surfaces may result and leaks could develop.
10   Note how it's fitted (which end is facing up or out), then lift out the thermostat **(see illustration)**.
11   Remove all traces of old gasket material and sealant from the housing and cover with a gasket scraper, then clean the gasket mating surfaces with lacquer thinner or acetone.
12   Refit the new thermostat in the housing. Make sure the correct end faces up - the spring is normally directed into the housing **(see illustration)**. Fit a new gasket on the thermostat **(see illustration)**. On models with a gasket, apply a thin layer of RTV sealant to the gasket mating surfaces of the housing and cover, then install.
13   Position a new gasket on the housing and make sure the bolt holes line up.
14   Carefully position the cover on the housing and refit the bolts. Tighten them a little at a time to the specified torque - don't overtighten them or the cover may be distorted!
15   Reattach the radiator hose to the cover fitting and tighten the hose clamp. Now is a good time to check and renew all of the cooling system hoses and clamps (see Chapter 1).
16   Refer to Chapter 1 and refill the system, then run the engine and check carefully for leaks and proper operation.

4   Engine cooling fan and clutch - check and renewal

Refer to illustrations 4.4 and 4.7
Note: *Do not attempt to repair fan blades - renew any fan which is damaged.*

Check

1   With the engine off and ignition key removed, rock the fan back and forth by hand to check for excessive bearing play. Visually inspect for substantial fluid leakage. Either problem calls for renewal of the clutch assembly.
2   With the engine fully warmed up, shut off the engine and remove the key for safety. Turn the fan by hand. Some drag should be evident. If the fan freewheels too easily or is completely locked up, renew the fan clutch.

Renewal

3   Disconnect the negative cable from the battery.
4   Remove the nuts attaching the fan/clutch assembly to the water pump hub **(see illustration)**.
5   Lift the fan/clutch assembly out of the engine compartment. If the shroud interferes,

unbolt it and lift it out with the fan. **Caution:** *Be careful not to let the fan hit the radiator.*
6   Carefully inspect the fan blades for any damage or defects. Renew if necessary.
7   At this point, the fan may be unbolted from the clutch, if desired **(see illustration)**.
8   Refitting is the reverse of removal. It may be necessary to temporarily loosen the drivebelt (see Chapter 1) in order to start the fan clutch hub nuts. Tighten clutch-to-water pump nuts securely.

4.4 Location of the fan clutch-to-pulley bolts

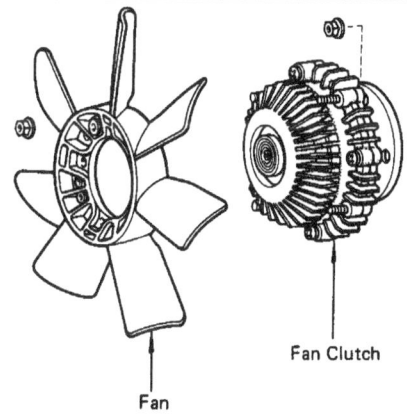

4.7 Typical fan/clutch assembly

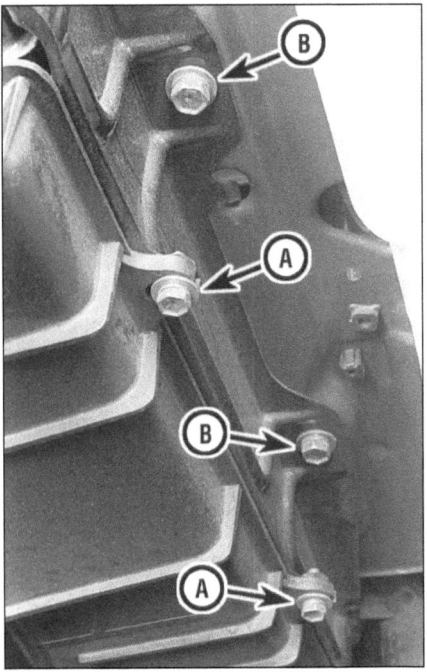

5.4 Right side view of radiator shows:

A   Location of shroud bolts
B   Location of radiator mounting bolts

5   Radiator - removal and refitting

Refer to illustration 5.4
Warning: *The engine must be completely cool before starting this procedure.*
1   Remove the engine undercover, if equipped.

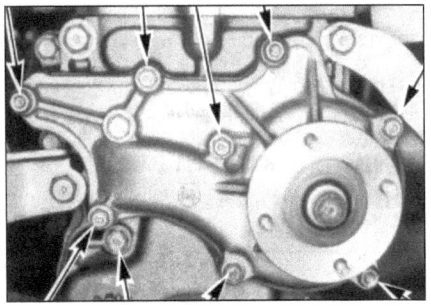

8.8a Water pump bolt locations - R-series petrol engines

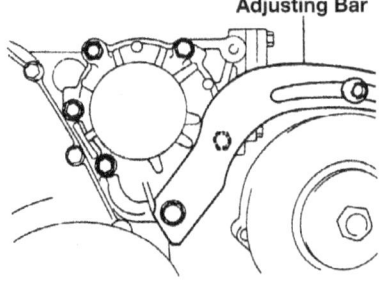

8.8b Water pump bolt locations - Y-series petrol engines

6.1 View of typical coolant reservoir shows locations of overflow hose and mounting bolts (arrows)

2   Drain the cooling system (see Chapter 1).
3   Disconnect the coolant hoses and overflow hose from the radiator.
4   Remove the fan shroud attaching bolts **(see illustration)**. Lay the shroud back over and then remove the fan (see Section 4).
5   On models with automatic transmissions, place a drain pan under the radiator and disconnect the transmission cooler lines from the radiator. Use a flare-nut wrench, if available, to prevent damaging the fittings.
6   Unscrew the mounting bolts and lift the radiator from the vehicle **(see illustration 5.4)**.
7   Refitting is the reverse of removal.
8   Refill the cooling system and on automatic transmission models, check transmission fluid level (see Chapter 1).

6   Coolant reservoir - removal and refitting

Refer to illustration 6.1
1   Disconnect the coolant overflow hose at the radiator neck **(see illustration)**.
2   Remove the screws attaching the reservoir to the inner fender.
3   Lift the reservoir straight up off its mounting bracket.
4   Refitting is the reverse of removal.

7   Water pump - check

1   Water pump failure can cause overheating of and serious damage to the engine. There are three ways to check the operation of the water pump while it's fitted on the engine. If any one of the three following quick checks indicates water pump failure, it should be renewed immediately.
2   Start the engine and warm it up to normal operating temperature. Squeeze the upper radiator hose. If the water pump is working properly, a pressure surge should be felt as the hose is released.
3   A seal protects the water pump impeller shaft bearing from contamination by engine coolant. If the seal fails, weep holes in the top and bottom of the water pump snout will leak coolant under the vehicle. If the weep hole is leaking, shaft bearing failure will follow. Renew the water pump immediately.
4   Besides contamination by coolant after a seal failure, the water pump impeller shaft bearing can also be prematurely worn out by an improperly tensioned drivebelt. When the bearing wears out, it emits a high pitched squealing sound. If noise is coming from the water pump during engine operation, the shaft

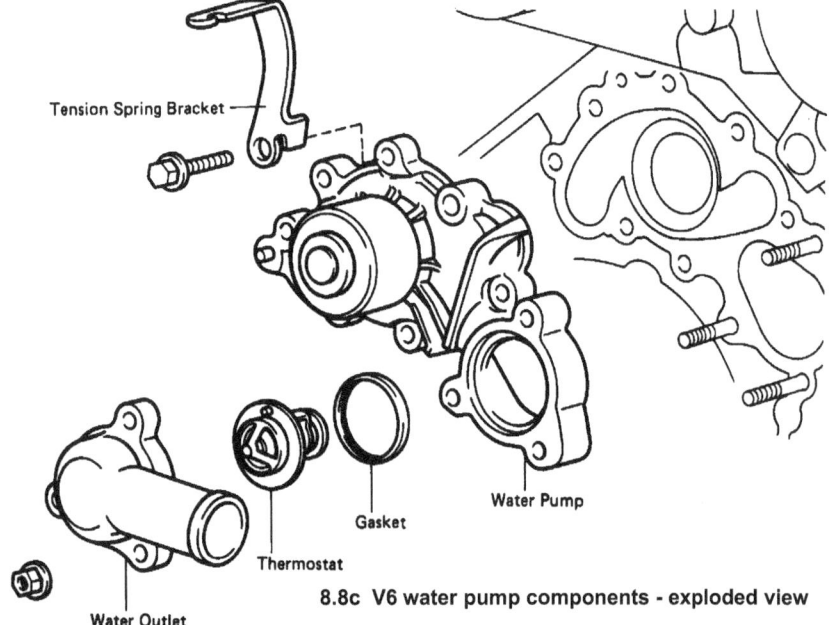

Tension Spring Bracket

Water Pump

Gasket

Thermostat

Water Outlet

8.8c V6 water pump components - exploded view

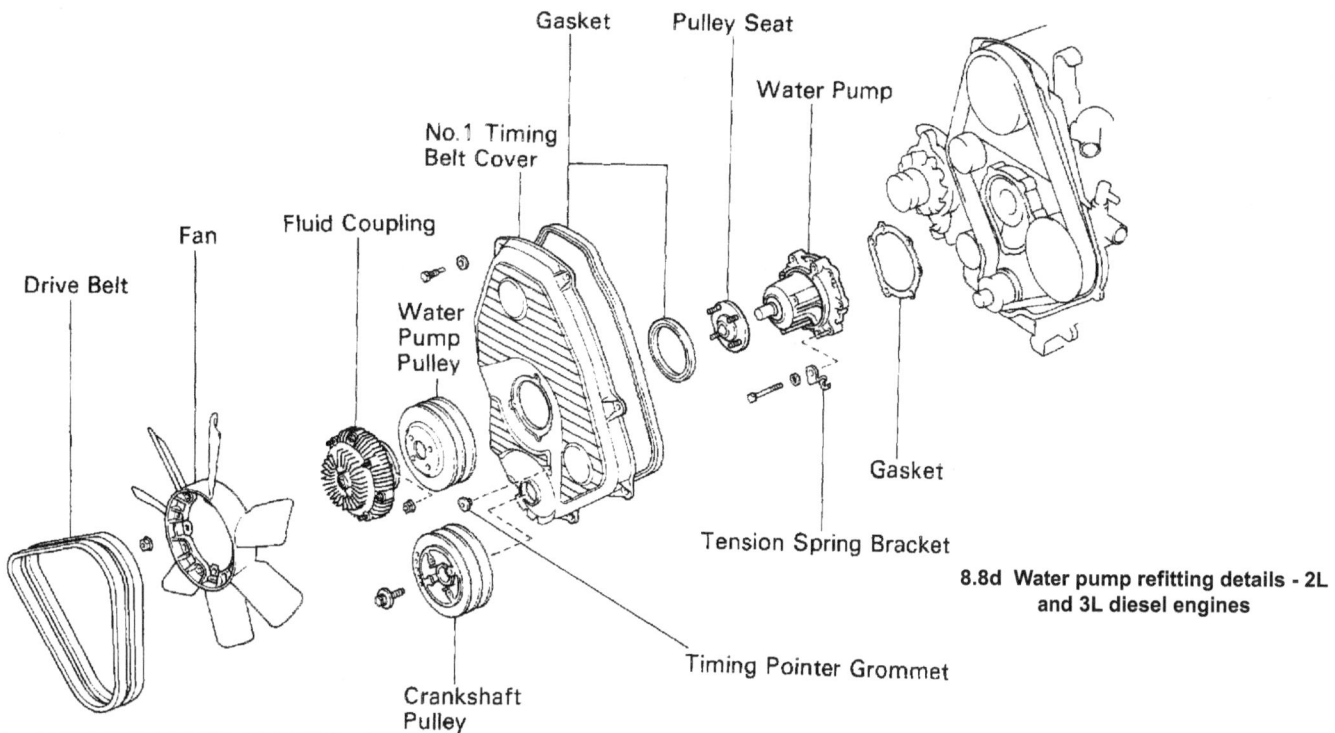

8.8d Water pump refitting details - 2L and 3L diesel engines

8.8e Water pump mounting bolts (arrows) - 3L (2.8 litre) diesel engine

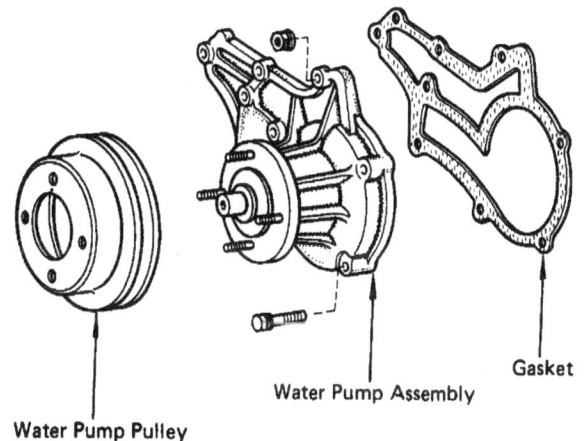

8.10a Water pump components - R-series petrol engines

bearing has failed. Renew the water pump immediately.

5   To identify excessive bearing wear before the bearing actually fails, grasp the water pump pulley and try to force it up-and-down or from side-to-side. If the pulley can be moved either horizontally or vertically, the bearing is nearing the end of its service life. Renew the water pump.

8   Water pump - removal and refitting

Refer to illustrations 8.8a and 8.8b
Warning: *Wait until the engine is completely cool before beginning this procedure.*
1   Disconnect the negative cable from the battery.

2   Drain the cooling system (see Chapter 1).
3   Remove the drivebelts (see Chapter 1).
4   Remove the cooling fan (Section 4) and lift the shroud out of the engine compartment.
5   Remove the timing belt cover (see Chapter 2C) or (see Chapter 2D).
6   On diesel engines remove the timing belt tension spring (see Chapter 2D).
7   Where fitted, cover the lower part of the timing belt so coolant doesn't spill on it when the pump is removed.
8   Unbolt and remove the water pump, noting the length and types of bolts as they are removed to ensure correct refitting **(see illustrations)**.
9   Thoroughly clean all gasket surfaces.
10   Position a new gasket onto the engine (four-cylinder engines), or a bead of RTV

sealant (V6 engines) **(see illustrations)**.
11   Refit the pump and tighten the bolts to the torque listed in this Chapter's Specifications.

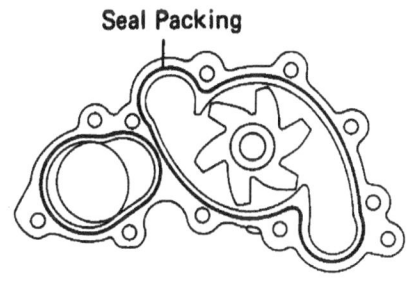

8.10b Apply sealer as shown to V6 water pump

9.9a On four-cylinder engines, the coolant temperature sending unit is located near the thermostat (arrow) - it has a single-wire connector

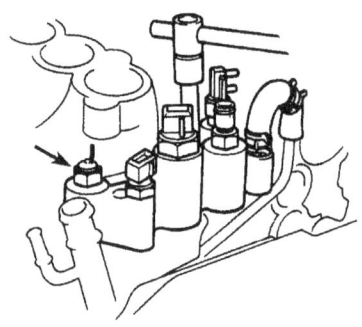

9.9b The coolant temperature sending unit on V6 engines is located at the rear of the inlet manifold (arrow)

9.9c On diesel engines, the coolant temperature sending unit is located in the thermostat housing (arrow) - it has a single-wire connector

12 Refit all parts removed in the reverse order of removal.

13 Refill the cooling system and check the belt tension (see Chapter 1). Run the engine and check for leaks.

9 Coolant temperature sending unit - check and renewal

Refer to illustration 9.9a, 9.9b and 9.9c

Warning: *The engine must be completely cool before removing the sending unit.*

Check

1 If the coolant temperature gauge is inoperative, check the fuses first (Chapter 12).
2 If the temperature gauge shows excessive temperature after running a while, see the *Troubleshooting* section in the front of the manual.
3 If the temperature gauge indicates "Hot" shortly after the engine is started cold, disconnect the wire at the coolant temperature sensor. If the gauge reading drops, renew the sending unit. If the reading remains high, the wire to the gauge may be shorted to earth or the gauge is faulty.
4 If the coolant temperature gauge fails to show any indication after the engine has been warmed up, (approximately 10 minutes) and the fuses checked out OK, shut off the engine. Disconnect the wire at the sending unit and using a jumper wire, connect it to a clean earth on the engine. Turn on the ignition

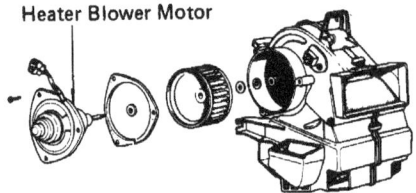

Heater Blower Motor

10.2 Typical heater blower unit - exploded view

without starting the engine. If the gauge now indicates "Hot", renew the sending unit.
5 If the gauge still does not work, the circuit may be open or the gauge may be faulty.

Renewal

6 With the engine completely cool, remove the cap from the radiator to release any pressure and then renew the cap. This reduces coolant loss during sender renewal.
7 Disconnect the electrical connector from the sending unit.
8 Prepare the new sending unit for refitting by applying a light coating of sealant to the threads.
9 Unscrew the sending unit from the engine **(see illustration)** and quickly fit the new one to prevent coolant loss.
10 Tighten the switch securely and connect the electrical connector.
11 Refill the cooling system, if necessary, and run the engine. Check for leaks and proper gauge operation.

10 Blower unit - removal and refitting

Refer to illustration 10.2

1 Locate the main heater unit, which is readily accessible beneath the dashboard of your vehicle. On early models, the blower is above the throttle pedal; later models have the unit mounted below the glove box.
2 The blower motor is located near the heater unit **(see illustration)**. On some models it is necessary to remove the left-side kick panel for access.
3 Disconnect the blower motor electrical connector.
4 Remove the three screws holding the blower motor to the heater unit housing. Remove the kick panel if it is in the way.
5 If you are renewing the motor, detach the fan and transfer it to the new motor.
6 Refitting procedures are the reverse of those for removal. Run the fan and check for proper operation.

11 Heater core - removal and refitting

Refer to illustrations 11.4, 11.9, 11.12a and 11.12b

1 Disconnect the cable from the negative battery terminal.
2 Open the radiator drain cock and drain the coolant into a suitable container (see Chapter 1).
3 Remove the glove compartment by removing the retaining screws.
4 Under the dash, locate the defroster hoses on either side of the heater unit and remove them by pulling straight up **(see illustration)**.
5 Locate the air damper assembly under the dash on the right side.
6 Remove the air damper by removing the retaining screws, then pull the air duct from the air damper and heater unit inlets.
7 Remove the two side defroster ducts.
8 Remove the heater control assembly as described in Section 12.
9 Locate the two heater hoses on the engine compartment side of the firewall and disconnect them by loosening their retaining clamps **(see illustration)**. Pull the hoses off the heater core pipes, then plug the pipes and hoses to prevent coolant leakage.
10 Remove the heater unit by removing the three retaining bolts. Guide the unit out the passenger side of the vehicle.
11 Unclamp and remove the two pipes leading to the heater core.
12 Remove the set screw and unfasten the six clips from the heater unit housing **(see illustrations)**.
13 Pull the heater core from the heater unit.
14 Refitting procedures are the reverse of those for removal.
15 Refill the cooling system, run the engine and check for proper operation and leaks.

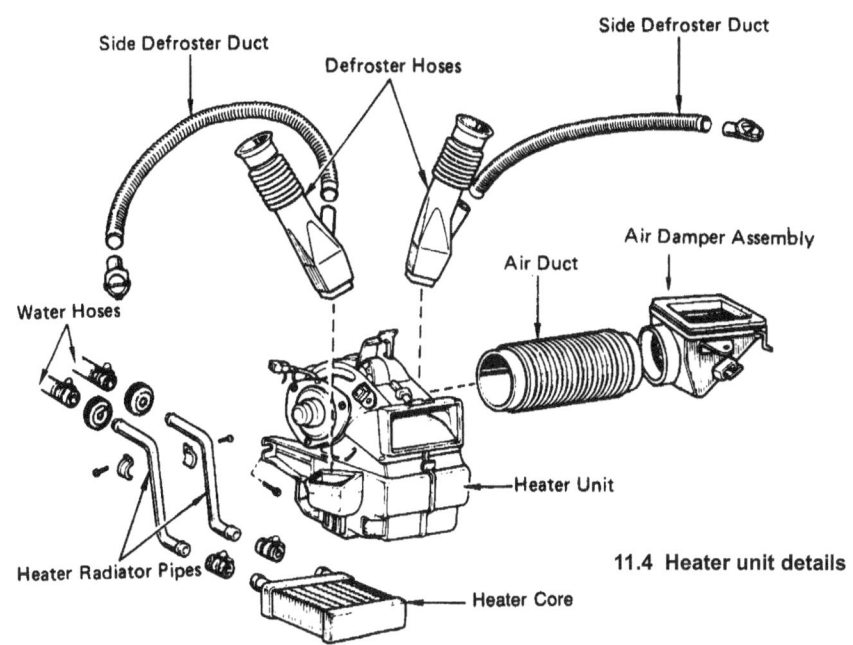

11.4 Heater unit details

11.9 The heater hoses connect to the heater core on the engine side of the firewall. Arrows point to the clamps

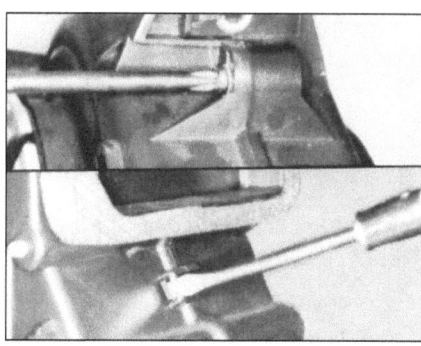

11.12a Locations of the screws and clips on the heater housing (typical)

12   Air conditioning and heater control assembly - removal and refitting

Refer to illustrations 12.2, 12.6, 12.7, 12.8 and 12.10

1   Disconnect the cable from the negative battery terminal.

Early models

2   Remove the steering column cover by removing the retaining screws (**see illustration**).

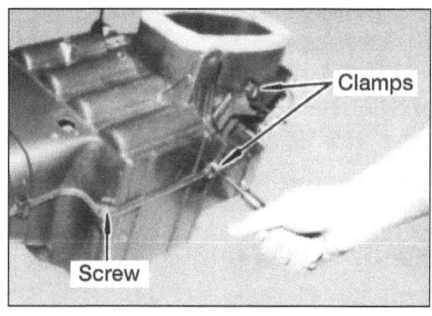

11.12b Locations of the screws and clips on the heater housing (typical)

3   Remove the radio by pulling off the volume and tuning knobs and removing the retaining screws (two at the side mounting tabs and one from underneath).

4   Disconnect the four heater control cables from their clamps. Note the positions of the cables relative to the clamps to facilitate proper refitting.

5   Unplug the air conditioning control switch, if equipped.

6   Remove the cable leading to the air inlet damper (**see illustration**).

7   Remove the cable leading to the water control valve (**see illustration**).

8   Remove the vent/heat mode select damper cable (**see illustration**).

9   Remove the heat/defroster mode select cable.

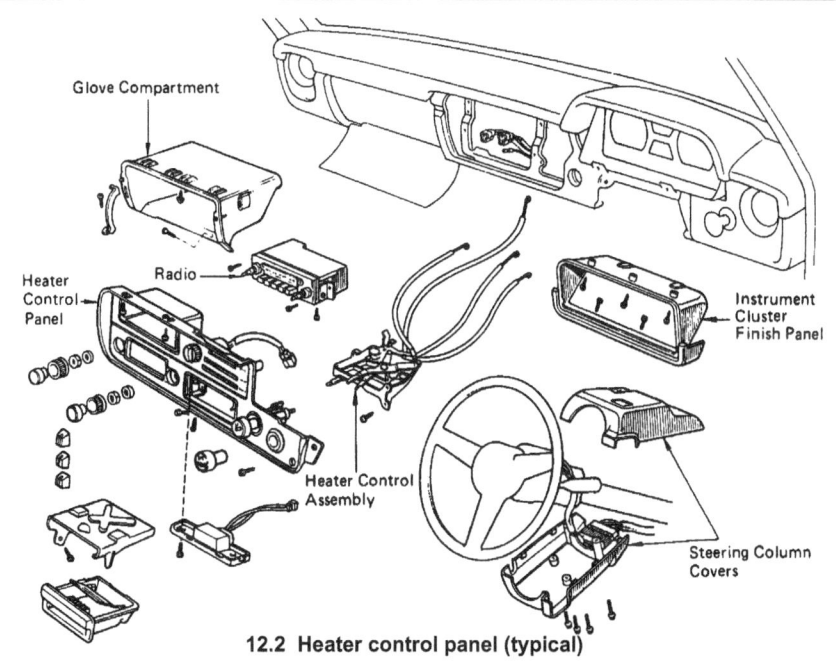

12.2 Heater control panel (typical)

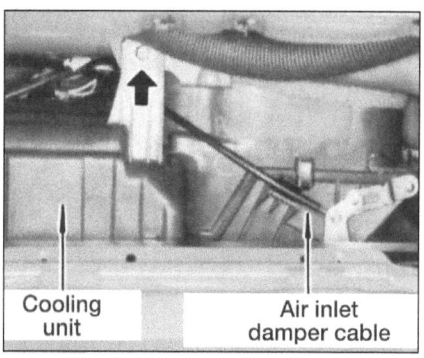

12.6 Location of the air inlet damper cable behind the glove box (typical)

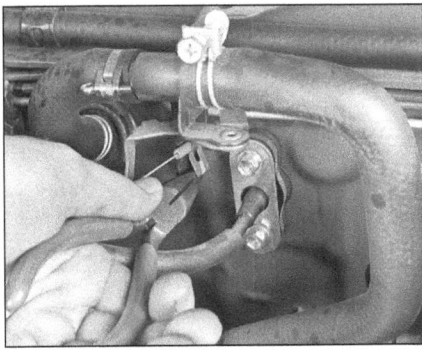

12.7 The water control valve cable is held in place by a clip located at the middle of the firewall in the engine compartment

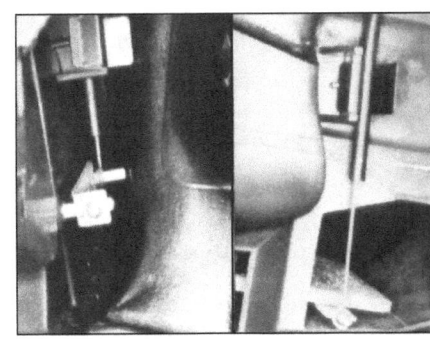

12.8 Location of vent/heat selector cable (left) and heat/defroster selector cable (right) - typical

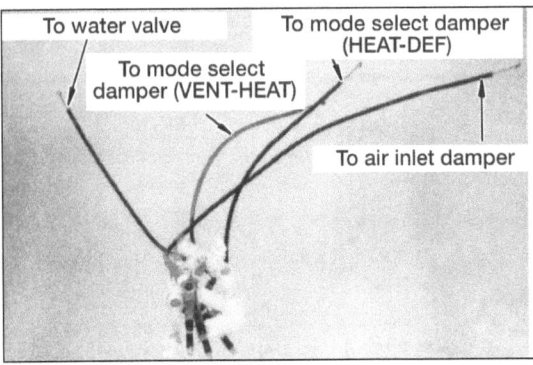

To water valve

To mode select damper (HEAT-DEF)

To mode select damper (VENT-HEAT)

To air inlet damper

12.10 Heater control assembly - typical

10   Remove the two screws holding the heater control assembly, then remove the assembly **(see illustration)**.

11   Before refitting the heater control, lubricate the cables with penetrating oil and the pivot points of the heater control valves with multi-purpose grease.

12   To refit the controls, connect the four cables to the heater control assembly.

13   Refit the heater control assembly.

14   To complete the refitting, reverse the steps above.

15   Test the control cable operation by moving the control levers back and forth, checking for stiffness, binding and proper operation through the levers' full range.

Later models

16   Detach the cable from the negative battery terminal.

17   Pull off the heater control knobs.

18   If the vehicle has air conditioning, prise off the A/C switch.

19   Using a screwdriver, prise out the heater control plate.

20   Remove the mounting screws and pull out the heater and air conditioner control assembly. Unplug all connectors and remove the control assembly.

21   Refitting is the reverse of removal.

---

13   Air conditioning system - check and maintenance

Refer to illustrations 13.3 and 13.9

Warning: *If any component of the air conditioning system requires removal, the system must first be depressurized by a qualified technician. Because the system contains refrigerant under very high pressure, do not attempt to disconnect any part of the system yourself This could result in physical injury as well as damage to the system.*

Caution: *The air conditioning system on later models uses the non-ozone depleting refrigerant, referred to as R-134a. The R-134a refrigerant and its lubricating oil are not compatible with the R-12 system, and under no circumstances should the two types of refrigerant and/or lubricating oils be intermixed. If mixed, it could result in costly compressor failure due to improper lubrication.*

1   Because of the special tools, equipment and skills required to service air conditioning systems, and the differences between the various systems that may be fitted on these vehicles, in-depth air conditioner servicing cannot be covered in a manual of this size.

2   We will cover component removal, as the home mechanic may realize a substantial savings in repair costs if he removes components himself, takes them to a professional for repair, and/or replaces them with new or rebuilt ones.

3   These vehicles are equipped with air conditioning systems available from a number of different sources. This and the following Sections will deal with the factory fitted system only **(see illustration)**.

4   Determine what type of system is on your vehicle by looking at the data plate usually found on the compressor, radiator support, firewall or on the underside of the bonnet. If you can't find the type of system, it would be best to consult an air conditioning specialty shop for repair information or help. Problems in the air conditioning system should be diagnosed, and the system refrigerant evacuated, by an air conditioning technician.

5   Once the new or reconditioned component has been fitted, the system should then be charged and checked by an air conditioning technician.

6   Before indiscriminately removing air conditioning system components, get more than one estimate of repair costs from reputable air conditioning service centres. You may find it

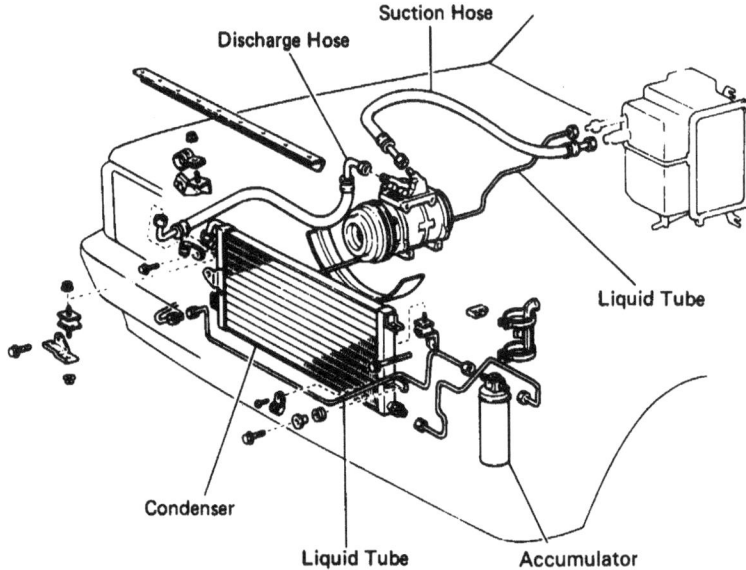

Suction Hose

Discharge Hose

Liquid Tube

Condenser

Liquid Tube

Accumulator

13.3 Air conditioning system components - typical

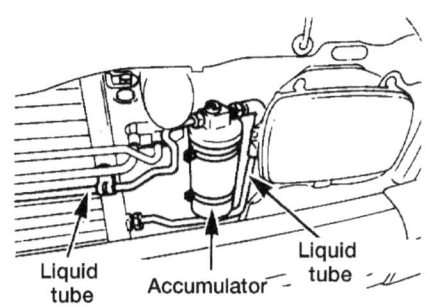

14.1 On most models, the accumulator is mounted next to the condenser

the condenser (**see illustration**) in the engine compartment.

2   Disconnect the two liquid lines from the accumulator. Cap the open fittings immediately to prevent moisture from entering the system.

3   Remove the accumulator from its bracket.

4   Refitting procedures are the reverse of those for removal.

5   Have the system evacuated, charged and leak tested. If a new accumulator was fitted, add 20cc of refrigerant oil.

cheaper and less trouble to let the entire operation be performed by someone else.

7   The following maintenance steps should be performed on a regular basis to ensure that the air conditioner continues to operate at peak efficiency.

a) *Check the tension of the drivebelt and adjust it if necessary (Chapter 1).*

b) *Check the condition of the hoses. Look for cracks, hardening and deterioration.* **Warning:** *Don't renew air conditioning system hoses until the system has been discharged by a dealer service department or repair shop.*

c) *Check the fins of the condenser for leaves, bugs and any other foreign material. A soft brush and compressed air can be used to remove them.*

d) *Maintain the correct refrigerant charge.*

8   The system should be run for about 10 minutes at least once a month. This is par-

ticularly important during the winter months because long term non-use can cause hardening and failure of the seals.

14   Air conditioning accumulator - removal and refitting

Refer to illustration 14.1

Warning: *Before removing the accumulator, the system must be discharged by an air conditioning technician. Do not attempt to do this yourself. The refrigerant should be discharged in to an approved recovery/recycling unit by a dealer service department or an automotive air conditioning repair facility. Always wear eye protection when disconnecting air conditioning system fittings.*

1   The accumulator, which acts as a reservoir, dryer and filter for the refrigerant, is the canister-shaped object mounted to the left of

15   Air conditioning compressor - removal and refitting

Refer to illustration 15.6

Warning: *Before removing the compressor, the system must be discharged by an air conditioning technician. Do not attempt to do this yourself. The refrigerant should be discharged in to an approved recovery/recycling unit by a dealer service department or an automotive air conditioning repair facility. Always wear eye protection when disconnecting air conditioning system fittings.*

1   The compressor is located at the right side of the engine and is engine driven by a pulley and belt.

2   Disconnect the cable from the negative battery terminal.

3   Disconnect the clutch lead wire from the wiring harness.

4   Disconnect the two flexible hoses from

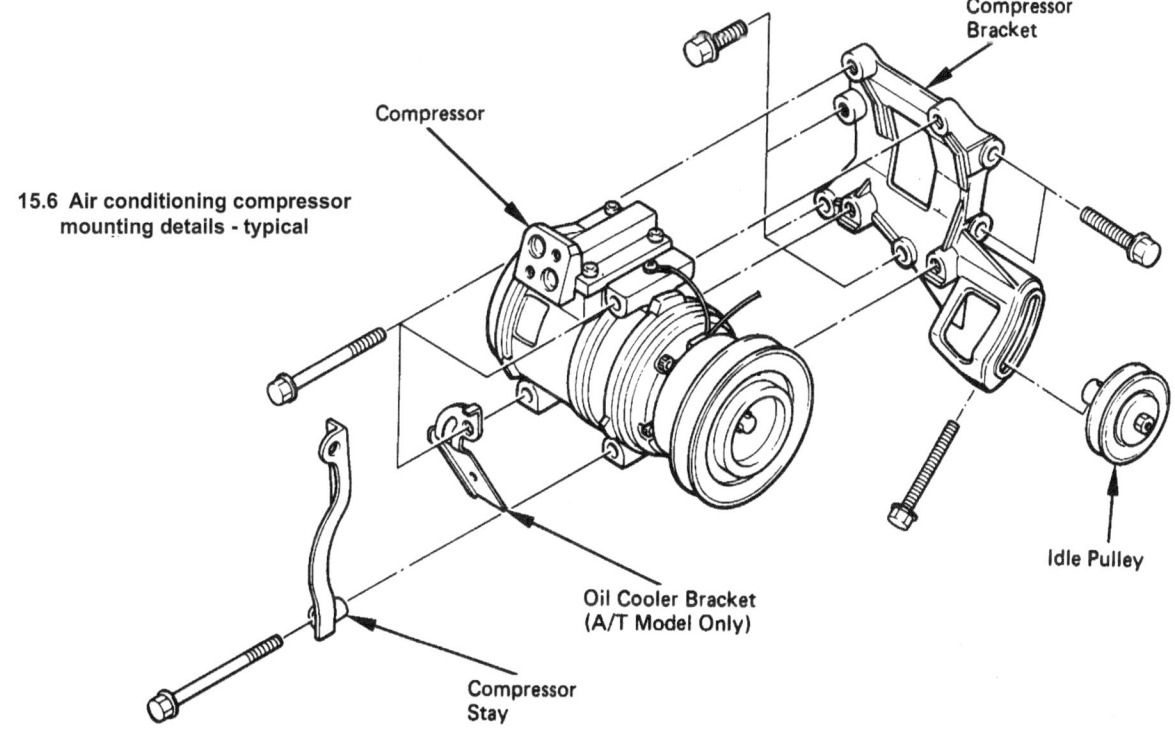

15.6 Air conditioning compressor mounting details - typical

the compressor service valves. Cap the openings immediately to prevent moisture from entering the system.

5   Loosen the drivebelt by loosening the adjustment and pivot bolts on the compressor mount. Unbolt the fan shroud and move it aside if necessary.

6   Remove the compressor mounting bolts and the compressor **(see illustration)**.

7   Refitting procedures are the reverse of those for removal. If a new or rebuilt compressor is being fitted, follow the directions supplied with the compressor regarding the proper level of oil prior to refitting.

8   Have the system evacuated, charged and leak tested by the shop that discharged it.

16   Air conditioning condenser - removal and refitting

Refer to illustration 16.5

Warning: *Before removing the condenser, the system must be discharged by an air conditioning technician. Do not attempt to do this yourself. The refrigerant should be discharged in to an approved recovery/recycling unit by a dealer service department or an automotive*

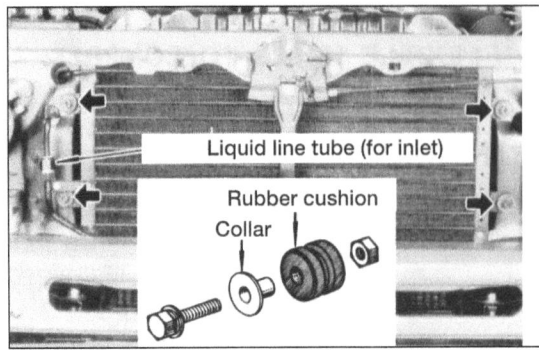

Liquid line tube (for inlet)

Rubber cushion

Collar

16.5 Arrows indicate locations of condenser mounting bolts

air conditioning repair facility. Always wear eye protection when disconnecting air conditioning system fittings.

1   The condenser is located in front of the radiator.

2   Remove the front grille (see Chapter 11) and the bonnet lock brace, if necessary.

3   Disconnect the flexible discharge hose from the condenser.

4   Disconnect the liquid line tube from the condenser, and remove the tube clip. **Note:** *Cap the open fittings immediately to prevent moisture from entering the system.*

5   Remove the four bolts holding the condenser to the front panel, making note of the cushion and collar arrangement **(see illustration)** so that proper refitting of the condenser is assured. Carefully lift the condenser out of the vehicle; do not bend the cooling fins or coil.

6   Refitting procedures are the reverse of those for removal.

7   Have the system evacuated, charged and leak tested. If the condenser was renewed, add 40 to 50cc of refrigerant oil.

Chapter 4 Part A
Fuel and exhaust systems - Petrol models

Contents

Specifications

Carburettor

Fast idle speed
12R engine	N/A
18R engine	2600 rpm
20R engine	2600 rpm
22R engine	2600 rpm
Y-series engine	2600 rpm

Idle speed
12R engine	700 rpm
18R engine	750 rpm
20R engine	800 rpm
22R engine	800 rpm

Y-series engine
Except 4Y-E with automatic transmission	700 rpm
4Y-E with automatic transmission	750 rpm

Carburettor (continued)

Idle mixture speed
- 12R engine... 700 rpm
- 18R, 20R engines .... 740 rpm
- 22R engine... 850 rpm
- Y-series engines
  - Through 1988
    - Manual transmission
      - Without power steering.. 700 rpm
      - With power steering... 800 rpm
    - Automatic transmission
      - Without power steering.. 800 rpm
      - With power steering... 900 rpm
  - 1989 on
    - Without power steering.. 750 rpm
    - With power steering... 850 rpm

Idle mixture adjusting screw (initial setting)
- 12R, 18R engines .... 2 turns out
- 20R, 22R engines .... 3-1/2 turns out
- Y-series .... 2-1/2 turns out

Float level **(see illustration 7.59a)**
- 12R engine... 3.5 mm
- 18R, 20R engines .... 5.0 mm
- 22R engine... 9.8 mm
- Y-series engines... 11.0 mm

Float drop **(see illustration 7.59b)**
- 12R engine... 1.2 mm
- 18R, 20R engines .... 1.0 mm
- 22R engine... 0.9 to 1.1 mm
- Y-series engines... 1.2 mm

Fuel pressure.. 27 to 62 kPa

Electronic fuel injection

Fuel pressure
- 22R-E and V6 engines
  - Engine stopped, fuel pump activated... 265 to 304 kPa
  - Engine idling
    - Vacuum hose disconnected .... 265 to 304 kPa
    - Vacuum hose connected .... 226 to 255 kPa
- 4Y-E engine
  - Engine stopped, fuel pump activated... 265 to 304 kPa
  - Engine idling
    - Vacuum hose disconnected .... 265 to 304 kPa
  - Vacuum hose connected
    - Through 1988.. 226 to 255 kPa
    - 1989 on .... 206 to 227 kPa

Fuel injector resistance
- 22R-E engine .... 13.4 to 14.2 ohms
- 4Y-E engine
  - Through 1988 .... 1.5 to 3 ohms
  - 1989 on.. 0.9 to 1.8 ohms

Cold start injector resistance
- 22R-E engine .... 2 to 4 ohms
- 4Y-E engine... 3 to 5 ohms
- V6 engine .... 2 to 4 ohms

Torque specifications   Nm

Throttle body mounting nuts/bolts
- 22R-E engine 18
- 4Y-E engine 12
- V6 engine 18

Cold start injector tube banjo bolt.. 18

Delivery pipe (fuel rail) bolts/nuts
- Four-cylinder engines... 19
- V6 engine 13

1 General information

The fuel system consists of a rear mounted tank, combination metal and flexible fuel hoses, an engine-mounted mechanical pump or an in-tank electric pump, and either a two-stage, two-venturi carburettor or an electronic fuel injection system.

The exhaust system is composed of an exhaust manifold or manifolds, the catalytic converter and a combination muffler and tailpipe assembly.

The emissions control systems modify the functions of both the exhaust and fuel systems. There are cross-references throughout this Chapter to Sections in Chapter 6 because the emissions control systems are integral to the induction and exhaust systems.

Extreme caution should be exercised when dealing with either the fuel or the exhaust system. Fuel is a primary element for combustion. Be very careful! The exhaust system is also an area for exercising caution as it operates at very high temperatures, particularly with the use of emissions control systems. Serious burns can result from even momentary contact with any part of the exhaust system and the fire potential is ever present. **Warning:** *Petrol is extremely flammable, so take extra precautions when you work on any part of the fuel system. Don't smoke or allow open flames or bare light bulbs near the work area, and don't work in a garage where a natural gas-type appliance (such as a water heater or a clothes dryer) with a pilot light is present. Since petrol is carcinogenic, wear latex gloves when there's a possibility of being exposed to fuel, and, if you spill any fuel on your skin, rinse it off immediately with soap and water. The fuel system on fuel-injected models is under constant pressure, so, if any fuel lines are to be disconnected, the fuel pressure in the system must be relieved first. Mop up any spills immediately and do not store fuel-soaked rags where they could ignite. When you perform any kind of work on the fuel system, wear safety glasses and have a Class B type fire extinguisher on hand.*

2 Fuel tank - removal and refitting

Refer to illustration 2.1

Warning 1: *Petrol is extremely flammable, so take extra precautions when you work on any part of the fuel system. See the Warning at the end of Section 1.*
Warning 2: *Repairs to the fuel tank or filler neck should be performed by a professional with the proper training to carry out this critical and potentially dangerous work. Even after cleaning and flushing, explosive fumes can remain and could explode during repair of the tank.*
Warning 3: *If the fuel tank is removed from the vehicle, it should not be placed in an area where sparks or open flames could ignite the*

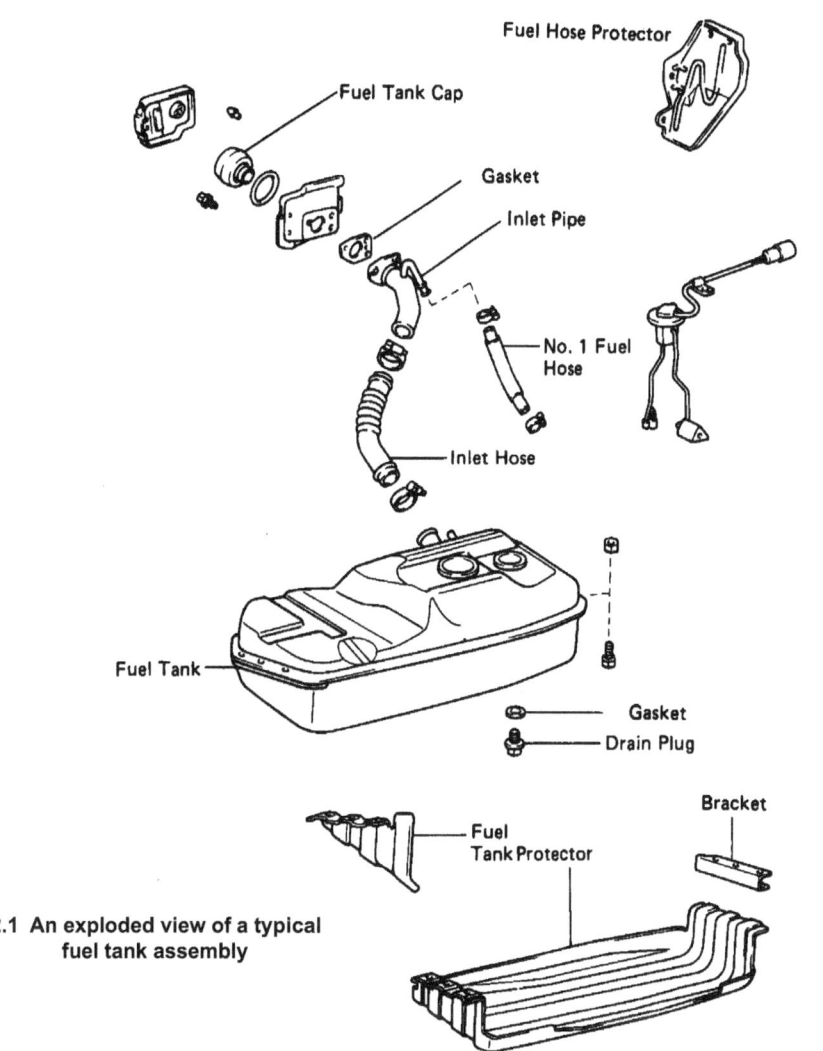

2.1 An exploded view of a typical fuel tank assembly

fumes coming out of the tank. Be especially careful inside garages where a natural gas appliance is located because the pilot light could cause an explosion.

1   The fuel tank **(see illustration)** is mounted at the rear of the vehicle. If it becomes necessary to work on it or its associated fittings, either in or out of the vehicle, the ignition switch must be Off and the battery earth cable disconnected. Before removing the tank, unscrew the drain plug and empty any remaining fuel into a suitably sized container.
2   Disconnect the electrical connector from the fuel level sending unit and (if your vehicle has an electric pump), the fuel pump.
3   Disconnect the vapour, feed and return hoses.
4   Disconnect the two filler pipes from the fuel tank.
5   Remove the fuel tank shield.
6   Remove the six retaining bolts at the ends of the tank and carefully remove it.
7   Refitting is the reverse of the removal procedure. Be sure to tighten all bolts, clamps and the plug securely.

3 Fuel pump/fuel pressure - check

Warning: *Petrol is extremely flammable, so take extra precautions when you work on any part of the fuel system. See the Warning at the end of Section 1.*
Note 1: *The following checks assume the fuel filter is in good condition. If you doubt its condition, fit a new one (see Chapter 1).*
Note 2: *All fuel-injected models are equipped with an electric in-tank fuel pump. Most carburetted models are equipped with a mechanical fuel pump mounted on the engine, although some later carburetted models have an electric pump mounted in the fuel tank.*
1   Make sure there's adequate fuel in the fuel tank.

Mechanical pump

Refer to illustration 3.2

Note: *In addition to the following pressure check, make sure there is no oil leaking out of the vent hole on the side of the fuel pump. If there's an oil leak from the vent hole, the oil seal inside the pump is broken and the fuel pump must be renewed.*

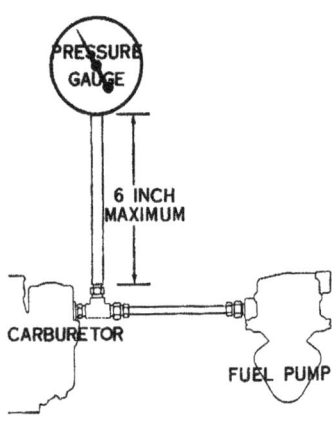

3.2 Attach the T-fitting as close to the carburettor as possible and use a 15 cm (maximum) length of hose when hooking up the pressure gauge to check the fuel pressure

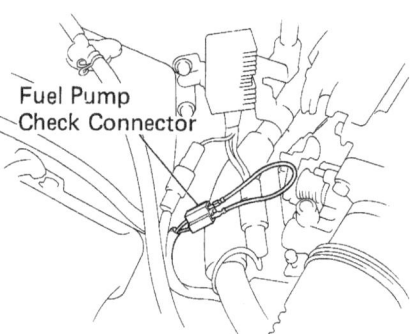

3.7 On fuel-injected models, bridge the terminals of the fuel pump check connector to actuate the fuel pump

3.12 If you don't have the special fuel pressure gauge adaptor, get an 8 mm bolt, place it in a vice, cut off the head, drill it out, add a locknut and wrap the threads with Teflon tape

2   Disconnect the fuel line from the carburettor and attach a T-fitting **(see illustration)**. Connect a fuel pressure gauge to the T-fitting with a section of fuel hose that's no longer than 15 cm.

3   Disconnect the gauge from the end of the fuel hose and direct the end of the hose into an approved fuel container. Operate the starter for a few seconds, until fuel spurts out of the hose, to vent pump (this eliminates any air in the fuel chamber, which could affect the pressure reading). Reattach the hose to the gauge.

4   Start the engine and allow it to idle. The pressure on the gauge should be within the range listed in this Chapter's Specifications. It should remain constant and return to zero slowly when the engine is shut off.

5   An instant pressure drop indicates a faulty outlet valve. If this occurs, or if the pressure is too high or low, renew the fuel pump. **Note:** *If the pressure is too high, check the air vent to see if it's plugged before renewing the pump.*

Electric pump

Refer to illustration 3.7

6   Turn on the ignition switch (but do not start the engine).

7   On fuel-injected models, bridge both terminals of the fuel pump check connector with a jumper wire **(see illustration)**.

8   On carburetted models, a check connector is not provided. The fuel pump circuit normally incorporates an oil pressure switch designed to shut off the fuel pump when the engine is not running (and there's no oil pressure). When testing the fuel pump on these models, disconnect the oil pressure switch.

9   Remove the fuel filler cap. Place your ear near the opening - you should be able to hear a whirring sound as the fuel pump is operating.

a) *On fuel-injected models, listen for fuel return noises from the fuel pressure*

regulator and check for fuel pressure in the hose between the fuel filter and the engine by pinching the hose. There should be fuel return noises and pressure. If there's no return noise or pressure, but you can hear the pump running, there's probably a restriction or leak in the fuel lines, fuel filter, pressure regulator, fuel injector(s) or pulsation damper. check the fuel pressure (see Step 12).*

b) *On carburetted models, turn the ignition switch to Off, disconnect the fuel line from the carburettor, extend the line using approved fuel hose, fittings and hose clamps, and direct the hose into an approved fuel container. Turn the ignition switch On but don't start the engine. Fuel should be expelled into the container at a rate no less than 1.2 litres per minute. If fuel flow is insufficient, the pump is malfunctioning or there's a restriction or leak in the fuel lines or fuel filter.*

10   Remove the jumper wire or reconnect the oil pressure switch. Turn off the ignition switch.

11   If the fuel pump is not operating, inspect the following components: the EFI 15-amp fuse and main relay (if equipped), the ignition fuse, the circuit opening relay, the fuel pump, wiring and electrical connectors.

Fuel pressure check (fuel-injected models)

Refer to illustrations 3.12, 3.17, 3.18a and 3.18b

12   A fuel pressure gauge equipped with an 8 mm banjo fitting on the end of the hose (Toyota tool no. 09268-45011) is required for the following procedure. There are a couple of alternatives to buying the special fuel pressure gauge setup:

a) *Buy an 8 mm banjo fitting and attach it to a fuel pressure gauge hose with a hose clamp.*

b) *If you can't find the correct size banjo fitting, buy an 8 mm bolt, cut the head off and drill a hole through it lengthwise.*

Add a locknut with the same thread pitch and wrap the threads with Teflon tape **(see illustration)**.

13   Relieve the fuel pressure (see Section 10).

14   Verify that the battery voltage is 12 volts or more.

15   Detach the cable from the negative terminal of the battery.

16   Detach the electrical connector from the cold start injector.

17   Put a metal container or shop towel under the cold start injector pipe banjo bolt at the fuel rail **(see illustration)**, then remove the banjo bolt and detach the cold start injector pipe from the fuel rail.

18   To attach the fuel pressure gauge to the fuel rail:

a) *If you are using the factory setup, or obtained an 8 mm banjo fitting for your pressure gauge kit, use the banjo bolt from the cold start injector pipe to attach the pressure gauge to the fuel rail. Be sure to use sealing washers on both sides of the banjo fitting.*

b) *If you are using a drilled-out 8 mm bolt, attach the bolt to the fuel rail ,tighten the locknut and attach the fuel pressure gauge hose with a hose clamp* **(see illustrations)**.

19   Wipe off any petrol that has leaked out of the fuel delivery pipe and attach the cable to the negative terminal of the battery.

20   Place the transmission in Neutral (manual) or Park (automatic) and apply the parking brake.

21   Start the engine, detach the vacuum sensing hose from the pressure regulator and plug it with a golf tee or pencil.

22   Measure the fuel pressure at idle and compare it to the values listed in this Chapter's Specifications.

a) *If the pressure is too high, the fuel pressure regulator is faulty or the fuel return line is plugged.*

b) *If the pressure is too low, look for leaks in the fuel hoses, lines and fittings, in the fuel filter and the pulsation damper.*

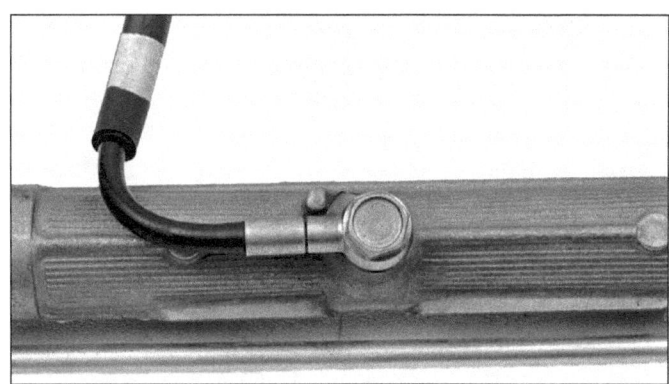

3.17 Remove the banjo bolt which attaches the lower end of the cold start injector pipe to the fuel rail and, using the banjo bolt and two sealing washers, attach the banjo fitting of the fuel pressure gauge to the fuel rail (fuel rail removed for clarity)

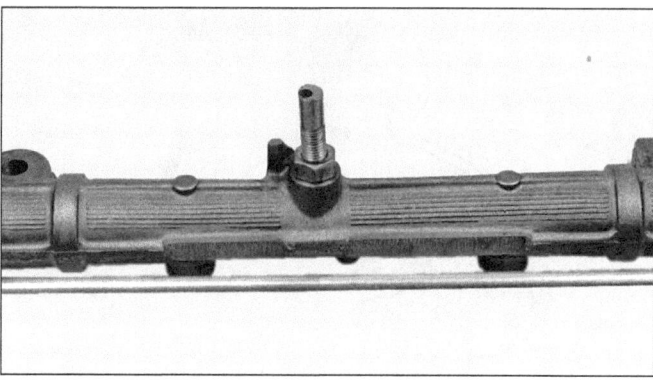

3.18a If you're using a makeshift adaptor bolt, screw it into the fuel rail and tighten the locknut . . .

3.18b . . . then attach the fuel pressure gauge hose with a hose clamp (fuel rail removed for clarity)

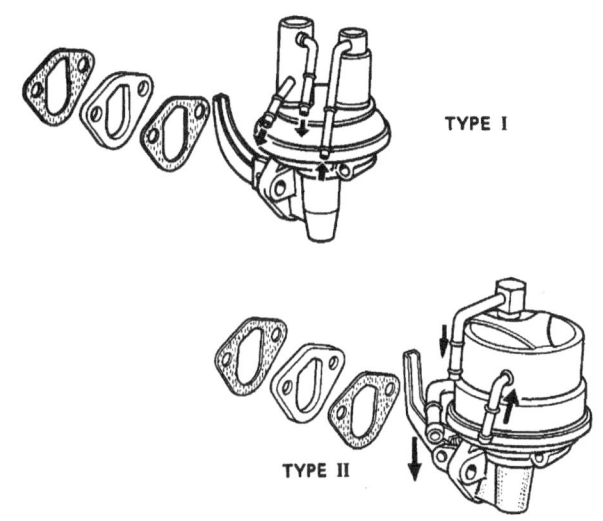

4.4a An exploded view of the Type I and Type II mechanical fuel pumps

If they all check out, pinch the fuel return hose. If the pressure rises sharply, the fuel pressure regulator is faulty. If the fuel pressure does not rise, the fuel pump is probably defective.

23   Reattach the vacuum hose to the fuel pressure regulator, measure the fuel pressure at idle and compare your reading to the fuel pressure listed in this Chapter's Specifications. Stop the engine. If the pressure drops quickly, a fuel line or hose, the pulsation damper, the fuel pump, pressure regulator and/or one or more fuel injectors is leaking.

24   Verify that the fuel pressure remains at 14 kPa or more for five minutes after the engine is turned off. If the pressure is not as specified, one of the components is leaking.

25   Relieve the fuel pressure.

26   Detach the cable from the negative terminal of the battery.

27   Carefully remove the fuel pressure gauge.

28   Using new sealing washers, reattach the cold start injector pipe banjo fitting to the fuel rail.

29   Reattach the electrical connector to the cold start injector. Be sure to wipe up any spilled petrol.

30   Attach the cable to the negative terminal of the battery.

31   Start the engine and check for leaks.

4   Fuel pump - removal and refitting

Note: *If the required pressure gauge is available, hook it up to the pump outlet with a T-fitting and check the pump outlet pressure before removing it from the engine.*

Warning: *Petrol is extremely flammable, so extra precautions must be taken when working on any part of the fuel system. See the Warning at the end of Section 1.*

Mechanical (carburetted vehicles)

Refer to illustrations 4.4a and 4.4b

1   Disconnect the cable from the negative terminal of the battery. Remove the air cleaner (see Section 5).

2   Exercise caution regarding flammable fuel and mark the location of the fuel hoses before performing the following step.

3   Remove the fuel pump line clamps and lines.

4   Remove the two bolts holding the fuel pump and heat shield to the cylinder head **(see illustrations)**.

5   Remove the fuel pump and gasket.

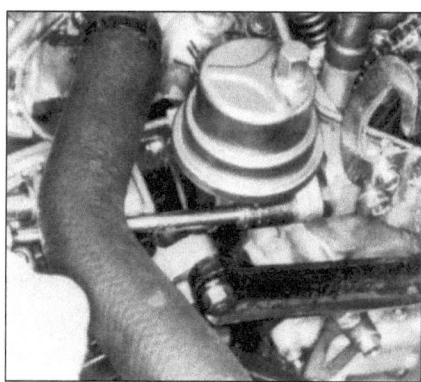

4.4b Removing the mounting bolts from a typical mechanical fuel pump (Type II shown)

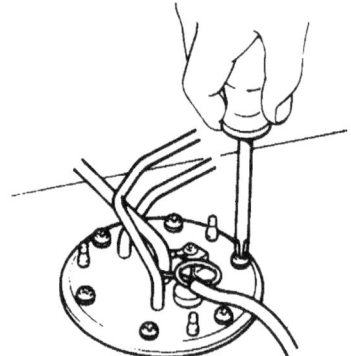

4.9 To remove the fuel pump/sending unit assembly from the fuel tank, remove all of the screws from the flange in the top of the fuel tank

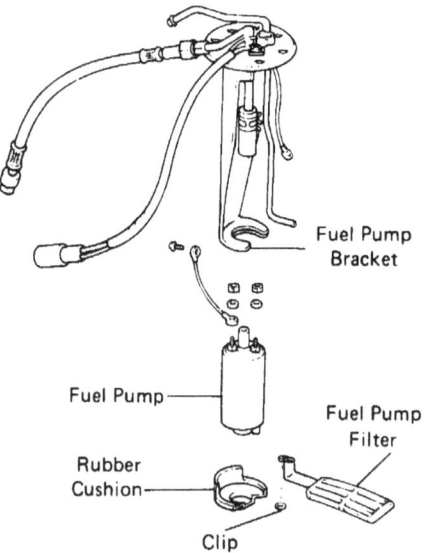

4.10 An exploded view of the fuel pump/ sending unit assembly

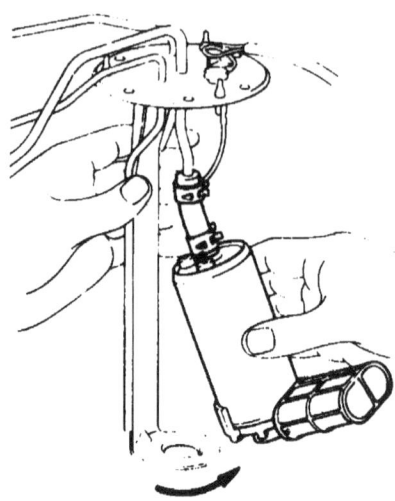

4.11 To detach the fuel pump from the pump/sending unit bracket, pull the lower end of the pump away from the bracket

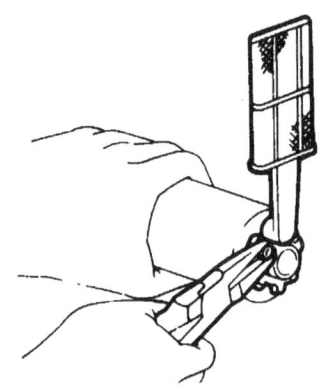

4.12 To detach the fuel pump filter from the pump, remove the rubber cushion, remove the clip with a pair of pliers and pull out the filter

6   Refitting is the reverse of removal. Use new gaskets when fitting the fuel pump. Check for oil leaks at the pump-to-cylinder head mating surface and for fuel leaks at the pipe-to-hose connections.

Electric pump (fuel-injected vehicles)

Refer to illustrations 4.9, 4.10, 4.11 and 4.12

7   Relieve the fuel pressure, then disconnect the cable from the negative terminal of the battery. Drain all fuel from the fuel tank (see Section 2).
8   Remove the fuel tank (see Section 2).
9   Remove the screws from the fuel pump/ sending unit mounting flange **(see illustration)** and pull the pump/sending unit assembly from the fuel tank.
10   Remove the two nuts **(see illustration)** and detach the wires from the fuel pump.
11   Pull the lower end of the pump from the bracket **(see illustration)**.
12   Remove the rubber cushion, remove the clip and pull out the filter from the fuel pump **(see illustration)**.
13   Refitting is the reverse of removal.

5   Air cleaner assembly (carburettor) - removal and refitting

Note: *See Chapter 1 for air filter renewal procedures.*
1   Disconnect the cable from the negative terminal of the battery.
2   Disconnect and label the emission control hoses at the base of the air cleaner.
3   Disconnect the air intake hoses.
4   Remove the mounting nuts and the wing nut from the air cleaner.
5   Lift the air cleaner off the carburettor or from the inner fender panel.
6   Refitting is the reverse of the removal procedures.

6   Carburettor - removal and refitting

Warning: *Petrol is extremely flammable, so extra precautions must be taken when working on any part of the fuel system. See the Warning at the end of Section 1.*
1   Remove the air cleaner (see Section 5)
2   Disconnect the accelerator linkage from the carburettor.
3   On automatic transmission equipped models, disconnect the throttle valve linkage from the carburettor (see Chapter 7B).
4   From the carburettor, disconnect and label all vacuum hoses; the two coolant hoses from the choke housing (early models with a water-heated choke); the PCV hose from the flange; the fuel hose(s); and the electrical connectors.
5   Remove the mounting flange nuts and bolts and lift off the carburettor. Cover the inlet

hole of the inlet manifold with a cloth.
6   Refitting is the reverse of the removal procedure, but make sure that the flange surfaces are clean and that a new gasket is used. Be sure to tighten the carburettor mounting bolts/nuts securely. After refitting, perform all of the adjustments described in this Chapter and Chapter 1. Also, refit the air cleaner, start the engine and check carefully for fuel leaks.

7   Carburettor - servicing and overhaul

Warning: *Petrol is extremely flammable, so extra precautions must be taken when working on any part of the fuel system. See the Warning at the end of Section 1.*

Servicing

1   A thorough road test and check of carburettor adjustments should be done before any major carburettor service. Specifications for some adjustments are listed on the Vehicle Emissions Control Information label found in the engine compartment.
2   Some performance complaints directed at the carburettor are actually a result of loose, misadjusted or malfunctioning engine or electrical components. Others develop when vacuum hoses leak, are disconnected or are incorrectly routed. The proper approach analysing carburettor problems should include a routine check of the following areas:
3   Inspect all vacuum hoses and devices for leaks and proper refitting.
4   Tighten the inlet manifold nuts and carburettor mounting nuts evenly and securely.
5   Perform a cylinder compression test.
6   Clean or renew the spark plugs as necessary.

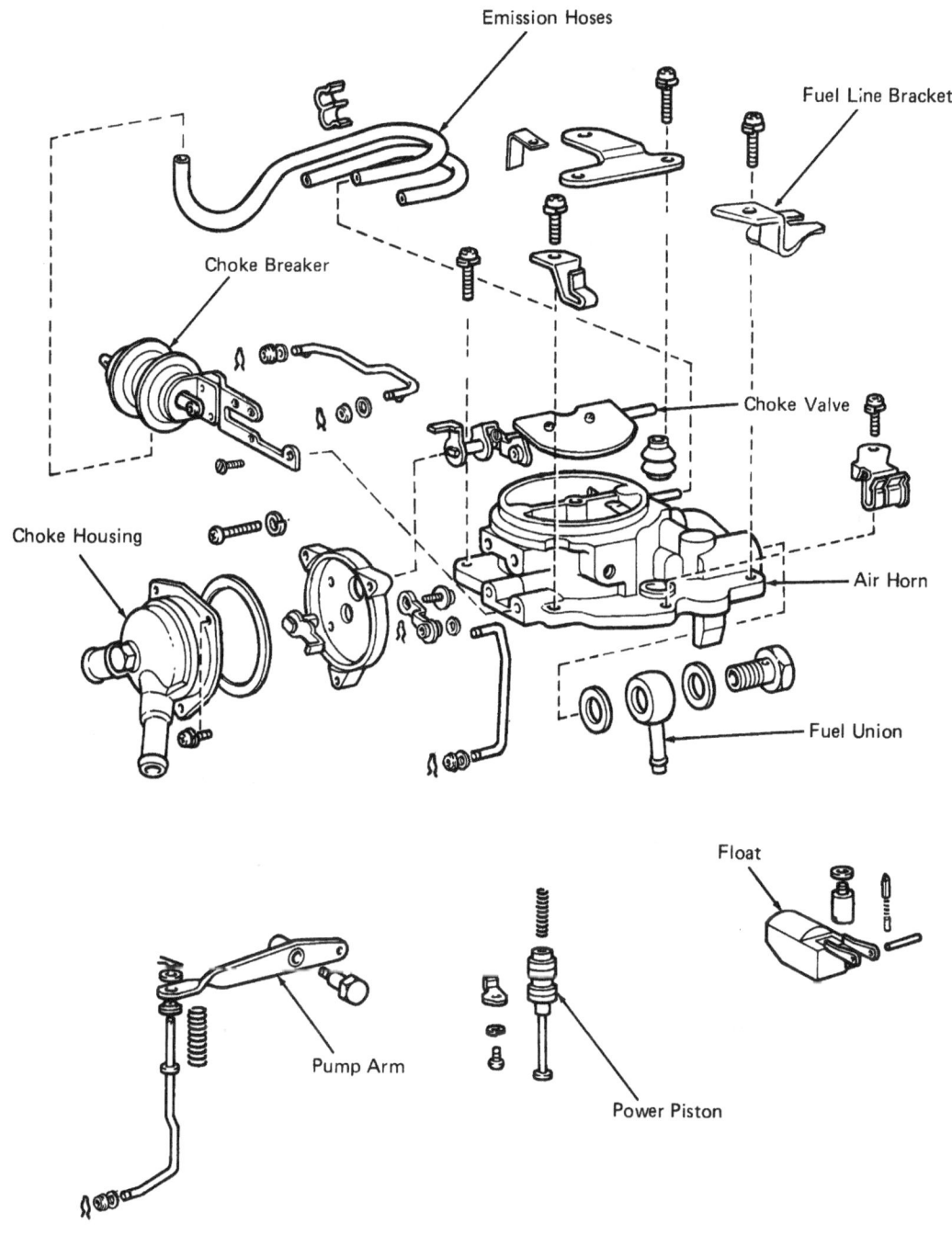

7.21a Carburettor air horn components - 18R and 20R engines

7   Check the spark plug wires (see Chapter 1).
8   Inspect the ignition primary wires and check the vacuum advance operation. Renew any defective parts.
9   Check the ignition timing (see Chapter 1).
10   Have the carburettor idle fuel/air mixture checked by a dealer service department or reputable repair facility.
11   Inspect the heated air intake system in the air cleaner for proper operation (see Chapter 6).

12   Remove the carburettor air filter element and blow out any dirt with compressed air. If the filter is extremely dirty, renew it (see Chapter 1).
13   Inspect the crankcase ventilation system (see Chapter 6).
14   Carburettor problems usually show up as flooding, hard starting, stalling, severe backfiring, poor acceleration and lack of response to idle mixture screw adjustments. A carburettor that is leaking fuel and/or covered with wet looking deposits definitely needs attention.

15   Diagnosing carburettor problems may require that the engine be started and run with the air cleaner removed. While running the engine without the air cleaner it is possible that it could backfire. A backfiring situation is likely to occur if the carburettor is malfunctioning, but removal of the air cleaner alone can lean the air/fuel mixture enough to produce an engine backfire. **Warning:** *Do not place your face or any parts of your body directly over the carburettor during diagnosis.*
16   Once it is determined that the carburettor is indeed at fault, it should be either

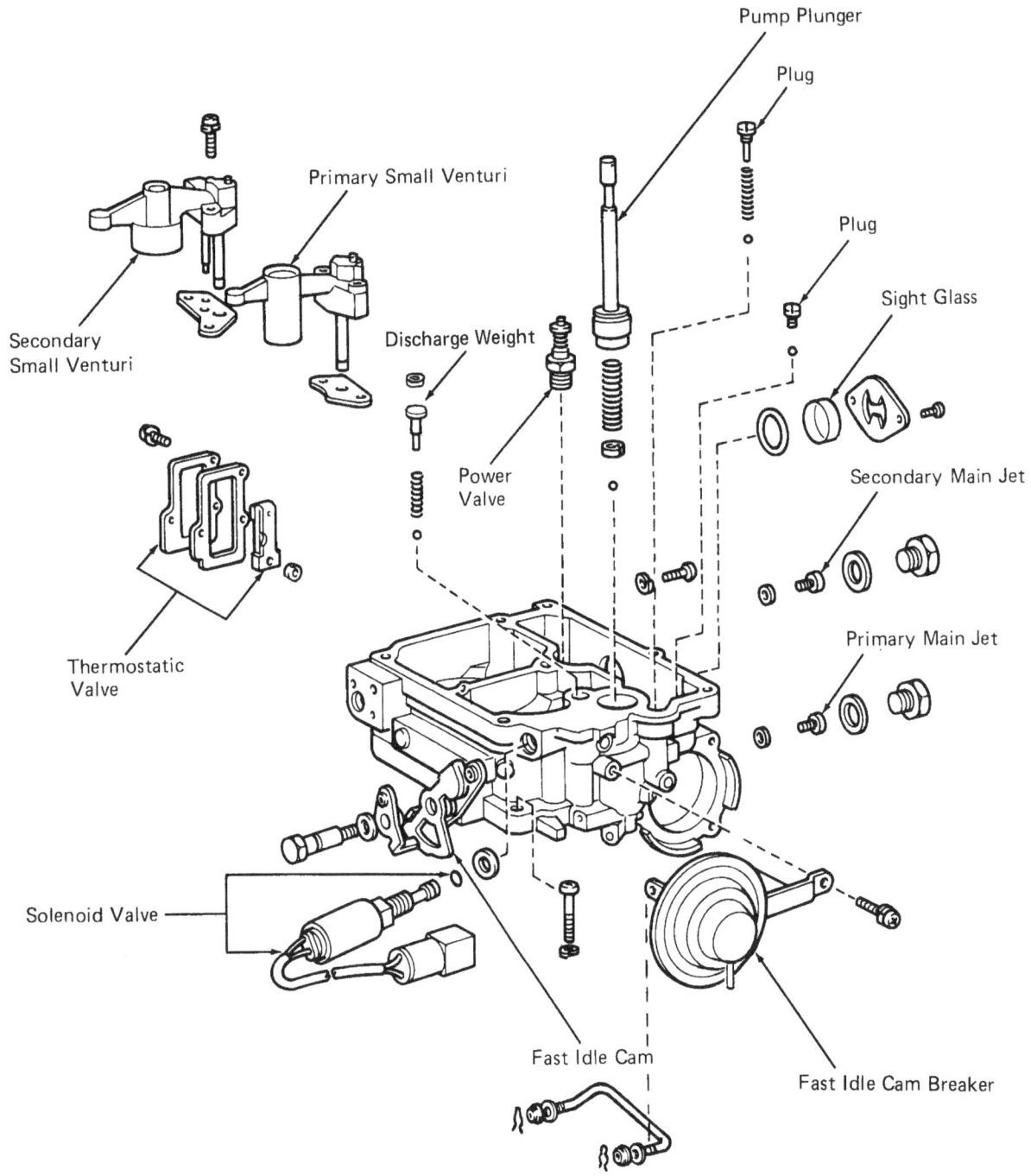

7.21b Carburettor body components - 18R and 20R engines

renewed with a new or factory-rebuilt unit or overhauled using new parts where necessary.

Overhaul

Refer to illustrations 7.21a through 7.21f

17 If you are going to overhaul the carburettor yourself, first obtain a good quality carburettor rebuild kit (which will include all necessary gaskets, internal parts, instructions and a parts list). You will also need some solvent and a means of blowing out the internal passages of the carburettor with air.

18 Because carburettor designs are constantly modified by the manufacturer in order to meet emissions regulations, it is best to refer to the specific instructions included in your carburettor overhaul kit. These instructions, which will be provided with any quality carburettor overhaul kit, will apply in a more specific manner to the carburettor on your vehicle.

19 An alternative is to obtain a new or rebuilt carburettor. They are readily available from dealers and auto parts stores. Make

sure the exchange carburettor is identical to the original. A tag is usually attached to the top of the carburettor, or a number is stamped onto the side of the main body of the carburettor. It will aid in determining the exact type of carburettor you have.

20 When obtaining a rebuilt carburettor or a rebuild kit, take time to make sure that the kit or carburettor matches your application exactly. Seemingly insignificant differences can make a large difference in the performance of your engine.

21 If you choose to overhaul your own car-

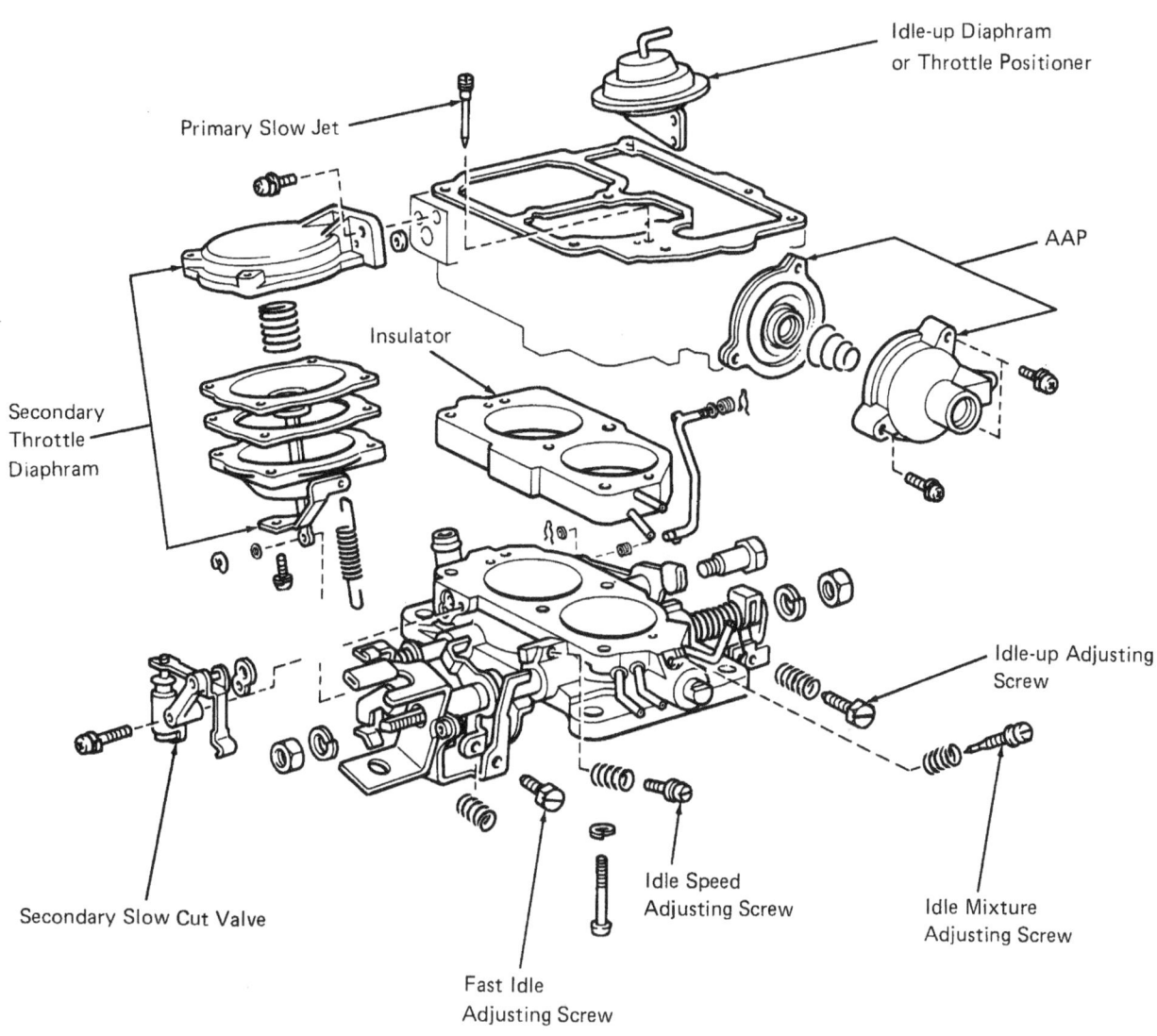

7.21c Carburettor base components - 18R and 20R engines

burettor, allow enough time to disassemble the carburettor carefully, soak the necessary parts in the cleaning solvent (usually for at least one-half day or according to the instructions listed on the carburettor cleaner) and reassemble it, which will usually take much longer than disassembly. When disassembling the carburettor, lay the parts out in order on a clean work surface **(see illustrations)**.

Disassembly

Note: *Not all steps in this procedure will apply to all carburettors. Refer to the exploded views* **(illustrations 7.21a through 7.21f)** *for parts identification.*

22 Use a small standard screwdriver to lift up the tab inside the electrical connector plastic housing, then pull the electrical connector terminal out of the housing.

23 Disconnect the hose from the choke vacuum break.

24 Pull the circlip off the fast-idle link with

needle-nose pliers, then disconnect the link from the choke mechanism. On 18R, 20R and Y-series carburettors, also detach the link for the secondary throttle valve diaphragm.

25 If you're working on a carburettor from a 22R engine, remove the metering needle valve from the air horn assembly (top of the carburettor). The needle valve is secured with a screw that has an Allen or Torx head.

26 Unclip the wire from the guide, then unscrew all the screws that secure the air horn to the carburettor. Lift off the air horn and overturn it for servicing. **Caution:** *When lifting off the air horn, be careful not to damage the float assembly.*

27 Remove the screws from underneath the carburettor, then lift the throttle body assembly off the carburettor main body.

28 Slide out the pin, then lift the float out of the air horn assembly.

29 Grasping the clip, lift the fuel inlet needle valve out of the seat assembly.

30 Using a large screwdriver or a socket, as appropriate, unscrew the fuel inlet needle valve seat from the carburettor air horn assembly. **Note:** *The fuel inlet needle seat may have a small filter screen attached to the end. If it does, be sure to remove it and clean it thoroughly before refitting it. If the screen is damaged in any way, renew it.*

31 On R-series carburettors, unscrew the small screw, then lift off the retainer and spacer (where applicable). Lift out the power valve piston. **Note:** *The power valve piston should move smoothly in and out of its bore. If it is stuck, use some penetrating oil and gentle force to pull it out. During reassembly, be sure the piston moves smoothly in and out of its bore.*

32 Unscrew the three screws and pull off the choke coil housing and gasket.

33 Unscrew the three screws and remove the choke breaker assembly from the air horn assembly. Pull off the circlip on the end of the

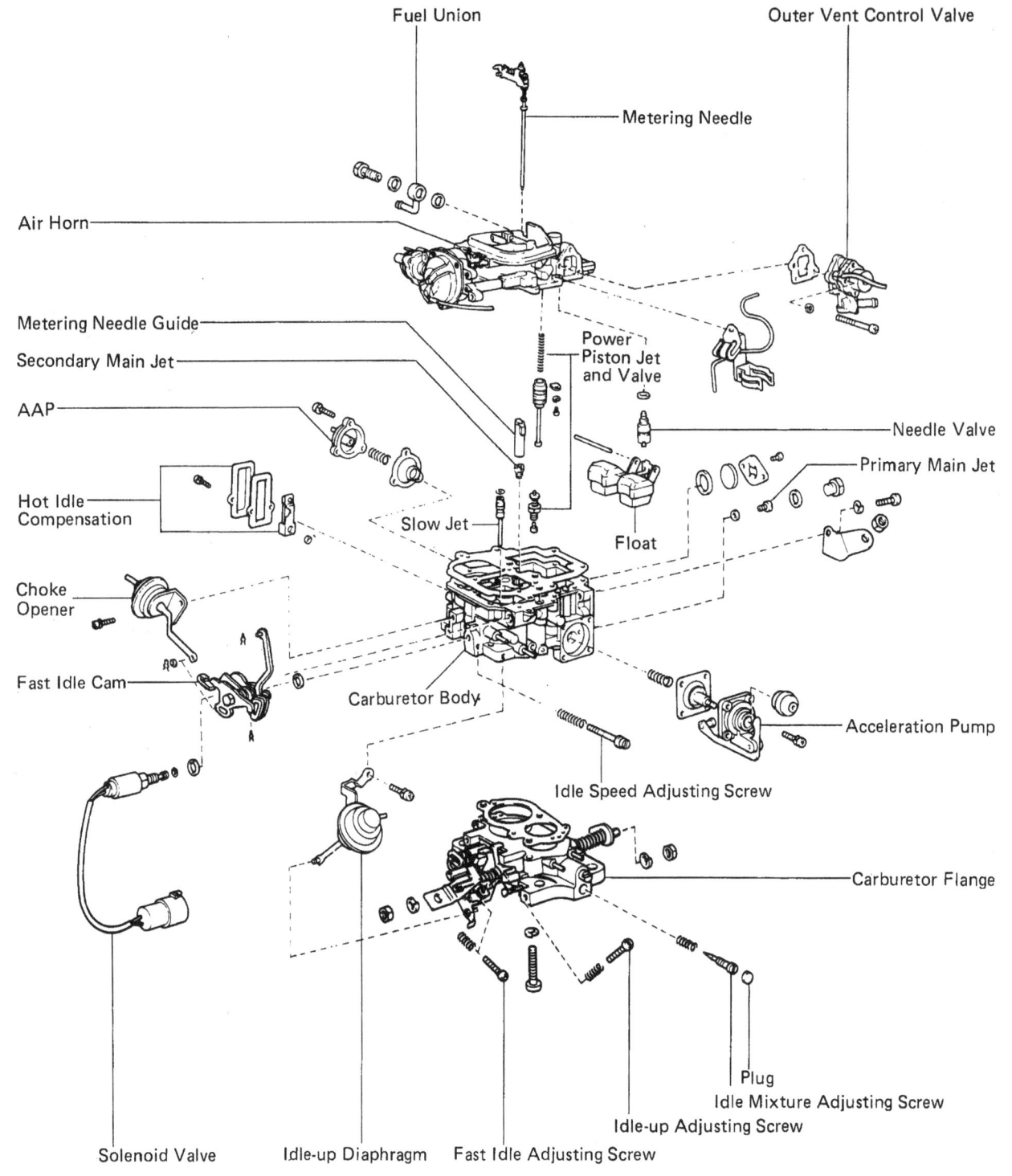

7.21d An exploded view of the 22R engine carburettor

breaker rod, then pull the assembly off the air horn.

34   Unscrew the three screws, then pull off the outer vent control valve and gasket.

35   Unscrew the screw(s) and lift the throttle position switch off the throttle body.

36   If equipped, remove the idle-up dia-phragm after unscrewing the single screw.

37   If equipped, drill out the plug covering the idle mixture screw, fully seat the screw by turning it clockwise, then thread an appropriately sized sheet-metal screw into the hole in the plug and use pliers on the screw to pull the plug out.

38   Remove the throttle opener off the main body by unscrewing the screw(s).

39   Unscrew the two screws that secure the sight glass cover, then remove the cover, glass and seal.

40   Remove the slow jet from the top of the main body by unscrewing it.

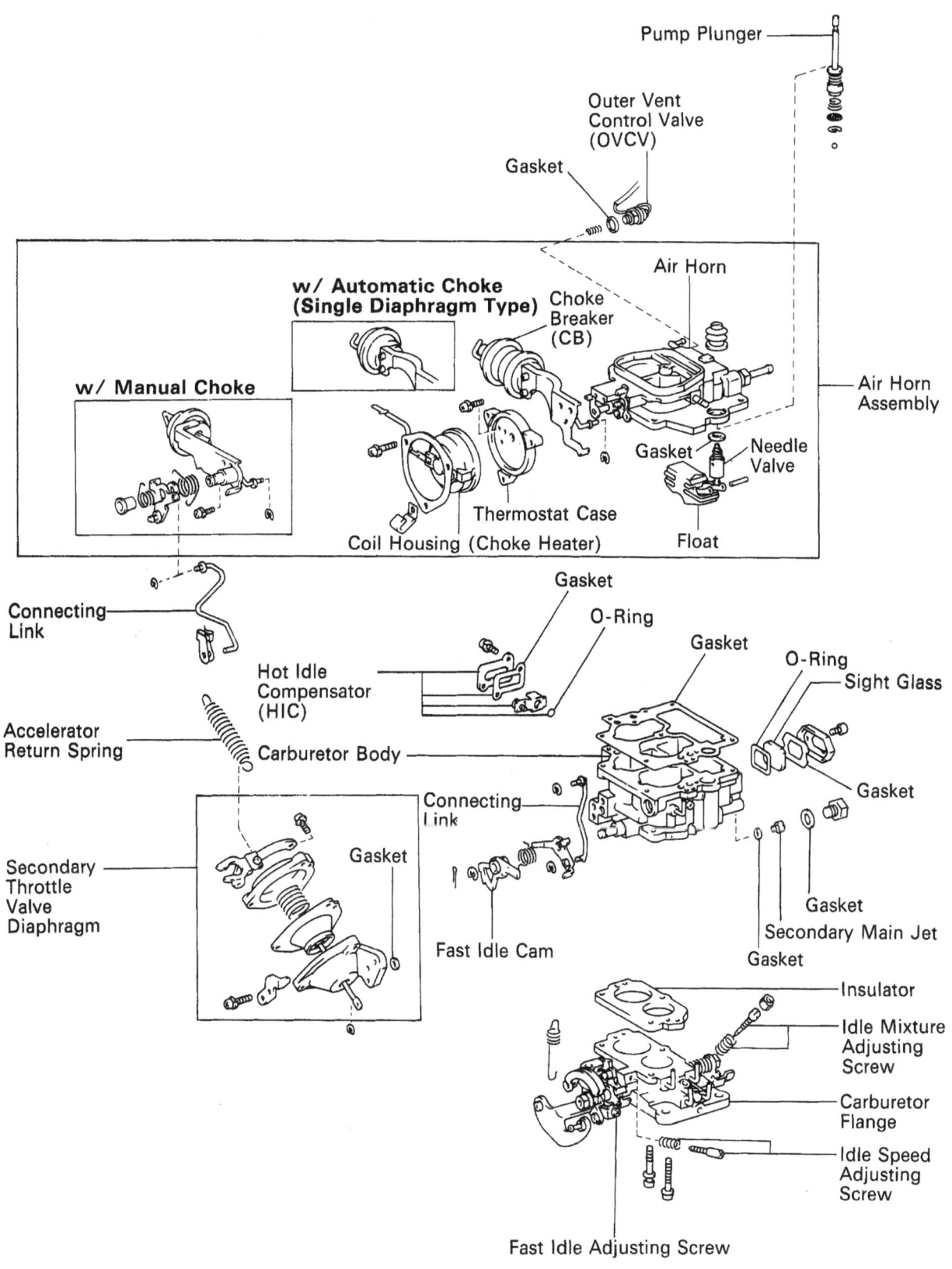

7.21e Exploded view of the Y-series engine carburettor

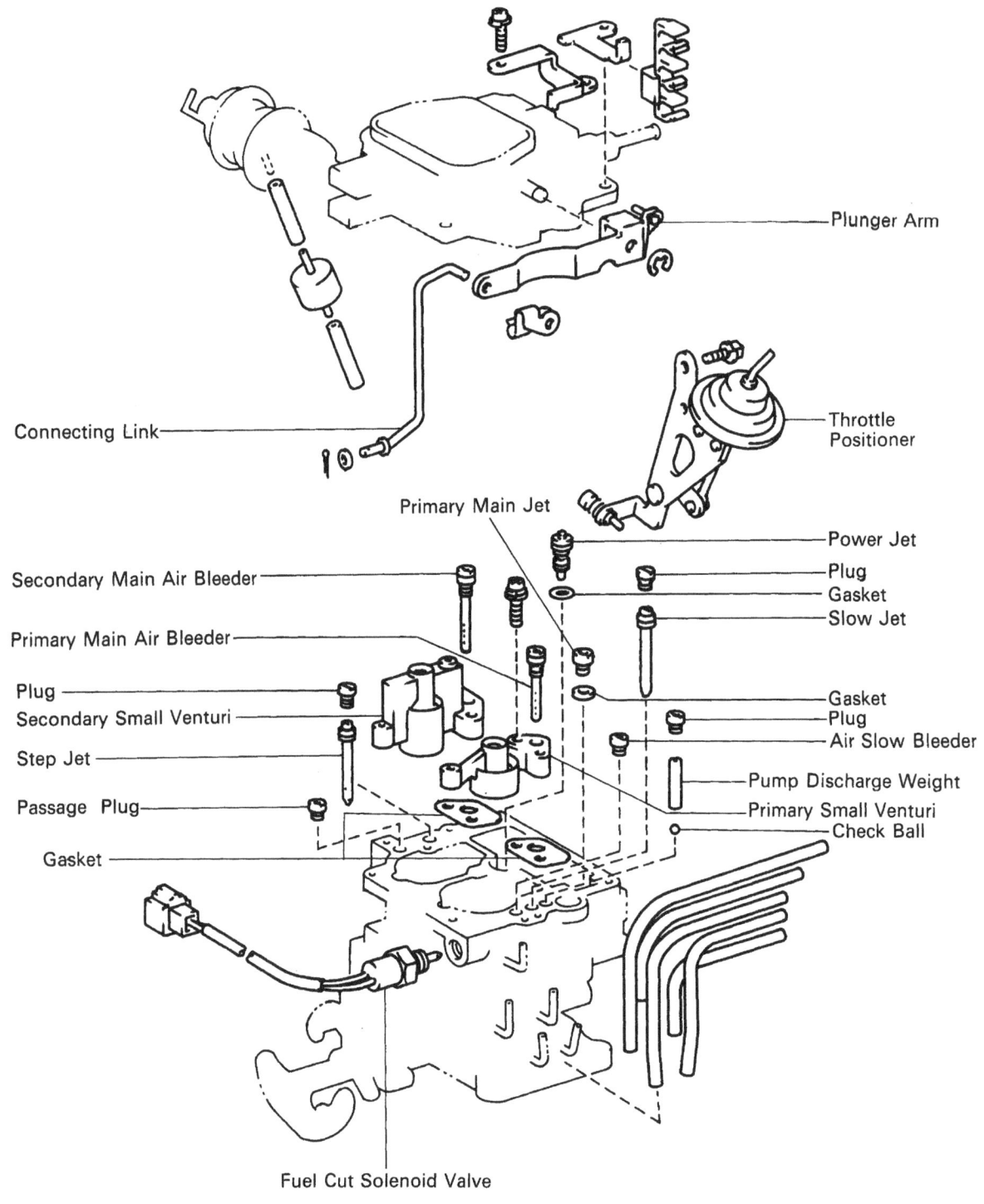

7.21f Air horn components - Y-series engine carburettor

41   Unscrew and remove the power valve (has a spring on top). It is located at the bottom of the float bowl.

42   Remove the metering needle guide by pulling it up, then remove the secondary main jet by unscrewing it.

43   Unscrew the large hex-head bolt from the side of the main body, next to where the sight glass was. Placing a screwdriver through the bolt hole, unscrew the primary main jet.

44   Unscrew the four screws securing the acceleration pump housing, then pull off the housing, plunger, rubber diaphragm and spring (R-series).

45   Remove the three screws securing the auxiliary acceleration pump housing, then pull off the housing, rubber diaphragm and spring (R-series).

46   Unscrew the screws, then remove the vent control valve.

47   Using needle-nose pliers, remove the circlip that secures the rod on the choke opener to the fast-idle cam assembly. Unscrew the two screws, then pull off the choke opener.

48   Using a wrench on the hex-shaped boss, unscrew the solenoid valve from the side of the main body, if equipped. Be sure to use a new gasket and O-ring on reassembly.

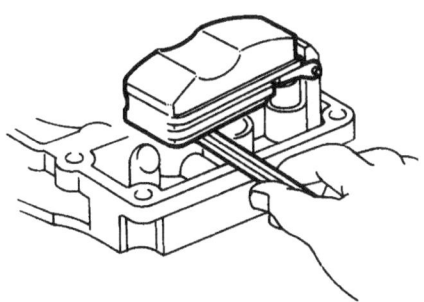

7.59a Measuring the float level (Y-series carburettor shown, R-series similar)

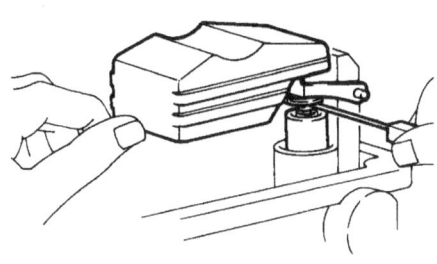

7.59b Measuring the float drop (Y-series carburettor shown, R-series similar)

Cleaning and inspection

49   Clean all metal carburettor parts thoroughly. It is best to use a "dip bucket" filled with caustic carburettor cleaning solution. These buckets, filled with cleaning solution, are available from most auto parts stores. Let the parts soak in the solution overnight (or as long as the solution manufacturer recommends), then rinse them off with water. DO NOT immerse openers, positioners and other solenoids and diaphragms in this solution, since the solution will destroy them. Clean them individually with a mild solution.

50   After all parts are clean, inspect them thoroughly for wear, scoring and other damage. Renew any parts that show excessive wear.

51   Check all needle valves for breakage and damage and renew as necessary. The idle mixture adjusting screw is frequently damaged from overtightening. If an idle mixture screw has a step on its tapered end, renew it.

52   Check the choke coil inside the choke coil housing to be sure it is not broken or damaged. The coil is a spring and should be wound evenly and have tension, springing back after it is coiled tighter. If the spring coils are distorted or if the coil lacks tension, renew the coil housing assembly

53   Scrape all traces of old gasket material off all gasket mating surfaces. Be sure to renew all gaskets, sealing washers and rubber O-rings on reassembly.

54   Inspect all drilled passages in the carburettor main body, throttle body and air horn for plugging with debris. Blow out all passages with filtered, unlubricated compressed air. **Warning:** *Always wear eye protection when using compressed air!* If an air compressor is not available, cans of compressed air are available from computer stores for a reasonable price (they're designed for cleaning computer keyboards).

55   Check the float for signs of fuel intrusion, which would cause the float to sink. It is best to routinely renew the float at overhaul time.

56   Check the vent control valve(s), choke breaker, power piston and power valve for smooth operation. The plungers in these devices should move smoothly in and out without binding. If any of these parts does not

operate smoothly, renew it.

57   Check the solenoid valve and vent control valve by momentarily connecting battery voltage to them and verify that they operate. There should be an audible "click" as the plunger moves. To connect battery voltage, connect fused jumper wires from the vehicle's battery terminals to the two wires (solenoid valve) or between the wire and component case (vent control valve). Be sure to connect the positive battery voltage to the wire on the vent control valve or the black wire with the orange stripe on the solenoid valve. **Caution:** *Do not perform this test for any longer than necessary to verify operation of components or component damage will result. Also, do not perform these tests near fuel or other combustibles since sparks may be created.*

Reassembly and adjustment

Refer to illustrations 7.59a and 7.59b

58   Reassemble parts in the reverse order of disassembly, using new gaskets, seals and O-rings. Use a removable thread locking compound on the throttle body attaching screws to ensure they will not come loose and possibly drop into the inlet manifold and engine.

59   When the float is fitted (remember - it's best to use a new one!), measure the distance from the air horn machined surface to the top of the float with the air horn inverted **(see illustration)**. This distance can be measured with measuring calipers, a steel rule, or the paper gauge that's generally included with rebuild kits. The distance should be as listed in this Chapter's Specifications. If the level is not correct, bend the tab on the float. Next, check the float drop; gently lift the float up and measure the gap between the float tip and the needle valve plunger **(see illustration)**. **Note:** *A drill bit of the proper size can be used as a gauge.* If the float drop is not as specified, bend the down stop portion of the float tang. After the carburettor is reassembled, refitted, operate the starter until fuel is visible in the sight glass and check that the fuel level is correct.

60   When refitting the idle mixture adjusting screw, turn the screw clockwise until it is lightly seated, then unscrew it 2-1/2 turns (Y-series), 3-1/2 turns (20R and 22R) or 2

turns (12R and 18R). **Caution:** *Do not tighten the screw when seating it as damage to the screw will occur.* This will provide an initial setting that will allow the engine to start and run after overhaul. Then, adjust the idle speed and mixture as described in Section 8. Final mixture adjustment will need to be done by a dealer service department or other qualified repair shop, since a CO meter should be used - do not fit a new plug until this adjustment has been accomplished.

61   Make an initial choke setting during reassembly by rotating the choke coil housing until the mark on the edge of the housing aligns with the centre mark on the thermostat case. Refer to Section 8 to make the final choke adjustment after the carburettor is refitted on the vehicle.

62   After the carburettor is refitted, adjust the carburettor, as described in Section 8. If it is necessary to adjust the choke breaker, choke opener or secondary throttle valve, it is best to have these operations performed by a dealer service department or other qualified shop, since a special angle meter is required. If the initial settings were not changed during overhaul, it is not usually necessary to make these adjustments at overhaul time.

8   Carburettor - on-vehicle adjustments

Refer to illustrations 8.1, 8.2, 8.3a, 8.3b, 8.3c, 8.3d, 8.9, 8.12, 8.14a, 8.14b, 8.14c and 8.14d

Warning: *Petrol is extremely flammable, so extra precautions must be taken when working on any part of the fuel system. See the Warning at the end of Section 1.*

Idle speed and idle mixture (lean drop method)

1   The following conditions should be met before beginning the adjustment:

a) *Air cleaner refitted.*
b) *Choke valve fully open.*
c) *Accessories switched Off.*
d) *All vacuum lines connected.*
e) *Ignition timing set correctly (see Chapter 5).*
f) *Transmission in Neutral (parking brake set and wheels blocked to prevent movement).*

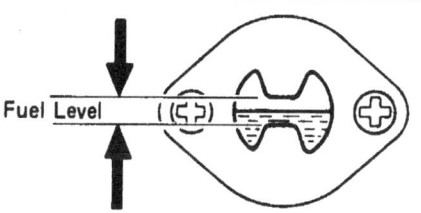

8.1 Always check the sight glass window on the carburettor float bowl to verify that the fuel level in the float bowl is correct before adjusting the idle speed

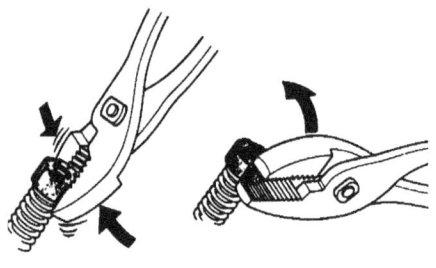

8.2 Use pliers to break off the limiter caps on the idle mixture and idle adjusting screws

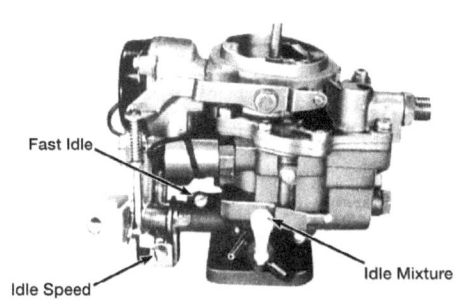

8.3a The idle mixture and idle speed adjusting screws (12R engine)

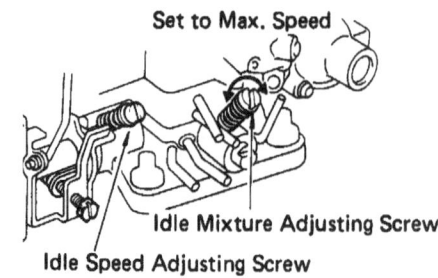

8.3b The idle mixture and idle speed adjusting screws (18R and 20R engines)

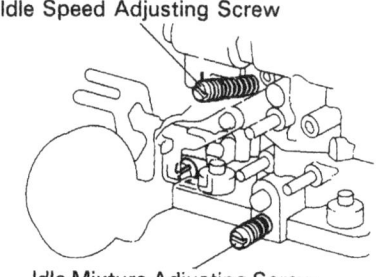

8.3c The idle mixture and idle speed adjusting screws (22R engine)

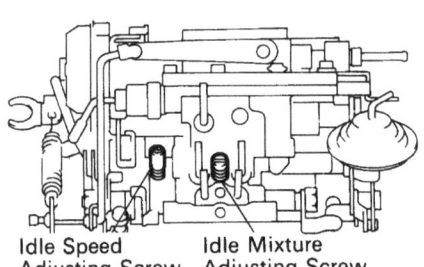

8.3d The idle mixture and idle speed adjusting screws (Y-series engines)

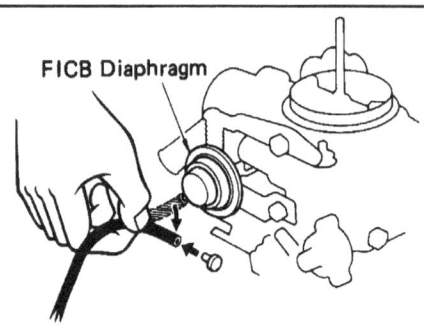

8.9 Detach the vacuum hose from the fast idle cam breaker (FICB) diaphragm and plug the hose end

g) *Engine idling at normal operating temperature.*
h) *A hand-held tachometer attached according to the manufacturer's recommendations.*
i) *Fuel level correct in sight glass* **(see illustration)**.

2   If idle limiter caps are refitted on the idle mixture and idle speed adjusting screws, break them off **(see illustration)**.
3   Turn the idle mixture adjusting screw **(see illustration)** to obtain the maximum engine rpm.
4   Turn the idle speed adjusting screw until the specified idle mixture speed is obtained.
5   Repeat the two Steps above until engine rpm cannot be increased by turning the idle mixture adjusting screw.
6   Turn the idle mixture adjusting screw until the idle speed listed in the Specifications is obtained.
7   If originally so equipped, fit new limiter caps on the idle mixture and idle speed adjusting screws.

Fast idle

8   Stop the engine and remove the air cleaner.
9   If so equipped, disconnect and plug the hose from the fast idle cam breaker diaphragm and plug the hose end **(see illustration)**.
10   Disconnect the hose(s) from the distributor and plug the hose end(s), cutting out the vacuum advance.
11   Disconnect the hose from the EGR valve, shutting off the EGR system.
12   While holding the throttle valve slightly open, pull up the fast idle cam linkage fully, then release the throttle **(see illustration)**.
13   Start the engine, but do not touch the accelerator pedal.
14   Check that the engine is operating at its specified fast idle speed. If not, bend the fast idle adjusting lever (models with a manual choke) **(see illustration)** or turn the fast idle adjustment screw **(see illustrations)** until the specified speed is reached.
15   Disconnect the tachometer and reconnect the distributor, EGR and fast idle cam

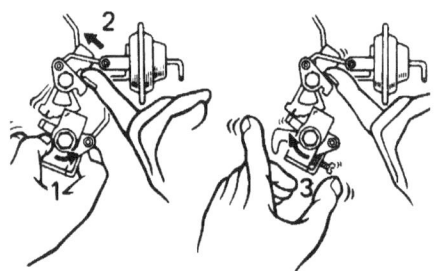

8.12 During the fast idle check, hold the throttle valve slightly open (1) while pulling up on the fast idle cam linkage (2), then release the throttle valve (3)

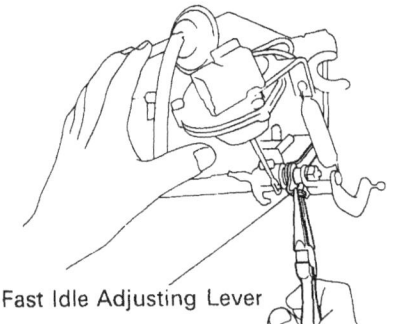

8.14a On models with a manual choke, bend this lever to adjust the fast idle speed

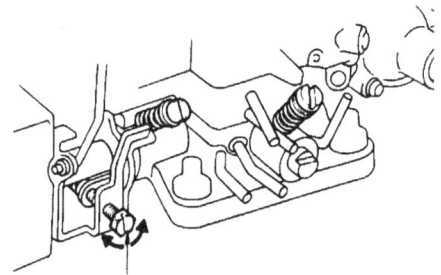

8.14b Location of the fast idle adjusting screw (18R and 20R engines)

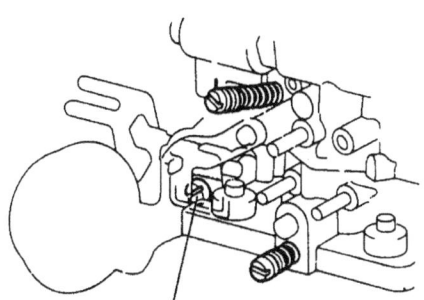

Fast Idle Adjusting Screw

8.14c Location of the fast idle adjusting screw (22R engine)

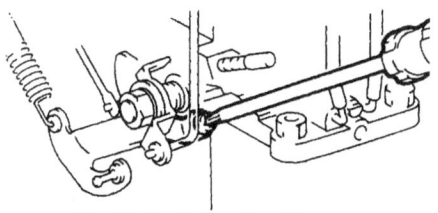

Fast Idle Adjusting Screw

8.14d Location of the fast idle adjusting screw (Y-series engines)

breaker (if so equipped) hoses. When the hoses are reconnected, the engine speed should drop noticeably. If it does not, check the choke opener diaphragm and fast idle linkage.

Choke adjustment

16 The choke on these models is adjustable by rotating the choke coil housing. Refer to the exploded-view drawings of the carburettor to locate the choke coil housing.

17 Generally the choke will need adjustment if the engine runs too lean or rich during warm-up. An excessively lean mixture is characterised by backfiring (popping and/ or flames coming through the carburettor) and a tendency to surge or stall. Lean-running engines will often start and run better when the accelerator pedal is pumped. An excessively rich mixture is characterised by black smoke from the tailpipe and an engine that "chugs" and runs slowly. Flooding is an extreme rich-mixture condition.

18 With the engine cold (approximately 10 to 20-degrees C), remove the air cleaner assembly and check the choke plate. The choke should be fully closed, but not excessively tight. Press down on the choke plate to verify it opens smoothly, without binding and that it springs back shut when released. If the choke plate does not respond as described, remove the three screws and the choke coil housing and inspect the coiled bimetal spring inside. Most problems with automatic chokes are caused by a spring that has broken or lost its tension. Renew the choke coil housing and spring, if necessary. If the spring is good but the choke plate does not open and close smoothly, inspect the choke linkage and lubricate or repair it, as necessary.

19 Loosen the three choke coil housing screws, then rotate the choke coil housing - clockwise to open the choke plate and lean the mixture or counterclockwise to close the choke plate and richen the mixture. If you're making an initial setting, rotate the housing counter-clockwise until the choke plate just begins to open, then rotate it clockwise to barely close the choke plate. Tighten the choke coil housing screws.

9 EFI system - general information and special precautions

General information

Some models are equipped with an Electronic Fuel Injection (EFI) system, also known as Multiport Fuel Injection (MFI). Electronic fuel injection provides optimum mixture ratios at all stages of combustion, and this, together with the immediate response characteristics of fuel injection, permits the engine to run on the weakest possible fuel/air mixture, which vastly reduces exhaust emissions. The EFI system is interrelated with and works in conjunction with the emission control and exhaust systems.

The EFI system consists of three subsystems; the fuel system, the air induction system and the electronic control system. The various components that make up the entire EFI system are detailed later in another Section.

Fuel from the tank is delivered under pressure from the electric fuel pump, through the filter and, to avoid pulsation, is fed through a mechanical damper. After passing through the damper and a pressure regulator, it is injected into the inlet manifold. The pressure regulator is designed to maintain a constant pressure difference between the fuel line pressure and the inlet manifold vacuum. Where manifold conditions are such that the fuel pressure would be beyond that specified, the pressure regulator returns surplus fuel to the tank.

An injection of fuel occurs once every rotation of the crankshaft. Because the injection signal comes from the control unit, all injectors operate simultaneously and independent of the engine stroke. Each injection supplies half the amount of fuel required by the cylinder and the length of the injection period is determined by information fed to the control unit by the various sensors included in the system.

Elements affecting the injection duration include engine rpm, quantity and temperature of the intake air, throttle valve opening, temperature of the engine coolant, position of the ignition switch, inlet manifold vacuum and amount of oxygen in the exhaust gases.

Because the EFI system operates at high fuel pressure, a slight leak can affect system efficiency and present a serious fire risk. Also, since the intake air flow is critical to the operation of the system, even a slight air leak will cause wrong air/fuel mixtures to occur.

The electric fuel pump in the EFI system uses two relays located in the passenger compartment. This set-up is designed so that if the engine accidentally stops, causing the alternator to turn off and the oil pressure to drop, the fuel pump will not operate.

Special precautions

Warning: *Petrol is extremely flammable, so extra precautions must be taken when working on any part of the fuel system. See the Warning at the end of Section 1.*

Prior to any operation in which a fuel line will be disconnected the pressure in the fuel system must first be relieved. This procedure is described later in this Chapter.

Prior to removing an EFI component be sure the ignition switch is off and the negative battery cable is disconnected.

The EFI wiring harness should be kept at least 20 cm away from adjacent harnesses. This includes a CB aerial feeder cable as well. This will prevent electrical pulses in other systems from interfering with the EFI operation.

Be sure all ignition and EFI wiring connections are clean and secure.

Check carefully for intake air leaks and make sure ignition system components are in good condition before assuming that the EFI system is malfunctioning. The drivebelt tension must be properly maintained and the battery must be kept fully charged as well.

Do not use a high pressure washer to clean the engine compartment. Water and caustic detergents may damage or corrode EFI system components.

Handle all EFI components with care when removing and refitting them. The oxygen sensor is particularly susceptible to damage from impact.

While some basic checks of the EFI components are included in this Chapter, the complexity of the system prevents many problems from being accurately diagnosed by the home mechanic. If a problem develops in the system which cannot be pinpointed by the checks listed here, take the vehicle to a Toyota dealer or other qualified repair shop to locate the fault.

10 Fuel pressure relief procedure

Warning: *Petrol is extremely flammable, so extra precautions must be taken when working on any part of the fuel system. See the Warning at the end of Section 1.*

1 Before servicing any component on a fuel injected vehicle, it is necessary to relieve the fuel pressure to minimise the risk of fire or personal injury.

2 Start the engine and allow it to idle.

3 Disconnect the electrical connector to

the fuel pump (white wire with black tracer and light blue wire).

4   Wait for the engine to stall, then crank it over two or three more times.

5   Turn the ignition switch off and reconnect the fuel pump wires. The fuel system is now ready to be serviced.

6   Whenever loosening a fuel fitting, wrap a rag around it to absorb any fuel that spills out. It's also a good idea to wear safety glasses when disconnecting fuel lines and fittings.

11.1 Location of the ECU (behind the left kick panel)

11   EFI components - general description

Control unit

Refer to illustration 11.1

The control unit (or ECU) **(see illustration)** is mounted under the left side kick panel in the cab on most models. The essential role of this unit is to generate a pulse to the injectors. Upon receiving inputs from each sensor, the control unit generates a pulse whose duration (injector open time period) is controlled to provide the exact amount of fuel needed, according to engine operating conditions at that particular time.

Airflow meter

The airflow meter measures the volume and temperature of the intake air and sends the signal to the control unit. This is achieved by a potentiometer which is linked to the air intake flap shaft. The more air that enters the flow meter the further the flap valve rotates which in turn rotates the potentiometer wiper through a variable resistance coil. This increasing or decreasing resistance (depending on the flap signal) changes the signal to the control unit. In order to dampen excessive movement of the flap due to vacuum depressions in the inlet manifold a helical spring and compensating plate in a damper chamber are provided. Also built into the airflow meter is an air temperature sensor which senses air temperature and sends a signal to the control unit. This signal will define the duration of the injection time. Air that flows into the meter is first passed through the air cleaner assembly.

Air valve

The air valve, also known as the Idle Air Control (IAC) valve, bypasses the throttle valve to control the quantity of air required for increasing the engine idle speed when starting the engine at a coolant temperature below a predetermined level. A bimetal spring and heater are built into the valve. When the ignition switch is turned to the Start position, or when the engine is running electric current, flows through the heater and the bimetal spring. As the heater warms up, the bimetal spring will close the air passage. The air passage will remain closed until the engine is stopped or the coolant temperature drops below the predetermined level.

Injectors

An injector is mounted on each branch of the inlet manifold. Each injector is actuated by a small solenoid valve built into the injector body. Actuating the solenoid valve pulls a needle valve into the open position to allow the fuel to inject. The duration of the pulse sent from the control unit defines the period of time that the solenoid valve is actuated. Air intake chamber

The air intake chamber is mounted over the inlet manifold and is equipped with a throttle body which controls the intake airflow in response to accelerator pedal movement. The shaft of this throttle valve is connected to the throttle position sensor. The valve remains closed during engine idling and the air required for idling passes through a bypass port, into the inlet manifold. Idle adjustment is made by the idle speed adjusting screw. A second line in the air intake chamber passes air through the air valve into the inlet manifold when the engine is started cold.

Fuel pump

The fuel pump is mounted in the fuel tank at the right side of the vehicle. Built into the outlet pipe of the pump is a check valve. The check valve prevents abrupt drops in fuel pressure when the engine is stopped.

Throttle position sensor

The throttle position sensor is attached to the throttle body and responds to accelerator pedal movement. This switch has two sets of contact points. One set monitors the idle position and the other set monitors the full throttle position. The idle contacts close when the throttle valve is positioned at idle and open when it is at any other position. The full throttle contacts close only when the throttle is positioned at full throttle. The contacts are open while the throttle valve is at any other position. The idle switch compensates for enrichment during idle and after idle sends a signal to the control unit to modify the fuel supply. The full throttle switch compensates for enrichment at the full throttle position.

Fuel filter

The fuel filter, which is mounted in the engine compartment, insures that only clean fuel reaches the injectors. A clogged fuel filter will stop the flow of fuel and cause the engine to stall. This is usually preceded by hesitation and sluggish operation.

Fuel damper

The fuel damper which is mounted on the fuel delivery pipe is designed to suppress pulsations in fuel flow from the fuel pump.

Pressure regulator

The pressure regulator, which is attached to the inlet manifold in the fuel supply line, maintains a constant fuel pressure at all stages of acceleration and deceleration. Under extreme manifold vacuum conditions, the full pressure delivered by the fuel pump combined with a high vacuum could cause excessive pressure in the fuel line. If such a condition occurs the pressure regulator opens to return excess fuel to the fuel tank.

Water thermo sensor

This device, which is located in the thermostat housing, monitors changes in the engine coolant temperature. As soon as a temperature change is sensed, a signal is sent to a control unit where a modified injector pulse duration will be computed.

Solenoid resistor

The solenoid resistor protects the injectors from alternator surges and effects of other electrical components by lowering the source voltage.

Cold start injector

This valve is designed to enrich the fuel/air mixture during cold engine operation by injecting fuel into the inlet manifold independently of the cylinder injectors. It receives electrical signals from the cold start injector time switch.

Cold start injector time switch

The switch, mounted in the thermostat housing, uses a bimetal contact to sense the engine coolant temperature for proper operation of the cold start injector.

Oxygen sensor

The oxygen sensor, which works in conjunction with the EFI system and the catalytic converter, measures the amount of oxygen present in the exhaust gases. This information is fed to the control unit, which adjusts the air/fuel mixture to compensate.

12   Fuel lines - repair and renewal

Warning: *Petrol is extremely flammable, so extra precautions must be taken when working on any part of the fuel system. See the Warning at the end of Section 1.*

1   The fuel injection system is designed to

13.15 Measure the resistance between main relay terminals 1 and 2 and 3 and 4 - if your readings are not within the ranges specified in the above table, renew the relay (4Y-E and 22R-E)

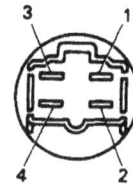

Between terminals	Resistance (Ω)
1 – 2	60 ohms +/- 20 ohms
3 – 4	Infinity

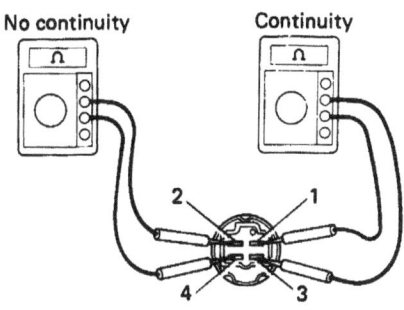

13.16 Verify that there is continuity between terminals 1 and 3, but not between terminals 2 and 4 and 3 and 4 - if continuity is not as specified, renew the relay (V6 and 1989 and later 22R-E)

operate at a pressure much higher than conventional fuel systems, so even slight leakage at a fuel joint can become a major problem. Ignoring a leaking joint is a serious fire risk and the pressure loss is certain to affect the system operation. From time-to-time check the security of all the fuel joints. Make sure that the rigid lines are not kinked or bent in any way. If a rubber hose shows signs of deterioration, renew it. **Caution:** *Do not disconnect any fuel lines without first eliminating the pressure from the system as described in Section 10.*

2   Since the EFI system accurately meters the intake air through the airflow meter, even a slight air leak will cause an improper fuel/air mixture, resulting in poor engine performance. For this reason a thorough inspection for leaks should he made at the oil filler cap, dipstick seal, PCV hoses, airflow meter-to-throttle body air duct, etc.

3   If a section of metal fuel line must be renewed, only brazed seamless steel tubing should be used, as copper or aluminium tubing does not have enough durability to withstand vibrations encountered during normal engine operation.

4   If only one section of a metal fuel line is damaged it can be cut out and renewed with a piece of rubber fuel hose. The rubber hose should be cut 10 cm longer than the section to be renewed, so there is about 50 mm of overlap between the rubber and metal lines at either end of the section. Hose clamps should be used to secure both ends of the repaired section.

5   If a section of metal line longer than 15 cm is being removed, use a combination of metal tubing and rubber hose so that the hose lengths are no longer than 7.5 cm.

6   Never use rubber hose within 10 cm of any part of the exhaust system.

13 EFI system - Electronic Control System

Note: *In most markets, an extended warranty covers the control unit, the information sensors and all components under its control. Damage to the ECU, the sensors and/or the control devices caused by the vehicle owner during diagnosis may void the warranty. Before proceeding, check with your dealer to inquire about the status of this extended warranty and how it pertains to your vehicle.*

ECU

1   This check employs a miniature test lamp, sometimes referred to as a "noid" light, to determine whether the open-injector pulse for cranking the engine is actually applied to the injectors (should the engine fail to start). To carry out this check, the engine must be cranked at a speed of more than 80 rpm. The battery must be fully charged.

2   Turn the ignition switch to the Off position.

3   Disconnect the wire harness from the cold start injector.

4   Disconnect the electrical connector from the number one cylinder injector.

5   Connect the test light to the number one cylinder injector wire harness terminals.

6   Turn the ignition switch to the Start position to crank the engine and note whether or not the lamp flashes. If the lamp flashes, the electrical pulse is present. If it does not, the control unit may be defective. Check all wires and connections carefully.

7   It must be emphasised that this check only proves whether or not a signal pulse is reaching the injectors. If the control unit is still suspect, there are numerous other circuits inside the unit that could be at fault, so have it checked by a Toyota dealer service department or other qualified repair shop.

8   The control unit is mounted under the left side kick panel in the cab (see illustration 11.1) and can be renewed as follows.

9   Turn the ignition switch to the Off position and then disconnect the battery earth cable.

10   Remove the screws and detach the control unit cover (if equipped).

11   Carefully disconnect the electrical connector from the control unit.

12   Remove the bolts that hold the control unit to the mounting bracket and detach the control unit.

13   Refitting is the reverse of the removal procedure. **Note:** *Be careful when refitting the electrical connector not to bend or break any of the terminals.*

Main relay

Refer to illustrations 13.15 and 13.16

14   Locate the main relay on 4Y-E and pre-1989 22R-E models by removing the right side kick panel in the cab (it's the relay that's lowest on the fuse/relay panel. On 1989 and later 22R and all V6 models, the relay is located in the fuse/relay panel on the right

side of the engine compartment. Turn on the ignition switch and listen for a clicking noise at the relay.

15   If your vehicle is equipped with a four-cylinder engine, remove the relay and measure the resistance between the terminals **(see illustrations)**. On 1988 and earlier models, the resistance between terminals 1 and 2 should be approximately 60 ohms, plus or minus 20 ohms. The resistance between terminals 3 and 4 should be infinite.

16   If the vehicle is equipped with a V6 or a 1989 or later four-cylinder, remove the relay and verify that there is continuity between terminals 1 and 3, that there is no continuity between 2 and 4 and that there is no continuity between terminals 3 and 4 **(see illustration)**. If continuity is not as specified, renew the relay. Then apply battery voltage across terminals 1 and 3 and verify that there is continuity between terminals 2 and 4. If relay operation is not as specified, renew it.

Circuit opening relay

Refer to illustrations 13.18a, 13.18b and 13.19

17   Locate the relay by removing the left side kick panel and on some models, the glove box and speaker.

18   If your vehicle is equipped with a four cylinder engine, check for voltage at terminal Fp **(see illustration)** when the engine is being cranked and when it is running. Stop

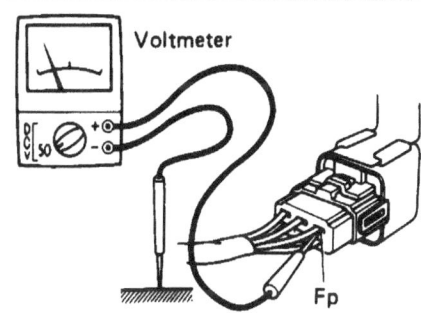

13.18a Verify that there is voltage at terminal Fp of the circuit opening relay while the engine is cranking and running (22R-E shown)

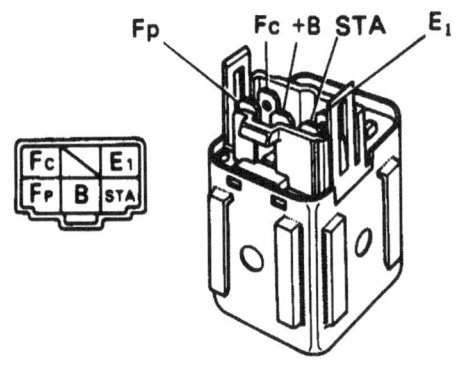

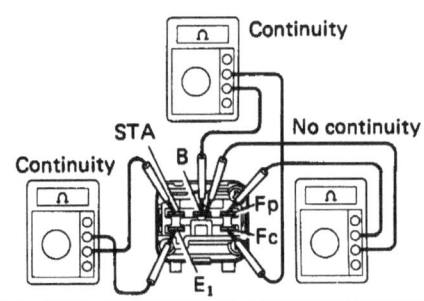

13.19 Verify that the continuity between the indicated terminals of the circuit opening relay is as specified (V6 engine)

Between terminals	Resistance (Ω)
STA — E₁	17 — 25
+B — Fc	88 — 132
+B — Fp	Infinity

13.18b Measure the resistance between the indicated terminals of the relay and compare your readings to the respective specified resistance range for each pair (22R-E shown)

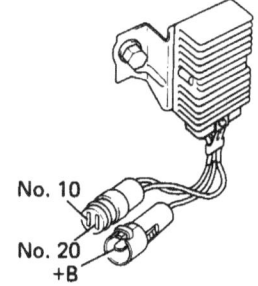

13.22a Measure the resistance between terminal + B and the other two terminals of the solenoid resistor (four-cylinder)

the engine and disconnect the relay wire harness. Using an ohmmeter, check the resistance between the relay terminals (see illustration). If the indicated resistance is not as specified, renew the relay.

19   If your vehicle is powered by a V6 engine, unplug the relay harness and verify that there is continuity between terminals STA and E1, and between terminals B and Fc, but not between terminals B and Fp (see illustration). If continuity is not as specified, renew the relay. Apply battery voltage across terminals SAT and E and verify that there is continuity between terminals B and Fp. Apply battery voltage across terminals B and Fp and verify that there is continuity between terminals B and Fp. If the relay does not operate as specified, renew it.

Solenoid resistor

Refer to illustrations 13.22a and 13.22b

20   Disconnect the cable from the negative terminal of the battery.
21   Locate the solenoid resistor on the right side of the engine compartment. Disconnect the solenoid resistor electrical connector.
22   Using an ohmmeter, check the resistance between terminal + B and the other two terminals (see illustrations). The resistance should be 2 to 3 ohms for each check.
23   If the measured resistance is not as specified, the solenoid resistor must be renewed as discussed below.
24   To renew the solenoid resistor, disconnect the battery negative cable. Disconnect the solenoid resistor electrical connector. Remove the screws and detach the resistor.

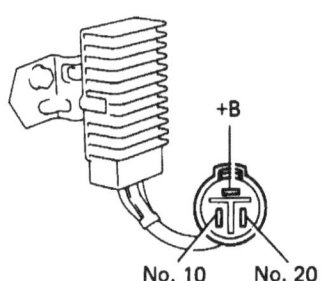

13.22b Measure the resistance between terminal + B and the other two terminals of the solenoid resistor (V6)

25   Refitting is the reverse of the removal procedure.

Start injector time switch (thermo-time switch)

Refer to illustrations 13.28a and 13.28b

26   Disconnect the battery earth cable.
27   Disconnect the wire harness from the cold start injector time switch (located in the thermostat housing on four-cylinder engines and in the water bypass outlet at the rear of the inlet manifold on the V6 engine.
28   Using an ohmmeter, measure the resistance between the terminals as shown in the accompanying tables (see illustrations).
29   If the resistance readings do not fall within the specified range, the cold start injector time switch will have to be renewed.
30   To renew the start injection time switch, drain the coolant, unplug the switch electrical connector and unscrew the switch. **Warning:** *The engine must be completely cool before draining the coolant.* Be sure to coat the threads of the new switch with Teflon tape to prevent leaks. Refitting is the reverse of removal. Refill the cooling system (see Chapter 1).

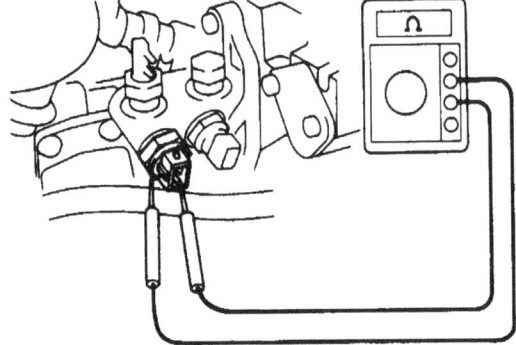

13.28a Measure the resistance between the start injector time switch terminals indicated in this table and compare your readings to the specified ranges (4Y-E engine)

Between terminals	Resistance (Ω)	Coolant temp.
STA — STJ	20 — 40	below 30°C (86°F)
	40 — 60	above 40°C (104°F)
STA — Ground	20 — 80	–

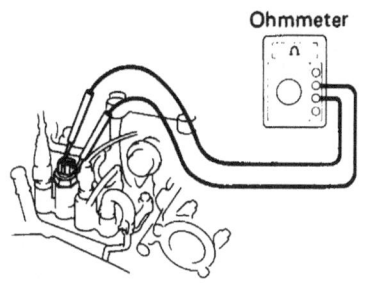

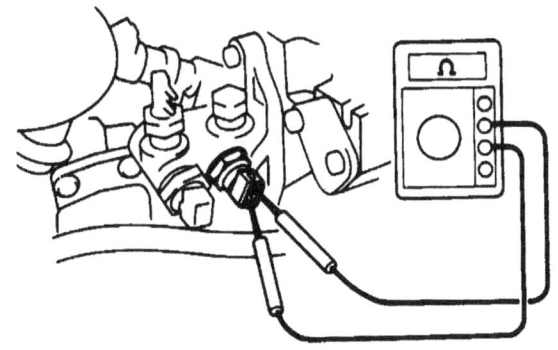

Between terminals	Resistance (Ω)	Coolant temperature
STA – STJ	30 – 50	Below 10°C (50°F)
	70 – 90	Above 20°C (68°F)
STA – Ground	30 – 90	–

13.28b Measure the resistance between the start injector time switch terminals indicated in this table and compare your readings to the specified ranges (V6 and 22R-E engines)

13.34a To check the coolant temperature sensor on a four-cylinder (located on the thermostat housing next to the cold start injector time switch) touch the leads of an ohmmeter to the water temperature sensor terminals and note the resistance readings at different temperatures (22R-E shown)

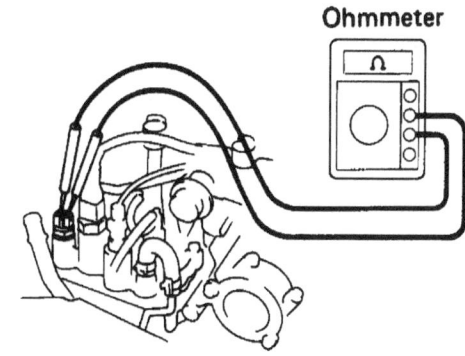

13.34b To check the coolant temperature sensor on the V6 (located on the water by-pass outlet next to the cold start injector time switch), touch the leads of an ohmmeter to the water temperature sensor terminals and note the resistance readings at different temperatures

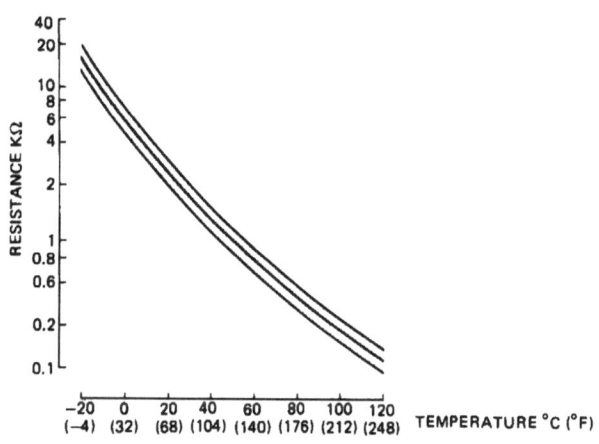

13.35 Compare your indicated coolant temperature sensor readings at various temperatures to the correct values indicated on this coolant temperature sensor resistance/temperature table

Coolant temperature sensor

Refer to illustrations 13.34a, 13. 34b and 13.35

Note: *The coolant temperature sensor is designed to have certain resistance values over a given temperature range. It can be checked after removal from the engine using containers of hot and cold water, but the procedure described here is for one that is in place in the engine.*

31   Run the engine until it is at normal operating temperature.
32   Locate the coolant temperature sensor (next to the start injector time switch). Disconnect the sensor wiring harness.
33   By placing a thermometer on the cylinder head, next to the sensor, the temperature can be monitored.
34   Connect the probes of the ohmmeter to the terminals of the sensor **(see illustrations)**. Watch the thermometer and note the resistance readings as the engine cools.

35   Compare the resistance readings at the various temperatures to the accompanying chart. If they are not as specified, the sensor may be faulty.
36   To renew the sensor, drain the coolant, detach the cable from the negative terminal of the battery, unplug the electrical connector from the sensor and unscrew the sensor. **Warning:** *The engine must be completely cool before draining the coolant.* Refitting is the reverse of removal.

High temperature line pressure up system

Refer to illustration 13.39

37   Locate the vacuum switching valve (VSV) (left side of valve cover on 22R-E; right side of engine compartment on V6).
38   Unplug the electrical connector from the VSV and attach a pair of jumper wires directly from the battery to the VSV terminals.
39   Blow into pipe E and verify that air

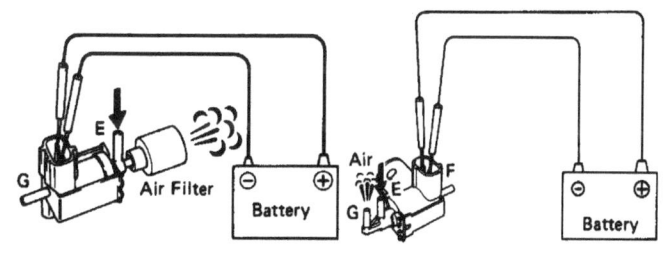

13.39 Checking the VSV - pre-1989 on left and 1989 and later on right

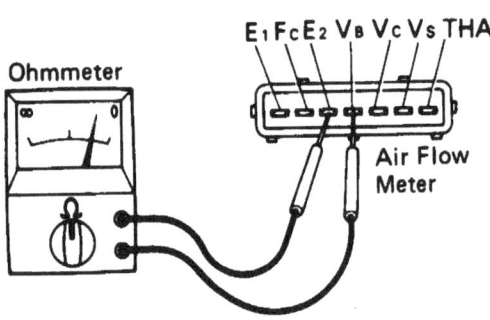

Between terminals	Resistance	Temperature
$E_2 - V_S$	20 — 400 Ω	—
$E_2 - V_C$	100 — 300 Ω	—
$E_2 - V_B$	200 — 400 Ω	—
$E_2 - THA$	10 — 20 KΩ 4 — 7 KΩ 2 — 3 KΩ 0.9 — 1.3 KΩ 0.4 — 0.7 KΩ	−20°C (4°F) 0°C (32°F) 20°C (68°F) 40°C (104°F) 60°C (140°F)
$E_1 - F_C$	Infinity	—

14.3a Airflow meter terminal locations (four-cylinder models)

14.3b Airflow meter terminal resistance table (four-cylinder models)

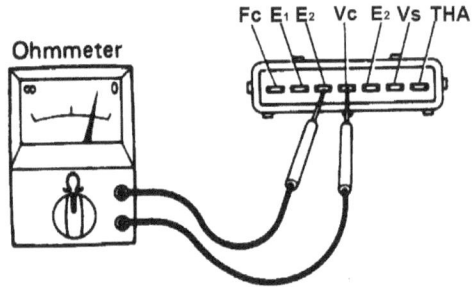

Terminals	Resistance	Temperature
$V_S - E_2$	200 — 600 Ω	—
$V_C - E_2$	200 — 400 Ω	—
$THA - E_2$	10 — 20 kΩ 4 — 7 kΩ 2 — 3 kΩ 0.9 — 1.3 kΩ 0.4 — 0.7 kΩ	−20°C (4°F) 0°C (32°F) 20°C (68°F) 40°C (104°F) 60°C (140°F)
$F_C - E_1$	Infinity	—

14.3c Airflow meter terminal locations (V6 models)

14.3d Airflow meter terminal resistance table (V6 models)

comes out of the air filter (or pipe G on 1989 and later models) **(see illustration)**.

40   Detach the cable from the negative terminal of the battery.

41   Blow into pipe E again and verify that air comes out of pipe G (or pipe F on 1989 and later models).

42   If the VSV fails either of the above tests, renew it.

43   To check for a short circuit in the VSV, use an ohmmeter to verify that there is no continuity between the terminal and the VSV body. If there is continuity, renew the VSV.

44   Measure the resistance between the terminals. It should be between 30 and 50 ohms at 20° C. If resistance is not within specification, renew the VSV.

45   To renew the VSV, simply detach the cable from the negative terminal of the battery, unplug the VSV electrical connector and detach the VSV valve from its mounting bracket. Refitting is the reverse of removal.

14 Airflow meter - check and renewal

Refer to illustrations 14.3a 14.3b, 14.3c and 14.3d

Note: *The following checks can be carried out without removing the airflow meter from the vehicle. An ohmmeter is needed for this check.*

1   Disconnect the battery earth cable.

2   Disconnect the wire harness electrical connector from the airflow meter.

3   Using an ohmmeter, measure the resistance between the indicated terminals **(see illustrations)**. **Note:** *Measure the first three pairs of terminals in the table for fours; measure the first two pairs of terminals in the table for V6s. The airflow meter should be renewed as an assembly if it is defective.*

4   To check the insulation resistance between the airflow meter body and the potentiometer terminals, hold one of the ohmmeter probes to the case and touch each of the terminals with the other probe. If continuity exists between any terminal and the body, the airflow meter is faulty and should be renewed as an assembly.

5   Connect the ohmmeter probes to terminals E2 and THA.

6   Using a normal household thermometer, measure the air temperature as near to the sensor as possible.

7   The accompanying tables give the correct resistance ranges at various temperatures. **Note:** *The air temperature sensor is part of the airflow meter and cannot be renewed as a unit. If the resistance readings are outside the ranges listed in the chart, the airflow meter must be renewed as an assembly.*

8   Disconnect the battery earth cable.

9   Remove the air duct and air hoses.

10   Disconnect the airflow meter wire harness connector.

11   Remove all fasteners and carefully

detach the airflow meter assembly and gasket. Discard the gasket.

12   Refitting is the reverse of the removal procedure. Be sure to use a new gasket when refitting the airflow meter.

15 Air valve - check and renewal

Refer to illustrations 15.1, 15.2 and 15.10

1   If you have a four-cylinder engine, start it and pinch off the throttle body-to-air valve hose to cut off the air flow **(see illustration)**.

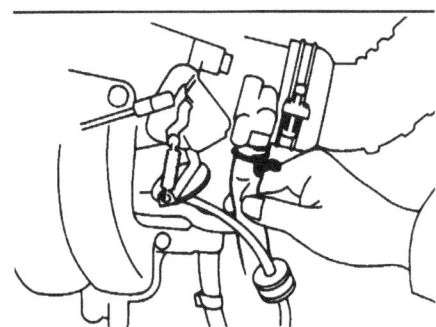

15.1 To check the operation of the air valve on a four-cylinder model, start the engine, then pinch off the air valve-to-throttle body hose - while the engine is still cold, rpm should drop; when the engine is warmed up, rpm should not drop more than 50 rpm (22R-E shown)

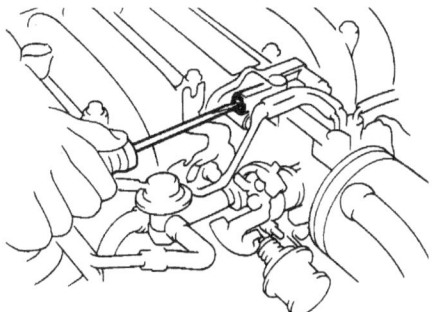

15.2 To check the operation of the air valve on a V6, start the engine, then turn the idle speed adjusting screw all the way in - while the engine is still cold, rpm should drop; when the engine is warmed up, rpm should not drop

15.10 To remove the air valve, detach the electrical connector, the coolant by-pass hose and the two air valve hoses, then remove the two mounting bolts (22R-E shown)

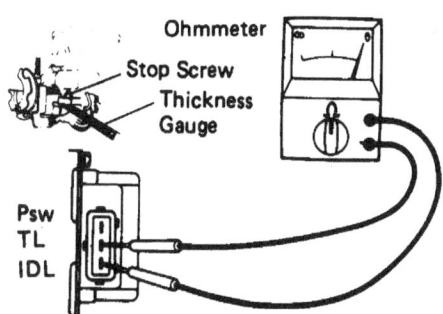

16.3a Throttle position sensor terminal locations (4Y-E engine)

Clearance between lever and stop screw		Continuity of terminals		
		IDL — TL	Psw — TL	IDL — Psw
0.50 mm	(0.0197 in.)	Continuity	No continuity	No continuity
0.70 mm	(0.0276 in.)	No continuity	No continuity	No continuity
Throttle valve fully opened position		No continuity	Continuity	No continuity

16.3b Throttle position sensor terminal resistance table (4Y-E engine)

The engine rpm should drop. Allow the engine to reach normal operating temperature. Repeat the check described above. This time, the engine rpm should not drop more than 50 rpm.

2 If you have a V6, start it up and let it reach a steady idle. Check the air valve operation by fully screwing in the idle speed adjusting screw **(see illustration)**. The engine rpm should drop while the engine is still cold. After the engine has warmed up, the engine should not drop with the idle speed adjusting screw all the way in.

3 If the air valve is still suspect after carrying out these checks, it is possible to visually check whether or not it is working.

4 With the engine stopped and completely cool, disconnect the hose from each end of the air valve.

5 By looking through the air valve it is possible to see if the bypass port is open. If it is, reconnect the hoses and run the engine until normal operating temperature is reached.

6 Now disconnect the hoses again. This time the bypass port should be completely closed.

7 To renew the air valve, disconnect the battery earth cable.

8 Drain three to four quarts of engine coolant. **Warning:** *Tho engine must be completely cool before starting this procedure.*

9 If you're working on a 4Y-E engine, remove the air intake chamber (plenum). Disconnect the coolant hoses and the inlet and outlet air hoses. Unplug the electrical connector.

10 Remove the two bolts **(see illustration)** from the air valve and detach it from the air intake chamber.

11 Refitting is the reverse of the removal procedure.

16 Throttle position sensor - check and renewal

Refer to illustrations 16.3a, 16.3b, 16.3c, 16.3d and 16.11

1 Disconnect the battery earth cable.

2 Unplug the throttle position sensor connector.

3 In two of the following tests you must insert a thickness gauge between the throttle stop screw and stop lever. The two gauge sizes used must correspond to the clearance between the lever and stop screw specified in the accompanying table. Using an ohmmeter, check the sensor at each of the indicated throttle settings **(see illustrations)**. If the results are not as specified, the throttle position sensor may require adjustment or renewal.

4 Disconnect the battery earth cable.

5 Disconnect the wire harness at the sensor.

6 Remove the two screws that hold the throttle position sensor to the throttle body and detach the sensor.

7 Refitting is the reverse of the removal procedure. After refitting, the throttle position sensor must be adjusted as follows:

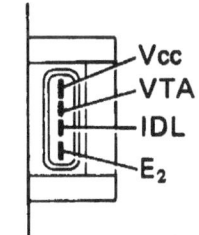

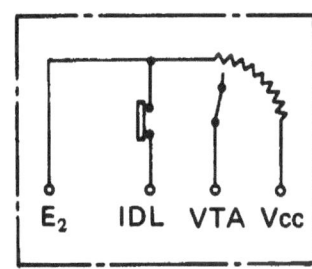

16.3c Throttle position sensor terminal locations (22R-E and V6)

Clearance between lever and stop screw	Between terminals	Resistance
* 0 mm (0 in.)	$VTA - E_2$	$0.2 - 0.8$ kΩ
** 0.57 mm (0.0224 in.)	$IDL - E_2$	Less than 2.3 kΩ
0.85 mm (0.0335 in.)	$IDL - E_2$	Infinity
Throttle valve fully opened position	$VTA - E_2$	$3.3 - 10$ kΩ
—	$Vcc - E_2$	4 - 9 k Ohms

* 0.50mm (0.0197 in) on V6
** 0.77mm (0.0303 in) on V6

16.3d Throttle position sensor terminal resistance table (22R-E and V6)

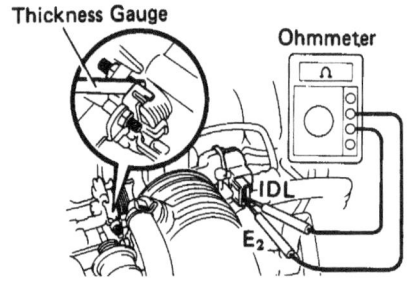

16.11 To adjust the throttle position sensor on a 22R-E or V6 engine, insert a thickness gauge of the specified thickness between the throttle lever and throttle stop screw and attach the probes of an ohmmeter to terminals IDL and E2 (V6 shown, 22R-E)

Port No.	At idling	At 3,000 rpm *
A	Vacuum	Vacuum
E	No vacuum	Vacuum
R	No vacuum	No vacuum
P	No vacuum	Vacuum

* at 3500 rpm on V6 models

17.2a To check the vacuum at each port, start the engine, pull off each vacuum hose (on top of the throttle body) and check for vacuum at the specified rpm with your finger (22R-E and V6 engines)

Port No.	At idling	At 3,000 rpm *
A	Vacuum	Vacuum
E	No vacuum	Vacuum
R	No vacuum	No vacuum
P	No vacuum	Vacuum

* at 3500 rpm on V6 models

17.2b Throttle body vacuum table for the 4Y-E engine

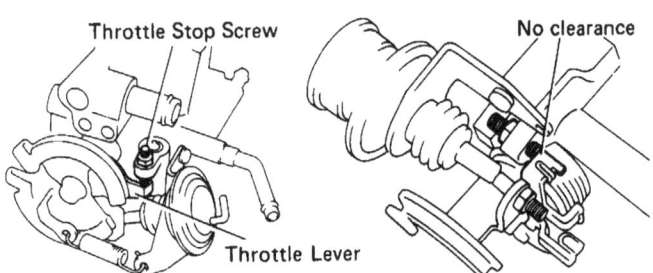

17.13 There should be no clearance between the throttle stop screw and the throttle lever when the throttle valve is fully closed (four-cylinder left, V6 right)

4Y-E engine

8   With the mounting screws loose, insert a thickness gauge (0.7 mm) between the throttle stop screw and lever and connect the ohmmeter to terminals IDL and TL.
9   Gradually turn the sensor counterclockwise until the ohmmeter deflects, then tighten the two screws.
10   Recheck the continuity between the terminals of the sensor (see Step 3).

22R-E and V6 engines

11   The procedure is identical to the one for the 4Y-E, but a 0.47 mm feeler gauge (22R-E) or a 0.62 mm gauge (V6) must be used and the ohmmeter must be connected to terminals IDL and E2 **(see illustration)**.

17   Throttle body - check, removal, adjustment and refitting

Refer to illustrations 17.2a, 17.2b, 17.13 and 17.14

On-vehicle check

1   Verify that the throttle linkage operates smoothly by grasping it with the thumb and forefinger and opening and closing it a few times. If it doesn't, renew the throttle body.
2   Start the engine, detach the vacuum hose from each of the ports on top of the throttle body and check the vacuum at each port with your finger. Compare your findings with the accompanying table **(see illustrations)**.

3   Check the throttle position sensor (see Section 16).
4   If your vehicle is powered by a V6, check the operation of the air valve (see Section 15).

Removal

5   Drain the engine coolant from the throttle body.
6   Remove the air intake duct.
7   Unplug the electrical connector to the throttle position sensor.
8   Label, then detach, all vacuum lines, the coolant hoses and the air valve hose.
9   If your vehicle is equipped with an automatic transmission, detach the throttle valve cable (see Chapter 7B).
10   Detach the accelerator cable and bracket.

17.14 When the throttle valve is fully closed, verify that the vacuum advance port is visible at the edge of the valve

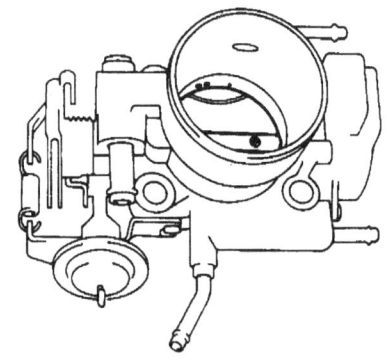

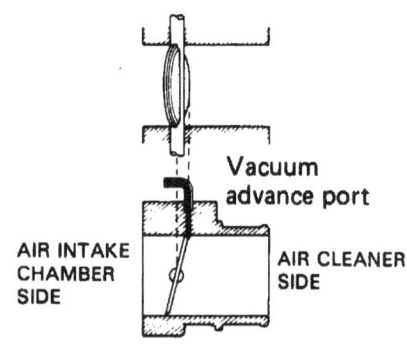

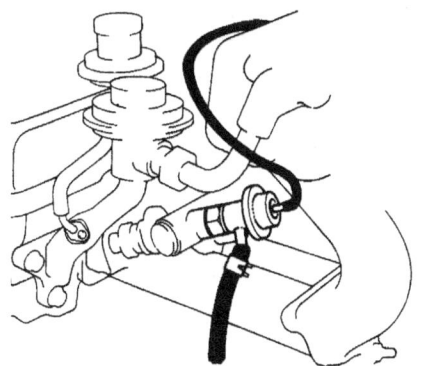

19.5a Typical pressure regulator (22R-E engine)

19.5b Typical pressure regulator (V6 engine)

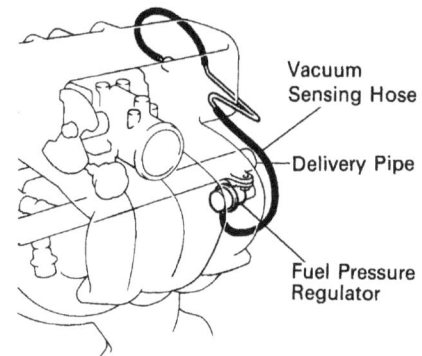

19.5c Pressure regulator details (4Y-E engine)

11   Remove the throttle body mounting fasteners and remove the throttle body and gasket. Discard the gasket.

Inspection

12   Thoroughly wash and clean the throttle body casting with a soft brush in carburettor cleaner. Do not, however, clean the throttle position sensor with anything-just wipe it off with a clean, soft rag. Using compressed air, blow out all passageways in the throttle body.
13   To check the throttle valve, verify that there is no clearance between the throttle stop screw and the throttle lever when the throttle valve is fully closed. When the throttle valve is fully closed, verify that the advancer port is visible on the air cleaner side of the throttle body intake bore **(see illustration)**. If it's not, adjust the throttle valve closing angle by adjusting the throttle stop screw.
14   To adjust the throttle stop screw, loosen the throttle stop screw locknut and loosen the screw until it's just barely touching the throttle lever, then screw it in another 1/4-turn and lock it in place with the locknut. The vacuum advance port **(see illustration)** should be barely visible at the edge of the throttle valve. **Caution:** *Do NOT adjust the throttle valve closing angle unless absolutely necessary.*
15   If necessary, adjust the throttle position sensor (see Section 16).

Refitting

16   Refitting is the reverse of removal. Be sure to use a new gasket and tighten the mounting fasteners to the specified torque.

18   Cold start injector - check and renewal

Note: *The procedure described below is an on-vehicle check of the cold start injector. If the test results are inconclusive, have the system checked by a dealer service department or other qualified repair shop.*

Check

1   This check must be done with the engine cold.

2   Start the engine and, using the procedure described in Section 20, listen to the cold start injector (located on the air intake chamber). You should hear a clicking noise, meaning the injector is functioning.
3   If a clicking sound is heard, let the engine reach operating temperature and repeat the check. No clicking should be heard.
4   If no clicking is heard in Step 2, a resistance check of the cold start injector should be performed. To do this, turn the ignition switch to the Off position.
5   Disconnect the battery earth cable.
6   Disconnect the wire harness from the cold start injector.
7   Using an ohmmeter, measure the resistance between the injector terminals. It should be 2 to 4 ohms. If the resistance is not as specified, the injector is most likely defective. Further testing is beyond the scope of the home mechanic. Remove the injector and have it bench-tested by a dealer.

Renewal

8   Release the fuel pressure in the system (see Section 10).
9   Disconnect the cold start injector wire harness.
10   Remove the cold start injector fuel line banjo fitting bolt and sealing washers. Discard the washers.
11   Remove the two mounting bolts and detach the injector.
12   Refitting is the reverse of the removal procedure. Be sure to use new sealing washers for the banjo fitting. Tighten the injector mounting bolts securely. Tighten the cold start injector tube banjo bolt to the specified torque.

19   Pressure regulator - check and renewal

Refer to illustrations 19.5a, 19.5b and 19.5c

Check

1   The fuel pressure regulator check is part of the fuel system pressure check (see Section 3).

Renewal

2   Eliminate the pressure in the fuel system (see Section 10).
3   Remove the EGR pipe (four cylinder only).
4   Disconnect the vacuum sensing hose and the fuel return hose **(see illustrations)**. Place a suitable container or shop rag under the fuel hose fitting to catch the leaking fuel.
5   Carefully loosen the locknut and remove the pressure regulator.
6   Refitting is the reverse of the removal procedure. Be sure to position the regulator with the return hose outlet pointing in the right direction. Tighten the locknut securely.

20   Air intake chamber - removal and refitting

Refer to illustration 20.14

Warning: *Petrol Is extremely flammable, so extra precautions must be taken when working on any part of the fuel system. See the Warning at the end of Section 1.*

1   Detach the cable from the negative terminal of the battery.
2   Drain the engine coolant from the throttle body.
3   Remove the air intake duct.
4   Detach the accelerator cable and bracket.
5   If your vehicle is equipped with an automatic transmission, detach the throttle valve cable (see Chapter 7B).
6   Label, then detach, the following hoses:
a) Both PCV hoses
b) Brake booster hose
c) Air control valve hoses (if equipped with power steering)
d) VSV hoses (if equipped with air conditioning)
e) EVAP hose
f) EGR vacuum modulator hose
g) Fuel pressure up VSV and hose and reed valve hose
h) Both air valve hoses from throttle body
i) Both coolant by-pass hoses from throttle body

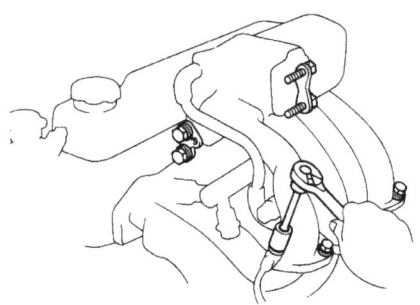

20.14 Air intake chamber mounting details - 4Y-E engine

7   Remove the EGR vacuum modulator (see Chapter 6).
8   Unplug the electrical connectors from the throttle position sensor and the cold start injector.
9   Label, then detach, all vacuum lines and hoses from the throttle body and air intake chamber.
10   Detach the cold start injector from the air intake chamber (see Section 18).
11   Remove the EGR pipe bolts (see Chapter 6) from the air intake chamber.
12   Remove the bolts holding the manifold stay to the air intake chamber.
13   Remove the bolts, nuts, bond strap and fuel hose clamp.
14   Remove the air intake chamber with the throttle body, resonator and gasket **(see accompanying illustration and illustrations 21.12a and 21.12b)**. Discard the old gasket.
15   Refitting is the reverse of removal. Be sure to use new gaskets.

21   Injector - check and renewal

Refer to illustrations 21.5, 21.12a, 21.12b, 21.13a, 21.13b and 21.13c
Warning: *Petrol is extremely flammable, so*

extra precautions must be taken when working on any part of the fuel system. See the Warning at the end of Section 1.

Check

1   If more than one injector is suspect, the control unit should be checked as previously described (see Section 13).
2   To trace a single faulty injector with the engine running, use a screwdriver as a stethoscope. Position the blade of the screwdriver on the injector and hold the handle against your ear. You should hear a click every time the injector operates. Compare the noise of the suspect injector with the remaining injectors. If the volume of the click is noticeably less than at the other injectors, that particular injector is faulty and should be renewed.
3   Once you have isolated a possibly faulty injector it can be verified by carrying out a resistance check. To do this, first disconnect the battery earth cable.
4   Disconnect the wiring harness from the suspect injector.
5   Attach the leads from an ohmmeter to the terminals on the injector **(see illustration)** and note the ohmmeter reading. Compare your reading to the specified resistance. If the resistance is not correct, renew the injector.

Renewal

6   Release the fuel pressure as described earlier in this Chapter.
7   Disconnect the battery earth cable.
8   Remove the air intake chamber (see Section 20).
9   Disconnect the fuel return hose.
10   Disconnect the following wires:
 a)   *Auxiliary air valve wire*
 b)   *Knock sensor wire*
 c)   *Oil pressure sender gauge or switch wire*
 d)   *Starter wire (terminal 50)*
 e)   *Transmission wires*
 f)   *Compressor wires (if equipped with A/C)*
 g)   *Injector wires*

 h)   *Water temperature sender gauge wire*
 I)   *Overdrive temperature switch wire (if equipped with automatic transmission)*
 j)   *Oxygen sensor wire*
 k)   *Igniter wire*
 l)   *VSV wire (if equipped with A/C)*
 m)   *Cold start injector time switch wire*
 n)   *Water temperature sensor wire*

11   Disconnect the fuel hose banjo bolt and remove the bolt, pulsation damper and sealing washers from the delivery pipe.
12   Remove the mounting bolts, then remove the delivery pipe and the injectors as an assembly. **Note:** *When moving the delivery pipe be careful not to drop any of the injectors, spacers or insulators* **(see illustrations)**.
13   Refitting is the reverse of the removal procedure with the following notes:
 a)   *Fit a new grommet and O-ring* **(see illustration)** *on each injector.*
 b)   *Apply petrol to the O-rings and refit the injectors in the delivery pipe.*
 c)   *On a four cylinder engine, refit the four insulators in the injector holes of the inlet manifold. On a V6, refit the six insulators and spacers into the injector holes of the inlet manifold.*
 d)   *Attach the injectors with the delivery pipe to the manifold. On the V6, don't forget the spacers for the inlet manifold mounting bolts.*
 e)   *Make sure the injectors rotate smoothly* **(see illustrations)** *and refit the bolts in the delivery pipe. Tighten the bolts/nuts to the specified torque.* **Note:** *If the injectors do not rotate smoothly, the probable cause may be incorrect refitting of the O-rings. Renew the O-ring after removing the injector.*
 f)   *Use new sealing washers on the pulsation damper banjo bolts and tighten it securely.*

14   After refitting is complete, check for fuel leaks.

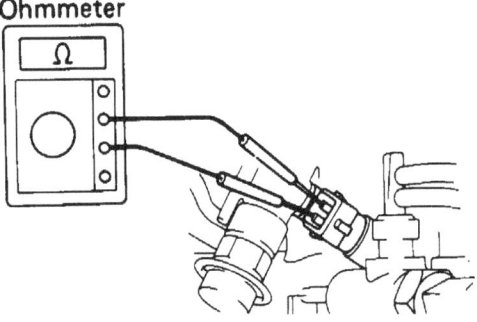

21.5 To check an injector, unplug the electrical connector, touch the probes of an ohmmeter to the terminals and compare your reading to the specified resistance - if the indicated resistance doesn't match the specified resistance, renew the injector

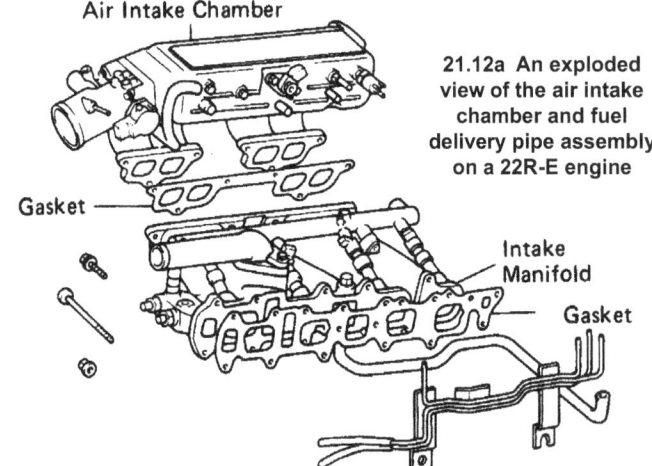

21.12a An exploded view of the air intake chamber and fuel delivery pipe assembly on a 22R-E engine

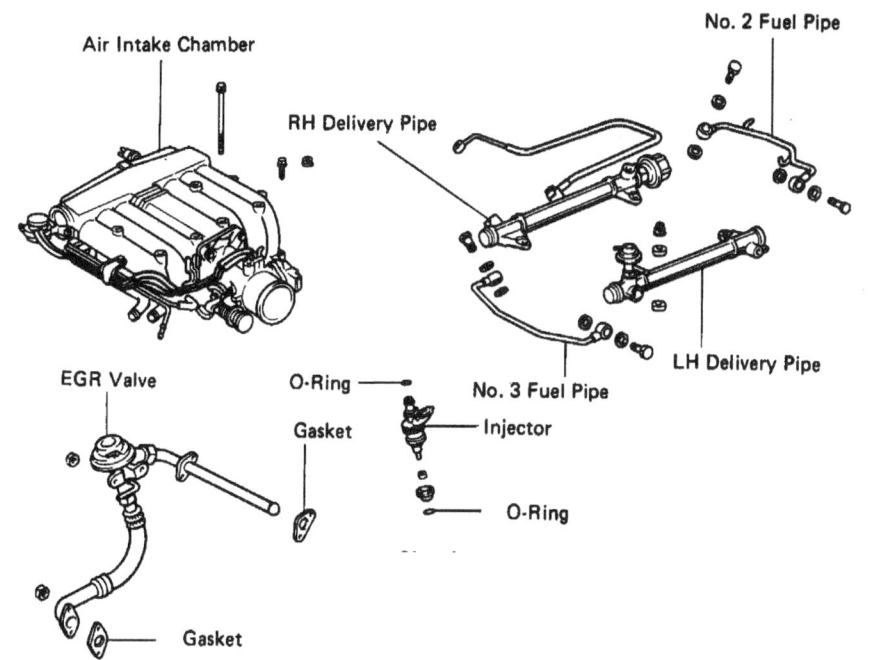

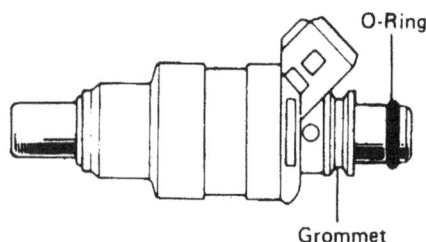

21.13a Always renew the O-ring every time an injector is removed and make sure that the grommet and O-ring are refitted correctly

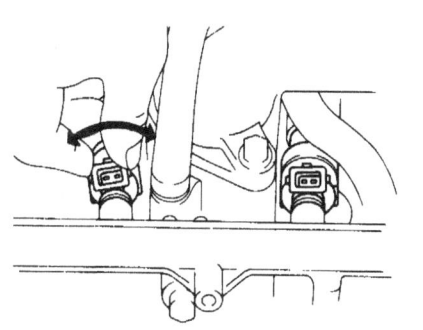

21.12b An exploded view of the air intake chamber and fuel delivery pipe assembly on a V6

21.13b After the delivery pipe is refitted, check the refitting of each injector by rotating it like this - if it doesn't rotate smoothly . . .

22 Exhaust system - servicing

Warning: *Inspection and repair of exhaust system components should be done only after enough time has elapsed after driving the vehicle to allow the system components to cool completely. Also, when working under the vehicle, make sure it is securely supported on jackstands.*

1   The exhaust system consists of the exhaust manifold, the catalytic converter, the muffler, the tailpipe and connecting pipes, brackets, hangers and clamps. The entire exhaust system is attached to the body with mounting brackets and rubber hangers. If any one of the parts are improperly refitted, excessive noise and vibration will be transmitted to the body.
2   Regular inspection of the exhaust system should be made to keep it safe and quiet. Look for any damaged or bent parts, open seams, holes, loose connections, excessive corrosion or other defects which could allow exhaust fumes to seep into the vehicle. Deteriorated exhaust system components should not be repaired; they should be renewed with new parts.
3   If the components are extremely corroded or rusted together, it may be a good idea to have the work performed by a reputable muffler shop, since welding equipment will probably be required to remove the components.
4   Always work from the back to the front when removing exhaust system components. Penetrating oil applied to mounting bolts and nuts will make them much easier to remove. Always use new gaskets, hangers and clamps and apply anti-seize compound to mounting bolt threads when putting everything back together. Also, when renewing any exhaust system parts, be sure to allow enough clearance from all points on the underbody to avoid overheating the floor pan.

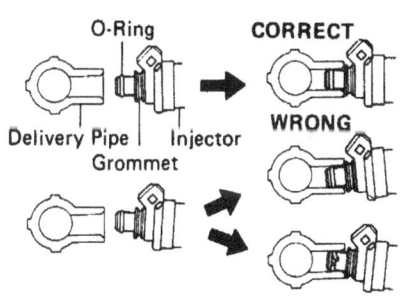

21.13c . . . chances are that it has been refitted incorrectly and must be refitted (be sure to use another new O ring)

Chapter 4 Part B
Fuel and exhaust systems - Diesel models

Contents

Specifications

Injection pump timing (plunger stroke)

L engine	1.0 mm
1988 and earlier 2L engine	1.14 mm
Later 2L and 3L engines	
With ACSD	0.54 to 0.66 mm
Without ACSD	0.84 to 0.96 mm

Torque specifications — Nm

	Nm
Fuel injectors	64
Injector nozzle leakage pipe nuts	29
Injection pipe fittings	25
Injection pump mounting nuts	21
Injection pump bracket bolts	18
Injection pump sprocket bolt	64
Distributive head plug bolt	17

1   General information, precautions and fuel system cleaning

General information

The fuel system comprises a fuel tank, a fuel injection pump, an engine compartment mounted fuel filter, a sediment catcher (L engine only), a fuel heater (some 2L and 3L engines), fuel supply and return lines and four fuel injectors.

The injection pump is driven at half crankshaft speed by the camshaft timing belt. Fuel is drawn from the fuel tank, through the filter (and sediment catcher on models with the L engine) by the injection pump, which then distributes the fuel under very high pressure to the injectors via separate delivery lines.

The injectors are spring-loaded mechanical valves which open when the pressure of the fuel supplied to them exceeds a specific limit. Fuel is then sprayed from the injector nozzle into the cylinder combustion chamber. The high compression developed by the rising piston superheats the mixture to the point of combustion.

The basic injection timing is set by the position of the injection pump on the engine. When the engine is running, the injection pump is advanced and retarded mechanically by the pump itself and is influenced primarily by the accelerator position and engine speed.

The engine is stopped by means of a fuel cut solenoid which interrupts the flow of fuel to the injection pump when de-activated.

The engine idle speed on some models can be raised manually by means of a hand throttle cable, controlled via a knob on the dash.

Precautions

Many of the operations described in this Chapter involve the disconnection of fuel lines, which may cause an amount of fuel spillage. Before commencing work, refer to the **Warnings and Cautions** given below and the information in Safety first at the beginning of this manual.

Warning 1: *Diesel fuel is flammable, so take extra precautions when you work on any part of the fuel system. Don't smoke or allow open flames or bare light bulbs near the work area, and don't work in a garage where a natural gas-type appliance (such as a water heater or a clothes dryer) with a pilot light is present. Since diesel fuel is carcinogenic, wear latex gloves when there's a possibility of being exposed to fuel, and, if you spill any fuel on your skin, rinse it off immediately with soap and water. Mop up any spills immediately and do not store diesel fuel-soaked rags where they could ignite. When you perform any kind of work on the fuel system, wear safety glasses and have a Class B type fire extinguisher on hand.*

Warning 2: *Fuel injectors operate at extremely high pressures and the jet of fuel produced at the nozzle is capable of piercing the skin, with potentially fatal results. Never work with pressurized injectors - any pressure testing of the fuel system components must be carried out by a diesel fuel systems specialist.*

Caution: *Under no circumstances should diesel fuel be allowed to come into contact with coolant hoses - wipe off accidental spillage immediately. Hoses that have been contaminated with fuel for an extended period should be renewed. Diesel fuel systems are particularly sensitive to contamination from dirt, air and water. Pay particular attention to cleanliness when working on any part of the fuel system to prevent the entry of dirt. Thoroughly clean the area around fuel fittings before disconnecting them. Store dismantled components in sealed containers to prevent contamination and the formation of condensation. Use only lint-free rags and clean fuel for component cleaning. Avoid using compressed air when cleaning components in place.*

Diesel fuel contamination

Before you renew an injection pump or some other expensive component, find out what caused the failure. If water contamination is present, buying a new or rebuilt pump or other component won't do much good. The following procedure will help you pinpoint whether water contamination is present:

a) *Remove the fuel filter and inspect the contents for the presence of water or petrol (see Chapter 1).*
b) *If the vehicle has been stalling, performance has been poor or the engine has been knocking loudly, suspect fuel contamination. Petrol or water must be removed by flushing (see below).*
c) *If you find a lot of water in the fuel filter, remove the injection pump fuel return line and check for water there. If the pump has water in it, flush the system.*
d) *Small quantities of surface rust won't create a problem. If contamination is excessive, the vehicle will probably stall.*
e) *Sometimes contamination in the system becomes severe enough to cause physical damage to the internal parts in the pump. If the damage reaches this stage, have the damaged parts renewed and the pump rebuilt by an authorized fuel injection shop, or buy a rebuilt pump.*

Storage

Good quality diesel fuel contains inhibitors to stop the formation of rust in the fuel lines and the injectors, so as long as there are no leaks in the fuel system, it's generally safe from water contamination. Diesel fuel is usually contaminated by water as a result of careless storage. There's not much you can do about the storage practices of service stations where you buy diesel fuel, but if you keep a small supply of diesel fuel on hand at home, as many diesel owners do, follow these simple rules:

a) *Diesel fuel "ages" and goes stale. Don't store containers of diesel fuel for long periods of time. Use it up regularly and renew it with fresh fuel.*
b) *Keep fuel storage containers out of direct sunlight. Variations in heat and humidity promote condensation inside fuel containers.*
c) *Don't store diesel fuel in galvanized containers. It may cause the galvanizing to flake off, contaminating the fuel and clogging filters when the fuel is used.*
d) *Label containers properly, as containing diesel fuel.*

Fighting fungi and bacteria with biocides

If there's water in the fuel, fungi and/or bacteria can form in diesel fuel in warm or humid weather. Fungi and bacteria plug fuel lines, fuel filters and injection nozzles; they can also cause corrosion in the fuel system.

If you've had problems with water in the fuel system and you live in a warm or humid climate, have your dealer correct the problem. Then, use a diesel fuel biocide to sterilize the fuel system in accordance with the manufacturer's instructions. Biocides are available from your dealer, service stations and auto parts stores. Consult your dealer for advice on using biocides in your area, and for recommendations on which ones to use.

Cleaning fuel system

Water in the fuel system

1   Disconnect the earth cable from the negative terminals of the battery.
2   Drain the fuel tank into an approved container and dispose of it properly.
3   Remove the fuel level sending unit (see Section 6).
4   Thoroughly clean the fuel tank. If it's rusted inside, send it to a repair shop or renew it. Clean or renew the fuel pick-up filter.
5   Refit the fuel tank but don't connect the fuel lines to the fuel tank yet.
6   Remove the fuel filter (see Chapter 1). Using low air pressure, blow out the line toward the rear of the vehicle. **Warning:** *Wear eye protection when using compressed air.*
7   Temporarily disconnect the fuel return fuel line at the injection pump and again, using low air pressure, blow out the line toward the rear of the vehicle.
8   Reconnect the main fuel and return lines at the tank. Fill the tank to a fourth of its capacity with clean diesel fuel. refit the cap on the fuel filler neck.
9   Discard the fuel filter.
10   Connect the fuel line to the fuel pump.
11   Reconnect the battery cable.
12   Purge the fuel pump and pump-to-filter line by cranking the engine until clean fuel is pumped out. Catch the fuel in a closed metal container.
13   Refit a new fuel filter.
14   Refit a hose from the fuel return line (from the injection pump) to a closed metal container with a capacity of at least two gallons.

2.1 Loosen the hose clamp and pull the air intake duct from the inlet manifold

2.2a Unscrew the air cleaner housing mounting bolts (arrows) . . .

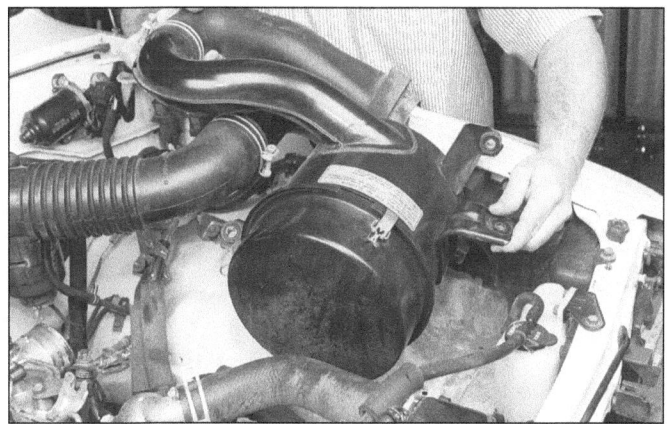

2.2b . . . then lift the housing and ducts from the engine compartment

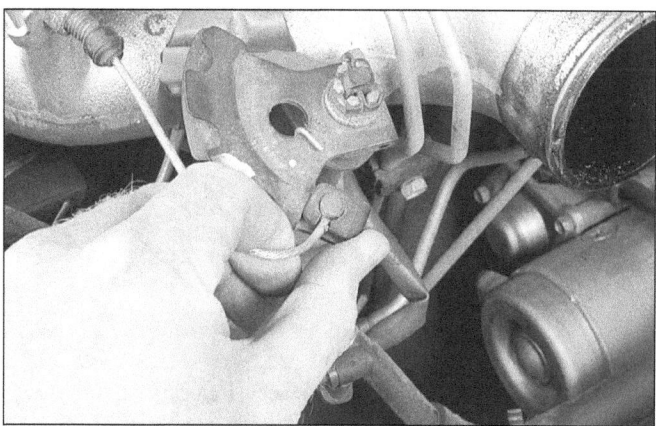

3.2 Detach the accelerator cable from the throttle lever

15   Crank the engine until clean fuel appears at tho roturn line. Don't crank tho ongino for more than 30 seconds at a time. If it's necessary to crank it again, allow a three-minute interval before resuming.

16   Using a flare-nut wrench, loosen each high pressure line at the injector nozzles.

17   Crank the engine until clean fuel appears at each nozzle. Don't crank the engine for more than 30 seconds at a time. If it's necessary to crank it again, allow a three-minute interval before resuming.

Petrol in the fuel system

Warning: *Diesel fuel is flammable, so take extra precautions when you work on any part of the fuel system. Refer to the Warnings earlier in this Section.*

If petrol has been accidentally pumped into the fuel tank, it should be drained immediately. Petrol in the fuel in small amounts, up to 30 percent, isn't usually noticeable. At higher ratios, the engine may make a knocking noise, which will get louder as the ratio of petrol increases. Here's how to rid the fuel system of petrol:

18   Drain the fuel tank into an approved container and fill the tank with clean, fresh diesel fuel.

19   Detach the fuel line between the fuel filtor and tho injoction pump.

20   Connect a short pipe and hose to the fuel filter outlet and run it to a closed metal container.

21   Crank the engine to purge petrol out of the fuel pump and fuel filter. Don't crank the engine more than 30 seconds. Allow two or three minutes between cranking intervals for the starter to cool.

22   Remove the short pipe and hose and refit the fuel line between the fuel filter and the injection pump.

23   Try to start the engine. If it doesn't start, purge the injection pump and lines: Crack the fuel line fittings a little, just enough for fuel to leak out. Depress the accelerator pedal to the floor and, holding it there, crank the engine until all petrol is removed, i.e. diesel fuel leaks out of the fittings. Tighten the fittings. Limit cranking to 30 seconds with two or three minute intervals between cranking. **Warning:** *Avoid sources of ignition and have a fire extinguisher handy.*

24   Start the engine and run it at idle for 15 minutes.

2   Air cleaner housing - removal and refitting

Refer to illustrations 2.1, 2.2a and 2.2b

1   Loosen the hose clamp and detach the air intake duct from the inlet manifold **(see illustration)** (the ducts connected to the air cleaner housing are easier to detach after the housing has been removed).

2   Unscrew the bolts and remove the air cleaner housing and ducts from the engine compartment **(see illustrations)**.

3   Refitting is the reverse of the removal procedure.

3   Accelerator cable and hand throttle cable - removal, refitting and adjustment

Accelerator cable

Refer to illustrations 3.2, 3.3, 3.5 and 3.9

Removal

1   Disconnect the cable from the negative terminal of the battery.

2   Rotate the throttle bellcrank and pass

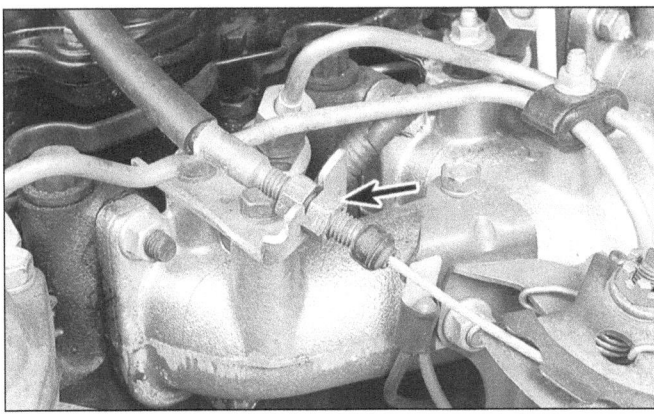

3.3 Loosen the cable locknut and detach the accelerator cable from the bracket

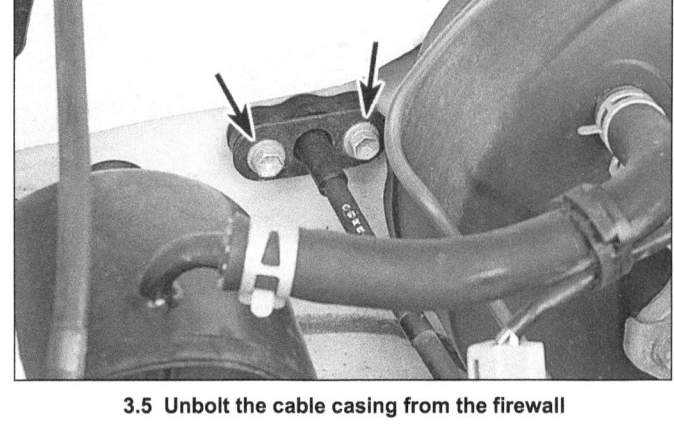

3.5 Unbolt the cable casing from the firewall

3.9 With a helper depressing the accelerator pedal, turn the adjusting nut on the cable casing until the throttle bellcrank just touches the maximum speed stop screw (arrow)

3.14 Squeeze the tang on the retainer and detach the hand throttle cable from the accelerator pedal arm

the accelerator cable through the slot to disconnect it **(see illustration)**.

3   Unscrew the cable locknut and pull the cable and casing from the bracket **(see illustration)**.

4   Detach the cable from the brackets on the valve cover and the right wheel well.

5   Unbolt the cable casing from the firewall **(see illustration)**.

6   Detach the cable from the accelerator pedal by pulling the inner cable retainer from the top of the pedal arm, then pass the cable through the slot in the pedal.

7   Pull the cable through the firewall into the engine compartment.

Refitting and adjustment

8   To refit the cable, reverse the removal procedure.

9   To adjust the cable, have a helper depress the accelerator pedal to the floor. Turn the adjusting nut on the cable casing until the throttle bellcrank on the injection pump just contacts the maximum speed stop screw **(see illustration)**.

10   Have your assistant release the accelerator pedal - the throttle bellcrank on the injection pump should now be resting against the idle speed adjusting screw, and the cable should have about 3 to 5 mm of slack when pushed.

11   Tighten the cable locknut securely.

Hand throttle cable

Refer to illustration 3.14

Removal

12   Remove the knob from the dash end of the cable by pushing in on the tab, then pull it off.

13   Unscrew the nut from the cable casing.

14   Detach the inner cable from the accelerator pedal arm **(see illustration)**.

Refitting and adjustment

15   Refitting is the reverse of removal. The cable should have approximately 3 to 5 mm of slack in it when the knob is screwed all the way in. If not, adjust it with the adjusting nut on the cable casing.

---

4   Fuel tank - removal and refitting

Refer to illustration 4.1

Warning 1: *Diesel fuel is flammable, so take extra precautions when you work on any part of the fuel system. See the* **Warnings** *in Section 1.*

Warning 2: *Repairs to the fuel tank or filler neck should be performed by a professional*

with the proper training to carry out this critical and potentially dangerous work. Even after cleaning and flushing, fumes can remain and could explode during repair of the tank.

Warning 3: *If the fuel tank is removed from the vehicle, it should not be placed in an area where sparks or open flames could ignite the fumes coming out of the tank. Be especially careful inside garages where a natural gas appliance is located because the pilot light could cause an explosion.*

1   The fuel tank **(see illustration)** is mounted at the rear of the vehicle. If it becomes necessary to work on it or its associated fittings, either in or out of the vehicle, the ignition switch must be Off and the battery earth cable disconnected. Before removing the tank, unscrew the drain plug and empty any remaining fuel into a suitably sized container.

2   Disconnect the electrical connector from the fuel level sending unit.

3   Mark and disconnect the fuel lines.

4   Disconnect the filler pipe(s) from the fuel tank.

5   Remove the fuel tank shield.

6   Support the fuel tank with a floor jack. Remove the retaining bolts at the ends of the tank and carefully remove it.

7   Refitting is the reverse of the removal procedure. Be sure to tighten all bolts, clamps and the plug securely.

5   Fuel tank cleaning and repair - general information

1   All repairs to the fuel tank or filler neck should be carried out by a professional who has experience in this critical and potentially dangerous work. Even after cleaning and flushing the tank, explosive fumes can remain and ignite during repair of the tank.
2   If the fuel tank is removed from the vehicle, it should not be placed in an area where sparks or open flames could ignite the fumes coming out of the tank. Be especially careful inside garages where a natural gas type appliance is located, because the pilot light could cause an explosion.

6   Fuel level sending unit - check and renewal

Warning: *Diesel fuel is flammable, so take extra precautions when you work on any part of the fuel system. See the* **Warnings** *in Section 1.*

Check

1   Raise the vehicle and support it securely on jackstands.
2   If the fuel level gauge on he instrument panel hasn't been working properly, first check the operation of the gauge. If the gauge works in accordance with the following tests, the gauge and its circuit are OK - the problem must lie in the fuel level sending unit.
3   Disconnect the electrical connector for the fuel level sending unit. Turn on the ignition key. The needle on the gauge should deflect past the Empty mark on the gauge.
4   Next, using a test light, probe the terminals on the electrical connector to find the one with battery voltage present. Using a jumper wire, earth the terminal without battery voltage - the needle on the gauge should now swing past the Full mark. If the gauge works as described, it is functioning properly.

5   A more accurate check of the sending unit can be made by removing it from the fuel tank and checking its resistance while manually operating the float arm. With the float arm hanging down (empty), the resistance should be approximately 110 ohms. With the float arm all the way up, the resistance should be approximately 3 ohms.

Renewal

6   Remove the fuel tank from the vehicle (see Section 4).
7   Remove the screws securing the sending unit to the tank. Lift the sending unit from the tank, being careful not to bend the float arm.
8   Refitting is the reverse of removal. Be sure to use a new gasket between the tank and the sending unit flange.

7   Fuel lines and fittings - inspection and renewal

Warning: *Diesel fuel is flammable, so extra precautions must be taken when working on any part of the fuel system. See the* **Warnings** *in Section 1.*
1   From time-to-time check the security of all the fuel joints. Make sure that the rigid lines are not kinked or bent in any way. If a rubber hose shows signs of deterioration, renew it.
2   If a section of metal fuel line must be renewed, only brazed seamless steel tubing should be used, as copper or aluminium tubing does not have enough durability to withstand vibrations encountered during normal engine operation.
3   If only one section of a metal fuel line is damaged it can be cut out and renewed with a piece of rubber fuel hose. The rubber hose should be cut 10 cm longer than the section to be renewed, so there is about 50 mm of overlap between the rubber and metal lines at either end of the section. Hose clamps should be used to secure both ends of the repaired section.
4   If a section of metal line longer than 15 cm is being removed, use a combination of

metal tubing and rubber hose so that the hose lengths are no longer than 7.5 cm.
5   Never use rubber hose within 10 cm of any part of the exhaust system.
6   If an injection pipe requires renewal, use only genuine factory spare parts (due to the extremely high pressures generated by the injection pump).

8   Fuel sedimenter (L engine) - removal, inspection and refitting

The sedimenter is a device mounted on the firewall which collects water and other impurities in the fuel system. It should be cleaned at the interval listed in Chapter 1. Refer to Chapter 1 for the sedimenter servicing procedure.

9   Fuel heater system (2L and 3L engines) - component check and renewal

Refer to illustrations 9.2, 9.3, 9.6 and 9.7
Warning: *Diesel fuel is flammable, so extra precautions must be taken when working on any part of the fuel system. See the* **Warnings** *in Section 1.*
Note: *The fuel heater system preheats the fuel to prevent it from thickening in cold weather operation. Not all 2L and 3L models are equipped with this system.*
1   The fuel heater system consists of the fuel heater in the fuel filter adapter, a vacuum switch (also in the filter adapter), a relay and a fuse. Before checking the individual components in the system, always check the IGN fuse first if the system is inoperative.

Fuel heater

2   Unplug the electrical connector for the fuel heater. Using an ohmmeter, check the resistance between the two terminals; there should be 0.7 ohms at 20-degrees C **(see illustration)**. If not, renew the fuel filter cap/ fuel heater assembly.

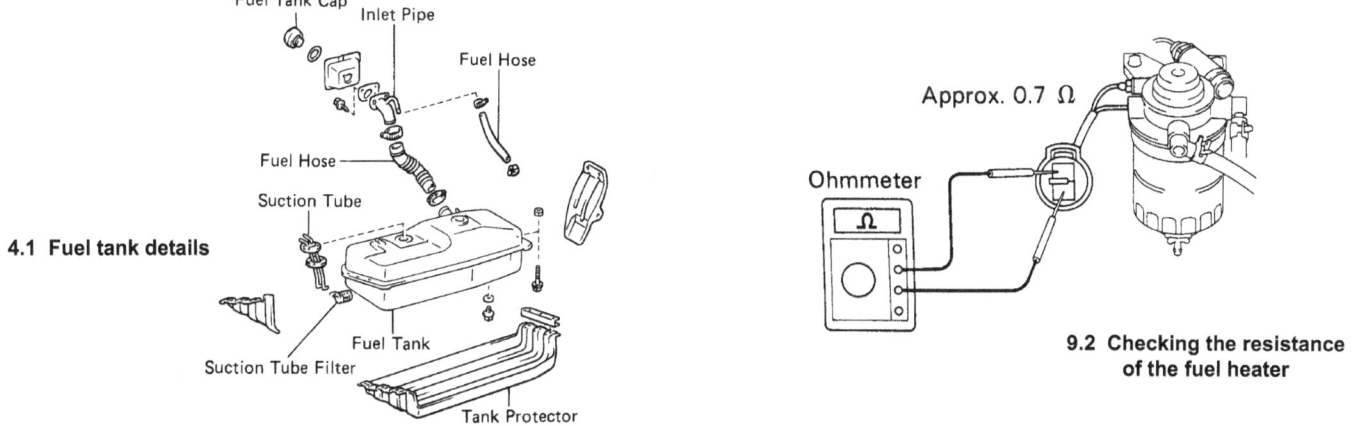

4.1 Fuel tank details

9.2 Checking the resistance of the fuel heater

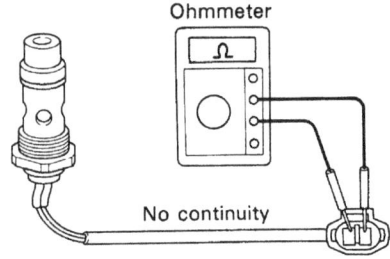

9.3 There should be no continuity across the vacuum switch terminals when no vacuum is applied

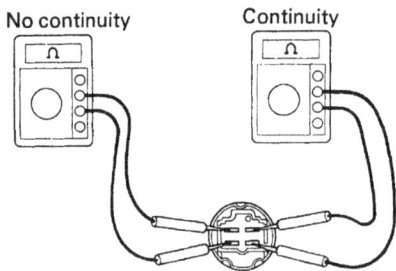

9.6 When checking the fuel heater relay, there should be continuity between one pair of terminals but not the other

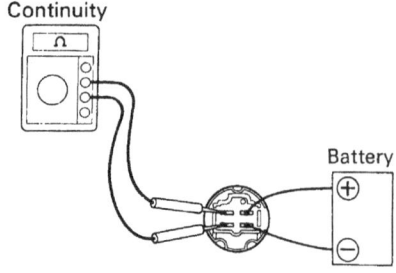

9.7 Apply battery voltage to the terminals of the fuel heater relay that have continuity; the terminals that didn't have continuity should now show 0 ohms resistance

Vacuum switch

3   Unplug the electrical connector for the vacuum switch. Using an ohmmeter, check for continuity between the two terminals in the connector **(see illustration)**. There should be no continuity. If there is continuity, renew the switch.

4   Unscrew the switch and connect a hand-held vacuum pump to the port on the bottom of the switch. Apply a vacuum of approximately 200 mm-Hg and check for continuity between the terminals. There should be continuity.

5   If the vacuum switch failed either test, renew it.

Fuel heater relay

6   The fuel heater relay is located in the underbonnet relay box. To check it, unplug it and check for continuity between each pair of terminals **(see illustration)**; there should be continuity between one pair but not the other. If there is continuity between both pairs, or no continuity on either pair, renew the relay.

7   If there is continuity between one pair but not the other, check the operation of the relay. Using fused jumper wires, apply battery voltage to the terminals that do have continuity and check for continuity between the other two terminals **(see illustration)**; there should be continuity, and the relay should make a click as the voltage is applied.

8   If the relay doesn't operate as described, renew it.

10   Fuel injectors - removal and refitting

Refer to illustrations 10.2, 10.5 and 10.8

Warning: *Diesel fuel is flammable, so extra precautions must be taken when working on any part of the fuel system. See the* **Warnings** *in Section 1.*

Removal

1   Disconnect the cable from the negative terminal of the battery. Remove the glow plug strap (see Chapter 6).

2   Loosen the hose clamp and detach the hose from the front of the nozzle leakage pipe **(see illustration)**.

3   Unscrew the injection pipe fittings at the fuel injectors and at the injection pump.

4   Remove the nuts securing the injection pipes to the inlet manifold, then remove the injection pipes.

5   Remove the nut from the top of each injector and detach the nozzle leakage pipe from the injectors **(see illustration)**. Recover the sealing washers from the top of each injector.

6   Using a deep socket, unscrew the injectors. Recover the seats and gaskets.

7   If necessary, take the injectors to a dealer service department or diesel engine specialist for testing. Do not attempt to disassemble the injectors, as this is also a job that should be left to a specialist.

Refitting

8   Make sure the seating areas on the head are clean. refit the injectors in their bores, threading them in by hand. Be sure to use new sealing washers and gaskets, and tighten the injectors to the torque listed in this Chapter's Specifications. If you're working on an L engine, refit new nozzle seats, making sure the correct side is facing up **(see illustration)**.

10.2 Loosen the hose clamp and detach the hose from the nozzle leakage pipe

9   Refit new sealing washers to the tops of the injectors, then refit the nozzle leakage pipe. Tighten the nuts to the torque listed in this Chapter's Specifications. Connect the hose to the front of the nozzle leakage pipe.

10   Refit the injection pipes. Before tightening any of the fitting nuts, make sure all fittings are threaded onto the injectors and the pump. Tighten the clamp nuts securely, then tighten the injection pipe-to-injection pump fitting nuts to the torque listed in this Chapter's Specifications. Leave the fitting nuts at the fuel injectors loose at this time. Connect the battery cable.

11   Before starting the engine, the injector pipes must be bled of air. Begin by depressing the priming pump plunger on the filter adapter (2L and 3L engines) or the sedimenter (L engines) about 30 or 40 times, or until the plunger feels harder to push.

12   If the injection pipe fitting nuts are not loose, loosen them now. Remove the glow plug fuse from the underbonnet fuse box.

13   Crank the engine over until fuel flows from the injection pipe fittings. Tighten the fittings to the torque listed in this Chapter's Specifications. refit the glow plug fuse.

14   Start the engine and check for fuel leaks.

11   Fuel injection pump - removal and refitting

Refer to illustrations 11.2, 11.6 and 11.8

Warning: *Diesel fuel is flammable, so extra precautions must be taken when working on any part of the fuel system. See the* **Warnings** *in Section 1.*

Caution: *Do not attempt to disassemble the injection pump. All repairs to the pump should be carried out by a dealer service department or a diesel engine specialist.*

Removal

1   Set the engine to top dead centre (TDC) for the number one piston, then remove the timing belt (see Chapter 2D).

2   Detach the accelerator linkage from the throttle lever **(see illustration)**. Loosen the

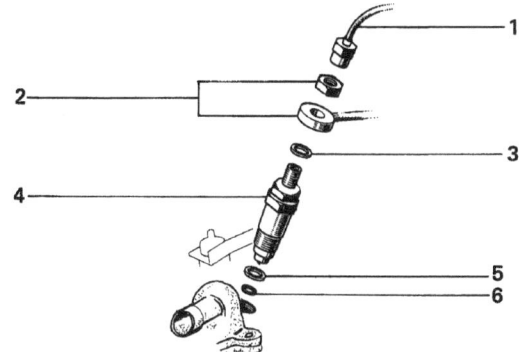

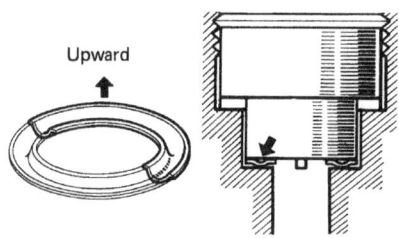

10.5 Fuel injector refitting details

1 *Injection pipe*
2 *Leakage pipe*
3 *Washer*
4 *Fuel injector*
5 *Injector nozzle seat*
6 *Gasket*

10.8 Make sure the dished side of the nozzle seat faces up (L engines)

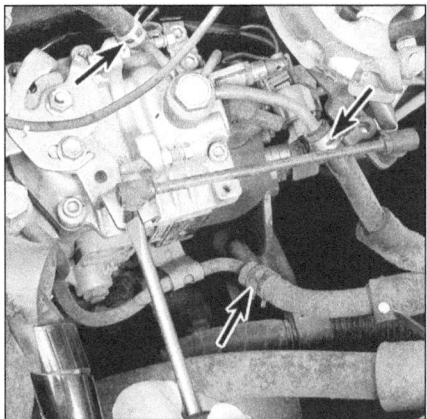

11.2 Prise the linkage from the injection pump, then detach the hoses (arrows)

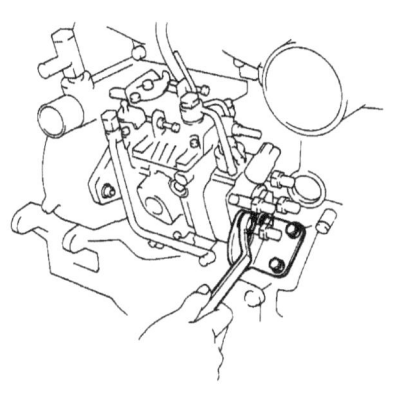

11.6 Unscrew the four bolts and remove the injection pump bracket from the rear of the pump

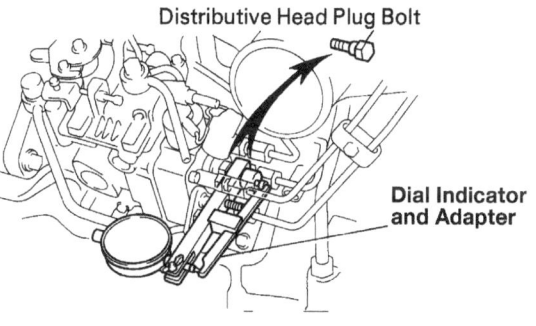

11.8 Make sure the marks on the pump and the engine are aligned (arrow), then unscrew the two mounting nuts (if there are no matchmarks, or if they aren't aligned, use a sharp scribe or a marking pen and apply new ones)

12.1 Remove the distributive head plug bolt from the rear of the injection pump and fit a dial indicator and adapter (tool no. 09275-54010 or equivalent)

clamps and disconnect the fuel hoses from the injection pump.
3   If equipped, detach the water bypass hoses from the pump.
4   Remove the injection pipes.
5   Remove the drive sprocket from the pump. To prevent the sprocket from turning when loosening the nut, thread two bolts into the threaded holes in the sprocket and wedge a screwdriver or lever across them. If the sprocket is stuck on the shaft, remove it with a two-jaw puller.
6   Remove the injection pump bracket **(see illustration)**.
7   Detach the electrical connectors for the fuel cut solenoid and tachometer pickup sensor.
8   Look for matchmarks on the pump and the engine **(see illustration)**. If there are no marks, make them with a sharp scribe.
9   Unscrew the two mounting nuts and remove the pump.

Refitting

10   Refitting is basically the reverse of removal. It is very important to align the matchmarks before tightening the mounting nuts.
11   Before attempting to start the engine after everything has been assembled, bleed the injector pipes as described in Section 10, Steps 11 through 13.
12   If the engine is sluggish or puts out an excessive amount of black smoke, the injection pump timing must be set (see Section 12).

12   Injection timing - check and adjustment

Refer to illustrations 12.1 and 12.3
Note: *This procedure requires the use of Toyota special tool no. 09275-54010, or equivalent. If you can't obtain this tool, have this procedure performed by a Toyota dealer service department or other qualified repair shop.*
1   Unscrew the distributive head plug bolt from the rear of the pump and fit special tool no. 09275-54010 (or equivalent) and a dial indicator into the hole **(see illustration)**.

2   Set the engine to 45-degrees before top dead centre (BTDC) for cylinder no. 1 or no. 4. In other words, the timing mark on the crankshaft pulley should be 1/8-turn before it reaches the timing pointer (the engine rotates clockwise, looking at it from the front of the vehicle).

3   If you are working on a 2L or 3L engine with an Automatic Cold Start Device (ACSD), turn the cold start lever approximately 20-degrees counterclockwise, then insert a piece of metal or wood, approximately 8.5 to 10 mm thick, between the ACSD plunger and the lever **(see illustration)**.

4   Zero the dial indicator, then slowly rotate the engine (using a spanner on the crankshaft pulley bolt) until the timing mark on the pulley is aligned with the timing pointer.

5   Check the plunger stroke on the dial indicator and compare your reading with the value listed in this Chapter's Specifications.

6   If the plunger stroke is out of specification, loosen the injection pipe fittings at the back of the pump, loosen the two bolts at the rear of the pump that hold it to the bracket, then loosen the two injection pump mounting nuts **(see illustrations 11.6 and 11.8)**.

7   Turn the injection pump slightly to adjust the plunger stroke. Rotating the pump toward the engine increases the plunger stroke; rotating it away from the engine reduces the plunger stroke.

8   After the timing has been set, tighten the pump mounting nuts securely, making sure the dial indicator reading does not change.

9   Tighten all fasteners to the torque values listed in this Chapter's Specifications. If equipped with an ACSD, remove the spacer fitted in Step 3.

10   Remove the dial indicator and adapter, then refit the distributive head plug bolt, using a new sealing washer. Tighten the bolt to the torque listed in this Chapter's Specifications.

11   Run the engine and check for fuel leaks and proper operation.

13   Fuel cut solenoid - check and renewal

Refer to illustrations 13.2 and 13.7

Warning: *Diesel fuel is flammable, so extra precautions must be taken when working on any part of the fuel system. See the* **Warnings** *in Section 1.*

Note: *The fuel cut solenoid is the device that shuts off the engine. If the engine won't turn off, or if it dies suddenly, suspect the fuel cut solenoid.*

Check

1   Place your finger on the fuel cut solenoid and have an assistant turn the ignition key on and off (without starting the engine). You should be able to feel and hear the solenoid operate.

2   If you can't feel or hear the solenoid, use a test light and check for voltage at the solenoid terminal with the ignition key in the On

position (you'll have to peel back the rubber boot on the solenoid to do this) **(see illustration)**.

3   If power is available at the terminal, renew the fuel cut solenoid.

4   If no voltage is present, check the IGN fuse and the circuit to the solenoid (refer to the wiring diagrams at the back of this manual if necessary).

Renewal

5   Disconnect the cable from the negative terminal of the battery.

6   Unbolt the bracket from the rear of the injection pump, then peel back the rubber boot on the top of the solenoid and unscrew the terminal nut.

7   Unscrew the solenoid and recover the spring, plunger and O-ring **(see illustration)**.

8   Also recover the filter and washer from the bottom of the hole (a thin pair of tweezers or a small pick can be used).

9   To refit the solenoid, place the washer and filter into the hole in the pump (be sure to renew the filter if it is dirty).

10   Fit a new O-ring to the solenoid, lubricating it with clean diesel fuel.

11   Assemble the spring and plunger to the solenoid.

12   Carefully thread the solenoid into its bore by hand, then tighten it to the torque listed in this Chapter's Specifications. Connect the wire to the terminal, refit the nut, then push the rubber boot over the solenoid and into place.

13   Reconnect the negative battery cable.

14   Exhaust system servicing - general information

Warning: *Inspection and repair of exhaust system components should be done only after enough time has elapsed after driving the vehicle to allow the system components to cool completely. Also, when working under the vehicle, make sure it is securely supported on jackstands.*

1   The exhaust system consists of the exhaust manifold, the muffler, the tailpipe and connecting pipes, brackets, hangers and clamps. The entire exhaust system is attached to the body with mounting brackets and rubber hangers. If any one of the parts are improperly fitted, excessive noise and vibration will be transmitted to the body.

2   Regular inspection of the exhaust system should be made to keep it safe and quiet. Look for any damaged or bent parts, open seams, holes, loose connections, excessive corrosion or other defects which could allow exhaust fumes to seep into the vehicle. Deteriorated exhaust system components should not be repaired; they should be renewed.

3   If the components are extremely corroded or rusted together, it may be a good idea to have the work performed by a reputable muffler shop, since welding equipment

will probably be required to remove the components.

4   Always work from the back to the front when removing exhaust system components. Penetrating oil applied to mounting bolts and nuts will make them much easier to remove. Always use new gaskets, hangers and clamps and apply anti-seize compound to mounting bolt threads when putting everything back together. Also, when renewing any exhaust system parts, be sure to allow enough clearance from all points on the underbody to avoid overheating the floor pan.

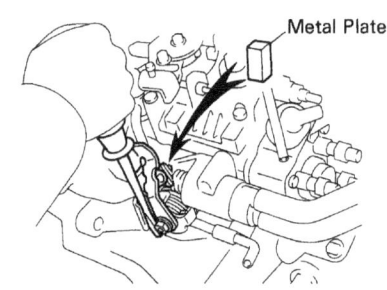

12.3 If your vehicle is equipped with an Automatic Cold Start Device (ACSD), prise the cold start lever counterclockwise and place a spacer (approximately 8.5 to 10 mm thick) between the lever and plunger

13.2 Peel back the rubber boot on the fuel cut solenoid, then check for voltage at the electrical terminal when the ignition key is turned to the On position

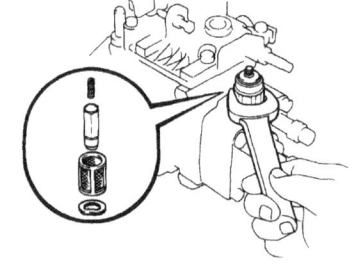

13.7 Fuel cut solenoid details

Chapter 5
Engine electrical systems

Contents

Specifications

Ignition system - petrol models

General

Cylinder numbers (front-to-rear)	
Four-cylinder	1-3-4-2
V6	
Right (driver's side)	1-3-5
Left (passenger side)	2-4-6
Firing order	
Four-cylinder	1-3-4-2
V6	1-2-3-4-5-6
Timing mark location (all engines)	Crankshaft pulley
Ignition timing	See Chapter 1
Distributor	
Direction of rotation	Clockwise
Air gap (all models with electronic ignition)	0.2 to 0.4 mm
Signal generator (pickup coil) resistance	
R-series engines	140 to 180 ohms
Y-series engines	140 to 180 ohms
V6 engine	
Through 1990	140 to 180 ohms
1991 on	205 to 255 ohms

Ignition coil

Primary resistance

    R-series engines .... 0.8 to 1.0 ohms

    Y-series engines

        Conventional coil .... 1.3 to 1.6 ohms

        Integral coil (in distributor)

            All except 4Y-E .... 1.3 to 1.6 ohms

            4Y-E .... 0.4 to 0.5 ohms

    V6 engine .... 0.4 to 0.5 ohms

Secondary resistance

    R-series engines .... 10.7 to 14.5 k-ohms

    Y-series engines

        Conventional coil .... 10.7 to 14.5 k-ohms

        Integral coil (in distributor)

            All except 4Y-E .... 10.4 to 14.0 k-ohms

            4Y-E .... 7.7 to 10.4 k-ohms

    V6 engine .... 10.2 to 13.8 k-ohms

Insulation resistance.. Infinity (at least more than 10 M ohms)

Alternator

Drivebelt tension... See Chapter 1

Rated output

    Petrol models

        12R engine .... 35 A

        18R engine 40A

        20R engine 45A

        22R engine 40A, 45A, 50A, 55A, 90A

        22R-E engine.. 60A

        Y-series engines 40A, 45A, 50A, 55A, 60A, 70A

        V6 engine.. 60A, 70A

    Diesel models

        L engine 55A

        2L and 3L engines

            Conventional type (external regulator).................................... 40A, 45A, 50A, 55A

            Compact, high-speed type (internal regulator)........................ 70A

Standard amperage

    No load .... Less than 10 amps

    With load .... More than 30 amps

Regulated voltage

    Petrol models .... 13.5 to 15.1 volts

    Diesel models (approximate)

        With external regulator.. 13.8 to 14.8 volts

        With internal regulator.. 13.8 to 15.1 volts

Brush length (minimum)

    Petrol models

        12R, 18R, 20R, 22R engines.. 5.5 mm

        22R-E engine.. 1.5 mm

        Y-series engines

            Conventional alternator .... 5.5 mm

            Compact, high-speed alternator............................ 1.5 mm

    Diesel models

        L engine .... 8 mm

        2L and 3L engines

            Conventional type (external regulator).................................... 5.5 mm

            Compact, high-speed type (internal regulator)........................ 1.5 mm

1 General information and precautions

The engine electrical systems include the charging and starting components, and the ignition system (petrol models). They are considered separately from the rest of the electrical system because of their proximity and importance to the engine. Exercise caution when working around any of these components for several reasons: they are easily damaged, if tested, connected or stressed incorrectly.

The alternator is driven by an engine drivebelt which could cause serious bodily harm if your fingers become entangled in it while the engine is running. The starter and alternator are both sources of direct battery voltage which could arc or even cause a fire if overloaded or shorted.

Never leave the ignition on for longer than ten minutes with the engine not running. Do not disconnect the battery cable while the engine is running. Do not cross connect the battery cables from another source (such as another vehicle) when jump starting. Don't earth either of the ignition coil terminals, even momentarily. Make sure that the igniter is properly earthed to the body.

Many of the procedural steps in this Chapter require the use of a multimeter, familiarity with its operation and a working knowledge of the basics of electricity. If you do not have these skills, it would be wise to have an authorised dealership or shop specialising in electrical systems diagnose your problem. You can often save money by removing and refitting the various components of the engine electrical system even if you are having someone else do the actual diagnosis and/or repairs.

2 Battery - removal and refitting

Refer to illustration 2.2

1   Disconnect both cables from the battery terminals, the negative first and then the positive.
2   Remove the bolt and nut from the battery hold-down clamp and remove the clamp **(see illustration)**.
3   Lift out the battery.
4   Refitting is the reverse of removal.

3 Battery - emergency jump starting

Refer to the *Booster battery (jump)* starting procedure at the front of this manual.

4 Battery cables - check and renewal

1   Periodically inspect the entire length of each battery cable for damage, cracked or burned insulation and corrosion. Poor battery cable connections can cause starting problems and decreased engine performance.
2   Check the cable-to-terminal connections at the ends of the cables for cracks, loose wire strands and corrosion. The presence of white, fluffy deposits under the insulation at the cable terminal connection is a sign that the cable is corroded and should be renewed. Check the terminals for distortion, missing mounting bolts and corrosion.
3   If only the positive cable is to be renewed, be sure to disconnect the negative cable from the battery first.
4   Disconnect the positive cable from the starter and/or the negative cable from the earth connection. Remove the cable. Make sure that the new cable is the same length and diameter.
5   Clean the threads of the starter or earth connection with a wire brush to remove rust and corrosion. Apply a light coat of petroleum jelly to the threads to ease refitting and prevent future corrosion.
6   Attach the cable to the starter or earth connection and tighten the mounting nut securely.
7   Before connecting the new cable to the battery, make sure that it reaches the terminal without having to be stretched.
8   Connect the positive cable first, followed by the negative cable.

5 Charging system - description

Two basic types of charging systems are used on the vehicles covered in this manual. The most obvious difference between the two is the type of regulator employed - external or integrated circuit (IC) type, which is mounted inside the alternator.

Both charging systems mount the alternator on the right front of the engine and utilize a V-belt and pulley drive system. Drivebelt tension and battery service are the two primary maintenance requirements for these systems. See Chapter 1 for the procedures regarding engine drivebelt checking and battery servicing.

6 Alternator - on-vehicle check

Refer to illustrations 6.8 and 6.12

1   As indicated at the beginning of this Chapter, basic electrical knowledge and skills, plus a working knowledge of a multimeter, are necessary for the successful performance of the following procedures. If you attempt the procedures in this Section and the ones that follow, relating to the alternator, be aware that other parts of the engine electrical system may also affect the alternator's performance. Check and test the system carefully before beginning any repairs.

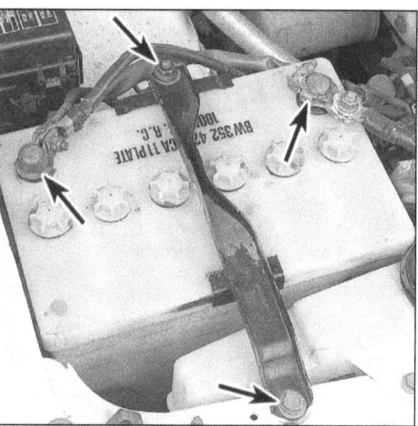

2.2 Detach the negative cable (left arrow) and the positive cable (right arrow), then unscrew the hold-down bolt and nut (upper and lower arrows) and remove the battery

General check

2   Check the battery, battery terminals and drivebelt tension according to the instructions found in Chapter 1. Check the battery cables (see Section 4). Check the fusible link for continuity.
3   Check the engine, gauge and turn signal fuses located in the combination fuse relay box and the interior fuse box (see Chapter 12).
4   Check the connections on the rear of the alternator and at the regulator. Make sure they are tight and corrosion free.
5   Use caution during the following step because the engine must be running. Keep hands and tools away from the drivebelts and pulleys. Perform this test with the engine at normal operating temperature. Allow the engine to run at normal idling speed and listen carefully to the alternator. It should make a smooth whirring sound if it makes any discernible noise at all. There should be no abnormal noises or grinding sounds. If unusual noises exist, remove the alternator and check it internally for bad bearings and brushes or take it to an alternator rebuilding shop or dealership. Do not disassemble the unit if you do not have the knowledge and tools required for this process.
6   While the engine is running, see that the charge light is off. Turn the engine off and turn the ignition switch back to On but don't start the engine. The charge light should be on. If it isn't, check the charge light circuit and bulb.

Output test

7   Perform the following steps with the engine off. Make certain all connections are tight and making good contact. Damage to the charging system components and test equipment or injury to the operator may result if the connections are improperly made.
8   Disconnect the wire from terminal B of the alternator and connect it to the negative terminal of an ammeter. Connect the positive

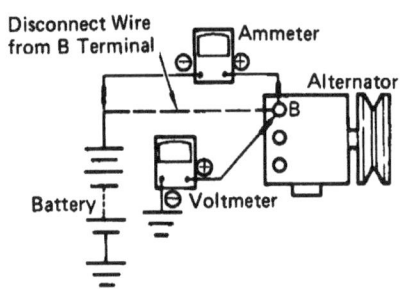

6.8 The correct hook-up for testing alternator output

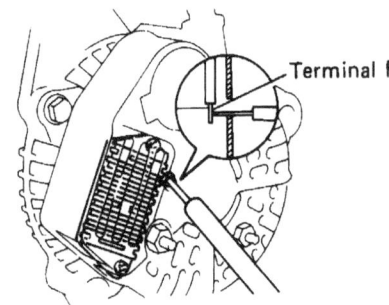

6.12 Earth terminal F before checking the voltage at terminal B on the alternator

7.3 Detach the electrical connectors (arrows), the vacuum and lubrication hoses (not visible in this photo), the adjustment bolt (arrow) and pivot bolt (not visible), then remove the alternator from its bracket

lead of the ammeter to terminal B. Connect the positive lead of the voltmeter to terminal B. Connect the negative lead of the voltmeter to earth **(see illustration)**.

9   Start the engine. Turn on the headlights (high beams) and all electrical accessories, then advance the engine speed from idle to 2000 rpm and check the alternator output under load. Check the ammeter and voltmeter readings throughout the range. Next turn off the lights and all of the accessories and run the engine at 2000 rpm until the ammeter reading is back down to approximately 10 amps. The battery voltage should register in the regulated voltage range listed in this Chapter's Specifications.

10   If the system uses an external regulator and the readings do not match the Specifications listed at the front of the chapter, it must be checked further (see Section 9).

11   If the alternator is equipped with an internal regulator, check the IC regulator and alternator as follows:

12   With terminal F earthed **(see illustration)**, start the engine and check the voltage reading of terminal B.

13   If the voltage is greater than the specified voltage, renew the IC regulator.

14   If the voltage is less than the specified voltage, have the alternator checked by a qualified electrical technician.

15   With the engine running at 2000 rpm, turn on the high beam headlights, place the heater fan control switch on the Hi position and check the reading on the ammeter.

16   If the ammeter reading is significantly less than specified, have the alternator checked and repaired by a qualified electrical technician. **Note:** *Sometimes the indicated ammeter reading will be slightly less than the*

specified amperage with a fully charged battery.

7   Alternator - removal, refitting and overhaul

Removal

Refer to illustration 7.3

1   Disconnect the negative cable from the battery.

2   On some later four-cylinder petrol models with power steering, the coolant must be drained, the engine compartment bottom shroud must be removed and the coolant

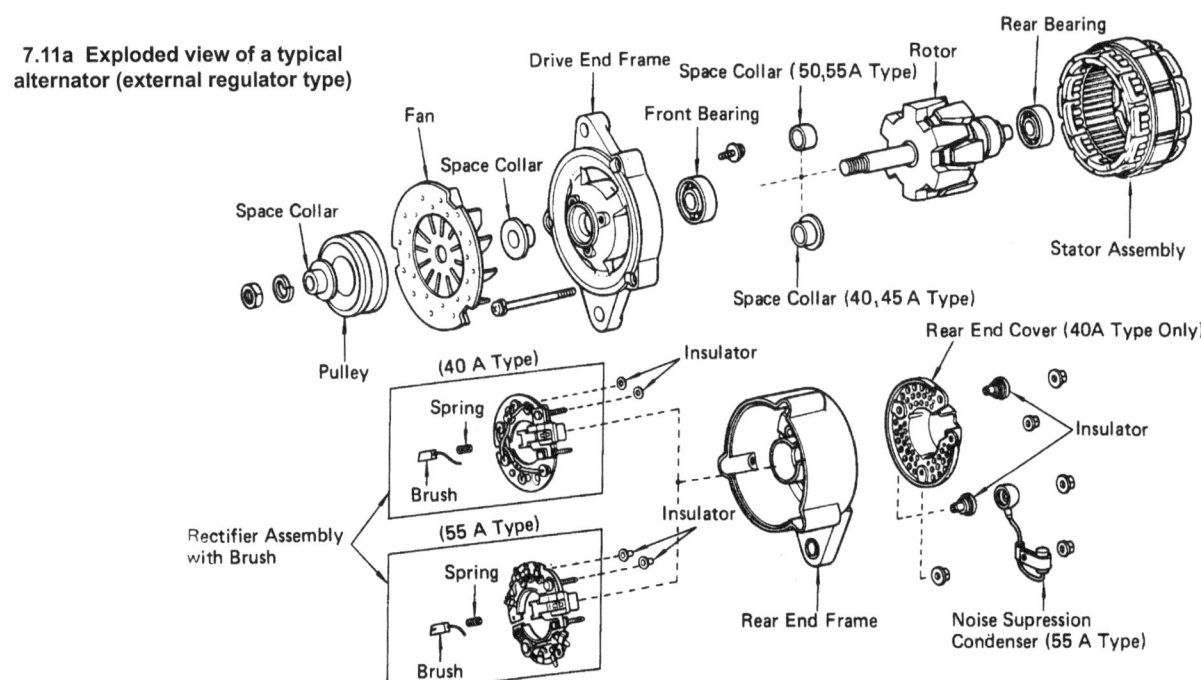

7.11a Exploded view of a typical alternator (external regulator type)

inlet hose must be detached from the engine before the alternator bolts are removed. Check carefully to see if this hose will interfere with alternator removal on your model before draining the coolant. If you find it necessary to drain the coolant and detach the hose, refer to Routine Maintenance (see Chapter 1).

Warning: *Wait until the engine is completely cool before draining the coolant.*

3   Label, then disconnect the wires at the rear of the alternator **(see illustration)**. On diesel models, also detach the vacuum hoses from the ports on the vacuum pump.

4   Remove the lower alternator swivel retaining bolt and nut.

5   Remove the adjustment bolt and nut.

6   Release the drivebelt and remove the alternator from its mounting bracket. If the alternator is a tight fit in its bracket, it may be helpful to unbolt the adjustment bracket from the engine block to give you more working room.

Refitting

7   If you are renewing the alternator with a new or rebuilt unit, take the old one with you when purchasing a spare unit. Make sure the new/rebuilt unit looks identical to the old alternator. Look at the terminals - they should be the same in number, size and location as the terminals on the old alternator. Finally, look at the identification numbers - they will be stamped into the housing or printed on a tag attached to the housing. Make sure the numbers are the same on both alternators.

8   Many new alternators do not have a pul-

ley fitted, so you may have to switch the pulley from the old unit to the renewal one. When buying an alternator, find out the shop's policy regarding pulleys - some shops will perform this service free of charge. You'll also have to remove the vacuum pump and transfer it to the new/rebuilt unit (see Chapter 9).

9   Refitting is the reverse of removal. Adjust the drivebelt (see Chapter 1).

Overhaul

Refer to illustrations 7.11a and 7.11b

10   Alternators are not commonly overhauled due to the special tools and knowledge necessary for the job and the unavailability of certain replacement parts. Ordinarily, new or rebuilt alternators are purchased and fitted.

11   If it is decided to dismantle the alternator for overhaul, refer to the exploded view drawings included in this section **(see illustrations)**.

12   Note the following:

Scribe a line across the alternator sections to insure alignment upon reassembly.

A press will be required to remove/refit the rotor assembly and bearing.

Where necessary a soldering iron should be used to separate parts such as the diode pack, rectifier and/or regulator. Do not apply unnecessary heat to these components as damage will occur.

Always use new brushes or insure the old brushes are of acceptable length.

8   Alternator - inspection and brush renewal

Models with an external regulator

Refer to illustrations 8.7, 8.9, 8.11 and 8.12

1   Remove the alternator as described in the previous Section. Detach the vacuum pump (see Chapter 9).

2   Remove the three alternator through bolts **(see illustration 7.11a)**.

3   Clamp the alternator in a vise equipped with soft jaws. Clamp on the mounting flange only.

4   Remove the four nuts, two terminal insulators and the noise suppression condenser.

5   Remove the rear end frame from the stator by gently levering it loose with two levers or screwdrivers. **Note:** *Be very careful not to damage any internal wiring or the external housing.*

6   Remove the stator assembly.

7   Measure the exposed brush length **(see illustration)** and compare it to the Specifications. If the brushes are worn beyond the specified limits, renew them as follows.

8   Unsolder the brushes at their connecting points.

9   Pull the brushes out of their respective slots in the brush holder **(see illustration)**.

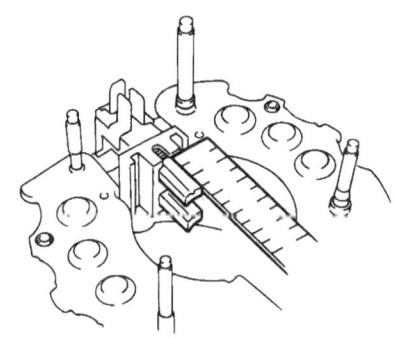

8.7 Measuring the exposed brush length on a typical alternator rectifier/brush holder assembly

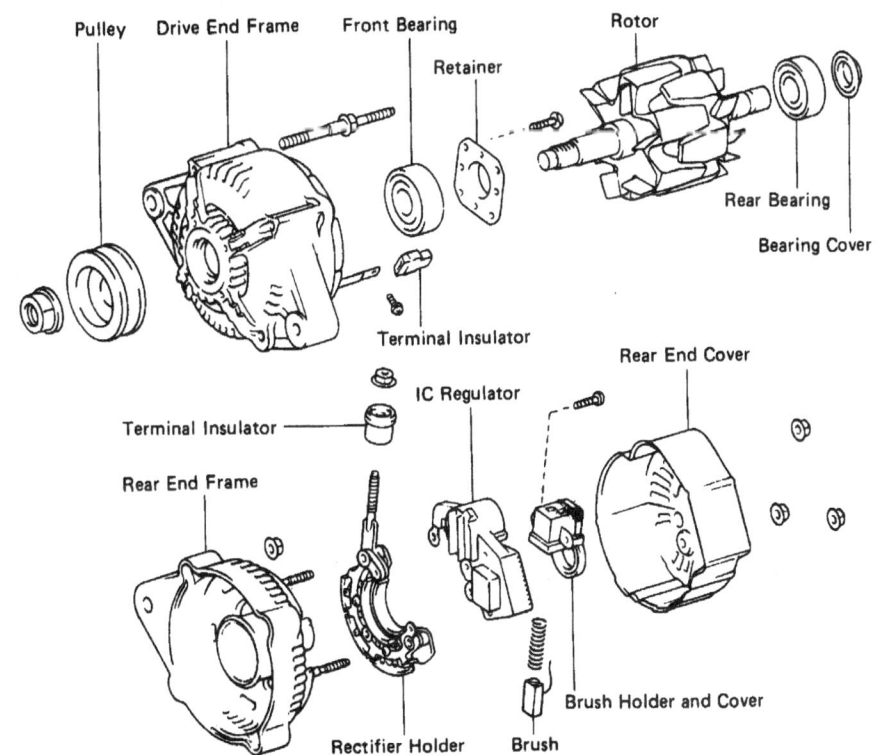

7.11b Exploded view of a typical alternator with an integral (IC) regulator

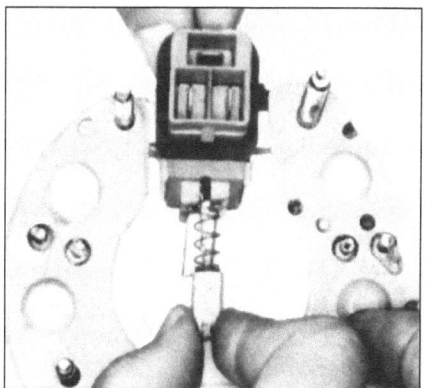

8.9 Removing the alternator brushes from the brush holder

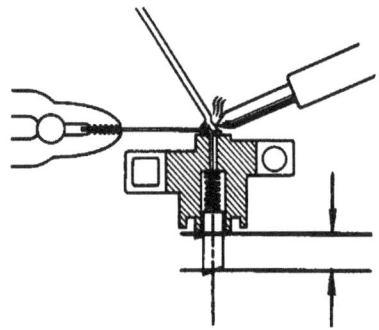

8.11 Soldering new alternator brushes in place

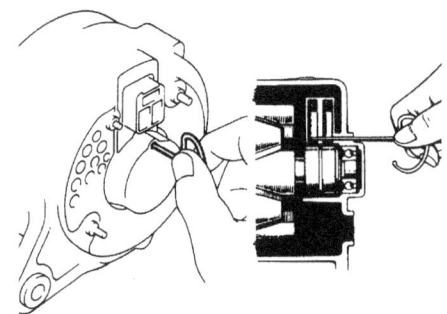

8.12 Insert a wire as shown to retain the brushes when assembling the alternator

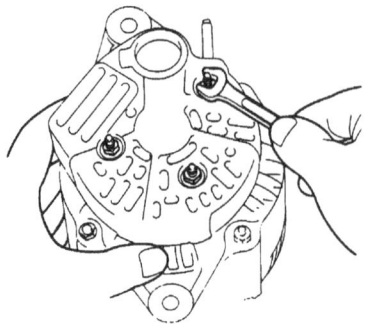

8.14 Removing the alternator rear end cover nuts

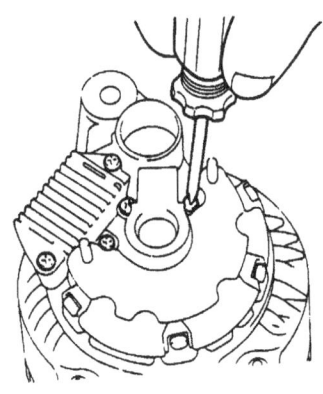

8.15 Removing the brush holder screws

10   Position the new brushes in the holder.

11   Solder the new brushes to the connecting points **(see illustration)**. Make sure that the exposed length of the brush is correct.

12   Reassembly is the reverse of disassembly. **Note:** *Take care that the housing is realigned in the same manner that it was when disassembled.* Using a small piece of wire, fashion a brush holder to fit through the slots provided in the retainer **(see illustration)**. This will hold the brushes in the retracted position while refitting the stator.

Models with an internal (IC) regulator

Refer to illustrations 8.14, 8.15, 8.16 and 8.19

13   Remove the alternator (see Section 7).

14   Remove the nut and terminal insulator, then remove the three end cover nuts **(see illustrations)** and separate the end cover from the rear of the alternator.

15   Remove the two screws and detach the brush holder and cover from the alternator **(see illustration)**.

16   Measure the exposed length of the brushes **(see illustration)**. If they are shorter than the specified length, renew them as follows.

17   Unsolder the leads and pull out the brushes and springs.

18   Insert the leads of the new brushes through the springs and fit them in the holder.

19   Make sure the brushes protrude the specified standard length, then solder the leads to the holder **(see illustration)**. Make sure the brushes move smoothly in the holder, then cut off any excess lead wire.

20   Refitting is the reverse of removal. Make sure the brush holder-to-wire connector clearance is at least one millimetre.

9   Voltage regulator - check and renewal

External regulator

Refer to illustration 9.5

Check

1   Check the regulator connections for a good tight fit and good electrical continuity.

2   Unplug the electrical connector and remove the two regulator mounting bolts. Remove the regulator and the regulator cover.

3   Inspect the point surfaces for burning and/or pitting.

4   If defective, renew the regulator. If the points appear to be in good condition, perform the following checks.

5   The following tests require the use of an ohmmeter. Measure the resistance between terminals IG and F **(see illustration)**. There should be zero resistance with the points open and 11 ohms resistance with the points closed.

6   Measure the resistance between terminals L and E. There should be zero resistance with the points open and 100 ohms resistance with the points closed.

7   Measure the resistance between terminals B and E. Resistance should be infinity with the points open and 100 ohms resistance with the points closed.

8   Measure the resistance between terminals B and L. The resistance should be infinity with the points open and zero with the points closed.

9   Measure the resistance between terminals N and E. Resistance should be 23 ohms.

10   If the regulator fails any of the above checks, renew it.

11   If the regulator checks described above indicate that the regulator is in good condition, but the charging system output is not as spec-

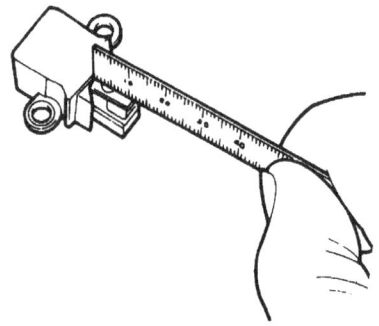

8.16 Measuring the exposed brush length

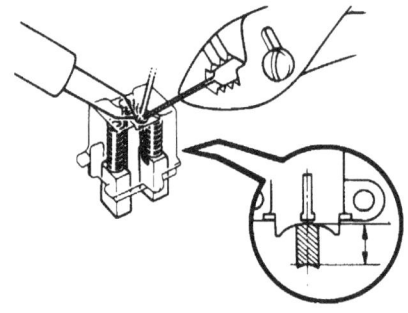

8.19 Make sure the brush protrudes the specified amount before soldering the leads

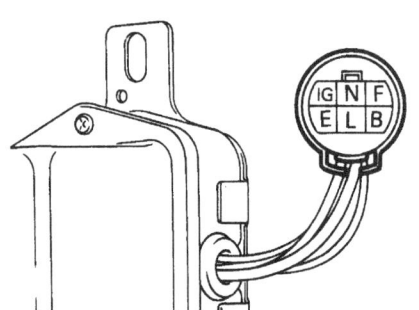

9.5 The terminals of a typical external voltage regulator

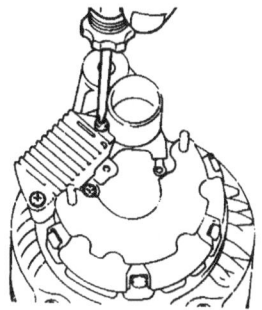

9.21 To remove an internal-type IC regulator from the alternator, remove the alternator, remove the brush holder, then unscrew the regulator mounting screws

ified, the regulator can be adjusted (a job that should be left to an automotive electrician). It is usually easier and maybe cheaper to simply renew the regulator.

Renewal

12 Detach the cable from the negative terminal of the battery.
13 Unplug the electrical connector.
14 Remove the two mounting bolts.
15 Refitting procedures are the reverse of those for removal.

Internal (IC) type regulators

Refer to illustration 9.21

Check

16 Connect the probes of a voltmeter across the terminals of the battery and check the voltage; the reading should be approximately 12 to 13.4 volts.
17 Now start the engine and check the meter; there should now be a reading of 13.5 to 15.1 volts.
18 If the voltage reading didn't go up when the engine was started, chances are that the regulator is defective.

Renewal

19 Remove the alternator (see Section 7).
20 Remove the brush holder (see Section 8).
21 Remove the IC regulator **(see illustration)**.
22 Refitting is the reverse of removal.

10 Starting system - description

Two types of starting systems are used. A conventional starter with direct drive, which is readily identifiable by its top mounted solenoid (magnetic switch) is one type **(see illustration 12.7a)**. The second type of starter is a gear reduction type with bottom mounted solenoid switch **(see illustration 12.17b)**. It is also identifiable by the side terminals on the bottom mounted solenoid switch.

The gear reduction type starter is further subdivided into different power outputs; 1.0 kW and 1.4 kW on petrol models and a

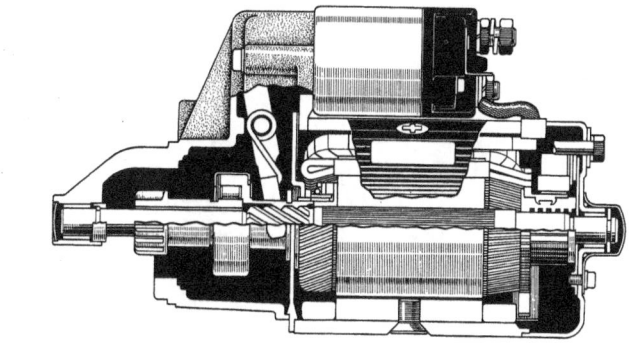

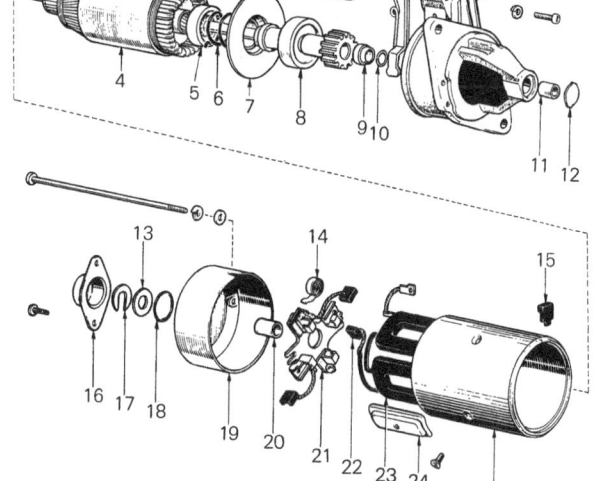

12.7a Standard starter motor components - exploded view

1	Solenoid	10	Snap-ring	19	Commutator end frame
2	Drive lever	11	Bush	20	Bush
3	Drive housing	12	Bush cover	21	Brush holder
4	Armature	13	Shim	22	Brush
5	Spring holder	14	Brush spring	23	Field coil
6	Spring	15	Rubber plate	24	Pole shoe
7	Centre bearing	16	End frame cap	25	Field frame
8	Clutch assembly	17	Lockplate		
9	Collar	18	O-ring		

2.0 kW, 2.5 kW, or a 2.7 kW starter on diesel models.

The 1.0 kW model is identifiable by its removable field frame end cover, while the field frame cover assembly on the remaining types is one piece.

The starter is activated through the starter switch, and a Neutral safety switch is provided on automatic transmission equipped vehicles. Direct battery current is provided to the starter motor by the solenoid, which also engages the drive pinion with the engine flywheel.

It should be noted that rebuilt starter units are often available from wholesale and retail auto parts outlets on an exchange basis, and that the utilization of these rebuilt units can often save the vehicle owner time and money.

11 Starter motor - testing in-vehicle

1 If the starter motor does not turn at all when the switch is operated, make sure that the shift lever is in Neutral or Park (automatic transmission) or that the clutch pedal is depressed (manual transmission).
2 Make sure that the battery is charged and that all cables, both at the battery and starter solenoid terminals, are secure.
3 If the starter motor spins but the engine is not cranking, the overrunning clutch in the starter motor is slipping and the motor must be removed from the engine for renewal.
4 If, when the switch is actuated, the starter motor does not operate at all but the solenoid clicks, then the problem lies with either the battery, the main solenoid contacts

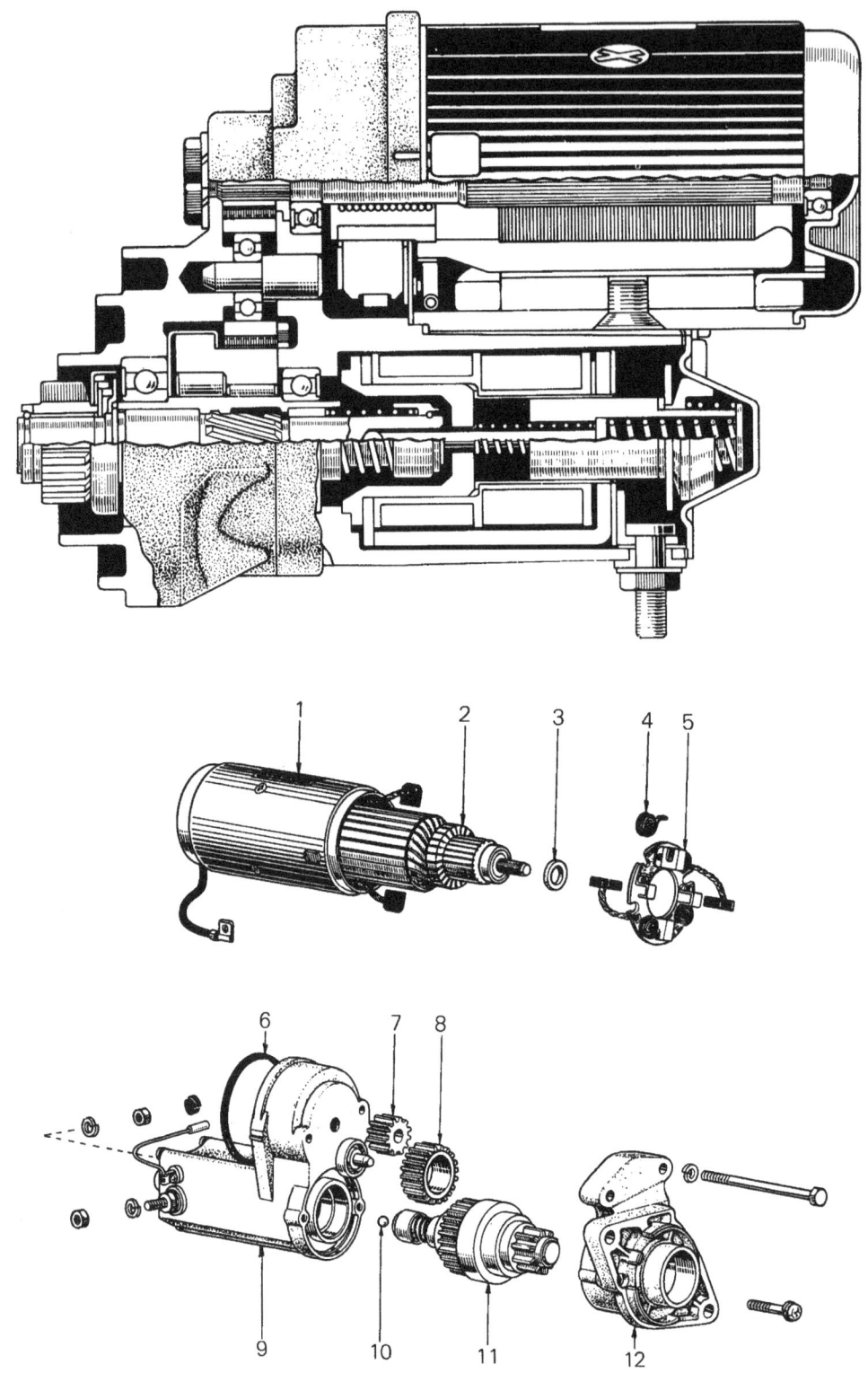

12.7b Reduction gear type starter motor components - exploded view

1	Field frame assembly	5	Brush holder	9	Solenoid assembly
2	Armature	6	O-ring	10	Steel ball
3	Felt seal	7	Pinion gear	11	Clutch assembly
4	Brush spring	8	Idler gear	12	Starter housing

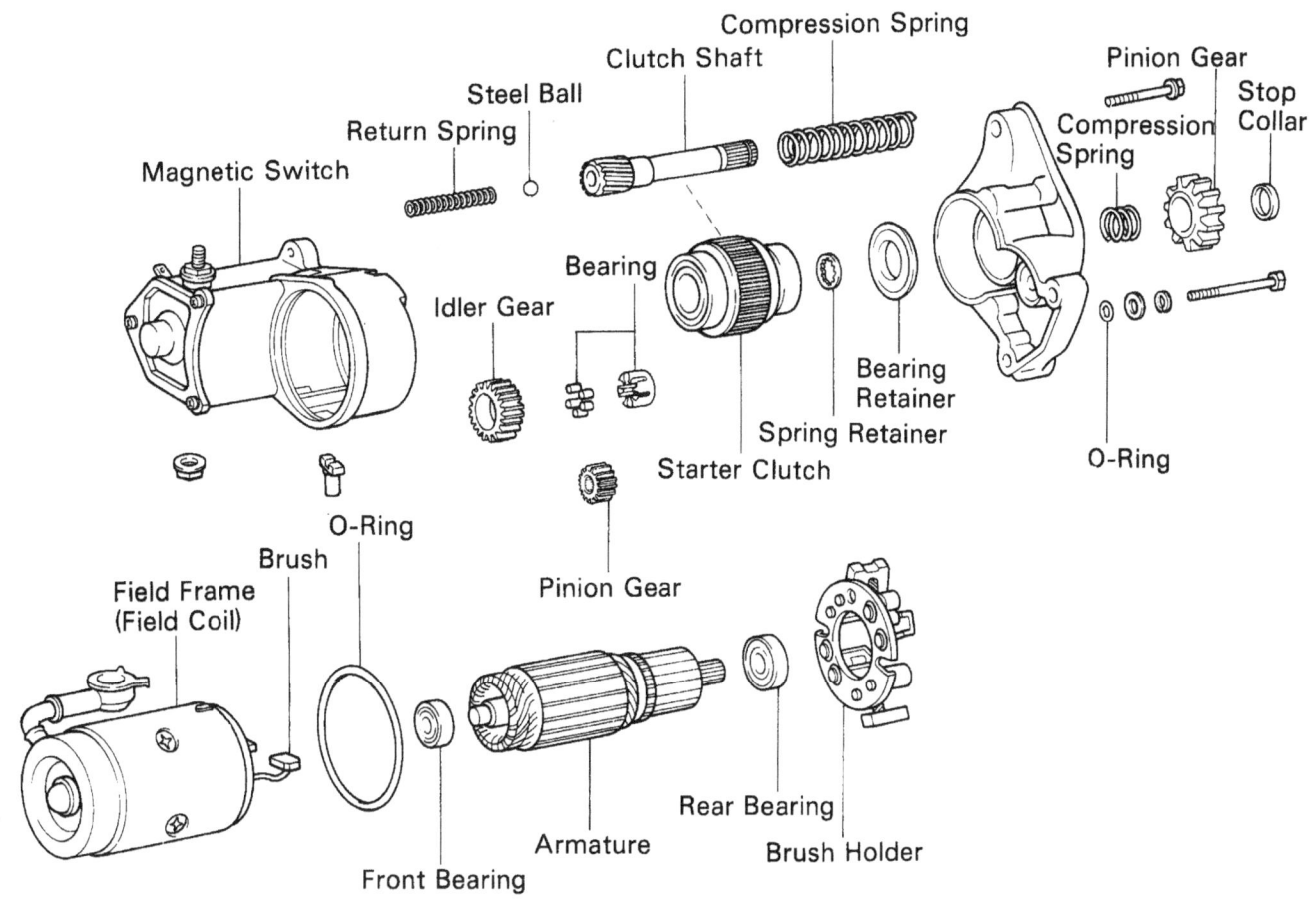

Magnetic Switch

Return Spring
Steel Ball

Clutch Shaft
Compression Spring

Pinion Gear
Compression Spring
Stop Collar

Idler Gear

Bearing

Bearing Retainer

Spring Retainer

Starter Clutch

O-Ring

Field Frame
(Field Coil)

Brush

O-Ring

Pinion Gear

Armature

Front Bearing

Rear Bearing

Brush Holder

12.7c Exploded view of a 2.0 kW starter motor

or the starter motor itself. **Note:** *Before diagnosing starter problems, make sure that the battery is fully charged.*

5   If the solenoid plunger cannot be heard when the switch is actuated, the solenoid itself is defective or the solenoid circuit is open.

6   To check the solenoid, connect a jumper lead between the battery positive terminal and the terminal on the solenoid. If the starter motor now operates, the solenoid is OK and the problem is in the ignition switch, neutral start switch or in the wiring.

7   If the starter motor still does not operate, renew it and exchange it for a rebuilt unit.

8   If the starter motor cranks the engine at an abnormally slow speed, first make sure that the battery is charged and that all terminal connections are tight. If the engine is partially seized, or has the wrong viscosity oil in it, it will crank slowly.

9   Run the engine until normal operating temperature is reached, then disconnect the coil wire from the distributor cap and earth it on the engine, on petrol models, or disconnect the wire from the fuel cut-off solenoid (see Chapter 4B) on diesel models.

10   Connect a voltmeter positive lead to the

starter motor terminal of the solenoid and then connect the negative lead to earth.

11   Crank the engine and take the voltmeter readings as soon as a steady figure is indicated. Do not allow the starter motor to turn for more than 15 seconds at a time. A reading of 9 volts or more, with the starter motor turning at normal cranking speed, is normal. If the reading is 9 volts or more but the cranking speed is slow, the motor is faulty. If the reading is less than 9 volts and the cranking speed is slow, the solenoid contacts are probably burned.

---

12 Starter motor - removal, refitting and overhaul

Removal

1   Disconnect the negative battery cable from the battery.

2   Raise the vehicle and place it securely on jackstands.

3   Disconnect the leads from the starter. There is one clip connection and one terminal held by a nut and washer.

4   Remove the bolts retaining the starter to the bellhousing.

5   Remove the starter.

Refitting

6   Refitting procedures are the reverse of those for removal. **Note:** *On some models there is a tab on the clip which connects to the starter that must be properly aligned.*

Overhaul

Refer to illustrations 12.7a, 12.7b, 12.7c and 12.7d

Note: *Starter motor overhaul requires certain tools and techniques which can be out of the scope for some home mechanics. Often, the fitting of a new or rebuilt starter is the preferred choice. For more information, see your local auto parts dealer.*

7   Remove the through bolts and separate the starter housing **(see illustrations)**.

8   Disassemble the remaining components.

9   Reassembly is the reverse of disassembly. Replace any worn brushes and and fit new brushes.

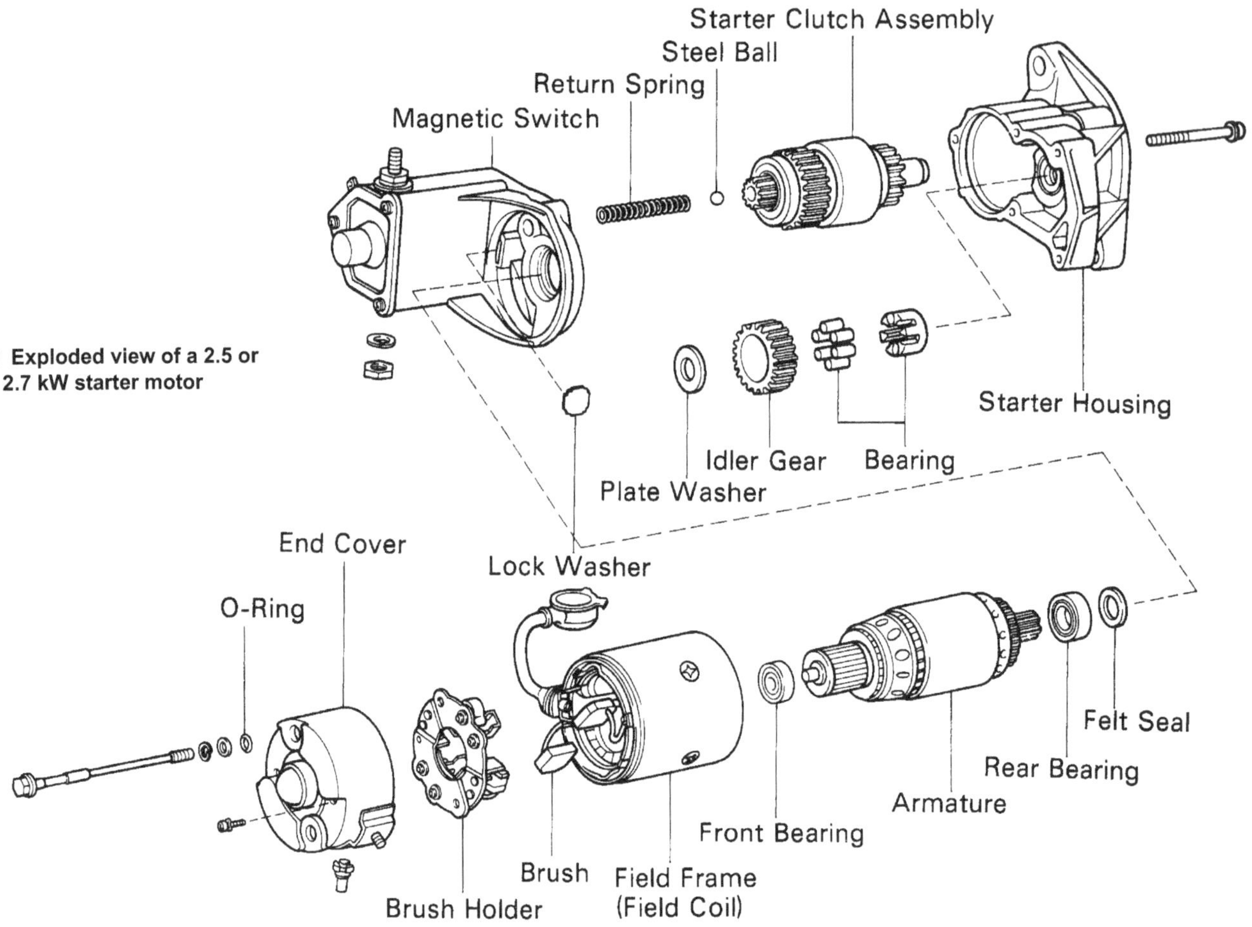

Starter Clutch Assembly

Steel Ball

Return Spring

Magnetic Switch

12.7d Exploded view of a 2.5 or 2.7 kW starter motor

Starter Housing

Idler Gear   Bearing

Plate Washer

End Cover

Lock Washer

O-Ring

Felt Seal

Rear Bearing

Armature

Front Bearing

Brush   Field Frame
(Field Coil)

Brush Holder

---

13   Starter relay - check and renewal

Refer to illustrations 13.1 and 13.2

Check

1   Unplug the electrical connectors from the relay. On some models the relay is located in the left rear corner of the engine compartment **(see illustration)**; on other models it's mounted on the right side of the engine compartment.

2   Using an ohmmeter, check for continuity between terminals ST and E **(see illustration)**. Continuity should exist.

3   Check for continuity between terminals MG and B - no continuity should exist.

4   Using fused jumper wires, apply battery voltage to terminals ST and E, while checking for continuity between terminals MG and B. Continuity should exist.

5   If the relay fails any of these checks, renew it.

Renewal

6   To renew the relay, disconnect the electrical connector(s) and unscrew the mounting bolt. Refitting is the reverse of removal.

14   Ignition system - description

The ignition system is designed to ignite the fuel/air charge entering the cylinder at just

13.1 On some models the starter relay is mounted on the left side of the engine compartment (arrow)

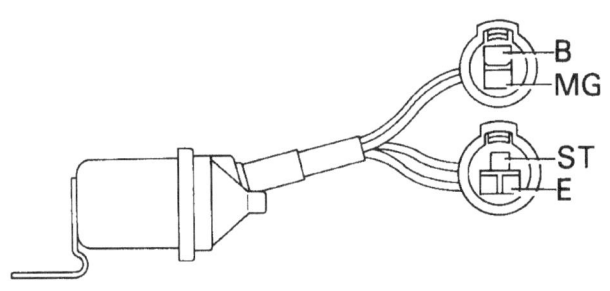

B
MG

ST
E

13.2 Starter solenoid terminal designations

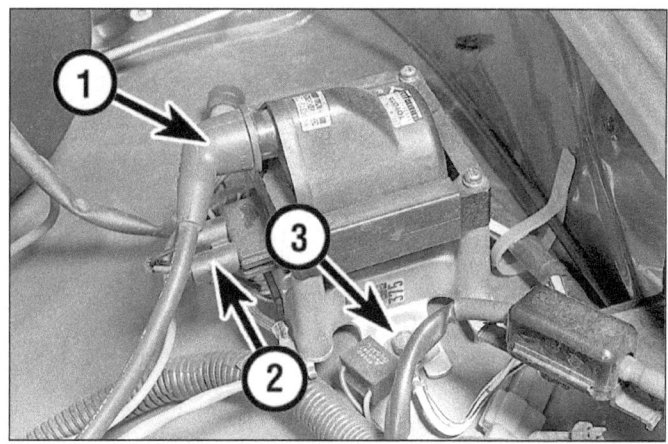

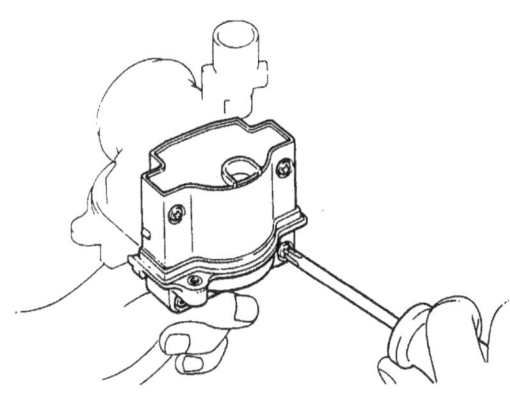

16.2a To remove a conventional coil, detach the cable from the negative terminal of the battery, detach the coil high tension lead (1), unplug the primary leads (2) and remove the mounting bracket bolts (3 - other bolt not shown)

16.2b Distributor-mounted coils are retained by four screws

the right moment. It does so by producing a high voltage electrical spark between the electrodes of the spark plug. The timing of the spark (when it occurs in the engine cycle) is automatically varied to meet the requirements of engine load and speed.

Some of the models covered in this manual are equipped with electronic ignition systems which provide relatively trouble and maintenance free operation. Others are equipped with a conventional breaker-point type ignition system.

The typical system consists of an ignition switch, ignition coil, distributor, electronic control unit (igniter) (on electronic ignition systems only), spark plugs and wires, and the battery. Although some components may differ slightly in detail, the ignition systems on later models are essentially the same as earlier systems. On some models the ignition coil is mounted on the distributor body. There are two variations of this design; one type uses a centrifugal advance mechanism, while the other incorporates an Electronic Spark Advance (ESA) system.

15   Ignition system - check

Warning: *Because of the high voltage generated by the ignition system, extreme care should be taken whenever an operation is performed involving ignition components. This not only includes the igniter, coil, distributor and spark plug wires, but related components such as spark plug connectors, tachometer and other test equipment.*

Ignition tester method

1   If the engine turns over but will not start, disconnect the spark plug wire from any spark plug and attach it to a spark tester (available at most auto parts stores).
2   Connect the clip on the tester to a earth such as a metal bracket, crank the engine and observe the tip of the tester to see if a spark occurs.
3   If a spark occurs, sufficient voltage is reaching the plugs to fire the engine. If no spark occurs, one of the ignition components - coil, distributor cap, rotor, pick-up

coil or breaker points, igniter, ECU or spark plug wires - is defective. Check them all thoroughly.

Alternative method

Note: *If you are unable to obtain a spark tester, the following method will enable you to determine whether the ignition system has spark but it will not tell you if there is enough voltage present to actually initiate combustion.*

4   Disconnect the spark plug boot from a spark plug. Using an insulated tool, hold the wire about 7 mm from a good earth and have an assistant crank the engine.
5   If there is no spark, check another wire in the same manner. A few sparks followed by no spark is the same condition as no spark at all.
6   If there is good spark, check the spark plugs (refer to Chapter 1) and the fuel system (refer to Chapter 4).

16   Ignition coil - check and renewal

Refer to illustrations 7.2a, 7.2b, 7.4a, 7.4b, 5.5a and 5.5b

Caution: *If the coil terminals touch an earth source, the coil and/or igniter could be damaged.*

1   Mark the wires and terminals with pieces of numbered tape, then remove the primary wires and the high-tension lead from the coil.
2   On conventional coils, remove the coil or coil/igniter assembly **(see illustration)** from its mount, clean the outer case and check it for cracks and other damage. On models with integral coils (mounted in the distributor), remove the distributor cap, mark and disconnect the wires then remove the coil mounting screws **(see illustration)**.
Note: *It isn't necessary to remove the coil from the distributor to check the resistance values, but it is a good idea to remove it to*

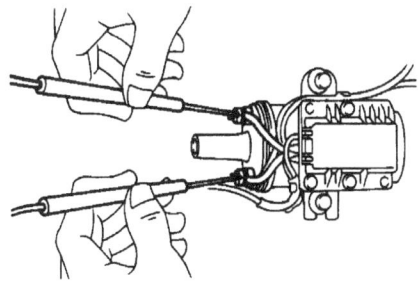

16.4a To check coil primary resistance, measure the resistance between the positive and negative terminals and compare your reading to the specified coil primary resistance (four-cylinder with electronic ignition shown)

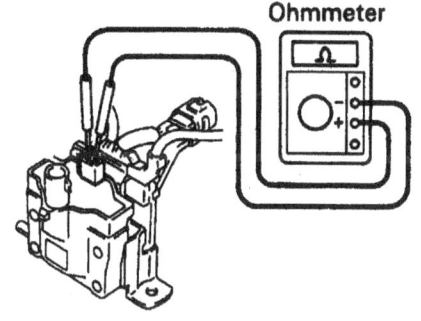

Ohmmeter

16.4b To check the primary resistance of the coil, measure the resistance between the positive and negative terminals (V6 coil shown)

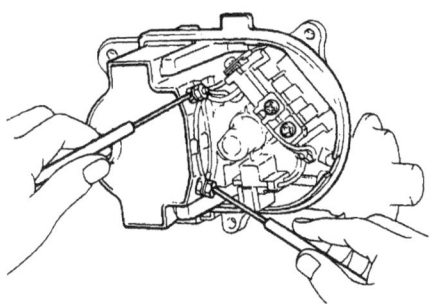

16.4c Checking the primary resistance of a distributor-mounted coil

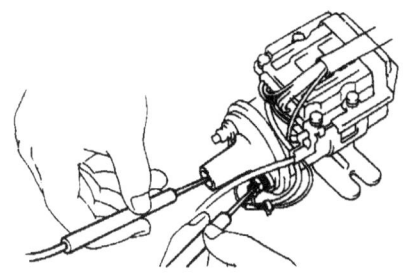

16.5a To check secondary coil resistance, measure the resistance between the positive primary terminal and the high tension terminal and compare your reading to the specified coil secondary resistance (four-cylinder engine with electronic ignition shown)

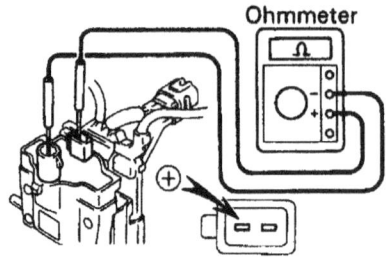

16.5b To check the secondary resistance of the coil, measure the resistance between the positive and high tension terminals (V6 coil shown)

check for carbon tracking and other signs of damage.

3   Inspect the primary coil terminals and the coil tower terminal for corrosion. Clean them with a wire brush if any corrosion is found.

4   Check the primary coil resistance by attaching the leads of an ohmmeter to the positive and negative primary terminals **(see illustrations)**. Compare the measured resistance to the Specifications.

5   Check the secondary coil resistance by hooking one of the ohmmeter leads to one of the primary terminals and the other ohmmeter lead to the high-tension coil tower terminal **(see illustrations)**. Compare the measured resistance to the Specifications.

6   Measure the insulation resistance by attaching the leads of an ohmmeter to the positive terminal and earth (the igniter body). Compare the measured resistance to the Specifications.

7   If the measured resistances are not as specified, the coil is probably defective and should be renewed.

8   It is essential for proper ignition system operation that all coil terminals and wire leads to be kept clean and dry.

9   Refit the coil in its mount and hook up the wires.

17 Igniter - removal and refitting

1   If, after the ignition coil, distributor cap, rotor, spark plug wires and fuel system have been checked out, the vehicle still won't start, is hard to start, idles roughly or stalls, the igniter (located on top of the coil) should be suspect. It can be renewed as follows.

2   Remove the coil/igniter assembly as a unit (see Section 7), then unbolt and separate the igniter from the coil.

3   Visually inspect all components for obvious damage, burning, etc.

4   Refitting is the reverse of removal. **Caution:** *Remember that if the coil terminals touch earth, the coil and/or igniter could be damaged.*

18 Distributor - on-vehicle inspection

Refer to illustrations 9.3a, 9.3b, 9.3c, 9.7a, 9.7b, 9.7c and 9.9

1   Detach the cable from the negative terminal of the battery.

2   Remove the distributor cap (see Chapter 1).

Air gap check

3   Using a feeler gauge, measure the gap between the signal rotor tooth and the pickup coil projection **(see illustrations)**.

4   Check that the gap is within specifications.

5   On models with a 22R engine, if the gap is not within specifications, loosen the two screws that hold the signal generator and adjust the signal generator plate until the gap is within specifications. Tighten the screws and recheck the gap.

6   On models with Y-series engines and on V6 models, if the gap is not within specifications, renew the distributor.

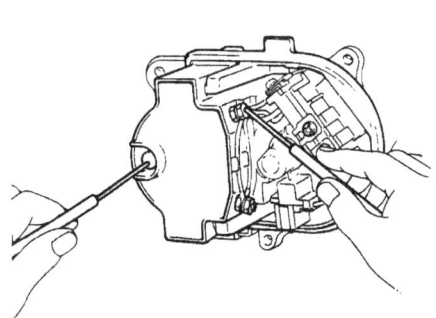

16.5c Checking the secondary resistance of a distributor-mounted coil

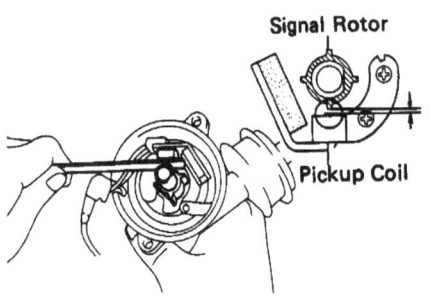

18.3a To check the air gap on a distributor for a four cylinder engine, insert a feeler gauge between the signal rotor and the signal generator (pickup coil) projection

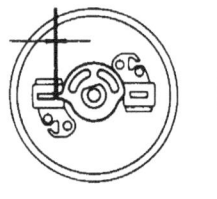
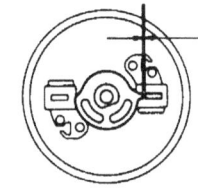
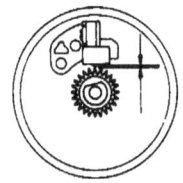

18.3b To check the air gap on a distributor for a V6, insert a feeler gauge between the signal rotor and the pickup coil projection at the indicated points

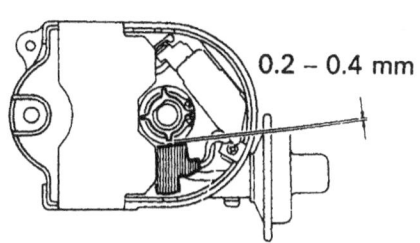

18.3c Checking the air gap on a distributor with an integral coil

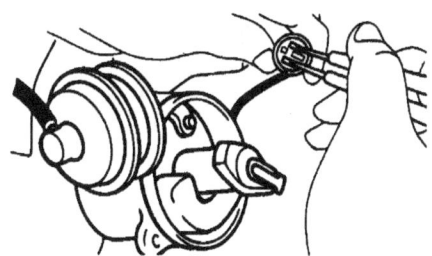

18.7a Use an ohmmeter to measure the resistance between the two terminals of the pickup coil lead electrical connector for the distributor on an R-series engine

18.7b On a V6, use an ohmmeter to measure the resistance between terminal G and each of the other three terminals

Signal generator (pick-up coil) check

7   Using an ohmmeter **(see illustrations)**, check that the resistance of the signal generator is within specifications.
8   If the resistance is not correct, renew the signal generator (see Section 10).

Vacuum advance check (if equipped)

9   If you do not have a vacuum pump, go to Step 11. If you do have one, disconnect the vacuum hose from the vacuum advance unit and connect the pump to the vacuum pipe on the diaphragm **(see illustration)**.
10   Apply vacuum and verify that the vacuum advance moves. If it doesn't, renew the vacuum advance unit.
11   Hook up a timing light in accordance with the manufacturer's instructions, as if you were adjusting the ignition timing.
12   Start the engine and set it at approximately 2500 rpm.
13   Observe the timing marks at the front of the engine and remove the vacuum hose(s) from the vacuum advance control unit on the distributor. When the hose(s) are removed, the timing mark on the crankshaft pulley should appear to move closer to the stationary mark on the timing tab. When the hose(s) are reconnected, the mark should move away

again.
14   If reconnecting the vacuum hose(s) produces an abrupt increase in advance, or none at all, the vacuum advance control unit is probably defective. Renew it.

Centrifugal advance check (if equipped)

15   To statically check the centrifugal advance mechanism, simply turn the rotor shaft clockwise, release it and note whether it returns slightly (turns counterclockwise).
16   Grasp the rotor shaft with your thumb and index finger and try to twist it from side to side to verify that it's not excessively loose.
17   To dynamically check the centrifugal advance mechanism, hook up a timing light in accordance with the manufacturer's instructions, as if you were adjusting the ignition timing.
18   With the engine running at idle speed and the timing light properly connected, remove the vacuum hose(s) from the vacuum advance control unit on the distributor.
19   Observe the timing marks on the front of the engine and slowly accelerate the engine. The timing mark on the crankshaft pulley should appear to move smoothly in a direction away from the stationary mark on the timing tab. Then when the engine is slowed down,

the mark should return to its original position.
20   If the above conditions are not met, the advance mechanism inside the distributor should be checked for broken governor springs, corrosion or other problems.
21   Reconnect the vacuum hose(s).

19   Signal generator (pickup coil) - removal and refitting

Refer to illustrations 10.1 and 10.4
1   Remove two screws and pull off the distributor cap and O-ring **(see illustration)**.
2   Remove the distributor rotor by pulling it off.
3   If equipped, remove the dust cover from the signal generator by levering it up with a screwdriver.
4   Remove the signal generator by removing the two retaining screws **(see illustration)**.
5   Refitting procedures are the reverse of those for removal.
6   Check the air gap (see Section 9).

20   Distributor - removal and refitting

1   After carefully marking them, remove the coil wire and plug wires from the distributor cap.
2   Remove the number one spark plug.
3   Manually rotate the engine to top dead centre on the compression stroke for number one piston (see Chapter 2).
4   Carefully mark the vacuum hoses if more than one is present on your model.
5   Disconnect the vacuum hose(s).
6   Disconnect the electrical wires to the distributor.
7   Use paint or a scribe to mark the rotor position in relation to the body of the distributor. Scribe a similar mark between the distributor body and the mating surface on the engine.
8   Remove the hold down bolt and clamp.
9   Remove the distributor. **Note:** *Do not rotate the engine with the distributor out.*

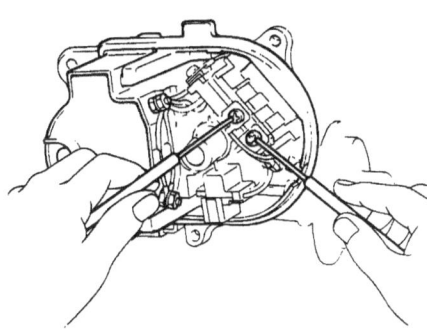

18.7c Measuring the pickup coil resistance on a Y-series engine distributor

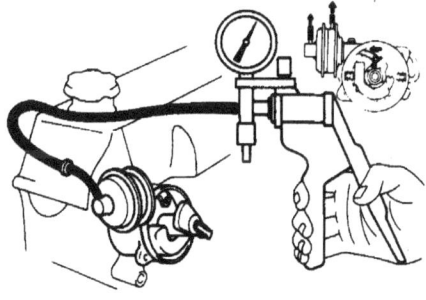

18.9 If the distributor on your vehicle has a vacuum advance unit, detach the vacuum hose from the diaphragm, attach a vacuum pump and apply some vacuum to the advance unit - if it's working properly, it should move the breaker plate slightly

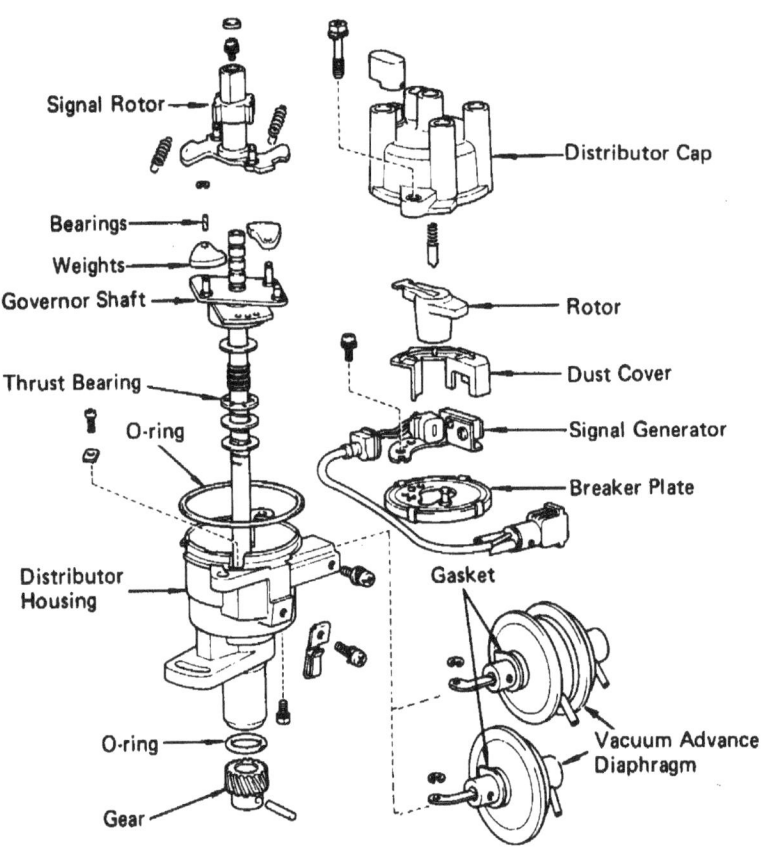

Signal Rotor

Distributor Cap

Bearings

Weights

Governor Shaft

Rotor

Thrust Bearing

Dust Cover

O-ring

Signal Generator

Breaker Plate

Distributor
Housing

Gasket

O-ring

Vacuum Advance
Diaphragm

Gear

19.1 An exploded view of a typical distributor with centrifugal and vacuum advance mechanisms

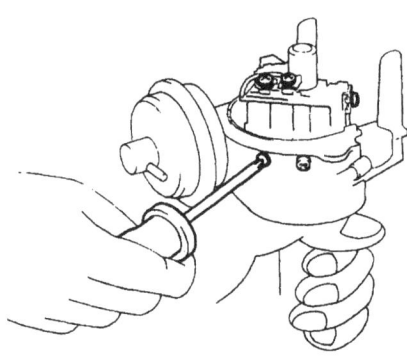

**19.4 Removing the pickup coil on a
Y-series engine distributor**

10   Before starting refitting of the distributor, make certain the number one piston is at top dead centre on the compression stroke.

11   Align the drilled mark on the driven gear with the centre of the number one spark plug terminal on the distributor cap. Insert the distributor into the engine with the adjusting clamp centred over the hold-down hole. Make sure that the gear does not turn as the distributor is inserted.

12   Refit the hold-down bolt. The marks previously made on the distributor housing and on the rotor and engine should line up before the bolt is tightened.

13   Refit the distributor cap.

14   Connect the wiring for the distributor.

15   Refit the spark plug wires.

16   Refit the vacuum hoses as previously marked.

17   Time the engine as described in Chapter 1, *Ignition timing check and adjustment.*

Chapter 6
Emissions control and pre-heating systems

Contents

Specifications

Fuel Evaporative Emission Control (EVAP) system

Outer vent control valve solenoid resistance	63 to 73 ohms

Throttle Positioner (TP) system

Setting speed	1050 rpm
VSV resistance (cold)	
Early models	48 to 60 ohms
Later models	18 to 23 ohms

Oxidation Catalyst (OS)

Thermo sensor resistance	2 to 200 K ohms

Automatic choke system

Heating coil resistance (cold)	20 ohms (approximately)

Dashpot (DP) system

Setting speed	
Carburetted four-cylinder	3000 rpm
Fuel-injected four-cylinder and V6	2000 rpm

Torque specifications — **Nm**

Glow plugs	13

1   General information

Refer to illustrations 1.1a and 1.1b

To prevent pollution of the atmosphere from burned and evaporating gases, a number of major and auxiliary emission control systems are incorporated on Toyota trucks. The combination of systems used depends on the year in which the vehicle was manufactured, the locality to which it was originally delivered and the engine type. Check the Vehicle Emissions Control Information (VECI) label **(see illustration)** in your engine compartment to determine which systems are used on your vehicle. A vacuum schematic is also located under the bonnet on most models **(see illustration)**. The major systems incorporated on the trucks with which this manual in concerned include:

Positive Crankcase Ventilation (PCV) system
Fuel Evaporative Emission Control (EVAP) system
Throttle Positioner (TP) system
Spark Control (SC) system
Exhaust Gas Recirculation (EGR) system
Air Injection (AI) system
Air Suction (AS) system
Catalytic Converter (CCo) system
Mixture Control (MC) system
High Altitude Compensation (HAC) system

The auxiliary systems incorporated include:

Automatic Hot Air Intake (HAI) system
Auto choke system - including Choke Breaker (CB), Choke
Opener (CO) and Fast Idle Cam Breaker (FICB) systems
Auxiliary Accelerator Pump (AAP)
Deceleration fuel cut system
Air bleed system

The Sections in this Chapter include general descriptions. checking procedures (where possible) and component renewal procedures (where applicable) for each of the systems listed above.

Before assuming that an emission control system is malfunctioning, check the fuel and ignition systems carefully. In some cases, special tools and equipment, as well as specialised training, are required to accurately diagnose the causes of a rough running or difficult to start engine. If checking and servicing become too difficult or if a procedure is beyond the scope of the home mechanic, consult a Toyota dealer service department. This does not necessarily mean however, that the emission control systems are particularly difficult to maintain and repair. You can quickly and easily perform many checks and do most (if not all) of the regular maintenance at home with common tune-up and hand tools. **Note:** *The most frequent cause of emission system problems is simply a loose or broken vacuum hose or wiring connection. Therefore, always check hose and wiring connections first (refer to the accompanying emissions control system layout illustrations).*

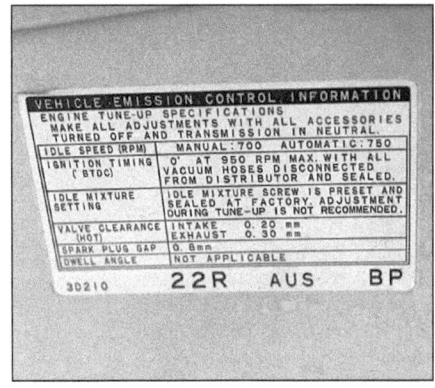

1.1a The Vehicle Emission Control Information (VECI) label is a handy reference guide for tune-up information and for the types of emission devices used on your vehicle

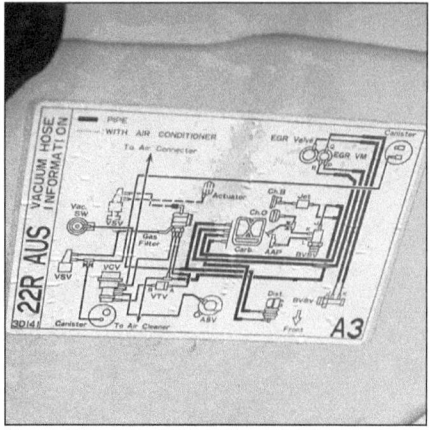

1.1b Another label provides a vacuum schematic showing the location of all emissions hoses and devices

Pay close attention to any special precautions outlined in this Chapter (particularly those concerning the catalytic converter). It should be noted that the illustrations of the various systems may not exactly match the systems refitted in your particular vehicle, due to changes made by the manufacturer during production or from year to year.

2   Positive Crankcase Ventilation (PCV) system

Refer to illustrations 2.1a, 2.1b and 2.1c

General description

1   This system is designed to reduce hydrocarbon emission (HC) by routing blow-by gases (fuel/air mixture that escapes from the combustion chamber past the piston rings into the crankcase) from the crankcase to

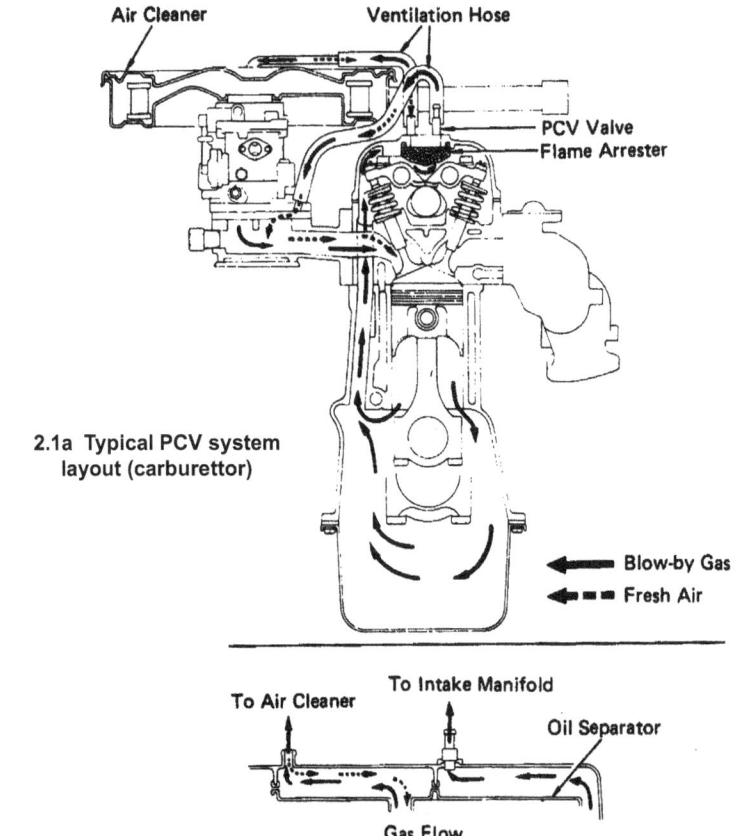

2.1a Typical PCV system layout (carburettor)

◀━━━ Blow-by Gas
◀ ━ ━ Fresh Air

Gas Flow

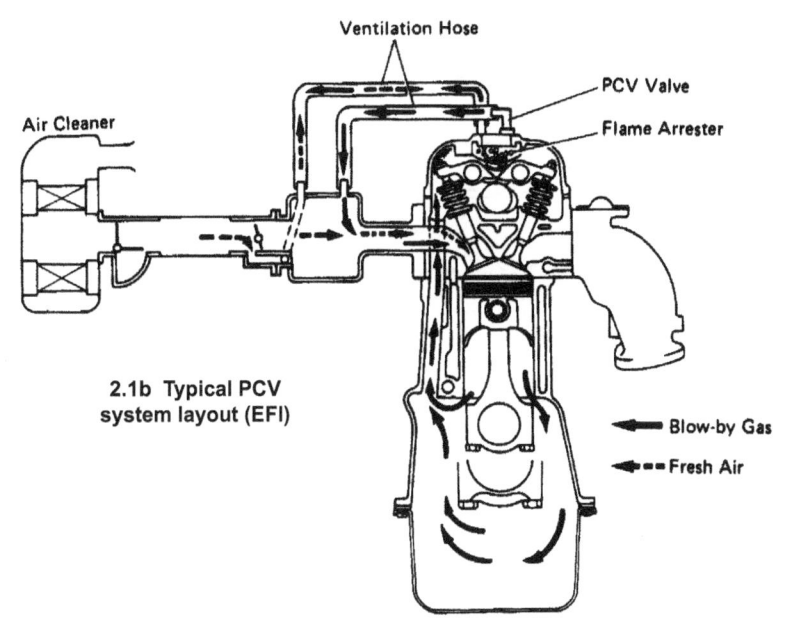

2.1b Typical PCV system layout (EFI)

← Blow-by Gas

←-- Fresh Air

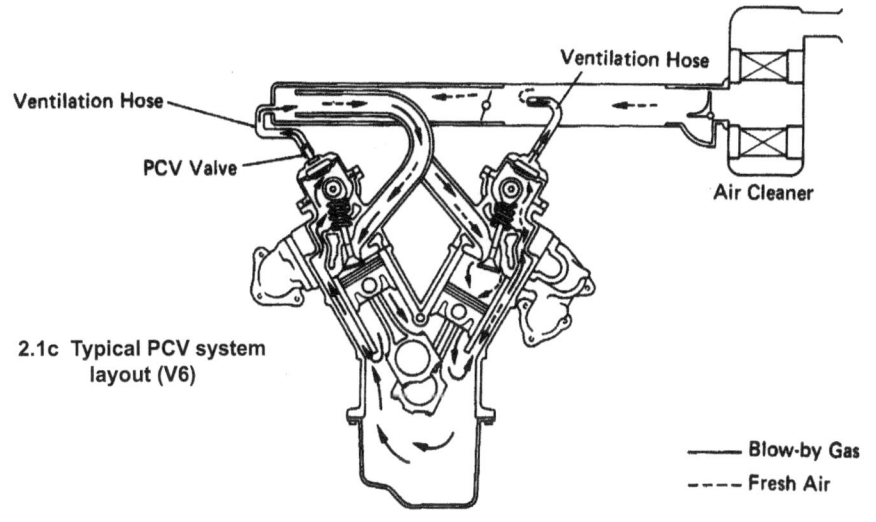

2.1c Typical PCV system layout (V6)

——— Blow-by Gas

---- Fresh Air

the inlet manifold and combustion chamber, where they are burned during engine operation. It is included on all year and engine models **(see illustrations)**.

2   The system is very simple and consists of rubber hoses and a small renewable metering valve (PCV valve).

Checking and component renewal

3   Checking, cleaning and renewal of the PCV system components is a routine maintenance procedure. Refer to Chapter 1 for details .

3   Fuel Evaporative Emission Control (EVAP) system

Refer to illustrations 3.3, 3.4, 3.5, 3.17, 3.19 and 3.24

General description

1   This system is designed to trap and store fuel that evaporates from the fuel tank and carburettor float chambers which would normally enter the atmosphere and contribute to hydrocarbon (HC) emissions. EVAP systems are incorporated on all engine and year models.

2   The system on a carburetted vehicle consists of an outer vent control valve, charcoal-filled canister(s), thermo switch, speed sensor, TVSV, VSV, jet check valves, VCV and connecting lines and hoses, although not all components are incorporated on all systems. On EFI equipped vehicles, the EVAP system is considerably simpler. It has a charcoal canister with an integral check valve and the connecting hoses between the canister, fuel tank and inlet manifold. V6 vehicles also have a bimetal vacuum switching valve (BVSV)

3   When the engine is off and high pressure begins to build in the fuel tank and carburettor float chambers, fuel vapours are absorbed by the charcoal in the canister(s) **(see illustration)**. When the engine is started (cold), the charcoal continues to absorb and

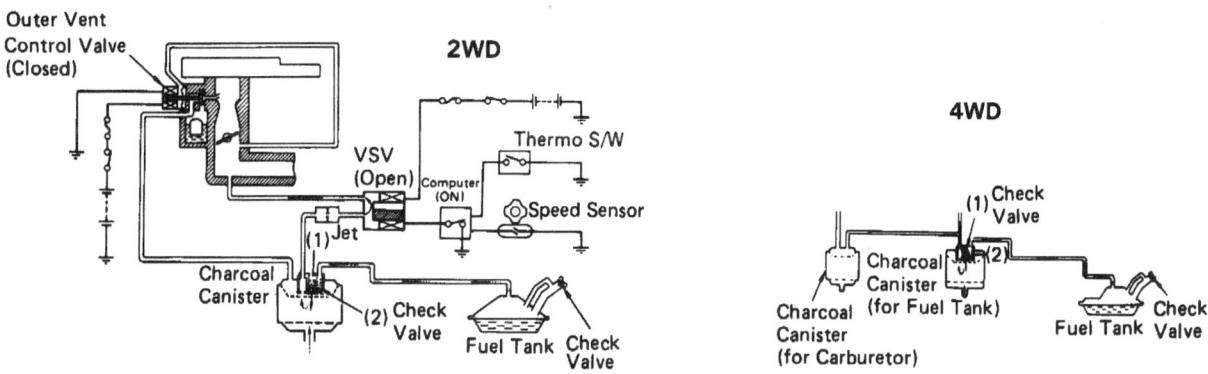

3.3 A typical EVAP system on a carburetted model

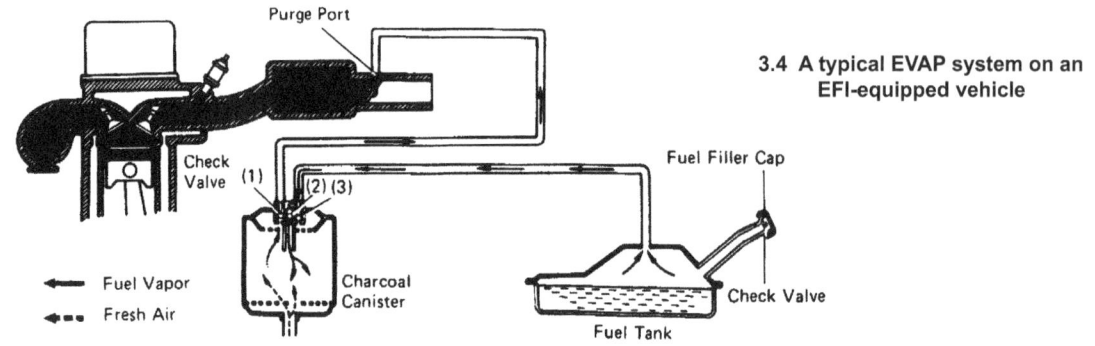

3.4 A typical EVAP system on an EFI-equipped vehicle

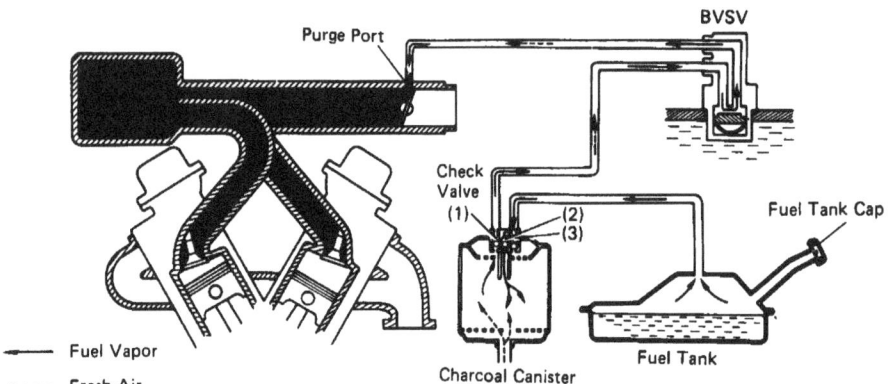

3.5 The EVAP system on a model with a V6 engine

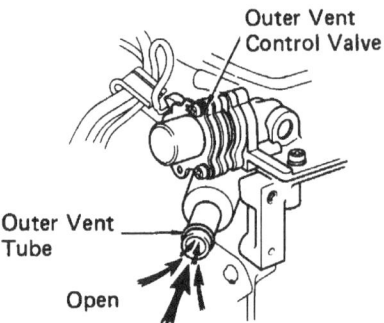

3.17 Detach the outer vent hose from the carburettor, blow air into the outer vent pipe and verify that the outer vent control valve is open - then start the engine, blow air into the outer vent pipe again and verify that the outer vent control valve is closed

store fuel vapour. As the engine coolant warms up, the stored fuel vapours are routed to the inlet manifold and combustion chamber where they are burned during normal engine operation. The VSV and outer vent control valve direct the fuel vapours to the appropriate place. The VSV is activated by the coolant temperature and/or the speed sensor, via a microcomputer, while the outer vent control valve is activated by inlet manifold pressure changes. The check valve mounted in the fuel tank filler cap is calibrated to open when the tank vacuum reaches a certain level, allowing outside air to enter the tank and relieve the high vacuum. The check valve in the charcoal canister operates in a similar manner.

4   On a vehicle with EFI **(see illustration)**, the EVAP system is considerably less complex:

a) *At idle and low speed, fuel vapours from the tank are absorbed by the ;canister. A check valve integrated into the top of the canister closes, preventing these vapours from being drawn out of the canister and into the intake chamber.*

b) *During medium and high speed driving, this check valve opens, allowing the high manifold vacuum of the intake to draw the fuel vapours from the canister into the intake chamber.*

c) *When there is high pressure in the tank (the vehicle is parked, with the engine off, for example), the check valve that regulates the line between the fuel tank and the canister opens, allowing the canister to absorb fuel vapours from the tank. A third check valve prevents these vapours from escaping the canister and flowing back to the tank. A fourth check valve, located in the fuel filler cap, closes to prevent the pressurised vapours from escaping into the atmosphere.*

d) *When there is high vacuum in the tank, these check valves in the canister reverse themselves: The first one closes and the other one opens, preventing fuel vapours from being drawn out of the canister by the vacuum in the tank. And the check valve in the fuel filler cap opens to allow air into the tank to relieve the vacuum .*

5   On V6-equipped models **(see illustration)**, the EVAP system is similar to the one described above for EFI-equipped fours. The fuel vapours are still routed either from the tank into the canister or from the canister into the air intake chamber through the same three check valves integrated into the top of the canister, but vapour flow into the intake chamber is also controlled by a bimetal vacuum switching valve (BVSV), which in turn is opened and closed by coolant temperature:

a) *When the BVSV is closed (the coolant temperature is below 35-degrees*

C), *or when it's open (coolant exceeds 54-degrees C) but the upper edge of the throttle valve is positioned downstream from the purge port in the roof of the intake, fuel vapours from the tank are absorbed by the canister.*

b) *When the BVSV is open and the throttle valve is positioned above the purge port, fuel vapours from the canister are drawn into the intake chamber.*

Check

Canister

6   Label the lines and their respective canister pipes before detaching them. The following test requires that you be able to identify the tank and purge pipes.

7   Remove the charcoal canister(s) (some models have one canister, some have two).

8   Inspect the canister(s) for cracks or damage.

9   To check the canister(s) for a clogged filter, blow into the fuel tank pipe with low pressure compressed air and verify that the air flows out the other pipes without resistance.

10   Blow into the purge pipe and verify that air flows without resistance from the other pipes.

11   If the canister fails either of the above tests, renew it.

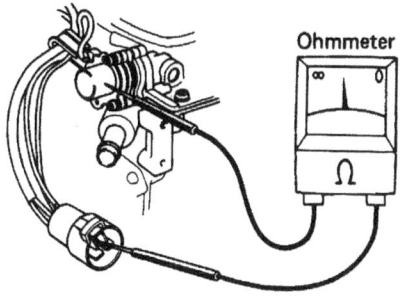

3.19 Unplug the wiring connector to the outer vent control valve and measure the resistance between the positive terminal and the solenoid body - compare your reading to the specified resistance and renew the valve if it's out of specification

12   To clean the filter, blow low pressure compressed air into each pipe while closing off the other canister pipes. No activated charcoal should come out. If it does, renew the canister. **Caution:** *Do not attempt to wash the canister.*

Fuel filler cap and check valves

13   Checking the canister and lines is a routine maintenance procedure. Refer to Chapter 1 for details.
14   To check the filler cap and check valve, remove the cap and detach the retainer (it is held in place with screws). The retainer is not removable on newer caps.
15   Look for a damaged or deformed gasket and make sure that the check valve is not stuck open. If the valve or gasket is not in good condition, renew the cap.

Outer vent control valve

16   Disconnect the outer vent hose from the carburettor.
17   Blow air into the outer vent pipe **(see illustration)** and see if the outer vent control valve is open.
18   Start the engine and, with the engine idling, blow air into the outer vent pipe again. The outer vent control valve should now be closed.

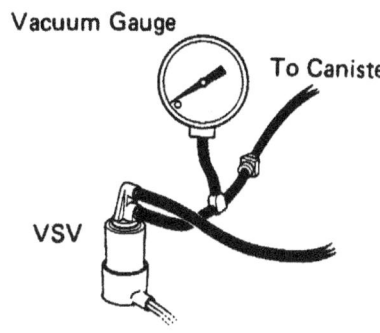

3.24 To check the speed sensor-to-VSV circuit, hook up a vacuum gauge to the hose between the VSV and the canister with a T-fitting and, with the engine warmed up and running, verify that the vacuum is zero at low speed (under 11 km/h) - then verify that there is manifold vacuum above 20 km/h

19   Unplug the wiring connector and, using an ohmmeter, measure the resistance between the positive terminal and the solenoid body **(see illustration)**. Make sure it is within specifications. If a problem is found, renew the outer vent control valve.

Thermo switch (1)

20   Make sure that the engine is cool (under 43-degrees C).
21   Using an ohmmeter, check for continuity between the switch terminal and the switch body.
22   Start the engine and warm it up to operating temperature (55-degrees C).
23   Make sure there is no continuity. If a problem is found, renew the thermo switch.

Speed sensor

24   Using a T-fitting, connect a vacuum gauge to the hose between the VSV and canister **(see illustration)**.
25   Place the connected vacuum gauge in the driver's compartment.
26   Warm up the engine to operating temperature.
27   Check that the vacuum gauge reads

zero at low driving speed (below 11 km/h).
28   Check that the vacuum gauge indicates inlet manifold vacuum at middle and high speed driving (above 20 km/h).
29   Disconnect the vacuum gauge and reconnect the hose.

Component renewal

Canister(s), lines, hoses, fuel filler cap gasket

30   Renewal of the canister(s), lines, hoses and fuel filler cap gasket is straightforward. Be sure to label all hoses and lines to ensure proper reassembly.

Thermo switch

Warning: *Wait until the engine is completely cool before starting this procedure.*
31   Drain sufficient coolant from the radiator (see Chapter 1) to drain the inlet manifold, then disconnect the wires from the switch. Unscrew the old switch and renew it. Be sure to use thread sealant or Teflon tape to seal the threads. Reconnect the wires and refill the radiator.

Speed sensor

32   The speed sensor is an integral part of the speedometer assembly; if the sensor is inoperative, the speedometer must be renewed (see Chapter 12).

VSV, outer vent control valve, jet and VCV

33   Renewal of these components is accomplished by disconnecting the hoses and/or wires from the faulty components and reconnecting them to the new ones. Remove and fit one wire or hose at a time to avoid mixing them up.

---

4   Throttle Positioner (TP) system

Refer to illustration 4.1

General description

1   To reduce HC and CO emissions, this system **(see illustrations)** opens the throttle valve slightly more when decelerating than at idle. This causes the air-fuel mixture to burn more completely. This system is used on some 1979 through 1981 models only.
2   The system consists of a throttle positioner, a VSV and connecting hoses. It operates in conjunction with the vehicle's speed sensor.
3   With the vehicle at speeds above 26 km/h, inlet manifold vacuum acts on the TP diaphragm and the TP is set. The throttle valve is in the medium or high speed position. Upon deceleration of the vehicle above 11 km/h, the throttle valve is held in a position that is slightly more open than at idle. Upon deceleration below 11 km/h, atmospheric pressure acts on the TP diaphragm to release the TP and the throttle valve is returned to the idle position.

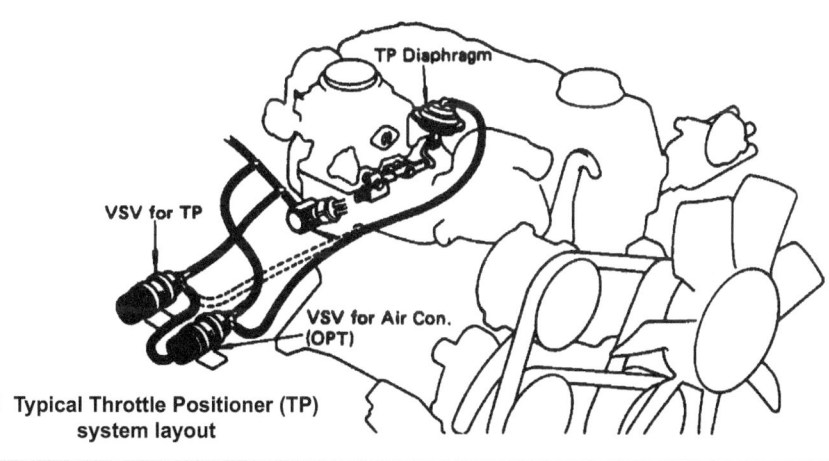

4.1 Typical Throttle Positioner (TP) system layout

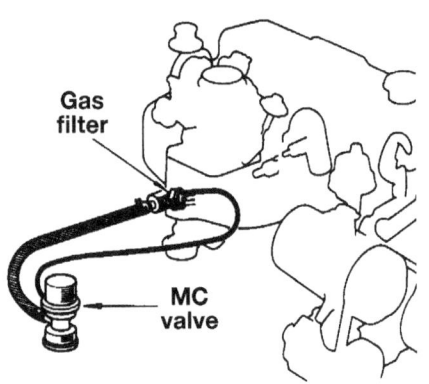

5.2a A typical Mixture Control (MC) system layout (early models)

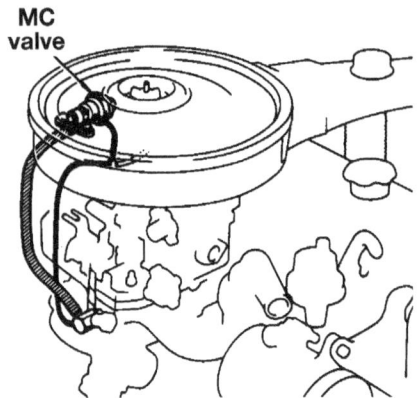

5.2b A typical Mixture Control (MC) system layout (later models)

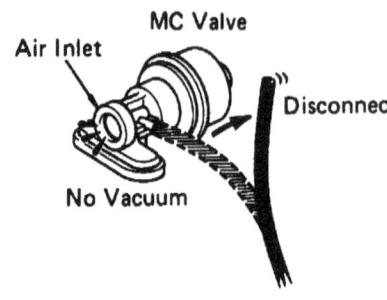

5.6 To check the MC valve, start the engine, detach the vacuum hose from the valve, place your finger over the air inlet and verify that there is no vacuum

Check

4   Have the engine running at idle speed, then disconnect the vacuum hose from the throttle positioner diaphragm. Increase the engine speed, then release the accelerator pedal.

5   The throttle positioner adjusting screw should be hard against the throttle valve lever, boosting the idle speed higher than normal.

6   Immediately connect the vacuum capsule directly to the inlet manifold, which should have the effect of releasing the throttle positioner screw and allow the engine to return to normal idle speed. If this does not happen, check for a faulty linkage. If the linkage is good, the vacuum unit is probably at fault.

7   With the engine at normal operating temperature and the vacuum hose disconnected from the throttle positioner vacuum unit, accelerate the engine, then release the accelerator pedal. The engine speed should be between 1300 and 1500 rpm on models with a manual transmission, and between 950 and 1150 rpm on models with an automatic transmission. Turn the positioner adjusting screw as necessary, then reconnect the vacuum hose.

Component renewal

Throttle positioner

8   Disconnect the hose and remove the mounting screws which hold the faulty TP in place. Fit the new TP, tighten the screws and reconnect the hose.

VSV and speed sensor

9   See Section 3.

---

5   Mixture Control (MC) system

Refer to illustrations 5.2a, 5.2b and 5.6

General description

1   To reduce HC and CO emissions, this system allows fresh air to enter the inlet manifold on sudden deceleration. MC systems are incorporated on 1980 and later carburetted,

manual transmission equipped vehicles.

2   The system consists of a mixture control valve and its connecting hoses **(see illustrations)**.

3   At constant rpm, the MC valve is closed and no air flows through it. Upon sudden deceleration, high vacuum acts on chamber B of the valve, forcing it open and allowing fresh air to be routed through the valve into the inlet manifold. This allows the fuel/air mixture to burn completely. After a few seconds, vacuum in both chambers of the MC valve equalises through a balancing port and the valve is closed.

Check

4   Start the engine.

5   Disconnect the vacuum hose from the MC valve.

6   Place your fingers over the air inlet of the MC valve and check that no vacuum is felt **(see illustration)**.

7   Reconnect the vacuum hose and check that vacuum is felt momentarily at the outlet. **Note:** *At this time, the engine will idle roughly or die, but this is normal.*

8   If any problem is encountered, renew the MC valve.

Component renewal

9   Disconnect the attached hoses, renew the faulty MC valve and refit the hoses.

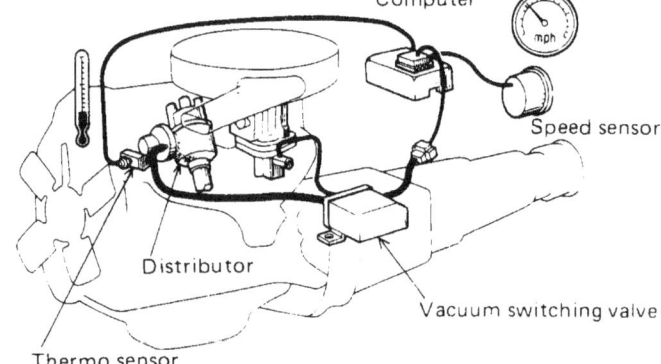

6.1 A typical Spark Control (SC) system layout

---

6   Spark Control (SC) system

Refer to illustration 6.1

General description

1   The spark control system **(see illustration)** is designed to reduce HC and NOx emissions by advancing the ignition timing only when the engine is cold.

2   The SC system includes a distributor mounted vacuum unit, a thermo sensor, a speed sensor, a vacuum switching valve and a computer, and the associated wires and hoses connecting the components.

3   Depending on the engine coolant temperature, altitude and the position of the throttle, vacuum is applied to either one or both sides of the diaphragms in the distributor vacuum unit and the ignition timing is changed to reduce emissions and improve cold engine driveability.

Check

4   With the engine running at normal operating temperature, disconnect the wire from the thermo sensor several times. You should be able to feel the vacuum switching valve operate as this is done.

5   If the valve does not actuate, disconnect the wire from the thermo sensor and insert

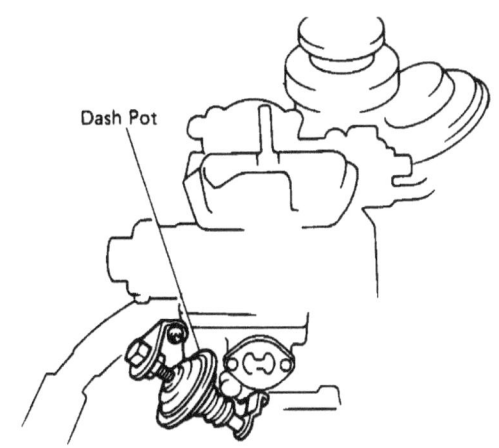

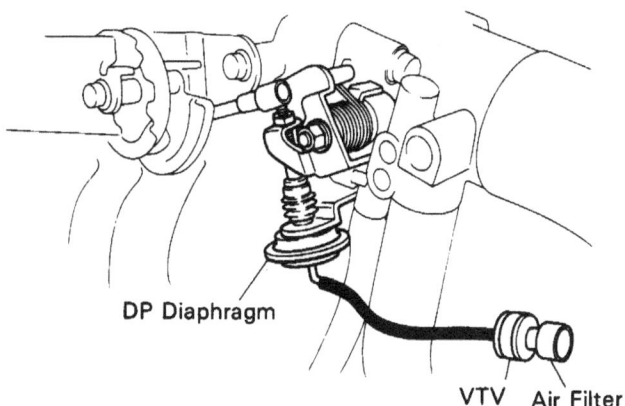

7.1a Dashpot location on a carburetted engine (typical)   7.1b Dashpot location on an EFI-equipped engine (typical)

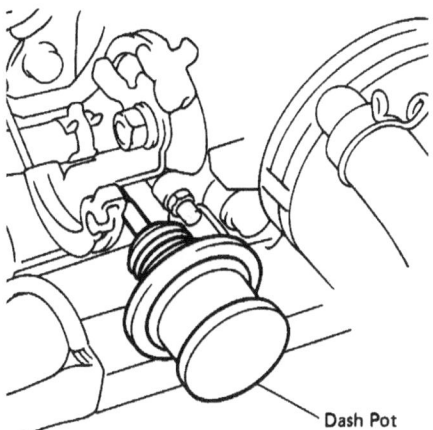

7.1c Dashpot location on a V6 (typical)

the test light probe in the vacuum switching valve electrical connector. Withdraw and insert the test light several times and feel if the vacuum switching valve actuates and the test light lights up. If neither happens, renew the switching valve.

6   Turn off the engine and disconnect the wire from the thermo sensor. Use an ohmmeter to check the resistance of the thermo

7.4a To check the DP setting speed on a carburetted engine, open the throttle valve until the throttle lever arm is no longer touching the dashpot plunger, then release the throttle valve, note the DP setting speed and compare it to the specified DP setting speed

sensor - it should be about 2000 ohms (with the coolant temperature at 81-degrees C). If outside the specified resistance, renew the thermo sensor. **Warning:** *The engine must be completely cool before renewing the sensor.* If the vacuum switching valve still doesn't operate, the computer (mounted under the instrument panel) is probably at fault.

Component renewal

Vacuum advance unit

7   Remove the distributor cap, remove the advance unit mounting screws and detach the pullrod from the breaker plate. Refitting is the reverse of removal.

Thermo sensor

Warning: *The engine must be completely cool before starting this procedure.*
8   Drain the coolant from the engine block (see Chapter 1), remove the vacuum hoses from the sensor, then remove the sensor and renew it. Refitting is the reverse of the removal procedures.

Note: *Be sure to apply liquid sealer to the threads of the new sensor before fitting it.*

7   Dashpot (DP) system

Refer to illustrations 7.1a, 7.1b, 7.1c, 7.4a, 7.4b, 7.4c, 7.4d, 7.6a, 7.6b and 7.6c

General description

1   The dashpot (DP) system **(see illustrations)**, used on some 1985 through 1987 vehicles with carburetted engines and an automatic transmission, on some 1985 and later EFI-equipped four-cylinder vehicles with a manual transmission and on some V6 powered vehicles, reduces HC and CO emissions by opening the throttle valve slightly more during deceleration than at idle. This causes the air-fuel mixture to burn completely.
2   The three DP systems used on various vehicles differ slightly. All three systems utilise a diaphragm and plunger assembly that dampens the closing rate of the throttle valve. The DP system used on EFI equipped vehicles also

uses an air filter and vacuum transmitting valve (VTV), which are connected to the dashpot by a vacuum hose. The diaphragm and plunger assembly, VTV and air filter are integrated into a single unit on the V6.
3   All three DP systems share the same operation principles:
   a) *When the engine is idling and the throttle valve is in the idle position, the throttle shaft lever arm pushes against the plunger with sufficient force to overcome the pressure of the diaphragm spring and expel the air from the diaphragm housing, pushing the plunger into the housing.*
   b) *During normal driving, the throttle valve is open and the throttle shaft lever arm is not touching the DP plunger, so the plunger is extended by the diaphragm spring.*
   c) *During deceleration, the throttle shaft lever arm pushes against the plunger, but the expulsion of air behind the diaphragm is delayed slightly preventing the plunger from retracting instantly, which slightly delays the throttle valve's return to its normal idle position .*

Check

Dashpot

4   Warm up the engine/ check the idle speed and, if necessary, adjust it.
   a) *If you are checking the DP on a carburetted vehicle with an automatic transmission, open the throttle valve until the throttle lever arm no longer touches the DP plunger* **(see illustration)**.
   b) *If you are checking the DP on an EFI-equipped vehicle with a manual transmission, push on the throttle lever arm, open the throttle valve enough to maintain engine speed at a steady 2500 rpm and pinch the vacuum hose between the DP and the VTV* **(see illustration)**.
   c) *If you are checking the DP on a V6, remove the cap and filter* **(see illustration)** *from the DP, race the engine at 2500 rpm for a few seconds and plug the VTV hole* **(see illustration)**.

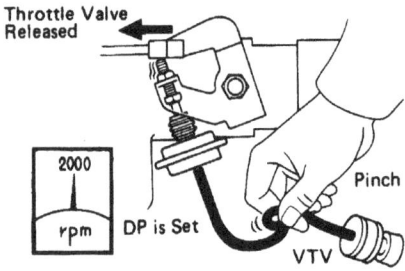

7.4b To check the DP setting speed on a 1985 through 1988 EFI-equipped 4-cylinder engine, maintain the engine speed at 2500 rpm, pinch the vacuum hose between the DP and the VTV, release the throttle valve, note the DP setting speed and compare it to the specified DP setting speed

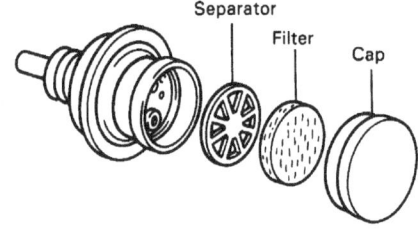

7.4c To check the DP setting speed on a V6 or a 1989 and later EFI-equipped 4-cylinder, remove the cap, filter and separator from the DP . . .

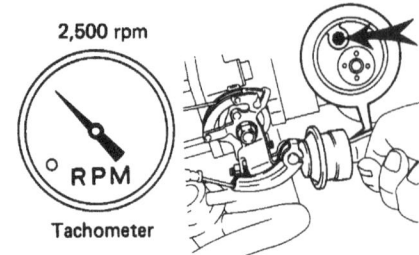

7.4d . . . race the engine at 2500 rpm for a few seconds, the VTV hole, release the throttle valve, note the DP setting speed and compare it to the specified DP setting speed

5   Release the throttle valve, note the DP "setting speed" (the rpm at which the throttle lever arm touches the DP plunger) and compare it to the specified DP setting speed.

6   If the observed rpm is not as specified:

a) *On a carburetted vehicle, unlock the lock nut on the DP diaphragm housing and adjust the setting speed by turning the housing* (**see illustration**).

b) *On an EFI-equipped vehicle or a V6, unlock the lock nut on the DP diaphragm housing and adjust the setting speed by turning the DP adjusting screw with an Allen wrench* (**see illustrations**).

VTV (EFI-equipped four-cylinder engines and V6 only)

7   Set the DP speed using the procedure outlined above.

8   Release the pinched hose and verify that the engine returns to idle speed in about one second.

9   If the VTV performs as specified, the DP system is okay. If it doesn't, disassemble and inspect it.

10   Check the filter for contamination or damage. Using compressed air, clean the filter.

11   Check the VTV by blowing air into each side. It should flow without resistance in one direction and with difficulty from the opposite.

12   If the VTV doesn't perform as specified, renew it.

7.6a If the DP setting speed needs to be readjusted on a carburetted vehicle, loosen the locknut and turn the DP diaphragm housing until the speed is correct, then tighten the locknut

8   Exhaust Gas Recirculation (EGR) system

Refer to illustrations 8.1a, 8.1b, 8.1c and 8.6

General description

Note: *On all 1993 and later models, the designation for the BVSV (Bimetal Vacuum Switching Valve) was changed to TVV (Thermal Vacuum Valve). The valve operates the same within the EGR system, only the name has been changed.*

1   To reduce NOx emissions, part of the exhaust gases are recirculated through the EGR valve into the inlet manifold to lower the

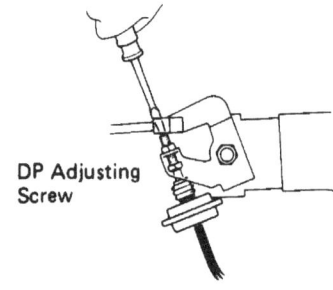

7.6b If the DP setting speed needs to be adjusted on an EFI-equipped vehicle, loosen the locknut and, using a screwdriver (earlier model) or an Allen wrench (later model), adjust the DP adjusting screw until the speed is correct, then tighten the locknut

maximum combustion temperature (**see illustrations**).

2   The main component of the system is the EGR valve. It operates in conjunction with a wide variety of devices, such as the EGR vacuum modulator, the BVSV, the VSV(s) and the VTV, although not all components are incorporated on all models.

3   At low engine temperatures, the VSV or BVSV and EGR valves are shut and the exhaust gas is not being recirculated. At higher engine temperatures, the VSV or BVSV opens. When the throttle valve is pivoted open enough to expose the EGR port, and the pressure in the EGR valve is low, the pressure increases, closing the modulator and causing the EGR valve to open. The pressure then drops, reopening the modulator and closing the EGR valve, cutting off exhaust gas recirculation. The VSV(s) and VTV, where incorporated, serve the EGR system in various capacities, depending on coolant temperature, exhaust gas pressure, fuel flow pressure and ignition switch position.

Check

4   If the engine runs roughly at idle, hesitates under acceleration, accelerates poorly or gets poor fuel economy, the EGR system is probably not shutting off.

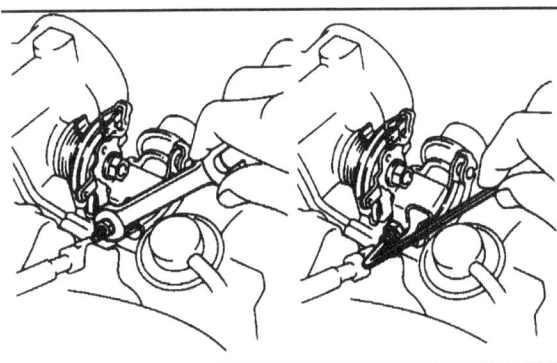

7.6c If the DP setting speed needs to be adjusted on a V6 or a 1989 and later EFI-equipped 4-cylinder, loosen the locknut (left) and, using an Allen wrench, turn the DP adjusting screw until the speed is correct (right), then tighten the locknut

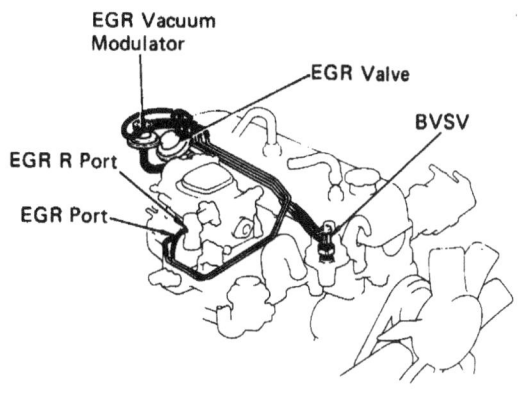

8.1a EGR system layout - typical for 4-cylinder models with carburettor

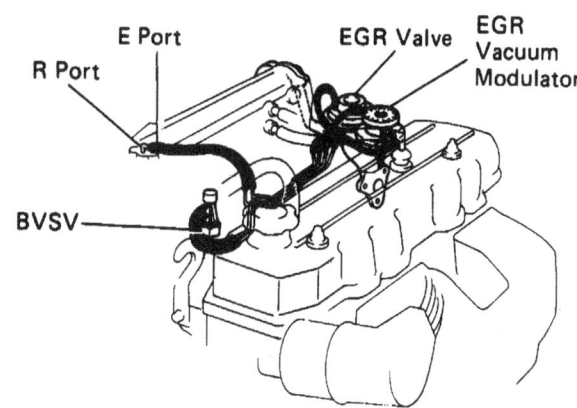

8.1b EGR system layout - typical for 4-cylinder models with EFI

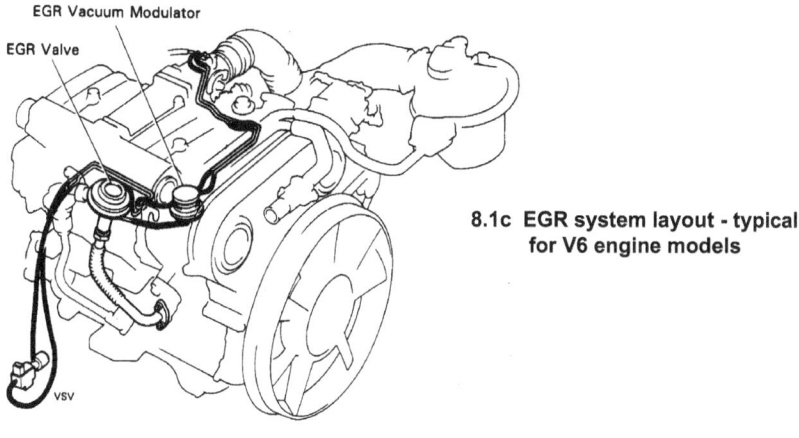

8.1c EGR system layout - typical for V6 engine models

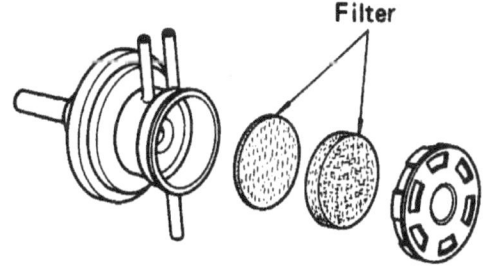

8.6 A typical EGR vacuum modulator and filter assembly

unburned hydrocarbons and carbon monoxide before they are allowed to exit the exhaust system.

2   This system **(see illustration)** is composed of various configurations of any of the following devices: an air pump, check valve(s), thermo switch(es), thermo sensor(s), an oxygen sensor, restrictor jets, plus ABV, ACV, ASV, EACV, TVSV, VCS, VCV, VSV AND VTV components . Note that not all components are included on every system. To determine which components are employed on the AI system on your vehicle, refer to the VECI label (see Section 1).

3   The check valve mounted on the manifold prevents the reverse flow of exhaust gases into the system. The other components control the injection of the air into the ports based on catalytic converter temperatures and engine load.

Check

4   Visually check the hoses, tubes and connections for cracks, loose fittings and separated parts.
5   Check the drivebelt condition and tension (refer to Chapter 1 for this procedure).

Air pump, ABV, ACV, ASV and EACV

6   These components require special tools and/or checking procedures for checking and servicing. It is therefore recommended that you have these components inspected by your Toyota dealer.

Check valves

7   Inspect the check valve that is located between the ASV and the manifold by disconnecting the hose from the inlet side and remove the ACV, ASV or EACV from the manifold. Next, blow into the check valve from the manifold side and verify that air does not flow through the check valve, then reverse the check valve and verify that air does flow through the valve when blowing into the inlet side.
8   If a problem is found, renew the check valve.

5   Before checking the EGR valve, always inspect the condition of all vacuum hoses in the system. Make sure they're all properly attached and are in good condition. If any of the hoses are cracked or otherwise damaged, renew them.
6   Also inspect the EGR vacuum modulator filter **(see illustration)** for contamination or damage. If it's dirty, clean it with compressed air.
7   Disconnect the vacuum hose from the EGR valve and connect a vacuum pump to it.
8   Apply vacuum directly to the EGR valve. The engine should run roughly or die. If it doesn't, renew the EGR valve.

Component renewal

EGR valve

9   Disconnect the vacuum hose, remove the retaining bolts and the valve, renew the faulty valve, fit the bolts and reconnect the vacuum hoses.

9   Air injection (AI) system

Refer to illustration 9.2

General description

1   This system supplies air under pressure to the exhaust port to promote combustion of

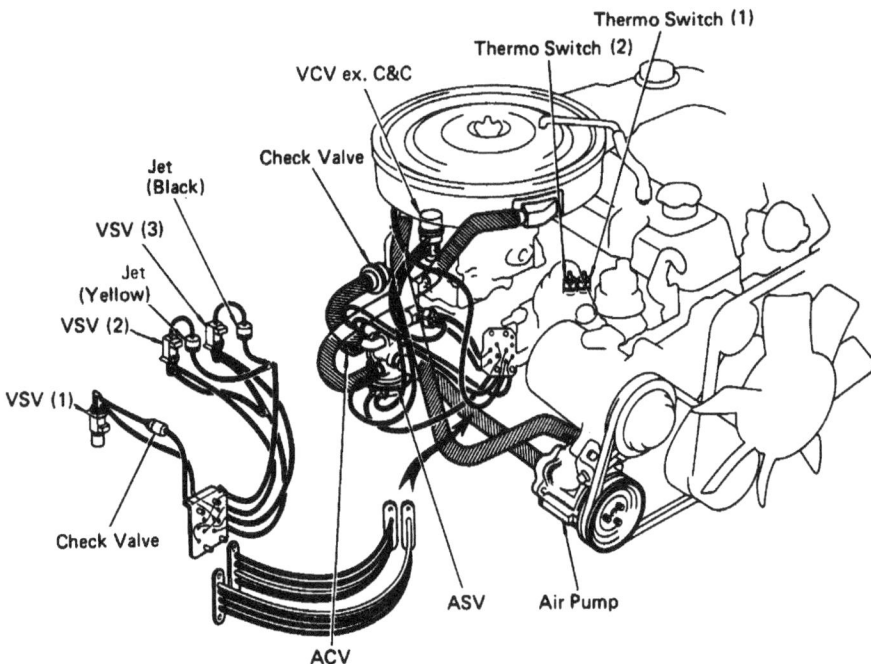

9.2 Typical Air Injection (AI) system layout

9   Inspect the check valve that is found between the VSV and the manifold by disconnecting the hoses from both ends. Next blow air into the white pipe of the valve and verify that air flows through the valve. Reverse the valve and verify that air does not flow through the valve when blowing air into it from the black side.
10   If a problem is found, renew the check valve.

Component renewal

Manifold check valve
11   Renew the valve by disconnecting the hose and unscrewing the check valve, then reverse the procedure, fitting the new part.
Note: *It's a good idea to spray some penetrating oil on the threads of the valve before attempting removal.*

In-line check valve
12   Renew these parts by disconnecting the hoses and/or wires from the faulty part, then reverse the procedure, fitting the new part.

10   Air Suction (AS) system

Refer to illustrations 10.1a, 10.1b, 10.1c and 10.13

General description
1   This system (see illustrations) is used on many Toyota pick-ups to reduce HC and CO emissions.
2   AS systems employ various combinations of an air suction valve, an ASV, a VSV, a check valve, a VCV, a thermo switch, a reed valve and other emissions devices.
3   The AS system draws air into the exhaust manifold to accelerate oxidation, using vacuum generated by the exhaust pulsation in the exhaust manifold.

Check

Early models
4   Visually check the hoses and tubes for cracks, kinks, damage or loose connections.
5   Disconnect the air suction hose from the air cleaner.
6   Verify that the engine is cold.
7   Start the engine and check that a bubbling noise is not heard from the air suction hose at idle.
8   Let the engine warm up to normal operating temperature and check that a bubbling noise is heard from the air suction hose at idle.
9   Disconnect the vacuum hose between the check valve and vacuum pipe bracket at the check valve side and plug the hose end.
10   Check that a bubbling noise is heard from the air suction hose at idle with the engine at normal operating temperature.
11   Reconnect the vacuum hose.
12   With the engine at normal operating temperature, race the engine and quickly close the throttle valve, checking that the bubbling noise at the air suction hose stops momentarily.
13   With the engine idling, connect a wire to

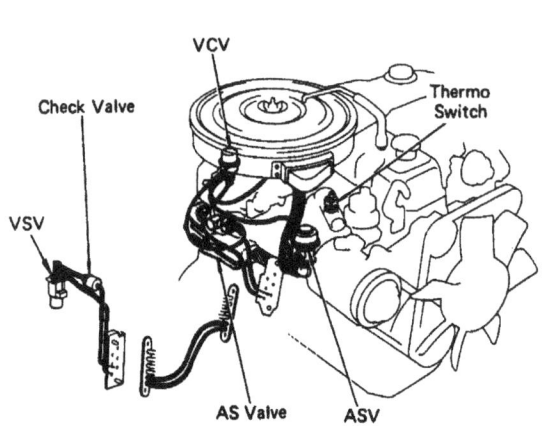

10.1a Typical Air Suction (AS) system layout
(models with remotely mounted air cleaner similar)

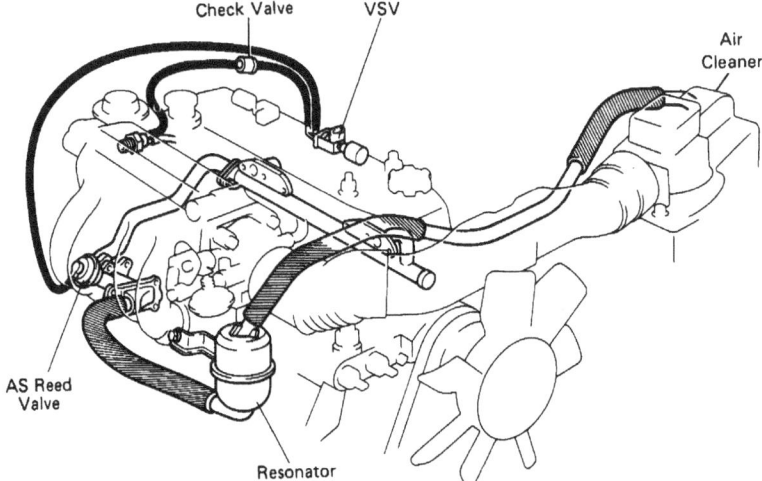

10.1b Typical Air Suction (AS) system layout - four-cylinder EFI vehicles

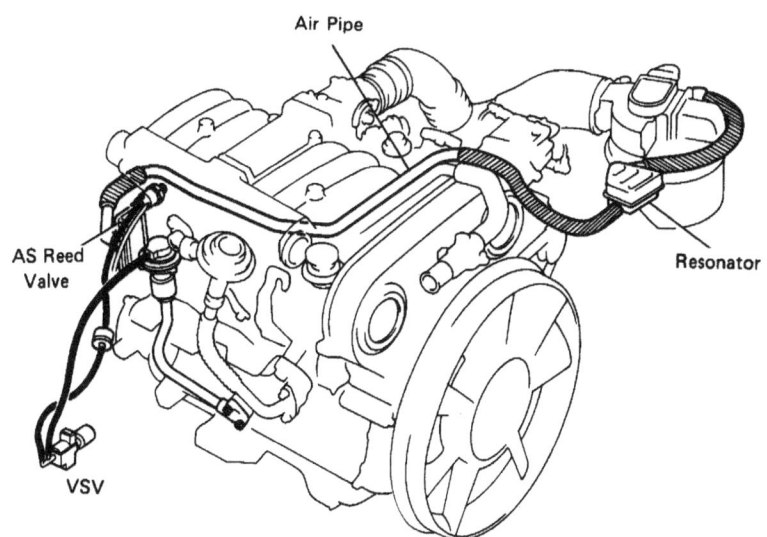

10.1c Typical Air Suction (AS) system layout - V6 vehicles

Air Pipe

AS Reed Valve

VSV

Resonator

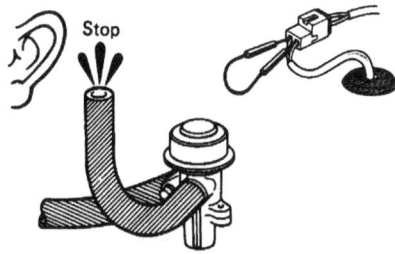

Stop

10.13 Checking the oxidation catalyst (OC) thermo sensor during the general check of the AS system

both terminals of the Oxidation Catalyst (OC) thermo sensor (**see illustration**).

14   Check that the bubbling noise at the air suction hose stops.

15   Disconnect the wire from the terminals.

16   If no problem has been found thus far, the AS system is okay. If any problem is encountered, take the vehicle to a dealer.

1988 and later EFI-equipped models

37   Visually inspect the hoses and tubes for cracks, kinks, damage or loose connections.

38   With the engine running but the coolant still cold (below 30-degrees C), disconnect the AS system hose from the air cleaner housing and verify that there is a bubbling noise coming from the hose.

39   Warm up the engine to above 40-degrees C. With the engine idling, verify that a bubbling noise is not coming from the same hose.

40   Race the engine, then quickly snap the throttle shut. Verify that the bubbling noise stops momentarily.

41   If the AS system performs as described, it's okay. If it doesn't, take the vehicle to a dealer.

V6 models

42   Visually inspect all hoses and tubes for cracks, kinks, damage or loose connections.

43   With the engine running but the coolant still cold (below 35-degrees C), disconnect the AS system hose from the air pipe and verify that there is a bubbling noise coming from the hose.

44   Warm up the engine to above 35-degrees C. With the engine idling, verify that a bubbling noise is not coming from the same hose.

45   Race the engine above 2000 rpm and verify that a bubbling noise is heard from the pipe within 2 to 6 seconds.

46   If the AS system performs as described, it's okay. If it doesn't, take the vehicle to a dealer.

11   Catalytic converter system

General description

1   Two types of catalysts are used to convert outgoing exhaust from the engine into other chemicals. The oxidation catalyst converts hydrocarbons and carbon monoxide to water and carbon dioxide. The 3-way catalyst reduces hydrocarbons, carbon monoxide and oxides of nitrogen emissions to dinitrogen, carbon dioxide and water.

Check

2   Visual inspection of either type of catalyst is the main form of checking it. Any type of dents, damage, loose connections, or cracks can affect the operation of the catalyst. In addition, the heat insulator which is situated between the vehicle body and the catalyst must be in place and not touching the catalytic converter. Serious damage to the vehicle

or the occupants can result if the heat insulator is loose or missing.

3   The 3-way catalyst can be checked by lightly slapping the housing and listening for any loose, rattling noises inside (this method can only be used if the catalyst is cold). If it's hot, place a block of wood against the bottom and tap the block lightly. This is a sign that the beads of catalyst material have come loose and renewal of the converter is necessary.

Component renewal

4   Do not attempt to remove the catalytic converter until the complete exhaust system is cool. Raise the vehicle and support it securely on jackstands. Apply some penetrating oil to the clamp bolts and allow it to soak in. Disconnect the thermo sensor wiring connector (if so equipped) from under the driver's seat. Push the grommet through the floor pan to free the wire.

5   Remove the bolts and the rubber hangers, then separate the converter from the exhaust pipes. Remove the old gaskets if they are stuck to the pipes.

6   If the thermo sensor is being renewed, position the converter with the sensor up and remove the bolts. Withdraw the sensor and remove the gasket. Position a new gasket on the converter and slide the new thermo sensor into place. Tighten the bolts securely.

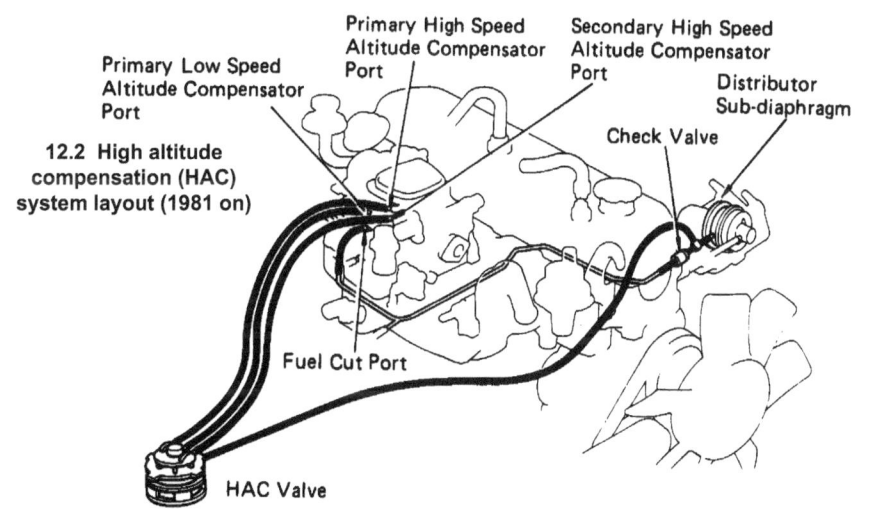

Primary High Speed Altitude Compensator Port

Secondary High Speed Altitude Compensator Port

Primary Low Speed Altitude Compensator Port

Distributor Sub-diaphragm

Check Valve

12.2 High altitude compensation (HAC) system layout (1981 on)

Fuel Cut Port

HAC Valve

7   Refitting of the converter is the reverse of removal. Use new exhaust pipe gaskets and tighten the clamp bolts securely. Renew the rubber hangers if the originals are deteriorated. Reconnect the thermo sensor wires (if so equipped), start the engine and check carefully for exhaust leaks.

12   High Altitude Compensation (HAC) system

Refer to illustrations 12.2, 12.4 and 12.12

General description

1   Starting with some 1980 Toyota Hi-Lux models, HAC systems were incorporated to ensure that the proper air/fuel mixture is supplied by the carburettor at altitudes of 1200 meters and above.
2   The main components of this system include the carburettor altitude compensator ports (primary high and low speed ports in 1980; primary high and low speed ports, a secondary high speed port and a fuel cut port in 1981 through 1988), a HAC valve and a check valve, plus connecting hoses **(see illustration)**.
3   The high altitude compensation is accomplished by two methods: Additional air is supplied to the primary high and low and secondary high speed circuits of the carburettor and the ignition timing is advanced for improved driveabilty above 1200 meters. At lower altitudes, the additional air is cut off and the initial advance occurs only at idle.

Check (1980 vehicles)

HAC valve

4   Above 1200 meters, check that air flows into either of the two ports on top of the HAC valve **(see illustration)** with the engine idling.
5   Below 800 meters, check that air does not flow into either of the two ports on top of the HAC valve with the engine idling.
6   Depending on the atmospheric pressure between 800 meters and 1200 meters, the HAC valve may be either opened or closed. Therefore, attempt to check the valve at either altitude listed in paragraphs 4 and 5.

Carburettor

7   Disconnect the hoses from the pipes on top of the HAC valve.
8   Blow air into each hose and make sure that air flows into the carburettor.

Check valve

9   Disconnect the hoses from the check valve.
10   Blow air into the white pipe and make sure that air flows through the valve.
11   Blow air into the black pipe and make sure that air does not flow through the valve. If a problem is encountered renew the valve.

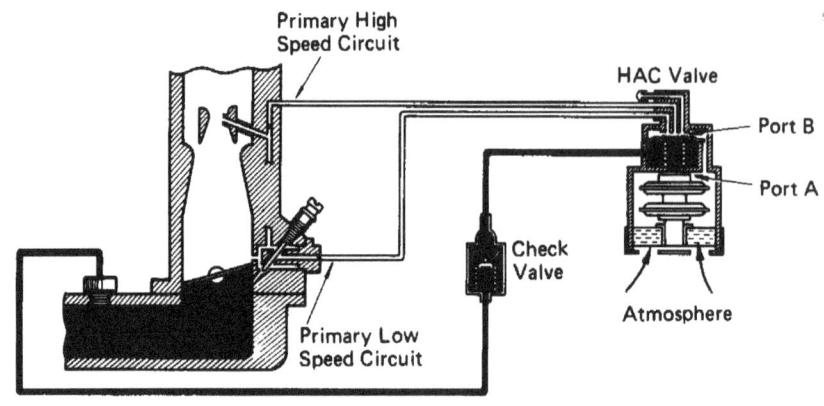

12.4 Details of HAC system layout (1980)

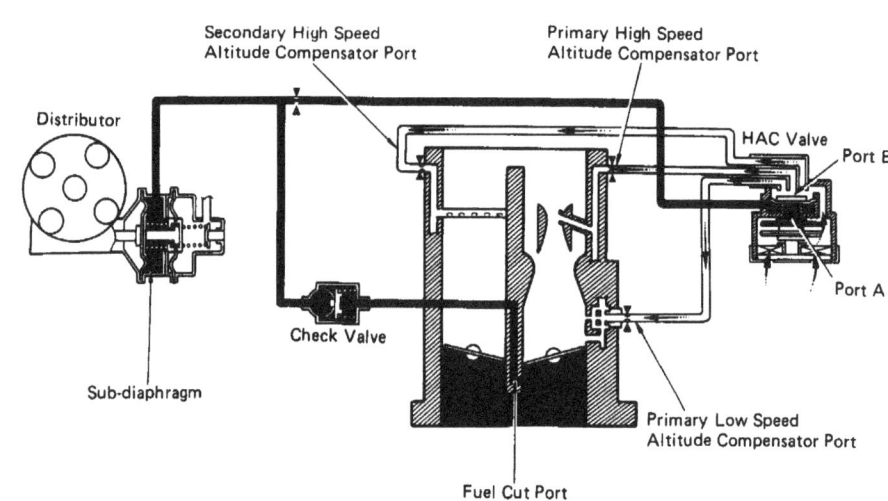

12.12 Details of the HAC system layout (1981 on)

Check (1981 and later vehicles)

12   Determine the position of the HAC valve by blowing into any one of the three ports on top of the valve **(see illustration)**. If the passage is open, the valve is in the high altitude position. If it is closed, the valve is in the low altitude position.
13   If the HAC valve is in the high altitude position, warm up the engine to normal operating temperature.
14   Disconnect the hose from the distributor sub-diaphragm and plug the hose end.
15   Check the ignition timing at idle (see Chapter 1).
16   Reconnect the hose to the sub-diaphragm.
17   With the engine still idling at 950 rpm, verify that the ignition advances slightly (approximately 7-degrees).
18   Disconnect the vacuum hose between the check valve and the vacuum pipe at the vacuum pipe side and plug the pipe end.
19   Check that the ignition timing remains stationary for more than one minute.

20   Stop the engine and reconnect the hose to the vacuum pipe, then go to Step 25.
21   If the HAC valve is in the low altitude position, check the ignition timing and advance as described above in Steps 15 through 17.
22   Disconnect the vacuum hose from the lower port of the HAC valve, plug the hose end and perform the checks below.
23   Disconnect the vacuum hose between the check valve and the vacuum pipe at the vacuum pipe side and plug the pipe end.
24   Check that the ignition timing remains stationary for more than one minute.
25   Stop the engine and reconnect the hoses to their proper locations.
26   Disconnect the three hoses from the pipes on top of the HAC valve.
27   Blow air into each hose and make sure that air flows into the carburettor.
28   Reconnect the hoses to their proper locations.
29   If no problems have been encountered in these tests, the HAC system is okay.

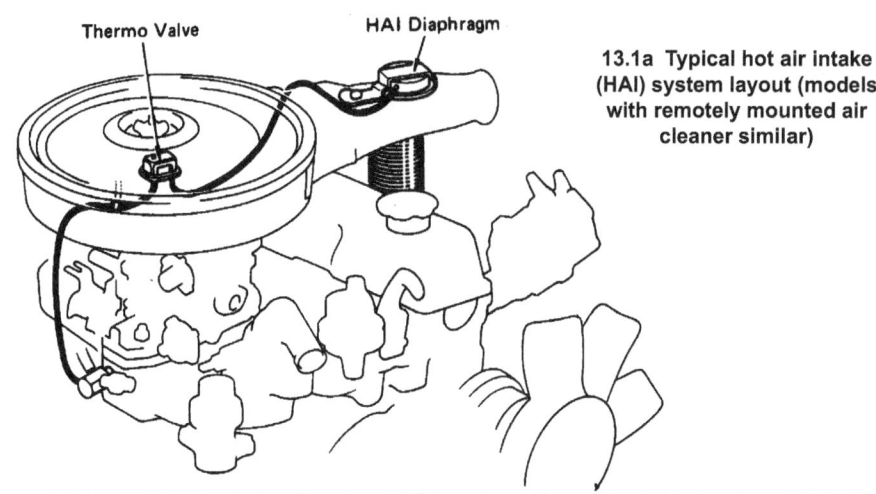

13.1a Typical hot air intake (HAI) system layout (models with remotely mounted air cleaner similar)

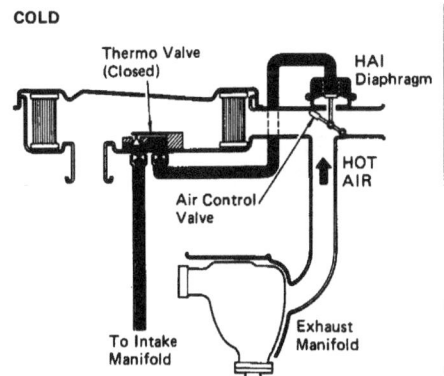
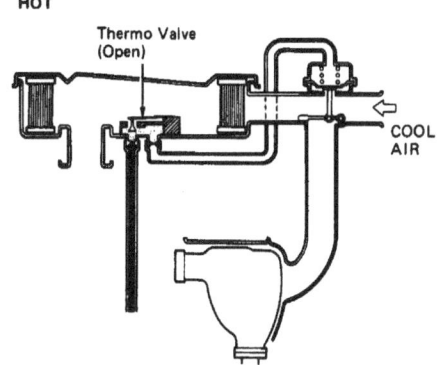

13.1b Details of typical HAI system layout

HAC valve

30   Remove the cover from the bottom of the HAC valve and clean and visually check the filter.

Check valve

31   Disconnect the hoses from the check valve.
32   Check the air flows through the valve from the inlet side.
33   Check that air does not flow through the valve from the outlet side.

Distributor

34   Remove the distributor cap and rotor (see Chapter 5, if necessary).
35   Apply vacuum to the diaphragm and make sure that the vacuum advancer moves in accordance with the vacuum.
36   Refit the rotor and distributor cap.

Component renewal

37   The HAC valve and check valve can be renewed by removing the hoses from the faulty component and renewing it.
38   If problems are encountered with the distributor, see Chapter 5.

13   Hot Air Intake (HAI) system

Refer to illustrations 13.1a and 13.1b

General description

1   This system **(see illustrations)** is designed to improve driveability and prevent carburettor icing in extremely cold weather by directing hot air from around the exhaust manifold to the air cleaner intake.
2   The system is composed of a diaphragm-activated air control valve located in the air cleaner intake, a thermo valve, an exhaust manifold shroud and interconnecting hoses and ducts.
3   When the underbonnet temperature is below 38 degrees on 1979 and 1980 vehicles, or below 30 degrees on later models, the thermo valve allows manifold vacuum to act on the air cleaner diaphragm, which closes the control valve, or baffle, and allows hot air to enter the air cleaner. As temperature rises above 41 degrees on 1979 and 1980 models, or 45 degrees on later models, the thermo valve cuts off the vacuum to the diaphragm and spring pressure opens the air control valve. Intake air is then drawn from under the bonnet, rather than from around the exhaust manifold.

Check

Air control valve

4   Remove the air cleaner cover or the air intake duct (on models with remotely mounted air cleaners).
5   Make sure the underbonnet temperature is below the low temperature listed in paragraph 3.
6   Verify that the air control valve closes the cool air passage with the engine running at idle.
7   Refit the air cleaner cover and warm up the engine until the underbonnet temperature is above the high temperature listed in paragraph 3.
8   Verify that the air control valve opens the cool air passage at idle.

Hoses and connections

9   Visually check the hoses and connections for cracks, leaks or damage.

Component renewal

10   Renewal of all of the component(s) in this system is a simple matter of removing the faulty component and renewing it. Make sure the hoses are correctly fitted and tighten all hose clamps and mounting bolts securely. If a new air control valve is fitted, make sure it moves freely before checking the system operation.

14   Automatic choke system

Refer to illustrations 14.1, 14.2, 14.3, 14.6, 14.9 and 14.10.

General description

1   The automatic choke system **(see illustration)** temporarily supplies a rich fuel/air mixture to the engine by closing the choke valve during cold engine starting. Typical automatic choke systems may include various combinations of any of the following components: a water or electrically heated coil, a choke breaker diaphragm, a choke opener diaphragm, a fast idle cam breaker, a VSV, a TVSV, a BVSV and connecting hoses and linkage, although not all components are employed on every model. The components employed in a specific system are dependent upon year, model and territorial motor vehicle regulations. Your local Toyota dealer can supply you with information on your particular vehicle should you be in doubt as to which components make up your system.
2   The choke breaker **(see illustration)** opens the choke valve slightly when the engine starts, preventing an overly rich mixture and the resulting increase in emissions discharge to the atmosphere.
3   After the engine reaches a pre-determined temperature, the choke opener holds the choke valve open and releases the fast idle cam to the 4th step which lowers the engine speed and prevents an overly rich mixture condition. On some early models, a fast idle cam breaker diaphragm is

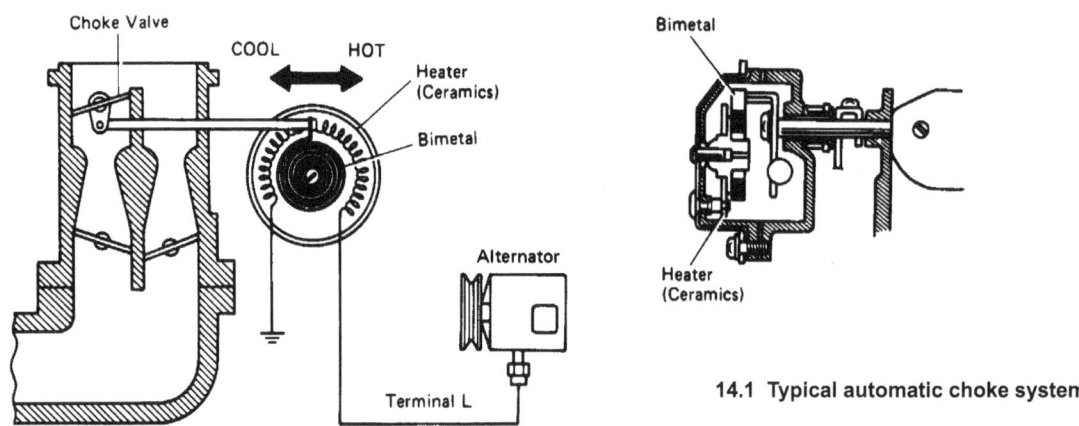

14.1 Typical automatic choke system

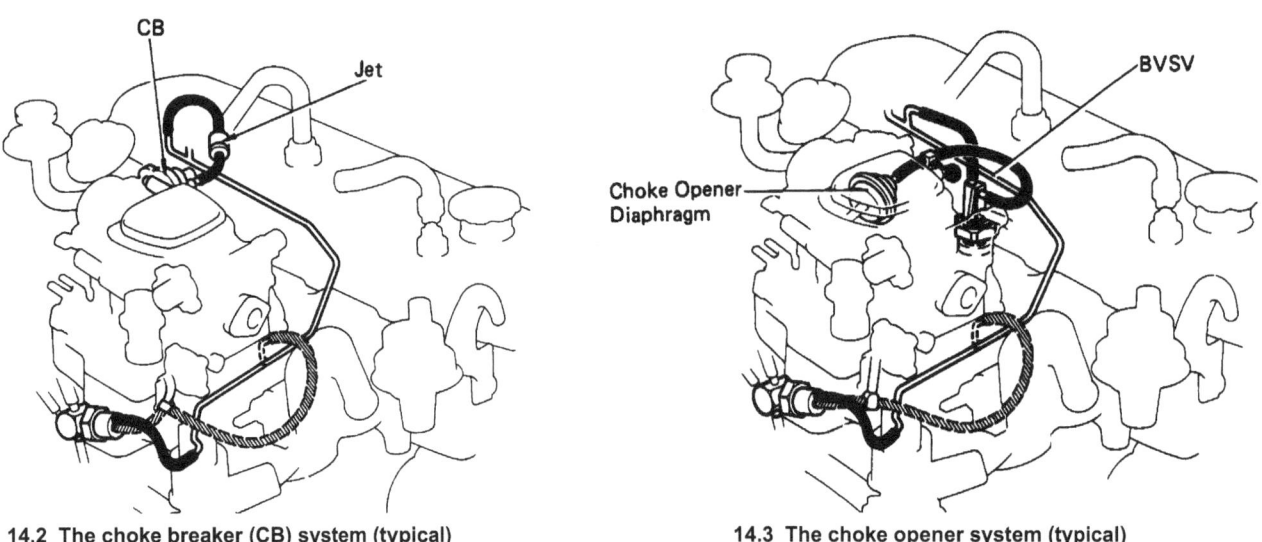

14.2 The choke breaker (CB) system (typical)   **14.3 The choke opener system (typical)**

employed to perform this latter function **(see illustration)**.

Check

Automatic choke system

4   Refer to Chapter 1, for the general carburettor choke check procedures. If the choke is determined to be malfunctioning, check the hoses for cracks, kinks and broken sections and make sure all wiring connections are tight before checking the other system components.

Heater housing (water heated) (1980 models)

5   Look for water leaks. Check the hoses for cracks and damage. Make sure that the middle mark on the thermostatic case is aligned with the mark on the coil housing. If not, correct it by loosening the three screws around the circumference of the housing, aligning the marks and re-tightening the screws. **Caution:** *Do not loosen the bolt at the centre of the case, as this will allow coolant to leak out.*

Heater housing (electrically heated) (1981 and later models)

6   Unplug the wiring connector and, using an ohmmeter, measure the resistance of the connector terminal **(see illustration)** and compare your reading to the resistance value listed in this Chapter's Specifications.

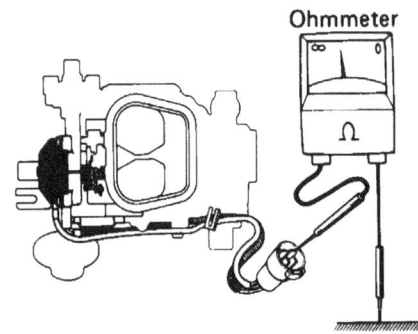

14.6 Measuring the resistance of an electrically heated choke housing

7   Start the engine. Shortly after starting it, note whether the choke is starting to open, then touch the choke housing and verify that it is heating up.

Choke breaker

8   While holding the throttle slightly open, push the choke valve closed and hold it closed as you release the throttle valve.
9   On 1981 and later models, disconnect the vacuum hose between the jet and the vacuum pipe at the jet side. then apply vacuum to the jet and verify that the choke valve opens slightly **(see illustration)**.

Choke opener

10   Check the thermostatic vacuum switching valve (TVSV) (1981 and 1982) or bimetal vacuum switching valve (BVSV) (1983 on) with a cold engine:

a) *The coolant temperature must be below 60-degrees C.*
b) *Detach the vacuum hose from the choke opener diaphragm* **(see illustration)**.
c) *Step down on the accelerator pedal and release it, then start the engine.*

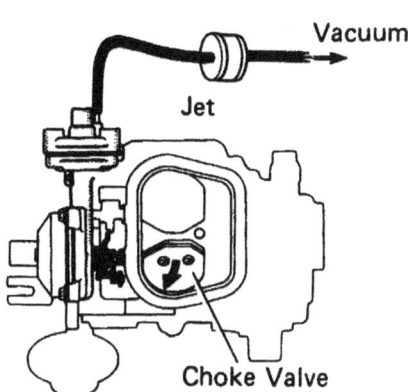

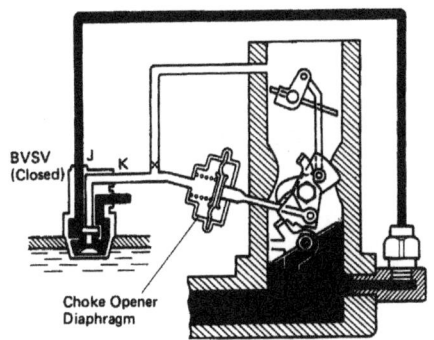

14.10 Choke opener system details

14.9 To check choke breaker operation, hold the throttle open slightly, push the choke valve closed, hold it closed and release the throttle valve, then disconnect the vacuum hose from the jet, apply vacuum to the jet port and note whether the choke valve opens slightly

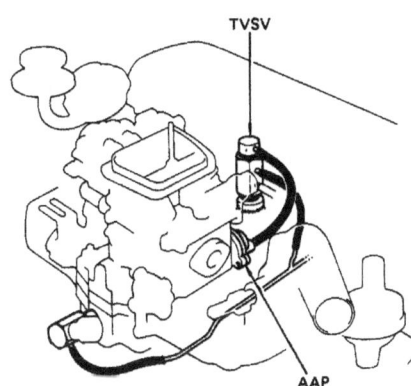

15.1 Auxiliary Accelerator Pump (AAP) system (typical)

d)   *Reattach the vacuum hose and verify that the choke linkage does not move.*

11   Check the TVSV or BVSV with a warm engine:

a)   *Warm up the engine to normal operating temperature.*
b)   *Detach the vacuum hose from the choke opener diaphragm.*
c)   *Set the fast idle cam by holding the throttle slightly open, pushing the choke valve closed and holding it closed as you release the throttle valve.*
d)   *Start the engine but do not touch the accelerator pedal.*
e)   *Reattach the vacuum hose and verify that the choke linkage moves and that the fast idle cam is released to the 4th step.*

12   If the choke opener does not perform as described, proceed to the steps below.
13   Apply vacuum to the diaphragm and verify that the linkage moves. If it doesn't, renew the diaphragm.

BVSV

14   Be sure that the coolant temperature is below 60-degrees C (1981 through 1983) or 55 degrees C (1984 on).
15   Remove the hoses from the BVSV pipes.
16   Blow air into pipe J and verify that air comes out of pipe L.
17   Warm up the engine to above 75-degrees C.
18   Blow air into pipe J and verify that air comes out of pipe K.
19   If any problem is encountered renew the BVSV.

Component renewal

20   Because renewal of the heater housing, choke breaker, choke opener and/or fast idle cam breaker requires partial disassembly of the carburettor, refer to the instructions included with the carburettor rebuild kit for your carburettor. Be sure to make any adjustments required after the components are renewed.
21   To renew the VSV or TVSV, see Section 3.
22   To renew the BVSV, remove the hoses from the pipes, then use a wrench to remove the BVSV from the inlet manifold. Refitting is the reverse of the removal procedure.

15   Auxiliary Accelerator Pump (AAP) system

Refer to illustrations 15.1 and 15.7

General description

1   The AAP system **(see illustrations)** is designed to improve cold engine acceleration performance.
2   The system is composed of an auxiliary accelerator pump, a TVSV on all models through 1982, renewed with a BVSV in 1983, and various vacuum hoses.
3   A typical air/fuel mixture is very lean. When accelerating with a cold engine, the main accelerator pump capacity is insufficient to provide good acceleration. At constant RPM the diaphragm in the AAP is pulled by vacuum and fuel is drawn into the AAP chamber. Upon acceleration, the

diaphragm is returned by spring pressure and the stored fuel in the AAP chamber is forced into the acceleration nozzle, enriching the air/fuel mixture. Once the engine is sufficiently warmed up, The AAP system becomes inoperative.

Check

General

4   Be sure that the coolant temperature is below 50-degrees C (1979 and 1980), 60-degrees C (1981 through 1983) or 55-degrees C (1984 on).
5   Remove the air cleaner cover.
6   Start the engine.
7   Pinch the AAP hose **(see illustration)** and stop the engine.
8   Release the hose and verify that petrol spurts from the accelerator nozzle.
9   Warm up the engine to normal operating temperature.
10   Pinch the hose and stop the engine.
11   Verify that petrol does not spurt from the accelerator nozzle.
12   If no problem is encountered in the above check, the AAP system is okay, otherwise inspect the components as follows.

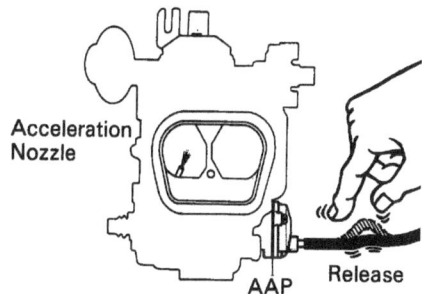

15.7 To check the AAP system, remove the air cleaner, start the engine and, with the coolant temperature below the prescribed level, pinch the AAP hose and stop the engine, then release the hose and verify that petrol spurts from the accelerator nozzle - then warm the engine up to operating temperature, pinch the hose, stop the engine and verify that petrol does not spurt from the accelerator nozzle

AAP diaphragm

13 Start the engine.

14 Disconnect the vacuum hose from the AAP.

15 Apply and release vacuum to the diaphragm with the engine idling, observing that the engine rpm changes when the vacuum is released.

16 Reconnect the AAP hose.

17 If a problem is encountered, renew the diaphragm.

Component renewal

Warning: *Petrol is extremely flammable, so take extra precautions when you work on any part of the fuel system. Don't smoke or allow open flames or bare light bulbs near the work area, and don't work in a garage where a natural gas-type appliance (such as a water heater or a clothes dryer) with a pilot light is present. Since petrol is carcinogenic, wear latex gloves when there's a possibility of being exposed to fuel, and, if you spill any fuel on your skin, rinse it off immediately with soap and water. Mop up any spills immediately and do not store fuel-soaked rags where they could ignite. When you perform any kind of work on the fuel system, wear safety glasses and have a Class B type fire extinguisher on hand.*

18 To renew the AAP diaphragm, remove the hoses from the pipes, unscrew the AAP housing and renew the diaphragm. Reassembly is the reverse of the disassembly procedure.

19 To renew the TVSV or BVSV, see Section 3 or Section 14, as applicable.

---

16 Deceleration fuel cut system

Refer to illustrations 16.1 and 16.7

General description

1 This system **(see illustration)** serves to prevent overheating and after-burning in the exhaust system.

2 The system is made up of a fuel cut solenoid valve, a vacuum switch and attaching vacuum hose.

3 The system cuts off part of the fuel in the slow circuit of the carburettor at low rpm under high and low vacuum conditions and at high rpm under low vacuum conditions. At high rpm under high vacuum conditions, the system is off and the slow circuit in the carburettor is closed.

Check

General

4 For vehicles with HAC systems, disconnect the vacuum hoses from the lower port of the HAC valve and plug the hose end (refer to Section 12).

5 Connect a tachometer to the engine according to the instructions supplied by the tachometer manufacturer.

6 Start the engine and observe that it runs normally.

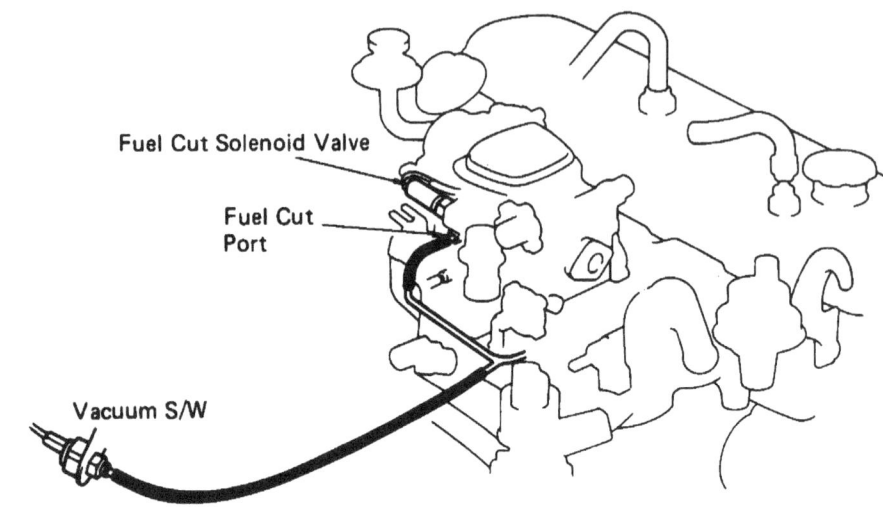

16.1 A typical deceleration fuel cut system layout (all years)

7 Pinch off the hose to the vacuum switch **(see illustration)**.

8 Gradually increase the engine speed and observe that the engine misfires slightly between 1800 and 3000 rpm. **Caution:** *Perform this check quickly to avoid overheating the catalytic converter.*

9 Release the pinched hose.

10 Gradually increase the rpm to 3000 again and observe that the engine operation returns to normal.

11 With the engine idling, unplug the wiring connector to the solenoid valve and confirm that the engine idles roughly or dies.

Note: *Perform this check quickly to avoid overheating the catalytic converter.*

12 Stop the engine and reconnect the wiring.

13 Remove the tachometer.

14 If no problem was encountered in the checks above, the system is okay, otherwise inspect the components as follows.

Fuel cut solenoid valve

15 Disconnect the connector and remove the fuel cut solenoid valve.

16 Using jumper wires, connect battery volt-

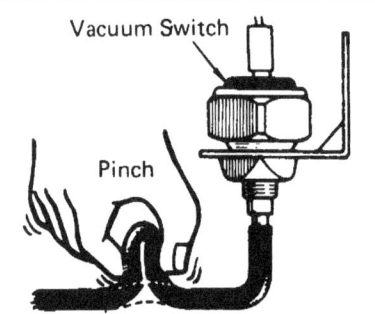

16.7 Checking the decel fuel cut system

age to the two terminals inside the connector that are attached to the wires that lead to the solenoid valve **(see illustration)**.

17 Confirm that you can feel a click from the solenoid when the battery is connected and disconnected.

18 Check the O-ring for damage.

19 Refit the valve and hook up the wiring connector.

20 If a problem was encountered, renew the solenoid valve or O-ring.

Vacuum switch

21 Using an ohmmeter, check for continuity between the switch terminal and body.

22 Start the engine.

23 Using an ohmmeter, check that there is no continuity between the switch terminal and the body.

24 If a problem is encountered, renew the vacuum switch.

Component renewal

25 The fuel cut solenoid valve and vacuum switch can be renewed by disconnecting the connector and hoses, removing the faulty component and fitting a new one, reversing the removal procedures.

---

17 Idle advance system

Refer to illustration 17.5

General description

1 The purpose of the idle advance system is to improve fuel economy at idle. The system advances the ignition timing only while the engine is idling.

Check

2 Warm up the engine to its normal operating temperature.

3 Hook-up a timing light in accordance

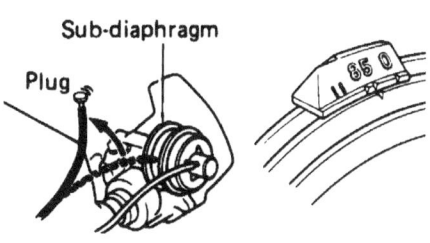

17.5 Checking the idle advance system

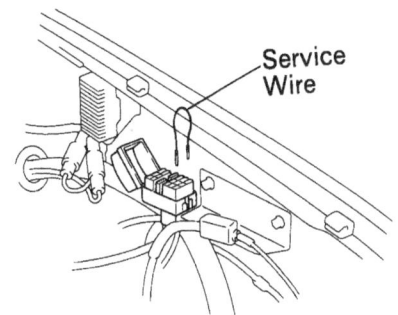

18.3a Location of the check connector on models with a 4Y-E engine (along the left inner fender panel)

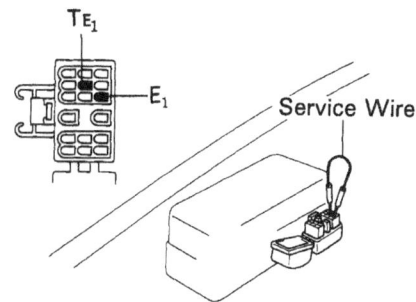

18.3b Location of the check connector - V6 models through 1989 and models with a 22R-E engine (along the right inner fender panel)

with the manufacturer's instructions.
4   Check the ignition timing at idle (see Chapter 1).
5   Detach the vacuum hose from the distributor sub-diaphragm **(see illustration)** and plug the hose end.
6   Check the ignition timing at idle again and verify that the timing has changed slightly.
7   Reattach the vacuum hose and disconnect the timing light.
8   If the system does not perform as specified, inspect and repair or, if necessary, renew the vacuum advance unit.

18   EFI system self diagnosis capability - general information

Refer to illustrations 18.3a, 18.3b, 18.3c, 18.6a and 18.6b

The EFI system control unit (computed hac a built-in self diagnosis system which detects malfunctions in the system sensors and alerts the driver by illuminating a CHECK ENGINE warning light on the instrument panel. The computer stores the failure code until the diagnostic system is cleared by removing the EFI fuse with the ignition switch off. The warning light goes out automatically when the malfunction is repaired.

The CHECK ENGINE warning light should come on when the ignition switch is placed in the On position. When the engine is started, the warning light should go out. If the light remains on, the diagnostic system has detected a malfunction or abnormality in the system.

To determine which sensor or system component is malfunctioning, connect a jumper wire across terminals T and E (4Y-E models) or TE1 and E1 (22R-E and V6 models) of the check connector located along the inner fender panel **(see illustrations)**. Make sure the battery voltage is greater than 11 volts, the transmission is in Neutral, the accessories are off, the throttle valve is closed and the engine is at normal operating temper-

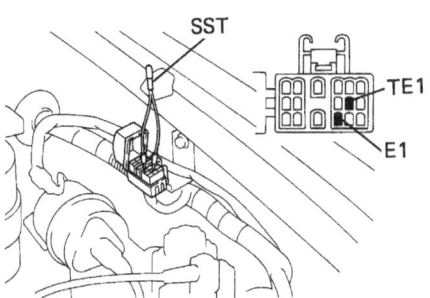

18.3c Location of the check connector - 1990 and later V6 models (along the left inner fender panel)

ature, then turn the ignition switch to the On position but do not start the engine.

The diagnostic code is the number of flashes indicated on the CHECK ENGINE light. Normal system operation is represented by continuos blinking of the light. If any malfunction has been detected, the light will blink from two to seven times every three seconds (two to thirteen times every 4-1/2 seconds for later models). The accompanying tables explain the code that will be flashed for each of the malfunctions. The accompanying charts indicate the diagnostic code - in flashes - along with the system, diagnosis and specific areas. With codes above 10, the flashes appear with a pause between the two numbers, i.e. code 21 will have two quick flashes, then a short pause followed by one flash. The code will be repeated as long as the jumper wire is attached.

After the diagnosis check, remove the jumper wire and close the cover on the check connector. Check the indicated system or component or take the vehicle to a dealer service department to have the malfunction repaired.

After repairs have been made, the diagnostic code must be cancelled by removing the EFI fuse for 30 seconds or more with the ignition switch off **(see illustrations)**. The

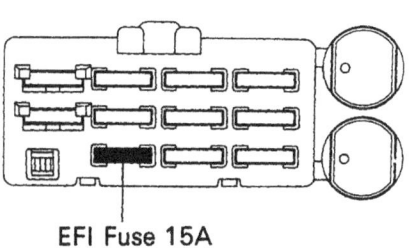

18.6a To clear trouble codes, remove the EFI fuse for at least 30 seconds (4Y-E shown)

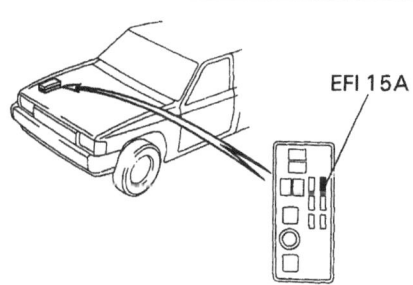

18.6b Location of the EFI fuse on models with a 22R-E or V6 engine

lower the air temperature, the longer the fuse must be left out.

After cancellation, perform a road test and make sure the warning light does not come on. If desired, the check can be repeated to confirm that code 1 (system normal) is flashed. If the original trouble code is repeated, additional repairs are required.

19   EFI system fault code lists

See diagnostic code charts on the following pages.

Code No.	Number of CHECK ENGINE blinks	System	Diagnosis	Trouble area
1	ON ON ON ON ON OFF OFF OFF OFF FI0840	Normal	This appears when none of the other codes (2 thru 11) are identified	–
2	FI0841	Air flow meter signal	• VC circuit open or VS–E2 short circuited. • E2 circuit open or VC–VS short circuited.	1. Air flow meter circuit 2. Air flow meter 3. ECU
3	FI0842	Ignition signal	No signal from igniter four times in succession.	1. Ignition circuit (+B, IGF, IGT) 2. Igniter 3. ECU
4	FI0843	Water temp. sensor signal	Open or short circuit in water temp. sensor signal.	1. Water temp. sensor circuit 2. Water temp. sensor 3. ECU
5	FI0844	Oxygen sensor signal	Open circuit in oxygen sensor signal (only lean indication)	1. Oxygen sensor circuit 2. Oxygen sensor 3. ECU
6	FI0845	RPM signal	No NE signal to ECU while cranking, or NE value over 1,500 rpm in spite of no NE signal to ECU	1. Distributor circuit 2. Distributor 3. Igniter 4. Starter signal circuit 5. ECU
7	FI0846	Throttle position sensor signal	Open or short circuit in throttle position sensor signal.	1. Throttle position sensor circuit 2. Throttle position sensor 3. ECU
8	FI0847	Intake air temp. sensor signal	Open or short circuit in intake air temperature sensor.	1. Air temp. sensor circuit 2. ECU
9	FI0848	Vehicle speed sensor signal	No signal for over 8 seconds when vehicle is travelling 0 km/h and engine running over 2,800 rpm.	1. Vehicle speed sensor circuit 2. Vehicle sensor 3. ECU
10	FI0849	Starter signal	No STA signal to ECU when vehicle stopped and engine running over 800 rpm	1. Starter relay circuit 2. IG switch circuit (starter) 3. IG Switch 4. ECU
11	FI0850	Switch signal	Air conditioner switch ON, idle switch OFF or shift position in any position other than P or N range during diagnosis check.	1. Air conditioner switch 2. Throttle position sensor circuit 3. Throttle position sensor 4. Neutral start switch 5. ECU

Trouble code chart for models with a 4Y-E engine (through 1988)

Code No.	Number of Check engine blinks	System	Diagnosis	Trouble area
—	FI1604	Normal	This appears when none of the other codes are identified.	—
12	FI1606	RPM Signal	No "NE" signal to ECU within 2 seconds after engine has been cranked.	• Distributor circuit • Distributor • Stater signal circuit • Igniter circuit • Igniter • ECU
13	FI1607	RPM Signal	No "NE", signal to ECU when engine speed is above 1,500 rpm.	• Distributor circuit • Distributor • Igniter circuit • Igniter • ECU
14	FI1608	Ignition Signal	No "IGF" signal to ECU 4-5 times in succession.	• Igniter and ignition coil circuit • Igniter and ignition coil • ECU
21	FI1609	Oxygen Sensor Signal	Detection of oxygen sensor detrioration.	• Oxygen sensor circuit • Oxygen sensor • ECU
		Oxygen Sensor Heater Signal	Open or short circuit in oxygen sensor heater.	• Oxygen sensor heater circuit • Oxygen sensor heater • ECU
22	FI1610	Water Temp. Sensor Signal	Open or short circuit in water temp. sensor signal.	• Water temp. sensor circuit • Water temp. sensor • ECU
24	FI1611	Intake Air Temp. Sensor Signal	Open or short circuit in intake air temp. sensor signal.	• Intake air temp sensor circuit • Intake air temp. sensor • ECU
25	FI2562	Air-fuel Ratio Lean Malfunction	(1) When air-fuel ratio feedback compensation value or adaptive control value continues at the upper (lean) or lower (rich) limit renewed for a certain period of time. (2) When air-fuel ratio feedback compensation value or addptive control value feedback frequency is abnormally high during feed-back condition. HINT: For condition (2), since neither a lean (Code No. 25) nor a rich (Code No. 26) diagnosis displayed consecutively.	• Injector circuit • Injector • Fuel line pressure • Air flow meter • Air intake system • Oxygen sensor circuit • Oxygen sensor • Ignition system • ECU
26	FI2563	Air-fuel Ratio Rich Malfunction		• Injector circuit • Injector • Fuel line pressure • Air flow meter • Cold start injector • ECU

Trouble code chart for models with a 4Y-E engine (1989 on) - part 1 of 2

Code No.	Number of Check engine blinks	System	Diagnosis	Trouble area
27	FI2617	Sub-oxygen Sensor Signal	Open or short circuit in sub-oxygen sensor signal.	● Sub-oxygen sensor circuit ● Sub-oxygen sensor ● ECU
31	FI1612	Air Flow Meter Signal	(1) Short circuit between VC and VB, VC and E2, or VS and VC. (2) Open circuit between VC and E2.	● Air flow meter circuit ● Air flow meter ● ECU
41	FI1614	Throttle Position Sensor Signal	(1) Open or short circuit in throttle position sensor signal. (2) IDL ON and PSW ON condition continues for several seconds.	● Throttle position sensor circuit ● Throttle position sensor ● ECU
42	FI1615	Vehicle Speed Sensor Signal	No "SPD" signal for 8 seconds when engine speed is between 1,500 rpm and 5,000 rpm and coolant temp. is below 80°C (176°F) except when racing the engine	● Vehicle speed sensor circuit ● Vehicle speed sensor ● ECU
43	FI1616	Starter Signal	No "STA" signal to ECU until engine speed reaches 800 rpm with vehicle not moving	● Ignition switch circuit ● Ignition switch ● ECU
51	FI1617	Switch Signal	No "IDL" signal, "NSW" signal to ECU, with the check terminals E1 and T connected.	● Throttle position sensor circuit ● Throttle position senor ● Neutral start switch circuit ● Neutral start switch ● Accelerator pedal and cable ● ECU

Trouble code chart for models with a 4Y-E engine (1989 on) - part 2 of 2

DIAGNOSTIC CODES

Code No.	Number of blinks "CHECK ENGINE"	System	Diagnosis	Trouble area
–	ON ⎍⎍⎍⎍⎍⎍⎍ OFF FI1401	Normal	This appears when none of the other codes are identified.	–
12	⎍⎍⎍ FI1389	RPM Signal	NO "Ne" signal to ECU within 2 seconds after engine has been cranked.	• Distributor circuit • Distributor • Igniter circuit • Igniter • Starter signal circuit • ECU
13	⎍⎍⎍⎍ FI1390	RPM Signal	NO "Ne signal to ECU when engine speed is above 1,500 rpm.	• Distributor circuit • Distributor • Igniter circuit • Igniter • ECU
14	⎍⎍⎍⎍⎍ FI1391	Ignition Signal	NO "IGf" signal to ECU 4–5 times in succession.	• Igniter and ignition coil circuit • Igniter and ignition coil • ECU
21	⎍⎍⎍ FI1400	Oxygen Sensor	• Detection of oxygen sensor detrioration.	• Oxygen sensor circuit • Oxygen sensor • ECU
21	⎍⎍⎍ FI1400	Oxygen Sensor Heater	• Open or short circuit in oxygen sensor heater.	• Oxygen sensor heater circuit • Oxygen sensor heater • ECU
22	⎍⎍⎍⎍ FI1392	Water Temp. Sensor Signal	• Open or short circuit in water temp. sensor signal.	• Water temp. sensor circuit • Water temp. sensor • ECU
24	⎍⎍⎍⎍⎍⎍ FI1611	Intake Air Temp. Sensor Signal	• Open or short circuit in intake air temp. sensor signal.	• Intake air temp. sensor circuit • Intake air temp. sensor • ECU
25	⎍⎍⎍⎍⎍⎍⎍ FI2562	Air-fuel Ratio Lean Malfunction	• Open or short circuit in oxygen sensor	• Oxygen sensor circuit • Oxygen sensor • ECU
26	⎍⎍⎍⎍⎍⎍⎍⎍ FI2563	Air-fuel Ratio Rich Malfunction		• Oxygen sensor circuit • Oxygen sensor • ECU
31	⎍⎍⎍⎍ FI1394	Air flow. Meter Signal	• Short circuit between V_C and V_D, V_C and E_2, or V_S and V_C. • Open circuit between V_B and E_2.	• Air flow meter circuit
41	⎍⎍⎍⎍⎍ FI1396	Throttle Position Sensor Signal	• Open or short circuit in throttle position sensor signal.	• Throttle position sensor circuit • Throttle position sensor
42	⎍⎍⎍⎍⎍⎍ FI1397	Vehicle Speed Sensor Signal	• NO "SPD" signal for 5 seconds when engine speed is above 2,500 rpm.	• Vehicle speed sensor circuit • Vehicle speed sensor • ECU
43	⎍⎍⎍⎍⎍⎍⎍ FI1398	Starter Signal	• NO "STA" signal to ECU until engine speed reaches 800 rpm with vehicle not moving.	• IG switch circuit • IG switch • ECU

Trouble code chart for models with a 22R-E engine - part 1 of 2

Code No.	Number of blinks "CHECK ENGINE"	System	Diagnosis	Trouble area
52	FI1618	Knock Sensor Signal	• Open or short circuit in knock sensor signal.	• Knock sensor circuit • Knock sensor • ECU
53	FI1619	Knock Control Signal in ECU	• Knock control in ECU faulty.	• ECU
51	FI1399	Switch Signal	• NO "IDL" signal or "A/C" signal to ECU, with the check connector TE_1 and E_1 connected.	• A/C switch circuit • A/C switch • A/C Amplifire • Throttle position sensor circuit • Throttle position sensor • ECU

Trouble code chart for models with a 22R-E engine - part 2 of 2

Code No.	Number of blinks "CHECK ENGINE"	System	Diagnosis	Trouble area
—	ON OFF FI1401	Normal	This appears when none of the other codes are identified.	—
12	FI1389	RPM Signal	No "NE and G" signal to ECU within 2 seconds after the engine is cranked.	• Distributor circuit • Distributor • Starter signal circuit • ECU
13	FI1390	RPM Signal	No "NE" signal to ECU when engine speed is above 1,000 rpm.	• Distributor circuit • Distributor • ECU
14	FI1391	Ignition Signal	No "IGF" signal to ECU 6 — 8 times in succession.	• Igniter and ignition coil circuit • Igniter and ignition coil
21	FI1400	Oxygen Sensor Signal	• During air-fuel ratio feedback correction, voltage output from the oxygen sensor does not exceed a set value on the lean side and the rich side continuously for certain period.	• Oxygen sensor circuit • Oxygen sensor • ECU
21		Oxygen Sensor Heater Signal	• Open or short circuit in oxygen sensor heater signal (HT).	• Oxygen sensor heater circuit • Oxygen sensor heater • ECU
22	FI1392	Water Temp. Sensor Signal	• Open or short circuit in water temp. sensor signal (THW).	• Water temp. sensor circuit • Water temp. sensor • ECU
24	FI1611	Intake Air Temp. Sensor Signal	• Open or short circuit in intake air temp. sensor signal (THA).	• Intake air temp. sensor circuit • Intake air temp. sensor • ECU
25	FI2562	• Fuel Malfunction • Oxygen Sensor Signal	• When the air-fuel ratio feedback correction value or adaptive control valve feedback frequency is abnormally high during feed-back condition. • Open circuit in oxygen sensor signal (OX).	• Injector circuit • Injector • Fuel line pressure • Ignition system • Oxygen sensor circuit • Oxygen sensor • Air flow meter • Water temp. sensor • ECU
26	FI2563	• Fuel Malfunction • Oxygen Sensor Signal		• Oxygen sensor circuit • Oxygen sensor

Trouble code chart for models with a V6 engine - part 1 of 2

Code No.	Number of blinks "CHECK ENGINE"	System	Diagnosis	Trouble area
31	FI1394	Air Flow Meter Signal	• Open circuit in VC signal or short circuit between VS and E2. • When idle contacts are closed.	• Air flow meter circuit • Air flow meter • ECU
32	FI1395	Air Flow Meter Signal	• Open circuit in E2 or short circuit between VC and VS.	• Air flow meter circuit • Air flow meter • ECU
41	FI1396	Throttle Position Sensor Signal	• Open or short circuit in throttle position sensor signal (VTA).	• Throttle position sensor circuit • Throttle position sensor • ECU
42	FI1397	Vehicle Speed Sensor Signal	• No "SPD" signal to ECU for 8 seconds when engine speed is between 1,500 rpm and 4,000 rpm and coolant temp. is above 80°C (176°F) except when revving the engine.	• Vehicle speed sensor circuit • Vehicle speed sensor • ECU
43	FI1398	Starter Signal	• No "STA" signal to ECU until engine speed reaches 800 rpm with vehicle not moving.	• IG switch circuit • IG switch • ECU
52	FI1618	Knock Sensor Signal	• Open circuit in knock sensor signal (KNK).	• Knock sensor circuit • Knock sensor • ECU
53	FI1619	Knock Control Signal in ECU	• Knock control program faulty.	• ECU
51	FI1399	Switch Condition Signal	• Air conditioner switch ON, idle switch OFF during diagnosis check.	• A/C switch circuit • A/C switch • A/C Amplifier • Throttle position sensor circuit • Throttle position sensor • ECU

Trouble code chart for models with a V6 engine - part 2 of 2

20 Diesel engine pre-heat system - general information

To assist cold starting, diesel engines are equipped with a pre-heating system, which comprises four glow plugs, a pre-heating timer, a dash-mounted warning lamp and the associated relays and electrical wiring.

The glow plugs are miniature electric heating elements, encapsulated in a metal case with a probe at one end and electrical connection at the other. Each intake port has a glow plug threaded into it; the glow plug probe is positioned directly in line with the incoming spray of fuel. When the glow plug is energized, the fuel passing over it is heated, allowing its optimum combustion temperature to be achieved more readily when it reaches the cylinder.

The duration of the pre-heating period is governed by the pre-heating timer, which monitors the temperature of the engine via the water temperature sensor and alters the pre-heating time to suit the conditions.

Pre-heating is triggered by the ignition key being turned to the second position. A dash mounted warning lamp informs the

driver that pre-heating is taking place. The lamp turns off when sufficient pre-heating has taken place to allow the engine to be started, but power will still be supplied to the glow plugs for a further period until the engine is started. If no attempt is made to start the engine, the power supply to the glow plugs is

21.1 Voltage should be present at the glow plug strap when the ignition key is turned to the On position (the duration will vary depending on the temperature)

switched off to prevent battery drain and glow plug burn-out.

After the engine has been started, the glow plugs continue to operate for a further period of time. This helps to improve fuel combustion whilst the engine is warming up, resulting in quieter, smoother running and reduced exhaust emissions.

21.2 The glow plug pre-heating timer is located behind the left kick panel

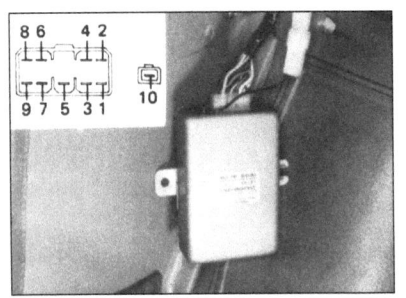

Check for	Tester connection	Condition	Specified value
Voltage	2 - ground	Ignition off	Battery voltage
Voltage	3 - ground	Ignition off	1 volt
Voltage	9 - ground	Ignition off	1 volt
Voltage	2 - ground	Engine started	No voltage
Voltage	7 - ground	Ignition on	Battery voltage
Voltage	8 - ground	Ignition at ST	Battery voltage

21.3a Terminal guide and voltage table for the pre-heating timer electrical connector (L [21.2 litre] engine)

Wire Harness Side

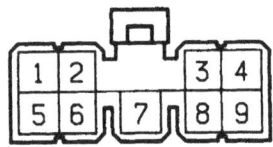

21.3b Terminal guide and voltage/continuity table for the pre-heating timer electrical connector (variable delay system)

Check for	Tester connection	Condition	Specified value
Voltage	1 – Ground	Turn starter switch OFF	No voltage
		Turn starter switch START	Battery voltage
Voltage	3 – Ground	Turn starter switch OFF	No voltage
		Turn starter switch ON	Battery voltage
Continuity	7 – Ground	–	Continuity
Voltage	8 – Ground	Turn starter switch OFF	No voltage
		Turn starter switch ON	Battery voltage

21 Diesel engine pre-heating timer - check and renewal

Refer to illustrations 21.1, 21.2, 21.3a, 21.3b and 21.3c

Check

1   The pre-heating timer itself can't be checked, but the voltage inputs to it can be checked, as well as harness continuity checks. By performing these checks, the timer can be diagnosed by process of elimination. If the engine has been having difficulty starting, especially when cold, check for voltage at the glow plug strap when the ignition key is turned to the On position **(see illustration)**. If no voltage is present, check the glow plug fuse in the underbonnet fuse/relay box. If the fuse is OK, check the pre-heating timer by using the following procedure. If all of the tests pass, check the glow plug relay(s) (see Section 3), the glow plugs (see Section 4), and the water temperature sensor (see Section 7). On mod-

els with an L engine, also check the current sensor. On models with two glow plug relays, check the glow plug resistor (see Section 5).

2   Remove the left kick panel and unplug the electrical connector from the timer **(see illustration)**.

3   Refer to the accompanying charts and check for voltage or continuity on the indicated terminals of the electrical connector (not on the pre-heating timer) **(see illustrations)**. If all of the checks are as indicated, renew the timer. **Note:** *There are three different types of pre-heating systems used on the vehicles covered by this manual, with different electrical connector configurations at the pre-heating timer. Compare the electrical connector on your vehicle with the connectors shown in the accompanying charts, then perform the checks shown in that chart.*

Renewal

4   Unplug the electrical connector, remove the two bolts and detach the unit from the vehicle. Refitting is the reverse of removal.

22 Diesel engine glow plug relay(s) - check and renewal

Note: *Some models use two glow plug relays; others have only one. On early models with two relays, the No. 1 relay is located on the left side of the engine compartment and the No. 2 relay is located on the right side of the engine compartment. On later models with two relay systems, both relays are mounted on the left rear corner of the engine compartment.*

Check

No. 1 glow plug relay

Refer to illustrations 22.2a and 22.2b

Note: *If your system uses only 1 relay, skip to the No. 2 glow plug relay check.*

1   Unplug the relay electrical connector.

2   Using an ohmmeter, check for continuity between terminals g and E **(see illustrations)**; continuity should exist. Now check for

---

Wire Harness Side

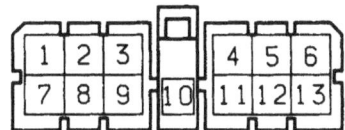

21.3c Terminal guide and voltage/continuity table for the pre-heating timer electrical connector (Super Glow system)

Check for	Tester connection	Condition	Specified value
Continuity	1 – Ground	–	Continuity
Voltage	3 – Ground	Turn starter switch OFF	No voltage
		Turn starter switch ON	Battery voltage
Voltage	4 – Ground	Turn starter switch OFF	No voltage
		Turn starter switch ON	Battery voltage
Continuity	5 – Ground	–	Continuity
Continuity	6 – Ground	–	Continuity
Continuity	7 – Ground	–	Continuity
Continuity	10 – Ground	–	Continuity
Voltage	11 – Ground	Turn starter switch OFF	No voltage
		Turn starter switch START	Battery voltage

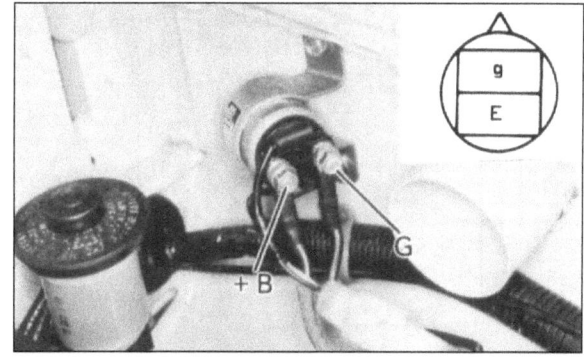

22.2a No. 1 glow plug relay terminals (early models)

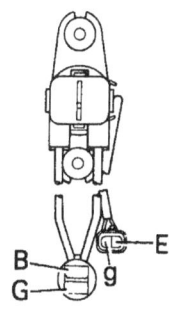

22.2b No. 1 glow plug relay terminals (later models)

22.4 On some models the glow plug relay is located in the left rear corner of the engine compartment (arrow)

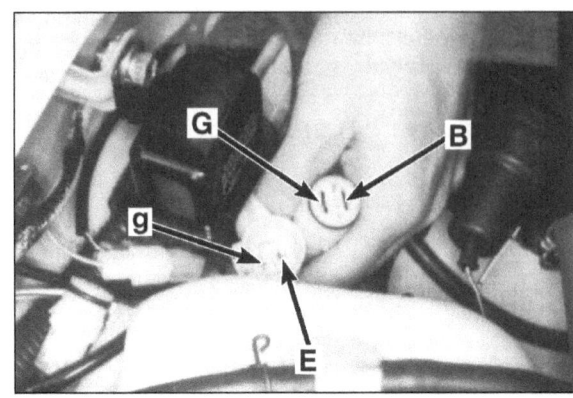

22.5a No. 2 glow plug relay terminals (early models)

continuity between terminals B and G; continuity should not exist.

3   To check the operation of the relay, use fused jumper wires and apply battery voltage to terminals E and g; the relay should click and continuity should exist between terminals B and G.

No. 2 glow plug relay

Refer to illustrations 22.4, 22.5a and 22.5b

4   Unplug the relay electrical connector **(see illustration)**.
5   Using an ohmmeter, check for continuity between terminals g and E **(see illustrations)**; continuity should exist. Now check for continuity between terminals B and G; continuity should not exist.
6   To check the operation of the relay, use fused jumper wires and apply battery voltage to terminals E and g; the relay should click and continuity should exist between terminals B and G.

Renewal

7   To renew the relay, simply unplug the electrical connector(s) and remove the mounting screw. Refitting is the reverse of removal.

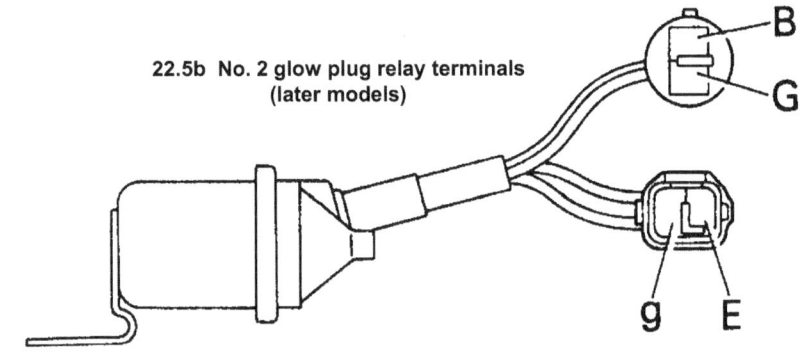

22.5b No. 2 glow plug relay terminals (later models)

23   Diesel engine glow plugs - check and renewal

Refer to illustrations 23.2 and 23.3

Check

1   Disconnect the cable from the negative terminal of the battery.
2   Remove the nut holding the feed cable and the glow plug strap to the insulated post on the inlet manifold, then remove the four nuts holding the glow plug strap to the tops of the glow plugs **(see illustration)**. Remove the glow plug strap.
3   Using an ohmmeter or a self-powered test light, check to see if there is continuity between the glow plug post and earth **(see illustration)**. Continuity should exist; if not, the glow plug must be renewed.

23.2 The glow plug strap is secured to the insulated post on the inlet manifold by one nut, and to each glow plug by a slotted nut (arrows)

23.3 There should be continuity between the glow plug post and earth

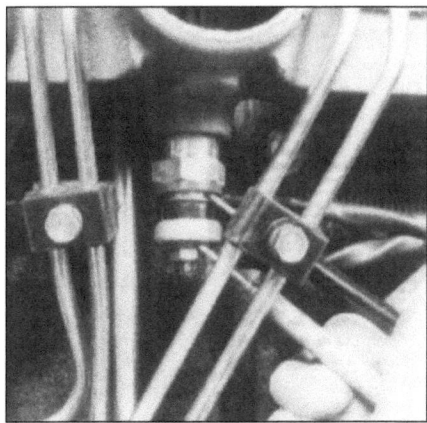

24.3 Continuity should exist between the terminals of the glow plug resistor

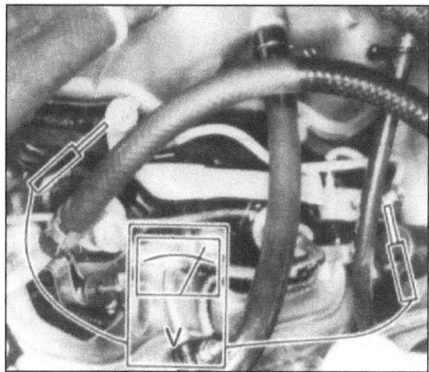

25.1 Continuity should exist between the terminals of the glow plug current sensor (L [2.2 litre] engine)

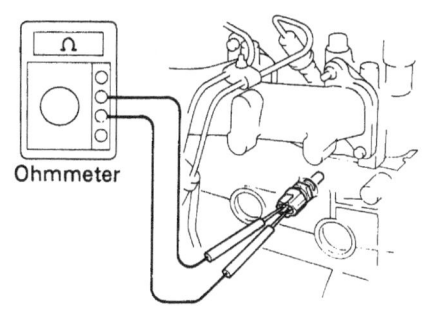

26.2a Checking the resistance of the water temperature sensor

Renewal

4   Remove the glow plug strap, if not already done (see Steps 1 and 2).
5   Using a deep socket, unscrew the glow plug(s).
6   Refitting is the reverse of removal. Be careful not to allow the socket to cock to one side, as this could damage the glow plug.
7   When connecting the strap and the feed cable to the post on the manifold, make sure the insulators are properly positioned (there should be no contact between the strap/feed wire and the post. Tighten the nut securely.

24 Diesel engine glow plug resistor - check and renewal

Refer to illustration 24.3

Note: Only systems that have two glow plug relays use a glow plug resistor.
1   Disconnect the cable from the negative terminal of the battery.
2   Detach the wire from the resistor.
3   Using an ohmmeter or a self-powered test light, check for continuity between the terminals of the resistor **(see illustration)**; continuity should exist. If not, renew the resistor.
4   To renew the resistor, unscrew it from the inlet manifold and thread the new one in, tightening it securely.

25 Diesel engine glow plug current sensor (L engine) - check and renewal

Refer to illustration 25.1

Note: *The glow plug resistor is located above the no. 3 glow plug.*
1   Using an ohmmeter or a self-powered test light, check for continuity between the

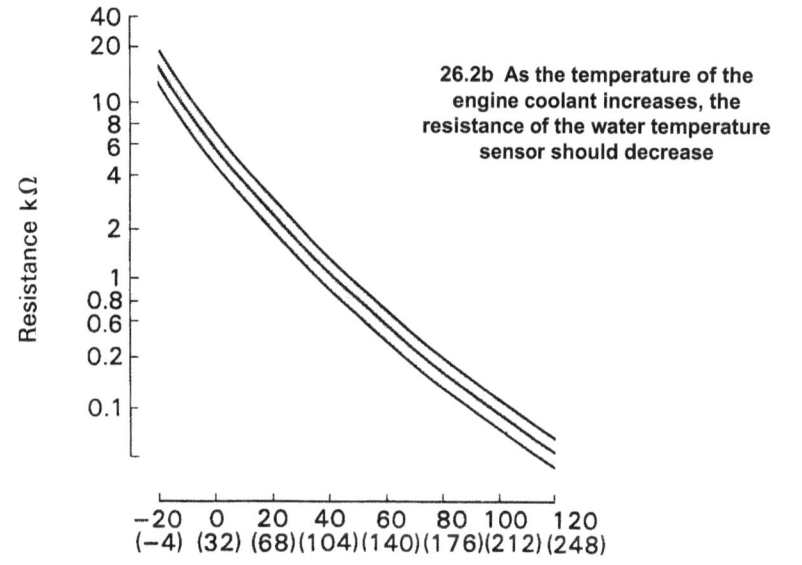

26.2b As the temperature of the engine coolant increases, the resistance of the water temperature sensor should decrease

terminals of the current sensor **(see illustration)**. If there is no continuity, the sensor is burned out and must be renewed.
2   To renew the resistor, remove the fasteners, detach the terminals from each end and fit the new one.

26 Diesel engine water temperature sensor - check and renewal

Refer to illustrations 26.2a and 26.2b

Check

1   Disconnect the electrical connector from the water temperature sensor, located on the engine block under the inlet manifold.
2   The water temperature sensor is a thermistor - a resistor that changes its resistance value with changes in temperature. Using an ohmmeter, check the resistance of the sensor **(see illustration)**. Compare your resistance

reading with the accompanying chart **(see illustration)**.
3   If the resistance values of the sensor are out of range, renew it.

Renewal

Warning: *The engine must be completely cool before beginning this procedure.*
4   Prepare the new sensor for refitting by wrapping its threads with Teflon tape or by applying a thread sealant.
5   Unscrew the radiator cap to relieve any residual pressure in the system, then refit the cap.
6   Unscrew the sensor from the block and fit the new one as quickly as possible. Be prepared for coolant spillage.
7   Tighten the new sensor securely, then reattach the electrical connector.
8   Check the coolant level and add some, if necessary (see Chapter 1).

Notes

Chapter 7 Part A
Manual transmission

Contents

Specifications

General

Fifth gear thrust clearance	
G40, G52, G54 and G58 series	
Standard clearance...	0.10 to 0.30 mm
Maximum clearance..	0.30 mm
W50, W52 and W56 series	
Standard clearance...	0.10 to 0.41 mm
Maximum clearance..	0.46 mm
Counter gear thrust clearance	
L40, L42 and L43	
Standard clearance...	0.10 to 0.30 mm

Torque specifications

	Nm
Back-up light switch	
G series..	37
W series	40
Case covor bolts (L-series)..	19
Case plug bolt..	37
Clutch housing bolts (L-series)...	59
Clutch housing bolts (all others)	37
Extension housing bolts..	37
Front bearing retainer bolts	
G series..	17
W series	25
L series	7.4
Locking ball plugs	25
Rear bearing retainer bolts	18
Restrict pins	
G series..	27
W series	40
Reverse idler shaft stop bolt	
G series..	17
W series	25
Reverse shift arm bracket bolts..	18
Shift fork set bolts	
G series..	20
W series	12
Shift lever control retainer bolts	18
Shift lever retainer bolts (L-series)...................................	20
Shift lever housing set bolt	38
Speedometer lock plate bolt...	11
Stiffener plate bolts..	37
Torx screw plugs..	19
Transfer case adaptor housing bolts	37
Transmission/clutch housing-to-engine bolt	72

1.1a Typical 4WD transmission and related components

1	Transmission housing bolts	4	Rear support member bolts	7	Transfer case	10	Clutch release cylinder
2	Exhaust pipe clamp	5	Rear driveshaft	8	Transmission drain plug	11	Starter
3	Transmission	6	Rear mounting bolts	9	Front driveshaft		

1.1b Typical 2WD transmission and related components

1	Transmission housing bolts	4	Rear mounting bolts	7	Transmission drain plug
2	Exhaust pipe clamp	5	Rear bracket bolts	8	Clutch release cylinder
3	Back-up light switch connector	6	Speedometer cable	9	Starter

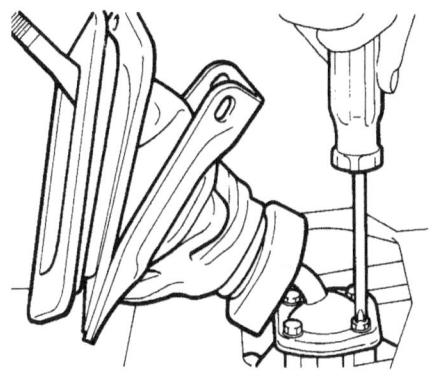

3.3 On some models a screwdriver can be used to remove the shift lever bolts/screws

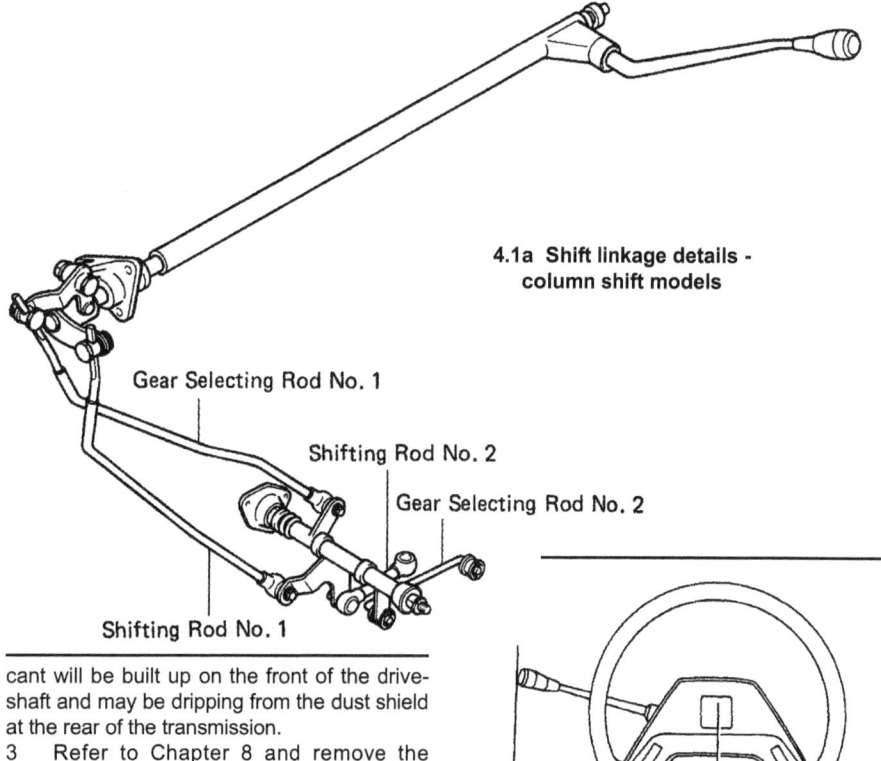

4.1a Shift linkage details - column shift models

Gear Selecting Rod No. 1

Shifting Rod No. 2

Gear Selecting Rod No. 2

Shifting Rod No. 1

1 General information

Refer to illustrations 1.1a and 1.1b

All vehicles covered in this manual are equipped with either a 4 or 5-speed manual transmission or an automatic transmission **(see illustrations)**. All information on the manual transmission is included in this Part of Chapter 7. Information on the automatic transmission can be found in Part B. Information on the transfer case used on 4WD models can be found in Part C.

Due to the complexity, unavailability of spare parts and the special tools necessary, internal repair of the manual transmission is not recommended for the home mechanic, however, general procedures and illustrations have been.

Depending on the expense involved in having a faulty transmission overhauled, it may be an advantage to consider renewing the unit with either a new or rebuilt one. Your local dealer, transmission shop or wrecking yard should be able to supply you with information concerning cost, availability and exchange policy. Regardless of how you decide to remedy a transmission problem, you can still save considerable expense by removing and installing the unit yourself.

2 Oil seal renewal

1   Oil leaks frequently occur due to wear of the extension housing oil seal and bush, and/or the speedometer drive gear oil seal and O-ring. Renewal of these seals is relatively easy, since the repairs can usually be performed without removing the transmission from the vehicle.

Extension housing

2   The extension housing oil seal is located at the extreme rear of the transmission, where the driveshaft is attached. If leakage at the seal is suspected, raise the rear of the vehicle and support it securely on jackstands. Be sure to block the front wheels to keep the vehicle from rolling. If the seal is leaking, transmission lubri-

cant will be built up on the front of the driveshaft and may be dripping from the dust shield at the rear of the transmission.
3   Refer to Chapter 8 and remove the driveshaft.
4   Using a soft-faced hammer carefully tap the dust shield to the rear and remove it from the transmission. Be careful not to distort it.
5   Using a screwdriver or lever, carefully prise the oil seal and bush out of the rear of the transmission. Do not damage the splines on the transmission output shaft.
6   If the oil seal and bush cannot be removed with a screwdriver or lever, it may be necessary to obtain a special seal removal tool, available at your dealer or an auto parts store.
7   Using a large section of pipe or a very large deep socket as a drift, install the new oil seal. Drive it into the bore squarely and make sure that it is completely seated. Install a new bush using the same method.
8   Reinstall the dust shield by carefully tapping it into place. Lubricate the splines of the transmission output shaft and the outside of the driveshaft sleeve yoke with lightweight grease, then install the driveshaft. Be careful not to damage the lip of the new seal.

Speedometer driven gear

9   The speedometer cable and driven gear housing is located on the side of the extension housing. Look for transmission oil around the cable housing to determine if the seal and O-ring are leaking.
10   Disconnect the cable housing with pliers.
11   Using a spanner, remove the speedometer driven gear housing.
12   Remove the driven gear from the housing.
13   Using a hook, remove the seal.
14   Using a small socket of the appropriate diameter or other similar tool as a drift, install the new seal.

4.1b The shift lever should be positioned so that when at rest, in neutral, the tip of the lever is approximately 300 mm from the centerline of the steering column

15   Install a new O-ring to the driven gear housing and reinstall the driven gear housing and cable assembly to the extension housing.

3 Shift lever (floor-shift models) - removal and installation

Refer to illustration 3.3

1   Remove the console (if equipped) and shift boot screws.
2   Place the shift lever in Neutral.
3   Remove the shift lever retainer-to-transmission bolts/screws **(see illustration)**.
4   To disconnect the shift lever from the transmission on some older models, a special tool, available from Toyota dealers, is needed.
5   Lift the shift lever assembly from the transmission.
6   Installation is the reverse of removal.

4 Shift linkage (column-shift models) - adjustment

Refer to illustrations 4.1a, 4.1b, 4.2 and 4.3

1   The shift lever should be positioned so that when at rest, in neutral, the tip of the lever is approximately 300 mm from the centre of the steering column, measured horizontally **(see illustrations)**.

2   If this dimension is not correct, loosen the swivel nut for shifting rod no. 1 **(see illustration)**, adjust the linkage as necessary to obtain the position shown in **illustration 4.1b**, then tighten the swivel nut securely.

3   Also, when the transmission is in neutral, the shift lever should positioned so that the clearance between the shift lever and the steering wheel is approximately 95 mm **(see illustration)**. If it isn't, loosen the swivel nut for shifting rod no. 2 **(see illustration 4.2)**, adjust the linkage as necessary to obtain this dimension, then tighten the swivel nut.

5   Manual transmission - removal and installation

Removal

1   Disconnect the negative cable at the battery.

2   Remove the fan shroud.

3   From inside the vehicle, remove the shift lever (floor-shift models) (see Section 3). On 4WD models, use pliers to disengage the snapring and remove the transfer case shift lever.

4   Raise the vehicle and support it securely on jackstands.

5   Disconnect the speedometer cable and electrical connections from the transmission and, if equipped, the transfer case **(see illustrations 1.1a and 1.1b)**. Disconnect the shift linkage from the transmission (column shift models).

6   Remove the driveshaft (Chapter 8).

7   Drain the transmission and, if equipped, the transfer case.

8   Remove the starter motor, if possible. On some later models you may not be able to remove the starter until the clutch release cylinder and various mounting brackets are out of the way and the transmission is partially lowered.

9   Unbolt the clutch release cylinder and fasten it out of the way.

10   Remove the exhaust system components as necessary for clearance (Chapter 4).

11   Support the engine. This can be done from above by using an engine hoist, or by placing a jack (with a block of wood as an insulator) under the engine sump. The engine should remain supported at all times while the transmission is out of the vehicle.

12   Support the transmission with a jack - preferably a special jack made for this purpose. Safety chains will help steady the transmission on the jack.

13   Remove the rear transmission support-to-crossmember nuts and bolts.

14   Remove the nuts from the crossmember bolts. Raise the transmission slightly and remove the crossmember.

15   Remove the bolts securing the transmission clutch housing to the engine.

16   Make a final check that all wires and hoses have been disconnected from the transmission and transfer case (4WD models) and then move the transmission and jack toward the rear of the vehicle until the clutch

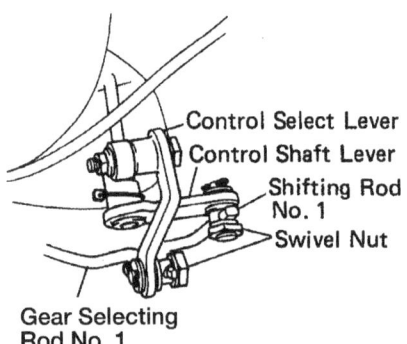

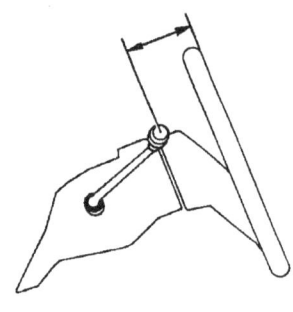

4.2 The shift rods are adjusted at the bellcranks at the base of the steering column, where it exits the firewall

4.3 The shift lever, when in neutral, should be positioned approximately 95 mm from the rear edge of the steering wheel

housing is clear of the engine dowel pins. Keep the transmission level as this is done. Be careful not to damage the extension housing dust deflector (4WD models).

17   Lower the transmission and remove it from under the vehicle. **Caution:** *Do not depress the clutch pedal while the transmission is removed from the vehicle.*

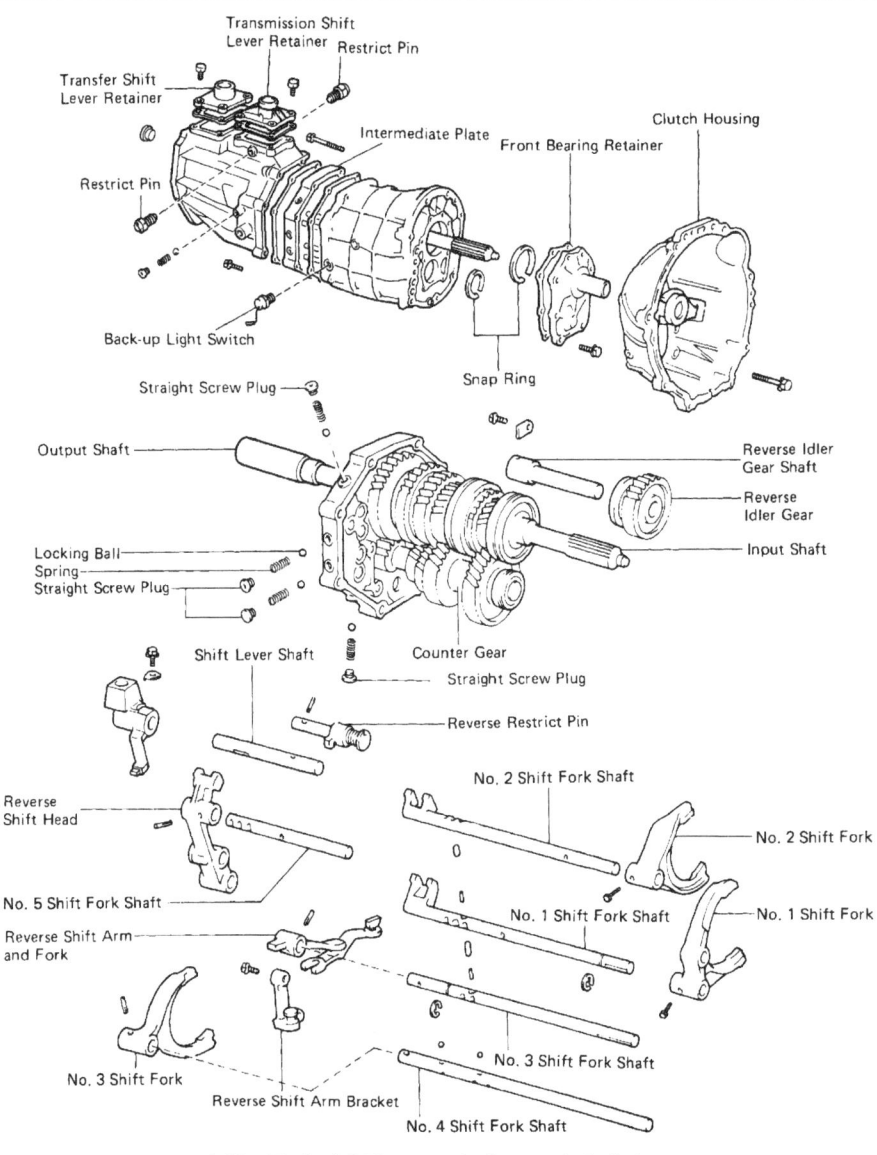

6.10a Typical G52 transmission exploded view

18   The clutch components now can be inspected (see Chapter 8). In most cases, new clutch components should be installed as a matter of course if the transmission is removed.

Installation

19   If removed, install the clutch components (see Chapter 8).

20   With the transmission secured to the jack as on removal, raise it into position behind the engine and then carefully slide it forward, engaging the clutch housing over the dowel pins. Do not use excessive force to install the transmission; if it does not slide into place, readjust the angle of the transmission so it is level.

21   Install the transmission/clutch housing-to-engine bolts. Tighten the bolts to the torque listed in this Chapter's Specifications.

22   Install the crossmember and trans-mission support. Tighten all nuts and bolts securely.

23   Remove the jacks supporting the transmission and the engine.

24   Install the various items removed previously, referring to Chapter 8 for the installation of the driveshaft and Chapter 4 for information regarding the exhaust system components.

25   Make a final check that all wires, hoses and the speedometer cable have been connected and that the transmission and if equipped, transfer case have been filled with lubricant to the proper level (see Chapter 1). Lower the vehicle.

26   Connect the shift lever (floor-shift models) (see Section 3) or connect and adjust the shift linkage (column-shift models) (see Section 4).

27   On 4WD models, install the transfer case shift lever.

28   Connect the negative battery cable.

Road test the vehicle for proper operation and check for leakage.

---

6   Manual transmission - overhaul

General information

1   If your transmission reaches the end of its service life, you can save a great deal of money by removing and refitting it yourself, but you're better off leaving the overhaul to a transmission repair shop. Better yet, buy a rebuilt unit from a dealer parts department or an auto parts store. Rebuilding a manual transmission is a difficult job involving the disassembly and reassembly of many small parts. The cost in time and money to overhaul a transmission yourself will almost surely exceed the cost of a rebuilt unit.

2   Nevertheless, it's not impossible for an inexperienced mechanic to rebuild a transmission if the special tools are available and the job is done in a deliberate step-by-step manner so nothing is overlooked.

3   The tools necessary for an overhaul include internal and external snap-ring pliers, a bearing puller, a slide hammer, a set of pin punches, a dial indicator and possibly a hydraulic press. In addition, a large, sturdy workbench and a vise or transmission stand will be required.

4   During disassembly of the transmission, make careful notes of how each piece comes off, where it fits in relation to other pieces comes off, where it fits in relation to other pieces and what holds it in place. When removing parts, note how they're fitted; this will make it easier to reassemble the transmission correctly.

5   Before taking the transmission apart for repair, it will help if you have some idea what area of the transmission is malfunctioning. Certain problems can be closely tied to specific areas in the transmission, which can make component examination and renewal easier. Refer to the *Troubleshooting* section at the front of this manual for information regarding possible sources of trouble.

G40, G52, G54 and G58 series

Disassembly

Refer to illustrations 6.10a, 6.10b, 6.10c, 6.11, 6.14, 6.20, 6.21, 6.22, 6.23, 6.24, 6.25, 6.27, 6.29 and 6.30

7   Remove the transmission from the vehicle (see Section 5) and clean the exterior of the transmission. Remove the transmission drain plug and drain the excess lubricant into a drain pan.

8   Remove the release fork and bearing.

9   On 2WD models, remove the speedometer gear and the back-up light switch.

10   Remove the nine clutch housing retaining bolts and separate the housing from the case **(see illustrations)**.

11   Using a Torx socket remove the plug from the side of the case **(see illustration)**.

12   Remove the four shift lever retaining

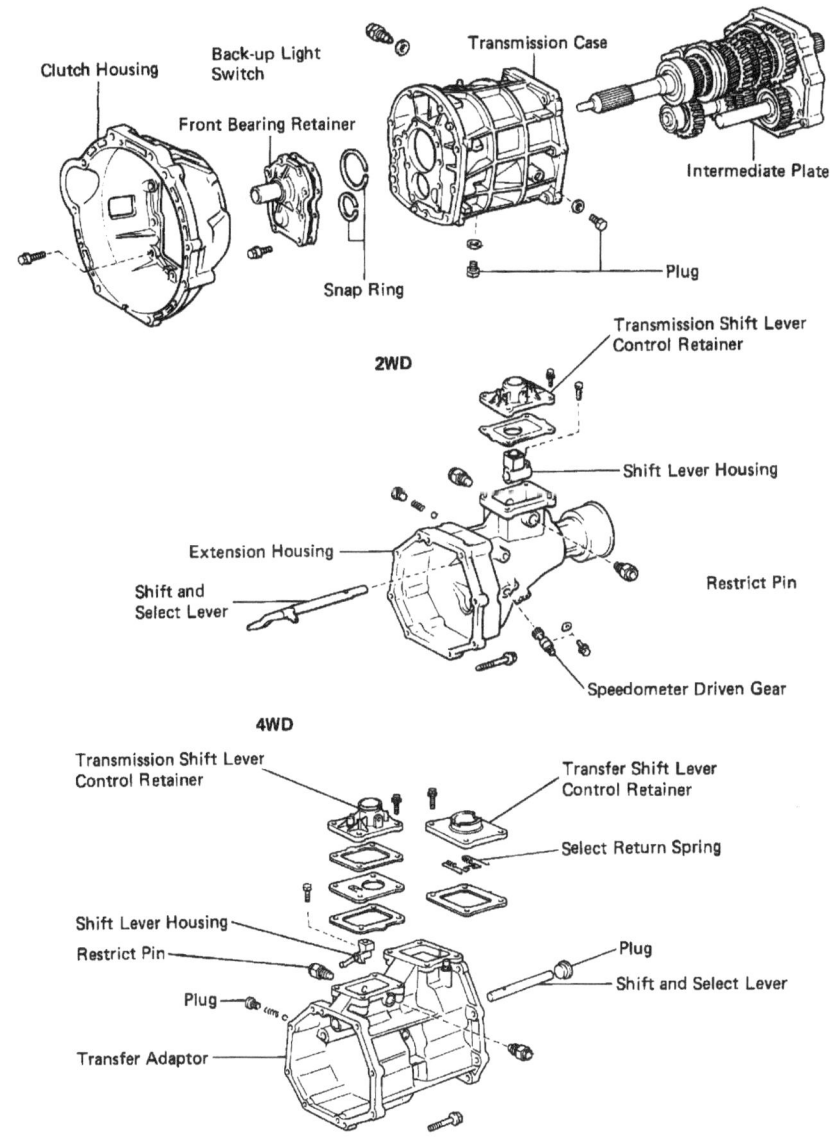

6.10b Typical G40, G54 and G58 series transmission case exploded view

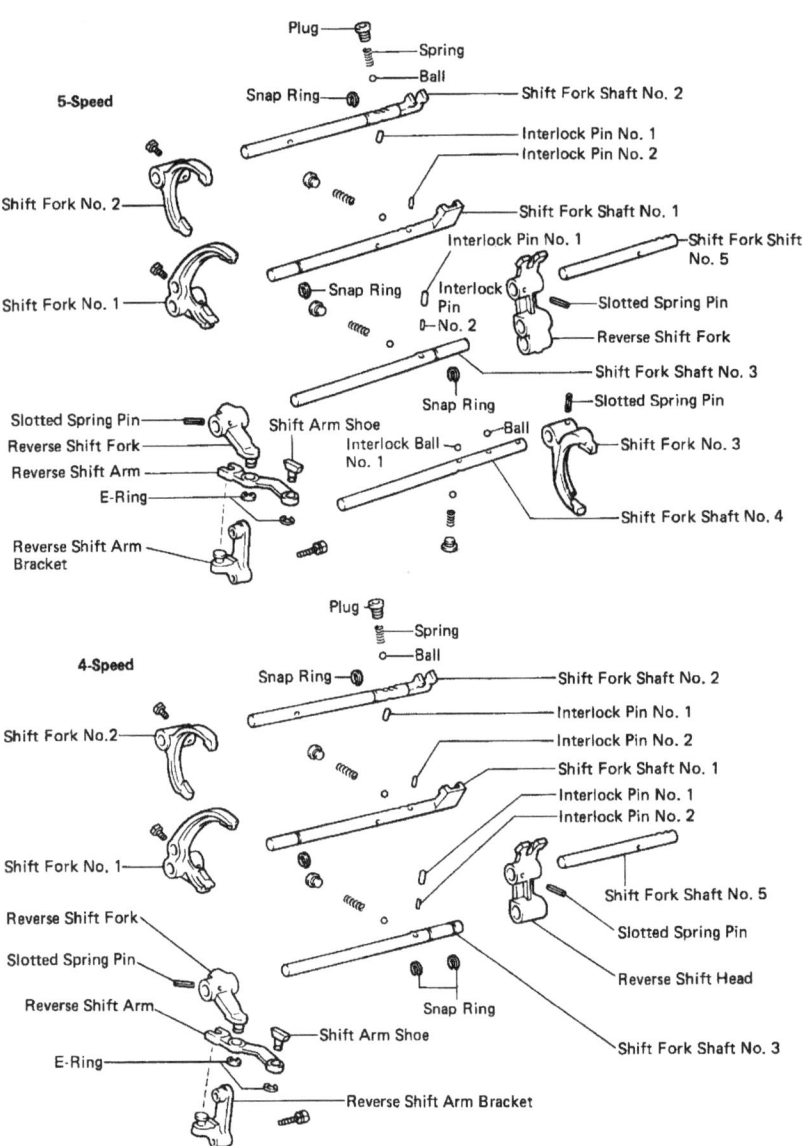

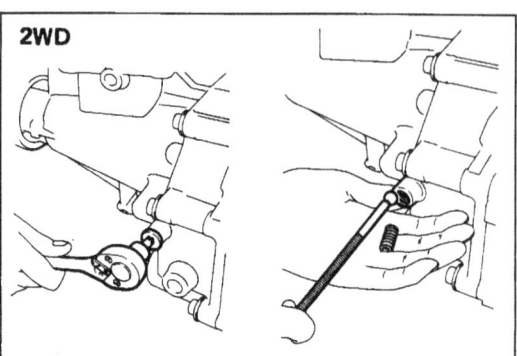

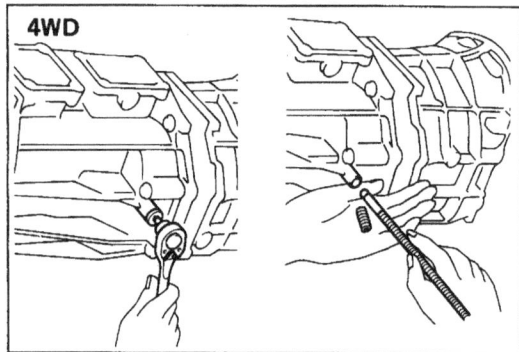

6.11 Remove the plug from the case and use a magnet to pull the spring and ball from the case

6.10c Typical G40, G54 and G58 series transmission shift assemblies exploded view

bolts and remove the retainer. On 4WD models remove the four transfer case shift lever retainer bolts.

13 Remove the two restrict pins using an open end spanner.

14 On 2WD models, remove the eight extension housing bolts and the shift lever housing set bolt (on the end of the select lever) and lightly tap the extension housing off with a plastic hammer. As the extension housing sepa-

rates, pull the shift lever and housing out with the housing (**see illustration**).

15 On 4WD models, remove the access plug from the rear of the transfer case adaptor using an Allen wrench. Remove the shift lever housing set bolt and slide the shift lever shaft out through the access hole in the case-housing adaptor. Remove the eight case housing retaining bolts and lightly separate the case housing with a plastic hammer.

16 Remove the eight front bearing retainer bolts and remove the retainer.

17 Using a pair of external snap ring pliers remove the input shaft and counter shaft bearing snap rings.

18 Set the transmission case on end. Hold the input shaft while carefully taping up on the case and remove the case from the intermediate plate.

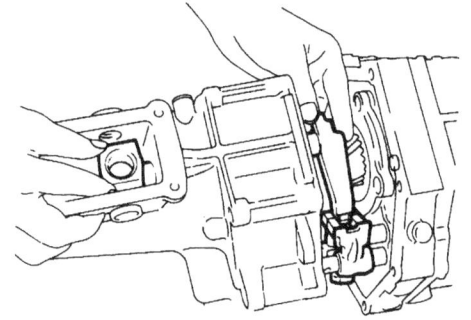

6.14 Slowly pull the extension housing and shift select lever away from the case

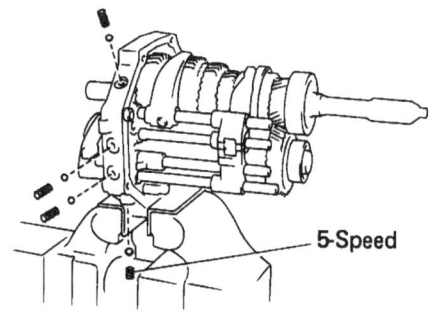

6.20 Remove the plugs from the plate, use a magnet to pull the springs and balls from the plate

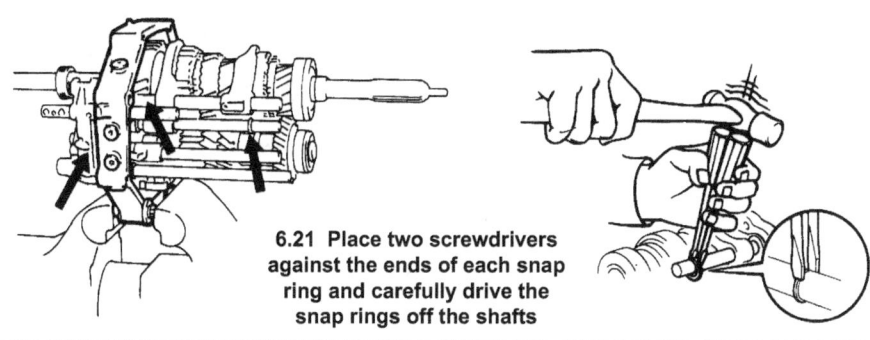

6.21 Place two screwdrivers against the ends of each snap ring and carefully drive the snap rings off the shafts

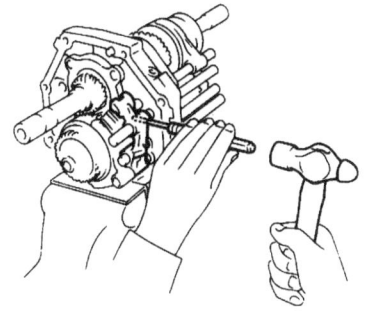

6.22 Drive the roll pin in towards output shaft and remove it from the back side of the shift fork - for exploded view see illustration 6.10

19 Once the case has been removed from the intermediate plate install two nuts, bolts with washers and tighten them securely. Using the heads of the nuts and bolts as a mounting surface set the plate assembly in a vise and tighten the vise down on the nuts and bolts.
20 Using a Torx socket slowly remove the intermediate plate plugs **(see illustration)**. **Note:** *4-speed models use three plugs and 5-speed models use four plugs.*
21 Remove the shift shaft fork snap rings. 4-speed models have three snap rings and 5-speed models have four snap rings **(see illustration)**.
22 Using a pin punch drive the roll pin out of shift fork No.5 and remove the No.5 shift shaft fork **(see illustration)**.
23 Using a pin punch drive the roll pin out of shift fork No.3 and remove the No.4 shift shaft fork and the reverse shift head **(see illustration)**.

24 Using a magnet remove the interlock pin from the No.3 shift fork **(see illustration)**, then use a pin punch drive the roll pin out of shift fork No.3 and remove the No.3 shift shaft fork
25 Using a magnet remove the interlock pin No.1 **(see illustration)**, and remove the reverse shift arm and fork.
26 Using a magnet remove the interlock pin No.2 from shift shaft fork No.2 **(see illustration 6.27)**.
27 Remove the No.1 shift fork set bolt and remove the No.1 shift shaft fork. While removing the No.1 shift shaft fork use a magnet to remove the No.1 interlock **(see illustration)**.
28 Remove the No.2 shift fork set bolt and remove the No.1 shift fork and No.2 shift shaft.
29 On 5-speed models, measure the 5th gear thrust clearance **(see illustration)**.
30 On 5-speed models, remove the 5th gear snap ring and 5th gear using a puller **(see illustration)**.

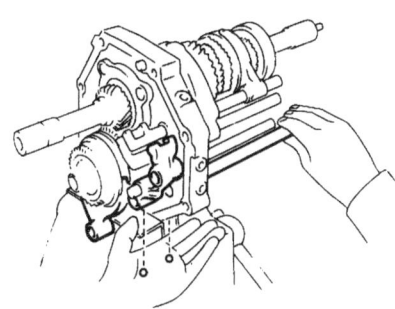

6.23 Remove the No.3 shift fork and reverse shift head - when the shaft is pulled all the way out two lock balls will fall out

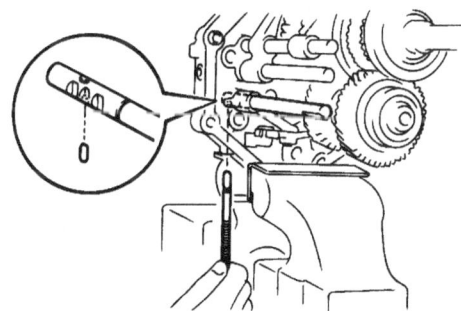

6.24 Use a long pencil type magnet to remove the interlock pin from the intermediate plate

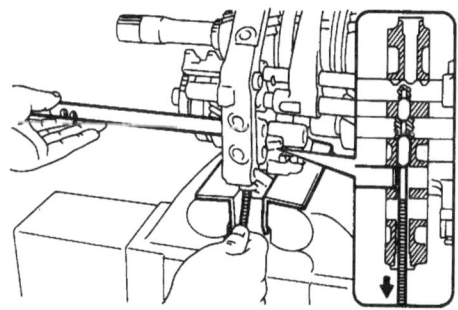

6.25 Before the No.3 shift shaft can be removed insert a long pencil type magnet into the intermediate plate to remove the No.1 interlock pin

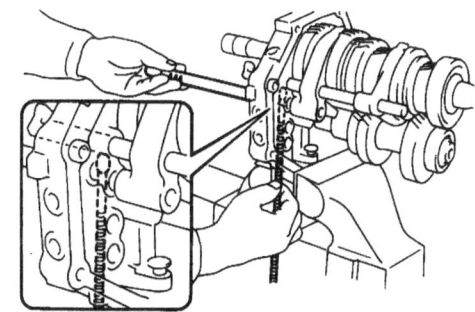

6.27 Pull on the shift shaft while using the magnet - this will make removal of the interlock pin easier

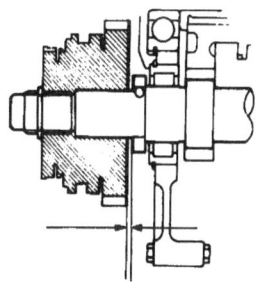

6.29 Using a feeler gauge check the 5th gear thrust clearance (arrows) the clearance should be 0.10 to 0.30 mm

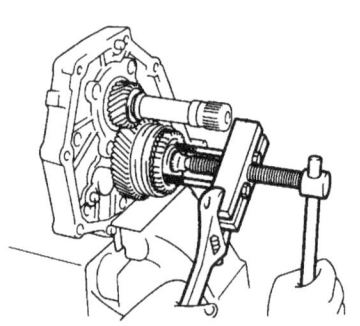

6.30 Use a puller designed to remove this type of gear - DO NOT use a two jaw gear puller

31 On 5-speed models, remove the spacer and lock ball from the counter shaft.

32 On 4-speed models, remove the oil separator snap ring from the counter shaft and remove the separator.

33 Remove the two reverse shift arm bracket retaining bolts from the backside of the intermediate plate.

34 Remove the reverse idler gear shaft stop set bolt and remove the stopper, idler gear and shaft.

35 Remove the four Torx rear bearing retainer mounting bolts and remove the retainer.

36 Remove the counter shaft bearing snap ring using snap ring pliers. Once the snap ring is removed use a two jaw puller that will fit into the snap ring groove. Remove the bearing and counter gear from the intermediate plate.

37 Place your hand under the input shaft to catch any of the 13 needle bearing that might fall out as you pull the input shaft and synchronizer away from the output shaft assembly.

38 Using a pair of external type snap ring pliers remove the output shaft snap ring from the intermediate plate. Hold the output shaft in one hand and carefully tap on the intermediate plate with a plastic hammer to remove the shaft from the plate.

Inspection

Refer to illustrations 6.39a and 6.39b

39 Wash the transmission components thoroughly with solvent. Inspect the transmission cases for cracks in the bores, sides, bosses and bolt holes and stripped threads in the bolt holes. Check the geartrain and shift mechanisms for broken, chipped or worn gear teeth, bent or broken inserts, weak or broken insert springs, damaged roller or needle bearings and bearing bores in the countershaft and hub, output shaft, reverse idler shaft **(see illustrations)**. Check the snap-rings for distortion and lack of tension. Inspect the front and rear bearings for galling, damage and roughness. Inspect the shift mechanisms for worn, damaged or bent inserts, forks, rails, arms, plates, interlocks and levers.

Reassembly

Refer to illustrations 6.43, 6.50, 6.54, 6.56, 6.58, 6.61, 6.64, 6.65 and 6.68

Note: *Before reassembling the transmission components lubricate all bearings, gears, synchronizer rings, shafts, seals, clutch hub assemblies with transmission fluid.*

40 Refit the output shaft in the intermediate plate, it may be necessary to lightly tap on the intermediate plate with a plastic hammer to fully seat the bearing. Once the output shaft assembly is seated in the plate refit the output shaft bearing snap ring flush with the intermediate plate.

41 Coat the 13 input shaft roller bearings with grease and fit them in a circle inside of the input shaft.

42 Coat the synchronizer ring with transmission fluid and refit the ring on the input shaft.

43 Refit the input shaft to the output shaft **(see illustration)**.

44 Refit the counter shaft bearing snap ring on the bearing.

45 Refit the counter shaft assembly in the intermediate plate and slide the countershaft bearing onto the countershaft. Seat the bearing and countershaft into the intermediate plate using a hammer and long sleeve or tube that only contacts the bearing outer race.

46 Refit the rear bearing retainer and tighten to the Torx bolts to the torque listed at the beginning of this Chapter's Specifications Section.

47 Refit the reverse idler shaft through the intermediate plate and into the reverse idler gear.

48 Refit the idler shaft stop and bolt and tighten the bolt to the torque listed at the

Rear Bearing Retainer ─ Sleeve

Snap Ring

Snap Ring

5th Gear

Synchronizer Ring

Input Shaft

No. 5 Gear Spline Piece

Counter 5th Gear

Spacer

Counter Rear Bearing

Counter Gear

Synchronizer Ring

No. 3 Hub Sleeve

Needle Roller Bearing

Rear Bearing

Needle Roller Bearing

Synchronizer Ring

Inner Race

1st Gear

No. 1 Hub Sleeve

Snap Ring

Synchronizer Ring

2nd Gear

Needle Roller Bearing

Output Shaft

3rd Gear

Needle Roller Bearing

Synchronizer Ring

Snap Ring

No. 2 Hub Sleeve

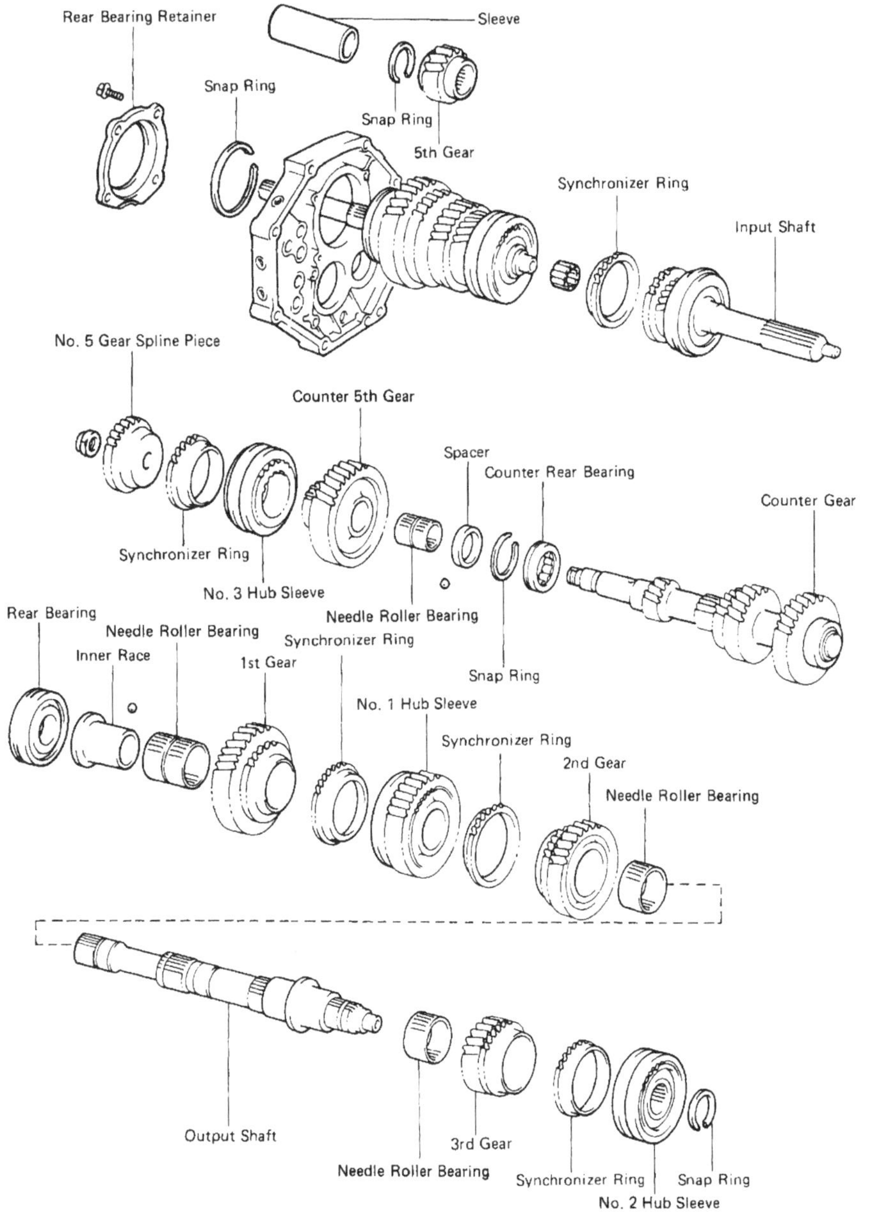

6.39a Typical G52 transmission shaft and geartrain exploded view

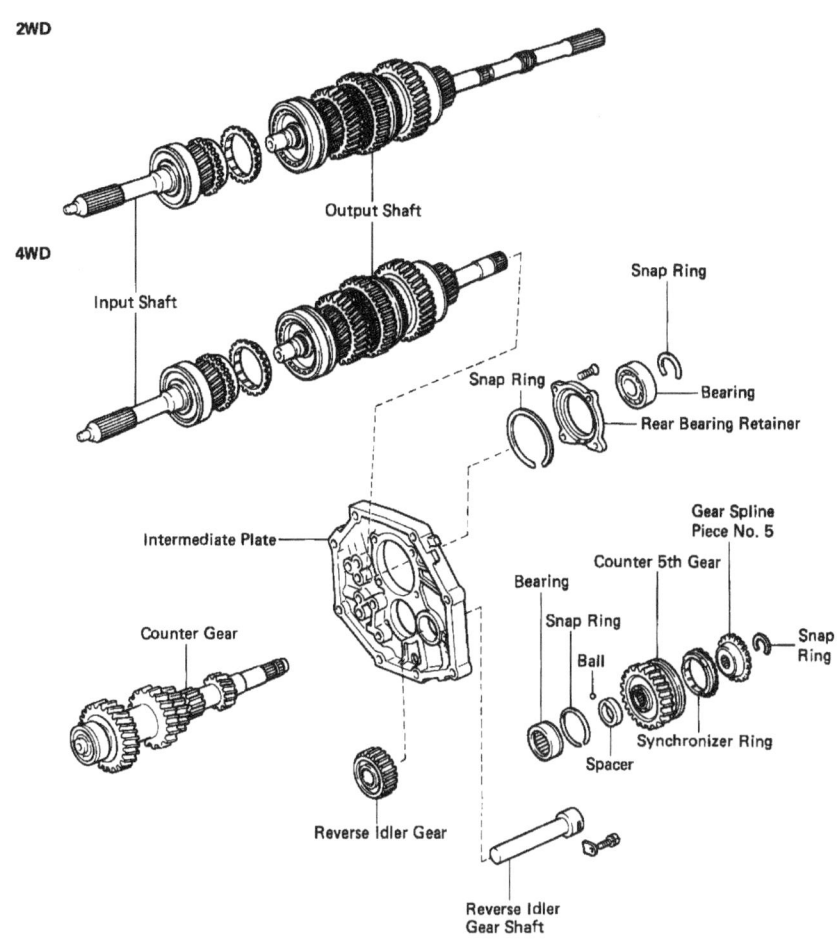

2WD

Output Shaft

4WD

Input Shaft

Snap Ring

Snap Ring

Bearing

Rear Bearing Retainer

Intermediate Plate

Gear Spline
Piece No. 5

Counter 5th Gear

Bearing

Counter Gear

Snap Ring

Snap
Ring

Ball

Synchronizer Ring

Spacer

Reverse Idler Gear

Reverse Idler
Gear Shaft

6.39b Typical G40, G54 and G58 series transmission shaft and geartrain exploded view

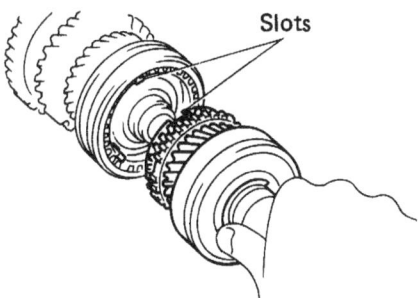

Slots

6.43 Align the slots in the synchronizer ring with the shifting keys on the output shaft

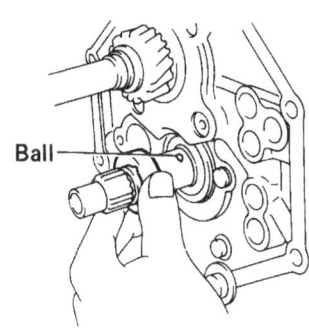

Ball

6.50 Refit the ball into the counter shaft and slide the spacer onto the shaft and over the ball

beginning of this Chapter's Specifications Section.

49 Refit the reverse shift arm bracket and tighten the two bolts to the torque listed at the beginning of this Chapter's Specifications Section.

50 On 5-speed models refit the lock ball and spacer **(see illustration)**.

51 On 5-speed models coat the 5th gear needle bearings with transmission fluid and refit the 5th gear, No. 3 sleeve and needle bearings onto the counter shaft.

52 On 5-speed models refit the synchronizer ring and splined gear piece No.5 onto

the counter shaft. Remove the assembly and stand on end.

53 On 5-speed models press the splined gear piece No.5 onto the counter shaft and refit the snap ring.

54 On 5-speed models, measure the 5th gear thrust clearance between the spacer and 5th gear **(see illustration 6.29)**, if incorrect remove the snap ring holding splined gear piece No.5 and fit the correct thickness of snap ring.

55 On 4-speed models refit the oil separator and snap ring.

56 Refit the No.1 and No.2 shift forks onto

the output shaft and slide the No.2 shift shaft through the intermediate case and both shift forks **(see illustration)**.

57 Refit the No.2 shift fork set bolt and tighten the bolt to the torque listed at the beginning of this Chapter's Specifications Section.

58 Coat the interlock pin No.2 with grease and refit it into the shift shaft fork No.1 **(see illustration)**.

59 Using a magnet refit the interlock pin No.1 into the intermediate plate and refit the No.1 shift shaft fork through the intermediate plate and into the No.1 shift fork **(see illustration 6.27)**.

60 Refit the No.1 shift fork set bolt and tighten the bolt to the torque listed at the beginning of this Chapter's Specifications Section.

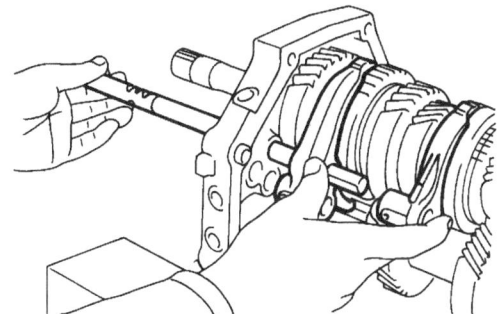

6.56 Lubricate the No.2 shift shaft and slide the shaft through the plate and No.1 and 2 shift forks

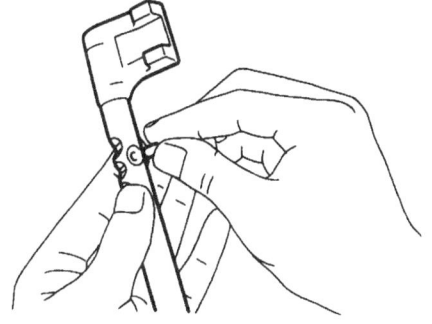

6.58 Refit the No.2 interlock pin into the No.1 shift shaft using grease to hold it in place

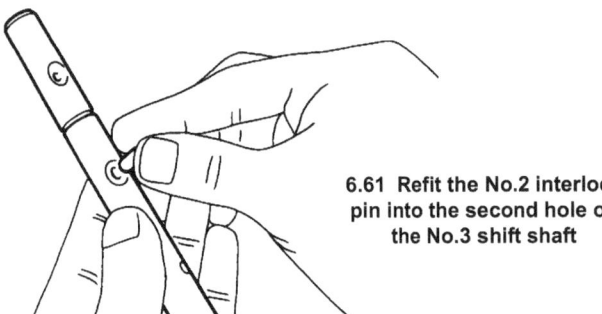

6.61 Refit the No.2 interlock pin into the second hole on the No.3 shift shaft

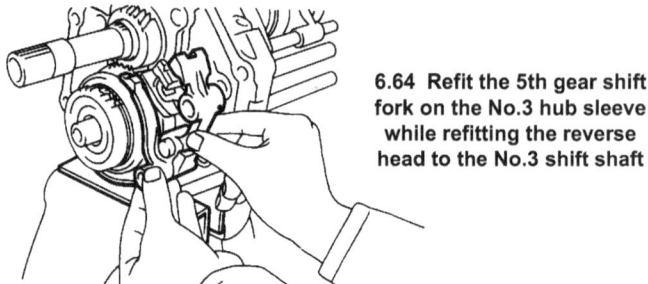

6.64 Refit the 5th gear shift fork on the No.3 hub sleeve while refitting the reverse head to the No.3 shift shaft

61   Coat the interlock pin No.2 with grease and refit it into the shift shaft fork No.3 **(see illustration)**.

62   Using a magnet refit the interlock pin No.1 into the intermediate plate and refit the No.3 shift shaft fork through the intermediate plate and into the reverse shift fork **(see illustration 6.25)**.

63   Refit the roll pin into the reverse shift fork using a pin punch and hammer.

64   On 5-speed models, refit the reverse shift head onto the No.3 shift shaft and refit the No.3 shift fork **(see illustration)**.

65   On 5-speed models, use a magnet and refit the ball into the reverse shift head and refit the No.4 shift shaft fork through the shift fork No.3 and the reverse shift head **(see illustration)**. Use a magnet and refit the interlock ball No.1 into the intermediate plate and slide the No.4 shift shaft fork through the intermediate plate.

66   On 5-speed models, align the hole in the No.4 shift shaft fork with hole in the No.3 shift fork and refit the roll pin using a hammer and pin punch.

67   On 5-speed models, refit the No.5 shift shaft through the reverse head and intermediate plate. Align the holes in the No.5 shift shaft with the reverse head and refit the roll pin using a hammer and punch.

68   On 4-speed models, refit the reverse shift head onto the shift shaft No.3 and refit the No.5 shift shaft through the reverse shift head and intermediate plate. Refit the roll pin into the reverse shift head using a hammer and pin punch **(see illustration)**.

69   Refit the shift shaft fork snap rings, locking balls, springs and intermediate screw plugs **(see illustrations 6.21 and 6.20)**. Tighten the intermediate screw plugs to the torque listed at the beginning of this Chapter's Specifications Section.

70   Remove the transmission from the vise and remove the nuts and bolts used to hold the assembly in the vise.

71   Apply non-hardening gasket sealant to the case mounting surfaces of the transmission. Lower the case onto the intermediate plate dowel pins while aligning the input bearing and counter bearings through the case. Refit the input and counter shaft front bearing snap rings.

72   Refit the front bearing retainer and gasket and tighten the eight retaining bolts to the torque listed at the beginning of this Chapter's Specifications Section.

73   On 2WD models, apply non-hardening gasket sealant to the extension housing mounting surface.

74   On 2WD models, refit the shift and select lever into the extension housing. Refit the extension housing to the case while guiding the lever into the shift fork and the No.5 shift shaft into the extension housing **(see illustration 6.14)**.

75   On 2WD models, refit the extension housing bolts and tighten the bolts to the torque listed at the beginning of this Chapter's Specifications Section.

76   On 2WD models, refit the shift lever housing set bolt and tighten the bolt to the torque listed at the beginning of this Chapter's

Specifications Section.

77   On 4WD models, apply non-hardening gasket sealant to the transfer case adaptor mounting surface. Refit the transfer case adaptor to the intermediate plate and tighten the eight retaining bolts to the torque listed at the beginning of this Chapter's Specifications Section.

78   On 4WD models, refit the shift lever through the top of the transfer case adaptor and align the lever with shift forks.

79   On 4WD models, refit the shift lever shaft through the transfer case adaptor plug, shift lever and intermediate plate. Refit the shift lever housing set bolt and tighten the bolt to the torque listed at the beginning of this Chapter's Specifications Section.

80   On 4WD models, refit the transfer case adaptor access plug using an Allen wrench and tighten the plug to the torque listed at the beginning of this Chapter's Specifications Section.

81   Refit the locking ball, spring and plug **(see illustration 6.11)** and tighten the plug to the torque listed at the beginning of this Chapter's Specifications Section.

82   Refit the restrict pins and shift lever retainer bolts and tighten to the torque listed at the beginning of this Chapter's Specifications Section.

83   Coat the clutch housing mounting bolts with thread sealer then slowly tighten the bolts in a clockwise direction until all the bolts and housing are seated. Then tighten the bolts to the torque listed at the beginning of this Chapter's Specifications Section.

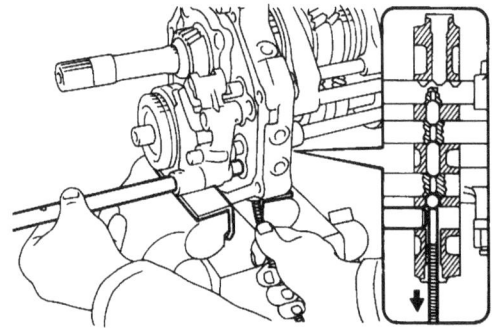

6.65 Slide the No.4 shift shaft through the No.3 shift fork, reverse head and into the intermediate plate - the check ball should rest on top of the shaft

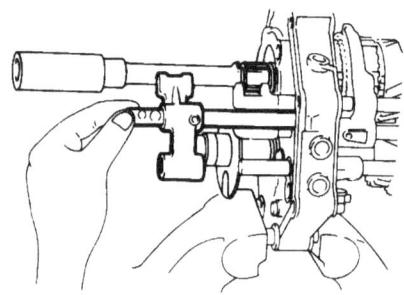

6.68 Refit the reverse shift head on the No.3 shift shaft - once the roll pin holes are aligned refit the roll pin using a hammer and pin punch

84   Refit the back-up light switch, speedometer gear and drain plug.

85   Refit the transmission in the vehicle and fill with the proper lubricant (see Chapter 1).

W50, W52 and W56 series

Disassembly

Refer to illustrations 6.88, 6.97, 6.102, 6.103, 6.106 and 6.110

86   Remove the transmission from the vehicle and clean the exterior of the transmission. Remove the transmission drain plug and drain the excess lubricant into a drain pan.

87   Remove the back-up light switch.

88   Remove the nine clutch housing retaining bolts and separate the housing from the case **(see illustration)**.

89   Remove the six shift lever retaining bolts and remove the lever and oil deflector.

90   Remove the two restrict pins using an open end spanner.

91   Remove the shift lever set bolt.

92   Remove the nine transfer case adaptor bolts and lightly tap the adaptor housing off with a plastic hammer.

93   Remove the seven front bearing retainer bolts and carefully prise the retainer from the case.

94   Using external type snap rings remove the input bearing and counter shaft bearing snap rings.

95   Using a plastic hammer lightly tap the case from the intermediate plate.

96   Once the case has been removed from the intermediate plate install two nuts, bolts with washers and tighten them securely. Using the heads of the nuts and bolts as a mounting surface set the plate assembly in a vise and tighten the vise down on the nuts and bolts.

97   Remove the locking ball and spring plugs **(see illustration)**, use a magnet to remove the springs and locking balls.

98   Remove the No.1 and No.2 shift fork lock washer and set bolts.

99   Remove the No.1 and No.2 shift shaft snap rings with two screwdrivers and a hammer **(see illustration 6.21)**.

100   Remove the reverse idler gear stop bolt then the idler gear and shaft.

101   Remove the No.1 shift shaft and fork.

102   Using a pencil type magnet remove the

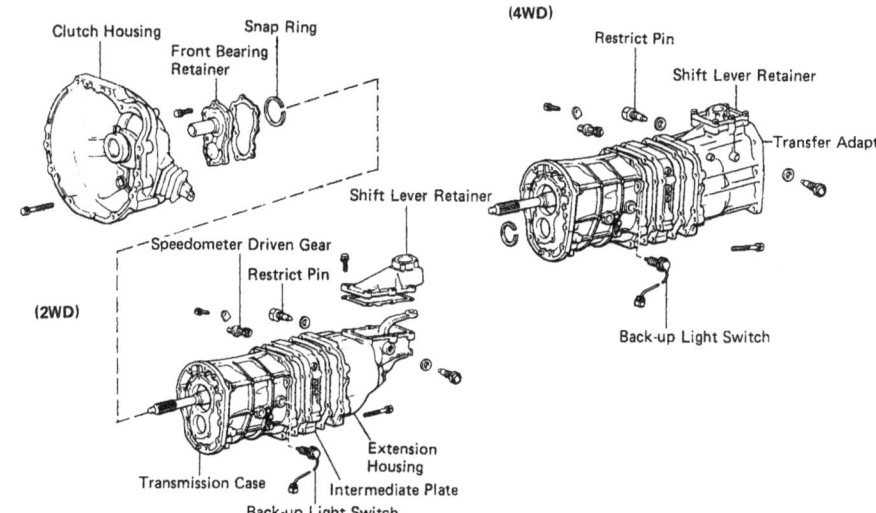

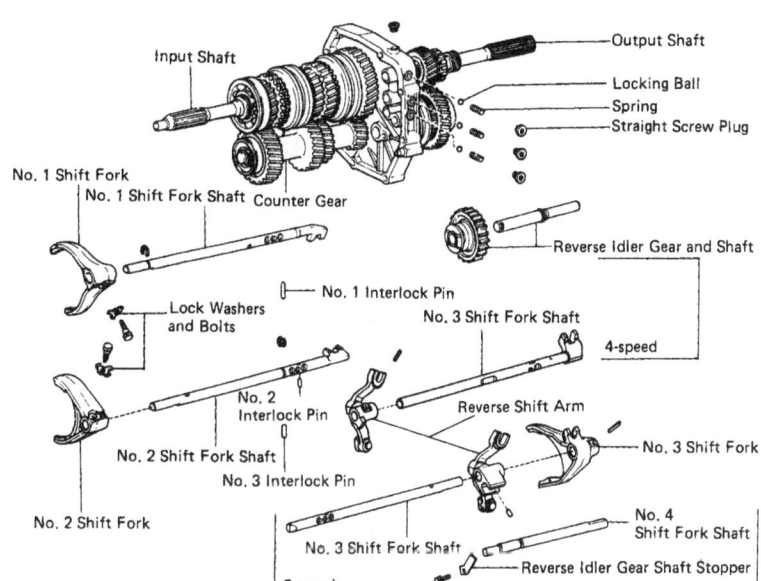

6.88 Typical W50, W52 and W56 series transmission exploded view

interlocking pins from the intermediate plate **(see illustrations)**.

103   Remove the No.2 shift fork.

104   Using a pin punch drive the roll pin out of the No.3 shift fork and remove the No.4 shift

shaft.

105   Remove the No.3 shift shaft, fork and reverse arm as an assembly.

106   Measure the 5th gear thrust clearance **(see illustration)**.

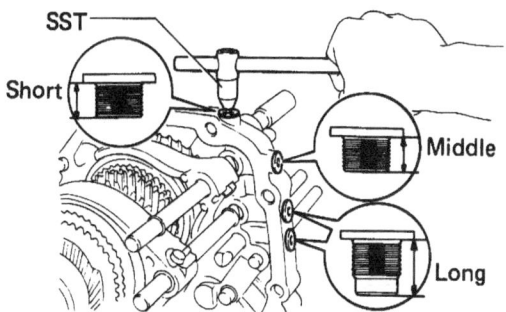

6.97 The locking ball plugs come in three different lengths 1 short, 1 medium and 2 long

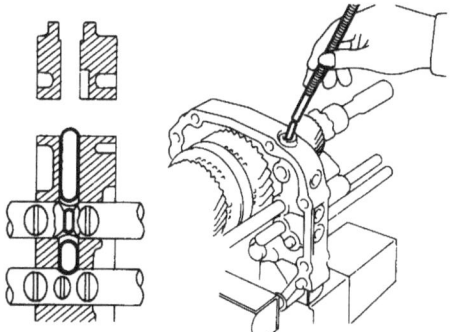

6.102a Typical location of the No.1 and No.2 interlock pins

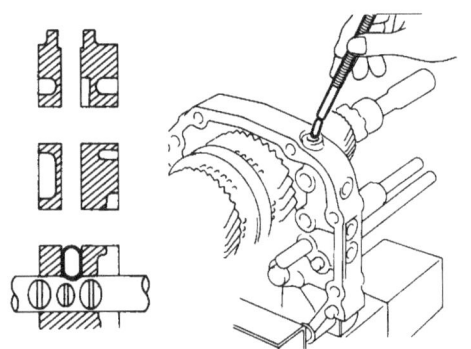

6.102b Typical location of the No.3 interlock pin

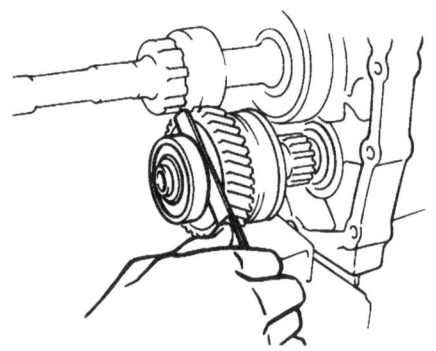

6.106 Using a feeler gauge check the 5th gear thrust clearance
the clearance should be 0.10 to 0.41 mm

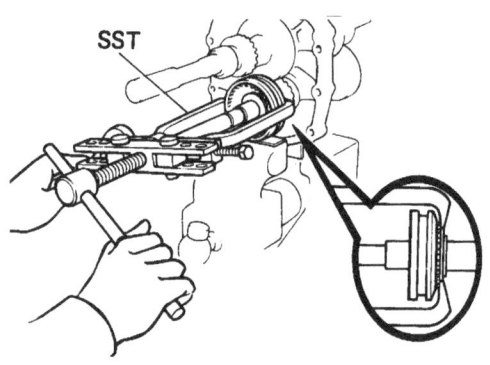

6.110 The puller jaws must contact the
hub not the shifter sleeve

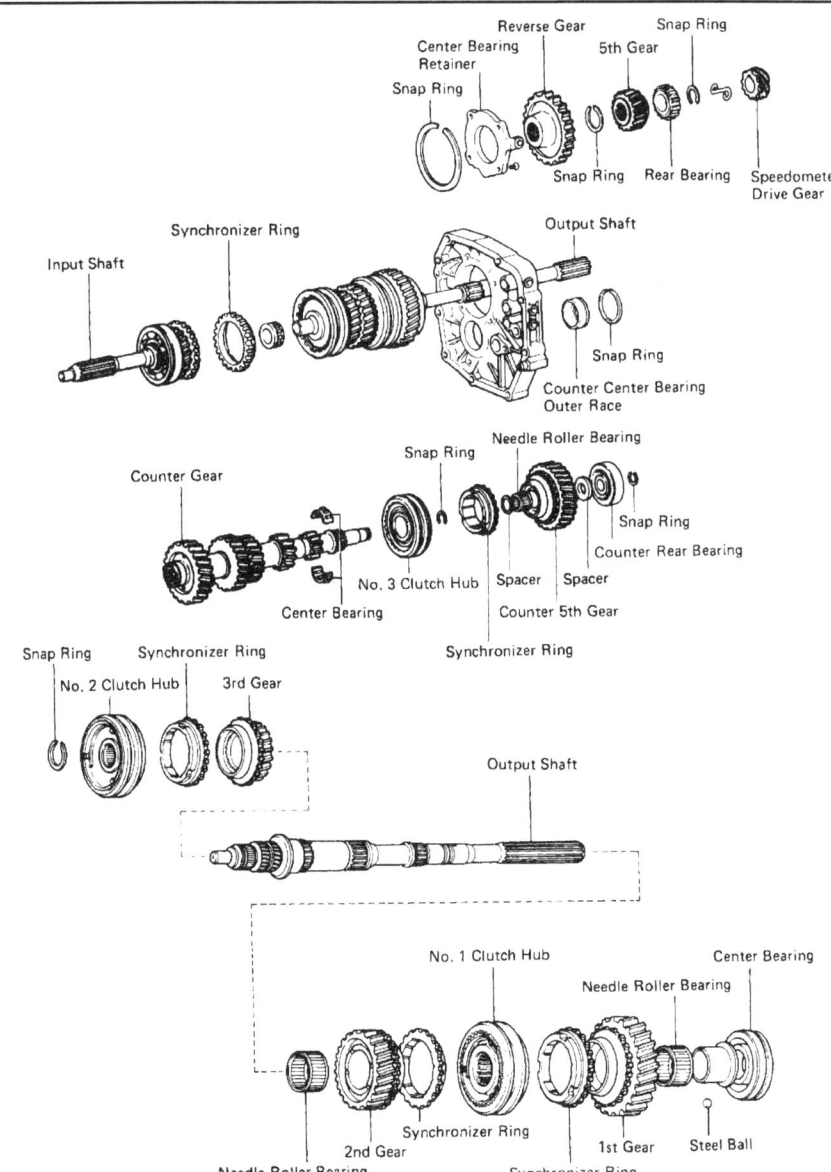

6.117 Typical W50, W52 and W56 series transmission shaft and geartrain exploded view

107 Using a pair of external type snap ring pliers remove the counter shaft rear bearing snap ring.

108 Remove the 5th gear, spacer and countershaft bearing using a two jaw gear puller.

109 Remove the No.3 hub assembly snap ring with two screwdrivers and a hammer **(see illustration 6.21)**.

110 Remove the No.3 clutch hub with a two jaw gear puller **(see illustration)**.

111 Remove the output shaft bearing snap ring with two screwdrivers and a hammer **(see illustration 6.21)**.

112 Use a three jaw type gear puller to remove the 5th gear and rear counter shaft bearing.

113 Remove the reverse gear snap ring with a pair of external snap ring pliers.

114 Remove the reverse gear with a long three jaw gear puller.

115 Using a Torx socket remove the four center bearing retainer Torx screws.

116 Remove the two center bearing snap rings and tap the counter shaft and then the main shaft out with a plastic hammer.

Inspection

Refer to illustration 6.117

117 Wash the transmission components thoroughly with solvent. Inspect the transmission cases for cracks in the bores, sides, bosses and bolt holes and stripped threads in the bolt holes. Check the geartrain and shift mechanisms for broken, chipped or worn gear teeth, bent or broken inserts, weak or broken insert springs, damaged roller or needle bearings and bearing bores in the countershaft and hub, output shaft, reverse idler shaft **(see illustration)**. Check the snap-rings for distortion and lack of tension. Inspect the front and rear bearings for galling, damage and roughness. Inspect the shift mechanisms for worn,

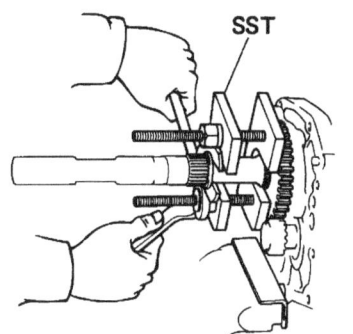

6.122 Refit the reverse gear using a suitable press

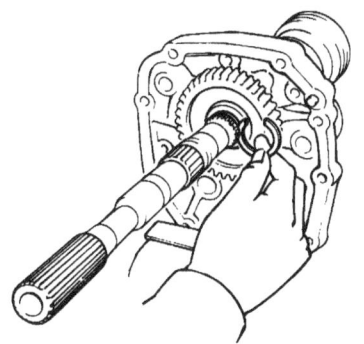

6.123 Check the clearance using the snap ring

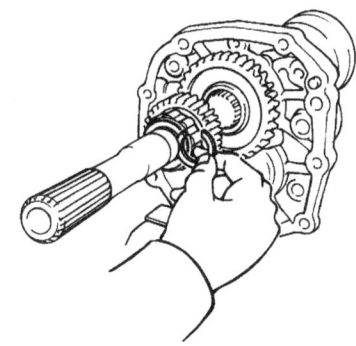

6.125 Check the clearance at the output shaft rear bearing snap ring

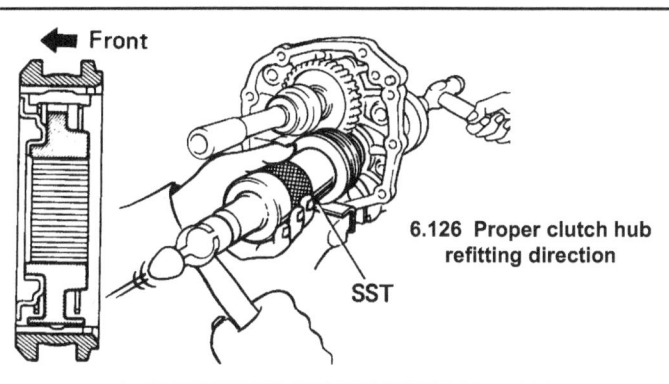

6.126 Proper clutch hub refitting direction

6.143 Guide the shift select lever into the shift fork

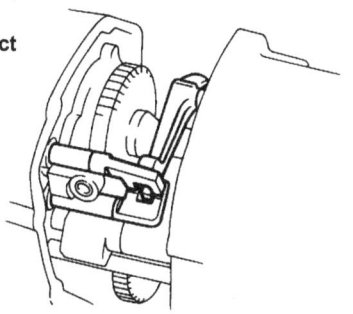

damaged or bent inserts, forks, rails, arms, plates, interlocks and levers.

Reassembly

Refer to illustrations 6.122, 6.123, 6.125, 6.126 and 6.143

Note: *Before reassembling the transmission components lubricate all bearings, gears, synchronizer rings, shafts, seals and clutch hub assemblies with transmission fluid.*

118 Refit the output shaft into the intermediate plate using a plastic hammer. Tap the intermediate plate with the plastic case while pulling the output shaft into the plate.

119 Coat the input shaft roller bearing cage with grease and fit it into the input shaft.

120 Refit the counter shaft and input shaft together make sure to align the slots in the synchronizer ring with the shifting keys on the output shaft.

121 Refit the center bearing snap rings and center bearing retainer and tighten the Torx screws to the torque listed at the beginning of this Chapter's Specification Section.

122 Refit the reverse gear using a press **(see illustration)**.

123 Use the snap ring as a feeler gauge to check the clearance **(see illustration)** and fit the correct snap ring to the output shaft using snap ring pliers.

124 Refit the 5th gear, spacer and output shaft bearing together.

125 Check the clearance at the output shaft rear bearing **(see illustration)** and refit the snap ring.

126 Refit the No.3 clutch hub **(see illustration)** with a long tube and hammer.

127 Check the clearance at the No.3 clutch

hub snap ring and fit the proper snap ring on the shaft.

128 Refit the 5th counter shaft gear, needle bearings and synchronizer ring make sure to align the slots in the synchronizer ring with the shifting keys.

129 Refit the bearing and spacer and bearing snap ring check the clearance the 5th gear counter shaft thrust clearance it should be between 0.10 to 0.41 mm **(see illustration 6.106)**. If the clearance is incorrect fit a new snap ring.

130 Refit the reverse idler gear and shaft apply grease to the pin and refit the pin into the reverse shift head. Refit the No.3 shift shaft through the No.3 shift fork and reverse arm. Set the No.3 shift fork on the No.3 clutch hub sleeve, insert the reverse shift arm into the pivot and slide the No.3 shift shaft into the intermediate plate.

131 Using a screwdriver push the pin through the reverse shift head and into the No.3 shift shaft. Refit the No.4 shift shaft over the reverse shift head and through the intermediate plate. Align the roll pin hole in the No.3 shift shaft with the roll pin hole in the No.3 shift fork and refit the roll pin using a hammer and pin punch.

132 Refit the No.3 interlock pin **(see illustration 6.102b)** into the intermediate plate.

133 Refit the No.2 shift shaft and fork and interlock pin No.2 **(see illustration 6.102a)** into the intermediate plate. Refit the No.2 shift shaft snap ring.

134 Using grease refit interlock pin No.1 into the intermediate plate **(see illustration 6.102a)**.

135 Refit the No.1 shift fork into the No.1

clutch hub then the No.1 shift shaft through the fork and into the intermediate plate. Refit the No.1 shift shaft snap ring.

136 Refit the No.1 and No.2 shift fork set bolts and lock washers and tighten the bolts to the torque listed at the beginning of this Chapter's Specification Section. Bend the lock washers around the bolt head using pliers.

137 Refit the locking balls, springs and plugs **(see illustration 6.97)** and tighten the plugs to the torque listed at the beginning of this Chapter's Specification Section..

138 Refit the reverse idler stop and tighten the bolt to the torque listed at the beginning of this Chapter's Specification Section.

139 Remove the transmission from the vise and remove the nuts and bolts used to hold the assembly in the vise.

140 Apply non-hardening gasket sealant to the case mounting surfaces of the transmission. Lightly tap the case with a plastic hammer to help seat the case to the intermediate plate and refit the input and counter shaft bearing snap rings.

141 Apply non-hardening gasket sealant to the front bearing retainer mounting surfaces. Refit the retainer to the case and tighten the retainer bolts to the torque listed at the beginning of this Chapter's Specification Section.

142 Refit the shift and select lever into the transfer case adaptor.

143 Apply non-hardening gasket sealant to the transfer case adaptor mounting surfaces and start to refit the adaptor to the intermediate plate **(see illustration)**.

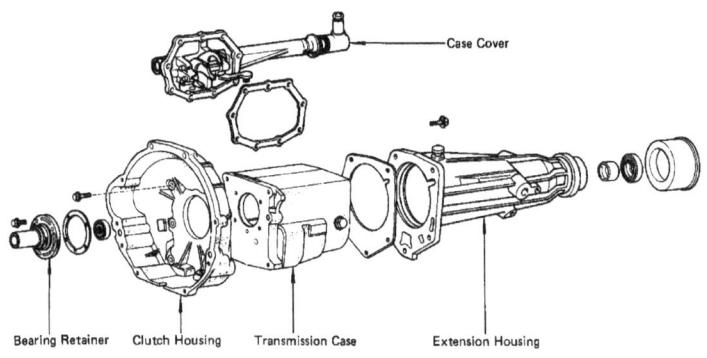

6.153 Typical L40, L42 and L43 transmission exploded view

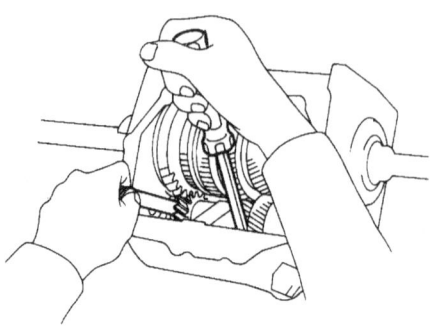

6.158 Use a screwdriver to push the counter shaft to the front of the case and measure the clearance using a feeler gauge - the clearance should be 0.10 to 0.30 mm

144 Refit the shift lever housing to the shift select lever and seat the adaptor to the intermediate plate.

145 Refit the shift lever set bolt and tighten the bolt to the torque listed at the beginning of this Chapter's Specification Section.

146 Refit the nine transfer case adaptor mounting bolts and tighten the bolts to the torque listed at the beginning of this Chapter's Specification Section.

147 Refit the restrict pins and shift lever retainer bolts and tighten to the to the torque listed at the beginning of this Chapter's Specifications Section.

148 Refit the clutch housing and tighten the nine bolts to the to the torque listed at the beginning of this Chapter's Specifications Section.

149 Refit the back-up light switch, speedometer gear and drain plug.

150 Refit the transmission in the vehicle and fill with the proper lubricant (see Chapter 1).

L40, L42 and L43 series

Disassembly

Refer to illustrations 6.153 and 6.158

151 Remove the transmission from the vehicle (see Section 5) and clean the exterior of the transmission. Remove the transmission drain plug and drain the excess lubricant into a drain pan.

152 Remove the release fork and bearing, speedometer gear and the back-up light switch.

153 Remove the two shift lever retaining bolts and nine case cover bolts, then slowly pull the case cover from the transmission case **(see illustration)**.

154 Remove the four clutch housing mounting bolts use a plastic hammer to lightly tap the clutch housing apart if needed.

155 Remove the four front bearing retainer bolts and remove the retainer and gasket.

156 Remove the five extension housing bolts and slide the extension from the transmission case. Use a plastic hammer to lightly tap the extension housing apart if needed.

157 Push the reverse idler shaft to the rear of the case and remove the half moon shaped key from the bottom of the shaft and pull the shaft from the case. Once the idler shaft is

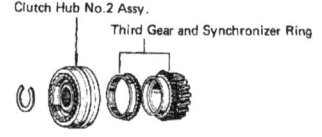

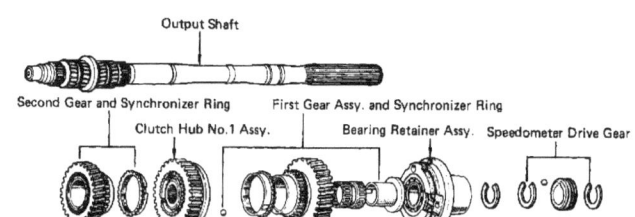

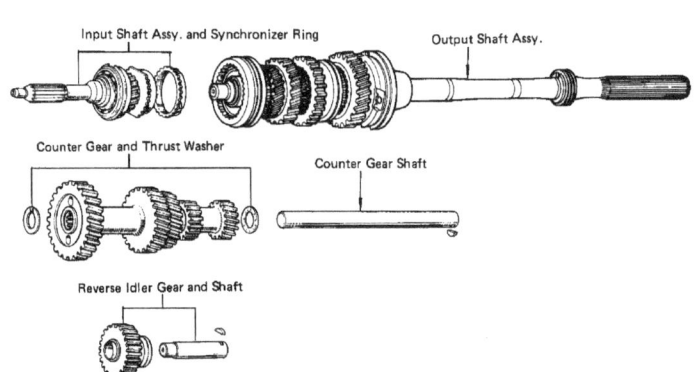

6.163a Typical L40, L42 and L43 transmission geartrain exploded view

removed remove the reverse idler gear from the case.

158 Check the counter gear thrust clearance **(see illustration)**.

159 From the front of the case, drive the counter gear shaft out (to the rear) using a long brass punch and allow the counter shaft to drop into the case and remove the key.

160 Pull the output shaft to the rear of the case and remove it from the case through the top.

161 Once the output shaft has been removed rotate the input shaft until the flat spot on the input shaft can clear the counter shaft and remove the input shaft through the top of the case.

162 Remove the counter shaft, thrust washers and needle bearings from the case.

Inspection

Refer to illustrations 6.163a and 6.163b

163 Wash the transmission components thoroughly with solvent. Inspect the transmission cases for cracks in the bores, sides, bosses and bolt holes and stripped threads in the bolt holes. Check the geartrain and shift mechanisms for broken, chipped or worn gear teeth, bent or broken inserts, weak or broken insert springs, damaged roller or needle bearings and bearing bores in the countershaft and hub, output shaft, reverse idler shaft **(see illustrations)**. Check the snap-rings for distortion and lack of tension. Inspect the front and rear bearings for galling, damage and roughness. Inspect the shift mechanisms for worn, damaged or bent inserts, forks, rails, arms, plates, interlocks and levers.

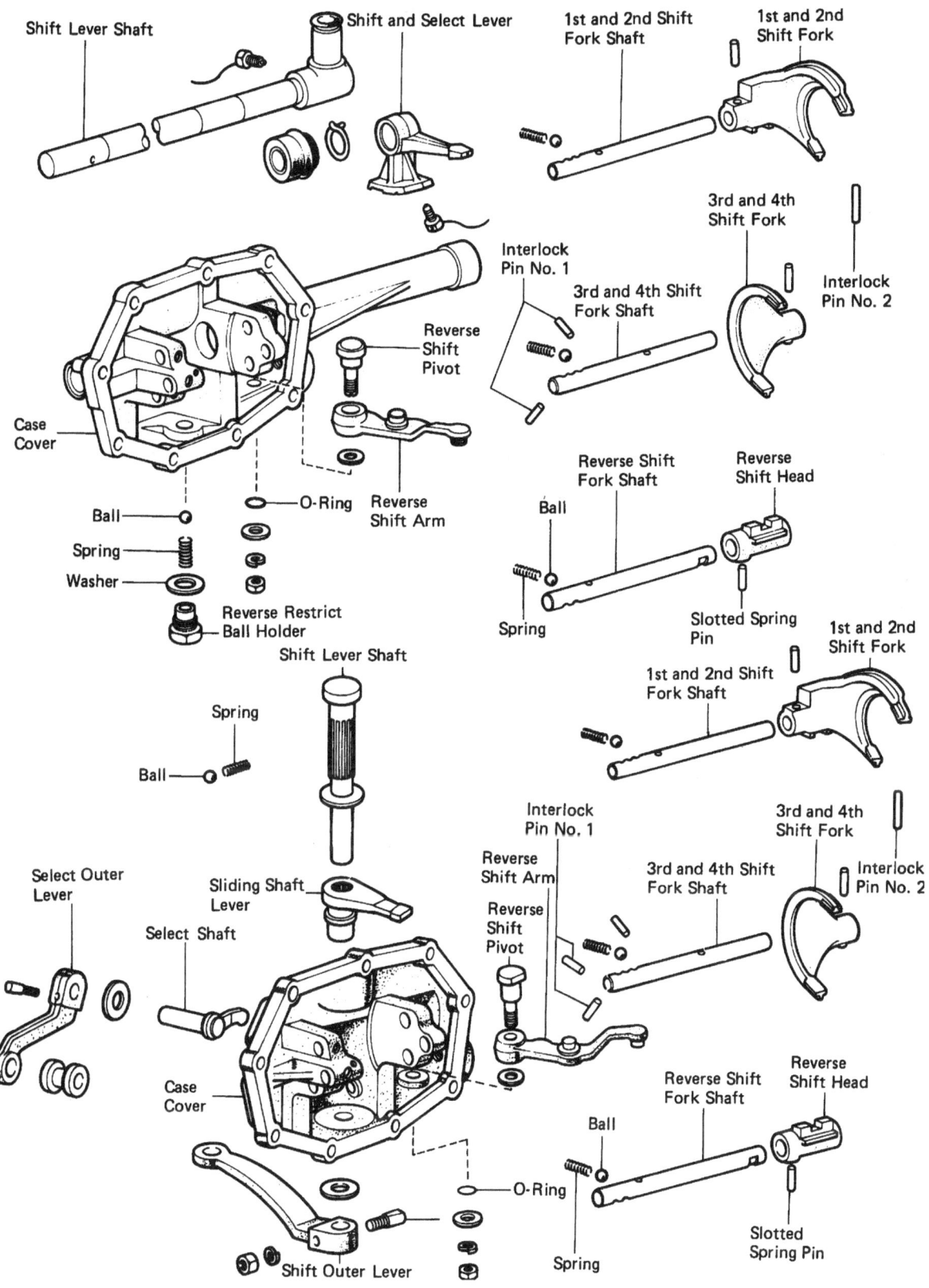

6.163b Typical L40, L42 and L43 transmission shift assembly exploded view

Reassembly

Refer to illustrations 6.175

Note: *Before reassembling the transmission components lubricate all bearings, gears, synchronizer rings, shafts, seals, clutch hub assemblies with transmission fluid.*

164 Coat the counter shaft needle bearings with grease and refit the bearings into the counter shaft.

165 Coat the counter shaft thrust washers with grease and refit them into the case. There is a difference between the front and rear thrust washer. The rear washer is slightly smaller than the front washer and has a mark on the back of the washer.

166 Refit the counter shaft into the case. Make sure the thrust washer tangs are fitted into the slots in the case.

167 Coat the input shaft needle bearings with grease and refit them into the input shaft. Rotate the input shaft until the flat spot on the input shaft can clear the counter shaft and refit the input shaft into the case.

168 Refit the front bearing retainer and gasket to the case with the oil return hole at the bottom. Coat the retainer bolt threads with sealant and refit the bolts. Tighten the bolts to the torque listed in this Chapter's Specification Section.

169 Refit the output shaft assembly into the case. Align the rear bearing roll pin with the

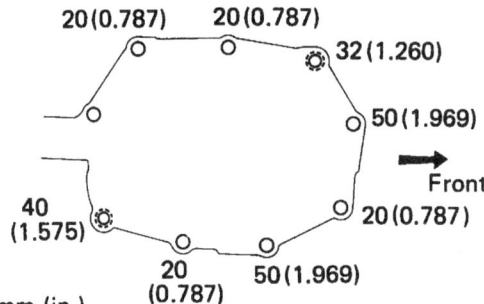

6.175 Refit the case cover bolts into the correct bolt hole locations as shown

groove in the rear of the case.

170 Refit the counter gear shaft through the rear of the case, thrust washers, counter gear and needle bearings and refit the half moon shaped key and seat the shaft into the case.

171 Check the thrust clearance **(see illustration 6.158)**. If the thrust clearance is incorrect replace the thrust washers with the appropriate size.

172 Refit the reverse idler gear and shaft into the case and Refit the half moon shaped key into the bottom of the shaft.

173 Refit a new gasket on the extension housing and fit the housing onto the case. Tighten the bolts to the torque listed in this Chapter's Specification Section.

174 Refit the clutch housing to the case and tighten the four bolts to the torque listed in this Chapter's Specification Section.

175 Fit a new case cover gasket onto the case and place the shift forks in the neutral position. Refit the cover onto the case **(see illustration)** and tighten the bolts to the torque listed in this Chapter's Specification Section.

176 Refit the two shift lever retaining bolt and tighten the bolts to the torque listed in this Chapter's Specification Section.

177 Refit the back-up light switch, speedometer gear and the release fork and bearing.

178 Refit the transmission in the vehicle and fill with the proper lubricant (see Chapter 1).

Chapter 7 Part B
Automatic transmission

Contents

Specifications

Torque specifications

	Nm
Transmission-to-engine bolt	64
Torque converter-to-driveplate bolt	
YN/LN50, 60 series	18
YN/RN/LN80, 90, 105, 106, 110	41
4Runner	27
Rear engine mount-to-crossmember	25
Rear engine mount-to-extension housing	19 to 30

1 General information

All vehicles covered in this manual are equipped with either a 4- or 5-speed manual transmission or an automatic transmission. All information on the automatic transmission is included in this Part of Chapter 7. Information for the manual transmission can be found in Part A. Information on the transfer case used on 4WD models can be found in Part C.

Specialised techniques and equipment are required when working on the automatic transmissions, due to their complexity. Consequently, this Chapter addresses only those procedures concerning routine maintenance, general diagnosis and removal and refitting.

If the transmission requires major repair work, it should be left to a dealer service department or an automotive transmission repair shop. You can, however, remove and refit the transmission yourself and save the expense, even if the repair work is done by a transmission specialist.

2 Diagnosis - general

Note: *Automatic transmission malfunctions may be caused by five general conditions: poor engine performance, improper adjustments, hydraulic malfunctions, mechanical malfunctions or malfunctions in the computer or its signal network. Diagnosis of these problems should always begin with a check of the easily repaired items: fluid level and condition (Chapter 1), shift linkage adjustment and throttle linkage adjustment. Next, perform a road test to determine if the problem has been corrected or if more diagnosis is necessary. If the problem persists after the preliminary tests and corrections are completed, additional diagnosis should be done by a dealer service department or transmission repair shop.*

Preliminary checks

1 Drive the vehicle to warm the transmission to normal operating temperature.
2 Check the fluid level as described in Chapter 1:

a) *If the fluid level is unusually low, add enough fluid to bring the level within the designated area of the dipstick, then check for external leaks (see below).*
b) *If the fluid level is abnormally high, drain off the excess, then check the drained fluid for contamination by coolant. The presence of engine coolant in the automatic transmission fluid indicates that a failure has occurred in the internal radiator walls that separate the coolant from the transmission fluid (see Chapter 3).*
c) *If the fluid is foaming, drain it and refill the transmission, then check for coolant in the fluid or a high fluid level.*

3 Check the engine idle speed. **Note:** *If the engine is malfunctioning, do not proceed with the preliminary checks until it has been repaired and runs normally.*
4 Check the throttle valve cable for freedom of movement. Adjust it if necessary (Section 3). **Note:** *The throttle valve cable may function properly when the engine is shut off and cold, but it may malfunction once the*

engine is hot. Check it cold and at normal engine operating temperature.

5   Inspect the shift control linkage (Section 4). Make sure that it's properly adjusted and that the linkage operates smoothly.

Fluid leak diagnosis

6   Most fluid leaks are easy to locate visually. Repair usually consists of renewing a seal or gasket. If a leak is difficult to find, the following procedure may help.

7   Identify the fluid. Make sure it's transmission fluid and not engine oil or brake fluid.

8   Try to pinpoint the source of the leak. Drive the vehicle several kilometres, then park it over a large sheet of cardboard. After a minute or two, you should be able to locate the leak by determining the source of the fluid dripping onto the cardboard.

9   Make a careful visual inspection of the suspected component and the area immediately around it. Pay particular attention to gasket mating surfaces. A mirror is often helpful for finding leaks in areas that are hard to see.

10   If the leak still cannot be found, clean the suspected area thoroughly with a degreaser or solvent, then dry it.

11   Drive the vehicle for several kilometres at normal operating temperature and varying speeds. After driving the vehicle, visually inspect the suspected component again.

12   Once the leak has been located, the cause must be determined before it can be properly repaired. If a gasket is renewed but the sealing flange is bent, the new gasket will not stop the leak. The bent flange must be straightened.

13   Before attempting to repair a leak, check to make sure that the following conditions are corrected or they may cause another leak. **Note:** *Some of the following conditions (a leaking torque converter, for instance) cannot be fixed without highly specialised tools and expertise. Such problems must be referred to a transmission shop or a dealer service department.*

Gasket leaks

14   Check the pan periodically. Make sure the bolts are tight; no bolts are missing, the gasket is in good condition and the pan is flat (dents in the pan may indicate damage to the valve body inside).

15   If the pan gasket is leaking, the fluid level or the fluid pressure may be too high, the vent may be plugged, the pan bolts may be too tight, the pan sealing flange may be warped, the sealing surface of the transmission housing may be damaged, the gasket may be damaged or the transmission casting may be cracked or porous. If sealant instead of gasket material has been used to form a seal between the pan and the transmission housing, it may be the wrong sealant.

Seal leaks

16   If a transmission seal is leaking, the fluid level or pressure may be too high, the vent may be plugged, the seal bore may be damaged, the seal itself may be damaged or

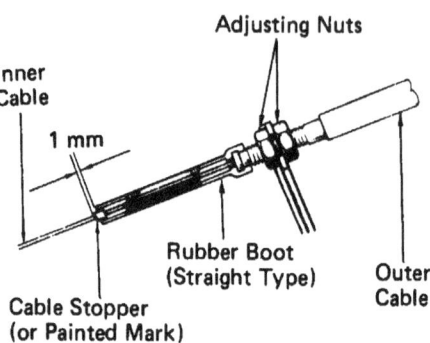

3.3 Throttle Valve (TV) linkage adjustment details

improperly fitted, the surface of the shaft protruding through the seal may be damaged or a loose bearing may be causing excessive shaft movement.

17   Make sure the dipstick tube seal is in good condition and the tube is properly seated. Periodically check the area around the speedometer gear or sensor for leakage. If transmission fluid is evident, check the O-ring for damage.

Case leaks

18   If the case itself appears to be leaking, the casting is porous and will have to be repaired or renewed.

19   Make sure the oil cooler hose fittings are tight and in good condition.

Fluid comes out vent pipe or fill tube

20   If this condition occurs, the transmission is overfilled, there is coolant in the fluid, the dipstick is incorrect, the vent is plugged or the drain-back holes are plugged.

3   Throttle Valve (TV) linkage - adjustment

Refer to illustration 3.3

1   Make sure the throttle cable bracket is not bent or loose before attempting to make this adjustment. Also, the rubber boot must be seated properly on the adjuster.

2   Press the accelerator pedal all the way to the floor (an assistant would be helpful here).

Note: *The throttle plate on the carburettor or bellcrank on the injection pump must be against the maximum speed stop; check and adjust if necessary.*

3   Check the distance between the end of the rubber boot and the stopper (or painted mark) on the cable **(see illustration)**. It must be 1 mm.

4   If the boot-to-stopper clearance is not as specified, loosen and back off the outer adjusting nut. Turn the inner adjusting nut to remove the cable housing as required to produce the specified clearance. Be sure to tighten the outer nut to lock the housing in position.

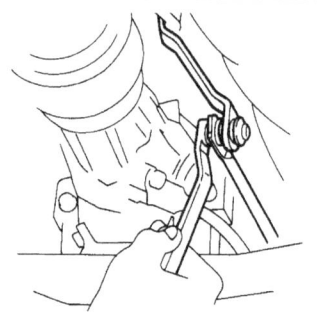

4.6 Shift linkage adjustment point

4   Shift linkage - adjustment

Refer to illustration 4.6

1   This adjustment should not be considered routine and is not required unless wear in the linkage or misalignment of the shift position indicator occurs.

2   Position the shift lever in Drive, Second, Low and Reverse and make sure the transmission responds accordingly. Place the lever in Neutral, then verify that the transmission lever shifts to Neutral. Check to see if the shift position indicator registers correctly with the lever in each detent position.

3   If adjustment is required, the vehicle must be raised and supported securely on jackstands.

4   Push the lever on the transmission all the way to the rear, then return it two notches to the Neutral position.

5   In the passenger compartment, place the shift lever in the Neutral position.

6   With the assistant holding the shift lever tightly against the stop (toward Reverse gear), tighten the linkage nut securely **(see illustration)**.

5   Neutral start switch - adjustment and renewal

Refer to illustration 5.5, 5.8a, 5.8b and 5.11

1   The neutral start switch is located on the side of the transmission housing. Its purpose is to allow the starter to operate only when

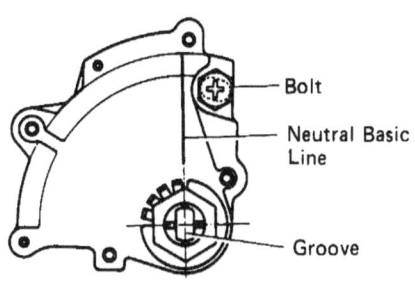

5.5 Neutral start switch
adjustment details

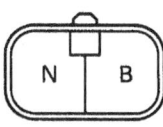

	B	N	RB	RL
P	o—————o			
R			o—————o	
N	o—————o			

5.8a Continuity should exist between the
indicated start switch terminals when the
switch is correctly aligned (Hi-lux models)

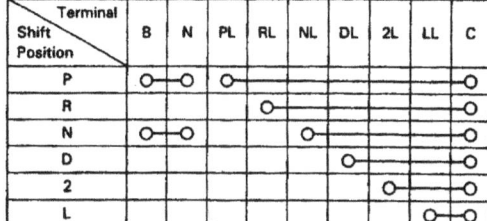

Terminal Shift Position	B	N	PL	RL	NL	DL	2L	LL	C
P	o—o	o							o
R			o						o
N	o—o		o						o
D					o				o
2					o				o
L							o—o		

5.8b The switch connector and
the continuity table look like
this on 4Runner models

the selector lever is in Neutral or Park. It also
operates the back-up lights when the lever is
in Reverse.
2   If the engine can be started with the shift
lever in any position other than Park or Neutral, the neutral start switch should be checked
and adjusted and, if necessary, renewed.

Adjustment

3   Place the shift lever in Neutral.
4   Raise the vehicle and place it securely
on jackstands.
5   Loosen the neutral start switch bolt **(see
illustration)**.
6   Align the groove in the end of the control
shaft with the vertical index line on the switch
by pivoting the switch.

7   Tighten the switch bolt.
8   To verify that you've adjusted the switch
properly, check for continuity between the
indicated terminals of the switch electrical
connector **(see illustrations)**.
9   If the switch fails the continuity check,
renew it.

Renewal

10   Detach the cable from the negative battery terminal.
11   Remove the control shaft nut and washer
(see illustration).
12   Detach the lever.
13   Bend the lock washer tangs open and
unscrew the switch retaining nut. Remove the
washer and grommet behind the nut.

14   Remove the switch mounting bolt.
15   Unplug the switch electrical connector, if
you haven't already done so.
16   Remove the neutral start switch.
17   Refitting is the reverse of removal. Make
sure the grooved side of the grommet faces
toward the transmission. Don't forget to bend
down the tangs on the lock washer.
18   Adjust the switch as previously
described.

6   Automatic transmission - removal and refitting

*Refer to illustrations 6.10a, 6.10b, 6.18a,
6.18b, 6.20 and 6.21*

1   Disconnect the cable from the negative
battery terminal.
2   Drain the cooling system and disconnect
the radiator top hose, then remove the fan
shroud.
3   Remove the air cleaner assembly and
disconnect the throttle linkage cable at the
carburettor or throttle body on petrol models, or at the injection pump linkage on diesel
models.
4   Remove the upper mounting nut on the
starter.
5   Raise the vehicle and support it securely
on jackstands.
6   Drain the fluid from the transmission
(Chapter 1).
7   Disconnect the wiring connectors to
the solenoid, Neutral start and back-up light
switches located near the starter.
8   Remove the starter motor (see Chapter 5).
9   Remove the driveshaft(s).
10   On 4WD models, disconnect the transfer
case shift linkage and then unbolt and remove
the cross shaft **(see illustrations)**.
11   Disconnect the speedometer drive cable.
12   Disconnect the manual shift linkage
at the rear connection. Disconnect the fluid
cooler lines from the transmission and plug
them.
13   Disconnect the exhaust pipe clamp.
14   On 4WD models, disconnect and plug
the two oil cooler lines.

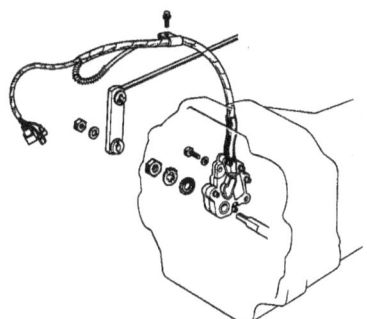

5.11 Typical neutral start switch
refitting details

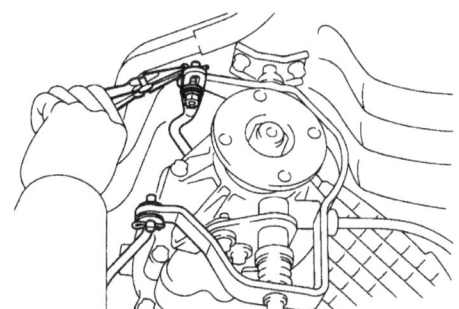

6.10a Use needle-nose pliers to
disconnect the transfer case linkage by
pulling out the retaining pins

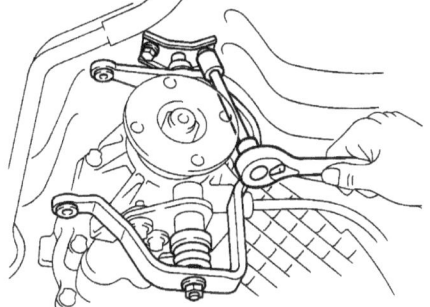

6.10b Remove the two transfer case
shift cross shaft bolts with a
socket and extension

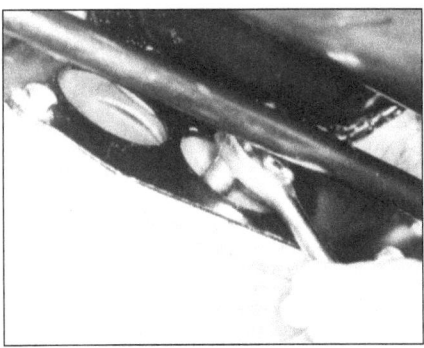

6.18a Use a socket and ratchet to remove each of the six torque converter bolts in turn by rotating the crankshaft pulley bolt with a spanner

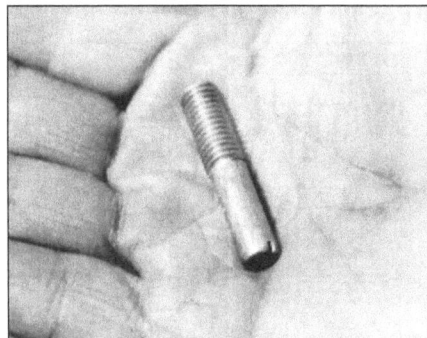

6.18b Guide pins (like this one made by cutting the head off a bolt) aid in removal of the transmission

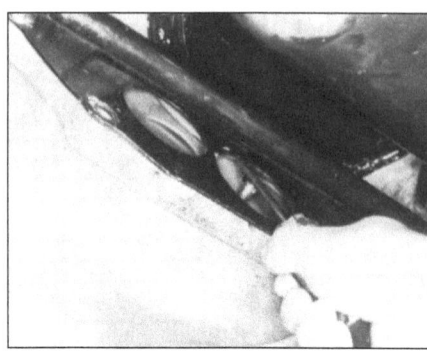

6.20 Use a large screwdriver to prise between the engine rear plate and the guide pins to move the transmission away from the engine

15   Remove the bolt and pull the fluid filler tube from the transmission, taking care not to lose the O-rings.
16   Remove the driveplate cover.
17   Remove the splash shield from below the radiator (if equipped).
18   Support the automatic transmission with a jack, then remove the rear support cross-member and mount. Through the open lower half of the torque converter housing, remove the six bolts which join the driveplate and converter together. Remove them one at a time by rotating the driveplate **(see illustration)**. To do this, turn the crankshaft with a spanner attached to the front pulley securing bolt. Now screw two guide pins (easily made from two old bolts) into opposite bolt holes in the front of the driveplate, then rotate the engine until they are horizontal **(see illustration)**. These pins will act as levering points during removal of the transmission.
19   Place a jack under the engine sump (use a block of wood to protect it), and remove the bolts which attach the torque converter housing to the engine.

20   Lower both jacks progressively until the transmission will clear the lower edge of the firewall. Use a large lever or screwdriver, between the engine rear plate and the temporary guide pins and prise the transmission away from the engine **(see illustration)**. Make sure the torque converter stays with the transmission. Never position the lever between the driveplate and the torque converter as damage or distortion will result.
21   The torque converter can now be pulled forward to remove it from the housing **(see illustration)**. The driveplate can be unbolted from the crankshaft flange if it has to be renewed because of a worn starter ring gear or for access to the rear main oil seal (see Chapter 2).
22   The refitting procedure is basically the reverse of removal. Before refitting the transmission, make sure the torque converter is completely seated by pushing it toward the transmission and turning it until it "clunks" into place on the input shaft and the front pump splines (it may make more than one "clunk").

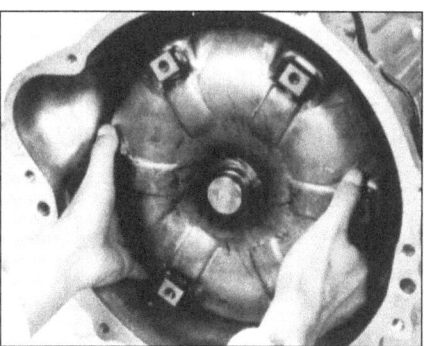

6.21 Grasp the torque converter securely and pull it from the transmission; be careful, it is quite heavy

23   Tighten all bolts and nuts securely. using a torque wrench where necessary. Be sure to refill the cooling system and the transmission with the required fluids (see Chapter 1). Adjust the shift and throttle valve linkages as described in this Chapter before road testing the vehicle.

Chapter 7 Part C
Transfer case

Contents

Specifications

Torque specifications

	Nm
Companion flange nuts	
Counter gear type	123
Planetary gear type	118
Extension housing bolts	
Counter gear type	39
Planetary gear type	11
Front bearing retainer bolts	
Counter gear type	18
Planetary gear type	11
Gear reduction case bolts	39
Oil pump body bolts	11
Oil strainer bolts	18
Output shaft bearing retainer bolts	18
Rear case bolts	39
Torx screw plugs	12 to 19
Transfer case cover bolts	8.8
Transfer case-to-transmission bolts	39
Transfer case indicator switch	34
Upper cover bolts	18

2.2 Mark the relationship of the driveshaft to the transfer case companion flange before removing the bolts (this will ensure correct alignment of the shaft during installation)

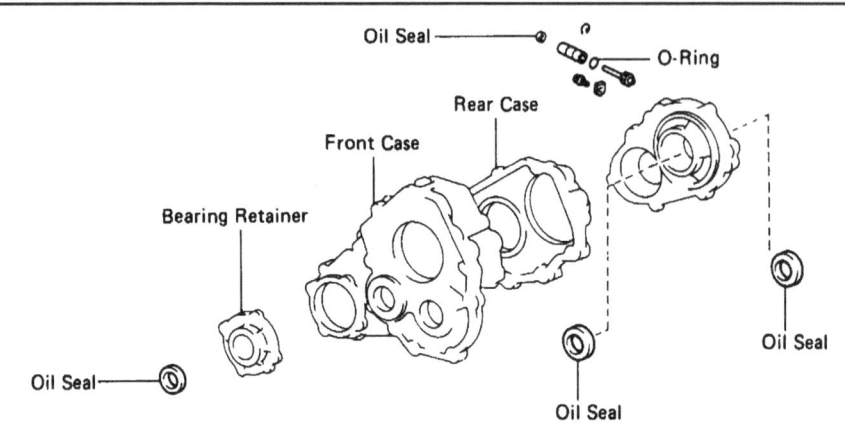

2.5 Exploded view of transfer case seals (typical)

1   General information

Four-wheel drive models are equipped with a transfer case mounted on the rear of the transmission. Drive is passed from the engine through the transmission and the transfer case to the front and rear wheels by the driveshafts.

2   Transfer case oil seals - renewal

Refer to illustrations 2.2 and 2.5

1   Raise the vehicle and support it on jack-stands. Remove the transfer case rock guard and drain the oil (see Chapter 1).
2   Mark the positions of the driveshaft flanges in relation to the transfer case flanges **(see illustration)**. Remove the bolts and disconnect the driveshafts.
3   Remove the locknut from the transfer case companion flange. To keep the flange from turning, reinstall two of the driveshaft mounting bolts and engage a lever between them.
4   Using a puller, remove the companion flange.
5   Carefully prise the oil seal out with a screwdriver or seal removal tool, being sure not to scratch or damage the seal bore in the case **(see illustration)**. A block of wood placed between the screwdriver and case can provide additional leverage.
6   Lubricate the lip of the seal with gear oil and tap it into position with a seal driver or a large socket or block of wood.
7   Place the companion flange into position. Install the locknut and tighten it to the torque listed in this Chapter's Specifications.
8   Reinstall the driveshaft, being sure the flange marks made during removal are aligned.
9   Refill the transfer case with oil, referring to Chapter 1 if necessary.
10   Reinstall the rock guard and lower the vehicle to the ground.

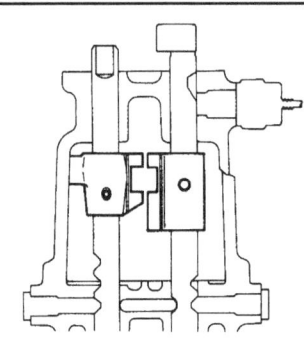

3.5 Move the shift fork shafts to the high/four position before installing the transfer case to the transmission

3   Transfer case - removal and refitting

Refer to illustrations 3.5, 3.8, 3.9a and 3.9b

Removal

1   Remove the transmission and transfer case from the vehicle as a unit, referring to the removal procedures in either Part A or Part B of this Chapter.
2   Carefully clean off the assembly, removing all mounts, dampers and dust covers from the transfer case.
3   Stand the transfer case/transmission in a vertical position, with the transfer case pointed up and remove the transfer case-to-transmission bolts.
4   Pull the transfer case straight up and remove it from the transmission, taking care not to damage the adapter rear oil seal with the transfer case input shaft gear spline.

Refitting

Manual transmission

5   Shift the two shift forks to the high/four position **(see illustration)**.
6   Lubricate the transfer case adapter oil seal with multi-purpose grease.
7   Fit a new gasket.
8   With the transmission in a vertical position, carefully insert the input gear straight

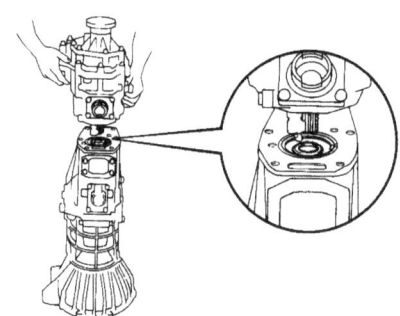

3.8 Lower the transfer case input shaft carefully into the transmission, taking care not to damage the oil seal

into the adapter rear oil seal, fit the transfer case to the transmission **(see illustration)**. Refit the bolts. Tighten the bolts to the specified torque listed in this Chapters Specification Section.

Automatic transmission

9   Carefully clean the contact surfaces of the transmission and transfer case, making sure that all traces of sealer are removed. Apply a 3 mm wide bead of sealant such as Loctite 518 or equivalent to the transmission contact surface and fit the two gaskets **(see illustrations)**. Carefully lower the transfer case onto the transmission and refit the seven retaining bolts. Tighten the bolts to the specified torque listed in this Chapters Specification Section.

4   Transfer case - overhaul

General information

1   If your transfer case reaches the end of its service life, you can save a great deal of money by removing and fitting it yourself, but you're better off leaving the overhaul to a transmission repair shop. Better yet, buy a rebuilt unit from a dealer parts department or an auto parts store. Rebuilding a transfer is a difficult job involving the disassembly and reassembly of many small parts. The cost in

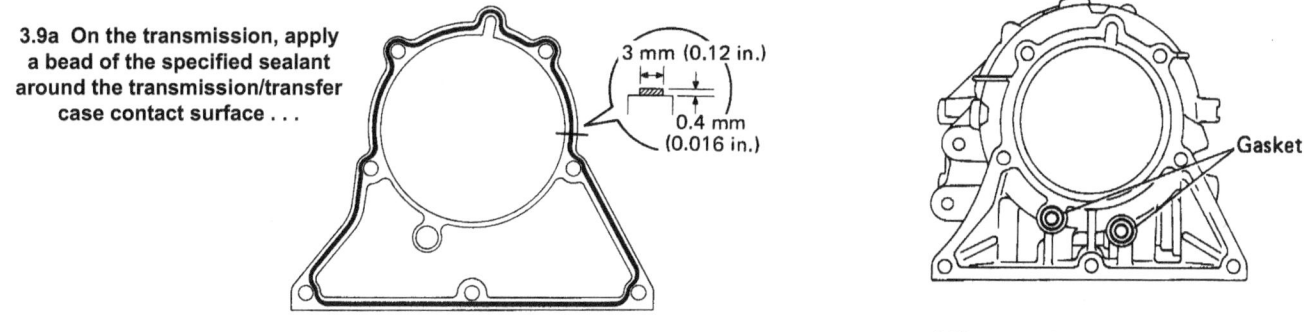

3.9a On the transmission, apply a bead of the specified sealant around the transmission/transfer case contact surface . . .

3 mm (0.12 in.)

0.4 mm (0.016 in.)

Gasket

3.9b . . . and then fit the two gaskets

time and money to overhaul a transfer case yourself will almost surely exceed the cost of a rebuilt unit.

2   Nevertheless, it's not impossible for an inexperienced mechanic to rebuild a transfer case if the special tools are available and the job is done in a deliberate step-by-step manner so nothing is overlooked.

3   The tools necessary for an overhaul include internal and external snap-ring pliers, a bearing puller, a slide hammer, a set of pin punches, a dial indicator and possibly a hydraulic press. In addition, a large, sturdy workbench and a vise or transmission stand will be required.

4   During disassembly of the transfer case, make careful notes of how each piece comes off, where it fits in relation to other pieces comes off, where it fits in relation to other pieces and what holds it in place. When removing parts, note how they're refitted; this will make it easier to reassemble the transfer case correctly.

5   Before taking the transfer case apart for repair, it will help if you have some idea what area of the transfer case is malfunctioning. Certain problems can be closely tied to specific areas in the transfer case, which can make component examination and renewal easier. Refer to the *Troubleshooting* section at the front of this manual for information regarding possible sources of trouble.

Counter gear type

Disassembly

Refer to illustrations 4.6, 4.7 and 4.19

6   Remove the speedometer gear and transfer indicator switch **(see illustration)**.

7   Remove the front and rear companion flange nuts, washers and remove the flanges **(see illustration)**.

8   Remove the seven extension housing bolts and detach the extension housing.

9   Remove the speedometer (drive) gear and the steel lock ball. Then remove the oil pump screw and output shaft rear bearing.

10   Remove the ten rear case mounting bolts and detach the rear case. **Caution:** *Keep the front case upright to prevent the clutch hub and steel ball from falling out.*

11   Remove idler gear bearing snap ring and detach the assembly from the case with a soft faced hammer.

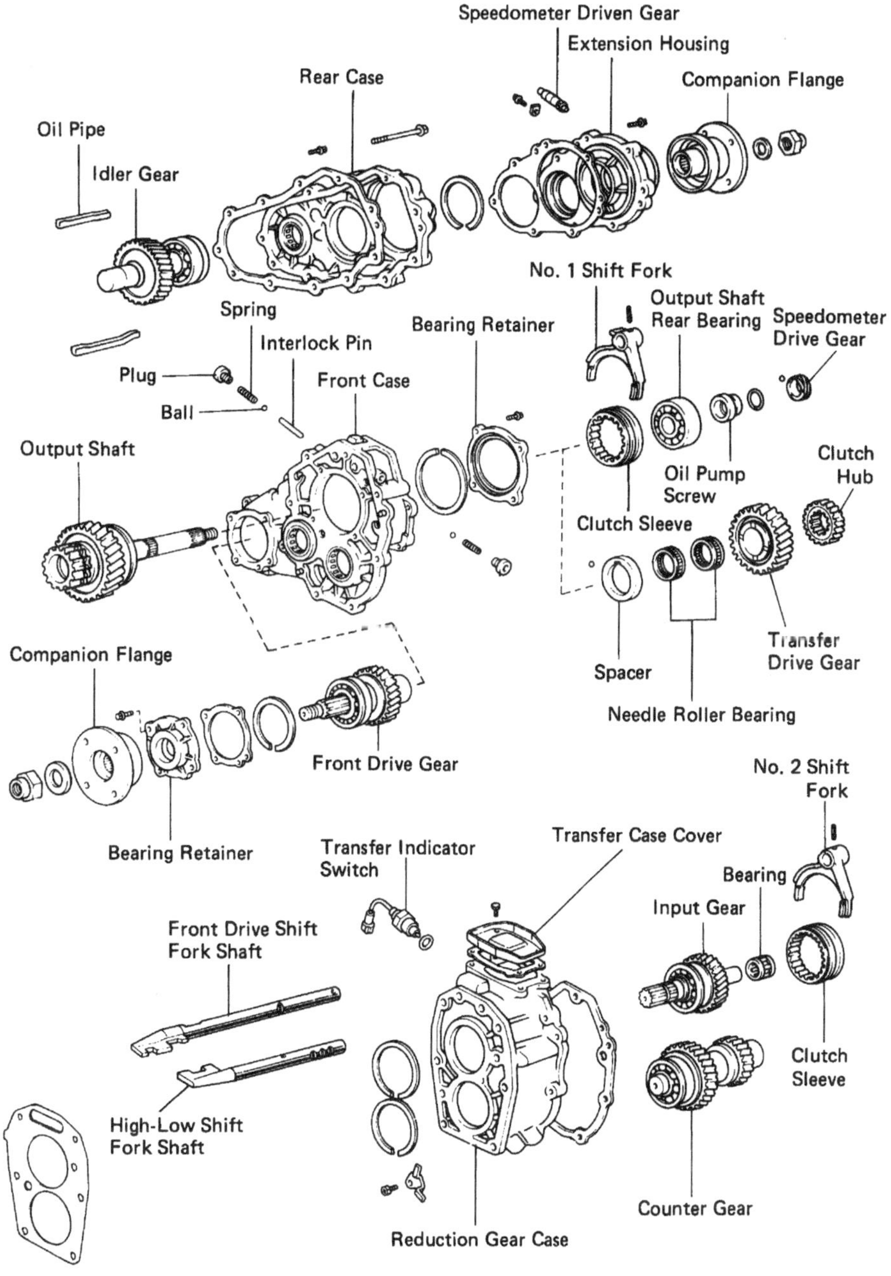

Speedometer Driven Gear

Extension Housing

Rear Case

Companion Flange

Oil Pipe

Idler Gear

No. 1 Shift Fork

Output Shaft Rear Bearing

Speedometer Drive Gear

Spring

Interlock Pin

Bearing Retainer

Plug

Front Case

Ball

Clutch Hub

Output Shaft

Oil Pump Screw

Clutch Sleeve

Clutch Sleeve

Spacer

Transfer Drive Gear

Needle Roller Bearing

Companion Flange

No. 2 Shift Fork

Bearing Retainer

Transfer Indicator Switch

Transfer Case Cover

Bearing

Input Gear

Front Drive Shift Fork Shaft

High-Low Shift Fork Shaft

Front Drive Gear

Clutch Sleeve

Reduction Gear Case

Counter Gear

4.6 Typical counter gear type transfer case exploded view

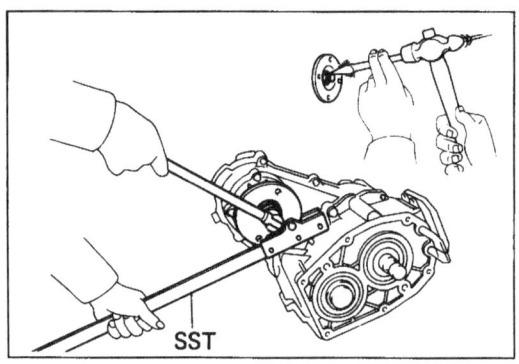
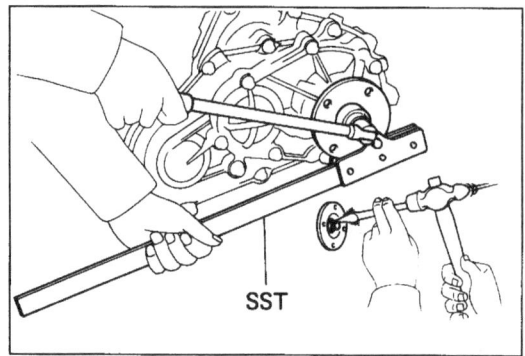

4.7 Hold the flange from turning with a chain wrench (or flange holding tool) and loosen the retaining nut

12   Remove the four front bearing housing bolts and detach the bearing housing.

13   Remove front drive gear bearing snap ring and detach the assembly from the case with a soft faced hammer.

14   Remove the oil pipes with a pair of needle nose pliers **(see illustration 4.45)**

15   Place the transfer case in the neutral position and remove the No.1 shift fork roll pin using a hammer and pin punch.

16   Remove the No.1 shift fork and clutch sleeve as an assembly.

17   Remove the clutch hub and transfer drive gear using a puller. Remove the needle bearings, No.2 spacer and steel ball.

18   Remove the four case cover bolts and detach the cover and gasket.

19   Remove the Torx screw plugs, springs and locking balls **(see illustration)**.

20   Remove the front drive shift fork. Remove the interlock pin using a pencil type magnet.

21   Remove the high-low shift fork shaft roll pin using a hammer and pin punch and remove the shaft.

22   Remove the four front case mounting bolts and detach the case using a soft-faced hammer.

23   Remove the No.2 fork and clutch sleeve and the needle bearings from the end of the input shaft.

24   Place the reduction gear case on two blocks of wood. Remove the input gear and counter gear snap rings. Tap the input gear and counter gear out of the case with a soft faced hammer.

25   Remove the four output shaft bearing retainer bolts from the front case. Remove the

output shaft snap ring. Tap the output shaft out of the front case with a soft faced hammer.

Inspection

26   Wash the transfer case components thoroughly with solvent. Inspect the cases for cracks in the bores, sides, bosses and bolt holes and stripped threads in the bolt holes. Check the geartrain and shift mechanisms for broken, chipped or worn gear teeth, bent or broken inserts, weak or broken insert springs, damaged roller or needle bearings and bearing bores in the counter gear and hub, output shaft. Check the snap-rings for distortion and lack of tension. Inspect the front and rear bearings for galling, damage and roughness. Inspect the shift mechanisms for worn, damaged or bent inserts, forks, rails, arms, plates, interlocks and levers.

Reassembly

Refer to illustrations 4.32, 4.45 and 4.47

Note: *Before reassembling the transfer case components lubricate all bearings, gears, shafts, seals and clutch hub assemblies with transmission fluid.*

27   Refit the output shaft to the front case with a soft faced hammer. Refit the output shaft rear bearing snap ring.

28   Refit the bearing retainer to the front case and tighten the bolts to the torque listed at the beginning of this Chapter's Specification Section.

29   Refit the input and counter gear into the reduction case with a soft faced hammer and refit the snap rings.

30   Coat the input shaft needle bearing with grease and refit the bearing on the input shaft.

31   Refit the No.2 hub and shift fork onto the input shaft.

32   Fit a new gasket to the front case and refit the reduction case assembly. Tighten the reduction case mounting bolts **(see illustration)** to the torque listed at the beginning of this Chapter's Specification Section.

33   Refit the front drive gear assembly into the front case with a soft faced hammer. Refit the snap ring.

34   Fit a new gasket to the front case with the oil return hole in the gasket to the bottom.

35   Refit the front bearing retainer and tighten the front bearing retainer bolts to the torque listed at the beginning of this Chapter's Specification Section.

36   Refit the high-low shift fork into the No.2 shift fork.

37   Align the roll pin holes and refit the roll pin with a hammer and pin punch.

38   Refit the interlock pin into the front case. Refit the front drive shift fork with the two grooves facing away from the interlock pin.

39   Refit the locking balls, springs and Torx screw plugs **(see illustration 4.19)**.

40   Coat the Torx screw threads with LOC-TITE or equivalent and tighten the plugs to the torque listed at the beginning of this Chapter's Specification Section.

41   Refit the steel ball and No.2 spacer.

42   Coat the needle bearings with oil and refit the bearings into the transfer drive gear. Refit the transfer gear and clutch hub onto the output shaft.

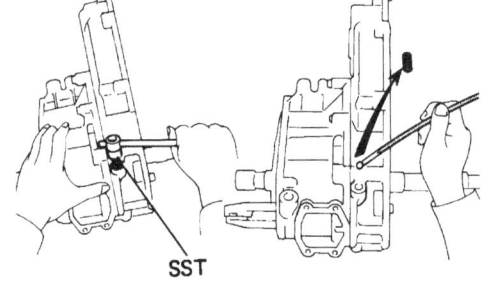

4.19 Remove the spring and ball using a pencil type magnet (left side shown right side is the same)

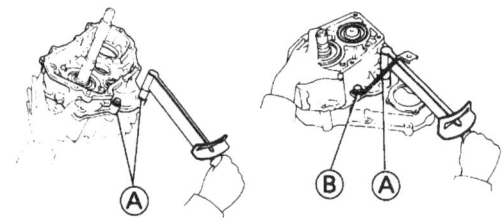

4.32 Refit the reduction case mounting bolts into the correct locations

A   47 mm bolt length   *B   49 mm bolt length*

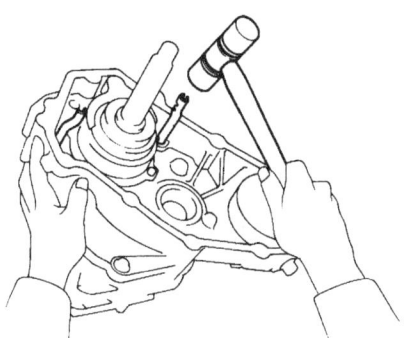

4.45 Use a soft faced hammer to seat the oil pipes into the case

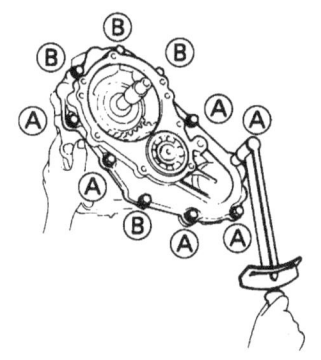

4.47 Refit the rear case mounting bolts into the correct locations

A   47 mm bolt length
B   112 mm bolt length

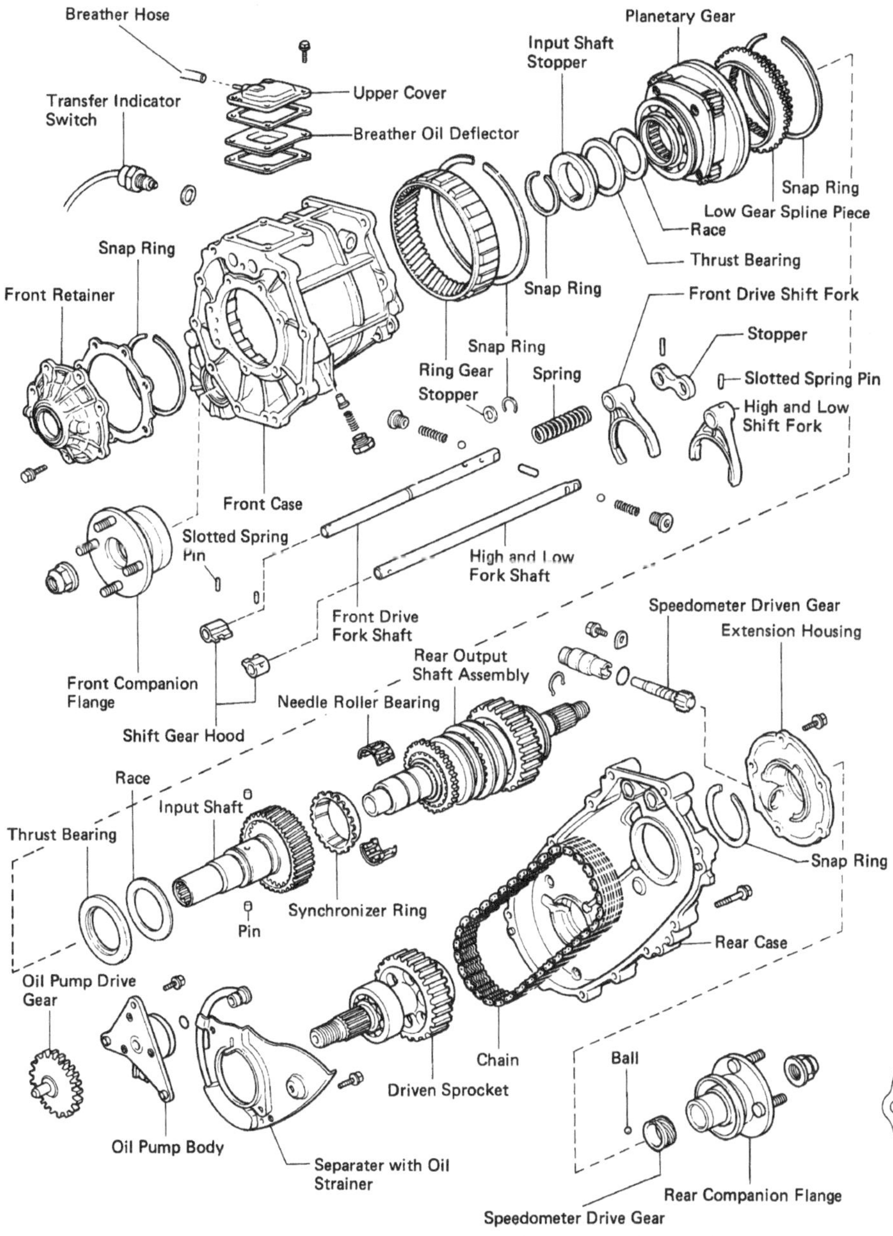

43   Refit the No.1 shift fork and clutch sleeve on the output shaft and through the front drive shift shaft.

44   Align the roll pin holes in the shift shaft with the shift fork and refit the roll pin with a hammer and pin punch.

45   Refit the oil pipes into the case **(see illustration)**.

46   Refit the idler gear into the rear case with a soft faced hammer and refit the snap ring.

47   Fit a new gasket on the front case and refit the rear case to the front case. Refit the rear case mounting bolts **(see illustration)**, and tighten the bolts to the torque listed at the beginning of this Chapter's Specification Section.

48   Refit the oil pump screw, locking ball and speedometer gear to the output shaft.

49   Refit the extension housing with a new gasket and tighten the extension housing bolts to the torque listed at the beginning of this Chapter's Specification Section.

50   Refit the transfer case cover with a new gasket and tighten the cover bolts to the torque listed at the beginning of this Chapter's Specification Section.

51   Refit the companion flanges. Apply silicone sealer or equivalent to the center of the companion flange and shaft end.

52   Refit companion shaft washer and nut. Tighten the nut to the torque listed at the beginning of this Chapter's Specification Section.

53   Refit the transfer indicator switch with washer and speedometer gear. Tighten the switch to the torque listed at the beginning of this Chapter's Specification Section.

54   Refit the transfer case in the vehicle and fill with the proper lubricant (see Chapter 1).

Planetary gear type

Disassembly

Refer to illustrations 4.55, 4.56, 4.66 and 4.79

55   Remove the speedometer gear and transfer indicator switch **(see illustration)**.

56   Remove the No.1 and No.2 gear shift heads **(see illustration)**.

57   Remove the seven front retainer bolts and detach the retainer from the front case.

58   Remove the four upper cover bolts detach the covers and oil deflector from the front case.

4.55 Typical planetary gear type transfer case exploded view

Breather Hose
Transfer Indicator Switch
Snap Ring
Front Retainer
Front Companion Flange
Shift Gear Hood
Race
Thrust Bearing
Input Shaft
Oil Pump Drive Gear
Pin
Oil Pump Body
Separater with Oil Strainer
Speedometer Drive Gear
Synchronizer Ring
Driven Sprocket
Chain
Front Case
Slotted Spring Pin
Front Drive Fork Shaft
Needle Roller Bearing
Rear Output Shaft Assembly
Upper Cover
Breather Oil Deflector
Snap Ring
Ring Gear Stopper
Spring
High and Low Fork Shaft
Input Shaft Stopper
Planetary Gear
Snap Ring
Low Gear Spline Piece
Race
Thrust Bearing
Front Drive Shift Fork
Stopper
Slotted Spring Pin
High and Low Shift Fork
Speedometer Driven Gear
Extension Housing
Snap Ring
Rear Case
Ball
Rear Companion Flange

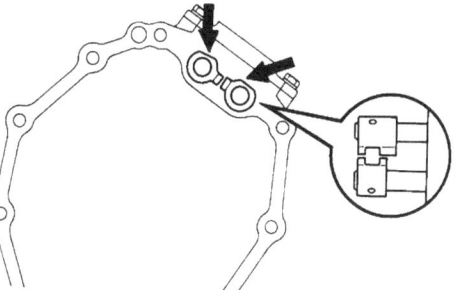

4.56 Align the shift heads and remove with the roll pins using a hammer and pin punch

59 Remove the front and rear companion flange nuts, washers and remove the flanges **(see illustration 4.7)**.

60 Remove the companion flanges with an appropriate puller.

61 Remove the five extension housing bolts and detach the extension housing with a soft faced hammer.

62 Remove the speedometer (drive) gear and ball from the output shaft.

63 Remove the twelve rear case to front case mounting bolts.

64 Separate the case halves using a soft faced hammer. **Caution:** *Don't attempt to prise the case halves apart along the mating surfaces. Damage to matting surfaces could cause leaks.*

65 Remove the Torx straight screw plugs from the case using a Torx socket available at most auto parts stores.

66 Remove the spring and locking balls **(see illustration)**.

67 Remove the front fork roll pins using a hammer and pin punch.

68 The front drive fork is spring loaded hold the fork in hand to prevent it from springing out once the pin punch is removed.

69 Remove the front fork shaft spring and fork from the case.

70 Remove the straight pin from the rear case using a pencil magnet.

71 Remove the high-low shift shaft, fork and stopper from the rear case.

72 Remove the output shaft bearing snap ring with a pair of snap ring pliers.

73 Mount the rear case in a soft jawed vise. Remove the output shaft and driven sprocket from the rear case with a soft faced hammer and remove the chain

74 Remove the synchronizer ring from the input shaft.

75 Remove the three separator bolts and detach the separator, oil strainer and O-rings.

76 Remove the three oil pump bolts and detach the oil pump body assembly from the case.

77 Remove the oil pump drive gear from the planetary gear assembly.

78 Remove the planetary gear assembly snap ring from the front case using a pair of external snap ring pliers.

79 Remove the planetary gear assembly from the case **(see illustration)**.

Inspection

80 Wash the transfer case components thoroughly with solvent. Inspect the cases for cracks in the bores, sides, bosses and bolt holes and stripped threads in the bolt holes. Check the geartrain and shift mechanisms for broken, chipped or worn gear teeth, bent or broken inserts, weak or broken insert springs, damaged roller or needle bearings and bearing bores in the counter gear and hub, output shaft and chain. Check the snap-rings for distortion and lack of tension. Inspect the front and rear bearings for galling, damage and roughness. Inspect the shift mechanisms for worn, damaged or bent inserts, forks, rails, arms, plates, interlocks and levers.

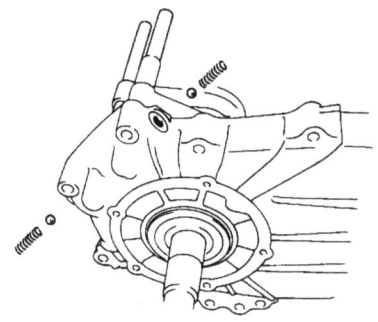

4.66 Remove the springs and balls using a pencil type magnet

Reassembly

Refer to illustration 4.96

Note: *Before reassembling the transfer case components lubricate all bearings, gears, shafts, seals, clutch hub assemblies and chain with transmission fluid.*

82 Refit the planetary gear assembly into the rear case **(see illustration 4.79)**.

83 Refit the planetary gear assembly snap ring using external type snap ring pliers.

84 Refit the oil pump drive gear into the planetary gear assembly.

85 Refit the oil pump body to the rear case. Tighten the three mounting bolts to the torque listed at the beginning of this Chapter's Specification Section.

86 Fit new O-ring to the oil strainer pipe. **Caution:** *If you damage the O-ring during assembly, it could result in pump failure.*

87 Coat the O-ring and strainer with oil and refit the separator and oil strainer. Tighten the oil separator bolts to the torque listed at the beginning of this Chapter's Specification Section.

88 Coat the synchronizer ring with grease. Align the slots in the synchronizer ring with the shifting keys on the high and low clutch hub and refit the ring to the hub.

89 Refit the rear output shaft and driven sprocket to the chain.

90 Refit the chain assembly into the rear case using a soft faced hammer.

91 Refit the driven sprocket snap ring with a pair of external snap ring pliers.

92 Refit the high and low shift fork into the high and low hub sleeve.

93 Refit the high low shift shaft through the shift fork and stopper.

94 Refit the straight pin into the case.

95 Refit the front drive shift fork into the front drive hub sleeve. Slide the spring onto the shift shaft and refit the shift shaft through the front drive fork and into the stopper.

96 Refit the roll pins **(see illustration)**.

97 Refit the locking balls and springs into the case. Apply sealer to the Torx screw plugs **(see illustration 4.66)** and tighten the screw plugs to the torque listed at the beginning of this Chapter's Specification Section.

98 Apply non-hardening gasket sealant to the rear case, shift the high and low sleeve to the low side position and refit the rear case to the front case. Refit the twelve rear case bolts

4.79 Twist and pull the planetary gear assembly from the case

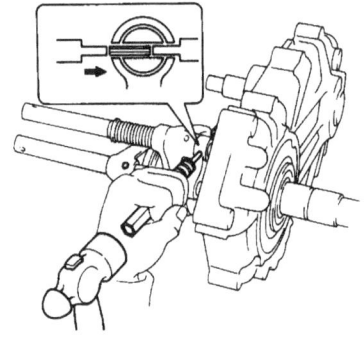

4.96 Align the roll pin holes and refit the roll pins with a hammer and pin punch.

and tighten the bolts to the torque listed at the beginning of this Chapter's Specification Section.

99 Refit the ball and speedometer (drive) gear onto the output shaft.

100 Apply non-hardening gasket sealant to the extension housing and refit the housing to the rear case. Refit the five housing bolts and tighten the bolts to the torque listed at the beginning of this Chapter's Specification Section.

101 Refit the front and rear companion flanges. Tighten the flange nuts to the torque listed at the beginning of this Chapter's Specification Section and stake the nuts to the shafts.

102 Fit new upper cover gaskets and refit the oil deflector and upper cover to the case. Refit the upper cover bolts and tighten the bolts to the torque listed at the beginning of this Chapter's Specification Section.

103 Fit a new gasket to the front retainer and refit the retainer to the case. Apply liquid sealer to the retainer bolts and tighten the bolts to the torque listed at the beginning of this Chapter's Specification Section.

104 Refit the No.1 and 2 gear shift heads. Align the roll pin holes and refit the roll pins with a hammer and pin punch **(see illustration 4.56)**.

105 Refit the transfer indicator switch with washer and speedometer gear. Tighten the switch to the torque listed at the beginning of this Chapter's Specification Section.

106 Refit the transfer case in the vehicle and fill with the proper lubricant (see Chapter 1).

Chapter 8
Clutch and driveline

Contents

Specifications

Clutch

Pedal height and freeplay	See Chapter 1
Fluid type	DOT 3 brake fluid
Disc rivet head depth limit (minimum)	0.3 mm
Diaphragm spring tip out-of-alignment limit	0.6 mm

Driveshaft

Runout limit	0.8 mm
U-joint spider bearing axial play	Less than 0.05 mm

Driveaxle standard length
393.9 to 403.9 mm

Rear axleshaft

Maximum shaft runout	2.0 mm
Maximum flange runout	0.2 mm

Differential

Drive pinion preload (within backlash)

7.5 inch ring gear	0.59 to 0.98 Nm
8.0 inch ring gear	
2 pinion type	0.88 to 1.28 Nm
4 pinion type	0.49 to 0.78 Nm

Torque specifications

	Nm
Clutch pressure plate-to-flywheel	15 to 20
Bellhousing-to-engine	50 to 77
Clutch master cylinder reservoir mounting bolt	20 to 28
Driveshaft centre support bearing-to-front shaft (3-joint type)	
Step one	167 to 195
Step two	Loosen
Step three	
Petrol	
1/2-ton	30
3/4-ton	34
Diesel	
LN30, 40, 50, 60	34
LN80, 90	44
Others	69

Torque specifications (continued)

	Nm
Driveshaft centre support bearing-to-rear shaft (3-joint type)	30 to 49
Driveshaft-to-transfer case companion flanges (4WD)	30 to 49
Driveshaft-to-companion flange on differential	30 to 49
Centre support bearing flange-to-crossmember (3-joint type)	15 to 19
Freewheel hub body-to-axle hub	28 to 34
Freewheel hub body-to-driveaxle	17
Automatic locking hub drum adjusting nut	7
Automatic locking hub centre bolt/washer	18
Automatic locking hub cover bolts	10
Freewheel hub cover-to-hub	8 to 12
Spindle mounting bolts	39 to 53
Differential carrier cover bolts	20 to 28
Differential tube-to-carrier	65
Rear axle shaft-to-rear axle housing nuts	60 to 77
Drive pinion nut	
7.5 inch ring gear	
Standard	108
Maximum	236
8.0 inch ring gear	
Standard	196
Maximum	343
Driveaxle-to-side gear shaft nuts	83
Front differential mounting bolts	
Front	146
Left and right	167
Wheel nuts	See Chapter 1

1   General information

The information in this Chapter deals with the components from the rear of the engine to the rear wheels (and to the front wheels on 4WD models), except for the transmission and transfer case (4WD models), which are dealt with in the previous Chapter. For the purposes of this Chapter, these components are grouped into four categories; clutch, driveshaft, front axle and rear axle. Separate Sections within this Chapter offer general descriptions and checking procedures for each of these four groups.

Since nearly all the procedures covered in this Chapter involve working under the vehicle, make sure it's securely supported on sturdy jackstands or on a hoist where the vehicle can be easily raised and lowered.

2   Clutch - description and check

Refer to illustration 2.1

1   All models equipped with a manual transmission feature a single dry plate, diaphragm spring-type clutch **(see illustration)**. The actuation is through a hydraulic system.

2   When the clutch pedal is depressed, hydraulic fluid (under pressure from the clutch master cylinder) flows into the release cyl-

inder. Because the release cylinder is connected to the clutch fork, the fork moves the release bearing into contact with the pressure plate release fingers, disengaging the clutch plate.

3   The hydraulic system locates the clutch pedal and provides clutch adjustment automatically, so no adjustment of the linkage is required.

4   Terminology can be a problem regarding the clutch components because common names have in some cases changed from that used by the manufacturer. For example, the driven plate is also called the clutch plate or disc, the clutch release bearing is sometimes called a throwout bearing, and the release cylinder is sometimes called the operating or slave cylinder.

5   Due to the slow wearing qualities of the clutch, it is not easy to decide when to go to the trouble of removing the transmission in order to check the wear on the friction lining. The only positive indication that something should be done is when it starts to slip or when squealing noises during engagement indicate that the friction lining has worn down to the rivets. In such instances it can only be hoped that the friction surfaces on the flywheel and pressure plate have not been scored or badly worn.

6   A clutch will wear according to the way in which it is used. Much intentional slipping of the clutch while driving - rather than the cor-

rect selection of gears - will accelerate wear. It is best to assume, however, that the disc will need renewal at about 64,000 km.

7   Because of the clutch's location between the engine and transmission, it cannot be worked on without removing either the engine or transmission. If repairs which would require removal of the engine are not needed, the quickest way to gain access to the clutch is by removing the transmission, as described in Chapter 7.

8   Other than to renew components with obvious damage, some preliminary checks should be performed to diagnose a clutch system failure.

a) *The first check should be of the fluid level in the clutch master cylinder. If the fluid level is low, add fluid as necessary and re-test. If the master cylinder runs dry, or if any of the hydraulic components are serviced, bleed the hydraulic system as described in Section 8.*

b) *To check "clutch spin down time", run the engine at normal idle speed with the transmission in Neutral (clutch pedal up-engaged). Disengage the clutch (pedal down), wait nine seconds and shift the transmission into Reverse. No grinding noise should be heard. A grinding noise would indicate component failure in the pressure plate assembly or the clutch disc.*

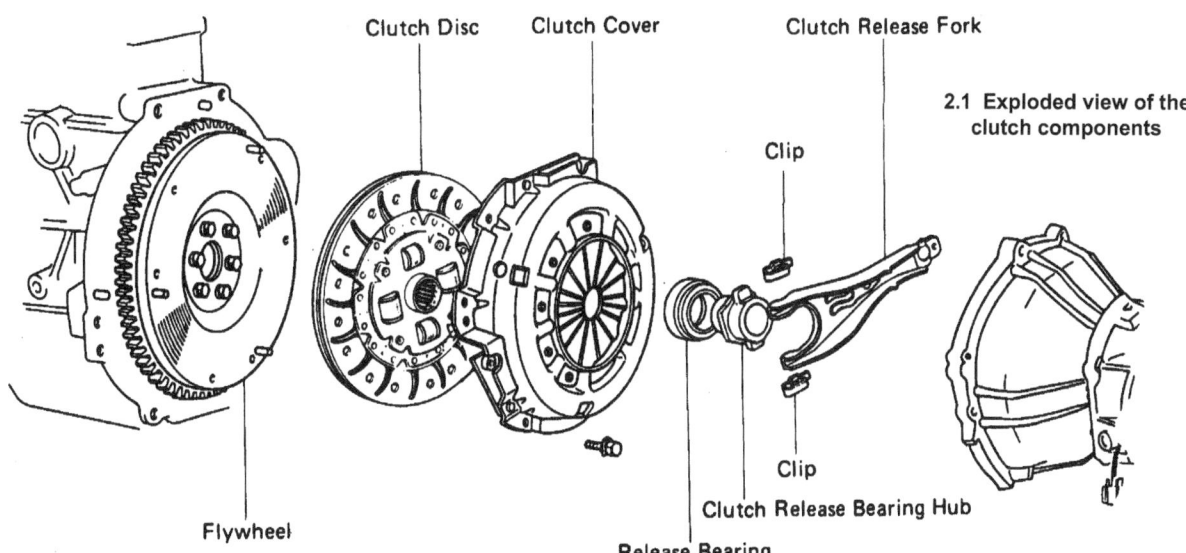

2.1 Exploded view of the clutch components

Clutch Disc · Clutch Cover · Clutch Release Fork · Clip · Clip · Clutch Release Bearing Hub · Release Bearing · Flywheel

c) To check for complete clutch release, run the engine (with the brake on to prevent movement) and hold the clutch pedal approximately 13 mm from the floor mat. Shift the transmission between 1st gear and Reverse several times. If the shift is not smooth, component failure is indicated. Measure the release cylinder pushrod travel. With the clutch pedal completely depressed the release cylinder pushrod should extend substantially. If the pushrod will not extend very far or not at all, check the fluid level in the clutch master cylinder. If the level is OK, the clutch master cylinder or release cylinder is probably faulty.

d) Visually inspect the clutch pedal bush at the top of the clutch pedal to make sure there is no sticking or excessive wear.

e) Under the vehicle, check that the clutch fork is solidly mounted on the ball stud.

Note: *Because access to the clutch components is an involved process, any time either the engine or transmission is removed, the clutch disc, pressure plate assembly and release bearing should be carefully inspected and, if necessary, renewed. Since the clutch disc is normally the item of highest wear, it should be renewed as a matter of course if there is any question about its condition.*

3 Clutch components - removal, inspection and refitting

Refer to illustrations 3.4, 3.5, 3.8, 3.10, 3.12a, 3.12b and 3.14

Warning: *Dust produced by clutch wear and deposited on clutch components may contain asbestos, which is hazardous to your health. DO NOT blow it out with compressed air and DO NOT inhale it. DO NOT use petrol or petroleum-based solvents to remove the dust. Brake system cleaner should be used to flush*

3.4 A clutch alignment tool can be used to prevent the disc from dropping out as the pressure plate is removed

the dust into a drain pan. After the clutch components are wiped clean with a rag, dispose of the contaminated rags and cleaner in a marked, sealed container.

Removal

1 Access to the clutch components is normally accomplished by removing the transmission, leaving the engine in the vehicle. If, of course, the engine is being removed for major overhaul, then the opportunity should always be taken to check the clutch for wear and renew worn components as necessary. The following procedures assume that the engine will stay in place.

2 Remove the release cylinder (see Section 7).

3 Referring to Chapter 7 Part A, remove the transmission from the vehicle. Support the engine while the transmission is out. Preferably, an engine hoist should be used to support it from above. However, if a jack is used underneath the engine, make sure a piece of wood is used between the jack and sump to spread the load. **Caution:** *The pickup for the oil pump is very close to the bottom of the sump. If the*

3.5 Be sure to mark the pressure plate and flywheel to ensure proper alignment during refitting

pan is bent or distorted in any way, engine oil starvation could occur.

4 To support the clutch disc during removal, fit a clutch alignment tool through the clutch disc hub **(see illustration)**.

5 Carefully inspect the flywheel and pressure plate for indexing marks. The marks are usually an X, an O or a white letter. If they cannot be found, apply marks yourself so the pressure plate and the flywheel will be in the same alignment during installation **(see illustration)**.

6 Turning each bolt only 1/2-turn at a time, slowly loosen the pressure plate-to-flywheel bolts. Work in a diagonal pattern and loosen each bolt a little at a time until all spring pressure is relieved. Then hold the pressure plate securely and completely remove the bolts, followed by the pressure plate and clutch disc.

Inspection

7 Ordinarily, when a problem occurs in the clutch, it can be attributed to wear of the clutch driven disc assembly. However, all components should be inspected at this time.

3.8 Check the flywheel for cracks, hot spots (as seen in this photo) and other obvious defects. Slight imperfections can be removed by a machine shop

3.10 Once the clutch disc is removed, the rivet depth can be measured and compared to the Specifications

3.12a Examine the pressure plate friction surface for score marks, cracks and evidence of overheating

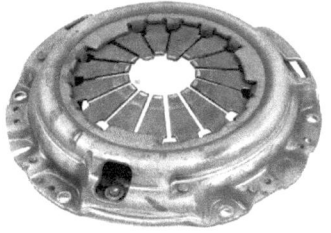

BROKEN OR BENT FINGERS

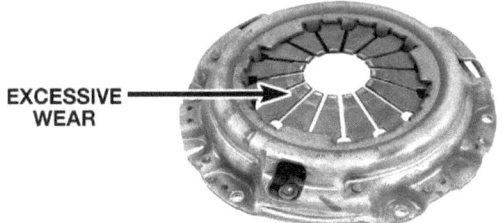

EXCESSIVE WEAR

EXCESSIVE FINGER WEAR

NORMAL FINGER WEAR

3.12b Renew the pressure plate if excessive wear is noted

8   Inspect the flywheel for cracks, heat checking, grooves or other signs of obvious defects (see illustration). If the imperfections are slight, a machine shop can machine the surface flat and smooth, which is highly recommended regardless of the surface appearance. Refer to Chapter 2 for the flywheel removal and refitting procedure.

9   Inspect the pilot bearing (Section 5).

10   Inspect the lining on the clutch disc. There should be at least 0.6 mm of lining above the rivet heads. Check for loose rivets, warpage, cracks, distorted springs or damper bushes and other obvious damage (see illustration). As mentioned above, ordinarily the clutch disc is renewed as a matter of course, so if in doubt about the condition, renew it.

11   Ordinarily, the release bearing is also renewed along with the clutch disc (see Section 4).

12   Check the machined surfaces and the diaphragm spring fingers of the pressure plate (see illustrations). If the surface is grooved or otherwise damaged, renew the pressure plate. Also check for obvious damage, distortion, cracking, etc. Light glazing can be removed with medium grit emery cloth. If a new pressure plate is indicated, new or factory-rebuilt units are available.

Refitting

13   Before installing, carefully wipe the flywheel and pressure plate machined surfaces

clean with brake system cleaner or a rubbing-alcohol dampened rag. It's important that no oil or grease is on these surfaces or the lining of the clutch disc. Handle these parts only with clean hands.

14   Position the clutch disc and pressure plate with the clutch held in place with an alignment tool (see illustration). Make sure it's installed properly (most replacement clutch discs will be marked "flywheel side" or something similar - if not marked, install the clutch with the damper springs or bushes toward the transmission).

15   Tighten the pressure plate-to-flywheel bolts only finger tight, working around the pressure plate.

16   Centre the clutch disc by ensuring the alignment tool is through the splined hub and into the pilot bearing in the crankshaft. Wiggle the tool up, down or side-to-side as needed to bottom the tool in the pilot bush. Tighten the pressure plate-to-flywheel bolts a little at a time, working in a criss-cross pattern to prevent distorting the cover. After all of the bolts are snug, tighten them to the torque listed in this Chapter's Specifications. Remove the alignment tool.

17   Using high-temperature grease, lubricate the inner groove of the release bearing (see Section 4). Also place grease on the fork fingers.

18   Install the clutch release bearing as described in Section 4.

3.14 Insert a clutch alignment tool or metal bar through the middle of the clutch and move the disc until it is centered

19   Install the transmission, release cylinder and all components removed previously, tightening all fasteners to the proper torque specifications.

4　Clutch release bearing - renewal

Refer to illustration 4.5

1   The sealed release bearing, although designed for long life, is worth renewing at the same time that the other clutch components are being renewed or serviced.

4.5 Removing the retaining clips from the clutch release bearing

5.10 . . . then force the bearing out hydraulically with a steel rod slightly smaller than the bore in the bearing - when the hammer strikes the rod, the grease will transmit force to the backside of the bearing and push it out

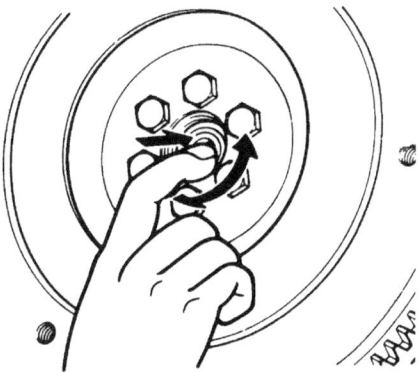

5.5 Turn the pilot bearing by hand while pressing in on it - if it is rough or noisy, a new one should be fitted

5.11 Using a hammer and socket, carefully drive the new bearing into place

5.9 Fill the opening behind the bearing with grease . . .

2   Deterioration of the release bearing should be suspected when there are signs of grease leakage or if the unit is noisy when spun with the fingers.

3   Remove the rubber dust boot which surrounds the release lever at the bellhousing opening.

4   Using a screwdriver, unhook and detach the retaining spring from the pivot stud in the bellhousing.

5   Remove the retaining clips (**see illustration**).

6   The clutch release bearing and hub assembly can now be removed. **Note:** *Make sure that the release fork has not been cracked or bent. Slowly turn the front face of the release bearing, making sure it turns freely and without any noise. The release bearing is pre-lubricated and should not be washed in solvent.*

7   If necessary, remove the release bearing from its hub using a two- or three-jaw puller.

8   Press on the new bearing, but apply pressure only to the centre race. If necessary, take the bearing and hub to a local repair shop, as considerable force may be needed to press the bearing on.

9   Reassembly is the reverse of disassembly but apply multi-purpose grease to the internal recess of the release bearing hub.

10   Also apply similar grease to the pivot

points of the clutch release lever, the sliding surface of the bearing sleeve and the splines on the transmission input shaft. **Note:** *Apply only a thin coat of grease to these points, as too much grease will run onto the friction lining when hot, causing damage to the clutch disc surfaces.*

5   Pilot bearing - inspection, removal and refitting

Refer to illustrations 5.5, 5.9, 5.10 and 5.11

1   The clutch pilot bearing is a needle roller type bearing which is pressed into the rear of the crankshaft. Its primary purpose is to support the front of the transmission input shaft. The pilot bearing should be inspected whenever the clutch components are removed from the engine. Due to its inaccessibility, if you are in doubt as to its condition, install a new one. **Note:** *If the engine has been removed from the vehicle, disregard the following steps which do not apply.*

2   Remove the transmission (see Chapter 7A).

3   Remove the clutch components (see Section 3).

4   Using a clean rag, wipe the bearing clean and inspect for any excessive wear, scoring or obvious damage. A flashlight will be helpful to direct light into the recess.

5   Check to make sure the pilot bearing turns smoothly and quietly (**see illustration**). If the transmission input shaft contact surface is worn or damaged, install a new bearing.

6   Removal can be accomplished with a slide hammer and a blind-hole puller attachment, but an alternative method sometimes works:

7   Find a solid steel bar which is slightly smaller in diameter than the bearing. Alternatives to a solid bar would be a wood dowel or a socket with a bolt fixed in place to make it solid.

8   Check the bar for fit - it should slide into the bearing with very little clearance.

9   Pack the bearing and the area behind it (in the crankshaft recess) with heavy grease (**see illustration**). Pack it tightly to eliminate as much air as possible.

10   Insert the bar into the bearing bore and hammer on the bar, which will force the grease to the backside of the bearing and push it out (**see illustration**). **Note:** *It's a good idea to place a rag over the bearing and bar to catch any grease that might squirt out.* Remove the bearing and clean all the grease from the crankshaft recess.

11   To fit the new bearing, lubricate the outside surface with oil, then drive it into the recess with a hammer and a socket with an outside diameter that matches the bearing outer race (**see illustration**).

12   Install the clutch components, transmission and all other components removed to gain access to the pilot bearing.

6   Clutch master cylinder - removal, overhaul and refitting

Refer to illustrations 6.2, 6.4 and 6.5

Caution: *Do not allow brake fluid to contact any painted surfaces of the vehicle, as damage to the finish may result. Rinse off any spills immediately with plenty of water.*

Removal

1   Disconnect the master cylinder pushrod from the clutch pedal.

2   Disconnect the hydraulic line from the master cylinder and drain the fluid into a suitable container **(see illustration)**.

3   Remove the master cylinder flange mounting nuts and withdraw the unit from the engine compartment.

Overhaul

4   Remove the hold-down bolt and pull off the reservoir tank **(see illustration)**. Newer models use a slotted spring pin to attach the reservoir. To remove, drive out the pin with a small punch.

5   Pull back the boot and remove the snap-ring **(see illustration)**.

6   Pull out the pushrod, washer and piston.

7   Examine the inner surface of the cylinder bore. If it is scored or exhibits bright wear areas, the entire master cylinder should be renewed.

8   If the cylinder bore is in good condition, obtain a clutch master cylinder rebuild kit, which will contain all of the necessary renewal parts.

9   Prior to refitting any parts, first dip them in brake fluid to lubricate them.

10   Refitting of the parts in the cylinder is the reverse of removal.

Refitting

11   Refitting is the reverse of removal, but check the pedal height and freeplay as described in Chapter 1 and bleed the hydraulic system (Section 8).

---

7   Clutch release cylinder - removal, overhaul and refitting

Refer to illustrations 7.2 and 7.4

Removal

1   The clutch release cylinder is located at the right side of the transmission bellhousing.

2   Using a flare-nut wrench, disconnect the clutch line union **(see illustration)**.

3   Remove the two bolts and pull off the release cylinder.

Overhaul

4   Pull off the dust boot and pushrod and then tap the cylinder gently on a block of wood to extract the piston and spring **(see illustration)**.

5   Unscrew and remove the bleeder screw.

6   Examine the surfaces of the piston and

cylinder bore for scoring or bright wear areas. If any are found, discard the cylinder and purchase a new one.

7   If the components are in good condition, wash them in clean brake fluid. Remove the seal and discard it, noting carefully which way the seal lips face.

8   Obtain a repair kit which will contain all the necessary new items.

9   Install the new seal using your fingers only to manipulate it into position. Be sure the lips face in the proper direction.

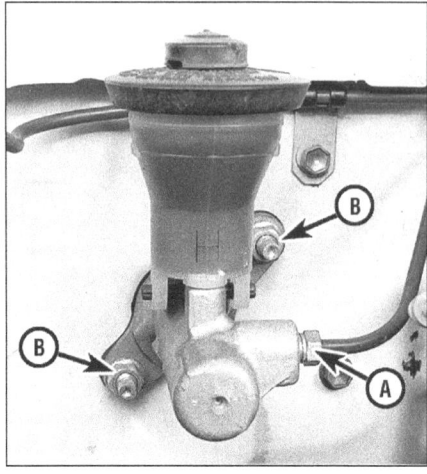

6.2 Unscrew the fitting (A) then remove the mounting nuts (B) and detach the clutch master cylinder from the firewall

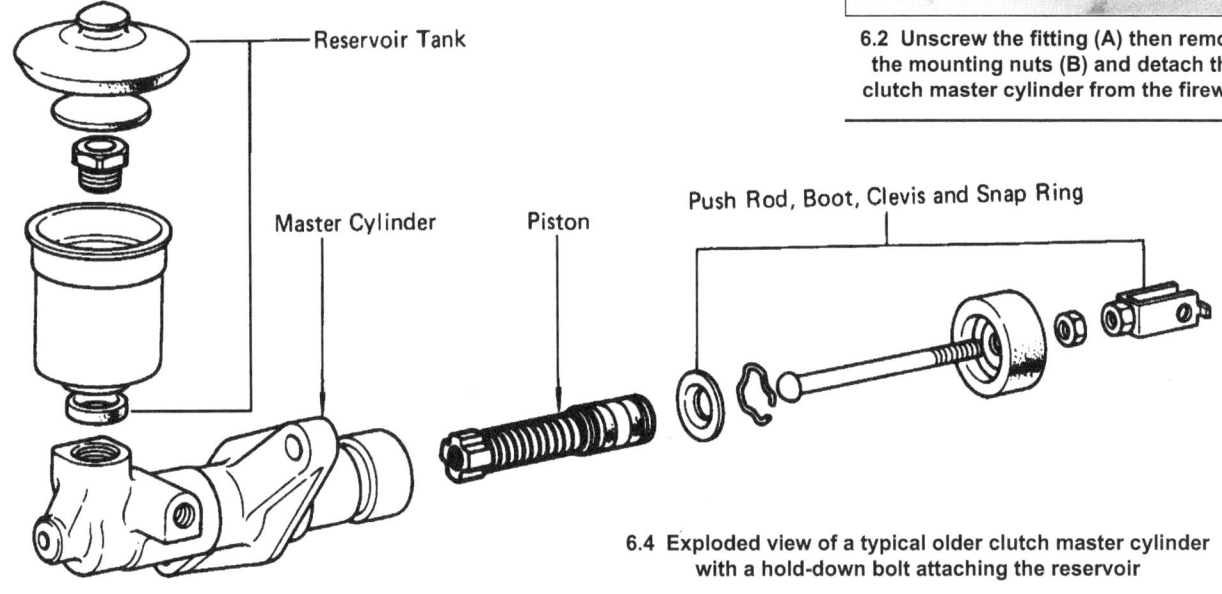

6.4 Exploded view of a typical older clutch master cylinder with a hold-down bolt attaching the reservoir

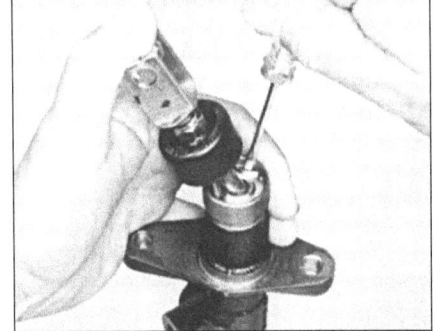

6.5 Prise the snap-ring from the clutch master cylinder using a small screwdriver

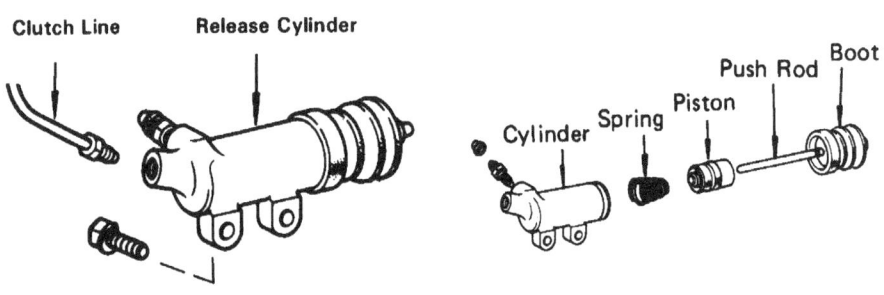

7.2 Clutch release cylinder mounting details

7.4 Exploded view of the clutch release cylinder

10   Dip the piston assembly in clean brake fluid before fitting it and the spring into the cylinder.

11   Install the bleeder.

12   Complete the reassembly by refitting the pushrod and the dust cover. Be sure the dust cover is secure on the cylinder housing.

Refitting

13   Refitting is the reverse of the removal procedure. After the cylinder has been installed, bleed the clutch hydraulic system as described in Section 8.

8   Clutch hydraulic system - bleeding

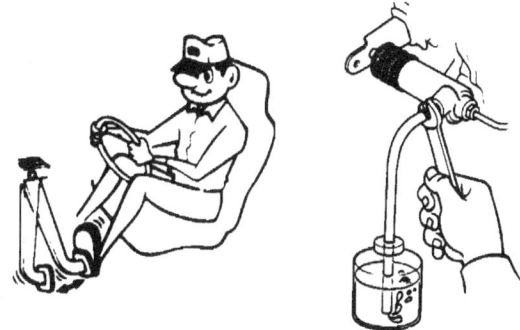

8.3 When bleeding the clutch hydraulic system, a hose is connected to the bleeder valve at the release cylinder and then submerged in brake fluid. Air will be seen as bubbles in the container and the tube

Refer to illustration 8.3

Caution: *Do not allow the brake fluid to contact any painted surface of the vehicle, as damage to the finish will result. Rinse off any spills immediately with plenty of water.*

1   Bleeding will be required whenever the hydraulic system has been dismantled and reassembled and air has entered the system.

2   First fill the fluid reservoir with clean brake fluid which has been stored in an airtight container. Never use fluid which has drained from the system or has bled out previously, as it may contain grit.

3   Attach a rubber or plastic bleed tube to the bleeder screw on the release cylinder and immerse the open end of the tube in a glass jar containing an inch or two of fluid **(see illustration)**.

4   Open the bleeder screw about half a turn and have an assistant quickly depress the clutch pedal completely. Tighten the screw and then have clutch pedal slowly released with the foot completely removed. Repeat this sequence of operations until air bubbles are no longer ejected from the open end of the tube beneath the fluid in the jar.

5   After two or three strokes of the pedal, make sure the fluid level in the reservoir has not fallen too low. Keep it full of fresh fluid, otherwise air will be drawn into the system.

6   Tighten the bleeder screw on a pedal down stroke (do not overtighten it), remove the bleed tube and jar, top-up the reservoir and install the cap.

7   If an assistant is not available, alternative 'one-man' bleeding operations can be carried out using a bleed tube equipped with a one-way valve or a pressure bleed kit, both of which should be used in accordance with the manufacturer's instructions.

9   Clutch pedal assembly - removal and refitting

Refer to illustration 9.1

1   Remove the pedal return spring **(see illustration)**.

2   Disconnect the master cylinder pushrod from the pedal by removing the spring clip and pulling out the pushrod pin.

3   Remove the pedal shaft.

4   Remove the clutch pedal with its bushes and collar.

5   Clean the parts in solvent and renew any that are damaged or excessively worn.

6   Refitting is the reverse of the removal procedure. During refitting, apply multi-purpose grease to the pedal boss, return spring, pedal shaft and pushrod pin.

10   Driveshafts, differentials and rear axles - general information

Refer to illustrations 10.1a, 10.1b and 10.1c

Three different driveshaft assemblies are used on the vehicles covered in this manual **(see illustrations)**. Standard wheelbase 2WD models use a one-piece driveshaft which incorporates two universal joints, one at either end of the shaft.

Long wheelbase 2WD models use a two-piece driveshaft which incorporates a centre

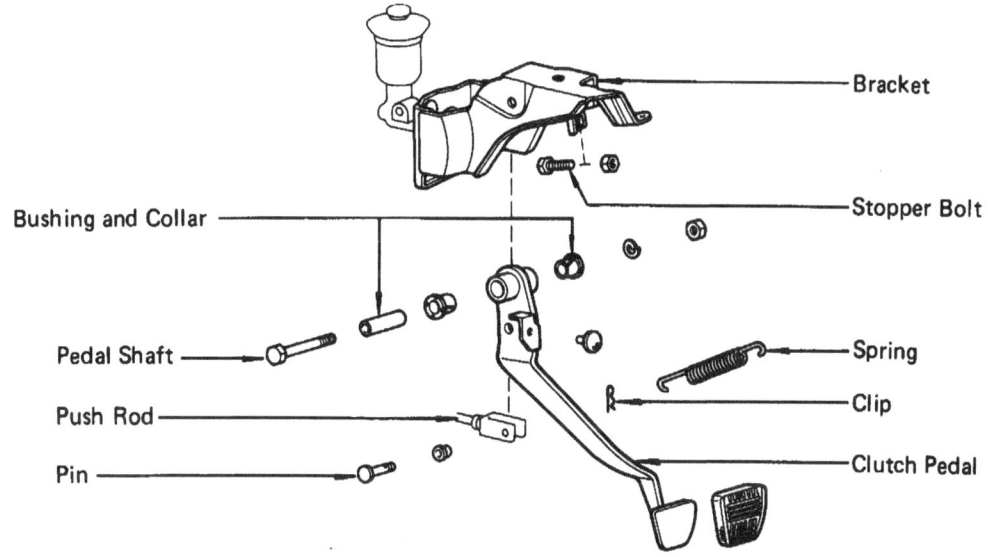

9.1 Clutch pedal mounting details

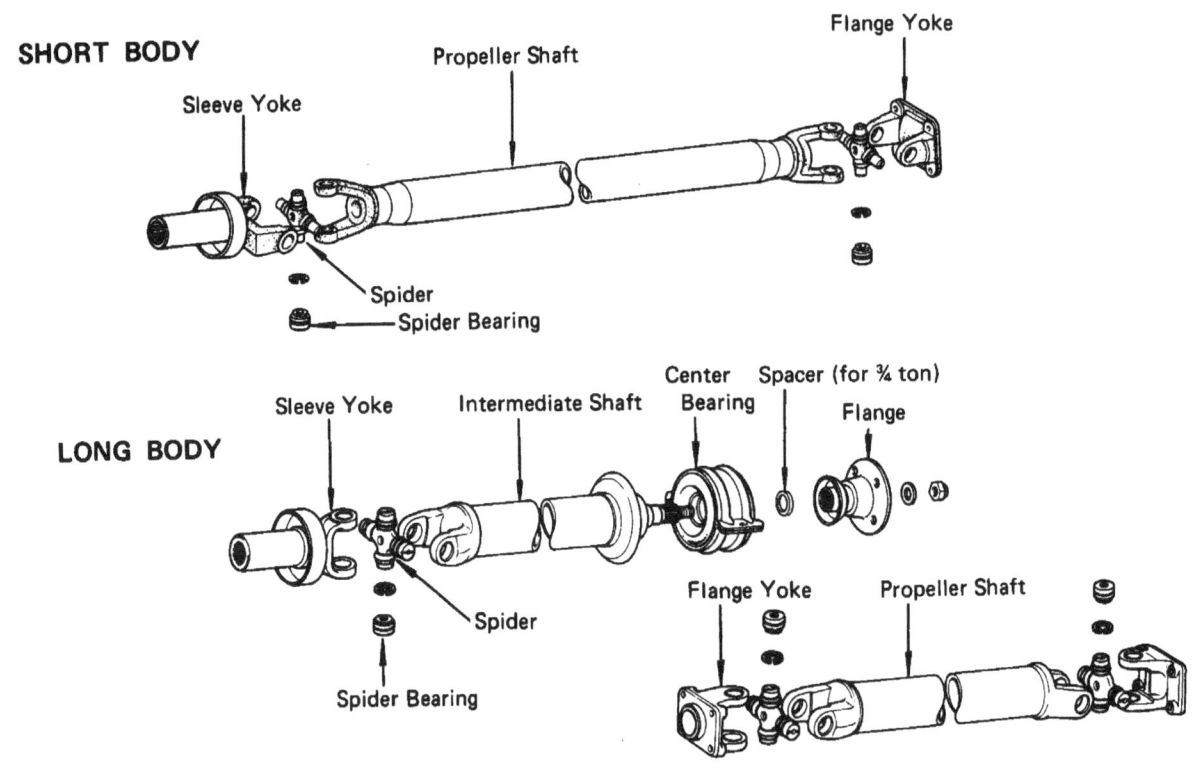

10.1a 2WD driveshaft assemblies - exploded view

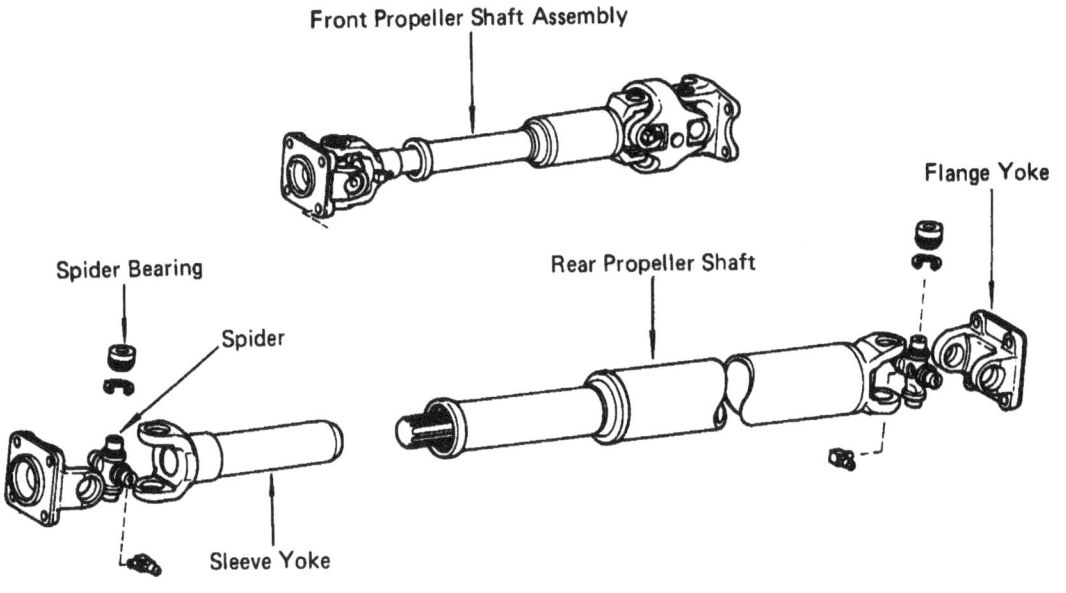

10.1b 4WD driveshaft assemblies - exploded view

bearing at the rear of the front shaft. This driveshaft uses three universal joints; one at the transmission end, one behind the centre bearing and one at the differential flange.

The 4WD models use two driveshafts; the front shaft runs between the transfer case and the front differential and the rear driveshaft runs between the transfer case and the rear differential. Long wheelbase models use a two-piece rear driveshaft with a centre support bearing.

All universal joints are of the solid type and can be renewed separate from the driveshaft.

The driveshafts are finely balanced during production and whenever they are removed or disassembled, they must be reassembled and refitted in the exact manner and positions they were originally in, to avoid excessive vibration.

The rear axle is of the semi-floating type, having a 'banjo' design axle housing, which is held in proper alignment with the body by the rear suspension.

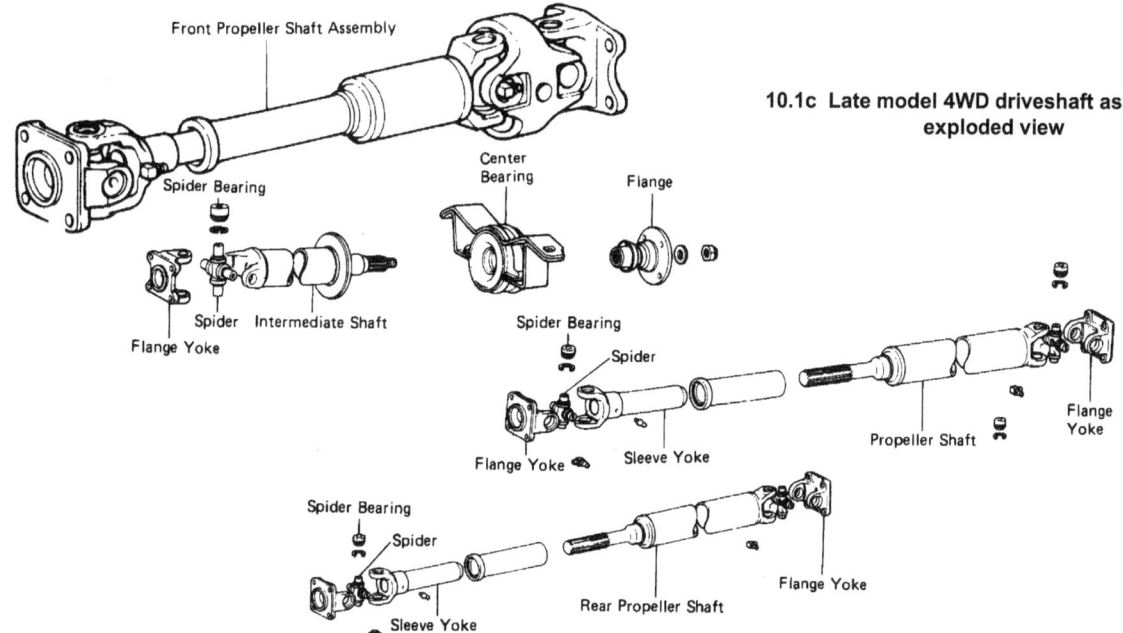

10.1c Late model 4WD driveshaft assemblies - exploded view

Mounted in the centre of the rear axle is the differential, which transfers the turning force of the driveshaft to the rear axleshafts, on which the rear wheels are mounted.

The axleshafts are splined at their inner ends to fit into the splines in the differential gears; outer support for the shaft is provided by the rear wheel bearing.

Because of the complexity and critical nature of the differential adjustments, as well as the special equipment needed to perform the operations, we recommend any disassembly of the differential be done by a Toyota dealer service department or other qualified repair facility.

11 Driveline inspection

1   Raise the rear of the vehicle and support it securely on jackstands.
2   Slide under the vehicle and visually inspect the condition of the driveshaft. Look for any dents or cracks in the tubing. If any are found, the driveshaft must be renewed.
3   Check for any oil leakage at the front and rear of the driveshaft. Leakage where the driveshaft enters the transmission indicates a defective rear transmission seal (see Chapter 7) . Leakage where the driveshaft enters the differential indicates a defective pinion seal (see Section 15).
4   While still under the vehicle, have an assistant turn the rear wheel so the driveshaft will rotate. As it does, make sure that the universal joints are operating properly without binding, noise or looseness. On long bed models, listen for any noise from the centre bearing, indicating it is worn or damaged. Also check the rubber portion of the centre bearing for cracking or separation, which will necessitate renewal.

5   The universal joint can also be checked with the driveshaft motionless, by gripping your hands on either side of the joint and attempting to twist the joint. Any movement at all in the joint is a sign of considerable wear. Lifting up on the shaft will also indicate movement in the universal joints.
6   Finally, check the driveshaft mounting bolts at the ends to make sure they are tight.
7   On 4WD models, the above driveshaft checks should be repeated on all driveshafts. In addition, check for grease leakage around the sleeve yoke, indicating failure of the yoke seal.
8   Check for leakage at each connection of the driveshafts to the transfer case and front differential. Leakage indicates worn oil seals.
9   At the same time, check for looseness in the joints of the front driveaxles. Also check for grease or oil leakage from around the driveaxles by inspecting the rubber boots and both ends of each axle. Oil leakage at the differential junction indicates a defective side oil seal. Leakage at the wheel side indicates a defective front hub seal, while leakage at the boots means a damaged rubber boot. For servicing of these components, see the appropriate Sections.

12 Driveshafts - removal and refitting

Refer to illustrations 12.2 and 12.15

Front driveshaft (4WD)

Caution: *Do not disassemble the front drive-shaft of 4WD vehicles.*
1   Raise the front of the vehicle and place it on jackstands.
2   Mark the edges of both front and both rear flanges so they can be realigned upon refitting **(see illustration)**.

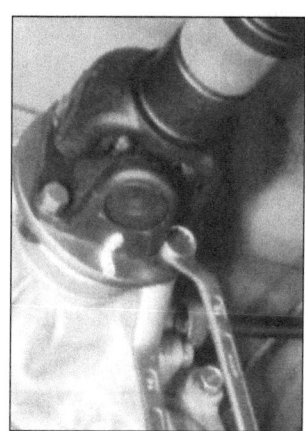

12.2 Mark the relationship of the driveshaft flanges to the transfer case and differential companion flanges to facilitate realignment

3   Remove the four bolts at both front and rear flanges.
4   Push the shaft slightly to the rear to disconnect the front flange and lower the driveshaft.

Rear driveshaft

5   Raise the rear of the vehicle and support it on jackstands.
6   Remove the two bolts holding the centre support bearing to the frame (3-joint type).
7   Mark the edges of the driveshaft rear flange and the differential pinion flange so they can be realigned upon refitting **(see illustration 12.2)**.
8   Remove the four nuts and bolts.
9   Push the shaft forward slightly to disconnect the rear flange (2WD).
10   Pull the yoke from the transmission while supporting the driveshaft with your hand (2WD).

12.15 Correct alignment of the centre bearing centre line and the centre of the bracket hole

13.1 Mark the relationship of the centre flange to the front section of a 3-joint driveshaft

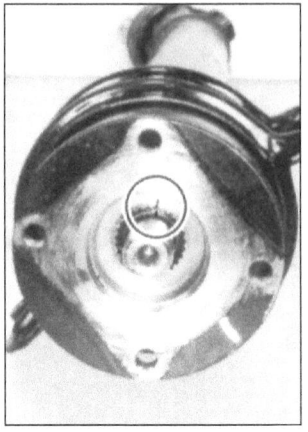

13.3 Mark the relationship of the companion flange to the shaft

11   Mark the driveshaft flange and the flange on the transfer case so they can be realigned upon refitting (4WD).

12   Remove the four nuts and bolts (4WD).

13   Push the shaft slightly to the rear to disconnect the front flange and gently lower the driveshaft (4WD).

14   While the driveshafts are removed, insert a plug in the transmission to prevent lubricant leakage.

15   Refitting is the reverse of the removal procedures. During refitting, make sure all flange marks line up. When connecting the centre bearing support to the frame, first finger-tighten the two mounting bolts, then make sure that the bearing bracket is at right angles to the driveshaft and that the bearing centre line is in the centre of the bracket hole (see illustration). Tighten all nuts and bolts to the torque values listed in this Chapter's Specifications.

13 Centre bearing - renewal

Refer to illustrations 13.1, 13.3 and 13.11

Note: *This procedure requires the use of a hydraulic press. If access to a press is not available, take the disassembled driveshaft to a dealer service department or other repair shop to have the centre bearing removed.*

1   Remove the driveshaft (Section 12). Mark the relationship of the centre flange to the front section of the driveshaft (see illustration).

2   Remove the four bolts that attach the centre flange to the companion flange (see illustration 13.1).

3   Mark the companion flange in relation to the slot in the shaft (see illustration).

4   The centre joint nut is staked to prevent it from working loose. To remove it, first use a punch to knock the staking back out, then unscrew it from the shaft. To keep the flange from turning, either obtain a special tool designed for this purpose, or one can be made using a flat steel bar and old bolts inserted through the flange holes. The bar should be drilled to match at least two of the flange holes.

5   Using an appropriate puller, remove the companion flange.

6   The centre bearing can be removed from the front section of the driveshaft by using a hydraulic press and appropriate support plate.

7   Using a dial indicator, inspect all driveshafts for damage and runout. If the shaft runout is greater than the specified maximum, install a new driveshaft.

8   Inspect the yokes and flanges for damage and wear. If damage or wear is found, renew the appropriate parts.

9   Inspect the centre support bearing for

wear or damage and make sure that the bearing turns freely. If any faults are found, renew the centre bearing.

10   For inspection procedures for the universal joints, see Section 14.

11   Begin reassembly of the driveshaft by coating the splines of the intermediate shaft with multi-purpose grease and placing the bearing on the shaft (see illustration).

12   Place the flange on the shaft and align the marks. **Note:** *On 3/4-ton models, attach the spacer to the rear side of the bearing before refitting the flange.*

13   Using the special tool or the one you have fabricated (see Step 4) to hold the flange, tighten a new centre joint nut to press the bearing into position.

14   Tighten the nut to 167 to 195 Nm.

15   Loosen the nut, then tighten it to the specified torque.

16   Using a hammer and punch, stake the centre joint nut.

17   Attach the rear shaft to the centre support bearing flange by aligning the marks on the flanges and connecting the four bolts and nuts.

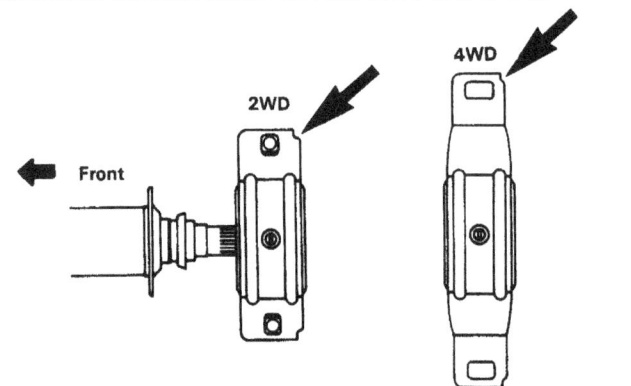

13.11 Refit the centre bearing with the notches in the flange facing the rear of the vehicle

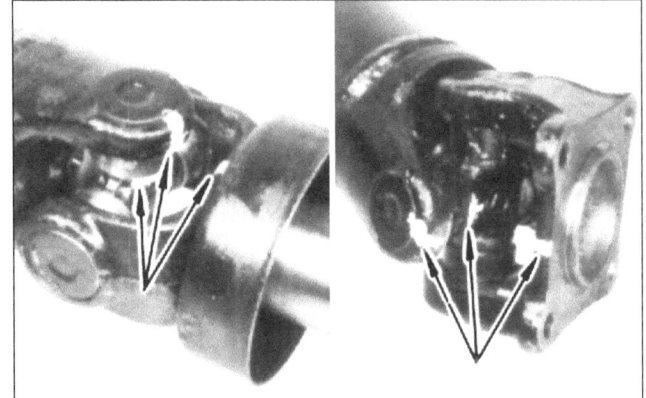

14.5 Mark the relationship of the driveshaft, universal joint spider and yoke or flange before disassembling the joint

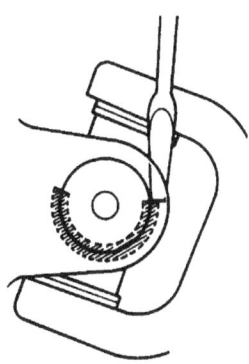

14.7 Push the snap-rings from the U-joint bearings with a small screwdriver,

14.9a Use a vice, a large socket (left) and a small socket (right) to press the bearing out of the universal joint

14.9b Pliers may be needed to finish removing the bearing

14 Universal joints - inspection and renewal

Refer to illustrations 14.5, 14.7, 14.9a, 14.9b, 14.17a and 14.17b

1   Wear in the needle roller bearings is characterised by vibration in the transmission, noise during acceleration, and in extreme cases of lack of lubrication, metallic squeaking and ultimately grating and shrieking sounds as the bearings disintegrate.

2   It is easy to check if the needle bearings are worn with the driveshaft (3-joint) in position by trying to turn the shaft with one hand, the other hand holding the rear axle flange when the rear universal joint is being checked or the front half coupling when the front universal joint is being checked. Any movement between the driveshaft and the front half couplings, and around the rear half couplings, is indicative of considerable wear.

3   On one-piece driveshafts, try turning the shaft with one hand, with the other hand holding the rear axle flange when the rear universal joint is being checked and the front half coupling when the front universal joint is being checked. Any movement between the shaft and the couplings is indicative of wear and the universal joints should be renewed.

4   With the driveshafts removed, the uni-versal joints may be checked by holding the shaft in one hand and turning the yoke or flange with the other. If the axial movement is more than specified, renew the bearings.

5   To renew the universal joints, with the driveshaft removed, place alignment marks on each shaft, universal joint spider and yoke or flange **(see illustration)**.

6   Using a ratchet extension or similar tool and hammer, tap lightly on the bearing outer races of the universal joint to relieve pressure on the snap-rings.

7   Using a screwdriver, remove the snap-rings from their grooves **(see illustration)**.

8   To remove the bearings from the yokes, you will need two sockets. One should be large enough to fit into the yoke where the snap-rings were fitted and the other should have an inside diameter just large enough for the bearings to fit into when they are forced out of the yoke.

9   Mount the universal joint in a vice with the large socket on one side of the yoke and the small socket on the other side, pushing against the bearing. Carefully tighten the vice until the bearing is pushed out of the yoke and into the large socket **(see illustration)**. If it cannot be pushed all the way out, remove the universal joint from the vice and use pliers to finish removing the bearing **(see illustration)**.

10   Reverse the sockets and push out the bearing on the other side of the yoke. This time, the small socket will be pushing against the cross-shaped universal joint spider end.

11   Before pressing out the two remaining bearings, make sure the spider is marked so it can be fitted in the same relative position during reassembly.

12   The remaining universal joints can be disassembled following the same procedure. Be sure to mark all components for each universal joint so they can be kept together and reassembled in the proper position.

13   Check the spider journals for scoring, needle roller impressions, rust and pitting. Renew it if any of the above conditions exist.

14   Check the sleeve yoke splines for wear and damage.

15   When reassembling the universal joints, renew all needle bearings, dust seals and snap-rings.

16   Before reassembly, pack each grease cavity in the spiders with a small amount of grease. Also, apply a thin coat of grease to the new needle bearing rollers and the roller contact areas on the spiders.

17   Apply a thin coat of grease to the dust seal lips and fit the bearings and spider into the yoke using the vice and sockets that were used to remove the old bearings. Work slowly

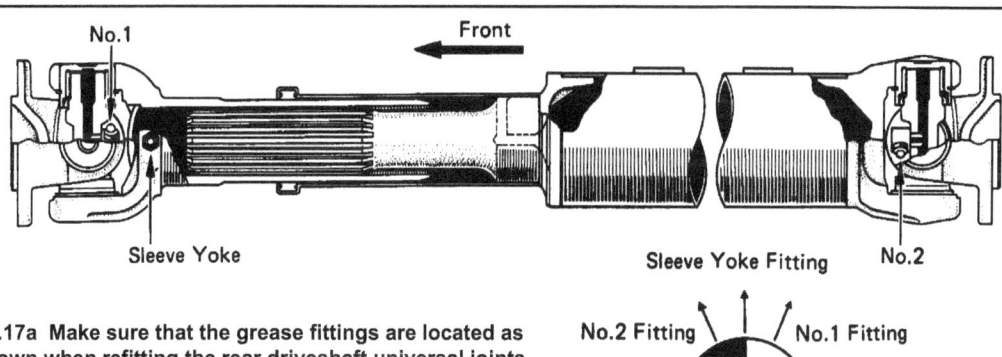

14.17a Make sure that the grease fittings are located as shown when refitting the rear driveshaft universal joints on 1983 and earlier 4WD models

and be very careful not to damage the bearings as they are being pressed into the yokes. **Note:** *When fitting the rear universal joint on 4WD vehicles, be sure that the grease fitting hole is facing in the proper direction* (see illustrations).

18   Press the bearings in until the width of the snap-ring grooves is approximately 2.5 mm. Install snap-rings of the same thickness on each side (various sizes are available for different models) and make sure there is no clearance between the bearing cups and the snap-rings. **Note:** *If there is clearance, check with your Toyota dealer or auto parts store for other available snap-ring thicknesses.* Tap the yoke with a hammer to move the cups slightly.

19   Make sure that the spider moves freely in the bearings, then check the axial play. If it is excessive, thicker snap-rings must be used to reduce the play.

20   Assemble the remaining universal joint(s) and, in the case of 3-joint shafts, rejoin the two driveshafts.

15   Pinion oil seal - renewal

Refer to illustrations 15.1, 15.5 and 15.6

1   A pinion shaft oil seal failure results in the leakage of differential gear lubricant past the seal and onto the driveshaft yoke or flange. The seal is replaceable without removing or disassembling the differential (see illustration).

2   Raise the vehicle and place it on jackstands.

3   Remove the drain and fill plugs from the differential housing and allow the differential lubricant to drain into a suitable container. When the draining is complete, loosely fit the drain plug.

4   Disconnect the driveshaft from the companion flange (Section 12).

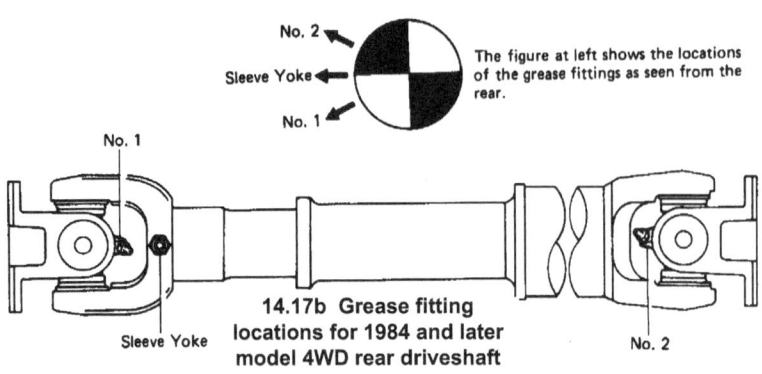

14.17b Grease fitting locations for 1984 and later model 4WD rear driveshaft

5   Using a torque wrench, slowly turn the pinion shaft nut and measure the preload (see illustration) within the backlash of the drive pinion gear and the ring gear (if the axles and wheels turn, the backlash has been exceeded and the torque figure is incorrect). The preload should be within the Specifications. If it is not, the preload must be adjusted with shims prior to fitting of the new oil seal. This procedure should be performed by a dealer service department or a reputable repair shop, as special tools are required.

6   Mark the relationship of the pinion shaft, flange and nut (see illustration).

7   Using a hammer and chisel, loosen the staked part of the companion flange nut. Using a flange holder to hold the flange, remove the nut.

8   Using a hammer, tap the companion flange off the shaft. **Caution:** *Do not hammer on the shaft.*

9   After noting what the visible side of the oil seal looks like, carefully prise it out of the differential with a screwdriver or seal removal tool. Be careful not to damage the splines on the pinion shaft.

10   Lubricate the new seal lip with multi-pur-

pose grease and carefully fit it in position in the differential. Using a short section of pipe of the proper circumference and a hammer, carefully drive the seal into a depth of 1.0 mm to 1.5 mm.

11   Clean the sealing lip contact surface of the differential companion flange. Apply a thin coat of multi-purpose grease to the seal contact surface and the shaft spines and fit the companion flange onto the shaft, making sure the matchmarks on the shaft and flange are aligned.

12   Fit the companion flange nut and, using the holder to hold the flange, tighten the nut until the mark on the nut is aligned with the mark on the companion flange.

13   Turn the companion flange several times.

14   Using a torque wrench, see how much torque is required to turn the pinion shaft within the range of gear backlash (if the axles and wheel turn, the backlash has been exceeded and the torque figure is incorrect). This torque is the drive pinion bearing preload. If the preload is greater than that specified, the bearing spacer will have to be renewed by an authorised dealer service department

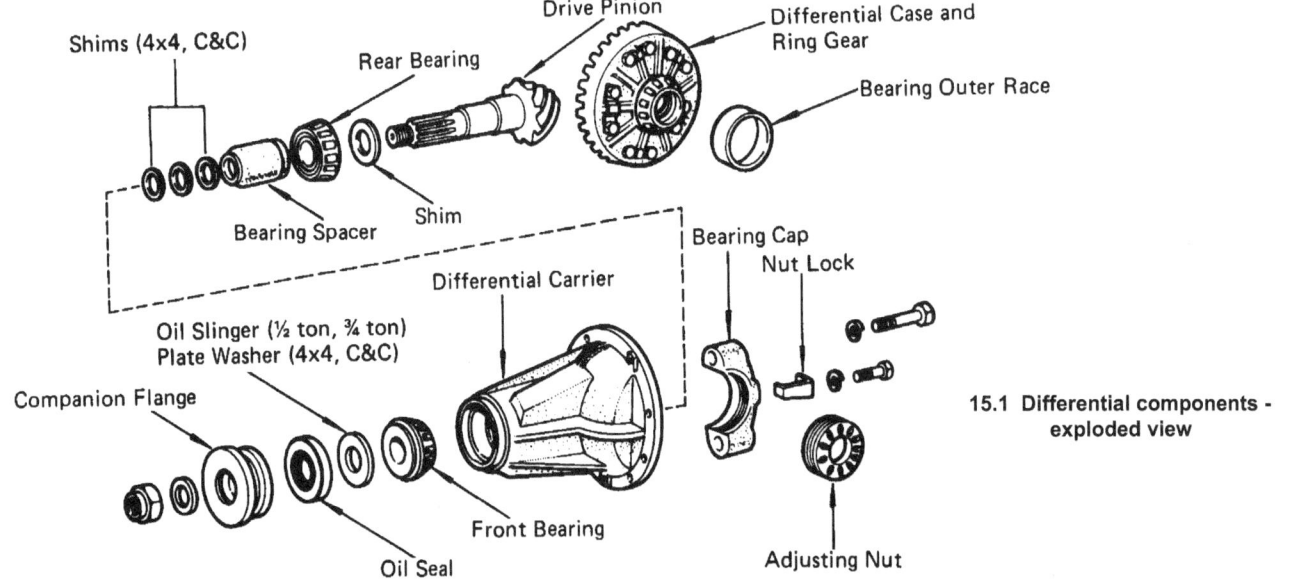

15.1 Differential components - exploded view

15.5 A torque wrench is used to measure drive pinion preload

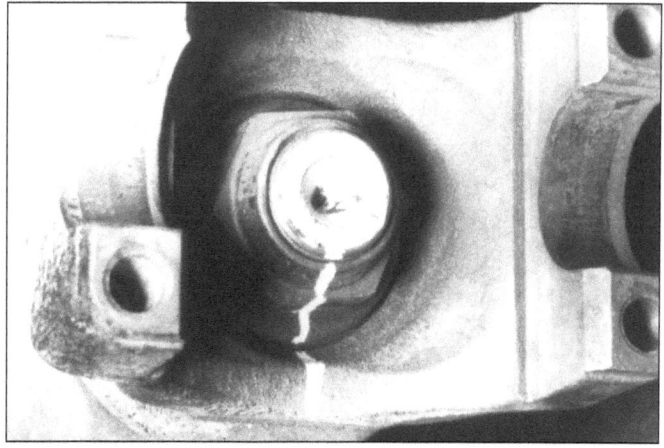

15.6 Mark the relative positions of the pinion shaft, nut and flange before removing the nut

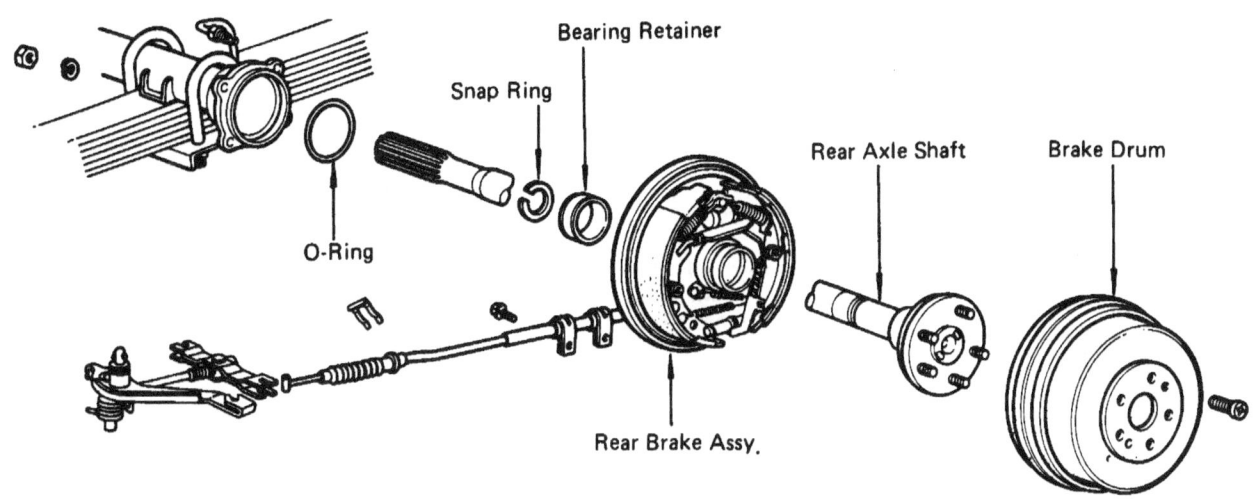

16.1 Rear axleshaft assembly - exploded view

or reputable repair shop. If the preload is less than that specified, retighten the nut a little at a time until the specified preload is reached. If the maximum torque specified is reached before the preload figure is obtained, the bearing spacer must be renewed by a qualified repair facility. **Note:** *Do not back off the pinion nut to reduce the preload.*

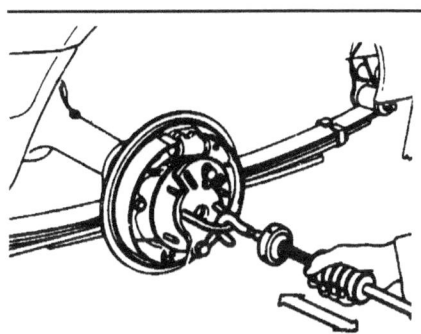

16.7 A rear axle adapter plate and slide hammer may be needed to remove the rear axle assembly

15   When the preload is ascertained, stake the nut with a punch and hammer.
16   Connect the driveshaft to the companion flange (Section 12).
17   Tighten the drain plug and fill the housing to the proper level with the recommended gear lubricant (see *Recommended lubricants and fluids* at the front of Chapter 1).
18   Fit the filler plug and tighten it fully.
19   Lower the vehicle to the ground, test drive it and check for evidence of leakage.

16   Rear axleshafts, bearings and oil seals - removal and refitting

Refer to illustrations 16.1, 16.7, 16.9, 16.14 and 16.20

1   The axleshafts can be removed without disturbing the differential assembly. They must be removed in order to renew the bearings and oil seals and when removing the differential carrier from the rear axle housing **(see illustration)**. **Note:** *Read the entire Section before starting work.*

2   Raise the rear of the vehicle and support it securely on jackstands. Block the front wheels to keep the vehicle from rolling.
3   Remove the rear wheels and release the parking brake, then remove the brake drums (see Chapter 9 for details).
4   Remove the drain plug and drain the differential oil into a suitable container. When the draining is complete, finger-tighten the drain plug in place.
5   Disconnect the brake line (see Chapter 9 for details).
6   Remove the brake backing plate mounting nuts.
7   The axleshaft, complete with the brake assembly, can now be pulled out from the rear axle. If the axleshaft will not pull out by hand, a slide hammer can be attached to the wheel studs using an adapter plate **(see illustration)**.
8   Since the wheel bearing is press-fitted onto the axleshaft, its removal and refitting will require the use of special tools and either a special puller or a hydraulic press. If the necessary equipment is not available, this operation should be left to a dealer or other

16.9 Remove the snap-ring from the axleshaft

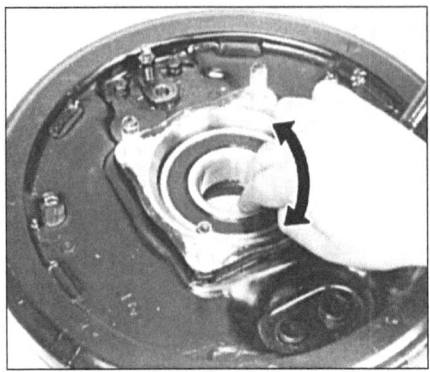

16.14 Rotate the inner race of the bearing to feel for roughness or sticking. If it doesn't turn smoothly, renew it

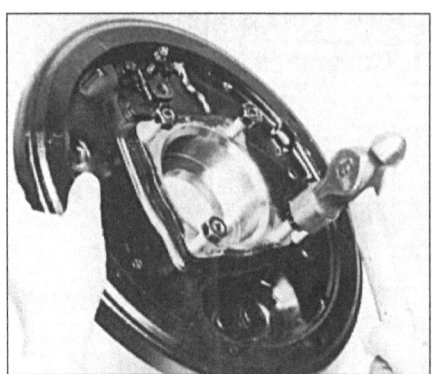

16.20 Knock the backing plate mounting lugs from the backing plate, then remove the bearing case

suitably equipped shop. If the equipment is available, proceed as follows.

9   Using snap-ring pliers, remove the snap-ring from the axleshaft **(see illustration)**.

10   Using either a special puller designed for this purpose or a hydraulic press equipped with the necessary supports, press the axleshaft from the backing plate.

11   Inspect the axleshaft for wear or damage.

12   Inspect the outer seal for wear or damage.

13   To renew the outer seal, remove it with a puller, then use a seal driver or section of appropriately sized pipe and a hammer to drive in the new seal.

14   Check the rear axle bearing for wear or damage **(see illustration)**.

15   To renew the bearing, first remove the bearing oil seal.

16   Using a driver and collar and with the brake assembly properly supported, press the bearing out.

17   Using the collar and driver, press in the new bearing and fit a new oil seal (see Step 13).

18   Inspect the bearing case for damage or cracks.

19   To renew the bearing case, first remove the oil seal and bearing (Steps 13 and 16).

20   Fit nuts on the backing plate mounting lugs, then tap on the nuts to remove the lugs. Remove the bearing case **(see illustration)**.

21   To fit the new bearing case, position the backing plate on the new case and, using two sockets placed one on either side of the mounting lug, press in the lugs. **Note:** *Position the flat side of the bearing case and two longer lugs at the upper side of the bearing case.*

22   Fit a new bearing and oil seal (see Steps 13 and 17).

23   Inspect the inner oil seal for wear or damage.

24   To renew the inner oil seal, first use a puller to remove the old seal.

25   Use a driver or section of appropriately sized pipe and a hammer to drive in the new seal.

26   To refit the axleshaft, first apply multi-purpose grease to the inner lip of the oil seal.

27   Place the backing plate and bearing retainer on the axleshaft.

28   Using a collar and press, press the axleshaft into the backing plate assembly.

29   Using snap-ring pliers, fit the snap-ring on the axle.

30   Attach the axle and backing plate assembly to the axle housing and tighten the four nuts at the back of the backing plate to the specified torque.

31   Following fitting, tighten the drain plug and fill the differential with the proper grade and amount of lubricant as specified in Chapter 1.

17 Rear differential - removal and refitting

1   Raise the rear of the vehicle and support it securely on jackstands. Block the front wheels to keep the vehicle from rolling.

2   Remove the drain plug and drain the differential oil into a suitable container, then install the drain plug finger-tight.

3   Remove the rear axleshafts (see Section 16).

4   Disconnect the driveshaft flange from the companion flange (see Section 12).

5   Remove the nuts from the differential carrier assembly and pull out the differential assembly. The mounting nuts should be loosened in steps, following a criss-cross pattern.

6   The overhaul of the rear axle differential unit is not within the scope of the home mechanic, due to the specialised gauges and tools which are required. Where the unit requires servicing or repair, due to wear or excessive noise, it is most economical to exchange it for a factory reconditioned assembly.

7   Before installing the rear differential, scrape all traces of old gasket from the mating surfaces of the axle housing. Position a new gasket on the housing (use a silicone-type gasket sealant).

8   Refitting is the reverse of the removal procedure.

9   Following refitting, fill the differential with the proper grade and quantity of lubricant (see Chapter 1).

18 Rear axle assembly - removal and refitting

1   Loosen the rear Wheel nuts, raise the vehicle and support it securely on jackstands placed underneath the frame. Remove the wheels.

2   Support the rear axle assembly with a floor jack placed underneath the differential.

3   Remove the shock absorber lower mounting nuts and compress the shocks to get them out of the way (Chapter 10).

4   Disconnect the driveshaft from the differential companion flange and hang it with a piece of wire from the underbody (Section 12).

5   Unbolt the stabiliser bar from the stabiliser bar link, if so equipped (Chapter 10).

6   Disconnect the parking brake cables from the equaliser (2WD models). On 4WD models, unbolt the equaliser from the rear axle housing and disconnect the rear cable ends from the adjusting levers on the brake backing plates (Chapter 9). Unbolt the load sensing proportioning valve control rod from the axle housing.

7   Disconnect the flexible brake hose from the junction block on the rear axle housing. Plug the end of the hose or wrap a plastic bag tightly around it to prevent excessive fluid loss and contamination.

8   Remove the U-bolt nuts from under the leaf spring seats (Chapter 10).

9   Raise the rear axle assembly off of the leaf spring and carefully manoeuvre it out from between the leaf spring and the frame (2WD models). It would be a good idea to have an assistant on hand, as the assembly is very heavy. On 4WD models, lower the assembly from the vehicle.

10   Refitting is the reverse of the removal procedure. Be sure to tighten the U-bolt nuts and the driveshaft companion flange bolts to the specified torque.

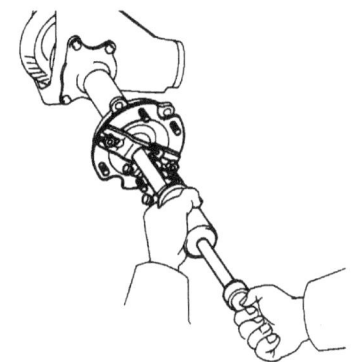

19.9 Pull the side gear shafts from the differential with a slide hammer and adapter plate

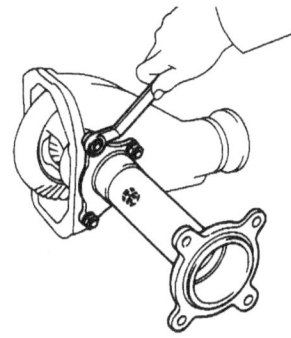

19.10 Remove the four differential tube-to-differential carrier mounting nuts and separate the tube from the carrier

20.7 Remove the U-bolt nuts only after the axle assembly has been supported with a floor jack

19   Front differential (4WD) - removal and refitting

Models with solid front axle

1   Raise the front end of the vehicle and place it securely on jackstands.
2   Remove the differential drain plug and drain the lubricant into a suitable container, then install the drain plug finger-tight.
3   Remove the front axleshafts (see Section 23).
4   Disconnect the front driveshaft flange from the companion flange (see Section 12).
5   Remove the nuts from the differential housing and pull out the differential carrier assembly.
6   Refitting is the reverse of the removal procedures. Be sure to tighten all bolts and nuts to the specified torque. Use the correct amount and type of lubricant when refilling the differential (see Chapter 1).

Models with independent front suspension

Refer to illustrations 19.9 and 19.10

7   Unscrew the plug at the bottom of the differential and allow the lubricant to drain. Remove the front axle assembly following the procedure outlined in Section 20.
8   Remove the differential cover from the carrier.
9   Using a slide hammer and axle flange adapter, remove the differential side gear shafts **(see illustration)**.
10   Unbolt the differential tube from the carrier **(see illustration)**.
11   Refitting is the reverse of the removal procedure. When refitting the cover to the carrier, apply a bead of silicone gasket sealer to the mating surface on the cover, position the cover on the carrier and install the bolts. Tighten the bolts to the specified torque while the sealer is still wet. Be sure to tighten the remainder of the fasteners to the specified

torque and use the correct type and amount of lubricant when refilling the differential.

20   Front axle assembly (4WD) - removal and refitting

1   Loosen the Wheel nuts, raise the front of the vehicle and support it securely on jackstands placed under the frame rails. Remove the wheels.

Models with solid front axle

Refer to illustration 20.7

2   Disconnect the drag link from the left side steering knuckle arm (Chapter 10).
3   Disconnect the brake hoses from the calipers (Chapter 9). Plug the ends of the hoses to prevent excessive fluid loss and contamination.
4   Remove the shock absorber lower mounting bolts and compress the shocks to get them out of the way.
5   Remove the stabiliser bar-to-axle housing nuts and bolts, if so equipped (see Chapter 10). Take note as to how the washers, bushes and spacers are arranged.
6   Unbolt the torque rod from its mounting bracket on the axle housing (Chapter 10).
7   Support the axle housing with two floor jacks, one placed under each axle tube. Remove the U-bolt nuts from under the leaf spring seats **(see illustration)**.
8   Carefully lower the assembly from the vehicle.
9   Refitting is the reverse of the removal procedure. Be sure to tighten the U-bolt nuts to the torque listed in this Chapter's Specifications.

Models with independent front suspension

Refer to illustration 20.11

10   Unbolt the driveaxles from the differential side gear shafts (see Section 24). Support the inner ends of the driveaxles with pieces of wire - don't let them hang unsupported, as damage to the outboard constant velocity (CV) joint may occur.
11   Support the differential with a floor jack. Remove the differential front mounting bolt and nut **(see illustration)**.

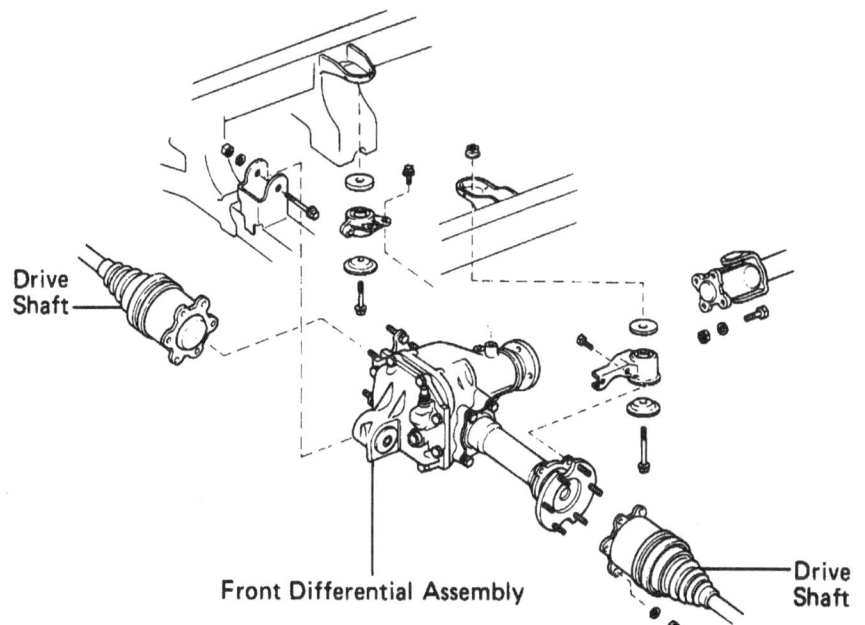

Drive Shaft

Front Differential Assembly

Drive Shaft

20.11 Front axle assembly mounting details (4WD models with independent front suspension)

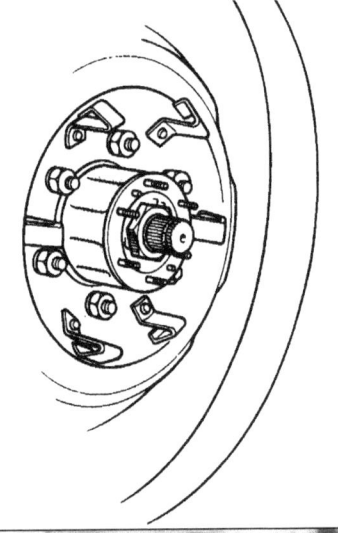

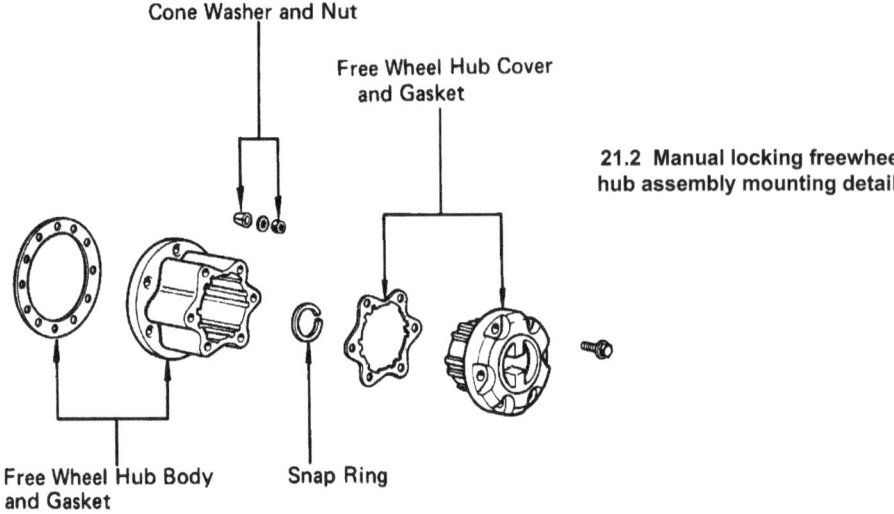

21.2 Manual locking freewheel hub assembly mounting details

Cone Washer and Nut

Free Wheel Hub Cover and Gasket

Free Wheel Hub Body and Gasket

Snap Ring

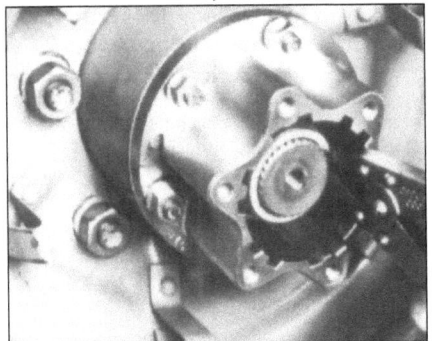

21.3 Remove the snap-ring from the end of the axle

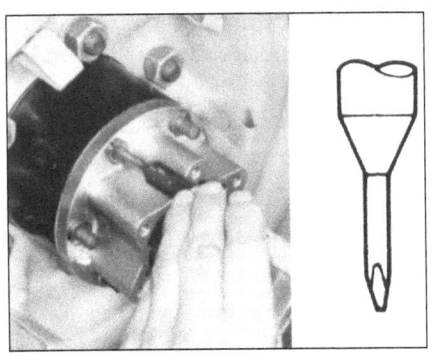

21.5 Use a tapered punch to remove the cone washers

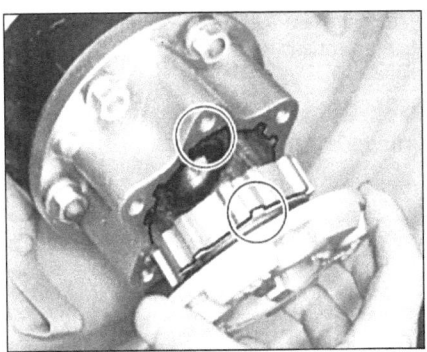

21.7 When refitting the hub assembly, align the follower pawl tabs with the non-toothed portion of the hub body

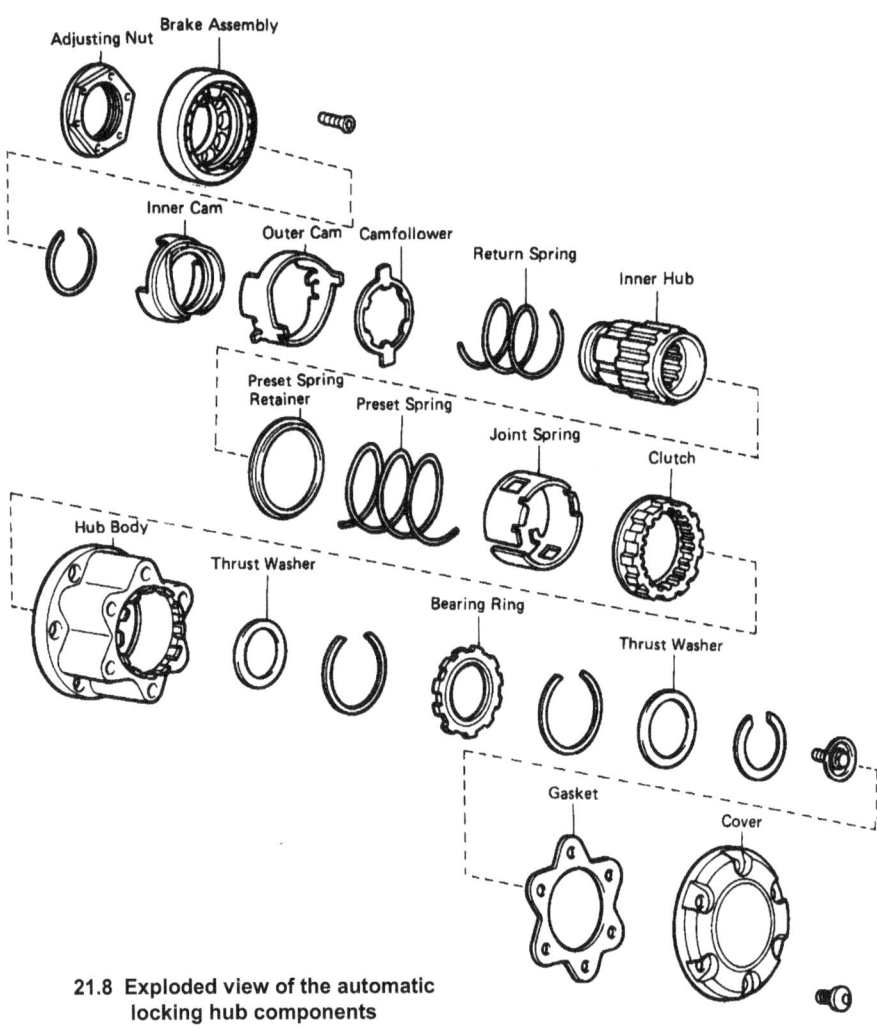

21.8 Exploded view of the automatic locking hub components

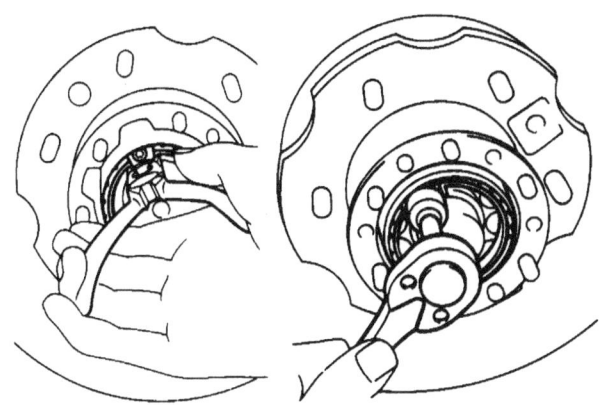

21.10 Compress the brake spring and align the gap with one of the screws, then remove the screw (repeat the procedure for the remaining screws)

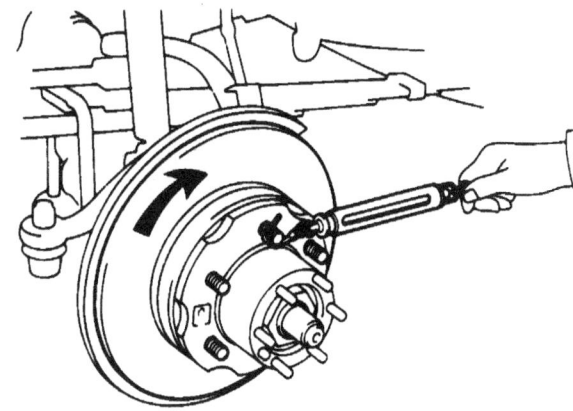

21.14 Checking the oil seal frictional drag with a spring scale

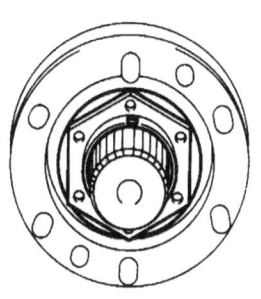
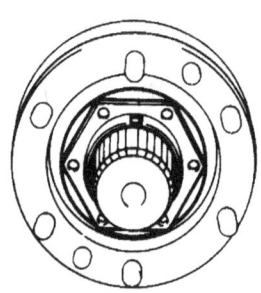

21.15 Make sure the hub nut is aligned in one of the two ways shown

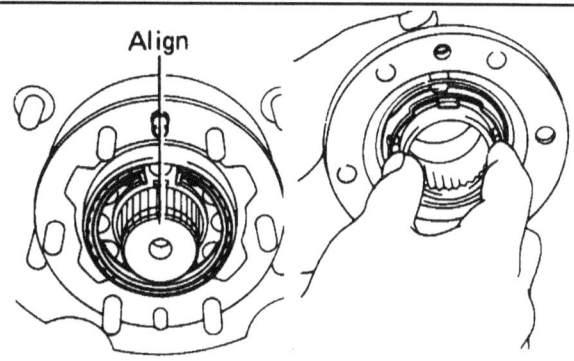

21.16 Align the spring claw of the brake assembly with the pin and the inner cam protrusion with the pin hole when the hub body is refitted

12 Remove the bolt that fastens the axle tube bracket to the frame **(see illustration 20.11)**.
13 Remove the differential rear mounting bolt **(see illustration 20.11)**.
14 Carefully lower the assembly from the vehicle.
15 Refitting is the reverse of the removal procedure. Be sure to tighten all of the fasteners to the torque values listed in this Chapter's Specifications.

21 Freewheel hub (4WD) - removal and refitting

Manual locking hubs

Refer to illustrations 21.2, 21.3, 21.5 and 21.7

Removal

1 Set the hub cover to the Free position.
2 Remove the hub cover mounting bolts and pull off the cover with the clutch **(see illustration)**.
3 Using snap-ring pliers, remove the snap-ring from the end of the axle **(see illustration)**.
4 Remove the mounting nuts from the freewheel hub body.
5 Using a tapered punch, tap on the slits

of the cone washers and remove them **(see illustration)**.
6 Pull the freewheel hub body from the axle hub.

Refitting

7 Refitting is the reverse of the removal procedure. Use new gaskets and apply multi-purpose grease to the inner hub splines. The control handle should be set to the Free position and the cover should be attached to the body with the following pawl tabs aligned with the non-toothed portions of the body **(see illustration)**.

Automatic locking hubs

Refer to illustrations 21.8, 21.10, 21.14, 21.15 and 21.16

Removal

8 Remove the bolts and detach the hub cover, then remove the bolt and washer from the centre of the hub **(see illustration)**.
9 Refer to Steps 4 through 7 above.
10 Using needle-nose pliers, compress the brake spring and align the gap with one of the screws **(see illustration)**. **Note:** *Do not remove the shoe from the drum and do not compress the spring excessively.*
11 Using a Torx socket, remove the screw,

then align the spring gap with the next screw and remove it **(see illustration 21.10)**. Finally, align the spring gap with the remaining screw, remove it and detach the brake assembly.
12 The hub nut can be removed if necessary, but it requires a very large socket.

Refitting

13 Install the hub nut (if removed), then tighten it to 58 Nm and turn the hub several times in both directions to seat the bearings.
14 Loosen the nut until it can be turned by hand, then attach a spring scale to one of the hub wheel studs and measure the frictional drag of the oil seal **(see illustration)**. Record the measurement for use later.
15 Tighten the hub nut to the torque listed in this Chapter's Specifications. Make sure the nut is positioned properly **(see illustration)**. If it isn't, tighten it slightly until it is.
16 Align the brake assembly with the groove in the axle and slip it into place **(see illustration)**. It must bottom against the nut and the holes must be aligned.
17 Check the preload with the scale (preload is the force required to start the hub turning). It must be 3 to 12 Nm greater than the oil seal frictional drag measured previously. If it isn't, the hub nut must be loosened or tightened until it is.

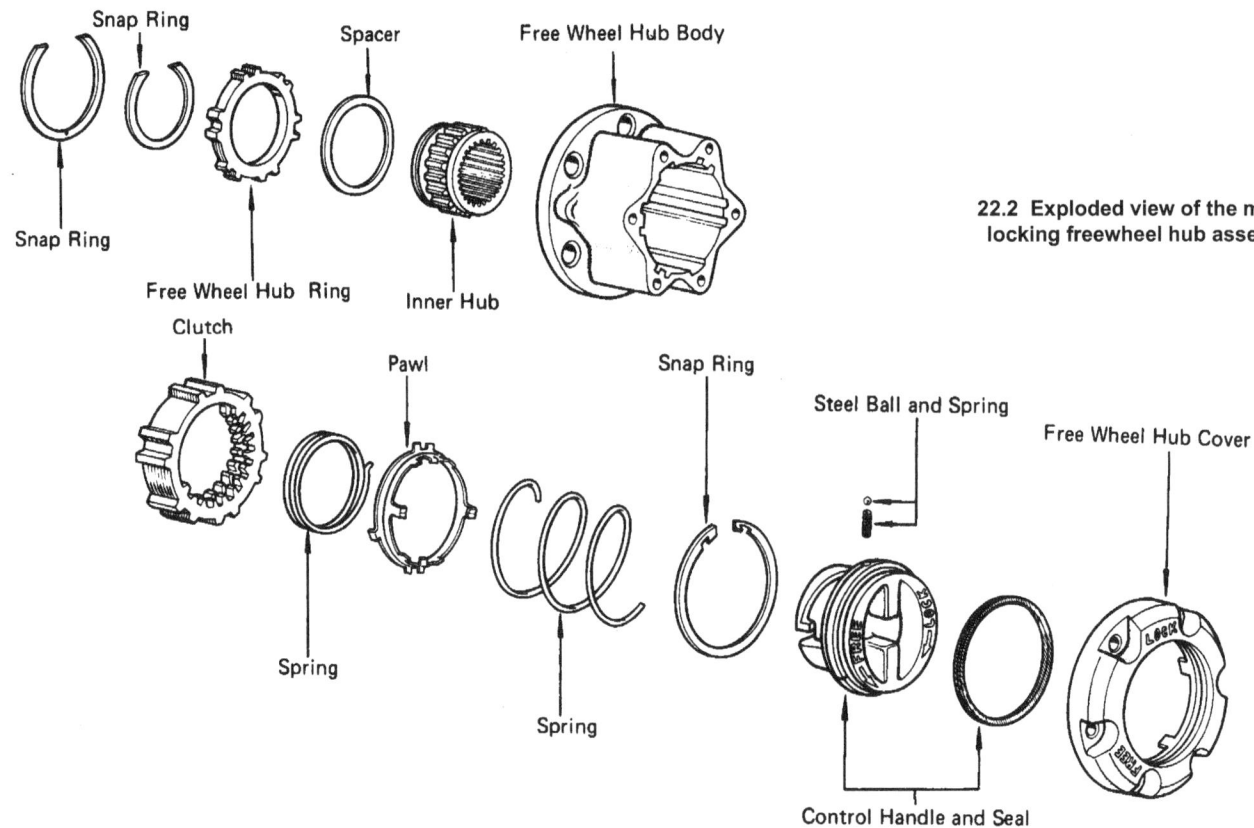

22.2 Exploded view of the manual locking freewheel hub assembly

18   Install the Torx screws and tighten them to the torque listed in this Chapter's Specifications. **Caution:** *Do not deviate from the specified torque and make sure the brake shoe is as far back in the drum as it will go.*
19   Align the spring claw of the brake assembly with the knock pin, then align the inner cam protrusion with the hub body knock pin hole and install the hub body. Make sure the hub body bottoms on the axle hub, then install the cone washers and nuts. Tighten the nuts to the torque listed in this Chapter' Specifications.
20   Install the washer and bolt in the centre of the hub and tighten the bolt to the torque listed in this Chapter's Specifications. Install the cover and tighten the bolts to the torque listed in this Chapter's Specifications.

22   Freewheel hub (4WD) - disassembly, inspection and reassembly

Note: *When disassembling the freewheel hub, pay very close attention to the way the parts fit together. If confusion is a possibility, make a sketch as they are disassembled and lay them out in the order of removal.*

Manual locking hubs

Refer to illustrations 22.2, 22.4, 22.5, 22.9, 22.13 and 22.14

1   Remove the freewheel hub (Section 21).
2   Using snap-ring pliers, remove the snap-ring from the inside of the hub cover, then remove the control handle from the cover **(see illustration).**

3   Remove the steel ball and spring from the control handle.
4   On 1991 and earlier models, using a screwdriver, remove the snap-ring that retains the inner hub and freewheel hub ring to the freewheel hub body **(see illustration)**, then remove the inner hub and ring from the body.
5   On 1991 and earlier models, using snap-ring pliers, remove the snap-ring that retains the freewheel hub ring to the inner hub **(see illustration)**, then remove the ring and spacer from the inner hub.
6   Inspect the cover, handle and seal for wear or damage. If wear or damage is found, renew the appropriate parts.
7   Temporarily attach the handle to the cover and see if the handle moves smoothly and freely.
8   Inspect the hub body, clutch spring,

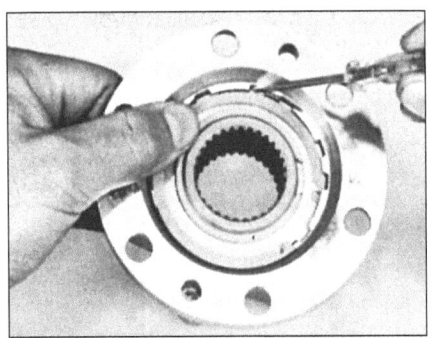

22.4 Removing the snap-ring retaining the inner hub and ring to the hub body (1991 and earlier models)

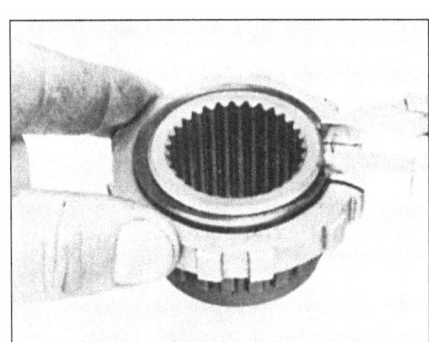

22.5 Remove the snap-ring retaining the hub ring to the inner hub (1991 and earlier models)

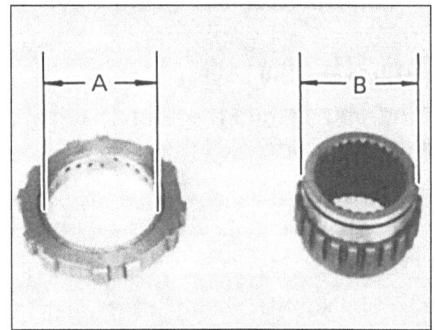

22.9 Oil clearance between the hub ring (A) and the inner hub (B) should be 0.012 in (0.3 mm) (1991 and earlier models)

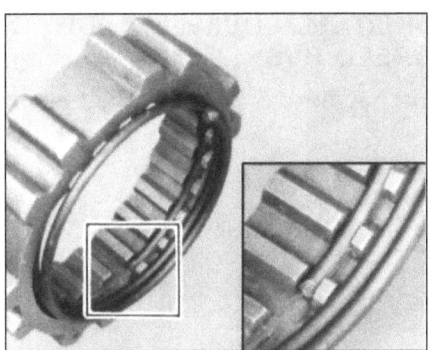

22.13 Proper alignment of the tension spring in the clutch

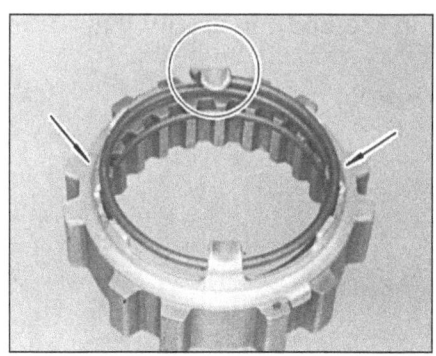

22.14 Spring end abuts one of the large tabs, and the top ring rests on the small tabs of the follower pawl

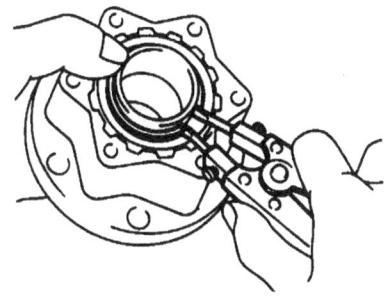

22.23a Remove the snap-ring and detach the inner hub

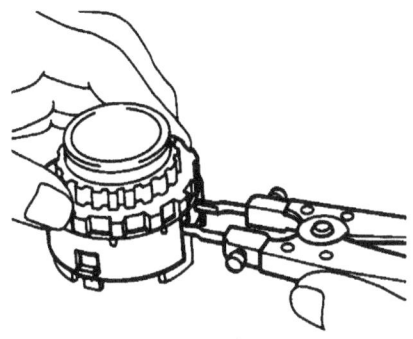

22.23b Extend the joint spring and release it from the cam follower tabs

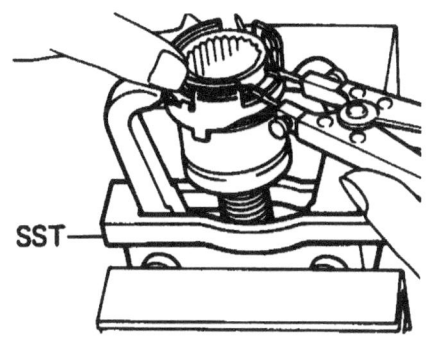

22.25 Remove the snap-ring after compressing the return spring with a gear puller

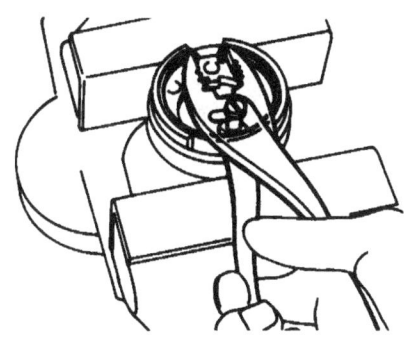

22.26a Compress the brake spring with pliers and pull the shoe part out

clutch body and follower pawl for wear and make sure that the clutch moves smoothly in the hub body. Renew any worn parts.

9   On 1991 and earlier models, inspect the inner hub and free wheel ring for wear or damage, and check the oil clearance between the hub and ring **(see illustration)**. It should be as specified. Renew any worn parts.

10   To begin assembly of the freewheel hub, apply multi-purpose grease to the contact surfaces of all parts.

11   Attach a new seal and the spring and ball to the control handle.

12   Insert the handle into the cover and install the snap-ring.

13   Install the tension spring in the clutch, with the spring end aligned with the initial groove **(see illustration)**.

14   Place the follower pawl over the tension spring, with one of the large tabs positioned against the bent spring end. The top coil of the spring should rest on the small tabs of the pawl **(see illustration)**.

15   Place the spring between the hub cover and clutch, with the large end of the spring toward the cover.

16   Compress the spring and install the clutch with the pawl tab fitted into the handle cam.

17   On 1991 and earlier models, install the spacer and freewheel hub ring in the inner hub, then install the snap-ring with snap-ring pliers.

18   On 1991 and earlier models, insert the inner hub and freewheel hub ring into the hub body. Using a screwdriver, install the snap-ring.

19   Set the control handle and clutch to the Free position.

20   Insert the cover in the hub body and verify that the inner hub turns freely.

21   Before attaching the freewheel hub to the vehicle, remove the cover from the body.

22   Install the freewheel hub (Section 21).

Automatic locking hubs

Refer to illustrations 22.23a, 22.23b, 22.25, 22.26a, 22.26b and 22.28

23   Using snap-ring pliers, remove the snap-ring and detach the inner hub from the hub. Extend the joint spring and release it from the cam follower tabs **(see illustrations)**. Do not stretch the spring excessively.

24   Remove the clutch, joint spring, preset spring and spring retainer.

25   Compress the return spring with a gear puller (hook the puller jaws over the cam follower tabs), then remove the snap-ring **(see illustration)**. Remove the outer cam, inner cam, cam follower and return spring.

26   Compress the brake spring with pliers and draw the shoe part out of the drum (don't remove it) **(see illustration)**. Measure the shoe thickness with a dial or Vernier caliper **(see illustration)**. If it is less than 1 mm,

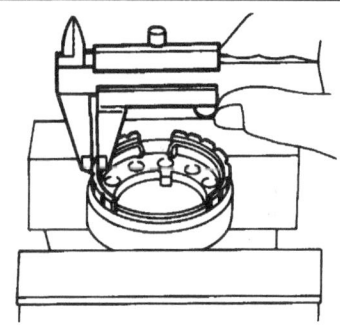

22.26b Measuring the brake shoe thickness

replace the brake shoes as a complete set. Compress the spring and push the shoe back into the drum. Make sure the hub body and clutch engage and disengage smoothly. If they don't, renew the hub assembly. Look for evidence of excessive wear and galling on each part. If wear or damage is noted, renew the hub assembly.

27   Apply Benton Plus Guard SG grease (available from your Toyota dealer) to the sliding surfaces of the components (do not use any other grease). **Note:** *The hubs are maintenance-free and do not require regreasing unless foreign matter has entered them or they have been washed out with solvent.*

28   Assemble the inner hub and cam follower in the jaws of the gear puller. The cam

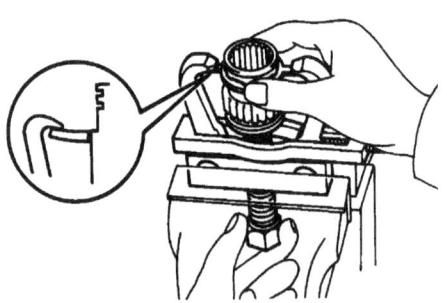

22.28 Align the cam follower with the step on the hub and adjust the gear puller jaws before beginning reassembly

23.4 Remove the eight knuckle spindle mounting bolts then remove the dust seal and cover

23.6 Tap the knuckle spindle off the steering knuckle with a brass drift and hammer

23.7 Turn the axleshaft so the flat faces up, then pull the axle from the housing

23.10 Dislodge the outer joint and shaft with a brass drift and hammer (be careful not to let the joint fall)

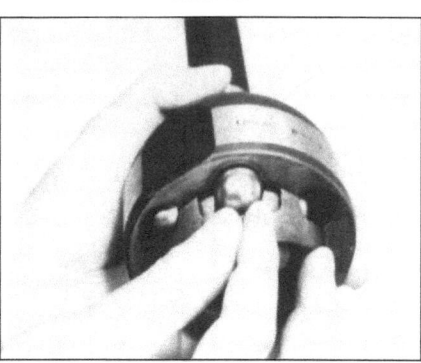

23.11 Tilt the inner race and cage and remove the balls from the joint one at a time

follower must mesh with the splines of the hub. Adjust the gear puller until the cam follower is aligned with the step on the hub **(see illustration)**. The jaws of the puller must bear against the cam follower tabs.

29   Remove the cam follower, then assemble the outer and inner cams. Align the inner cam notch with the outer cam tab, then align the inner cam tab in the opening of the outer cam.

30   Install the return spring on the hub, then attach the cam follower to the cam assembly and slip them onto the hub. Compress the return spring and install the cam follower tabs under the gear puller jaws. install the snapring.

31   Assemble the joint spring, preset spring and spring retainer on the clutch, then attach them to the inner hub. Expand the joint spring and attach it to the cam follower.

32   The remaining steps are the reverse of removal.

---

23   Front axleshaft (4WD models with solid front axle) - removal, overhaul and refitting

---

Removal

Refer to illustrations 23.4, 23.6, 23.7, 23.10, 23.11, 23.12, 23.13, 23.17, 23.18, and 23.20

1   Loosen the Wheel nuts, raise the front of the vehicle and support it securely on jackstands. Remove the wheel.

2   Remove the freewheel hub (Section 21).
3   Remove the front axle hub (see Chapter 1).
4   Remove the knuckle spindle mounting bolts **(see illustration)**.
5   Remove the dust seal and dust cover from the knuckle spindle.
6   Using a brass bar, tap the knuckle spindle off the knuckle **(see illustration)**.
7   Position one flat of the axleshaft outer end facing up and carefully pull the axleshaft out of the housing **(see illustration)**.
8   Inspect the constant velocity joint for excessive wear and looseness. If the joint feels sloppy and worn out, disassemble and inspect it, renewing any parts that may be questionable.

Overhaul

9   Place the inner axleshaft in a vice with soft jaws or blocks of wood, so as not to mar the shaft.
10   Place a brass drift against the inner race of the joint and drive off the joint and outer shaft with a hammer **(see illustration)**.
11   Tilt the inner race and cage and remove the ball bearings one at a time **(see illustration)**.
12   Tilt the two large openings in the cage around the lands of the outer shaft and pull out the cage and inner race **(see illustration)**.
13   Remove the inner race from the cage by positioning it so that two of its lands line up with the large openings in the cage, turn-

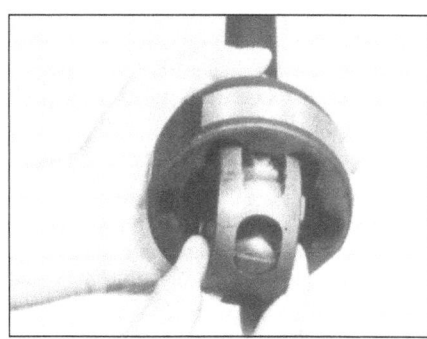

23.12 Tilt the inner race and cage 90 degrees, then align the windows of the cage with the lands of the housing and rotate the inner race up and out of the outer race

ing the race 90-degrees and pulling it out **(see illustration)**.
14   Clean and inspect the inner parts of the joint for wear or damage. If necessary, renew any worn or damaged parts.
15   To reassemble the joint, coat the inner parts of the joint and the inside of the outer shaft with moly-based grease.
16   Insert the inner race into the cage by reversing Step 13.
17   Position the protruding end of the inner race toward the wide side of the cage **(see illustration)**.
18   Assemble the cage and inner race to the outer shaft by reversing Step 12. **Note:** *Make sure to position the wide side of the cage and*

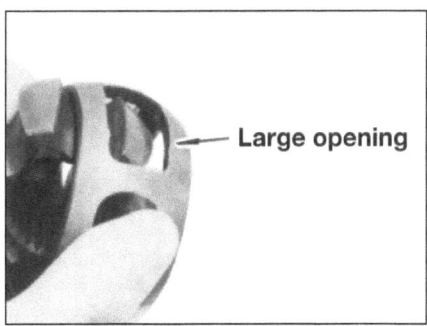

23.13 Align the inner race lands with the cage windows and rotate the inner race out of the cage

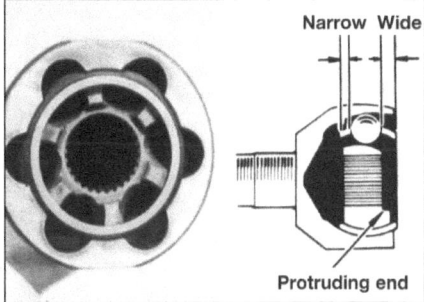

23.18 The wide side of the cage and the protruding end of the inner race must face the open end of the joint when refitted

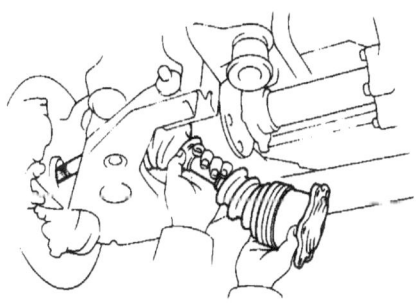

24.5 Carefully guide the driveaxle out from the steering knuckle, between the side gear shaft and the lower control arm

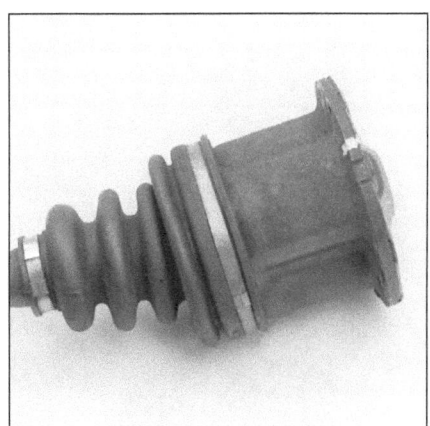

25.2 Paint (do not punch) match marks on the inboard joint tulip and the driveaxle

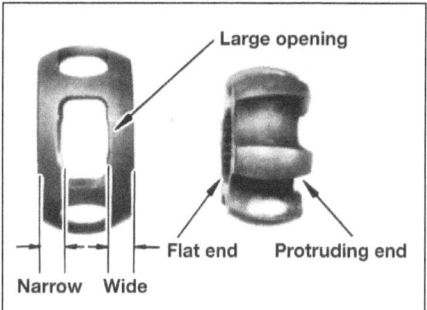

23.17 The protruding end of the inner race and the wide side of the cage must be on the same side when assembled

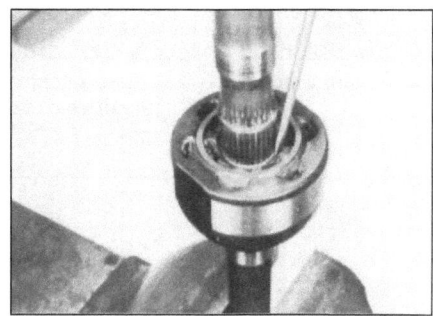

23.20 Compress the inner snap-ring with a screwdriver and slide the inner shaft into the inner race of the joint and outer shaft assembly

the protruding end of the inner race facing out **(see illustration)**.
19   Install new snap-rings on the inner axle-shaft.
20   Place the outer shaft in the vice (still lined with soft jaws or wood) and install the inner shaft to the outer shaft while compressing the inner snap-ring with a screwdriver **(see illustration)**.
21   Verify that the inner axleshaft can't be pulled out of the joint.

Refitting

22   To install the axleshaft in the axle housing, reverse the removal procedure.

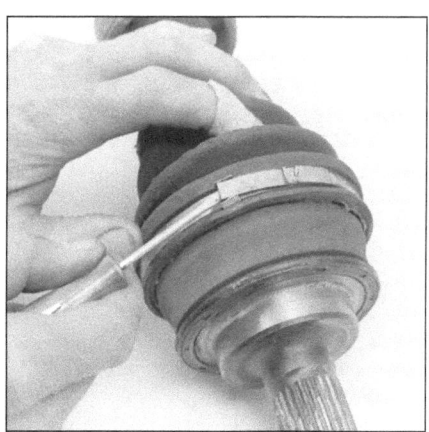

25.3 The large boot clamps can be pried open with a small screwdriver

24   Front driveaxle (4WD models with independent front suspension) - removal and refitting

Refer to illustration 24.5

Removal

1   Loosen the Wheel nuts, raise the front of the vehicle and support it securely on jack-stands. Remove the wheel.
2   Remove the six driveaxle-to-differential side gear flange nuts. Have an assistant step on the brake to prevent the axle from turning.
3   Remove the freewheeling hub (see Section 21).
4   Using a pair of snap-ring pliers, remove the snap-ring from the outer end of the drive-axle. Slide the spacer off the axle.
5   Separate the inboard joint from the differential side gear flange then carefully pull the driveaxle outer end from the steering knuckle/hub **(see illustration)**.

Refitting

6   Apply a coat of moly-based grease to the outboard CV joint shaft.
7   Insert the outer end of the shaft into the steering knuckle/hub. Position the inboard CV joint housing onto the differential side gear flange, making sure all six studs protrude through the CV joint flange holes. Install the nuts, but don't tighten them at this time.
8   Install the spacer and the snap-ring to the outer end of the axle.
9   Install the freewheeling hub (Section 21).
10   Tighten the six driveaxle-to-side gear shaft nuts to the torque listed in this Chapter's Specifications, again having an assistant depress the brake pedal to prevent the axle from turning.
11   Install the wheel and wheel nuts. Lower the vehicle and tighten the wheel nuts to the torque listed in the Chapter 1 Specifications.

25   Driveaxle boot renewal and CV joint inspection

Refer to illustrations 25.2, 25.3, 25.5, 25.6, 25.7, 25.11, 25.12a, 25.12b and 25.14

Note: *If the CV joints exhibit signs of wear indicating need for an overhaul (usually due to torn boots), explore all options before beginning the job. Complete rebuilt driveaxles are available on an exchange basis, which eliminates much time and work. Whichever route you choose to take, check on the cost and availability of parts before disassembling your vehicle.*

1   Remove the driveaxle (refer to Section 24).
2   Paint a pair of match marks on the joint tulip and the driveaxle **(see illustration)**.
3   Prise the outer (larger) clamps loose with a small screwdriver **(see illustration)** and slide them off the ends of the driveaxle. Cut the inner (smaller) clamps and the drive

25.5 Remove the snap-ring that retains the inboard joint tripod with a pair of snap-ring pliers

25.6 Use a centre-punch to place match marks on the tripod and the driveaxle to insure that they are reassembled properly

25.7 Drive the tripod from the driveaxle with a brass drift and hammer - be careful not to damage the bearing surfaces or the splines on the shaft

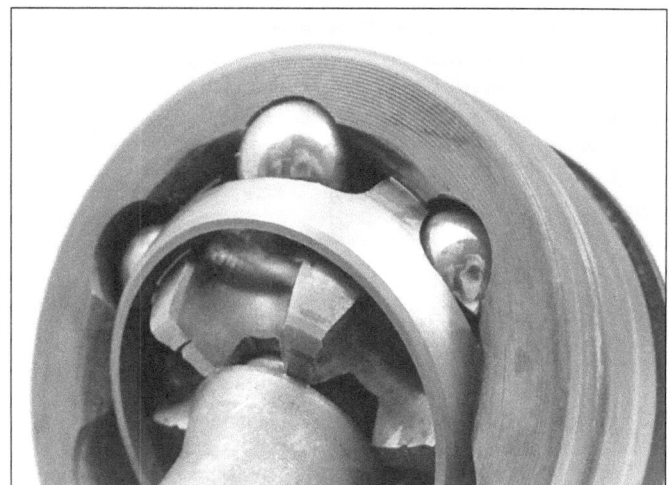

25.11 After the old grease has been rinsed away and the cleaning solvent has been blown out with compressed air, rotate the outboard joint housing through its full range of motion and inspect the bearing surfaces for wear or damage - if any of the balls, the race or the cage look damaged, renew the driveaxle/ outboard joint assembly

25.12a To fit the new clamps. bend the tang downward and . . .

25.12b . . . tap the tabs down to hold it in place

shaft damper clamp with a pair of diagonal cutters and discard them.

4   Separate the inboard joint tulip from the tripod joint.

5   Remove the tripod joint snap-ring with a pair of snap-ring pliers (see illustration).

6   Punch match marks on the tripod and the driveaxle (see illustration).

7   Using a hammer and brass punch, drive the tripod joint from the driveaxle (see illustration).

8   Slide the inboard joint boot and the outboard joint boot off the driveaxle.

9   Thoroughly wash the inboard and outboard CV joints in clean solvent and blow them dry with compressed air, if available. Note: *Because the outboard joint cannot be disassembled, it is difficult to wash away all the old grease and to rid the bearing of solvent once it's clean. But it is imperative that the job be done thoroughly, so take your time and do it right.*

10   Inspect the inboard tripod joint for signs of wear or damage. If the tripod is obviously worn or damaged, renew it, along with the tulip, as an assembly.

11   Bend the outboard CV joint housing at an angle to the driveaxle to expose the bearings, inner race and cage (see illustration). Inspect the bearing surfaces for signs of wear. If the bearings are damaged or worn, renew the driveaxle.

12   Slide the new outboard boot onto the driveaxle. It's a good idea to wrap vinyl tape

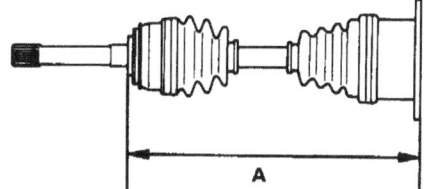

25.14 The driveaxle standard length (A) should be as specified and the boots shouldn't be compressed or stretched out

around the spline of the shaft to prevent damage to the boot. When the boot is in position, add the specified amount of grease (included in the boot renewal kit) to the outboard joint and the boot (pack the joint with as much grease as it will hold and put the rest into the boot). Slide the boot on the rest of the way and install the new clamps (see illustrations).

13   Slide the inboard boot onto the driveaxle. Align the match marks you made before removing the joint and, using a brass bar and hammer, tap the tripod onto the driveaxle. Install the snap ring. Fill the inboard joint tulip with grease and install it over the tripod joint. Slide the boot into place and install the boot clamps, but don't tighten them yet.

14   Measure the driveaxle standard length, comparing it to the dimension listed in this Chapter's Specifications, and make sure that

the boot is not stretched, contracted or distorted in any way (see illustration). Insert a small screwdriver under the edge of the boot to equalise the pressure inside. Tighten the boot clamps as shown in illustrations 25.12a and 25.12b.

15   Install the driveaxle (see Section 24).

---

26   Front differential side gear shaft oil seals (4WD models with independent front suspension) - renewal

Refer to illustrations 26.3 and 26.4

1   Remove the front axle assembly following the procedure described in Section 20.

2   Remove the side gear shaft and differential tube from the differential carrier (see Section 19).

3   Using a seal puller attached to a slide hammer, remove the seal from the differential carrier (see illustration).

4   Using an appropriately sized seal driver or large socket, drive the new seal into the differential carrier until it is flush with the carrier surface (see illustration).

5   Install the differential tube to the differential carrier and install the side gear shaft (Section 19).

6   Install the front axle assembly (see Section 20).

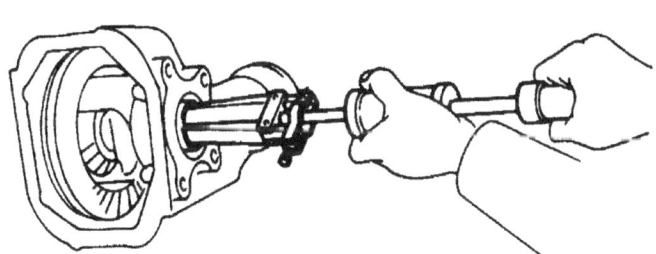

26.3 Pop the seal from the differential carrier with a seal puller and slide hammer. Note: *Sometimes the seals can be pried out with a large screwdriver or lever*

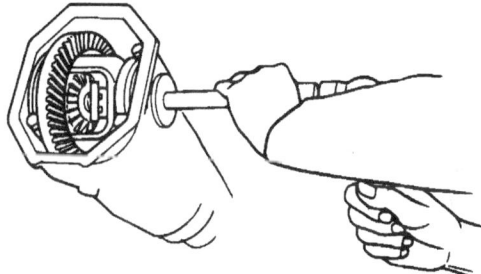

26.4 A seal driver is the preferred tool for fitting the new seals into the differential carrier, but a socket or section of pipe with an outside diameter slightly less than that of the seal can be used

Chapter 9 Brakes

Contents

Specifications

General

Brake fluid type...	See Chapter 1
Power brake booster pushrod-to-master cylinder	
piston clearance	0.60 to 0.65 mm

Disc brakes

Minimum brake pad thickness..	See Chapter 1
Disc minimum thickness..	Refer to the marks cast or stamped on the disc
Disc runout (maximum)	0.15 mm

Drum brakes

Minimum brake shoe lining thickness...................................	See Chapter 1
Drum inside diameter	Refer to the marks cast or stamped on the drum

Torque specifications

	Nm
Brake booster mounting nuts	13
Master cylinder-to-brake booster	13
Brake hose banjo fitting bolt	18
Brake caliper mounting bolts	
Petrol models	
RN30, 40 series	
S-16 type caliper	92 to 116
K-type caliper	39 to 53
YN50, 60 series	
PD60 type caliper (2WD)	35 to 44
FS17 type caliper (2WD)	84 to 93
S12+8 type caliper (4WD)	74 to 102
YN/RN80, 90, 105, 106, 110 series	
PD60 type caliper (2WD)	39
FS18 type caliper (2WD)	88
S12+8 type caliper (4WD)	123
4Runner	123
Diesel models	
PD60 type caliper (2WD)	35 to 44
FS17 type caliper (2WD)	84 to 93
FS18 type caliper (2WD)	88
S12+8 type caliper (4WD)	
LN30, 40, 50, 60 series	74 to 102
LN80, 90, 105, 106, 110 series, 4Runner	123
Caliper torque plate-to-steering knuckle bolts	
YN/LN50, 60 series (2WD)	99 to 117
YN/RN/LN80, 90, 105, 106, 110 series (2WD)	64
Brake disc-to-front axle hub	
LN30, 40, 50, 60 series/4Runner	64
LN80, 90. 105, 106, 110 series	46
Vacuum pump oil/vacuum fitting bolt	14
Wheel cylinder-to-backing plate	
Leading/trailing type drum brake	10
Duo-servo type drum brake	14
Wheel lug nuts	See Chapter 1

1 General information

The braking system in the vehicles covered by this manual is either a single circuit (early models) or a split circuit design. Split circuit systems incorporate two separate circuits, one for the front brakes and one for the rear brakes. With this system, if one circuit fails, the other circuit will still function. On models with a single circuit, all braking power will be lost if there is a failure in any part of the system.

The master cylinder on models with a split system incorporates a primary piston for one circuit and a secondary piston for the other.

A vacuum booster unit, used on most models, draws vacuum from the inlet manifold to add power assistance to the normal brake pressure.

The Load Sensing Proportioning Valve (LSPV) is designed to prevent the rear wheels from locking under severe braking conditions. The valve operates by changing rear brake fluid pressure distribution in response to vehicle loading.

The front wheels on most models are equipped with disc brakes. These consist of a flat, disc-like rotor which is attached to the axle and wheel. Around one section of the rotor is mounted caliper assembly, either floating or fixed, which houses one or four hydraulically operated disc brake pads. When the brake pedal is applied, brake fluid pressure forces both pads against the rotor. The pressure and resultant friction on the rotor is what slows the wheel.

Some models are equipped with front drum brakes, either of the dual-leading type or the dual-trailing type.

The rear brakes on some models use the conventional drum brakes of the dual-servo type. Other models employ a single action, leading/ trailing shoe type with a pivot point at the bottom of each shoe. With either of these designs, fluid pressure from the master cylinder forces the rear wheel cylinder pistons outward, which in turn forces the brake shoes against the spinning brake drum attached to the rear wheel. The force of the brake shoes against the drum is what slows the wheel. The wheel cylinders contain two operating pistons which contact both brake shoes. Adjustment is automatic, occurring when the parking brake is applied.

Precautions

There are some general notes and cautions involving the brake system on this vehicle:

a) Use only DOT 3 brake fluid in this system.

b) The brake pads and linings may contain asbestos fibres which are hazardous to your health if inhaled. Whenever you work on brake system components, wear an approved filtering mask and carefully clean all parts with brake system cleaner. Do not allow the fine asbestos dust to become airborne.

c) Safety should be paramount whenever any servicing of the brake components is performed. Do not use parts or fasteners which are not in perfect condition, and be sure that all clearances and torque specifications are adhered to. If you are at all unsure about a certain procedure, seek professional advice. Upon completion of any brake system work, test the brakes carefully in a controlled area before putting the vehicle into normal service. If a problem is suspected in the brake system, do not drive the vehicle until the fault is corrected.

d) Tyres, load and front end alignment are factors which also affect braking performance.

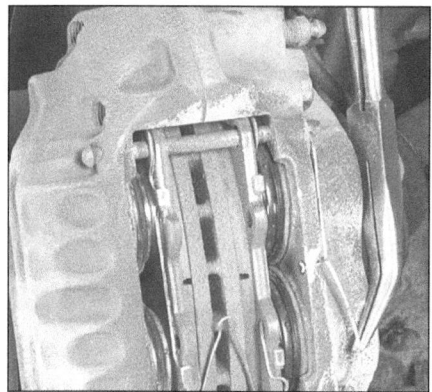

2.3a Remove the retaining clip then pull out the pins and remove the anti-rattle springs

2 Front brake pads - renewal

Warning: *Disc brake pads must be renewed on both front wheels at the same time- never renew the pads on only one wheel. Also, the dust created by the brake system may contain asbestos, which is harmful to your health. Never blow it out with compressed air and don't inhale any of it. An approved filtering mask should be worn when working on the brakes. Do not, under any circumstances, use petroleum-based solvents to clean brake parts. Use brake system cleaner or denatured alcohol only!*
Note: *It is a good idea to work on only one side at a time so that the other brake can be used as a guide if difficulties are encountered during reassembly.*

Fixed calipers

Refer to illustrations 2.3a, 2.3b and 2.7

1   Remove the cover from the brake fluid reservoir, siphon off about two-thirds of the brake fluid into a container and discard it.
2   Loosen the wheel lug nuts, raise the front of the vehicle and support it securely on jackstands. Remove the front wheels. Wash down the brake assembly with brake system cleaner.

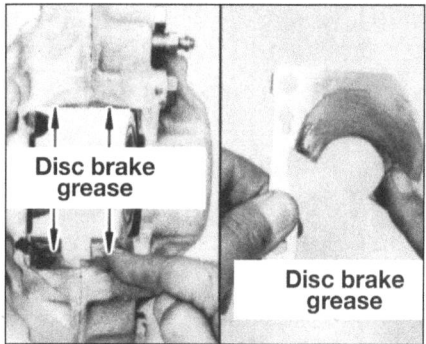

2.7 When applying disc brake grease to the caliper and the anti-squeal shims, apply a thin coat only - an excessive amount may contaminate the pad linings

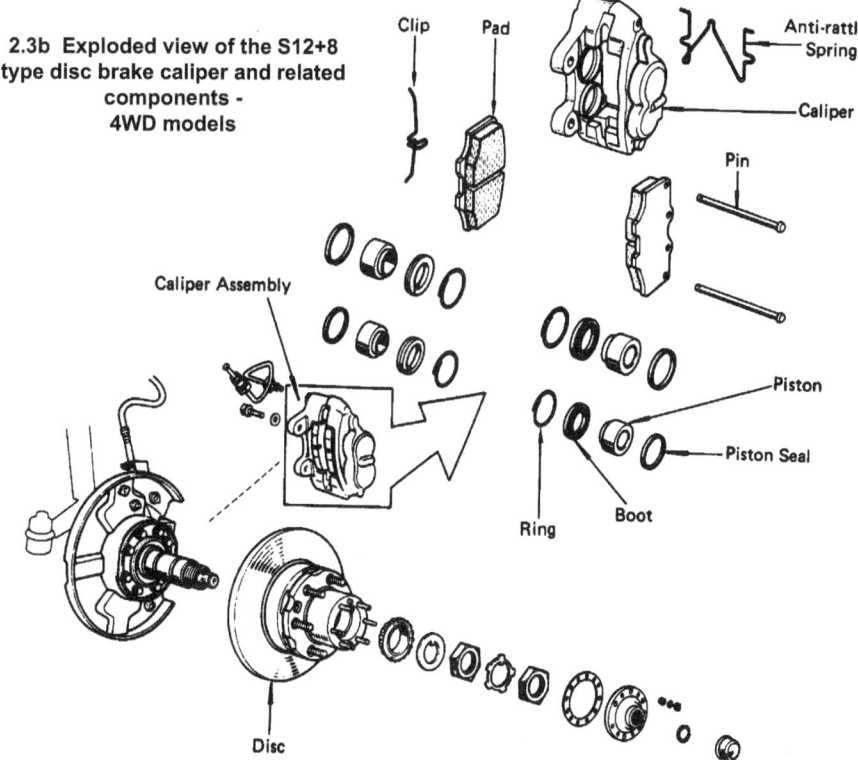

2.3b Exploded view of the S12+8 type disc brake caliper and related components - 4WD models

3   Remove the pin retaining clip, then pull the pins out with a pair of pliers **(see illustrations)**. **Warning:** *While pulling out the pins, cover the anti-rattle spring with your hand so it doesn't fly out.*
4   Using a pair of large pliers, squeeze one pad against the caliper housing to push the pistons into their bores, making room for the new brake pad. Do this slowly, alternating between each end of the pad, to ensure the pistons are compressed evenly and don't become cocked in the bores.
5   Slide the two pad and anti-squeal shims (if equipped) out of the caliper.
6   Inspect the brake disc as described in Section 4.

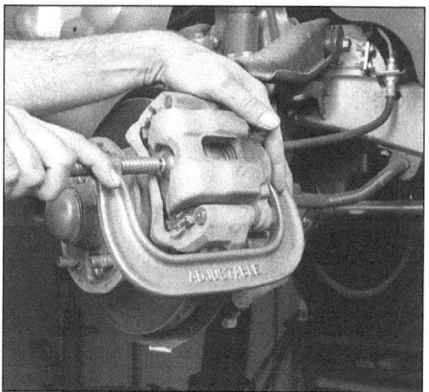

2.12 Using a large C-clamp, push the piston back into the caliper bore - note that one end of the clamp is on the flat area near the brake hose fitting and the other end (screw end) is pressing against the outer brake pad

7   Apply a thin coat of disc brake grease to the upper and lower openings of the caliper and to the anti-squeal shims, if so equipped **(see illustration).**
8   Insert the brake pad and anti-squeal shim(s) into the caliper, making sure the arrows on the shims point in the direction of forward wheel rotation. Repeat the procedure to remove and fit the other pad.
9   Refit the anti-rattle spring and the pad retaining pins and clip. Mount the front wheel and tighten the lug nuts to the specified torque.
10   Perform the same steps to the other side.
Warning: *Pump the brake pedal several times before driving the vehicle to bring the pads in contact with the brake disc. Check the brake fluid level, topping it off if necessary. Make sure the brakes are working smoothly and make several low speed stops before taking the vehicle into a traffic situation.*

Floating calipers (FS17, FS18, PD60 and PD66 types)

Refer to illustrations 2.12, 2.13a, 2.13b, 2.13c, 2.14, 2.15, 2.17, 2.18 and 2.19

11   Perform Steps 1 and 2 of this Section.
12   Using a large C-clamp, push the piston back into its bore **(see illustration)**.
13   On FS17 or FS18 style calipers **(see illustration)**, remove one of the slide pins and pivot the caliper on the other slide pin. Remove the caliper from the torque plate and hang it by a piece of wire from the top of the shock absorber **(see illustrations)**.
14   On PD60 and PD66 type calipers **(see illustration)**, remove both refitting bolts and lift the caliper off the torque plate, but

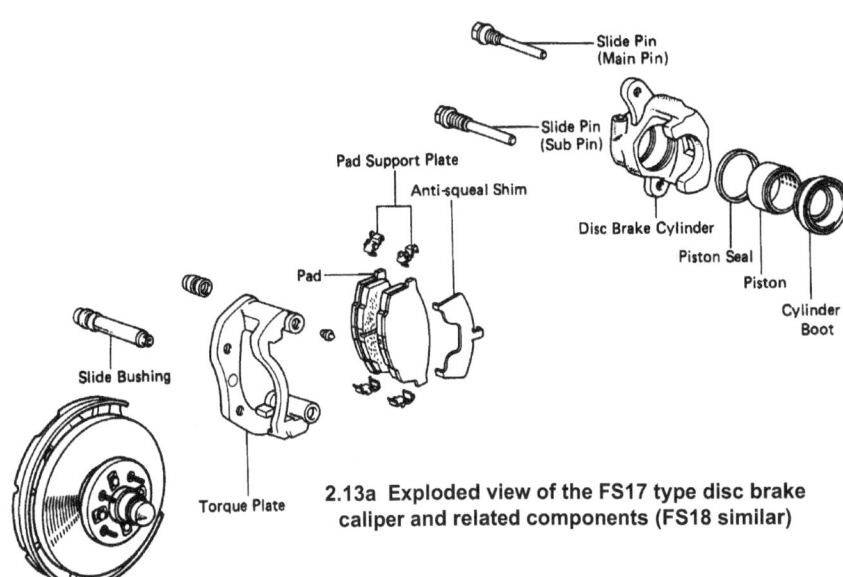

2.13a Exploded view of the FS17 type disc brake
caliper and related components (FS18 similar)

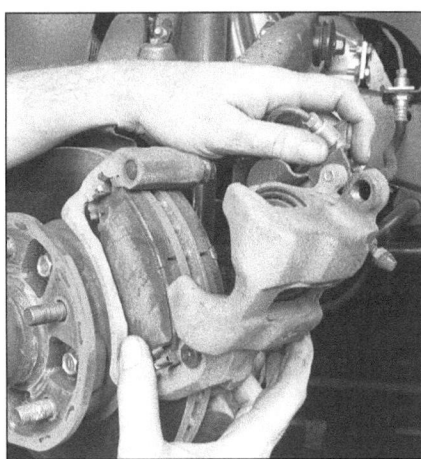

2.13b Remove a slide pin and tilt the
caliper far enough to detach it from the
torque plate

2.13c Place the caliper on top of the
upper control arm and secure it with a
piece of wire looped through the caliper
and over the top of the shock absorber
- never let the caliper hang by the brake
hose

be careful not to lose the anti-rattle springs. Hang it by a piece of wire - don't let it hang by the brake hose.

15   Remove the two pads from the torque plate **(see illustration)**.

16   Refer to Section 4 and inspect the brake disc.

17   Apply disc brake grease to the anti-squeal shim and fit it to the outer pad **(see illustration)**.

18   Refit the pad support plates in the torque plate **(see illustration)**. **Note:** *It's a good idea to fit new pad support plates.*

19   Fit new wear indicators to the lower side of each pad **(see illustration)**.

20   Place the pads (and anti-rattle springs, if equipped) in the torque plate and refit the caliper, tightening the slide pin or mounting bolts to the specified torque. Refit the front wheel and tighten the lug nuts to the specified torque.

21   Repeat the procedure on the other front brake. **Warning:** *Pump the brake pedal several times before driving the vehicle to bring the pads into contact with the brake disc. Check the brake fluid level, topping it off if necessary. Make sure the brakes are working smoothly and make several low speed stops before taking the vehicle into a traffic situation.*

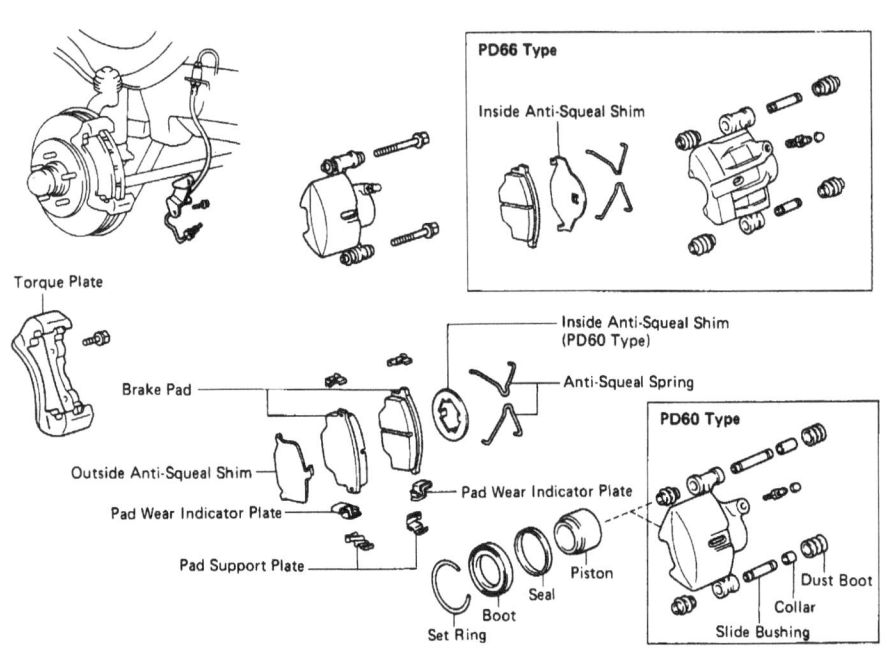

2.15 Tilt the pads and remove them from
the torque plate. As this is done, notice
the position of the pad components, such
as the wear indicator, anti-squeal shim(s)
and pad support plates

2.14 Exploded view of the PD60 and PD66 type
disc brake caliper and related components

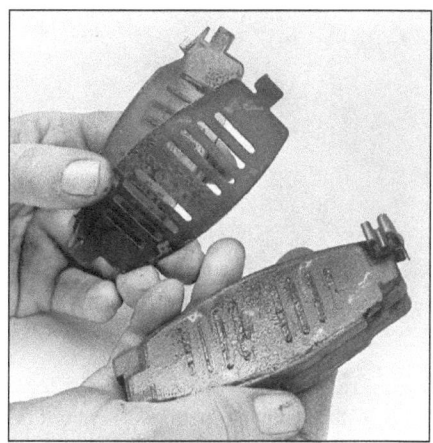

2.17 Apply disc brake grease to the pad backing plate and assemble the anti-squeal shim(s) to the backing plate (some calipers use two shims, others only one)

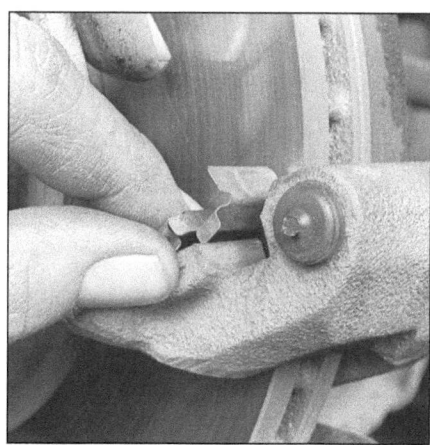

2.18 Refit the pad support plates into the torque plate

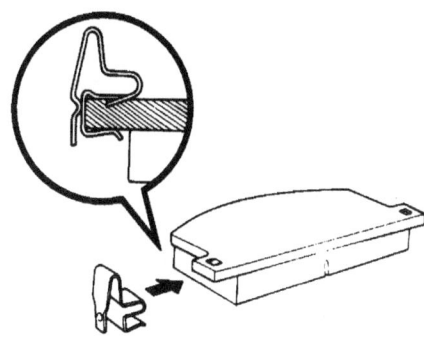

2.19 Push new wear indicators onto the lower edge of the pad

Floating caliper (K type)

Refer to illustration 2.24

22   Perform Steps 1 and 2 of this Section.
23   Using a large C-clamp, push the piston back into its bore **(see illustration 2.12)**.
24   Unscrew the two bolts and remove the guide plates and support springs **(see illustration)**. Lift the caliper off.
25   Prise the outer pad from the caliper frame, noting how the anti-rattle spring is refitted.

26   Remove the inner pad from the steering knuckle. Inspect the anti-squeal shims, support plates and springs for signs of wear or fatigue. Renew parts as necessary.
27   Apply high-temperature brake grease to the areas where the caliper contacts the steering knuckle.
28   Also apply high-temperature brake grease to the anti-squeal shims and refit them on the pads.
29   Refit the inner pad and shim onto the steering knuckle.

30   Refit the outer pad onto the caliper frame, retaining it with the anti-rattle spring.
31   Refit the caliper and outer pad assembly over the disc and inner pad. Refit the guide plates and support springs and bolts, using new lock washers. Tighten the bolts to the torque listed in this Chapter's Specifications.
32   Repeat the procedure on the other front brake. **Warning:** *Pump the brake pedal several times before driving the vehicle to bring the pads into contact with the brake disc. Check the brake fluid level, topping it off if necessary. Make sure the brakes are working smoothly and make several low speed stops before taking the vehicle into a traffic situation.*

3   Disc brake caliper - removal. overhaul and refitting

Refer to illustrations 3.4a, 3.4b, 3.5, 3.7, 3.8a and 3.8b
Note: *The following procedure applies to all caliper designs used on the vehicles covered by this manual. On multiple piston caliper designs, simply repeat the necessary Steps to complete the rebuild procedure. If an overhaul is indicated (usually because of fluid leakage) explore all options before beginning the job. New and factory rebuilt calipers are available on an exchange basis, which makes this job quite easy. If it is decided to rebuild the calipers, make sure that a rebuild kit is available before proceeding.*

Removal

1   Disconnect the brake line from the caliper and plug it to keep contaminants out of the brake system and to prevent losing any more brake fluid than is necessary. Unbolt the brake line bracket from the caliper (on models so equipped). **Note:** *If you are removing the caliper for access to other components, don't disconnect the brake line.*

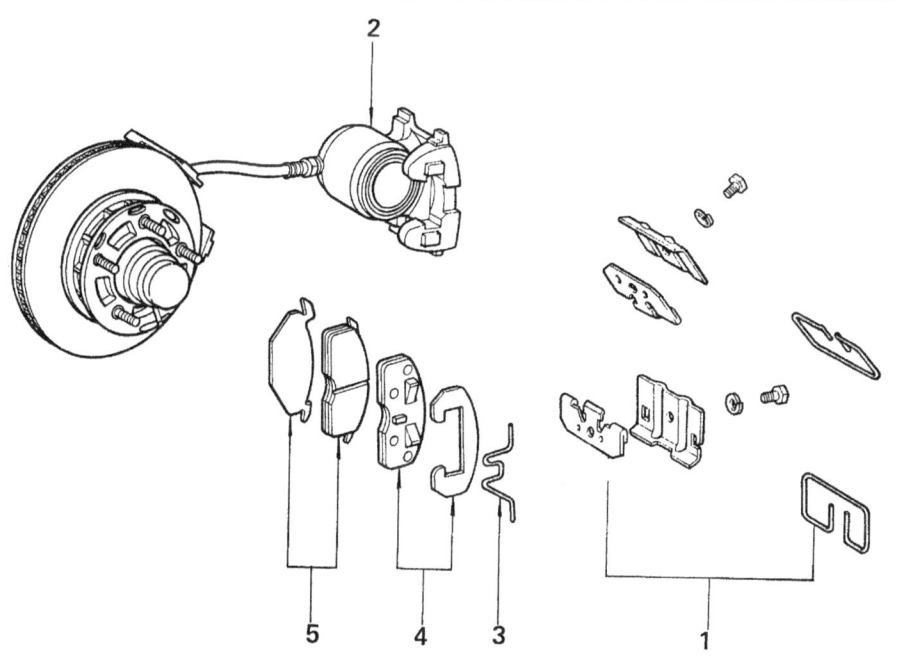

2.24 Exploded view of the K-type disc brake

1 Guide plate, support spring and pad support plate
2 Caliper
3 Anti-rattle spring
4 Outer brake pad and anti-squeal shim
5 Inner brake pad and anti-squeal shim

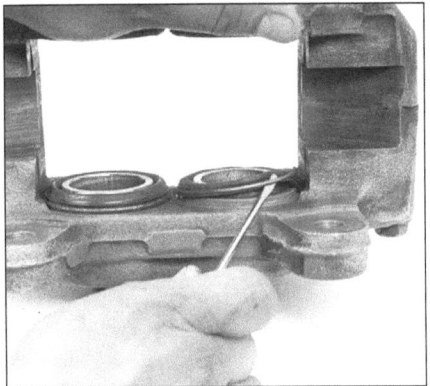

3.4a Using a small screwdriver, remove the boot retaining ring(s)

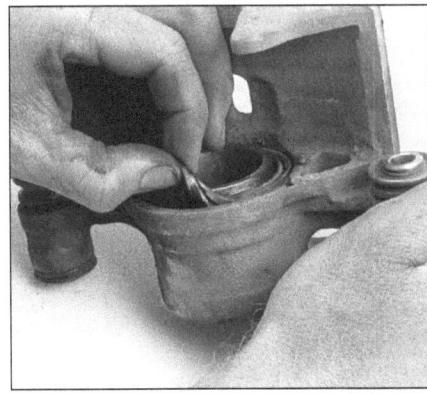

3.4b Remove the boot(s) from the cylinder

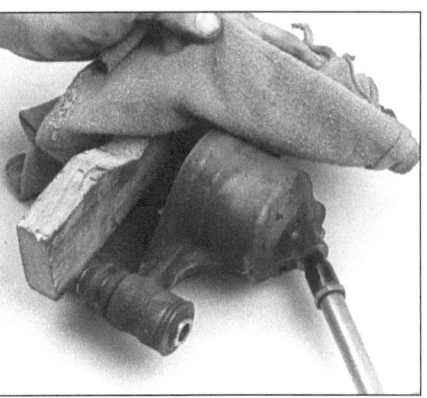

3.5 With the caliper padded to catch the piston(s), use compressed air to force the piston(s) out of the bore(s) - make sure your hands and fingers are not between the piston and caliper

2   On models with fixed calipers, remove the pads from the caliper (see Section 2). Remove the two caliper mounting bolts and lift the caliper off the brake disc (see the previous Section).

3   On FS17, FS18, PD60 and PD66 types, remove the brake pads from the caliper; on K type calipers, remove the outer pad (see Section 2).

Overhaul

Warning: *Do not, under any circumstances, use petroleum-based solvents to clean brake parts. Use only clean brake fluid or denatured alcohol. Allow all parts to dry, preferably using compressed air to blow out all passages. Make sure the compressed air is filtered, as a harmful lubricant residue will be present in unfiltered systems.*

4   To overhaul the caliper, remove the rubber boot retaining ring(s) and the rubber boot(s) **(see illustrations)**. Before you remove the piston(s), place a wood block in the centre of the caliper to prevent damage to the piston upon removal.

5   To remove the piston(s) from the caliper, apply compressed air to the brake fluid hose connection on the caliper body **(see illustration)**. Use only enough air pressure to ease the piston(s) out of the bore. **Warning:** *Be careful not to place your fingers between the piston and the caliper as the piston may come*

out with some force. **Note:** *On calipers with multiple pistons (fixed calipers), it may be difficult to remove the remaining pistons once the first piston has been ejected. If this is the case, cover the open bore(s) with a piece of wood held in place with a C-clamp and proceed to remove the other piston(s).*

6   Inspect the mating surfaces of the piston and caliper bore wall. If there is any scoring, rust, pitting or bright areas, renew the complete caliper unit with a new one.

7   If these components are in good condition, remove the rubber seal from the caliper bore using a wooden or plastic tool (metal tools may cause bore damage). Be careful not to damage the cylinder bore **(see illustration)**.

8   On PD60 style calipers, push the sliding bush out of the caliper housing **(see illustration)** and remove the two rubber boots from both ends. Slide the bush sleeve out of the caliper housing **(see illustration)**. On FS17 models the slide bushes and boots are located in the torque plate.

9   Wash all the components in brake system cleaner, clean brake fluid or rubbing alcohol.

10   To reassemble the caliper, you should already have the correct rebuild kit for your vehicle. **Note:** *During reassembly apply silicone based grease (supplied with the rebuild kit) between the sliding bush and the bush sleeve (on models so equipped).*

11   Submerge the new piston seal(s) and the piston(s) in brake fluid and fit them into the caliper bore(s). Do not force the piston into the bore, but make sure that it is squarely in place, then apply firm (but not excessive) pressure to refit it.

12   Fit the new rubber boot(s) and retaining ring(s).

Refitting

13   To refit the caliper, reverse the removal procedure. Be sure to bleed the system by following the procedure described in Section 10.

---

4   Brake disc - inspection, removal and refitting

Inspection

Refer to illustrations 4.4a, 4.4b and 4.5

1   Loosen the wheel nuts, raise the vehicle and support it securely on jackstands. Remove the wheel.

2   Remove the brake caliper as outlined in Section 3. It's not necessary to disconnect the brake hose. After removing the caliper bolts, suspend the caliper out of the way with a piece of wire. Don't let the caliper hang by the hose and don't stretch or twist the hose. On

3.7 Use a non-metallic tool to remove the piston(s) seal from the groove in the cylinder - a pencil works well (metal tools can scratch the bore surface)

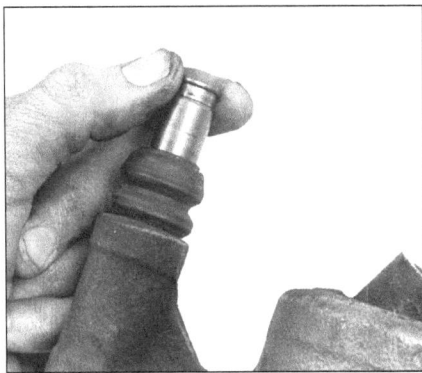

3.8a On each side of the caliper, push the sliding bush up through the boot and pull it free, then remove the dust boots (PD60 caliper only)

3.8b Push the bush sleeve out of the caliper (PD60 caliper only)

4.4a Check disc runout with a dial indicator - if the reading exceeds the maximum allowable runout, the disc will have to be resurfaced or renewed

4.4b Using a swirling motion, remove the glaze from the disc with emery cloth or sandpaper

4.5 Measure the disc thickness at several points with a micrometer

single piston caliper models, also remove the two torque plate-to-steering knuckle bolts and the torque plate **(see illustrations 2.13a and 2.14)**.

3 Visually check the disc surface for score marks and other damage. Light scratches and shallow grooves are normal after use and may not always be detrimental to brake operation, but deep score marks - over 0.38 mm - require disc removal and refinishing by an automotive machine shop. Be sure to check both sides of the disc. If pulsating has been noticed during application of the brakes, suspect disc runout.

4 To check disc runout, place a dial indicator at a point about 13 mm from the outer edge of the disc **(see illustration)**. Set the indicator to zero and turn the disc. The indicator reading should not exceed the specified allowable runout limit. If it does, the disc should be refinished by an automotive machine shop. **Note:** *Professionals recommend resurfacing of brake discs regardless of the dial indicator reading (to produce a smooth, flat surface that will eliminate brake pedal pulsations and other undesirable symptoms related to questionable discs).* At the very least, if you elect not to have the discs resurfaced, deglaze the brake pad surface with medium grit emery cloth (use a swirling motion to ensure a non-directional finish) **(see illustration)**.

5 The disc must not be machined to a thickness less than the specified minimum refinish thickness. The minimum wear (or discard) thickness is cast into the inside of the disc. The disc thickness can be checked with a micrometer **(see illustration)**.

Removal and refitting

Refer to illustrations 4.11, 4.12 and 4.14

6 If it has been determined while performing the inspection procedures in this Section that the brake disc must be removed and/or renewed, perform the following procedure. **Note:** *If the disc is to be taken to a machine shop to be refinished, do not remove the disc from the axle hub. Take the entire disc/hub assembly.*

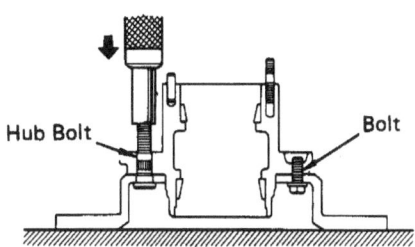

4.11 Knock the hub bolts out of the hub using a large brass punch and hammer

7 Remove the axle hub (see Chapter 1).

2WD models

8 Remove the disc from the axle hub by removing the five retaining bolts.
9 Refit a new disc and tighten the five bolts, following a criss-cross pattern, to the specified torque.
10 Refit the axle hub and adjust the front bearing preload (see Chapter 1).

4WD models

11 Using a hydraulic press or a large brass punch and hammer, drive the hub bolts out of the axle hub **(see illustration)**.
12 Remove the two disc retaining bolts and separate the disc and hub **(see illustration)**.
13 Refit a new disc to the axle hub and tighten the two retaining bolts to the specified torque.
14 Using a collar positioned under the hub and a large brass punch (or a hydraulic press), drive the hub bolts into the hub **(see illustration)**.
15 Refit the axle hub and adjust the front wheel bearings (see Chapter 1).

5 Drum brake shoes - renewal

Warning: *Drum brake shoes must be renewed on both wheels at the same time - never renew the shoes on only one wheel. Also, the dust created by the brake system may contain asbestos, which is harmful to your health. Never blow it out with compressed air and do not inhale any of it.*

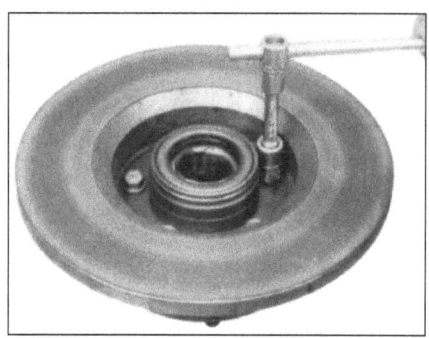

4.12 The disc on 4WD models is retained to the hub by two bolts

An approved filtering mask should be worn whenever servicing the brake system. Do not, under any circumstances, use petroleum-based solvents to clean brake parts. Use brake system cleaner only.
Caution: *Whenever the brake shoes are renewed, the retractor and hold-down springs should also be renewed. Due to the continuous heating/cooling cycle that the springs are subjected to, they lose their tension over a period of time and may allow the shoes to drag on the drum and wear at a much faster rate than normal.*

1 Loosen the wheel lug nuts, raise the vehicle and support it securely on jackstands. Remove the wheels. Remove the drums according to the brake check instructions in Chapter 1. Perform all drum brake checks as described in Chapter 1. It is a good idea to disassemble only one brake at a time so that

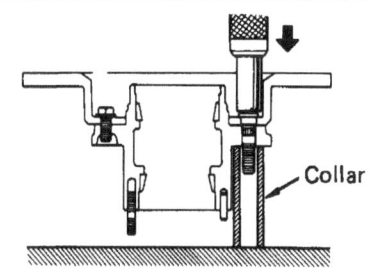

4.14 Place a collar (or an appropriately sized piece of tubing) under the hub to support it while the hub bolt is being driven in

the other brake can be used as a guide if difficulties are encountered during reassembly.

Rear drum brakes

Leading/trailing drum brake - 2WD LN30, 40 series, LN50, 60 series, LN80, 90, 105, 106, 110 series, 4Runner with 4-link rear suspension

Refer to illustrations 5.2a, 5.2b, 5.6, 5.7, 5.10, 5.20 and 5.23

2   Using a brake spring tool, detach the ends of the adjuster spring from the brake shoes **(see illustrations)**.
3   Using a hold-down tool, remove the front shoe hold-down spring and pin.
4   Remove the front brake shoe and tension spring that goes between the front and rear shoes. Remove the adjuster and spring assembly. Note the locations of the adjuster assembly components to facilitate refitting. Also note that the right-side adjuster screw has right-hand threads and the left-side adjuster has left-hand threads.
5   Remove the rear shoe hold-down spring and pin, then remove the rear shoe.
6   Remove the automatic adjusting strut and tension spring from the automatic adjusting lever **(see illustration)**.
7   Disconnect the parking brake cable from the parking brake lever **(see illustration)**.
8   Using a screwdriver, remove the C-clips, parking brake lever and automatic adjusting lever from the rear shoe.
9   Be sure to check the wheel cylinders. Even if no leakage is found coming from the cylinders, it is advisable to rebuild or renew them when new linings are fitted (see Section 6).
10   Refitting is basically the reverse of removal. Lubricate the brake shoe contact points with a brake lube designed specifically for this purpose **(see illustration)**. Use grease sparingly and take care not to get it on the brake shoe lining material. Make sure the brake lining material is clean. Use brake cleaner for this purpose if any oil or grease has contacted the friction surface.

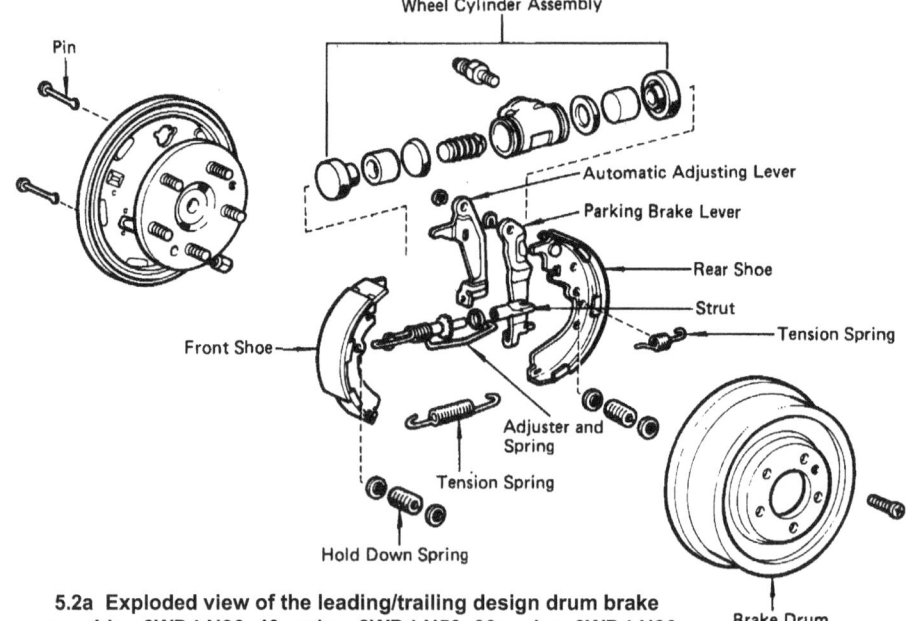

5.2a Exploded view of the leading/trailing design drum brake assembly - 2WD LN30, 40 series, 2WD LN50, 60 series, 2WD LN80, 90, 105, 106, 110 series, 4Runner with 4-link rear suspension

11   Using pliers, attach the parking brake lever and automatic adjusting lever to the new rear shoe with new C-clips.
12   Connect the parking brake cable to the parking brake lever.
13   Connect the strut and shorter tension spring to the automatic adjusting lever.
14   Set the rear brake shoe in place with the end of the shoe inserted in the wheel cylinder.
15   Using a hold-down spring tool, refit the rear shoe hold-down spring and pin.
16   Refit the longer tension spring between the front and rear shoes.
17   Position the adjuster, then set the front brake shoe in place with the end of the shoe inserted in the wheel cylinder. Make sure that the adjuster is properly seated in both brake shoes.
18   Refit the front hold-down spring and pin with a hold-down spring tool.

19   Using a brake spring tool, refit the adjuster return spring.
20   Move the bottom of the adjuster lever back and forth, checking to see that the adjust-

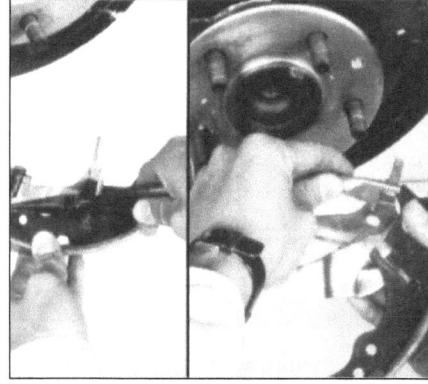

5.6 Unhook the tension spring and adjusting strut from the adjusting lever

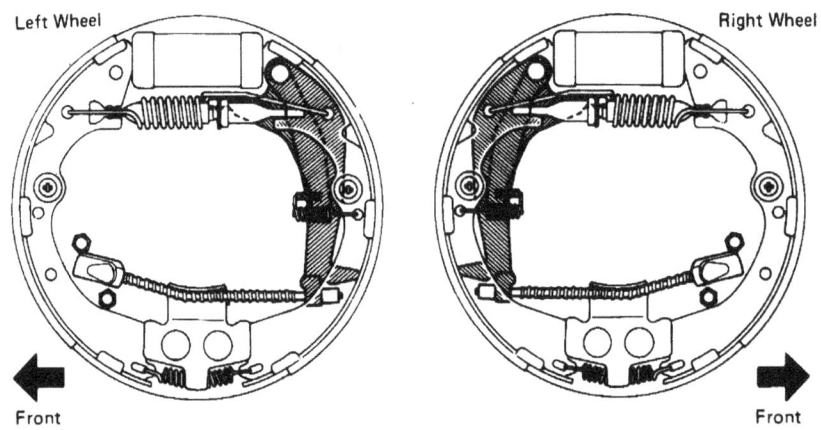

5.2b Assembled view of the leading/trailing design drum brake assembly - 2WD LN30, 40 series, 2WD LN50, 60 series, 2WD LN80, 90, 105, 106, 110 series, 4Runner with 4-link rear suspension

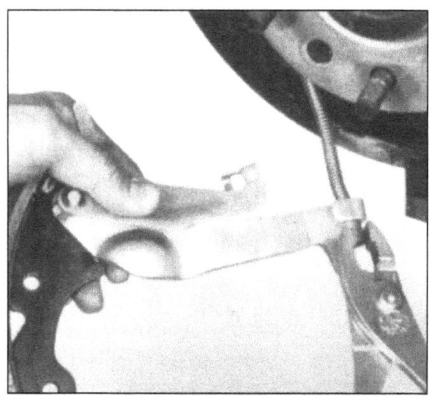

5.7 Grip the end of the parking brake cable with a pair of pliers, pull on it to compress the spring then unhook it from the lever

ing bolt turns **(see illustration)**. If the adjuster bolt does not turn, recheck all components you have just fitted for binding or improper refit and make adjustments as necessary.

21 Before refitting the drum it should be checked for cracks, score marks, deep scratches and hard spots, which will appear as small discolored areas. If the hard spots cannot be removed with fine emery cloth or if any of the other conditions listed above exist, the drum must be taken to an automotive machine shop to have it turned. **Note:** *Professionals recommend resurfacing the drums whenever a brake job is done. Resurfacing will eliminate the possibility of out-of-round drums. If the drums are worn so much that they can't be resurfaced without exceeding the maximum allowable diameter (stamped into the drum), then new ones will be required.* At the very least, if you elect not to have the drums resurfaced, remove the glazing from the surface with emery cloth or sandpaper using a swirling motion.

22 Adjust the brake shoes so the drum just slips over them with very little clearance. refit the wheel and tighten the lug nuts to the torque listed in the Chapter 1 Specifications.

23 Rotate the wheel slowly, listening for the brake shoes dragging on the drum. If they don't, turn the adjuster screw star wheel with a screwdriver inserted through the backing plate until a slight dragging sound is heard. Then, using another small screwdriver, hold the adjuster lever off the star wheel while turning the star wheel in the opposite direction, until no brake shoe drag can be detected when the drum is rotated **(see illustration)**.

5.10 Lubricate the shoe contact points on the backing plate with high temperature brake grease

Actuate the parking brake a few times and make a number of forward and reverse stops to fine-tune the self-adjuster mechanism. Test the brakes carefully before returning the vehicle to normal service.

Duo-servo drum brakes

Refer to illustrations 5.24a, 5.24b, 5.24c, 5.25 and 5.27

Note: *This procedure applies to both types of duo-servo drum brakes. One design uses a cable-actuated self-adjuster; the other design, used on the rear of models with front drum brakes, is not self-adjusting. If you are working on one of these modes, ignore the steps which do not apply.*

24 Using a brake spring remover, remove the two shoe return springs from the pin above the wheel cylinder **(see illustrations)**.

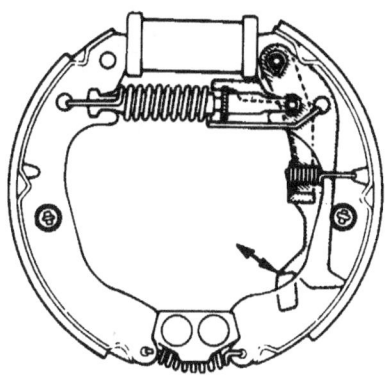

5.20 Check to see if the adjuster bolt turns by moving the bottom of the adjuster lever (arrow)

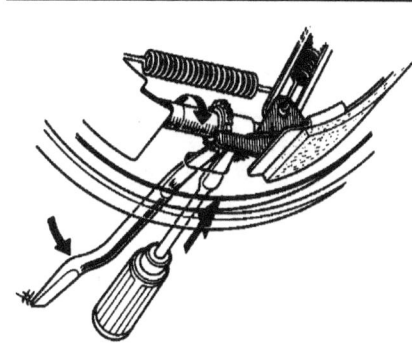

5.23 A screwdriver and brake adjuster tool (or two screwdrivers) are used to adjust the rear brake shoes - to retract the shoes, push the adjuster lever off the star wheel and turn the wheel in the proper direction

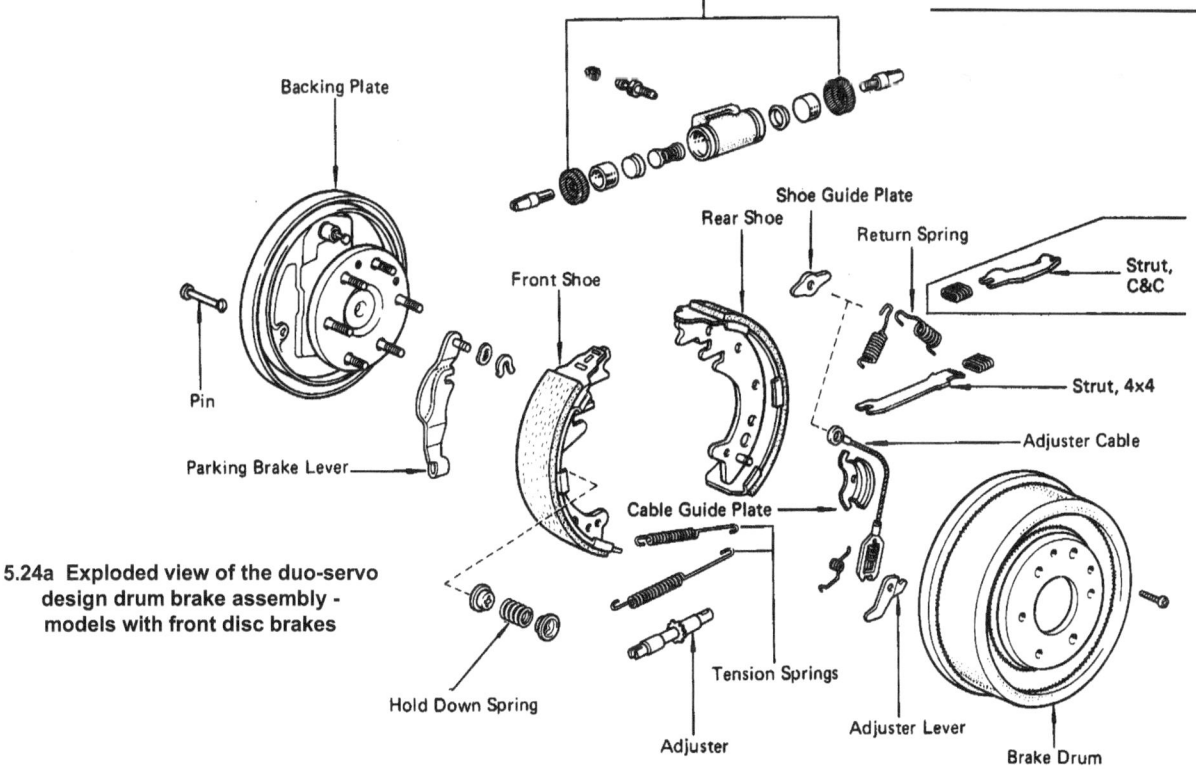

5.24a Exploded view of the duo-servo design drum brake assembly - models with front disc brakes

Backing Plate

Wheel Cylinder Assembly

Pin

Parking Brake Lever

Front Shoe

Rear Shoe

Shoe Guide Plate

Return Spring

Strut, C&C

Strut, 4x4

Adjuster Cable

Cable Guide Plate

Hold Down Spring

Tension Springs

Adjuster

Adjuster Lever

Brake Drum

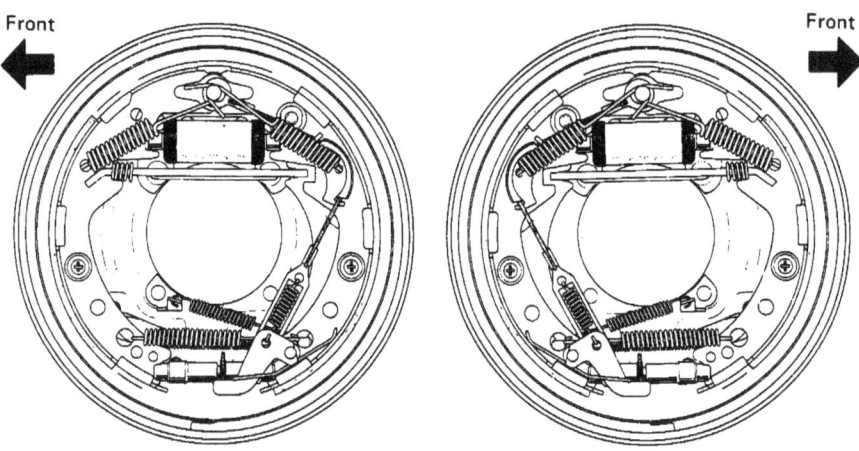

5.24b Assembled view of the duo-servo design drum brake assembly - models with front disc brakes

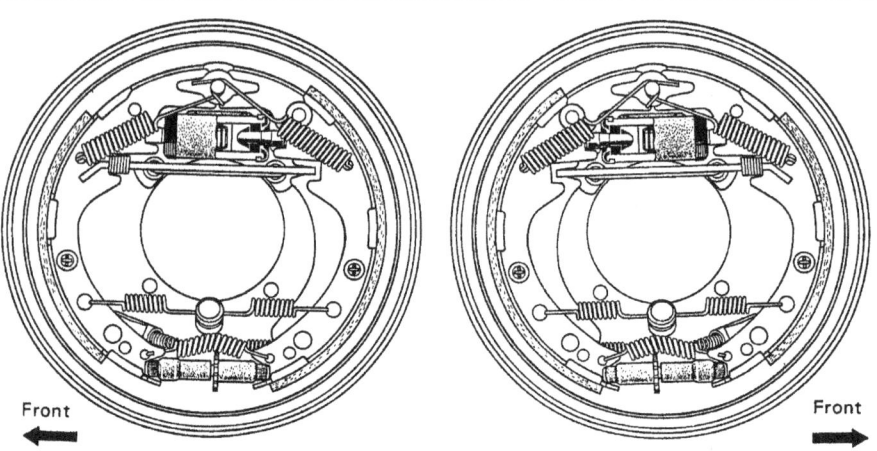

5.24c Assembled view of the duo-servo design drum brake assembly - models with front drum brakes

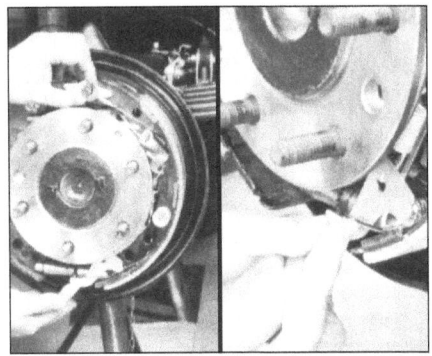

5.25 Push up on the adjuster lever and disconnect the cable, cable guide and the shoe guide plate

5.27 Remove the tension springs with a pair of pliers

25   Push up on the adjuster lever located between the bottoms of the two brake shoes and remove the adjusting cable, cable guide and shoe guide plate **(see illustration)**. **Note:** *This Step does not apply to models with front drum brakes.*
26   Take the adjusting lever tension spring off the adjusting lever and remove the lever and spring.
27   Using pliers, remove the two shoe ten-

sion springs **(see illustration)**.
28   Using a hold-down spring tool, remove the shoe hold-down springs and pins from the front and rear brake shoes.
29   The shoes are now loose from their mountings. Remove both shoes, the adjuster assembly and the strut, taking careful notice of their locations to assist you during refitting.
30   Disconnect the parking brake cable from the parking brake lever.

31   Using a screwdriver, remove the C-clip from the rear shoe, then remove the parking brake lever.
32   Perform Steps 9 and 10.
33   Connect the parking brake cable to the parking brake lever.
34   Set the brake shoes in place with the ends of the shoes inserted in the wheel cylinder piston rods and the strut in place.
35   Using a hold-down spring tool, refit the shoe hold-down springs and pins.
36   Apply brake grease to the adjuster.
37   Refit the adjuster assembly, making sure that the adjuster is properly seated in both brake shoes.
38   Using pliers, refit the two tension springs.
39   Refit the shoe guide plate, cable guide and adjusting cable.
40   Using a brake spring tool, refit the front shoe return spring, then the rear shoe return spring.
41   Attach the adjusting lever tension spring to the rear shoe.
42   Hook the adjuster cable to the adjusting lever and refit the lever in place.
43   Refit the adjusting lever tension spring to retain the lever.
44   Pull the adjusting lever backward with your thumb and release it. If the adjusting bolt does not turn, recheck all components you have just refitted for binding or improper fit and make adjustments as necessary.
45   Follow steps 21 through 23.

Leading/trailing drum brake - 4WD LN80, 90, 105, 106, 110 series, 4Runner with leaf spring rear suspension

Refer to illustrations 5.46a, 5.46b, 5.46c, 5.49, 5.50 and 5.55

46   Using a brake spring tool, remove the return spring from between the front and rear shoes **(see illustrations)**.
47   Remove the rear shoe hold down spring and pin, then remove the shoe.
48   Remove the front shoe hold down spring and pin.
49   Remove the front shoe/parking brake lever assembly from the backing plate and unhook the No. 1 parking brake cable from the No. 3 bellcrank **(see illustration)**.
50   Remove the adjusting lever spring and adjuster from the front shoe **(see illustration)**.
51   Perform Step 8 of this Section.
52   Perform Steps 9 and 10.
53   Apply grease to the adjuster bolt threads and end. Assemble the parking brake lever, adjuster screw and automatic adjuster lever to the front brake shoe **(see illustration 5.50)**.
54   Hook the No. 1 parking brake cable to the No. 3 bellcrank, position the front brake shoe assembly on the backing plate and refit the hold down pin and spring.
55   Connect the anchor spring between the bottom of each shoe and place the rear brake shoe on the backing plate **(see illustration)**. Push the rear shoe into the slot in the adjuster screw end. Also, make sure the anchor spring is routed under the anchor plate.

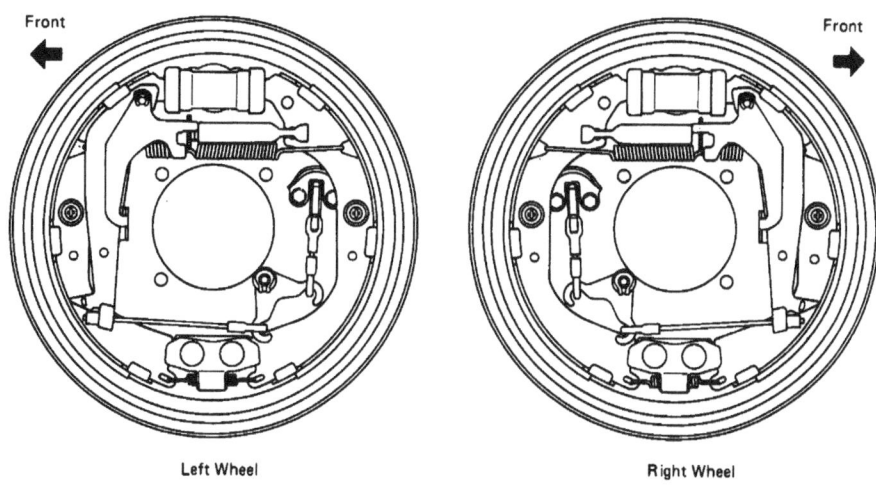

5.46a Assembled view of the leading/trailing drum brake assembly - 4WD LN80, 90, 105, 106, 110 series, 4Runner with leaf spring rear suspension

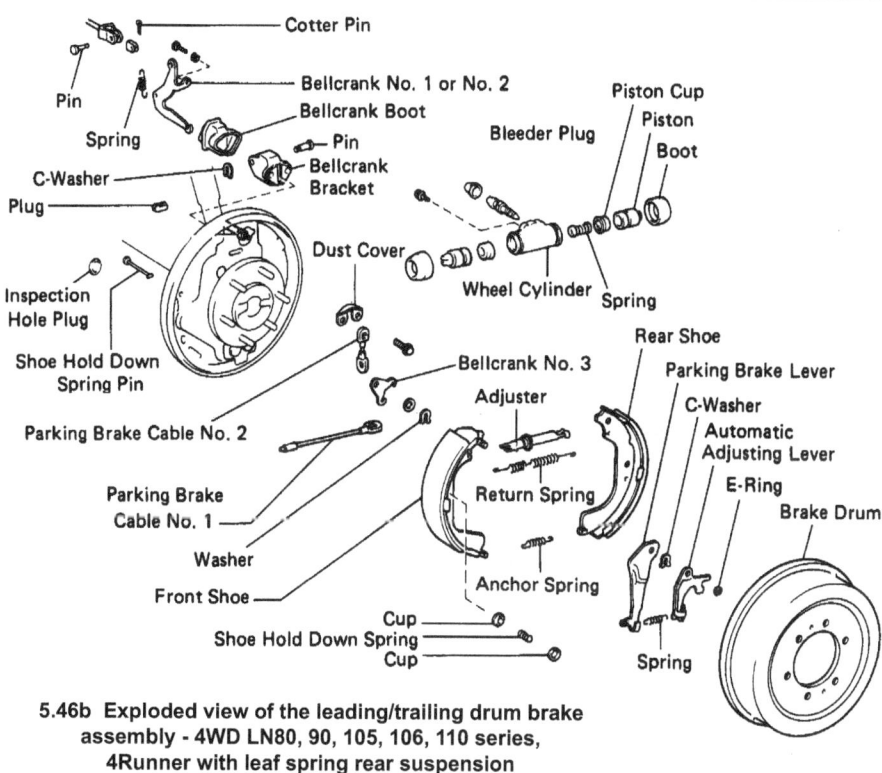

5.46b Exploded view of the leading/trailing drum brake assembly - 4WD LN80, 90, 105, 106, 110 series, 4Runner with leaf spring rear suspension

56 Refit the rear shoe hold down pin and spring.

57 Stretch the tension spring from the front shoe to the rear shoe, hooking the end of the spring into the proper hole in the rear shoe.

58 Check the operation of the automatic adjuster mechanism by pulling up on the parking brake handle and verifying that the adjuster screw turns.

59 Perform Steps 21 through 23.

60 Pull the parking brake handle through its full range of motion several times to adjust the brake shoes.

Front drum brakes

Refer to illustrations 5.61a and 5.61b

Note: *There are two types of front drum brakes on the models covered by this manual. One type uses two leading shoes; the other uses two trailing shoes. Service procedures for both types are identical.*

61 Using a hold-down spring tool, remove the hold-down springs and pins from both shoes **(see illustrations)**.

62 Allow the shoes to fold outward, then remove the return springs.

63 Remove the shoes from the backing plate.

64 Clean the threads and rotating portions of the adjuster screws, then lubricate them with a light coat of high-temperature brake grease. Reassemble the adjuster screws.

65 Apply a light film of high-temperature brake grease to the shoe contact areas on the backing plate **(see illustration 5.10)**.

66 Place the shoes against the backing plate and refit the hold-down pins, springs and retainers.

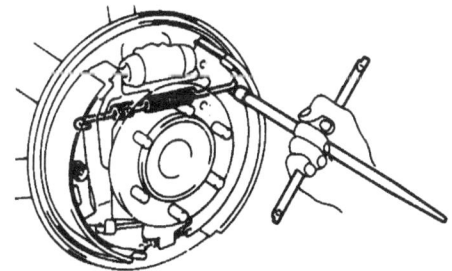

5.46c Use a brake spring tool to unhook the return spring from the brake shoe

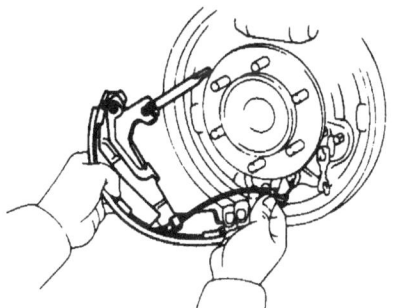

5.49 Lift the front shoe off the backing plate and unhook the parking brake cable from the bellcrank

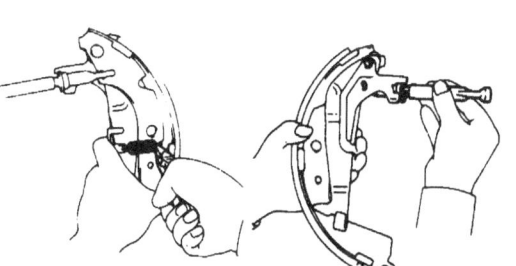

5.50 Unhook the adjusting lever spring and remove the adjuster

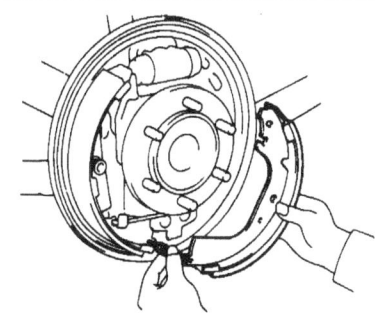

5.55 Refit the anchor spring between the two shoes then mount the rear shoe on the backing plate

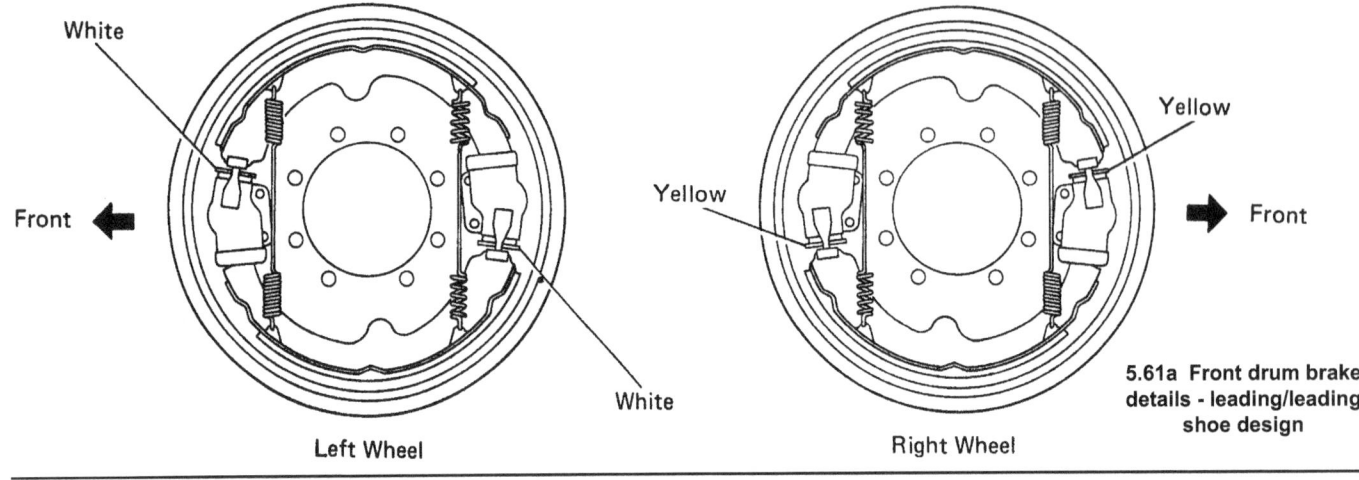

Left Wheel   **Right Wheel**

**5.61a   Front drum brake
details - leading/leading
shoe design**

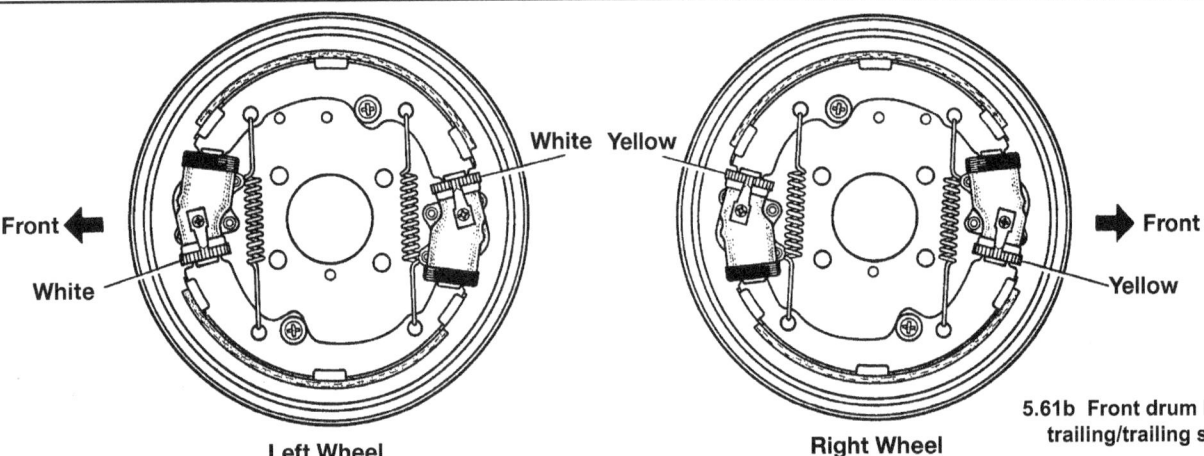

Left Wheel   **Right Wheel**

**5.61b   Front drum brake details -
trailing/trailing shoe design**

67   Refit the return springs.

68   Refit the brake drum. Adjust each brake shoe, one at a time, by placing a screwdriver through the backing plate and turning each adjuster screw star wheel, until the shoe drags on the drum as the drum is turned. Then, back-off the star wheel until the shoe doesn't drag.

69   Refit the wheels and lug nuts, lower the vehicle and tighten the lug nuts to the torque listed In the Chapter 1 Specifications. Test the brakes carefully before returning the vehicle to normal service.

6   Wheel cylinder - removal, overhaul and refitting

Note: *If an overhaul is indicated (usually because of fluid leakage or sticky operation) explore all options before beginning the job. New wheel cylinders are available, which makes this job quite easy. If it's decided to rebuild the wheel cylinder, make sure that a rebuild kit is available before proceeding. Never overhaul only one wheel cylinder - always rebuild both of them at the same time.*

Removal

Refer to illustration 6.4

1   Raise the rear of the vehicle and sup-port it securely on jackstands. Block the front wheels to keep the vehicle from rolling.

2   Remove the brake shoe assembly (Section 5).

3   Remove all dirt and foreign material from around the wheel cylinder.

4   Disconnect the brake line **(see illustration)**. Don't pull the brake line away from the wheel cylinder.

5   Remove the wheel cylinder mounting bolts.

6   Detach the wheel cylinder from the brake backing plate and place it on a clean workbench. Immediately plug the brake line to prevent fluid loss and contamination.

Overhaul

Refer to illustrations 6.7a and 6.7b

7   Remove the bleeder valve, seals, pistons, boots and spring assembly from the wheel cylinder body **(see illustrations)**.

8   Clean the wheel cylinder with brake fluid, denatured alcohol or brake system cleaner. **Warning:** *Do not, under any circumstances, use petroleum based solvents to clean brake parts!*

9   Use filtered, unlubricated compressed air to remove excess fluid from the wheel cylinder and to blow out the passages.

10   Check the cylinder bore for corrosion and score marks. Crocus cloth can be used

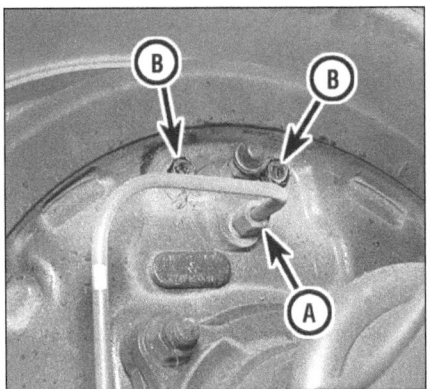

**6.4   Completely loosen the brake line
fitting (A) then remove the two wheel
cylinder mounting bolts (B)**

to remove light corrosion and stains, but the cylinder must be renewed with a new one if the defects cannot be removed easily, or if the bore is scored.

11   Lubricate the new seals with brake fluid.

12   Assemble the brake cylinder components. Make sure the seal lips face in.

Refitting

13   Place the wheel cylinder in position and refit the bolts.

6.7a Exploded view of the wheel cylinder - rear drum brake

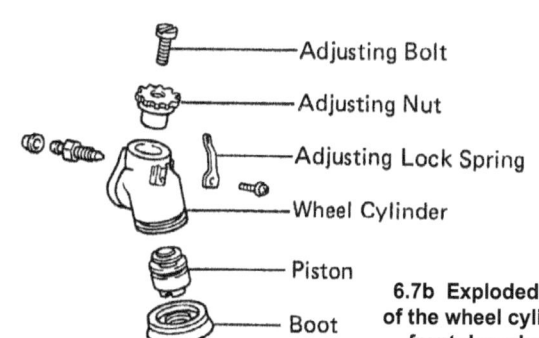

6.7b Exploded view
of the wheel cylinder -
front drum brake

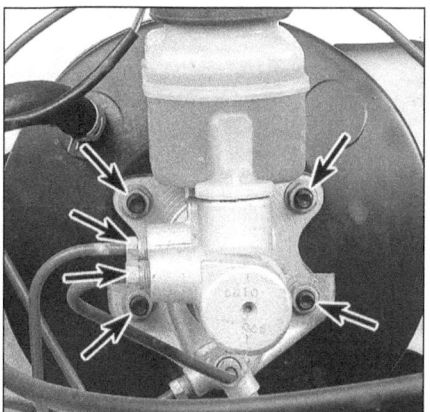

7.6 Unscrew the brake line fittings at the master cylinder, then remove the four mounting bolts

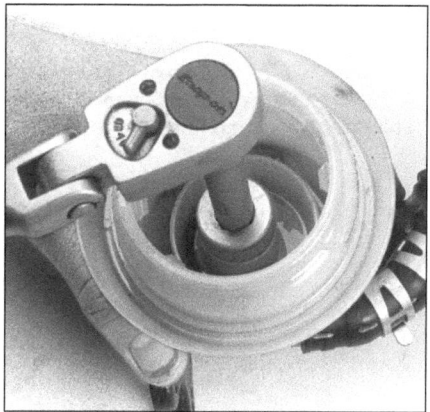

7.8a Remove the set bolt inside the reservoir, if equipped

7.8b Use pliers to release the hose clamp, then separate the reservoir hose from the master cylinder and remove the reservoir (single reservoir, dual-circuit type)

14   Connect the brake line and refit the brake shoe assembly.
15   Bleed the brakes following the procedure described in Section 10.

7   Master cylinder - removal, overhaul and refitting

Refer to illustrations 7.6, 7.8a, 7.8b, 7.8c, 7.9, 7.10, 7.11a, 7.11b, 7.11c, 7.11d, 7.11e and 7.26

Note 1: *Before deciding to overhaul the master cylinder, check on the availability and cost*

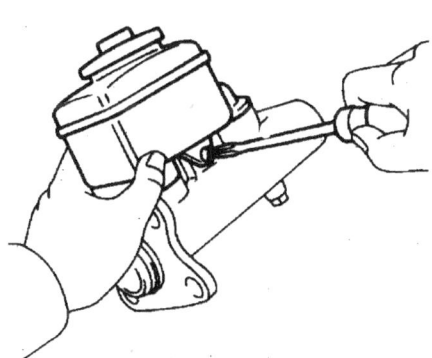

7.8c Remove the set screw and pull off the reservoir (dual reservoir, dual-circuit type)

of a new or factory rebuilt unit and also the availability of a rebuild kit.
Note 2: *Some early models use a single-circuit master cylinder. If you are rebuilding one of these, simply ignore the Steps in this procedure which do not apply.*

Removal

1   The master cylinder is located in the engine compartment, mounted to the power brake booster.
2   Remove as much fluid as you can from the reservoir with a syringe.
3   Place rags under the fluid fittings and prepare caps or plastic bags to cover the ends of the lines once they are disconnected. **Caution:** *Brake fluid will damage paint. Cover all body parts and be careful not to spill fluid during this procedure.*
4   Loosen the tube nut(s) at the ends of the brake line(s) at the master cylinder. To prevent rounding off the flats of the nut(s), the use of a flare nut wrench, which wraps around the nut, is preferred.
5   Pull the brake line(s) slightly away from the master cylinder and plug the end(s) to prevent contamination.
6   Disconnect the electrical connector at the master cylinder if equipped, then remove the nuts attaching the master cylinder to the power booster **(see illustration)**. Pull the master cylinder off the studs and out of the engine compartment. Again, be careful not to spill the fluid as this is done.

Overhaul

7   Before attempting the overhaul of the master cylinder, obtain the proper rebuild kit, which will contain the necessary spare parts and also any instructions which may be specific to your model.
8   Inspect the reservoir grommet(s) for indications of leakage near the base of the reservoir. Remove the reservoir **(see illustrations)**.
9   Place the cylinder in a vise and use a punch or Phillips screwdriver to fully depress the pistons until they bottom against the other end of the master cylinder **(see illustration)**. Hold the pistons in this position and remove the stop bolt on the side of the master cylinder. Remove the two outlet plugs and the copper gaskets.
10   Carefully remove the snap-ring at the end of the master cylinder **(see illustration)**.
11   The internal components can now be removed from the cylinder bore **(see illustrations)**. Make a note of the proper order of the components so they can be returned to their original locations. **Note:** *The two springs are of different tension, so pay particular attention to their order.*
12   Carefully inspect the inside bore of the master cylinder. Any deep scoring or other damage will mean a new master cylinder is required.
13   Renew all parts included in the rebuild

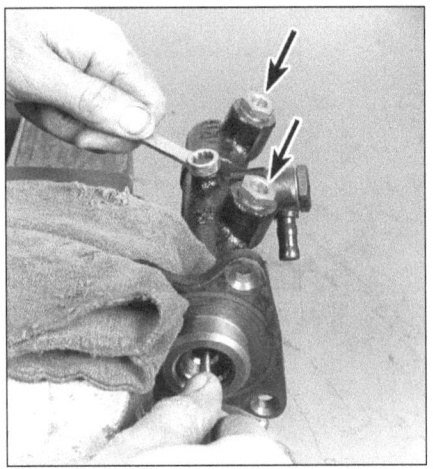

7.9 Push the pistons in all the way and remove the piston stop bolt and the copper gasket (also remove the two outlet plugs [arrows] and gaskets)

7.10 Push the pistons in and use snap-ring pliers to remove the snap-ring

7.11a Tilt the cylinder and remove the No. 1 piston and spring

7.11b To free a stuck piston, tap the cylinder firmly against a block of wood

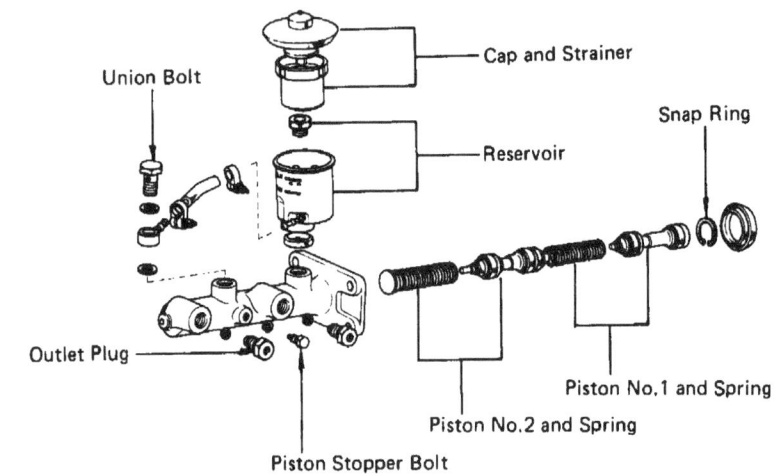

7.11c Exploded view of the single reservoir, dual-circuit master cylinder

kit, following any instructions in the kit. Clean all reused parts with clean brake fluid or denatured alcohol. Do not use any petroleum-based cleaners. During assembly, lubricate all parts liberally with clean brake fluid. Be sure to tighten all fittings and connections to the specified torque.

14   Push the assembled components into the bore, bottoming them against the end of the master cylinder, then refit the stop bolt.

15   Refit the new snap-ring, making sure it is seated properly in the groove.

16   Before fitting the new master cylinder it should be bench bled. Because it will be necessary to apply pressure to the master cylinder piston and, at the same time, control flow from the brake line outlets, it is recommended that the master cylinder be mounted in a vise, with the jaws of the vise clamping on the mounting flange.

17   Insert threaded plugs into the brake line outlet holes and snug them down so that there will be no air leakage past them, but not so tight that they cannot be easily loosened.

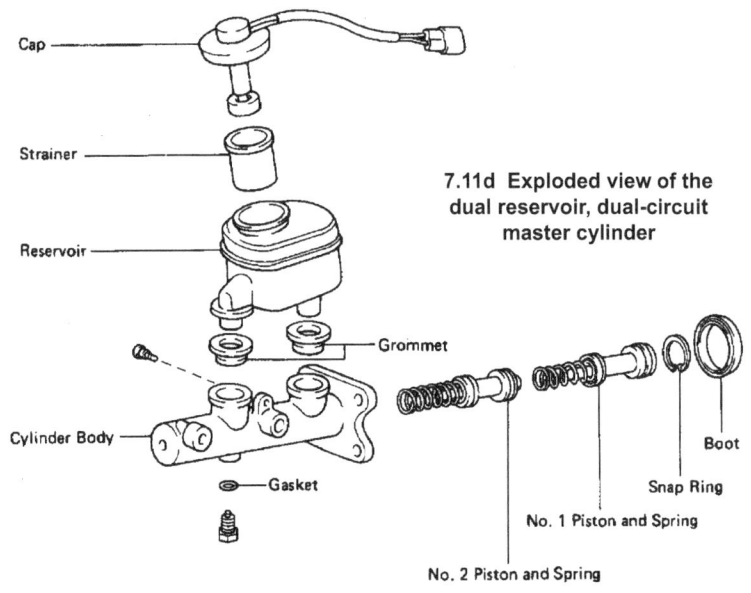

7.11d Exploded view of the dual reservoir, dual-circuit master cylinder

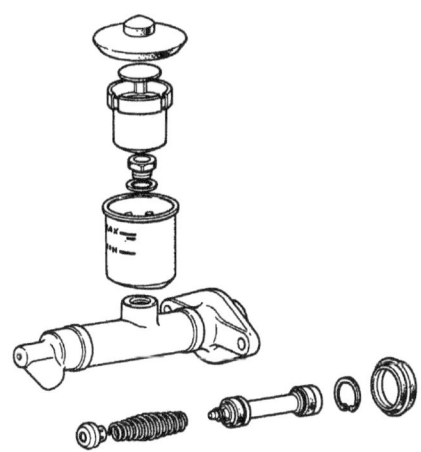

7.11e Exploded view of the single-circuit master cylinder

7.26 Have an assistant pump the brake pedal several times, then hold it to the floorboard. Loosen the fitting nut, allowing the air and fluid to escape. Repeat this procedure on both fittings until the fluid is clear of air bubbles

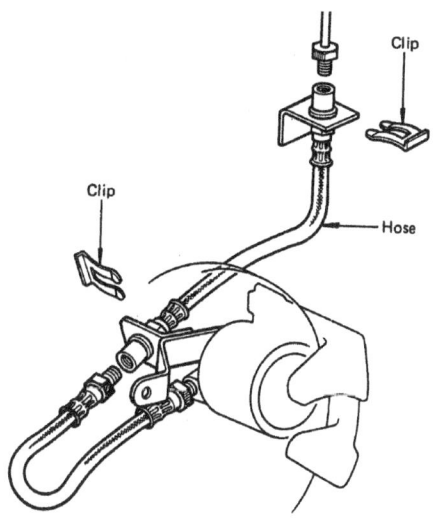

8.1 Flexible brake hoses should be inspected about every six months

18   Fill the reservoir with brake fluid of the recommended type (see Chapter 1).

19   Remove one plug and push the piston assembly into the master cylinder bore to expel the air from the master cylinder. A large Phillips screwdriver can be used to push on the piston assembly.

20   To prevent air from being drawn back into the master cylinder the plug must be renewed and snugged down before releasing the pressure on the piston assembly.

21   Repeat the procedure until only brake fluid is expelled from the brake line outlet hole. When only brake fluid is expelled, repeat the procedure with the other outlet hole and plug. Be sure to keep the master cylinder reservoir filled with brake fluid to prevent the introduction of air into the system.

22   Since high pressure is not involved in the bench bleeding procedure, an alternative to the removal and renewal of the plugs with each stroke of the piston assembly is available. Before pushing in on the piston assembly, remove the plug as described in Step 19. Before releasing the piston, however, instead of renewing the plug, simply put your finger tightly over the hole to keep air from being drawn back into the master cylinder. Wait several seconds for brake fluid to be drawn from the reservoir into the piston bore, then depress the piston again, removing your finger as brake fluid is expelled. Be sure to put your finger back over the hole each time before releasing the piston, and when the bleeding procedure is complete for that outlet, renew the plug and snug it before going on to the other port.

Refitting

23   Refit the master cylinder over the studs on the power brake booster and tighten the attaching nuts only finger tight at this time.

24   Thread the brake line fittings into the master cylinder. Since the master cylinder is still a bit loose, it can be moved slightly in order for the fittings to thread in easily. Do not strip the threads as the fittings are tightened.

25   Fully tighten the mounting nuts and the brake fittings.

26   Fill the master cylinder reservoir with fluid, then bleed the master cylinder (only if the cylinder has not been bench bled) and the brake system as described in Section 10. To bleed the cylinder on the vehicle, have an assistant pump the brake pedal several times and then hold the pedal to the floor. Loosen the fitting nut to allow air and fluid to escape. Repeat this procedure on both fittings until the fluid is clear of air bubbles **(see illustration)**. Test the operation of the brake system carefully before placing the vehicle in normal service.

8   Brake lines and hoses - inspection and renewal

Refer to illustrations 8.1 and 8.4

1   About every six months the flexible hoses which connect the steel brake lines with the rear brakes and front calipers **(see illustration)** should be inspected for cracks, chafing of the outer cover, leaks, blisters, and other damage (see Chapter 1).

2   Renewal steel and flexible brake lines are commonly available from dealer parts departments and auto parts stores. Do not, under any circumstances, use anything other than genuine steel brake lines or approved flexible brake hoses as renewal items.

3   When fitting the brake line, leave at least 19 mm clearance between the line and any moving or vibrating parts.

4   When disconnecting a hose and line, first remove the spring clip. Then, using a normal spanner to hold the hose and a flare-nut wrench to hold the tube, make the disconnection (see illustration). Use the wrenches in the same manner when making a connection, then refit a new clip. Note: Make sure the tube passes through the centre of its grommet.

5   When disconnecting two hoses, use normal wrenches on the hose fittings. When connecting two hoses, make sure they are not bent, twisted or strained.

6   Steel brake lines are usually retained along their span with clips. Always remove these clips completely before removing a fixed brake line. Always refit these clips, or new ones if the old ones are damaged, when fitting a brake line, as they provide support and keep the lines from vibrating, which can eventually break them.

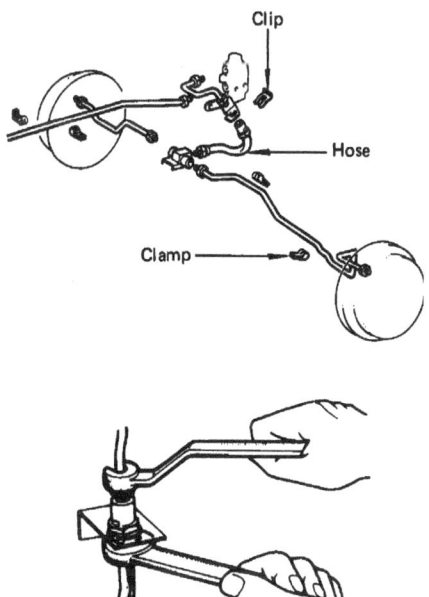

8.4 A backup wrench must be used to hold the hose from turning, otherwise the steel brake line will twist

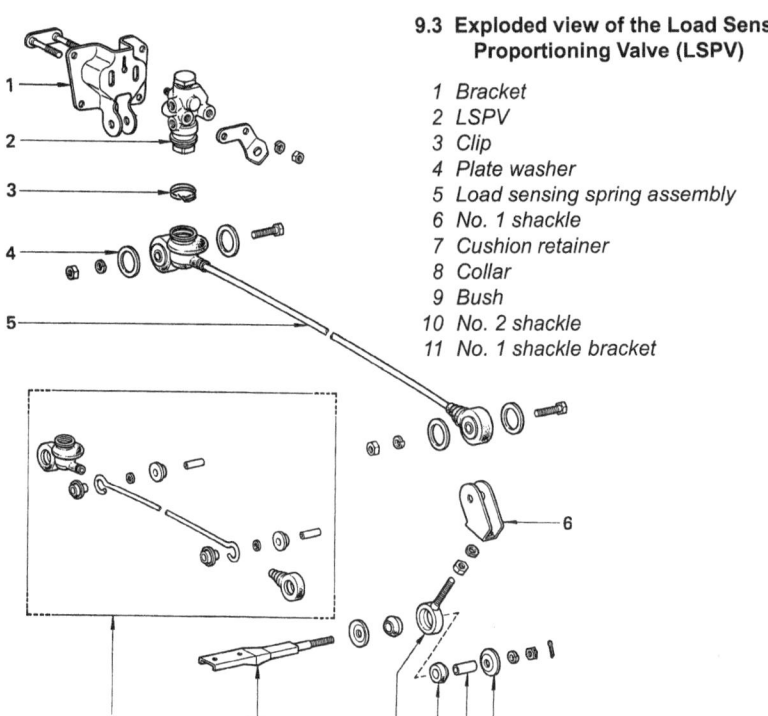

9.3 Exploded view of the Load Sensing Proportioning Valve (LSPV)

1 Bracket
2 LSPV
3 Clip
4 Plate washer
5 Load sensing spring assembly
6 No. 1 shackle
7 Cushion retainer
8 Collar
9 Bush
10 No. 2 shackle
11 No. 1 shackle bracket

10.7 When bleeding the brakes, a clear piece of tubing is attached to the bleeder screw fitting and submerged in brake fluid - air bubbles can be see in the tube and container when the bleeder valve is opened (when no more bubbles appear, all of the air has been purged)

9   Load Sensing Proportioning Valve (LSPV) - general information

Refer to illustration 9.3

1   Due to the fact that disc brakes are non-self-energizing, they require more hydraulic pressure than drum brakes to function properly. Added to the fact that, conversely, drum brakes require less hydraulic pressure to be efficient in an automotive system is the fact that they are usually fitted to the rear of vehicles, requiring even less pressure than the front discs because most of the vehicle's weight is transferred forward during braking.

2   If the hydraulic pressure were the same to the front and rear brakes, the rear drums would be locked up almost every time the brakes were applied with force. The load sensing proportioning valve (LSPV) allows a portion of the rear brake hydraulic pressure to be applied to the front brakes, thus providing for smoother, more controlled stops.

3   Due to the special tools, test equipment and skills required to diagnose the LSPV system, it is not recommended that the home mechanic attempt the procedures. If the valve has been determined to be faulty, it can be renewed by unscrewing the hydraulic lines and unbolting it from the frame bracket **(see illustration)**. It may, however, be necessary to have the hydraulic pressures adjusted after renewal of the valve.

10   Brake system - bleeding

Refer to illustration 10.7

1   If the brake system has air in it, operation

of the brake pedal will be spongy and imprecise. Air can enter the brake system whenever any part of the system is dismantled or if the fluid level in the master cylinder reservoir runs low. Air can also leak into the system through a leak too slight to allow fluid to leak out. In this case, it indicates that a general overhaul of the brake system is required.

2   To bleed the brakes, you will need an assistant to pump the brake pedal, a supply of new brake fluid, an empty jar or bottle, a plastic or vinyl tube which will fit over the bleeder nipple, and a spanner for the bleeder screw.

3   There are five locations at which the brake system is bled; the master cylinder, the front brake caliper assemblies and the rear brake wheel cylinders. After bleeding the master cylinder (see Section 7), bleed the brakes in this sequence: left rear, right rear, left front, right front.

4   Check the fluid level at the master cylinder reservoir. Add fluid, if necessary, to bring the level up to the Full or Max mark. Use only the recommended brake fluid and do not mix different types. Never use fluid from a container that has been standing uncapped. You will have to check the fluid level in the master cylinder reservoir often during the bleed procedure. If the level drops too far, air will enter the system through the master cylinder.

5   Raise the vehicle and set it securely on jackstands, as instructed in the front of the book.

6   Remove the bleeder screw cap from the wheel cylinder or caliper assembly that is being bled. If more than one wheel must be bled, start with the one farthest from the master cylinder.

7   Attach one end of the clear plastic or vinyl tube to the bleeder screw nipple and

place the other end in the glass or plastic jar submerged in a small amount of clean brake fluid **(see illustration)**.

8   Loosen the bleeder screw slightly. then tighten it to the point where it is snug yet easily loosened.

9   Have the assistant pump the brake pedal several times and hold it in the fully depressed position.

10   With pressure on the brake pedal, open the bleeder screw approximately one-half turn. As the brake fluid is flowing through the pedal, hold it in the fully depressed position, and loosen the bleeder screw momentarily. Do not allow the brake pedal to be released with the bleeder screw in the open position.

11   Repeat the procedure until no air bubbles are visible in the brake fluid flowing through the tube. Be sure to check the brake fluid level in the master cylinder reservoir while performing the bleeding operation.

12   Fully tighten the bleeder screw, remove the plastic or vinyl tube and refit the bleeder screw cap.

13   Follow the same procedure to bleed the other wheel cylinder or caliper assemblies.

14   Check the brake fluid level in the master cylinder to make sure it is adequate, then test drive the vehicle and check for proper brake operation.

11   Power brake booster - check. removal and refitting

Refer to illustrations 11.7a, 11.7b, 11.14a and 11.14b

Note: *Before condemning a power brake booster, check the vacuum reservoir for leaks* (see Section 16).

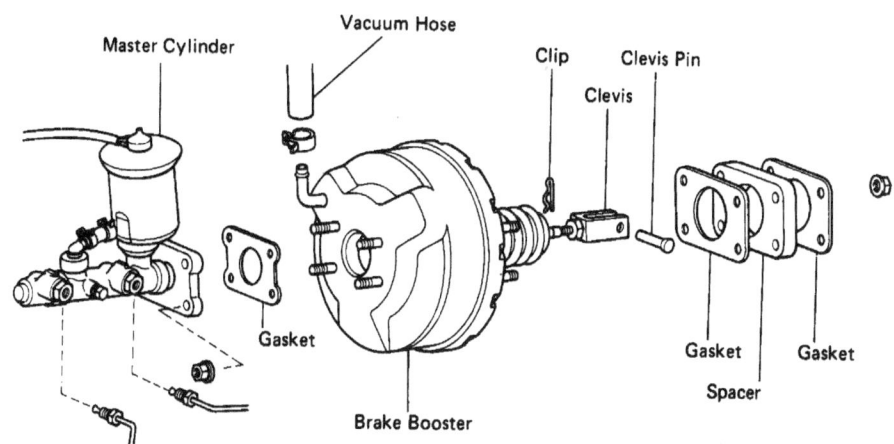

Master Cylinder · **Vacuum Hose** · **Clip** · **Clevis Pin** · **Clevis** · **Gasket** · **Gasket** · **Gasket** · **Spacer** · **Brake Booster**

11.7a Power brake booster refitting details (gasket and spacer arrangement may vary from model-to-model)

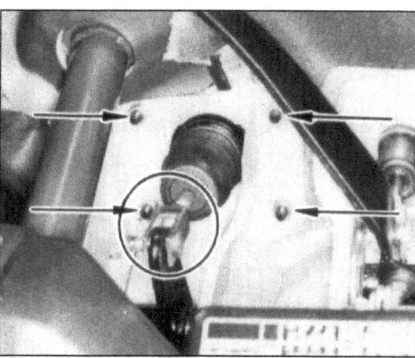

11.7b Arrows indicate the nuts holding the brake booster to the firewall - the pushrod clevis is circled

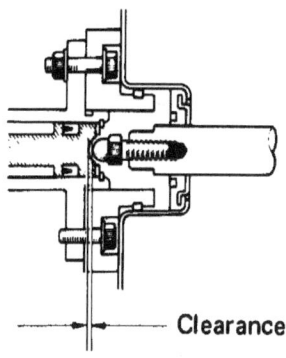

Clearance

11.14a The booster pushrod-to-master cylinder piston must be as specified - if there is little or no clearance, the brakes may drag; if there is too much clearance, there will be excessive brake pedal travel

Operating check

1   Depress the brake pedal several times with the engine off and make sure that there is no change in the pedal reserve distance.
2   Depress the pedal and start the engine. If the pedal goes down slightly, operation is normal.

Airtightness check

3   Start the engine and turn it off after one or two minutes. Depress the brake pedal several times slowly. If the pedal goes down farther the first time but gradually rises after the second or third depression, the booster is airtight.
4   Depress the brake pedal while the engine is running, then stop the engine with the pedal depressed. If there is no change in the pedal reserve travel after holding the pedal for 30 seconds, the booster is airtight.

Removal

5   Power brake booster units should not be disassembled. They require special tools not normally found in most automotive repair stations or shops. They are fairly complex and because of their critical relationship to brake performance it is best to renew a defective booster unit with a new or rebuilt one.
6   To remove the booster, first remove the brake master cylinder as described in Section 7.
7   Locate the pushrod clevis connecting the booster to the brake pedal (see illustrations). This is accessible from the interior in front of the driver's seat.
8   Remove the clevis pin retaining clip with pliers and pull out the pin.
9   Holding the clevis with pliers, disconnect the clevis locknut with a spanner. The clevis is now loose.
10   Disconnect the hose leading from the engine to the booster. Be careful not to damage the hose when removing it from the booster fitting.

11   Remove the four nuts and washers holding the brake booster to the firewall. You may need a light to see these, as they are up under the dash area (see illustration 11.7b).
12   Slide the booster straight out from the firewall until the studs clear the holes and pull the booster, brackets and gaskets from the engine compartment area.

Refitting

13   Refitting procedures are basically the reverse of those for removal. Tighten the clevis locknut and booster mounting nuts to the specified torque figures.
14   If the power booster unit is being renewed, the clearance between the master cylinder piston and the pushrod in the vacuum booster must be measured. Using a depth micrometer or vernier calipers, measure the distance from the seat (recessed area) in the master cylinder to the master cylinder mounting flange. Next, measure the distance from the end of the vacuum booster pushrod to the mounting face of the booster (including gasket) where the master cylinder mounting flange seats. Subtract the two measurements to get the clearance (see illustration). If the clearance is more or less than specified, turn the adjusting screw on the end of the power booster pushrod until the clearance is within the specified limit (see illustration).
15   After the final refitting of the master cylinder and brake hoses and lines, the brake pedal height and free play must be adjusted and the system must be bled. See the appropriate Sections of this Chapter for the procedures.

12 Parking brake - check and adjustment

Refer to illustrations 12.1a, 12.1b, 12.1c and 12.3

1   The parking brake system is activated by

a handle assembly in the middle of the vehicle's interior. A pulley bracket attached to the end of the handle assembly activates a front cable, which in turn acts on an intermediate lever (see illustration). Attached to this lever via an equalizer are cables that run to each rear brake drum and hold the vehicle stationary by expanding the rear shoes in the brake drums (see illustrations). Adjustment for cable stretch is accomplished by a threaded nut at the equalizer bar and is accessible from

11.14b To adjust the length of the booster pushrod, hold the serrated portion of the rod with a pair of pliers and turn the adjusting screw in or out, as necessary, to achieve the desired setting

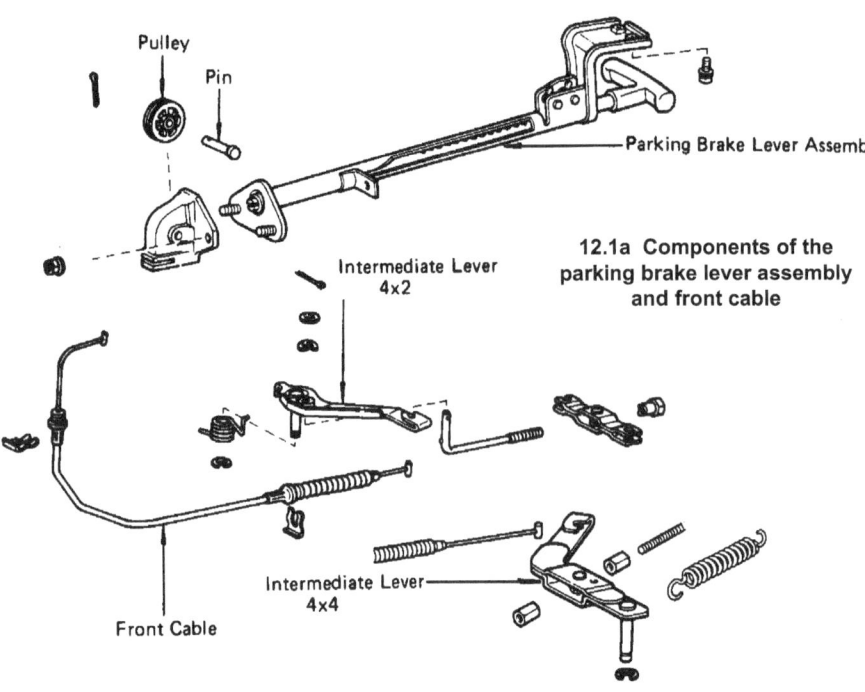

12.1a Components of the parking brake lever assembly and front cable

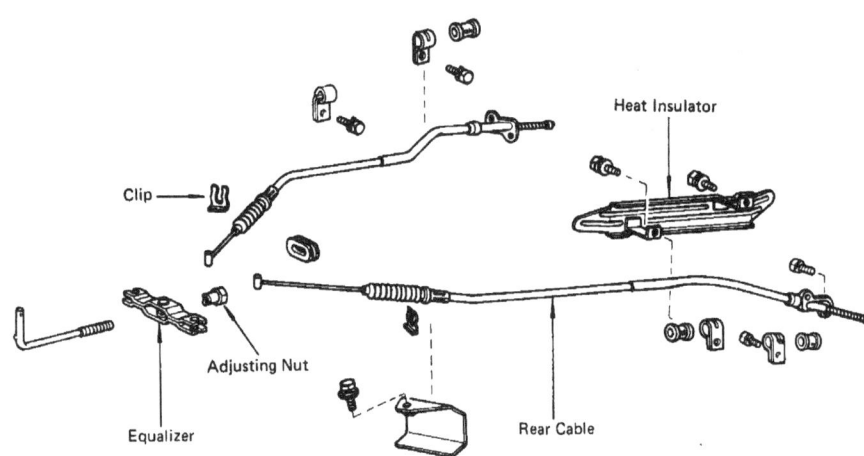

12.1b Components of the parking brake rear cable assembly - 2WD models

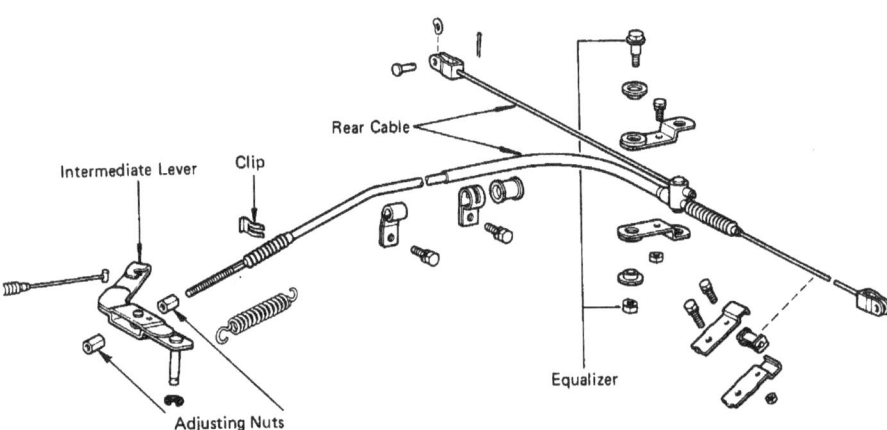

12.1c Components of the parking brake rear cable assembly - 4WD models

under the vehicle. The parking brake system also is used to activate the automatic brake adjusters on the rear brake shoes. When the parking brake is activated, it adjusts the rear adjuster one notch until all of the slack is taken up in the brake system (if the brake shoes have worn down enough to permit this).

2   If the parking brake will not hold the vehicle while parked on an incline, or if the parking brake lever does not respond within the lever click travel limit as designated in the Specifications while pulling the lever all the way up, check to confirm that the rear brake shoe adjustment is correct (see Section 5). If the adjustment is incorrect, adjust the shoes and recheck the parking brake operation. If the adjustment is correct, adjust the parking brake as follows after raising the vehicle and placing it on jackstands.

Adjustment - 2WD models

3   Tighten the intermediate lever adjusting nut until the travel is correct (**see illustration**). This may require several trial-and-error adjustments to get the correct lever travel.

4   After adjusting the parking brake, confirm that the rear brakes are not dragging.

Adjustment - 4WD models

5   Locate the bellcrank stopper screws at the back of the rear brake backing plates.

6   Tighten the bellcrank stopper screws until the play of the rear brake links is zero, then loosen the screws one turn and tighten the screw locknut.

7   Tighten one of the adjusting nuts of the intermediate lever while loosening the other until the travel is correct, then tighten both nuts.

8   After adjusting the parking brake, confirm that the bellcrank stopper screws come in contact with the backing plates.

---

13   Parking brake cables - renewal

Refer to illustration 13.7

1   It is not necessary to remove the entire parking brake system to renew an individual part such as a parking brake cable. Determine the part in need of renewal through visual inspection before dismantling the entire

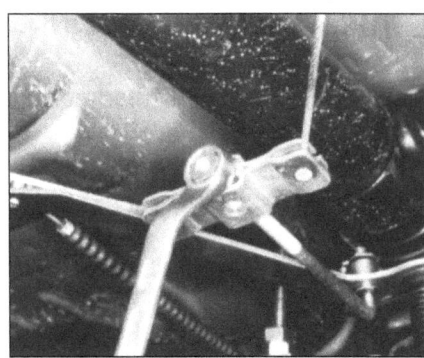

12.3 Turn the adjusting nut at the equalizer to take up slack in the parking brake cables (2WD models)

system. A helper is beneficial in this process to operate the system while you observe its operation from under the vehicle. Jack up the vehicle and support it on jackstands. Remove the adjuster nut from the lever under the centre of the vehicle. When unthreading this nut, it will probably be helpful to spray the exposed pullrod threads with a rust penetrant.

Brake lever front cable - all models

2   To remove the brake lever and front cable, begin by disconnecting the front cable from the intermediate lever.
3   Remove the parking brake indicator light switch.
4   Push the parking brake pawl with your finger to unlock the lever and completely push in the parking brake lever.
5   Remove the pulley bracket by removing the two bolts.
6   Disconnect the front cable from the parking brake lever shaft by pulling the end of the cable from the slot in the side of the shaft.
7   Remove the pulley pin **(see illustration)**.
8   Remove the pulley **(see illustration 13.7)**.
9   Remove the cable retaining clip with pliers, releasing the front cable from the pulley bracket.

Rear cable - 2WD models

10   To remove the rear cable, first disconnect the rear cable from the equalizer by turning the cables until the ends line up with the slots in the equalizer bracket, then slide the cables out.
11   Remove the cable retaining clips and clamps.
12   To remove the cables from the brake shoes and backing plates, first remove the drum and brake shoes as described in Section 5 of this Chapter, then unbolt the rear cable from the backing plate.
13   Refitting is the reverse of removal. Before refitting the brake cables, thoroughly lubricate them with a good quality cable lube or penetrating oil if necessary. Check the cable for signs of stretching or fraying. Put a small amount of light grease on the handle ratchet assembly.
14   Adjust the parking brake as described in Section 12 of this Chapter.

Rear cable - 4WD models

15   Disconnect the rear cable leader from the intermediate lever by unscrewing the two adjusting nuts.
16   Remove the cable retaining clip and clamps.
17   Unbolt the equalizer and cable guide from the rear axle housing, then disconnect the rear cable from the bellcrank.
18   Disassemble the rear brakes as described in Section 5 of this Chapter, then remove the adjusting cable from the adjusting lever on each backing plate.
19   Using pliers, remove the spring from the bellcrank on the rear side of each backing plate.

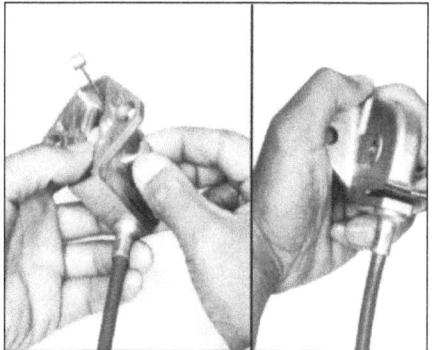

13.7 Removing the pulley pin (left) and pulley (right) from the parking brake lever assembly

20   Remove the front and rear bellcranks and the parking brake cable from each backing plate.
21   To refit the rear cables, first coat the front bellcrank with multi-purpose grease.
22   Using pliers, refit the front bellcrank on each backing plate.
23   Refit the cable, rear bellcrank and spring on each backing plate.
24   Assemble the rear brakes as described in Section 5 of this Chapter.
25   On each rear brake, tighten the bellcrank stopper screw until the play of the rear brake link becomes zero, then loosen the screw one turn and tighten the screw locknut.
26   Connect the rear cables to the rear bellcranks.
27   Refit the equalizer and cable guide on the rear axle housing.
28   Connect the rear cable leader to the intermediate lever.
29   Refit the cable retaining clamps and clip.
30   Adjust the parking brake as described in Section 12 of this Chapter.

14   Brake pedal - removal and refitting

Refer to illustration 14.3
1   Remove the floor mat.
2   Disconnect the brake light switch at the plastic connector. Pull it apart at the junction rather than pulling on the wires.
3   Remove the clip from the end of the pushrod pin **(see illustration)**.
4   Pull out the pushrod pin.
5   Remove the pedal spring.
6   Remove the nut from the left end of the pedal shaft while holding the right end of the shaft with a spanner.
7   Remove the pedal shaft. The brake pedal will pull down and out of the mounting bracket.
8   Disassemble the bushes and collar from the brake pedal.
9   Inspect all parts for wear or damage and renew them with new parts as needed.
10   Refitting procedures are the reverse of those for removal. Coat all the bushes, the

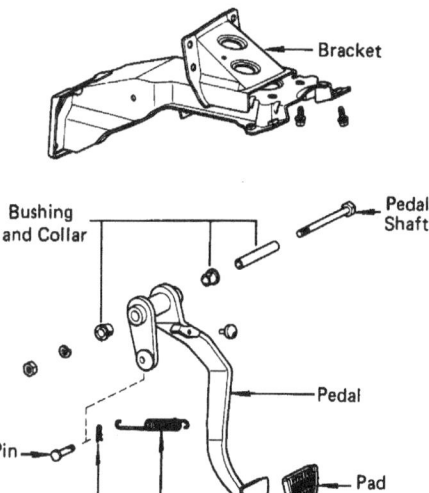

14.3 Brake pedal mounting details

collar, the spring and the pedal pin with multi-purpose light grease before refitting. Before connecting the brake light switch, adjust the pedal height (see Chapter 1).

15   Vacuum pump - removal and refitting

Refer to illustrations 15.1, 15.4a, 15.4b, 15.4c and 15.5
1   Disconnect the cable from the negative terminal of the battery. Loosen the hose clamps and detach the oil outlet hose and the vacuum hose from their ports on the vacuum pump **(see illustration)**. Plug the oil hose and its port to prevent oil leakage. Also unscrew the fitting and detach the oil inlet hose. Wrap a plastic bag tightly around the hose fitting to prevent leakage.
2   Detach any other vacuum hoses from the pump.

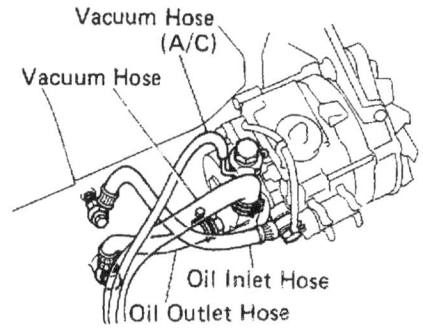

15.1 Vacuum pump details (rear-mounted pump)

15.4a Mark the relationship of the vacuum
pump to the alternator
to facilitate reassembly

15.5 On front-mounted pumps, check the
seal for signs of leakage or deterioration
and renew it if necessary

3   If you're working on a model with a front-
mounted vacuum pump, remove the alternator from the engine (see Chapter 5).
4   Mark the relationship of the pump to

15.4b Unbolting a rear-mounted vacuum
pump from the alternator

the alternator (see illustration). Remove the
pump mounting bolts (see illustrations) and
detach the pump from the alternator. On rear-
mounted pumps, discard the O-ring.
5   Check the pump seal for signs of leakage, renewing it if necessary (see illustration).
6   Refitting is the reverse of removal. If
you're working on a rear-mounted pump, fit
a new O-ring. On either type, be sure to use
new sealing washers on the oil inlet hose fitting and vacuum hose fitting (where equipped)
and tighten the fitting bolts to the torque listed
in this Chapter's Specifications.

16 Vacuum reservoir - removal and refitting

Refer to illustration 16.1

Note: If the brake pedal feels "hard," the
power brake booster or the vacuum reservoir
could be the problem. Check the reservoir for
leaks before condemning the brake booster.
1   To remove the vacuum reservoir, detach
the vacuum hoses and the electrical connec-

15.4c Front-mounted vacuum pumps
are retained by four bolts

16.1 Loosen the hose clamps and detach
the hoses from the vacuum reservoir,
unplug the electrical connector, then
unscrew the mounting bolts

tor, then unscrew the two mounting bolts (see
illustration).
2   Refitting is the reverse of removal.

Chapter 10 Part A
Suspension and steering systems (2WD models)

Contents

Specifications

General

Steering wheel freeplay	Less than 30 mm
Power steering fluid type	See Chapter 1
Power steering pump drivebelt tension	See Chapter 1

Torque specifications

Nm

Front suspension

Strut bar-to-lower suspension arm bolts	95
Strut bar-to-bracket nut	123
Torque arm-to-lower suspension arm	49
Lower balljoint-to-lower suspension arm	
RN30, 40 series	
8 mm bolts	20 to 28
10 mm bolts	39 to 53
YN/LN50, 60 series	69
YN/LN80, 90, 106, 110; RN/LN80, 90, 105, 110 series	127
Lower suspension arm shaft nut	
RN30, 40, 80, 90, RN/LN105, 110;	
YN/LN80, 90, 106, 110 series	226
YN/LN50, 60 series	270
Lower balljoint-to-steering knuckle	142

Torque specifications (continued)

	Nm
Upper arm mounting bolts	
Petrol models	
RN30, 40 series..	88
YN50, 60, 80, 90, 106, 110; RN80, 90, 105, 110 series	96
Diesel models...	96
Upper balljoint-to-steering knuckle	108
Upper suspension arm shaft bolts	
Petrol models	
RN30, 40 series (screw-type bush)	300
YN50, 60, 80, 90, 106, 110; RN80, 90,	
105, 110 series (rubber bush)......................................	126
Diesel models	
Screw-type bush..	230
Rubber bush	126
Upper balljoint-to-upper suspension arm..............................	30

Rear suspension

Leaf spring hanger pin bolts	
RN30, 40; YN/LN50, 60 series......................................	15
YN80, 90, 106, 110; RN/LN80, 90, 105, 106, 110............................	25
U-bolt mounting nuts	
RN30, 40; YN/LN50, 60 series......................................	98
YN80, 90, 106, 110; RN/LN80, 90, 105, 106, 110 series	123
Hanger pin mounting nuts	
Rubber bush type..	91 to 108
Press-fitted type	157
Shackle pin mounting nuts	91

Steering

Steering shaft-to-coupling pinch bolt	
YN/LN50, 60 series...	26
All except YN/LN50, 60 series	35
Steering wheel nut..	34
Steering gear housing mounting bolts	
RN30, 40 series	42
YN/LN50, 60 series	65
YN/RN/LN80, 90, 105, 106, 110 series	
2WD...	118
4WD (Independent Front Suspension).........................	142
4Runner (all)	142
Pitman arm-to-sector shaft nut	123
Pitman arm-to-relay rod	90
Tie-rod tube clamps	25
Tie-rod end nuts	90
Relay rod mounting nuts (idler arm end)...............................	59
Relay rod mounting nuts (Pitman arm end)...........................	90
Knuckle arm-to-steering knuckle	108
Steering damper-to-relay rod...	59
Steering damper-to-frame	13
Wheel nuts...	See Chapter 1

1 General information

Refer to illustrations 1.1a, 1.1b, 1.1c and 1.1d

Toyota two wheel drive (2WD) and four wheel drive (4WD) vehicles share many common components in their suspension and steering systems; however, due to the few distinct differences that do exist, this Chapter is divided into two Parts.

In Chapter 10A, you will find information on the suspension and steering components and procedures that pertain exclusively to 2WD vehicles **(see illustrations)**, plus all information on components and procedures that are identical relative to the 4WD's suspension and steering.

Chapter 10B deals only with those components and procedures that are exclusive to 4WD vehicles. Some 4WD components that share functions in the 4WD's driveline system, such as the front axle, are dealt with in Chapter 8. Such components are noted and referenced in this Chapter.

Complete specifications for each vehicle type are listed at the beginning of each sub-Chapter.

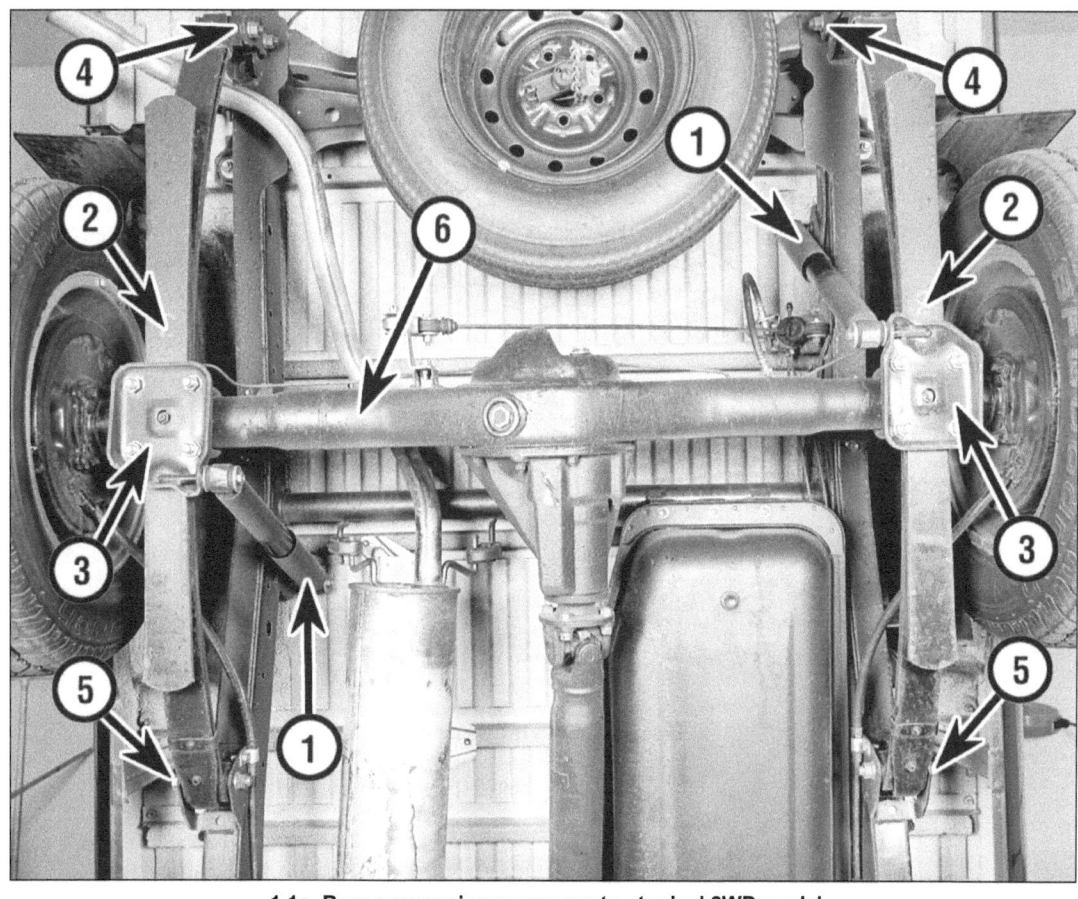

1.1a Rear suspension components - typical 2WD model

1 Shock absorber
2 Leaf spring
3 Spring seat
4 Shackle
5 Hanger pin
6 Rear axle housing

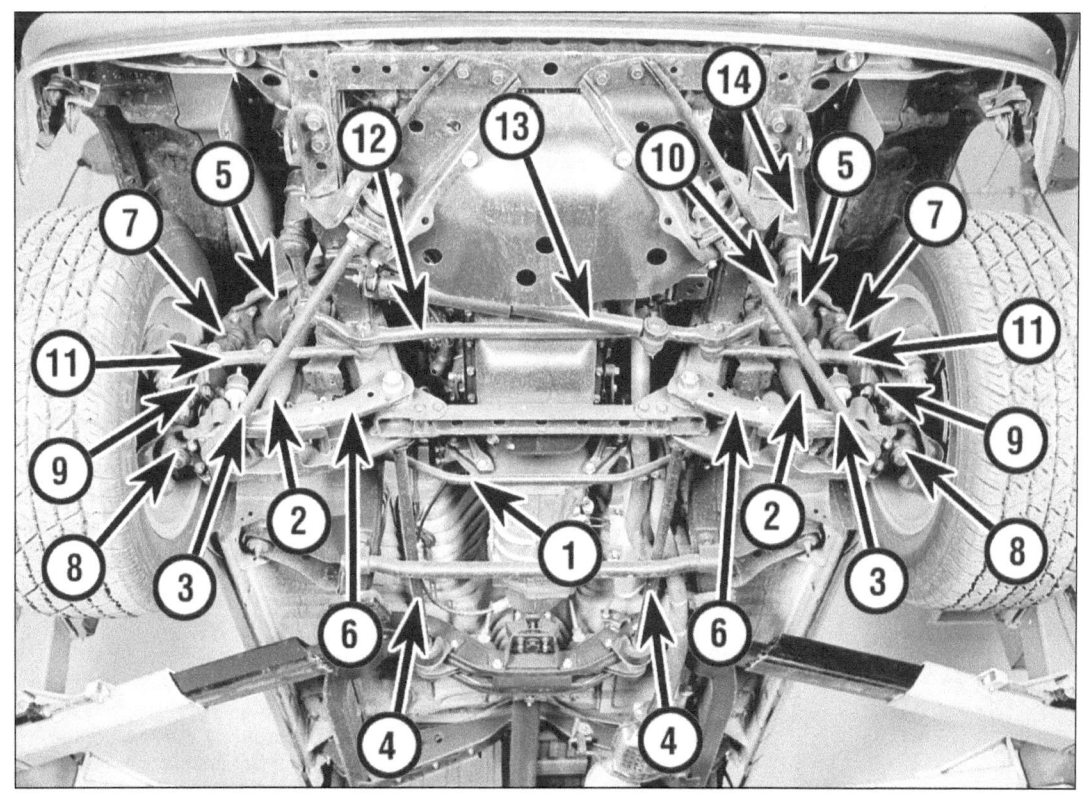

1.1b Front suspension components - typical 2WD model

1 Stabiliser bar
2 Shock absorber
3 Strut bar
4 Torsion bar
5 Upper suspension arm
6 Lower suspension arm
7 Upper balljoint
8 Lower balljoint
9 Steering knuckle
10 Pitman arm
11 Tie-rod
12 Relay rod
13 Steering damper
14 Steering gear

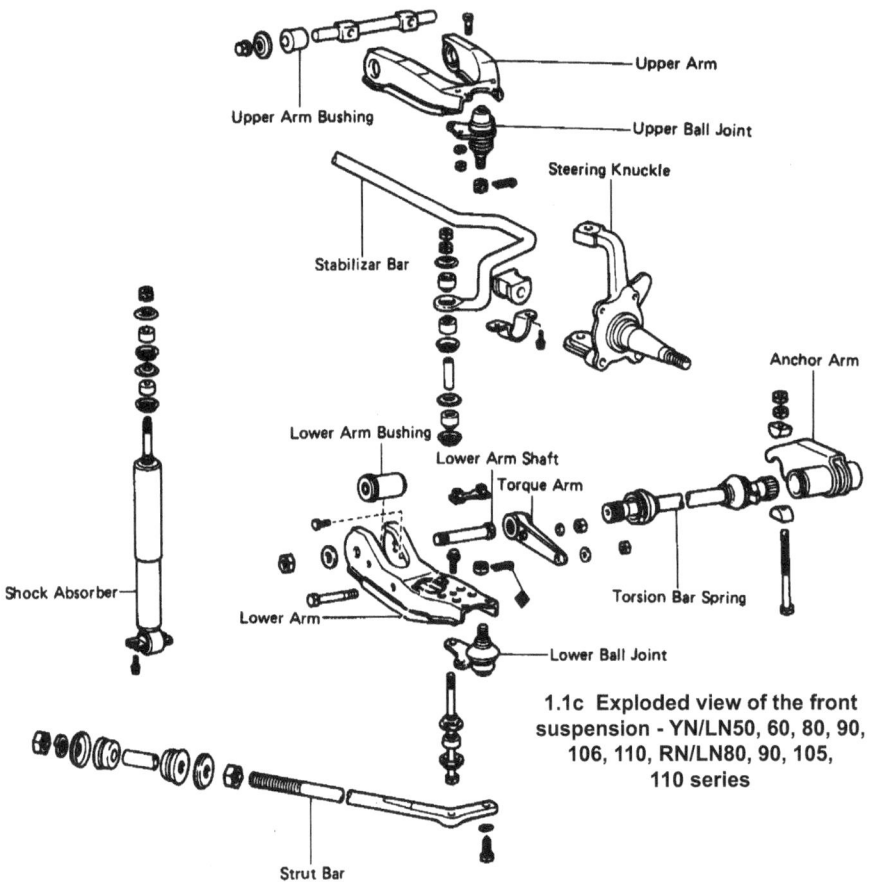

1.1c Exploded view of the front suspension - YN/LN50, 60, 80, 90, 106, 110, RN/LN80, 90, 105, 110 series

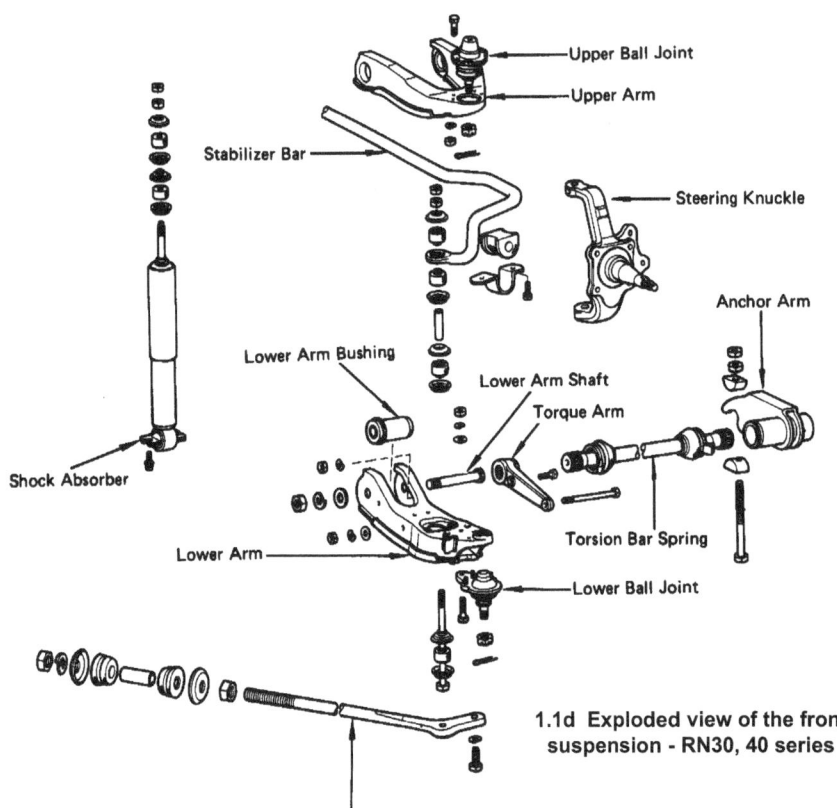

1.1d Exploded view of the front suspension - RN30, 40 series

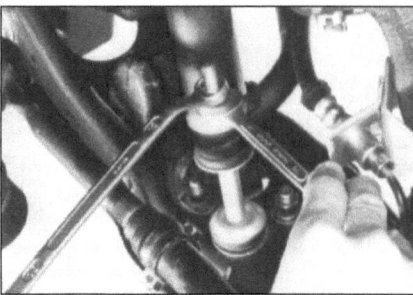

2.2 Remove the nuts from the stabiliser bar link bolts and remove the bolts, washers, spacers and bushes

2.3 A bracket, bush and two bolts connect the stabiliser bar to each side of the frame

2   Front stabiliser bar - removal and refitting

Refer to illustrations 2.2, 2.3 and 2.5

1   Jack up the front of the vehicle and place it securely on jackstands.

2   Remove the nuts, bolts and cushions from both ends of the stabiliser bar at the lower suspension arms and disconnect the stabiliser bar **(see illustration)**.

3   Remove the stabiliser bar bushes and brackets from the frame and remove the stabiliser bar **(see illustration)**.

4   Inspect all parts for wear or damage. Renew parts as necessary.

5   Refitting is the reverse of the removal procedures. Make sure the bolts, cushions and nuts are assembled in their proper order **(see illustration)** and tighten all bolts and nuts securely.

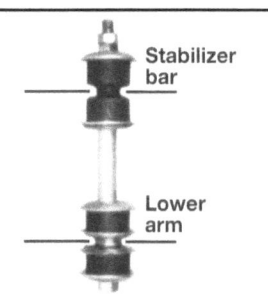

2.5 When properly assembled, the stabiliser bar links should be arranged like this

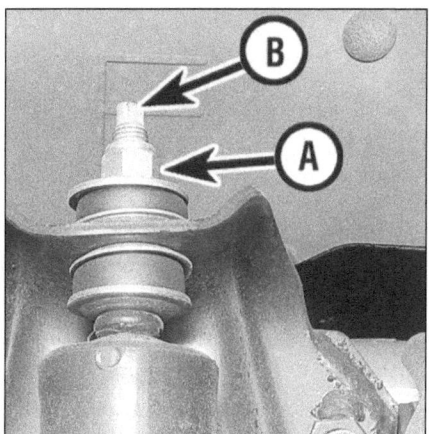

3.3 When removing the shock absorber upper mounting nut (A), hold the flats on the shock rod (B) to prevent the rod from

turning (some models use two nuts in place of a lock nut)

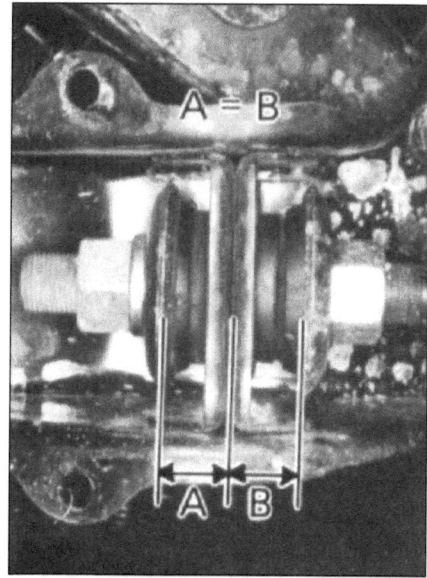

3.5 The shock absorber is fastened to the lower suspension arm by two bolts

3 Front shock absorbers - removal and refitting

Refer to illustrations 3.3 and 3.5

1   Loosen the wheel lug nuts. Jack up the front of the vehicle and place it securely on jackstands.
2   Remove the wheels.
3   Remove the nut(s) holding the shock absorber to the frame **(see illustration)**. Clamp a pair of locking pliers to the flats at the top of the shock rod to prevent it from turning.
4   Remove the washers and the cushions from the shaft of the shock absorber.
5   Disconnect the shock from the lower arm by removing the two bolts **(see illustration)**.
6   Tilt the shock forward, turn it 90-degrees so the bush is at right angles to the vehicle and pull it out.
7   Inspect the shock components for wear, damage or oil leaks. Renew parts as necessary.
8   Refitting is the reverse of the removal procedure. Make sure the washers and bushes are assembled in the proper order. Tighten the bolts and nuts securely.

4 Strut bar - removal and refitting

Refer to illustration 4.6

1   When fitting the strut bar, do so with the vehicle unloaded and the weight of the vehicle on the tyres.
2   Place alignment marks on the threaded portion of the strut bar and the inner nut.
3   Remove the outer nut from the strut bar.
4   Remove the bolts holding the strut bar to the lower arm and remove the strut bar.
5   Inspect the strut bar and components for wear or damage. Renew parts as necessary.
6   Refitting is the reverse of the removal procedure. Be sure to first thread the inside nut onto the strut bar and align marks made before removal. If a new strut bar is being fitted, measure the distance from the end of the old bar to the previously applied marks, then thread the nut onto the new bar the same distance. Tighten the bolts according to the torque figures listed in the Specifications. Make sure distances A and B are equal **(see illustration)**, when the specified torque is attained. If the distances aren't equal, loosen the outer nut slightly and tighten the inner

nut slightly until the bushes are compressed an equal amount, and the torque applied to finally tighten the outer nut is as listed in this Chapter's Specifications.

5 Torsion bar - removal, refitting and adjustment

Refer to illustrations 5.2, 5.3, 5.4 and 5.5

Removal

1   Jack up the front of the vehicle and place it securely on jackstands.
2   Slide back the rubber boots and place alignment marks on the torsion bar, anchor arm and torque arm to facilitate proper alignment upon refitting **(see illustration)**.
3   Remove the locknut securing the anchor arm and torsion bar and measure the protruding bolt end A **(see illustration)**. Record the measurement.

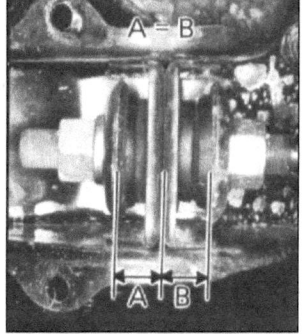

4.6 When tightened to the specified torque, the strut bar bushes should be equally compressed

5.2 Apply alignment marks to the torsion bar, anchor arm and torque arm to ensure proper realignment

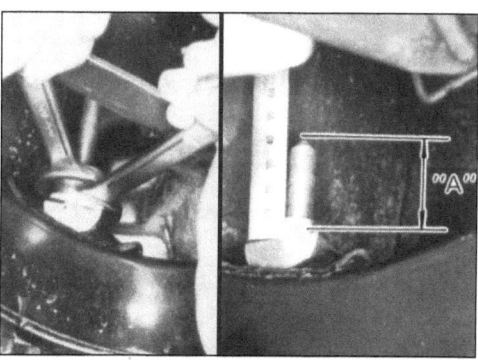

5.3 Remove the locknut while holding the adjusting nut with another spanner (left), then measure the anchor arm bolt protrusion (right)

5.4 The torque arm is held to the lower suspension arm by two bolts and nuts. Don't loosen these nuts unless the anchor arm bolt adjusting nut has been completely loosened

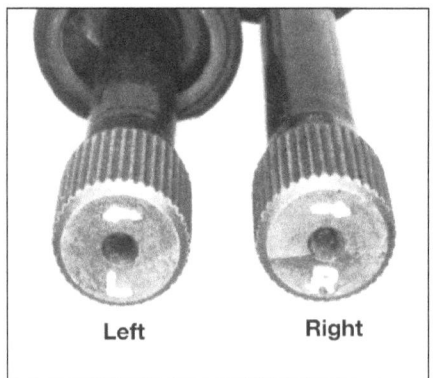

5.5 The torsion bars are marked on the rear ends - don't mix them up

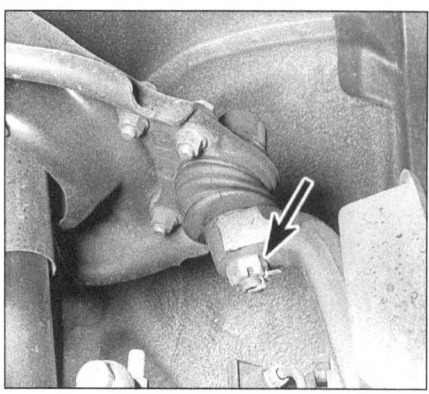

6.4 Remove the upper balljoint- to-steering knuckle nut

4   Unbolt the torque arm from the lower suspension arm **(see illustration)**. Loosen the adjusting nut completely and remove the anchor arm, torque arm and torsion bar.
5   Inspect the parts for wear or damage, including the splines on the torque arm **(see illustration)**. **Note:** *There are left and right identification marks on the rear end of the torsion bars* **(see illustration)**. *Be careful not to interchange them. Renew any damaged or worn parts.*

Refitting and adjustment

6   Apply a light coat of multi-purpose grease to the torsion bar splines.
7   Set the alignment marks and attach the torsion bar to the torque arm, tightening the nuts to the torque listed in this Chapter's Specifications.
8   Set the alignment marks and attach the anchor arm to the torsion bar.
9   Tighten the adjusting nut until the bolt protrusion is equal to that recorded before removal.
10   Measure the vehicle's ride height on each side, from equal points on the frame to the earth. If the side that has been worked on is higher or lower than the other side, turn the

torsion bar adjusting nut accordingly until the vehicle sits level. This may take a few tries, and it is important to roll the vehicle back-and-forth and jounce the front end between adjustments, to settle the suspension and get an accurate reading.
11   Apply multi-purpose grease to the lips of the boots and refit them on the torque arm and anchor arm.
12   Tighten the locknut to the specified torque, using another wrench to prevent the adjusting nut from turning.
13   When refitting is correct, the front wheel alignment and ride height should be checked by a front end alignment and repair shop.

---

6   Upper suspension arm - removal and refitting

Refer to illustrations 6.4, 6.5, 6.7 and 6.12

Removal

1   Jack up the front of the vehicle and place it securely on jackstands.
2   Remove the front wheels. Support the lower suspension arm with a floor jack and raise it slightly.

3   Remove the brake caliper and hang it out of the way with a piece of wire (see Chapter 9).
4   Remove the split pin and castle nut retaining the upper balljoint to the steering knuckle **(see illustration)**.
5   Using a balljoint separator, remove the upper balljoint from the steering knuckle **(see illustration)**.
6   Remove the bolts and nuts retaining the upper balljoint to the upper suspension arm, noting how it is refitted.
7   Remove the upper arm mounting bolts and the adjusting shims **(see illustration)**. **Note:** *Do not lose the shims. Record the position and the thickness of the shims so that they can be refitted in their original locations.*
8   Inspect the upper arm for damage. Renew it with a new one if damage is found.
9   Inspect the bushes for wear or damage. If wear or damage is found, renew them. A hydraulic press is needed to perform this job, so it is advisable to take the arm to a repair shop or an auto parts store equipped for this type of work.

Refitting

10   If the bushes have been refitted, don't tighten the upper arm shaft bolts yet (make sure they are loose enough for the shaft to turn).

6.5 Use a balljoint separator to pop the balljoint out of the steering knuckle - make sure the lower suspension arm is supported by a floor jack before doing this!

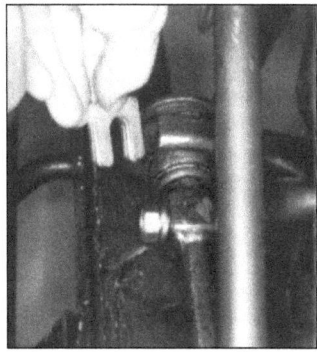

6.7 Record the positions and number of adjusting (alignment) shims as they are removed

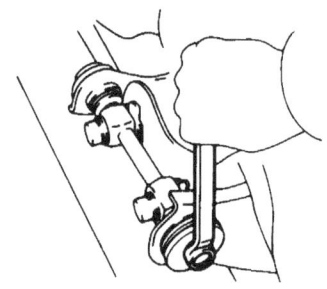

6.12 Tighten the upper arm shaft bolts only when the vehicle is at normal ride height

7.5 Remove the lower balljoint-to-lower suspension arm retaining bolts

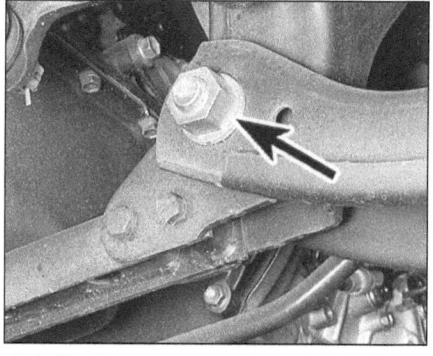

7.6 The lower suspension arm is held to the frame by the lower arm shaft, which is splined to the torque arm on the other end

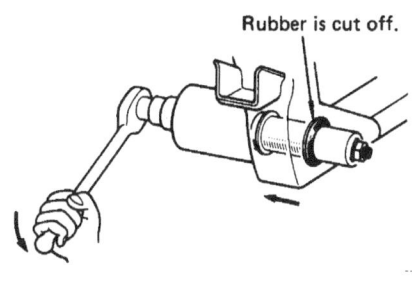

Rubber is cut off.

7.10 As the bolt is tightened, the smaller socket will push the bush out of the lower arm and into the larger socket

11   To complete the refitting, reverse the remaining removal steps, tightening all bolts, except the upper arm shaft bolts, to the specified torque **(see illustrations 1.1c and 1.1d if necessary)**.
12   Raise the lower suspension arm to simulate normal ride height, then tighten the upper arm shaft bolts to the specified torque **(see illustration)**.

7 Lower suspension arm - removal and refitting

Refer to illustrations 7.5, 7.6, 7.10 and 7.11

Removal

1   Remove the torsion bar (see Section 5).
2   Disconnect the stabiliser bar from the lower suspension arm (see Section 2).
3   Disconnect the strut bar from the lower suspension arm (see Section 4).
4   Remove the front shock absorber (see Section 3).
5   Disconnect the lower balljoint from the lower suspension arm by removing the retaining bolts **(see illustration)**.
6   Remove the lower suspension arm shaft nut **(see illustration)**.
7   Remove the torque arm and lower arm shaft from the lower suspension arm, then pull down on the lower suspension arm to remove it.

8   Inspect the lower suspension arm and its related components for wear or damage. Renew parts as necessary.
9   Inspect the lower suspension arm bush for wear or damage. If the bush is worn or damaged, renew it as follows.
10   Using a heavy, threaded bolt, nut, two washers, a socket to fit the head of the bolt and two large sockets - one slightly smaller in diameter than the bush, the other large enough to fit over the bush rubber - remove the bush from the crossmember. **Note:** *As the bush is removed, the rubber on the rear side will be cut off* **(see illustration)**.
11   Apply soapy water to the front rubber part of the new bush, reverse the position of the removal apparatus and fit the new bush **(see illustration)**.

Refitting

12   To refit the lower suspension arm, place the arm in position and insert the lower shaft into the arm.
13   Finger tighten, but do not torque the mounting nut at this time.
14   Refit the torque arm to the lower suspension arm and tighten the torque arm nuts and bolts to the specified torque.
15   To complete the refitting, reverse the remaining removal steps, except for the tightening of the lower suspension arm shaft nut.
16   Remove the jackstands and lower the vehicle.
17   Bounce the vehicle several times to stabilise the lower suspension arm bush.

18   Tighten the lower suspension arm shaft to the torque listed in this Chapter's Specifications, then refer to Section 5 and adjust the vehicle ride height.

8 Balljoints - renewal

Note: *This procedure applies to all 2WD models and 4WD models with independent front suspension.*

Upper balljoint

1   For removal of the upper balljoint, refer to Section 6, Steps 1 through 6.
2   To refit the upper balljoint, attach it to the upper suspension arm and tighten the mounting nuts and bolts to the specified torque **(see illustrations 1.1c and 1.1d)**.
3   Connect the upper balljoint to the steering knuckle and refit and tighten the castle nut to the specified torque.
4   Refit a new split pin.
5   The remainder of the procedure is the reverse of removal.

Lower balljoint

Refer to illustrations 8.8, 8.9 and 8.10

6   Raise the vehicle and support it on jackstands placed underneath the frame rails. Remove the wheel.
7   Using a jack, support the lower control arm, as close to the balljoint as possible, while still allowing enough room to work.

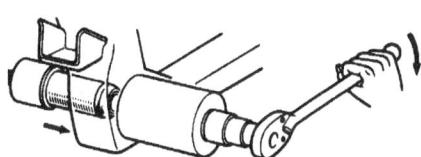

7.11 The new bush is fitted in the lower arm by reversing the positions of the sockets - be sure to lubricate the bush with soapy water (don't use oil or grease)

8.8 Remove the lower balljoint-to-steering knuckle nut (arrow) - on some models the balljoint faces upward; on others, it faces downward

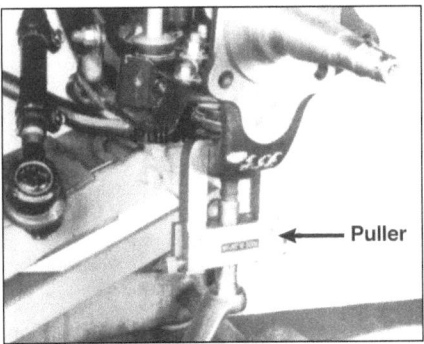

8.9 Use a two-jaw puller or balljoint separator to separate the balljoint from the steering knuckle (on models with upward-facing balljoints this tool may not work - as an alternative, you can strike the steering knuckle in the vicinity of the balljoint stud with a hammer or use a "picklefork" type balljoint separator)

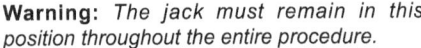

Warning: *The jack must remain in this position throughout the entire procedure.*

8   Remove the split pin and castle nut securing the lower balljoint to the steering knuckle **(see illustration)**.

9   Using a balljoint separator or a two-jaw puller, disconnect the lower balljoint from the steering knuckle **(see illustration)**.

10   Remove the retaining nuts and bolts, then remove the lower balljoint from the lower suspension arm **(see illustration)**.

11   Renew the balljoint.

12   Fit the new balljoint between the lower arm and steering knuckle.

8.10 The balljoint is fastened to the lower arm with three bolts and nuts

13   Tighten the lower balljoint mounting nuts and bolts to the specified torque.

14   Connect the balljoint to the steering knuckle, then tighten the castle nut to the specified torque and secure it with a new split pin.

9   Steering knuckle - removal and refitting

Refer to illustration 9.5

Removal

1   Remove the brake caliper and front axle hub (see Chapter 9).

2   Unbolt and remove the dust cover, then remove the knuckle arm (see Section 15).

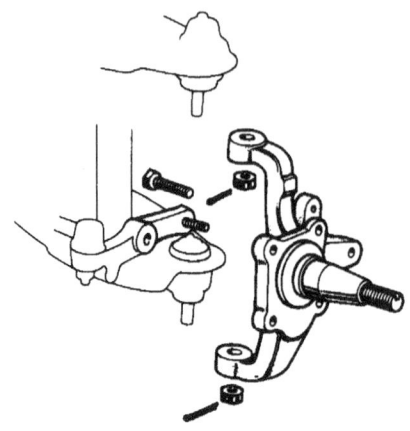

9.5 Steering knuckle refitting details

3   Place a jack under the lower arm to support it.

4   Using a balljoint puller, disconnect the lower balljoint from the steering knuckle after removing the split pin and castle nut (see Section 8).

5   Using a balljoint puller, disconnect the upper balljoint from the steering knuckle after removing the split pin and castle nut (Section 8). Remove the steering knuckle from the balljoints **(see illustration)**.

6   Take the steering knuckle to an automotive machine shop and have it inspected for damage or cracks.

Refitting

7   Refitting is the reverse of the removal procedures. Be sure to refer to the Specifications for the correct torque when tightening bolts. When refitting is complete, the front wheel alignment should be checked by a reputable front end alignment and repair shop.

10   Rear shock absorber - removal and refitting

Refer to illustration 10.3

1   If the shock absorber is to be renewed, it is recommended that both shocks on the rear of the vehicle be renewed at the same time.

2   Raise the rear of the vehicle and support it securely on jackstands placed under the frame rails. Support the rear axle with a floor jack (one side at a time) when removing a shock absorber. Do not attempt to remove the shock absorbers with the vehicle raised and the axle unsupported.

3   Unscrew and remove the lower shock absorber mounting bolt to disconnect it at the spring seat **(see illustration)**.

4   Unscrew and remove the upper mounting nuts at the frame and remove the shock absorber.

5   Check the shock absorber for worn bushes, leaking oil, sticking, and "dead spots" while compressing it. If the unit is defective, it must be renewed.

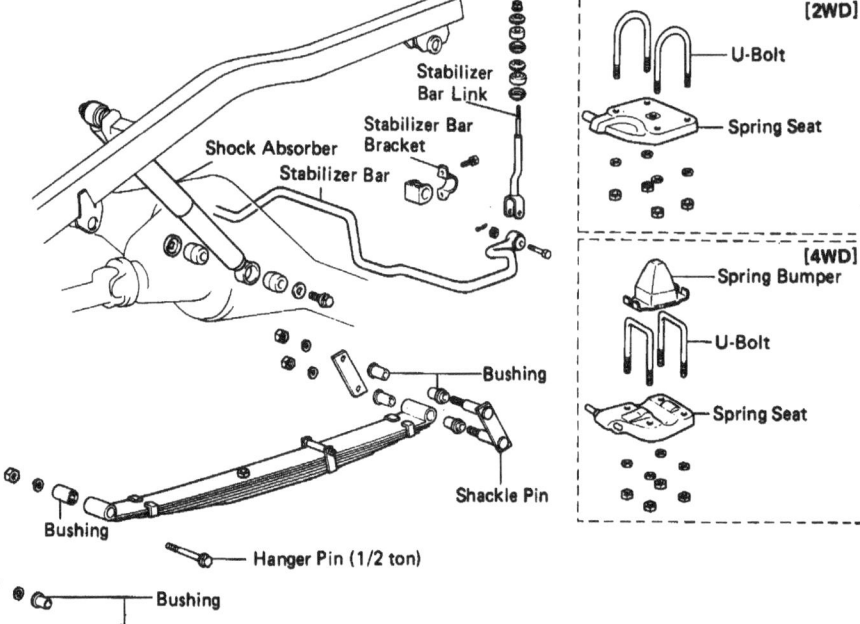

10.3 Exploded view of the rear suspension

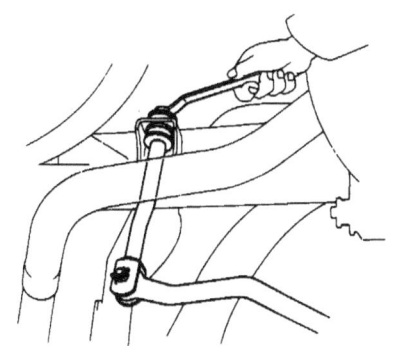

11.2 Removing the stabiliser bar link-to-frame nut

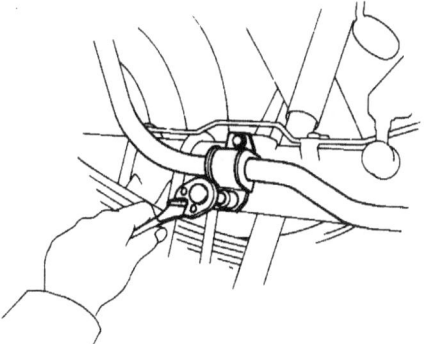

11.3 Remove the bolts that retain the stabiliser bar brackets to the rear axle housing

12.6 The spring seat is retained by the four U-bolt nuts

6   Refit the shocks in the reverse order of removal, but let the vehicle be free-standing before tightening the mounting bolts and nuts.
7   Bounce the rear of the vehicle a couple of times to settle the bushes into place, then tighten the nuts and bolt securely.

11 Rear stabiliser bar - removal and refitting

Refer to illustrations 11.2 and 11.3

1   Raise the vehicle and support it securely on jackstands.
2   Remove the stabiliser bar link-to-body nuts **(see illustration)**.
3   Unbolt the stabiliser bar brackets from the axle housing and remove the bar from the vehicle **(see illustration)**.
4   Inspect the rubber bushes for hardness, cracking and general deterioration, renewing them if necessary.
5   If it is necessary to remove a stabiliser bar link, pull out the split pin, remove the nut and bolt then separate the link from the bar.
6   To refit the stabiliser bar, reverse the removal steps.

12 Rear leaf spring - removal and refitting

Refer to illustrations 12.6, 12.8a and 12.8b

1   Loosen the rear wheel lug nuts, raise the rear of the vehicle and support the frame securely on jackstands.
2   Remove the rear wheels.
3   Place a jack under the rear differential housing.
4   Lower the axle housing until the leaf spring tension is relieved, and lock the jack in this position.
5   Disconnect the shock absorber from the spring seat.
6   Remove the U-bolt mounting nuts **(see illustration)**.
7   Remove the spring seat and U-bolts.
8   Unbolt and remove the shackle pin and hanger pin assemblies **(see illustrations)**.
9   Remove the spring. If the bushes need to be renewed, they can be pressed out in a similar manner to that shown in **illustration 7.10.**
10   Refitting is the reverse of the removal procedure. When refitting the hanger pin and shackle pin nuts, finger tighten them until all

other components are refitted, then raise the jack under the differential until the vehicle is just free of the stands and tighten the hanger pin and shackle pin nuts to the specified torque. The U-bolts should be tightened to the specified torque as well.

13 Steering wheel - removal and refitting

Refer to illustration 13.4

Removal

1   Disconnect the cable from the negative battery terminal.
2   Remove the screws from the back of the steering wheel and pull off the horn button or centre pad.
3   Mark the steering wheel hub and the column shaft with paint to ensure correct repositioning during reassembly.
4   Unscrew the steering wheel nut and remove the wheel using a steering wheel puller **(see illustration)**.

12.8a Remove the shackle pin nuts, pull the inner shackle plate off the pins and remove the rear end of the leaf spring

12.8b Remove the hanger pin nut (arrow), push the pin out of the frame bracket using a punch or drift and pull the leaf spring out of the bracket

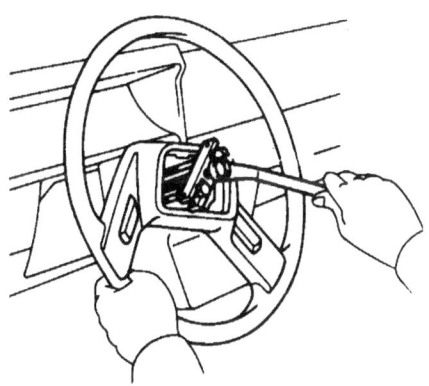

13.4 Remove the wheel from the shaft with a puller - DO NOT hammer on the shaft

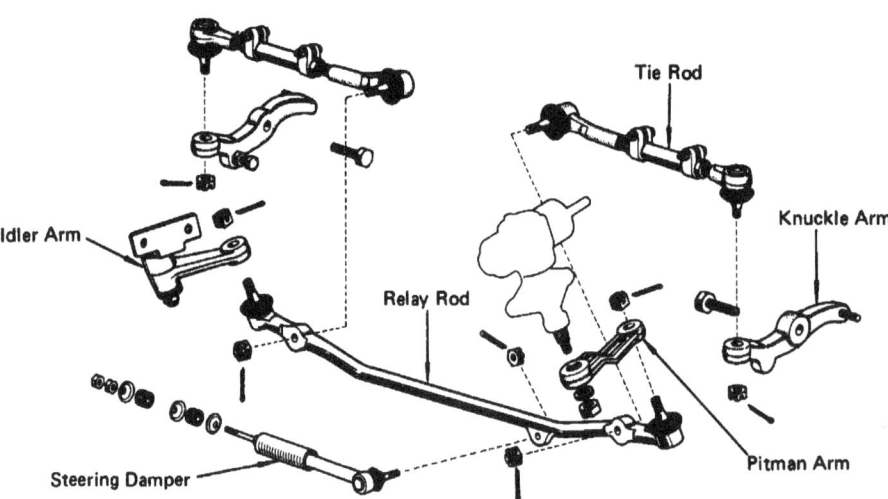

14.4 Exploded view of the steering linkage

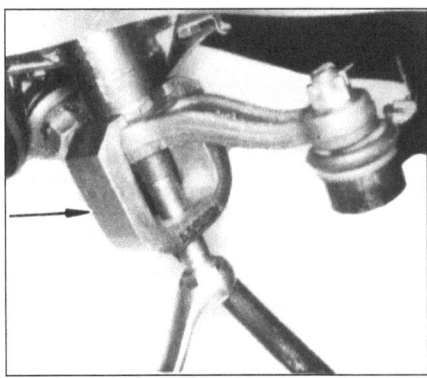

14.6 Use a puller to remove the Pitman arm - don't attempt to prise it off the sector shaft

Note: *Do not hammer on the wheel or the shaft to separate them.*

Refitting

5   Realign the steering wheel and the column shaft using the match marks. refit and tighten the retaining nut to the specified torque, then attach the horn button or centre pad.
6   Hook up the negative battery cable to the battery.

---

14   Steering linkage - removal and refitting

---

1   All steering linkage removal and refitting procedures should be performed with the front end of the vehicle raised and placed securely on jackstands.
2   Before removing any steering linkage components, obtain a balljoint separator. It may be a screw-type puller or a wedge-type tool, although the wedge-type tool tends to damage the balljoint seals. It is possible to jar a balljoint taper pin free from its eye by strik-ing opposite sides of the eye simultaneously with two large hammers, but the space available to do so is usually very limited.
3   After refitting any of the steering linkage components, the front wheel alignment should be checked by a reputable front end alignment and repair shop.

Pitman arm

Refer to illustrations 14.4 and 14.6

4   Remove the nut securing the Pitman arm to the steering gearbox sector shaft **(see illustration)**.
5   Scribe or paint match marks on the arm and shaft.
6   Using a puller, disconnect the Pitman arm from the shaft splines **(see illustration)**.
7   Remove the split pin and castle nut securing the Pitman arm to the relay rod.
8   Using a puller, disconnect the Pitman arm from the relay rod.
9   Refitting is the reverse of the removal procedure. Be sure to tighten the nuts to the specified torque.

Tie-rod

Refer to illustrations 14.12 and 14.13

10   Remove the split pins and castle nuts

securing the tie-rod to the relay rod and knuckle arm **(see illustration 14.4)**.
11   Separate the tie-rod from the relay rod and knuckle arm with a puller.
12   Before refitting, if both tie-rods have been removed and disassembled, adjust the tie-rod ends in the adjusting clamps until the measurements are equal **(see illustration)**. The tie-rods should be approximately 314 mm long, on 2WD models or 328.5 mm on 4Runner models **(see illustration)**.
13   Turn the tie-rod ends so they are at approximately 90-degree angles to each other, then tighten the adjusting tube clamps to lock the ends in position **(see illustration)**.
14   The remaining refitting steps are the reverse of those for removal. Make sure to tighten the nuts to the specified torque.

Relay rod

15   Remove the split pins and castle nuts securing the tie-rod ends to the relay rod **(see illustration 14.4)**.
16   Remove the split pin and castle nut securing the steering damper to the relay rod.
17   Remove the split pin and castle nut securing the relay rod to the Pitman arm.
18   Remove the split pin and castle nut securing the relay rod to the idler arm.
19   Using a puller, separate the relay rod from the tie-rod ends, steering damper, Pitman arm and idler arm.

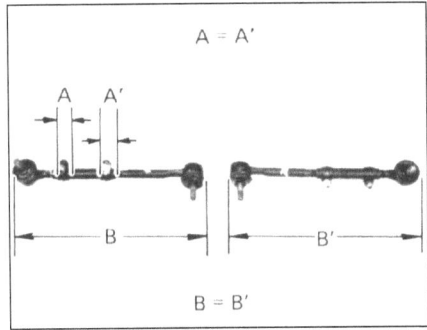

14.12 The exposed thread area (A) and the adjusting clamp position should be equal on both sides of the sleeve. The overall length of the tie-rods (B) should be approximately 314 mm (2WD models) or 328.5 mm (4Runner models)

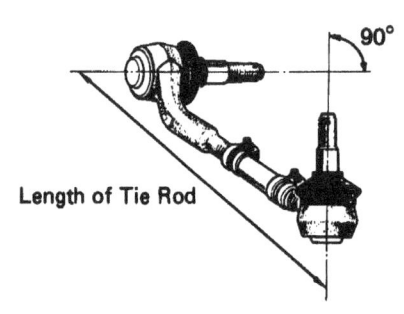

14.13 The tie-rod balljoint studs should be situated at 90-degrees to each other

14.24 Unbolting the knuckle arm from the steering knuckle

15.2 Apply an alignment mark from the steering shaft coupling to the steering gear worm shaft

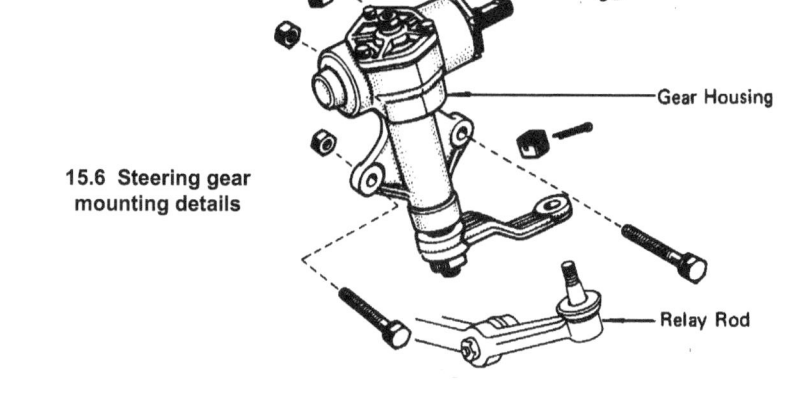

15.6 Steering gear mounting details

Coupling

Gear Housing

Relay Rod

20   Refitting is the reverse of the removal procedures. Be sure to tighten all nuts to the specified torque.

Knuckle arm

Refer to illustration 14.24

21   Remove the split pin and castle nut securing the tie-rod end to the knuckle arm.
22   Using a puller, separate the tie-rod end from the knuckle arm.
23   Remove the front axle hub (see Chapter 1).
24   Unbolt the knuckle arm from the steering knuckle and remove the knuckle arm **(see illustration)**.
25   Refitting is the reverse of the removal procedure. Be sure to tighten all nuts and bolts to the specified torque.

Steering damper

26   Remove the split pin and castle nut securing the damper to the relay rod **(see illustration 14.4)**.
27   Using a puller, separate the damper end from the relay rod.
28   Using two wrenches, remove the locknut and mounting nut securing the damper to the front axle and remove the damper.
29   When refitting, connect the damper to the tie-rod first, then attach the damper to the front axle. Make sure the cushions and washers are refitted in the proper order and tighten all nuts to the specified torque.

---

15   Steering gear - removal and refitting

Refer to illustrations 15.2 and 15.6

Note: *If you find that the gearbox is defective, it is not recommended that you overhaul it. Because of the special tools needed to do the job, it is best to let a dealer service department or other qualified repair shop overhaul it for you (or you can renew it with a factory*

rebuilt unit). However, you can remove and refit it yourself by following the procedure outlined here.*

The removal and refitting procedures for manual steering and power steering gear housings are identical except that the inlet and outlet lines must be removed from the steering gear housing on power steering equipped models before the housing can be removed.

The steering system should be filled and power steering systems should be bled after the gear housing is refitted (see Section 18).
1   Raise the front of the vehicle and place it securely on jackstands.
2   Place an alignment mark on the steering coupling and the gear housing worm shaft to assure correct reassembly **(see illustration)**, then remove the coupling bolt.
3   Loosen the Pitman arm set nut at the bottom of the steering gear housing.
4   Remove the split pin and castle nut securing the relay rod end to the Pitman arm.
5   Using a puller, disconnect the relay rod end from the Pitman arm **(see illustration 14.6)**.
6   Remove the bolts securing the gear housing to the chassis and pull the gear housing from the coupling **(see illustration)**.
7   Refitting is the reverse of the removal procedure except that the Pitman arm nut should be tightened before the Pitman arm is connected to the relay rod end. Be sure to tighten all nuts and bolts to the specified torque.

---

16   Steering freeplay - adjustment

Refer to illustration 16.6

1   Raise the vehicle with a jack so that the front wheels are off the ground and place the vehicle securely on jackstands.
2   Point the wheels straight ahead. Turn the steering wheel back-and-forth in its freeplay. If

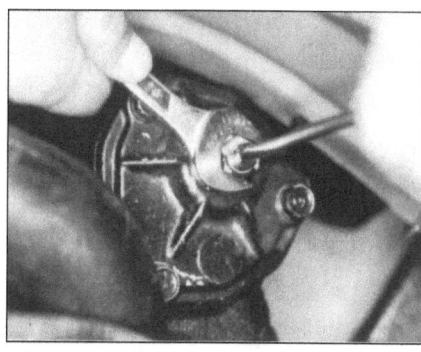

16.6 The adjusting screw must be held stationary while tightening the locknut

the freeplay is greater than that listed in this Chapter's Specifications, adjust the steering freeplay.
3   Using a spanner, loosen the locknut on the steering gearbox.
4   Turn the adjusting screw clockwise to decrease steering wheel freeplay and counterclockwise to increase it. **Note:** *Turn the adjusting screw in small increments, checking the steering wheel freeplay between them.*
5   Turn the steering wheel halfway around in both directions, checking that the freeplay is correct and that the steering is smooth.
6   Hold the adjusting screw so that it will not turn, then tighten the locknut securely **(see illustration)**.
7   Remove the jackstands and lower the vehicle.

---

17   Power steering pump - removal and refitting

Refer to illustrations 17.2, 17.3, 17.5, 17.7a and 17.7b

Note: *If you find that the steering pump is defective, it is not recommended that you overhaul it. Because of the special tools needed to do the job, it is best to let a dealer*

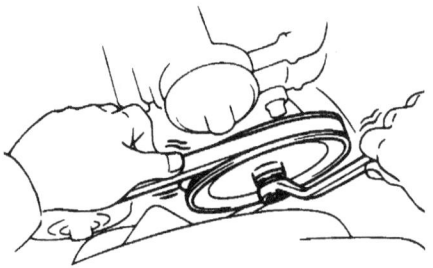

17.2 Push down on the drivebelt sufficiently to prevent the pump pulley from turning when the pulley nut is loosened

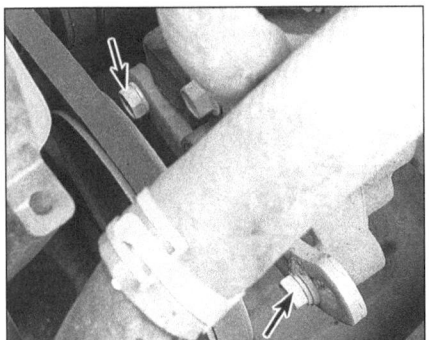

17.3 Location of the power steering pump adjustment (lower arrow) and pivot (upper arrow) bolts

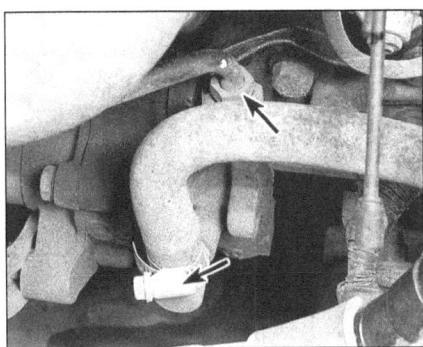

17.5 Location of the power steering pump pressure (upper arrow) and return (lower arrow) lines

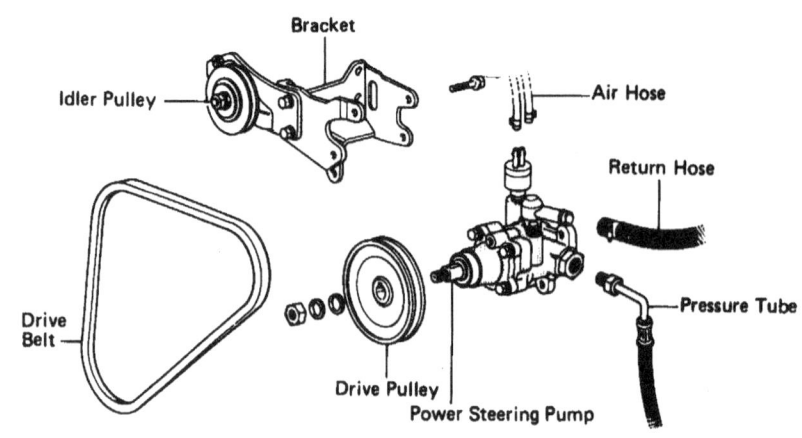

17.7a Power steering pump mounting details - four-cylinder engine (typical)

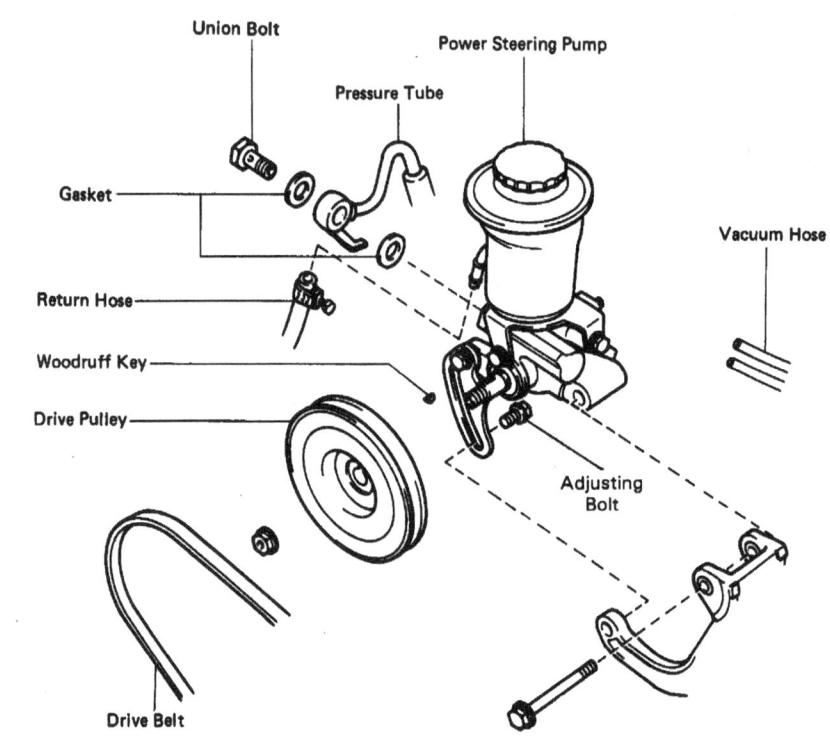

17.7b Power steering pump mounting details - V6 engine

service department or other qualified repair shop overhaul it for you (or you can renew it with a factory rebuilt unit). However, you can remove it yourself using the procedures which follow.

Removal

1   Disconnect the cable from the negative terminal of the battery.
2   Push on the drivebelt to increase its tension sufficiently to prevent the pulley from turning and loosen the drive pulley nut **(see illustration)**.
3   Loosen the adjusting bolt and remove the drivebelt **(see illustration)**.
4   Remove the drive pulley nut and the drive pulley.

5   Using a flare nut-wrench (except V6 models), loosen and disconnect the pressure hose **(see illustration)**. Position a suitable container so as to catch the pump fluid and plug the hose to prevent contamination. On V6 models, remove the union bolt.
6   Loosen the return line hose clamp, pull off the hose and plug it to prevent contamination. On later models, also mark and disconnect the hoses from the air control valve.
7   Remove the pump mounting bolts and lift the pump out of the engine compartment **(see illustrations)**.

Refitting

8   Refitting is the reverse of the removal procedure. When refitting the pressure

line, make sure there is sufficient clearance between the line and the exhaust manifold.
9   To adjust the drivebelt tension, see Chapter 1.
10   Fill the power steering fluid reservoir with the specified fluid and bleed the power steering system (see Section 18).
11   Check for fluid leaks.

18 Power steering system - bleeding

1   Check the fluid in the reservoir and add fluid of the specified type if it is low.
2   Jack up the front of the vehicle and place it securely on jackstands.

3   With the engine off, turn the steering wheel fully in both directions two or three times.

4   Recheck the fluid in the reservoir and add more fluid if necessary.

5   Start the engine and turn the steering wheel fully in both directions two or three times. The engine should be running at 1000 rpm or less.

6   Remove the jackstands and lower the vehicle completely.

7   With the engine running at 1000 rpm or less, turn the steering wheel fully in both directions two or three times.

8   Return the steering wheel to the centre position.

9   Check that the fluid is not foamy or cloudy.

10   Measure the fluid level with the engine running.

11   Turn the engine and again measure the fluid level. It should rise no more than 5 mm when the engine is turned off.

12   If a problem is encountered, repeat Steps 7 through 11.

13   If the problem persists, remove the pump (see Section 17), and have the pump repaired by a qualified service facility, or renew it.

19   Front end alignment - general information

Refer to illustration 19.1

A front end alignment refers to the adjustments made to the front wheels so they are in proper angular relationship to the suspension and the ground. Front wheels that are out of proper alignment not only affect steering control, but also increase tyre wear. The front end adjustments normally required are camber, caster and toe-in (**see illustration**).

Getting the proper front wheel alignment is a very exacting process, one in which complicated and expensive machines are necessary to perform the job properly. Because of this, you should have a technician with the proper equipment perform these tasks. We will, however, use this space to give you a basic idea of what is involved with front end alignment so you can better understand the process and deal intelligently with the shop that does the work.

Toe-in is the turning in of the front wheels. The purpose of a toe specification is to ensure parallel rolling of the front wheels. In a vehicle with zero toe-in, the distance between the front edges of the wheels will be

the same as the distance between the rear edges of the wheels. The actual amount of toe-in is normally only a couple of millimeters or so. Toe-in adjustment is controlled by the tie-rod end position on the inner tie rod. Incorrect toe-in will cause the tyres to wear improperly by making them scrub against the road surface.

Camber is the tilting of the front wheels from the vertical when viewed from the front of the vehicle. When the wheels tilt out at the top, the camber is said to be positive (+). When the wheels tilt in at the top the camber is negative (-). The amount of tilt is measured in degrees from the vertical and this measurement is called the camber angle. This angle affects the amount of tyre tread which contacts the road and compensates for changes in the suspension geometry when the vehicle is cornering or travelling over an undulating surface. Camber on some models is adjusted by adding or subtracting shims equally from each end of the upper control arm mount. On other models it's adjusted by turning the cam bolts on the lower suspension arm.

Caster is the tilting of the front steering axis from the vertical. A tilt toward the rear is positive caster and a tilt toward the front is negative caster. Caster angle affects the self-centering action of the steering, which governs straight-line stability. Caster is adjusted on some models by moving shims from one end of the upper control arm mount to the other. On other models it's adjusted by turning the cam bolts on the lower suspension arm.

20   Wheels - general information

Wheels can be damaged by an impact with a curb or other solid object. If the wheels are bent, the result is a hazardous condition which must be corrected. To check the wheels, raise the vehicle and set it on jackstands. Visually inspect the wheels for obvious signs of damage such as cracks and deformation.

Tyre and wheel balance is very important to the overall handling, braking and ride performance of the vehicle. Whenever a tyre is dismounted for repair or renewal, the tyre and wheel assembly should be balanced before being refitted on the vehicle.

Wheels should be periodically cleaned, especially on the inside, where mud and road salts accumulate and eventually cause rust and, ultimately, possible wheel failure.

Tyres are extremely important from a safety standpoint. The tread should be

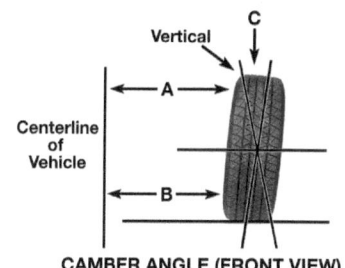

CAMBER ANGLE (FRONT VIEW)

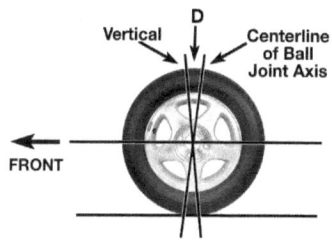

CASTER ANGLE (SIDE VIEW)

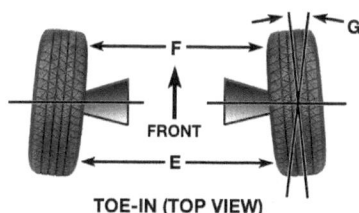

TOE-IN (TOP VIEW)

19.1 Front end alignment details

A minus B = C (degrees camber)
D = caster (measured in degrees)
E minus F = toe-in (measured in inches or millimeters)
G = toe-in (expressed in degrees)

checked periodically to see that the tyres have not worn excessively, a condition which can be dangerous, especially in wet weather.

To equalize wear and add life to a set of tyres, it is recommended that they be rotated periodically. When rotating, check for signs of abnormal wear and foreign objects in the tread or sidewalls (refer to Chapter 1, Routine Maintenance).

Proper tyre inflation is essential for maximum life of the tread and for proper handling and braking.

Tyres that are wearing in an abnormal way are an indication that their inflation is incorrect or that the front end components are not adjusted properly. Take the vehicle to a reputable front end alignment and repair shop to correct the situation.

Chapter 10 Part B
Suspension and steering systems (4WD)

Contents

Specifications

General

Steering wheel free play	Less than 30 mm
Steering gearbox oil level	See Chapter 1
Drivebelt tension	See Chapter 1
Stub axle alternate spacer available thickness (4WD models with independent front suspension)	1.80 mm and 2.25 mm

Torque specifications   Nm

Front suspension (models with a solid front axle)

Torque rod mounting bolts	
RN/LN 30, 40 series	166
YN/RN/LN50, 60, 80, 90, 105, 106, 110 series	142
Leaf spring hanger pin bolts	11 to 15
U-bolt nuts	
RN/LN 30, 40 series	146
YN/RN/LN50, 60, 80, 90, 105, 106, 110 series	123
Hanger pin and shackle pin mounting nuts	
RN/LN 30, 40 series	107
YN/RN/LN50, 60, 80, 90, 105, 106, 110 series	
Rubber bush type	91
Pressed-in bush type	157

Front suspension (models with independent front suspension)

Lower suspension arm-to-frame bolt nuts	196
Upper suspension arm-to-frame bolts	178
Upper balljoint-to-steering knuckle	142
Lower suspension arm-to-lower balljoint	142
Lower balljoint-to-steering knuckle	58
Upper suspension arm-to-upper balljoint	
Hi-Lux	25
4Runner	33
Steering knuckle arm-to-steering knuckle	183

Rear suspension (leaf-spring rear suspension)

Hanger pin lock bolts	
YN/LN50, 60 series	13
YN/RN/LN80, 90, 105, 106, 110 series	25
U-bolt mounting nuts	123
Hanger pin/shackle pin nut	
RN/LN 30, 40 series	107
YN/LN50, 60 series	
With bolt-type hanger pin	108
Hanger pin with two lock bolts	91

Rear suspension (leaf-spring rear suspension) (continued)

YN/RN/LN 80, 90, 105, 106, 110 series/4Runner

Rubber bush type	91
Pressed-in bush type	157

Rear suspension (four-link [coil spring] rear suspension)

Control arm nuts/bolts (upper and lower)	201
Lateral control rod bolts/nuts	
Upper	137
Lower	113
Shock absorber	
Upper nut	25
Lower bolt...	64
Stabiliser bar	
Bracket bolts	13
Link-to-bar nuts	95
Link-to-frame nuts	17

Steering

Intermediate shaft joint yoke bolts...	43
Steering gear mounting bolts	
RN/LN30, 40 series...	63
YN/RN/LN50, 60, 80, 90, 105, 106, 110 series	56
Pitman arm-to-sector shaft	
RN/LN30, 40 series...	185
YN/RN/LN50, 60, 80, 90, 105, 106, 110 series	172
Tie-rod tube clamps	
RN/LN30, 40 series/4Runner..	28
YN/RN/LN50, 60 series..	37
YN/RN/LN80, 90, 105, 106, 110 series	69
Tie-rod mounting bolts..	75 to 107
Wheel lug nuts...	See Chapter 1

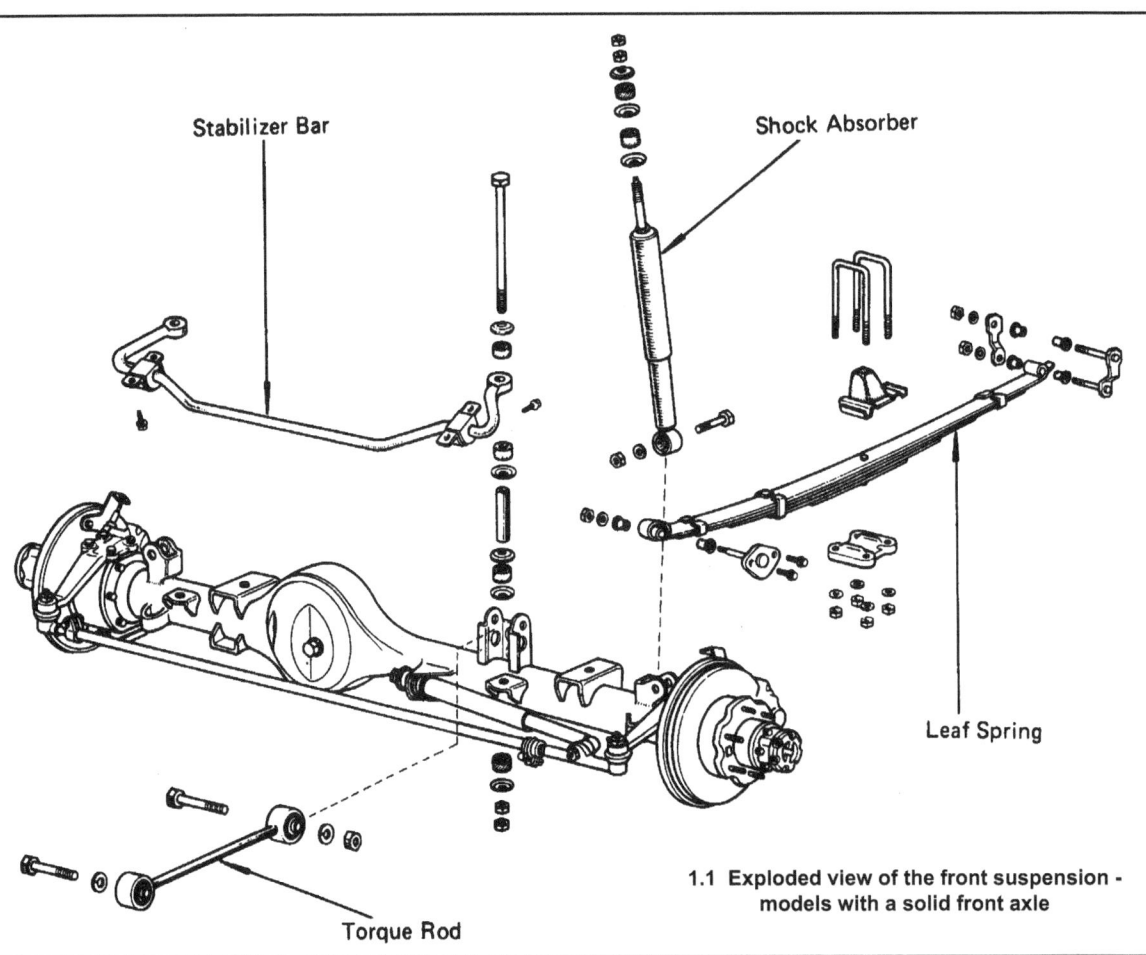

Stabilizer Bar

Shock Absorber

Leaf Spring

Torque Rod

1.1 Exploded view of the front suspension - models with a solid front axle

1   General information

Refer to illustrations 1.1 and 1.2

This Chapter deals solely with the suspension and steering components which are unique to vehicles equipped with four-wheel drive (4WD). All procedures and specifications dealing with suspension and steering that are common between the two-wheel drive (2WD) and 4WD vehicles can be found in Part A of this chapter (see Chapter 10A).

Some 4WD models utilize a conventional solid axle/leaf spring front suspension configuration **(see illustration)**. Others are equipped with a fully independent front suspension **(see illustration)**, which employs upper and lower suspension arms, torsion bar springs and driveaxles with two constant velocity (CV) joints per side.

The rear suspension on all Hi-Lux models and some 4Runner models is composed of leaf springs, shock absorbers and a solid rear axle. Other 4Runners are equipped with a four-link type rear suspension that uses coil springs, shock absorbers, and a lateral control rod and four control arms to locate the solid rear axle. A stabiliser bar is used to control body roll.

2   Front shock absorber - removal and refitting

1   Loosen the front wheel lug nuts. Raise the front of the vehicle and place it securely on jackstands.
2   Remove the front wheels.
3   Remove the two upper nuts holding the shock absorber to the frame bracket **(see illustration 1.1 or 1.2)**.
4   Remove the washers and cushions from the shaft of the shock absorber .
5   Disconnect the shock from the lower arm (or axle housing on models with a solid front axle) and remove it from the vehicle.

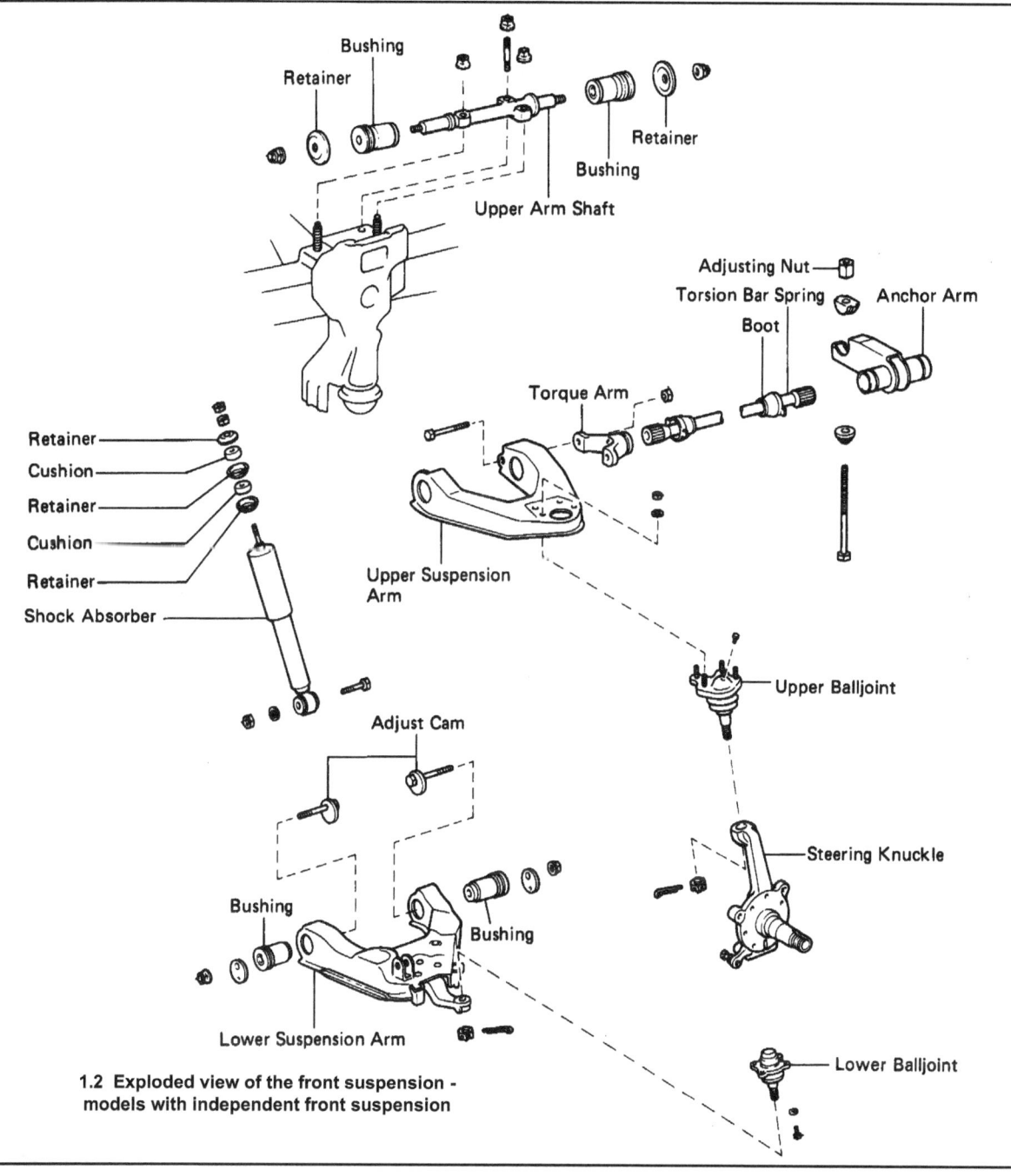

1.2 Exploded view of the front suspension - models with independent front suspension

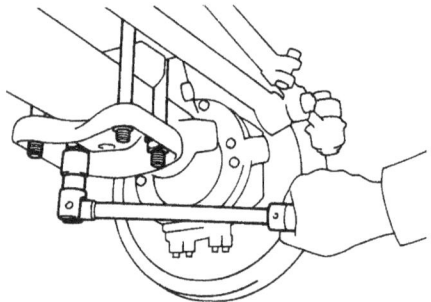

5.8 Removing the U-bolt nuts - don't do this unless the axle assembly is supported with a jack

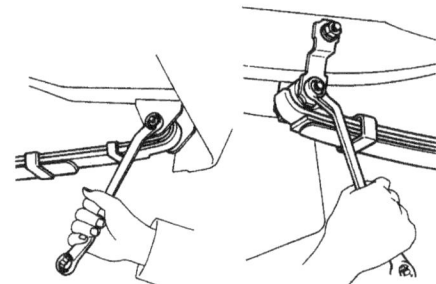

5.10 Removing the hanger pin (left) and shackle pin (right) nuts

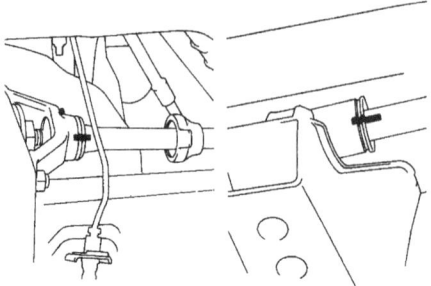

6.2 Applying match marks on the torsion bar, torque arm and anchor arm will ensure correct positioning and easy refitting of the torsion bar

6　Inspect the components for wear, damage or oil leaks. Renew parts as necessary.
7　Refitting is the reverse of the removal procedure. Make sure the washers and bushes are assembled in the proper order.

3　Front stabiliser bar - removal and refitting

1　Raise the front of the vehicle and place it securely on jackstands.
2　Remove the nuts, cushions and bolts from both ends of the stabiliser bar where it attaches to the axle housing **(see illustration 1.1)**.
3　Unbolt and remove the two stabiliser bar brackets from the frame and remove the stabiliser bar from the vehicle.
4　Inspect all parts for wear or damage. Renew parts as necessary.
5　Refitting is the reverse of the removal procedure. Make sure that the cushions are assembled and installed in the proper order and that all nuts and bolts are tightened securely.

4　Torque rod - removal and refitting

Note: *This procedure applies to models with a solid front axle only.*
1　Raise the front of the vehicle and place it securely on jackstands.
2　Remove the nut and bolt that attach the torque rod to the bracket on top of the front axle **(see illustration 1.1)**.
3　Remove the bolt retaining the torque rod to the frame and remove the torque rod from the vehicle.
4　Inspect the torque rod for damage. If necessary, renew the torque rod.
5　Inspect the bushes for wear or damage.
6　If it is necessary to renew the torque rod bushes, use a press and collar to remove the old bushes.
7　Using a press and collar, fit the new bushes. **Note:** *Position the bush holes at a right angle to the rod and press the bush in from the bevelled end.*
8　Attach the torque rod to the axle and

frame and tighten the mounting bolts finger-tight.
9　Lower the vehicle and bounce the front of it several times to stabilise the bushes.
10　Tighten the mounting bolts to the torque listed in this Chapter's Specifications.

5　Front leaf spring - removal and refitting

Refer to illustrations 5.8 and 5.10
Note: *This procedure applies to models with a solid front axle only.*

Removal

1　Loosen the wheel lug nuts, raise the front of the vehicle and support it securely on jackstands placed under the frame rails. Remove the wheels.
2　Disconnect the shock absorber from the axle housing (see Section 2 for details).
3　Disconnect the stabiliser bar from the front axle (see Section 3 for details).
4　Remove the split pin from the drag link end (see Section 12).
5　Using a screwdriver, remove the plug from the drag link end.
6　Disconnect the drag link from the knuckle arm.
7　Using a floor jack, support the axle housing.
8　Unbolt and remove the U-bolts, spring seat and spring bumper from the leaf spring **(see illustration)**.
9　Lower the jack enough to relieve tension on the leaf spring.
10　Remove the hanger pin and shackle pin from the front and rear of the front spring, respectively, and remove the spring **(see illustration)**.

Refitting

11　To refit the spring, first insert the bushes into both ends of the leaf spring.
12　Place the spring in position on the vehicle.
13　Install the hanger pin to the leaf eye and tighten the two bolts on the bracket to the specified torque.
14　Finger tighten the nut on the end of the hanger pin.

15　Install the shackle pin and finger tighten both nuts.
16　Raise the axle housing with the jack.
17　Install the spring bumper, spring seat and U-bolts.
18　Tighten the U-bolt mounting nuts to the specified torque in a criss-cross pattern. The threaded ends of the U-bolts should protrude an equal amount past each nut.
19　Raise the front axle housing until the vehicle is just clear of the jackstands. This will simulate normal ride height.
20　Tighten the front hanger pin nut and both shackle pin nuts to the specified torque, then lower the vehicle back on the jackstands.
21　Connect the stabiliser bar to the axle housing and tighten the nuts securely.
22　Connect the shock absorber to the axle housing and tighten the nut securely.
23　Insert the drag link on the knuckle arm and install the ball stud seat, spring, spring seat and plug in the drag link end.
24　Tighten the plug until it is snug, then loosen it 1-1/3 turns.
25　Secure the plug with a split pin.
26　Install the wheels, remove the jackstands and lower the vehicle. Be sure to tighten the lug nuts to the torque listed in the Chapter 1 Specifications.

6　Torsion bar - removal, refitting and adjustment

Refer to illustrations 6.2 and 6.3
Note: *This procedure applies to models with independent front suspension only.*

Removal

1　Loosen the wheel lug nuts, raise the vehicle and support it securely on jackstands. Remove the wheel.
2　Apply match marks from the torsion bar to the anchor arm and the torque arm **(see illustration)**.
3　Measure the amount of bolt protrusion from the top of the adjusting bolt nut **(see illustration)**. Record this figure for use on refitting.
4　Remove the anchor arm adjusting bolt lock nut while holding the adjusting nut with a spanner to prevent it from turning.

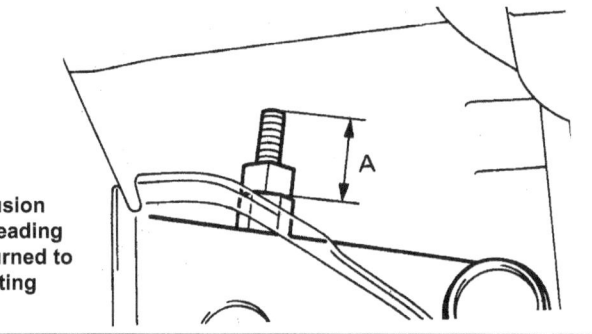

6.3 Measure the bolt protrusion distance (A) and record the reading so the suspension can be returned to the same height upon refitting

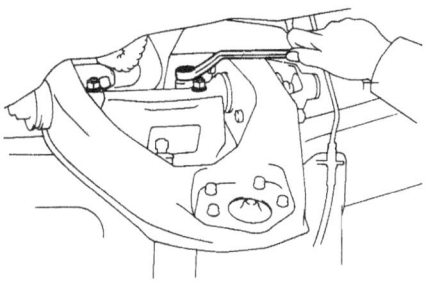

7.6 The upper suspension arm shaft is held to the frame by three bolts

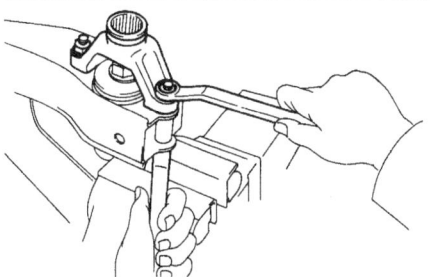

7.7 Check the torque arm splines for damage and renew it if necessary. It must also be removed if the upper arm bushes are to be renewed

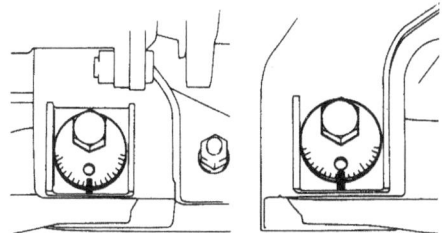

8.5 The adjusting cam bolts must be marked so they can be returned to their original settings

5   Remove the adjusting nut and bolt, then remove the anchor arm and torsion bar from the vehicle.

Refitting and adjustment

Note: *There are left and right side identification marks on the rear ends of the torsion bars* **(see illustration 5.5 in Chapter 10A)** - if both bars have been removed, be careful not to get them mixed up.

6   Apply a thin coat of moly-based grease to the splines on each end of the torsion bar.
7   Line up the match marks and insert the torsion bar into the torque arm. If you're fitting a new torsion bar, turn the torsion bar slowly until the large spline on the bar finds the large slot in the torque arm.
8   Line up the match marks on the bar with the marks on the anchor arm and slide the anchor arm onto the torsion bar. If you're fitting a new torsion bar, line-up the large spline on the anchor arm with the large spline on the torsion bar.
9   Refit the adjusting bolt and nut. Tighten the nut until the previously recorded bolt protrusion figure has been attained. Install the lock nut and tighten it securely.
10   Install the wheel and lower the vehicle. Tighten the lug nuts to the torque listed in the Chapter 1 Specifications.
11   Bounce the front end of the vehicle several times to settle the suspension.
12   Measure the vehicle's ride height on each side, from equal points on the frame to the ground. If the side that has been worked on is higher or lower than the other side, turn the torsion bar adjusting nut accordingly until the vehicle sits level. This may take a few tries, and it is important to roll the vehicle back-and-forth and jounce the front end

between adjustments, to settle the suspension and get an accurate reading. Tighten the locknut when the adjustment is correct.

7   Upper suspension arm - removal and refitting

Refer to illustrations 7.6 and 7.7

Note: *This procedure applies to models with independent front suspension only.*

Removal

1   Loosen the wheel lug nuts, raise the front of the vehicle and support it securely on jackstands. Remove the wheel.
2   Following the procedure described in Section 6, remove the torsion bar.
3   Place a floor jack under the lower suspension arm and raise it until the upper arm isn't resting on the rubber bumper stop.
4   Remove the split pin and castle nut from the upper balljoint stud and separate the balljoint from the steering knuckle with a puller (see Chapter 10 Part A, Section 8).
5   Remove the shock absorber-to-frame nut, bushes and retainers.
6   Remove the three bolts retaining the upper suspension arm shaft to the frame **(see illustration)**. It may be necessary to disconnect the steering intermediate shaft from the steering gear if you are working on the driver's side.
7   If necessary, unbolt the torque arm from the upper arm **(see illustration)**.
8   Inspect the upper arm bushes for separation, cracking and hardness. These bushes are replaceable, but due to the special tools required, it is recommended that the upper

arm be taken to an automotive machine shop or garage to have the new bushes pressed in.

Refitting

9   Position the upper arm on the frame rail and refit the three bolts, tightening them to the specified torque.
10   Insert the balljoint stud into the steering knuckle and refit the castle nut, tightening it to the specified torque. Fit a new split pin.
11   Insert the shock absorber rod through its hole in the frame and refit the retainers, bush and nut. Tighten the nut securely.
12   Install the torsion bar.
13   Install the wheel and lug nuts. Lower the vehicle and tighten the nuts to the torque listed in the Chapter 1 Specifications.

8   Lower suspension arm - removal and refitting

Refer to illustrations 8.5 and 8.7

Note: *This procedure applies to models with independent front suspension only.*

Removal

1   Loosen the wheel lug nuts, raise the vehicle and support it securely on jackstands. Remove the wheel.
2   Unbolt the stabiliser bar link from the lower arm (see Section 3).
3   Disconnect the shock absorber from the lower arm (Section 2).
4   Remove the split pin and castle nut from the lower balljoint stud. Separate the balljoint from the steering knuckle using a puller or balljoint separator (see Chapter 10 Part A, Section 8).
5   Using white paint or a sharp scribe, mark the positions of the front and rear adjusting cam bolts **(see illustration)**.
6   Remove the nuts from the adjusting cam bolts and remove the lower arm from the vehicle.
7   Inspect the lower arm bushes for hardness, cracking and general deterioration. If they are worn out, it is possible to press them out using two sockets and a large vice. Position one socket against the smaller diameter side of the bush (the socket should have an outside diameter slightly smaller than the diameter of the bush) and the other socket

over the other side of the bush. Place the assembly in a vice and tighten the vice until the small socket forces the bush into the large socket **(see illustration).**

8   To fit the new bush, reverse the removal procedure and press the bush into the lower arm until it is completely seated.

Refitting

9   Position the lower arm in the frame brackets and refit the adjusting cam bolts and nuts, but don't fully tighten the nuts yet.

10   Insert the balljoint stud into the steering knuckle and refit the castle nut, tightening it to the specified torque. Install a new split pin.

11   Connect the stabiliser bar link to the lower arm.

12   Install the lower end of the shock absorber to the lower arm.

13   Install the wheel and lug nuts. Lower the vehicle and tighten the nuts to the torque listed in the Chapter 1 Specifications.

14   Bounce the vehicle several times to settle the suspension. Align the match marks on the adjusting cams and tighten the nuts to the specified torque.

15   It is a good idea to drive the vehicle to an alignment shop to have the front end alignment checked and, if necessary, adjusted.

---

9   Balljoints - renewal

Refer to Chapter 10 Part A, Section 8 for the balljoint renewal procedure for models with independent front suspension, as it is the same as the procedure for 2WD models.

---

10   Steering knuckle - removal and refitting

Refer to illustrations 10.4, 10.5, 10.6 and 10.12

Removal

Independent front suspension

1   Loosen the wheel lug nuts, raise the vehicle and support it securely on jackstands. Remove the wheel.

2   Remove the disc brake caliper and hang it out of the way with a piece of wire (see Chapter 9).

3   Remove the front axle hub (see Chapter 1, *Front wheel bearing check, repack and adjustment*).

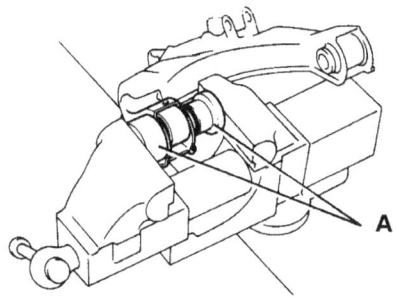

8.7 Two sockets (A) and a vice are used to press the bushes out of the lower suspension arm. The smaller socket on the inside of the bush will push the bush out of the arm and into the large socket

4   Remove the dust cover and oil seal from the steering knuckle **(see illustration).**

5   Disconnect the steering knuckle arm from the steering knuckle **(see illustration)** .

6   At this point, the steering knuckle bush thrust clearance must be measured. Thread a bolt into the end of the stub axle, grasp the bolt with a pair of pliers and pull outward on it. Using a feeler gauge, measure the clearance between the steering knuckle outside bush and the spacer on the stub axle **(see illustration)**. If the clearance is greater than 1.0 mm, the steering knuckle bushes (both outside and inside) must be renewed.

7   Unbolt the lower end of the shock absorber from the lower suspension arm.

8   Remove the stabiliser bar link-to-lower arm bolt.

9   Using a pair of snap-ring pliers, remove the snap-ring from the stub axle. Slide the spacer off the stub axle, too.

10   Remove the castle nuts from the upper and lower balljoint studs then separate the balljoints from the steering knuckle using a puller or balljoint separator (see Chapter 10 Part A, Section 8 if necessary).

11   Push the knuckle and lower arm down to disconnect the knuckle from the upper balljoint. Disconnect the knuckle from the lower balljoint stud, then slide the knuckle off the stub axle. **Note:** *Make sure the driveaxle is supported by the lower arm or hang it by a piece of wire once it has been freed from the knuckle - don't let it hang unsupported, as the inner CV joint may be damaged.*

12   Prise the dust deflector from the steering knuckle **(see illustration).**

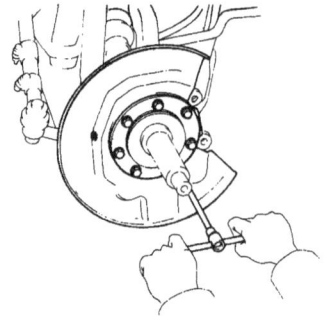

10.4 Remove the dust cover bolts and the oil seal

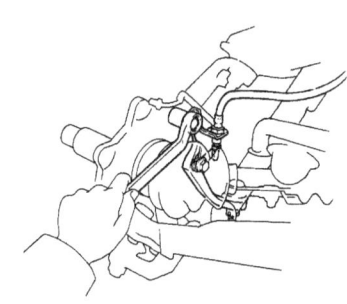

10.5 Unbolt the knuckle arm from the steering knuckle

13   If, after the measurement taken in Step 6, it has been determined that the steering knuckle bushes are in need of renewal, take the knuckle to an automotive repair shop or dealer service department to have the new bushes fitted.

Refitting

14   Apply a moly-based grease to the steering knuckle inside and outside bushes.

15   Refit a new dust deflector by gently tapping around the outer circumference until it is seated.

16   Lubricate the stub axle splines with moly-based grease. Slide the knuckle over the axle and insert the upper and lower balljoint studs into the knuckle. refit the castle nuts and tighten them to the specified torque. refit new split pins.

17   Refit the spacer and snap-ring on the stub axle, making sure the snap-ring seats in the groove.

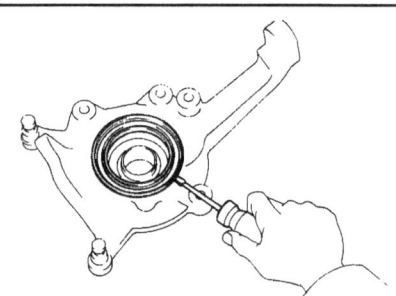

10.12 The dust deflector can be pried out of the knuckle with a screwdriver

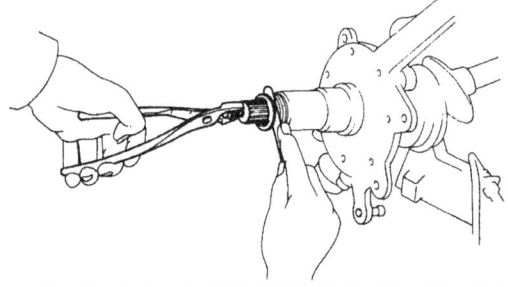

10.6 Pull outward on the axle shaft and measure the gap between the outside steering knuckle bush and the spacer

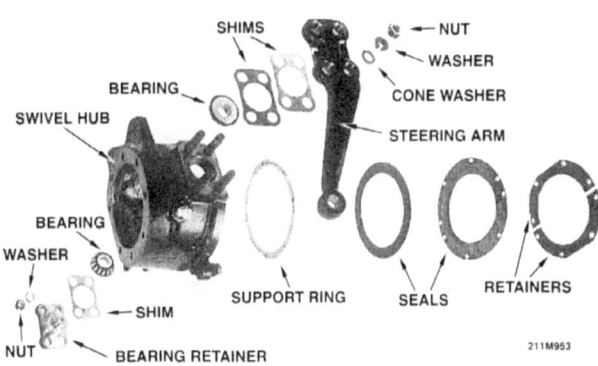

10.30 Typical swivel hub components

18 If the knuckle inside and outside bushes have been renewed, check the drive-axle thrust clearance using the technique described in Step 6. The clearance should be 0.075 to 0.690 mm. If it isn't within this range, change the spacer with one of a different thickness (refer to the Specifications at the front of this Chapter).
19 Connect the stabiliser bar to the lower arm.
20 Attach the shock absorber to the lower arm and tighten the nut securely .
21 Apply a thread sealant to the threads of the steering knuckle arm bolts and refit the arm, tightening the bolts to the specified torque.
22 Refit the dust cover and new oil seal. Tighten the bolts securely.
23 Refit the front axle hub (Chapter 1).
24 Refit the brake caliper and bleed the brakes if the brake line was disconnected (Chapter 9).
25 Refit the wheel and lug nuts. Lower the vehicle and tighten the lug nuts to the torque listed in the Chapter 1 Specifications.

Solid axle front suspension

To remove and install

26 Loosen the front wheel nuts.
27 Raise the front of the vehicle and support it on chassis stands positioned under the chassis side rails. Remove the front wheel.
28 Remove the front hub and axle shaft as previously described.
29 Remove the split pin and castellated nut retaining the tie rod end ball joint to the swivel hub steering arm. Disconnect the ball joint stud from the steering arm using a separator or by placing a dolly or a hammer against the steering arm eye and striking the opposite side with a hammer.
30 If the right hand swivel hub is being removed, withdraw the split pin from the front of the steering drag link and unscrew the plug in the end of the drag link until it can be disconnected from the swivel hub steering arm (see illustration).
31 Working at the rear of the swivel hub, remove the bolts and withdrawl the oil seal retainers.

32 Remove the nuts retaining the steering arm and the bearing cap to the swivel hub.
33 Where applicable, remove the cone washers from the steering arm retaining studs by tapping the end of the studs using a hammer and brass drift.
34 Remove the steering arm and the bearing retainer from the swivel hub, using a hammer and punch where necessary. Ensure that the shims are kept with the steering arm or bearing retainer to ensure correct installation.
35 Manoeuvre the swivel hub from the axle housing ensuring that the upper and lower bearing cones are kept separate to ensure that they are installed to their original positions during assembly.
36 Remove the swivel hub seals and support ring from the axle housing.
37 If the bearing cups are being renewed, drive the upper and lower bearing cups from the axle housing using a hammer and punch.

To clean and inspect

38 Clean all components except the seals in cleaning solvent and dry with compressed air, if available. **Note:** *Do not spin the bearings with compressed air as damage to the bearings or injury to the operator may result.*
39 Check the bearing cones and cups for wear, pitting and damage, renew as necessary.
40 Inspect the swivel hub and the axle housing for wear, cracks and damage. Remove and burrs on the housing with an oil stone.
41 Check the seals for cracks and deterioration. It is recommended that the swivel hub seals be renewed.
42 Renew any components that are unserviceable.

To assembly and install

Note: *When grease is referred to in the assembly and installation procedure, use molybdenum disulphide lithium base grease unless otherwise stated.*
Assembly and installation is a reverse of the dismantling procedure with attention to the following points:
43 Where removed, install the bearing cups to the axle housing using a suitable tubular drift.

44 Using the heel of the hand, pack the swivel hub bearing cones with molybdenum disulphide lithium based grease.
45 Install the upper bearing cone to the axle housing.
46 Install the lower bearing cone to the axle housing, hold it in position and manoeuvre the swivel hub onto the axle housing.
47 Install the steering arm, the bearing retainer and their shims to the swivel hub and gently tap the bearing retainer and steering arm into position, ensuring that the bearing cones are centralised. **Note:** *If the original shims were not kept with the bearing retainer and steering arm, or if inspection of the axle shaft seal running surface in an earlier procedure indicated that the swivel hub was not centralised, it is recommended that shimming of the swivel hub be entrusted to an authorised dealer. Special tools are required to shim the swivel hub.*
48 Where applicable, install the cone washers and tighten the nuts or bolts to the specified torque.
49 With the swivel hub in the straight ahead position, connect a spring gauge to the steering arm eye at a right angle to the steering arm and measure the effort required to rotate the swivel hub on the axle housing. If the turning effort is not to Specifications, alter the thickness of the swivel hub bearing shims located under the steering arm and lower retainer. **Note:** *Shims are available in thicknesses of 0.1, 0.2, 0.5 and 1.0 mm. The turning effort will be altered by 1-2 N with each 0.1 mm alteration in thickness. Thinner shims will increase the turning effort. To ensure that the swivel hub remains centralised on the axle housing, ensure that shims of the same thickness are installed to or removed from the upper and lower bearings.*
50 Install the support ring, rubber seal and the felt seal into the swivel housing, install the retainers and tighten the bolts securely.
a51 Connect the tie rod end to the steering arm, tighten the castellated nut to the specified torque and install a new split pin.

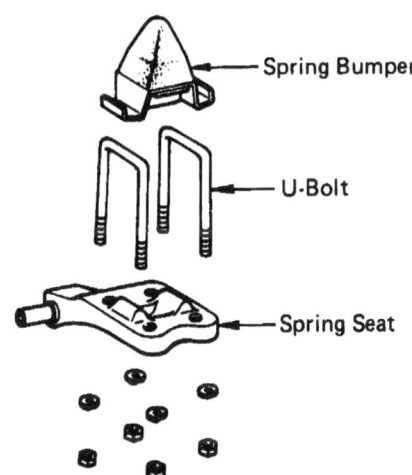

11.1 The rear spring bumper is retained by the U-bolts

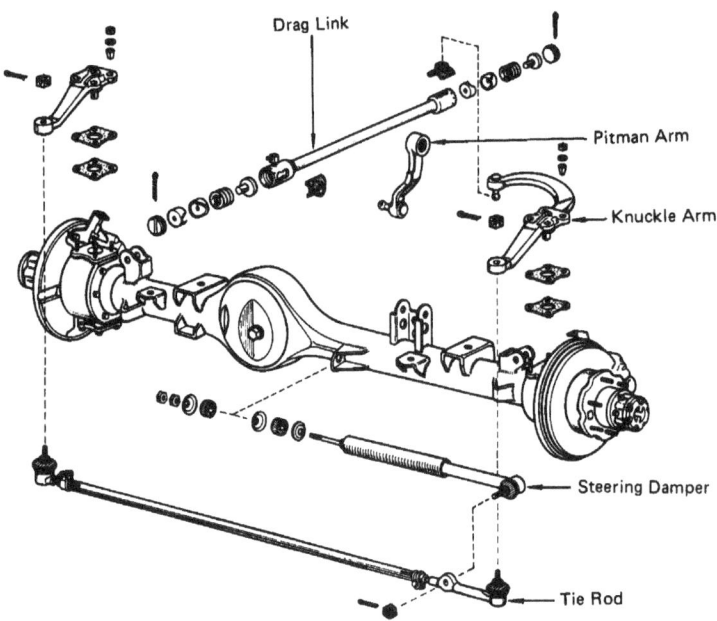

12.2 Exploded view of the steering linkage - models with a solid front axle

12.7 Mark the relationship of the Pitman arm to the steering gear sector shaft

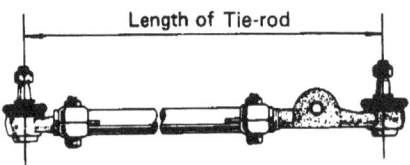

12.14 The tie-rod should be adjusted to the specified length before fitting it. An equal number of threads should be showing on each tie-rod end

52   If the right hand swivel hub was removed, connect the drag link to the steering arm as described in Part 2 of the Steering section.
53   Install the front hub and axle shaft as previously described.

---

11 Rear leaf spring - removal and refitting

Refer to illustration 11.1

Note: *The components involved and the removal and refitting procedures are the same for 4WD vehicles as for 2WD vehicles, except that a spring bumper is added to 4WD vehicles* **(see illustration)**. *The bumper is removed and installed with the spring seat and U-bolts. See Section 12 in Chapter 10 Part A.*

---

12 Steering linkage - removal and refitting

Refer to illustration 12.2

Note: *This Section pertains to 4WD models with solid front axles only. For information regarding the steering linkage on 4WD models with independent front suspension, refer to Chapter 10 Part A, as it is similar to the 2WD steering linkage.*

1   All steering linkage removal and refitting procedures should be performed with the front end of the vehicle raised and placed securely on jackstands.
2   Before removing any steering linkage components **(see illustration)**, obtain a balljoint separator. It may be a screw-type puller

or a wedge-type tool, however the latter usually tears the balljoint seal. It is possible to jar a balljoint taper pin free from its eye by striking opposite sides of the eye simultaneously with two large hammers, but the space available to do so is usually very limited.
3   After refitting any of the steering linkage components, the front wheel alignment should be checked by a reputable front end alignment and repair shop.

Pitman arm

Refer to illustration 12.7

4   Remove the split pin from the drag link end.
5   Using a screwdriver, remove the drag link plug, spring seat, spring and ball stud seat.
6   Remove the nut securing the Pitman arm to the sector shaft.
7   If none are visible, scribe alignment marks on the arm and shaft **(see illustration)**.
8   Using a puller, remove the Pitman arm from the sector shaft.
9   Refitting is the reverse of the removal procedures. Be sure to tighten the nut to the specified torque. When installing the drag link end, tighten the end until it is snug, then unscrew it 1-1/3 turns.

Tie-rod

Refer to illustrations 12.14 and 12.17

10   Remove the split pin and castle nut securing the steering damper to the tie-rod **(see illustration 12.2)**.
11   Using a puller, remove the steering damper end from the tie-rod.
12   Remove the split pins and castle nut securing the tie-rod ends to the knuckle arms.

13   Using a puller, remove the tie-rod ends from the knuckle arms.
14   When refitting the tie-rod, turn the tie-rod ends equal amounts into the tie-rod tube. The tie-rod length should be approximately 120 cm, measured from centre-to-centre of the tie-rod ends **(see illustration)**.
15   Connect the tie-rod ends to the steering arms and tighten the castle nuts to the specified torque, then fit the split pins.
16   Connect the steering damper and tighten the castle nut to the specified torque, then fit the split pin.
17   Tighten the clamp bolts securing the ends to the tie-rod. **Note:** *The clamp at the steering damper end of the tie-rod must be positioned at the front of the tie-rod and face within 45-degrees from straight down* **(see illustration)**.

Steering damper

18   Remove the split pin and castle nut connecting the steering damper to the tie-rod **(see illustration 12.2)**.
19   Using a puller, disconnect the damper from the tie-rod.
20   Using two spanneres, remove the locknut and mounting nut securing the damper to the front axle.
21   Refitting is the reverse of the removal procedure. Be sure to tighten all nuts to the specified torque.

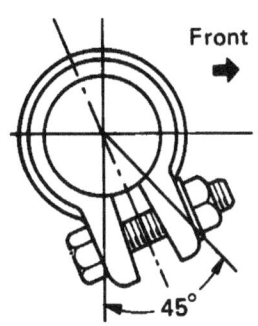

12.17 Proper clamp alignment of the steering damper end of the tie-rod when installed on the vehicle

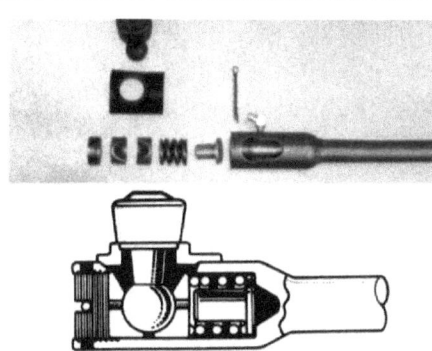

12.24a Proper assembly of drag link-to-Pitman arm components

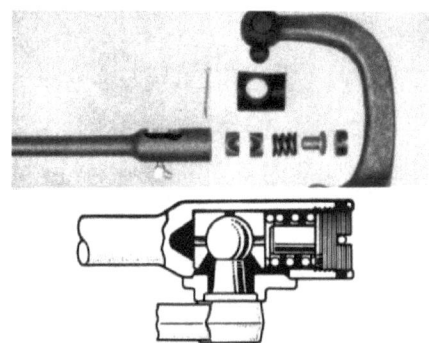

12.24b Proper assembly of drag link-to-knuckle arm components

Drag link

Refer to illustrations 12.24a and 12.24b

22   Disconnect the drag link from the Pitman arm and knuckle arm (see Steps 4 and 5).

23   Remove the drag link.

24   Refitting is the reverse of the removal procedure. Drag link-to-Pitman arm assembly order is: spring seat, spring, ball stud seal and plug **(see illustration)**. Drag link-to-knuckle arm assembly order is: ball stud seat, spring, spring seat and plug **(see illustration)**. When refitting the drag link ends, tighten the plugs until they are snug, then unscrew them 1-1/3 turns. Apply chassis grease to both grease fittings after refitting the drag link.

13   Steering intermediate shaft - removal and refitting

Refer to illustrations 13.2 and 13.6

Removal

1   Turn the front wheels to the straight ahead position.

2   Remove the joint protector **(see illustration)**.

3   Using white paint, place alignment marks on the upper universal joint, the steering shaft, the lower universal joint and the steering gear input shaft.

4   Remove the upper and lower universal joint yoke pinch bolts.

5   Prise the intermediate shaft off the steering gear shaft with a large screwdriver, then pull the shaft from the steering column.

Refitting

6   Refitting is the reverse of the removal procedure. When refitting the shaft to the upper joint, adjust the depth of the shaft so that approximately 15 mm of splined area is exposed **(see illustration)**. When connecting the lower end of the shaft, the steering gear worm shaft should penetrate 27 mm (34 mm on power steering models). Be sure to align the marks and tighten the yoke bolts to the specified torque.

14   Steering gear - removal and refitting

Refer to illustrations 14.7a and 14.7b
Note: *This procedure applies to models with*

a solid front axle only. For information pertaining to the steering gear on 4WD models with independent front suspension, refer to Chapter 10, Part A. If you find that the gearbox is defective, it is not recommended that you overhaul it. Because of the special tools needed to do the job, it is best to let your dealer service department overhaul it for you (or renew it with a factory rebuilt unit). However, you can remove and refit it yourself by following the procedure outlined here.

The removal and refitting procedures for manual steering and power steering gear housings are identical except that the pressure and return lines must be removed from the steering gear housing on power steering equipped models before the housing can be removed.

The steering system should be filled and bled after the housing is installed, (see Chapter 10A).

Removal

1   Place an alignment mark on the joint yoke and steering gear housing worm shaft to ensure correct reassembly.

2   Loosen the joint yoke bolt and compress the intermediate shaft.

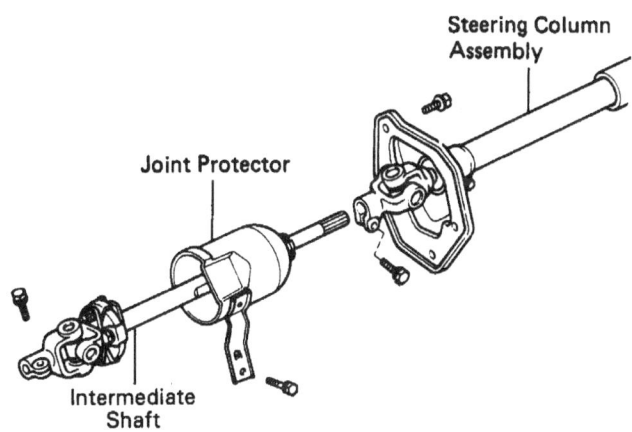

13.2 Steering intermediate shaft refitting details

Steering Column Assembly

Joint Protector

Intermediate Shaft

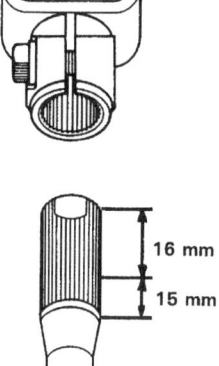

16 mm
15 mm

13.6 After attaching the intermediate shaft to the upper joint yoke, 15 mm of the spline should appear outside the yoke

14.7a Removing the steering gear mounting nuts

3   Remove the split pin and unscrew the plug from the drag link/Pitman arm connection (see Section 12).
4   Disconnect the drag link from the Pitman arm.
5   Remove the Pitman arm set nut at the end of the sector shaft.
6   Using a puller, disconnect the Pitman arm from the gear housing.
7   Remove the four bolts and take the gear housing out of the engine compartment **(see illustrations)**.

Refitting

8   When refitting the steering gear housing, first refit the gear housing with four bolts and tighten the bolts to the specified torque.
9   Align the matching marks on the joint yoke and worm shaft.
10   Compress and refit the intermediate shaft onto the worm shaft. **Note:** *The fitted depth should be 27 mm on manual steering models and 34 mm on power steering models.*
11   Tighten the joint yoke bolt to the specified torque.
12   Align the matching marks on the Pitman arm sector shaft, refit the Pitman arm and tighten the set nut to the specified torque.
13   Insert the Pitman arm into the drag link after inserting the spring retainer, spring and ball stud seat.
14   Insert the plug into the drag link end, tighten it until it is snug, then loosen it 1-1/3 turns.
15   Secure the plug with a split pin.

15 Shock absorbers (rear) - removal and refitting

Refer to illustrations 15.2 and 15.3
Note: *This procedure applies to 4Runner models with four-link (coil spring) rear suspension only.*
1   Loosen the rear wheel lug nuts, raise the rear of the vehicle and support it securely on jackstands placed under the frame rails. Remove the wheels.
2   Support the rear axle with a floor jack. Unscrew the shock absorber lower mounting bolt **(see illustration)**.

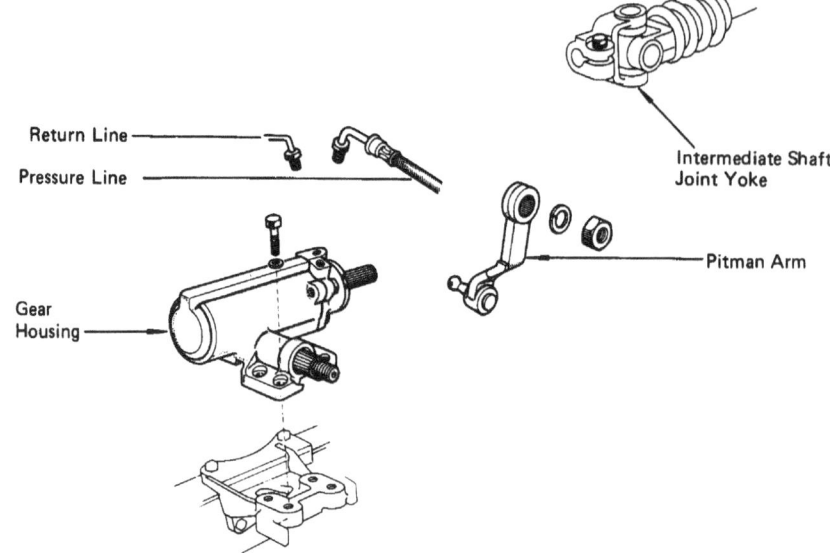

14.7b Steering gear mounting details - models with a solid front axle

3   Remove the upper mounting nut from the damper rod. It will probably be necessary to prevent the rod from turning by placing a small spanner on the flats of the rod **(see illustration)**.
4   Remove the shock absorber, noting how the bushes and washers are arranged.
5   Refitting is the reverse of removal. Tighten the mounting nuts to the torque listed in this Chapter's Specifications.

16 Coil spring (rear) - removal and refitting

Refer to illustration 16.5
Note: *This procedure applies to 4Runner models with four-link (coil spring) rear suspension only.*
1   Loosen the rear wheel lug nuts, raise the rear of the vehicle and support it securely on jackstands placed under the frame rails. Remove the wheels.

2   Support the rear axle with a floor jack placed under the axle tube nearest the coil spring to be removed, then unscrew the shock absorber lower mounting bolt from the same side **(see illustration 15.2)**.
3   Unbolt the upper end of the lateral control rod from the frame (see Section 17).
4   Disconnect the stabiliser bar from the rear axle housing (see Section 18).
5   Slowly lower the floor jack until the coil spring is fully extended. Remove the coil spring and insulators **(see illustration)**. **Caution:** *Be careful not to stretch the brake hose or parking brake cables while doing this.*
6   Inspect the coil spring for nicks and rust, which could cause premature failure. Inspect the insulators for cracking and general deterioration. Renew parts as required.
7   Refitting is the reverse of removal. Make sure the upper insulator is properly seated on the top of the coil spring, and that the lower insulator is resting properly on the rear axle housing.

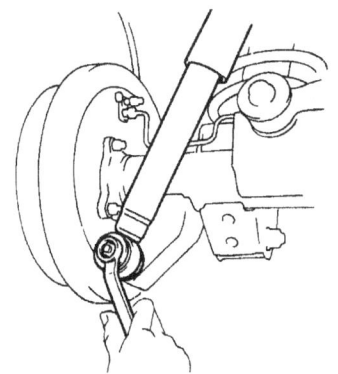

15.2 Remove the shock absorber lower mounting nut . . .

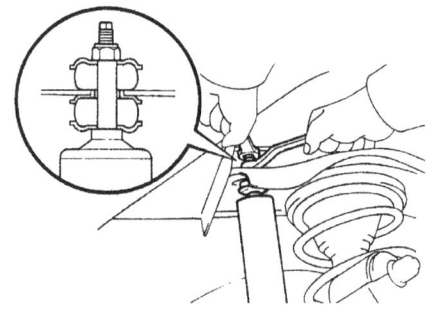

15.3 . . . followed by the upper nut (prevent the damper rod from turning by holding it with a spanner while loosening the nut with another spanner)

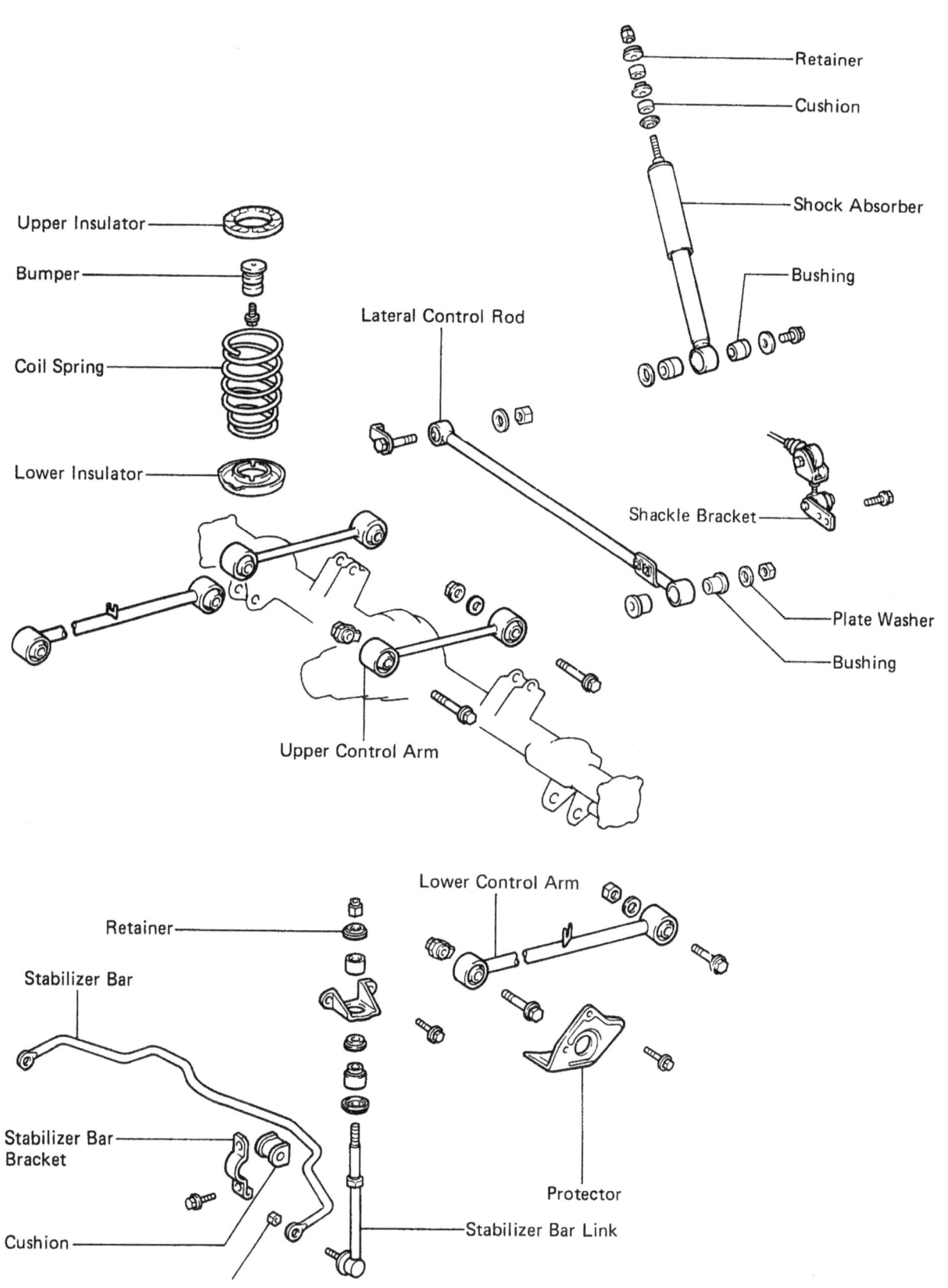

16.5 Four-link (coil spring) type rear suspension - exploded view

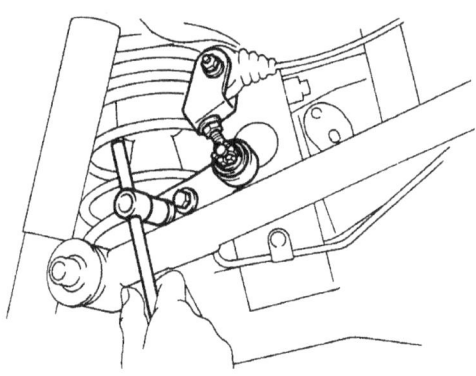

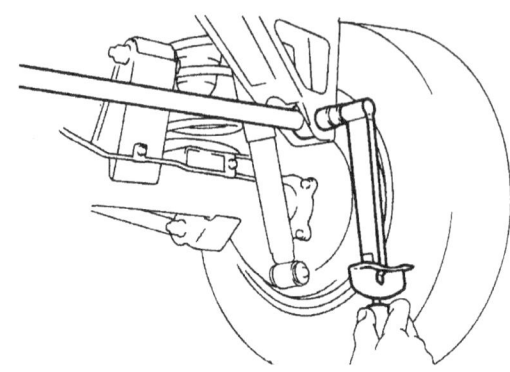

17.4 Remove these two bolts to detach the LSPV from the lateral control rod, then remove the nut from the lower (left end) of the rod

17.5 Unscrew the bolt from the upper (right end) of the lateral control rod and remove the rod from the vehicle

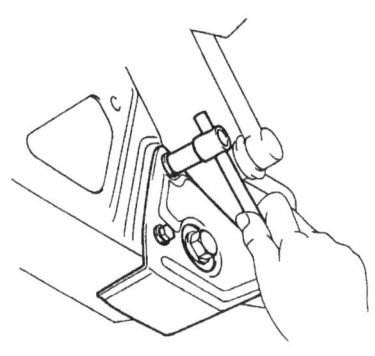

17.8 If you're removing a lower control arm, you'll have to remove this protector for access to the front mounting bolt

17   Rear suspension control arms and lateral control rod - removal and refitting

Note: *This procedure applies to 4Runner models with four-link (coil spring) rear suspension only.*
1   Loosen the rear wheel lug nuts, raise the rear of the vehicle and support it securely on jackstands placed under the frame rails. Remove the wheels.
2   Support the rear axle with a jack placed under the differential.

Lateral control rod

Refer to illustrations 17.4 and 17.5
3   Disconnect the lower end of the right-side shock absorber from the rear axle.
4   Unbolt the shackle bracket for the Load Sensing Proportioning Valve (LSPV) linkage **(see illustration)**.
5   Remove the nut securing the lower end of the lateral control rod from the rear axle housing, then remove the bolt securing the arm to the frame **(see illustration)**. Remove the rod, noting how the bushes and washers are arranged.
6   Refitting is the reverse of removal. Tighten the nut and bolt to the torque values listed in this Chapter's Specifications. Be sure to tighten the wheel lug nuts to the torque listed in the Chapter 1 Specifications.

Upper and lower control arms

Refer to illustration 17.8
Note: *Remove and refit only one arm at a time.*
7   If you're removing a lower control arm, unbolt the parking brake cable from the lower control arm.
8   If you're removing a lower control arm, unscrew the two bolts and detach the protector from the front of the lower control arm **(see illustration)**.
9   Remove the bolts, washers and nuts from each end of the arm, then detach the arm from the vehicle **(see illustration 16.5)**.
10   Refitting is the reverse of removal, but before tightening the fasteners to the torque values listed in this Chapter's Specifications,

lower the vehicle, jounce the suspension a few times, then raise the vehicle and support it securely on jackstands once again. Raise the rear axle with a floor jack to simulate normal ride height, then tighten the bolts to the torque listed in this Chapter's Specifications.
11   Be sure to tighten the wheel lug nuts to the torque listed in the Chapter 1 Specifications.

18   Stabiliser bar (rear) - removal and refitting

Note: *This procedure applies to 4Runner models with four-link (coil spring) rear suspension only.*
1   Raise the rear of the vehicle and support it securely on jackstands placed under the frame rails. Remove the wheels.
2   Support the rear axle with a jack placed under the differential. Unbolt the stabiliser bar links from each end of the bar **(see illustration 16.5)**.
3   If the bushes at the upper ends of the links look deteriorated, unscrew the nuts and remove the links from the frame, noting how the bushes and washers are arranged.
4   Unbolt the stabiliser bar brackets from the rear axle housing and remove the bar from the vehicle. Check the bracket bushes for hardness, cracking and other signs of deterioration, renewing them if necessary.
5   Refitting is the reverse of removal. Tighten the fasteners to the torque values listed in this Chapter's Specifications.

Chapter 11   Body

Contents

Specifications

Door glass trailing edge-to-channel clearance
  RN/LN30, 40 Series
    With ventilator window .... 82 mm
    Without ventilator window .... 114 mm
  YN/LN50, 60 series
    With ventilator window .... 213.5 mm
    Without ventilator window .... 276 mm
  YN/LN80, 90, 106, 110, RN/LN80, 90, 105, 110 series
    Front door (with or without vent window) .... 278.4 mm
    Rear door 80.3mm
  YN130, RN125, 130 series, 4Runner
    Without ventilator window
      Two door .... 278.4 mm
      Four door .... 170.2 mm
    With ventilator window
      Two door .... 278.4 mm
      Four door .... 175 mm

1   General information

All models covered by this manual are constructed on a separate channel-section frame and all cabs are of welded steel construction.

Short and long wheelbase models are available in a variety of trim levels and in two-wheel drive (2WD) and four-wheel drive (4WD) types.

2   Body exterior - maintenance

1   The condition of your vehicle's body is of considerable importance as it is on this that the resale value will mainly depend. It is much more difficult to repair neglected bodywork than to renew mechanical components.

The hidden portions of the body, such as the wheel arches, fender skirts, frame and engine compartment, are equally important, although obviously not requiring as frequent attention as the exterior paint.
2   Once a year or every 20,000 kilometres it is a good idea to have the underside of the body steam cleaned. All traces of dirt and oil will have to be removed and the underside can then be inspected carefully for rust, damaged hydraulic brake lines, frayed electrical wiring and similar problems. The front suspension should be greased after completion of this job.
3   At the same time, clean the engine and the engine compartment with a water-soluble cleaner.
4   The fender wells should be given particular attention, since undercoating can easily come away and stones and dirt thrown up from the wheels can soon cause the paint to

chip and flake and allow rust to set in. If rust is found, clean down to the bare metal and apply an anti-rust paint.
5   The body should be washed once a week or when dirty. Thoroughly wet the vehicle to soften the dirt and then wash it down with a soft sponge and plenty of clean water. If the surplus dirt is not washed off very gently, in time it will wear the paint down.
6   Spots of tar thrown up from the road surfaces are best removed with a cloth soaked in a cleaner made especially for this purpose.
7   Once every six months, or more frequently, depending on the weather conditions, give the body and chrome trim a thorough wax job. If a chrome cleaner is used to remove rust on any of the vehicle's plated parts, remember that the cleaner can also remove part of the chrome, so use it sparingly.

These photos illustrate a method of repairing simple dents. They are intended to supplement *Body repair - minor damage* in this Chapter and should not be used as the sole instructions for body repair on these vehicles.

1 If you can't access the backside of the body panel to hammer out the dent, pull it out with a slide-hammer-type dent puller. In the deepest portion of the dent or along the crease line, drill or punch hole(s) at least one inch apart . . .

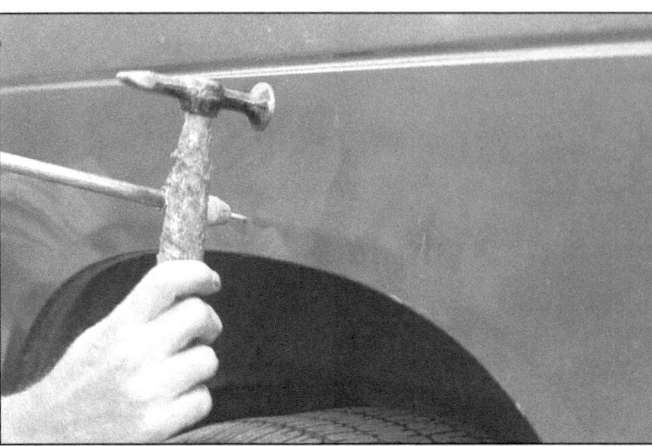

2 . . . then screw the slide-hammer into the hole and operate it. Tap with a hammer near the edge of the dent to help 'pop' the metal back to its original shape. When you're finished, the dent area should be close to its original contour and about 3 mm below the surface of the surrounding metal

3 Using coarse-grit sandpaper, remove the paint down to the bare metal. Hand sanding works fine, but the disc sander shown here makes the job faster. Use finer (about 320-grit) sandpaper to feather-edge the paint at least one inch around the dent area

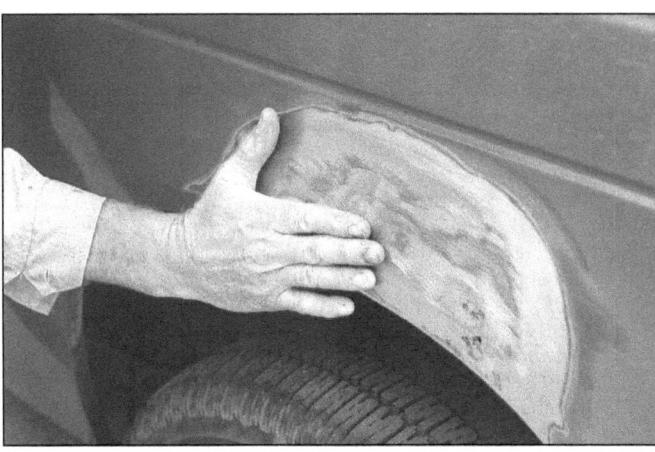

4 When the paint is removed, touch will probably be more helpful than sight for telling if the metal is straight. Hammer down the high spots or raise the low spots as necessary. Clean the repair area with wax/silicone remover

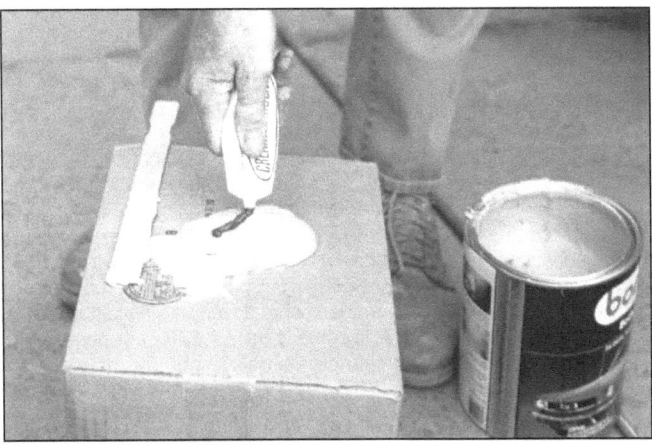

5 Following label instructions, mix up a batch of plastic filler and hardener. The ratio of filler to hardener is critical, and, if you mix it incorrectly, it will either not cure properly or cure too quickly (you won't have time to file and sand it into shape)

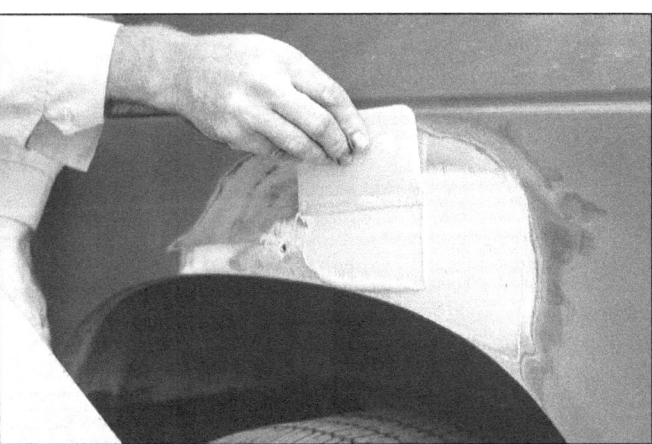

6 Working quickly so the filler doesn't harden, use a plastic applicator to press the body filler firmly into the metal, assuring it bonds completely. Work the filler until it matches the original contour and is slightly above the surrounding metal

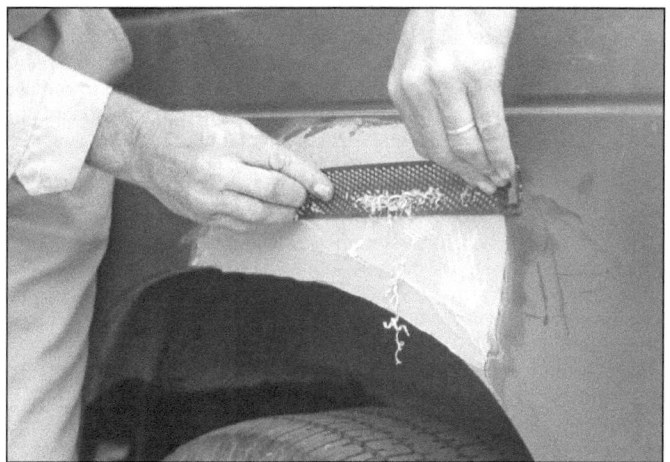

7 Let the filler harden until you can just dent it with your fingernail. Use a body file or Surform tool (shown here) to rough-shape the filler

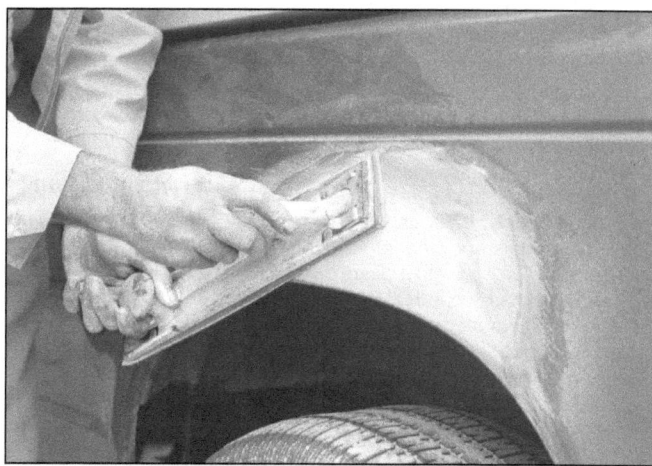

8 Use coarse-grit sandpaper and a sanding board or block to work the filler down until it's smooth and even. Work down to finer grits of sandpaper - always using a board or block - ending up with 360 or 400 grit

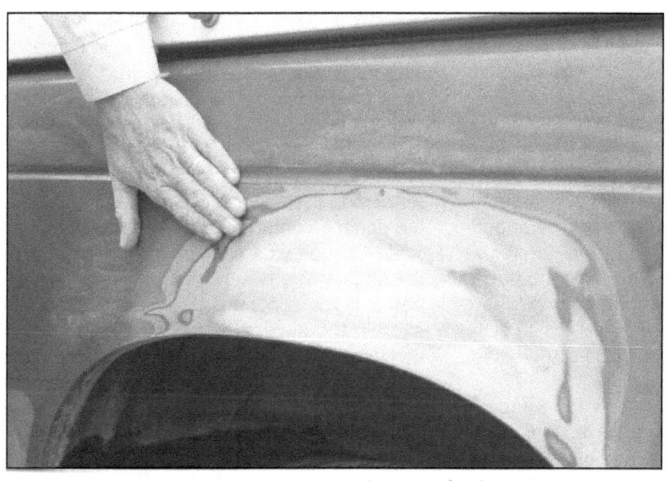

9 You shouldn't be able to feel any ridge at the transition from the filler to the bare metal or from the bare metal to the old paint. As soon as the repair is flat and uniform, remove the dust and mask off the adjacent panels or trim pieces

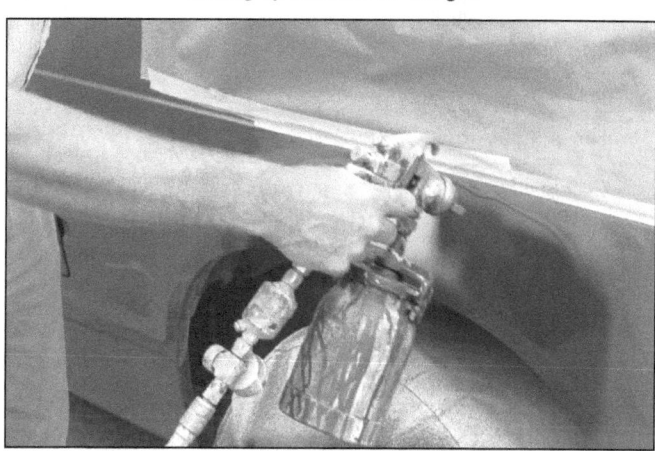

10 Apply several layers of primer to the area. Don't spray the primer on too heavy, so it sags or runs, and make sure each coat is dry before you spray on the next one. A professional-type spray gun is being used here, but aerosol spray primer is available inexpensively from auto parts stores

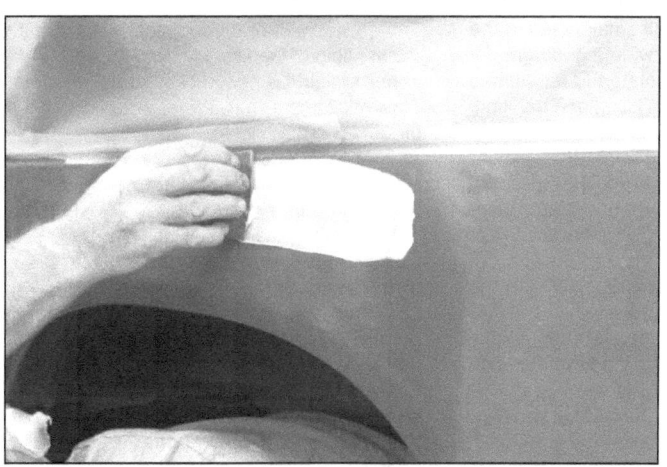

11 The primer will help reveal imperfections or scratches. Fill these with glazing compound. Follow the label instructions and sand it with 360 or 400-grit sandpaper until it's smooth. Repeat the glazing, sanding and respraying until the primer reveals a perfectly smooth surface

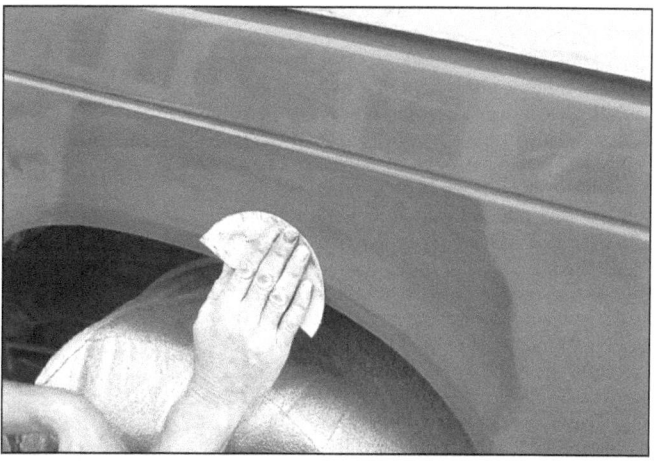

12 Finish sand the primer with very fine sandpaper (400 or 600-grit) to remove the primer overspray. Clean the area with water and allow it to dry. Use a tack rag to remove any dust, then apply the finish coat. Don't attempt to rub out or wax the repair area until the paint has dried completely (at least two weeks)

3   Upholstery and carpets - maintenance

1   Remove the carpets or mats and thoroughly vacuum the interior of the vehicle every three months (more frequently if necessary).
2   Beat out the carpets and vacuum them if they are very dirty. If the upholstery is soiled, apply an upholstery cleaner with a damp sponge and wipe it off with a clean, dry cloth.
3   Consult your local dealer or auto parts store for cleaners made especially for newer automotive upholstery fabrics. Always test the cleaner in an inconspicuous place.

4   Vinyl trim - maintenance

Vinyl trim should not be cleaned with detergents, caustic soaps or petroleum based cleaners. Plain soap and water or a mild vinyl cleaner is best for stains. Test a small area for colour fastness. Bubbles under the vinyl can be corrected by piercing them with a pin and then working the air out.

5   Hinges and locks - maintenance

Every 5000 kilometres or three months, the door, bonnet and tailgate hinges and locks should be lubricated with a few drops of oil. The door striker plates should also be given a thin coat of grease to reduce wear and ensure free movement.

6   Body repair - minor damage

See photo sequence

Repair of minor scratches

1   If the scratch is superficial and does not penetrate to the metal of the body, repair is very simple. Lightly rub the scratched area with a fine rubbing compound to remove loose paint and built up wax. Rinse the area with clean water.
2   Apply touch-up paint to the scratch, using a small brush. Continue to apply thin layers of paint until the surface of the paint in the scratch is level with the surrounding paint. Allow the new paint at least two weeks to harden, then blend it into the surrounding paint by rubbing with a very fine rubbing compound. Finally, apply a coat of wax to the scratch area.
3   If the scratch has penetrated the paint and exposed the metal of the body, causing the metal to rust, a different repair technique is required. Remove all loose rust from the bottom of the scratch with a pocket knife, then apply rust inhibiting paint to prevent the formation of rust in the future. Using a rubber or nylon applicator, coat the scratched area with glaze-type filler. If required, the filler can be mixed with thinner to provide a very thin paste, which is ideal for filling narrow scratches. Before the glaze filler in the scratch

hardens, wrap a piece of smooth cotton cloth around the tip of a finger. Dip the cloth in thinner and then quickly wipe it along the surface of the scratch. This will ensure that the surface of the filler is slightly hollow. The scratch can now be painted over as described earlier in this section.

Repair of dents

4   When repairing dents, the first job is to pull the dent out until the affected area is as close as possible to its original shape. There is no point in trying to restore the original shape completely as the metal in the damaged area will have stretched on impact and cannot be restored to its original contours. It is better to bring the level of the dent up to a point which is about 3 mm below the level of the surrounding metal. In cases where the dent is very shallow, it is not worth trying to pull it out at all.
5   If the back side of the dent is accessible, it can be hammered out gently from behind using a soft-face hammer. While doing this, hold a block of wood firmly against the opposite side of the metal to absorb the hammer blows and prevent the metal from being stretched.
6   If the dent is in a section of the body which has double layers, or some other factor makes it inaccessible from behind, a different technique is required. Drill several small holes through the metal inside the damaged area, particularly in the deeper sections. Screw long, self tapping screws into the holes just enough for them to get a good grip in the metal. Now the dent can be pulled out by pulling on the protruding heads of the screws with locking pliers.
7   The next stage of repair is the removal of paint from the damaged area and from an inch or so of the surrounding metal. This is easily done with a wire brush or sanding disk in a drill motor, although it can be done just as effectively by hand with sandpaper. To complete the preparation for filling, score the surface of the bare metal with a screwdriver or the tang of a file or drill small holes in the affected area. This will provide a good grip for the filler material. To complete the repair, see the sub-Section, below, on filling and painting.

Repair of rust holes or gashes

8   Remove all paint from the affected area and from an inch or so of the surrounding metal using a sanding disk or wire brush mounted in a drill motor. If these are not available, a few sheets of sandpaper will do the job just as effectively.
9   With the paint removed, you will be able to determine the severity of the corrosion and decide whether to renew the whole panel, if possible, or repair the affected area. New body panels are not as expensive as most people think and it is often quicker to fit a new panel than to repair large areas of rust.
10   Remove all trim pieces from the affected area except those which will act as a guide to the original shape of the damaged body, such as headlight shells, etc. Using metal snips or

a hacksaw blade, remove all loose metal and any other metal that is badly affected by rust. Hammer the edges of the hole inward to create a slight depression for the filler material.
11   Wire brush the affected area to remove the powdery rust from the surface of the metal. If the back of the rusted area is accessible, treat it with rust-inhibiting paint.
12   Before filling is done, block the hole in some way. This can be done with sheet metal riveted or screwed into place, or by stuffing the hole with wire mesh.
13   Once the hole is blocked off, the affected area can be filled and painted. See the following sub-Section on filling and painting.

Filling and painting

14   Many types of body fillers are available, but generally speaking, body repair kits which contain filler paste and a tube of resin hardener are best for this type of repair work. A wide, flexible plastic or nylon applicator will be necessary for imparting a smooth and contoured finish to the surface of the filler material. Mix up a small amount of filler on a clean piece of wood or cardboard (use the hardener sparingly). Follow the manufacturer's instructions on the package, otherwise the filler will set incorrectly.
15   Using the applicator, apply the filler paste to the prepared area. Draw the applicator across the surface of the filler to achieve the desired contour and to level the filler surface. As soon as a contour that approximates the original one is achieved, stop working the paste. If you continue, the paste will begin to stick to the applicator. Continue to add thin layers of paste at 20-minute intervals until the level of the filler is just above the surrounding metal.
16   Once the filler has hardened, the excess can be removed with a body file. From then on, progressively finer grades of sandpaper should be used, starting with a 180-grit paper and finishing with 600-grit wet-or-dry paper. Always wrap the sandpaper around a flat rubber or wooden block, otherwise the surface of the filler will not be completely flat. During the sanding of the filler surface, the wet-or-dry paper should be periodically rinsed in water. This will ensure that a very smooth finish is produced in the final stage.
17   At this point, the repair area should be surrounded by a ring of bare metal, which in turn should be encircled by the finely feathered edge of good paint. Rinse the repair area with clean water until all of the dust produced by the sanding operation is gone.
18   Spray the entire area with a light coat of primer. This will reveal any imperfections in the surface of the filler. Repair the imperfections with fresh filler paste or glaze filler and once more smooth the surface with sandpaper. Repeat this spray-and-repair procedure until you are satisfied that the surface of the filler and the feathered edge of the paint are perfect. Rinse the area with clean water and allow it to dry completely.

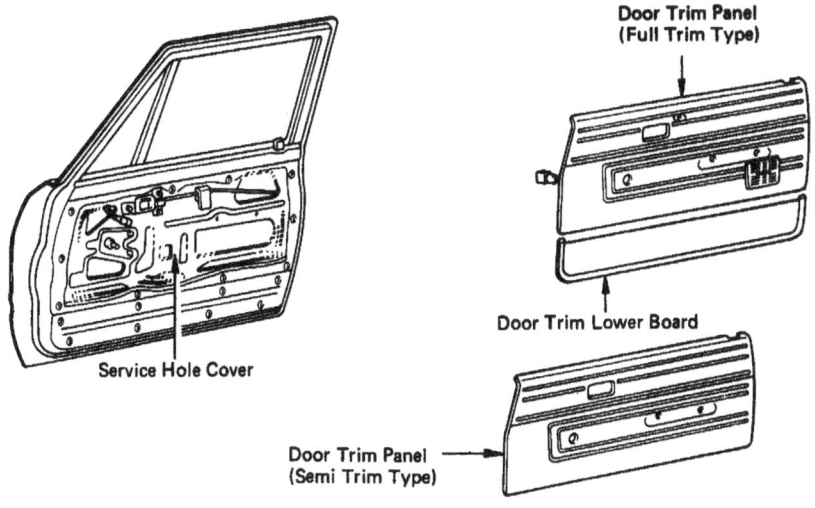

8.1 Typical door trim panel component layout

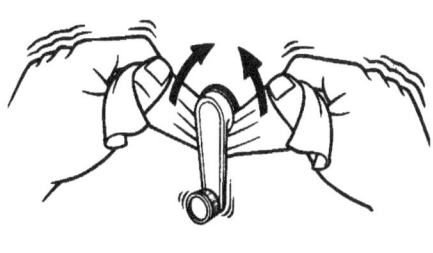

8.2 Use a cloth to push upwards and remove the window crank snap-ring

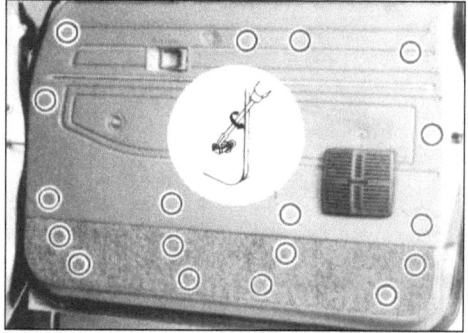

8.3 Location of door panel retainers (circled, early model shown): inset shows the method for disengaging the retainers by levering with a screwdriver

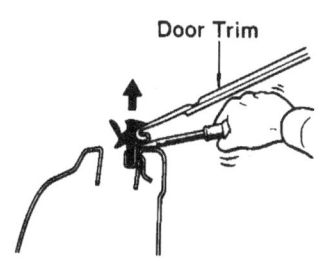

8.5 Use a screwdriver to prise the weatherstripping channel from the door

19   The repair area is now ready for painting. Spray painting must be carried out in a warm, dry, windless and dust free atmosphere. These conditions can be created if you have access to a large indoor work area, but if you are forced to work in the open, you will have to pick the day very carefully. If you are working indoors, dousing the floor in the work area with water will help settle the dust which would otherwise be in the air. If the repair area is confined to one body panel, mask off the surrounding panels. This will help minimise the effects of a slight mismatch in paint colour. Trim pieces such as chrome strips, door handles, etc., will also need to be masked off or removed. Use masking tape and several thicknesses of newspaper for the masking operations.
20   Before spraying, shake the paint can thoroughly, then spray a test area until the spray painting technique is mastered. Cover the repair area with a thick coat of primer. The thickness should be built up using several thin layers of primer rather than one thick one. Using 600-grit wet-or-dry sandpaper, rub down the surface of the primer until it is very smooth. While doing this, the work area should be thoroughly rinsed with water and the wet-or-dry sandpaper periodically rinsed as well. Allow the primer to dry before spraying additional coats.

21   Spray on the top coat, again building up the thickness by using several thin layers of paint. Begin spraying in the centre of the repair area and then, using a circular motion, work out until the whole repair area and about two inches of the surrounding original paint is covered. Remove all masking material 10 to 15 minutes after spraying on the final coat of paint. Allow the new paint at least two weeks to harden, then use a very fine rubbing compound to blend the edges of the new paint into the existing paint. Finally, apply a coat of wax.

7 Body and frame repair - major damage

1   Major damage must be repaired by an auto body/frame repair shop with the necessary welding and hydraulic straightening equipment.
2   If the damage has been serious, it's vital that the frame be checked for proper alignment or the vehicle's handling characteristics may be adversely affected. Other problems, such as excessive tyre wear and wear in the driveline and steering, may occur.

3   Due to the fact that all of the major body components (bonnet, fenders, etc.) are separate and replaceable units, any seriously damaged components should be renewed rather than repaired. Sometimes these components can be found in a wrecking yard that specialises in used vehicle components, often at considerable savings over the cost of new parts.

8 Door trim panel - removal and refitting

Refer to illustrations 8.1, 8.2, 8.3, 8.5 and 8.8
1   Unscrew and remove the inside door handle bezel and the arm rest (**see illustration**).
2   Using a piece of cloth placed between the window crank and the window crank trim ring, remove the window crank snap-ring retainer and pull off the crank (**see illustration**).
3   Using a screwdriver, prise carefully between the door trim panel and the retainers to loosen the panel (**see illustration**).
4   If so equipped, reach behind the loosened door panel and disconnect the wires to the radio speakers and/or power window switch.

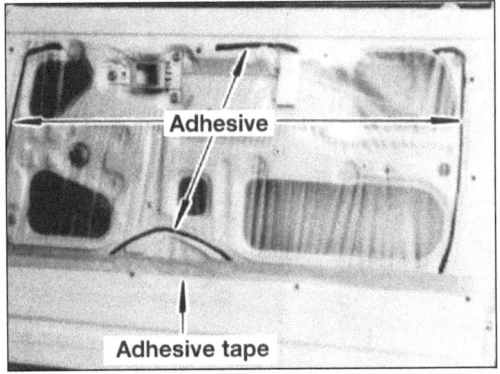

8.8 Service hole cover adhesive refitting details

5   Tilt the loosened door trim up and, with a screwdriver, prise the weatherstripping channel from the door, working from front to rear, freeing the trim panel **(see illustration)**. **Note:** *Be careful not to damage the door trim panel as you are removing it.*
6   Peel off the outer ridges of the service hole cover.
7   All of the inside door components are now accessible, but be careful not to tear the service hole cover.
8   Refitting is the reverse of the removal procedure. When refitting the service cover, apply adhesive and tape as shown **(see illustration)**. Refit the window crank, with the glass fully raised, in the same position as the crank on the opposite door.

9   Door glass (without ventilator) - removal and refitting

Refer to illustrations 9.3, 9.4 and 9.8
1   Lower the window completely.
2   Remove the door trim panel and peel off the outer ridges of the service hole cover (see Section 8).
3   Remove the outer weatherstripping from the door by levering it out carefully with a screwdriver **(see illustration)**.
4   Remove the two glass channel mounting bolts **(see illustration)**.
5   Remove the door glass by pulling it up and out.

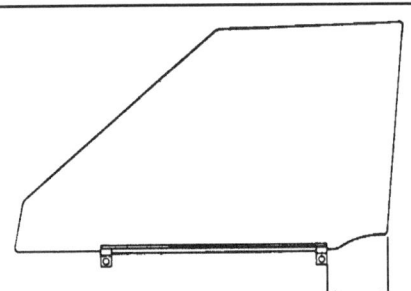

9.8 The distance between the end of the channel and the end of the glass must be as listed in the Specifications section at the front of this Chapter

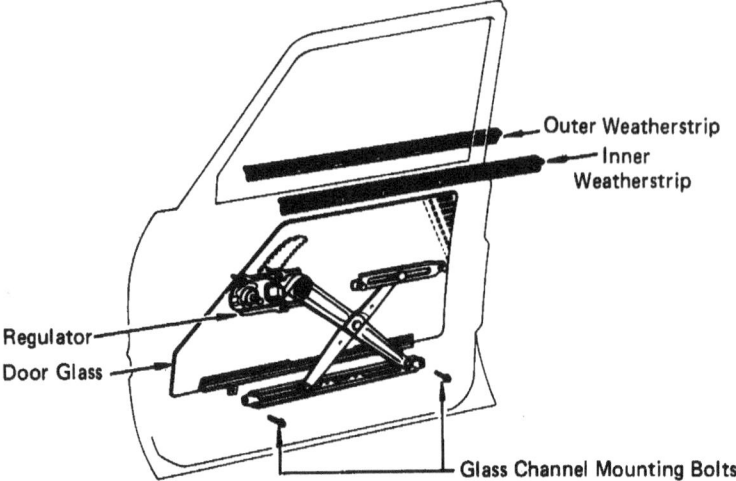

9.3 Typical door glass component layout (non-ventilator earlier models shown)

6   Remove the glass channel from the glass with a putty knife or similar tool, taking care not to damage the glass if it is to be refitted.
7   To refit the glass, apply soapy water to the inside of the weatherstripping in the channel.
8   Tap the channel onto the glass with a plastic hammer. **Note:** *The glass should be fitted in the channel so that the trailing bottom edge of the glass is the proper distance from the trailing edge of the channel* **(see illustration** and refer to the Specifications).
9   The remaining refitting procedures are the reverse of those for removal.

10   Door glass (with ventilator) - removal and refitting

Refer to illustrations 10.4a and 10.4b
1   Lower the window completely.
2   Remove the door trim panel and peel up

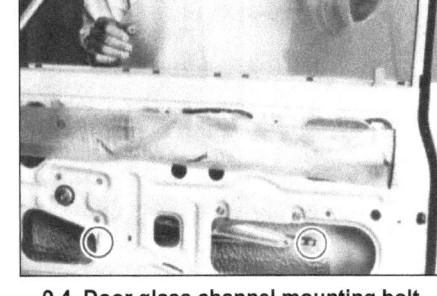

9.4 Door glass channel mounting bolt locations (circled)

the outer ridges of the service hole cover (see Section 8).
3   Remove the bolt and detach the lower door glass frame (if equipped). Remove the outer weather stripping from the door by levering it out carefully with a screwdriver.
4   Remove the two glass channel mounting bolts and place the glass in the bottom of the door cavity **(see illustrations)**.
5   Remove the three screws retaining the

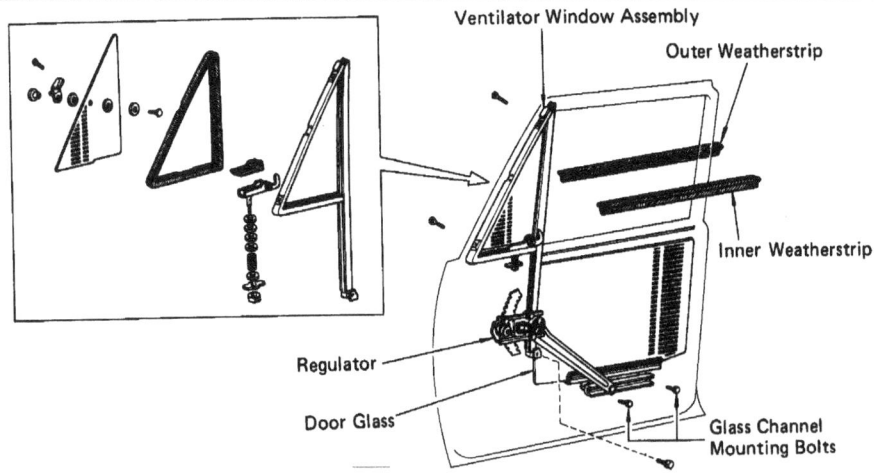

10.4a Ventilator-equipped window glass refitting details (LN80, 90, 105, 106, 110 series and 4Runner)

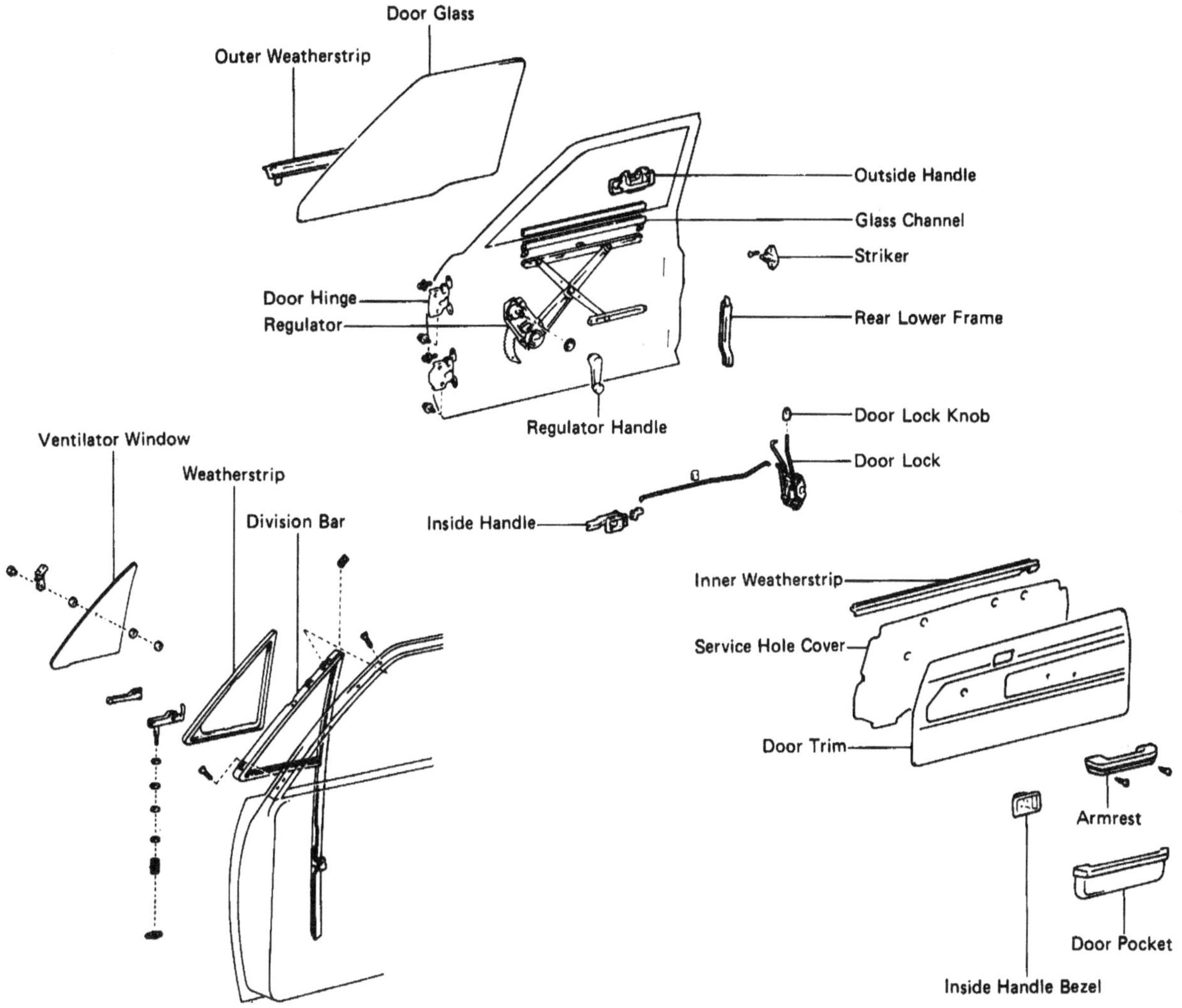

Door Glass

Outer Weatherstrip

Outside Handle

Glass Channel

Striker

Door Hinge

Regulator

Rear Lower Frame

Regulator Handle

Door Lock Knob

Door Lock

Ventilator Window

Weatherstrip

Division Bar

Inside Handle

Inner Weatherstrip

Service Hole Cover

Door Trim

Armrest

Door Pocket

Inside Handle Bezel

10.4b Door and glass details (LN30, 40, 50 and 60 series)

vent window frame and remove the division bar bolts (if equipped).

6   Tilt the vent window assembly in and pull it up and out of the door.

7   Remove the door glass by pulling it up.

8   Remove the glass channel from the glass with a putty knife or similar tool, taking care not to damage the glass if it is to be refitted.

9   To refit the glass, apply soapy water to the inside of the weatherstripping in the channel.

10   Tap the glass into the channel with a plastic hammer. **Note:** *The glass should be fitted in the channel so that the trailing bottom edge of the glass is the proper distance from the trailing edge of the channel* **(see illustration 9.8 and refer to Specifications)**.

11   The remaining refitting procedures are the reverse of those for removal.

11   Window regulator - removal and refitting

Refer to illustrations 11.2a and 11.2b

1   Remove the door trim panel and peel off the outer ridges of the service hole cover (see Section 8).

2   Remove the two glass channel mounting bolts and support the glass with one hand while removing the regulator mounting bolts with the other **(see illustrations)**.

3   On models so equipped, remove the two equaliser arm bracket mounting bolts.

4   Remove the regulator through the service hole.

5   Check the gears for wear and the spring for weakness. Renew parts as necessary.

6   Before refitting the regulator, lubricate the sliding parts with multi-purpose grease.

7   Refitting is the reverse of the removal procedure. For proper refitting of the door glass, see Section 9 or 10.

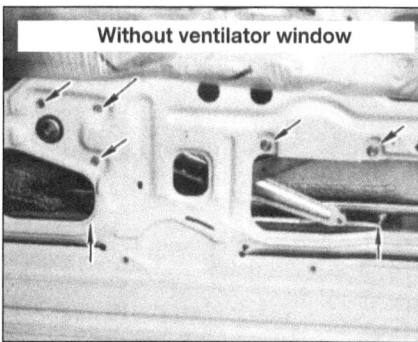

11.2a Typical non-ventilator window equipped glass regulator bolt locations (arrows)

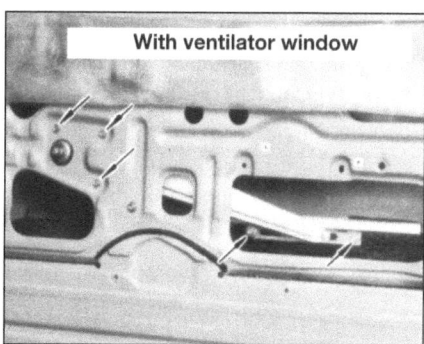

11.2b Window regulator bolt location (arrows) (ventilator-equipped model)

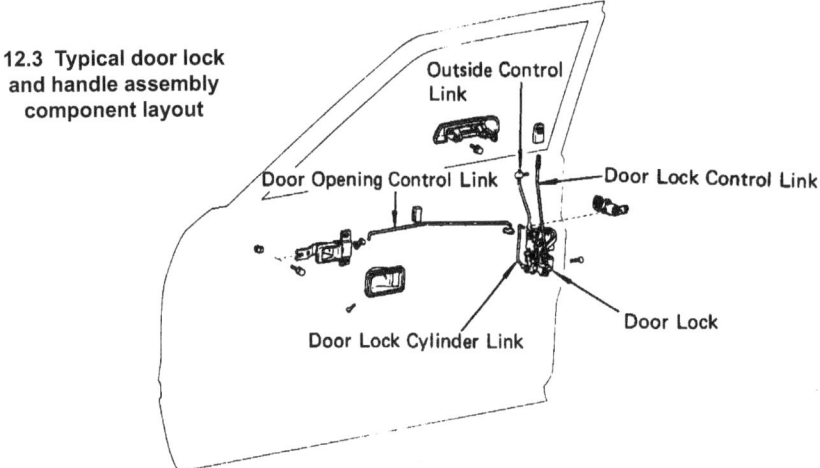

12.3 Typical door lock and handle assembly component layout

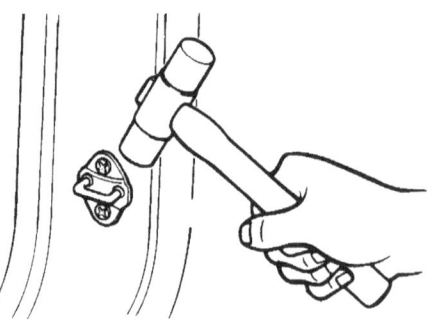

12.17 Loosen the lock striker bolts and adjust its position by tapping with a plastic hammer

12 Door lock and handle assembly - removal, refitting and adjustment

Refer to illustrations 12.3 and 12.17

1   Remove the door trim panel and peel off the outer ridges of the service hole cover (see Section 8).
2   Unthread the door lock button from the door control link.
3   Using a screwdriver, disconnect the door opening the control link, outside control link, door lock control link and door lock cylinder link **(see illustration)**.
4   Using a screwdriver, remove the door lock assembly.
5   Inspect the linkage arms for wear or damage. Renew parts as necessary.
6   Check the operation of the door lock. Lubricate all contact points with multi-purpose grease.
7   Refitting is the reverse of the removal procedures.
8   To adjust the inside door handle on models with slotted mounting holes, after all linkages have been connected, loosen the handle assembly mounting screws and push the handle forward until light resistance is felt. Move the handle back 0.5 to 1.0 mm and tighten the mounting screws. (On models without slotted holes the handle does not require adjustment.)
9   To adjust the outside door handle, dis-

connect the outside control link by removing the retaining clip.
10   Loosen the handle mounting bolts.
11   Raise the handle 0.5 to 1.0 mm from the rest position.
12   Tighten the outside door handle mounting bolts.
13   Fit the pin to the handle assembly mounting hole by turning the adjuster, then refit the retaining clip.
14   To renew the key lock cylinder, disconnect the cylinder link from the cylinder tang by removing the retaining clip.
15   Slide the lock cylinder retaining clip out of the groove in the cylinder and remove the cylinder from the outside of the door.
16   To fit a new cylinder, reverse the two Steps immediately above. **Note:** *If a cylinder lock is to be renewed, it should be renewed in both doors and in the ignition switch (see Chapter 12), as these cylinders come in sets. Or the new door lock cylinder can be coded to the same key as the others, by a dealer service department or other qualified repair shop.*
17   The lock striker is attached to the door opening by two screws. Loosening the screws allows the striker to be moved vertically and horizontally to adjust the closed position of the door **(see illustration)**. Tighten the screws after the proper door positioning has been obtained.

13 Door - removal, refitting and adjustment

Refer to illustrations 13.1a and 13.1b

1   Remove the door by first placing a jack under the centre of the door for support. Use a pencil or sharp scribe to draw around the hinges and bolts to help position the door properly upon refitting. Remove the door stopper pin **(see illustration)**. Remove the four door hinge bolts, unplug any electrical connectors and carefully lift off the door **(see illustration)**.
2   Refitting is the reverse of removal.
3   Adjust the new door for a good fit by referring to the following procedure.
4   Loosen the body hinge bolts and move the door in the direction desired (forward or backward, up or down).
5   Loosen the door hinge bolts and move the door in the direction desired (left or right; up or down).
6   Adjust the lock striker as described in Section 12.

14 Back door (4Runner) - disassembly and reassembly

Refer to illustrations 14.2, 14.10a and 14.10b

1   Remove the door trim, the plate and the service hole cover.
2   Disconnect the control link on the regu-

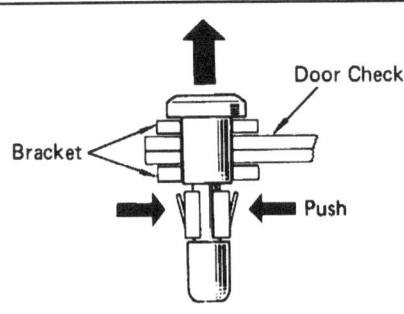

13.1a Door stopper pin details; after removal, leave the claw raised

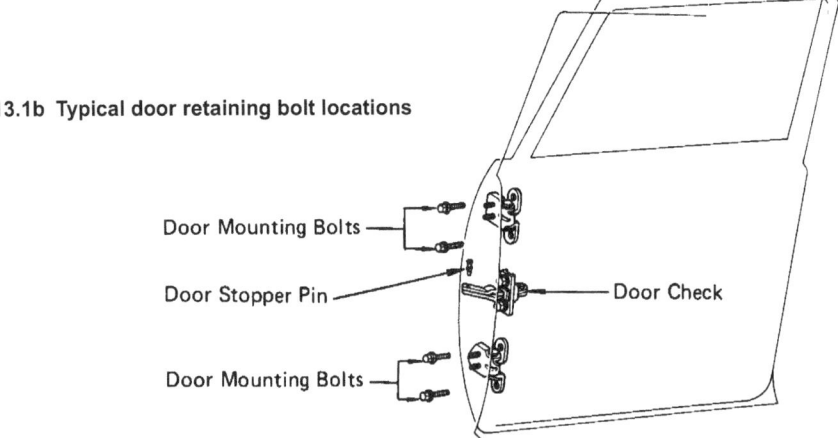

13.1b Typical door retaining bolt locations

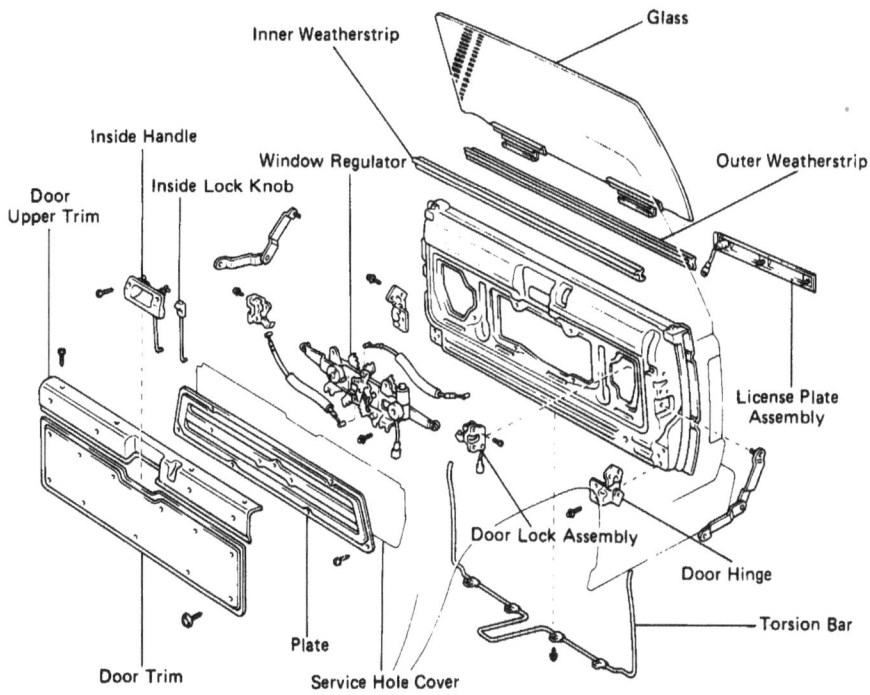

14.2 4Runner back door - exploded view

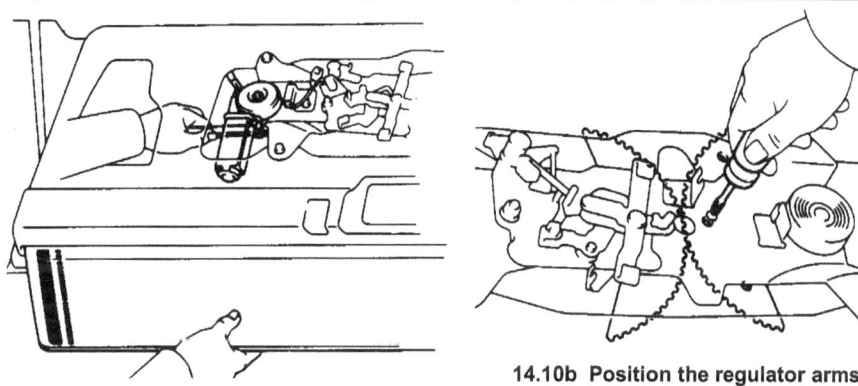

14.10a If the window is not operational,
hold the glass and remove the regulator

14.10b Position the regulator arms
horizontally and insert a screwdriver into
the hole to secure the arms

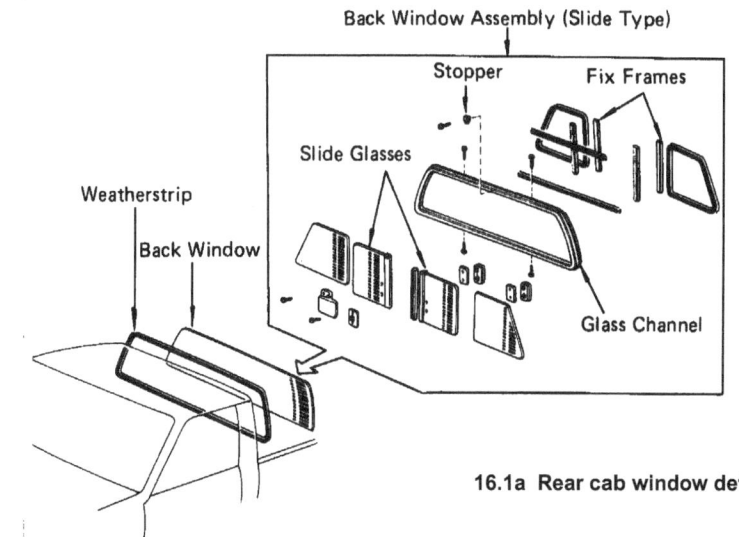

16.1a Rear cab window details

lator side, then remove the two screws and
detach the inside handle assembly (see illustration).

3   Remove the inside lock knob and disconnect the link on the regulator side.

4   Remove the upper trim and the inner weatherstrip.

5   If the electric window is operative, use a screwdriver to move the lock assembly to the lock position, then raise the window glass until the regulator arms are in a straight line.

6   Unplug the window regulator wire harness connector.

7   If the window is not operative, disconnect both wires at the regulator, then remove the bolt and detach the earth cable.

8   Disconnect the door lock cables.

9   If the window is operative, disconnect both wires at the regulator, then remove the bolt and detach the earth cable.

10   If the window is not operative, hold the door glass and remove the regulator. Caution: Never attempt to remove the regulator motor without holding the glass (the regulator arm may swing up). Lower the glass all the way and open the door by pulling on the door lock control cables. Raise the glass to position the regulator arms horizontally, then insert a screwdriver into the hole to secure the arms (see illustrations).

11   Remove the three regulator mount bolts, then slide the regulator from side-to-side to free the arms from the glass channel.

12   Remove the glass, then shift the regulator into the cavity and pull it out.

13   Remove the outer weatherstrip, then unplug the outer power window switch electrical connector.

14   The door lock assembly can be removed after unplugging the electrical connector on the left side and removing the three mounting screws.

15   Place a protective pad between the door and bumper, then remove the hinge bolts and detach the door.

16   Reassembly is the reverse of disassembly.

15 Windscreen - removal and refitting

Due to the possibility of glass breakage when fitting a new windscreen and/or possible damage to the surrounding body panels and paint, it is recommended that a damaged windscreen be renewed by a dealership or an auto glass specialist.

16 Rear cab window - removal, disassembly and refitting

Refer to illustrations 16.1a, 16.1b, 16.3, 16.5, 16.10 and 16.12

1   Using a screwdriver from the inside of the cab, prise carefully around the weatherstrip lip, forcing the weatherstripping out (see illustrations). Have an assistant pull on the window assembly to remove it, with the weatherstripping attached.

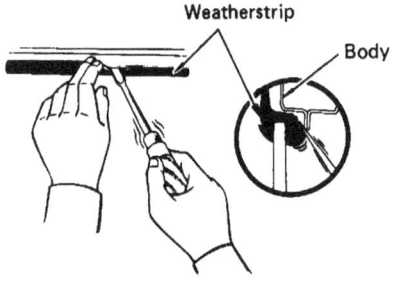

16.1b Use a screwdriver to prise the weatherstripping up and force it out of the groove

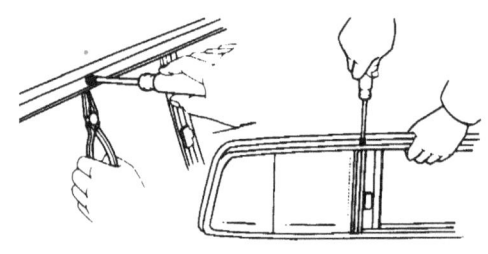

16.3 On sliding windows, remove the four screws retaining the two fix frames

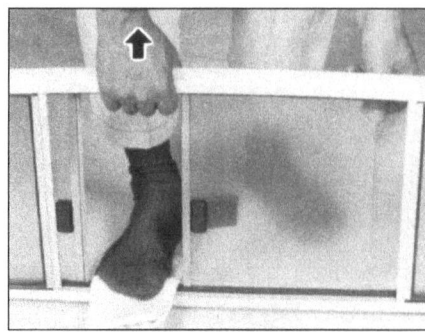

16.5 Hold the centre of the frame with your foot while pulling up on the top edge of the frame

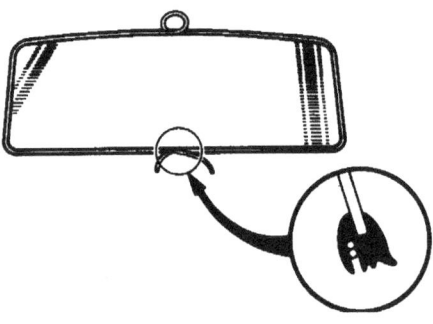

16.10 Place the cord as shown when fitting the rear window

16.12 With an assistant pushing on the outside of the glass and weatherstripping, pull the cord out of the weatherstripping on the inside, which will correctly position the weatherstripping around the body channels

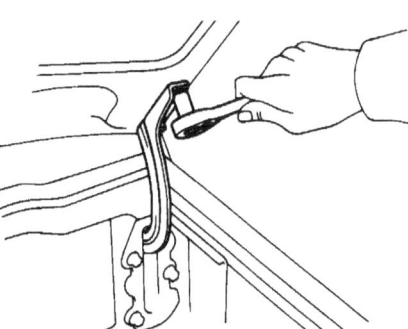

17.1 With an assistant supporting the weight of the bonnet, remove the four retaining bolts with a socket

2   On sliding type rear windows, using a screwdriver and pliers, remove the sliding glass stopper from the channel.

3   From the channel track, remove the four screws holding the two fix frames **(see illustration)**.

4   With the window assembly standing vertically on its lower edge, place a folded rag near the centre of the window frame to protect the channel.

5   Stand on the rag with one foot and gently lift the top edge of the frame and remove the sliding windows and fix frames **(see illustration)**.

6   Move the rag toward either end of the channel frame and remove the two non-sliding windows in the same manner.

7   To refit the rear window, first transfer the weatherstripping from the non-sliding window(s) being renewed to the new window(s).

8   Apply soapy water to the contact face of the weatherstripping surrounding the glass channel and to the glass channel flange.

9   The remaining refitting procedures are the reverse of those for removal. It is probable that the old weatherstripping has become weather hardened and may develop water leaks. Renew the weatherstripping with new material if any such deterioration is indicated.

10   Once the rear window is assembled, apply a working cord along the weatherstripping groove **(see illustration)**.

11   Begin the refitting in the centre of the lower part of the glass.

12   Attach the window assembly to the body by pulling on the cord from the inside while an assistant pushes along the weatherstripping from the outside **(see illustration)**.

13   Seat the window assembly by tapping around the circumference of the glass with your open hand.

17 Bonnet - removal, refitting and adjustment

Refer to illustrations 17.1, 17.5, 17.6 and 17.7

1   To remove the bonnet, scribe a line (or use paint) around the hinge bolt heads to ensure correct alignment when the bonnet is refitted. Have an assistant hold the bonnet

while the bolts are loosened. Finish removing the bolts while supporting the bonnet on both sides, then carefully lift it off **(see illustration)**.

2   Refitting is the reverse of removal.

3   To adjust the bonnet for a good fit, refer to the following procedure.

4   Loosen the bonnet hinge bolts and move the bonnet in the desired direction (left or right; forward or backward).

5   Loosen the body hinge bolts and move the rear of the bonnet in the desired direction (up or down) **(see illustration)**.

6   Loosen the adjustment cushions at the front corners of the bonnet to raise or lower the front of the bonnet until it is even with the tops of the fenders **(see illustration)**.

7   Loosen the bonnet lock bolts and move the lock in the desired direction to obtain a snug fit when closed **(see illustration)**.

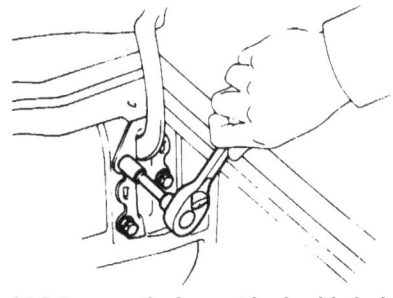

17.5 Loosen the bonnet body side bolts to adjust the rear edge up and down

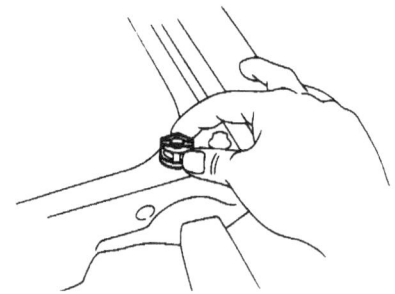

17.6 Screw the bonnet bumpers in or out to adjust the front edge of the bonnet

17.7 Loosen the bonnet lock bolts to adjust how tightly the bonnet closes

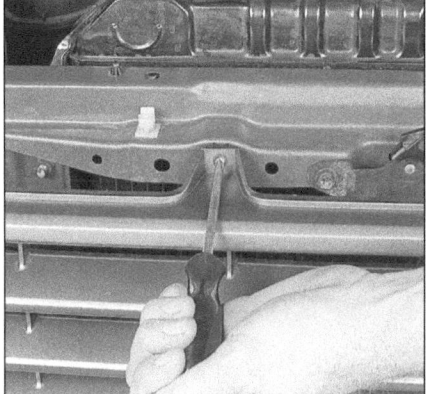

18.5 Use a Phillips head screwdriver to remove the grille retaining screws (later models)

18.2a Location of the screws retaining the top of the grille (arrows) (early models)

18.2b Lower grille retaining screws (arrow) (early models)

18 Grille - removal and refitting

Refer to illustrations 18.2a, 18.2b, 18.5 and 18.6

1   Open the bonnet.

Early models

2   Remove the four screws along the top edge of the grille and the three screws along

the bottom **(see illustrations)**.

3   Pull the grille out.

4   Refitting is the reverse of the removal procedure

Later models

5   Remove the two grille retaining screws **(see illustration)**.

6   Use a screwdriver to prise on the retaining clips while pulling out on the grille until it is disengaged and then lift it from the vehicle **(see illustration)**.

7   To refit, place the grille into position and push it in until the clips are engaged. Refit the retaining screws.

19 Tailgate lock - removal and refitting

Refer to illustration 19.2

1   Using a spanner, remove the tailgate stay from the tailgate lock and body.

2   Using a screwdriver, remove the service hole cover **(see illustration)**.

3   Disconnect the tailgate lock link from the

tailgate lock control.

4   Remove the three set screws from the tailgate lock.

5   Pull the tailgate lock from the tailgate.

6   To refit the lock, place it in the tailgate and refit the three set screws.

7   Bolt the tailgate stay to the body and to the tailgate lock.

8   Connect the tailgate lock link to the tailgate lock control.

9   Refit the service hole cover.

20 Tailgate lock control - removal and refitting

1   Using a screwdriver, remove the service hole cover **(see illustration 19.2)**.

2   Disconnect the two tailgate lock links from the lock control.

3   Using a socket, remove the tailgate lock handle.

4   Using a socket, remove the tailgate lock control.

5   Refitting is the reverse of the removal procedure.

18.6 Disengage the grille by levering on the retaining clips while pulling out on the grille

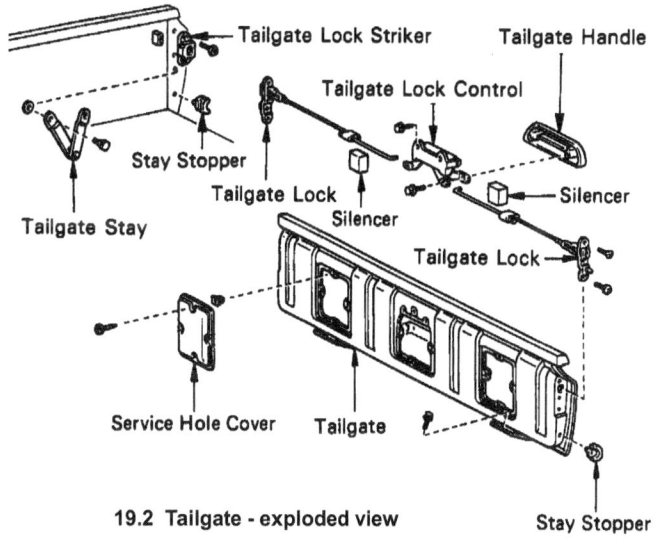

19.2 Tailgate - exploded view

Notes

Chapter 12
Chassis electrical system

Contents

1 General information

This Chapter covers the repair and service procedures for the various lighting and electrical components not associated with the engine, as well as general information on troubleshooting the vehicle's various electrical circuits. Information on the battery, alternator, distributor (petrol) and starter motor can be found in Chapter 5.

The electrical system is a 12 volt, negative earth type with power supplied by a lead/acid battery which is charged by the alternator.

It should be noted that whenever portions of the electrical system are worked on, the negative battery cable should be disconnected to prevent electrical shorts and/or fires.

2 Electrical troubleshooting - general information

A typical electrical circuit consists of an electrical component, any switches, relays, motors, etc. related to that component and the wiring and connectors that connect the component to both the battery and the chassis. To aid in locating a problem in any

electrical circuit, wiring diagrams are included at the end of this Chapter.

Before tackling any troublesome electrical circuit, first study the appropriate diagrams to get a complete understanding of what makes up that individual circuit. Trouble spots, for instance, can often be narrowed down by noting if other components related to that circuit are operating properly or not. If several components or circuits fail at one time, chances are the problem lies in the fuse or earth connection, as several circuits often are routed through the same fuse and earth connections.

Electrical problems often stem from simple causes, such as loose or corroded connections, a blown fuse, melted fusible link or popped circuit breaker. Prior to any electrical troubleshooting, always visually check the condition of the fuse or circuit breaker, wires and connections of the problem circuit.

If testing instruments are going to be utilised, use the diagrams to plan ahead of time where you will make the necessary connections in order to accurately pinpoint the trouble spot.

The basic tools needed for electrical troubleshooting include a circuit tester or voltmeter (a 12 volt bulb with a set of test leads can also be used), a continuity tester (which includes a bulb, battery and set of test leads)

and a jumper wire, preferably with a circuit breaker incorporated, which can be used to bypass electrical components.

Voltage checks should be performed if a circuit is not functioning properly. Connect one lead of a circuit tester to either the negative battery terminal or a known good earth. Connect the other lead to a connector in the circuit being tested, preferably nearest to the battery or fuse. If the bulb of the tester lights, voltage is reaching that point (which means the part of the circuit between that connector and the battery is problem free). Continue checking along the entire circuit in the same fashion. When you reach a point where no voltage is present, the problem lies between there and the last good test point. Most of the time the problem is due to a loose connection. Keep in mind that some circuits receive voltage only when the ignition key is in the Accessory or Run position.

A method of finding shorts in a circuit is to remove the fuse and connect a test light or voltmeter in its place to the fuse terminals. There should be no load in the circuit. Move the wiring harness from side-to-side while watching the test light. If the bulb lights, there is a short to earth somewhere in that area, probably where insulation has rubbed off a wire. The same test can be performed on other components of the circuit, including the switch.

An earth check should be done to see if a component is earthed properly. Disconnect the battery and connect one lead of a self-powered test light, such as a continuity tester, to a known good earth. Connect the other lead to the wire or earth connection being tested. If the bulb lights, the earth is good. If the bulb does not light, the earth is not good.

A continuity check is performed to see if a circuit, section of circuit or individual component is passing electricity through it properly. Disconnect the battery, and connect one lead of a self-powered test light, such as a continuity tester, to one end of the circuit being tested and the other lead to the other end of the circuit. If the bulb lights, there is continuity, which means the circuit is passing electricity through it properly. Switches can be checked in the same way.

Remember that all electrical circuits are composed basically of electricity running from the battery, through the wires, switches, relays, etc. to the electrical component (light bulb, motor, etc.). From there it is run to the body (earth) where it is passed back to the battery. Any electrical problem is basically an interruption in the flow of electricity to and from the battery.

3   Fuses, fusible links and circuit breakers - general information

Refer to illustrations 3.2a, 3.2b, 3.2c, 3.9 and 3.11

1 The electrical circuits of the vehicle are protected by a combination of fuses, fusible links and a circuit breaker.

Fuses

2 The fusebox is located under the dash on the left side on some models and under the dash on the right side on other models. Some models have them in both places. Additionally, some models also have one in the engine compartment **(see illustration)**. Access is gained by simply snapping off the plastic cover.

3 Each of the fuses is designed to protect a specific circuit, as identified on the fuse cover. Spare fuses and a special removal tool are included in the fuse box cover.

4 If an electrical component has failed, your first check should be the fuse. A fuse which has 'blown' can be readily identified by inspecting the metal element inside the housing **(see illustrations)**. If this element is broken, the fuse is inoperable and should be renewed. You can also check the fuses without removing them. Probe each side of the fuse with a test light. If power is available on one side of the fuse but not the other, the fuse is blown

5 Fuses are renewed by simply pulling out the old one and pushing in the new one.

6 It is important that the correct fuse be refitted. The different electrical circuits need varying amounts of protection, indicated by

3.2a On some models, a fuse box is located in the engine compartment, behind the battery

3.9 The fusible links on later models are located in the engine compartment fuse box and can be checked visually

the amperage rating on the fuse. A fuse with too low a rating will blow prematurely, while a fuse with too high a rating may not blow soon enough to avoid serious damage to other components or the wiring.

7 At no time should the fuse be bypassed with metal or foil. Serious damage to the electrical system could result.

8 If the renewal fuse immediately fails, do not renew it with another until the cause of the problem is isolated and corrected. In most cases the cause will be a short circuit in the wiring caused by a broken or deteriorated wire. In addition to fuses, the wiring system incorporates fusible links for overload protection. These links are used in circuits which are not ordinarily fused.

Fusible links

9 The fusible links are located near the positive battery terminal and are easily removed by unplugging the connectors at either end. On later models the fusible links are located in the engine compartment fuse box and the check and renewal procedures are similar to fuses **(see illustration)**.

10 If an electrical failure occurs in one of the circuits covered by a fusible link, these

3.2b Early model fuses are tubular in shape with a glass tube covering the filament

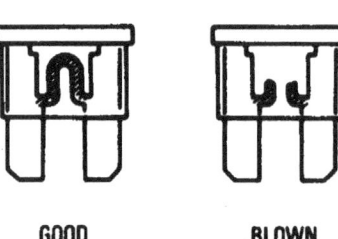

3.2c Later model fuses are plastic with blade terminals

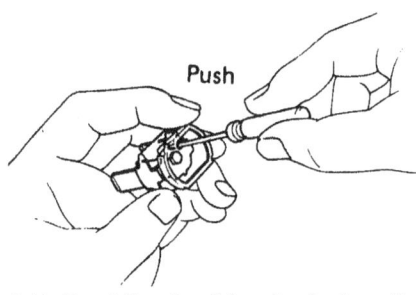

3.11 Reset the circuit breaker by inserting a pin through the hole

should be the first check. If the link is melted, the entire fusible link should be renewed, but only after checking and correcting the electrical fault that caused it.

Circuit breaker

11 Some models are equipped with a circuit breaker, which is usually located in the junction block behind the left-side kick panel. If the circuit breaker pops, it can be reset by inserting a pin or thin pick into the hole in the top of it **(see illustration)**.

4   Ignition switch - check, removal and refitting

Refer to illustrations 4.2, 4.4a, 4.4b, 4.4c, 4.4d, 4.6 and 4.9

1 Remove the negative cable from the battery.

2   Remove the upper and lower steering column trim **(see illustration)**.
3   Unplug the ignition switch electrical connector.

Check

4   Using an ohmmeter, check the continuity of the ignition switch in each position. Refer to the accompanying terminal diagrams and continuity charts **(see illustrations)**. If the switch fails any of the checks, it must be renewed.

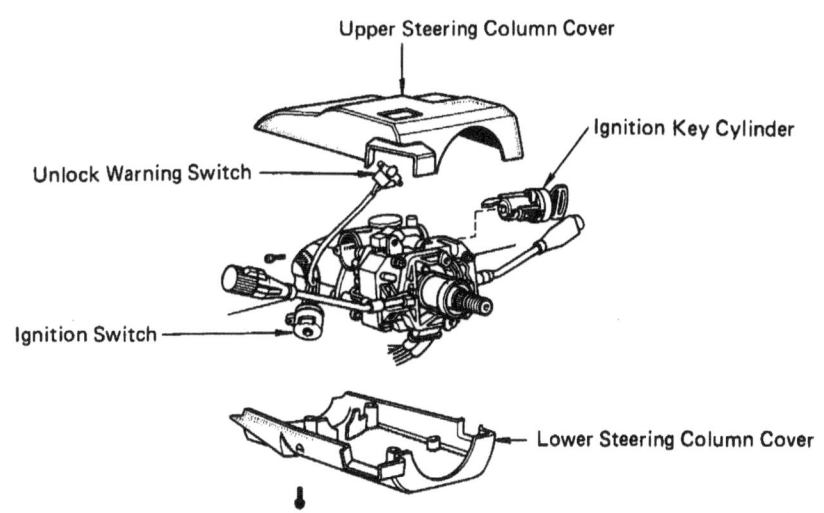

4.2 Steering column cover and ignition switch component layout

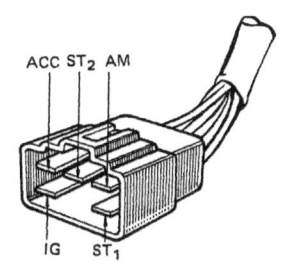

(Terminal (Wire color) / Switch position	AM (BR)	ACC (LR)	IG (BY)	ST1 (BW)	ST2 (B)
OFF					
ACC	o—o				
ON	o—o—o				
START	o———o—o—o				

4.4a Ignition switch terminal guide and continuity chart (LN30, 40 series)

Terminal (wire color) / Switch position	AM₁ (B-R)	ACC (L-R)	IG₁ (B-Y)	ST₁ (B-W)	AM₂ (BR)	IG₂ (BR-W)	ST₂ (BR-R)	H (G-W)	I (G-W)
LOCK									
ACC	o—o								
ON	o—o—o			o—o				
START	o——o—o			o—o—o				
warning normal									
warning push								o—o	

4.4b Ignition switch terminal guide and continuity chart (LN50, 60 series)

	AM₁	ACC	IG₁	ST₁
	AM₂	IG₂		ST₂

	H
	I

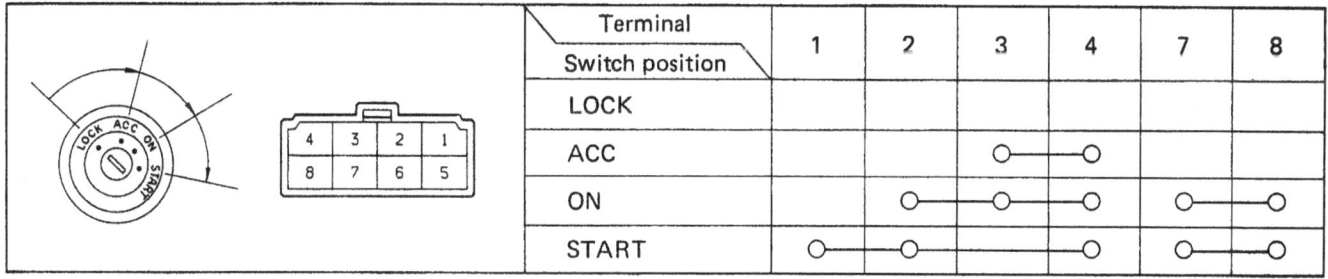

Terminal / Switch position	1	2	3	4	7	8
LOCK						
ACC			o—o			
ON			o—o—o	o—o	
START	o——o		o	o—o	

4.4c Ignition switch terminal guide and continuity chart (LN80, 90, 105, 106, 110 series)

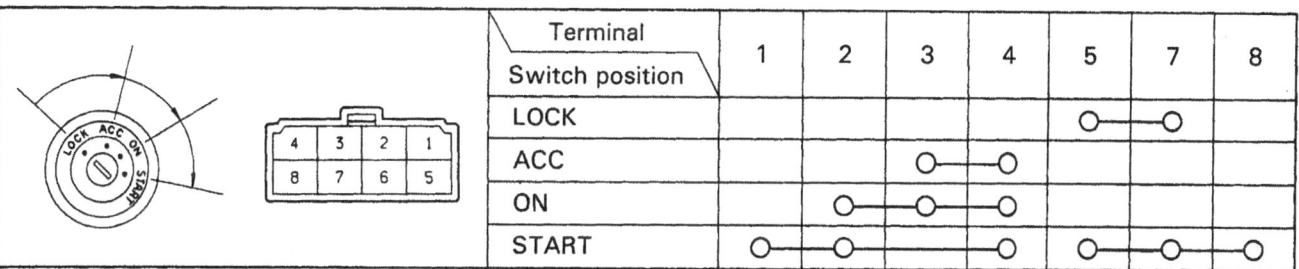

Terminal / Switch position	1	2	3	4	5	7	8
LOCK					o—o		
ACC			o—o				
ON		o—o—o					
START	o—o——o			o—o—o	

4.4d Ignition switch terminal guide and continuity chart (4Runner models)

4.6 Push in on the retaining pin while pulling the ignition switch and key out

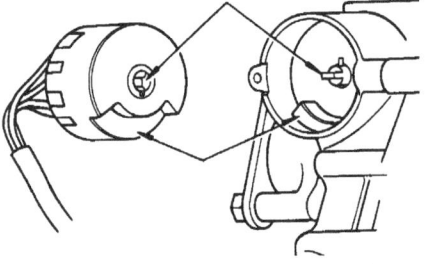

4.9 Prior to refitting, align the bracket with the ignition switch

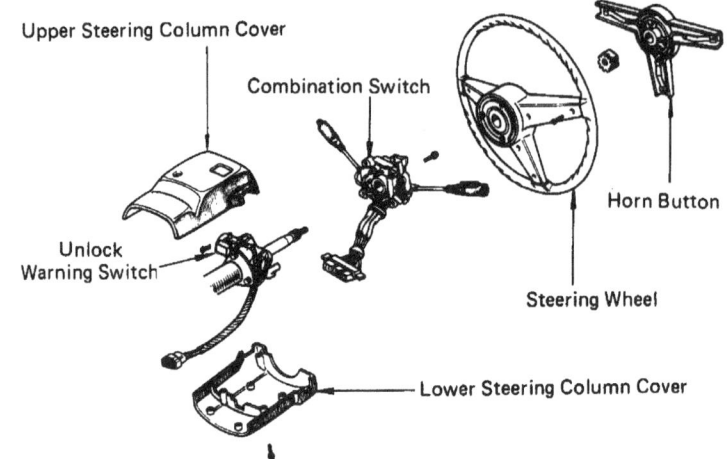

5.3 Combination switch and steering column details

Removal and refitting

5　Turn the ignition key to the Accessory position.

6　Push in the retaining pin with a paper clip and pull out the ignition key and cylinder **(see illustration)**.

7　Remove the unlock warning switch by removing the two screws.

8　Remove the ignition switch by removing the retaining screw and pulling the switch out of the housing.

9　Refitting is the reverse of the steps for

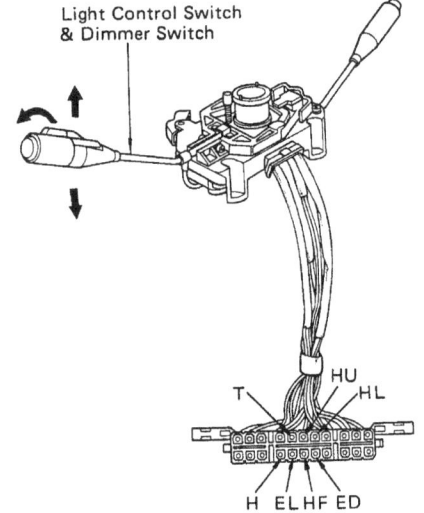

Terminal (Wire color) / Switch position		T (W)	H (R)	EL (W)	ED (WB)	HU (RY)	HL (RG)	HF (RW)
Light control	OFF							
	ONE STEP	O		O				
	TWO STEP	O	O	O				
Dimmer	Headlight U.					O	O	
	Headlight L.					O		O
	Headlight F.					O	O	O

5.4a Headlight switch/dimmer switch terminal guide and continuity chart (LN30, 40 series)

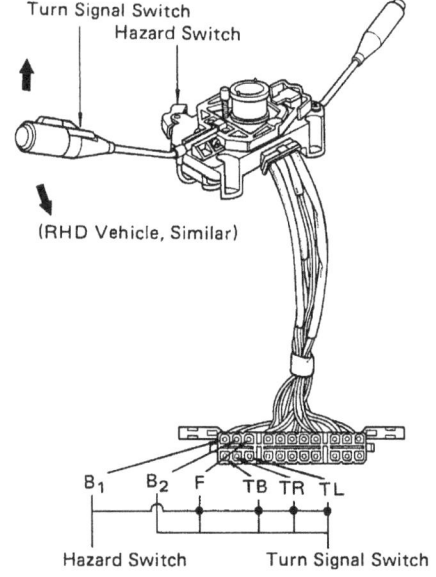

Terminal (Wire color) / Switch position		TL (GB)	TB (GW)	TR (GY)	B₁ (GL)	F (G)	B₂ (GO)
Turn signal	R		O	O	O	O	
	N				O	O	
	L	O	O		O	O	
Hazard		O	O	O		O	O

5.4b Turn signal switch/hazard flasher switch terminal guide and continuity chart (LN30, 40 series)

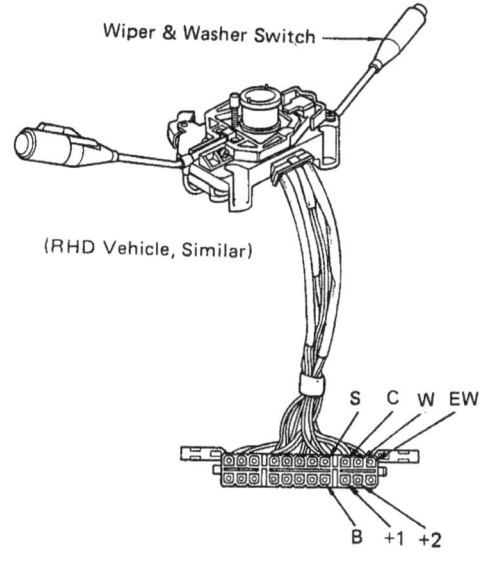

Wiper & Washer Switch

(RHD Vehicle, Similar)

S C W EW

B +1 +2

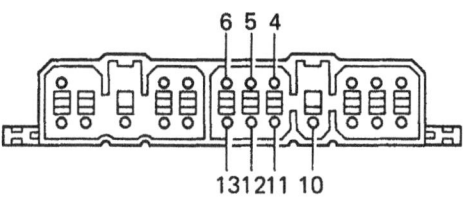

Light Control Switch and Headlight Dimmer Switch

6 5 4

13 12 11 10

Terminal (Wire color) Switch position	B (LW)	+1 (LB)	+2 (LO)	S (LR)	W (L)	EW (B)
OFF		O——————O				
LOW	O——O					
HI	O——————O					
WASHER					O——O	

Standard type

Terminal (Wire color) Switch position	B (LW)	S (LR)	+1 (LB)	+2 (LO)	C (LgR)	EW (B)	W (L)
OFF		O——O					
INT		O——O			O——O		
LO	O——————O						
HI	O——————————O						
WASHER						O——O	

Intermittent type

5.4c Wiper/washer switch terminal guide and continuity chart (LN30, 40 series)

Light control switch

Switch position	Terminal (Wire color) 10 or 11 EL (W)	10 or 11 T (W)	4 H (R)
OFF			
TAIL	O——————O		
HEAD	O——————O		O

Headlight dimmer switch

Switch position	Terminal (Wire color) 13 ED (W-B)	6 HL (R-G)	5 HU (R-Y)	12 HF (R-W)
Flash	O——————————————O		O——————O	
Low Beam	O——————O			
High Beam	O——————————————O			

5.4d Headlight switch/dimmer switch terminal guide and continuity chart (LN50/60 series)

removal. Make sure that the switch recess and bracket tab are aligned when refitting the switch in the housing **(see illustration)**.

5 Combination switch - check, removal and refitting

Refer to illustrations 5.3, 5.4a, 5.4b, 5.4c, 5.4d, 5.4e, 5.4f, 5.4g and 5.4h

1 Disconnect the cable from the negative terminal of the battery. From the back of the steering wheel, remove the screws secur-

ing the horn button assembly. Remove the assembly and disconnect it from the wiring harness.

2 Remove the steering wheel as described in Chapter 10.

3 Remove the steering column trim and the upper and lower parts of the switch cover **(see illustration)**.

Check

4 Using an ohmmeter, check the continuity of the various switches in each position. Refer to the accompanying terminal diagrams and continuity charts **(see illustrations)**. If

any switch fails any of the checks, it must be renewed.

Removal and refitting

5 Disconnect the combination switch leads at the connector by pressing down on the connector locks and separating the plug and socket parts.

6 Unscrew and remove the switch assembly mounting screws. Note the position of the switch assembly in relation to the cancelling pawl and then remove the switch assembly.

7 When refitting the switch assembly (by reversing the removal operation), make sure

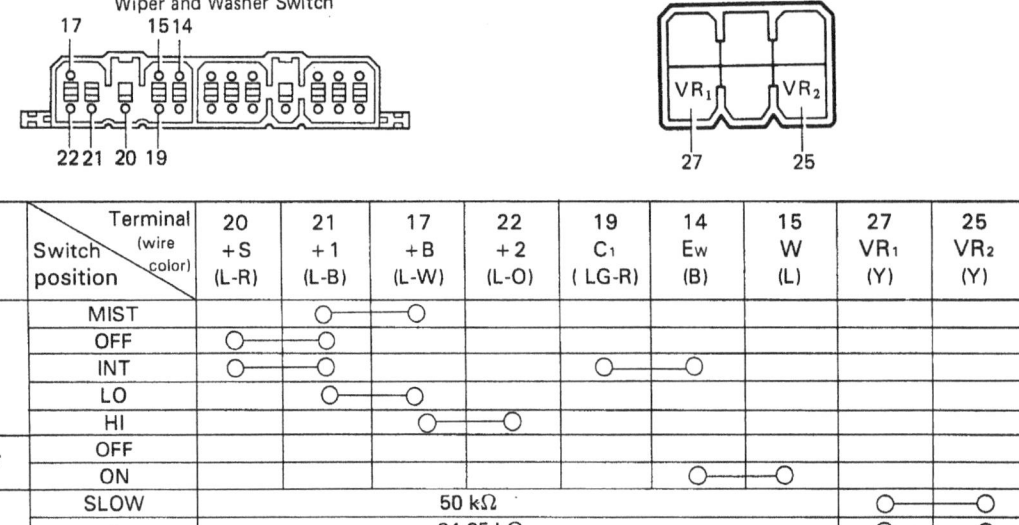

Wiper and Washer Switch

Switch	Switch position	Terminal (wire color)	20 +S (L-R)	21 +1 (L-B)	17 +B (L-W)	22 +2 (L-O)	19 C₁ (LG-R)	14 Ew (B)	15 W (L)	27 VR₁ (Y)	25 VR₂ (Y)
Wiper	MIST			o——o	o						
	OFF		o——o	o							
	INT		o——o	o			o——o	o			
	LO			o——o	o						
	HI				o——o	o					
Washer	OFF										
	ON							o——o	o		
INT Time Control	SLOW		50 kΩ							o——o	o
	•		34.25 kΩ							o——o	o
	•		15.75 kΩ							o——o	o
	FAST		0 kΩ							o——o	o

5.4e Wiper/washer switch terminal guide and continuity chart (LN50/60 series)

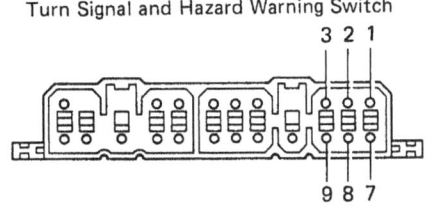

Turn Signal and Hazard Warning Switch

Switch Position		Terminal (Wire color)	9 TL (G-B)	3 TB (G-W)	8 TR (G-Y)	2 B₁ (G-L)	7 F (G)	1 B₂ (G-O)
Turn signal	L		o——o	o		o——o	o	
	N					o——o	o	
	R			o——o	o	o——o	o	
Hazard	ON		o——o	o——o	o		o——o	o

5.4f Turn signal switch/hazard flasher switch terminal guide and continuity chart (LN50/60 series)

Headlight switch

Terminal (Color) Switch position	10/13 (W)	11/13 (W)	4/13 (R)
OFF			
TAIL	o——o	o	
HEAD	o——o	o——o	o

Headlight dimmer switch

Terminal (Color) Switch position	5/13 (R-Y)	6/13 (R-G)	12/13 (R-W)	13/13 (W-B)
Flash	o		o——o	o
Low beam		o		o
High beam	o		o——o	o

Turn signal switch

Terminal (Color) Switch position	3/13 (G-W)	8/13 (G-Y)	9/13 (G-B)
Left turn	o———————o		o
Neutral			
Right turn	o——o	o	

5.4g Headlight switch/dimmer switch/turn signal switch terminal guide and continuity chart (LN80, 90, 105, 106, 110 series, 4Runner)

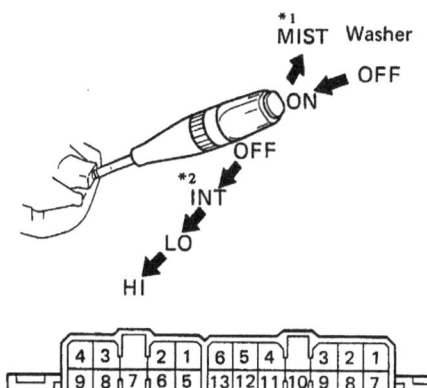

*1 MIST   Washer
OFF
ON
OFF
*2 INT
LO
HI

*1 w/ Mist Wiper
*2 w/ Intermittent Wiper

5.4h Headlight switch/dimmer switch terminal guide and continuity chart (LN80, 90, 105, 106, 110 series, 4Runner)

w/ Mist Wiper

Terminal (Color)		1/9 (B)	2/9 (L)	4/9 (L-W)	7/9 (L-R)	8/9 (L-B)	9/9 (L-O)
Switch position							
Wiper	MIST			o———		———o	
	OFF				o———	———o	
	LO			o———		———o	
	HI			o———			———o
Washer	OFF						
	ON	o———	———o				

w/ Intermittent Wiper

Terminal (Color)		1/9 (B)	2/9 (L)	4/9 (L-W)	7/9 (L-R)	8/9 (L-B)	9/9 (L-O)
Switch position							
Wiper	OFF				o———	———o	
	INT				o———	———o	
	LO			o———		———o	
	HI			o———			———o
Washer	OFF						
	ON	o———	———o				

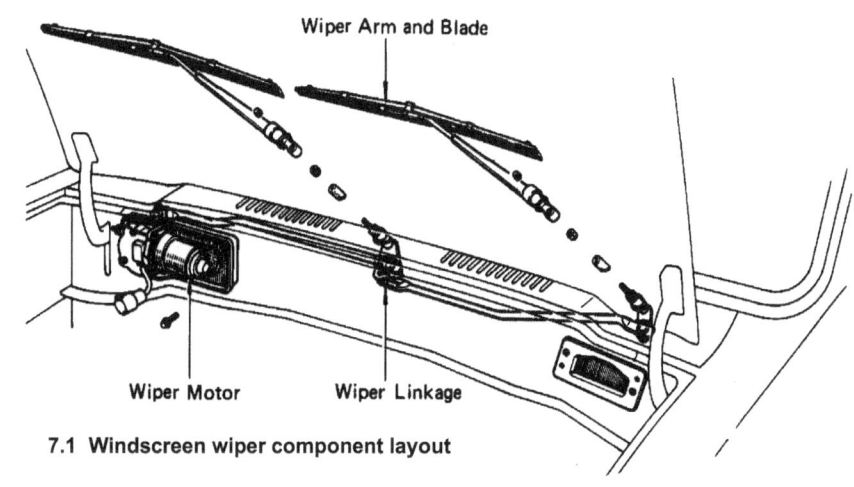

Wiper Arm and Blade

Wiper Motor   Wiper Linkage

7.1 Windscreen wiper component layout

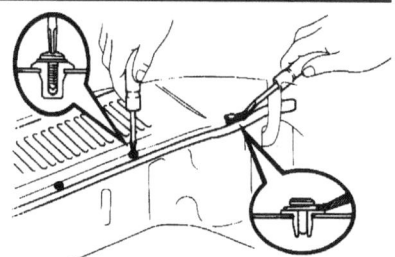

7.2 Remove the screws, prise the clips out and remove the cowl louver

7   Windscreen wipers - removal and refitting

Refer to illustrations 7.1, 7.2, 7.3 and 7.4

1   Lift up the covers on the wiper arms and use a spanner to remove the nuts, then remove the arms **(see illustration)**.
2   Remove the screws and clips and remove the cowl louvre **(see illustration)**.
3   Disconnect the electrical connector from the wiper motor, then remove the wiper motor by removing the mounting bolts **(see illustration)**.

that the switch and the automatic cancelling pawl are in their correct relative positions before refitting the steering wheel. After reconnecting the wiring harness plug, make sure that the switch functions correctly before refitting the column trim.

6   Hazard warning and turn signal lights - checking and renewal

1   If the flashers fail to work properly, first check the bulbs, then make sure that the nuts which hold the light units to the vehicle are tight and free from corrosion. These complete the circuit and any resistance here could affect the operation of the flasher unit.
2   Check the security of all wiring connectors after referring to the proper wiring diagram.
3   If everything is secure after making the above checks, then the hazard warning/turn signal flasher unit itself must be faulty. Since it cannot be repaired, it must be renewed. It is located under the left side of the dash behind

the kick panel on RN/LN30, 40 series, under the right side of the dash on the fuse/relay block on YN/LN50, 60 series, under the left side of the dash near the fuse/relay block on YN/RN/LN80, 90, 105, 106, 110 series and 4Runner. To renew it, slide it from its bracket mount or fuse/relay block, disconnect the electrical connector and fit a new unit.

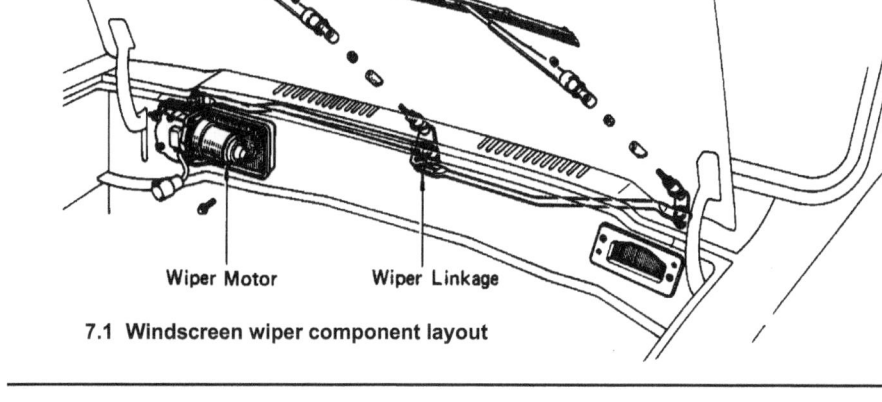

7.4 Prise the wiper arm link off with a screwdriver using a twisting motion as shown

7.3 Detach the electrical connector, then unscrew the wiper motor mounting bolts (arrows)

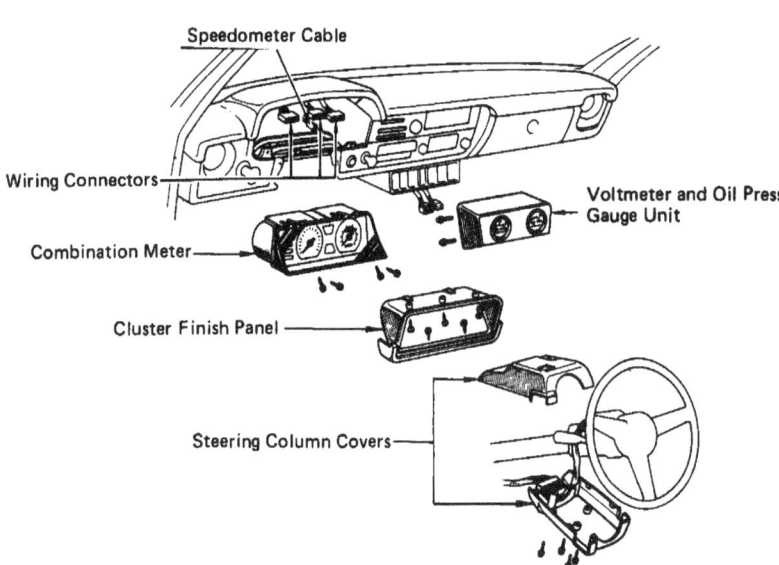

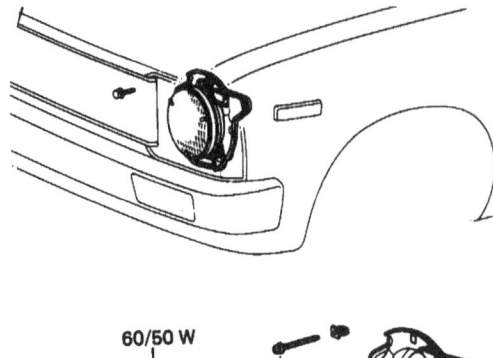

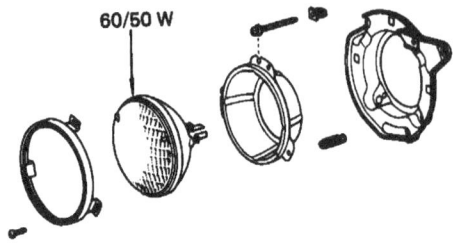

8.2 Typical combination meter refitting details

9.2 Round headlight refitting details

4   Insert a screwdriver between the link and the arm and prise the link from the arm **(see illustration)**.
5   Remove the nuts holding the pivot arms, then remove the wiper linkage through the access hole.
6   Refitting is the reverse of removal. Be sure that the wiper motor is in the auto-stop position before attaching the wiper arms.

8   Combination meter - removal and refitting

Refer to illustration 8.2
1   Disconnect the negative cable from the battery.
2   Remove the steering column covers **(see illustration)**.
3   Remove the screws holding the cluster finish panel in place, then remove the finish panel.
4   While pushing the lock lever, pull out the speedometer cable.
5   Remove the retaining screws, then pull out the combination meter and disconnect the wiring connectors.
6   To renew any faulty components within the combination meter, simply unbolt or unscrew them and renew them with new units.
7   Refitting is the reverse of removal.

9   Headlights - removal and refitting

Refer to illustrations 9.2 and 9.4
1   On vehicles with round headlights, remove the screws securing the headlight housing, then remove the housing.
2   Loosen, but do not remove the three screws in the keyhole slots in the light bezel.

Do not disturb the adjusting screws. Turn the bezel clockwise, then lift the bezel off the screw heads **(see illustration)**.
3   Hold the head light and disconnect the plug from the contacts at the rear.
4   On vehicles with rectangular headlights, remove the screws holding the headlight trim ring, then lift off the trim ring **(see illustration)**. On later models, it will be necessary to remove the grille to provide access to the headlight retaining screws (see Chapter 11).
5   Pull out the headlight and disconnect the plug from the contacts at the rear.
6   Refitting is the reverse of removal.

10   Headlights - adjustment

Refer to illustrations 10.1 and 10.3
Note: *The headlights must be aimed correctly. If adjusted incorrectly they could blind the driver of an oncoming vehicle and cause a serious accident or seriously reduce your ability to see the road. The headlights should be checked for proper aim every 12 months and any time a new headlight is fitted or front end body work is performed. It should be emphasised that the following procedure is*

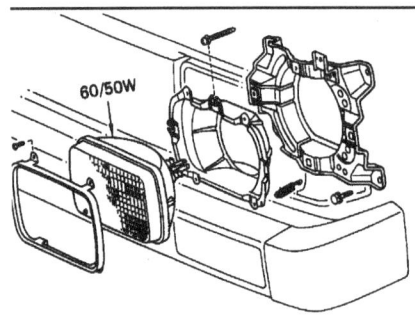

9.4 Rectangular headlight details

only an interim step which will provide temporary adjustment until the headlights can be adjusted by a properly equipped shop.
1   Sealed beam headlights have two spring-loaded adjusting screws, one on the top controlling up-and-down movement and one on the side controlling left-and right movement **(see illustration)**.
2   There are several methods of adjusting the headlights. The simplest method requires a blank wall 7.5 meters in front of the vehicle and a level floor.
3   Position masking tape vertically on the wall in reference to the vehicle centerline and the centerlines of both headlights **(see illustration)**.
4   Position a horizontal tape vertically on the wall in reference to the centerline of the headlights. **Note:** *It may be easier to position the tape on the wall with the vehicle parked only a few centimeters away.*
5   Adjustment should be made with the vehicle sitting level, the fuel tank half-full and no unusually heavy load in the vehicle.

10.1 The headlight vertical adjustment screw is located at the top of the headlight and the horizontal screw is on the side of the headlight (arrows)

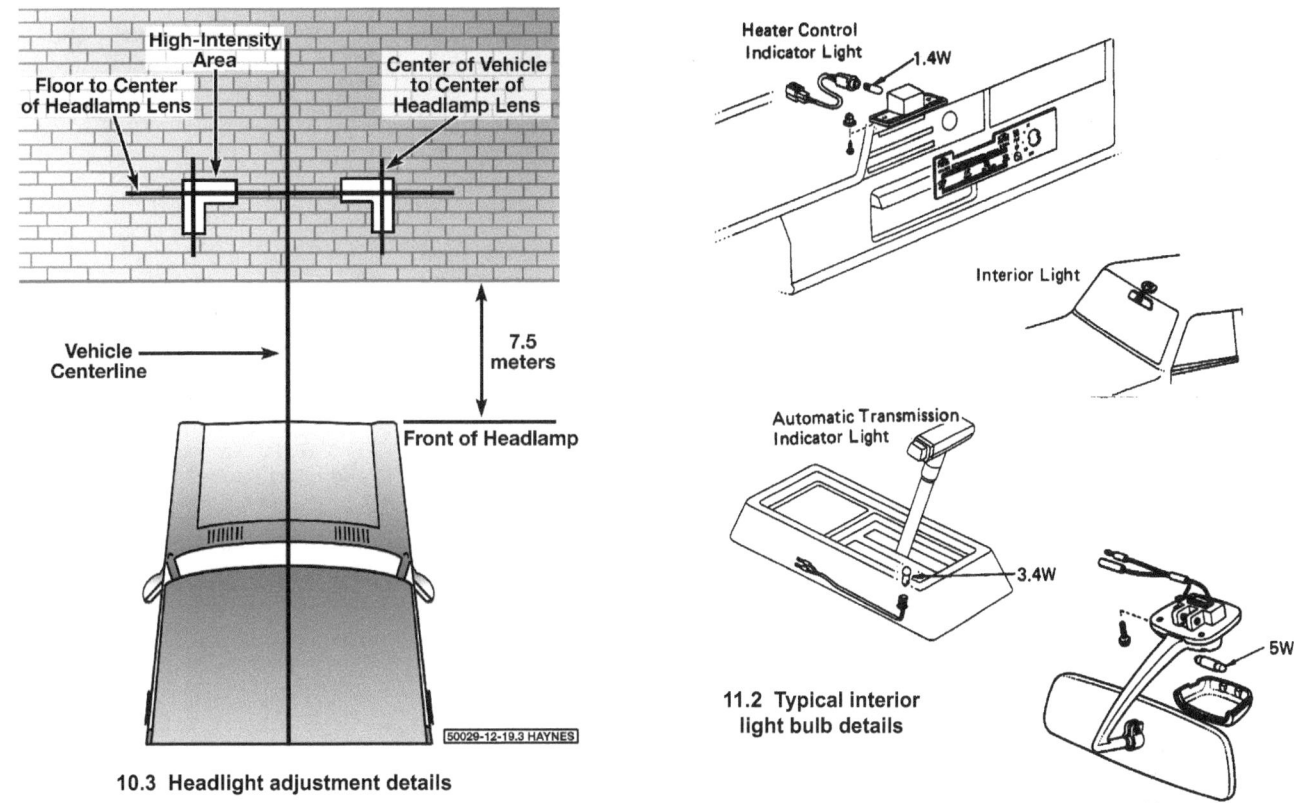

10.3 Headlight adjustment details

11.2 Typical interior light bulb details

6   Starting with the low beam adjustment, position the high-intensity zone so it's five centimeters below the horizontal line and five centimeters to the side of the headlight vertical line, away from oncoming traffic. Adjustment is made by turning the top adjustment screw clockwise to raise the beam and counterclockwise to lower it. The adjusting screw on the side is used in the same manner to move the beam left or right.

7   With the high beams on, the high-intensity zone should be vertically centered with the exact centre just below the horizontal line. **Note:** *It may not be possible to position the headlight aim exactly for both high and low beams. If a compromise must be made, keep in mind that the low beams are the most used and have the greatest effect on driver safety.*
8   Have the headlights adjusted by a dealer service department or service station at the earliest opportunity.

11   Bulb renewal

Refer to illustrations 11.2, 11.5 and 11.8

1   Make sure that replacement bulbs are the correct wattage, according to your owners manual or the number on the burned out bulb, before refitting them. Also, be sure to refit all pertinent gaskets when refitting the lenses.

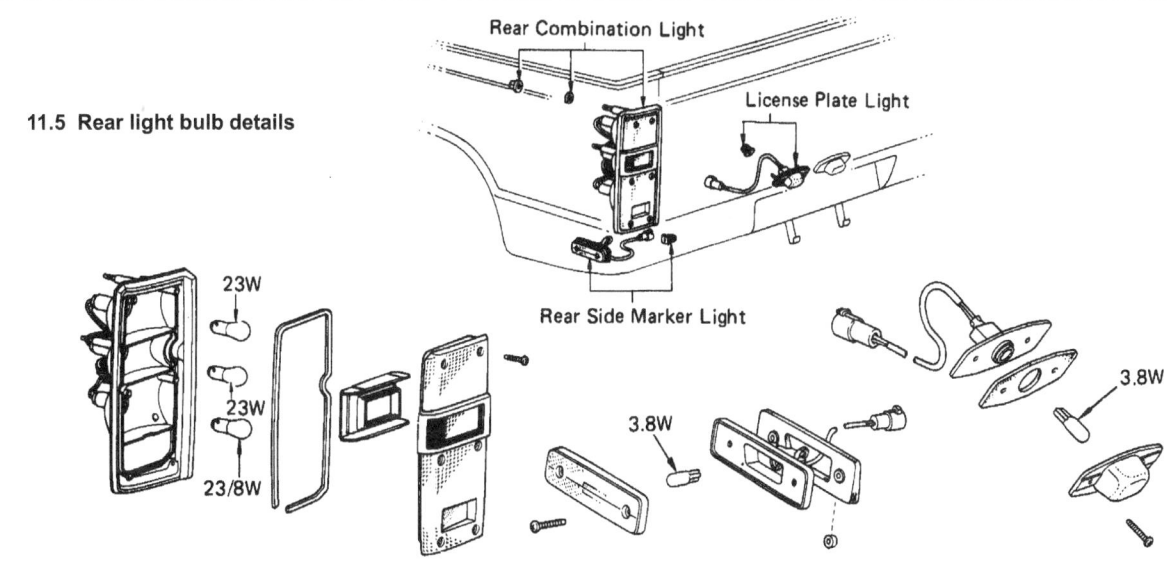

11.5 Rear light bulb details

Interior

Heater control indicator light

2   Remove the two screws above the heater control panel that hold the heater control indicator light housing in place to gain access to the bulb. Pull straight out on the bulb to remove it **(see illustration)**.

Dome light

3   Insert a flat-bladed screwdriver into the recess at the right side of the dome light lens and prise down gently to remove the lens, exposing the bulb.

Automatic transmission indicator light (if so equipped)

4   Remove the control lever trim plate to gain access to the indicator bulb. It is of the bayonet type.

Exterior

Rear combination light

5   Remove the screws securing the lens over the light assembly to remove the lens. The individual bulbs may be released from their bayonet mounts by pushing in on the bulbs and twisting them counterclockwise **(see illustration on previous page)**.

Rear side marker light

6   Remove the screws securing the lens and remove the lens. Pull straight out on the bulb to remove it.

Number plate light

7   The number plate light bulb is renewed in the same manner as the rear side marker light.

Front turn signal, parking and side marker lights

8   The lights are similar in that the lens in each of them is held in place by two screws. Remove the screws and pull off the lens to gain access to the bulbs. The turn signal and parking bulbs are bayonet mount and the side marker bulb is a push-pull type **(see illustration)**.

11.8 On later models, remove the screws and rotate the front parking light housing out for access to the bulb

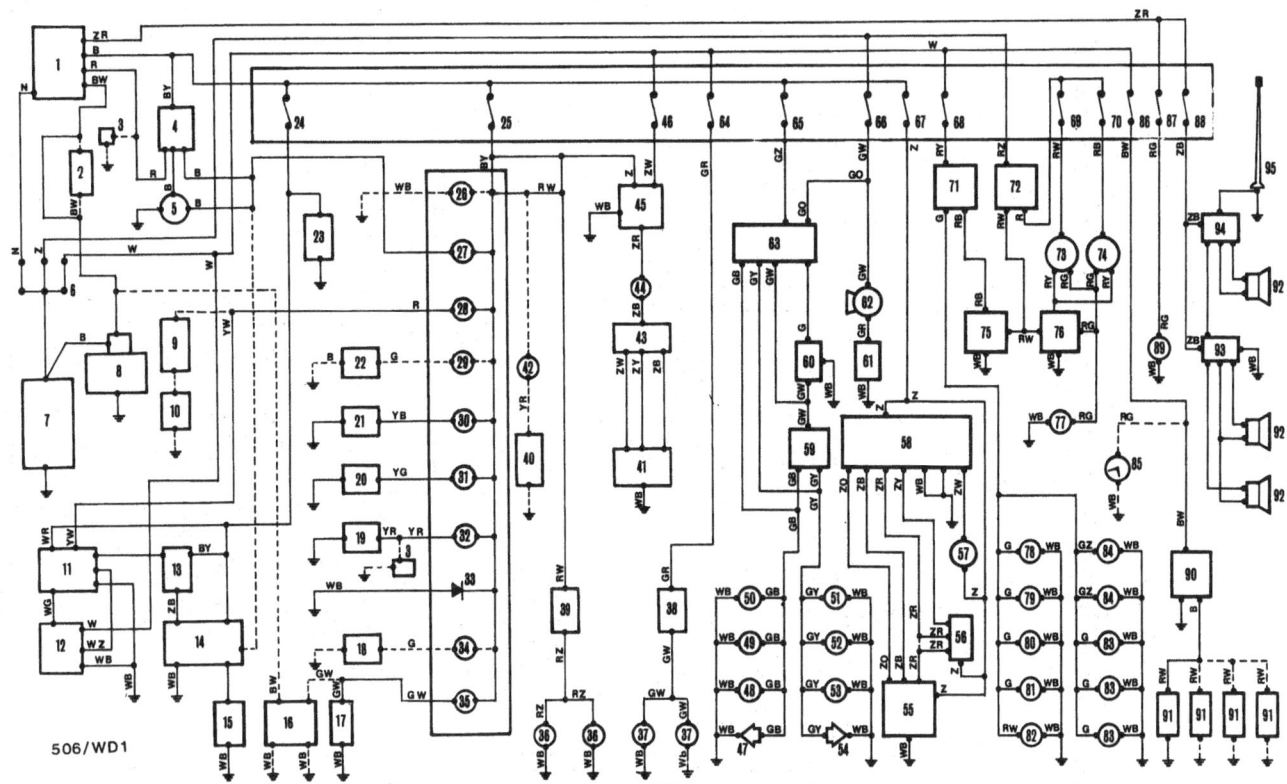

506/WD1

COLOUR CODE

The first letter of the code represents the main wire colour, the other letters represent the trace colours.

B = BLACK
L = BLUE
G = GREEN
R = RED
Y = YELLOW
W = WHITE
N = BROWN
O = ORANGE
K = PINK
S = GREY
V = VIOLET
P = PURPLE
X = LIGHT GREEN
Z = LIGHT BLUE
M = DARK GREEN
T = DARK BLUE
A = LIGHT BROWN
E = SLATE
D = TAN

KEY
1. Ignition switch
2. Neutral safety switch
3. Capacitor
4. Ignition coil
5. Distributor
6. Fusible links
7. Battery
8. Starter motor
9. Choke heater coil
10. Thermistor
11. Alternator regulator
12. Alternator
13. Vacuum switching valve
14. Emission control computer
15. Speed sensor
16. Bulb check relay
17. Brake fluid level switch
18. Four wheel drive warning switch
19. Fuel level sender
20. Water temperature sender
21. Oil pressure switch
22. Hand brake warning lamp switch
23. Fuel cut solenoid
24. Engine fuse
25. Warning lamp fuse
26. Voltmeter
27. Tachometer
28. Charge warning lamp
29. Hand brake warning lamp
30. Oil pressure lamp

31. Water temperature gauge
32. Fuel gauge
33. Diode
34. Four wheel drive warning lamp
35. Brake fluid level warning lamp
36. Reverse lamp
37. Stop lamp
38. Stop lamp switch
39. Reverse lamp switch
40. Oil pressure sender
41. Heater blower switch
42. Oil pressure gauge
43. Heater resistor
44. Heater blower motor
45. Heater relay
46. Heater fuse
47. LH turn signal warning lamp
48. LH front turn signal lamp
49. LH rear turn signal lamp
50. LH side turn signal lamp
51. RH side turn signal lamp
52. RH rear turn signal lamp
53. RH front turn signal lamp
54. RH turn signal warning lamp
55. Windscreen wiper motor
56. Windscreen wiper intermittent relay
57. Windscreen washer motor
58. Windscreen wiper/washer switch
59. Turn signal switch
60. Flasher unit

61. Horn push
62. Horn
63. Hazard switch
64. Stop lamp fuse
65. Turn signal fuse
66. Horn fuse
67. Wiper fuse
68. Tail lamp fuse
69. LH headlamp fuse
70. RH headlamp fuse
71. Tail lamp relay
72. Headlamp relay
73. LH headlamp
74. RH headlamp
75. Light control switch
76. Headlamp dip switch
77. High beam warning lamp
78. LH front parking lamp
79. RH front parking lamp
80. LH tail lamp
81. RH tail lamp
82. Heater control illumination lamp
83. Instrument cluster illumination lamp
84. Number plate lamp
85. Clock
86. Interior dome lamp fuse
87. Cigar lighter fuse
88. Radio fuse
89. Cigar lighter
90. Interior lamp and switch
91. Interior lamp and courtesy switch
92. Radio/cassette speaker
93. Radio cassette
94. Radio
95. Radio antenna

RN36 and RN46 starting, charging, ignition, interior and exterior lighting, climate control, wipers/washers, accessory circuits
1979 to 1989 models - petrol models

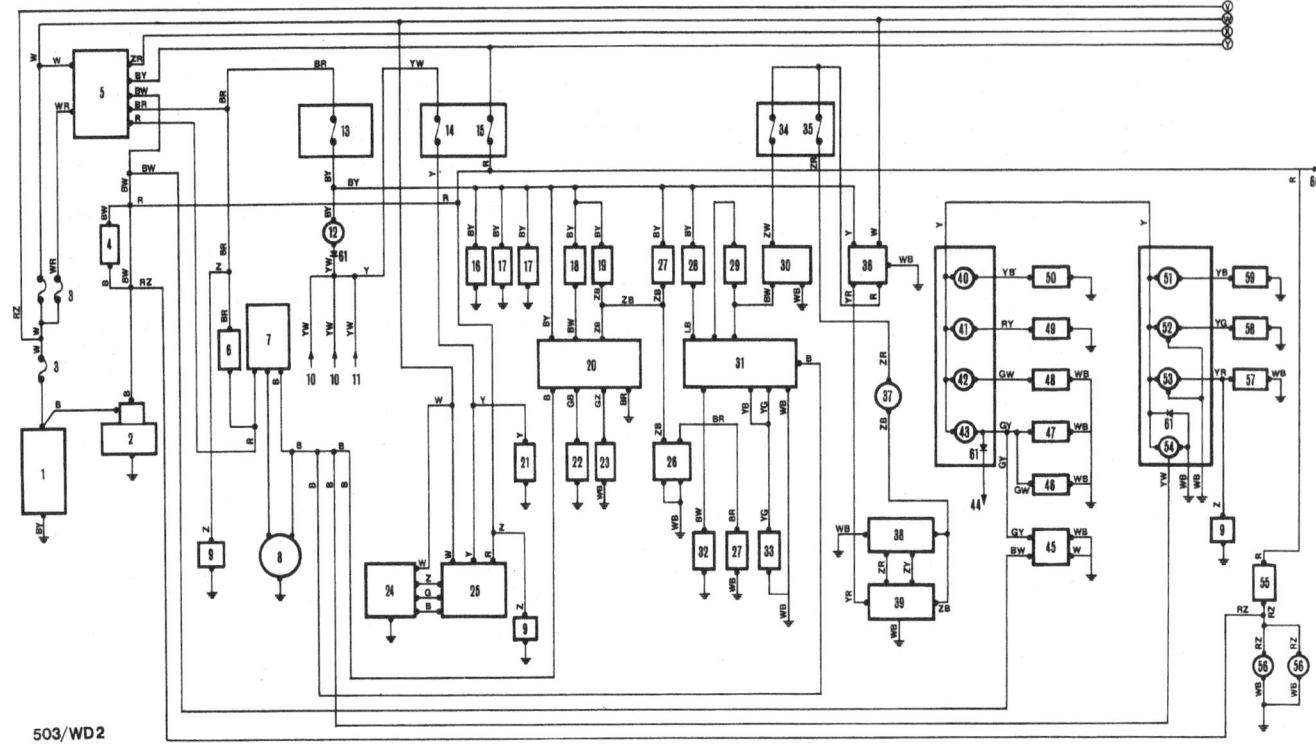

503/WD2

COLOUR CODE

The first letter of the code represents the main wire colour, the other letters represent the trace colours.

B — BLACK
L — BLUE
G — GREEN
R — RED
Y — YELLOW
W — WHITE
N — BROWN
O — ORANGE
K — PINK
S — GREY
V — VIOLET
P — PURPLE
X — LIGHT GREEN
Z — LIGHT BLUE
M — DARK GREEN
T — DARK BLUE
A — LIGHT BROWN
E — SLATE
D — TAN

KEY

1. Battery
2. Starter motor
3. Fusible link
4. Neutral safety switch, automatic transmission
5. Ignition switch
6. Resistor
7. Coil
8. Distributor
9. Condenser
10. To instrument cluster
11. To pre-heating timer
12. Charge warning lamp
13. Ignition fuse
14. Charge fuse
15. Engine fuse
16. Fuel cut solenoid
17. Bowl/outer vent valve
18. Fuel cut solenoid
19. Vacuum switching valve
20. Emission control computer
21. Choke heater coil
22. Vacuum switch
23. Speed sensor
24. Alternator
25. Alternator regulator
26. Idle up relay
27. Idle up vacuum switch
28. Vacuum switching valve
29. Low pressure switch
30. Air conditioner switch and warning lamp
31. Air conditioner control amplifier
32. Air conditioner compressor

33. Thermistor
34. Air conditioner fuse
35. Heater fuse
36. Heater relay
37. Heater blower motor
38. Resistor resistor
39. Heater blower switch
40. Oil pressure warning lamp
41. Four wheel drive warning lamp
42. Parking brake warning lamp
43. Brake fluid level warning lamp
44. To charge fuse
45. Bulb check relay
46. Vacuum switch
47. Brake fluid level switch
48. Parking brake warning switch
49. Four wheel drive control switch
50. Oil pressure switch
51. Oil pressure gauge
52. Coolant temperature gauge
53. Fuel gauge
54. Tachometer
55. Reverse lamp switch
56. Reverse lamps
57. Fuel level sender
58. Coolant temperature sender
59. Oil pressure sender
60. To turn signal switch
61. Diode

YN63, YN65, YN67 starting, charging, emission control, climate control, warning lamps, stop and reverse lamps
1979 to 1989 models - petrol models

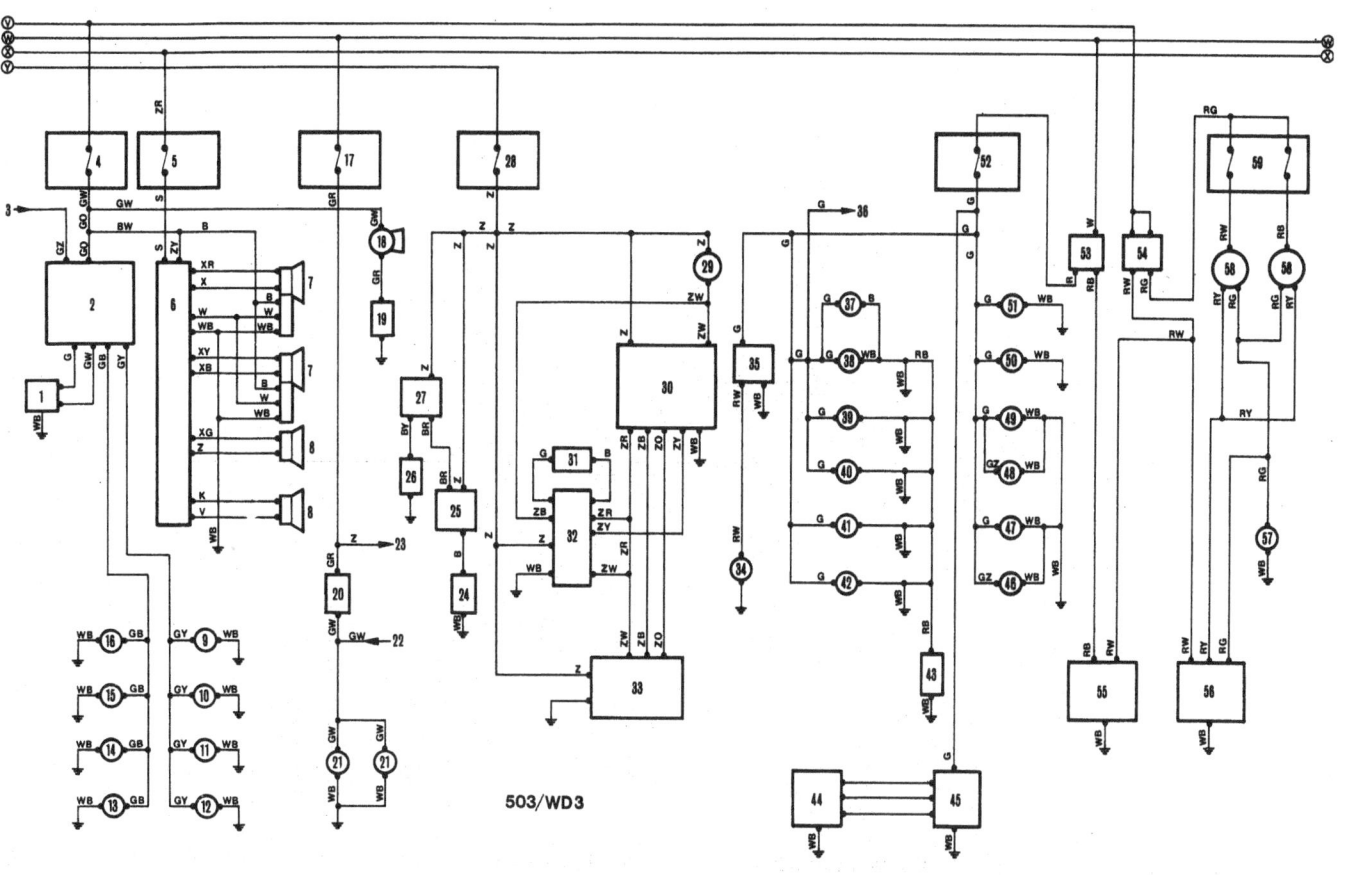

503/WD3

COLOUR CODE

The first letter of the code represents the main wire colour, the other letters represent the trace colours.

B — BLACK
L — BLUE
G — GREEN
R — RED
Y — YELLOW
W — WHITE
N — BROWN
O — ORANGE
K — PINK
S — GREY
V — VIOLET
P — PURPLE
X — LIGHT GREEN
Z — LIGHT BLUE
M — DARK GREEN
T — DARK BLUE
A — LIGHT BROWN
E — SLATE
D — TAN

KEY

1. Flasher unit
2. Turn signal control switch
3. To engine fuse
4. Turn signal lamp/horn fuse
5. Cigar lighter/radio fuse
6. Radio cassette
7. R H rear speakers
8. L H rear speakers
9. R H turn signal warning lamp
10. R H front turn signal lamp
11. R H side turn signal lamp
12. R H rear turn signal lamp
13. L H rear turn signal lamp
14. L H side turn signal lamp
15. L H front turn signal lamp
16. L H turn signal warning lamp
17. Stop lamp fuse
18. Horn
19. Horn push
20. Stop lamp switch
21. Stop lamps
22. To cruise control computer
23. To cruise control computer
24. Overdrive main switch (2 WD only)
25. Overdrive warning lamp (2 WD only)
26. Overdrive solenoid (2 WD only)
27. Overdrive relay (2 WD only)
28. Wiper fuse

29. Windscreen washer motor
30. Windscreen wiper/ washer control switch
31. Intermittent time switch
32. Windscreen wiper relay
33. Windscreen wiper motor
34. Work lamp
35. Work lamp switch
36. To digital clock
37. Inclinometer illumination lamp
38. Heater control illumination lamp
39. Automatic Transmission quadrant illumination lamp
40. Overdrive switch illumination lamp
41. Instrument cluster illumination lamp
42. Demister switch illumination lamp
43. Rheostat
44. Luggage compartment lamp and switch
45. Deck lamp and switch
46. Number plate lamp
47. L H rear parking lamp
48. Number plate lamp
49. R H rear parking lamp
50. L H front parking lamp
51. R H front parking lamp
52. Tail lamp fuse
53. Tail lamp relay
54. Headlamp relay
55. Light control switch
56. Headlamp dip switch
57. High beam warning lamp
58. Headlamps
59. Headlamp fuses

YN63, YN65, YN67 interior and exterior lighting, automatic transmission overdrive control, horn, audio system
1979 to 1989 models - petrol models

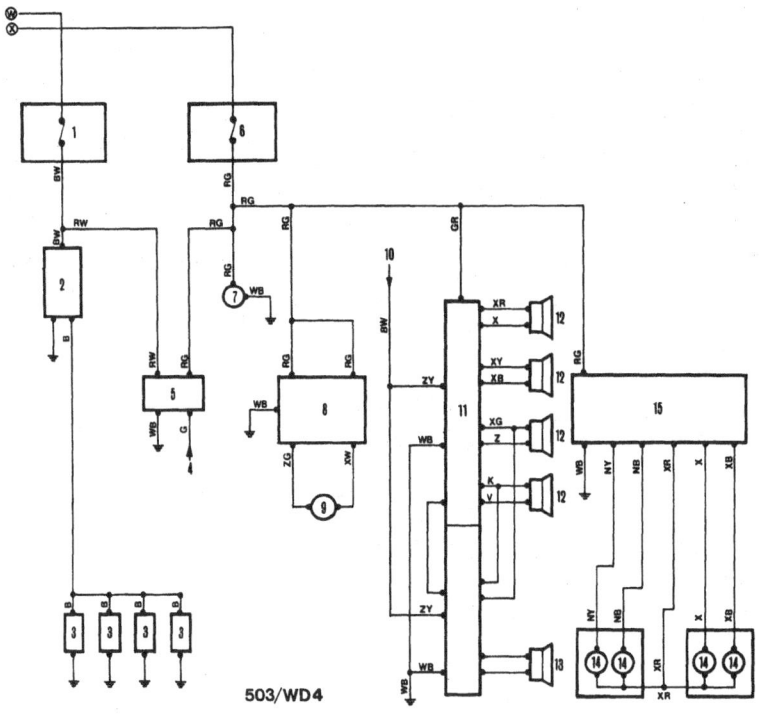

503/WD4

COLOUR CODE	KEY

COLOUR CODE

The first letter of the code represents the main wire colour, the other letters represent the trace colours.

B — BLACK
L — BLUE
G — GREEN
R — RED
Y — YELLOW
W — WHITE
N — BROWN
O — ORANGE
K — PINK
S — GREY
V — VIOLET
P — PURPLE
X — LIGHT GREEN
Z — LIGHT BLUE
M — DARK GREEN
T — DARK BLUE
A — LIGHT BROWN
E — SLATE
D — TAN

KEY

1. Interior dome lamp fuse
2. Interior lamp and switch
3. Interior lamp courtesy switches
4. To tail lamp fuse
5. Digital clock
6. Cigar lighter fuse
7. Cigar lighter
8. Radio antenna control switch
9. Radio antenna motor
10. To turn signal/horn fuse
11. Radio cassette
12. Speakers
13. Woofer speaker
14. Exterior mirror motors
15. Exterior mirror control switch

YN63, YN65, YN67 interior illumination, digital clock, audio system, power mirror circuits
1979 to 1989 models - petrol models

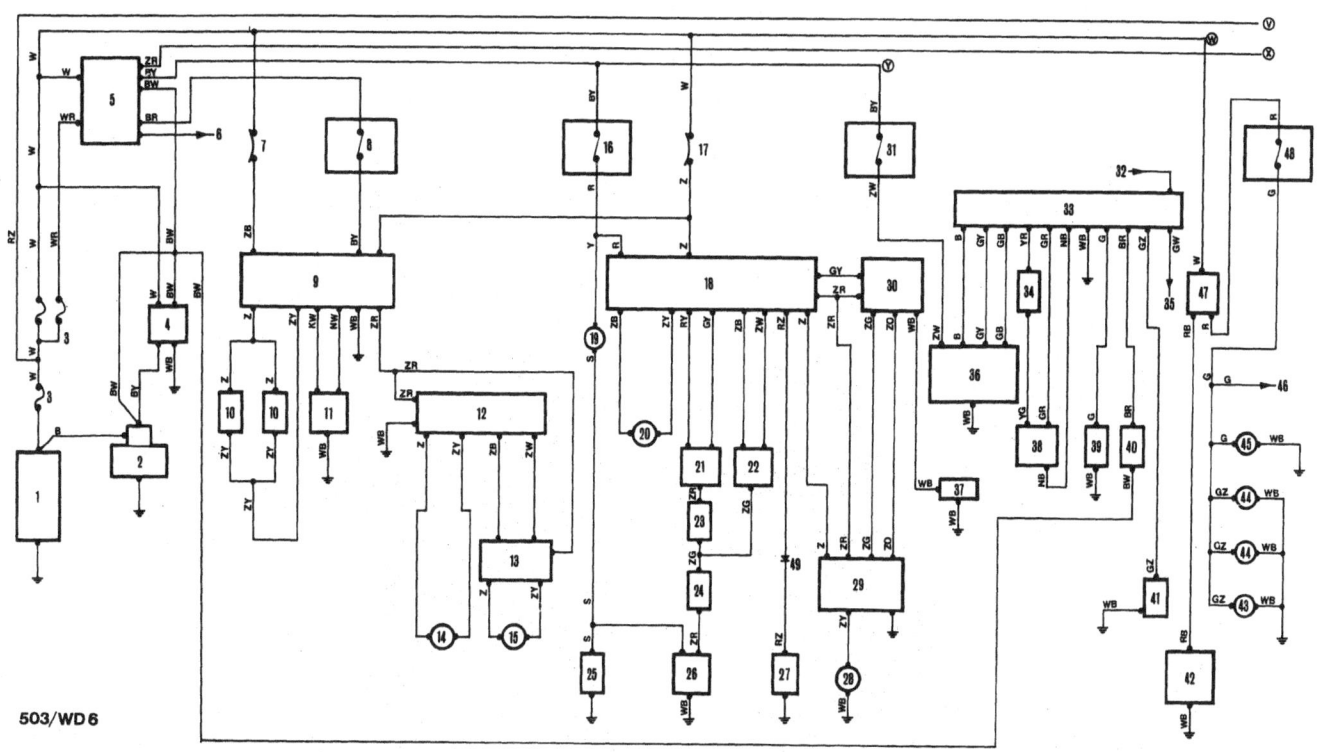

503/WD 6

COLOUR CODE

The first letter of the code represents the main wire colour, the other letters represent the trace colours.

B — BLACK
L — BLUE
G — GREEN
R — RED
Y — YELLOW
W — WHITE
N — BROWN
O — ORANGE
K — PINK
S — GREY
V — VIOLET
P — PURPLE
X — LIGHT GREEN
Z — LIGHT BLUE
M — DARK GREEN
T — DARK BLUE
A — LIGHT BROWN
E — SLATE
D — TAN

KEY

1. Battery
2. Starter motor
3. Fusible link
4. Starter relay
5. Ignition switch
6. To glow plug circuit (diesel)
7. Power operated door lock circuit breaker
8. Ignition fuse
9. Door lock control relay
10. Door lock solenoids
11. Door lock control switch
12. Power operated window master control switch
13. L H power operated window control switch
14. R H power operated window motor
15. L H power operated window motor
16. Engine fuse
17. Power operated window circuit breaker
18. Power operated rear window and wiper relay
19. Tailgate unlock warning lamp
20. Tailgate rear window motor
21. Rear window control switch
22. Rear window inner control switch
23. Rear window lock switch
24. Canopy off window safety switch
25. Tailgate lock/window warning switch

26. Tailgate lock detection switch
27. Rear window limit switch
28. Rear window washer motor
29. Rear window wiper/washer control switch
30. Rear wiper motor
31. Wiper fuse
32. To stop lamp fuse
33. Cruise control computer
34. Cruise control stop switch
35. To stop lamp
36. Cruise control main switch
37. Rear window wiper retention detection switch
38. Cruise control clutch switch
39. Parking brake switch
40. Cruise control clutch switch
41. Speed sensor
42. Light control switch
43. Rear window wiper/washer control switch illumination lamp
44. Rear window control switch illumination lamp
45. Cruise control switch illumination lamp
46. To deck lamp
47. Tail lamp relay
48. Tail lamp fuse
49. Diode

YN63 power door locks, power windows, rear window wiper/washers, cruise control
1979 to 1989 models - petrol models

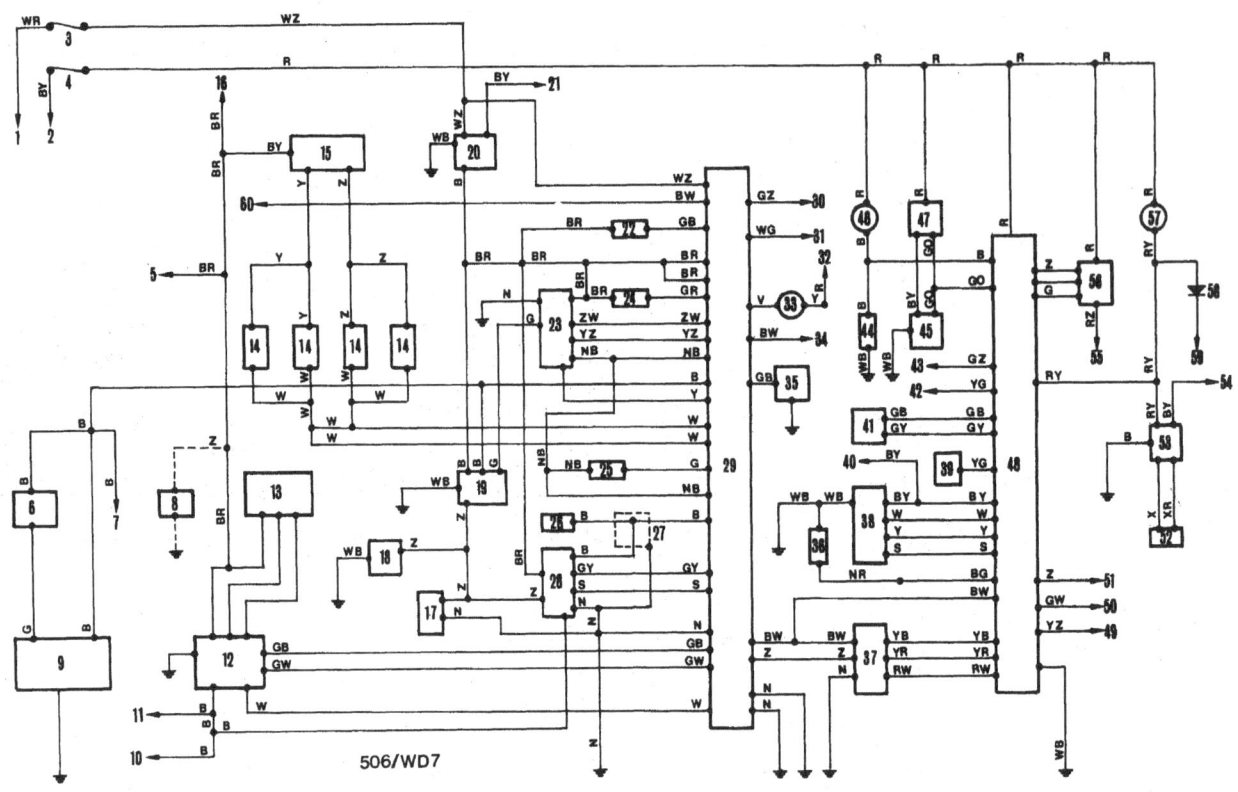

506/WD7

COLOUR CODE

The first letter of the code represents the main wire colour, the other letters represent the trace colours.

B = BLACK
L = BLUE
G = GREEN
R = RED
Y = YELLOW
W = WHITE
N = BROWN
O = ORANGE
K = PINK
S = GREY
V = VIOLET
P = PURPLE
X = LIGHT GREEN
Z = LIGHT BLUE
M = DARK GREEN
T = DARK BLUE
A = LIGHT BROWN
E = SLATE
D = TAN

KEY

1. To fusible link
2. To ignition switch
3. Electronic fuel injection fuse
4. Engine fuse
5. To ignition switch
6. Cold start injector
7. To starter motor
8. Capacitor
9. Cold start injector time switch
11. To air conditioner amplifier
12. Distributor
13. Ignition coil
14. Injector
15. Resistor
16. To ignition fuse
17. Air valve
18. Fuel pump
19. Circuit opening relay
20. Electronic fuel injection main relay
21. To ignition fuse
22. Fuel pressure vacuum switching valve
23. Air flow meter
24. Idle speed control valve
25. Water temperature sensor
26. Oxygen sensor
27. Shielded cable
28. Check connector
29. Electronic fuel injection control unit
30. To speed sensor
31. To air conditioner amplifier
32. To engine fuse
33. Check engine indicator lamp

34. To air conditioner compressor
35. Water temperature switch
36. Transmission speed sensor
37. Throttle position sensor
38. Transmission solenoid
39. Check connector
40. To cruise control computer
41. Automatic transmission fluid temperature sensor
42. To overdrive relay
43. To vehicle speed sensor
44. Overdrive main switch
45. Automatic transmission indicator
46. Overdrive OFF indicator lamp
47. Transmission pattern selector switch
48. Transmission control unit
49. To four wheel drive indicator switch
50. To stop lamp switch
51. To stop fuse
52. Automatic transmission fluid temperature sensor
53. Transmission control computer
54. To ignition fuse
55. To reverse lamps
56. Neutral safety switch
57. Automatic transmission fluid temperature warning lamp
58. Diode
59. To Charge fuse
60. To ignition switch

YN61 starting, ignition, EFI, automatic transmission control module
1979 to 1989 models - petrol models

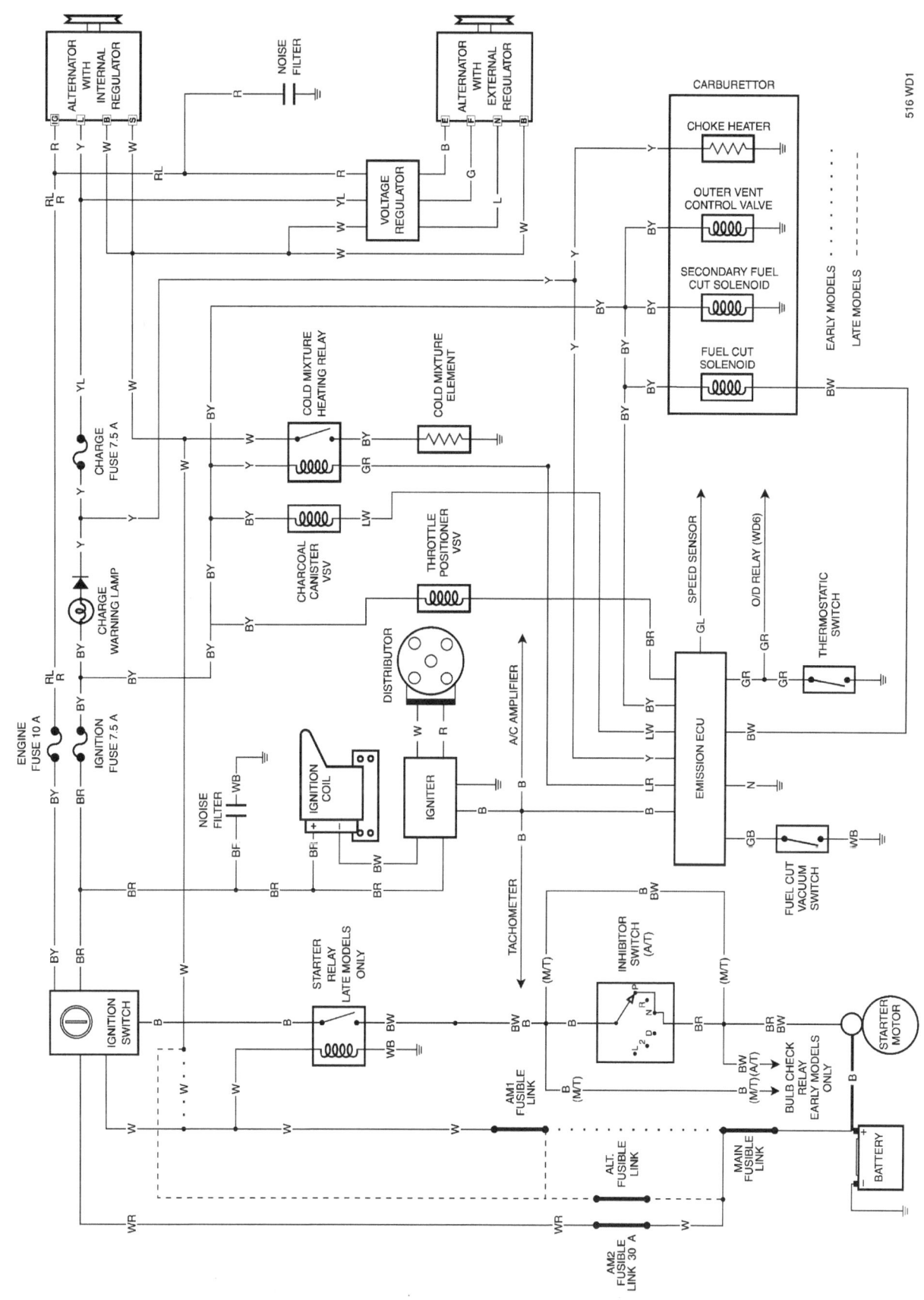

Starting, charging, ignition, carburettor and emission control systems
Models from 1990 - petrol models

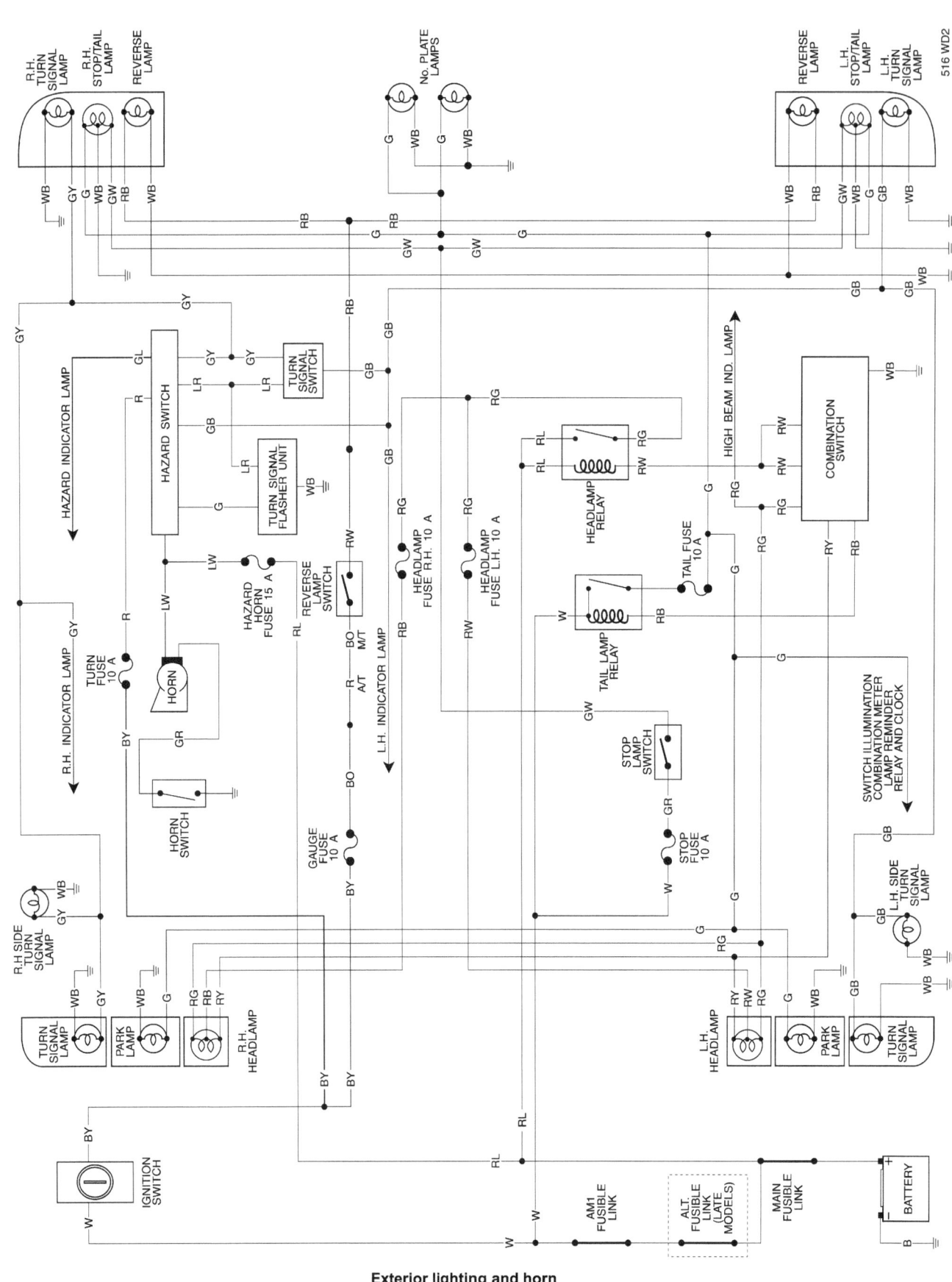

Exterior lighting and horn
Models from 1990 - petrol models

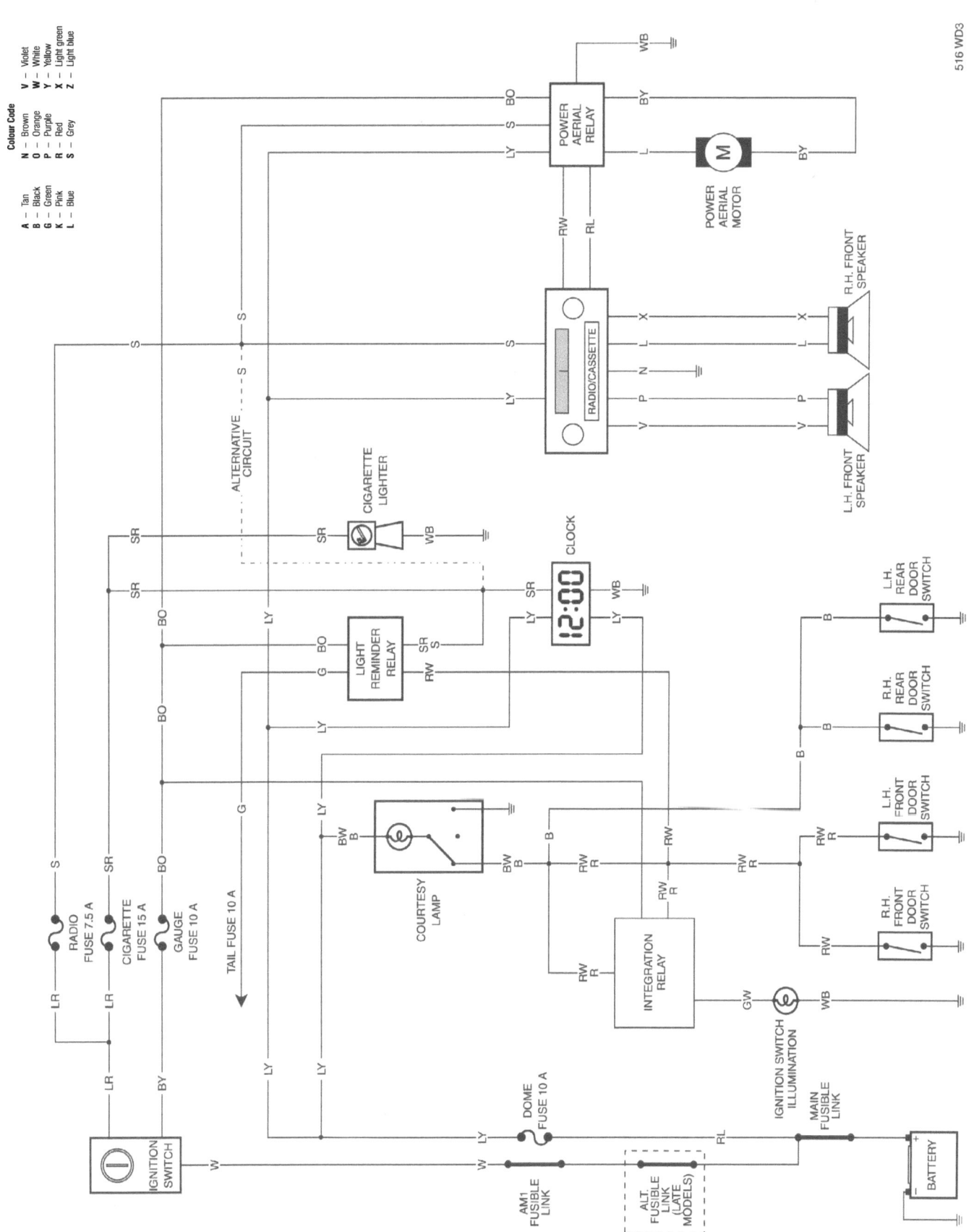

Courtesy lamp, clock, cigarette lighter and sound system
Models from 1990 - petrol models

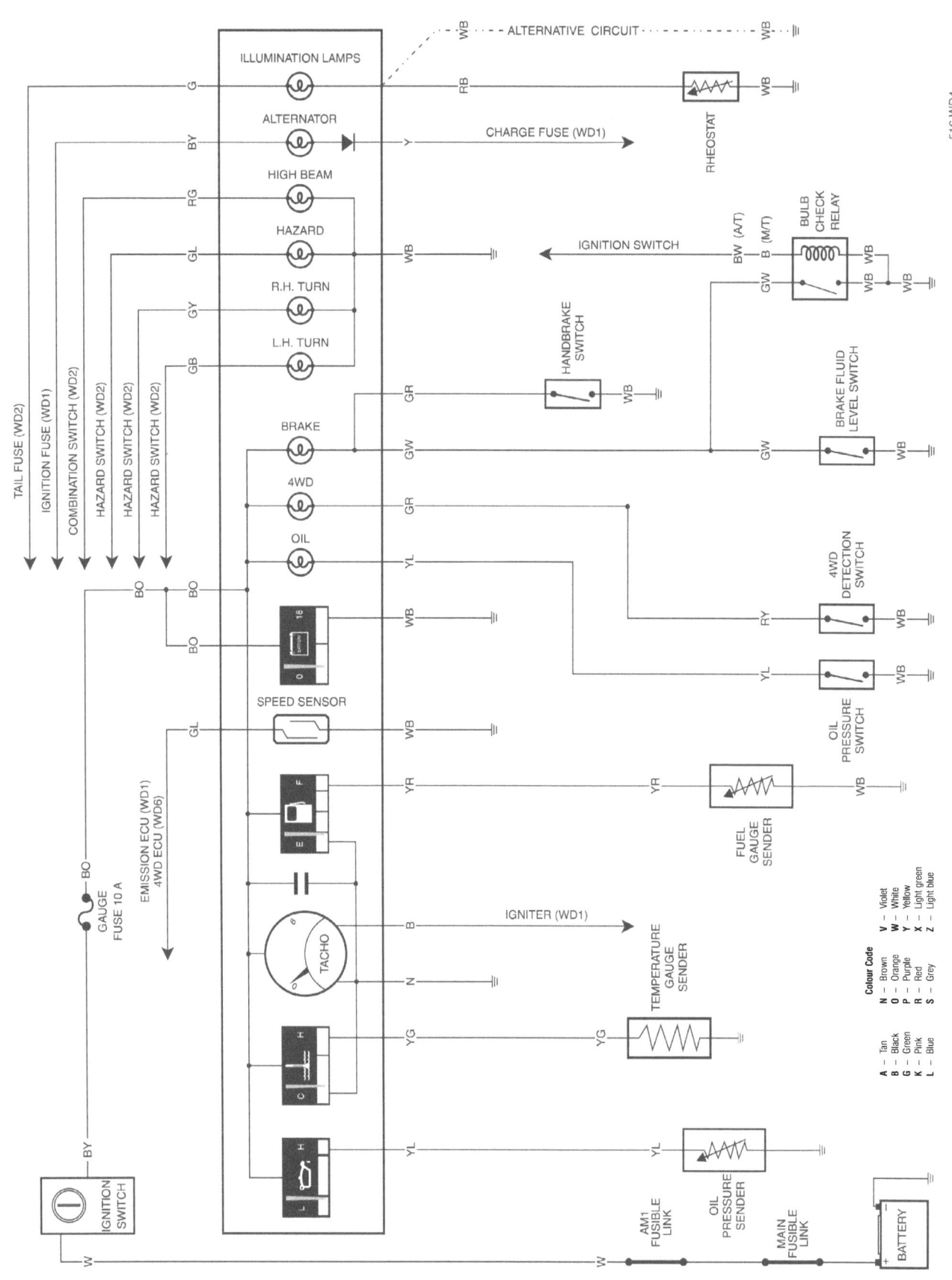

Instrument cluster
Models prior to August 1991 - petrol models

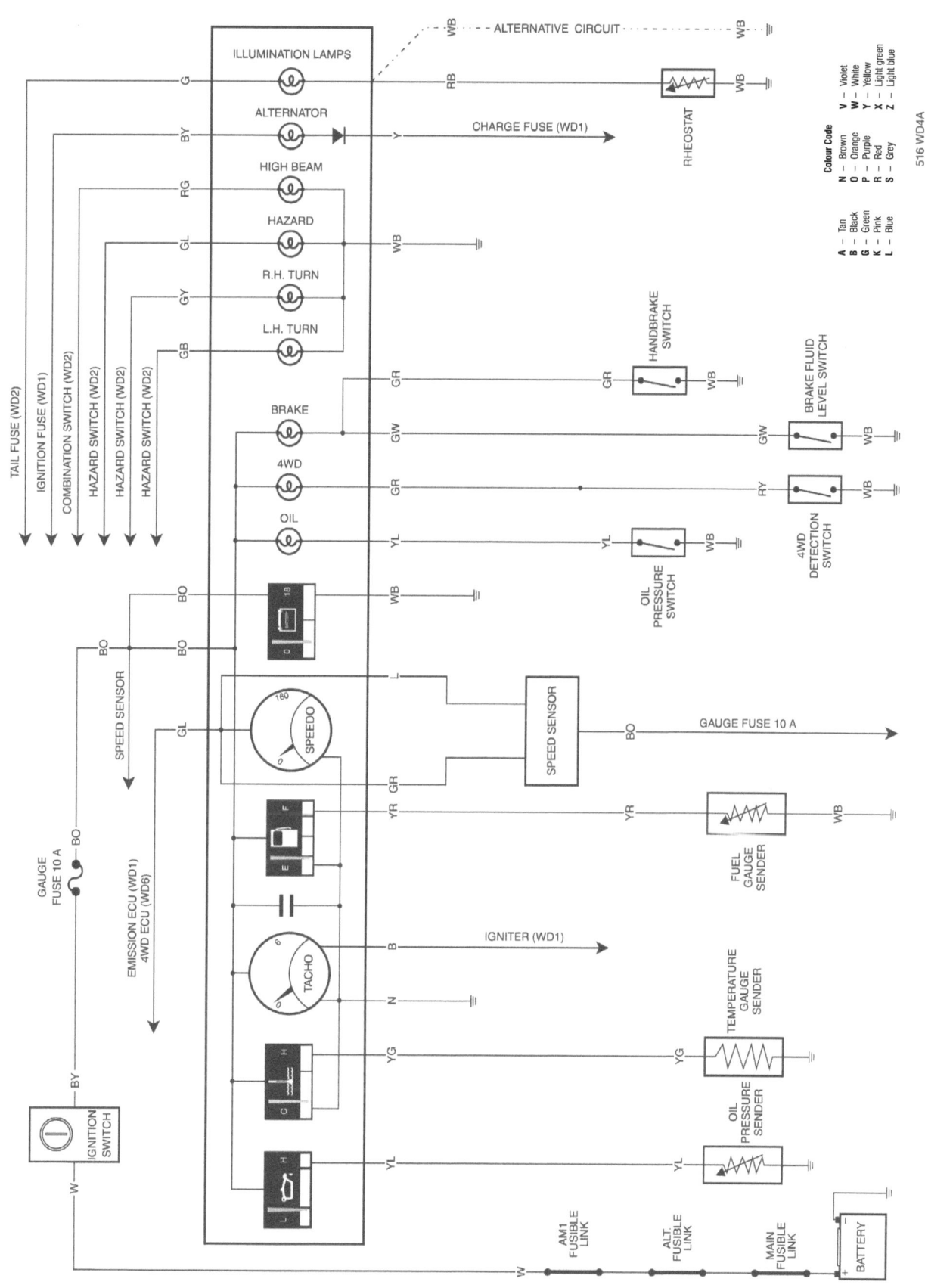

Instrument cluster
Models from August 1991 - petrol models

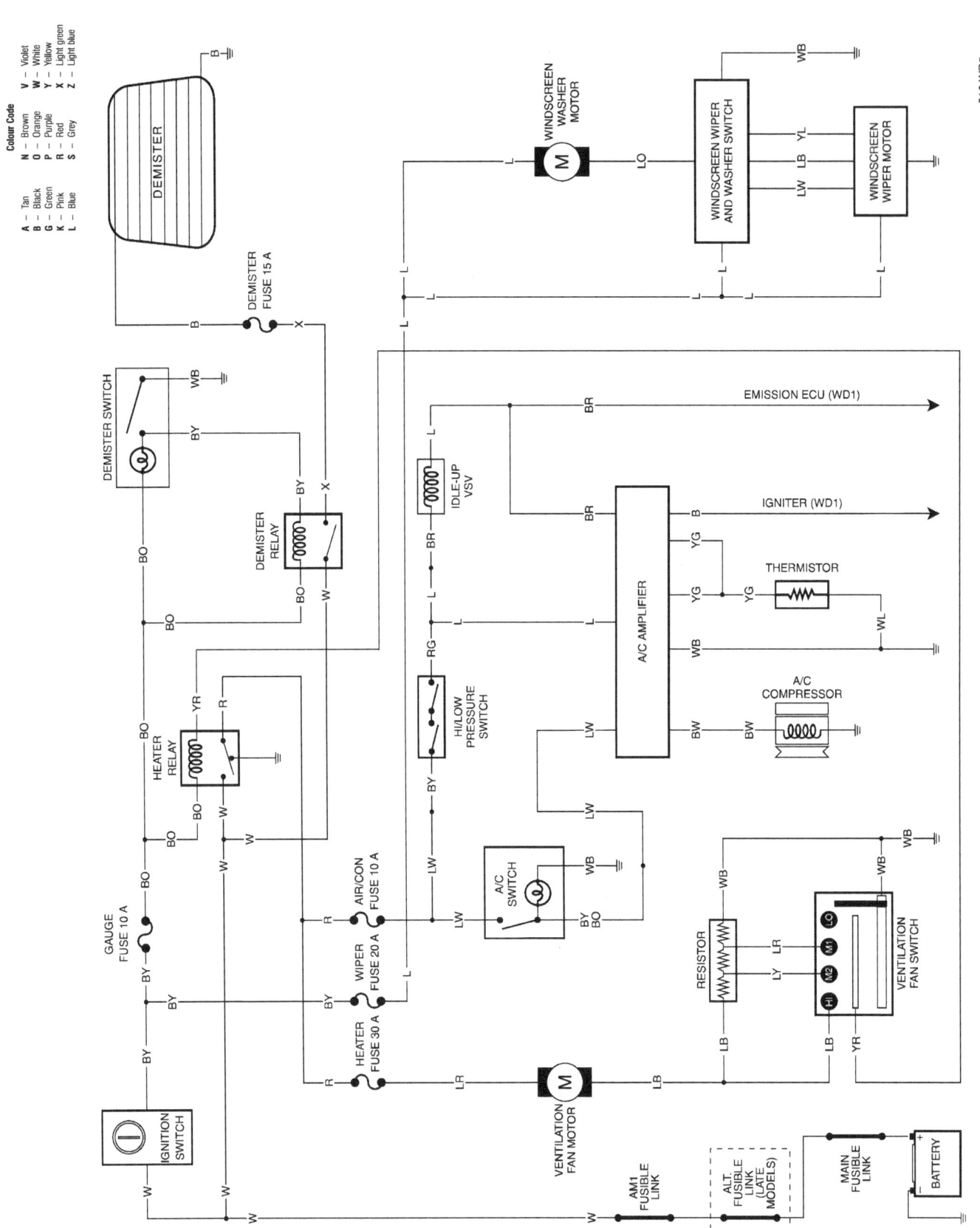

Ventilation system, air conditioning, demister and windscreen wiper and washer
Models from 1990 - petrol models

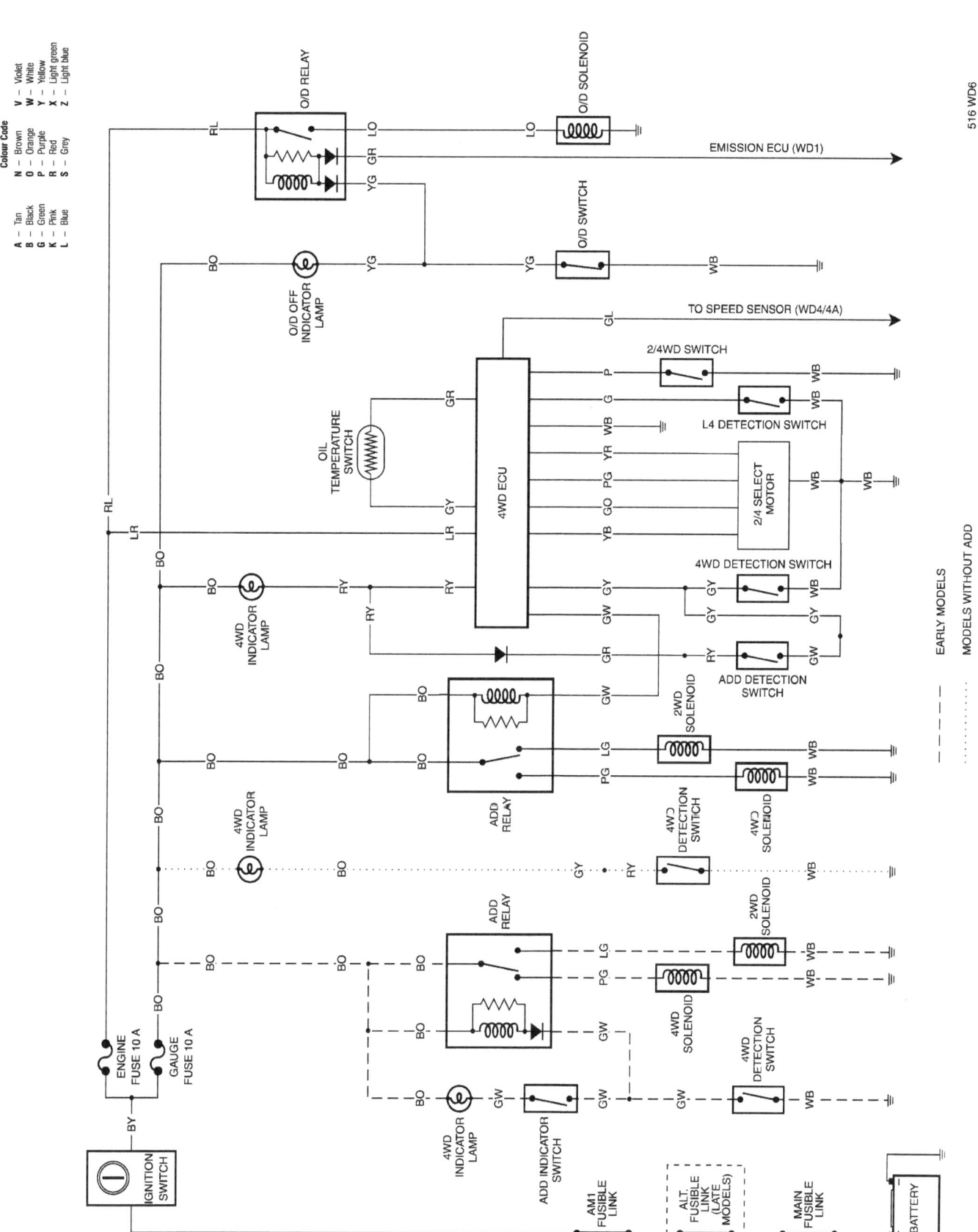

516 WD6

Automatic disconnecting differential (ADD) system, 4WD lamp and automatic transmission overdrive
Models from 1990 - petrol models

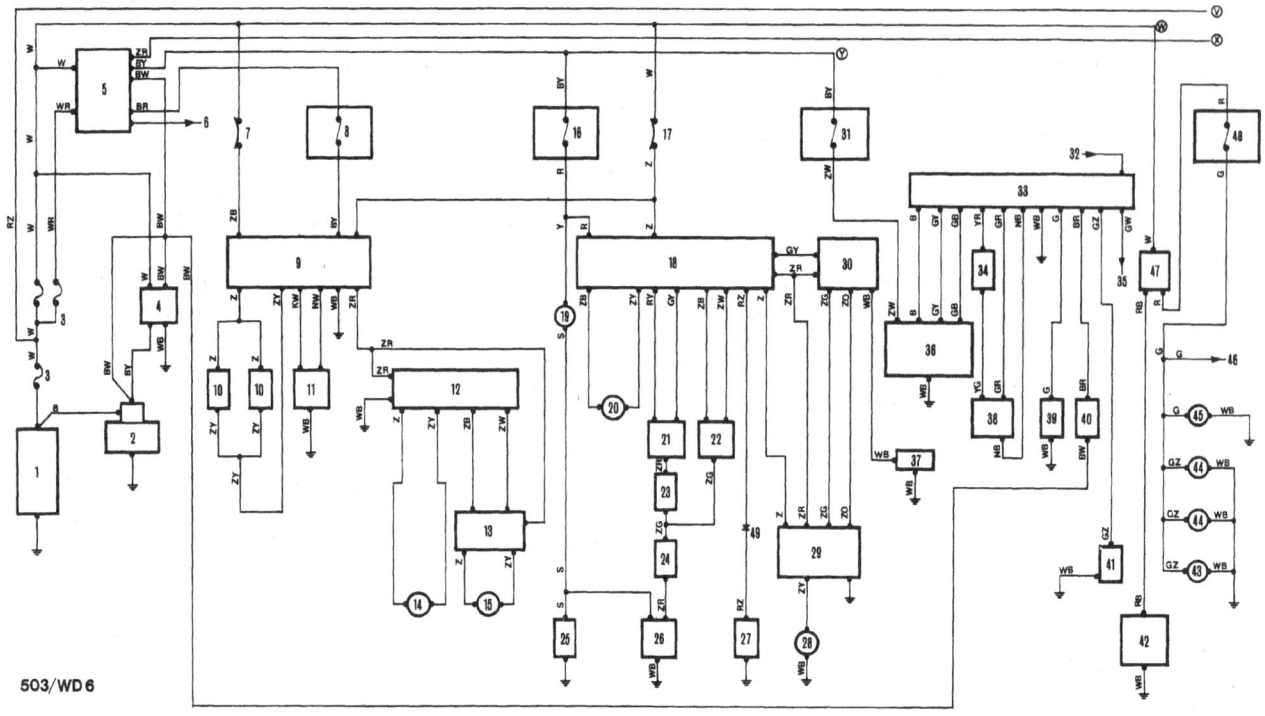

503/WD 6

COLOUR CODE

The first letter of the code represents the main wire colour, the other letters represent the trace colours.

B — BLACK
L — BLUE
G — GREEN
R — RED
Y — YELLOW
W — WHITE
N — BROWN
O — ORANGE
K — PINK
S — GREY
V — VIOLET
P — PURPLE
X — LIGHT GREEN
Z — LIGHT BLUE
M — DARK GREEN
T — DARK BLUE
A — LIGHT BROWN
E — SLATE
D — TAN

KEY

1. Battery
2. Starter motor
3. Fusible link
4. Starter relay
5. Ignition switch
6. To glow plug circuit
7. Power operated door lock circuit breaker
8. Ignition fuse
9. Door lock control relay
10. Door lock solenoids
11. Door lock control switch
12. Power operated window master control switch
13. L H power operated window control switch
14. R H power operated window motor
15. L H power operated window motor
16. Engine fuse
17. Power operated window circuit breaker
18. Power operated rear window and wiper relay
19. Tailgate unlock warning lamp
20. Tailgate rear window motor
21. Rear window control switch
22. Rear window inner control switch
23. Rear window lock switch
24. Canopy off window safety switch
25. Tailgate lock/window warning switch
26. Tailgate lock detection switch

27. Rear window limit switch
28. Rear window washer motor
29. Rear window wiper/washer control switch
30. Rear wiper motor
31. Wiper fuse
32. To stop lamp fuse (petrol engine)
33. Cruise control computer (petrol engine)
34. Cruise control stop switch (petrol engine)
35. To stop lamp (petrol engine)
36. Cruise control main switch (petrol engine)
37. Rear window wiper retention detection switch
38. Cruise control clutch switch (petrol engine)
39. Parking brake switch (petrol engine)
40. Cruise control clutch switch (petrol engine)
41. Speed sensor (petrol engine)
42. Light control switch
43. Rear window wiper/washer control switch illumination lamp
44. Rear window control switch illumination lamp
45. Cruise control switch illumination lamp (petrol engine)
46. To deck lamp
47. Tail lamp relay
48. Tail lamp fuse
49. Diode

Power door locks, power windows, rear wiper/washer, cruise control.
LN61 4Runner models and Hi-Lux models to 1998 - diesel models

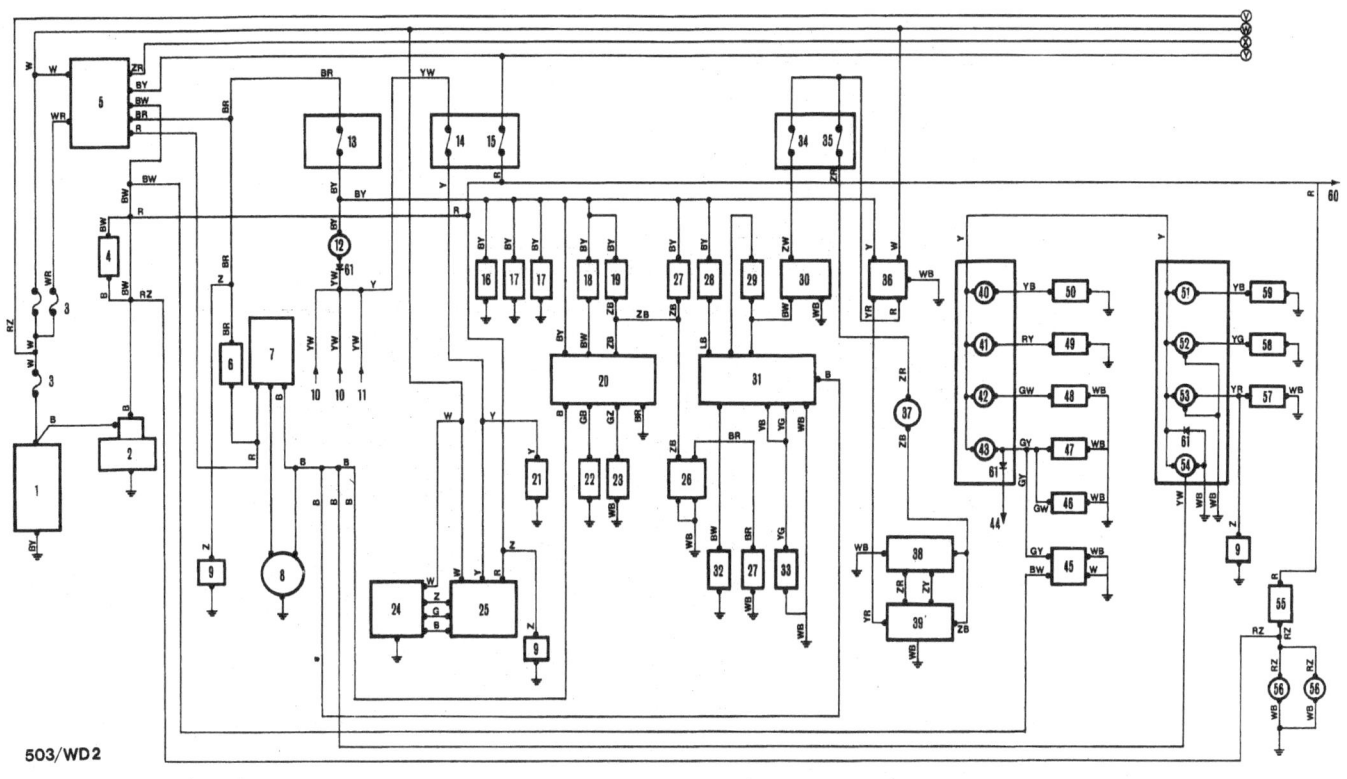

503/WD2

COLOUR CODE

The first letter of the code represents the main wire colour, the other letters represent the trace colours.

B — BLACK
L — BLUE
G — GREEN
R — RED
Y — YELLOW
W — WHITE
N — BROWN
O — ORANGE
K — PINK
S — GREY
V — VIOLET
P — PURPLE
X — LIGHT GREEN
Z — LIGHT BLUE
M — DARK GREEN
T — DARK BLUE
A — LIGHT BROWN
E — SLATE
D — TAN

KEY

1. Battery
2. Starter motor
3. Fusible link
4. Neutral safety switch, automatic transmission
5. Ignition switch
6. Resistor (petrol engine)
7. Coil (petrol engine)
8. Distributor (petrol engine)
9. Condenser (petrol engine)
10. To instrument cluster
11. To pre-heating timer
12. Charge warning lamp
13. Ignition fuse
14. Charge fuse
15. Engine fuse
16. Fuel cut solenoid
17. Bowl/outer vent valve (petrol engine)
18. Fuel cut solenoid (petrol engine)
19. Vacuum switching valve (petrol engine)
20. Emission control computer (petrol engine)
21. Choke heater coil (petrol engine)
22. Vacuum switch (petrol engine)
23. Speed sensor (petrol engine)
24. Alternator
25. Alternator regulator
26. Idle up relay
27. Idle up vacuum switch
28. Vacuum switching valve
29. Low pressure switch
30. Air conditioner switch and warning lamp

31. Air conditioner control amplifier
32. Air conditioner compressor
33. Thermistor
34. Air conditioner fuse
35. Heater fuse
36. Heater relay
37. Heater blower motor
38. Heater resistor
39. Heater blower switch
40. Oil pressure warning lamp
41. Four wheel drive warning lamp
42. Parking brake warning lamp
43. Brake fluid level warning lamp
44. To charge fuse
45. Bulb check relay
46. Vacuum switch
47. Brake fluid level switch
48. Parking brake warning switch
49. Four wheel drive control switch
50. Oil pressure switch
51. Oil pressure gauge
52. Coolant temperature gauge
53. Fuel gauge
54. Tachometer
55. Reverse lamp switch
56. Reverse lamps
57. Fuel level sender
58. Coolant temperature sender
59. Oil pressure sender
60. To turn signal switch
61. Diode

Starting, charging, emission control, air conditioning, warning lamps, stop lamps, reverse lamps.
LN61 and LN65 4Runner models and Hi-Lux models to 1998 - diesel models

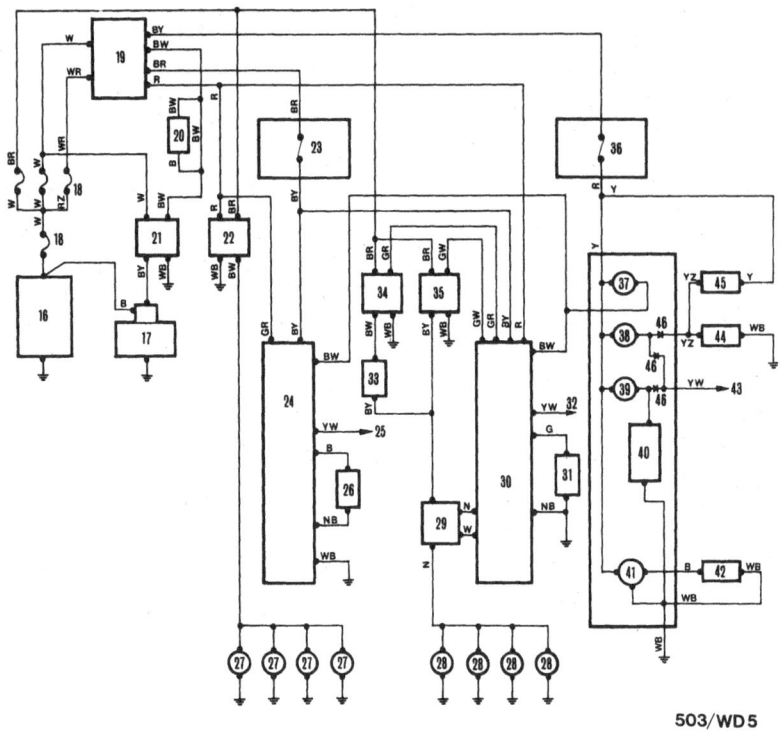

503/WD 5

COLOUR CODE

The first letter of the code represents the main wire colour, the other letters represent the trace colours.

B — BLACK
L — BLUE
G — GREEN
R — RED
Y — YELLOW
W — WHITE
N — BROWN
O — ORANGE
K — PINK
S — GREY
V — VIOLET
P — PURPLE
X — LIGHT GREEN
Z — LIGHT BLUE
M — DARK GREEN
T — DARK BLUE
A — LIGHT BROWN
E — SLATE
D — TAN

KEY

16. Battery
17. Starter motor
18. Fusible link
19. Ignition switch
20. Neutral safety switch automatic transmission
21. Starter relay
22. Glow plug relay, variable delay type
23. Ignition fuse
24. Preheating timer variable delay type
25. To charge fuse
26. Water thermo sensor, variable delay type
27. Glow plugs, variable delay type
28. Glow plugs, super glow type
29. Glow plug current sensor, super glow type.
30. Preheating timer, super glow type

31. Water thermo sensor, super glow type
32. To charge fuse
33. Glow plug resistor. Super glow type
34. Afterglow glow plug relay, super glow type
35. Glow plug relay, super glow type
36. Engine fuse
37. Glow plug warning lamp
38. Fuel filter warning lamp
39. Timing belt warning lamp
40. Timing belt warning control switch
41. Tachometer
42. Tachometer pick up sensor
43. To charge fuse
44. Fuel filter warning control switch
45. Fuel filter warning buzzer
46. Diode

Starting, pre-heat system.
LN61 and LN65 4Runner models and Hi-Lux models to 1998 - diesel models

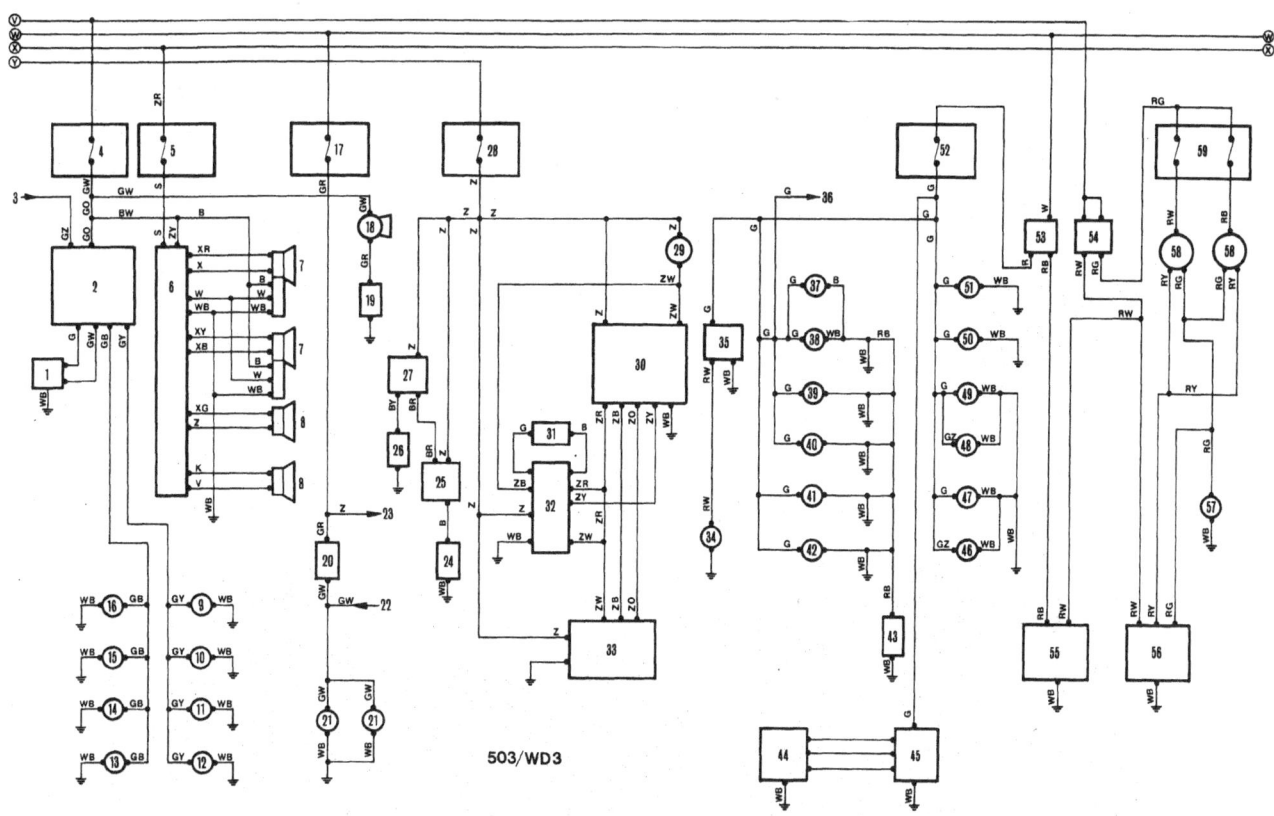

503/WD3

COLOUR CODE

The first letter of the code represents the main wire colour, the other letters represent the trace colours.

B — BLACK
L — BLUE
G — GREEN
R — RED
Y — YELLOW
W — WHITE
N — BROWN
O — ORANGE
K — PINK
S — GREY
V — VIOLET
P — PURPLE
X — LIGHT GREEN
Z — LIGHT BLUE
M — DARK GREEN
T — DARK BLUE
A — LIGHT BROWN
E — SLATE
D — TAN

KEY

1. Flasher unit
2. Turn signal control switch
3. To engine fuse
4. Turn signal lamp/horn fuse
5. Cigar lighter/radio fuse
6. Radio cassette
7. R H rear speakers
8. L H rear speakers
9. R H turn signal warning lamp
10. R H front turn signal lamp
11. R H side turn signal lamp
12. R H rear turn signal lamp
13. L H rear turn signal lamp
14. L H side turn signal lamp
15. L H front turn signal lamp
16. L H turn signal warning lamp
17. Stop lamp fuse
18. Horn
19. Horn push
20. Stop lamp switch
21. Stop lamps
22. To cruise control computer (petrol engine)
23. To cruise control computer (petrol engine)
24. Overdrive main switch
25. Overdrive warning lamp
26. Overdrive solenoid
27. Overdrive relay
28. Wiper fuse
29. Windscreen washer motor
30. Windscreen wiper/ washer control switch
31. Intermittent time switch
32. Windscreen wiper relay
33. Windscreen wiper motor
34. Work lamp
35. Work lamp switch
36. To digital clock
37. Inclinometer illumination lamp
38. Heater control illumination lamp
39. Automatic Transmission quadrant illumination lamp
40. Overdrive switch illumination lamp
41. Instrument cluster illumination lamp
42. Demister switch illumination lamp
43. Rheostat
44. Luggage compartment lamp and switch
45. Deck lamp and switch
46. Number plate lamp
47. L H rear parking lamp
48. Number plate lamp
49. R H rear parking lamp
50. L H front parking lamp
51. R H front parking lamp
52. Tail lamp fuse
53. Tail lamp relay
54. Headlamp relay
55. Light control switch
56. Headlamp dip switch
57. High beam warning lamp
58. Headlamps
59. Headlamp fuses

Exterior lighting, interior lighting, instrument illumination, horn, audio system, automatic transmission control.
LN61 and LN 65 4Runner models and Hi-Lux models to 1998 - diesel models

COLOUR CODE

The first letter of the code represents the main wire colour, the other letters represent the trace colours.

B — BLACK
L — BLUE
G — GREEN
R — RED
Y — YELLOW
W — WHITE
N — BROWN
O — ORANGE
K — PINK
S — GREY
V — VIOLET
P — PURPLE
X — LIGHT GREEN
Z — LIGHT BLUE
M — DARK GREEN
T — DARK BLUE
A — LIGHT BROWN
E — SLATE
D — TAN

KEY

1. Battery
2. Starter motor
3. Starter relay
4. Fusible links
5. Ignition switch
6. Glow plug warning lamp
7. Glow plug timer
8. Glow plug relay
9. Glow plugs
10. Coolant temperature sender
11. Resistor solenoid
12. Fuel cut solenoid
13. Alternator
14. Alternator regulator
15. Engine fuse
16. Four wheel drive warning control switch
17. Fuel level sender
18. Condenser
19. Coolant temperature sender
20. Oil pressure switch
21. Sedimenter switch
22. Vacuum switch
23. Brake fluid level switch
24. Brake fluid level warning lamp
25. Timing belt warning lamp
26. Timing belt warning cancelling switch
27. Charge warning lamp
28. Sedimenter warning buzzer
29. Oil pressure warning lamp
30. Coolant temperature gauge
31. Fuel gauge
32. Four wheel drive warning lamp
33. Instrument cluster warning lamp fuse
34. Heater fuse
35. Heater relay
36. Air conditioner controls amplifier
37. Heater blower motor
38. Heater resistor
39. Thermal switch
40. Thermistor
41. Heater blower switch
42. Stop lamp switch
43. Air conditioner compressor
44. Reverse lamp switch
45. Reverse lamps
46. Stop lamps
47. L H turn signal warning lamp
48. L H front turn signal lamp
49. L H rear turn signal lamp
50. L H side turn signal lamp
51. R H side turn signal lamp
52. R H rear turn signal lamp
53. R H front turn signal lamp
54. R H turn signal warning lamp
55. Windscreen wiper motor
56. Windscreen wiper intermittent relay
57. Windscreen washer motor
58. Windscreen washer switch
59. Turn signal switch
60. Flasher unit
61. Horn push
62. Horn
63. Hazard switch
64. Stop lamp fuse
65. Turn signal fuse
66. Horn fuse
67. Wiper fuse
68. Tail lamp relay
69. L H headlamp
70. R H headlamp
71. Tail lamp relay
72. Headlamp relay
73. L H headlamp
74. R H headlamp
75. Light control switch
76. Headlamp dip switch
77. High beam warning lamp
78. L H front parking lamp
79. R H front parking lamp
80. L H rear parking lamp
81. R H rear parking lamp
82. Heater control illumination lamp
83. Instrument cluster illumination lamps
84. Number plate lamps
85. Clock
86. Interior dome lamp fuse
87. Cigar lighter fuse
88. Radio fuse
89. Cigar lighter
90. Interior lamp and switch
91. Interior lamp courtesy switches
92. Radio/cassette speakers
93. Radio cassette
94. Radio
95. Radio antenna

Key for the wiring diagrams on the opposite page - diesel models

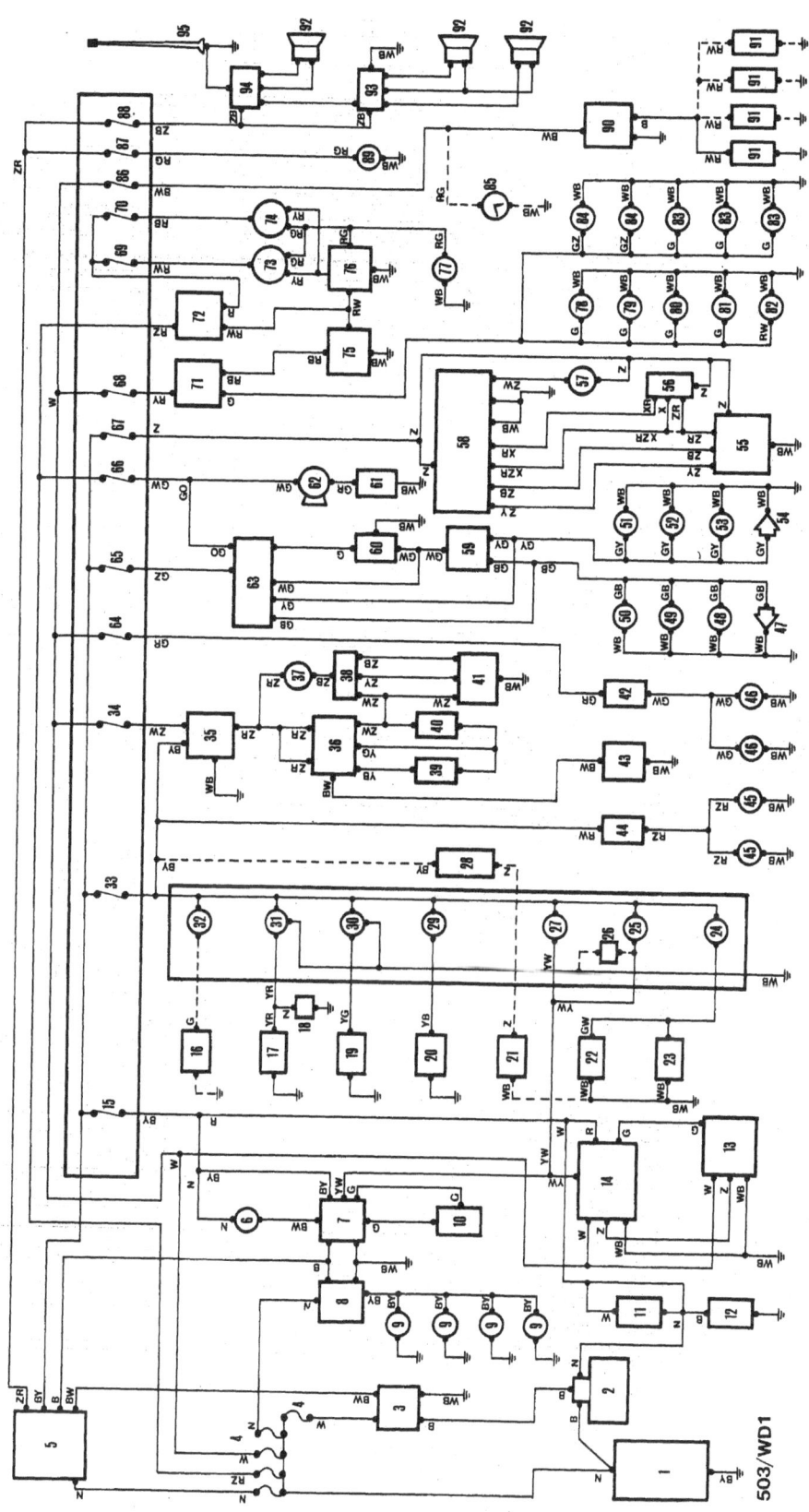

Starting, charging, pre-heat system, instrument illumination, air conditioning, wiper/washer, accessory circuits.
LN46 4Runner models and Hi-Lux models to 1998 - diesel models

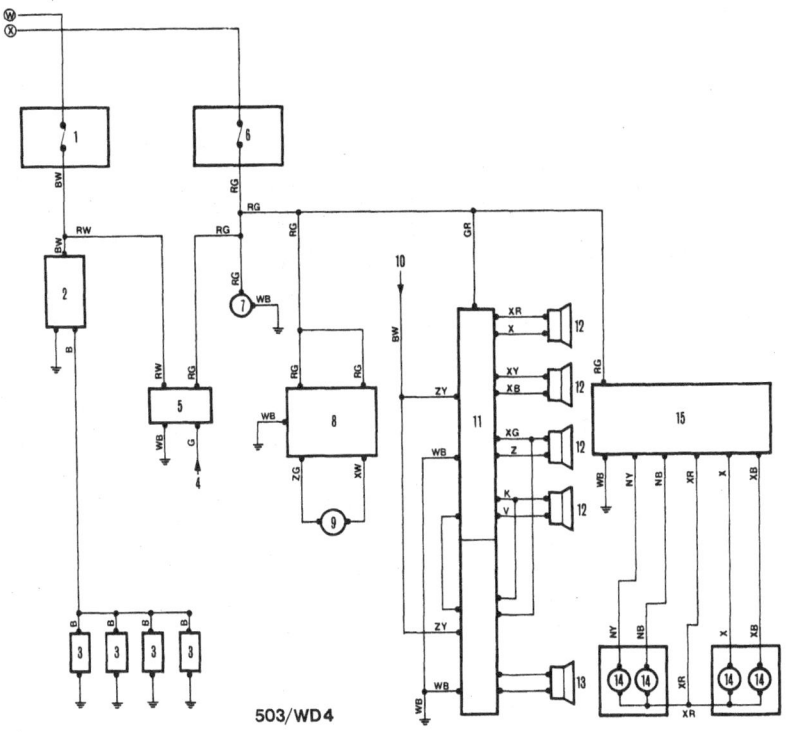

503/WD4

COLOUR CODE

The first letter of the code represents the main wire colour, the other letters represent the trace colours.

B — BLACK
L — BLUE
G — GREEN
R — RED
Y — YELLOW
W — WHITE
N — BROWN
O — ORANGE
K — PINK
S — GREY
V — VIOLET
X — LIGHT GREEN
Z — LIGHT BLUE
M — DARK GREEN
T — DARK BLUE
A — LIGHT BROWN
E — SLATE
D — TAN

KEY

1. Interior dome lamp fuse
2. Interior lamp and switch
3. Interior lamp courtesy switches
4. To tail lamp fuse
5. Digital clock
6. Cigar lighter fuse
7. Cigar lighter
8. Radio antenna control switch
9. Radio antenna motor
10. To turn signal/horn fuse
11. Radio cassette
12. Speakers
13. Woofer speaker
14. Exterior mirror motors
15. Exterior mirror control switch

Interior illumination, digital clock, radio cassette, power mirrors.
LN61 and LN 65 4Runner models and Hi-Lux models to 1998 - diesel models

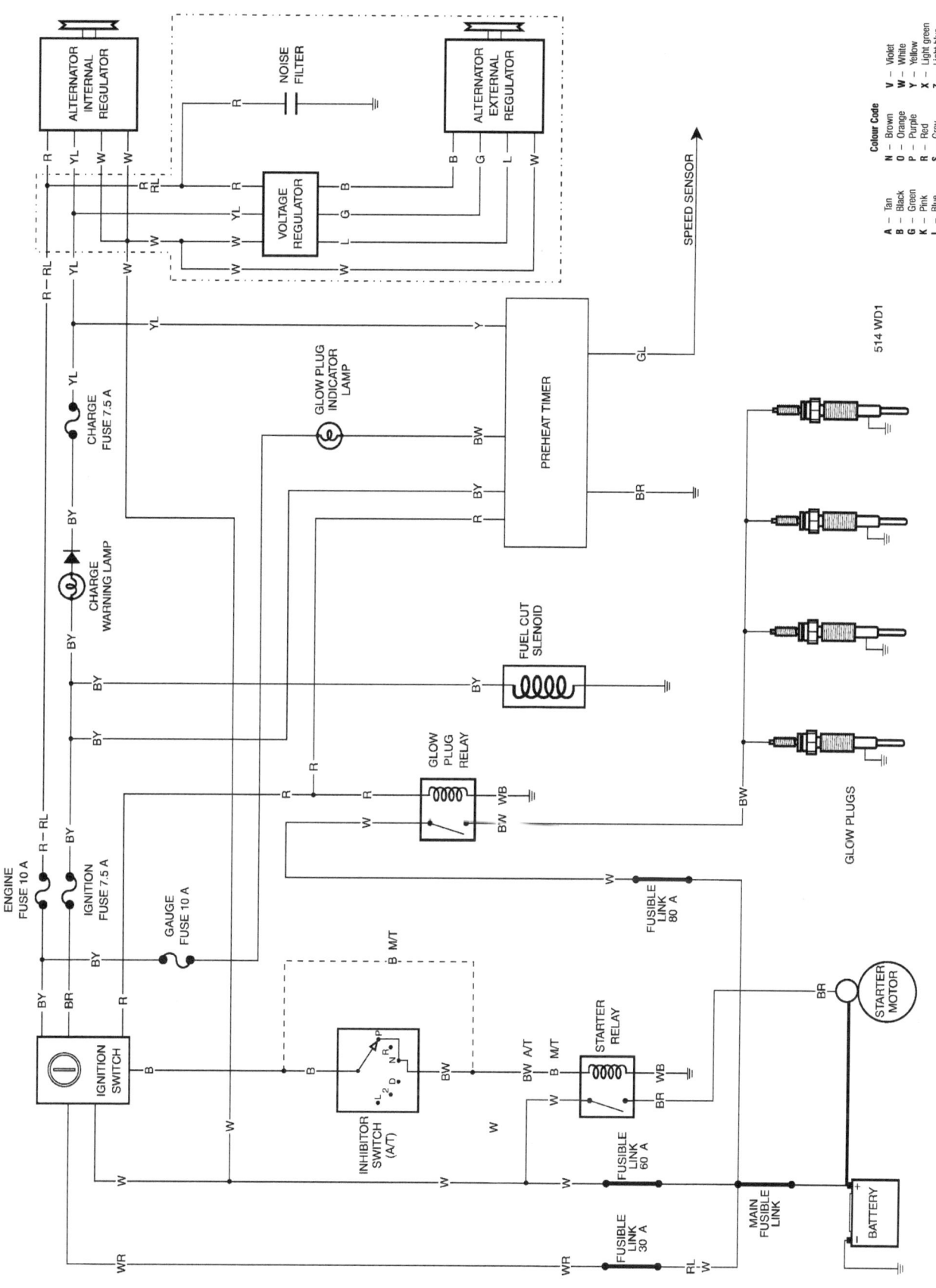

Power supply, alternator, starter motor and preheat system.
Hi-Lux models from 1988 - diesel models

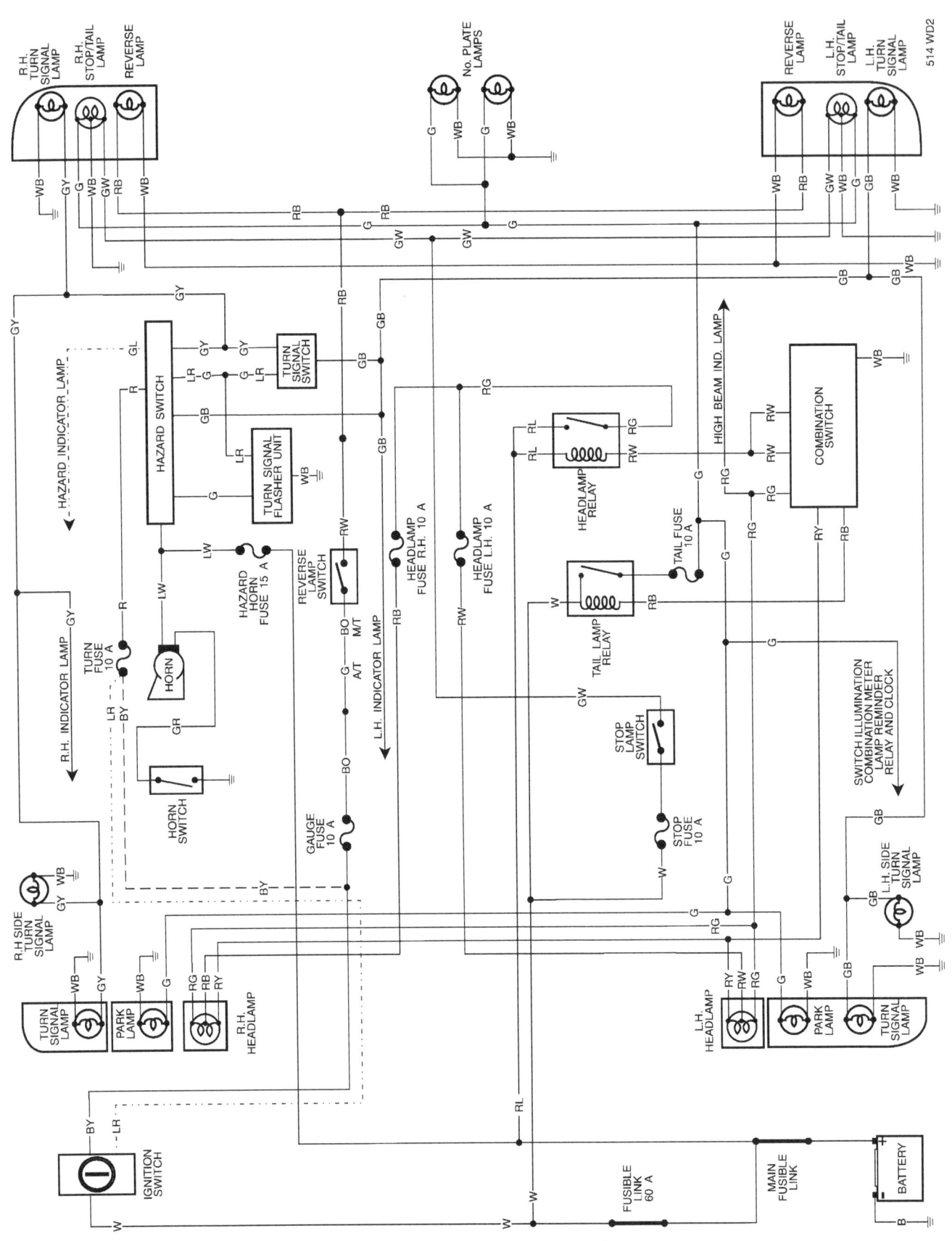

Exterior lighting.
Hi-Lux models from 1988 - diesel models

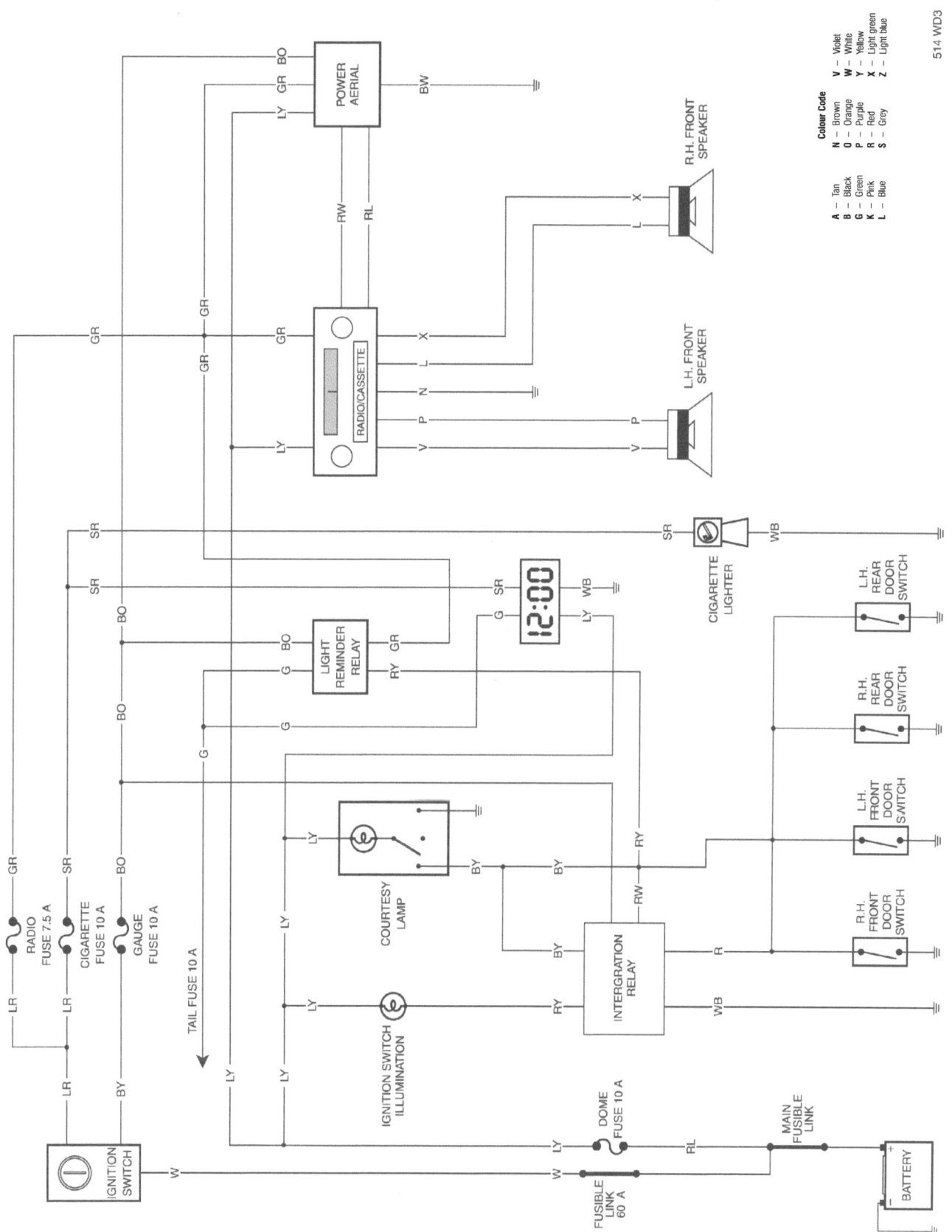

Courtesy lamp, clock and sound system. Early models.
Hi-Lux models from 1988 - diesel models

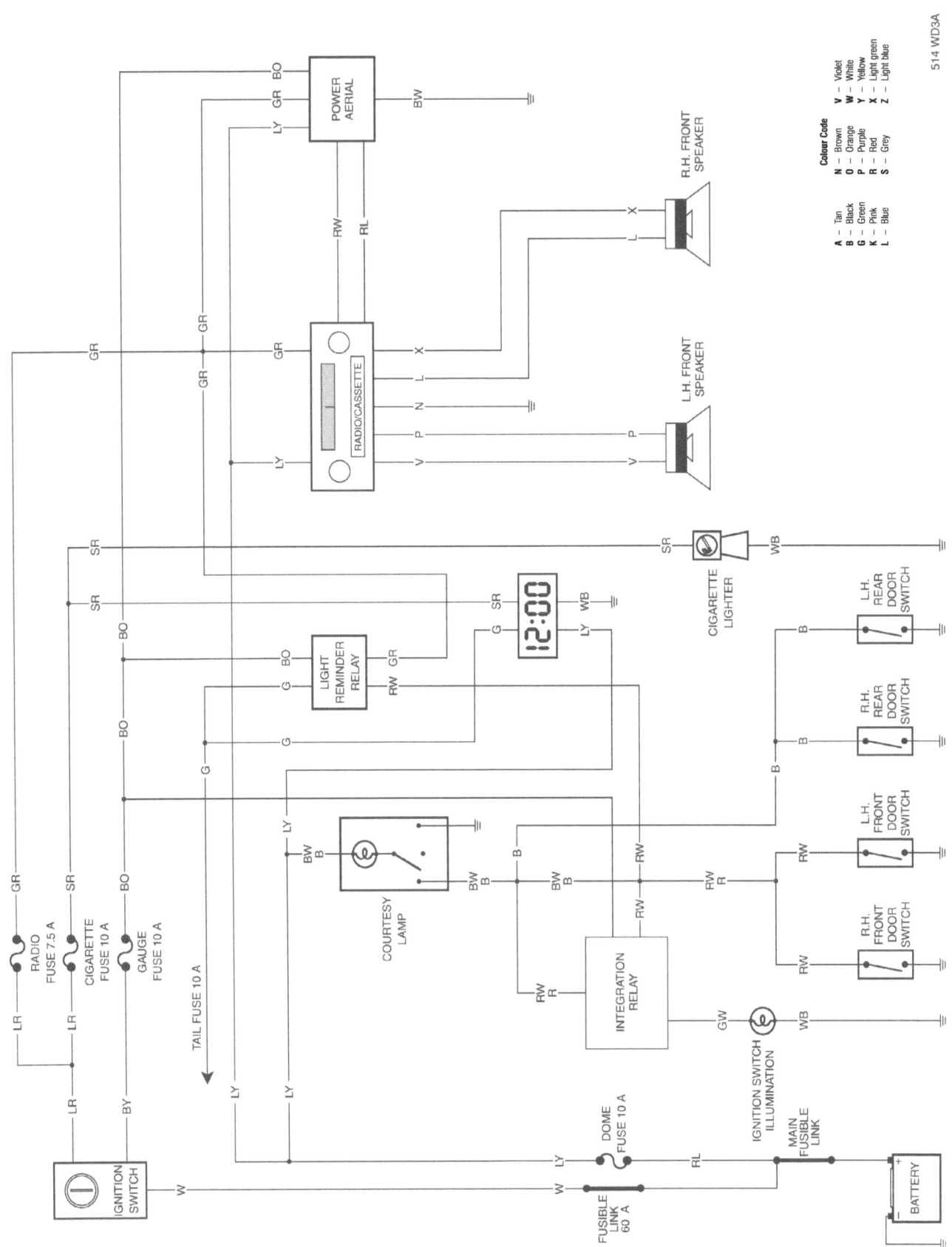

Courtesy lamp, clock and sound system. Late models.
Hi-Lux models from 1988 - diesel models

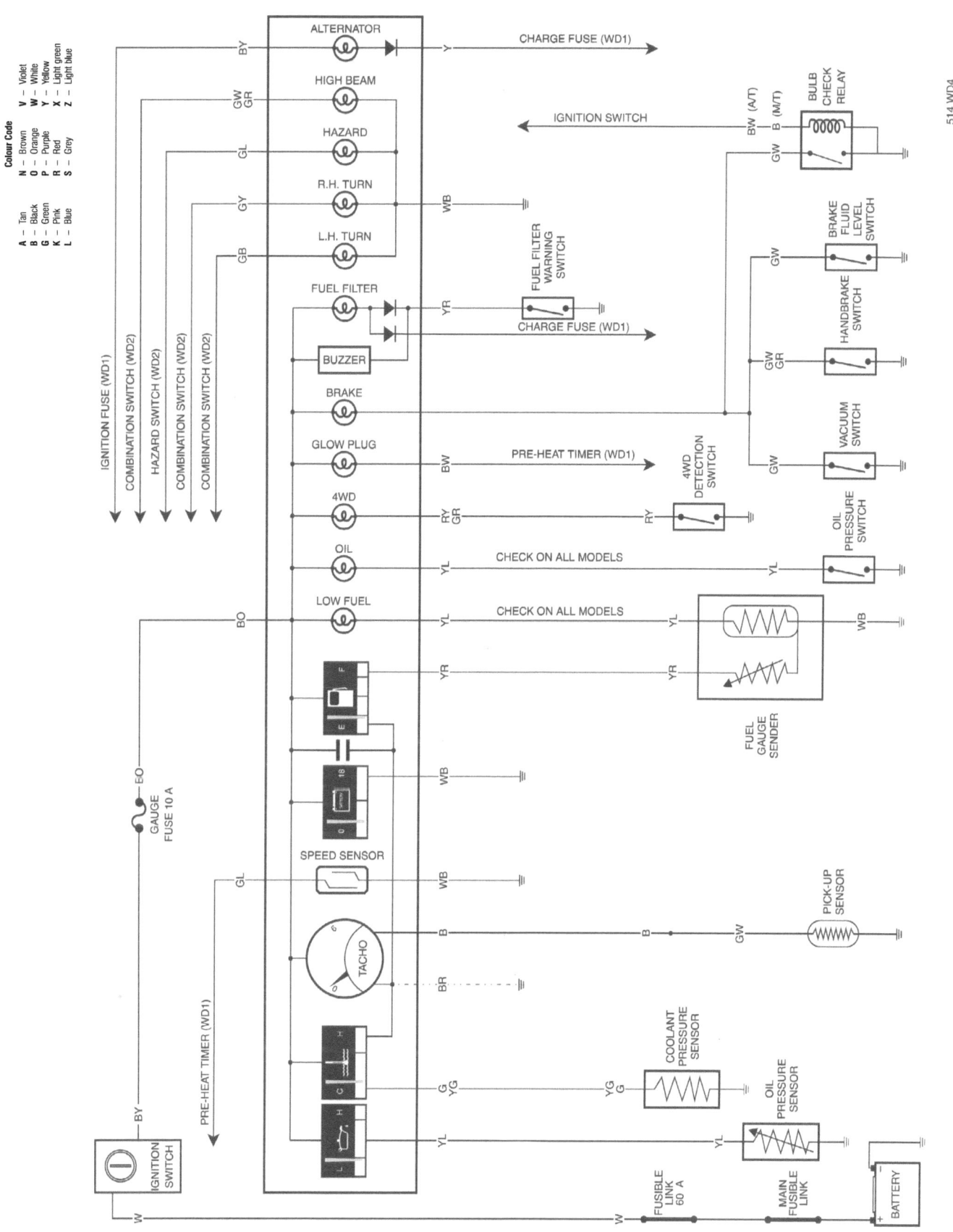

Instrument cluster.
Hi-Lux models from 1988 - diesel models

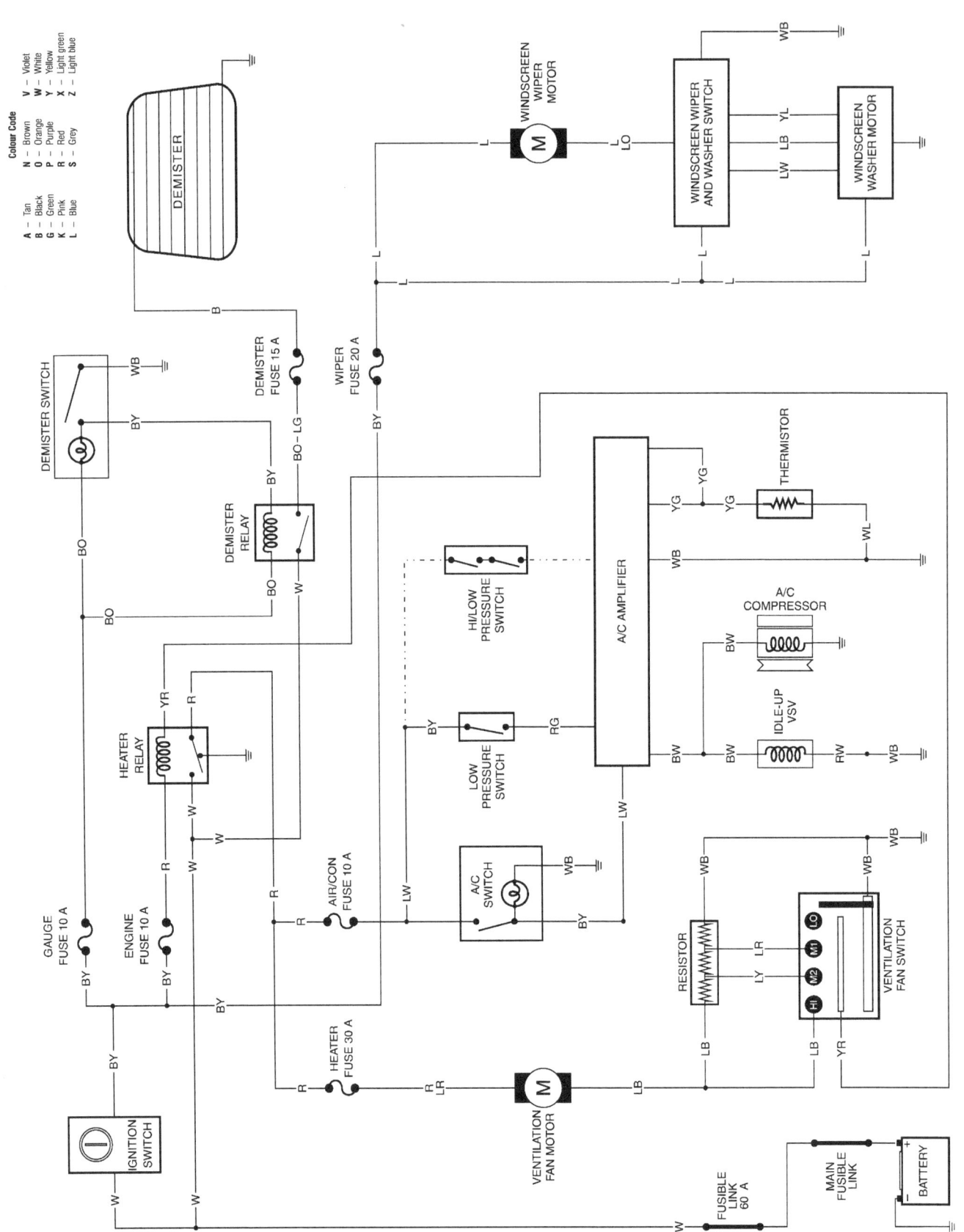

Ventilation system, air conditioning, demister and windscreen wiper and washer.
Hi-Lux models from 1988 - diesel models

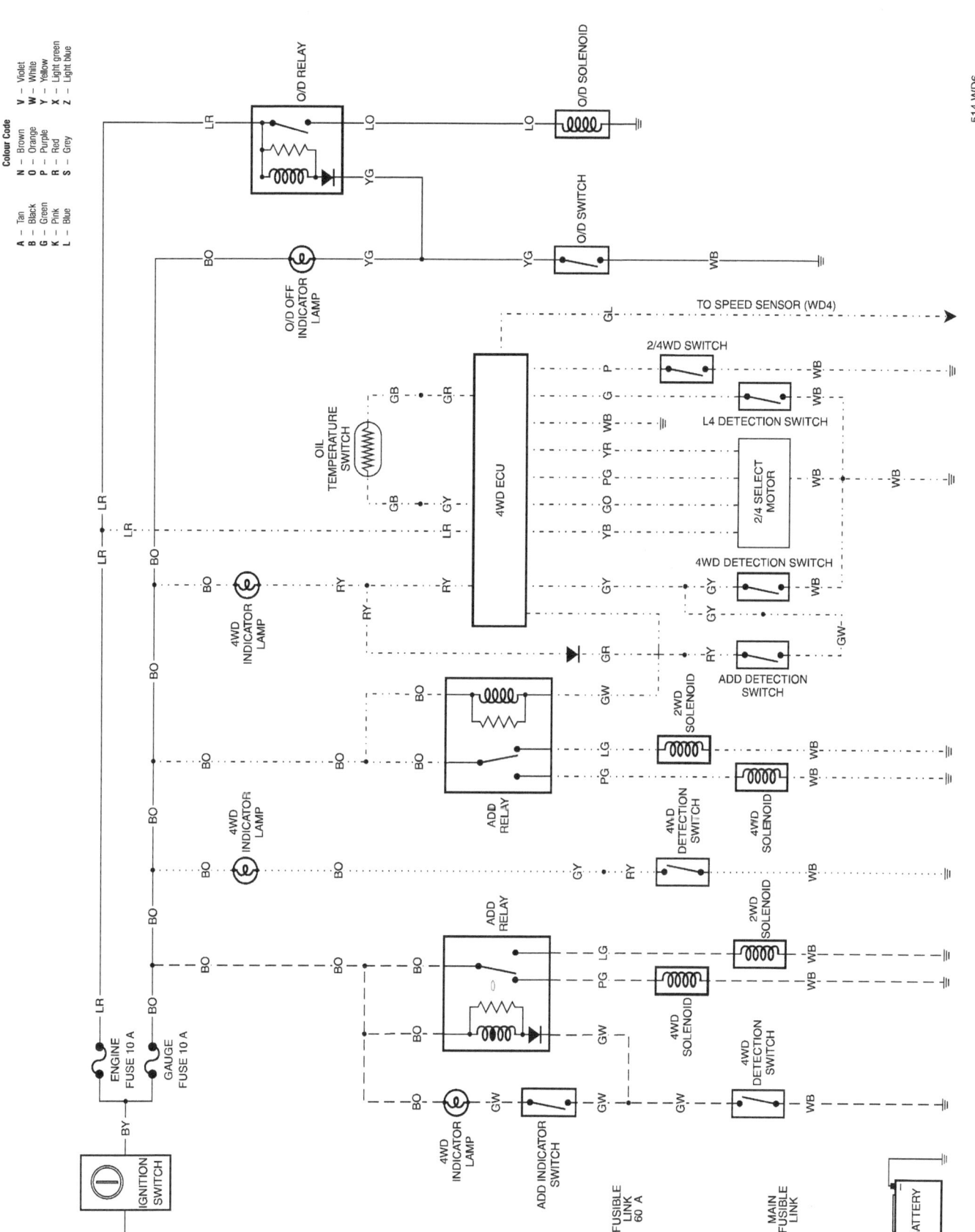

514 WD6

**Automatic disconnecting differential (ADD) system and automatic transmission overdrive.
Hi-Lux models from 1988 - diesel models**

Index

Zeitfracht Medien GmbH
Ferdinand-Jühlke-Straße 7
99095 Erfurt, Deutschland
produktsicherheit@kolibri360.de